2015 Wiley CPAexcel® EXAM REVIEW STUDY GUIDE JULY 2015

2015

Wiley

CPAexcel®
EXAM REVIEW
STUDY GUIDE
JULY 2015

REGULATION

O. Ray Whittington, CPA, PhD

WILEY

Cover Design: John Wiley & Sons, Inc.
Cover image: © iStockphoto/turtleteeth

The following items, copyright © by the American Institute of Certified Public Accountants, Inc., are reprinted (or adapted) with permission.

1. Material from *Uniform CPA Examination Questions and Answers*, 1978 through 2014.

2. *Information for Uniform CPA Examination Candidates*, Board of Examiners, 2013.

3. Definitions, examples, etc. from *The Code of Professional Conduct*.

Material from the Certified Internal Auditor Examination, Copyright © 1994 through 1997 by the Institute of Internal Auditors, Inc., are reprinted and/or adapted with permission.

Material from the Certified Management Accountant Examinations, Copyright © 1993 through 1997 by the Institute of Certified Management Accountants, are reprinted and/or adapted with permission.

Material adapted, with permission, from *Writing for Accountants*, Aletha Hendrickson, South-Western Publishing Co., 1993.

Published by John Wiley & Sons, Inc., Hoboken, New Jersey.
Published simultaneously in Canada.

For general information on our other products and services or for technical support, please contact our Customer Care Department within the US at 800-762-2974, outside the US at 317-572-3993 or fax 317-572-4002.

Wiley also publishes its books in a variety of electronic formats. Some content that appears in print may not be available in electronic books. For more information about Wiley products, visit our Web site at www.wiley.com.

ISBN 978-1-119-11993-7 (paperback); 978-1-119-12822-9 (ebk); 978-1-119-12823-6 (ebk)

Printed in the United States of America

10 9 8 7 6 5 4 3 2 1

CONTENTS

PREFACE

Passing the CPA exam upon your first attempt is possible! The *Wiley CPAexcel Exam Review 2015 Study Guide July: Regulation* preparation materials provide you with the necessary materials (visit our website at www.wiley.com/cpa for more information). It's up to you to add the hard work and commitment. Together we can beat the pass rate on each section of about 50% All Wiley CPA products are continuously updated to provide you with the most comprehensive and complete knowledge base. Choose your products from the Wiley preparation materials and you can proceed confidently. You can select support materials that are exam-based and user-friendly. You can select products that will help you pass!

Remaining current is one of the keys to examination success. Here is a list of what's new in the *Wiley CPAexcel Exam Review 2015 Study Guide July: Regulation* text:

- The new AICPA Content Specification Outlines on Regulation for the Computerized CPA Examination beginning in 2014
- AICPA questions released in 2015
- Tax law changes for 2014 (tested on the 2015 examination)
- Coverage of latest business law legislation
- New outlines and questions for material tested in 2015

The objective of this work is to provide you with the knowledge to pass the Regulation portion of the Uniform Certified Public Accounting (CPA) Exam. The text is divided up into 17 areas of study called modules. Each module contains written text with discussion, examples, and demonstrations of the key exam concepts. Following each text area, actual American Institute of Certified Public Accountants (AICPA) unofficial questions and answers are presented to test your knowledge. We are indebted to the AICPA for permission to reproduce and adapt examination materials from past examinations. Author-constructed questions and task-based simulations are provided for new areas or areas that require updating. All author-constructed questions and task-based simulations are modeled after AICPA question formats. The multiple-choice questions are grouped into topical areas, giving candidates a chance to assess their areas of strength and weakness. Selection and inclusion of topical content is based upon current AICPA Content Specification Outlines. Only testable topics are presented. If the CPA exam does not test it, this text does not present it.

The CPA exam is one of the toughest exams you will ever take. It will not be easy. But if you follow our guidelines and focus on your goal, you will be thrilled with what you can accomplish.

—Ray Whittington
July 2015

DON'T FORGET TO VISIT OUR WEBSITE AT WWW.WILEY.COM/GO/ CPAERRATA FOR SUPPLEMENTS AND UPDATES.

ABOUT THE AUTHOR

Ray Whittington, PhD, CPA, CMA, CIA, is the dean of the Driehaus College of Business at DePaul University. Prior to joining the faculty at DePaul, Professor Whittington was the Director of Accountancy at San Diego State University. From 1989 through 1991, he was the Director of Auditing Research for the American Institute of Certified Public Accountants (AICPA), and he previously was on the audit staff of KPMG. He previously served as a member of the Auditing Standards Board of the AICPA and as a member of the Accounting and Review Services Committee and the Board of Regents of the Institute of Internal Auditors. Professor Whittington has published numerous textbooks, articles, monographs, and continuing education courses.

ABOUT THE CONTRIBUTORS

Edward C. Foth, PhD, CPA, is a faculty member at DePaul University. Professor Foth is the author of CCH Incorporated's *Federal Tax Study Manual,* and is a contributing author to the *CCH Federal Taxation: Comprehensive Topics* textbook as well as CCH's *S Corporations Guide*. Professor Foth prepared the answer explanations to the multiple-choice and other objective questions in Federal Taxation, wrote new questions, selected the mix of questions, and updated the outlines and exam items to reflect revisions in the tax law.

Brad McDonald, JD, is an instructor of Business Law and Statistics at Northern Illinois University. He has taught business law since 1987 and has taught the Business Law section of the Northern Illinois CPA review course since 1998. He wrote and revised most of the Business Law modules. He prepared and revised answer explanations for the multiple-choice and simulation questions.

INTRODUCTION

To maximize the efficiency of your review program, begin by studying (not merely reading) Chapters 1 through 5 of this volume. They have been carefully organized and written to provide you with important information to assist you in successfully completing the Regulation section of the CPA exam. Beyond providing a comprehensive outline to help you organize the material tested on the Regulation section of the exam, Chapter 1 will assist you in organizing a study program to prepare for the Regulation portion. Self-discipline is essential.

Chapter 1: Beginning Your CPA Review Program

GENERAL COMMENTS ON THE EXAMINATION

The Uniform CPA Examination is delivered using computer-based testing (CBT). Computer-based testing has several advantages. You may take the exam one section at a time. As a result, your studies can be focused on that one section, improving your chances for success. In addition, you may take the exam on your schedule, eight months of the year, six days a week, and in the morning or in the afternoon.

Successful completion of the Regulation section of the CPA Examination is an attainable goal. Keep this point foremost in your mind as you study the first four chapters in this volume and develop your study plan.

Purpose of the Examination[1]

The Uniform CPA Examination is designed to test the entry-level knowledge and skills necessary to protect the public interest. These knowledge and skills were identified through a Practice Analysis performed in 2008, which served as a basis for the development of the content specifications for the exam.

The CPA examination is one of many screening devices to assure the competence of those licensed to perform the attest function and to render professional accounting services. Other screening devices include educational requirements, ethics examinations, and work experience.

The examination appears to test the material covered in accounting programs of the better business schools. It also appears to be based upon the body of knowledge essential for the practice of public accounting and the audit of a medium-sized client. Since the examination is primarily a textbook or academic examination, you should plan on taking it as soon as possible after completing your accounting education.

Examination Content

Guidance concerning topical content of the computer-based exam in Regulation can be found in a document prepared by the Board of Examiners of the AICPA entitled *Content and Skill Specifications for the Uniform CPA Exam*. We have included the content outline for Regulation at the beginning of Chapter 5. The outline should be used as an indication of the topics' relative emphasis on the exam.

The Board's objective in preparing this detailed listing of topics tested on the exam is to help "in assuring the continuing validity and reliability of the Uniform CPA Examination." These outlines are an excellent source of guidance concerning the areas and the emphasis to be given each area on future exams.

The new Content and Skill Specification Outlines for the CPA examination went into effect January 1, 2014. In addition, the AICPA adopted CBT-e, which is a new computer platform. The major change from your standpoint is that simulations are smaller in size and a larger number of these "task-based simulations" are included on the Auditing and Attestation, Financial Accounting and Reporting, and Regulation exams. In addition, all questions that test writing skills have been moved to the Business Environment and Concepts exam.

The exam covers the Internal Revenue Code and federal tax regulations in effect six months before the particular testing window. For the Regulation section, federal laws are tested six months following their *effective* date and for uniform acts one year after their adoption by a simple majority of jurisdictions. This section deals with federal and widely adopted uniform laws. If there is no federal or uniform law on a topic, the questions are intended to test knowledge of the law of the majority of jurisdictions. Professional ethics questions are based on the AICPA *Code of Professional Conduct* because it is national in its application, whereas codes of other organizations and jurisdictions may be limited in their application. The AICPA posts content changes regularly on its Internet site. The address is www.cpa-exam.org.

Nondisclosure and Computerization of Examination

Beginning May 1996, the Uniform CPA Examination became nondisclosed. For each exam section, candidates are required to agree to a *Statement of Confidentiality*, which states that they will not divulge the nature and content of any

---

[1]More information may be obtained from the AICPA's *Uniform CPA Examination Candidate Bulletin*, which you can find on the AICPA's website at www.cpa-exam.org.

exam question. The CPA exam is computer-based, and candidates take the exam at Prometric sites in the 55 jurisdictions in which the exam is offered. The CPA exam is offered continually during the testing windows shown below.

Testing Window (Exam Available)	January through February	April through May	July through August	October through November
AICPA Review and Update (Exam Unavailable)	March	June	September	December

One or more exam sections may be taken during any exam window, and the sections may be taken in any desired order. **However, no candidate will be allowed to sit for the same section more than once during any given testing window.** In addition, a candidate must pass all four sections of the CPA exam within a "rolling" eighteen-month period, which begins on the date he or she passes a section. In other words, you must pass the other three sections of the exam within eighteen months of when you pass the first section. If you do not pass all sections within the eighteen-month period, credit for any section(s) passed outside the eighteen-month period will expire and the section(s) must be retaken.

Types of Questions

The computer-based Uniform CPA Examination consists of two basic question formats.

1. Multiple-Choice—questions requiring the selection of one of four responses to a short scenario.
2. Task-Based Simulations—short case studies that are used to assess knowledge and skills in a context approximating that found on the job through the use of realistic scenarios and tasks, and access to normally available and familiar resources.

The multiple-choice questions are much like the ones that have constituted a majority of the CPA examination for years. **And the good news is that these types of questions constitute 60% of the Regulation section.**

Process for Sitting for the Examination

While there are some variations in the process from state to state, the basic process for sitting for the CPA examination may be described as follows.

1. Apply to take the examination (request, complete, and submit an application)
2. Pay the examination fees
3. Review the tutorial and sample tests
4. Receive your Notice to Schedule (NTS)
5. Schedule your examination
6. Take your examination(s)
7. Receive your Score Report(s)

Applying to Take the Examination

The right to practice public accounting as a CPA is governed by individual state statutes. While some rules regarding the practice of public accounting vary from urisdiction to jurisdiction, all State Boards of Accountancy use the Uniform CPA Examination and AICPA advisory grading service as one of the requirements to practice public accounting. Every candidate should contact the applicable State Board of Accountancy to determine the requirements to sit for the exam (e.g., education requirements). For comparisons of requirements for various state boards and those policies that are uniform across jurisdictions you should refer to the website of the National Association of State Boards of Accountancy (NASBA) at www.nasba.org.

A frequent problem candidates encounter is failure to apply by the deadline. **Apply to sit for the examination early. Also, you should use extreme care in filling out the application and mailing required materials to your State Board of Accountancy.** If possible, have a friend review your completed application before mailing with check and other documentation. The name on your application must appear exactly the same as it appears on the identification you plan to use at the testing center. Candidates may miss a particular CPA examination window simply because of minor technical details that were overlooked (check not signed, items not enclosed, question not answered on application, etc.). **Because of the**

very high volume of applications received in the more populous states, the administrative staff does not have time to call or write to correct minor details and will simply reject your application.

The NASBA website has links to the registration information for all 55 jurisdictions. It is possible for candidates to sit for the examination at a Prometric site in any state or territory. Candidates desiring to do so should refer to the registration information for the applicable State Board of Accountancy.

International Applicants

International administration of the CPA Exam is currently offered in Brazil, Japan, Bahrain, Kuwait, Lebanon, and the United Arab Emirates. If you live in one of these testing locations, or other select countries, you may be able to take the Exam without traveling to the U.S. The Exam is only offered in English, and is the same computerized test as the one administered in the U.S. You are required to meet the same eligibility requirements and complete the same licensure requirements as your U.S. counterparts.

Applicants from countries other than the U.S. must follow the same basic steps as U.S. applicants. This means they must select the jurisdiction in which they wish to qualify and file an application with the board of accountancy (or its designated agent) in that jurisdiction. Any special instructions for candidates who have completed their education outside the U.S. are included in the board of accountancy requirements. For more information on the international administration of the CPA Examination, visit the International section of the NASBA website.

Obtaining the Notice to Schedule

Once your application has been processed and you have paid all fees, you will receive a Notice to Schedule (NTS) from NASBA. The NTS will list the section(s) of the examination that you are approved to take. When you receive the NTS, verify that all information is correct. **Be certain that the name appearing on the NTS matches EXACTLY the name on the identification documents that you will use during check-in at the testing center. If the information is incorrect or the name does not match, immediately contact your board of accountancy or its designated agent to request a correction. You must bring your NTS with you to the examination.**

Exam Scheduling

Once you have been cleared to take the exam by the applicable state board, you will receive by mail a Notice to Schedule (NTS) and may then schedule to sit for one or more sections of the exam.

You have the following two options for scheduling your examination:

1. **Visit www.prometric.com/cpa on the Internet**

   This is the easiest and quickest way to schedule an examination appointment (or cancel and reschedule an appointment, if necessary). Simply go to the website, select "Schedule your test," and follow the directions. It is advised that you print and keep for your records the confirmation number for your appointment.

2. **Call 800-580-9648 (Candidate Services Call Center)**

   Before you call, you must have your NTS in front of you, and have in mind several times, dates, and locations that would work for you. You will not receive written confirmation of your appointment. Be sure to write down the date, time, location, and confirmation number for each of your appointments.

You should also be aware that if you have to cancel or reschedule your appointment, you may be subject to a cancellation/rescheduling fee. The AICPA's Uniform CPA Examination Candidate Bulletin lists the rescheduling and cancellation fees.

To assure that you get your desired location and time period it is imperative that you schedule early. To get your first choice of dates, you are advised to schedule at least 45 days in advance. You will not be scheduled for an exam fewer than 5 days before testing.

ATTRIBUTES OF EXAMINATION SUCCESS

Your primary objective in preparing for the Regulation section is to pass. Other objectives such as learning new and reviewing old material should be considered secondary. The six attributes of examination success discussed below are **essential**. You should study the attributes and work toward achieving/developing each of them **before** taking the examination.

1. **Knowledge of Material**

   Two points are relevant to "knowledge of material" as an attribute of examination success. **First,** there is a distinct difference between being familiar with material and knowing the material. Frequently candidates confuse familiarity with knowledge. Can you remember when you just could not answer an examination question or did poorly on an examination, but maintained to yourself or your instructor that you knew the material? You probably were only familiar with the material. On the CPA examination, familiarity is insufficient; you must know the material. Remember, the exam will test your ability to analyze data, make judgments, communicate, perform research, and demonstrate understanding of the material. Knowledgeable discussion of the material is required on the CPA examination. This text contains outlines of the topical areas in regulation. Return to the original material (e.g., your business law and tax textbooks, Code Sections, etc.) only if the outlines do not reinforce material you already know. **Second,** the Regulation exam tests a literally overwhelming amount of material at a rigorous level. **Furthermore,** as noted earlier, the CPA exam will test new material, sometimes as early as six months after issuance. In other words, you are not only responsible for material you learned in your business law and tax courses, but also for all new developments in business law and income tax.

2. **Commitment to Exam Preparation**

   Your preparation for the CPA exam should begin at least two months prior to the date you plan to schedule your seating for an exam section. If you plan to take more than one section, you should start earlier. Over the course of your preparation, you will experience many peaks and valleys. There will be days when you feel completely prepared and there will also be days when you feel totally overwhelmed. This is not unusual and, in fact, should be expected.

   The CPA exam is a very difficult and challenging exam. How many times in your college career did you study months for an exam? Probably not too many. Therefore, candidates need to remain focused on the objective—succeeding on the CPA exam.

   Develop a personal study plan so that you are reviewing material daily. Of course, you should schedule an occasional study break to help you relax, but don't schedule too many breaks. Candidates who dedicate themselves to studying have a much greater chance of going through this process only one time. On the other hand, a lack of focus and piecemeal preparation will only extend the process over a number of exam sittings.

3. **Solutions Approach**

   The solutions approach is a systematic approach to solving the questions and task-based simulations found on the CPA examination. Many candidates know the material fairly well when they sit for the CPA exam, but they do not know how to take the examination. Candidates generally neither work nor answer questions efficiently in terms of time or grades. The solutions approach permits you to avoid drawing "blanks" on CPA exam questions; using the solutions approach coupled with grading insights (see below) allows you to pick up a sizable number of points on test material with which you are not familiar. Chapter 3 outlines the solutions approach for multiple-choice questions and task-based simulations.

4. **Grading Insights**

   Your score on each section of the exam is determined by the sum of points assigned to individual questions and simulation parts. Thus, you must attempt to maximize your points on each individual item.

   The multiple-choice questions within each section are organized into three groups which are referred to as testlets. Each multiple-choice testlet is comprised of approximately 24 multiple-choice questions. The multiple-choice testlets vary in overall difficulty. A testlet is labeled either "medium difficult" or "difficult" based on its makeup. A "difficult" testlet has a higher percentage of hard questions than than a "medium difficult" testlet. Every candidate's first multiple-choice testlet in each section will be a "medium difficult" testlet. If a candidate scores well on the first testlet, he or she will receive a "difficult" second testlet. Candidates that do not perform well on the first testlet receive a second "medium difficult" testlet. Because the scoring procedure takes the difficulty of the testlet into account, candidates are scored fairly regardless of the type of testlets they receive.

   Each multiple-choice testlet contains "operational" and "pretest" questions. The operational questions are the only ones that are used to determine your score. Pretest questions are not scored; they are being tested for future use as operational questions. However, you have no way of knowing which questions are operational and which questions are pretest questions. Therefore, you must approach each question as if it will be used to determine your grade.

   Task-based simulations on the Regulation exam include more extensive scenarios and requirements. For example, the requirements may involve calculations, form completion, or research. The points assigned to the requirements will vary according to their difficulty. The task-based simulations make use of a number of commonly used tools such as spreadsheets and electronic research databases. Therefore, you need to become proficient in the use of these tools to maximize your score on the simulations.

CPA Exam scores are reported on a scale from 0 to 99. The total score is not a percent correct score. It is a combination of scores from the multiple-choice and simulation portions of the exam considering the relative difficulty of the items. A total score of 75 is required to pass each section.

The AICPA includes a tutorial and sample examinations on its website that allow you to get experience with the use of the actual computer tools used on the CPA exam. Also, more experience with computer testing can be obtained by using *Wiley CPAexcel Exam Review Test Bank.*

5. **Examination Strategy**

Prior to sitting for the examination, it is important to develop an examination strategy (i.e., an approach to working efficiently throughout the exam). Your ability to cope successfully with three hours of examination can be improved by

a. Recognizing the importance and usefulness of an examination strategy
b. Using Chapter 4, Taking the Examination, and previous examination experience to develop a "personal strategy" for the exam
c. Testing your "personal strategy" on example examinations under conditions similar to those at the testing centers (using similar tools and databases and with a time limit)

6. **Examination Confidence**

You need confidence to endure the physical and mental demands of three hours of test-taking under tremendous pressure. Examination confidence results from proper preparation for the exam which includes mastering the first four attributes of examination success. Examination confidence is necessary to enable you to overcome the initial frustration with questions for which you may not be specifically prepared.

This study manual, when properly used, contributes to your examination confidence. Build confidence by completing the questions contained herein.

Common Candidate Mistakes

The CPA Exam is a formidable hurdle in your accounting career. With a pass rate of about 45% on each section, the level of difficulty is obvious. The good news, though, is that about 75% of all candidates (first-time and re-exam) sitting for each examination eventually pass. The authors believe that the first-time pass rate could be higher if candidates would be more careful. Seven common mistakes that many candidates make are

1. Failure to understand the exam question requirements
2. Misunderstanding the supporting text of the problem
3. Lack of knowledge of material tested, especially recently issued pronouncements
4. Failure to develop proficiency with computer-based testing and practice tools such as electronic research databases and spreadsheets
5. Inability to apply the solutions approach
6. Lack of an exam strategy (e.g., allocation of time)
7. Sloppiness and computational errors

These mistakes are not mutually exclusive. Candidates may commit one or more of the above items. Remind yourself that when you decrease the number of common mistakes, you increase your chances of successfully becoming a CPA. Take the time to read carefully the exam question requirements. Do not jump into a quick start, only to later find out that you didn't understand what information the examiners were asking for. Read slowly and carefully. Take time to recall your knowledge. Respond to the question asked. Apply an exam strategy such as allocating your time among all question formats. Do not spend too much time on the multiple-choice testlets, leaving no time to spend on preparing your simulation responses. Answer questions quickly but precisely, avoid common mistakes, and increase your score.

PURPOSE AND ORGANIZATION OF THIS REVIEW TEXTBOOK

This book is designed to help you prepare adequately for the Regulation Examination. There is no easy way to prepare for the successful completion of the CPA Examination; however, through the use of this manual, your approach will be systematic and logical.

The objective of this book is to provide study materials supportive to CPA candidates. While no guarantees are made concerning the success of those using this text, this book promotes efficient preparation by

1. Explaining how to **maximize your score** through analysis of examination grading and illustration of the solutions approach.

2. **Defining areas tested** through the use of the content specification outlines described. Note that predictions of future exams are not made. You should prepare yourself for all possible topics rather than gambling on the appearance of certain questions.

3. **Organizing your study program** by comprehensively outlining all of the subject matter tested on the examination in 17 easy-to-use study modules. Each study module is a manageable task which facilitates your exam preparation. Turn to Chapter 5 and peruse the contents to get a feel for the organization of this book.

4. **Providing CPA candidates with previous examination questions** organized by topic (e.g., contracts, negotiable instruments, etc.) Questions have also been developed for new areas and in simulation format.

5. **Explaining the AICPA unofficial answers** to the examination questions included in this text. The AICPA publishes unofficial answers for all questions from exams administered prior to 1996 and for any released questions from exams administered on or after May 1996. However, no explanation is made of the approach that should have been applied to the examination questions to obtain these unofficial answers. Relatedly, the AICPA unofficial answers to multiple-choice questions provide no justification and/or explanation.

As you read the next few paragraphs which describe the contents of this book, flip through the chapters to gain a general familiarity with the book's organization and contents. Chapters 2, 3, and 4 are to help you "maximize your score."

Chapter 2	Examination Grading
Chapter 3	The Solutions Approach
Chapter 4	Taking the Examination

Chapters 2, 3, and 4 contain material that should be kept in mind throughout your study program. Refer back to them frequently. Reread them for a final time just before you sit for the exam.

The Regulation Modules contain

1. AICPA Content Specification Outlines of material tested on the Regulation Examination
2. Multiple-choice questions
3. Task-based simulation problems
4. AICPA unofficial answers with the author's explanations for the multiple-choice questions
5. Author answers to task-based simulations

Also included at the end of this text is a complete Sample Regulation Examination. The sample exam is included to enable candidates to gain experience in taking a "realistic" exam. While studying the modules, the candidate can become accustomed to concentrating on fairly narrow topics. By working through the sample examination near the end of their study programs, candidates will be better prepared for taking the actual examination. Because some task-based simulations require the use of research materials, it is useful to have the appropriate electronic research database (Internal Revenue Code and Income Tax Regulations) or printed versions of the Internal Revenue Code and Income Tax Regulations to complete the sample examination. **Remember that this research material will not be available to answer the multiple-choice questions.**

Other Textbooks

This text is a comprehensive compilation of study guides and outlines; it should not be necessary to supplement them with accounting textbooks and other materials for most topics. You probably already have business law and tax textbooks. In such a case, you must make the decision whether to replace them and trade familiarity (including notes therein, etc.), with the cost and inconvenience of obtaining the newer texts containing a more updated presentation.

Before spending time and money acquiring a new book, begin your study program with the *Wiley CPAexcel Exam Review 2015 Study Guide July: Regulation* to determine your need for a supplemental text.

Ordering Other Textual Materials

If you want to order AICPA materials, locate an AICPA educator member to order your materials, since educator members are entitled to a discount and may place website or telephone orders.

AICPA (CPA2Biz)

Telephone: 888-777-7077

website: www.CPA2Biz.com

A variety of supplemental CPA products is available from John Wiley & Sons, Inc. By using a variety of learning techniques, such as software, computer-based learning, and audio CDs, the candidate is more likely to remain focused during the study process and to retain information for a longer period of time. Visit our website at **www.wiley.com/cpa** for other products, supplements, and updates.

Working CPA Questions

The AICPA content outlines, study outlines, etc., will be used to acquire and assimilate the knowledge tested on the examination. This, however, should be only **one-half** of your preparation program. The other half should be spent practicing how to work questions. Some candidates probably spend over 90% of their time reviewing material tested on the CPA exam. Much more time should be allocated to working previous examination questions **under exam conditions**. Working examination questions serves two functions. First, it helps you develop a solutions approach as well as solutions that will maximize your score. Second, it provides the best test of your knowledge of the material.

The multiple-choice questions and answer explanations can be used in many ways. First, they may be used as a diagnostic evaluation of your knowledge. For example, before beginning to review negotiable instruments you may wish to answer 10 to 15 multiple-choice questions to determine your ability to answer CPA examination questions on negotiable instruments. The apparent difficulty of the questions and the correctness of your answers will allow you to determine the necessary breadth and depth of your review. Additionally, exposure to examination questions prior to review and study of the material should provide motivation. You will develop a feel for your level of proficiency and an understanding of the scope and difficulty of past examination questions. Moreover, your review materials will explain concepts encountered in the diagnostic multiple-choice questions.

Second, the multiple-choice questions can be used as a poststudy or postreview evaluation. You should attempt to understand all concepts mentioned (even in incorrect answers) as you answer the questions. Refer to the explanation of the answer for discussion of the alternatives even though you selected the correct response. Thus, you should read the explanation of the unofficial answer unless you completely understand the question and all of the alternative answers.

Third, you may wish to use the multiple-choice questions as a primary study vehicle. This is probably the quickest but least thorough approach in preparing for the exam. Make a sincere effort to understand the question and to select the correct response before referring to the unofficial answer and explanation. In many cases, the explanations will appear inadequate because of your lack of familiarity with the topic. Always refer back to an appropriate study source, such as the outlines and text in this volume, your business law and tax textbooks, Code Sections, etc.

The multiple-choice questions outnumber the task-based simulations by greater than 10 to 1 in this book. This is similar to the proposed content of the new computer-based examination. One problem with so many multiple-choice questions is that you may overemphasize them. Candidates generally prefer to work multiple-choice questions because they are

1. Shorter and less time-consuming
2. Solvable with less effort
3. Less frustrating than task-based simulations

Another problem with the large number of multiple-choice questions is that you may tend to become overly familiar with the questions. The result may be that you begin reading the facts and assumptions of previously studied questions into the questions on your examination. Guard against this potential problem by reading each multiple-choice question with **extra** care.

Beginning with the introduction of the computer-based examination, the AICPA began testing with simulations. Simulations released by the AICPA, prepared by the author, and revised from prior CPA exam problems are incorporated in the modules to which they pertain. (See the listing of question material at the beginning of Chapter 5.)

The questions and solutions in this volume provide you with an opportunity to diagnose and correct any exam-taking weaknesses prior to sitting for the examination. Continually analyze your incorrect solutions to determine the cause of the error(s) during your preparation for the exam. Treat each incorrect solution as a mistake that will not be repeated (especially on the examination). Also attempt to generalize your weaknesses so that you may change, reinforce, or develop new approaches to exam preparation and exam taking.

SELF-STUDY PROGRAM

CPA candidates generally find it difficult to organize and complete their own self-study programs. A major problem is determining **what** and **how** to study. Another major problem is developing the self-discipline to stick to a study program. Relatedly, it is often difficult for CPA candidates to determine how much to study (i.e., determining when they are sufficiently prepared.) The following suggestions will assist you in developing a **systematic**, **comprehensive**, and **successful** self-study program to help you complete the Regulation exam.

Remember that these are only suggestions. You should modify them to suit your personality, available study time, and other constraints. Some of the suggestions may appear trivial, but CPA candidates generally need all the assistance they can get to systemize their study programs.

Study Facilities and Available Time

Locate study facilities that will be conducive to concentrated study. Factors that you should consider include

1. Noise distraction
2. Interruptions
3. Lighting
4. Availability (e.g., a local library is not available at 5:00 A.M.)
5. Accessibility (e.g., your kitchen table vs. your local library)
6. Desk or table space

You will probably find different study facilities optimal for different times (e.g., your kitchen table during early morning hours and local libraries during early evening hours).

Next review your personal and professional commitments from now until the exam to determine regularly available study time. Formalize a schedule to which you can reasonably commit yourself. At the end of this chapter, you will find a detailed approach to managing your time available for the exam preparation program.

Self-Evaluation

The *Wiley CPAexcel Exam Review 2015 Study Guide July: Regulation* self-study program is partitioned into 17 topics or modules. Since each module is clearly defined and should be studied separately, you have the task of preparing for the CPA Regulation exam by tackling 17 manageable tasks. Partitioning the overall project into 17 modules makes preparation psychologically easier, since you sense yourself completing one small step at a time rather than seemingly never completing one or a few large steps.

By completing the following "Preliminary Estimate of Your Present Knowledge of Subject" inventory below, organized by the 17 modules in this program, you will tabulate your strong and weak areas at the beginning of your study program. This will help you budget your limited study time. Note that you should begin studying the material in each module by answering up to 1/4 of the total multiple-choice questions covering that module's topics (see instruction 4.A. in the next section). This "mini-exam" should constitute a diagnostic evaluation as to the amount of review and study you need.

PRELIMINARY ESTIMATE OF YOUR PRESENT KNOWLEDGE OF SUBJECT

No.	Module	Proficient	Fairly Proficient	Generally Familiar	Not Familiar
	Professional Responsibilities and Business Law				
23	Professional and Legal Responsibilities				
24	Federal Securities Acts				
25	Business Structure				
26	Contracts				
27	Sales				
28	Negotiable Instruments				
29	Secured Transactions				
30	Bankruptcy				
31	Debtor-Creditor Relationships				

No.	Module	Proficient	Fairly Proficient	Generally Familiar	Not Familiar
32	Agency				
33	Regulation of Business, Employment, Environment, and Antitrust				
34	Property				
	Federal Taxation				
35	Individual Taxation				
36	Transactions in Property				
37	Partnership Taxation				
38	Corporate Taxation				
39	Other Taxation Topics				

NOTE: The numbering of modules in this text commences with number 23 to correspond with the numbering system used in our two-volume set.

Time Allocation

The study program below entails an average of 68 hours (Step 5. below) of study time. The breakdown of total hours is indicated in the left margin.

[2 1/2 hrs.] 1. Study Chapters 2–4 in this volume. These chapters are essential to your efficient preparation program. (Time estimate includes candidate's review of the examples of the solutions approach in Chapters 2 and 3.)

[1/2 hr.] 2. Begin by studying the introductory material at the beginning of Chapter 5.

3. Study one module at a time. The modules are listed above in the self-evaluation section.

4. For each module:

[6 hrs.] A. First, review the listing of key terms at the end of the module. Then, work 1/4 of the multiple-choice questions (e.g., if there are 40 multiple-choice questions in a module, you should work every 4th question). Score yourself.

This diagnostic routine will provide you with an index of your proficiency and familiarity with the type and difficulty of questions.

The outlines for each module are broken into smaller sections that refer you to multiple-choice questions to test your comprehension of the material. You may find this organization useful in breaking your study into smaller bites.

Time estimate: 3 minutes each, not to exceed 1 hour total.

[22 hrs.] B. Study the outlines and illustrations. Where necessary, refer to your business law and tax textbooks and original authoritative pronouncements (e.g., code sections). (This will occur more frequently for topics in which you have a weak background.)

Time estimate: 1 hour minimum per module with more time devoted to topics less familiar to you.

[15 hrs.] C. Work the remaining multiple-choice questions. Study the explanations of the multiple-choice questions you missed or had trouble answering.

Time estimate: 3 minutes to answer each question and 2 minutes to study the answer explanation of each question missed.

[18 hrs.] D. Under exam conditions, work at least 6 simulations per module and the questions and task-based simulations in Appendices B and C. Work additional questions and simulations as time permits.
Time estimate: 2 minutes for each multiple-choice question, 15 minutes for each simulation, and 10 minutes to review the solution for each simulation worked.

[4 hrs.]   E.   Work through the sample CPA examination presented as Appendix A. Each exam should be taken in one sitting.

         Take the examination under simulated exam conditions (i.e., in a strange place with other people present [your local municipal library or a computer lab]). Apply your solutions approach to each question and your exam strategy to the overall exam.

         You should limit yourself to the time you will have when taking the actual CPA exam section (3 hours for the Regulation section). Spend time afterwards grading your work and reviewing your effort.

         Time estimate: To take the exam and review it later, approximately 4 hours.

5.   The total suggested time of 68 hours is only an average. Allocation of time will vary candidate by candidate. Time requirements vary due to the diverse backgrounds and abilities of CPA candidates. Allocate your time so you gain the most proficiency in the least time. Remember that while 68 hours will be required, you should break the overall project down into 17 more manageable tasks. Do not study more than one module during each study session.

Using Notecards

Below are one candidate's notecards on business law topics which illustrate how key definitions, lists, etc., can be summarized on index cards for quick review. Since candidates can take these anywhere they go, they are a very efficient review tool.

<table>
<tr>
<td valign="top">

1) Consideration of <u>Land</u> (i.e., mortgages, leases)
2) Agreements > <u>1 year</u> (From "date" of agreement)
3) Answer for <u>Debt of another</u>
4) Consideration of <u>Marriage</u>
5) Sale of goods > $500
    NOTE: a) Any form will do
              b) Can be in more than one document
              c) Writing need not occur at time of contract

</td>
<td valign="top">

<u>Negotiable Instruments → Requirement of Negotiability</u>

1) Must be in writing (written)
2) Must be signed by person who is ordering payment (signed)
3) Promise (note) or order (draft) to pay (promise or order)
4) Must be unconditional
5) State a specific amount of money (sum certain)
6) Contain no other promises or orders
7) Be payable on demand or at a definite time
8) Be payable "To Order" or "Bearer"

</td>
</tr>
</table>

Prepared by Maureen McBeth, Northern Illinois University CPA Law Faculty member

Level of Proficiency Required

What level of proficiency must you develop with respect to each of the topics to pass the exam? You should work toward a minimum correct rate on the multiple-choice questions of 80%. Working toward a correct rate of 80% or higher will give you a margin.

    Warning: Disproportional study time devoted to multiple-choice (relative to task-based simulations) can be disastrous on the exam. You should work a substantial number of simulation problems under exam conditions, even though multiple-choice questions are easier to work and are used to gauge your proficiency. The authors believe that practicing simulation problems will also improve your proficiency on the multiple-choice questions.

Multiple-Choice Feedback

One of the benefits of working through previous exam questions is that it helps you to identify your weak areas. Once you have graded your answers, your strong areas and weak areas should be clearly evident. Yet, the important point here is that you should not stop at a simple percentage evaluation. The percentage only provides general feedback about your knowledge of the material contained within that particular module. The percentage **does not** give you any specific feedback regarding the concepts which were tested. In order to get this feedback, you should look at the questions missed on an individual basis because this will help you gain a better understanding of **why** you missed the question.

    This feedback process has been facilitated by the fact that within each module where the multiple-choice answer key appears, two blank lines have been inserted next to the multiple-choice answers. As you grade the multiple-choice questions, mark those questions which you have missed. However, instead of just marking the questions right and wrong, you should now focus on marking the questions in a manner which identifies **why** you missed the question. As an example, a candidate could mark the questions in the following manner: ✓ for math mistakes, x for conceptual mistakes, and ? for areas which the candidate was unfamiliar with. The candidate should then correct these mistakes by reworking through the marked questions.

The objective of this marking technique is to help you identify your weak areas and thus, the concepts which you should be focusing on. While it is still important for you to get between 75% and 80% correct when working multiple-choice questions, it is more important for you to understand the concepts. This understanding applies to both the questions answered correctly and those answered incorrectly. Remember, questions on the CPA exam will be different from the questions in the book; however, the concepts will be the same. Therefore, your preparation should focus on understanding concepts, not just getting the correct answer.

Conditional Candidates

If you have received conditional status on the examination, you must concentrate on the remaining section(s). Unfortunately, many candidates do not study after conditioning the exam, relying on luck to get them through the remaining section(s). Conditional candidates will find that material contained in Chapters 1–5 and the information contained in the appropriate modules will benefit them in preparing for the remaining section(s) of the examination.

PLANNING FOR THE EXAMINATION

Overall Strategy

An overriding concern should be an orderly, systematic approach toward both your preparation program and your examination strategy. A major objective should be to avoid any surprises or anything else that would rattle you during the examination. In other words, you want to be in complete control as much as possible. Control is of paramount importance from both positive and negative viewpoints. The presence of control on your part will add to your confidence and your ability to prepare for and take the exam. Moreover, the presence of control will make your preparation program more enjoyable (or at least less distasteful). However, a lack of organization will result in inefficiency in preparing for and taking the examination, with a highly predictable outcome. Likewise, distractions during the examination (e.g., inadequate lodging, long drive) are generally disastrous.

In summary, establishing a systematic, orderly approach to taking the examination is of paramount importance.

1. Develop an overall strategy at the beginning of your preparation program (see below)
2. Supplement your overall strategy with outlines of material tested on the Regulation exam
3. Supplement your overall strategy with an explicitly stated set of question-and problem solving-procedures—the solutions approach
4. Supplement your overall strategy with an explicitly stated approach to each examination session (see Chapter 4)
5. Evaluate your preparation progress on a regular basis and prepare lists of things "to do" (see Weekly Review of Preparation Program Progress on following page)
6. RELAX: You can pass the exam. About 40 to 45% of the candidates taking a section of the CPA examination pass. But if you take out the individuals that did not adequately prepare, these percentages increase substantially. You will be one of those who pass if you complete an efficient preparation program and execute well (i.e., solutions approach and exam strategy) while taking the exam.

The following outline is designed to provide you with a general framework of the tasks before you. You should tailor the outline to your needs by adding specific items and comments.

A. **Preparation Program (refer to Self-Study Program discussed previously)**

1. Obtain and organize study materials
2. Locate facilities conducive for studying and block out study time
3. Develop your solutions approach (including solving task-based simulations as well as multiple-choice questions)
4. Prepare an examination strategy
5. Study the material tested recently and prepare answers to actual exam questions on these topics under examination conditions
6. Periodically evaluate your progress

B. **Physical Arrangements**

1. Apply to and obtain acceptance from your State Board
2. Schedule your test location and time

C. **Taking the Examination (covered in detail in Chapter 4)**

1. Become familiar with location of the test center and procedures
2. Implement examination strategies and the solutions approach

Weekly Review of Preparation Program Progress

The following pages contain a hypothetical weekly review of program progress. You should prepare a similar progress chart. This procedure, taking only 5 minutes per week, will help you proceed through a more efficient, complete preparation program.

Make notes of materials and topics

1. That you have studied
2. That you have completed
3. That need additional study

Weeks to go	Comments on progress, "to do" items, etc.
8	1) Read RESP, FEDE → made notecards 2) Worked some MC Questions and Simulation Problems
7	1) Read CONT and SALES → made notecards 2) Worked some MC Questions and Simulation Problems in these areas
6	1) Read NEG and SECU → made notecards 2) Worked some MC Questions and Simulation Problems in these areas 3) Reviewed remedies for breach
5	1) Read BANK, DBCR, AGEN → made notecards 2) Worked some MC Questions and Simulation Problems in these areas 3) Reviewed firm offer examples and battle of forms
4	1) Read RBUS, PROP → made notecards 2) Worked some MC Questions and Simulation Problems in these areas
3	1) Read ITAX, PTAX → made notecards 2) Worked some MC Questions and Simulation Problems in these areas
2	1) Read CTAX, GETX → made notecards 2) Worked some MC Questions and Simulation Problems in these areas
1	1) Worked Complete task-based simulations in Appendices B and C 2) Reviewed weak modules
0	1) Took sample exam in Regulation 2) Reviewed exam policies and procedures 3) Reviewed notecards

Time Management of Your Preparation

As you begin your CPA exam preparation, you obviously realize that there is a large amount of material to cover over the course of the next two to three months. Therefore, it is very important for you to organize your calendar, and maybe even your daily routine, so that you can allocate sufficient time to studying. An organized approach to your preparation is much more effective than a last week cram session. An organized approach also builds up the confidence necessary to succeed on the CPA exam.

An approach which we have already suggested is to develop weekly "to do" lists. This technique helps you to establish intermediate objectives and goals as you progress through your study plan. You can then focus your efforts on small tasks and not feel overwhelmed by the entire process. And as you accomplish these tasks you will see yourself moving one step closer to realizing the overall goal, succeeding on the CPA exam.

Note, however, that the underlying assumption of this approach is that you have found the time during the week to study and thus accomplish the different tasks. Although this is an obvious step, it is still a very important step. Your exam preparation should be of a continuous nature and not one that jumps around the calendar. Therefore, you should strive to find available study time within your daily schedule, which can be utilized on a consistent basis. For example, everyone has certain hours of the day which are already committed for activities such as jobs, classes, and, of course, sleep. There is also going to be the time you spend relaxing because CPA candidates should try to maintain some balance in their lives. Sometimes too much studying can be counterproductive. But there will be some time available to you for studying and working through the questions. Block off this available time and use it only for exam prep. Use the time to accomplish your weekly tasks and to keep yourself committed to the process. After a while your preparation will develop into a habit and the preparation will not seem as overwhelming as it once did.

NOW IS THE TIME TO MAKE YOUR COMMITMENT

Chapter 2: Examination Grading

All State Boards of Accountancy use the AICPA advisory grading service. As your grade is to be determined by this process, it is very important that you understand the AICPA grading process and its **implications for your preparation program and for the solution techniques you will use during the examination**.

The AICPA has a full-time staff of CPA examination personnel under the supervision of the AICPA Board of Examiners, which has responsibility for the CPA examination.

This chapter contains a description of the AICPA grading process including a determination of the passing standard.

Setting the Passing Standard of the Uniform CPA Examination

As a part of the development of any licensing process, the passing score on the licensing examination must be established. This passing score must be set to distinguish candidates who are qualified to practice from those who are not. After conducting a number of studies of methods to determine passing scores, the Board of Examiners decided to use candidate-centered methods to set passing scores for the computer-based Uniform CPA Examination. In candidate-centered methods, the focus is on looking at actual candidate answers and making judgments about which sets of answers represent the answers of qualified entry-level CPAs. To make these determinations, the AICPA convened panels of CPAs to examine candidate responses and set the passing scores for multiple-choice questions and simulations. The data from these panels provide the basis for the development of question and problem points (relative weightings). **As with the previous pencil-and-paper exam, a passing score on the computer-based examination is 75%.**

Grading the Examination

All of the responses on the Regulation section of the computer-based CPA examination are objective in nature. Obviously, this includes the responses to the multiple-choice questions. However, it also includes the responses to the requirements of simulations. Requirements of simulations include responses involving check boxes, entries into spreadsheets, form completion, graphical responses, and drag and drop. All of these responses are computer graded. Therefore, no consideration is given to any comments or explanations outside of the structured responses.

Multiple-Choice Grading

Regulation exams contain three multiple-choice testlets of 24 questions each. **A few of these questions will be pretest questions that will not be considered in the candidate's score, but there is no way of identifying those questions.** Also, the possible score on a question and on a testlet will vary based on the difficulty of the questions. The makeup of the second testlet provided to a candidate will be determined based upon the candidate's performance on the first testlet, and the makeup of the third testlet will be determined by the candidate's performance on the first two testlets. Therefore, you should not be discouraged if you a get a difficult set of questions; it may merely mean that you performed very well on the previous testlet(s). Also, you will receive more raw points for hard and medium questions than for easy questions.

Your answers to the multiple-choice questions are graded by the computer. Your grade is based on the total number of correct answers weighted by their difficulty, and with no penalty for incorrect answers. As mentioned earlier, four of the multiple-choice questions are pretest items that are not included in the candidate's grade.

Task-Based Simulation Grading

As indicated previously, the responses to the simulations are also computer graded. They will typically involve checking a box, selecting a response from a list, or dragging and dropping an answer.

As with the multiple-choice questions, a small percentage of the simulations will be pretest items that will not be included in the candidate's grade.

Chapter 3 will provide detailed suggestions on ways that you may use the information about grading to maximize your score.

Requesting a Score Review

For an additional fee, you may request a score review. A score review is a verification of your score making certain that the approved answer key was used. Because the AICPA grades your exam at least twice as a part of its normal process, it is unlikely that you will get an adjustment to your score. You should contact the applicable board of accountancy to request a score review.

NOW IS THE TIME TO MAKE YOUR COMMITMENT

Chapter 3: The Solutions Approach

The **solutions approach** is a systematic problem-solving methodology. The purpose is to assure efficient, complete solutions to CPA exam questions, some of which are complex and confusing relative to most undergraduate accounting problems. This is especially true with regard to the new simulation type problems. Unfortunately, there appears to be a widespread lack of emphasis on problem-solving techniques in accounting courses. Most accounting books and courses merely provide solutions to specific types of problems. Memorization of these solutions for examinations and preparation of homework problems from examples is "cookbooking." "Cookbooking" is perhaps a necessary step in the learning process, but it is certainly not sufficient training for the complexities of the business world. Professional accountants need to be adaptive to a rapidly changing complex environment. For example, CPAs have been called on to interpret and issue reports on new concepts such as price controls, energy allocations, and new taxes. These CPAs rely on their problem-solving expertise to understand these problems and to formulate solutions to them.

The steps outlined below are only one of many possible series of solution steps. Admittedly, the procedures suggested are **very** structured; thus, you should adapt the suggestions to your needs. You may find that some steps are occasionally unnecessary, or that certain additional procedures increase your own problem-solving efficiency. Whatever the case, substantial time should be allocated to developing an efficient solutions approach before taking the examination. You should develop your solutions approach by working previous CPA questions and problems.

Note that the steps below relate to any specific question or problem; overall examination or section strategies are discussed in Chapter 4.

Multiple-Choice Screen Layout

The following is a computer screenshot that illustrates the manner in which multiple-choice questions will be presented:

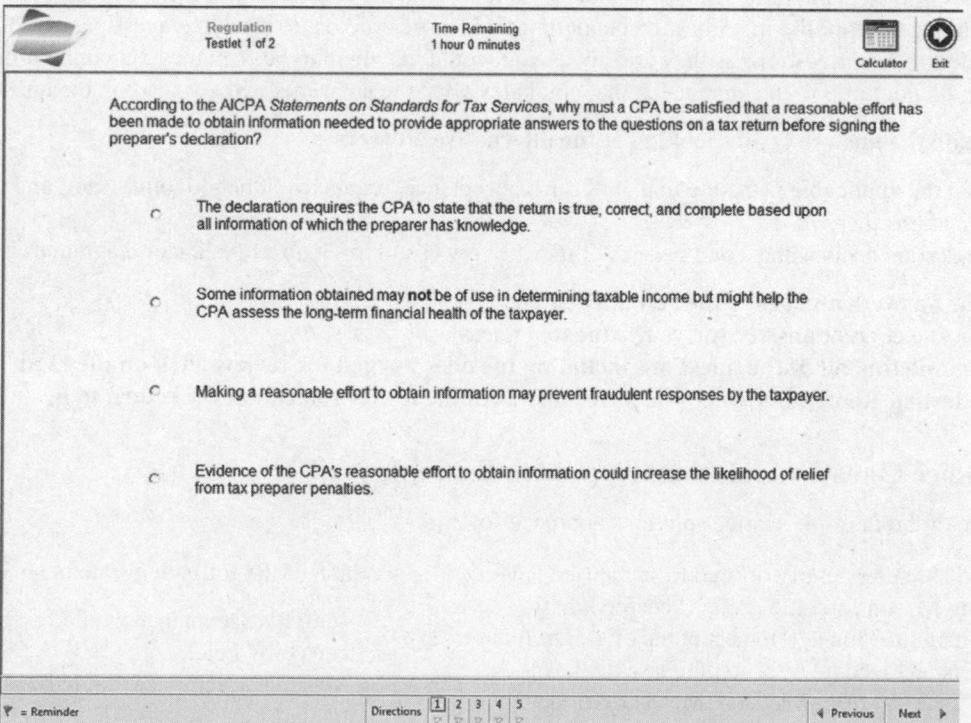

As indicated previously, multiple-choice questions will be presented in three individual testlets of 24 questions each. Characteristics of the computerized testlets of multiple-choice questions include the following:

1. You may move freely within a particular testlet from one question to the next or back to previous questions until you quit the testlet by clicking the "Exit" button. Once you have exited a testlet, you can never return to that set of questions.

2. A button on the screen will allow you to "flag" a question for review if you wish to come back to it later.
3. A four-function computer calculator with an electronic tape is available as a tool.
4. The time remaining for the entire exam section is shown on the screen.
5. The questions will be shown at the bottom of the screen. You may navigate between questions by simply clicking on the question number.
6. The "Help" button will provide you with help in navigating and completing the testlet.

The screenshot above was obtained from the AICPA's sample examinations at www.cpa-exam.org. Candidates are urged to complete the tutorial and other example questions on the AICPA's website to obtain additional experience with the computer-based testing.

Multiple-Choice Question Solutions Approach

1. **Work individual questions in order.**

   a. If a question appears lengthy or difficult, skip it until you can determine that extra time is available. Mark it for review to remind you to return to a question that you have skipped or need to review.

2. **Read the stem of the question without looking at the answers.**

   a. The answers are sometimes misleading and may cause you to misread or misinterpret the question.

3. **Read each question *carefully* to determine the topical area.**

   a. Study the requirements **first** so you know which data are important.
   b. Note keywords and important data.
   c. Identify pertinent information.
   d. Be especially careful to note when the requirement is an **exception** (e.g., "Which of the following is **not** an effective disclaimer of the implied warranty of merchantability?").
   e. If a set of data is the basis for two or more questions, read the requirements of each of the questions first before beginning to work the first question (sometimes it is more efficient to work the questions out of order).
   f. Be alert to read questions as they are, not as you would like them to be. You may encounter a familiar looking item; do not jump to the conclusion that you know what the answer is without reading the question completely.

4. **Anticipate the answer before looking at the alternative answers.**

   a. Recall the applicable principle (e.g., offer and acceptance, requisites of negotiability, etc.) and the respective applications thereof.
   b. If a question deals with a complex area, it may be very useful to set up a timeline or diagram using abbreviations.

5. **Read the answers and select the *best* alternative.**
6. **Click on the correct answer (or your educated guess).**
7. **After completing all of the questions including the ones flagged for review click on the "Exit" button to close out the testlet. Remember, once you have closed out the testlet you can never return to it.**

Multiple-Choice Question Solutions Approach Example

A good example of the multiple-choice solutions approach follows.

13. On June 15, Peters orally offered to sell a used lawn mower to Mason for $125. Peters specified that Mason had until June 20 to accept the offer. On June 16, Peters received an offer to purchase the lawn mower for $150 from Bronson, Mason's neighbor. Peters accepted Bronson's offer. On June 17, Mason saw Bronson using the lawn mower and was told the mower had been sold to Bronson. Mason immediately wrote to Peters to accept the June 15 offer.

Which of the following statements is correct?

a. Mason's acceptance would be effective when received by Peters.
b. Mason's acceptance would be effective when mailed.
c. Peters' offer had been revoked and Mason's acceptance was ineffective.
d. Peters was obligated to keep the June 15 offer open until June 20.

Step 3:

Topical area? Contracts—Revocation and Attempted Acceptance

Step 4:

Principle? An offer may be revoked at any time prior to acceptance and is effective when received by offeree

Step 5:

a. Incorrect — Mason's acceptance was ineffective because the offer had been revoked prior to Mason's acceptance.
b. Incorrect — Same as a.
c. Correct — Peters' offer was effectively revoked when Mason learned that the lawn mower had been sold to Bronson.
d. Incorrect — Peters was not obligated to keep the offer open because no consideration had been paid by Mason. Note that if consideration had been given, an option contract would have been formed and the offer would have been irrevocable before June 20.

Currently, all multiple-choice questions are scored based on the number correct, weighted by a difficulty rating (i.e., there is no penalty for guessing). The rationale is that a "good guess" indicates knowledge. Thus, you should answer all multiple-choice questions.

Task-Based Simulations

Task-based simulations are short case-based problems designed to

- Test integrated knowledge
- More closely replicate real-world problems
- Assess research and other skills

Any of the following types of responses might be required on task-based simulations:

- Multiple selection
- Drop-down selection
- Numeric and monetary inputs
- Formula answers
- Check box response
- Enter spreadsheet formulas
- Research results

The screenshot below illustrates a simulation that requires the candidate to make a selection from a drop list.

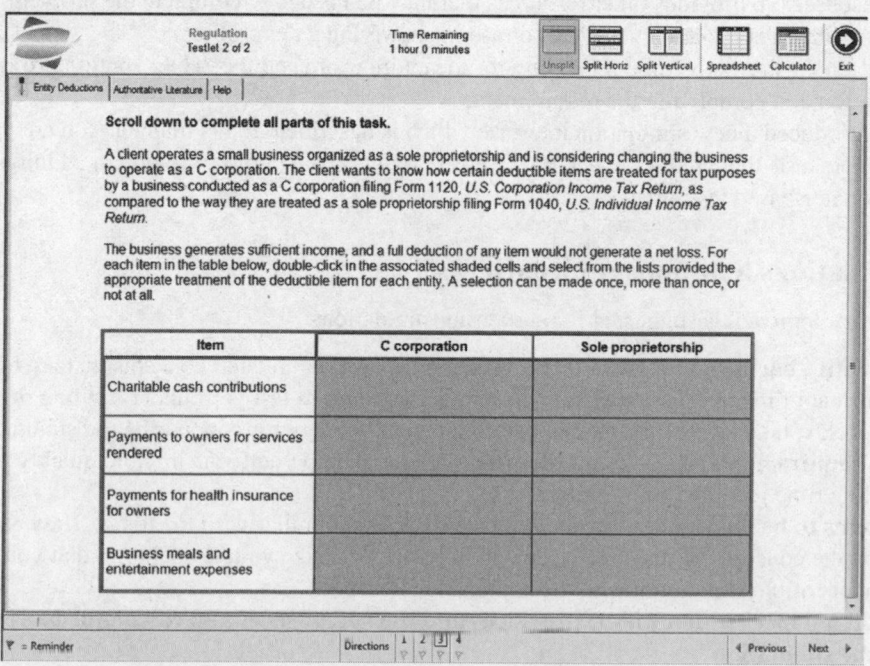

The screenshot below illustrates a requirement to complete a tax form.

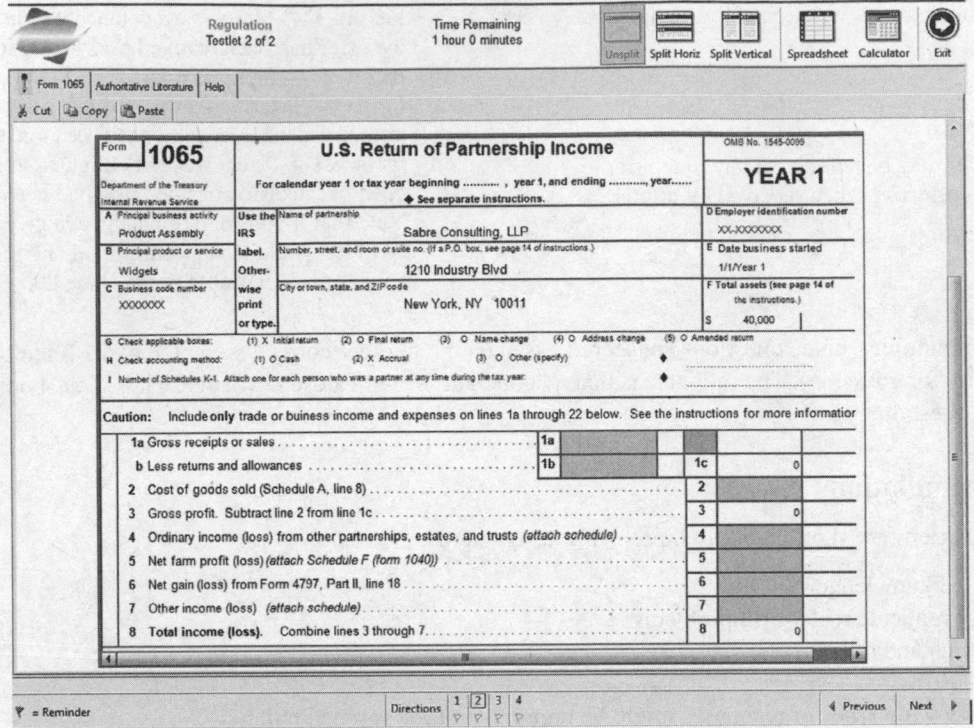

To complete the simulations, candidates are provided with a number of tools, including

- A four-function computer calculator with an electronic tape
- Scratch spreadsheet
- The ability to split windows horizontally and vertically to show two tabs on the screen (e.g., you can examine the situation tab in one window and a particular requirement in a second window)
- Access to professional literature databases to answer research requirements
- Copy and paste functions

In addition, the resource tab provides other resources that may be needed to complete the problem. For example, a resource tab might contain a depreciation schedule for use in answering a tax problem.

A window on the screen shows the time remaining for the entire exam and the "Help" button provides instructions for navigating the simulation and completing the requirements.

The AICPA has introduced a new simulation interface which is described in this manual. You are urged to complete the tutorial and other sample tests that are on the AICPA's website (www.cpa-exam.org) to obtain additional experience with the interface and computer-based testing.

Task-Based Simulations Solutions Approach

The following solutions approach is suggested for answering simulations:

1. **Review the entire background.** Get a feel for the topical area and related concepts that are being tested. Even though the format of the question may vary, the exam continues to test your understanding of applicable principles or concepts. Relax, take a deep breath, and determine your strategy for conquering the simulation.
2. **Identify the requirements of the simulation.** This step will help you focus in more quickly on the solution(s) without wasting time reading irrelevant material.
3. **Study the items to be answered.** As you do this and become familiar with the topical area being tested, you should review the concepts of that area. This will help you organize your thoughts so that you can relate logically the requirements of the simulation with the applicable concepts.
4. **Use the scratch paper (which will be provided) and the spreadsheet and calculator tools to assist you in answering the simulation.**

The screenshots below explain how the spreadsheet operates. Notice that mathematical operations can be input directly into a cell. A mathematical operation must be entered using a function in one of the two ways shown.

Figure 4

Figure 5

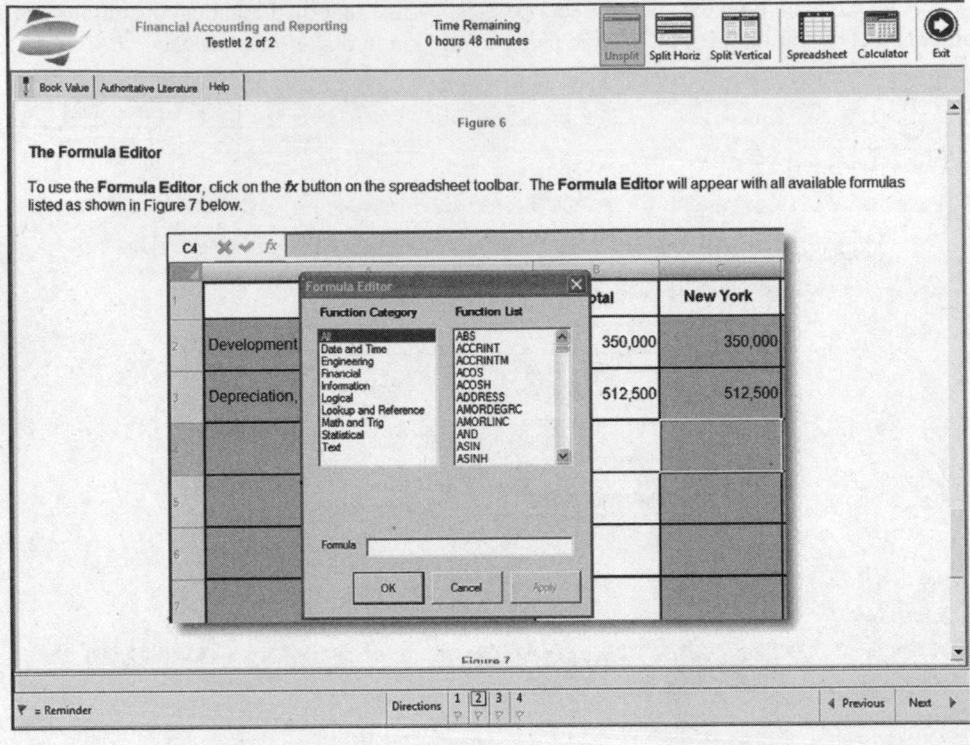

Figure 6

The Formula Editor

To use the **Formula Editor**, click on the *fx* button on the spreadsheet toolbar. The **Formula Editor** will appear with all available formulas listed as shown in Figure 7 below.

Figure 7

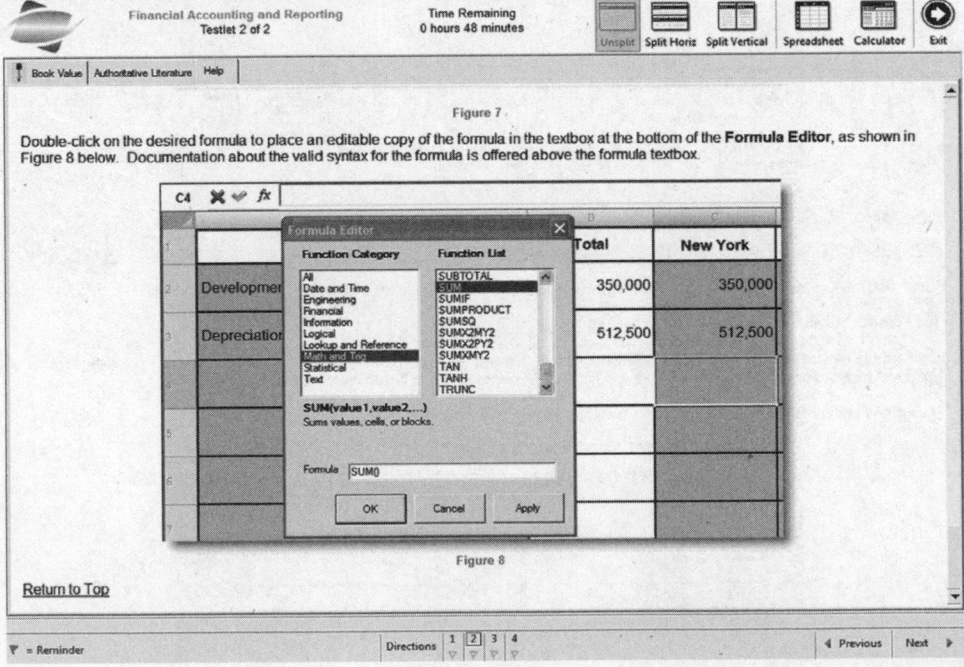

Figure 7

Double-click on the desired formula to place an editable copy of the formula in the textbox at the bottom of the **Formula Editor**, as shown in Figure 8 below. Documentation about the valid syntax for the formula is offered above the formula textbox.

Figure 8

Return to Top

Research Simulations

One simulation on the Regulation section will be a research simulation. Research simulations require candidates to search the professional literature in electronic format and interpret the results. In the Regulation section the professional literature database includes

- Internal Revenue Code and Income Tax Regulations (IRC)
- Statements on Responsibilities in Tax Practice (TS)

Shown below is a screenshot of a task-based research simulation for the Regulation section of the CPA examination.

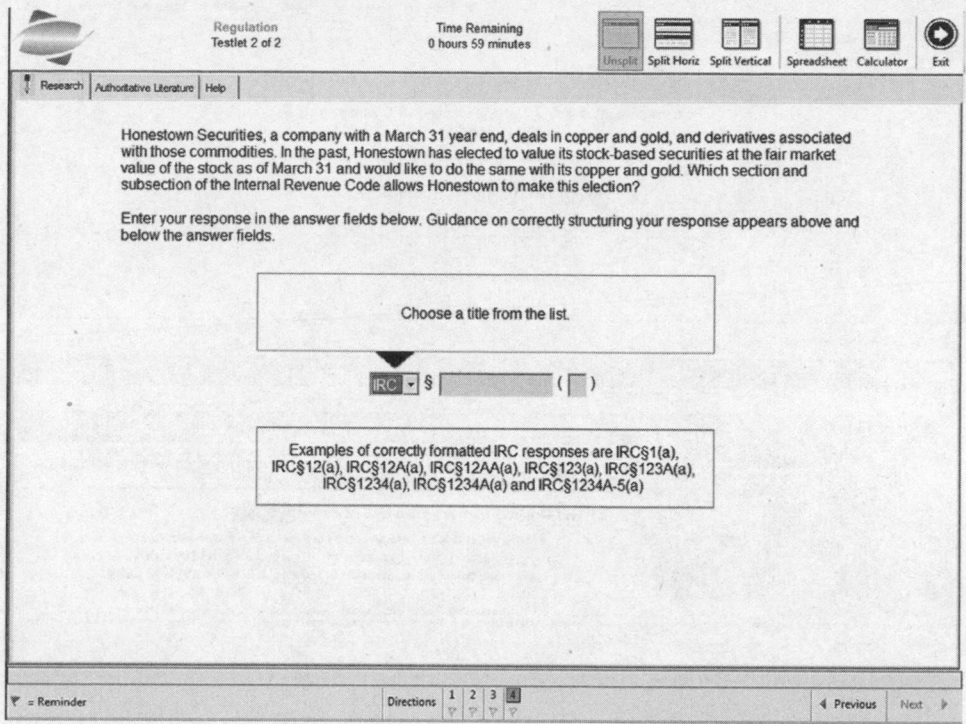

The literature may be searched using the table of contents or a keyword search. Therefore, knowing important code sections may speed up your search. If you use the search function, you must spell the term or terms correctly.

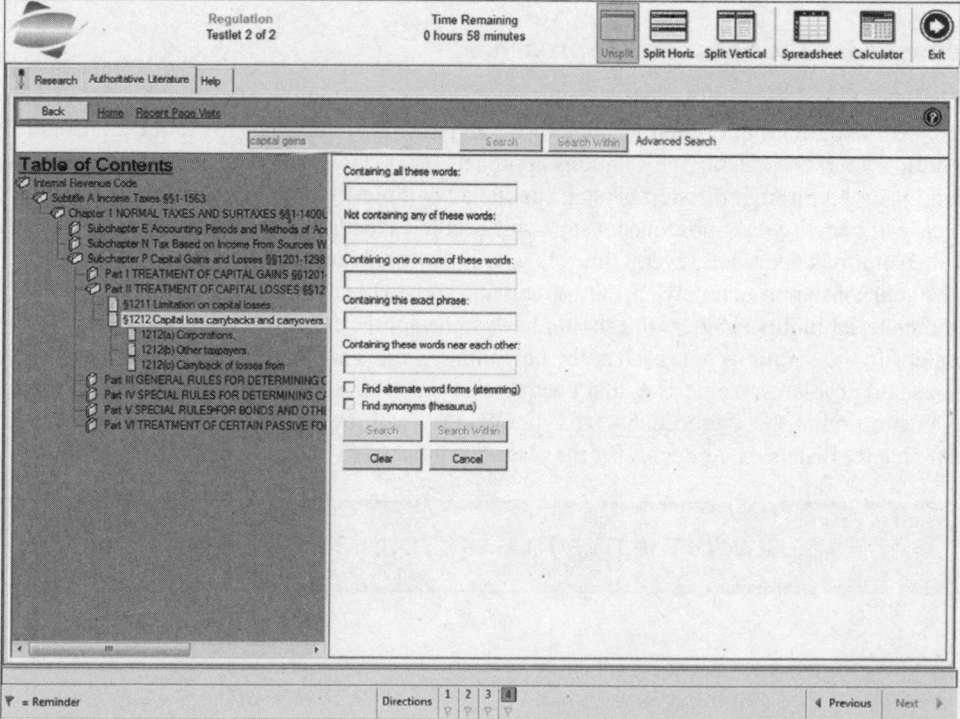

Once you have found the correct passage in the literature, you must input the citation in the answer box. To facilitate this process you should use the split screen function to view the literature in one screen and the answer box in the other as shown below.

If possible, it is important to get experience using the electronic version of the Internal Revenue Code to sharpen your skills. If that is not available, you should use the printed copy of the professional standards to answer the simulation problems in the manual.

Chapter 5 of this manual contains guidance on how to perform research on the Internal Revenue Code.

Time Requirements for the Solutions Approach

Many candidates bypass the solutions approach, because they feel it is too time-consuming. Actually, the solutions approach is a time-saver and, more importantly, it helps you prepare better solutions to all questions and simulations.

Without committing yourself to using the solutions approach, try it step-by-step on several questions and simulations. After you conscientiously go through the step-by-step routine a few times, you will begin to adopt and modify aspects of the technique which will benefit you. Subsequent usage will become subconscious and painless. The important point is that you must try the solutions approach several times to accrue any benefits.

In summary, the solutions approach may appear foreign and somewhat cumbersome. At the same time, if you have worked through the material in this chapter, you should have some appreciation for it. Develop the solutions approach by writing down the steps in the solutions approach at the beginning of this chapter, and keep them before you as you work CPA exam questions and problems. Remember that even though the suggested procedures appear **very structured** and **time-consuming,** integration of these procedures into your own style of problem solving will help improve **your** solutions approach. The next chapter discusses strategies for the overall examination.

NOW IS THE TIME TO MAKE YOUR COMMITMENT

Chapter 4: Taking the Examination

This chapter is concerned with developing an examination strategy (e.g., how to cope with the environment at the test center, time management, etc.).

EXAMINATION STRATEGIES

Your performance during the examination is final and not subject to revision. While you may sit for the examination again if you are unsuccessful, the majority of your preparation will have to be repeated, requiring substantial, additional amounts of time. Thus, examination strategies (discussed in this chapter) that maximize your exam-taking efficiency are very important.

Getting "Psyched Up"

The CPA exam is quite challenging and worthy of your best effort. Explicitly develop your own psychological strategy to get yourself "up" for the exam. Pace your study program such that you will be able to operate at peak performance when you are actually taking the exam. A significant advantage of the computerized exam is that if you have scheduled early in a testing window and do not feel well, you can reschedule your sitting. However, once you start the exam, you cannot retake it in the same testing window, so do not leave the exam early. Do the best you can.

Lodging, Meals, Exercise

If you must travel to the test center, make advance reservations for comfortable lodging convenient to the test center. Do not stay with friends, relatives, etc. Both uninterrupted sleep and total concentration on the exam are a must. Consider the following in making your lodging plans:

1. Proximity to the test center
2. Availability of meals and snacks
3. Recreational facilities

Plan your meal schedule to provide maximum energy and alertness during the day and maximum rest at night. Do not experiment with new foods, drinks, etc., around your scheduled date. Within reasonable limits, observe your normal eating and drinking habits. Recognize that overconsumption of coffee during the exam could lead to a hyperactive state and disaster. Likewise, overindulgence in alcohol to overcome nervousness and to induce sleep the night before might contribute to other difficulties the following morning.

Tenseness should be expected before and during the examination. Rely on a regular exercise program to unwind at the end of the day. As you select your lodging for the examination, try to accommodate your exercise pleasure (e.g., running, swimming etc.).

To relieve tension or stress while studying, try breathing or stretching exercises. Use these exercises before and during the examination to start and to keep your adrenaline flowing. Remain determined not to have to sit for the section another time.

In summary, the examination is likely to be both rigorous and fatiguing. Expect it and prepare for it by getting in shape, planning methods of relaxation during the exam and in the evening before, and finally, building the confidence and competence to complete the exam (successfully).

Test Center and Procedures

If possible, visit the test center before the examination to assure knowledge of the location. Remember: no surprises. Having a general familiarity with the facilities will lessen anxiety prior to the examination. Talking to a recent veteran of the examination will give you background for the general examination procedures. **You must arrive at the testing center 30 minutes before your scheduled time.**

Upon completion of check-in at the test location, the candidate

- Is seated at a designated workstation
- Begins the exam after proctor launches the session

- Is monitored by a Test Center Administrator
- Is videotaped

If you have any remaining questions regarding examination procedure, call or write your state board or go to Prometric's website at www.prometric.com/cpa.

Allocation of Time

Budget your time. Time should be carefully allocated in an attempt to maximize points per minute. While you must develop your own strategy with respect to time allocation, some suggestions may be useful. Allocate 5 minutes to reading the instructions. When you begin the exam you will be given an inventory of the total number of testlets, including the suggested times. Budget your time based on this inventory.

Plan on spending 1½ minutes working each of the individual multiple-choice questions. Plan on spending about 1¼ to 1½ hours on the simulation testlet.

Techniques for Time Management

The Regulation exam has three testlets of multiple-choice questions with 24 questions each. As you complete each testlet keep track of how you performed in relation to the AICPA suggested time. The Regulation section will also have a testlet containing six task-based simulations. After you finish the multiple-choice testlets, budget your time for the simulations testlet based on your remaining time and the AICPA suggested times. Remember that you alone control watching your progress towards successfully completing this exam.

Examination Rules

1. Prior to the start of the examination, you will be required to accept a *Confidentiality and Break Policy Statement.*
2. You must not bring any personal/unauthorized items into the testing room. Such items include but are not limited to outerwear, hats, food, drinks, purses, briefcases, notebooks, pagers, watches, cellular telephones, recording devices, and photographic equipment. You will be asked to empty and turn your pockets inside out prior to every entry into the test room to confirm that you have no prohibited items. Lockers are provided for storage of personal items.
3. Breaks may be taken at any time between testlets. **However, your exam time continues to run while you take the break.**
4. If you need access to an item stored in the test center during a break such as food or medicine, you must inform the Test Center Administrator before you retrieve the item. You are not allowed to access a prohibited item.
5. Any reference during the examination to books or other materials or the exchange of information with other persons shall be considered misconduct sufficient to bar you from further participation in the examination.
6. Penalties will be imposed on any candidate who is caught cheating before, during, or after the examination. These penalties may include expulsion from the examination, denial of applications for future examinations, and civil or criminal penalties.
7. You may not leave the examination room with any notes about the examination.

Refer to the *CPA Candidate Bulletin* for other rules.

CPA EXAM CHECKLIST

One week before you are scheduled to sit

___ 1. Review law and taxation notecards, and other law and taxation notes for important terms, lists, and key phrases.

___ 2. If time permits, work through a few questions in your weakest areas so that the applicable principles and concepts are fresh in your mind.

___ 3. Assemble materials listed under 1. above into a "last review" notebook to be taken with you to the exam.

What to bring

___ 1. *Notice to Schedule (NTS)*—You must bring the proper NTS with you.

___ 2. *Identification*—Bring two valid forms of ID. One must be government issued. The name on the ID must match exactly the name on the NTS. The *CPA Candidate Bulletin* lists valid primary and secondary IDs.

___ 3. *Hotel confirmation*—(if you must travel).

___ 4. *Cash*—Payment for anything by personal check is rarely accepted.

___ 5. *Major credit card*—American Express, Master-Card, Visa, etc.

___ 6. *Alarm clock*—This is too important an event to trust to a hotel wake-up call that might be overlooked.

___ 7. *Clothing*—Should be comfortable and layered to suit the possible temperature range in the testing room.

___ 8. *Earplugs*—Even though examinations are being given, there may be constant activity in the testing room (e.g., people walking around, rustling of paper, clicking of keyboards, people coughing, etc.). The use of earplugs may block out some of this distraction and help you concentrate better.

___ 9. *Other*—Any "Last review" materials.

Evening before exam

1. Reviewing the evening before the exam could earn you the extra points needed to pass a section. Just keep this last-minute effort in perspective and do **not** panic yourself into staying up all night trying to cover every possible point. This could lead to disaster by sapping your body of the endurance needed to attack questions creatively during the next day.

2. Reread key outlines or notecards for Regulation the evening before, reviewing important terms, key phrases, and lists (i.e., essential elements for a contract, requirements for a holder in due course, computation of taxable income, etc.).

3. Go over mnemonics and acronyms you have developed as study aids. Test yourself by writing out the letters on paper while verbally giving a brief explanation of what the letters stand for.

4. **Set your alarm and get a good night's rest!** Being well rested will permit you to meet each day's challenge with a fresh burst of creative energy. **You must plan to arrive 30 minutes before your scheduled time.**

Exam-taking strategy

1. Review the AICPA suggested times for the testlets to plan your time allocation during the exam.

2. Do not spend an excess amount of time on the introductory screens. If you take longer than 10 minutes on these screens, the test session will automatically terminate. If the exam session terminates, it will not be possible to restart the examination and you will have to reapply to take the section.

3. Report equipment/software issues to the test center staff immediately. Do not attempt to correct the problem yourself and do not use examination time thinking about it before reporting it. Remind the test center staff to file a report describing the problem. The test center staff should be able to handle any equipment or software problems. However, if you believe the problem was not handled appropriately, contact NASBA at candidatecare@nasba.org.

4. Report any concerns about test questions to test center staff after you have completed the session. The members of the test center staff know nothing about the CPA Examination content. The test center staff can report the issues to the AICPA. You should also report concerns about the questions in writing to the AICPA (FAX to [609] 671-2922). If possible, the question and testlet numbers should be included in the FAX.

5. In the event of a power outage or incident requiring a restart, the computer clock will stop and you will not lose examination time. Your responses up to the time of the restart will not be lost as responses are saved at frequent intervals throughout the examination.

6. If you have questions about the examination software functions (e.g., the transfer function), you should read the instructions and "Help" tab information. The test center staff is not familiar with the functioning of the examination software and, therefore, will not be able to help you.

7. The crucial technique to use for multiple-choice questions is to read through each question stem **carefully,** noting keywords such as "oral," "without disclosing," "qualified pension plan," etc. Then **read each choice** carefully before you start eliminating inappropriate answers. Often the first or second answer may **sound** correct, but a later answer may be **more correct.** Be discriminating! Reread the question and choose the **best** answer.

8. If you are struggling with questions beyond a minute or two, use the strategy of dividing multiple-choice questions into two categories.

   a. Questions for which you **know** you lack knowledge to answer: Drawing from any responses you have, narrow answers down to as few as possible, then make an **educated guess**.

   b. Questions for which you feel you should be getting the correct answer: Mark the question for review. Your mental block may clear, or you may spot a simple error in logic that will be corrected when you rereview the question.

9. Remember: **Never** change a first impulse answer later unless you are absolutely certain you are right. It is a proven fact that your subconscious often guides you to the correct answer.

10. Begin the task-based simulations, carefully monitoring your time. Read the information and requirement tabs and organize your thoughts around the concepts, mnemonics, acronyms, and buzzwords that are responsive to the requirements. Constantly compare your progress with the time remaining. Fight the urge to **complete** one simulation at the expense of others.

11. Each test may include a simulation requirement or question for which you may feel unprepared. Accept the challenge and go after the points! Draw from all your resources. Every simulation (no matter how impossible it may look at first glance) contains some points that are yours for the taking. Make your best effort. You may be on the right track and not even know it!

12. Constantly compare your progress with the time remaining. **Never** spend excessive amounts of time on one testlet or simulation.

13. The cardinal rule is **never,** but **never,** leave an answer blank.

After taking the examination

1. Retain the Confirmation of Attendance form issued after the examination because it provides valuable contact information.

2. Report any examination incidents/concerns in writing, even if the issues were already reported to test center staff.

3. If you feel that the circumstances surrounding your test administration prevented you from performing at a level consistent with your knowledge and skills, immediately contact NASBA at candidatecare@nasba.org.

HAVE YOU MADE YOUR COMMITMENT?

Chapter 5: Exam Content Overview

Preparing for the Regulation Exam

Regulation is a section of the exam that includes both business law and taxation topics. **In preparing for the Regulation exam, you should take a systematic approach such as the one detailed in Chapter 1.**

First, in approaching your study, you should become acquainted with the nature of the Regulation exam itself. The content specification outlines are printed below.

Relatedly, you should evaluate your competence by working 10 to 20 multiple-choice questions from each of the modules (23–39). This diagnostic routine will acquaint you with the specific nature of the questions tested on each topic as well as indicate the amount of study required per topic. You should work toward an 80% correct response rate as a minimum on each topic.

Second, study the content of modules 23–39 emphasizing the concepts of each topic such as legal liability of accountants, elements of a contract, and taxable income. You may have to refer to your textbooks, etc., for topics to which you have had no previous exposure.

Third, work the multiple-choice and task-based simulations under examination conditions.

AICPA CONTENT AND SKILLS SPECIFICATIONS

The AICPA Content and Skills Specifications for the Uniform CPA Exam sets forth the coverage of topics on the Regulation exam. This outline was issued by the AICPA and is effective beginning in 2014. The first part of the outline describes the topical coverage of the Regulation exam, and the second part provides some insights into the skills tested on all sections of the Uniform CPA exam.

Content Specification Outlines (CSOs)

The Regulation section tests knowledge and understanding of ethics, professional and legal responsibilities, business law, and federal taxation.

Ethics, Professional and Legal Responsibilities, and Business Law

These topics test knowledge and understanding of professional and legal responsibilities of certified public accountants. Professional ethics questions relate to tax practice issues and are based on the AICPA Code of Professional Conduct, Treasury Department Circular 230, and rules and regulations for tax return preparers. Business law topics test knowledge and understanding of the legal implications of business transactions, particularly as they relate to accounting, auditing, and financial reporting. This section deals with federal and widely adopted uniform state laws or references identified in this CSO.

In addition to demonstrating knowledge and understanding of these topics, candidates are required to demonstrate the skills required to apply that knowledge in performing their responsibilities as certified public accountants. To demonstrate such knowledge and skills, candidates will be expected to perform the following tasks:

- Identify situations that might be unethical or a violation of professional standards, perform research and consultations as appropriate, and determine the appropriate action.
- Recognize potentially unethical behavior of clients and determine the impact on the tax services being performed.
- Demonstrate the importance of identifying and adhering to requirements, rules, and standards that are established by licensing boards within their state, and which may place additional professional requirements specific to their state of practice.
- Apply business law concepts in evaluating the economic substance of client transactions, including purchase agreements, loans and promissory notes, sales contracts, leases, side agreements, commitments, contingencies, and assumption of liabilities.
- Evaluate the legal structure of an entity to determine the implications of applicable laws and regulations on how a business is organized, governed, and operates.

Federal Taxation

These topics test knowledge and understanding of concepts and laws relating to federal taxation (income, gift, and estate). The areas of testing include federal tax process, procedures, accounting, and planning, as well as federal taxation of property transactions, individuals, and entities (which include sole proprietorships, partnerships, limited liability entities, C corporations, S corporations, joint ventures, trusts, estates, and tax-exempt organizations).

In addition to demonstrating knowledge and understanding of these topics, candidates are required to demonstrate the skills required to apply that knowledge in providing tax preparation and advisory services and performing other responsibilities as certified public accountants. To demonstrate such knowledge and skills, candidates will be expected to perform the following tasks:

- Evaluate the tax implications of different legal structures for business entities.
- Apply analytical reasoning tools to assess how taxes affect economic decisions related to the timing of income/expense recognition and property transactions.
- Consider the impact of multijurisdictional tax issues on federal taxes.
- Identify the differences between tax and financial accounting.
- Analyze information and identify data relevant for tax purposes.
- Identify issues, elections, and alternative tax treatments.
- Research issues and alternative tax treatments.
- Formulate conclusions.
- Prepare documentation to support conclusions and tax positions.
- Research relevant professional literature.

The outline below specifies the knowledge in which candidates are required to demonstrate proficiency.

I. Ethics, Professional, and Legal Responsibilities (15%–19%)

    A. Ethics and Responsibilities in Tax Practice

      1. Treasury Department Circular 230
      2. AICPA Statements on Standards for Tax Services
      3. Internal Revenue Code of 1986, as amended, and Regulations related to tax return preparers

    B. Licensing and Disciplinary Systems

      1. Role of state boards of accountancy
      2. Requirements of regulatory agencies

    C. Legal Duties and Responsibilities

      1. Common law duties and liability to clients and third parties
      2. Federal statutory liability
      3. Privileged communications, confidentiality, and privacy acts

II. Business Law (17%–21%)

    A. Agency

      1. Formation and termination
      2. Authority of agents and principals
      3. Duties and liabilities of agents and principals

    B. Contracts

      1. Formation
      2. Performance
      3. Third-party assignments
      4. Discharge, breach, and remedies

    C. Uniform Commercial Code

      1. Sales contracts
      2. Negotiable instruments

      3. Secured transactions
      4. Documents of title and title transfer

    D. Debtor-Creditor Relationships

      1. Rights, duties, and liabilities of debtors, creditors, and guarantors
      2. Bankruptcy and insolvency

    E. Government Regulation of Business

      1. Federal securities regulation
      2. Other federal laws and regulations (antitrust, copyright, patents, money-laundering, labor, employment, and ERISA)

    F. Business Structure (Selection of a Business Entity)

      1. Advantages, disadvantages, implications, and constraints
      2. Formation, operation, and termination
      3. Financial structure, capitalization, profit and loss allocation, and distributions
      4. Rights, duties, legal obligations, and authority of owners and management

III. Federal Tax Process, Procedures, Accounting, and Planning (11%–15%)

    A. Federal Tax Legislative Process
    B. Federal Tax Procedures

      1. Due dates and related extensions of time
      2. Internal Revenue Service (IRS) audit and appeals process
      3. Judicial process
      4. Required disclosure of tax return positions
      5. Substantiation requirements
      6. Penalties
      7. Statute of limitations

C. Accounting Periods
D. Accounting Methods

1. Recognition of revenues and expenses under cash, accrual, or other permitted methods
2. Inventory valuation methods, including uniform capitalization rules
3. Accounting for long-term contracts
4. Installment sales

E. Tax Return Elections, Including Federal Status Elections, Alternative Treatment Elections, or Other Types of Elections Applicable to an Individual or Entity's Tax Return
F. Tax Planning

1. Alternative treatments
2. Projections of tax consequences
3. Implications of different business entities
4. Impact of proposed tax audit adjustments
5. Impact of estimated tax payment rules on planning
6. Role of taxes in decision making

G. Impact of Multijurisdictional Tax Issues on Federal Taxation (Including Consideration of Local, State, and Multinational Tax Issues)
H. Tax Research and Communication

1. Authoritative hierarchy
2. Communications with or on behalf of clients

IV. Federal Taxation of Property Transactions (12%–16%)

A. Types of Assets
B. Basis and Holding Periods of Assets
C. Cost Recovery (Depreciation, Depletion, and Amortization)
D. Taxable and Nontaxable Sales and Exchanges
E. Amount and Character of Gains and Losses, and Netting Process
F. Related Party Transactions
G. Estate and Gift Taxation

1. Transfers subject to the gift tax
2. Annual exclusion and gift tax deductions
3. Determination of taxable estate
4. Marital deduction
5. Unified credit

V. Federal Taxation of Individuals (13%–19%)

A. Gross Income

1. Inclusions and exclusions
2. Characterization of income

B. Reporting of Items from Pass-Through Entities
C. Adjustments and Deductions to Arrive at Taxable Income
D. Passive Activity Losses
E. Loss Limitations
F. Taxation of Retirement Plan Benefits
G. Filing Status and Exemptions

H. Tax Computations and Credits
I. Alternative Minimum Tax

VI. Federal Taxation of Entities (18%–24%)

A. Similarities and Distinctions in Tax Treatment among Business Entities

1. Formation
2. Operation
3. Distributions
4. Liquidation

B. Differences between Tax and Financial Accounting

1. Reconciliation of book income to taxable income
2. Disclosures under Schedule M-3

C. C Corporations

1. Determination of taxable income/loss
2. Tax computations and credits, including alternative minimum tax
3. Net operating losses
4. Entity/owner transactions, including contributions and distributions
5. Earnings and profits
6. Consolidated returns

D. S Corporations

1. Eligibility and election
2. Determination of ordinary income/loss and separately stated items
3. Basis of shareholder's interest
4. Entity/owner transactions, including contributions and distributions
5. Built-in gains tax

E. Partnerships

1. Determination of ordinary income/loss and separately stated items
2. Basis of partner's/member's interest and basis of assets contributed to the partnership
3. Partnership and partner elections
4. Transactions between a partner and the partnership
5. Treatment of partnership liabilities
6. Distribution of partnership assets
7. Ownership changes and liquidation and termination of partnership

F. Trusts and Estates

1. Types of trusts
2. Income and deductions
3. Determination of beneficiary's share of taxable income

G. Tax-Exempt Organizations

1. Types of organizations
2. Obtaining and maintaining tax-exempt status
3. Unrelated business income

References—Regulation

Ethics, Professional and Legal Responsibilities, and Business Law

- AICPA Statements on Standards for Tax Services
- Revised Model Business Corporation Act
- Revised Uniform Limited Partnership Act
- Revised Uniform Partnership Act
- Securities Act of 1933
- Securities Exchange Act of 1934
- Sarbanes-Oxley Act of 2002
- Uniform Accountancy Act
- Uniform Commercial Code
- Current textbooks covering business law, auditing, accounting, and ethics

Federal Taxation

- Internal Revenue Code of 1986, as amended, and Regulations
- Treasury Department Circular 230
- Other administrative pronouncements
- Case law
- Public Law 86-272
- Uniform Division of Income for Tax Purposes Act (UDITPA)
- Dodd-Frank Wall Street Reform and Consumer Protection Act of 2010
- Current Federal tax textbooks

Skill Specification Outlines

The Skill Specification Outlines (SSOs) identify the skills to be tested on the Uniform CPA Examination. There are three categories of skills, and the weightings will be implemented through the use of different question formats in the exam. For each of the question formats, a different set of tools will be available as resources to the candidates, who will need to use those tools to demonstrate proficiency in the applicable skills categories.

Weights

The percentage range assigned to each skill category will be used to determine the quantity of each type of question, as described below. The percentage range assigned to each skill category represents the approximate percentage to which that category of skills will be used in the different sections of the CPA Examination to assess proficiency. The ranges are designed to provide flexibility in building the examination, and the midpoints of the ranges for each section total 100%. No percentages are given for the bulleted descriptions included in these definitions. The presence of several groups within an area or several topics within a group does not imply equal importance or weight will be given to these bullets on an examination.

Skills Category	Weights (FAR, REG, AUD)	Weights (BEC)
Knowledge and Understanding	50%–60%	80%–90%
Application of the Body of Knowledge	40%–50%	–
Written Communication	–	10%–20%

Knowledge and Understanding. Multiple-choice questions will be used as the proxy for assessing knowledge and understanding, and will be based upon the content topics as outlined in the CSOs. Candidates will not have access to the authoritative literature, spreadsheets, or database tools while answering these questions. A calculator will be accessible for the candidates to use in performing calculations to demonstrate their understanding of the principles or subject matter.

Application of the Body of Knowledge. Task-based simulations will be used as the proxy for assessing application of the body of knowledge and will be based upon the content topics as outlined in the CSOs. Candidates will have access to the authoritative literature, a calculator, spreadsheets, and other resources and tools which they will use to demonstrate proficiency in applying the body of knowledge.

Written Communication (BEC section only) will be assessed through the use of responses to essay questions, which will be based upon the content topics as outlined in the CSOs. Candidates will have access to a word processor, which includes a spell-check feature.

Outlines

The outlines below provide additional descriptions of the skills that are represented in each category.

Knowledge and Understanding. Expertise and skills developed through learning processes, recall, and reading comprehension. Knowledge is acquired through experience or education and is the theoretical or practical understanding of a subject; knowledge is also represented through awareness or familiarity with information gained by experience of a fact or situation. Understanding represents a higher level than simple knowledge and is the process of using concepts to deal adequately with given situations, facts, or circumstances. Understanding is the ability to recognize and comprehend the meaning of a particular concept.

Application of the Body of Knowledge, including Analysis, Judgment, Synthesis, Evaluation, and Research. Higher-level cognitive skills that require individuals to act or transform knowledge in some fashion. These skills are inextricably intertwined and thus are grouped into this single skill area.

- Assess the Business Environment

  - Business Process Evaluation: Assess and integrate information regarding a business's operational structure, functions, processes, and procedures to develop a broad operational perspective; identify the need for new systems or changes to existing systems and/or processes.
  - Contextual Evaluation: Assess and integrate information regarding client's type of business or industry.
  - Strategic Analysis—Understand the Business: Obtain, assess, and integrate information on the entity's strategic objectives, strategic management process, business environment, the nature of and value to customers, its products and services, extent of competition within its market space, etc.).
  - Business Risk Assessment: Obtain, assess, and integrate information on conditions and events that could impede the entity's ability to achieve strategic objectives.
  - Visualize Abstract Descriptions: Organize and process symbols, pictures, graphs, objects, and other information.

- Research

  - Identify the appropriate research question.
  - Identify key search terms for use in performing electronic searches through large volumes of data.
  - Search through large volumes of electronic data to find required information.
  - Organize information or data from multiple sources.
  - Integrate diverse sources of information to reach conclusions or make decisions.
  - Identify the appropriate authoritative guidance in applicable financial reporting frameworks and auditing standards for the accounting issue being evaluated.

- Application of Technology

  - Use electronic spreadsheets to perform calculations, financial analysis, or other functions to analyze data.
  - Integrate technological applications and resources into work processes.
  - Use a variety of computer software and hardware systems to structure, utilize, and manage data.

- Analysis

  - Review information to determine compliance with specified standards or criteria.
  - Use expectations, empirical data, and analytical methods to determine trends and variances.
  - Perform appropriate calculations on financial and nonfinancial data.
  - Recognize patterns of activity when reviewing large amounts of data or recognize breaks in patterns.
  - Interpret financial statement data for a given evaluation purpose.
  - Forecast future financial statement data from historical financial statement data and other information.
  - Integrate primary financial statements: using data from all primary financial statements to uncover financial transactions, inconsistencies, or other information.

- Complex Problem Solving and Judgment

  - Develop and understand goals, objectives, and strategies for dealing with potential issues, obstacles, or opportunities.

- Analyze patterns of information and contextual factors to identify potential problems and their implications.
- Devise and implement a plan of action appropriate for a given problem.
- Apply professional skepticism, which is an attitude that includes a questioning mind and a critical assessment of information or evidence obtained.
- Adapt strategies or planned actions in response to changing circumstances.
- Identify and solve unstructured problems.
- Develop reasonable hypotheses to answer a question or resolve a problem.
- Formulate and examine alternative solutions in terms of their relative strengths and weaknesses, level of risk, and appropriateness for a given situation.
- Develop creative ways of thinking about situations, problems, and opportunities to create insightful and sound solutions.
- Develop logical conclusions through the use of inductive and deductive reasoning.
- Apply knowledge of professional standards and laws, as well as legal, ethical, and regulatory issues.
- Assess the need for consultations with other professionals when gray areas, or areas requiring specialized knowledge, are encountered.

- Decision Making

  - Specify goals and constraints.
  - Generate alternatives.
  - Consider risks.
  - Evaluate and select the best alternative.

- Organization, Efficiency, and Effectiveness

  - Use time effectively and efficiently.
  - Develop detailed work plans, schedule tasks and meetings, and delegate assignments and tasks.
  - Set priorities by determining the relevant urgency or importance of tasks and deciding the order in which they should be performed.
  - File and store information so that it can be found easily and used effectively.

Written Communication (BEC section only). The various skills involved in preparing written communication, including

- Basic writing mechanics, such as grammar, spelling, word usage, punctuation, and sentence structure.
- Effective business writing principles, including organization, clarity, and conciseness.
- Exchange technical information and ideas with coworkers and other professionals to meet goals of job assignment.
- Documentation

  - Prepare documents and presentations that are concise, accurate, and supportive of the subject matter.
  - Document and cross-reference work performed and conclusions reached in a complete and accurate manner.

- Assist client to recognize and understand implications of critical business issues by providing recommendations and informed opinions.
- Persuade others to take recommended courses of action.
- Follow directions.

RESEARCHING INCOME TAX ISSUES[1]

Research components of the Regulation section will involve a research database that includes the Internal Revenue Code (IRC) or the Statements of Standards for Tax Services (TS).

The Internal Revenue Code of 1986, as Amended (commonly called IRC, or simple the Code) is the most important source of federal income tax law. The IRC is actually Title 26 of the United States Code. The US Code is the complete set of laws passed by Congress. All laws dealing with one topic are consolidated under one title of the US Code. For example, Title 10 of the US Code contains all of the military laws of the United States.

Any changes when Congress passes a new tax law are integrated in the Code. The Code has been amended almost every year since it was reformed in 1986. Prior to that, the Code was reorganized in 1954, and from then until 1986, it was known as the Internal Revenue Code of 1954, as Amended. Before the IRC of 1954, the tax law was contained in the Internal Revenue Code of 1939, the first IRC. Before 1939, the tax law was an unorganized series of tax acts.

---

[1]This section was prepared by Gerald E. Whittenburg, Ph.D., CPA. For more information about tax research refer to West's *Federal Tax Research*, 6th Edition (Thomson South-Western)

Code Organization

There are many different subdivision to the Code, each with a different purpose and name. The Code is divided into subtitles, chapters, parts, subparts, and sections. Some common subtitles of the Code are

Subtitle A	Income Taxes
Subtitle B	Estate and Gift Taxes
Subtitle C	Employment Taxes
Subtitle D	Miscellaneous Excise Taxes
Subtitle E	Alcohol, Tobacco, and Certain Excise Taxes
Subtitle F	Procedures and Administration

Each Subtitle is divided into chapters. The chapters contained in Subtitle A are

Chapter 1	Normal and Surtaxes
Chapter 2	Tax on Self-Employment Income
Chapter 3	Withholding Tax and Nonresident Aliens and Foreign Corporations
Chapter 4	[Repealed]
Chapter 5	Tax on Transfers to Avoid Income Tax
Chapter 6	Consolidated Returns

The chapters are again subdivided into numerous subchapters. Some of the notable subchapters of Chapter 1 are

Subchapter A	Determination of Tax Liability
Subchapter B	Computation of Taxable Income
Subchapter C	Corporate Distributions and Adjustments
Subchapter E	Accounting Periods and Methods
Subchapter I	Natural Resources
Subchapter K	Partners and Partnerships
Subchapter N	International Taxation
Subchapter S	Tax Treatment of S Corporations

Each subchapter may be further divided into parts and subparts, as needed.

The smallest unique part of the Code is the section. The section is normally the basic reference when citing a provision of the Internal Revenue Code. In day-to-day tax practice, reference to larger divisions of the Code such as subtitles and chapters is generally disregarded. Currently, the sections in the Code are numbered from 1 to over 9,000, albeit many numbers are skipped to allow for future expansion of the tax law. Each Code section may be further subdivided into subsections, paragraphs, subparagraphs, and clauses. As an example, the following Code section reference is to the definition of the term medical for purposes of the medical care deduction:

Citation: Section 213(d)(1)(A), where

213 is the Section Number
(d) is the Subdivision
(1) is the Paragraph
(A) is the Subparagraph

The tax practitioner can be assured that there is only one Section 213 in the Code and that this is a specific tax reference that cannot be confused with any other provision of the Code.

Database Searching

Searching a database consists of the following five steps:

1. Define the issue. What is the research question to be answered?
2. Select the database to search (e.g., the IRC).
3. Choose a keyword or table of contents search.
4. Execute the search. Enter the keyword(s) or click on the appropriate table of contents item and complete the search.
5. Evaluate the results. Evaluate the research to see if an answer has been found. If not, try a new search.

EXAMPLE

Bill and Betty support their 18-year old daughter and her husband who live with and are supported by them. Both the daughter and her husband are full-time students at a local community college and have no income. Bill and Betty would like to know if their daughter's husband qualifies as a dependent on their tax return. The research database search would be as follows:

1. Define the issue. Does a daughter's husband qualify as a relative for dependent purposes?
2. Select the database to search. Internal Revenue Code.
3. Choose appropriate keywords. "Son-in-law," or "dependent."
4. Execute the search. A search should find Section 152(a)(8).
5. Evaluate the results. A son-in-law is a qualified relative.

Advanced Searches

On the Regulation exam you can also perform advanced searches, including

1. Searching for citations that contain two or more keywords.
2. Searching for citations that contain either or both keywords.
3. Searching for citations that contain the first set of keyword(s) but not the second.
4. Searching for citations that contain an exact phrase.
5. Searching for citations that contain words near each other.

The advanced search also allows you to select options for the search. One alternative allows you to retrieve alternative word terms. For example, using this approach with a search on the word "cost" would also retrieve sections containing the word "costing." A synonyms option allows you to retrieve sections that contain words that mean the same as the specified word. You also have the option to search only on the selected sections of the literature.

PROFESSIONAL RESPONSIBILITIES AND BUSINESS LAW

As indicated previously, this section consists of 12 modules designed to facilitate your study for the Professional Responsibilities and Business Law portion of the Regulation section of the Uniform CPA Examination. The table of contents at the right describes the content of each module.

Module 23: Professional and Legal Responsibilities

Overview

This module covers the general standards of care and ethics that must be followed by CPAs. CPAs are authorized to practice by the various state boards of accountancy. They must follow the rules of these bodies which generally follow the AICPA *Code of Professional Conduct*. The AICPA and the state societies cooperate on enforcing the ethics of the profession.

Accountants' civil liability arises primarily from contract law, the law of negligence, fraud, the Securities Act of 1933, and the Securities Exchange Act of 1934. The first three are common law and largely judge-made law, whereas the latter two are federal statutory law.

The agreement between an accountant and his/her client is generally set out in a carefully drafted engagement letter. Additionally, the accountant has a duty to conduct his/her work with the same reasonable care as an average accountant. This duty defines the standard used in a negligence case. It is important to understand

1. When an accountant can be liable to his/her client.
2. When an accountant can be liable to third parties.
3. That an accountant is liable to the client and to all third parties that relied on the financial statements when the accountant committed fraud, constructive fraud, or was grossly negligent; furthermore in these cases, the accountant can be assessed punitive damages.
4. The extent of liability under the Securities Act of 1933 and the Securities Exchange Act of 1934 as well as how they differ from each other and from common law. The CPA examination also tests the dual nature of the ownership of the accountant's working papers. Although the accountant owns the working papers and retains them as evidence of his/her work, confidentiality must be maintained. Therefore, the CPA cannot allow this information to reach another without the client's consent. In general, privileged communications between a CPA and the client are not sanctioned under federal statutory law or common law, but the privilege is in existence in states that have passed statutes granting such a right.

CPAs also have specific rules and regulations that affect their practice as tax preparers which are covered in this module. Before beginning the reading you should review the key terms at the end of the module.

A. Regulation of the Profession

Permits to practice for CPA firms and licenses to practice for individual CPAs are granted by the boards of accountancy in the various states and other jurisdictions. These boards also regulate the profession and may suspend or revoke a CPA or a CPA firm's right to practice. While all boards require successful completion of the CPA examination, the requirements for education and experience vary.

1. To audit issuers (public companies) the CPA in charge of the engagement must have a license to practice issued by a state board of accountancy. In addition, that individual's firm must have a permit to practice issued by the appropriate state board of accountancy, and the firm must be registered with the Public Company Accounting Oversight Board (PCAOB).
2. State boards have their own codes of professional ethics. However, they generally follow the AICPA Code of Professional Conduct. Therefore, violation of an AICPA rule also generally involves violation of a state board rule.

41

3. AICPA *Code of Professional Conduct* is applicable to all AICPA members, not merely those in public practice.
4. The Code provides minimum levels of acceptable conduct relating to all services performed by CPAs, unless wording of a standard specifically excludes some members.

      The AICPA has developed the Uniform Accountancy Act (UAA) to provide state jurisdictions a model act to regulate CPAs. Key provisions of the UAA include

1. The state board of accountancy of the state will issue the "certified public accountant" credential to individuals meeting the experience, education, and examination requirements.

   a. A bachelors degree is required for the first 5 years after the act becomes effective.
   b. After 5 years from the effective date, 150 semester hours of college education is required, including a bachelors or higher degree.

2. The UAA provides that the state board issues licenses to individual CPAs and permits to CPA firms to practice in the state. Individuals and firms that perform certain services or hold themselves out as CPAs must be licensed and permitted. The only professional services for which licensing is required are

   a. Attest services

      (1) Audits of financial statements performed in accordance with AICPA Statements on Auditing Standards (SAS).
      (2) Reviews of financial statements performed in accordance with AICPA Statements on Standards for Accounting and Review Services (SSARS).
      (3) An examination of prospective financial statements performed in accordance the AICPA Statements on Standards for Attestation Engagements (SSAE).
      (4) An engagement performed in accordance with standards of the Public Company Accounting Oversight Board (PCAOB).

   b. Compilation of financial statements under SSARS.

3. To renew licenses and permits the UAA includes periodic peer review and continuing education requirements.
4. To facilitate interstate practice and free movement of CPAs between states, the UAA provides that individuals that have met "substantial equivalency" shall be allowed to be licensed in the state.
5. The state board will regulate and enforce the practice of accountancy in the state.
6. The UAA has ethical provisions that are typically included in the code of ethics of state societies and the AICPA, such as the requirements for confidentiality, working papers, etc.

B. Disciplinary Systems of the Profession and Regulatory Bodies

1. The AICPA *Code of Professional Conduct* is interpreted and enforced by the Professional Ethics Executive Committee (PEEC), a senior technical committee of the AICPA.
2. State accountancy boards ethics rules are enforced by the various state boards of accountancy.
3. If CPAs are members they must also adhere to the ethics requirements of their state societies of CPAs. The codes of ethics of these bodies are also very similar to the AICPA Code of Professional Conduct. Virtually all state societies have agreements with AICPA to allow joint enforcement of ethics complaints through the Joint Ethics Enforcement Program (JEEP). This means there is a single investigation and, if warranted, a single settlement agreement or joint trial board hearing.

   a. Enforcement of rules regarding competitive bidding is excluded from the JEEP process.

4. Joint trial board may discipline CPAs—possible results include

   a. No violation/dismissal
   b. Admonishment (publication of the admonishment is mandatory)
   c. Corrective action required (e.g., additional continuing professional education)
   d. Suspension for up to two years
   e. Expulsion from AICPA

      (1) The CPA may still practice public accounting using valid license issued by a state

         (a) Violation of state board code, however, can result in revocation of CPA certificate and loss of ability to practice public accounting. State board codes generally mirror the AICPA *Code of Professional Conduct*.

(2) Any member who departs from rulings or interpretations has burden justifying it in any disciplinary proceedings.

(3) A member of the AICPA may be expelled or suspended without hearing for any of the following:

    (a) The member's CPA certificate or license or permit to practice is revoked by state as a disciplinary measure.

    (b) The member is convicted of a crime punishable by imprisonment for more than one year.

    (c) The member files or aids in filing a fraudulent tax return for client or self.

    (d) The member intentionally fails to file his or her required tax return.

(4) AICPA Professional Ethics Division may investigate ethics violations and may sanction those that are less serious using less severe remedies.

(5) In addition, court decisions have consistently held that even if an individual is not a member of AICPA, that individual is still expected to follow profession's *Code of Professional Conduct*.

5. Securities and Exchange Commission actions against accountants.

  a. After a hearing, the SEC can revoke or suspend an accountant from practicing before the SEC if the accountant willfully violated federal securities laws or regulations, or has acted unethically or unprofessionally. If a CPA is suspended from practicing before the SEC, he or she cannot serve as auditor for issuer (public company).

  b. The SEC can revoke or suspend an accountant from practicing before the SEC upon conviction of felony or misdemeanor in which moral turpitude was involved.

  c. The SEC can penalize accountants with civil fines and mandates to pay profits gained from violations of securities laws and regulations.

6. Disciplinary actions against CPA firms.

  a. A state board of accountancy has the power to bar a CPA firm from practicing in the state.

  b. The SEC can prohibit an accountant or an accounting firm from doing work for an issuer (public company).

  c. The PCAOB investigates and sanctions registered firms for violations of standards of performance. Firms must be registered with the PCAOB to perform audits or reviews of the financial statements of issuer (public company) clients.

    (1) Registered CPA firms must have inspections by the PCAOB staff.

      (a) Firms with more than 100 publicly traded clients (issuers) must be inspected each year.

      (b) Firms with 100 or less publicly traded clients must be inspected every three years.

    (2) When investigations lead to alleged violations a hearing will be held by the PCAOB.

    (3) The PCAOB hearing may result in sanctions being imposed on the firm or the individuals involved, including suspension or revocation of a firm's registration, suspension or bar of an individual from associating with a registered public accounting firm, or civil monetary penalties.

    (4) The PCAOB may also impose other remedial measures, such as

      (a) Improvements in the firm's quality control or training.

      (b) Independent monitoring of the audit work of a firm or individual within a firm.

NOW REVIEW MULTIPLE-CHOICE QUESTIONS 1 THROUGH 5

C. Accountant's Legal Liabilities

1. Common Law Liability to Clients
Common law is law that has historically been derived from court interpretations of what is fair and equitable. Most of common law has now been codified in state statutes. CPAs have responsibilities to their clients that are codified in common law.

  a. Liability to clients for breach of contract

    (1) The relationship between the client and the CPA is that of an employer and an independent contractor. A CPA may be held liable to a client if the accountant fails to perform substantially as agreed under contract (the engagement letter).

(a) Duties under contract may be

    (1) Implied—The accountant owes duty in contract to perform in nonnegligent manner.

    (2) Express—The accountant owes duty to perform under terms of the contract.

       (a) This duty can extend liability beyond that which is standard under a normal audit.

       (b) Typically, the terms are expressed in engagement letter that should specify clearly and in writing the following:

          (i) The nature and scope of engagement to avoid misunderstandings between the CPA and client.

          (ii) The procedures and tests to be used.

          (iii) That the engagement will not necessarily uncover fraud, defalcations, errors, or illegal actions, unless the CPA agrees to greater responsibility.

          (iv) Engagement letter should be signed by at least the client (accountant will typically sign also) but oral contract for audit still enforceable without engagement letter.

(b) An accountant (CPA) is said to be in privity of contract with client when contract exists between them.

    (1) The reverse is also true (i.e., client is in privity of contract with CPA).

(c) An accountant is not an insurer of financial statements and thus does not guarantee against losses from error or fraud.

    (1) A "normal" financial statement audit is not intended to uncover fraud, shortages, or defalcations, in general but is meant to provide audit evidence needed to express opinion on fairness of financial statements. The audit is designed to provide reasonable assurance of detecting material errors and fraud.

(d) An accountant is not normally liable for failure to detect fraud, etc. unless

    (1) "Normal" audit or review would have detected it

    (2) The accountant by agreement has undertaken greater responsibility such as a fraud audit

    (3) The wording of audit report indicates greater responsibility

---

EXAMPLE

A CPA has been hired by a client to perform an audit. A standard engagement letter is used. During the course of the audit, the CPA fails to uncover a clever embezzlement scheme by one of the client's employees. The CPA is not liable for the losses unless a typical, reasonable audit should have resulted in discovery of the scheme.

(e) In an audit or review of financial statements, the accountant is under duty to investigate when he or she discovers or becomes aware of suspicious items.

    (1) The investigation should extend beyond management's explanations.

(2) The client should not interfere or prevent accountant from performing.

EXAMPLE

A CPA firm issues its opinion a few days late because of its client's failure to supply needed information. The CPA firm is entitled to the full fee agreed upon under the contract (engagement).

---

(3) When a breach of contract occurs

    (a) The accountant is not entitled to compensation if breach is major.

EXAMPLE

Miller failed to complete the audit by the agreed date. If time is of the essence so that the client receives no benefit from the audit, Miller is not entitled to compensation.

    (b) The accountant is entitled to compensation if there are only minor errors but the client may deduct from fees paid any damages caused by breach.

    (c) The client may recover any damages caused by breach even if accountant is not entitled to fee.

    (d) In general, punitive damages are not awarded for breach of contract.

b. Liability to clients based on negligence

    (1) Elements needed to prove negligence against accountant

        (a) The accountant has a duty to perform with same degree of skill and judgment possessed by average (reasonable) accountant.

            (1) This is the standard used in cases involving ordinary negligence (or simply called negligence).

            (2) Different phrases are used for this standard, including duty to exercise due care, duty of skill of an average, reasonable accountant (or CPA), duty to act as an average (or reasonable) accountant (or CPA) would under the circumstances, or duty of judgment of an ordinary, prudent accountant (or CPA).

            (3) Standard for accountants is guided by

                (a) State and federal statutes

                (b) Court decisions

                (c) Contract with client

                (d) GAAS and GAAP (persuasive but not conclusive)

                    (i) Failure to follow GAAS virtually establishes lack of due care but reverse not true (i.e., following GAAS does not automatically preclude negligence but is strong evidence for presence of due care)

                (e) Customs of the profession (persuasive but not conclusive)

EXAMPLE

Will, a CPA, issued an unqualified opinion on the financial statements of X Company. Included in the assets was inventory stated at cost when the market was materially below cost. This violation of GAAP can be used to establish that Will was negligent. Also, the client can sue under contract law because Will has an implied duty in the contract to not be negligent.

A CPA, while performing the annual audit, detects material errors in the previously issued audit report. The CPA has a duty to correct these material errors.

A CPA failing to warn a client of known internal control deficiency is falling below this standard.

        (b) The accountant breached duty owed of average reasonable accountant.

        (c) Damages or losses resulted from the breach.

            (1) Damages are limited to actual losses that use of reasonable care would have avoided.

            (2) Punitive damages are not normally allowed for ordinary negligence.

            (3) Contributory negligence may be a complete defense by CPA in many states if client's own negligence substantially contributed to the accountant's failure to perform audit adequately.

> **EXAMPLE**
>
> A CPA failed to detect a material fraud in an audit of the client's financial statements. However the CPA had communicated to the client for a number of years a significant deficiency in internal control that allowed the fraud to occur. The client ignored the recommendations and failed to correct the deficiency in internal control. The client's contributory negligence may in some states prevent the client from recovering losses from the CPA for negligence. In other states it will reduce the liability of the CPA.

(d) A causal relationship must exist between fault of accountant and damages of plaintiff and the cause must be proximate (i.e., foreseeable).

> **EXAMPLE**
>
> A CPA negligently fails to discover during an audit that several expensive watches are missing from the client's inventory. Subsequently, an employee is caught stealing some watches. He confesses to stealing several before the audit and more after the audit when he found out he did not get caught. Only 5 of the watches can be recovered from the employee, who is unable to pay for those stolen. The CPA may be liable for those losses sustained after the audit if discovery could have prevented them. However, the CPA normally would not be liable for the watches taken before the audit when the loss is not the proximate result of the negligent audit. But if there were watches that could have been recovered at the time of the audit but can't be now, the CPA could be liable for those watches even though they were taken before the audit.

c. The accountant's liability is not based solely on honest errors of judgment; liability requires at least negligence under common law.

d. Liability to client for fraud, gross negligence, or constructive fraud

   (1) Common law fraud of accountant is established by the following elements:

      (a) Misrepresentation of material fact or accountant's expert opinion
      (b) Scienter, shown by either

         (1) Intent to mislead with accountant's knowledge of falsity, or
         (2) Reckless disregard of the truth.

      (c) Reasonable or justifiable reliance by injured party
      (d) Actual damages

   (2) Called constructive fraud or gross negligence if when proving above four elements, reckless disregard of the truth is established instead of knowledge of falsity.

> **EXAMPLE**
>
> During the course of an audit, a CPA fails to verify the existence of the company's investments which amounted to a substantial portion of the assets. Many of these, it is subsequently found, were nonexistent. Even in the absence of intent to defraud, the CPA is liable for constructive fraud based on reckless disregard of the truth.
>
>   Care and Less Co., CPAs, uncover suspicious items during the course of their audit of Blue Co. Because their audit steps did not require the additional steps needed to check into these suspicious items, the CPAs failed to uncover material errors. Even if a typical audit would not have required these additional audit steps, the CPAs are liable for the damages that result because they have a duty to look into such circumstances when they come to their attention.

(3) Contributory negligence of client is not a defense available for accountant in cases of fraud, constructive fraud, or gross negligence.

(4) Privity of contract is not required for plaintiff to prove fraud, constructive fraud, or gross negligence.

(5) Punitive damages may be added to actual damages for fraud, constructive fraud, or gross negligence.

NOW REVIEW MULTIPLE-CHOICE QUESTIONS 6 THROUGH 16

---

2. Common Law Liability to Third Parties (Nonclients)

   a. Privity of contract.

      (1) In typical accountant-client relationship, there usually is no privity of contract between the accountant and third parties who rely on the financial statements. However, in some cases the client is not the company being audited.

> **EXAMPLE**
>
> Dudley Company is considering acquiring Tyler Company. Dudley engages Wilson, CPA to audit Tyler to obtain assurance that Tyler's financial statements are not materially misstated. Dudley is the client because it engaged Wilson. Accordingly, Dudley would be able to hold Wilson liable for breach of contract or ordinary negligence.

      (2) Traditionally, accountants could use the defense of no privity against suing third parties in contract and negligence cases.

         (a) Ultramares decision is leading case in which the accountants were held liable for ordinary negligence only to parties who primarily benefit from the audit or the audited financial statement.

> **EXAMPLE**
>
> First Bank requested Goodman Company to obtain an audit to receive a needed loan. Adam, CPA audited the financial statements of Goodman knowing that the Goodman was obtaining the audit to satisfy the request of First Bank. In this case, First Bank would be considered a primary beneficiary of the audit and, therefore, First Bank would have the same rights as the client under common law.

         (1) This generally means only the client or third-party beneficiaries since these are in privity of contract with accountant.

         (2) However, a third party who can prove fraud or constructive fraud (gross negligence) may recover from the accountant.

         (b) This is a significant **minority** rule today.

   b. More recently, many courts have expanded liability to other some third parties. The following distinctions should be understood:

      (1) Foreseen party —A third party who the accountant knew would rely on financial statements, or member of limited class that accountant knew would rely on financial statements, for specified transaction.

         (a) The **majority rule** is that the accountant is liable to foreseen third parties for ordinary negligence.

            (1) The rationale for not allowing liability to more third parties is that accountants should not be exposed to liability in indeterminate amount to indeterminate class.

> **EXAMPLE**
>
> A CPA agrees to perform an audit for ABC Client knowing that the financial statements will be used to obtain a loan from XYZ Bank. Relying on the financial statements, XYZ Bank loans ABC $100,000. ABC goes bankrupt. If XYZ can establish that the financial statements were not fairly stated, thus causing the bank to give the loan, and if negligence can be established, most courts will allow XYZ Bank to recover from the CPA.
>
> Assume the same facts as in the example above except that XYZ Bank was not specified. Since the CPA knew that some bank would rely on these financial statements, the actual bank is a foreseen party since it is a member of a limited class and most courts will allow for liability.

    (b) The accountant is liable for fraud, constructive fraud, or gross negligence to all parties whether foreseen or not.

  (2) Distinguish foreseen party and foreseeable party

    (a) Foreseeable party —Any party that accountant could reasonably foresee would receive financial statements and use them.

      (1) The **majority rule** is that accountant **not** liable to foreseeable parties for negligence.

> **EXAMPLE**
>
> A CPA is informed that financial statements after being audited will be used to obtain a loan from a bank. The audited financial statements are also shown to trade creditors and potential investors. The bank is a foreseen third party but these other third parties are not actually foreseen parties and generally cannot recover from the CPA for ordinary negligence. They may qualify as foreseeable third parties since creditors or investors are the types of parties whom an accountant should reasonably foresee as users of the audited financial statements.

      (2) Some courts now hold that accountant is liable for negligence to parties that are merely foreseeable.

  c. To be awarded damages against the accountant a third party must prove

    (1) Losses (damages),

    (2) Negligence (either ordinary or gross negligence depending on the type of party and nature of state law) by the CPA,

    (3) Proximate cause (i.e., reliance on the work of the CPA caused the losses).

  d. Concepts of liability

    (1) In many cases in which third-parties sue the accountant, the accountant is not the only party at fault. Typically, management of the company is also responsible for the losses of third parties. It is common that both the accountant and management are named as defendants in these cases. If the defendants lose the case, state courts vary in how the obligation to pay damages is allocated.

      (a) **Joint liability.** In a state that applies joint liability, both the accountant and management are liable up to the full amount of the obligation. If management has no funds, the entire amount may be collected from the accountant

      (b) **Several liability.** In a state that applies several (proportionate liability), the accountant and management are only obligated to pay their respective share of the damages based on the degree of responsibility for the losses. This is the liability standard that is included in the AICPA Uniform Accountancy Act.

> **EXAMPLE**
>
> First bank extended a line of credit in the amount of $1,000,000 to Carey Corporation in reliance on financial statements audited by Gordon, CPA. The financial statements were materially misstated by management, and Gordon did not detect the misstatement. Assume that First Bank prevailed in a lawsuit against management and Gordon. Management was found to be 60% responsible and Gordon was found to be 40% responsible for First Bank's losses of $1,000,000. In a state that applies the concept of several liability, management would be obligated to pay $600,000 (60% × $1,000,000) and Gordon would be obligated to pay $400,000 (40% × $1,000,000). Gordon would not be obligated to pay more even if management had no ability to pay its obligation.

    (c) Joint and several liability. In a state that applies joint and several liability, each of the parties are responsible for the full amount of the obligation but may seek to get reimbursement from the other parties. Most state courts apply joint and several liability.

> **EXAMPLE**
>
> If the state in the previous example applies the concept of joint and several liability, First Bank could seek to collect the entire $1,000,000 from Gordon. Gordon would then have to pursue management for its $600,000 share.

NOW REVIEW MULTIPLE-CHOICE QUESTIONS 17 THROUGH 22

---

3. Statutory Liability to Third Parties—Securities Act of 1933

  a. General information on the Securities Act of 1933

    (1) Covers regulation of initial sales of securities registered under 1933 Act

      (a) Requires registration of initial issuances of securities with SEC and makes it unlawful for registration statement to contain untrue **material** fact or to omit **material** fact.

        (1) Material fact—One about which average prudent investor should be informed.
        (2) Most potential accountant liability occurs because registration statement (and prospectus) includes audited financial statements.
        (3) Accountant's legal liability arises for untrue material fact or omission of material fact in registration statement (or prospectus).
        (4) Securities Act of 1933 does not include periodic reports to SEC or annual reports to stockholders (these are in the 1934 Act below).

  b. Parties that may sue

    (1) Any purchaser of registered securities

      (a) Plaintiff need not be initial purchaser of security.
      (b) Purchaser generally must prove that specific security was offered for sale through registration statement.

        (1) Exchange and issuance of stock based on a merger counts as a sale.

    (2) Third parties can sue without having privity of contract with accountant under Federal Securities Acts.

  c. Liability under Section 11 of the 1933 Act.

    (1) This imposes liability on auditors (and other experts) for misstatements or omissions of material fact in certified financial statements or other information provided in registration statements. The registration statement is the document that is used to sell the securities and, in general, includes

(a) A description of the company's properties and business
(b) A description of the security to be offered for sale
(c) Information about the management of the company
(d) Financial statements certified by independent accountants

(2) To be awarded damages against the accountant, the plaintiff (purchaser of the securities) must prove

(a) Damages were incurred.
(b) There was material misstatement or omission in financial statements or included in registration statement.
(c) If these two facts are proven, it is sufficient to win against the CPA and shifts burden of proof to the CPA accountant who may escape liability by proving one of the following defenses:

(1) "Due diligence," that is, after reasonable investigation, the accountant had reasonable grounds to believe and did believe that statements were not materially misstated.

> **NOTE:** Although the basis of liability is not negligence, an accountant who was at least negligent will probably not be able to establish "due diligence."

(2) Plaintiff knew financial statements were incorrect when investment was made.
(3) Lack of causation—loss was due to factors other than the misstatement or omission in the financial statements.
(4) Following generally accepted auditing standards is generally valid as a defense for CPA.

(d) The plaintiff **need not** prove reliance on financial statements unless security was purchased at least twelve months after effective date of registration statement.
(e) The plaintiff **need not** prove negligence or fraud.

d. Damages

(1) The difference between amount paid and market value at time of suit.
(2) If sold, difference between amount paid and sale price.
(3) Damages cannot exceed price at which security was offered to public.
(4) The plaintiff cannot recover decrease in value after suit is brought and the accountant is given the benefit of any increase in market value during the suit.

e. Statute of limitations

(1) Action must be brought against accountant within one year from discovery (or when discovery should have been made) of false statement or omission in financial statements.
(2) Or if earlier, action must be brought within three years after security offered to public.

f. This liability can arise from negligence in reviewing events subsequent to date of certified balance sheet. The CPA firm is responsible for reviewing for material events that occur up until the effective date of the registration statement.

(1) This is referred to as S-1 review when made for registration statement under securities regulations.

EXAMPLE

An accountant performed an audit and later performed an S-1 review to review events subsequent to the balance sheet date. The accountant did not detect certain material events during this S-1 review even though there was sufficient evidence to make the accountant suspicious. Further investigation was required to avoid liability.

NOW REVIEW MULTIPLE-CHOICE QUESTIONS 23 THROUGH 30

4. Statutory Liability to Third Parties—Securities Exchange Act of 1934

    a. The Securities Exchange Act of 1934 regulates securities sold on national stock exchanges.

        (1) Includes securities traded over-the-counter and other equity securities where the corporation has more than $10 million in total assets and the security is held by 500 or more persons at the end of a fiscal year.
        (2) Requires each company to furnish to SEC an annual report (Form 10-K) which includes financial statements (not necessarily the same as an annual report to shareholders) to be audited in accordance with PCAOB standards by a registered firm. It also requires the company to file quarterly reports (Form 10-Qs) which include quarterly financial statements reviewed by a registered firm.
        (3) Accountant civil liability comes from two sections—10 and 18.

            (a) Section 10 (including Rule 10b-5)—makes it unlawful to

                (1) Employ any device, scheme, or artifice to defraud.
                (2) Make untrue statement of material fact or omit material fact.
                (3) Engage in act, practice, or course of business to commit fraud or deceit in connection with purchase or sale of security.

            (b) Section 18—makes it unlawful to make false or misleading statement with respect to a material statement unless done in "good faith."

    b. Purchasers **and** sellers of registered securities may sue under these sections. Note that under the 1933 Act only purchasers may sue.
    c. Proof requirements—Section 10, including Rule 10b-5

        (1) The plaintiff (purchaser or seller) must prove damages resulted in connection with purchase or sale of a registered security in interstate commerce.
        (2) The plaintiff must prove there was a material misstatement or omission in information released by the issuer (public company).

            (a) Information may, for example, be in the form of audited financial statements in report to stockholders or in Form 10-K.

        (3) The plaintiff must prove justifiable reliance on financial information.
        (4) The plaintiff must prove existence of **scienter** (the intent to deceive, manipulate, or defraud).

            (a) Includes reckless disregard of truth or knowledge of falsity.
            (b) Negligence alone will not subject accountant to liability under this section but lack of good faith will.

        (5) Note that these proof requirements differ in very significant ways from proof requirements under the 1933 Act.
        (6) The plaintiff cannot recover if he or she is reckless or fraudulent.

    d. Proof requirements—Section 18

        (1) The plaintiff (purchaser or seller) must prove

            (a) That damages were incurred.
            (b) There was a material misstatement or omission on report (usually Form 10-K) filed with SEC.
            (c) The plaintiff read and relied on defective report.

        (2) Then the burden of proof is shifted to the accountant who may escape liability by proving s/he acted in "good faith."

            (a) Although basis of liability here is not negligence, an accountant who has been grossly negligent typically will not be able to establish "good faith."
            (b) An accountant who has been only negligent will probably be able to establish "good faith."

    e. Damages

        (1) Generally, damages are calculated as the difference between amount paid by the plaintiff and market value at time of suit.
        (2) If sold, damages are calculated as the difference between amount paid and sale price.

5. Summary of auditors' defenses under Securities Act of 1933 and Securities Exchange Act of 1934

- **Defenses** available to auditors:

	1934 Act	1933 Act
1. Audit was performed with **due care**	Yes	Yes
2. Misstatement was immaterial	Yes	Yes
3. Plaintiff had prior knowledge of misstatement	Yes	Yes
4. Plaintiff did not rely on information	Yes	No
5. Misstatement was not cause of loss	Yes	Yes

Prepared by Debra R. Hopkins, Northern Illinois University

- Due diligence is a defense for the 1933 Act **only**. (Do not use for liability under the 1934 Act.)

NOW REVIEW MULTIPLE-CHOICE QUESTIONS 31 THROUGH 34

D. Legal Considerations Affecting the Accountant's Responsibility

1. Accountant's working papers

    a. Consist of evidence, notes, computations, etc. that accountant accumulates when doing professional work for client.
    b. Working papers are owned by accountant unless there is agreement to the contrary.
    c. Ownership is essentially custodial in nature and it serves two purposes:

       (1) To preserve confidentiality of client information. Without client consent, an accountant cannot allow transmission of information in working papers to another party. However, an accountant must produce working papers upon being given an enforceable subpoena, or if agreeing to provide access to working papers to a government agency is part of the agreement with the client.

          (a) Subpoenas should be limited in scope and for a specific purpose.
          (b) The accountant may challenge a subpoena as being too broad and unreasonably burdensome.

2. Privileged communications between accountant and client generally is not provided by state or federal laws.

    a. Only a few states have enacted laws providing for privileged communications.
    b. Federal law does not recognize privileged communications.
    c. If the accountant is acting as agent for (hired by) an individual who has privileged communication such as an attorney, then accountant's communications are privileged.
    d. To be considered privileged, an accountant-client communication must

       (1) Be located in a jurisdiction where privileged communication is recognized.
       (2) Have been intended to be confidential at time of communication.
       (3) Not have privilege waived by the client.

    e. If considered privileged, valid grounds exist for the accountant to refuse to testify in court concerning these matters.

       (1) This privilege is, in general, for benefit of client.
       (2) Can be waived by client.
       (3) If part of the privileged communication is allowed, all of privilege is lost.

    f. ACIPA *Code of Professional Conduct* prohibits disclosure of confidential client data unless

       (1) The client consents. If the client is a partnership, each partner is actually a client and therefore must give consent.
       (2) To comply with GAAS and GAAP.
       (3) To comply with enforceable subpoena (e.g., courts where privilege is not recognized).

(4) Disclosure is made in conjunction with a quality (peer) review of the CPA firm's practice.
(5) The AICPA is responding an investigation by the AICPA ethics division or trial board.

g. An interpretation of the *Code of Professional Conduct* allows a CPA to provide confidential client information to a third-party service provider (e.g., a tax return preparation provider) without the client's permission. However, the CPA must enter into a contractual agreement with the service provider to maintain the confidentiality of the information and be reasonably assured that the third-party service provider has appropriate procedures in place to prevent the unauthorized release of confidential information to others.

h. US Supreme Court has held that tax accrual files are not protected by accountant-client privilege.

3. Accountants also should be familiar with privacy laws that may affect their practice. Privacy is defined as "the rights and obligations of individuals and organizations with respect to the collection, use, retention, and disclosure of personal information."

a. Accountants that prepare individual tax returns or provide nonbusiness tax or financial advice must be familiar with the provisions of the Gramm-Leach Bliley (Financial Modernization) Act of 1999.

(1) Accountants are prohibited from disclosing to a nonaffiliated third party any nonpublic personal information about their clients.
(2) Related FTC regulations require accountants to develop, implement, and maintain a comprehensive information security program that outlines the ways in which they protect client information.
(3) Accountants are responsible for maintaining the confidentiality of information that is outsourced for processing (e.g., outsourced tax return preparation to a firm in a foreign country).

b. The Internal Revenue Code prohibits tax preparers from "knowingly" or "recklessly" disclosing or using tax-related information other than in connection with the preparation of the return. Treasury Department regulations allow information to be used for certain other purposes but only if a consent is obtained from the individual.

4. Illegal acts by clients

a. Situations in which there may be a duty to notify parties outside the client

(1) Form 8-K disclosures. When a change is auditor is reported by a Form 8-K (as required by securities laws), the client must disclose the reason for the change and the auditor must agree with the reason stated by the client or indicate how the auditor disagrees.
(2) Disclosure to successor auditor. Upon a change in auditor, the predecessor auditor must accurately and completely respond to inquiries by the successor auditor after the client has given consent.
(3) Disclosure in response to subpoena.
(4) Disclosure to funding agency for entities receiving governmental financial assistance.

5. CPA certificates are issued under state (not federal) jurisdiction.
6. Acts of employees.

a. Accountant is liable for acts of employees in the course of employment.

EXAMPLE

XYZ, a partnership of CPAs, hires Y to help perform an audit. Y is negligent in the audit, causing the client damage. The partners cannot escape liability by showing they did not perform the negligent act.

---

b. Professional liability insurance typically is used to cover such losses.

7. The duty to perform an audit is not delegable because it is a contract for personal services unless client agrees to delegation.
8. Generally, the basis of relationship of accountant to his or her client is that of independent contractor.
9. Insurance

a. The accountants' professional liability (malpractice) insurance covers their negligence.
b. A fidelity bond protects client from accountant's fraud.

c. A client's insurance company is subrogated to client's rights (i.e., has same rights of recovery of loss against accountant that client had).

d. The portions of debts incurred in violation of securities laws not covered by insurance are not dischargeable in bankruptcy by the accountant.

10. Reliance by an auditor on other auditor's work

a. The principal auditor is still liable for all work unless the audit report clearly indicates divided responsibility.

b. The principal auditor cannot rely on unaudited data; must disclaim or qualify opinion.

11. Subsequent events and subsequent discovery

a. The accountant is generally not liable for the effect of events occurring subsequent to the date of the audit report.

(1) Liability extends to effective date of registration for reports filed with SEC.

b. The accountant may be held liable if subsequently discovered facts that existed at report date indicate statements were misleading **unless**

(1) An immediate investigation is conducted
(2) Prompt revision of statements is possible
(3) The SEC and persons known to be relying on statements are notified by the client or the accountant

c. The accountant is liable if he or she makes assurances that there are no material changes after fieldwork or report date when in fact there are material changes. Therefore, the accountant should perform sufficient audit procedures before giving this assurance.

12. Liability from preparation of unaudited financial statements, including compiled and reviewed financial statements for nonissuers (nonpublic companies)

a. Financial statements are unaudited if

(1) No auditing procedures have been applied.
(2) Insufficient audit procedures have been applied to express an opinion (e.g., inquiries and analytical procedures applied in a review engagement).

b. The accountant may liable in these types of engagements

(1) Failure to mark each page, "unaudited," or "See Accountant's Compilation Report," or "See Accountant's Review Report."
(2) Failure to issue a disclaimer of opinion, or an appropriately worded compilation or review report.
(3) Failure to follow appropriate AICPA Statements on Standards for Accounting and Review Services.
(4) Failure to inform client of any discovery of indications of major issues; for example, circumstances indicating presence of fraud.

> **NOW REVIEW MULTIPLE-CHOICE QUESTIONS 35 THROUGH 42**

E. Criminal Liability

1. Sources of liability

a. Securities Act of 1933 and Securities Exchange Act of 1934

(1) An accountant can be held criminally liable for **willful** illegal conduct.

(a) Intentional misleading omission of material facts
(b) Putting false information in registration statement

(2) Subject to fine of up to $10,000 and/or up to five years prison
(3) Examples of possible criminal actions include

       (a) CPA aids management in a fraudulent scheme.
       (b) CPA covers up prior year financial statement misstatements.

  b. Criminal violations of the Internal Revenue Code

    (1) For willfully preparing false return (perjury)
    (2) For willfully assisting others to evade taxes (tax evasion)

  c. Criminal liability under RICO (Racketeer Influenced and Corrupt Organizations) Act

    (1) Covers individuals affiliated with businesses or associations involved in a pattern of racketeering.

       (a) Racketeering includes organized crime but also includes fraud under the federal securities laws as well as mail fraud.

          (1) Accountants are subject to criminal penalty through affiliation with accounting firm or business involved in racketeering.

       (b) A pattern of racketeering means at least two illegal acts of racketeering in previous ten years.

    (2) RICO has also been expanded to allow civil suit by private parties.

       (a) Treble damages allowed (to encourage private enforcement).
       (b) It has been held to apply against accountants even without a criminal indictment or conviction.

EXAMPLE

A CPA firm is convicted of a number of violations of securities laws in a short period of time. The CPA firm could potentially be held liable under RICO for a pattern of violations of laws.

NOW REVIEW MULTIPLE-CHOICE QUESTIONS 43 AND 44

F. Responsibilities of Auditors under Private Securities Litigation Reform Act

1. Auditors who audit financial statements under Federal Securities Exchange Act of 1934 are required to establish procedures to

  a. Detect material illegal acts,
  b. Identify material related-party transactions, and
  c. Evaluate ability of firm to continue as going concern.

2. If auditor detects possible illegal activity, he or she must inform audit committee or board of directors.

  a. If senior management or board fails to take remedial action and if illegal activities are material so that departure from standard audit report or auditor resignation is indicated, the auditor shall report this to board of directors.

    (1) Board has one day to notify SEC of this report.

       (a) If not done, auditor must furnish SEC with copy of auditor's report to board and/or resign from audit.

3. Civil liability may be imposed by SEC for the auditor's failures under the Act.

  a. Auditors are protected from private civil suits for these reports to SEC under this Act.

4. Amends Federal Securities Act of 1933 and Federal Securities Exchange Act of 1934.

  a. Law passed to reduce lawsuits against accounting firms and issuers of securities

    (1) SEC's enforcement of securities laws not affected by the Act because the law governs private litigation.

5. The act creates a "safe harbor" from legal liability for preparation of forward-looking statements.

    a. Including projections of income, revenues, EPS, and company plans for products and services.

    b. To fall within safe harbor, written or oral forward-looking statement should include cautions and identify assumptions and conditions that may cause projections to vary.

    c. Purpose is to encourage company to give investors more meaningful information without fear of lawsuits.

6. Discourages class action lawsuits for frivolous purposes

    a. Accomplished by

       (1) Providing for stringent pleading requirements for many private actions under Securities Exchange Act of 1934

       (2) Awards costs and attorneys' fees against parties failing to fulfill these pleading requirements

7. Changes rules on joint and several liability, so that liability of defendants is generally proportionate to their degree of fault

    a. This relieves the accountants (and others) from being "deep pockets" beyond their proportional fault.

    b. Exception—joint and several liability is imposed if defendant **knowingly** caused harm.

EXAMPLE

Plaintiffs suffered $2 million in damages from securities fraud of a company. The auditors of the company are found to be 15% at fault. If the auditors did not act knowingly, they can be held liable for the 15% or $300,000. If they acted knowingly, they can be held liable for up to the full $2 million based on joint and several liability.

---

    c. Accountants may be held liable for the proportionate share of damages they actually (and unknowingly) caused plus an additional 50% where principal defendant is insolvent.

> **NOW REVIEW MULTIPLE-CHOICE QUESTIONS 45 THROUGH 50**

G. Responsibilities under Sarbanes-Oxley Act

1. Sarbanes-Oxley Act, also known as Public Company Accounting Reform and Investor Protection Act
2. New federal crimes involving willful nonretention of audit and review workpapers

    a. Retention required for five years (in some cases seven years).

    b. Makes illegal the destruction or falsifying of records to impede investigations.

    c. Provides for fines or imprisonment up to twenty years or both.

    d. Applies to an accountant who audits an issuer of securities (public company).

       (1) It also applies to others such as attorneys, consultants, and company employees.

    e. Act requires SEC to issue new rules and then periodically update its rules on details of retaining workpapers and other relevant records connected with audits or reviews.

3. Created the Public Company Accounting Oversight Board (PCAOB).

    a. PCAOB is a nonprofit corporation not federal agency.

       (1) Violation of rules of the PCAOB are treated as violation of Securities Exchange Act of 1934 with its penalties.

    b. The PCAOB consists of five members.

       (1) Two members must be or have been CPAs.

       (2) Three members cannot be or cannot have been CPAs.

       (3) None of Board members may receive pay or profits from CPA firms.

    c. Board regulates firms that audit SEC registrants, not accounting firms of private companies.

    d. Main functions of Board are to

    (1) Register and conduct inspections of public accounting firms

        (a) This replaces peer reviews for the part of a CPA firm's practice that involves audits of issuers (public company clients).

        (b) CPA firms that audit more than 100 issuers (public companies) are inspected annually.

        (c) CPA firms that audit from 1 to 100 issuers (public companies) are inspected every three years.

        (d) Special inspections may be performed in addition to the regular inspections.

    (2) Set standards on auditing, quality control, independence, or preparation of audit reports

        (a) May adopt standards of existing professional groups or new groups.

        (b) Accounting firm must have second partner review and approve each audit report.

        (c) Accounting firm must report on examination of internal control along with description of material weaknesses.

    (3) The PCAOB may regulate the nature and extent of nonaudit services that CPA firms may perform for issuer audit clients

    (4) Enforce compliance with professional standards, securities laws relating to accountants and audits

    (5) Perform investigations and disciplinary proceedings on registered public accounting firms

    (6) May perform any other duties needed to promote high professional standards and to improve auditing quality

    (7) Material services must receive preapproval by audit committee, and fees for those services must be disclosed to investors

4. Additional responsibilities and provisions

  a. A company must disclose whether it has adopted code of ethics for company's principal executive officer, principal accounting officer, principal financial officer or controller.

    (1) A company may have separate codes of ethics for different officers or may have broad code of ethics covering all officers and directors.

    (2) A company is not required to adopt code of ethics but if it has not, it must disclose the reasons why.

  b. Company officials found liable for fraud cannot use bankruptcy law to discharge that liability.

  c. Attorneys practicing before SEC representing issuers must report evidence of material violations by the company or its officers, directors, or agents of securities laws or breach of fiduciary duties

    (1) The report must be made to the chief legal officer or the chief executive officer.

        (a) If management does not respond appropriately, then the attorney must report the evidence "up the ladder" to audit committee of the board of directors, another committee of independent directors, or finally to the entire board of directors.

  d. The SEC adopted new rules requiring more events to be reported on Form 8-K and shortening filing deadlines for most reportable events to four business days after the date the event occurs.

    (1) If the company becomes directly or contingently liable for material obligation arising from an off-balance-sheet arrangement, it must describe this matter including its material terms and nature of arrangement.

  e. The company must disclose several items if a director has resigned or refused to stand for reelection because of disagreement with company's practices, operations or policies, or if the director has been removed for cause.

    (1) The company must disclose such items as circumstances regarding disagreement with company.

  f. If a new executive officer is appointed, the company must disclose information such as his or her name, the position, and description of any material terms of the employment agreement between company and officer.

5. The act lists several specific service categories that the issuer's public accounting firm cannot legally do, even if approved by audit committee, such as

  a. Bookkeeping or other services relating to financial statements or accounting records

  b. Financial information systems design and/or implementation

  c. Appraisal services

  d. Internal audit outsourcing services

e. Management functions
f. Actuarial services
g. Investment or broker-dealer services
h. Certain tax services, such as tax planning for potentially abusive tax shelters
i. Board permitted to exempt (on case by case basis) services of audit firm for audit client

Note that the act does **not** restrict the auditor from performing these services for to nonaudit clients or to private companies. Also, the act permits the auditor as a registered public accounting firm to perform nonaudit services not specifically prohibited (e.g., tax services) when approved by issuer's audit committee.

6. The act prohibits the audit partner having primary responsibility for the issuer's audit's and the audit partner who reviews the audits from serving for more than five consecutive years (i.e., the audit partners must be rotated every five years).

   a. If public company has hired an employee of an audit firm to be its CEO, CFO, or CAO within the previous year, the audit firm may not audit that public company.

7. The act requires increased disclosure of off-balance-sheet transactions.
8. The act mandates that pro forma financial disclosures be reconciled with figures done under GAAP.
9. The act creates new federal laws against destruction or tampering with audit workpapers or documents that are to be used in official proceedings.
10. The act increases protection of whistle-blowers from retaliation because of participation in proceedings against firms in securities fraud.

    a. Also, provides that employees may report securities fraud directly to the audit committee and may provide the information anonymously and confidentially.

11. Public Companies may not make or modify personal loans to officers or directors with few exceptions.
12. Annual reports filed with SEC that contain financial statements need to incorporate all material corrections noted by CPA firms.
13. Each company must disclose on a current basis information on financial condition that the SEC determines is useful to public.
14. The SEC is authorized to discipline professionals practicing before SEC.

    a. SEC may censure, temporarily bar or permanently bar him or her for

       (1) Lack of qualifications needed
       (2) Improper professional conduct
       (3) Willful violation of helping another violate securities laws or regulations

15. The auditor must report to the issuer's audit committee.
16. The auditors must retain workpapers for five years.

    a. Failure to do so is punishable by prison term of up to ten years.

17. Sarbanes-Oxley Act directed SEC to perform various tasks including several studies to formulate regulations; some of these studies have deadlines in the future and are expected to be used to promulgate new important regulations—others have been completed, resulted in regulations by SEC, and have force of law including the following:

    a. Require disclosure of differences between pro forma financial results and GAAP.
    b. Require that "critical" accounting policies be reported from auditors to audit committee.
    c. Companies are required to disclose if they have adopted a code of ethics.
    d. Disclosure of names of "financial experts" who serve on a company's audit committee.
    e. Actions are prohibited that fraudulently manipulate or mislead auditors.
    f. New conflict of interest rules were established for analysts.
    g. The SEC may petition courts to freeze payments by companies that are extraordinary.

18. CEOs and CFOs of most large companies listed on public stock exchanges are now required to certify financial statements filed with SEC.

    a. This generally means that they certify that information "fairly represents in all material respects the financial conditions and results of operations" of those companies and that

(1) The signing officer reviewed the report.
(2) The company's report does not contain any untrue statements of material facts or does not omit any statements of material facts to the best of his or her knowledge.
(3) The company has an internal control system in place to allow honest certification of financial statements.

(a) Or if any deficiencies in internal control exist, they must be disclosed to the auditors.

19. Blackout periods were established for issuers of certain security transaction types that limit companies' purchase, sale, or transfer of funds in individual accounts.
20. Stiffer penalties for other white-collar crimes including federal law covering mail fraud and wire fraud

H. Additional Statutory Liability Against Accountants

1. Auditors are required to use adequate procedures to uncover illegal activity of client.

2. Civil liability is proportional to degree of responsibility.

a. One type of responsibility is through the auditors' own carelessness.
b. Another type of responsibility is based on auditor's assisting in improper activities that he or she is aware or should be aware of.

NOW REVIEW MULTIPLE-CHOICE QUESTIONS 51 THROUGH 56

I. Responsibilities of Tax Return Preparers

1. **Preparer** —an individual who prepares for compensation, or who employs one or more persons to prepare for compensation, any federal tax return, or a substantial portion thereof, including income, employment, excise, exempt organization, gift, and estate tax returns.

a. Compensation must be received and can be implied or explicit (e.g., accountant who prepares individual return of the president of a company, for which he performs the audit, for no additional fee as part of a prior agreement **has** been compensated [implied]).

b. The performance of the following acts will not classify a person as a preparer:

(1) Preparation of a return for a friend, relative, or neighbor free of charge even though the person completing the return receives a gift of gratitude from the taxpayer;
(2) The furnishing of typing, reproducing, or other mechanical assistance in preparing a return; and
(3) Preparation by an employee of a return for his or her employer, or an officer of the employer, or for another employee if he or she is regularly employed by that employer.

c. Preparation of a tax return includes giving advice on events that have occurred at the time the advice is given if the advice is directly relevant to determining the existence, character, or amount of a schedule, entry, or other portion of a tax return.

2. **AICPA Statements on Standards for Tax Services**

a. **Tax Return Positions**

(1) With respect to tax return positions, a CPA

(a) Should determine and comply with the standards that are imposed by the applicable taxing authority with respect to recommending a tax return position, or preparing or signing a tax return.
(b) The CPA should

(1) Satisfy the reporting standard and disclosure requirements of the applicable taxing authority, or
(2) If the taxing authority has no written standard (or it is of lower level), the following should be applied:

(a) For undisclosed positions, realistic possibility of success
(b) For disclosed positions, reasonable basis

(c) In assisting the taxpayer in tax planning related to a tax shelter, the practitioner should inform the taxpayer of the penalty risks associated with the tax position recommended that does not possess sufficient authority to satisfy the more likely than not standard.

(d) Should not prepare or sign a tax return if the CPA knows the return takes a position that the CPA could not recommend under (b) above.

(e) Notwithstanding (b) and (c), a CPA may recommend a position for which there is a reasonable basis so long as the position is adequately disclosed on the return or claim for refund. In determining whether a given standard has been satisfied, a CPA should consider a well-reasoned construction of the applicable stature, well-reasoned articles or treatises, and pronouncements issued by the applicable taxing authority.

(f) Should advise the client of the potential penalty consequences of any recommended tax position.

(2) A CPA should not recommend a tax position that exploits the IRS audit process, or serves as a mere arguing position advanced solely to obtain leverage in bargaining with the IRS.

(3) A CPA has both the right and the responsibility to be an advocate for the client.

b. **Realistic Possibility and More Likely Than Not Standards**

(1) The CPA should consider the weight of each authority (e.g., Code, Regs., court decisions, well-reasoned treaties, article in professional tax publications, etc.) in determining whether these standards are met, and may rely on well-reasoned treatises and articles in recognized professional tax publications.

(2) Realistic possibility of success may require as much as a **one-third likelihood** of success.

(3) The more likely than not standard requires more than 50% probability of success.

c. **Answers to Questions on Returns**

(1) A CPA should make a reasonable effort to obtain from the client and provide appropriate answers to all questions on a tax return before signing as preparer.

(2) When reasonable grounds for omitting an answer exist, the CPA is not required to provide an explanation on the return of the reason for omission. Reasonable grounds for omitting an answer include

(a) Information is not readily available and the answer is not significant in terms of taxable income or tax liability.

(b) Uncertainty as to meaning of question.

(c) Answer is voluminous and return states that data will be supplied upon examination.

d. **Procedural Aspects of Preparing Returns**

(1) A CPA may in good faith rely without verification upon information furnished by the client or by third parties, and is not required to audit, examine, or review books, records, or documents in order to independently verify the taxpayer's information.

(a) However, the CPA should not ignore implications of information furnished and should make reasonable inquires if information appears incorrect, incomplete, or inconsistent.

(b) When feasible, the CPA should refer to the client's past returns.

(2) Where the IRS imposes a condition for deductibility or other treatment of an item (e.g., requires supporting documentation), the CPA should make appropriate inquiries to determine whether the condition for deductibility has been met.

(3) When preparing a tax return, a CPA should consider information known from the tax return of another client if that information is relevant to the return being prepared, and such consideration does not violate any rule regarding confidentiality.

e. **Use of Estimates**

(1) Where data is missing (e.g., result of a fire, computer failure), estimates of the missing data may be made by the client.

(2) A CPA may prepare a tax return using estimates if it is impracticable to obtain exact data, and the estimated amounts are reasonable.

(3) An estimate should not imply greater accuracy than actually exists (e.g., estimate $1,000 rather than $999.32).

f. **Departure from Position Previously Concluded in an IRS Proceeding or Court Decision**

(1) Unless the taxpayer is bound to a specified treatment in the later year, such as by a formal closing agreement, the treatment of an item as part of concluding an IRS proceeding or as part of a court decision in a prior year, does not restrict the CPA from recommending a different tax treatment in a later year's return.

(2) Court decisions, rulings, or other authorities more favorable to the taxpayer's current position may have developed since the prior proceeding was concluded or the prior court decision was rendered.

g. **Knowledge of Error: Return Preparation**

(1) The term "error" as used here includes any position, omission, or method of accounting that, at the time the return is filed, fails to meet the standards as outlined in a. and b. above. An error does not include an item that has an insignificant effect on the client's tax liability.

(2) A CPA should inform a client promptly upon becoming aware of a material error in a previously filed return or upon becoming aware of a client's failure to file a required return. A CPA

(a) Should recommend (either orally or in writing) measures to be taken.

(b) Is not obligated to inform the IRS of the error, and may not do so without the client's permission, except where required by law.

(3) If the CPA is requested to prepare the client's current return, and the client has not taken appropriate action to correct an error in a prior year's return, the CPA should consider whether to continue a professional relationship with the client or withdraw.

h. **Knowledge of Error: Administrative Proceedings**

(1) When a CPA is representing a client in an IRS proceeding (e.g., examination, appellate conference) with respect to a return that contains an error of which the CPA has become aware, the CPA should promptly inform the client and recommend measures to be taken.

(2) The CPA should request the client's permission to disclose the error to the IRS, and lacking such permission, should consider whether to withdraw from representing the client.

i. **Form and Content of Advice to Clients**

(1) No standard format is required in communicating written or oral advice to a client, but CPA should comply with standards of taxing authority

(2) In deciding on the form of advice provided (e.g., oral or written) the CPA should consider the importance of the transaction and the amounts, the specific or general nature or the inquiry, the technical complexity involved, the existence of authorities and precedents, the sophistication of the taxpayer, the type of transaction and whether it is subject to heightened reporting or disclosure, and the potential penalties involved.

(3) A CPA may choose to communicate with a client when subsequent developments affect previous advice. Such communication is only required when the CPA undertakes this obligation by specific agreement with the client.

3. **Treasury Department Circular 230**

a. **Rules Governing Authority to Practice**

(1) Practice before the IRS comprehends all matters connected with a presentation to the IRS including (but not limited to) preparing and filing documents, corresponding and communicating with the IRS, rendering written advice with respect to any entity, transactions, plan or arrangement, and representing a client at conferences, hearings, and meetings.

(2) Practice before the IRS is limited to CPAs, attorneys, enrolled agents (EAs), and for limited purposes enrolled actuaries, enrolled retirement plan agents, and registered tax return preparers (RTRP). Enrollment as an EA, retirement plan agent, or RTRP is granted if the individual is at least 18 years old and demonstrates competence in tax matters by passing an examination. Additionally, certain former employees of the IRS may be granted the right to practice as an enrolled agent by virtue of service and experience.

(a) Practice as a RTRP is limited to preparing and signing tax returns and claims for refund, and other documents for submission to the IRS. A RTRP may represent taxpayers before revenue agents, customer service representatives, or similar employees of the IRS during an examination if the RTRP signed the tax return or claim for refund for the taxable year or period under examination.

(b) A RTRP's right to practice does not permit such individual to represent the taxpayer before appeals officers, revenue officers, counsel, or similar employees of the IRS. Similarly, a RTRP is not authorized to provide tax advice to a client except as necessary to prepare a tax return, claim for refund, or other documents to be submitted to the IRS.

(3) All paid tax return preparers (including CPAs, attorneys, and EAs) must register with the IRS, pay an annual fee, and obtain a Preparer Tax Identification Number (PTIN) before preparing or signing taxpayers' tax returns or claims for refund. The IRS Office of Professional Responsibility oversees PTIN registrations, enrollment, and renewal processes.

(4) Individuals may appear on their own behalf before the IRS. Also, an individual who is not a practitioner may represent a taxpayer before the IRS in limited situations. This group includes members of the taxpayer's immediate family; full-time employees may represent their employers; an officer or full-time employee may represent a corporation; a general partner or full-time employee of a partnership may represent the partnership; and trusts, receiverships, guardianships, or estates may be represented by their trustees, receivers, guardians, or executors.

b. **Duties and Restrictions Relating to Practice Before the IRS**

(1) A practitioner must promptly submit records or information in any matter before the IRS unless the practitioner believes in good faith and on reasonable grounds that the records or information are privileged.

(2) A practitioner must, at the request of a client, promptly return the client's records. The client's records include all documents and electronic media provided to the practitioner. The existence of a dispute over fees generally does not allow the practitioner to retain records.

(3) A practitioner who becomes aware that a client has not complied with the revenue laws or has made an error in or omission from any return must advise the client promptly of the fact of such noncompliance, error, or omission, and must advise the client of the consequences under the law of such noncompliance, error, or omission.

(4) A practitioner must exercise due diligence in preparing returns and documents relating to IRS matters, as well as in determining the correctness of oral and written representations to clients and the Department of the Treasury. A practitioner may rely on the work product of another person if the practitioner used reasonable care in engaging, supervising, training, and evaluating the person.

(5) A practitioner may not charge an unconscionable fee and generally may not charge a contingent fee for preparing an original return. However, a contingent fee may be charged in connection with the IRS's examination of an original tax return, or an amended return or claim for refund or credit. Also, a contingent fee may be charged for services rendered in connection with any judicial proceeding arising under the Code.

(6) A practitioner may publish the availability of a written fee schedule including fixed fees for specific routine services, hourly rates, ranges of fees for specific services, and the fee charged for an initial consultation. The practitioner may charge no more than the published fees for at least 30 days after the last date on which the fee schedule was published.

(7) A practitioner may not use any form of public communication or private solicitation containing a false, fraudulent, or coercive statement or claim, nor a misleading or deceptive statement or claim. Enrolled agents may not utilize the word "certified" or imply an employer/employee relationship with the IRS.

(8) Tax advisors should provide clients with the highest quality representation concerning Federal tax issues by adhering to best practices in providing advice and in preparing or assisting in the preparation of a submission to the IRS.

(9) A practitioner who prepares returns may not endorse nor negotiate any federal tax refund check issued to a client by the government.

c. **Standards for Returns and Advising**

(1) A practitioner may not willfully, recklessly, or through gross incompetence sign a tax return or claim for refund that the practitioner reasonably should know contains a position that lacks a **reasonable basis**, is an unreasonable position, or is a willful attempt to understate tax liability or a reckless or intentional disregard of rules and regulations. The prohibition also applies to advising a client to take a position on a tax return or claim for refund that lacks a reasonable basis, or preparing a portion of a tax return or claim for refund containing a position that lacks a reasonable basis. The reasonable basis standard may require at least a 20% probability of a position being sustained on its merits.

(2) A practitioner may not advise a client to take a position on a document, affidavit, or other paper submitted to the IRS that is **frivolous**, nor advise a client to submit documents with the intent of delaying or

impeding the administration of federal tax laws. A frivolous position is one without basis in fact or law, or that espouses a position that the courts have held to be frivolous or groundless.

(3) A practitioner must inform a client of any penalties that are likely to apply to a position taken on a return, and must inform the client of any opportunity to avoid penalties by disclosure and the requirements of adequate disclosure.

(4) A practitioner may rely in good faith without verification upon information furnished by the client, but must make reasonable inquiries if the information furnished appears to be incorrect, incomplete, or inconsistent with other facts.

(5) Tax practitioners are required to possess the necessary competence to engage in practice before the IRS. Competence requires the appropriate level of knowledge, skill, thoroughness, and the preparation necessary for the matter at issue. A practitioner may become competent by consulting with experts or studying the applicable tax law.

(6) Practitioners with principal authority and responsibility for overseeing a firm's tax practice must take reasonable steps to ensure that their firm has adequate procedures to ensure compliance by all firm members, associates, and employees.

(7) Practitioners providing written advice must adhere to specific standards.

  (a) In providing written advice, the practitioner must:

    1) Base the advice on reasonable factual and legal assumptions.
    2) Reasonably consider all relevant facts that are known or reasonably should be known to the practitioner.
    3) Use reasonable efforts to identify and ascertain relevant facts.
    4) Not rely on unreasonable representations, statements, findings, or agreements provided by the taxpayer.
    5) Relate applicable law and authorities to facts.
    6) Not take into account that a tax return will not be audited or that the matter will not be raised on audit.

  (b) A practitioner may only rely on the advice of another person if the advice was reasonable and the reliance is in good faith considering all of the facts and circumstances.

  (c) In evaluating whether a practitioner providing written advice complied with the requirements of Circular 230, the IRS will apply a reasonable practitioner standard, considering all facts and circumstances. If the written advice is an opinion that will be used in promoting, marketing, or recommending to one or more taxpayers a partnership or other entity or arrangement with a significant purpose of avoidance or evasion of tax, the IRS will apply a reasonable practitioner standard, considering all facts and circumstances with emphasis given to the additional risk caused by the practitioner's lack of knowledge of the taxpayer's particular circumstances.

4. **Preparer Penalties**

  a. A preparer is subject to a penalty equal to the greater of $1,000, or 50% of the income derived (or to be derived) by the preparer with respect to the return or refund claim if any part of an understatement of liability with respect to the return or claim is due to an undisclosed position on the return or refund claim for which there is *not* **substantial authority**.

  (1) Substantial authority exists if the weight of authorities supporting the position is substantial in relation to the weight of those that take a contrary position. The substantial authority standard may require at least a 40% probability of being sustained on its merits.

  (2) The penalty can be avoided by

    (a) An adequate disclosure of the questionable position on the return or refund claim.
    (b) A showing that there was a **reasonable basis** for the position. The reasonable basis standard may require at least a 20% probability of being sustained on its merits.

  (3) A higher **more likely than not** standard applies if the position is with respect to a tax shelter as defined in Sec. 6662 (d)(2)(C)(ii) or a reportable transaction to which Sec. 6662A applies. This standard requires a more than 50% probability of being sustained on its merits.

  (4) The penalty can also be avoided if the preparer can show there was a reasonable cause for the understatement and that the return preparer acted in good faith.

b. If any part of an understatement of liability with respect to a return or refund claim is due (1) to a willful attempt to understate tax liability by a return preparer with respect to the return or claim, or (2) to any reckless or intentional disregard of rules or regulations, the preparer is subject to a penalty equal to the greater of $5,000, or 50% of the income derived (or to be derived) by the preparer with respect to the return or refund claim.

    (1) This penalty is reduced by the penalty paid in a. above.
    (2) Rules and regulations include the Internal Revenue Code, Treasury Regulations, and Revenue Rulings.

c. Additional penalties may be imposed on preparers if they fail to fulfill the following requirements (unless failure is due to reasonable cause):

    (1) Preparer must sign returns done for compensation.
    (2) Preparer must provide a copy of the return or refund claim to the taxpayer no later than when the preparer presents a copy of the return to the taxpayer for signing.
    (3) Returns and claims for refund must contain the social security number of preparer and identification number of preparer's employer or partnership (if any).
    (4) Preparer must either keep a list of those for whom returns were filed with specified information, or copies of the actual returns, for three years.
    (5) Employers of return preparers must retain a listing of return preparers and place of employment for three years.
    (6) Preparer must not endorse or negotiate a refund check issued to a taxpayer.
    (7) Preparer must not disclose information furnished in connection with the preparation of a tax return, unless for quality or peer review, or under an administrative order by a regulatory agency.

NOW REVIEW MULTIPLE-CHOICE QUESTIONS 57 THROUGH 80

KEY TERMS

Common Law. Law that has historically been established by judicial precedents. Much common law has now been codified in state statutes. This law is the source of liability to clients and third parties (not covered by securities laws).

Constructive fraud. Failure to even use slight care. Constructive fraud is often referred to as gross negligence.

Contributory negligence. Negligence on the part of the plaintiff that contributed to that party's losses. Contributory negligence will typically mitigate some or all of the defendant's damages.

Due diligence. The standard of care required under filings under the Securities Act of 1933. To establish "due diligence" an accountant must have made a reasonable investigation, and must have had reasonable grounds to believe and did believe that that the registration statement (including the financial statements) were not misleading.

Fraud. A misrepresentation intended to mislead another party or a representation made with a reckless disregard for its truth.

Joint and several liability. A concept of liability that is similar to joint liability except that if all of the judgment is recovered from one defendant that party may attempt to collect from other defendants their proportionate shares of the judgment. As an example, assume a bank files suit against both the CPA firm and management for misleading financial statements, and the CPA firm is found to be 30% liable and management is found to be 70% liable. The bank may recover 100% of the judgment from the CPA firm and it is up to the CPA firm to collect from management its share of the judgment.

Joint Ethics Enforcement Program (JEEP). A joint program of the American Institute of Certified Public Accountants (AICPA) and state CPA societies to jointly investigate ethics violations.

Joint liability. A liability concept in which any joint defendant may be forced to pay the entire amount of a judgment. As an example, if a bank files suit against both the CPA firm and management for misleading financial statements, the bank may recover the entire amount from management or the CPA firm.

Negligence. Failure to perform with the level of skill and judgment possessed by a typical professional. Negligence is often referred to as ordinary negligence.

Primary beneficiary. A party other than the client who primarily benefits from the contracted services provided by the CPA. As an example, if the CPA is aware that an audit is being performed at the request of the client's bank, the bank is a primary beneficiary of the contract between the CPA and the client. Under common law a primary beneficiary has the same rights as the client.

Privileged communication. Communication that is not subject to disclosure in court or administrative proceedings. Privilege must be established by law, and generally the communication between an accountant and a client is not privileged.

Privity. A mutual relationship established between parties typically established by a contract. The client and third-party beneficiaries are in privity with the CPA in a contract to provide services.

Public Company Accounting Oversight Board (PCAOB). A nonprofit organization created by the Sarbanes-Oxley Act to oversee the audits of public companies (issuers).

Public Company Accounting Reform and Investor Protection (Sarbanes-Oxley) Act. An act that set a new set of enhanced standards for public company boards, management, and public accounting firms. The Act established the Public Company Accounting Oversight Board (PCAOB).

Racketeer Influenced and Corrupt Organization (RICO) Act. An act designed to allow prosecution of organized criminals. However, the Act has been used to pursue CPA firms who engage in multiple instances (a pattern) of wrongful acts. Civil actions under the Act can result in recovery of treble damages.

Securities Act of 1933. A federal securities act that covers the initial registration of securities.

Securities Exchange Act of 1934. A federal securities act that covers the secondary purchase and sale of securities.

Several liability. A concept of liability in which joint defendants are responsible for only their proportionate share of the judgment. As an example, assume that a bank files suit against both the CPA firm and management for misleading financial statements, and the CPA firm is found to be 30% liable and management is found to be 70% liable. The bank may recover only 30% of the judgment from the CPA firm. The remaining amount must be recovered by the bank from management.

State boards of accountancy. State boards that regulate the practice of public accountancy in a state or jurisdiction. All individual CPAs and CPA firms must be licensed to practice in the states where they practice.

Statements on Standards for Tax Services. AICPA standards for CPAs that perform tax services for clients.

Treasury Department Circular 230. Regulatory requirements regarding the authority to practice before the Internal Revenue Service.

US Securities and Exchange Commission (SEC). A federal agency with primary responsibility for enforcing the federal securities laws and regulating the securities industry.

A.   *Regulation of the Profession*

1. Which of the following bodies issue permits to practice for CPAs?

    a. The AICPA.
    b. The SEC.
    c. The state boards of accountancy.
    d. The PCAOB.

2. Which of the following is **not** an accurate statement about the requirements of the AICPA Uniform Accountancy Act (UAA)?

    a. The UAA requires all accountants to be licensed.
    b. The UAA contains requirements for the issuance of CPA certificates.
    c. The UAA contains a substantial equivalency provision to allow for movement between states.
    d. The UAA contains provisions for continuing education.

B.   *Disciplinary Systems of the Profession and Regulatory Bodies*

3. Which of the following is **not** a possible result of an AICPA investigation of a member for an ethics violation?

    a. Revocation of right to prepare tax returns.
    b. Admonishment.
    c. Corrective action.
    d. Expulsion.

4. Which of the following may **not** result in automatic expulsion from the AICPA?

    a. Revocation of CPA certificate by an authorized body.
    b. Filing a fraudulent tax return.
    c. Failure to file a required tax return.
    d. Conviction for a felony or a misdemeanor.

5. A member of the AICPA is convicted of filing a fraudulent tax return. What is the likely consequence of this action?

    a. The CPA will likely be expelled or suspended from membership in the AICPA.
    b. The CPA will likely be admonished by the AICPA.
    c. The CPA will likely have his or her permit to practice revoked by the AICPA.
    d. The AICPA will take no action because the court has already taken sufficient action.

C.1.   *Common Law Liability to Clients*

6. Cable Corp. orally engaged Drake & Co., CPAs, to audit its financial statements. Cable's management informed Drake that it suspected the accounts receivable were materially overstated. Though the financial statements Drake audited included a materially overstated accounts receivable balance, Drake issued an unqualified opinion. Cable used the financial statements to obtain a loan to expand its operations. Cable defaulted on the loan and incurred a substantial loss.

If Cable sues Drake for negligence in failing to discover the overstatement, Drake's best defense would be that Drake did **not**

    a. Have privity of contract with Cable.
    b. Sign an engagement letter.
    c. Perform the audit recklessly or with an intent to deceive.
    d. Violate generally accepted auditing standards in performing the audit.

7. Which of the following statements best describes whether a CPA has met the required standard of care in conducting an audit of a client's financial statements?

    a. The client's expectations with regard to the accuracy of audited financial statements.
    b. The accuracy of the financial statements and whether the statements conform to generally accepted accounting principles.
    c. Whether the CPA conducted the audit with the same skill and care expected of an ordinarily prudent CPA under the circumstances.
    d. Whether the audit was conducted to investigate and discover all acts of fraud.

8. Ford & Co., CPAs, issued an unqualified opinion on Owens Corp.'s financial statements. Relying on these financial statements, Century Bank lent Owens $750,000. Ford was unaware that Century would receive a copy of the financial statements or that Owens would use them to obtain a loan. Owens defaulted on the loan.

To succeed in a common law fraud action against Ford, Century must prove, in addition to other elements, that Century was

    a. Free from contributory negligence.
    b. In privity of contract with Ford.
    c. Justified in relying on the financial statements.
    d. In privity of contract with Owens.

9. When performing an audit, a CPA

    a. Must exercise the level of care, skill, and judgment expected of a reasonably prudent CPA under the circumstances.
    b. Must strictly adhere to generally accepted accounting principles.
    c. Is strictly liable for failing to discover client fraud.
    d. Is **not** liable unless the CPA commits gross negligence or intentionally disregards generally accepted auditing standards.

10. When performing an audit, a CPA will **most** likely be considered negligent when the CPA fails to

a. Detect all of a client's fraudulent activities.
b. Include a negligence disclaimer in the client engagement letter.
c. Warn a client of known internal control weaknesses.
d. Warn a client's customers of embezzlement by the client's employees.

Items 11 through 14 are based on the following:

Edgar, CPA, reviewed the financial statements of Yoke Company (a nonissuer company). In performing the review Edgar failed to discover that a supplier had been overbilling Yoke for purchases for a number of years. Yoke filed a lawsuit against Edgar for negligence in performing the review.

11. Under which of the following sources of law would this lawsuit likely be filed?

a. The Securities Act of 1933.
b. The Securities Exchange Act of 1934.
c. Common law.
d. State securities law.

12. What would be essential to proving Yoke's case against Edgar?

a. Failure to adhere to generally accepted auditing standards.
b. Reckless disregard for professional standards.
c. Ordinary negligence in the performance of the review.
d. Gross negligence in the performance of the review.

13. Which of the following would not likely be part of Edgar's defense in this lawsuit?

a. Contributory negligence.
b. Performance of the engagement in accordance with Statement for Accounting and Review Services.
c. A review cannot be relied upon to detect fraud.
d. Misrepresentations by management.

14. Assuming that Yoke prevails in proving negligence by Edgar in this case, which of the following is the most accurate statement about the damages that would be awarded? Assume that no other party, including Yoke, was found to be partially responsible for the losses.

a. Edgar would be responsible for all of the overbillings that occurred.
b. Edgar would be responsible for overbillings occurring since the date he should have detected the scheme.
c. Edgar would be responsible only for returning the fees for the engagement.
d. Edgar would not be held responsible for any damages unless he is also found to be in violation of some criminal law.

15. A CPA's duty of due care to a client most likely will be breached when a CPA

a. Gives a client an oral instead of written report.
b. Gives a client incorrect advice based on an honest error of judgment.
c. Fails to give tax advice that saves the client money.
d. Fails to follow generally accepted auditing standards.

16. Which of the following elements, if present, would support a finding of constructive fraud on the part of a CPA?

a. Gross negligence in applying generally accepted auditing standards.
b. Ordinary negligence in applying generally accepted accounting principles.
c. Identified third-party users.
d. Scienter.

C.2. Common Law Liability to Third Parties (Nonclients)

17. If a CPA recklessly departs from the standards of due care when conducting an audit, the CPA will be liable to third parties who are unknown to the CPA based on

a. Negligence.
b. Gross negligence.
c. Strict liability.
d. Criminal deceit.

18. In a common law action against an accountant, lack of privity is a viable defense if the plaintiff

a. Is the client's creditor who sues the accountant for negligence.
b. Can prove the presence of gross negligence that amounts to a reckless disregard for the truth.
c. Is the accountant's client.
d. Bases the action upon fraud.

19. A CPA audited the financial statements of Shelly Company. The CPA was negligent in the audit. Sanco, a supplier of Shelly, is upset because Sanco had extended Shelly a high credit limit based on the financial statements which were incorrect. Which of the following statements is the **most** correct?

a. In most states, both Shelly and Sanco can recover from the CPA for damages due to the negligence.
b. States that use the Ultramares decision will allow both Shelly and Sanco to recover.
c. In most states, Sanco cannot recover as a mere foreseeable third party.
d. Generally, Sanco can recover but Shelly cannot.

20. Under the Ultramares rule, to which of the following parties will an accountant be liable for negligence?

	Parties in privity	Foreseen parties
a.	Yes	Yes
b.	Yes	No
c.	No	Yes
d.	No	No

Items 21 and 22 are based on the following:

While conducting an audit, Larson Associates, CPAs, failed to detect material misstatements included in its client's financial statements. Larson's unqualified opinion was included with the financial statements in a registration statement and prospectus for a public offering of securities made by the client. Larson knew that its opinion and the financial statements would be used for this purpose.

21. In a suit by a purchaser against Larson for common law negligence, Larson's best defense would be that the

- a. Audit was conducted in accordance with generally accepted auditing standards.
- b. Client was aware of the misstatements.
- c. Purchaser was **not** in privity of contract with Larson.
- d. Identity of the purchaser was **not** known to Larson at the time of the audit.

22. In a suit by a purchaser against Larson for common law fraud, Larson's **best** defense would be that

- a. Larson did **not** have actual or constructive knowledge of the misstatements.
- b. Larson's client knew or should have known of the misstatements.
- c. Larson did **not** have actual knowledge that the purchaser was an intended beneficiary of the audit.
- d. Larson was **not** in privity of contract with its client.

C.3. Statutory Liability to Third Parties— Securities Act of 1933

23. Quincy bought Teal Corp. common stock in an offering registered under the Securities Act of 1933. Worth & Co., CPAs, gave an unqualified opinion on Teal's financial statements that were included in the registration statement filed with the SEC. Quincy sued Worth under the provisions of the 1933 Act that deal with omission of facts required to be in the registration statement. Quincy must prove that

- a. There was fraudulent activity by Worth.
- b. There was a material misstatement in the financial statements.
- c. Quincy relied on Worth's opinion.
- d. Quincy was in privity with Worth.

24. Beckler & Associates, CPAs, audited and gave an unqualified opinion on the financial statements of Queen Co. The financial statements contained misstatements that resulted in a material overstatement of Queen's net worth. Queen provided the audited financial statements to Mac Bank in connection with a loan made by Mac to Queen. Beckler knew that the financial statements would be provided to Mac. Queen defaulted on the loan. Mac sued Beckler to recover for its losses associated with Queen's default. Which of the following must Mac prove in order to recover?

I. Beckler was negligent in conducting the audit.
II. Mac relied on the financial statements.

- a. I only.
- b. II only.
- c. Both I and II.
- d. Neither I nor II.

Items 25 and 26 are based on the following:

Dart Corp. engaged Jay Associates, CPAs, to assist in a public stock offering. Jay audited Dart's financial statements and gave an unqualified opinion, despite knowing that the financial statements contained misstatements. Jay's opinion was included in Dart's registration statement. Larson purchased shares in the offering and suffered a loss when the stock declined in value after the misstatements became known.

25. In a suit against Jay and Dart under the Section 11 liability provisions of the Securities Act of 1933, Larson must prove that

- a. Jay knew of the misstatements.
- b. Jay was negligent.
- c. The misstatements contained in Dart's financial statements were material.
- d. The unqualified opinion contained in the registration statement was relied on by Larson.

26. If Larson succeeds in the Section 11 suit against Dart, Larson would be entitled to

- a. Damages of three times the original public offering price.
- b. Rescind the transaction.
- c. Monetary damages only.
- d. Damages, but only if the shares were resold before the suit was started.

Items 27 and 28 are based on the following:

Under the liability provisions of Section 11 of the Securities Act of 1933, a CPA may be liable to any purchaser of a security for certifying materially misstated financial statements that are included in the security's registration statement.

27. Under Section 11, a CPA usually will **not** be liable to the purchaser

- a. If the purchaser is contributorily negligent.
- b. If the CPA can prove due diligence.
- c. Unless the purchaser can prove privity with the CPA.
- d. Unless the purchaser can prove scienter on the part of the CPA.

28. Under Section 11, which of the following must be proven by a purchaser of the security?

	Reliance on the financial statements	Fraud by the CPA
a.	Yes	Yes
b.	Yes	No
c.	No	Yes
d.	No	No

29. Ocean and Associates, CPAs, audited the financial statements of Drain Corporation. As a result of Ocean's negligence in conducting the audit, the financial statements included material misstatements. Ocean was unaware of this fact. The financial statements and Ocean's unqualified opin-ion were included in a registration statement and prospectus for an original public offering of stock by Drain. Sharp purchased shares in the offering. Sharp received a copy of the prospectus prior to the purchase but did not read it. The shares declined in value as a result of the misstatements in Drain's financial statements becoming known. Under which of the following Acts is Sharp **most** likely to prevail in a lawsuit against Ocean?

	Securities Exchange Act of 1934, Section 10(b), Rule 10b-5	Securities Act of 1933, Section 11
a.	Yes	Yes
b.	Yes	No
c.	No	Yes
d.	No	No

30. Danvy, a CPA, performed an audit for Lank Corporation. Danvy also performed an S-1 review to review events subsequent to the balance sheet date. If Danvy fails to further investigate suspicious facts, under which of these can he be found negligent?

    a. The audit but not the review.
    b. The review but not the audit.
    c. Neither the audit nor the review.
    d. Both the audit and the review.

C.4. Statutory Liability to Third Parties— Securities Exchange Act of 1934

31. Dart Corp. engaged Jay Associates, CPAs, to assist in a public stock offering. Jay audited Dart's financial statements and gave an unqualified opinion, despite knowing that the financial statements contained misstatements. Jay's opinion was included in Dart's registration statement. Larson purchased shares in the offering and suffered a loss when the stock declined in value after the misstatements became known.

In a suit against Jay under the antifraud provisions of Section 10(b) and Rule 10b-5 of the Securities Exchange Act of 1934, Larson must prove all of the following **except**

    a. Larson was an intended user of the false registration statement.
    b. Larson relied on the false registration statement.
    c. The transaction involved some form of interstate commerce.
    d. Jay acted with intentional disregard of the truth.

32. Under the antifraud provisions of Section 10(b) of the Securities Exchange Act of 1934, a CPA may be liable if the CPA acted

    a. Negligently.
    b. With independence.
    c. Without due diligence.
    d. Without good faith.

33. Under Section 11 of the Securities Act of 1933, which of the following standards may a CPA use as a defense?

	Generally accepted accounting principles	Generally accepted fraud detection standards
a.	Yes	Yes
b.	Yes	No
c.	No	Yes
d.	No	No

34. Dart Corp. engaged Jay Associates, CPAs, to assist in a public stock offering. Jay audited Dart's financial

statements and gave an unqualified opinion, despite knowing that the financial statements contained misstatements. Jay's opinion was included in Dart's registration statement. Larson purchased shares in the offering and suffered a loss when the stock declined in value after the misstatements became known.

If Larson succeeds in the Section 10(b) and Rule 10b-5 suit, Larson would be entitled to

    a. Only recover the original public offering price.
    b. Only rescind the transaction.
    c. The amount of any loss caused by the fraud.
    d. Punitive damages.

D.1. Accountant's Working Papers

35. Which of the following statements is correct with respect to ownership, possession, or access to a CPA firm's audit working papers?

    a. Working papers may **never** be obtained by third parties unless the client consents.
    b. Working papers are **not** transferable to a purchaser of a CPA practice unless the client consents.
    c. Working papers are subject to the privileged communication rule which, in most jurisdictions, prevents any third-party access to the working papers.
    d. Working papers are the client's exclusive property.

36. Which of the following statements is correct regarding a CPA's working papers? The working papers must be

    a. Transferred to another accountant purchasing the CPA's practice even if the client hasn't given permission.
    b. Transferred permanently to the client if demanded.
    c. Turned over to any government agency that requests them.
    d. Turned over pursuant to a valid federal court subpoena.

37. To which of the following parties may a CPA partnership provide its working papers, without being lawfully subpoenaed or without the client's consent?

    a. The IRS.
    b. The FASB.
    c. Any surviving partner(s) on the death of a partner.
    d. A CPA before purchasing a partnership interest in the firm.

38. To which of the following parties may a CPA partnership provide its working papers without either the client's consent or a lawful subpoena?

	The IRS	The FASB
a.	Yes	Yes
b.	Yes	No
c.	No	Yes
d.	No	No

D.2. Privileged Communications between Accountant and Client

39. A CPA is permitted to disclose confidential client information without the consent of the client to

I. Another CPA who has purchased the CPA's tax practice.
II. Another CPA firm if the information concerns suspected tax return irregularities.
III. A state CPA society voluntary quality control review board.

    a. I and III only.
    b. II and III only.
    c. II only.
    d. III only.

40. Thorp, CPA, was engaged to audit Ivor Co.'s financial statements. During the audit, Thorp discovered that Ivor's inventory contained stolen goods. Ivor was indicted and Thorp was subpoenaed to testify at the criminal trial. Ivor claimed accountant-client privilege to prevent Thorp from testifying. Which of the following statements is correct regarding Ivor's claim?

    a. Ivor can claim an accountant-client privilege only in states that have enacted a statute creating such a privilege.
    b. Ivor can claim an accountant-client privilege only in federal courts.
    c. The accountant-client privilege can be claimed only in civil suits.
    d. The accountant-client privilege can be claimed only to limit testimony to audit subject matter.

41. A violation of the profession's ethical standards **most** likely would have occurred when a CPA

    a. Issued an unqualified opinion on the 2002 financial statements when fees for the 2001 audit were unpaid.
    b. Recommended a controller's position description with candidate specifications to an audit client.
    c. Purchased a CPA firm's practice of monthly write-ups for a percentage of fees to be received over a three-year period.
    d. Made arrangements with a financial institution to collect notes issued by a client in payment of fees due for the current year's audit.

42. Which of the following statements concerning an accountant's disclosure of confidential client data is generally correct?

    a. Disclosure may be made to any state agency without subpoena.
    b. Disclosure may be made to any party on consent of the client.
    c. Disclosure may be made to comply with an IRS audit request.
    d. Disclosure may be made to comply with generally accepted accounting principles.

E. Criminal Liability

43. A CPA may be held criminally liable under any of the following, except:

    a. The Securities Act of 1933.
    b. Common law.

    c. The Racketeer Influenced and Corrupt Organizations Act.
    d. Federal tax laws.

44. Which of the following acts allows civil suits with the potential recovery of treble damages?

    a. The Racketeer Influenced and Corrupt Organizations Act.
    b. The Securities Act of 1933.
    c. The Securities Exchange Act of 1934.
    d. Federal tax acts.

F. Responsibilities of Auditors under Private Securities Litigation Reform Act

45. McGee is auditing Nevus Corporation and detects probable criminal activity by one of the employees. McGee believes this will have a material impact on the financial statements. The financial statements of Nevus Corporation are under the Securities Exchange Act of 1934. Which of the following is correct?

    a. McGee should report this to the Securities Exchange Commission.
    b. McGee should report this to the Justice Department.
    c. McGee should report this to Nevus Corporation's audit committee or board of directors.
    d. McGee will discharge his duty by requiring that a note of this be included in the financial statements.

46. Which of the following is an auditor not required to establish procedures for under the Private Securities Litigation Reform Act?

    a. To develop a comprehensive internal control system.
    b. To evaluate the ability of the firm to continue as a going concern.
    c. To detect material illegal acts.
    d. To identify material related-party transactions.

47. Which of the following is an auditor required to do under the Private Securities Litigation Reform Act concerning audits under the Federal Securities Exchange Act of 1934?

I. Establish procedures to detect material illegal acts of the client being audited.
II. Evaluate the ability of the firm being audited to continue as a going concern.

    a. Neither I nor II.
    b. I only.
    c. II only.
    d. Both I and II.

48. Lin, CPA, is auditing the financial statements of Exchange Corporation under the Federal Securities Exchange Act of 1934. He detects what he believes are probable material illegal acts. What is his duty under the Private Securities Litigation Reform Act?

    a. He must inform the principal shareholders within ten days.
    b. He must inform the audit committee or the board of directors.
    c. He need not inform anyone, beyond requiring that the financial statements are presented fairly.

d. He should not inform anyone since he owes a duty of confidentiality to the client.

49. The Private Securities Litigation Reform Act

a. Applies only to securities not purchased from a stock exchange.
b. Does not apply to common stock of a publicly held corporation.
c. Amends the Federal Securities Act of 1933 and the Federal Securities Exchange Act of 1934.
d. Does not apply to preferred stock of a publicly held corporation.

50. Bran, CPA, audited Frank Corporation. The shareholders sued both Frank and Bran for securities fraud under the Federal Securities Exchange Act of 1934. The court determined that there was securities fraud and that Frank was 80% at fault and Bran was 20% at fault due to her negligence in the audit. Both Frank and Bran are solvent and the damages were determined to be $1 million. What is the maximum liability of Bran?

a. $0
b. $200,000
c. $500,000
d. $1,000,000

G. Responsibilities under Sarbanes-Oxley Act

51. Which of the following nonattest services are auditors allowed to perform for a public company?

a. Bookkeeping services.
b. Appraisal services.
c. Tax services.
d. Internal audit services.

52. Which of the following Boards has the responsibility to regulate CPA firms that audit public companies?

a. Auditing Standards Board.
b. Public Oversight Board.
c. Public Company Accounting Oversight Board.
d. Accounting Standards Board.

53. The Sarbanes-Oxley Act includes all of the following provisions, **except:**

a. Penalties for failure to retain audit workpapers.
b. Requirement for registration of CPA firms to audit public companies.
c. Requirement for inspection of public-company audits.
d. Requirement for a minimum level of experience for audit partners.

54. Under the Sarbanes-Oxley Act, which of the following individuals are required personally to certify to the accuracy of financial statements filed with the SEC?

a. The chief financial officer and the chief executive officer.
b. The chief financial officer, the chief executive officer, and the controller.
c. The audit partner and the chief executive officer.

d. The chairman of the board, the chief executive officer, and the chief financial officer.

55. Generally a Form 8-K must be filed with the SEC

a. Annually.
b. Quarterly.
c. Within four days of the occurrence of a triggering event.
d. Within 10 days of the occurrence of a triggering event.

56. The Sarbanes-Oxley Act of 2002 requires rotation of the audit partner on a public company audit at least every

a. 3 years.
b. 5 years.
c. 7 years.
d. 10 years.

I. Responsibilities of Tax Return Preparers

57. Which of the following acts constitute(s) grounds for a tax preparer penalty?

I. Without the taxpayer's consent, the tax preparer disclosed taxpayer income tax return information under an order from a state court.
II. At the taxpayer's suggestion, the tax preparer deducted the expenses of the taxpayers' personal domestic help as a business expense on the taxpayer's individual tax return.

a. I only.
b. II only.
c. Both I and II.
d. Neither I nor II.

58. Vee Corp. retained Water, CPA, to prepare its 2014 income tax return. During the engagement, Water discovered that Vee had failed to file its 2009 income tax return. What is Water's professional responsibility regarding Vee's unfiled 2009 income tax return?

a. Prepare Vee's 2009 income tax return and submit it to the IRS.
b. Advise Vee that the 2009 income tax return has not been filed and recommend that Vee ignore filing its 2009 return since the statute of limitations has passed.
c. Advise the IRS that Vee's 2009 income tax return has not been filed.
d. Consider withdrawing from preparation of Vee's 2014 income tax return until the error is corrected.

59. To avoid tax return preparer penalties for a return's understated tax liability due to an intentional disregard of the regulations, which of the following actions must a tax preparer take?

a. Audit the taxpayer's corresponding business operations.
b. Review the accuracy of the taxpayer's books and records.
c. Make reasonable inquiries if the taxpayer's information is incomplete.
d. Examine the taxpayer's supporting documents.

60. Kopel was engaged to prepare Raff's 2014 federal income tax return. During the tax preparation interview, Raff told Kopel that he paid $3,000 in property taxes in 2014. Actually, Raff's property taxes amounted to only $600. Based on Raff's word, Kopel deducted the $3,000 on Raff's return, resulting in an understatement of Raff's tax liability. Kopel had no reason to believe that the information was incorrect. Kopel did not request underlying documentation and was reasonably satisfied by Raff's representation that Raff had adequate records to support the deduction. Which of the following statements is correct?

    a. To avoid the preparer penalty for willful understatement of tax liability, Kopel was obligated to examine the underlying documentation for the deduction.

    b. To avoid the preparer penalty for willful understatement of tax liability, Kopel would be required to obtain Raff's representation in writing.

    c. Kopel is **not** subject to the preparer penalty for willful understatement of tax liability because the deduction that was claimed was more than 25% of the actual amount that should have been deducted.

    d. Kopel is **not** subject to the preparer penalty for willful understatement of tax liability because Kopel was justified in relying on Raff's representation.

61. A penalty for understated corporate tax liability can be imposed on a tax preparer who fails to

    a. Audit the corporate records.

    b. Examine business operations.

    c. Copy all underlying documents.

    d. Make reasonable inquiries when taxpayer information appears incorrect.

62. A tax return preparer is subject to a penalty for knowingly or recklessly disclosing corporate tax return information, if the disclosure is made

    a. To enable a third party to solicit business from the taxpayer.

    b. To enable the tax processor to electronically compute the taxpayer's liability.

    c. For peer review.

    d. Under an administrative order by a state agency that registers tax return preparers.

63. A tax return preparer may disclose or use tax return information without the taxpayer's consent to

    a. Facilitate a supplier's or lender's credit evaluation of the taxpayer.

    b. Accommodate the request of a financial institution that needs to determine the amount of taxpayer's debt to it, to be forgiven.

    c. Be evaluated by a quality or peer review.

    d. Solicit additional nontax business.

64. Which, if any, of the following could result in penalties against an income tax return preparer?

  I. Knowing or reckless disclosure or use of tax information obtained in preparing a return.

  II. A willful attempt to understate any client's tax liability on a return or claim for refund.

    a. Neither I nor II.

    b. I only.

    c. II only.

    d. Both I and II.

65. Clark, a professional tax return preparer, prepared and signed a client's 2014 federal income tax return that resulted in a $600 refund. Which one of the following statements is correct with regard to an Internal Revenue Code penalty Clark may be subject to for endorsing and cashing the client's refund check?

    a. Clark will be subject to the penalty if Clark endorses and cashes the check.

    b. Clark may endorse and cash the check, without penalty, if Clark is enrolled to practice before the Internal Revenue Service.

    c. Clark may endorse and cash the check, without penalty, because the check is for less than $1,000.

    d. Clark may endorse and cash the check, without penalty, if the amount does **not** exceed Clark's fee for preparation of the return.

66. A CPA who prepares clients' federal income tax returns for a fee must

    a. File certain required notices and powers of attorney with the IRS before preparing any returns.

    b. Keep a completed copy of each return for a specified period of time.

    c. Receive client documentation supporting all travel and entertainment expenses deducted on the return.

    d. Indicate the CPA's federal identification number on a tax return only if the return reflects tax due from the taxpayer.

67. A CPA owes a duty to

    a. Provide for a successor CPA in the event death or disability prevents completion of an audit.

    b. Advise a client of errors contained in a previously filed tax return.

    c. Disclose client fraud to third parties.

    d. Perform an audit according to GAAP so that fraud will be uncovered.

68. In general, if the IRS issues a 30-day letter to an individual taxpayer who wishes to dispute the assessment, the taxpayer

    a. May, without paying any tax, immediately file a petition that would properly commence an action in Tax Court.

    b. May ignore the 30-day letter and wait to receive a 90-day letter.

    c. Must file a written protest within 10 days of receiving the letter.

    d. Must pay the taxes and then commence an action in federal district court.

69. A CPA will be liable to a tax client for damages resulting from all of the following actions **except**

    a. Failing to timely file a client's return.

    b. Failing to advise a client of certain tax elections.

c. Refusing to sign a client's request for a filing extension.

d. Neglecting to evaluate the option of preparing joint or separate returns that would have resulted in a substantial tax savings for a married client.

70. According to the AICPA Statement on Standards for Tax Services, which of the following statements is correct regarding the standards a CPA should follow when recommending tax return positions and preparing tax returns?

a. A CPA may recommend a position that the CPA concludes is frivolous as long as the position is adequately disclosed on the return.

b. A CPA may recommend a position in which the CPA has a good faith belief that the position has a realistic possibility of being sustained if challenged.

c. A CPA will usually **not** advise the client of the potential penalty consequences of the recommended tax return position.

d. A CPA may sign a tax return as preparer knowing that the return takes a position that will **not** be sustained if challenged.

71. According to the standards of the profession, which of the following statements is(are) correct regarding the action to be taken by a CPA who discovers an error in a client's previously filed tax return?

I. Advise the client of the error and recommend the measures to be taken.

II. Withdraw from the professional relationship regardless of whether or not the client corrects the error.

a. I only.
b. II only.
c. Both I and II.
d. Neither I nor II.

72. According to the profession's ethical standards, a CPA preparing a client's tax return may rely on unsupported information furnished by the client, without examining underlying information, **unless** the information

a. Is derived from a pass-through entity.
b. Appears to be incomplete on its face.
c. Concerns dividends received.
d. Lists charitable contributions.

73. Which of the following acts by a CPA will **not** result in a CPA incurring an IRS penalty?

a. Failing, without reasonable cause, to provide the client with a copy of an income tax return.

b. Failing, without reasonable cause, to sign a client's tax return as preparer.

c. Understating a client's tax liability as a result of an error in calculation.

d. Negotiating a client's tax refund check when the CPA prepared the tax return.

74. According to the standards of the profession, which of the following sources of information should a CPA consider before signing a client's tax return?

I. Information actually known to the CPA from the tax return of another client.

II. Information provided by the client that appears to be correct based on the client's returns from prior years.

a. I only.
b. II only.
c. Both I and II.
d. Neither I nor II.

75. According to Treasury Department Circular 230, a practitioner may

a. Charge a contingent fee for preparing a client's original tax return.

b. Charge any amount of fixed fee for tax work.

c. Retain a client's records for nonpayment of fees.

d. Charge a contingent fee for representing a client in connection with a judicial proceeding.

76. Circular 230 limits practice before the Internal Revenue Service to

a. Certified Public Accountants.
b. Attorneys.
c. Registered tax return preparers.
d. All of the above may practice before the IRS.

77. A practitioner is in violation of Circular 230 if the practitioner

a. Publishes the availability of a written schedule of fees containing hourly rates.

b. Charges a contingent fee for filing an original tax return.

c. Informs a client of the possible penalties that may apply to a position taken on a tax return.

d. Relies, without verification, upon information furnished by the client.

78. Circular 230 defines practice before the Internal Revenue Service to include

a. Preparing and filing documents with the IRS.

b. Corresponding and communicating with the IRS.

c. Representing a client during an examination at IRS offices.

d. All of the above are considered practice before the IRS.

79. According to Circular 230, practitioners must not sign a tax return if the return takes a position that does **not** have

a. A more-likely-than-not probability of being sustained.
b. Substantial authority.
c. A realistic possibility of being sustained.
d. A reasonable basis.

80. According to Treasury Circular 230, when providing written advice, a practitioner must do all of the following, except:

a. Base the advice on reasonable and legal assumptions.

b. Use reasonable efforts to identify and ascertain relevant facts.

c. Consider whether the matter will be raised on a tax audit.

d. Relate applicable law and authorities to facts.

Multiple-Choice Answers and Explanations

Answers

1.	c	__ __	18.	a	__ __	35.	b	__ __	52.	c	__ __	69.	c	__ __
2.	a	__ __	19.	c	__ __	36.	d	__ __	53.	d	__ __	70.	b	__ __
3.	a	__ __	20.	b	__ __	37.	c	__ __	54.	a	__ __	71.	a	__ __
4.	d	__ __	21.	a	__ __	38.	d	__ __	55.	c	__ __	72.	b	__ __
5.	a	__ __	22.	a	__ __	39.	d	__ __	56.	b	__ __	73.	c	__ __
6.	d	__ __	23.	b	__ __	40.	a	__ __	57.	b	__ __	74.	c	__ __
7.	c	__ __	24.	c	__ __	41.	a	__ __	58.	d	__ __	75.	d	__ __
8.	c	__ __	25.	c	__ __	42.	b	__ __	59.	c	__ __	76.	d	__ __
9.	a	__ __	26.	c	__ __	43.	b	__ __	60.	d	__ __	77.	b	__ __
10.	c	__ __	27.	b	__ __	44.	a	__ __	61.	d	__ __	78.	d	__ __
11.	c	__ __	28.	d	__ __	45.	c	__ __	62.	a	__ __	79.	d	__ __
12.	c	__ __	29.	c	__ __	46.	a	__ __	63.	c	__ __	80.	c	__ __
13.	d	__ __	30.	d	__ __	47.	d	__ __	64.	d	__ __			
14.	b	__ __	31.	a	__ __	48.	b	__ __	65.	a	__ __			
15.	d	__ __	32.	d	__ __	49.	c	__ __	66.	b	__ __			
16.	a	__ __	33.	b	__ __	50.	b	__ __	67.	b	__ __	1st:	__/80 =	__%
17.	b	__ __	34.	c	__ __	51.	c	__ __	68.	b	__ __	2nd:	__/80 =	__%

Explanations

1. (c) The requirement is to identify the body that issues permits to practice. Answer (c) is correct because only state boards of accountancy (or similar authorities) may issue permits to practice. The other organizations do not.

2. (a) The UAA only requires accountants who perform attest services or compilations of financial statements to be licensed. Answers (b), (c), and (d) are incorrect because they are all requirements of the UAA.

3. (a) The requirement is to identify the item that is **not** a possible result of an AICPA ethics investigation. Answer (a) is correct because the AICPA cannot revoke the right to prepare a tax return.

4. (d) The requirement is to identify the item that may **not** result in automatic expulsion from the AICPA. Answer (d) is correct because conviction for a misdemeanor would not result in automatic expulsion.

5. (a) The requirement is to identify the likely result of a member of the AICPA being convicted of filing a fraudulent tax return. Answer (a) is correct because this is one of the situations that can result in suspension or expulsion without a hearing.

6. (d) A CPA is not automatically liable for failure to discover a materially overstated account. The CPA can be liable if the failure to discover was due to the CPA's own negligence. Although performing an audit in accordance with GAAS does not guarantee that there is no negligence, it is normally a good defense against negligence. Answer (a) is incorrect because there was privity of contract with Cable. There was an oral agreement constituting a contractual relationship, therefore this would not be a good defense. Answer (b) is incorrect because an oral contract for an audit is still enforceable without a

signed engagement letter. Answer (c) is incorrect because a CPA does not have to perform an audit recklessly or with an intent to deceive to be liable for negligence. Negligence simply means that a CPA failed to exercise due care owed of the average reasonable accountant in performing an audit.

7. (c) In order to meet the required standard of due care in conducting an audit of a client's financial statements, a CPA has the duty to perform with the same degree of skill and judgment expected of an ordinarily prudent CPA under the circumstances. Answer (a) is incorrect because the client's expectations do not guide the standard of due care. Rather, the standard of due care is guided by state and federal statute, court decisions, the contract with the client, GAAS and GAAP, and customs of the profession. Answer (b) is incorrect because it is generally the client's responsibility to prepare its financial statements in accordance with generally accepted accounting principles. Answer (d) is incorrect because a CPA is not normally liable for failure to detect fraud or irregularities unless (1) a "normal" audit would have detected it, (2) the accountant by agreement has undertaken greater responsibility, or (3) the wording of the audit report indicates greater responsibility.

8. (c) The following elements are needed to establish fraud against an accountant: (1) misrepresentation of the accountant's expert opinion, (2) scienter shown by either the accountant's knowledge of falsity or reckless disregard of the truth, (3) reasonable reliance by injured party, and (4) actual damages. Answer (a) is incorrect because contributory negligence of a third party is not a defense available for the accountant in cases of fraud. Answers (b) and (d) are incorrect because privity of contract is not a requirement for an accountant to be held liable for fraud.

9. (a) In the performance of an audit, a CPA has the duty to exercise the level of care, skill, and judgment expected of a reasonably prudent CPA under the circumstances. Answer (b) is incorrect because a CPA performing an audit must adhere to generally accepted **auditing** standards. It is the client's responsibility to prepare its financial statements in accordance with generally accepted accounting principles. Answer (c) is incorrect because an accountant is not liable for failure to detect fraud unless (1) a "normal" audit would have detected it, (2) the accountant by agreement has undertaken greater responsibility such as a defalcation audit, or (3) the wording of the audit report indicates greater responsibility for detecting fraud. Answer (d) is incorrect because a CPA **can** be liable for negligence, which is simply a failure to exercise due care in performing an audit. The CPA does not have to be grossly negligent or intentionally disregard generally accepted auditing standards to be held liable for negligence.

10. (c) A CPA will be liable for negligence when s/he fails to exercise due care. The standard for due care is guided by state and federal statutes, court decisions, contracts with clients, conformity with GAAS and GAAP, and the customs of the profession. Per the AICPA Professional Standards, AU 325, requires that if the auditor becomes aware of weaknesses in the design or operation of the internal control structure, these weaknesses, termed reportable conditions, be communicated to the audit committee of the client. Answer (a) is incorrect because a CPA is not normally liable for failure to detect fraud. Answer (b) is incorrect because including a negligence disclaimer in an engagement letter has no bearing on whether the CPA is negligent. Answer (d) is incorrect because generally a CPA is not required to inform a client's customers of embezzlements although knowledge of the embezzlements may adversely affect the CPA's audit opinion.

11. (c) The requirement is to identify the source of law under which the lawsuit would likely be filed. Answer (c) is correct because lawsuits by clients for negligence are filed under common law. Answer (a) is incorrect because suits by investors in securities issued by a public company would be filed under this law. Answer (b) is incorrect because suits by individuals who purchase or sell securities of a public company would be filed under this law. Answer (d) is incorrect because suits by individuals who purchase or sell securities regulated by a state would be filed under these laws.

12. (c) Since Yoke is the client and in privity of contract with Edgar, Yoke need only prove ordinary negligence on the part of Edgar. Therefore, answer (c) is correct. Answer (a) is incorrect because Edgar was not performing an audit. Answer (b) is incorrect because this would not be necessary; ordinary negligence would be sufficient. Answer (d) is incorrect because this would not be necessary; ordinary negligence would be sufficient.

13. (d) The requirement is to identify the item that would not likely be part of Edgar's defense. Answer (d) is correct because there is no indication that management made any misrepresentations. Answer (a) is incorrect because if Edgar can show that management was negligent in establishing control, some of the responsibility for the losses may be shifted to management. Answer (b) is incorrect because performance

of the engagement in conformity with professional standards would establish that Edgar was not negligent. Answer (c) is incorrect because Edgar would try to establish the limitations of the engagement.

14. (b) The requirement is to identify the accurate statement about damages. The court tries to establish a link between (causation) the losses and the defendant's negligence. Therefore, answer (b) is correct because Edgar should be held responsible for the losses that have occurred since Edgar should have discovered the scheme. Answer (a) is incorrect because Edgar should not be held liable for losses that were incurred prior to the time he should have detected the scheme. Answer (c) is incorrect because Edgar would be responsible for more than just returning the fees. Answer (d) is incorrect because in civil proceedings there is no need to provide criminal liability.

15. (d) A CPA's duty of due care is guided by the following standards: (1) state and federal statutes, (2) court decisions, (3) contract with the client, (4) GAAS and GAAP, and (5) customs of the profession. Therefore, failure to follow GAAS constitutes a breach of a CPA's duty of due care. Answer (a) is incorrect because issuance of an oral rather than written report does not necessarily constitute a failure to exercise due care. Answers (b) and (c) are incorrect because the standard of due care requires the CPA to exercise the skill and judgment of an ordinary, prudent accountant. An honest error of judgment or failure to provide money saving tax advice would not breach the duty of due care if the CPA acted in a reasonable manner.

16. (a) A CPA's liability for constructive fraud is established by the following elements: (1) misrepresentation of a material fact, (2) reckless disregard for the truth, (3) reasonable reliance by the injured party, and (4) actual damages. Gross negligence constitutes a reckless disregard for the truth. Answer (b) is incorrect because ordinary negligence is not sufficient to support a finding of constructive fraud. Answer (c) is incorrect because the liability for constructive fraud does not depend upon the identification of third-party users. Answer (d) is incorrect because the presence of the intent to deceive is needed to satisfy the scienter requirement for fraud. However, even in the absence of the intent to deceive, the CPA can be liable for constructive fraud based on reckless disregard of the truth.

17. (b) A foreseeable third party is someone not identified to the CPA, but who may be expected to receive the accountant's audit report and rely upon it. Even though this party is unknown to the CPA, the CPA is liable for gross negligence or fraud.

18. (a) Lack of privity can be a viable defense against third parties in a common law case of negligence or breach of contract. A client's creditor is not in privity of contract with the accountant. Answers (b) and (d) are incorrect because plaintiffs who are suing for fraud, constructive fraud, or gross negligence, which involves a reckless disregard for the truth, need not show privity of contract. Answer (c) is incorrect because the accountant's client is in privity of contract with the accountant due to their contractual agreement.

19. (c) Since Sanco was a foreseeable third party instead of an actually foreseen third party by the CPA, Sanco in most states cannot recover. Answer (a) is incorrect because most states do not extend liability to mere foreseeable third parties for simple negligence. Answer (b) is incorrect because the Ultramares decision limited liability to parties in privity of contract with the CPA. Answer (d) is incorrect because the client can recover for damages caused to it when negligence is established.

20. (b) Under the Ultramares rule, the accountant is held liable only to parties whose primary benefit the financial statements are intended. This generally means only the client or third-party beneficiaries who are in privity of contract with the accountant. Many courts have more recently departed from the Ultramares decision to allow foreseen third parties to recover from the accountant. However, those courts that adhere to the Ultramares rule do not expand liability to foreseen parties.

21. (a) In order to establish common law liability against an accountant based upon negligence, it must be proven that (1) the accountant had the duty to exercise due care, (2) the accountant breached the duty of due care, (3) damage or loss resulted, and (4) a causal relationship exists between the fault of the accountant and the resulting damages. The accountant may escape liability if due care can be established. The standard for due care is guided by state and federal statute, court decisions, contract with client, GAAS and GAAP, and customs of the profession. Although following GAAS does not automatically preclude negligence, it is strong evidence for the presence of due care. Answer (b) is incorrect because although the client may be aware of the misstatement, the auditor has the responsibility to detect the material misstatement if it is such that an average, reasonable accountant should have detected it. Answer (c) is incorrect because the client and Larson intended for the opinion and the financial statements to be used by purchasers. Therefore, a purchaser is considered a third-party beneficiary and is in privity of contract. Answer (d) is incorrect because the accountant need not know the specific identity of a third-party beneficiary to be held liable for negligence.

22. (a) To establish a CPA's liability for common law fraud, the following elements must be present: (1) misrepresentation of a material fact or the accountant's expert opinion, (2) scienter, shown by either an intent to mislead or reckless disregard for the truth, (3) reasonable or justifiable reliance by injured party, and (4) actual damages resulted. If Larson did not have actual or constructive knowledge of the misstatements, the scienter element would not be present and thus Larson would not be liable. Answers (b) and (d) are incorrect because neither contributory negligence of the client nor lack of privity of contract are defenses available to the accountant in cases of fraud. Answer (c) is incorrect because an accountant is generally liable to all parties defrauded. Therefore, the accountant need not have actual knowledge that the purchaser was an intended beneficiary.

23. (b) The Securities Act of 1933 requires that a plaintiff need only prove that damages were incurred and that there was a material misstatement or omission in order to establish a prima facie case against a CPA. The Act does not require that

the plaintiff prove that s/he relied on the financial information or that there was negligence or fraud present. The Securities Act of 1933 eliminates the necessity for privity of contract.

24. (c) Mac is a third party that the accountant knew would rely on the financial statements. Queen's financial statements contained material misstatements. Mac can recover by showing that the accountant was negligent in the audit. Mac also needs to establish that it did rely on the financial statements in order to recover from the accountant for the losses on Queen.

25. (c) Under the Securities Act of 1933, a CPA is liable to any third-party purchaser of registered securities for losses resulting from misstatements in the financial statements included in the registration statement. The plaintiff (purchaser) must establish that damages were incurred, and that the misstatements were material misstatements of facts. Answer (a) is incorrect because under the 1933 Act it is not necessary for the purchaser of securities to prove "scienter," or knowledge of material misstatement, on the part of the CPA. Answers (b) and (d) are incorrect because under the 1933 Act, the plaintiff need not prove negligence on the part of the CPA or that there was reliance by the plaintiff on the financial statements included in the registration statement.

26. (c) In a Section 11 suit under the 1933 Act, the plaintiff may recover damages equal to the difference between the amount paid and the market value of the stock at the time of the suit. If the stock has been sold, then the damages are the difference between the amount paid and the sale price. Answer (a) is incorrect because damages of triple the original price are not provided for under this act. Answer (b) is incorrect because rescission is not a remedy under this act. Answer (d) is incorrect because if the shares have not been sold before the suit, then the court uses the difference between the amount paid and the market value at the time of the suit.

27. (b) Under Section 11 of the 1933 Act, if the plaintiff proves damages and the existence of a material misstatement or omission in the financial statements included in the registration statement, these are sufficient to win against the CPA unless the CPA can prove one of the applicable defenses. Due diligence is one of the defenses. Answer (a) is incorrect because contributory negligence is not a defense under Section 11. Answer (c) is incorrect because the purchaser need not prove privity with the CPA. Answer (d) is not correct because the purchaser needs to prove the above two elements but not scienter.

28. (d) To impose liability under Section 11 of the Securities Act of 1933 for a misleading registration statement, the plaintiff must prove the following: (1) damages were incurred, and (2) a material misstatement or omission was present in financial statements included in the registration statement. The plaintiff generally is not required to prove the defendant's intent to deceive nor must the plaintiff prove reliance on the registration statement.

29. (c) The proof requirements necessary to establish an accountant's liability under the Securities Act of 1933, Section 11 are as follows: (1) the plaintiff must prove damages were incurred, and (2) the plaintiff must prove there was a material misstatement or omission in financial statements included in the registration statement. To establish an accountant's liability under the Securities Exchange Act of 1934, Section 10(b), Rule 10b-5, the following elements must be proven: (1) damages resulted to the plaintiff in connection with the purchase or sale of a security in interstate commerce, (2) a material misstatement or omission existed in information released by the firm, (3) the plaintiff justifiably relied on the financial information, and (4) the existence of scienter. Because Sharp can prove that damages were incurred and that the statements contained material misstatements, Sharp is likely to prevail in a lawsuit under the Securities Act of 1933, Section 11. However, Sharp would be unable to prove justifiable reliance on the misstated information or the existence of scienter; thus, recovery under the Securities Exchange Act of 1934, Section 10(b), Rule 10b-5, is unlikely.

30. (d) If an accountant is negligent, s/he may have liability not only for a negligently performed audit but also for a negligently performed review when there were facts that should require the accountant to investigate further because of their suspicious nature. This is true even though a review is not a full audit.

31. (a) In order to establish a case under the antifraud provisions of Section 10(b) and Rule 10b-5 of the 1934 Act, the plaintiff has to prove that the defendant either had knowledge of the falsity in the registration statement or acted with reckless disregard for the truth. In addition, the plaintiff must show that the transaction involved interstate commerce so that there is a constitutional basis for using this federal law. S/he also must prove justifiable reliance. The plaintiff need not prove that s/he was an intended user of the false registration statement.

32. (d) Under Rule 10b-5 of Section 10(b) of the Securities Exchange Act of 1934, a CPA may be liable if s/he makes a false statement of a material fact or an omission of a material fact in connection with the purchase or sale of a security. Scienter is required which is shown by either knowledge of falsity or reckless disregard for the truth. Of the four answers given, lack of good faith best describes this scienter requirement. Answer (a) is incorrect because negligence is not enough under this rule. Answer (b) is incorrect because independence is not the issue under scienter. Answer (c) is incorrect because although due diligence can be a defense under Section 11 of the Securities Act of 1933, it is not the standard used under Section 10(b) of the Securities Exchange Act of 1934.

33. (b) Under Section 11 of the Securities Act of 1933, the CPA may be liable for material misstatements or omissions in certified financial statements. The CPA may escape liability by showing due diligence. This can often be proven by the CPA showing that s/he followed Generally Accepted Accounting Principles. There are not generally accepted fraud detection standards that the CPA can use as a defense.

34. (c) In a civil suit under Section 10(b) and Rule 10b-5, the damages are generally the difference between the amount paid and the market value at the time of suit, or the difference between the amount paid and the sales price if sold.

Answer (a) is incorrect because recovery of the full original public offering price is not used as the damages. Answer (b) is incorrect because the above described monetary damages are used. Answer (d) is incorrect because punitive damages are not given under this rule.

35. (b) In general, the accountant's workpapers are owned by the accountant. However, the CPA's ownership of the working papers is custodial in nature and the CPA is required to preserve confidentiality of the client's affairs. Normally, the CPA firm cannot allow transmission of information included in the working papers to third parties without the client's consent. This prevents a CPA firm from transferring workpapers to a purchaser of a CPA practice unless the client consents. Answer (c) is incorrect because the privileged communication rule does not exist at common law and has only been enacted by a few states. Additionally, the privileged communications rule only applies to communications which were intended to be privileged at the time of communication. Answer (a) is incorrect because working papers may be obtained by third parties without the client's consent when they appear to be relevant to issues raised in litigation (through a subpoena).

36. (d) The working papers are owned by the CPA, but the CPA must preserve confidentiality. They cannot be transmitted to another party unless the client consents or unless the CPA is required to under a valid court or governmental agency subpoena. Answers (a) and (c) are incorrect because these do not preserve the confidentiality. Answer (b) is incorrect because the CPA retains the working papers as evidence of the work done.

37. (c) Any of the partners of a CPA partnership can have access to the partnership's working papers. Third parties outside the firm need to have the client's consent or a legal subpoena.

38. (d) To preserve confidentiality, a CPA (including a CPA partnership) may not allow transmission of information in the working papers to other parties. Exceptions are consent of the client or the production of an enforceable subpoena. There are no exceptions for the IRS or the FASB, thus making answers (a), (b), and (c) incorrect.

39. (d) In a jurisdiction having an accountant-client privilege statute, the CPA generally may not turn over workpapers without the client's permission. It is allowable to do so, however, for use in a quality review under AICPA authorization or to be given to the state CPA society quality control panel. Answers (a), (b), and (c) are incorrect because the client would have to give permission for the CPA to turn over the confidential workpapers to the purchaser of the CPA practice, as well as to another CPA firm in regard to suspected tax return irregularities.

40. (a) Privileged communications between the accountant and client are recognized only in a few states. Therefore, if a state statute has been enacted creating such a privilege, Ivor will be able to prevent Thorp from testifying. Answer (b) is incorrect because federal law does not recognize accountant-client privileged communication. Answer (d) is incorrect because Ivor will not be able to prevent Thorp from testifying about the nature of the work performed in the audit unless a privileged communication statute has been enacted in that state. Answer (c) is incorrect because privileged communication does not exist at common law but must be created by state statute. Criminal law is based on common law and varies by state. However, as a general rule, in states that recognize accountant-client privilege, it can be claimed in both civil and criminal suits.

41. (a) The requirement is to identify the situation in which it is **most** likely that a violation of the profession's ethical standards would have occurred. Answer (a) is correct because independence is impaired if fees remain unpaid for professional services of the preceding year when the report on the client's current year is issued. Accordingly, no report should have been issued on the 2002 financial statements when fees for the 2001 audit were unpaid. Answer (b) is incorrect because CPAs may recommend a position description (ET 191) without violating the profession's ethical standards. Answer (c) is incorrect because a practice may be purchased for a percentage of fees to be received. Answer (d) is incorrect because the Code of Professional Conduct does not prohibit arrangements with financial institutions to collect notes issued by a client in payment of professional fees.

42. (b) A CPA must not disclose confidential information of a client unless the client gives consent to disclose it to that third party. Answer (a) is incorrect because state agencies need a subpoena before the CPA must comply. Answer (c) is incorrect because the IRS does not have the right to force a CPA to turn over confidential information of a client without either the client's consent or an enforceable subpoena. Answer (d) is incorrect because although the CPA can use the client information to defend a lawsuit, the CPA is not normally requested to disclose confidential information to comply with generally accepted accounting principles.

43. (b) The requirement is to identify the source of law which may not result in criminal liability. Answer (b) is correct because common law can only result in civil liability.

44. (a) The requirement is to identify the act that provides for possible treble damages. Answer (a) is correct because only the Racketeer Influenced and Corrupt Organizations Act provides for potential treble damages.

45. (c) Under the Private Securities Litigation Reform Act, the auditor should inform first the audit committee or the board of directors. Answer (a) is incorrect because the Securities Litigation Reform Act does not require that the SEC be informed unless after the audit committee or board of directors is informed, no remedial action is taken. Answer (b) is incorrect because the Justice Department need not be informed of this under the Private Securities Litigation Reform Act. Answer (d) is incorrect because inclusion of the problem in a note of the financial statements is not enough; the audit committee or the board of directors should be informed.

46. (a) The Private Securities Litigation Reform Act requires that auditors of firms covered under the Securities Exchange Act of 1934 establish procedures to do the items in (b), (c), and (d). Developing a comprehensive internal control system is not specifically mentioned, although part of this would be helpful in accomplishing the three stated items.

47. (d) Under the Private Securities Litigation Reform Act, an auditor who audits financial statements under the Federal Securities Exchange Act of 1934 is required to establish procedures to (1) detect illegal acts, (2) identify material related-party transactions, and (3) evaluate the ability of the firm to continue as a going concern.

48. (b) Under the Private Securities Litigation Reform Act, he is required to report this to the audit committee of the firm or the board of directors. Answer (a) is incorrect because he need not report this to the shareholders but to the audit committee or the board of directors. Answers (c) and (d) are incorrect because he is required under the Reform Act to inform the audit committee or the board of directors.

49. (c) The Private Securities Litigation Reform Act amends both the 1933 and 1934 Acts. Answer (a) is incorrect because it applies to the 1933 and 1934 Acts which apply to stocks sold on a stock exchange. Answers (b) and (d) are incorrect because this Reform Act applies to securities covered under the 1933 and 1934 Acts which may include both common and preferred stock of a publicly held corporation.

50. (b) Bran is liable under the Private Securities Litigation Reform Act for her proportionate fault of the liability since she acted unknowingly. Answer (a) is incorrect because Bran was determined to be 20% at fault. Answers (c) and (d) are incorrect because the Reform Act changes the joint and several liability for unknowing conduct and substitutes proportionate liability.

51. (c) The Sarbanes-Oxley Act of 2002 established a number of nonattest services that may not be performed by the auditor for a public company. Tax services may be performed but must be approved by the company's audit committee.

52. (c) The Sarbanes-Oxley Act established the Public Accounting Oversight Board to regulate CPA firms that audit public companies.

53. (d) The requirement is to identify the provision that is not part of the Sarbanes-Oxley Act of 2002. Answer (d) is correct because Sarbanes-Oxley does not contain a provision for minimum partner experience. All of the others items are provisions of Sarbanes-Oxley.

54. (a) The requirement is to identify the individuals who must personally certify to the accuracy of the financial statements filed with the SEC. Answer (a) is correct because only the chief financial officer and the chief executive officer must certify.

55. (c) The requirement is to identify when a Form 8-K must be filed with the SEC. Answer (c) is correct because the form generally must be filed within 4 days of the occurrence of the triggering event.

56. (b) The requirement is to identify the required partner rotation period under the Sarbanes-Oxley Act. Answer (b) is correct because the act requires rotation at least every 5 years.

57. (b) The requirement is to determine which act(s) constitute(s) grounds for a tax preparer penalty. A return preparer will be subject to penalty if the preparer knowingly or recklessly discloses information furnished in connection with the preparation of a tax return, unless such information is furnished for quality or peer review, under an administrative order by a regulatory agency, or pursuant to an order of a court. Additionally, a return preparer will be subject to penalty if any part of an understatement of liability with respect to a return or refund claim is due to the preparer's willful attempt to understate tax liability, or to any reckless or intentional disregard of rules and regulations.

58. (d) The requirement is to determine Water's responsibility regarding Vee's unfiled 2009 income tax return. A CPA should promptly inform the client upon becoming aware of the client's failure to file a required return for a prior year. However, the CPA is not obligated to inform the IRS and the CPA may not do so without the client's permission, except where required by law. If the CPA is requested to prepare the current year's return (2014) and the client has not taken action to file the return for the earlier year (2009), the CPA should consider whether to withdraw from preparing the current year's return and whether to continue a professional relationship with the client. Also, note that the normal statue of limitations for the assessment of a tax deficiency is three years after the due date of the return or three years after the return is filed, whichever is later. Thus, the statute of limitations is still open with regard to 2009 since there is no time limit for the assessment of tax if no tax return was filed.

59. (c) The requirement is to determine which action a tax return preparer must take to avoid tax preparer penalties for a return's understated tax liability due to a taxpayer's intentional disregard of regulations. A return preparer may, in good faith, rely without verification upon information furnished by the client or by third parties, and is not required to audit, examine, or review books, records, or documents in order to independently verify the taxpayer's information. However, the preparer should not ignore the implications of information furnished and should make reasonable inquiries if the furnished information appears incorrect, incomplete, or inconsistent.

60. (d) According to the Statements on Standards for Tax Services, in preparing a tax return a CPA may in good faith rely upon information furnished by the client or third parties without further verification.

61. (d) The requirement is to determine the correct statement regarding the imposition of a preparer penalty for understated corporate tax liability. A return preparer may in good faith rely without verification upon information furnished, and is not required to audit, examine, or review books, records, or documents in order to independently verify a taxpayer's information. However, the preparer should not ignore the implications of information furnished and should make reasonable inquiries if information appears incorrect, incomplete, or inconsistent.

62. (a) A tax return preparer is subject to a penalty for knowingly or recklessly disclosing corporate tax return information, if the disclosure is made to enable a third party to solicit business from the taxpayer. Taxpayer return information can be disclosed by the preparer without penalty if the disclosure is made to enable the tax processor to electronically compute the taxpayer's liability, for purposes of the tax return preparer's peer review, or if the disclosure is made under an administrative order by a state agency that registers tax return preparers.

63. (c) The requirement is to determine the correct statement regarding a tax return preparer's disclosure or use of tax return information without the taxpayer's consent. Generally, a tax return preparer who knowingly or recklessly discloses **any** information furnished to him in connection with the preparation of a return, or uses any such information other than to prepare, or to assist in preparing a return, is guilty of a misdemeanor, and upon conviction may be subject to fine and/or imprisonment. A limited exception permits the disclosure or use of tax return information for purposes of being evaluated by quality or peer reviews.

64. (d) A penalty of up to $1,000 may be assessed against a tax return preparer who knowingly or recklessly discloses or uses any tax return information other than to prepare, or assist in preparing a return. Additionally, a penalty equal to the greater of $5,000, or 50% of the income to be derived by the return preparer from the return or refund claim will be assessed against a return preparer who willfully attempts to understate any client's tax liability on a return or claim for refund.

65. (a) Under Internal Revenue Code Section 6695(f) any person who is an income tax return preparer who endorses or otherwise negotiates any check which is issued to a taxpayer shall pay a penalty of $500.

66. (b) A CPA who prepares a federal income tax return for a fee must keep a completed copy of the return for a minimum of three years. Answer (a) is incorrect because prior to preparing a tax return the CPA would not be required to file certain notices and powers of attorney with the IRS. Answer (c) is incorrect because a CPA would only be required to ask the client if documentation of these expenses exists. The CPA would not have to actually receive and examine this documentation. Answer (d) is incorrect because the CPA's federal identification number would be required on any federal income tax return prepared for a fee.

67. (b) A CPA generally does owe a duty to inform a client that there are errors in a previously filed tax return so that the client may file an amended tax return. Answer (a) is incorrect because the client chooses his/her own CPA. Answer (c) is incorrect because CPAs are not required to disclose fraud by the client but are usually engaged to give an opinion on the fairness of the financial statements. Answer (d) is incorrect because although the CPA has a duty to perform an audit in accordance with GAAS and consistent with GAAP, the CPA is not under a duty to discover fraud in the audit unless the fraud would have been uncovered in the process of an ordinary audit or unless the CPA agreed to greater responsibility to uncover fraud.

68. (b) If the IRS issues a 30-day letter to an individual taxpayer who wishes to dispute the assessment, the taxpayer may ignore the 30-day letter and wait to receive a 90-day letter. Answer (a) is incorrect because a taxpayer must receive a 90-day letter before a petition can be filed in Tax Court. Answer (c) is incorrect because a taxpayer has a 30-day period during which to file a written protest. Answer (d) is incorrect because a taxpayer is not required to pay the taxes and commence an action in federal district court.

Generally, upon the receipt of a 30-day letter, a taxpayer who wishes to dispute the findings has 30 days to (1) request a conference with an appeals officer or file a written protest letter, or (2) may elect to do nothing during the 30-day period and await a 90-day letter. The taxpayer would then have 90 days to file a petition with the Tax Court. Alternatively, a taxpayer may choose to pay the additional taxes and file a claim for refund. When the refund claim is disallowed, the taxpayer could then commence an action in federal district court.

69. (c) A CPA will be liable to a tax client for damages resulting from the following activities: (1) failure to file a client's return on a timely basis, (2) gross negligence or fraudulent conduct resulting in client losses, (3) erroneous advice or failure to advise client of certain tax elections, and (4) wrongful disclosure or use of confidential information. A CPA will **not** be liable to a tax client for refusing to sign a client's request for a filing extension, therefore answer (c) is correct.

70. (b) According to the AICPA Statements on Standards for Tax Services, a CPA should not recommend a position unless there is a realistic possibility of it being sustained if it is challenged. Furthermore, a CPA should not prepare or sign an income tax return if the CPA knows that the return takes a position that will not be sustained if challenged. Therefore, answer (d) is incorrect. Also, a CPA should advise the client of the potential penalty consequences of any recommended tax position. Therefore, answer (c) is incorrect. Answer (a) is incorrect as a CPA may not recommend a position that is frivolous even if the position is adequately disclosed on the return.

71. (a) While performing services for a client, a CPA may become aware of an error in a previously filed return. The CPA should advise the client of the error (as required by the Statements on Standards for Tax Services) and the measures to be taken. It is the client's responsibility to decide whether to correct the error. In the event that the client does not correct an error, or agree to take the necessary steps to change from an erroneous method of accounting, the CPA should consider whether to continue a professional relationship with the client.

72. (b) A CPA may in good faith rely without verification upon information furnished by the client when preparing the client's tax return. However, the CPA should not ignore implications of information furnished and should make reasonable inquiries if information appears incorrect, incomplete, or inconsistent.

73. (c) Answer (a) is incorrect because IRC §6695(a) imposes a $50 penalty upon income tax return preparers who fail to furnish a copy of the return to the taxpayer. Answer (b) is incorrect because IRC §6695(b) imposes a $50 penalty upon income tax return preparers who fail to sign a return, unless the failure is due to reasonable cause. Answer (d) is incorrect because IRC §6695(f) imposes a $500 penalty upon income tax return preparers who endorse or otherwise negotiate a client's tax refund checks. There is no code section imposing a penalty for the understating of a client's tax liability due to an error in calculation.

74. (c) A CPA should consider both: (1) information actually known to the CPA from the tax return of another client; and (2) information provided by the client that appears to be correct based on the client's returns from prior years. In preparing or signing a return, a CPA may in good faith rely without verification upon information furnished by the client or by third parties. However, the CPA should not ignore the implications of information furnished and should make reasonable inquires if the information furnished appears to be incorrect, incomplete, or inconsistent either on its face or on the basis of other facts known to the CPA.

75. (d) The requirement is to identify the correct statement regarding Treasury Department Circular 230. Answer (d) is correct because a practitioner may charge a contingent fee for representing a client in connection with a judicial proceeding. Answer (a) is incorrect because a practitioner may not charge a contingent fee for preparing a client's original tax return. Answer (b) is incorrect because a practitioner may not charge an unconscionable fee. Answer (c) is incorrect because a practitioner may not retain a client's records for nonpayment of fees.

76. (d) Circular 230 limits practice before the Internal Revenue Service to certified public accountants, attorneys, enrolled agents, enrolled actuaries, enrolled retirement plan agents, and registered tax return preparers.

77. (b) A practitioner is in violation of Circular 230 if the practitioner charges a contingent fee for preparing and filing an original tax return. However, a contingent fee may be charged in representing a client in connection with an IRS examination of an original return, or an amended return or claim for refund or credit. Additionally, a contingent fee may be charged for services rendered in connection with any judicial proceeding arising under the Code.

78. (d) Circular 230 defines practice before the IRS to include all matters connected with a presentation to the IRS relating to a taxpayer's rights, privileges, or liabilities including preparing and filing documents, corresponding and communicating with the IRS, rendering written advice with respect to any transaction having a potential for tax avoidance or evasion, and representing a client at conferences, hearings, and meetings.

79. (d) According to Circular 230, practitioners must not sign a tax return or claim for refund that the practitioner knows or reasonably should know contains a position that lacks a reasonable basis, is an unreasonable position, or is a willful attempt by the practitioner to understate tax liability. The reasonable basis standard comprehends at least a 20% probability of being sustained, while the more likely than not (more than 50% probability), substantial authority (40% probability), and realistic possibility (33% probability) are higher standards. Answer (b) is incorrect since a position lacking substantial authority can be taken so long as there is adequate disclosure and there is a reasonable basis for the position.

80. (c) The requirement is to identify the item that does not have to be done when providing written advice. Answer (c) is correct because Circular 230 specifically states that the practitioner should not take into account that the matter will not be raised in an audit.

Simulations

Task-Based Simulation 1

Analysis		
	Authoritative Literature	Help

Situation

Under Section 11 of the Securities Act of 1933 and Section 10(b), Rule 10b-5, of the Securities Exchange Act of 1934, a CPA may be sued by a purchaser of registered securities.

Items 1 through 6 relate to what a plaintiff who purchased securities must prove in a civil liability suit against a CPA. For each item determine whether the statement must be proven under Section 11 of the Securities Act of 1933, under Section 10(b), Rule 10b-5, of the Securities Exchange Act of 1934, both Acts, or neither Act.

	Only Section 11 (A)	Only Section 10(b) (B)	Both (C)	Neither (D)
The plaintiff security purchaser must allege or prove				
1. Material misstatements were included in a filed document.	○	○	○	○
2. A monetary loss occurred.	○	○	○	○
3. Lack of due diligence by the CPA.	○	○	○	○
4. Privity with the CPA.	○	○	○	○
5. Reliance on the document.	○	○	○	○
6. The CPA had scienter.	○	○	○	○

Task-Based Simulation 2

Preparer's Responsibility		
	Authoritative Literature	Help

A CPA sole practitioner has tax preparers' responsibilities when preparing tax returns for clients.

Items 1 through 9 each represent an independent factual situation in which a CPA sole practitioner has prepared and signed the taxpayer's income tax return. For each item, select from the following list the correct response regarding the tax preparer's responsibilities. A response may be selected once, more than once, or not at all.

Answer List

P. The tax preparer's action constitutes an act of tax preparer misconduct subject to the Internal Revenue Code penalty.

E. The Internal Revenue Service will examine the facts and circumstances to determine whether the reasonable cause exception applies; the good-faith exception applies; or both exceptions apply.

N. The tax preparer's action does **not** constitute an act of tax preparer misconduct.

                                                                                        (P) (E) (N)

1. The tax preparer disclosed taxpayer income tax return information under an order from a state court,   ○   ○   ○
    without the taxpayer's consent.

2. The tax preparer relied on the advice of an advisory preparer to calculate the taxpayer's tax liability.   ○   ○   ○
    The tax preparer believed that the advisory preparer was competent and that the advice was
    reasonable. Based on the advice, the taxpayer had understated income tax liability.

3. The tax preparer did **not** charge a separate fee for the tax return preparation and paid the taxpayer the   ○   ○   ○
    refund shown on the tax return less a discount. The tax preparer negotiated the actual refund check for
    the tax preparer's own account after receiving power of attorney from the taxpayer.

4. The tax preparer relied on information provided by the taxpayer regarding deductible travel expenses.   ○   ○   ○
    The tax preparer believed that the taxpayer's information was correct but inquired about the existence
    of the travel expense records. The tax preparer was satisfied by the taxpayer's representations that the
    taxpayer had adequate records for the deduction. Based on this information, the income tax liability
    was understated.

5. The taxpayer provided the tax preparer with a detailed check register to compute business expenses.   ○   ○   ○
    The tax preparer knowingly overstated the expenses on the income tax return.

6. The tax preparer disclosed taxpayer income tax return information during a quality review conducted   ○   ○   ○
    by CPAs. The tax preparer maintained a record of the review.

7. The tax preparer relied on incorrect instructions on an IRS tax form that were contrary to the regula-   ○   ○   ○
    tions. The tax preparer was **not** aware of the regulations or the IRS announcement pointing out the
    error. The understatement was immaterial as a result of the isolated error.

8. The tax preparer used income tax return information without the taxpayer's consent to solicit   ○   ○   ○
    additional business.

9. The tax preparer knowingly deducted the expenses of the taxpayer's personal domestic help as wages   ○   ○   ○
    paid in the taxpayer's business on the taxpayer's income tax return.

Simulation Solutions

Task-Based Simulation 1

Analysis		
	Authoritative Literature	**Help**

	Only Section 11 (A)	Only Section 10(b) (B)	Both (C)	Neither (D)
1. Material misstatements were included in a filed document.	○	○	●	○
2. A monetary loss occurred.	○	○	●	○
3. Lack of due diligence by the CPA.	○	○	○	○
4. Privity with the CPA.	○	○	○	●
5. Reliance on the document.	○	●	○	●
6. The CPA had scienter.	○	●	○	○

Explanations

1. (C) Section 11 of the Securities Act of 1933 imposes liability on auditors for misstatements or omissions of a material fact in certified financial statements or other information provided in registration statements. Similarly, under Section 10(b), Rule 10b-5 of the Securities Exchange Act of 1934, the plaintiff must prove there was a material misstatement or omission in information released by the firm such as audited financial statements. Actually, if the examiners wish to emphasize the phrase "filed document" in the question, then the answer would be (A). Under Section 10(b), the material misstatement may occur in information released by the firm rather than filed. Since the requirements state "...**must** allege or prove," technically the answer would be (D), since the plaintiff could allege or prove **omission** of material facts instead of material **misstatements** stated in the question. Therefore, this question depends upon how technical one decides to get on these points.

2. (C) Under both Section 11 of the 1933 Act and Section 10(b) of the 1934 Act, the plaintiff must allege or prove that s/he incurred monetary damages.

3. (D) Under Section 11 of the 1933 Act, the burden of proof is shifted to the defendant, accountant. The accountant may then defend him- or herself by establishing due diligence. The plaintiff does not have to show lack of due diligence by the CPA. Under Section 10(b), the plaintiff must prove scienter.

4. (D) The plaintiff does not have to prove that s/he was in privity with the CPA under either section.

5. (B) Under Section 10(b), the plaintiff must prove justifiable reliance on the financial information. This is not true under Section 11 in which the plaintiff need prove only the items in item **1.** and item **2.** discussed above.

6. (B) The plaintiff does have to prove that the CPA had scienter under Section 10(b) of the 1934 Act. Scienter is **not** needed under the 1933 Act, however.

Task-Based Simulation 2

Preparer's Responsibility		
	Authoritative Literature	Help

		(P)	(E)	(N)
1.	The tax preparer disclosed taxpayer income tax return information under an order from a state court, without the taxpayer's consent.	○	○	●
2.	The tax preparer relied on the advice of an advisory preparer to calculate the taxpayer's tax liability. The tax preparer believed that the advisory preparer was competent and that the advice was reasonable. Based on the advice, the taxpayer had understated income tax liability.	○	●	○
3.	The tax preparer did not charge a separate fee for the tax return preparation and paid the taxpayer the refund shown on the tax return less a discount. The tax preparer negotiated the actual refund check for the tax preparer's own account after receiving power of attorney from the taxpayer.	●	○	○
4.	The tax preparer relied on information provided by the taxpayer regarding deductible travel expenses. The tax preparer believed that the taxpayer's information was correct but inquired about the existence of the travel expense records. The tax preparer was satisfied by the taxpayer's representations that the taxpayer had adequate records for the deduction. Based on this information, the income tax liability was understated.	○	○	●
5.	The taxpayer provided the tax preparer with a detailed check register to compute business expenses. The tax preparer knowingly overstated the expenses on the income tax return.	●	○	○
6.	The tax preparer disclosed taxpayer income tax return information during a quality review conducted by CPAs. The tax preparer maintained a record of the review.	○	○	●
7.	The tax preparer relied on incorrect instructions on an IRS tax form that were contrary to the regulations. The tax preparer was not aware of the regulations or the IRS announcement pointing out the error. The understatement was immaterial as a result of the isolated error.	○	●	○
8.	The tax preparer used income tax return information without the taxpayer's consent to solicit additional business.	●	○	○
9.	The tax preparer knowingly deducted the expenses of the taxpayer's personal domestic help as wages paid in the taxpayer's business on the taxpayer's income tax return.	●	○	○

Explanations

1. (N) A return preparer will be subject to penalty if the preparer knowingly or recklessly discloses information furnished in connection with the preparation of a tax return, unless such information is furnished for quality or peer review, under an administrative order by a regulatory agency, or pursuant to an order of a court.

2. (E) The reasonable cause and good faith exception applies if the return preparer relied in good faith on the advice of an advisory preparer who the return preparer had reason to believe was competent to render such advice.

3. (P) A return preparer will be subject to penalty if the preparer endorses or otherwise negotiates (directly or through an agent) any refund check issued to a taxpayer (other than the preparer) if the preparer was the preparer of the return or claim for refund which gave rise to the refund check.

4. (N) A return preparer may in good faith rely without verification upon information furnished by the client or third parties, and is not required to audit, examine, or review books, records, or documents in order to independently verify the taxpayer's information. If the IRS requires supporting documentation as a condition for deductibility, the return preparer should make appropriate inquiries to determine whether the condition has been met.

5. **(P)** A return preparer will be subject to penalty if there is a willful attempt in any manner to understate the tax liability of any taxpayer. A preparer is considered to have willfully attempted to understate liability if the preparer disregards information furnished by the taxpayer to wrongfully reduce the tax liability of the taxpayer.

6. **(N)** A return preparer will be subject to penalty if the preparer knowingly or recklessly discloses information furnished in connection with the preparation of a tax return, unless such information is furnished for quality or peer review, under an administrative order by a regulatory agency, or pursuant to an order of a court.

7. **(E)** Under these facts, a position taken on a return which is consistent with incorrect instructions does not satisfy the realistic possibility standard. However, if the preparer relied on the incorrect instructions and was not aware of the announcement or regulations, the reasonable cause and good faith exception may apply depending upon the facts and circumstances.

8. **(P)** A return preparer will be subject to penalty if the preparer knowingly or recklessly discloses information furnished in connection with the preparation of a tax return, unless such information is furnished for quality or peer review, under an administrative order by a regulatory agency, or pursuant to an order of a court.

9. **(P)** A return preparer will be subject to penalty if there is a willful attempt in any manner to understate the tax liability of any taxpayer or there is a reckless or intentional disregard of rules or regulations. The penalty will apply if a preparer knowingly deducts the expenses of the taxpayer's domestic help as wages paid in the taxpayer's business.

Module 24: Federal Securities Acts

Overview

The bulk of the material tested on the exam from this area comes from the Securities Act of 1933, as amended, and the Securities Exchange Act of 1934, as amended. Topics included under the scope of the 1933 Act are registration requirements, exempt securities, and exempt transactions. The purposes of the 1933 Act are to provide investors with full and fair disclosure of a security offering and to prevent fraud. The basic prohibition of the 1933 Act is that no sale of a security shall occur in interstate commerce without registration and without furnishing a prospectus to prospective purchasers unless the security or the transaction is exempt from registration.

The purpose of the 1934 Act is the establishment of the Securities Exchange Commission to assure fairness in the trading of securities subsequent to their original issuance. The basic scope of the 1934 Act is to require periodic reports of financial and other information concerning registered securities, and to prohibit manipulative and deceptive devices in both the sale and purchase of securities.

The exam often tests on the Federal Securities Acts; however, this is sometimes combined with accountant's liability or is included within questions concerning corporate or limited partnership law. You should also expect questions on the Sarbanes-Oxley Act of 2002 and the Dodd-Frank Act of 2010. Before beginning the reading you should review the key terms at the end of the module.

A. **Securities Act of 1933** (Generally applies to initial issuances [primary offerings] of securities)

1. The purposes of the 1933 Act are to provide potential investors with full and fair disclosure of all material information relating to issuance of securities (such that a prudent decision to invest or refrain from investing can be made) and to prevent fraud or misrepresentation.

   a. This is accomplished by

      (1) Requiring a registration statement to be filed with Securities Exchange Commission (SEC) before either a public sale or an offer to sell securities in interstate commerce

         (a) This is the fundamental thrust of the 1933 Act.
         (b) The SEC is a government agency comprised of commissioners and its staff that was created to administer and enforce the Federal Securities Laws . The Commission interprets the acts, conducts investigations, adjudicates violations, and performs a rule-making function to implement the acts.

            (1) Can subpoena witnesses
            (2) Can obtain injunction preventing sale of securities
            (3) Cannot assess monetary penalties without court proceedings
            (4) Cannot prosecute criminal acts

      (2) Requiring prospectuses to be provided to investors with, or before, the sale or delivery of the securities to provide public with information given to the SEC in registration statement.
      (3) Providing civil and criminal liabilities for failure to comply with these requirements and for misrepresentation or fraud in the sale of securities even if not required to be registered.

   b. The SEC does not evaluate the merits or value of securities

    (1)   The SEC can only compel full and fair disclosure.

    (2)   In theory, the public can evaluate the merits of the security when provided with full and fair disclosure.

    (3)   The SEC's function is not to detect fraud or to stop offerings where fraud or unethical conduct is suspected.

    (4)   The SEC's functions are also to

        (a)   Regulate securities markets

        (b)   Maintain fair markets

        (c)   Protect investors

        (d)   Review corporate financial statements

        (e)   Enforce securities laws

        (f)   Provide guidance for accounting rules

c. The major items you need to know include

    (1)   That a registration statement and prospectus are usually required

    (2)   Which transactions are exempt from registration

    (3)   Which securities are exempt from registration

    (4)   What the liability is for false or misleading registration statements

2. Definitions

a. Security—any note, stock, bond, certificate of interest, debenture, investment contract, etc., or any interest or instrument commonly known as a security.

    (1)   The general idea is that investor intends to make a profit on the investment through the efforts of others rather than through his/her own efforts.

EXAMPLE

Ward is a general partner of WDC partnership in Washington, D.C. Usually, Ward's interest would not be considered a security because a general partner's interest typically involves participation in the business rather than mere investment.

        (a)   Includes limited partnership interests

        (b)   Includes rights and warrants to subscribe for the above

        (c)   Includes treasury stock

        (d)   Investment contract is a security when money is invested in a common enterprise with profits to be derived from the effort of others

---

EXAMPLE

Blue Corporation in Florida owns several acres of orange trees. Blue is planning on selling a large portion of the land with the orange trees to several individuals in various states on a row-by-row basis. Each purchaser gets a deed and is required to purchase a management contract whereby Blue Corporation maintains all the land and oranges and then remits the net profits to the various purchasers. Even though it may appear that each individual purchased separately the land with the oranges and a management contract, the law looks at the "big picture" here. Since in reality the individuals are investing their money, and the profits are derived from the efforts of others, the law treats the above fact pattern as involving securities. Therefore, the Securities Acts apply.

---

b. Person—individual, corporation, partnership, unincorporated association, business trust, government.

c. Controlling person—has power, direct/indirect, to influence the management and/or policies of an issuer, whether by stock ownership, contract, position, or otherwise.

EXAMPLE

A 51% stockholder is a controlling person by virtue of a majority ownership.

> **EXAMPLE**
>
> A director of a corporation also owns 10% of that same corporation. By virtue of the stock ownership and position on the board of directors, he has a strong voice in the management of the corporation. Therefore, he is a controlling person.

    d.   Insiders—(applies to the Securities Exchange Act of 1934) include officers, directors, and owners of more than 10% of any class of an issuer's equity securities.

        (1)   Note that debentures are not included because not equity securities.

        (2)   For purposes of this law to avoid a "loophole," insiders include "beneficial owners" of more than 10% of the equity stock of issuer.

            (a)   To determine the amount of "beneficial ownership," add to the individual's equity ownership, equity stock owned by

                (1)   Owner's spouse
                (2)   Owner's minor children
                (3)   Owner's relative in same house
                (4)   Owner's equity stock held in trust in which owner is beneficiary

> **EXAMPLE**
>
> Linda owns 6% of the common stock of ABC Company in Philadelphia. Her spouse owns 3% of ABC Company's common stock. The stock was also placed in the name of their two minor children, each owning 1% of ABC Company's common stock. Linda has beneficial ownership of 11% of the equity securities of ABC Company so she is an insider for the 1934 Act. Note that her husband also qualifies as an insider.

> **EXAMPLE**
>
> Use the same facts as in the previous example except that all four individuals owned debentures of ABC Company. Since these are not equity securities, none qualifies as an insider.

> **EXAMPLE**
>
> Robert is an officer who owns 4% of the common stock of XYZ Company in Washington, DC. Since Robert is an officer, he is an insider even though the ownership level is below 10%.

    e.   Underwriter—any person who has purchased from an issuer with a view to the public distribution of any security or participates in such undertaking.

        (1)   Includes any person who offers or sells for issuer in connection with the distribution of any security.

        (2)   Does not include person who sells or distributes on commission for underwriter (i.e., dealers).

    f.   Sales of securities are covered by the Securities Act of 1933

        (1)   Issuance of securities as part of business reorganization (e.g., merger or consolidation) constitutes a sale and must be registered with SEC unless the issue otherwise qualifies as an exemption from the registration requirements of 1933 Act.

        (2)   Issuance of stock warrants is considered a sale so that requirements of 1933 Act must be met.

        (3)   Employee stock purchase plan is a sale and therefore must comply with the provisions of the 1933 Act. The company must supply a prospectus to each employee to whom stock is offered.

        (4)   Stock dividends or splits are not sales.

   g.   Registration statement—the statement required to be filed with SEC before initial sale of securities in interstate commerce.

       (1)   Includes financial statements and all other relevant information about the registrant's property, business, directors, principal officers, together with prospectus, and any amendment, report, or document filed as part of the statement or incorporated therein by reference.

       (2)   It is against law to sell, offer to sell, or offer to purchase securities before filing a registration statement.

       (3)   The registration statement and prospectus becomes public upon filing.

          (a)   The effective date of registration statement is 20th day after filing.

          (b)   It is against the law to sell securities until the effective date but issuer may **offer** securities upon filing registration statement.

          (c)   Such offers may be made

             (1)   Orally

             (2)   By tombstone ads that identify security, its price, and who will take orders

             (3)   By a "red-herring prospectus"

                (a)   Legend in red ink (thus, red-herring) is printed on this preliminary prospectus indicating that the prospectus is "preliminary" and that a registration statement has been filed but has not become effective.

   h.   Prospectus—any notice, circular, advertisement, letter, or communication offering any security for sale (or merger).

       (1)   May be a written, radio, or television communication.

          (a)   SEC adopted new "plain English" rule for important sections of companies' prospectuses, including risk factor sections.

       (2)   After the effective date of the registration statement, communication (written or oral) will not be considered a prospectus if

          (a)   Prior to or at same time, a written prospectus was also sent.

          (b)   If it only states from whom written prospectus is available, identifies security, states price, and who will execute orders for it (i.e., tombstone ad).

3. Registration requirements

   a.   Registration is required under the Act if the securities are to be offered, sold, or delivered in interstate commerce or through the mail.

       (1)   Interstate commerce means trade, commerce, transportation, or communication (e.g., telephone call) among more than one state or territory of US. This is interpreted very broadly to include trade, commerce, etc. that is within one state but affects interstate commerce.

EXAMPLE

A corporation issues securities to individuals living only in Philadelphia. It is further shown that this issuance affects trade in Delaware. Interstate commerce is affected because although Philadelphia is of course in one state, the effects on at least one other state allow the Federal Securities Acts to take effect under our Constitution. Therefore, registration of these securities is required under the Federal Law unless exemptions are found as discussed later.

---

       (2)   Unless it is an exempted security or exempted transaction as discussed later.

   b.   The issuer has primary duty of registration

       (1)   Any person who sells unregistered securities that should have been registered may be liable to a purchaser (unless transaction or security is exempt).

       (2)   Liability cannot be disclaimed in writing or orally by the issuer.

       (3)   This liability not dischargeable in bankruptcy.

   c.   The information required, in general, in registration statements

       (1)   Financial statements audited by independent CPA

       (2)   Names of the issuer, directors, officers, general partners, underwriters , large stockholders, counsel, etc.

    (3) The risks associated with the securities
    (4) A description of property, business, and capitalization of issuer
    (5) Information about management of issuer
    (6) A description of security to be sold and use to be made by issuer of proceeds

d. The prospectus is also filed as part of registration statement

    (1) It generally must contain same information as registration statement, but it may be condensed or summarized.

e. The registration statement and prospectus are reviewed by SEC

    (1) Amendments are almost always required by SEC.
    (2) The SEC may issue stop-order suspending effectiveness of registration if statement appears incomplete or misleading.
    (3) Otherwise the registration becomes effective on 20th day after filing (or on 20th day after filing amendment). The twenty-day period is called the waiting period.
    (4) It is unlawful for company to sell the securities prior to approval (effective registration date). However, preliminary prospectuses are permitted once registration statement is filed.

f. Applies to both corporate and noncorporate issuers.
g. The registration covers a single distribution, so second distribution must also be registered.
h. The shelf registration is an exception to requirement that each new distribution of nonexempt securities requires a new filing.

    (1) It allows certain qualified issuers to register securities once and then offer and sell them on a delayed or continuous basis "off the shelf."
    (2) Advantage is that issuer can respond better to changing market conditions affecting stock.

i. Different registration forms are available

    (1) Form S-1 is basic long-form registration statement.
    (2) Additional forms now required based on Sarbanes-Oxley Act that require non-GAAP financial measures to be presented so that they reconcile to the most directly comparable GAAP financial measure. The goal is to reduce concerns regarding improper use of non-GAAP financial measures.
    (3) Forms S-2 and S-3

        (a) These forms were adopted by SEC to ease much of burden of disclosures required under federal securities regulation.
        (b) They require less detailed disclosures than Form S-1.
        (c) They integrate information required under 1933 and 1934 Acts. Firms already on file with SEC under 1934 Act may incorporate much information by reference to avoid additional disclosure.

    (4) Forms SB-1 and SB-2

        (a) These forms permitted for small businesses under Regulation S-B.

            (1) They reduce amount of financial and nonfinancial information required when registering under 1933 Act and when reporting quarterly information under 1934 Act.
            (2) A small business issuer is generally one that has revenues less than $25 million.

4. Exempt securities (need not be registered but still subject to antifraud provisions under the Act).

a. Commercial paper (e.g., note, draft, check, etc.) with a maturity of nine months or less.

    (1) Must be for commercial purpose and not investment.

EXAMPLE

OK Corporation in Washington, DC, wishes to finance a short-term need for more cash for current operations. OK will do this by issuing some short-term notes which all have a maturity of nine months or less. These are exempt from the registration requirements.

b.   Intrastate issues—securities offered and sold only within one state.

   (1)   The issuer must be resident of state and doing 80% of business in the state and must use at least 80% of sale proceeds in connection with business operations in the state.

   (2)   All offerees and purchasers must be residents of state.

   (3)   For nine months after last sale by the issuer, resales can only be made to residents of state.

   (4)   All of a particular issue must qualify under this rule or this exemption cannot be used for any sale of the issue.

EXAMPLE

A regional corporation in need of additional capital makes an offer to the residents of the state in which it is incorporated to purchase a new issue of its stock. The offer expressly restricts sales to only residents of the state and all purchasers are residents of the state.

---

c.   Small issues (Regulation A)—issuances up to $5,000,000 by issuer in 12-month period may be exempt if

   (1)   There is a notice filed with SEC.

   (2)   An offering circular (containing financial information about the corporation and descriptive information about offered securities) must be provided to offeree. Financial statements in offering circular need not be audited.

   (3)   Nonissuers can sell up to $1,500,000 in 12-month period.

> **NOTE:** An offering circular (statement) is required under Regulation A instead of the more costly and time-consuming prospectus.

d.   Securities of governments, banks, quasi governmental authorities (e.g., local hospital authorities), savings and loan associations, farmers, co-ops, and common carriers regulated by ICC. Public utilities are not exempt.

e.   Security exchanged by the issuer exclusively with its existing shareholders so long as

   (1)   No commission is paid.

   (2)   Both sets of securities must have been issued by the same person.

EXAMPLE

A stock split is an exempt transaction under the 1933 Act and thus, the securities need not be registered at time of split.

---

f.   Securities of nonprofit religious, educational, or charitable organizations.

g.   Certificates issued by receiver or trustee in bankruptcy.

h.   Insurance and annuity contracts.

5. Exempt transactions or offerings (still subject, however, to antifraud provisions of the Act; may also be subject to reporting requirements of the 1934 Act).

a.   Sale or offer to sell by any person **other than** an issuer, underwriter, or dealer

   (1)   Generally covers sales by individual investors on their own account.

   (2)   May be a transaction by broker on customer's order. It does not include solicitation of these orders.

   (3)   Exemption does not apply to sales by controlling persons because they are considered an underwriter or issuer.

b.   **Regulation D** establishes three important exemptions in Rules 504, 505, and 506 under the 1933 Act.

   (1)   Rule 504 exempts an issuance of securities up to $1,000,000 sold in 12-month period to any number of investors (this is also known as seed capital exemption).

    (a) General offering and solicitations are permitted under Rule 504 as long as they are restricted to "accredited investors," such as banks, insurance companies, high-worth individuals, etc.

    (b) The issuer need not restrict purchasers' right to resell securities.

    (c) No specific disclosure is required.

    (d) The issuer must send notice of offering to SEC within 15 days of first sale of securities.

(2) Rule 505 exempts issuance of up to $5,000,000 in 12-month period.

    (a) No general offering or solicitation is permitted within 12-month period.

    (b) Permits sales to 35 unaccredited (nonaccredited term sometimes used) investors and to unlimited number of accredited investors within 12 months.

        (1) Accredited investors are, for example, banks, savings and loan associations, credit unions, insurance companies, broker dealers, certain trusts, partnerships, and corporations, also natural persons having joint or individual net worth exceeding $1,000,000 (not including value of primary residence) or having individual net income of $200,000 or joint net income of $300,000 for two most recent years.

        (2) SEC must be notified within fifteen days of first sale.

    (c) The issuer must restrict the purchasers' right to resell the securities; in general must be held for two years or else exemption is lost.

    (d) These securities typically state that they have not been registered and that they have resale restrictions.

    (e) Unlike under Rule 504, if nonaccredited investor purchases these securities, audited balance sheet must be supplied (i.e., disclosure is required) as well as other financial statements or information, if readily available.

        (1) If purchased only by accredited investors, no disclosure required.

(3) Rule 506 allows private placement of unlimited amount of securities.

    (a) In general, the same rules apply here as outlined under Rule 505. Under the provisions of the Jumpstart Our Business Startups (JOBS) Act general solicitation and advertising for Rule 506 offerings is allowed providing that the issuer takes reasonable steps to determine that all of the purchasers are accredited investors. The issuer must also indicate whether it is relying on the provision that permits general solicitation and advertising.

    (b) However, an additional requirement is that the unaccredited investors (up to 35) must be sophisticated investors (individuals with knowledge and experience in financial matters) or be represented by individual with such knowledge and experience.

EXAMPLE

A growing corporation is in need of additional capital and decides to make a new issuance of its stock. The stock is only offered to 10 of the president's friends who regularly make financial investments of this sort. They are interested in purchasing the stock for an investment and each of them is provided with the type of information that is regularly included in a registration statement.

---

(4) Disclosures for offerings under $2,000,000 have been simplified to be similar to disclosures under Regulation A.

(5) A controlling person who sells restricted securities may be held to be an underwriter (and thus subject to the registration provisions) unless requirements of Rule 144 are met when controlling person is selling through a broker.

    (a) If the following are met, the security can be sold without registration:

        (1) The broker performs no services beyond those of typical broker who executes orders and receives customary fee.

        (2) Ownership (including beneficial ownership) for at least two years.

        (3) Only limited amounts of stock may be sold—based on a specified formula.

        (4) Public must have available adequate disclosure of the issuer corporation.

        (5) Notice of sale must be filed with SEC.

(6) Small issuers sometimes use offerings over Internet to investors and often use regulation to avoid registration. These types of offerings are referred to as crowdfunding. The JOBS Act of 2012 has provisions that make it easier for firms to make Internet offerings. However, the provision will not be effective or testable on the CPA exam until after the SEC develops the related rules. Recently, several states have developed their own crowdfunding regulations for offerings within those states.

c. Postregistration transactions by dealer (i.e., dealer is not required to deliver prospectus) if the transaction is made at least 40 days after first date security was offered to public, or after 90 days if it is issuer's first public issue. This exemption does not apply to sales of securities that are leftover part of an allotment from the public issue.

6. Antifraud provisions

a. Apply even if securities are exempt or the transactions are exempt as long as interstate commerce is used (use of mail or telephone qualifies) to sell or offer to sell securities.

b. Included are schemes to defraud purchaser or making sale by use of untrue statement of material fact or by omission of material fact.

(1) Proof of negligence is sometimes sufficient rather than proof of scienter.
(2) Protects purchaser, not seller.

7. Civil liability (i.e., private actions brought by purchasers of securities).

a. The purchaser may recover if he or she can establish that

(1) It was a purchase of a security issued under a registration statement containing a misleading statement or omission of a material fact, and purchaser may also recover if issuer or any person sold unregistered securities for which there is no exemption.
(2) Suffered economic loss.
(3) Privity of contract is **not** necessary.

EXAMPLE

Third parties who have never dealt with issuer but bought securities from another party have a right to recover when the above is established despite lack of privity.

---

(4) Need **not** prove that the defendant intended to deceive.
(5) The purchaser need **not** rely on registration statement to recover.

b. The purchaser of securities may recover from (1) the issuer, (2) any directors, partners or underwriters of the issuer, (3) anyone who signed the registration statement, and (4) experts of authorized statements (e.g., attorneys, accountants, engineers, appraisers). Liability is not discharged in bankruptcy.

c. The burden of proof is shifted to defendant in most cases; however, except for the issuer, defendant may use "due diligence" defense.

(1) The due diligence defense can be used successfully by defendant by proving that

(a) As an expert, s/he had reasonable grounds after reasonable investigation to believe that his/her own statements were true and/or did not contain any omissions of material facts by the time the registration statement became effective.

EXAMPLE

Whitewood, a CPA, performs a reasonable audit and discovers no irregularities.

(b) S/he relied on an expert for the part of the registration statement in question and did believe (and had reasonable grounds for such belief) that there were no misstatements or material omissions of fact.

> **EXAMPLE**
>
> Greenwood, a CPA, relies on an attorney's work as a foundation for his own work on contingent liabilities.

    (c)   S/he did reasonably believe that after a reasonable investigation, statements not in the province of an expert were true or that material omissions did not exist.

> **EXAMPLE**
>
> Lucky, an underwriter, made a reasonable investigation on the registration statement and did reasonably believe no impropriety existed even though misstatements and omissions of material facts existed. Note that the issuer is liable even if s/he exercised the same care and held the same reasonable belief because the issuer is liable without fault and cannot use the due diligence defense.

NOTE: The issuer is liable even if s/he exercised the same care and held the same reasonable belief because the issuer is liable without fault and cannot use the due diligence defense.

    d.   The seller of the security is liable to purchaser if interstate commerce or mail is used, and if the registration is not in effect and should be, or if the registration statement contains misstatements or omissions of material facts. The purchaser may recover the amount paid plus interest less any income received by the purchaser. The buyer may ask for rescission of sale instead of damages.

    e.   The statute of limitations is the earlier of these dates:

       (1)   Two years after discovery is made of fraud, deceit, or manipulation involving contravention of securities laws; or

       (2)   Five years after such violation of securities laws involving fraud, deceit, or manipulation

8. Criminal liability

    a.   If person intentionally (willfully) makes an untrue statement or intentionally omits a material fact, or willfully violates SEC Act or regulation.

       (1)   Reckless disregard of the truth may also qualify.

       (2)   Tampering with documents to be used in official proceedings do qualify.

    b.   If person uses interstate commerce or mail to fraudulently sell any security.

    c.   Person is subject to fine or imprisonment up to twenty years or both.

       (1)   Injunctions are also available.

    d.   Criminal liability results even if securities are exempt or transactions are exempt.

9. Increased protection for whistle-blowers of public companies

NOW REVIEW MULTIPLE-CHOICE QUESTIONS 1 THROUGH 26

B. Securities Exchange Act of 1934 (Generally applies to subsequent trading of securities—must comply separately with 1933 Act if applicable, that is, initial issuances rather than subsequent trading).

1. Purposes of the Act

    a.   To federally regulate securities exchanges and securities traded thereon

    b.   To require periodic disclosure by issuers of equity securities

    c.   To require adequate information be provided in various transactions

    d.   To prevent unfair use of information by insiders

    e.   To prevent fraud and deceptive practices

2. Following securities must be registered with SEC

    a.   Over-the-counter and other equity securities traded in interstate commerce where corporation has assets of more than $10 million and 500 or more shareholders. Equity securities include stock, rights to subscribe to stock, or securities convertible into stock. (Note that a provision of the Jumpstart Our Business Startups [JOBS] Act increases this threshold to 500 unaccredited shareholders or 2,000 total shareholders. It also provides that the threshold will not consider shares obtained by a shareholder as a part of a qualified employee compensation plan. This Act will be eligible for testing beginning in January 2013.)

    b.   Securities that are traded on any national securities exchange must be registered. Securities exempted under 1933 Act may still be regulated under 1934 Act.

    c.   Securities offered by issuer who was required to register under 1933 Act.

3. Required disclosures in registration include

    a.   Names of officers and directors

    b.   Nature of business

    c.   Financial structure of firm

    d.   Any bonus and profit-sharing provisions

4. Sanctions available to SEC under the 1934 Act

    a.   Revocation or suspension of registration

    b.   Denial of registration

    c.   Permanent or temporary suspension of trading of securities (injunction)

    d.   May order accounting and disgorgement of gains made illegally

    e.   May sanction individuals violating foreign laws

    f.   May require large traders to identify selves

5. Exempt securities

    a.   Obligations of US government, guaranteed by, or in which US government has interest.

    b.   Obligations of state or political subdivision, or guaranteed thereby.

    c.   Securities of federally chartered bank or savings and loan institution.

    d.   Securities of common carrier regulated by ICC.

    e.   Industrial development bonds.

6. Issuers of securities registered under the 1934 Act must file the following reports with SEC.

    a.   Annual reports (Form 10-K) must be certified by independent public accountant.

    b.   Quarterly reports (Form 10-Q) must be filed for each of first three fiscal quarters of each fiscal year of issuer.

        (1)   Must be reviewed by CPA.

        (2)   Not required to be reported on by CPA.

    c.   Event reports (Form 8-K) when material events occur such as change in corporate control, significant change or revaluation of assets, or change in amount of issued securities. In most cases the form must be filed within four days after the material event occurs.

    d.   Similar reports must be provided to shareholders. However, annual report need not be given if issuer had to disclose under 1934 Act only because it made a registered offering under 1933 Act.

7. Whether registered under 1934 Act or not, the securities registered during the previous year under 1933 Act must have periodic reports filed with SEC by issuers.

8. Proxy solicitations

    a.   Proxy—grant of authority by shareholder to someone else to vote his/her shares at a meeting.

    b.   A proxy solicitation provisions apply to solicitation (by any means of interstate commerce or the mails) of holders of securities required to be registered under the 1934 Act—must be reported to SEC.

    c.   A proxy statement must be sent with proxy solicitation.

        (1)   It must contain disclosure of all material facts concerning matters to be voted upon.

       (a)   Either misstatements or omissions of material facts are violations of proxy rules.

       (b)   Material means that it would likely affect vote of average shareholder on proposed action.

   (2)   The purpose is for fairness in corporate action and election of directors.

d.   The requirements of the proxy itself

   (1)   Indicate on whose behalf solicitation is made

   (2)   Identify clearly and impartially each matter to be acted on

e.   Some of inclusions in the proxy material

   (1)   Proposals by shareholders that are a proper subject for shareholders to vote on

   (2)   Financial statements for last two years, certified by independent accountant, if

       (a)   Solicitation is on behalf of management.

       (b)   It is for annual meeting at which directors are to be elected.

f.   Any person who owns at least 5% or has held stock for six months or more has right of access to lists of shareholders for lawful purpose.

g.   The proxy statement, proxy itself, and any other soliciting material must be filed with SEC.

h.   Brokers are required to forward proxies for customers' shares held by broker.

i.   Incumbent management is required to mail proxy materials of insurgents to shareholders if requested and expenses are paid by the insurgents.

j.   Remedies for violation of proxy solicitation rules

   (1)   Civil action by aggrieved shareholder for damages caused by material misinformation or omissions of material facts

   (2)   Or injunctions are possible

   (3)   Or the court may set aside vote taken and require a new proxy solicitation with full and fair disclosure

9. Tender offers

a.   A tender offer is invitation by buyer (bidder) to shareholders of targeted company to tender shares they own for sale for price specified over a period of time.

b.   Reporting and disclosure requirements apply to tender offers to provide shareholders full disclosure by both the bidder and targeted company.

10. Short-swing profits

a.   A corporation is entitled to recover profits from any insider who sells stock of company within six months of its purchase.

b.   Profits that can be recovered are calculated by matching highest sale price with lowest purchase price found within six months.

c.   Losses cannot be used to offset these profits.

11. Antifraud provisions—very broad scope

a.   It is unlawful to manipulate process and create appearance of active trading (not good-faith transactions by brokers).

b.   It is unlawful to use any manipulative or deceptive devices in purchase or sale of securities.

   (1)   Applies to all securities, whether registered or not (as long as either mail, interstate commerce, or a national stock exchange is used)—this is important.

   (2)   Includes any act, practice, or scheme which is deceptive or manipulative (against SEC rules and/or regulations)—most importantly, it is unlawful to make any false statement of a material fact or any omission of a material fact that is necessary to make statement(s) not misleading (in connection with purchase or sale of security, whether registered or not).

       (a)   This is Rule 10b-5 promulgated by the SEC under Section 10(b) of the Act.

NOTE: There are no exemptions under Rule 10b-5.

(3)   The plaintiff must prove

    (a)   The defendant made material false statement or omission of material fact in connection with purchase or sale of securities.

        (1)   The basic test of materiality is whether a reasonable person would attach importance to the fact in determining his/her choice of action in the transaction.

EXAMPLE

A broker offers to sell a stock and omits to tell the purchaser that the corporation is about to make an unfavorable merger.

    (b)   The defendant acted with scienter which is either knowledge of falsity, or reckless disregard for the truth.

        (1)   Negligence is not sufficient.
        (2)   Note that with antifraud provisions under the **1933** Act scienter need not necessarily be proven.

    (c)   The defendant must have relied upon false statements or omissions.
    (d)   The defendant who suffers damages may sue for monetary damages, or rescind the transaction.

(4)   Applies to brokers who intend to never deliver securities or who intend to misappropriate proceeds of sales. The SEC by US Supreme Court ruling has power to sue brokers for fraud.

(5)   Applies to any seller, buyer, or person who lends his/her name to statements used in the buying and selling of securities. Cross reference this to the 1933 Act that only applies to sellers or offerors of securities.

(6)   Applies to insider who buys or sells on inside information until it is disseminated to public.

    (a)   Includes a broad scope of insiders such as officers, directors, accountants, lawyers, employees at the various levels of firm, consultants, agents, representatives of firm, and any other persons owing a fiduciary duty to company.

(7)   Even if exempt from registration under 1934 Act, still subject to antifraud provisions.
(8)   Extensive potential liability for insiders

    (a)   Must forego trading if one has such knowledge until public has information

        (1)   Includes insiders and anyone with knowledge (e.g., accountant, attorney, engineer)
        (2)   Illegal for person (tipper) to give inside information to another person (called tippee)
        (3)   Tippee is liable if acts on inside information until information is known by public

            (a)   Tipper is liable for illegal profits of tippee.

12. Civil liability

    a.   Any person (including an accountant) who intentionally (willfully) manipulates a security may be liable to the buyer or seller of that security if the buyer or seller is damaged.

NOTE: Both buyers and sellers may recover under the 1934 Act.

    b.   Any person who makes a misleading (or of course false) statement about any material fact in any application, report, or document is liable to an injured purchaser or seller if s/he relied on the statement, and did not know it was false or misleading.

        (1)   Privity of contract is not necessary.
        (2)   However, the party sued can avoid liability if s/he can prove s/he acted in good faith, and had no knowledge that the statements were materially misleading or false. The SEC may collect liability funds for victims of securities fraud.

13. Criminal liability

    a.   Has been increased due to Sarbanes-Oxley Act

(1) Individuals in violation of Rule 10b-5 may be put in prison for up to 20 years and/or may be fined for up to five million dollars.

   (a)   May be put in prison for up to 25 years and/or fined for willful violation of 1934 Act.

(2) Corporations or partnerships are subject to fines of up to 25 million dollars.

b.   Criminal liability can also be used for intentional false or misleading statements on material facts provided in applications, reports, or other documents under this Act.

14. The Bankruptcy Abuse Prevention and Consumer Protection Act of 2005 prohibits discharge of any debts incurred in violation of securities laws.

15. Both private parties and SEC now have civil remedies against violators of 1934 Act.

   a.   Private parties may recover from those who violate rule 10b-5 as well as from others sharing responsibility such as attorneys, accountants, corporations.

   (1) Private parties may also rescind contracts to purchase contacts when violations hurt them.

   b.   SEC authorized to give awards to individuals that provide information leading to prosecution of insider-trading violators.

16. Statute of limitations extended for securities fraud

17. Reporting requirements of insiders under 1934 Act

   a.   Must file statement with SEC

   (1) Discloses amount of equity securities
   (2) Time of statement disclosure

      (a)   When securities registered
      (b)   When registration statement becomes effective
      (c)   Within ten days of person attaining insider status

   (3) Insider must report any changes in ownership within 10 days.

18. Foreign Corrupt Practices Act

   a.   Unlawful for any domestic company or its officers or employees or agents to offer or give to foreign officials or to political party or political officials something of value to influence decisions.

   (1) Excluded are routine governmental actions that do not involve official's discretion such as processing applications or permits.
   (2) Amendment includes attempt by supplier to obtain any improper advantage is unlawful.

   b.   Requires companies having registered securities to maintain system of internal control and to maintain accurate accounting and to protect integrity of independent audits.
   c.   Actions of foreign citizens or organizations committed within US also covered.

19. Regulation Fair Disclosure (Reg FD) from SEC requires corporation to disseminate its data equally among investors and analysts to help avoid conflicts of interest by analysts.

   a.   If one mistakenly gives out inside information s/he must disclose it publicly as soon as is practicable and always within 24 hours or less.
   b.   Applies also to giving nonpublic information to shareholders who are likely to trade based upon it.

NOW REVIEW MULTIPLE-CHOICE QUESTIONS 27 THROUGH 42

C.   The Sarbanes-Oxley Act of 2002

1. The act covers all public companies.
2. Section 906 certification provision of Act requires that each periodic report that contains financial reports of the issuer must be accompanied with written statement of CEO or CFO that certifies that reports comply fully with relevant securities laws and also fairly present the financial condition of company in all material aspects.

   a.   Any officer who makes certification while knowing it does not comply with SEC requirements can be fined up to $1,000,000 or imprisoned for up to 10 years, or both.

      (1)   Officers can be fined for up to $5,000,000 or imprisoned for up to 20 years, or both, for willful violation of this certification requirement.

      (2)   SEC now permitted to freeze payments to officers and directors during investigation of wrongdoings.

      (3)   SEC may now prevent unfit individuals from serving as officers or directors of public companies.

    b.   CEO and CFO must give up any bonuses , incentive-based pay and profits on sales of stock that they received during 12-month time before financial statements are required to be restated because of omissions or misstatements of material facts.

3.   Section 302 certification makes officers responsible for maintaining effective internal controls and requires principal executive and financial officers to disclose all significant internal control deficiencies to issuer's auditors and audit committee.

    a.   Management must now evaluate any changes in internal control methods.

    b.   Officers and directors of an issuer or their agents are prohibited from fraudulently influencing or coercing auditors to render financial statements materially misleading.

4.   Act amends Securities Exchange Act of 1934 to make it illegal for issuer to give various types of personal loans to or for any executive officer or director.

5.   CEO and CFO must give up any bonus, any compensation that is equity based or incentive based, or any profit from sale of corporation's securities during period when corporation was required to restate financial statements due to wrongdoings.

    a.   CEO and CFO must give up these bonuses and profits even if wrongdoings were not by them but also if they were by any other officer or employee.

    b.   Act requires that any wrongdoing officer give up profits from stock sales or bonuses received due to stock being overpriced because of false information.

      (1)   Act allows not only that improper gains be recovered but also any remedy needed to protect investors.

6.   Attorneys are required to report to chief legal counsel or CEO such things as material violations of securities laws or breach of fiduciary duties. Attorneys must report this to audit committee (or another committee) or board of directors if counsel or CEO does not take action.

7.   Companies must disclose material off-balance sheet liabilities and transactions.

    a.   Amendments require management disclosure of information needed by users of financial statements to better understand off-balance sheet arrangements involving such things as their business purpose, market risk, credit risk, liquidity, or other material effects.

8.   Pro forma information disclosed to public in financial reports, press releases, etc., must not contain any untrue statement of a material fact or omit any material fact.

    a.   Pro forma information must also be reconciled with financial statements prepared in accordance with GAAP.

9.   SEC now requires that reports by insiders that disclose their securities holdings must be filed electronically with SEC to result in earlier public notification and wider public availability of this information.

    a.   Issuers having corporate Web sites must also post such information quickly.

10.   New rules require disclosures, both financial and nonfinancial, to aid public in assessing risk better pertaining to companies (e.g., disclosing off-balance sheet financing).

    a.   Also, aid in purpose of Act to produce reports under Securities Acts that are timely and reliable.

D. The Wall Street Reform and Consumer Protection (Dodd-Frank) Act of 2010

The Dodd-Frank Act was passed as a reaction to the recent financial crisis. The Act was designed "to promote the financial stability of the United States by improving accountability and transparency in the financial system, to end "too big to fail," to protect the American taxpayer by ending bailouts, to protect consumers from abusive financial services practices, and for other purposes."

1.   The Act created the Financial Stability Oversight Council that is charged with identifying threats to the financial stability of the US, promoting market discipline, and responding to emerging risks. The Council will identify significant nonbank financial firms and regulate these institutions, and prescribe risk management standards for payment, clearing, and settlement activities by financial market institutions.

2. The Act increased the types of financial companies that could be seized and liquidated by the FDIC to include insurance companies and nonbank financial companies.
3. The Act requires previously exempt US and non-US advisors of hedge funds, private equity funds, and other private investment vehicles to register with the SEC under the Advisors Act. It also provides for additional reporting requirements for registered and nonregistered advisors.
4. The Act eliminated the Office of Thrift Supervision, distributing its responsibilities to other agencies.
5. The Act created the Federal Insurance Office to regulate insurance companies.
6. The Act created the Bureau of Consumer Financial Protection to regulate the offering of consumer products and services (e.g., credit counseling, check-cashing, etc.) under the federal consumer financial laws.
7. The Act prohibits any "banking entity" from engaging in proprietary trading, or sponsoring or investing in a hedge fund or private equity fund (the Volcher rule).
8. The Act gives authority to the Commodity Futures Trading Commission and the SEC to regulate the derivatives (swaps) markets, including the regulation of swap dealers and major swap participants.
9. The Act has provisions to help prevent conflicts of interests and increase transparency by credit rating agencies.
10. The Act includes broad changes in executive compensation policies for public companies, including

   a. Requiring the national exchanges to issue new listing rules requiring companies to develop and implement compensation-recovery arrangements (clawback policies). The Act states that when noncompliance with a financial-reporting requirement leads to an accounting restatement, the company is required to recover from any current or former executive officer all excessive incentive-based compensation paid over the preceding three-year period.
   b. Requiring that all members of the compensation committee of the board of directors be independent.
   c. Requiring a shareholder nonbinding vote on the prior year's executive compensation at least every three years, and a vote at least every six years as to whether the vote on compensation should be held more often.
   d. Requiring a nonbinding vote by shareholders on "golden parachutes" to be provided to executives as a result of major transactions.

11. The Act provides that the SEC will increase its compliance activities regarding securities trading, and will pay awards to whistle-blowers for providing information about violations of securities laws that result in aggregate monetary sanctions in excess of $1 million.

   a. A whistle-blower is eligible to receive 10 to 30% of the monetary penalty if the information is derived from independent knowledge or analysis of the whistle-blower and not known to the government from any other source.
   b. Tips can be made anonymously (through an attorney) with the whistle-blower only being identified to the SEC after determination that an award will be given.
   c. A broad group of individuals are eligible including employees, customers, and suppliers. Individuals that are generally excluded from eligibility include

      (1) Officers, directors, trustees, or partners of an entity, when those individuals learned of information about the misconduct in question from another person or in connection with the company's processes for identifying potential illegal conduct.
      (2) Employees whose main job functions involve compliance or internal audit, or persons who are employed by a firm hired to perform audit or compliance functions or to investigate possible violations of the law.
      (3) Employees of public accounting firms performing an engagement required by the securities laws.

      However, the above individuals may be still eligible if it appears that the company is attempting to behave in a way that would harm investors or inhibit an investigation, or 120 days have passed since they notified the company of the violation.

   d. Whistle-blowers are encouraged to report the information through the normal internal corporate governance system by an indication that doing so will be considered when determining the amount of the award.

12. The act requires mortgage securitizers or originators to retain an economic interest (at least 5%) in a portion of the credit risk of any securitized asset that they create and sell.

E. Exemptions for Smaller and Emerging Companies

1. Smaller reporting companies have reduced requirements for disclosure of financial and nonfinancial information for initial filings (1933 Act) and periodic reporting (1934 Act). Smaller reporting companies are those that

   a. Have a common equity public float (market capitalization) of less than $75 million, or
   b. Are unable to calculate their public float and have annual revenues of $50 million or less.

2. The Dodd-Frank Act permanently exempted these smaller reporting companies (nonaccelerated filers) from the requirement to have integrated audits of their internal controls.

3. The JOBS Act of 2012 significantly reduced the registration and reporting requirements of "emerging growth companies." Notably, these companies are exempt for at least 5 years from the requirement to have integrated audits of their internal controls, and the Dodd-Frank provisions regarding executive compensation. A company qualifies as an emerging growth company if its initial public offering (IPO) was after December 8, 2011, and it had less than $1 billion of total annual gross revenues during its last completed fiscal year. A company no longer qualifies as an emerging growth company after the earliest of (1) the completion of a fiscal year in which the company has gross revenues of $1 billion or more, (2) the completion of the fiscal year of the 5th anniversary of the company's IPO, (3) the issuance of $1 billion in nonconvertible debt in the prior 3-year period, or (4) the company becoming a larger accelerated filer under SEC guidelines.

F. **Internet Securities Offering (ISO)** (Direct Public Offerings [DPO])

1. ISO used primarily by small businesses to accumulate capital.
2. SEC created electronic database of corporate information.

   a. Allows access to much data formerly available only to big institutions.

      (1) Thus tends to level playing field between small investors and large investors.
      (2) Also, tends to level playing field between small and large businesses.

   b. Allows electronic filing.
   c. Companies may market securities faster and more cheaply by circumventing paperwork of investment bankers.
   d. These securities are typically riskier because often avoid screening processes of various professionals.

3. In general, securities laws and regulations apply to ISO.
4. Prospectuses may be placed online.
5. Secondary market for securities may also be accomplished on websites.

G. **Electronic Signatures and Electronic Records**

1. Federal law specifies that no agreement, record, or signature required by federal securities laws or state laws can be denied legal effect because it is electronic record or contains electronic signature.

   a. Also applies to electronic signatures between investment advisors, brokers, dealers, and customers.
   b. SEC may specify manner of file retention but may not discriminate against any specific technology in effort to promote advances in technology.

H. **State "Blue-Sky" Laws**

1. These are state statutes regulating the issuance and sale of securities.

   a. They contain antifraud and registration provisions.

2. Must be complied with **in addition** to federal laws.
3. Exemptions from federal laws are not exemptions from state laws.

> **NOW REVIEW MULTIPLE-CHOICE QUESTIONS 43 THROUGH 45**

KEY TERMS

Insiders. Includes officers, directors, and owners of more than 10% of any class of an issuer's equity securities.
Prospectus. Any notice, circular, advertisement, letter, or communication offering any security for sale (or merger).
Proxy. Grant of authority by a shareholder to someone else to vote the shareholder's shares at a meeting.
Registration statement. The statement required to be filed with the SEC before the initial sale of securities can occur.
Security. Any debt or equity interest in a company including a note, stock, bond, certificate of interest, debenture, investment contract, etc.
Underwriter. Any person who has purchased from an issuer with a view to the public distribution of any security, or a party who participates in such an undertaking.

Multiple-Choice Questions (1–45)

A. Securities Act of 1933

1. A preliminary prospectus, permitted under SEC Regulations, is known as the

    a. Unaudited prospectus.
    b. Qualified prospectus.
    c. "Blue-sky" prospectus.
    d. "Red-herring" prospectus.

2. Under the Securities Exchange Act of 1934, which of the following types of instruments is excluded from the definition of "securities"?

    a. Investment contracts.
    b. Convertible debentures.
    c. Nonconvertible debentures.
    d. Certificates of deposit.

3. A tombstone advertisement

    a. May be substituted for the prospectus under certain circumstances.
    b. May contain an offer to sell securities.
    c. Notifies prospective investors that a previously-offered security has been withdrawn from the market and is therefore effectively "dead."
    d. Makes known the availability of a prospectus.

4. Under the Securities Act of 1933, which of the following statements most accurately reflects how securities registration affects an investor?

    a. The investor is provided with information on the stockholders of the offering corporation.
    b. The investor is provided with information on the principal purposes for which the offering's proceeds will be used.
    c. The investor is guaranteed by the SEC that the facts contained in the registration statement are accurate.
    d. The investor is assured by the SEC against loss resulting from purchasing the security.

5. Which of the following statements concerning the prospectus required by the Securities Act of 1933 is correct?

    a. The prospectus is a part of the registration statement.
    b. The prospectus should enable the SEC to pass on the merits of the securities.
    c. The prospectus must be filed after an offer to sell.
    d. The prospectus is prohibited from being distributed to the public until the SEC approves the accuracy of the facts embodied therein.

Items 6 and 7 are based on the following facts:

Sandy Corporation is considering the following issuances:

I. Notes with maturities of three months to be used for commercial purposes and having a total aggregate value of $500,000.
II. Notes with maturities of two years to be used for investment purposes and having a total aggregate value of $300,000.

III. Notes with maturities of two years to be used for commercial purposes and having a total aggregate value of $200,000.

6. Which of the above notes is (are) exempt securities and need **not** be registered under the Securities Act of 1933?

    a. I only.
    b. II only.
    c. I and III only.
    d. I, II, and III.

7. Which of the above notes is (are) subject to the antifraud provisions of the Securities Act of 1933?

    a. I only.
    b. II only.
    c. I and III only.
    d. I, II, and III.

8. Which of the following is **not** a security under the definition for the Securities Act of 1933?

    a. Any note.
    b. Bond certificate of interest.
    c. Debenture.
    d. All of the above are securities under the Act.

9. Which of the following requirements must be met by an issuer of securities who wants to make an offering by using shelf registration?

	Original registration statement must be kept updated	The offer must be a first-time issuer of securities
a.	Yes	Yes
b.	Yes	No
c.	No	Yes
d.	No	No

10. Which of the following securities would be regulated by the provisions of the Securities Act of 1933?

    a. Securities issued by not-for-profit, charitable organizations.
    b. Securities guaranteed by domestic governmental organizations.
    c. Securities issued by savings and loan associations.
    d. Securities issued by insurance companies.

11. Which of the following securities is exempt from registration under the Securities Act of 1933?

    a. Shares of nonvoting common stock, provided their par value is less than $1.00.
    b. A class of stock given in exchange for another class by the issuer to its existing stockholders without the issuer paying a commission.
    c. Limited partnership interests sold for the purpose of acquiring funds to invest in bonds issued by the United States.
    d. Corporate debentures that were previously subject to an effective registration statement, provided they are convertible into shares of common stock.

12. Universal Corp. intends to sell its common stock to the public in an interstate offering that will be registered under the Securities Act of 1933. Under the Act,

    a. Universal can make offers to sell its stock before filing a registration statement, provided that it does **not** actually issue stock certificates until after the registration is effective.

    b. Universal's registration statement becomes effective at the time it is filed, assuming the SEC does **not** object within twenty days thereafter.

    c. A prospectus must be delivered to each purchaser of Universal's common stock unless the purchaser qualifies as an accredited investor.

    d. Universal's filing of a registration statement with the SEC does **not** automatically result in compliance with the "blue-sky" laws of the states in which the offering will be made.

13. If securities are exempt from the registration provisions of the Securities Act of 1933, any fraud committed in the course of selling such securities can be challenged by

	SEC	Person defrauded
a.	Yes	Yes
b.	Yes	No
c.	No	Yes
d.	No	No

14. Issuers of securities are normally required under the Securities Act of 1933 to file a registration statement with the Securities Exchange Commission before these securities are either offered or sold to the general public. Which of the following is a reason why the SEC adopted the registration statement forms called Form S-2 and Form S-3?

    a. To require more extensive reporting.

    b. To be filed along with Form S-1.

    c. To reduce the burden that issuers have under the securities laws.

    d. To reduce the burden of disclosure that issuers have for intrastate issues of securities.

A.5. *Exempt Transactions or Offerings*

15. Regulation D provides for important exemptions to registration of securities under the Securities Act of 1933. Which of the following would be exempt?

  I. Issuance of $500,000 of securities sold in a 12-month period to forty investors.

  II. Issuance of $2,000,000 of securities sold in a 12-month period to 10 investors. The issuer restricts the right of the purchasers to resell for two years.

    a. I only.

    b. II only.

    c. Both I and II.

    d. Neither I nor II.

16. Pix Corp. is making a $6,000,000 stock offering. Pix wants the offering exempt from registration under the Securities Act of 1933. Which of the following provisions of the

Act would Pix have to comply with for the offering to be exempt?

    a. Regulation A.

    b. Regulation D, Rule 504.

    c. Regulation D, Rule 505.

    d. Regulation D, Rule 506.

17. Eldridge Corporation is seeking to offer $7,000,000 of securities under Regulation D of the Securities Act of 1933. Which of the following is (are) true if Eldridge wants an exemption from registration under the Securities Act of 1933?

  I. Eldridge must comply with Rule 506 of Regulation D.

  II. These securities could be debentures.

  III. These securities could be investment contracts.

    a. I only.

    b. I and II only.

    c. II and III only.

    d. I, II, and III.

18. An offering made under the provisions of Regulation A of the Securities Act of 1933 requires that the issuer

    a. File an offering circular with the SEC.

    b. Sell only to accredited investors.

    c. Provide investors with the prior four years' audited financial statements.

    d. Provide investors with a proxy registration statement.

19. Which of the following facts will result in an offering of securities being exempt from registration under the Securities Act of 1933?

    a. The securities are nonvoting preferred stock.

    b. The issuing corporation was closely held prior to the offering.

    c. The sale or offer to sell the securities is made by a person other than an issuer, underwriter, or dealer.

    d. The securities are AAA-rated debentures that are collateralized by first mortgages on property that has a market value of 200% of the offering price.

20. Regulation D of the Securities Act of 1933

    a. Restricts the number of purchasers of an offering to 35.

    b. Permits an exempt offering to be sold to both accredited and nonaccredited investors.

    c. Is limited to offers and sales of common stock that do not exceed $1.5 million.

    d. Is exclusively available to small business corporations as defined by Regulation D.

21. Frey, Inc. intends to make a $2,000,000 common stock offering under Rule 505 of Regulation D of the Securities Act of 1933. Frey

    a. May sell the stock to an unlimited number of investors.

    b. May make the offering through a general advertising.

    c. Must notify the SEC within 15 days after the first sale of the offering.

    d. Must provide all investors with a prospectus.

22. Under Regulation D of the Securities Act of 1933, which of the following conditions apply to private placement offerings? The securities

    a. Cannot be sold for longer than a six-month period.
    b. Cannot be the subject of an immediate unregistered reoffering to the public.
    c. Must be sold to accredited institutional investors.
    d. Must be sold to fewer than twenty nonaccredited investors.

23. Which of the following statements concerning an initial intrastate securities offering made by an issuer residing in and doing business in that state is correct?

    a. The offering would be exempt from the registration requirements of the Securities Act of 1933.
    b. The offering would be subject to the registration requirements of the Securities Exchange Act of 1934.
    c. The offering would be regulated by the SEC.
    d. The shares of the offering could **not** be resold to investors outside the state for at least one year.

24. Pix Corp. is making a $6,000,000 stock offering. Pix wants the offering exempt from registration under the Securities Act of 1933. Which of the following requirements would Pix have to comply with when selling the securities?

    a. No more than 35 investors.
    b. No more than 35 nonaccredited investors.
    c. Accredited investors only.
    d. Nonaccredited investors only.

25. Which of the following transactions will be exempt from the full registration requirements of the Securities Act of 1933?

    a. All intrastate offerings.
    b. All offerings made under Regulation A.
    c. Any resale of a security purchased under a Regulation D offering.
    d. Any stockbroker transaction.

26. Under Rule 504 of Regulation D of the Securities Act of 1933, which of the following is (are) required?

  I. No general offering or solicitation is permitted.
  II. The issuer must restrict the purchasers' right to resell the securities.

    a. I only.
    b. II only.
    c. Both I and II.
    d. Neither I nor II.

B. Securities Exchange Act of 1934

27. Dean, Inc., a publicly traded corporation, paid a $10,000 bribe to a local zoning official. The bribe was recorded in Dean's financial statements as a consulting fee. Dean's unaudited financial statements were submitted to the SEC as part of a quarterly filing. Which of the following federal statutes did Dean violate?

    a. Federal Trade Commission Act.
    b. Securities Act of 1933.

    c. Securities Exchange Act of 1934.
    d. North American Free Trade Act.

28. The Securities Exchange Commission promulgated Rule 10b-5 under Section 10(b) of the Securities Exchange Act of 1934. Which of the following is (are) purpose(s) of the Act?

	To rate securities so investors can choose more wisely	To encourage disclosure of information relevant to investors	To deter fraud involving securities
a.	No	No	Yes
b.	No	Yes	Yes
c.	Yes	Yes	Yes
d.	Yes	Yes	No

29. Integral Corp. has assets in excess of $4 million, has 350 stockholders, and has issued common and preferred stock. Integral is subject to the reporting provisions of the Securities Exchange Act of 1934. For its 2014 fiscal year, Integral filed the following with the SEC: quarterly reports, an annual report, and a periodic report listing newly appointed officers of the corporation. Integral did not notify the SEC of stockholder "short swing" profits; did not report that a competitor made a tender offer to Integral's stockholders; and did not report changes in the price of its stock as sold on the New York Stock Exchange. Under SEC reporting requirements, which of the following was Integral required to do?

    a. Report the tender offer to the SEC.
    b. Notify the SEC of stockholder "short swing" profits.
    c. File the periodic report listing newly appointed officers.
    d. Report the changes in the market price of its stock.

30. Which of the following factors, by itself, requires a corporation to comply with the reporting requirements of the Securities Exchange Act of 1934?

    a. Six hundred employees.
    b. Shares listed on a national securities exchange.
    c. Total assets of $2 million.
    d. Four hundred holders of equity securities.

31. The registration provisions of the Securities Exchange Act of 1934 require disclosure of all of the following information **except** the

    a. Names of owners of at least 5% of any class of nonexempt equity security.
    b. Bonus and profit-sharing arrangements.
    c. Financial structure and nature of the business.
    d. Names of officers and directors.

32. Under the Securities Act of 1933, which of the following statements is correct concerning a public issuer of securities who has made a registered offering?

    a. The issuer is required to distribute an annual report to its stockholders.
    b. The issuer is subject to the proxy rules of the SEC.
    c. The issuer must file an annual report (Form 10-K) with the SEC.

d. The issuer is **not** required to file a quarterly report (Form 10-Q) with the SEC, unless a material event occurs.

33. Which of the following persons is **not** an insider of a corporation subject to the Securities Exchange Act of 1934 registration and reporting requirements?

    a. An attorney for the corporation.
    b. An owner of 5% of the corporation's outstanding debentures.
    c. A member of the board of directors.
    d. A stockholder who owns 10% of the outstanding common stock.

34. The Securities Exchange Commission promulgated Rule 10b-5 from power it was given the Securities Exchange Act of 1934. Under this rule, it is unlawful for any person to use a scheme to defraud another in connection with the

	Purchase of any security	Sale of any security
a.	Yes	Yes
b.	Yes	No
c.	No	Yes
d.	No	No

35. The antifraud provisions of Rule 10b-5 of the Securities Exchange Act of 1934

    a. Apply only if the securities involved were registered under either the Securities Act of 1933 or the Securities Exchange Act of 1934.
    b. Require that the plaintiff show negligence on the part of the defendant in misstating facts.
    c. Require that the wrongful act must be accomplished through the mail, any other use of interstate commerce, or through a national securities exchange.
    d. Apply only if the defendant acted with intent to defraud.

Items 36 through 38 are based on the following:

Link Corp. is subject to the reporting provisions of the Securities Exchange Act of 1934.

36. Which of the following situations would require Link to be subject to the reporting provisions of the 1934 Act?

	Shares listed on a national securities exchange	More than one class of stock
a.	Yes	Yes
b.	Yes	No
c.	No	Yes
d.	No	No

37. Which of the following documents must Link file with the SEC?

	Quarterly reports (Form 10-Q)	Proxy Statements
a.	Yes	Yes
b.	Yes	No
c.	No	Yes
d.	No	No

38. Which of the following reports must also be submitted to the SEC?

	Report by any party making a tender offer to purchase Link's stock	Report of proxy solicitations by Link stockholders
a.	Yes	Yes
b.	Yes	No
c.	No	Yes
d.	No	No

39. Which of the following events must be reported to the SEC under the reporting provisions of the Securities Exchange Act of 1934?

	Tender offers	Insider trading	Soliciting proxies
a.	Yes	Yes	Yes
b.	Yes	Yes	No
c.	Yes	No	Yes
d.	No	Yes	Yes

40. Adler, Inc. is a reporting company under the Securities Exchange Act of 1934. The only security it has issued is voting common stock. Which of the following statements is correct?

    a. Because Adler is a reporting company, it is **not** required to file a registration statement under the Securities Act of 1933 for any future offerings of its common stock.
    b. Adler need **not** file its proxy statements with the SEC because it has only one class of stock outstanding.
    c. Any person who owns more than 10% of Adler's common stock must file a report with the SEC.
    d. It is unnecessary for the required annual report (Form 10-K) to include audited financial statements.

41. Which of the following is correct concerning financial statements in annual reports (Form 10-K) and quarterly reports (Form 10-Q)?

    a. Both Form 10-K and Form 10-Q must be audited by independent public accountants and both must be filed with the SEC.
    b. Both Form 10-K and Form 10-Q must be audited by independent public accountants but neither need be filed with the SEC.
    c. Although both Form 10-K and Form 10-Q must be filed with the SEC, only Form 10-K need be audited by independent public accountants.
    d. Form 10-K must be audited by independent public accountants and must also be filed with the SEC; however, Form 10-Q need not be audited by independent public accountants nor filed with the SEC.

42. Burk Corporation has issued securities that must be registered with the Securities Exchange Commission under the Securities Exchange Act of 1934. A material event took place yesterday, that is, there was a change in the control of Burk Corporation. Which of the following statements is correct?

a. Because of this material event, Burk Corporation is required to file with the SEC, Forms 10-K and 10-Q.
b. Because of this material event, Burk Corporation is required to file Form 8-K.
c. Burk Corporation need not file any forms with the SEC concerning this material event if the relevant facts are fully disclosed in the audited financial statements.
d. Burk Corporation need not file any form concerning the material event if Burk Corporation has an exemption under Rules 504, 505, or 506 of Regulation D.

C. The Sarbanes-Oxley Act of 2002

43. Under the Sarbanes-Oxley Act which of the following officers must periodically certify that reports comply fully with relevant securities laws and also fairly present the financial condition of company in all material aspects?

a. The chairman of the board and the chief executive officer.
b. The secretary and the chief executive officer.
c. The chief financial officer and the chief executive officer.
d. The chief risk officer and the chief executive officer.

D. The Wall Street Reform and Consumer Protection (Dodd-Frank) Act of 2010

44. Which of the following is **not** an aspect of the Wall Street Reform and Consumer Protection (Dodd-Frank) Act of 2010?

a. The act increased the regulation of insurance companies.
b. The act prohibits banks from engaging in proprietary trading.
c. The act puts limits on the compensation of corporate chief executive officers.
d. The act requires mortgage originators to retain an economic interest in a portion of the credit risk of any securitized asset that they create and sell.

45. The Wall Street Reform and Consumer Protection (Dodd-Frank) Act of 2010 requires

a. All members of the compensation committee of the board of directors to be independent.
b. All members of the corporate governance committee of the board of directors to be independent.
c. All voting members of the board of directors to be independent.
d. All members of the risk management committee of the board of directors to be independent.

Multiple-Choice Answers and Explanations

Answers

1.	d	__ __	11.	b	__ __	21.	c	__ __	31.	a	__ __	41.	c	__ __
2.	d	__ __	12.	d	__ __	22.	b	__ __	32.	c	__ __	42.	b	__ __
3.	d	__ __	13.	a	__ __	23.	a	__ __	33.	b	__ __	43.	c	__ __
4.	b	__ __	14.	c	__ __	24.	b	__ __	34.	a	__ __	44.	c	__ __
5.	a	__ __	15.	c	__ __	25.	b	__ __	35.	c	__ __	45.	a	__ __
6.	a	__ __	16.	d	__ __	26.	d	__ __	36.	b	__ __			
7.	d	__ __	17.	d	__ __	27.	c	__ __	37.	a	__ __			
8.	d	__ __	18.	a	__ __	28.	b	__ __	38.	a	__ __			
9.	b	__ __	19.	c	__ __	29.	c	__ __	39.	a	__ __	1st:	__/45=	__%
10.	d	__ __	20.	b	__ __	30.	b	__ __	40.	c	__ __	2nd:	__/45=	__%

Explanations

1. (d) A preliminary prospectus is usually called a "red-herring" prospectus. The preliminary prospectus indicates that a registration statement has been filed but has not become effective.

2. (d) Securities include debentures, stocks, bonds, some notes, and investment contracts. The main idea is that the investor intends to make a profit on the investment through the efforts of others. A certificate of deposit is a type of commercial paper, not a security.

3. (d) A tombstone advertisement is allowed to inform potential investors that a prospectus for the given company is available. It is not an offer to sell or the solicitation of an offer to buy the securities. Answer (a) is incorrect because the tombstone ad informs potential purchasers of the prospectus and cannot be used as a substitute for the prospectus. Answer (b) is incorrect because it informs of the availability of the prospectus and cannot be construed as an offer to sell securities. Answer (c) is incorrect because the tombstone ad notifies potential purchasers of the prospectus. It does not notify that the securities have been withdrawn from the market.

4. (b) The registration of securities under the Securities Act of 1933 has as its purpose to provide potential investors with full and fair disclosure of all material information relating to the issuance of securities, including such information as the principal purposes for which the offering's proceeds will be used. Answer (a) is incorrect because information on the stockholders of the offering corporation is not required to be reported. Answer (c) is incorrect because the SEC does not guarantee the accuracy of the registration statements. Answer (d) is incorrect because although the SEC does seek to compel full and fair disclosure, it does not evaluate the securities on merit or value, or give any assurances against loss.

5. (a) If no exemption is applicable under the Securities Act of 1933, public offerings must be registered with the SEC accompanied by a prospectus. Answer (b) is incorrect because the SEC does not pass on nor rate the securities. Answer (c) is incorrect because the prospectus is given to prospective purchasers of the securities. Answer (d) is incorrect because the SEC does not pass on the merits or accuracy of the prospectus.

6. (a) Notes are exempt securities under the Securities Act of 1933 if they have a maturity of nine months or less and if they are also used for commercial purposes rather than investments. The actual dollar amounts in the question are not a factor. The notes described in II are not exempt for two reasons; they have a maturity of two years and are used for investment purposes. The notes in III are not exempt because the maturity is two years even though they are for commercial purposes.

7. (d) Whether the securities are exempt from registration or not, they are still subject to the antifraud provisions of the Securities Act of 1933.

8. (d) The definition of a security is very broad under the Securities Act of 1933. The basic idea is that the investor intends to make a profit through the efforts of others rather than through his/her own efforts. Notes, bond certificates of interest, and debentures are all considered securities.

9. (b) If an issuer of securities wants to make an offering by using shelf registration, the actual issuance takes place over potentially a long period of time. Therefore, s/he must keep the original registration statement updated. There is no requirement that the offeror must be a first-time issuer of securities.

10. (d) Under the 1933 Act, certain securities are exempt. Although insurance and annuity contracts are exempt, securities issued by the insurance companies are not. Answer (a) is incorrect because securities of nonprofit organizations are exempt. Answer (b) is incorrect because securities issued by or guaranteed by domestic government organizations are exempt. Answer (c) is incorrect because securities issued by savings and loan associations are exempt.

11. (b) Securities exchanged for other securities by the issuer exclusively with its existing shareholders are exempt from registration under the 1933 Act as long as no commission is paid and both sets of securities are issued by the same issuer. Answer (a) is incorrect because nonvoting common stock is not exempted under the Act. The amount of the par value is irrelevant. Answer (c) is incorrect because although the securities of governments are themselves exempt, the limited partnership interests are not. Answer (d) is incorrect because no such exemption is allowed.

12. (d) Even though the issuer may comply with the Federal Securities Act of 1933, it must also comply with any applicable state "blue-sky" laws that regulate the securities at the state level. Answer (a) is incorrect because it is unlawful for the company to offer or sell the securities prior to the effective registration date. Answer (b) is incorrect because registration becomes effective on the twentieth day after filing unless the SEC issues a stop order. Answer (c) is incorrect because a prospectus is any notice, circular, advertisement, letter, or communication offering the security for sale. No general offering or solicitation is allowed under Rules 505 or 506 of Regulation D whether the purchaser is accredited or not.

13. (a) Even if the securities are exempt under the Securities Act of 1933, they are still subject to the antifraud provisions. Both the person defrauded and the SEC can challenge the fraud committed in the course of selling the securities.

14. (c) The SEC adopted the Forms S-2 and S-3 to decrease the work that issuers have in preparing registration statements by permitting them to give less detailed disclosure under certain conditions than Form S-1 which is the basic long form. Answer (a) is incorrect because these forms decrease, not increase, reporting required. Answer (b) is incorrect because when permitted, these forms are used instead of Form S-1 which is the standard long-form registration statement. Answer (d) is incorrect because the purpose of the forms was not directed at intrastate issues.

15. (c) The issuance described in I is exempt because Rule 504 exempts an issuance of securities up to $1,000,000 sold in a 12-month period to any number of investors. The issuer is not required to restrict the purchasers' resale. The issuance described in II is also exempt because Rule 505 exempts an issuance up to $5,000,000 sold in a 12-month period. It permits sales to 35 unaccredited investors and to any number of accredited investors. Since there were only 10 investors, this is met. The issuer also restricted the purchasers' right to resell for two years as required.

16. (d) Under Regulation D, Rule 504 exempts an issuance of securities up to $1,000,000 sold in a 12-month period. Rule 505 exempts an issuance of up to $5,000,000 in a 12-month period. So Rule 506 has to be resorted to for amounts over $5,000,000. Regulation A can be used only for issuances up to $1,500,000.

17. (d) When more than $5,000,000 in securities are being offered, an exemption from the registration requirements of the Securities Act of 1933 is available under Rule 506 of Regulation D. Securities under the Act include debentures and investment contracts.

18. (a) Under Regulation A of the 1933 Act, the issuer must file an offering circular with the SEC. Answer (b) is incorrect because the rules involving sales to unaccredited and accredited investors are in Regulation D, not Regulation A. Answer (c) is incorrect because although financial information about the corporation must be provided to offerees, the financial statements in the offering circular need not be audited. Answer (d) is incorrect because the issuer is not required to provide investors with a proxy registration statement under Regulation A.

19. (c) Sales or offers to sell by any person **other than** an issuer, underwriter, or dealer are exempt under the 1933 Act. Answer (a) is incorrect because the Act covers all types of securities including preferred stock. Answer (b) is incorrect because closely held corporations are not automatically exempt. Answer (d) is incorrect because debentures, as debt securities, are covered under the Act even if they are highly rated or backed by collateral.

20. (b) Regulation D of the Securities Act of 1933 establishes three important exemptions in Rules 504, 505, and 506. Although Rules 505 and 506 have some restrictions on sales to nonaccredited investors, all three rules under Regulation D allow sales to both nonaccredited and accredited investors with varying restrictions. Answer (a) is incorrect because although Rules 505 and 506 allow sales to up to 35 nonaccredited investors, all three rules allow sales to an unlimited number of accredited investors. Answer (c) is incorrect because Rule 506 has no dollar limitation. Rule 505 has a $5,000,000 limitation in a 12-month period and Rule 504 has a $1,000,000 limitation in a 12-month period. Answer (d) is incorrect because Regulation D is not restricted to only small corporations.

21. (c) Under Rule 505 of Regulation D, the issuer must notify the SEC of the offering within 15 days after the first sale of the securities. Answer (a) is incorrect because under Rule 505, the issuer may sell to an unlimited number of **accredited** investors and to 35 unaccredited investors. Answer (b) is incorrect because no general offering or solicitation is permitted. Answer (d) is incorrect because the accredited investors need not receive any formal information. The unaccredited investors, however, must receive a formal registration statement that gives a description of the offering.

22. (b) The private placement exemption permits sales of an unlimited number of securities for any dollar amount when sold to accredited investors. This exemption also allows sales to up to 35 nonaccredited investors if they are also sophisticated investors under the Act. Resales of these securities are restricted for two years after the date that the issuer sells the last of the securities. Answer (a) is incorrect because there is no such restriction of sale. Answer (c) is incorrect because sales may be made to an unlimited number of accredited investors and up to 35 nonaccredited investors. Answer (d) is incorrect because sales can be made to up to 35 nonaccredited investors.

23. (a) When the issuer is a resident of that state, doing 80% of its business in that state, and only sells or offers the securities to residents of the same state, the offering qualifies for an exemption under the 1933 Act as an intrastate issue. Answer (b) is incorrect as the offering also qualifies for an exemption under the 1934 Act. Therefore, as the offering is exempted from both the 1933 and 1934 Acts, it would not be regulated by the SEC. Answer (d) is incorrect because resales can only be made to residents of that state nine months after the issuer's last sale.

24. (b) Rule 506 permits sales to 35 unaccredited investors and to an unlimited number of accredited investors. The unaccredited investors must also be sophisticated investors (i.e., individuals with knowledge and experience in financial matters).

25. (b) Under Regulation A, an offering statement is required instead of the more costly disclosure requirements of full registration under the Securities Act of 1933. Answer (a) is incorrect because not all intrastate offerings are exempt. They must meet specified requirements to be exempt. Answer (c) is incorrect because many securities sold under Regulation D cannot be resold for two years. Answer (d) is incorrect because there is no such exemption for stockbroker transactions.

26. (d) Under Rule 504 of Regulation D, general offerings and solicitations are permitted. Also, the issuer need not restrict the purchasers' right to resell. Note that both I and II are requirements of Rules 505 and 506 of Regulation D.

27. (c) Under the Securities Exchange Act of 1934, issuers of securities registered under this Act must file quarterly reports (Form 10-Q) for the first three quarters of each fiscal year. The financial data in these may be unaudited; however, material misinformation is a violation of the 1934 Act. Answer (a) is incorrect—the Federal Trade Commission Act does not apply to this action. Answer (b) is incorrect because the Securities Act of 1933 applies to the initial issuance of securities and not to the secondary market of publicly traded securities. Answer (d) is incorrect because NAFTA is an agreement designed to promote free trade between the US, Mexico, and Canada.

28. (b) Purposes of Section 10(b) of the Securities Exchange Act of 1934 include deterring fraud in the securities industry and encouraging disclosure of relevant information so investors can make better decisions. The SEC does not rate the securities.

29. (c) Under the Securities Exchange Act of 1934, issuers of securities registered under this Act must file annual and quarterly reports with the SEC. The company must also file current reports covering certain material events such as a change in the amount of issued securities, a change in corporate control, or a change in newly appointed officers. Answer (a) is incorrect because a competitor's making a tender offer need not be reported to the SEC. Answer (b) is incorrect because Integral Corp. need not notify the SEC of stockholder "short swing profits." Answer (d) is incorrect because the company need not report information on the market price of its stock to the SEC. This market price information is already public information because the stock is traded on the New York Stock Exchange.

30. (b) Securities must be registered with the SEC if they are traded on any national securities exchange. Securities must also be registered if they are traded in interstate commerce where the corporation has more than $10 million in assets **and** 500 or more shareholders.

31. (a) The Securities Exchange Act of 1934 has registration provisions that require specified disclosures including bonus and profit-sharing arrangements, the financial structure and nature of this business, and names of officers and directors.

32. (c) Under the Federal Securities Act of 1933, which incorporates the filing requirements of the Federal Securities Exchange Act of 1934, the issuer must file with the SEC an annual report on Form 10-K. Answer (a) is incorrect because the issuer must file the annual report with the SEC but is not required to distribute it to its stockholders. Answer (b) is incorrect because the solicitation of proxies triggers certain proxy solicitation rules. Answer (d) is incorrect because it is the current report on Form 8-K that is filed when material events occur. The Form 10-Q is filed each of the first three quarters of each year and is known as the quarterly report.

33. (b) Under the 1934 Act, insiders include officers and directors of the corporation as well as owners of 10% or more of the stock of the corporation. Accountants, attorneys, and consultants can also be insiders subject to further regulation under the 1934 Act. Creditors, that is, owners of debentures are not considered to be insiders.

34. (a) Under Rule 10b-5, it is unlawful to use schemes to defraud in connection with the purchase **or** sale of any security. Note that this rule was made from powers given the SEC under the Securities Exchange Act of 1934, which applies to purchases in addition to sales of securities.

35. (c) For the Securities Exchange Act of 1934 to apply, including the antifraud provisions of Rule 10b-5, there must be shown a federal constitutional basis such as use of the mail, interstate commerce, or a national securities exchange. Answer (a) is incorrect because the antifraud provisions apply whether or not the securities had to be registered under either the 1933 Act or the 1934 Act. Answer (b) is incorrect because under Rule 10b-5, the plaintiff must prove more than negligence (i.e., either knowledge of falsity or reckless disregard for the truth in misstating facts). Answer (d) is incorrect because the plaintiff could recover if the defendant acted with reckless disregard for the truth.

36. (b) If the shares are listed on a national securities exchange, they are subject to the reporting provisions of the 1934 Act. There is no provision concerning a corporation owning more than one class of stock that by itself requires that it be subject to the reporting provisions of the 1934 Act.

37. (a) Under the 1934 Act, Link must file with the SEC annual reports (Form 10-K), quarterly reports (Form 10-Q), current reports (Form 8-K) of certain material events, and proxy statements when proxy solicitations exist.

38. (a) When there is a proxy solicitation, Link must make a report of this to the SEC. Also, reports of tender offers to purchase securities need to be submitted to the SEC.

39. (a) A tender offer is a request to the shareholders of a given company to tender their shares for a stated price. If the tender offer was unsolicited, the corporation must report this to the SEC under the reporting provisions of the Securities Exchange Act of 1934. Also, trading by insiders such as officers, directors, or shareholders owning at least 10% of the stock of a corporation registered with the SEC must also be reported to the SEC under the 1934 Act. Likewise, solicitation of proxies must be reported to the SEC.

40. (c) Under the Securities Exchange Act of 1934 which applies if interstate commerce or the mail is used, any purchaser of more than 5% of a class of equity securities must file a report with the SEC. Answer (d) is incorrect because the required annual report (Form 10-K) must be certified by independent public accountants. Answer (a) is incorrect because each company must also comply with the filing requirements under the Securities Act of 1933. Answer (b) is incorrect because there is no exemption from filing proxy statements simply because the company has only one class of stock.

41. (c) Forms 10-K (annual reports) and 10-Q (quarterly reports) must be filed with the SEC. Forms 10-K containing financial statements must be audited by independent public accountants. However, this is not true of Forms 10-Q which cover the first three fiscal quarters of each fiscal year of the issuer. The financial statements in 10-Qs must be reviewed by public accountants.

42. (b) When certain material events take place, such as a change in corporate control, the corporation covered under the 1934 Act must file Form 8-K, a current report, with the SEC within four days after the material event occurs. Answer (a) is incorrect because Burk Corporation must file Forms 10-K, annual reports, and Forms 10-Q, quarterly reports, whether or not a material event has taken place. Answer (c) is incorrect because there is no such exception provided. Answer (d) is incorrect because Rules 504, 505, and 506 under Regulation D apply to the initial issuance of securities under the Securities Act of 1933 and do not relieve Burk Corporation from the filing requirements with the SEC under the 1934 Act.

43. (c) The requirement is to identify the officers that must certify to financial reports under the Sarbanes-Oxley Act. Answer (c) is correct because the chief financial officer and the chief executive officer must certify.

44. (c) The requirement is to identify the item that is not an aspect of the Wall Street Reform and Consumer Protection Act of 2010. Answer (c) is correct because the act does not put limits on CEO compensation. Answers (a), (b), and (d) are incorrect because they are all aspects of the Dodd-Frank Act.

45. (a) The requirement is to identify the requirement of the Dodd-Frank Act of 2010. Answer (a) is correct because the Dodd-Frank Act requires all members of the compensation committee to be independent. Answers (b), (c), and (d) are incorrect because they are not requirements of the Act.

Simulations

Task-Based Simulation 1

Rules 504, 505, and 506		
	Authoritative Literature	Help

Situation

You will have 15 questions based on the following information:

Butler Manufacturing Corp. planned to raise capital for a plant expansion by borrowing from banks and making several stock offerings. Butler engaged Weaver, CPA, to audit its December 31, 2009 financial statements. Butler told Weaver that the financial statements would be given to certain named banks and included in the prospectuses for the stock offerings.

In performing the audit, Weaver did not confirm accounts receivable and, as a result, failed to discover a material overstatement of accounts receivable. Also, Weaver was aware of a pending class action product liability lawsuit that was not disclosed in Butler's financial statements. Despite being advised by Butler's legal counsel that Butler's potential liability under the lawsuit would result in material losses, Weaver issued an unqualified opinion on Butler's financial statements.

In May 2010, Union Bank, one of the named banks, relied on the financial statements and Weaver's opinion in giving Butler a $500,000 loan.

Butler raised an additional $16,450,000 through the following stock offerings, which were sold completely:

- June 2010—Butler made a $450,000 unregistered offering of Class B nonvoting common stock under Rule 504 of Regulation D of the Securities Act of 1933. This offering was sold over one year to 20 accredited investors by general solicitation. The SEC was notified eight days after the first sale of this offering.
- September 2010—Butler made a $10,000,000 unregistered offering of Class A voting common stock under Rule 506 of Regulation D of the Securities Act of 1933. This offering was sold over one year to 200 accredited investors and 30 nonaccredited investors through a private placement. The SEC was notified 14 days after the first sale of this offering.
- November 2010—Butler made a $6,000,000 unregistered offering of preferred stock under Rule 505 of Regulation D of the Securities Act of 1933. This offering was sold during a one-year period to forty nonaccredited investors by private placement. The SEC was notified 18 days after the first sale of this offering.

Shortly after obtaining the Union loan, Butler began experiencing financial problems but was able to stay in business because of the money raised by the offerings. Butler was found liable in the product liability suit. This resulted in a judgment Butler could not pay. Butler also defaulted on the Union loan and was involuntarily petitioned into bankruptcy. This caused Union to sustain a loss and Butler's stockholders to lose their investments. As a result

- The SEC claimed that all three of Butler's offerings were made improperly and were not exempt from registration.
- Union sued Weaver for

    - Negligence
    - Common Law Fraud

- The stockholders who purchased Butler's stock through the offerings sued Weaver, alleging fraud under Section 10(b) and Rule 10b-5 of the Securities Exchange Act of 1934.

These transactions took place in a jurisdiction providing for accountant's liability for negligence to known and intended users of financial statements.

Items 1 through 5 are questions related to the June 2010 offering made under Rule 504 of Regulation D of the Securities Act of 1933. For each item, indicate your answer by choosing either Yes or No.

	Yes	No
1. Did the offering comply with the dollar limitation of Rule 504?	○	○
2. Did the offering comply with the method of sale restrictions?	○	○
3. Was the offering sold during the applicable time limit?	○	○
4. Was the SEC notified timely of the first sale of the securities?	○	○
5. Was the SEC correct in claiming that this offering was not exempt from registration?	○	○

Items 6 through 10 are questions related to the September 2010 offering made under Rule 506 of Regulation D of the Securities Act of 1933. For each item, indicate your answer by choosing either Yes or No.

		Yes	No
6.	Did the offering comply with the dollar limitation of Rule 506?	○	○
7.	Did the offering comply with the method of sale restrictions?	○	○
8.	Was the offering sold to the correct number of investors?	○	○
9.	Was the SEC notified timely of the first sale of the securities?	○	○
10.	Was the SEC correct in claiming that this offering was not exempt from registration?	○	○

Items 11 through 15 are questions related to the November 2010 offering made under Rule 505 of Regulation D of the Securities Act of 1933. For each item, indicate your answer by choosing either Yes or No.

		Yes	No
11.	Did the offering comply with the dollar limitation of Rule 505?	○	○
12.	Was the offering sold during the applicable time limit?	○	○
13.	Was the offering sold to the correct number of investors?	○	○
14.	Was the SEC notified timely of the first sale of the securities?	○	○
15.	Was the SEC correct in claiming that this offering was not exempt from registration?	○	○

Task-Based Simulation 2

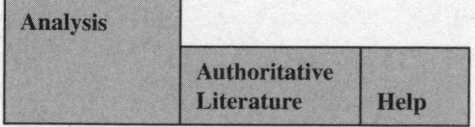

Situation

Coffee Corp., a publicly held corporation, wants to make an $8,000,000 exempt offering of its shares as a private placement offering under Regulation D, Rule 506, of the Securities Act of 1933. Coffee has more than 500 shareholders and assets in excess of $1 billion, and has its shares listed on a national securities exchange.

Items 1 through 5 relate to the application of the provisions of the Securities Act of 1933 and the Securities Exchange Act of 1934 to Coffee Corp. and the offering. For each item, select from List II whether only statement I is correct, whether only statement II is correct, whether both statements I and II are correct, or whether neither statement I nor II is correct.

List II

A. I only
B. II only
C. Both I and II
D. Neither I nor II

		(A)	(B)	(C)	(D)
1.	I. Coffee Corp. may make the Regulation D, Rule 506, exempt offering. II. Coffee Corp., because it is required to report under the Securities Exchange Act of 1934, may **not** make an exempt offering.	○	○	○	○
2.	I. Shares sold under a Regulation D, Rule 506, exempt offering may only be purchased by accredited investors. II. Shares sold under a Regulation D, Rule 506, exempt offering may be purchased by any number of investors provided there are **no** more than 35 nonaccredited investors.	○	○	○	○
3.	I. An exempt offering under Regulation D, Rule 506, must **not** be for more than $10,000,000. II. An exempt offering under Regulation D, Rule 506, has **no** dollar limit.	○	○	○	○

4. I. Regulation D, Rule 506, requires that all investors in the exempt offering be notified that   ○   ○   ○   ○
        for nine months after the last sale **no** resale may be made to a nonresident.
   II. Regulation D, Rule 506, requires that the issuer exercise reasonable care to assure that
        purchasers of the exempt offering are buying for investment and are **not** underwriters.

5. I. The SEC must be notified by Coffee Corp. within five days of the first sale of the exempt   ○   ○   ○   ○
        offering securities.
   II. Coffee Corp. must include an SEC notification of the first sale of the exempt offering
        securities in Coffee's next filed Quarterly Report (Form 10-Q).

Simulation Solutions

Task-Based Simulation 1

Rules 504, 505, and 506		
	Authoritative Literature	Help

		Yes	No
1.	Did the offering comply with the dollar limitation of Rule 504?	●	○
2.	Did the offering comply with the method of sale restrictions?	●	○
3.	Was the offering sold during the applicable time limit?	●	○
4.	Was the SEC notified timely of the first sale of the securities?	●	○
5.	Was the SEC correct in claiming that this offering was not exempt from registration?	○	●

Explanations

1. (Y) Rule 504 exempts an issuance of securities up to $1,000,000 sold in a 12-month period to any number of investors. Butler made the offering for $450,000.

2. (Y) This offering involved a general solicitation which is now allowed under Rule 504 providing the solicitation is to only accredited investors.

3. (Y) This offering was sold over the applicable 12-month period in Rule 504.

4. (Y) The SEC was sent notice of this offering eight days after the first sale. Under Rule 504, the SEC must be notified within 15 days of the first sale of the securities.

5. (N) Even though this stock was sold by general solicitation, this is allowed under Rule 504.

		Yes	No
6.	Did the offering comply with the dollar limitation of Rule 506?	●	○
7.	Did the offering comply with the method of sale restrictions?	●	○
8.	Was the offering sold to the correct number of investors?	●	○
9.	Was the SEC notified timely of the first sale of the securities?	●	○
10.	Was the SEC correct in claiming that this offering was not exempt from registration?	○	●

Explanations

6. (Y) Rule 506 allows private placement of an unlimited dollar amount of securities.

7. (Y) These securities were sold through private placement which is appropriate under Rule 506.

8. (Y) Rule 506 allows sales to up to 35 nonaccredited investors who are sophisticated investors with knowledge and experience in financial matters. It allows sales to an unlimited number of accredited investors.

9. (Y) The SEC was notified 14 days after the first sale of the offering which is within the 15-day rule.

10. (N) Since this offering met the requirements discussed in **6.** through **9.** above, the SEC was incorrect.

		Yes	No
11.	Did the offering comply with the dollar limitation of Rule 505?	○	●
12.	Was the offering sold during the applicable time limit?	●	○
13.	Was the offering sold to the correct number of investors?	○	●
14.	Was the SEC notified timely of the first sale of the securities?	○	●
15.	Was the SEC correct in claiming that this offering was not exempt from registration?	●	○

Explanations

11. (N) Rule 505 exempts an issuance of securities up to $5,000,000. Butler made a $6,000,000 unregistered offering of preferred stock.

12. (Y) The offering was sold during the applicable 12-month period.

13. (N) Rule 505 permits sales to 35 nonaccredited investors. Butler went over this limit by selling to 40 nonaccredited investors.

14. (N) The SEC was notified 18 days after the first sale of this offering which is over the 15-day requirement.

15. (Y) This offering was not exempt from registration because it went over the $5,000,000 limit and the stock was sold to more than 35 nonaccredited investors.

Task-Based Simulation 2

Analysis		
	Authoritative Literature	Help

		(A)	(B)	(C)	(D)
1.	I. Coffee Corp. may make the Regulation D, Rule 506, exempt offering. II. Coffee Corp., because it is required to report under the Securities Exchange Act of 1934, may **not** make an exempt offering.	●	○	○	○
2.	I. Shares sold under a Regulation D, Rule 506, exempt offering may only be purchased by accredited investors. II. Shares sold under a Regulation D, Rule 506, exempt offering may be purchased by any number of investors provided there are **no** more than 35 nonaccredited investors.	○	●	○	○
3.	I. An exempt offering under Regulation D, Rule 506, must **not** be for more than $10,000,000. II. An exempt offering under Regulation D, Rule 506, has **no** dollar limit.	○	●	○	○
4.	I. Regulation D, Rule 506, requires that all investors in the exempt offering be notified that for nine months after the last sale **no** resale may be made to a nonresident. II. Regulation D, Rule 506, requires that the issuer exercise reasonable care to assure that purchasers of the exempt offering are buying for investment and are **not** underwriters.	○	●	○	○
5.	I. The SEC must be notified by Coffee Corp. within five days of the first sale of the exempt offering securities. II. Coffee Corp. must include an SEC notification of the first sale of the exempt offering securities in Coffee's next filed Quarterly Report (Form 10-Q).	○	○	○	●

Explanations

1. (A) Statement I is correct because under Regulation D, Rule 506, the corporation may make a private placement of an unlimited amount of securities if it meets certain requirements. Statement II is incorrect. Coffee Corp. may still make an exempt offering under the Securities Act of 1933 even if it will be subject to the requirements of the Securities Exchange Act of 1934.

2. (B) Statement I is incorrect because up to 35 nonaccredited investors may purchase shares under Regulation D, Rule 506, if they are sophisticated investors. Statement II is correct because Rule 506 does allow sales to up to 35 nonaccredited investors **assuming they are also** sophisticated investors, that is, individuals with knowledge and experience in financial matters, or individuals represented by people with such knowledge and experience.

3. (B) Statement I is incorrect and Statement II is correct for the same reason. Regulation D, Rule 506, has no dollar limit on the placement of securities as long as other requirements are met.

4. (B) Statement I is incorrect because Regulation D has no requirements putting restrictions on resales to nonresidents. Statement II is correct because Regulation D requires that the issuer take reasonable steps to see that purchasers of the exempt offering are not underwriters and are buying for investment.

5. (D) Statement I is incorrect. Under Regulation D, the SEC must be notified within fifteen days of the first sale of the securities. Statement II is incorrect because the Quarterly Reports do not require SEC notification of the first sale of exempt securities.

Module 25: Business Structure

Overview

A sole proprietorship has only one owner, which creates both advantages and disadvantages. A partnership is an association of two or more persons to carry on a business as co-owners for profit. The major areas tested about partnerships are the characteristics of a partnership, comparisons with other structures, rights and liabilities of the partnership itself, the rights, duties, and liabilities of the partners among themselves and to third parties, the allocation of profits and losses, and the rights of various parties, including creditors, upon dissolution.

The law of joint ventures is similar to that of partnerships with some exceptions. Note that the joint venture is more limited in scope than the partnership form of business. The former is typically organized to carry out one single business undertaking or a series of related undertakings; whereas, the latter is formed to conduct ongoing business.

Subchapter S corporations are those corporations that elect to be taxed similar to partnerships under Subchapter S. Corporations that do not make this election are called Subchapter C corporations. In both cases, a corporation is an artificial person that is created by or under law and which operates under a common name through its elected management. It is a legal entity, separate and distinct from its shareholders. The corporation has the authority vested in it by statute and its corporate charter. The candidate should understand the characteristics and advantages of the corporate form over other forms of business organization.

Basic to preparation for questions on corporation law is an understanding of the following: the liabilities of a promoter who organizes a new corporation; the liability of shareholders; the liability of the corporation with respect to the preincorporation contracts made by the promoter; the fiduciary relationship of the promoter to the stockholders and to the corporation; the various circumstances under which a stockholder may be liable for the debts of the corporation; the rights of shareholders particularly concerning payment of dividends; the rights and duties of officers, directors, and other agents or employees of the corporation to the corporation, to stockholders, and to third persons; subscriptions; and the procedures necessary to merge, consolidate, or otherwise change the corporate structure.

State laws are now widely based on the Revised Business Corporation Act upon which changes to this module are based.

For all the business structures listed in this module you should know the basic characteristics of each. The Examiners expect you to understand the basic strengths and weaknesses of each business structure and to be able to select the appropriate business structure for given situations. Before beginning the reading you should review the key terms at the end of the module.

A. Nature of Sole Proprietorships

1. There is only one owner of business

    a. Business is not a separate legal entity apart from owner
    b. Owner does not share power or decision making with other owners

2. Advantages over other business structures

    a. Sole proprietorship is simplest type of business structure

        (1) Easy to form and to operate

            (a) Federal or state governments do not require formal filing or approval to begin operation

                (1) If business is operating under name other than that of sole proprietor, most states require that it file fictitious name statement with government

    b. Business can be sold without need to obtain approval from others such as shareholders or partners
    c. Owner has right to make all business decisions such as direction company should go, who to hire or fire, etc.
    d. If business generates profit, sole owner need not share it with other owners or investors
    e. The profits of the business are taxed on the personal tax return of the owner—profits are taxed only once

3. Disadvantages over other business structures

    a. If company has loss, sole proprietor suffers all of it
    b. Sole proprietorship cannot obtain capital from partners, shareholders, etc.

        (1) Capital is limited by funds the owner has or can borrow

    c. Sole proprietor has unlimited personal liability

> ## NOW REVIEW MULTIPLE-CHOICE QUESTION 1

B. Nature of Partnerships

1. A partnership is an association of two or more persons to carry on a business as co-owners for profit

    a. The phrase "to carry on a business" includes almost every trade, occupation, or profession

        (1) It does not include passive co-ownership of property (e.g., joint tenants of a piece of land)
        (2) Partnerships do not include nonprofit unincorporated associations (e.g., labor unions, charitable organizations, clubs)

    b. Co-ownership of the "business" (and not merely of assets used in a business) is an important element in determining whether a partnership exists

        (1) The most important and necessary element of co-ownership (and thereby partnership) is profit and loss sharing

            (a) Need not be equal, but is treated equally unless otherwise stated
            (b) Receipt of a share of profits is *prima facie evidence* (raises a presumption) of a partnership

                (1) Presumption rebutted by establishing that profit sharing was only for payment of debt, interest on loan, services performed, rent, etc.

        (2) Another important element of co-ownership is joint control

            (a) Each partner has an equal right to participate in management. Right to manage may be contracted away to a managing partner

        (3) Under Revised Uniform Partnership Act, now adopted by majority of states, partner is no longer co-owner of partnership property

2. Partnership relationship creates a fiduciary relationship between partners

   a. Fiduciary relationship arises because each partner is an agent for partnership and for each other in partnership business

3. Partnership relationship is based on contract but arrangements may be quite informal

   a. Agreement can be inferred from conduct (e.g., allowing someone to share in management and profits may result in partnership even though actual intent to become partner is missing)

4. Draws heavily on agency law because each partner is an agent as well as a principal of partnership

   a. Most rules can be changed in individual cases by agreement between parties affected (e.g., rights and duties between partners)

EXAMPLE

A, B, and C form a partnership in which all three partners agree that A is liable for all of the product liability cases against the partnership. This agreement is enforceable between A, B, and C but not against other parties that never agreed to this. Therefore, as long as A is solvent, B and C can collect from A even though a third party recovers from all of them for product liability .

---

5. Generally, any person (entity) who has the capacity to contract may become a partner

   a. Corporations
   b. Minors—but c
   c. Partnerships ca

6. Common characte

   a. Limited durati
   b. Transfer of ow
   c. May sue and b
   d. Unlimited liab
   e. Ease of format
   f. Partnership do   heir share of partnership operations on their individual tax

                                                            NS 2 THROUGH 4

C. Formation of Partr

1. By agreement, ex

   a. Agreement to   xists

      (1) Need not   share profits assumes sharing of losses
      (2) Sharing o

   b. Partnership n   ch as for payment of debt, wages, or lease

2. Creation of a par

   a. Written partne   Frauds (e.g., partnership that cannot be completed wi

---

EXAMPLE

A, B, and C form   years, has no time period specified. This partnership agreement may be oral.

EXAMPLE

X, Y, and Z organize XYZ partnership which by agreement will last at least five years. This partnership agreement must be in writing.

---

   b. Filing not required

3. Articles of copartnership (partnership agreement)—not legally necessary, but a good idea to have
4. Fictitious name statutes require partners to register fictitious or assumed names

   a. Failure to comply does not invalidate partnership but may result in fine
   b. The purpose is to allow third parties to know who is in partnership

D. Partner's Rights and Operation of Partnership

1. Partnership agreement, whether oral or written, is the controlling law for the partnership
2. The Revised Uniform Partnership Act (RUPA) is a law that fills in when relevant provisions are not contained in the partnership agreement
3. Look first to what the partnership agreement says; if the agreement is silent or the Examiners have not given you a relevant provision of the partnership agreement, then apply the RUPA rules that follow below. Remember the partnership agreement supersedes RUPA.
4. Partnership interest

   a. Refers to partner's right to share in profits and return of contribution on dissolution
   b. Is considered personal property
   c. Does not include specific partnership property, merely right to use it for partnership purposes
   d. Freely assignable without other partner's consent

     (1) Assignee is not substituted as a partner without consent of all other partners
     (2) Assignee does **not** receive right to manage partnership, to have an accounting, to inspect books, to possess or own any individual partnership property—merely receives rights in the assigning partner's share of profits and return of partner's capital contribution (unless partners agree otherwise)

       (a) Typically, assignments are made to secure a loan

EXAMPLE

C, a CPA, wishes to obtain a large loan. He is a member of a CPA firm and assigns his partnership interest to the bank to secure the loan.

---

     (3) Assignor remains liable as a partner
     (4) Does not create dissociation unless assignor also withdraws

5. Partnership property

   a. Includes

     (1) Property acquired with partnership funds unless different intent is shown
     (2) Property not acquired in partnership name is partnership property if

       (a) Partner acquires title to it in his/her capacity as a partner, or
       (b) Property acquired with partnership funds

   b. Not assignable or subject to attachment individually, only by a claim on partnership

     (1) Property may be assigned by agreement of all partners
     (2) Any partner can assign or sell property if for the apparent purpose of carrying on the business of the partnership in the usual way

    c. Upon partner's death, his/her estate is entitled to deceased partner's share of profits and capital, but not to any specific partnership property

       (1) Remaining partners have duty to account to the heirs of the deceased for value of interest
       (2) Heirs not automatically partners

6. Participate in management

    a. Right to participate equally in management

       (1) Ordinary business decisions by a majority vote
       (2) Unanimous consent needed to make fundamental changes, which include

          (a) Admitting new partners
          (b) Any action outside the scope of the normal partnership business
          (c) Any action contrary to the partnership agreement, or amending the partnership agreement

    b. Power to act as an agent for partnership in partnership business
    c. Also has right to inspect books and have full knowledge of partnership affairs
    d. Silent partner is one who does not help manage

       (1) Still has personal, unlimited liability

7. Share in profits and losses

    a. Profits and losses are shared equally unless agreement specifies otherwise

       (1) Even if contributed capital is not equal
       (2) For example, agreement may specify one partner to receive greater share of profits for doing more work, etc., while losses still shared equally

    b. If partners agree on unequal profit sharing but are silent on loss sharing, losses are shared per the profit-sharing proportions

       (1) May choose to share losses in a different proportion from profits

---

EXAMPLE

A, B, and C form a partnership with capital contributions as follows: A, $100,000; B, $20,000; and C, $20,000. Their agreement is silent on how to split profits or losses. Assume that the partnership loses $120,000. A, B, and C would each be liable for $40,000 of the losses.

EXAMPLE

Same as above except that they agree to give A 50% of the profits and B and C each get 25% of the profits. Profits as well as losses will be split based on these stated percentages. A is liable for $60,000 of the losses; B and C are liable for $30,000 each. Even though the partners had not allocated losses specifically, RUPA provides that losses are split the same as profits unless the partnership agreement states otherwise.

EXAMPLE

Assume that A, B, and C agree to a 50%, 25%, 25% split if there is a profit but to a 20%, 40%, 40% split, respectively, for any annual losses. If there is a $100,000 annual loss, A will suffer $20,000 and B and C each will suffer $40,000 of the loss.

8. Other rights

    a. Indemnification for expenses incurred on behalf of the partnership

    b. General partners may be creditors, secured or unsecured, of the partnership

        (1) May receive interest on loans

        (2) No interest on capital contributions unless stated in partnership agreement

    c. No right to salary for work performed because this is a duty unless they agree otherwise

        (1) It is common for partners to agree to pay salaries, especially if only one or two do most of the work, but do not assume this on the CPA exam; the Examiners must tell you that the partners have agreed to pay a partner a salary.

    d. May obtain formal accounting of partnership affairs

        (1) Each partner has the right if used reasonably

9. Every partner owes a fiduciary duty to every other partner (this is important). These fiduciary duties are essentially the same duties that are discussed in Module 32, section D.2.

    a. Each must act in best interest of others

        (1) May pursue own self-interest as long as it is not competition and does not interfere with partner's duty to partnership

        (2) Any wrongly derived profits must be held by partner for others

        (3) Must abide by partnership agreement

        (4) Liable to others partners for liability caused by going beyond actual authority

10. Incoming partners new to partnership have same rights as previous partners

    a. Requires consent of all partners to admit new partner unless otherwise stated in the partnership agreement

    b. Profit sharing, loss sharing, and capital contributions are by agreement between all partners

    c. A partnership may also be partner of separate partnership if all partners agree

---

> **NOW REVIEW MULTIPLE-CHOICE QUESTIONS 5 THROUGH 10**

E. Relationship to Third Parties

1. Partners are agents of the partnership; therefore the liability rules discussed in Module 32, section D. are applicable to partnerships

    a. Can bind partnership to contracts with third parties

        (1) Even where no actual authority, can bind partnership where there is apparent authority

        (2) Third parties are reasonable believing that a partner has authority to enter into contracts on the partnership's behalf

        (3) Contract must be for something related to the normal partnership business for apparent authority to exist

---

EXAMPLE

A, B, and C form a partnership to sell widgets. Contrary to the wishes of B and C, A decides to buy in the partnership name some "super-widgets" from T. Even though A did not have actual authority to buy these, T can enforce the contract based on apparent authority. A, of course, breached his fiduciary duty to B and C.

EXAMPLE

A and B have a partnership to sell furniture in a retail outlet. A and B agreed that neither would buy more than $10,000 of furniture from suppliers without the consent of the other. A, however, buys $20,000 of furniture from a regular supplier who was unaware of this limitation. When the supplier attempts to deliver, B refuses the furniture. Since A has apparent authority, the supplier can enforce the contract for the full $20,000.

If A had purchased $20,000, or any amount, of automotive supplies without B's consent, the partnership would not be liable since automotive supplies are unrelated to the furniture business.

b. Partnership is not liable for acts of partners outside the scope of the partnership business

EXAMPLE

A partner of a hardware store attempts to buy some real estate in the name of the partnership. Here apparent authority does not exist.

c. Partnership is liable for partner's torts committed in course and scope of business and for partner's breach of trust (i.e., misapplication of third party's funds)

EXAMPLE

A partner takes a third party's money on behalf of the partnership to invest in government bonds. Instead he uses it himself to build an addition onto his home. Both partner and partnership are liable to the investor.

EXAMPLE

A partner, while driving on partnership business, injures a third party. If the partner is negligent, the partnership is also liable.

2. Unanimous consent of partners is needed unless otherwise stated in the partnership agreement (so no apparent authority) for

a. Admission of a new partner
b. Amending the partnership agreement
c. Assignment of partnership property
d. Making partnership a surety or guarantor
e. Admitting to a claim against partnership in court
f. Submitting partnership claim to arbitrator
g. Any action outside the scope of the partnership business

3. Partner's liability is personal, that is, extends to all his/her personal assets (not just investment in partnership) to cover all debts and liabilities of partnership

a. Partners are jointly and severally liable for all debts

(1) RUPA requires creditors to first attempt collection from partnership before partners unless partnership is bankrupt

b. Partners may split losses or liability between themselves according to any proportion agreed upon; however, third parties can still hold each partner personally liable despite agreement

(1) If any partner pays more than his/her agreed share, s/he can get reimbursed from other partners

---

EXAMPLE

X, Y, and Z as partners agreed to split losses 10%, 20%, and 70% respectively. A third party recovers $100,000 from X only based on a partnership tort. X can get $20,000 from Y and $70,000 from Z so that X ends up paying only her 10%.

EXAMPLE

Same as before except that Y is insolvent. X can recover the proportionate share from Z or $87,500 ($100,000 × 70%/80%).

EXAMPLE

A, B, and C are partners who agree to split losses 10%, 10%, and 80%, respectively. Y sues the partners for a tort based on the partnership business. C files for bankruptcy. Y can recover from A and B and is not bound by the agreement between A, B, and C

---

   c. New partners coming into a partnership are liable for existing debts only to the extent of their capital contributions (i.e., the new partners have no personal liability on these preexisting debts)

      (1) Unless new partners assume personal liability for old debts

   d. Partners withdrawing are liable for existing liabilities
   e. Partners withdrawing are liable for subsequent liabilities unless notice of withdrawal or death is given to third parties

      (1) Actual notice to creditors who previously dealt with partnership
      (2) Constructive (e.g., published) notice is sufficient for others who merely knew of partnership's existence
      (3) Notice can also be provided by filing a statement of dissociation with the state's secretary of state

         (a) 90 days after statement is filed third parties have notice that partner is no longer affiliated with the partnership, regardless of whether the third party has actually seen the statement
         (b) Failure to file a statement, or give other adequate notice, may allow third parties to believe partner is still a partner for up to 2 years after the partner's departure

   f. Estates of deceased partners are liable for partners' debts
   g. Liability of withdrawing partner may be limited by agreement between partners but agreement is not binding on third parties (unless they join in on agreement)
   h. Partners are not criminally liable unless they personally participate in some way or unless statute prescribes liability to all members of management (e.g., environment regulation or sale of alcohol to a minor)

NOW REVIEW MULTIPLE-CHOICE QUESTIONS 11 THROUGH 15

F. Termination of a Partnership

  1. The process of termination begins when a partner dissociates from the partnership

   a. Dissociation occurs when a partner ceases to be associated with the partnership
   b. Actions that constitute dissociation are

      (1) Partner withdraws from the partnership

        (a) Partner leaves voluntarily in accordance with the partnership agreement

        (b) Partner leaves voluntarily in violation of the partnership agreement

        (c) Partner is forced to leave the partnership because of a vote by other partners or partner violated partnership agreement

    (2) Partner engages in conduct that interferes with the ability of the partnership to conduct business

    (3) Bankruptcy of a partner

    (4) Death of a partner

    (5) Incapacity of a partner

2. After dissociation occurs the partnership will either

    a. Commence dissolution and liquidation (winding up), or

    b. Continue the partnership business

3. Dissolution can occur by

    a. Prior agreement (e.g., partnership agreement)

    b. Present agreement of partners

    c. By decree of court in such cases as

        (1) Partner continually or seriously breaches partnership agreement

        (2) Partner guilty of conduct that harms business

    d. Assignment, selling, or pledging of partnership interest does **not** cause dissolution even if there is no consent of other partners; recall a partnership interest is only the partner's right to profits.

    e. Under RUPA, unlike previous law, partner's withdrawal, death, or bankruptcy does **not** automatically cause dissolution of partnership

        (1) Partners that own majority of partnership may choose to continue general partnership within ninety days of partners' withdrawal, death, or bankruptcy. If the partners fail to agree to continue partnership though, dissolution will occur.

        (2) Any partner has power to dissociate from partnership even if partner had agreed not to, but is liable for breach of such a contract

4. Winding up

    a. Remaining partners may elect to wind up and terminate partnership or not wind up and continue business

5. Order of distribution upon termination of general partnership

    a. To creditors including partners as creditors

    b. Capital contributions and profits or losses are calculated together

        (1) Partners may receive money or even need to pay money at this stage

6. Partners are personally liable to partnership for any deficits in their capital accounts and to creditors for insufficiency of partnership assets

---

EXAMPLE

A, B, and C formed the ABC partnership. The capital contributions were A $50,000, B $30,000, and C $20,000. After three years, the partners voted to dissolve the partnership. After liquidating its assets and paying off its creditors, ABC had $40,000 in cash. The $40,000 needs to be used to pay back the aforementioned capital contributions, but there is still $60,000 that will go unpaid. The $60,000 is treated as a loss. Each partner will have to pay his/her proportionate share of the $60,000. Since there is no information on how the partners agreed to split profits or losses, the RUPA rule of splitting profits and losses equally must apply. Therefore each partner will need to pay $20,000 to the partnership. Once that is done, the partnership will then pay each partner his/her capital contribution.

---

    a. Priority between partnership creditors and partner's personal creditors

        (1) Partnership creditors have first priority to partnership assets; any excess goes to personal creditors

        (2) Usually, personal creditors have first priority to personal assets; any excess goes to partnership creditors

7. During the winding up process all partners actual authority is terminated, other than those partners who are engaged in the winding up process

  a. No new business is permitted, other than transactions necessary to wind up

  b. Apparent authority can still exist, however

8. Partners can bind other partners and the partnership on contracts until third parties who have known of the partnership are given notice of dissolution

  a. Actual notice must be given to third parties who have dealt with the partnership prior to dissolution

  b. Constructive notice (e.g., notice in newspaper) is adequate for third parties who have only known of the partnership

  c. Partnership may also file a statement of dissolution with the state's secretary of state. All third parties are assumed to have knowledge of the dissolution 90 days after the filing, thus eliminating any apparent authority

9. The partnership may choose to continue instead of dissolving if either

  a. A majority of the remaining partners, after dissociation, vote to continue the partnership business, or

  b. A continuation agreement (clause) is contained in the partnership agreement

10. If the partnership continues, only the dissociated partner's actual authority is terminated

  a. Notice, however, must be provided to remove the apparent authority of the dissociated partner

    (1) Actual notice to creditors who previously dealt with partnership

    (2) Constructive (e.g., published) notice is sufficient for others who merely knew of partnership's existence

    (3) Notice can also be provided by filing a statement of dissociation with the state's secretary of state

      (a) 90 days after statement is filed, third parties have notice that partner is no longer affiliated with the partnership, regardless of whether the third party has actually seen the statement

      (b) Failure to file a statement, or give other adequate notice, may allow third parties to believe partner is still a partner for up to 2 years after the partner's departure

---

NOW REVIEW MULTIPLE-CHOICE QUESTIONS 16 THROUGH 18

G. Limited Partnerships

1. Revised Uniform Limited Partnership Act (RULPA) is designed to modernize law because today many limited partnerships are very large with many limited partners.

  a. RULPA has been adopted by majority of states

2. Creation of limited partnership

  a. Unlike a general partnership that requires no formal procedures to create it, a limited partnership requires compliance with state statute to create it

  b. Must file certificate of limited partnership with secretary of state; if the partnership does not, it will be treated as a general partnership

    (1) Must be signed by all general partners and include names of all general partners

      (a) Name and address of the limited partnership

      (b) Name and address of its agent

      (c) Latest date the partnership is to dissolve

      (d) Names of limited partners not required

      (e) Must amend certificate of partnership to show any additions or deletions of general partners

        (1) Must also amend certificate if any general partner becomes aware of false information in certificate

  c. Requires at least one general partner and at least one limited partner

    (1) Sole general partner may be a corporation

    (2) Liability of limited partner(s) is limited to amount of capital contributions (with some exceptions below)

    d. General or limited partners' capital contributions may not only be in cash, services performed, or property, but may also now be in promise to perform services, to give cash, or property in future

    e. Name of limited partner may not be used in name of limited partnership unless name is also name of a general partner.

        (1) If a limited partner **knowingly or negligently** allows his/her name to be part of limited partnership name, then the partner is personally liable to creditors who extend credit to business (unless creditors knew that limited partner was not a general partner)

    f. "Limited partnership" words or abbreviation must be in firm's name

    g. Partnership interests may be purchased with cash, property, services rendered, promissory note

    h. Defective formation of limited partnership causes limited partners to be liable as general partners

        (1) Under RULPA, partner who believes s/he is limited partner may avoid liability of general partner if upon learning of defective formation either

            (a) Withdraws from partnership and renounces all future profits

            (b) Files amendment or new certificate that cures defect

        (2) However, limited partner is liable for past transactions before withdrawal or amendment to any third party transacting business while believing partner was general partner

    i. Foreign limited partnership is one doing business in given state but was formed in another state

        (1) Foreign limited partnership must register with secretary of state before doing business in state

3. Rights of partners in limited partnership

    a. General partners manage partnership

    b. Limited partners invest

        (1) Limited partner who substantially manages partnership like general partner obtains liability like general partner to third parties who believed s/he was general partner

        (2) Limited partner allowed to do following without risking loss of limited liability

            (a) Acting as an agent or employee of limited partnership

            (b) Consulting with and advising general partner or limited partnership about partnership business

            (c) Approving or disapproving amendments to limited partnership agreement

            (d) Voting on dissolution or winding up of limited partnership

            (e) Voting on loans of limited partnership

            (f) Voting on change in nature of business

            (g) Voting on removal of a general partner

            (h) Bringing derivative lawsuit on behalf of limited partnership

            (i) Be surety for limited partnership

    c. Profit or loss sharing

        (1) Profits or losses are shared as agreed upon in certificate agreement

            (a) Losses and any liability are limited to capital contributions for limited partners

            (b) If no agreement on profit and losses exists, then shared based on percentages of capital contributions

                (1) Note how this differs from a general partnership in which losses and profits are shared equally unless agreed otherwise

    d. Admission of new partner requires written agreement of all partners unless partnership agreement provides otherwise

    e. Limited partnership interests (right to profits) may be assigned in part or in whole

        (1) Similar to general partnerships, assignee is only a creditor of the partner

        (2) Assignee acquires no rights of the limited partner other than the right to the limited partner's right to profits

    f. Limited partners have right to inspect partnership books and tax return information

    g. Can be a limited and general partner at same time

(1) Has rights, powers, and liability of a general partner
(2) Has rights against other partners with respect to contribution as a limited partner and also as a general partner

  h. Limited partners may own competing interests
  i. Limited partner may be a secured or unsecured creditor of partnership
  j. Limited partner may not withdraw capital contribution if it impairs creditors

4. Duties of partners

  a. General partners owe fiduciary duties to general and limited partners—limited partners in general do not owe fiduciary duties since they do not engage in the management of the business.

5. Dissolution of limited partnership takes place upon the following events :

  a. Completion of time period specified in certificate
  b. Upon event specified in partnership agreement
  c. Unanimous written consent of all partners
  d. Dissolution of court decree when not practical to continue partnership
  e. Event that causes partnership business to be illegal
  f. Withdrawal of general partner by retirement, removal, bankruptcy (but not mere insolvency), fraud against other partners, insanity, death

    (1) Unless all partners agree in writing to continue business
    (2) Unless partnership agreement allows partners to continue business
    (3) Withdrawal of limited partner does not cause dissolution
    (4) Death of limited partner does not cause dissolution

6. If partnership not continued, winding up takes place with the following distribution of assets of partnership in order of priority

  a. To creditors including partners who are creditors
  b. To partners and ex-partners to pay off unpaid distributions
  c. To partners to return capital contributions
  d. To partners for partnership interests in proportions they share in distributions
  e. Note that in these priorities general and limited partners share equally
  f. Also, note that partners can vary their rights by agreement of all parties affected

7. Upon dissolution, remaining partners typically complete winding-up process
8. Dissolution of a limited partnership requires the filing of a dissolution document with the state.

NOW REVIEW MULTIPLE-CHOICE QUESTIONS 19 THROUGH 29

H. Joint Ventures

1. Joint venture—An association of two or more persons (or entities) organized to carry out a single business undertaking (or series of related undertakings) for profit

  a. Generally, corporations may engage in joint ventures

EXAMPLE

X Corporation, O Corporation, and N Corporation decide to form a joint venture to bring oil from the north to the south of Alaska.

2. Law of joint ventures is similar to that of partnerships with some exceptions

a. Each joint venturer is not necessarily an agent of other joint venturers—limited power to bind others; there is no apparent authority for joint venturers

b. Joint venture is interpreted as special form of partnership

   (1) Fiduciary duties of partners in partnership law apply
   (2) Each member has right to participate in management
   (3) Liability is unlimited and each joint venturer is personally liable for debts of joint venture

3. Generally a joint venture is not required to file a document or certificate with the state

---

NOW REVIEW MULTIPLE-CHOICE QUESTION 30

I. Limited Liability Companies (LLC)

1. Laws for this form of business generally follow the Revised Uniform Limited Liability Company Act (RULLCA 2006)

2. LLC is not considered a corporation but a majority of states provide

  a. All owners (often called members) have limited liability and therefore no personal liability

    (1) Liability of owners limited to their capital contributions (including any obligation to make contributions) plus any equity in LLC

     (a) Typically, limited liability is retained even if members fail to follow usual formalities in conducting business

---

EXAMPLE

Members of LLC fail to keep minutes of the LLC's meetings. This failure does not expose them to personal liability for the debts of the LLC.

      1] Note that if a **corporation** does not follow the corporate formalities such as corporate meetings with relevant minutes, the corporate veil can be pierced, thus the corporate entity is disregarded and then shareholders of company obtain personal liability for corporation's debts

       (a) This is another important advantage of LLC

    (2) Compare with limited partnership in which only limited partners can have limited liability
    (3) In many states a sole proprietorship may be formed into LLC to obtain its advantages

  b. LLC must be formed according to limited liability company statute of the state in which it is formed

    (1) Some general partnerships or limited partnerships convert over to an LLC in which case partners retain liability they had in former partnership; they obtain benefits as new members of LLC only for transactions that take place after conversion date to LLC
    (2) LLC is foreign LLC in other states in which it does business, and laws of state where it was formed typically govern LLC in those other states

  c. LLC is separate legal entity so can sue or be sued in own name

    (1) Foreign LLC must register with secretary of state and obtain a certificate of authority to transact business in the state before doing business in another state, or cannot sue in state courts

  d. The name of a LLC must include the words "limited liability company" or "limited company" or the abbreviation "L.L.C.," "LLC," "L.C.," or "LC" to give notice to public

  e. To form LLC, one or more persons may act as organizers by filing a Certificate of Organization with secretary of state

    (1) May be amended by filing amendment with secretary of state

    (2) The Operating Agreement specifies the manner in which the company will conduct and wind up operations

  f. Think of an LLC as a large S corporation

    (1) There is no limit on the number of members (owners/shareholders)

    (2) The LLC itself is not taxed; the tax liability flows through the LLC to the individual members

3. Member (owner) of LLC has no interest in any specific property in LLC but has interest (personal property interest) in LLC in general

  a. Member has right to distributions according to profit and loss sharing agreed upon in operating agreement

    (1) Under the majority of state laws, in the absence of an agreement otherwise, members divide profits in proportion to their capital contributions

    (2) Under the RULLCA, in absence of agreement otherwise, members divide profits and losses equally

    (3) If the question does not specify RULLCA assume the majority state rule

    (4) Members may agree to divide profits differently than losses based on different formulas

---

EXAMPLE

The members agree that the various members each receive profits and losses on bases that are different for each member. Member Q, for example, receives 15% if there is a profit in a given year, but suffers a loss of 20% if the LLC were to suffer a loss. Member R, however, is allocated 12% whether there is a profit or a loss. This is enforceable since the members agree to it.

---

  b. Member has management interest

    (1) Includes rights to manage affairs of firm, vote within firm, and get information about LLC

    (2) Unless agreed otherwise, each member has equal voice in management

  c. Member may assign financial interest (right to profits) in LLC unless operating agreement specifies otherwise

    (1) Assignee does not become member, only receives assignor's share of profits assigned unless other members agree otherwise

    (2) Member may not assign any other right, including the right to be a member, without the consent of the other members

  d. Right to information

    (1) Members of member-managed companies (and managers in manager-managed companies) have right to receive (without demand) business information to properly exercise their rights and duties.

    (2) Other members, on demand, may inspect information (e.g., books and records) during reasonable times, at the business location and for appropriate purpose

  e. Members may be dissociated as members at any time, by notification of desire to dissociate, expulsion, sale of interest, etc.

4. Authority and duties in LLCs

  a. When LLC designated as member-managed LLC, all members have authority to bind LLC under agency law to contracts on behalf of LLC

  b. When LLC designated as manager-managed LLC, only managers have authority to bind LLC to contracts for LLC

    (1) LLC is bound only to contracts that

      (a) Either LLC has authorized under agency law, or

      (b) Are made in the ordinary course of business

  c. In either case

(1) Authority of both members and managers to bind LLC to contracts can be restricted in a statement of authority (filed with the Secretary of State) or in operating agreement

(2) Apparent authority of either members or managers to make contracts with third parties not affected for those who have proper notice of restrictions on contract-making authority

    (a) Restrictions in statement of authority are deemed proper notice to third parties if they are filed with Secretary of State

    (b) Restrictions in operating agreement are deemed to be proper notice to those third parties who actually receive direct notification of those restrictions

5. Other compensation

    a. Member who is not manager has no right to compensation for services performed

      (1) Exception is for services performed in winding up LLC

    b. Managers of LLCs receive compensation according to agreed contract

    c. LLC must reimburse members and managers for payments they made in name of LLC

    d. LLC is required to indemnify managers and/or members

6. Fiduciary duties owed by members and managers to LLC; these are essentially the same fiduciary duties discussed in Module 32, section C.2.

    a. Managers of manager-managed LLC and members of member-managed LLC owe LLC fiduciary duties

      (1) Both owe duty of loyalty and due care to LLC

        (a) Duty of loyalty includes

          (1) To account to the company and hold as trustee for it any property, profit, or benefit derived by the member

          (2) To refrain from dealing with the company on behalf of a party having an adverse interest in the company

          (3) To refrain from competing with the company

        (b) Duty of due care includes

          (1) Act with the care that a person in a like position would reasonably exercise and in a manner the member reasonably believes to be in the best interests of the company

        (c) The member shall discharge the duties under the operating agreement and exercise any rights consistently with the contractual obligations or good faith and fair dealings

    b. A member of a manager-managed company does not have any fiduciary duty to the company or other members solely as a result of being a member

7. Dissolution of LLC

    a. Most state LLC statutes cause LLC to dissolve when

      (1) All members agree in writing to dissolution

      (2) Time period passes or event happens as specified in operating agreement

      (3) Member withdraws, is voted out, dies, goes bankrupt, or becomes incompetent

        (a) Most states allow remainder of members to continue LLC if agreed upon unanimously

      (4) Court order dissolves it

8. Distribution of assets upon dissolution are made in following priorities:

    a. To creditors including managers and members except for their shares in the distribution of profits

    b. To members and past members for unpaid distributions unless agreed otherwise

    c. To members to receive back capital contributions, unless agreed otherwise

    d. To members for their distributions as agreed in operating agreement, or if not agreed upon, in proportion to contributions they had made

9. Dissolution of a LLC may require the filing of a dissolution document with the state.

> **NOW REVIEW MULTIPLE-CHOICE QUESTIONS 31 THROUGH 35**

J. Limited Liability Partnerships (LLP)

1. Majority of states now allow LLP
2. Formation of LLP

   a. Must file articles of LLP with Secretary of State
   b. Statutes of all jurisdictions require firm's name to include phrase of limited liability partnership or registered limited liability partnership or initials LLP or RLLP to notify public
   c. Majority of states require only majority, not unanimous, approval of partners to become LLP
   d. Generally, laws of state in which the LLP is formed govern affairs of the LLP in all other states
   e. The LLP often works well for professionals who want to do business as professionals in a partnership but still pass through tax benefits while limiting personal liability of the partners
   f. Most states allow an easy transition from conventional partnership into limited liability partnership
   g. Most common law and statutory law from partnership law applies to LLP

3. Liability provisions of partners in LLP

   a. Under traditional general partnerships and limited partnerships, big disadvantage is that general partners in both firms have unlimited personal liability for partnership obligations

      (1) Most states allow LLP to be formed so the general partners have no personal liability for the contractual obligations of the firm

> **EXAMPLE**
>
> The ABC LLP got a loan from 1st Bank. ABC subsequently defaulted on the loan. 1st Bank may only satisfy its claim against ABC; it may not go after the individual partners even if partnership assets are exhausted.

      (2) Partners also have no personal liability for the debts arising from the torts of the LLP. Partners do have personal liability, however

         (a) If the partner actually committed the tort
         (b) In most states for the torts committed by parties under the partners' supervision or control

> **EXAMPLE**
>
> Anson is a partner in the ABC LLP. Dietz is a junior partner at ABC and is under Anson's supervision. Dietz commits malpractice. Dietz has personal liability for the damages arising from the malpractice because Dietz committed the tort. Anson has personal liability because Anson is Dietz's supervisor.

   b. Popular for professionals such as accounting firms and law firms

> **NOW REVIEW MULTIPLE-CHOICE QUESTION 36**

K. Subchapter C Corporations

1. Under Federal Subchapter S Revision Act, all corporations are divided into two categories

   a. Subchapter S corporations are discussed later in this module
   b. Subchapter C corporations are all corporations that are not Subchapter S corporations

(1) Majority of this module covers "regular corporation" also referred to as Subchapter C corporation

  (a) In general, most provisions for Subchapter C corporations and Subchapter S corporations are similar such as limited liability of shareholders and structure of corporate management

    (1) Main distinction is tax treatment

NOW REVIEW MULTIPLE-CHOICE QUESTIONS 37 THROUGH 40

L. Characteristics and Advantages of Corporate Form

1. Limited liability

  a. Generally a shareholder in a corporation risks only his/her investment; creditors may not collect from shareholders' personal assets even if corporate assets are exhausted.

2. Transferability of ownership interest

  a. Shares in corporations are represented by stocks and can be freely bought, sold, or assigned unless shareholders have agreed to restrictions

3. Continuous life

  a. Unlike a partnership, a corporation is not terminated by death of a shareholder, or his/her incapacity

    (1) Regarded as perpetual, and continues to exist until dissolved, merged, or otherwise terminated

4. Separate entity

  a. A corporation is a legal entity in itself and is treated separately from its stockholders

    (1) Can take, hold, and convey property
    (2) Can contract in own name with shareholders or third parties
    (3) Can sue and be sued

5. Financing

  a. Often easier to raise large amounts of capital than in other business organizations by issuance of stock or other securities (e.g., bonds)
  b. More flexible because can issue different classes of stock and/or bonds to suit its needs and market demands

6. Corporate management

  a. Persons who manage corporations are not necessarily shareholders and therefore may be more qualified
  b. Management of a corporation is usually vested in board of directors elected by shareholders
  c. Directors could be removed from office before their elected term is finished only for cause under common law

    (1) Increasingly states have been passing laws that allow directors to be removed at any time with shareholders' consent

---

NOW REVIEW MULTIPLE-CHOICE QUESTIONS 41 THROUGH 45

M. Disadvantages of Corporate Business Structure

1. Tax treatment

  a. Tax burdens may be more than on other business structures because of double taxation

    (1) This often happens when income is taxed at corporate level and then dividends paid from after-tax income are taxed again at shareholder level
    (2) Corporation may alleviate double taxation as Subchapter S corporation by being taxed similar to partnership

2. Costs of incorporating, because must meet formal creation requirements

3. Formal operating requirements must be met
4. If the corporation goes public

    a. There substantial costs of compliance with federal securities laws
    b. May be subject to hostile takeover

NOW REVIEW MULTIPLE-CHOICE QUESTION 46

N. Types of Corporations

1. Domestic corporation is one that operates and does business within the state in which it was incorporated
2. Foreign corporation is one doing business in any state except the state in which it was incorporated

    a. Foreign corporations , if "doing business" in a given state, are not exempt from many requirements and details that domestic corporations must meet

        (1) Doing business in state is typically defined as maintaining an office or selling personal property in state

            (a) These are not considered doing business in state

                (1) Defending against a lawsuit
                (2) Holding bank account
                (3) Using mail to solicit orders
                (4) Collecting debts
                (5) Using independent contractors to make sales

        (2) Foreign corporations can be required to qualify to do business in state; accomplished by obtaining certificate of authority from state

            (a) Must appoint agent to receive service of process for suits against corporation
            (b) Must pay specified fees
            (c) Must file information with secretary of state

3. Professional corporations are ones under state laws that allow professionals to incorporate (e.g., doctors, accountants, attorneys)

    a. All states allow professional corporations
    b. Typically, shares may be owned only by licensed professionals
    c. Retain personal liability for their professional acts (i.e., personal liability for malpractice)
    d. Obtain other corporation benefits (e.g., limited liability for corporate debts, some tax benefits)

4. Model Statutory Close Corporation Supplement was passed to allow corporations to choose to be close corporations.

    a. Often helps corporations made up of entrepreneurial individuals
    b. Close corporations can also be called closely held corporations or closed corporations
    c. Only corporations having 50 or fewer shareholders may choose status of statutory close corporations

        (1) To choose such status, two-thirds of shares of each class of shares of corporation must approve it
        (2) Articles of corporation must contain a statement it is a statutory close corporation
        (3) All share certificates must clearly state they are issued by statutory close corporation

    d. Close corporations may function without some of formalities of operating corporations

        (1) If all shareholders approve, close corporation may function without board of directors

            (a) It is then managed by shareholders

        (2) Close corporation need not hold shareholders' meetings unless at least one shareholder demands in writing that meetings be held
        (3) Basically, shareholders may treat close corporation as a partnership for purposes of governing

            (a) Very importantly, statutory close corporation status allows shareholders to have limited liability

    (4) Usually the transfer of ownership interests (sale of stock) is restricted

5. **De facto** corporation has been formed in fact but has not been formed properly under the law

    a. Usually defective because of some small error
    b. Now, filing by secretary of state of Articles of Incorporation is deemed conclusive proof that incorporators did all that was necessary to incorporate

        (1) Third parties cannot now challenge that corporation exists
        (2) Only state can challenge existence and dissolve or cancel corporation

6. **De jure** corporation has been formed correctly in compliance with the incorporation statute

---

NOW REVIEW MULTIPLE-CHOICE QUESTIONS 47 THROUGH 51

O. Formation of Corporation

1. Promoters are persons who form corporations and arrange capitalization to begin corporations

    a. Promoter handles issuing of the prospectus, promoting stock subscriptions, and drawing up charter
    b. Promoter has a fiduciary relationship with corporation, and is not permitted to act against interests of corporation

        (1) Does not prevent personal profit if fully disclosed

    c. Promoter is not an agent of the corporation, because the corporation is still not in existence

        (1) Any agreements (preincorporation contracts) made by promoter are not binding on the future corporation unless adopted by the corporation after it comes into existence

            (a) Requires actual resolution of board of directors
            (b) Normally promoter is personally liable on contract. Adoption by corporation does not relieve promoter; **novation is required to relieve promoter**. The other party must agree to substituting the corporation

                (1) Promoter has liability even if promoter's name does not appear on contract
                (2) However, promoter is not liable if third party clearly states that s/he would look only to corporation for performance

            (c) Corporation is not liable to promoter for his/her services unless adopted by corporation

2. Formed only under state incorporation statutes ("Creature of statute")
3. Incorporation

    a. Articles of Incorporation (corporate charter) are filed with the state and contain

        (1) Proposed name of corporation and initial address
        (2) Purpose of corporation
        (3) Powers of corporation
        (4) Name of registered agent of corporation
        (5) Name and address of each incorporator

            (a) Incorporators may be promoters

        (6) Number of authorized shares of stock

    b. First shareholders' meeting

        (1) Stock certificates issued to shareholders
        (2) Resignation of temporary directors and election of new

    c. At same meeting or subsequent meeting, directors

        (1) Elect officers
        (2) Adopt or reject preincorporation contracts
        (3) Begin business of corporation
        (4) Adopt initial bylaws

      (a) These need not be filed with any government agency

      (b) Provide specific rules for management

  4. Articles of Incorporation may be subsequently amended

    a. Approval of any adversely affected shareholders of amendment needed

      (1) Majority vote required

        (a) Dissenting minority shareholders may assert right of appraisal and therefore receive fair value for shares

          1] Fair value is value just before vote

> **NOW REVIEW MULTIPLE-CHOICE QUESTIONS 52 THROUGH 57**

P. Corporate Financial Structure

  1. Definitions

    a. Uncertificated securities—securities not represented by written documents

    b. Authorized stock—amount permitted to be issued in Articles of Incorporation (e.g., amount and types)

    c. Issued stock—authorized and delivered to shareholders

    d. Unissued stock—authorized but not yet issued

    e. Outstanding stock—issued and not repurchased by the corporation (i.e., it is still owned by shareholders)

    f. Treasury stock—issued but not outstanding (i.e., corporation repurchased it)

      (1) Are not votable and do not receive dividends

      (2) Corporation does not recognize gain or loss on transactions with its own stock

      (3) Must be purchased out of unreserved or unrestricted earned surplus as defined below and as permitted by state law

        (a) If Articles of Incorporation so permit or if majority of voting shareholders permit, unrestricted capital surplus (see below) may also be used

      (4) May be distributed as part of stock dividend

      (5) May be resold without regard to par value

      (6) Can be resold without regard to preemptive rights

      (7) No purchase of treasury stock may be made if it renders corporation insolvent

    g. Canceled stock—stock purchased or received by corporation that is canceled

      (1) No longer issued or outstanding

      (2) Makes room for more stock to be issued

    h. Par-value stock

      (1) Par value is amount set in Articles of Incorporation

      (2) Stock should be issued for this amount or more

      (3) May subsequently be traded for any amount

      (4) Creditors may hold purchaser liable if stock originally purchased at below par

        (a) Contingently liable for difference between amount paid and par value

        (b) Subsequent purchaser also liable unless purchased in good faith without notice that sale was below par

    i. No-par stock—stock issued without a set par value

      (1) May have a stated value

    j. Stated capital (legal capital)—number of shares issued times par value (or stated value)

      (1) If no par or stated value, then includes total consideration received by corporation

        (a) Under limited circumstances, portion may be allocated by board of directors to capital surplus as permitted by law

(2) Dividends normally may not be declared or paid out of it

(3) Following also increase stated capital by number of shares increased times par value (or stated value)

  (a) Exercise of stock option
  (b) Small common stock dividend

(4) Following do not change stated capital

  (a) Acquisition or reissuance of treasury stock under cost method
  (b) Stock splits

    (1) Increase number of shares issued and decrease par or stated value (e.g., 2-for-1 stock split doubles the number of shares issued and cuts in half the par or stated value)
    (2) Do not distribute assets or capital

  (c) Payment of organization costs

k. Earned surplus (retained earnings)—cumulative amount of income (net of dividends) retained by the corporation during its existence or since a deficit was properly eliminated

(1) Note that under modern terminology, this is correctly referred to as retained earnings as indicated above; since laws written using old terms, CPA candidates should be familiar with old as well as new terms as learned in accounting

l. Net assets—excess of total assets over total debts
m. Surplus—excess of net assets over stated capital
n. Capital surplus—entire surplus of corporation less earned surplus

(1) Note that paid-in capital is considered capital surplus

o. Contributed capital—total consideration received by corporation upon issuance of stock

2. Classes of stock

a. Common stock usually gives each shareholder one vote per share and is entitled to dividends if declared by the directors

(1) Has no priority over other stock for dividends
(2) Shareholders entitled to share in final distribution of assets
(3) Votes may be apportioned to shares in other ways (e.g., one vote per ten shares)
(4) Corporation may issue more than one class of common stock with varying terms (e.g., class may have no voting rights or different par value, etc.)
(5) All stock is common stock unless specifically told otherwise

b. Preferred stock is given preferred status as to some characteristic of the stock, often liquidations and dividends, but the Examiners will state what the preference is

(1) Usually nonvoting stock; however, assume it is voting stock unless the Examiners specifically state otherwise
(2) Dividend rate is generally a fixed rate
(3) Cumulative preferred means that if a periodic dividend is not paid at the scheduled time, it accumulates and must be satisfied before common stock may receive a dividend

  (a) These arrearages are not liabilities of corporation until declared by board of directors

    (1) Disclosed in footnotes to financial statements

  (b) Noncumulative preferred means that if the dividend is passed, it will never be paid

(4) Participating preferred stock participates further in corporate earnings remaining after a fixed amount is paid to preferred shares

  (a) Participation with common shares is generally on a fixed percentage basis

c. Callable (or redeemable) stock may be redeemed at a fixed price by the corporation

(1) Call price is fixed in Articles of Incorporation or may be subject to agreement among shareholders themselves

d. Convertible preferred gives shareholder option to convert preferred stock to common stock at a fixed exchange rate

3. Marketing of stock

   a. Stock subscriptions are contracts to purchase a given number of shares in an existing corporation or one to be organized

      (1) Subscription to stock is a written offer to buy and is not binding until accepted by the corporation
      (2) Under the Model Business Corporation Act, preincorporation stock subscriptions are irrevocable for six months
      (3) Once accepted, the subscriber becomes liable

         (a) For the purchase
         (b) As a corporate shareholder

   b. Watered stock

      (1) Stock is said to be watered when the cash or property exchanged is less than par value or stated value
      (2) Stock must be issued for consideration equal to or greater than the par or stated value under most state laws

         (a) No-par stock may be issued for consideration that the directors determine to be reasonable

      (3) Creditors of the corporation may recover from the stockholders the amount of water in their shares; that is, the amount the stockholders would have paid to the corporation had they paid the full amount required (i.e., par value less amount paid)

         (a) If the corporation becomes insolvent
         (b) Subsequent purchaser of watered stock is not liable unless s/he had knowledge thereof

   c. Valid consideration or value for shares can be any benefit to corporation

      (1) Including cash, property, services performed, intangible property, promissory notes, other securities, or services contracted to be performed in future

         (a) Directors have duty to set value on property received

            (1) Directors' value set is conclusive unless fraud shown

4. Debt securities (holders are not owners but creditors)

   a. Debenture is instrument for long-term **unsecured** debt
   b. Bond is instrument for long-term **secured** debt

NOW REVIEW MULTIPLE-CHOICE QUESTIONS 58 THROUGH 69

Q. Powers and Liabilities of Corporation

1. Corporations generally have following powers

   a. To acquire their own shares (treasury stock) or retire their own shares

      (1) Typically limited to amount of surplus

   b. To make charitable contributions
   c. To guarantee obligations of others only if in reasonable furtherance of corporation's business
   d. Loans to directors require shareholder approval
   e. Loans to employees (even employees who are also directors) do not need shareholder approval and are appropriate if they benefit corporation
   f. Generally, a corporation may also be a partner of a partnership

2. Crimes

   a. Corporations are liable for crimes they are capable of committing
   b. Punishment generally consists of fines or forfeiture, although directors have been faced with prison sentences for crimes of the corporation

3. Contracts

    a. Rules under agency law apply in corporate dealings with third parties; see Module 32, Section D. 1—7

    b. The corporation is the principal

    c. Corporate officers, employees, and the board of directors are the agents

    d. Individual directors are not agents of the corporation; therefore an individual director cannot have apparent authority to enter into a contract on behalf of the corporation

4. Torts

    a. Corporations are liable for the damages resulting from torts committed by their officers, agents, or employees within the course and scope of their corporate duties

    b. Rules of agency law apply; see Module 32, section D. 8-15

5. *Ultra vires* acts

    a. Illegal and *ultra vires* acts are not the same

        (1) Illegal acts are acts in violation of statute or public policy

---

EXAMPLE

False advertising.

---

        (2) Whereas *ultra vires* acts are merely beyond the scope of the corporate powers (i.e., a legal act may be *ultra vires*)

EXAMPLE

Although legal to become a surety, the Articles of Incorporation may not allow it.

---

    b. The state's attorney general may dissolve corporation for *ultra vires* act

    c. Stockholders have right to object to ultra vires acts

    d. Directors or officers may be sued by shareholders, known as derivative action, behalf of the corporation or by the corporation itself if there are damages to the corporation for *ultra vires* acts

NOW REVIEW MULTIPLE-CHOICE QUESTIONS 70 THROUGH 72

R. Directors and Officers of Corporations

1. Directors are elected by shareholders
2. Directors' duties and powers

    a. A director as an individual has no power to bind the corporation—must act as a board member at a duly constituted meeting of the board

        (1) Majority vote of those present is needed for most business decisions if quorum is present

        (2) Action may be taken by board with no meeting

            (a) Unless prohibited by Articles of Incorporation or by corporate bylaws, and

            (b) There must be unanimous written consent by board members for action to be taken

    b. Powers and duties in general

        (1) Declaration of dividends

(2) Selection of officers

(3) Must comply with Articles of Incorporation. The Articles of Incorporation can only be amended by voting shareholders.

(4) Typically delegate some authority (e.g., day to day or routine matters to officers and agents)

(5) Directors are not entitled to compensation unless so provided in articles, bylaws, or by a resolution of the board passed before the services are rendered

    (a) May be reimbursed for expenses incurred on behalf of corporation

3. Director's liability

  a. General rule is that directors must exercise ordinary care, due diligence in performing the duties entrusted to them by virtue of their positions as directors, and acts in a manner he or she believes to be in the best interests of the corporation

    (1) Directors are liable for own torts committed even if acting for corporation

      (a) Corporation is **also** liable if committed within the scope of corporate duties

    (2) Business judgment rule—as long as director is acting in good faith s/he will not be liable for errors of judgment unless s/he is negligent

    (3) Directors are chargeable with knowledge of the affairs of the corporation

      (a) If director does not prevent (intentionally or negligently) wrongs of other directors, may be held liable

      (b) Normally may rely on reports of accountants, officers, etc. if reasonable judgment used

    (4) If corporation does not actually exist, then director as well as others in business have personal liability

  b. Directors liable for negligence if their action was the cause of the corporation's loss

    (1) Corporation may indemnify directors (also officers, employees, agents) against suits based on their duties for the corporation if acted in good faith and in best interests of corporation

      (a) Also applies to criminal actions if s/he reasonably believed that actions were lawful

    (2) Corporation may purchase liability insurance for officers and directors

      (a) Corporation pays premiums

      (b) Policies usually cover litigation costs as well as judgment or settlement costs

  c. Directors owe a fiduciary duty to the corporation

    (1) Owe fiduciary duties of loyalty, due care, and obedience to the corporation. These are the fiduciary duties of an agent. Even though individual directors are not considered agents of the corporation, directors owe the fiduciary duties of an agent.

    (2) Conflicts of interest

      (a) Transactions of a corporation with director(s) or other corporation in which director(s) has interest are valid as long as at least one of the following can be established

        (1) Conflict of interest is disclosed or known to board and majority of disinterested members approve of transaction

        (2) Conflict of interest is disclosed or known to shareholders and those entitled to vote approve it by a majority

        (3) Transaction is fair and reasonable to corporation

---

EXAMPLE

A plot of land already owned by a director is sold at the fair market value to the corporation. This contract is valid even without approval if the land is needed by the corporation.

d. Directors are personally liable for *ultra vires* acts of the corporation unless they specifically dissented on the record

e. Directors are personally liable to corporation for approving and paying dividends that are illegal

   (1) Directors who act in good faith may use defense of business judgment rule

4. Officers

   a. Typically operate day-to-day business

      (1) Delegated from directors

   b. An officer of the corporation is an agent and can bind corporation by his/her individual acts if within the scope of his/her authority as set forth in the bylaws

   c. Officers and directors may be the same persons

   d. Officers are selected by the directors for a fixed term under the bylaws

      (1) If a term is not definite, it is governed by the directors

   e. Officers have a fiduciary duty to corporation

   f. Courts recognize a fiduciary duty owed by majority shareholders to minority shareholders when the majority shareholders have de facto control over the corporation

5. Officers, like directors, are liable for own torts, even if committed while acting for corporation

   a. Corporation is also liable if officer was acting within the scope of his/her authority

6. Requirements of the Sarbanes-Oxley Act of 2002

   a. Requires all members of the audit committee of the board of directors to be independent and one must be a financial expert

   b. The audit committee must appoint, compensate, and oversee the work of the firm's public accounting firm

   c. The CEO and CFO must certify that the financial statements are fairly presented

   d. Prohibits officer or director from exerting improper influence on the conduct of the audit

   e. CEO and CFO must return compensation that was derived from misstated financial statements resulting from material noncompliance with the reporting requirements

NOW REVIEW MULTIPLE-CHOICE QUESTIONS 73 THROUGH 81

S. Stockholder's Rights

1. Right to transfer stock by endorsement and delivery or by separate assignment

   a. Stock certificates are negotiable instruments

   b. Limitations on transfer may be imposed, but they must be reasonable

      (1) UCC requires that any restrictions must be plainly printed on the certificate to be effective against third party

      (2) These limitations are most often imposed in closely held corporations

EXAMPLE

Existing shareholders of the corporation may have first option to buy.

2. Stockholder has no right to manage corporation unless s/he is also officer or director

   a. If stockholder is also an officer, the stockholder retains limited liability unlike limited partner who participates in management

3. Right to vote for election of directors, decision to dissolve the corporation, and any other fundamental corporate changes

   a. Governed by the charter and class of stock owned
   b. Annual meetings are required as specified in the bylaws
   c. Stockholders may have voting agreements that are enforceable which provide that they will vote a certain way on issues or vote for specified people for the board of directors
   d. Cumulative voting may be required (i.e., a person gets as many votes as s/he has shares times the number of directors being elected)

EXAMPLE

100 shares × 5 directors is 500 votes.

---

   (1) Gives minority shareholders an opportunity to get some representation by voting all shares for one or two directors

   e. Can vote by proxy—an assignment of voting rights
   f. Directors have the power to amend or repeal the bylaws unless reserved to the shareholders by the Articles of Incorporation
   g. Amendment of the Articles of Incorporation and approval of fundamental corporate changes such as a merger, consolidation, or sale of all assets generally require majority approval by shareholders

4. Right to dividends

   a. Shareholder generally has no right to dividends unless they are declared by the board of directors

      (1) Power to declare is discretionary based on the board's assessment of business needs

   b. Dividends become a liability of corporation only when declared

      (1) True for all types of stock such as common stock or even cumulative preferred stock

   c. Cash dividends may be paid out of unrestricted and unreserved earned surplus (retained earnings) unless corporation already is or will be insolvent because of dividend

      (1) Some states have other regulations, sometimes allowing reductions in other accounts, too
      (2) Under Model Business Corporation Act, dividends are prohibited that cause total liabilities to exceed total assets after effect of the distribution is considered. Dividends may not be declared if payment of same will cause the corporation to become insolvent.

5. Right of stockholders to inspect books and records exists

   a. These books and records include minute books, stock certificate books, stock ledgers, general account books
   b. Demand must be made in good faith and for a proper purpose

      (1) May get list of shareholders to help wage a proxy fight to attempt to control corporation
      (2) May not get list of shareholders or customers to use for business mailing list

6. Preemptive right

   a. This is the right to subscribe to new issues of stock (at fair market value) so that a stockholder's ownership will not be diluted without the opportunity to maintain it

---

EXAMPLE

A corporation has one class of common stock. Stockholder A owns 15%. A new issue of the same class of stock is to be made. Stockholder A has the right to buy 15% of it.

---

b. Usually only applies to common stock, not preferred

c. Not for treasury stock

d. There is no preemptive right to purchase stock unless Articles of Incorporation so provide; on the CPA exam the Examiners must tell you the shareholder has a preemptive right or it does not exist

7. Stockholder's right to sue

    a. Stockholder can sue in his/her own behalf where his/her interests have been directly injured, for example

        (1) Denial of right to inspect records

        (2) Denial of preemptive right if provided for

    b. Stockholders can sue on behalf of the corporation (i.e., a derivative suit)

        (1) In cases where a duty to the corporation is violated and corporation does not enforce, for example

            (a) Director violates his/her fiduciary duty to corporation

            (b) Illegal declaration of dividends (e.g., rendering corporation insolvent)

            (c) Fraud by officer on corporation

        (2) Unless demand would be futile, must first demand that directors sue in name of corporation and then may proceed if they refuse

            (a) Suit may be barred if directors make good faith business judgment that the suit is not in corporation's best interests

        (3) Damages go to corporation, not to the stockholders who sued; this is because the stockholders are suing on behalf of the injured corporation, not themselves.

8. Right to a pro rata share of distribution of assets on dissolution after creditors have been paid

---

> **NOW REVIEW MULTIPLE-CHOICE QUESTIONS 82 THROUGH 87**

T. Stockholder's Liability

1. Generally stockholder's liability is limited to his/her price paid for stock

2. May be liable to creditors for

    a. Original issue stock sold at below par value

        (1) Contingently liable for the difference between par value and original issuance price

    b. Unpaid balance on no-par stock

    c. Dividends paid which impair capital if the corporation is insolvent

3. Piercing the corporate veil—courts disregard corporate entity and hold stockholders personally liable

    a. Rarely happens but may occur if

        (1) Corporation used to perpetrate fraud (e.g., forming an undercapitalized corporation)

        (2) Owners/officers do not treat corporation as separate entity

        (3) Shareholders commingle assets, bank accounts, financial records with those of corporation

        (4) Corporate formalities not adhered to

4. Majority shareholders owe fiduciary duty to minority shareholders and to corporation

    a. Even shareholder who controls corporation (majority ownership not now needed) has fiduciary duty

---

> **NOW REVIEW MULTIPLE-CHOICE QUESTIONS 88 THROUGH 90**

U. Substantial Change in Corporate Structure

1. Merger

    a. Union of two corporations where one is absorbed by other

        (1) Surviving corporation issues its own shares (common and/or preferred) to shareholders of original corporations

2. Consolidation

    a. Joining of two (or more) corporations into a single new corporation
    b. All assets and liabilities are acquired by the new company
    c. New corporation is liable for debts of old corporations

3. Requirements to accomplish a merger or consolidation

    a. Boards of both corporations must prepare and submit plan to shareholders of both corporations
    b. Approval of board of directors of both companies

        (1) Exception for "short form" merger

            (a) parent corporation is acquiring subsidiary of which the parent owns 90% or more of the subsidiary
            (b) no vote required by either the parent or subsidiary shareholders

    c. Shareholders of both corporations must be given copy or summary of merger plan
    d. Majority vote of shareholders of each corporation
    e. Surviving corporation gets all assets and liabilities of merging corporations
    f. Dissatisfied shareholders of subsidiary may dissent and assert appraisal rights, thereby receiving the fair market value of their stock

4. Dissolution

    a. Once corporation is dissolved, it may do business only to wind up and liquidate business

        (1) Liquidation is the winding up of affairs and distribution of assets

            (a) Liquidation occurs in the following order

                (1) Expenses of liquidation and creditors
                (2) Preferred shareholders
                (3) Common shareholders

        (2) Termination occurs when winding up and liquidation are completed

    b. May be done by voluntary dissolution or involuntary dissolution by state for cause

        (1) Voluntary dissolution occurs when board of directors passes resolution to dissolve

            (a) Resolution must be ratified by majority of stockholders entitled to vote

    c. Shareholder may petition for judicial dissolution if directors or shareholders are deadlocked

5. Dissolution of a corporation requires the filing of a dissolution document with the state.
6. Stock purchases

    a. Where one corporation acquires a controlling interest in another corporation's stock.
    b. Not treated as a fundamental change; so

        (1) No resolution from the board of directors is needed.
        (2) No shareholder approval is needed.

NOW REVIEW MULTIPLE-CHOICE QUESTIONS 91 THROUGH 96

V. Subchapter S Corporation

1. When corporation elects to be Subchapter S corporation it can avoid double taxation by not paying tax at the corporate level

   a. Instead, the corporation income flows through to the income tax returns of the individual shareholders
   b. Shareholders report the income or loss even when income not distributed to them
   c. This flow-through may nevertheless be an advantage under some situations

2. Rules involving the criteria needed to be met to be taxed as a Subchapter S corporation can change to one's detriment, creating another potential disadvantage of needing to stay abreast of rule changes

   a. Some of the rules to watch out for involve

      (1) Corporation must be incorporated in the US and have only one class of stock
      (2) Number of shareholders Subchapter S corporation can have is limited to no more than 100 shareholders
      (3) Shareholders are limited to individuals, estates, qualified trusts, and similar entities
      (4) No foreign ownership of shares
      (5) The corporation cannot have excessive amounts of passive income

---

NOW REVIEW MULTIPLE-CHOICE QUESTION 97

KEY TERMS

Business judgment rule. Officers and/or directors of a corporation will not breach their fiduciary duty of care by simply making a poor business decision. Rather their action must be negligent to breach the duty of care.

C corporation. The assumed corporate form unless party affirmatively selects S corporation status. The typical form for large publically traded companies subject to double taxation. Generally, no personal liability for shareholders.

Derivative action. When a shareholder, or group of shareholders, sue, on behalf of the corporation a director or corporate officer for damages caused to the corporation.

Dissociation. When a partner is no longer affiliated with the partnership.

Dissolution. The process of ending a partnership.

General partnership. An association of two or more persons to carry on a business as co-owners for profit. Partners have unlimited personal liability.

Joint venture. An association of two or more persons/entities engaged in a business for a specific purpose.

Limited liability company (LLC). A business entity that is run primarily like a general partnership, but affords its members (owners) limited liability.

Limited liability partnership. A general partnership that affords its partners limited liability from the actions of the other partners.

Limited partner. In a limited partnership this partner has no personal liability; however, the limited partner is not allowed to participate in the running of the business.

Limited partnership. A partnership with two types of partners ; general and limited. General partners have unlimited liability; limited partners have no personal liability.

Partnership agreement. The rules by which a partnership is run. When a partnership agreement is silent about a particular rule, then the **Revised Uniform Partnership Act (RUPA)** will apply to the situation.

Partnership interest. The partner's right to profits. This is freely transferable. Contrast this with the ownership interest, the right to be a partner, which can only be transferred with the consent of all the other partners.

S-corporation. A type of corporation which must be affirmatively elected by the organizers. Taxed like a partnership, but the shareholders have no personal liability.

Sole proprietorship. One-owner business, owner has unlimited liability.

Ultra vires (Latin). An action that goes beyond the power or the authority of the corporation. Such actions violate the fiduciary duty of obedience.

Winding up. The liquidation of the partnership.

A. Nature of Sole Proprietorships

1. Which of the following statements is **not** true of a sole proprietorship?

  a. Federal and state governments typically require a formal filing with the appropriate government officials whether or not the sole proprietorship uses a fictitious name.
  b. The sole proprietorship is not a separate legal entity apart from its owner.
  c. The capital to start the business is generally limited to the funds the sole proprietor either has or can borrow.
  d. It is generally considered to be the simplest type of business structure.

B. Nature of Partnerships

2. A general partnership must

  a. Pay federal income tax.
  b. Have two or more partners.
  c. Have written articles of partnership.
  d. Provide for apportionment of liability for partnership debts.

3. Which of the following can be a partnership?

  a. Karen and Sharon form a charitable organization in which they received donations to give to their favorite charities.
  b. Frank and Pablo are members of a union at work that has 150 members.
  c. Janice and Stanley form a club to encourage business contacts for computer programmers.
  d. None of the above.

4. A silent partner in a general partnership

  a. Helps manage the partnership without letting those outside the partnership know this.
  b. Retains unlimited liability for the debts of the partnership.
  c. Both of the above are correct.
  d. None of the above is correct.

C. Formation of Partnership

5. A partnership agreement must be in writing if

  a. Any partner contributes more than $500 in capital.
  b. The partners reside in different states.
  c. The partnership intends to own real estate.
  d. The partnership's purpose **cannot** be completed within one year of formation.

D. Partner's Rights and Operation of Partnership

6. Sydney, Bailey, and Calle form a partnership under the Revised Uniform Partnership Act. During the first year of operation, the partners have fundamental questions regarding the rights and obligations of the partnership as well as the individual partners. Which of the following questions can correctly be answered in the affirmative?

  I. Is the partnership allowed legally to own property in the partnership's name?
 II. Do the partners have joint and several liability for breaches of contract of the partnership?
III. Do the partners have joint and several liability for tort actions against the partnership?

  a. I only.
  b. I and II only.
  c. II and III only.
  d. I, II, and III.

7. Which of the following is **not** true of a general partnership?

  a. Ownership by the partners may be unequal.
  b. It is a separate legal entity.
  c. An important characteristic is that the partners share in the profits equally.
  d. The partner may agree on unequal rights to participate in management.

8. The partnership agreement for Owen Associates, a general partnership, provided that profits be paid to the partners in the ratio of their financial contribution to the partnership. Moore contributed $10,000, Noon contributed $30,000, and Kale contributed $50,000. For the year ended December 31, 2012, Owen had losses of $180,000. What amount of the losses should be allocated to Kale?

  a. $40,000
  b. $60,000
  c. $90,000
  d. $100,000

9. Lark, a partner in DSJ, a general partnership, wishes to withdraw from the partnership and sell Lark's interest to Ward. All of the other partners in DSJ have agreed to admit Ward as a partner and to hold Lark harmless for the past, present, and future liabilities of DSJ. As a result of Lark's withdrawal and Ward's admission to the partnership, Ward

  a. Acquired only the right to receive Ward's share of DSJ profits.
  b. Has the right to participate in DSJ's management.
  c. Is personally liable for partnership liabilities arising before and after being admitted as a partner.
  d. Must contribute cash or property to DSJ to be admitted with the same rights as the other partners.

10. Cobb, Inc., a partner in TLC Partnership, assigns its partnership interest to Bean, who is **not** made a partner. After the assignment, Bean asserts the rights to

I. Participate in the management of TLC.
II. Cobb's share of TLC's partnership profits.
Bean is correct as to which of these rights?

a. I only.
b. II only.
c. I and II.
d. Neither I nor II.

E. Relationship to Third Parties

11. The apparent authority of a partner to bind the partnership in dealing with third parties

a. Will be effectively limited by a formal resolution of the partners of which third parties are aware.
b. Will be effectively limited by a formal resolution of the partners of which third parties are unaware.
c. Would permit a partner to submit a claim against the partnership to arbitration.
d. Must be derived from the express powers and purposes contained in the partnership agreement.

12. In a general partnership, which of the following acts must be approved by all the partners?

a. Dissolution of the partnership.
b. Admission of a partner.
c. Authorization of a partnership capital expenditure.
d. Hiring an employee.

13. Under the Revised Uniform Partnership Act, partners have joint and several liability for

a. Breaches of contract.
b. Torts committed by one of the partners within the scope of the partnership.
c. Both of the above.
d. None of the above.

14. Which of the following actions require(s) unanimous consent of the partners under partnership law?

I. Making partnership a surety.
II. Admission of a new partner.

a. I only.
b. II only.
c. Both I and II.
d. Neither I nor II.

15. Which of the following statements **best** describes the effect of the assignment of an interest in a general partnership?

a. The assignee becomes a partner.
b. The assignee is responsible for a proportionate share of past and future partnership debts.
c. The assignment automatically dissolves the partnership.
d. The assignment transfers the assignor's interest in partnership profits and surplus.

F. Termination of a Partnership

16. Under the Revised Uniform Partnership Act, in which of the following cases will property be deemed to be partnership property?

I. A partner acquires property in the partnership name.
II. A partner acquires title to it in his/her own name using partnership funds.
III. Property owned previously by a partner is used in the partnership business.

a. I only.
b. I and II only.
c. II only.
d. I, II, and III.

17. Wind, who has been a partner in the PLW general partnership for four years, decides to withdraw from the partnership despite a written partnership agreement that states, "no partner may withdraw for a period of five years." Under the Uniform Partnership Act, what is the result of Wind's withdrawal?

a. Wind's withdrawal causes a dissolution of the partnership by operation of law.
b. Wind's withdrawal has **no** bearing on the continued operation of the partnership by the remaining partners.
c. Wind's withdrawal is **not** effective until Wind obtains a court-ordered decree of dissolution.
d. Wind's withdrawal causes a dissolution of the partnership despite being in violation of the partnership agreement.

18. Dowd, Elgar, Frost, and Grant formed a general partnership. Their written partnership agreement provided that the profits would be divided so that Dowd would receive 40%; Elgar, 30%; Frost, 20%; and Grant, 10%. There was no provision for allocating losses. At the end of its first year, the partnership had losses of $200,000. Before allocating losses, the partners' capital account balances were: Dowd, $120,000; Elgar, $100,000; Frost, $75,000; and Grant, $11,000. Grant refuses to make any further contributions to the partnership. Ignore the effects of federal partnership tax law.

After losses were allocated to the partners' capital accounts and all liabilities were paid, the partnership's sole asset was $106,000 in cash. How much would Elgar receive on dissolution of the partnership?

a. $37,000
b. $40,000
c. $47,500
d. $50,000

G. Limited Partnerships

19. Which of the following statements is correct with respect to a limited partnership?

a. A limited partner may not be an unsecured creditor of the limited partnership.
b. A general partner may not also be a limited partner at the same time.

c. A general partner may be a secured creditor of the limited partnership.

d. A limited partnership can be formed with limited liability for all partners.

20. Sharif, Hirsch, and Wolff formed a limited partnership with Sharif and Hirsch as general partners. Wolff was the limited partner. They failed to agree upon a profit-sharing plan but put in capital contributions of $120,000, $140,000, and $150,000, respectively. At the end of the first year how should they divide the profits?

    a. Sharif and Hirsch each receives half and Wolff receives none.

    b. Each of the three partners receives one-third.

    c. The profits are shared in proportion to their capital contribution.

    d. None of the above.

21. Which of the following is (are) true of a limited partnership?

I. Limited partnerships must have at least one general partner.
II. The death of a limited partner terminates the partnership.

    a. I only.

    b. II only.

    c. Neither I nor II.

    d. Both I and II.

22. Alchorn, Black, and Chan formed a limited partnership with Chan becoming the only limited partner. Capital contributions from these partners were $20,000, $40,000, and $50,000, respectively. Chan, however, helped in the management of the partnership and Ham, who had several contracts with the partnership, thought Chan was a general partner. Ham won several breach of contract actions against the partnership and the partnership does not have sufficient funds to pay these claims. What is the potential liability for Alchorn, Black, and Chan?

    a. Unlimited liability for all three partners.

    b. Unlimited liability for Alchorn and Black; $50,000 for Chan.

    c. Up to each partner's capital contribution.

    d. None of the above.

23. To create a limited partnership, a certificate of limited partnership must be filed with the Secretary of State. Which of the following must be included in this certificate under the Revised Uniform Limited Partnership Act?

I. Names of all of the general partners.
II. Names of the majority of the general partners.
III. Names of all of the limited partners.
IV. Names of the majority of the limited partners.

    a. I only.

    b. II only.

    c. I and III only.

    d. I and IV only.

24. Mandy is a limited partner in a limited partnership in which Strasburg and Hua are the general partners. Which of the following may Mandy do without losing limited liability protection?

I. Mandy acts as an agent of the limited partnership.
II. Mandy votes to remove Strasburg as a general partner.

    a. I only.

    b. II only.

    c. Both I and II.

    d. Neither I nor II.

25. In a limited partnership, the limited partners' capital contribution may be in which of the following forms?

    a. A promise to perform services in the future for the partnership.

    b. An agreement to pay cash.

    c. A promise to give property.

    d. All of the above.

26. Hart and Grant formed Hart Limited Partnership. Hart put in a capital contribution of $20,000 and became a general partner. Grant put in a capital contribution of $10,000 and became a limited partner. During the second year of operation, a third party filed a tort action against the partnership and both partners. What is the potential liability of Hart and Grant respectively?

    a. $20,000 and $0.

    b. $20,000 and $10,000.

    c. Unlimited liability and $0.

    d. Unlimited liability and $10,000.

27. The admission of a new general partner to a limited partnership requires approval by

I. A majority of the general partners.
II. All of the general partners.
III. A majority of the limited partners.
IV. All of the limited partners.

    a. I only.

    b. II only.

    c. I and III only.

    d. II and IV only.

28. The admission of a new limited partner to a limited partnership requires approval by

I. A majority of the general partners.
II. All of the general partners.
III. A majority of the limited partners.
IV. All of the limited partners.

    a. I only.

    b. II only.

    c. I and III only.

    d. II and IV only.

29. Riewerts, Morgan and Stonk form a limited partnership. Riewerts is the one general partner. Which of the following events will cause this limited partnership to be dissolved?

I. Riewerts dies and is survived by the other two partners.
II. Morgan dies leaving Riewerts and Stonk.
III. Riewerts takes out personal bankruptcy.
IV. Stonk takes out personal bankruptcy.

    a. I only.

    b. I and II only.

    c. I and III only.

    d. III and IV only.

H.　Joint Ventures

30.　Which of the following is **not** true of a joint venture?

a.　Each joint venturer is personally liable for the debts of a joint venture.

b.　Each joint venturer has the right to participate in the management of the joint venture.

c.　The joint venturers owe each other fiduciary duties.

d.　Death of a joint venturer dissolves the joint venture.

I.　Limited Liability Companies (LLC)

31.　Which form(s) of a business organization can have characteristics common to both the corporation and the general partnership?

	Limited liability company	Subchapter S corporation
a.	Yes	Yes
b.	Yes	No
c.	No	Yes
d.	No	No

32.　Which of the following is true of a limited liability company under the laws of the majority of states?

a.　At least one of the owners must have personal liability.

b.　The limited liability company is a separate legal entity apart from its owners.

c.　Limited liability of the owners is lost if they fail to follow the usual formalities in conducting the business.

d.　All of the above are true.

33.　Which of the following is **not** characteristic of the typical limited liability company?

a.　Death of a member (owner) causes it to dissolve unless the remaining members decide to continue the business.

b.　All members (owners) are allowed by law to participate in the management of the firm.

c.　The company has, legally, a perpetual existence.

d.　All members (owners) have limited liability.

34.　Owners and managers of a limited liability company (LLC) owe

a.　A duty of due care.

b.　A duty of loyalty.

c.　Both a duty of due care and a duty of loyalty.

d.　None of the above.

35.　Which of the following is true of the typical limited liability company?

a.　It provides for limited liability for some of its members (owners), that is, those identified as limited members (owners).

b.　The members' (owners') interests are not freely transferable.

c.　Voting members (owners) but not all members can help choose the managers of the company.

d.　No formalities are required for its formation.

J.　Limited Liability Partnerships (LLP)

36.　In which of the following respects do general partnerships and limited liability partnerships **differ**?

I.　In the level of liability of the partners for torts they themselves commit.

II.　In the level of liability of the partners for torts committed by other partners in the same firm.

III.　In the amount of liability of the partners for contracts signed by other partners on behalf of the partnership.

a.　I only.

b.　II only.

c.　I and II only.

d.　II and III only.

K.　Subchapter C Corporations

37.　Under the federal Subchapter S Revision Act, all corporations are designated as

a.　Subchapter S corporations only.

b.　Either a Subchapter S corporation or a Subchapter C corporation.

c.　One of seven different types of corporations.

d.　Both a Subchapter S corporation and a Subchapter C corporation at the same time.

38.　Under the federal Subchapter S Revision Act all corporations are

a.　Now treated as Subchapter S corporations.

b.　Divided into either a Subchapter C corporation or a Subchapter S corporation.

c.　Divided into either a Subchapter C corporation, a Subchapter E corporation, or a Subchapter S corporation.

d.　None of the above.

39.　Which of the following statements is (are) true?

a.　Both Subchapter C corporations and Subchapter S corporations have limited liability for their shareholders.

b.　Both Subchapter C corporations and Subchapter S corporations are similar in their corporate management structure.

c.　All of the above are true.

d.　None of the above are true.

40.　The main difference between Subchapter S corporations and Subchapter C corporations is

a.　Their tax treatment.

b.　That the federal Subchapter S Revision Act covers Subchapter S corporations but does not cover Subchapter C corporations.

c.　Their limited liability of their shareholders.

d.　Their structure of their corporate management.

L.　Characteristics and Advantages of Corporate Form

41.　Which of the following statements **best** describes an advantage of the corporate form of doing business?

a. Day-to-day management is strictly the responsibility of the directors.
b. Ownership is contractually restricted and is **not** transferable.
c. The operation of the business may continue indefinitely.
d. The business is free from state regulation.

42. Which of the following is **not** considered to be an advantage of the corporate form of doing business over the partnership form?

   a. A potential perpetual and continuous life.
   b. The interests in the corporation are typically easily transferable.
   c. The managers in the corporation and shareholders have limited liability.
   d. Persons who manage the corporation are not necessarily shareholders.

43. Which of the following is **not** a characteristic of a corporation?

   a. It has a continuous life.
   b. Shares in the corporation can normally be freely transferred.
   c. A corporation is treated as a legal entity separate from its shareholders.
   d. A corporation is automatically terminated upon the death of a majority of its shareholders.

44. A corporation as a separate legal entity can do which of the following?

   a. Contract in its own name with its own shareholders.
   b. Contract in its own name with its own shareholders only if a majority of its shareholders agree that such a contract can be made.
   c. Contract in its own name with third parties.
   d. Both a. and c. are correct.

45. Which of the following are characteristics of the corporate form of doing business?

   a. Persons who manage corporations need not be shareholders.
   b. The corporation may convey or hold property in its own name.
   c. The corporation can sue or be sued in its own name.
   d. All of the above are true.

M. Disadvantages of Corporate Business Structure

46. Which of the following is a disadvantage of a Subchapter C corporation?

   a. It may face higher tax burdens than a Subchapter S corporation.
   b. The shareholders lose their limited liability when they switch from a general partnership to a corporation.
   c. A Subchapter C corporation is not well defined under the law.

d. A Subchapter C corporation does not protect its shareholders from liability as well as a Subchapter S corporation does.

N. Types of Corporations

47. Bond Company is incorporated in Florida but not in Georgia. Bond has branch offices in both states. Which of the following is correct?

I. Bond is a domestic corporation in Georgia.
II. Bond is a domestic corporation in Florida.
III. Bond needs to incorporate also in Georgia.

   a. I and II only.
   b. II only.
   c. II and III only.
   d. I, II, and III.

48. Colby formed a professional corporation along with two other attorneys. They took out loans in the name of the corporation. During the first year, Colby failed to file some papers on time for a client causing the client to lose a very good case. For which does Colby have the corporate protection of limited liability?

I. The negligence for failure to file the papers on time.
II. The corporate loans.

   a. I only.
   b. II only.
   c. Both I and II.
   d. Neither I nor II.

49. Macro Corporation was incorporated and doing business in Illinois. It is doing business in various other states including Nevada. Which of the following statements is (are) true?

   a. Macro must incorporate in Nevada.
   b. Macro is a domestic corporation in Nevada.
   c. Macro is a domestic corporation in Illinois.
   d. All of the above are true.

50. Cleanit Corporation was incorporated in Colorado. Cleanit wishes to perform some transactions in other states but does not want to incorporate or obtain a certificate of authority to qualify to do business in those other states. Which of the following normally would require Cleanit to obtain a certificate of authority in other states?

   a. Using the US mail to solicit orders in those states.
   b. Holding bank accounts in those states.
   c. Collecting debts in those states.
   d. None of the above.

51. Which of the following statements is true of professional corporations under the various state laws?

I. The professionals in the corporation have personal liability for their professional acts.
II. Normally under state laws, only licensed professionals are permitted to own shares in professional corporations.

   a. I only is true.
   b. II only is true.

c. Both I and II are true.
d. Neither I nor II is true.

O. Formation of Corporation

52. Which of the following statements is correct with respect to the differences and similarities between a corporation and a limited partnership?

a. Stockholders may be entitled to vote on corporate matters but limited partners are prohibited from voting on any partnership matters.
b. Stock of a corporation may be subject to the registration requirements of the federal securities laws but limited partnership interests are automatically exempt from those requirements.
c. Directors owe fiduciary duties to the corporation and limited partners owe such duties to the partnership.
d. A corporation and a limited partnership may be created only under a state statute and each must file a copy of its organizational document with the proper governmental body.

53. Under the Revised Model Business Corporation Act, which of the following must be contained in a corporation's Articles of Incorporation?

a. Quorum voting requirements.
b. Names of stockholders.
c. Provisions for issuance of par and nonpar shares.
d. The number of shares the corporation is authorized to issue.

54. Which of the following facts is (are) generally included in a corporation's Articles of Incorporation?

	Name of registered agent	Number of authorized shares
a.	Yes	Yes
b.	Yes	No
c.	No	Yes
d.	No	No

55. Absent a specific provision in its Articles of Incorporation, a corporation's board of directors has the power to do all of the following, **except**

a. Repeal the bylaws.
b. Declare dividends.
c. Fix compensation of directors.
d. Amend the Articles of Incorporation.

56. Which of the following statements is correct concerning the similarities between a limited partnership and a corporation?

a. Each is created under a statute and must file a copy of its certificate with the proper state authorities.
b. All corporate stockholders and all partners in a limited partnership have limited liability.
c. Both are recognized for federal income tax purposes as taxable entities.

d. Both are allowed statutorily to have perpetual existence.

57. Promoters of a corporation which is **not** yet in existence

a. Are persons that form the corporation and arrange for capitalization to help begin the corporation.
b. Are agents of the corporation.
c. Can bind the future corporation to presently made contracts they make for the future corporation.
d. Are shielded from personal liability on contracts they make with third parties on behalf of the future corporation.

P. Corporate Financial Structure

58. Johns owns 400 shares of Abco Corp. cumulative preferred stock. In the absence of any specific contrary provisions in Abco's Articles of Incorporation, which of the following statements is correct?

a. Johns is entitled to convert the 400 shares of preferred stock to a like number of shares of common stock.
b. If Abco declares a cash dividend on its preferred stock, Johns becomes an unsecured creditor of Abco.
c. If Abco declares a dividend on its common stock, Johns will be entitled to participate with the common stock shareholders in any dividend distribution made after preferred dividends are paid.
d. Johns will be entitled to vote if dividend payments are in arrears.

59. Gallagher Corporation issued 100,000 shares of $40 par value stock for $50 per share to various investors. Subsequently, Gallagher purchased back 10,000 of those shares for $30 per share and held them as treasury stock. When the price of the stock recovered somewhat, Gallagher sold this treasury stock to Thomas for $35 per share. Which of the following statements is correct?

I. Gallagher's purchase of the stock at below par value is illegal.
II. Gallagher's purchase of the stock at below par value is void as an ultra vires act.
III. Gallagher's resale of the treasury stock at below par value is valid.

a. I only.
b. II only.
c. III only.
d. I and II only.

60. An owner of common stock will **not** have any liability beyond actual investment if the owner

a. Paid less than par value for stock purchased in connection with an original issue of shares.
b. Agreed to perform services that were worth less than par value for the corporation in exchange for original issue par value shares.
c. Purchased treasury shares for less than par value.
d. Failed to pay the full amount owed on a subscription contract for no-par shares.

61. Which of the following securities are corporate debt securities?

	Convertible bonds	Debenture bonds	Warrants
a.	Yes	Yes	Yes
b.	Yes	No	Yes
c.	Yes	Yes	No
d.	No	Yes	Yes

62. All of the following distributions to stockholders are considered asset or capital distributions, **except**

    a. Liquidating dividends.
    b. Stock splits.
    c. Property distributions.
    d. Cash dividends.

63. Which of the following constitute(s) valid consideration or value to purchase shares of stock?

    a. Services performed.
    b. Intangible property.
    c. Services contracted to be performed in the future.
    d. All of the above.

64. Brawn subscribed to 1,000 shares of $1 par value stock of Caldo Corporation at the agreed amount of $20 per share. She paid $5,000 on April 1 and then paid $9,000 on August 1. Caldo Corporation filed for bankruptcy on December 1 and the creditors of the corporation sought to hold Brawn liable under her subscription agreement. Which of the following is true?

    a. Brawn has no liability to the creditors because subscription contract was with the corporation, not the creditors.
    b. Brawn has no liability to the creditors because she has paid more than $1,000 to the corporation which is the par value of the 1,000 shares.
    c. Brawn is liable for $6,000 to the creditors for the amount unpaid on the subscription price.
    d. Brawn is liable for $6,000 to the creditors based on the doctrine of ultra vires.

65. Pearl Corporation has some treasury stock on hand. Which of the following is (are) true?

    a. Pearl may not vote these shares of treasury stock.
    b. Pearl's treasury stock does not receive any dividends.
    c. Both of the above statements are true.
    d. None of the above statements are true.

66. Treasury stock of a corporation is stock that

    a. Has been issued by that corporation but is not outstanding.
    b. Was purchased from another corporation and is retained for a specified purpose.
    c. Has been cancelled.
    d. None of the above is true.

67. By law, a corporation

    a. Must issue both common stock and preferred stock.
    b. May issue more than one class of common stock as well as more than one class of preferred stock.

    c. Must issue dividends if it has earned a profit.
    d. Must issue at least some cumulative preferred stock.

68. Mesa Corporation is planning on issuing some debt securities. Which of the following statements is true?

    a. The holders of debt securities are owners of the corporation.
    b. A bond is an instrument for long-term secured debt.
    c. A debenture is an instrument for long-term secured debt.
    d. None of the above is true.

69. Stock of a corporation is called watered stock when the cash or property exchanged to acquire the stock is

    a. Less than the market value of the stock.
    b. More than the market value of the stock.
    c. Less than the par value or stated value of the stock.
    d. More than the par value or stated value of the stock.

Q. *Powers and Liabilities of Corporation*

70. Corporations generally have which of the following powers without shareholder approval?

  I. Power to acquire their own shares.
  II. Power to make charitable contributions.
  III. Power to make loans to directors.

    a. I only.
    b. I and II only.
    c. II and III only.
    d. I, II, and III.

71. Murphy is an employee of Landtry Corporation. Which of the following acts would make the corporation liable for Murphy's actions?

  I. Murphy deceived a customer to convince him to purchase one of Landtry's products.
  II. Murphy hit a customer with his fist, breaking his jaw. The management had warned Murphy that he and not the corporation would be responsible for any aggression against customers.

    a. I only.
    b. II only.
    c. Both I and II.
    d. Neither I nor II.

72. Which of the following statements is (are) true?

  I. Corporations can be found liable for crimes.
  II. Directors can face prison sentences for crimes committed by their corporations.
  III. Employees can be found guilty of crimes they commit while working for their corporation.

    a. I only.
    b. I and II only.
    c. III only.
    d. I, II, and III.

R. Directors and Officers of Corporations

73. Norwood was a promoter of Parker Corporation. On March 15, Norwood purchased some real estate from Burrows in Parker's name and signed the contract "Norwood, as agent of Parker Corporation." Parker Corporation, however, did not legally come into existence until June 10. Norwood never informed Burrows on or before March 15 that Parker Corporation was not yet formed. After the corporation was formed, the board of directors refused to adopt the preincorporation contract made by Norwood concerning the real estate deal with Burrows. Burrows sued Parker, Norwood, and the board of directors. Which of the following is correct?

   a. None of these parties can be held liable.
   b. Norwood only is liable.
   c. Norwood and Parker are liable but not the board of directors.
   d. Norwood, Parker, and the board of directors are all liable.

74. Under the Revised Model Business Corporation Act, which of the following statements is correct regarding corporate officers of a public corporation?

   a. An officer may **not** simultaneously serve as a director.
   b. A corporation may be authorized to indemnify its officers for liability incurred in a suit by stockholders.
   c. Stockholders always have the right to elect a corporation's officers.
   d. An officer of a corporation is required to own at least one share of the corporation's stock.

75. The officers of West Corporation wish to buy some used equipment for West Corporation. The used equipment is actually owned by Parks, a director of West Corporation. For this transaction to **not** be a conflict of interest for Parks, which of the following is (are) required to be true?

  I. Parks sells the used equipment to West Corporation in a contract that is fair and reasonable to the corporation.
  II. Parks' ownership of the used equipment is disclosed to the shareholders of West who approve it by majority vote.
  III. Parks' ownership of the used equipment is disclosed to the board of directors, who approve it by a majority vote of the disinterested directors.

   a. Any one of I, II, or III.
   b. I and II are both required.
   c. I and III are both required.
   d. All three of I, II, and III are required.

76. The following are two statements concerning a fiduciary duty in a corporation.

  I. Officers and directors of a corporation owe a fiduciary duty to that corporation.
  II. Majority shareholders of a corporation can owe a fiduciary duty to the minority shareholders.
   Which of the statements is (are) correct?

   a. I only.
   b. II only.
   c. Both I and II.
   d. Neither I nor II.

77. Hogan is a director of a large corporation. Hogan owns a piece of land that the corporation wishes to purchase and Hogan desires to sell this land at the fair market price. If he sells the land to the corporation, has he breached any fiduciary duty?

   a. No, a director does not owe a fiduciary duty to his corporation.
   b. No, since Hogan is selling the land to his corporation in a fair and reasonable contract.
   c. Yes, unless he discloses his conflict of interest to the shareholders who must then approve the sale of by a simple majority.
   d. Yes, unless he discloses his conflict of interest to the shareholders who must then approve the sale by a two-thirds vote.

78. Which of the following is **not** a power of the board of directors?

   a. May select the officers of the corporation.
   b. May declare the dividends to be paid to the shareholders.
   c. May amend the Articles of Incorporation.
   d. All of the above are powers of the board of directors.

79. Which of the following statements is (are) true under the law affecting corporations?

  I. A corporation may indemnify directors against lawsuits based on their good-faith actions for the corporation.
  II. A corporation may indemnify officers against lawsuits based on their good-faith actions for the corporation.
  III. A corporation is allowed to purchase liability insurance for its directors.

   a. I only.
   b. I and II only.
   c. I and III only.
   d. I, II, and III.

80. Which of the following is (are) true concerning corporations?

   a. Directors owe a fiduciary duty to the corporation.
   b. Officers owe a fiduciary duty to the corporation.
   c. Both of the above are true.
   d. None of the above are true.

81. McGarry is an officer of Norton Corporation. McGarry has committed a tort while acting for Norton Corporation within the scope of her authority. Which of the following is (are) true?

   a. Only McGarry is liable for the tort committed.
   b. Only Norton Corporation is liable for the tort committed.
   c. Both McGarry and Norton are liable for the tort committed.
   d. Neither McGarry nor Norton are liable for the tort committed.

S. Stockholders' Rights

82. Acorn Corp. wants to acquire the entire business of Trend Corp. Which of the following methods of business combination will **best** satisfy Acorn's objectives without requiring the approval of the shareholders of either corporation?

 a. A merger of Trend into Acorn, whereby Trend shareholders receive cash or Acorn shares.
 b. A sale of all the assets of Trend, outside the regular course of business, to Acorn for cash.
 c. An acquisition of all the shares of Trend through a compulsory share exchange for Acorn shares.
 d. A cash tender offer, whereby Acorn acquires at least 90% of Trend's shares, followed by a short-form merger of Trend into Acorn.

83. Price owns 2,000 shares of Universal Corp.'s $10 cumulative preferred stock. During its first year of operations, cash dividends of $5 per share were declared on the preferred stock but were never paid. In the second year, dividends on the preferred stock were neither declared nor paid. If Universal is dissolved, which of the following statements is correct?

 a. Universal will be liable to Price as an unsecured creditor for $10,000.
 b. Universal will be liable to Price as a secured creditor for $20,000.
 c. Price will have priority over the claims of Universal's bond owners.
 d. Price will have priority over the claims of Universal's unsecured judgment creditors.

84. Under the Revised Model Business Corporation Act, when a corporation's Articles of Incorporation grant stockholders preemptive rights, which of the following rights is (are) included in that grant?

	The right to purchase a proportionate share of a newly issued stock	The right to a proportionate share of corporate assets remaining on corporate dissolution
a.	Yes	Yes
b.	Yes	No
c.	No	Yes
d.	No	No

85. Under the Revised Model Business Corporation Act, which of the following actions by a corporation would entitle a stockholder to dissent from the action and obtain payment of the fair value of his/her shares?

I. An amendment to the articles of incorporation that materially and adversely affects rights in respect of a dissenter's shares because it alters or abolishes a preferential right of the shares.
II. Consummation of a plan of share exchange to which the corporation is a party as the corporation whose shares will be acquired, if the stockholder is entitled to vote on the plan.

 a. I only.
 b. II only.
 c. Both I and II.
 d. Neither I nor II.

86. To which of the following rights is a stockholder of a public corporation entitled?

 a. The right to have annual dividends declared and paid.
 b. The right to vote for the election of officers.
 c. The right to a reasonable inspection of corporate records.
 d. The right to have the corporation issue a new class of stock.

87. Which of the following is correct pertaining to the rights of stockholders in a corporation?

 a. Stockholders have no right to manage their corporation unless they are also directors or officers.
 b. Stockholders have a right to receive dividends.
 c. Stockholders have no right to inspect the books and records of their corporation.
 d. Stockholders have a right to get a list of their corporation's customers to use for the stockholder's personal business mailing list.

T. Stockholders' Liability

88. The limited liability of a stockholder in a closely held corporation may be challenged successfully if the stockholder

 a. Undercapitalized the corporation when it was formed.
 b. Formed the corporation solely to have limited personal liability.
 c. Sold property to the corporation.
 d. Was a corporate officer, director, or employee.

89. The corporate veil is **most** likely to be pierced and the shareholders held personally liable if

 a. The corporation has elected S corporation status under the Internal Revenue Code.
 b. The shareholders have commingled their personal funds with those of the corporation.
 c. An ultra vires act has been committed.
 d. A partnership incorporates its business solely to limit the liability of its partners.

90. Which of the following is correct about the law of corporations?

 a. Each shareholder owes a fiduciary duty to his or her corporation.
 b. Majority shareholders owe a fiduciary duty to their corporation.
 c. Majority shareholders do not owe a fiduciary duty to minority shareholders.
 d. All of the above are correct.

U. Substantial Change in Corporate Structure

91. A parent corporation owned more than 90% of each class of the outstanding stock issued by a subsidiary corporation and decided to merge that subsidiary into itself. Under the Revised Model Business Corporation Act, which of the following actions must be taken?

a. The subsidiary corporation's board of directors must pass a merger resolution.
b. The subsidiary corporation's dissenting stockholders must be given an appraisal remedy.
c. The parent corporation's stockholders must approve the merger.
d. The parent corporation's dissenting stockholders must be given an appraisal remedy.

92. Under the Revised Model Business Corporation Act, a merger of two public corporations usually requires all of the following **except**

a. A formal plan of merger.
b. An affirmative vote by the holders of a majority of each corporation's voting shares.
c. Receipt of voting stock by all stockholders of the original corporations.
d. Approval by the board of directors of each corporation.

93. Which of the following statements is a general requirement for the merger of two corporations?

a. The merger plan must be approved unanimously by the stockholders of both corporations.
b. The merger plan must be approved unanimously by the boards of both corporations.
c. The absorbed corporation must amend its articles of incorporation.
d. The stockholders of both corporations must be given due notice of a special meeting, including a copy or summary of the merger plan.

94. Which of the following must take place for a corporation to be voluntarily dissolved?

a. Passage by the board of directors of a resolution to dissolve.
b. Approval by the officers of a resolution to dissolve.
c. Amendment of the certificate of incorporation.
d. Unanimous vote of the stockholders.

95. A corporate stockholder is entitled to which of the following rights?

a. Elect officers.
b. Receive annual dividends.
c. Approve dissolution.
d. Prevent corporate borrowing.

96. When a consolidation takes place under the law of corporations, which of the following is true?

a. Two or more corporations are joined into one new corporation.
b. All assets are acquired by the new corporation.
c. The new corporation is liable for the debts of each of the old corporations.
d. All of the above are true.

V. Subchapter S Corporation

97. When a corporation elects to be a Subchapter S corporation, which of the following statements is (are) true regarding the federal tax treatment of the corporation's income or loss?

  I. The corporation's income is taxed at the corporate level and not the shareholders' level.
 II. The shareholders report the corporation's income on their tax returns when the income is distributed to them.
III. The shareholders report the corporation's income on their tax returns even if the income is not distributed to them.
IV. The shareholders generally report the corporation's loss on their tax returns.

a. I only is true.
b. II only is true.
c. III only is true.
d. III and IV only are true.

Multiple-Choice Answers and Explanations

Answers

1.	a	__ __	21.	a	__ __	41.	c	__ __	61.	c	__ __	81.	c	__ __
2.	b	__ __	22.	a	__ __	42.	c	__ __	62.	b	__ __	82.	d	__ __
3.	d	__ __	23.	a	__ . __	43.	d	__ __	63.	d	__ __	83.	a	__ __
4.	b	__ __	24.	c	__ __	44.	d	__ __	64.	c	__ __	84.	b	__ __
5.	d	__ __	25.	d	__ __	45.	d	__ __	65.	c	__ __	85.	c	__ __
6.	d	__ __	26.	d	__ __	46.	a	__ __	66.	a	__ __	86.	c	__ __
7.	c	__ __	27.	d	__ __	47.	b	__ __	67.	b	__ __	87.	a	__ __
8.	d	__ __	28.	d	__ __	48.	b	__ __	68.	b	__ __	88.	a	__ __
9.	b	__ __	29.	c	__ __	49.	c	__ __	69.	c	__ __	89.	b	__ __
10.	b	__ __	30.	d	__ __	50.	d	__ __	70.	b	__ __	90.	b	__ __
11.	a	__ __	31.	a	__ __	51.	c	__ __	71.	c	__ __	91.	b	__ __
12.	b	__ __	32.	b	__ __	52.	d	__ __	72.	d	__ __	92.	c	__ __
13.	c	__ __	33.	c	__ __	53.	d	__ __	73.	b	__ __	93.	d	__ __
14.	c	__ __	34.	c	__ __	54.	a	__ __	74.	b	__ __	94.	a	__ __
15.	d	__ __	35.	b	__ __	55.	d	__ __	75.	a	__ __	95.	c	__ __
16.	b	__ __	36.	d	__ __	56.	a	__ __	76.	c	__ __	96.	d	__ __
17.	d	__ __	37.	b	__ __	57.	a	__ __	77.	b	__ __	97.	d	__ __
18.	a	__ __	38.	b	__ __	58.	b	__ __	78.	c	__ __			
19.	c	__ __	39.	c	__ __	59.	c	__ __	79.	d	__ __	1st:	__/97 = __%
20.	c	__ __	40.	a	__ __	60.	c	__ __	80.	c	__ __	2nd:	__/97 = __%

Explanations

1. (a) Federal or state governments do not typically require any formal filing. If the business operates under a name different from that of the sole proprietor, most states require that a fictitious name statement be filed. Answer (b) is incorrect because the sole proprietorship and the sole proprietor are not separate legal entities. Answer (c) is incorrect because a sole proprietor does not have partners or shareholders from whom to obtain capital. Answer (d) is incorrect because the simplicity of this business structure is one of its advantages in its formation and operation.

2. (b) A general partnership is an association of two or more persons to carry on a business as co-owners for profit. There must be at least two partners involved in order for a partnership to exist. Answer (a) is incorrect because a general partnership is normally not recognized as a taxable entity under federal income tax laws. Answer (c) is incorrect because execution of written articles of partnership is not required to create a general partnership. A partnership agreement may be oral or in writing. Answer (d) is incorrect because a partnership does not have to provide for apportionment of liability for partnership debt. Note that even if the partners agreed to split partnership liability in a specified proportion, third parties can still hold each partner personally liable despite the agreement.

3. (d) A partnership involves two or more persons to carry on a business as co-owners for a profit. Partnerships do not include nonprofit associations such as charitable organizations, labor unions or clubs; therefore answers (a), (b), and (c) are incorrect.

4. (b) A silent partner does not help manage the partnership but still has unlimited liability.

5. (d) A partnership agreement may be expressed or implied based upon the activities and conduct of the partners. The expressed agreement may be oral or in writing with, in general, one exception. A partnership agreement that cannot be completed within one year from the date on which it is entered into must be in writing. Answer (b) is incorrect because the partners may reside in different states without having to put the partnership agreement in writing. Answer (a) is incorrect because the $500 amount applies to the sale of goods which must be in writing, not partnerships. Answer (c) is incorrect because the purpose of the partnership is irrelevant. Agreements to buy and sell real estate must be in writing, while an agreement to form a partnership whose principal activity will involve the buying and selling of real estate normally need not be in writing unless the stated duration exceeds one year.

6. (d) Under RUPA, the partnership is a legal entity that can own property in its own name. The partners also have joint and several liability for all debts whether they are based in contract or tort.

7. (c) The partners may agree to share profits as well as losses unequally. Answer (a) is incorrect because the partners may agree that ownership in the partnership is unequal. Answer (b) is incorrect because under RUPA, the partnership is a separate legal entity. Answer (d) is incorrect because the partners may agree to unequal management rights.

8. (d) Profits and losses in a general partnership are shared equally unless otherwise specified in the partnership agreement. If partners agree on unequal profit sharing but are silent on loss sharing, then losses are shared per the profit sharing proportions. The partnership agreement for Owen Associates provided that profits be paid to the partners in the ratio of their financial contribution to the partnership. The ratios are as follows:

Total contributed $10,000 + 30,000 + 50,000 = $90,000

Moore	$10,000	÷	90,000	=	1/9
Noon	$30,000	÷	90,000	=	1/3
Kale	$50,000	÷	90,000	=	5/9

For the year ended December 31, 2012, Owen had losses of $180,000. Therefore, Kale would be allocated $100,000 of the losses ($180,000 × 5/9).

9. (b) An incoming partner has the same rights as all of the existing partners. Thus, an incoming partner has the right to participate in the management of the partnership. Answer (a) is incorrect since the incoming partner acquires more than just the right to profits. Answer (c) is incorrect since a person admitted as a partner into an existing partnership is only liable for existing debts of the partnership to the extent of the incoming partner's capital contribution. Answer (d) is incorrect because a partner need not make a capital contribution to be admitted with the same rights as the other partners.

10. (b) A partner is free to assign his interest in any partnership to a third party. However, the assignee does not become a partner by virtue of this assignment, but merely succeeds to the assignor's rights as to profits and return of partner's capital contribution. The assignee does not receive the right to manage, to have an accounting, to inspect the books, or to possess or use any individual partnership property. Since Bean was not made a partner, he is entitled to Cobb's share of TLC's profits, but does not have the right to participate in the management of TLC.

11. (a) A partner's apparent authority is derived from the reasonable perceptions of third parties due to the manifestations or representations of the partnership concerning the authority each partner possesses to bind the partnership. However, if third parties are aware of a formal resolution which limits the partner's actual authority to bind the partnership, then that partner's apparent authority will also be limited. Answer (b) is incorrect because if third parties are unaware of such a resolution which limits the partner's actual authority, then the partner retains apparent authority to bind the partnership. Answer (c) is incorrect because third parties should be aware that in order for a partner to submit a claim against the partnership to arbitration, unanimous consent of the partners is needed. Therefore, a partner has no apparent authority to take such an action. Answer (d) is incorrect because as stated above, the apparent authority of a partner to bind the partnership is not derived from the express powers and purposes contained in the partnership agreement.

12. (b) In a general partnership, unanimous consent is required of all of the partners to admit a new partner. Answer (a) is incorrect because any one partner can cause a dissolution by

actions such as withdrawing. Answer (c) is incorrect because each partner is an agent of the general partnership and thus may purchase items for the business of the firm. Answer (d) is incorrect; an individual partner may hire an employee because such an action is viewed as within the regular course of business.

13. (c) Under the Revised Uniform Partnership Act, partners have joint and several liability for not only torts but also breaches of contract. This is a change from previous law and differs from the normal rules of agency law.

14. (c) Although individual partners normally have implied authority to buy and sell goods for the partnership; they do not have implied authority to do such things as making the partnership a surety or admitting a new partner. Such matters are not considered to be the ordinary business of the partnership, and thus require the consent of all partners.

15. (d) A partner's interest in a partnership is freely assignable without the other partners' consent. A partner's interest refers to the partners' right to share in profits and return of contribution. Answer (a) is incorrect because the assignee does not become a partner without the consent of all the other partners. Answer (b) is incorrect because the assignor remains liable as a partner. The assignee has only received the partner's right to share in profits and capital return. Answer (c) is incorrect because assignment of a partner's interest does not cause dissolution unless the assignor also withdraws.

16. (b) Under RUPA, partnership property not only includes property purchased in the partnership name but also includes property purchased by a partner, who is an agent of the partnership, with partnership funds. Note that a partner may use property in the partnership business without it becoming partnership property.

17. (d) Even if a partner has agreed not to withdraw before a certain period of time, s/he has the power to do so anyway. That partner's withdrawal is a break of contract and causes a dissolution of the partnership. If the remaining partners agreed to continue the partnership, this would prevent the dissolution, but there is no mention of such an agreement in the facts presented here. Answer (a) is incorrect because this dissolution is caused by an act of a partner rather than by operation of law. Answer (b) is incorrect because Wind's withdrawal does have an effect on the remaining partners because they must decide on what new terms they will operate or else wind up and terminate the partnership. Answer (c) is incorrect because the dissolution is effective once Wind does withdraw from the partnership. A court decree is not necessary.

18. (a) The best approach to answer this question is to make a chart as follows:

	Dowd 40%	Elgar 30%	Frost 20%	Grant 10%
Capital Balance	$120,000	$100,000	$75,000	$11,000
Allocation of Loss				
$200,000	(80,000)	(60,000)	(40,000)	(20,000)

	Dowd 40%	Elgar 30%	Frost 20%	Grant 10%
Remaining balance	40,000	40,000	35,000	(9,000)
Distribution of deficit of insolvent partner:				9,000
40/90 × 9,000	(4,000)			
30/90 × 9,000		(3,000)		
20/90 × 9,000			(2,000)	
Balance	36,000	37,000	33,000	0
Cash distribution $106,000	(36,000)	(37,000)	(33,000)	0
	0	0	0	0

A capital deficit may be corrected by the partner investing more cash or assets to eliminate the deficit or by distributing the deficit to the other partners in their resulting profit and loss sharing ratio. The latter was done in this case, as the facts in the question indicated that Grant refuses to make any further contributions to the partnership. The remaining cash is then used to pay the three partners' capital balances.

19. (c) A general partner has a voice in management and has unlimited personal liability. Anyone, including a secured creditor of the limited partnership, may be a general partner if he/she takes on these responsibilities. Answer (a) is incorrect because an unsecured creditor of the limited partnership may also be a limited partner. A limited partner is defined as having no voice in management and his/her liability is limited to the extent of his/her capital contribution. Answer (b) is incorrect because a general partner may also be a limited partner at the same time. This partner would have the rights, powers, and liability of a general partner, and the rights against other partners with respect to his/her contribution as both a limited and a general partner. Answer (d) is incorrect because every limited partnership must have at least one general partner who will be liable for the partnership obligations.

20. (c) Under the Revised Uniform Limited Partnership Act, when the partners do not agree how to split profits, the split is made in proportion to their capital contributions. Note that this is different for general partners under the Revised Uniform Partnership Act.

21. (a) Limited partnerships must have at least one general partner who has the unlimited personal liability of the firm. Unlike a general partner, the death of a limited partner does not cause a dissolution or termination of a partner.

22. (a) Since Chan acted like a general partner and Ham thought he was a general partner, Chan has the liability of a general partner to Ham. Answers (b), (c), and (d) are incorrect because Ham believed Chan was a general partner based on Chan's actions. Therefore, Chan had the liability of a general partner, that is, unlimited liability.

23. (a) Under the Revised Uniform Limited Partnership Act, none of the names of the limited partners need to be listed in the certificate of limited partnership that is filed with the Secretary of State. However, all of the general partners must be listed.

24. (c) A limited partner is allowed, without losing the protection of limited liability, to act as an agent of the limited partnership. The limited partner may also vote on the removal of a general partner.

25. (d) Partners' capital may not only be in cash, property, or services already performed, but also may be in the form of promises to give or perform these at a future date.

26. (d) If the liability is more than the partnership can pay, each partner loses its capital contribution and then the general partner has personal, unlimited liability for the debt.

27. (d) The admission of a new general partner to a limited partnership under the Revised Uniform Limited Partnership Act requires the approval of all partners, including limited partners.

28. (d) The admission of a new limited partner requires the approval of all the partners.

29. (c) Death or bankruptcy of a general partner in a limited partnership will cause dissolution of the limited partnership. However, this is not true if a limited partner dies or goes bankrupt.

30. (d) The death of a joint venturer does not automatically dissolve the joint venture. Answers (a), (b), and (c) are all incorrect because these are all characteristics of a joint venture.

31. (a) A limited liability company provides for limited liability of its members, similar to the limited liability of the shareholders of a corporation. However, it typically has a limited duration of existence, similar to that of a partnership in which the death or withdrawal of a member or partner causes the business to dissolve unless the remaining members or partners choose to continue the business. The limited liability company can also be taxed similar to a partnership if formed to do so. The Subchapter S corporation has the limited liability of the corporation but is taxed similar to a partnership.

32. (b) The limited liability company statutes provide that it is a separate legal entity apart from its owners. Thus it may sue or be sued in its own name. Answer (a) is incorrect because all owners have limited rather than personal liability. Answer (c) is incorrect because limited liability is normally retained even if the owners fail to follow the formalities usual in conducting the business. Answer (d) is incorrect because (b) is correct.

33. (c) Limited liability companies typically have a limited life. Provisions often provide that they exist for thirty years at most and dissolve if a member dies. Therefore (a) is an incorrect response. Answer (b) is also not chosen because members (owners) are permitted to participate in the management of the LLC or can choose the management. Answer (d) is an incorrect response because one of the main benefits of an LLC is the limited liability of its members (owners).

34. (c) Owners and managers of an LLC owe a duty of due care. They also owe a duty to be loyal to their LLC.

35. (b) In the typical limited liability company (LLC), unlike the common corporation, the interests of the members are not freely transferable. The other members have to agree to admit new members. Answer (a) is incorrect because it provides for limited liability of all of its members. Answer (c) is incorrect because all members have a voice in the management of the LLC. Answer (d) is incorrect because a limited liability company must be formed pursuant to the filing requirements of the relevant state statute.

36. (d) In most states a limited liability partnership (LLP), insulates partners from personal liability for all debts and obligations of the partnership regardless of whether those debts arose from contract or tort. Answer (a) is incorrect because both in the LLP and the general partnership, the partners have unlimited liability for their own torts. Answer (b) is incorrect because partners are insulated from contractual debts as well as debts arising from tort. Answer (c) is incorrect because partners have personal liability for their own actions.

37. (b) The federal Subchapter S Revision Act specifies that all corporations that do not meet the criteria of a Subchapter S corporation are categorized as a Subchapter C corporation. Answers (a), (c), and (d) are incorrect because the Act provides that a corporation is either a Subchapter S or Subchapter C corporation but not both at the same time.

38. (b) All corporations are divided under the federal Subchapter S Revision Act as being either a Subchapter C corporation or a Subchapter S corporation. Answer (a) is incorrect because the federal Subchapter S Revision Act provides that there are two categories of corporations: Subchapter C and Subchapter S corporations. Answer (c) is incorrect because this federal law provides for only two categories of corporations. A Subchapter E corporation is not one of these. Answer (d) is incorrect because answer (c) is correct.

39. (c) Both Subchapter C corporations and Subchapter S corporations are similar in their provisions for the limited liability of their shareholders and also in their corporate management structures. Answer (a) is incorrect because it does not include the similarity of the corporate management structures. Answer (b) is incorrect because it does not mention the similarity of the shareholders' limited liability. Answer (d) is incorrect for the reason that answer (c) is correct.

40. (a) Tax treatment is the main reason why Subchapter S corporations are formed instead of Subchapter C corporations. Answer (b) is incorrect because this federal Act covers both types of corporations. Answers (c) and (d) are incorrect because the provisions on the limited liability of shareholders and the provisions for the structure of corporate management are some of the ways that Subchapter C and Subchapter S corporations are generally similar.

41. (c) One advantage of the corporate form of business is that it has a continuous life and is not terminated by the death of a shareholder or manager. Answer (a) is incorrect because although the power to manage the corporation is vested in the board of directors, they usually delegate the day-to-day

management responsibilities to various managers. Answer (b) is incorrect because in most corporations, ownership is not contractually restricted. In fact, free transferability of the shares of stock is a major advantage of the corporate form of business. Answer (d) is incorrect because corporations are not free from state regulation.

42. (c) A major advantage is that shareholders have limited liability, that is, typically limited to what they paid for the stock. However, managers do not have limited liability for their actions as managers. If a manager is also a shareholder, that person has limited liability for the ownership in the stock but can still be sued for misdeeds as a manager. Answers (a), (b), and (d) are all considered to be advantages of a corporation. Note that since a person can manage a corporation without necessarily being an owner, this can encourage professional managers to get involved.

43. (d) The death of one or more of a corporation's shareholders does not automatically terminate it. Answer (a) is incorrect because a corporation continues to exist until it is dissolved, merged or otherwise terminated. Answer (b) is incorrect because shares in a corporation, represented by stocks, can be freely bought, sold, or assigned unless the shareholders have agreed to restrict this. Answer (c) is incorrect because a corporation is legally a separate entity apart from its shareholders.

44. (d) A corporation may make contracts in its own name with both its shareholders and third parties. Answer (a) is incorrect because it may also make contracts with third parties. Answer (b) is incorrect because corporations do not generally need the consent of other shareholders to contract with one shareholder. Answer (c) is incorrect because it may also contract with its shareholders.

45. (d) Persons who manage a corporation may be, but need not bc, shareholders of that corporation. Also, a corporation as a separate legal entity may convey or hold property. It may also sue or be sued in its own name. Answers (a), (b), and (c) are not comprehensive enough.

46. (a) A Subchapter S corporation is often formed to help avoid the double taxation that a Subchapter C corporation may face. Answer (b) is incorrect because partners in a general partnership have unlimited personal liability. Shareholders of a corporation have limited liability with few exceptions. Answer (c) is incorrect because a Subchapter C corporation is any corporation that is not a Subchapter S corporation. Answer (d) is incorrect because both Subchapter C and Subchapter S corporations provide their shareholders with limited liability with few exceptions.

47. (b) Bond is a domestic corporation in Florida since it incorporated there. It is a foreign corporation in Georgia since it did not incorporate there. Bond does not need to incorporate in Georgia but must qualify to do business there because it has branch offices in Georgia. This qualifying normally entails filing required documents with the state.

48. (b) In a professional corporation, the professional has most of the benefits of a corporation such as limited liability for corporate debts. However, the professional has personal liability for professional acts. Colby cannot avoid liability for the damage caused the client due to negligence in a professional act.

49. (c) A domestic corporation is one that operates and does business in the state in which it was incorporated. Answer (a) is incorrect because Macro, instead of incorporating in Nevada, may qualify to do business by obtaining a certificate of authority from Nevada. Answer (b) is incorrect because Macro is a foreign corporation in Nevada because it did not incorporate there. Answer (d) is incorrect because the statement in (c) is the only one that is true.

50. (d) None of the listed items are normally considered doing business in the other states such that Cleanit would be required to qualify to do business and thus have to obtain certificates of authority from those states. Therefore, answers (a), (b), and (c) are incorrect.

51. (c) Normally, under state laws, only licensed professionals may own shares in professional corporations. Furthermore, the licensed professionals retain personal liability for their professional acts in the professional corporation. Therefore (a), (b), and (d) are incorrect.

52. (d) Corporations and limited partnerships may only be created pursuant to state statutes. Normally, both the Articles of Incorporation and a Certificate of Limited Partnership must be filed with the Secretary of State. Answer (c) is incorrect since limited partners do not owe fiduciary duties to the partnership. Answer (a) is incorrect since limited partners have the right to vote on partnership matters such as the dissolution or winding up of the partnership, loans of the partnership, a change in the nature of the business of a partnership, and the removal of a general partner without jeopardizing their limited partner status. Answer (b) is incorrect since sale of limited partnership interests is not automatically exempted from the general securities laws' registration requirements.

53. (d) Under the Revised Model Business Corporation Act, a corporation's Articles of Incorporation generally must include the name of the corporation, the purpose of the corporation, the powers of the corporation, the name of the incorporators, the name of the registered agent of the corporation and the number of shares of stock the corporation is authorized to issue. Answers (a), (b), and (c) are incorrect because none of these items are required to be in the Articles of Incorporation.

54. (a) The Articles of Incorporation are filed with the state and contain the names of the corporation, registered agent, and incorporators. This document also contains the purpose and powers of the corporation as well as a description of the types of stock and number of authorized shares.

55. (d) Normally, the board of directors of a corporation has the power to adopt, amend, and repeal the bylaws. It also has the power to declare dividends and fix the compensation of the directors. Therefore, answers (a), (b), and (c) are incorrect. However, it does not have the power to amend the Articles of Incorporation. Amending the Articles of Incorporation is viewed as a fundamental change and is thus subject to a shareholder vote.

56. (a) Corporations and limited partnerships may only be created pursuant to state statutes. Normally, both the Articles of Incorporation and a Certificate of Limited Partnership must be filed with the Secretary of State. Answer (b) is incorrect because a limited partnership requires at least one general partner who retains unlimited personal liability. Answer (c) is incorrect because a limited partnership is treated the same as a general partnership for tax purposes in that it is not recognized as a separate taxable entity. Answer (d) is incorrect because a limited partnership is not statutorily allowed perpetual existence.

57. (a) The basic concept of a promoter is one who forms a corporation with the goal of the corporation eventually coming into existence. Answer (b) is incorrect because for there to be an agent, there must be a principal. There is no principal yet because the corporation is not yet formed. Answer (c) is incorrect because the promoters are not agents, since there is no principal yet, thus have no authority to bind the future corporations to contracts. Answer (d) is incorrect because the promoters are not agents and thus cannot use agency law to protect them.

58. (b) The Articles of Incorporation must include, among other things, the amount of capital stock authorized and the types of stock to be issued. Specific provisions applicable to stock must also be stated. Examples of stock provisions which must be authorized by the Articles of Incorporation include number of authorized shares, whether the stock is to be par value or no-par value, and classes of stock, including voting rights and dividend provisions. When, as here, a shareholder owns a cumulative stock the shareholder becomes an unsecured creditor of the corporation to the extent declared dividends are not paid; this includes dividends that were declared, but not paid, in previous years. Therefore, Johns becomes an unsecured creditor upon Abco's declaration of preferred stock dividend. In order for Johns to be entitled to convert his/her preferred shares to common shares, to participate with common shareholders in any dividend distribution made after preferred dividends are paid, or to be entitled to vote if dividend payments are in arrears, it must be stated in the Articles of Incorporation; therefore, (a), (c), and (d) are incorrect.

59. (c) Par value is the minimum amount that a corporation may sell stock initially. Par value does not apply to the corporation's purchase of stock; nor does par value apply to treasury stock. Gallagher originally sold the stock at above par value.

60. (c) A corporation may resell treasury shares without regard to par value. Therefore, an owner of common stock who purchased treasury shares for less than par value will not have any liability beyond actual investment. Answer (a) is incorrect because an owner of common stock who paid less than par value for stock purchased in connection with an original issue of shares is contingently liable in many states to creditors for the difference between the amount paid and par value. Answer (b) is incorrect because a promise to perform services is valid consideration, but only if it is for at least par value. Answer (d) is incorrect because once the corporation accepts an offer to buy stock subscriptions, the subscriber becomes liable for the purchase. Therefore, an owner of common stock who failed to pay the full amount owed on a subscription contract for no-par shares is liable for the difference between any amounts already paid and the full amount owed according to the contract.

61. (c) Corporate debt securities include the following: (1) registered bonds, (2) bearer bonds, (3) debenture bonds, (4) mortgage bonds, (5) redeemable bonds, and (6) convertible bonds. A warrant is not a corporate debt security, but rather is written evidence of a stock option which grants its owner the option to purchase a specified amount of shares of stock at a stated price within a specified period of time.

62. (b) A stock split increases the number of shares outstanding and proportionately decreases the par value per share. However, the total outstanding par value does not change and therefore no charge is made to retained earnings or capital. Answer (a) is incorrect because liquidating dividends represent a return of the stockholders' capital and are considered a capital distribution. Both cash and property distributions are considered asset distributions; therefore answers (c) and (d) are incorrect. Property distributions are recorded at the fair market value of the asset at the date of transfer.

63. (d) Valid consideration or value to purchase shares of stock can be any benefit to the corporation including any services contracted for that are yet to be performed in the future.

64. (c) Since Brawn had a contract to purchase 1,000 shares at $20 per share, this is binding. Therefore, the creditors can recover in bankruptcy the remainder of the price not paid. Answer (a) is incorrect because the creditors have the right to see that the bankruptcy estate includes this amount owed the corporation. Answer (b) is incorrect because the contract required that the full $20,000 be paid, not just the par value. Answer (d) is incorrect because ultra vires acts are acts that are beyond the scope of the powers of the corporation. These do not apply to this fact pattern.

65. (c) Treasury stock are not votable nor do they receive dividends. Therefore, answers (a), (b), and (d) are incorrect.

66. (a) Treasury stock is stock that a corporation issued previously but is no longer outstanding because the corporation repurchased it back. Answer (b) is incorrect because treasury stock is a corporation's own stock that it has repurchased. Answer (c) is incorrect because canceled stock is no longer issued or outstanding. Answer (d) is incorrect because (a) is correct.

67. (b) A corporation by law may issue one or more classes of common stock. This is also true for preferred stock. Answer (a) is incorrect because a corporation is not required to issue preferred stock. Answer (c) is incorrect because it is at the discretion of the board of directors to declare a dividend. They may wish to keep the earnings in the corporation for expansion purposes, etc. Answer (d) is incorrect because if it issues preferred stock, it may be either cumulative preferred stock or noncumulative preferred stock.

68. (b) A bond represents long-term secured debt. Answer (a) is incorrect because holders of debt securities are creditors rather than owners of the corporation. Answer (c) is incorrect because a debenture represents long-term unsecured debt not long-term secured debt. Answer (d) is incorrect because there was one correct answer.

69. (c) The definition of watered stock refers to when the stock is acquired by exchanging cash or property worth less than the par or stated value of the stock. Answers (a) and (b) are incorrect because watered stock deals with par value, not market value. Answer (d) is incorrect because watered stock is sold at less than par value, not more than.

70. (b) Corporations generally have the power to acquire or retire their own shares without shareholder approval. They can also make charitable contributions without such approval. Loans to directors require shareholder approval.

71. (c) A business is liable for the torts of its employees committed within the course and scope of employment. Intentional torts usually fall outside the scope of employment, but there are situations where intentional torts fall within the scope of employment. Principals can be held liable for the agent's fraud where the agent is authorized or appears to be authorized to make such statements. As an employee of Landtry, it can be assumed that Murphy has authority to discuss the features of Landtry's products. Torts involving violence can fall within the scope of employment if they are foreseeable. Here Lantry has previously warned Murphy not to engage in violent actions against customers, which provides evidence that Murphy's violent actions are foreseeable. The injured third party can hold both the employee and the corporation liable in either case.

72. (d) All three statements are true in the interest of punishing all parties who commit crimes.

73. (b) Norwood is personally liable on the contract because he signed the contract and agency law will not protect him. This is true because he was not an agent, even though he claimed to be, because there was no principal to authorize him when the contract was made on March 15. Answer (a) is incorrect since Norwood is liable. Answers (c) and (d) are incorrect; since the corporation never adopted the contract by words or actions, it is not liable. The board of directors is not personally liable either because they never agreed to the contract.

74. (b) Under the Revised Model Business Corporation Act, a corporation is authorized to indemnify its officers for expenses, attorney fees, judgments, fines and amounts paid in settlement incurred in a suit by stockholders when the liability is a result of the officer's good faith, nonnegligent actions on behalf of the best interest of the corporation. Answer (a) is incorrect because a corporate officer may also serve as a director. Answer (c) is incorrect because officers are appointed by the directors of a corporation who are in turn elected by the shareholders. Answer (d) is incorrect because there is no requirement that an officer must own any shares of the corporation's stock.

75. (a) The transaction the director wishes to have with the corporation is not a conflict of interest if any one of the following is true. (1) The transaction is fair and reasonable for the corporation. (2) The shareholders are given the relevant facts and they approve it by a majority vote. (3) The board of directors are given the relevant facts and they approve it by a majority vote of the disinterested members of the board of directors.

76. (c) Officers and directors are in important positions in a corporation. As such, they owe a fiduciary duty to the corporation to act in the best interests of the corporation. Courts have also recognized that because majority shareholders can exercise a lot of power in a corporation from their stockholdings and voting rights, they owe a fiduciary duty to the minority shareholders when these majority shareholders have de facto control over the corporation by virtue of their concentrated ownership.

77. (b) A contract between a director and his/her corporation is valid if it is reasonable to the corporation. Hogan has not breached his fiduciary duty with the corporation since he is selling the land at fair market value. Answer (a) is incorrect because a director does owe a fiduciary duty to his/her corporation to act in its best interests. Answers (c) and (d) are incorrect because since the transaction is fair and reasonable to the corporation, the shareholders need not approve it.

78. (c) The Articles of Incorporation may be amended by the shareholders' vote, not by the board of directors. Answer (a) is incorrect because one of the important powers of the directors is to select the officers of the corporation. Answer (b) is incorrect because it is up to the board of directors to declare any dividends to the shareholders. Answer (d) is incorrect because answer (c) is correct.

79. (d) A corporation may indemnify both its directors as well as its officers against suits based on their duties for the corporation if they acted in good faith and in the best interests of the corporation. A corporation may also purchase insurance to cover the liability for lawsuits lost based on actions of its directors and also its officers.

80. (c) Both directors as well as officers owe a fiduciary duty to their corporation.

81. (c) McGarry is liable for the tort she committed. Because she was acting within the scope of her authority in the corporation, Norton corporation is also liable. Note that McGarry is not relieved of liability even though Norton Corporation is also liable because McGarry is the one who committed the tort. Therefore, answers (a), (b), and (d) are incorrect.

82. (d) When Acorn pays cash and buys 90% or more of Trend's shares, it has control of the Trend stock. It can then accomplish a short-form merger of Trend Corp. into Acorn Corp. Answer (a) is incorrect because this can require the approval of Acorn shareholders. Answer (b) is incorrect because this is not a regular sale of Trend's assets and will require shareholder approval. Answer (c) is incorrect because the entire compulsory exchange for Acorn shares to accomplish the acquisition does require Trend's shareholder approval.

83. (a) Upon declaration, a cash dividend on preferred stock becomes a legal debt of the corporation, and the preferred shareholders become unsecured creditors of the corporation. However, any dividends not paid in any year concerning cumulative preferred stock are not a liability of the corporation until they are declared. Therefore, Universal will be liable to Price as an unsecured creditor for $10,000, which is the amount of the declared dividends. Answers (c) and (d) are incorrect because Price has become a general unsecured creditor for the declared dividends and will have the same priority as the debenture (unsecured) bond owners and the unsecured judgment creditors. Answer (b) is incorrect because

the undeclared dividends did not become a legal liability to Universal.

84. (b) The preemptive right gives the shareholder the right to purchase newly issued stock so as to keep the same overall percentage of ownership of the corporation. The Revised Model Business Corporation Act only provides this right if it is set forth in the Articles of Incorporation. The right to a proportionate share of assets upon dissolution is a right that all shareholders have and is not limited to preemptive shareholders.

85. (c) When the rights of individual shareholders may be adversely affected, the shareholder is given the right to dissent and receive payment of the fair value of his/her shares. This is true even if the dissenting shareholder has voting rights when s/he is being outvoted. In I., the shareholder has this right because his/her preference rights are being abolished. In II., the dissenting shareholder has this right because his/her shares being acquired by another corporation may affect the value and rights of the shares of stock.

86. (c) Shareholders have the right to inspect the corporate records if done in good faith for a proper purpose. Answer (a) is incorrect because shareholders do not have a right to dividends. It is the decision of the board of directors whether or not to declare dividends. Answer (b) is incorrect because although at least one class of stock must have voting rights to elect the **board of directors,** the **officers** may be selected by the board of directors. Answer (d) is incorrect because the shareholders cannot force an issuance of a new class of stock.

87. (a) Stockholders do not have the right to manage their corporation. However, stockholders who are also directors or officers do have the right to manage as part of their rights as directors and officers. Answer (b) is incorrect because stockholders generally have no right to receive dividends unless the board of directors declares such dividends. Answer (c) is incorrect because stockholders are given the right to inspect the books and records of their corporation. Answer (d) is incorrect because the stockholders may demand a list of shareholders for a proper purpose such as to help wage a proxy fight; however, they may not require the corporation to give them a list of its customers to use for a mailing list.

88. (a) Normally, the liability of shareholders of corporations is limited to their capital contribution. However, the court will "pierce the corporate veil" and hold the shareholders personally liable for the debts of the corporation if the corporate entity is being used to defraud people or to achieve other injustices. Thus, if the shareholders establish a corporation, knowing that it would have less capital than required for it to pay its debts, then the court will "pierce the corporate veil" and hold the shareholders personally liable. Answer (c) is incorrect because a shareholder may sell property to the corporation without becoming personally liable for the debts of the corporation. Answer (d) is incorrect because shareholders may also be corporate officers, directors or employees without jeopardizing their limited liability status. Answer (b) is incorrect because the formation of a corporation solely to limit personal liability is a valid purpose so long as it is done without intent to defraud.

89. (b) The court will disregard the corporate entity and hold the shareholders individually liable when the corporate form is used to perpetrate a fraud or is found to be merely an agent or instrument of its owners. An example of when the corporate veil is likely to be pierced is if the corporation and its shareholders commingle assets and financial records. In such a situation, the shareholders lose their limited liability and will be held personally liable for the corporation's legal obligations. Answer (a) is incorrect because the election of S corporation status is allowable under the law and is not, in itself, grounds for piercing the corporate veil. Answer (d) is incorrect because the desire of shareholders to limit their personal liability is a valid reason to form a corporation. Limited personal liability is one advantage of the corporate entity. Answer (c) is incorrect since the court will hold personally liable only those corporate officers responsible for the commission of an **ultra vires** act. The court will not pierce the corporate veil and hold the shareholders personally liable for such an act.

90. (b) Majority shareholders now owe a fiduciary duty to their corporation. Answer (a) is incorrect because minority shareholders do not owe a fiduciary duty to their corporation. Their main purpose normally is to be investors. Answer (c) is incorrect because majority shareholders now not only owe a fiduciary duty to their corporation but also to the minority shareholders. Answer (d) is incorrect because answer (b) is correct.

91. (b) Under the Revised Model Business Corporation Act, a corporation that owns at least 90% of the outstanding shares of each class of stock of the subsidiary may merge the subsidiary into itself without approval by the shareholders of the parent or subsidiary; thus answer (c) is incorrect. Answer (a) is incorrect because the approval of the shareholders or the subsidiary's board of directors is unnecessary since the parent owns 90% of the subsidiary. This ownership assures that the plan of the merger would be approved. The only requirement is a merger resolution by the board of directors of the parent corporation. Furthermore, the dissenting shareholders of the subsidiary must be given an appraisal remedy, which is the right to obtain payment from the parent for their shares. The shareholders of the parent do not have this appraisal remedy because the merger has not materially changed their rights; thus answer (d) is incorrect.

92. (c) In order for a merger of two public corporations to be accomplished, it is required that a formal plan of merger be prepared and that the merger plan be approved by a majority of the board of directors and stockholders of both corporations; therefore answers (a), (b), and (d) are incorrect.

93. (d) As one of the steps leading up to a merger of two corporations, the stockholders need to be given notice of the merger plan. This is true of the stockholders of both corporations, so a special meeting is called inviting both sets of stockholders. Answers (a) and (b) are incorrect because unanimous approval is not needed by either the stockholders or the boards of either corporation. Answer (c) is incorrect because the absorbed corporation will no longer exist after the merger plan is accomplished.

94. (a) A corporation voluntarily dissolves when its board of directors passes a resolution to dissolve and liquidate. Answer (d) is incorrect because this resolution must be ratified by a majority of stockholders who are entitled to vote. Following ratification, the corporation must file a certificate of dissolution with the proper state authority, cease business, wind up its affairs, and publish notice of its dissolution. Answers (b) and (c) are incorrect because they are not requirements of a voluntary dissolution.

95. (c) Shareholders have the right to vote on the dissolution of the corporation. Stockholders also have the right to elect the directors of the corporation, but the directors select the officers, not the shareholders; therefore, answer (a) is incorrect. Answer (b) is incorrect as shareholders do not have the right to receive dividends unless they are declared by the board of directors. Answer (d) is incorrect as shareholders are not necessarily involved in the management of the corporation and cannot prevent corporate borrowing.

96. (d) Under corporate law when a consolidation takes place, one new corporation comes from the joining of two or more corporations. Also, the assets and liabilities of the old corporations are acquired by the new corporation and the new corporation is liable for the debts of the old corporations.

97. (d) When a corporation elects to be a Subchapter S corporation, the corporate income and loss flow through to the income tax returns of the individual shareholders even when the income is not distributed to them. Answer (a) is incorrect because the corporation's income is not taxed at the corporate level when the Subchapter S election is made. Answer (b) is incorrect because the income flows through to the stockholders' tax returns regardless of when the distribution takes place. Answer (c) is incorrect because Statement IV as well as Statement III are both correct as discussed above.

Simulation

Task-Based Simulation 1

General Partnerships		
	Authoritative Literature	Help

Situation

In 2010 Anchor, Chain, and Hook created ACH Associates, a general partnership. The partners orally agreed that they would work full time for the partnership and would distribute profits based on their capital contributions. Anchor contributed $5,000: Chain $10,000; and Hook $15,000.

For the year ended December 31, 2011, ACH Associates had profits of $60,000 that were distributed to the partners. During 2012, ACH Associates was operating at a loss. In September 2012, the partnership dissolved.

In October 2012, Hook contracted in writing with Ace Automobile Co. to purchase a car for the partnership. Hook had previously purchased cars from Ace Automobile Co. for use by ACH Associates partners. ACH Associated did not honor the contract with Ace Automobile Co. and Ace Automobile Co. sued the partnership and the individual partners.

Required:

For each item, determine whether (A) or (B) is correct.

		(A)	(B)
1.	A. The ACH Associates oral partnership agreement was valid.	O	O
	B. The ACH Associates oral partnership agreement was invalid because the partnership lasted for more than one year.		
2.	A. Anchor, Chain, and Hook jointly owning and conducting a business for profit establishes a partnership relationship.	O	O
	B. Anchor, Chain, and Hook jointly owning income-producing property establishes a partnership relationship.		
3.	A. Anchor's share of ACH Associates' 2011 profits was $20,000.	O	O
	B. Hook's share of ACH Associates' 2011 profits was $30,000.		
4.	A. Anchor's capital account would be reduced by 1/3 of any 2012 losses.	O	O
	B. Hook's capital account would be reduced by 1/2 of any 2012 losses.		
5.	A. Ace Automobile Co. would lose a suit brought against ACH Associates because Hook, as a general partner, has no authority to bind the partnership.	O	O
	B. Ace Automobile Co. would win a suit brought against ACH Associates because Hook's authority continues during dissolution.		
6.	A. ACH Associates and Hook would be the only parties liable to pay any judgment recovered by Ace Automobile Co.	O	O
	B. Anchor, Chain, and Hook would be jointly and severally liable to pay any judgment recovered by Ace Automobile Co.		

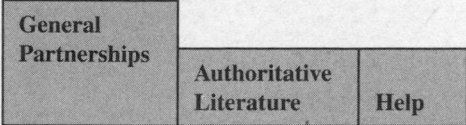

Simulation Solution

Task-Based Simulation 1

Explanations

1. (A) The creation of a partnership usually may be either oral or written. A written partnership agreement is not required unless it falls within the Statute of Frauds (e.g., the partnership cannot be completed within one year). Even though the partnership actually lasted longer than one year, the Statute of Frauds focuses on the term in the partnership agreement, not what actually happens. Since no term was specified in the oral agreement, it is possible that the partnership could have been completed in less than a year so no writing is required under the Statute of Frauds.

2. (A) A partnership is an association of two or more persons to carry on a business as co-owners for profit. Co-ownership of property is one element of a partnership; however, the most important and necessary element of a partnership is profit sharing. Another important element of co-ownership is joint control.

3. (B) Partnership profits and losses are shared equally unless the partnership agreement specifies otherwise. The agreement for ACH Associates specified that the partners would distribute profits based on their capital contributions. As such, Anchor's share of ACH Associates' 2011 profits would be

$$\frac{\$5,000}{15,000 + 10,000 + 5,000} \times \$60,000 = \$10,000$$

Hook's share of ACH Associates' 2011 profits would be

$$\frac{\$15,000}{15,000 + 10,000 + 5,000} \times \$60,000 = \$30,000$$

4. (B) Since the partners agreed on profit sharing in the creation of the partnership, but were silent on loss sharing, losses are shared on the same basis as profits. Therefore, Anchor's capital account would be reduced by

$$\frac{\$5,000}{15,000 + 10,000 + 5,000} = 16.6\% \text{ or } 1/6 \text{ of the 2012 losses}$$

Hook's capital account would be reduced by

$$\frac{\$15,000}{15,000 + 10,000 + 5,000} = 50\% \text{ or } 1/2 \text{ of the 2012 losses}$$

5. (B) During dissolution, partners can bind other partners and the partnership on contracts until third parties who have known of the partnership are given notice of dissolution. Actual notice must be given to third parties who have dealt with the partnership prior to the dissolution. Constructive notice is adequate for third parties who have only known of the partnership.

6. (B) Under the Revised Uniform Partnership Act, the partners are jointly and severally liable for all debts of the partnership. Creditors are required to first attempt collection from the partnership unless it is bankrupt. Once ACH Associates has paid off what it can, the partners are jointly and severally liable.

Module 26: Contracts

Overview

Contract rules provide a foundation for many other law topics; consequently, a good understanding of the material in this module will aid you in comprehending the material in other modules.

It is important to understand that there are two sets of contract rules to learn. The first is the group of common law contract rules that, in general, apply to contracts other than contracts for the sale of goods. Examples of contracts that are covered by the common law include real estate, insurance, employment, and professional services. The second set is the contract rules contained in Article Two of the Uniform Commercial Code (UCC). The UCC governs transactions involving the sale of goods (i.e., tangible personal property). Hence, if the contract is for the sale or purchase of tangible personal property, the provisions of the UCC will apply, and not the common law. For every contract question, it is important that you determine which set of rules to apply. Fortunately many of the rules under these two areas of law are the same. The best way for you to master this area is to first study the common law rules for a topic. Then review the rules that are different under the

UCC. Since the common law and the UCC rules have much in common, you will be learning contract law in the most understandable and efficient manner.

Contract law is tested by multiple-choice questions. You need to know the essential elements of a contract because the CPA examination tests heavily on offer and acceptance. Also, understand that an option is an offer supported by consideration. Distinguish between an option in the common law and a firm offer under the UCC; and understand how these are affected by revocations and rejections. You need to comprehend what consideration is and that it must be bargained for to be valid. The exam also requires that you understand that "past consideration" and moral obligations are not really consideration at all. You should have a solid understanding of the Statute of Frauds.

Once a contract is formed, third parties can obtain rights in the contract. An assignment is one important way this can happen.

If a contract is not performed, one of the parties may be held in breach of contract. Note that the possible remedies include monetary damages, specific performance, liquidated damages, and anticipatory repudiation. Before beginning the reading you should review the key terms at the end of the module.

A. Essential Elements of a Contract

1. Offer
2. Acceptance

    a. When offer and acceptance have occurred, an agreement, or mutual assent, is said to have been made

3. Consideration
4. Legal capacity
5. Legality (legal purpose)

6. Statute of Frauds

    a. Not a true element, but each factual situation should be examined to determine whether it applies because certain contracts must be in writing to be enforceable, as explained later

B. Types of Contracts

1. Express contract—terms are specifically stated orally or in writing
2. Implied contract—terms of contract not specifically stated, but some or all of terms are inferred from conduct of parties and/or circumstances

---

EXAMPLE

Hardy enters a fast food restaurant and orders a combo meal; there is an implied contract that Hardy will pay for the food and the restaurant will provide the food, even though those terms were never specifically stated.

---

3. Executed contract—terms have been fully performed
4. Executory contract—terms have not been fully performed by both parties
5. Unilateral contract

    a. One party gives promise for completion of requested act
    b. There is no legal obligation, no contract, unless the promisee undertakes the action

---

EXAMPLE

I promise to pay you $10 if you wash my car. If you wash my car, I must pay you $10. If you do not wash my car, I owe you nothing, but you are not under any obligation to wash my car.

---

6. Bilateral contract

    a. Each party exchanges promises
    b. Creates a legal obligation for both parties

EXAMPLE

You promise to wash my car next Friday and I promise to pay you $10. Each of us has a legal obligation: You must wash my car and I must pay you $10.

---

7. Voidable contract—one that is enforceable unless party that has right pulls out of contract
8. Void contract—one that is not enforceable by either party

C. Discussion of Essential Elements of a Contract

1. Offer

    a. May be either written or oral (or sometimes by actions)

EXAMPLE

Offeror takes can of soup to checkout stand and pays for it without saying anything.

---

    b. Requirements of a valid offer

(1) Intent: An indication that the offeror desired to enter into a bargain

  (a) Courts use an objective standard: Would reasonable person think that offer had been intended?
  (b) Subjective intent (what offeror actually intended or meant) is not considered
  (c) Promises made in apparent jest are not offers

EXAMPLE

A licensed real estate agent offers to sell your home for a 4% commission; if a reasonable person thinks that this is a serious offer, then an offer exists, even if the real estate agent was joking.

  (d) Statements of intent are not offers

EXAMPLE

"I am going to sell my car for $400." This is a statement of intent, not an offer.

  (e) Invitations to negotiate (preliminary negotiations) are not offers (e.g., price tags or lists, auctions, inquiries, general advertisements)

EXAMPLE

Mary offers to pay Lucas, an attorney, $500 to create an estate plan for her. Lucas responds that he would not create an estate plan for anything less than $1000. Mary says she accepts Lucas's offer to do the estate plan for $1000. There is no contract. Lucas did not intend to make an offer; rather, Lucas was letting Mary know that she needed to raise her offer considerably. These are only preliminary negotiations.

---

(2) Definite and/or certain: Sufficiently specific terms so that the offeror and the offeree know what their obligations are.

  (a) Courts allow some reasonable terms to be left open if customary to do so

---

EXAMPLE

C calls P, a plumber, to come and fix a clogged drain. No price is mentioned. However, upon P's completion of the work, he has the right to collect customary fee from C.

---

(3) Communicated: must be communicated to offeree by offeror or his/her agent

  (a) Offeree may learn of a public offer (e.g., reward) in any way; s/he merely needs knowledge of it
  (b) Offeror may limit who may accept the offer

EXAMPLE

This offer is only available to people 18 years of age and older. Even if Carlos, who is 17, heard the offer, he could not accept the offer because he does not satisfy the conditions of the offer.

---

c. Mistakes in transmission of offer are deemed to be offeror's risk because s/he chose method of communication; therefore, offer is effective as transmitted

d. Termination of offer can occur either by the actions of the parties or by operation of law

    (1) Actions of the contracting parties

        (a) Offeror's actions

            (1) Offeror specifically limits length of the offer

---

EXAMPLE

Offeror states that offer will remain open until June 9th. Offer ends on June 9th.

---

            (2) Revocation by the offeror

                (a) If offeree learns by reliable means that offeror has already sold subject of offer, it is revoked

                (b) Generally, offeror may revoke offer at any time prior to acceptance by offeree

                (c) Revocation is effective when received by offeree

                (d) An **option**, or an option contract, is an offer that is supported by consideration and cannot be revoked before stated time

---

EXAMPLE

On March 1, Madison offers to sell Potter a parcel of land for $50,000. Potter responds that he needs to think about it and asks Madison if she will hold the offer open for him. Madison writes on a note that she will hold the offer open for Potter until March 15. On, March 10, Bailey offers Madison $60,000 for the same parcel of land that she had offered to Potter. Madison agreed to sell the land to Bailey and immediately notified Potter that she revoked her offer to Potter. Madison's offer to Potter terminated as soon as she told Potter of the revocation. This is true despite her written promise to hold the offer open until March 15.

On March 1, if Potter had instead given Madison consideration, for example $50, if Madison would hold the offer open until March 15, then Madison cannot revoke the offer until after March 15, and she could not sell the property to Bailey during that same time period.

---

            (3) Offeree's actions

                (a) Rejection of the offer

                (b) Counteroffer: A rejection by the offeree coupled with a new offer

Warning: Be careful to distinguish a counteroffer from a mere inquiry. An inquiry does not terminate an offer, while a counteroffer will terminate an offer.

EXAMPLE

Madison offers to sell a parcel of land to Potter for $50,000. Potter asks Madison if she would be willing to take less than $50,000. Potter may still accept Madison's original offer to sell for $50,000. If, however, in response to Madison's original offer, Potter stated I'll give you $45,000 for the land, then that is a counteroffer and Madison's original offer is terminated.

                (c) Both rejections and counteroffers are effective when received by the offeror

    (2) Some offers terminate automatically by operation of law: If any of the following events occurs the offer is terminated:

        (a) Death of either party

        (b) Incapacity of either party

        (c) The subject matter of the offer is destroyed

        (d) The proposed contract becomes illegal

EXAMPLE

X offers to rent to Y an upstairs floor for a cabaret. Thereafter, the city adopts a fire code making use of the premises illegal without substantial rebuilding. The offer to rent is terminated automatically since renting the premises is now illegal.

---

2. Acceptance: When an offeree agrees to the offeror's terms

   a. May be written or oral

   b. Offer may be accepted only by person to whom it was directed

      (1) Use objective test—to whom would a reasonable person believe it to be directed?

      (2) Rewards can usually be accepted by anyone who knows of them, except for those who have a preexisting duty, such as a law enforcement officer.

   c. Offeree must have knowledge of offer in order to accept

---

EXAMPLE

D advertises a reward of $100 for the return of his pet dog. G, unaware of the offer, returns D's dog. G cannot require that D pay the $100 (if he later hears of the offer) because he was unaware of the offer when he returned the dog. He could not "accept" an offer he did not know existed.

---

   d. Intent to accept is required

      (1) Courts generally find click-on agreements legally enforceable when the offeree completes the contract online by clicking on a button that shows acceptance

         (a) Main issue is that offeree did clearly intend to accept offer by this action

   e. Acceptance must generally be in form specified by offer

   f. Acceptance must be unequivocal and unconditional (mirror image rule) under common law

      (1) An accceptance that attempts to change terms of offer is not acceptance, but is both a rejection and a counteroffer

---

EXAMPLE

O offers to sell some real estate for $100,000 cash. E says "I accept. I'll give you $50,000 now and $50,000 plus 13% interest one year from now." E's attempted acceptance is really a counteroffer since E altered the terms of the original offer.

         (a) Mere inquiry or request is not a counteroffer so offer remains in effect

---

EXAMPLE

O gives the same offer as above but this time E asks if O would accept $50,000 now and $50,000 plus 13% interest one year from now. The offer is neither accepted nor terminated.

         (b) An attempted counteroffer given to electronic agent such as web page or voice mail is not effective when it does not have ability to evaluate counteroffer

      (2) A condition which does not change or add to terms of contract is not a counteroffer (i.e., a condition that is already part of contract because of law, even though not expressed in previous negotiations)

g. Silence is not acceptance unless

    (1) Offer indicated silence would constitute acceptance (e.g., offer states "your silence is acceptance," and offeree intended his/her silence as acceptance)

    (2) Offeree has taken benefit of services or goods and exercised control over them when s/he had opportunity to reject them

    (3) Through prior dealings, by agreement between parties, or when dictated by custom, silence can be acceptance

h. Acceptances are valid when sent (Mailbox Rule)

    (1) If acceptance is made by method specified in offer or by same method used by offeror to communicate the offer, acceptance is effective when sent (e.g., when placed in mail or when telegram is dispatched)

EXAMPLE

Offeror mails a written offer without stating the mode of acceptance. Offeree mails acceptance. Offeror, before receipt, calls offeree to revoke the offer. The contract exists because acceptance was effective when mailed and revocation of offer came too late.

        (a) Exception: If offeree sends rejection and then acceptance, first received is effective even though offeree sent acceptance by same method used by offeror

        (b) If no method is specified, the acceptance will be valid when dispatched, if it is sent by a method normally used in similar transactions.

    (2) Methods of acceptance, other than those specified in the offer, implementing the same method used by the offeror, or those that are normally used are considered effective when actually received by offeror

    (3) Late acceptance does not create a contract—it is a counteroffer and a valid contract is formed only if original offeror then accepts the counteroffer

    (4) If acceptance is valid when sent, a lost or delayed acceptance does not destroy validity

---

EXAMPLE

R wires an offer to E asking her to accept by mail. The acceptance is correctly mailed but never arrives. There is a valid agreement.

---

    (5) Offeror can change above rules by stating other rule(s) in offer

---

EXAMPLE

Offeror mails a written offer to offeree stating that acceptance is valid only if received by the offeror within ten days. Offeree mails back the acceptance within ten days but it arrives late. Acceptance has not occurred even though the offeree used the same method.

---

i. Once there is an offer and acceptance, an agreement is formed

    (1) Details can be worked out later

    (2) Formalization often occurs later

    (3) Attempted revocations or rejections after agreement is formed are of no effect

j. Offers, revocations, rejections, and counteroffers are valid when received (under both common law and UCC)

    (1) Compare with rules for acceptances which are sometimes valid when sent and other times are valid when received

---

EXAMPLE

S offers to sell his land to B for $20,000. The offer is mailed to B. Later that same day, S changes his mind and mails B a revocation of this offer. When B receives the offer, she mails her acceptance. B receives the revocation the day after she mailed the acceptance. S and B have a valid contract because the acceptance was valid when sent but the revocation would have been valid when B received it. Once the offer is accepted, any attempted revocation will not be valid.

EXAMPLE

Use the same facts as above except that the offer required acceptance by mail; offeree uses a different method than the mailed acceptance. If B receives the revocation before S receives the acceptance, there is no contract.

---

k. Auctions

   (1) Bid is offer

   (2) Bidder may retract bid until auctioneer announces sale completed

   (3) If auction is "with reserve," auctioneer may withdraw goods before s/he announces completion of sale

   (4) If auction "without reserve," goods may not be withdrawn unless no bid made within reasonable time

   (5) Auctions are "with reserve" unless specified otherwise

l. Online auctions

   (1) Many individuals and businesses are conducting auctions online

      (a) Becoming increasingly popular as buyers and sellers rely on fluidity of contract-making abilities

---

NOW REVIEW MULTIPLE-CHOICE QUESTIONS 1 THROUGH 9

---

3. Formation Defenses: Although offer and acceptance appear to present, if one of the following formation defenses occurs, then there may not be an agreement.

  a. Fraud—includes following elements

   (1) Misrepresentation of a material fact

      (a) Can be falsehood or concealment of defect

      (b) Silence is not misrepresentation unless there is duty to speak, for example,

         (1) Fiduciary relationship between parties

         (2) Seller of property knows there is a dangerous latent (hidden) defect

      (c) Must be statement of past or present fact

         (1) Opinion (e.g., of value) is not fact

            (a) Experts' opinion, however, does constitute fraud

---

EXAMPLE

An expert appraiser of jewelry appraises a diamond to be worth $500 when he knows it is actually worth $1,500. This fulfills the "misrepresentation of a material fact" element and also scienter element. If the remaining elements of fraud are met, then there is fraud.

---

         (2) Opinions about what will happen in future (expert or not) do not satisfy fact requirement

---

EXAMPLE

A real estate agent tells a prospective buyer that the income property she is considering purchasing will earn at least 50% more next year than last year.

---

        (3) Puffing or sales talk is not fact

EXAMPLE

A seller claims her necklace is worth $1,000. The buyer pays $1,000 and later finds out that he can buy a very similar necklace from another seller for $700. Even if the other elements of fraud are present, this opinion does not constitute fraud.

---

        (4) Presently existing intention in mind of the speaker is fact

   (2) Intent to mislead—"scienter"

      (a) Need knowledge of falsity with intent to mislead, **or**
      (b) Reckless disregard for truth can be substituted

        (1) If all elements (1) through (4) are present but reckless disregard is proven instead of actual knowledge of falsity, then it is called constructive fraud

   (3) Reasonable reliance by injured party

      (a) One who knows the truth or might have learned it by a reasonable inquiry may not recover
      (b) One cannot reasonably rely on opinions about future

   (4) Resulting in injury
   (5) Remedies for fraud

      (a) Defrauded party may affirm agreement and sue for damages under tort of deceit, or if party is sued on contract, then s/he may set up fraud in reduction of damages, or
      (b) Defrauded party may rescind contract and sue for damages that result from the fraud

   (6) Fraud may occur

      (a) In the inducement

        (1) The misrepresentation occurs during contract negotiations
        (2) Creates voidable contract at option of defrauded party

---

EXAMPLE

A represents to B that A's car has been driven 50,000 miles when in fact it has been driven for 150,000 miles. If B purchases A's car in reliance on this misrepresentation, fraud in the inducement is present, creating a voidable contract at B's option.

      (b) In the execution

        (1) Misrepresentation occurs in actual form of agreement
        (2) Defrauded party does not know the true nature of the contract.
        (3) Creates void contract

EXAMPLE

Larry Lawyer represents to Danny that Danny is signing his will, when in fact he is signing a promissory note payable to Larry. This promissory note is void because fraud in the execution is present.

---

(7) Fraud is also called intentional misrepresentation

b. Negligent misrepresentation and innocent misrepresentation

    (1) Both involve an innocent misstatement made in good faith (i.e., no scienter)

    (2) All other elements same as fraud

    (3) Creates right of rescission (cancellation) in injured party—to return both parties to their precontract positions to extent practicably possible (i.e. the contract is voidable)

        (a) Does not allow aggrieved party to sue for damages

c. Mistake: Where at least one party to the agreement believes that a material fact is true, but the fact is not true.

    (1) Mutual mistake (i.e., by both parties) about material characteristics of subject matter in contract makes contract voidable by either party

---

EXAMPLE

S and B make a contract in which B agrees to buy a boat from S. Although neither party knew it at the time, this boat had been destroyed before this contract was made. This is a mutual mistake about the existence of the boat; therefore, either party may void this contract by law. Note that legally either party may pull out although usually only one party may wish to do so.

        (a) Also exists when both parties reasonably attach different meanings to word or phrase

        (b) Also called bilateral mistake

        (c) Mistake about value of subject matter is not grounds for voiding contract

    (2) Unilateral mistake generally does not allow party to void contract

        (a) Exception: If non-mistaken part knowingly takes advantage of the mistaken party

---

EXAMPLE

A subcontractor submits a bid to do the electrical work for a new building. The bid was $10,000; the fair value for such work is approximately $100,000 and the general contractor accepts the bid with knowledge of this error. The subcontractor can successfully use unilateral mistake as a defense and void the agreement.

---

d. Duress—a contract entered into because of duress can be voided because of invalid consent

    (1) Any acts or threats of violence or extreme pressure against party or member of party's family, which in fact deprives party of free will and causes him/her to agree, is duress

---

EXAMPLE

X threatens to criminally prosecute Y unless he signs a contract. This contract is made under duress; although threats of a civil lawsuit do not normally constitute duress.

        (a) May involve coercion that is social or economic that leaves him/her with no reasonable alternative

    (2) Physical duress in which party agrees to contract under physical force

    (3) Extreme duress causes agreement to be void

    (4) Ordinary duress creates voidable agreement; unless there is immediate risk of physical harm, duress is ordinary.

e. Undue influence—unfair persuasion of one person over another which prevents understanding or voluntary action

    (1) Usually occurs when very dominant person has extreme influence over weaker person

        (a) Weakness can result from physical, mental, or emotional weakness or combinations of these

(2) Also occurs through abuse of fiduciary relationship (e.g., CPA, attorney, guardian, trustee, etc.)

(3) Normally causes agreement to be voidable

4. Consideration—an act, promise, or forbearance that is offered by one party and accepted by another as inducement to enter into agreement

  a. Consideration requires an exchange of promises (i.e., each party must promise to undertake an obligation that he or she was not previously obligated to perform).

EXAMPLE

B pays S $500 for S's stereo that he hands over to B. B's consideration is the $500. S's consideration is the stereo.

EXAMPLE

S gives B a stereo today. B promises to pay S $500 in one week. The promise to pay $500, rather than the $500 itself, is the consideration. Thus, the element of consideration is met today.

EXAMPLE

A hits and injures P with his car. P agrees not to sue A when A agrees to settle out of court for $10,000. A's promise to pay the money is consideration. P's promise to refrain from bringing a lawsuit is consideration on his/her side.

EXAMPLE

Using the fact pattern above, further assume that it is not clear whether A is at fault. The settlement (contract) is still enforceable if made in good faith because of possible liability.

---

  b. Consideration must be legally sufficient, this includes

  (1) A promise to do something that one was not previously obligated to do

  (2) A promise to refrain from something that one has a legal right to do

---

EXAMPLE

Thomas promises his uncle that he will not drink alcohol for 10 months in exchange for his uncle's promise to pay him $1,000. If Thomas is a minor and prohibited by state law from drinking alcohol, then Thomas has not provided consideration, since Thomas has no legal right to drink. Conversely, if Thomas is legally allowed to drink, then his promise does constitute consideration.

---

  c. Legal sufficiency does not concern itself with the adequacy of consideration (i.e., the law is not concerned whether the exchanged consideration is a fair deal).

EXAMPLE

In the previous example involving Thomas and his uncle, the court does not care whether Thomas's act of not drinking is worth $1,000. Rather the court is concerned that each party provided some consideration.

---

d. Consideration must be bargained for (this is essential)

 (1) Agreement to accept from debtor a lesser sum than owed is unenforceable if the debt is a liquidated (undisputed) debt

---

EXAMPLE

C agrees to accept $700 for a $900 debt that D owes C. The amount is not disputed. D still owes C the additional $200.

 (a) But if debtor incurs a detriment in addition to paying, creditor's promise to accept lesser sum will be binding

---

EXAMPLE

X owes Y $1,000. Y agrees to accept $500 and X will also install Y's new furnace at no additional cost.

 (b) Note that agreement to accept a lesser sum is enforceable if amount of debt is unliquidated (disputed) because both parties give up right to more favorable sum

---

EXAMPLE

C claims that D owes him $1,000. D claims that the amount owed is $600. If C and D agree to settle this for $700, the agreement is supported by consideration since C gave up the right to attempt to collect more than $700 and D gave up the right to attempt settlement for a lesser sum.

---

 (2) Preexisting legal duty is not sufficient as consideration because no new legal detriment is suffered by performing prior obligation

---

EXAMPLE

Agreement to pay police officer $200 to recover stolen goods is unenforceable.

EXAMPLE

X promises to pay Y, a jockey, $50 to ride as hard as he can in the race. Y already owes his employer, Z, that duty so there is no consideration to enforce the agreement.

 (a) Agreement to pay more to finish a job, such as building a house, is unenforceable unless unforeseen difficulties are encountered (e.g., underground stream or marshy land under a house)

 (3) Past consideration (consideration for a prior act, forbearance, or agreement) is not sufficient for new contract because it is not bargained for

 (4) Moral obligation is not consideration

 (a) In majority of states the following need no consideration

 (1) Promise to pay debt barred by statute of limitations.

 (2) Promise to pay debt barred by bankruptcy. Promise must adhere to strict rules stated in Bankruptcy Reform Act of 1978 concerning reaffirmations of dischargeable debts.

(5) Modifying existing contracts

    (a) Modification of contract under the common law needs new consideration on both sides to be legally binding

---

EXAMPLE

S agrees in a written contract to sell a piece of land to P for $40,000. S later changes his mind and demands $50,000 for the same piece of land. The original contract is enforceable (at $40,000) even if P agrees to the increased price because although P has agreed to give more consideration, S has not given any new consideration.

    (b) Under UCC, a contract for sale of goods may be modified orally or in writing without consideration if in good faith

---

EXAMPLE

S agrees to sell P 300 pairs of socks for $1.00 each. Due to rapid price increases in S's costs, he asks P if he will modify the price to $1.20 each. P agrees. The contract as modified is enforceable because it is covered under the UCC and does not need new consideration on both sides.

---

    (6) Illusory contracts are not supported by consideration (e.g., party agrees to sell all he/she wishes)

  e. In majority of states, seals placed on contracts are not substitutes for consideration

  f. Best-efforts contracts are contacts which parties are to use best efforts to complete contract's objectives

  g. Promissory estoppel may act as substitute for consideration and renders promise enforceable—promisor is estopped from asserting lack of consideration

    (1) Elements

        (a) Detrimental reliance on promise
        (b) Reliance is reasonable and foreseeable
        (c) Damage results (injustice) if promise is not enforced

    (2) Usually applied to gratuitous promises but trend is to apply to commercial transactions. At least recovery of expenses is allowed.

EXAMPLE

A wealthy man in the community promises to pay for a new church if it is built. The church committee reasonably (and in good faith) relies on the promise and incurs the expenses.

---

  h. Mutuality of obligation—means both parties must be bound or neither is bound

    (1) Both parties must give consideration by paying or promising to pay for the act, promise, or forbearance of the other with something of legal value

  i. Promise to donate to charity is enforceable based on public policy reasons

5. Legal Capacity

  a. An agreement between parties in which one or both lack the capacity to contract is void or, in some cases, voidable

  b. Minors: In a majority of states these are people under the age of 18.

    (1) A minor may contract, but agreement is voidable by minor

        (a) Adult is held to contract unless minor disaffirms

(2) If minor has purchased nonnecessaries, when minor disaffirms, s/he is required to give back any part s/he still has

    (a) Minor may recover all of consideration given

    (b) In most courts, minor need not pay for what s/he cannot return

---

EXAMPLE

Alicia sells Martin, a minor, her car for $3,000. Later that day, the car is damaged when Martin is involved in an accident. Martin decides to return the damaged car to Alicia. In most states, Martin will get the entire $3,000 back from Alicia.

---

(3) Minor is liable for reasonable value of necessaries furnished to him/her

    (a) Minor may disaffirm contract if it is executory (i.e., not completed)

    (b) Necessaries include food, clothing, shelter, education, etc., considering his/her age and position in life

    (c) Many states have passed laws which make certain contracts enforceable against minors such as contracts which involve

        1] Medical care

        2] Life insurance

        3] Psychological care

        4] Loans for education

(4) Minor may disaffirm contract at any time until a reasonable time after reaching majority age

    (a) Failure to disaffirm within reasonable time after reaching majority acts as ratification (e.g., one year is too long in the absence of very special circumstances such as being out of the country)

(5) Minor may choose to ratify within a reasonable time after reaching age of majority

    (a) By words, either orally or in writing but must ratify all, or

    (b) By actions that indicate ratification

    (c) Ratification prior to majority is not effective

(6) If minor misrepresents his/her age when making contract, most states still allow minor to disaffirm

    (a) Some courts allow minor to disaffirm contract, but allow other party to sue for fraud

    (b) Some allow minor to disaffirm if minor returns consideration in similar condition

    (c) Other courts will not allow minor to disaffirm especially if it was a business contract

c. Incompetent persons

    (1) Contract by person adjudicated insane is void

        (a) Insane person need not return consideration

    (2) Contracts made by those with diminished capacity (e.g., compulsive spending disorder) are voidable

        (a) Where courts hold such agreements voidable, restitution is condition precedent to disaffirmance

d. Legal capacity of intoxicated person is determined by his/her ability to understand, and, by degree of intoxication

    (1) Contracts are enforceable, in general, unless extent of intoxication at time contract made was so great that intoxicated party did not understand terms or nature of contract—then contract voidable at option of one intoxicated if s/he returns items under contract

6. Legality

a. Agreement is generally unenforceable if it is illegal or violates public policy

b. When both parties are guilty, neither will be aided by court (i.e., if one party had already given some consideration, s/he will not get it back)

     (1) But if one party repudiates prior to performance, s/he may recover his/her consideration

---

EXAMPLE

X contracts to buy stolen goods from Y. If X pays Y but then repents and refuses to accept the stolen goods, X may recover the money he paid Y.

---

  c. When one party is innocent, s/he will usually be given relief

    (1) A member of a class of people designed to be protected by statute is considered innocent (e.g., purchaser of stock issued in violation of blue-sky laws)

  d. Types of illegal contracts (contracts that may not be enforceable due to public policy concerns)

    (1) Agreement to commit crime or tort

      (a) If agreement calls for intentional wrongful interference with a valid contractual relationship, it is an illegal agreement

    (2) An agreement to not press criminal charges for consideration is illegal

---

EXAMPLE

A has embezzled money from his employer. The employer agrees to not press charges if A pays back all of the money. Such an agreement is not enforceable, since employer has an obligation to cooperate with criminal investigations.

---

    (3) Services rendered without a license when statute requires a license

      (a) Two types of licensing statutes

        (1) Regulatory licensing statute—one that seeks to protect public from incapable, unskilled, or dishonest persons

          (a) Contract is unenforceable by either party
          (b) Even if party performs work, the other party need not pay since this is an illegal bargain

---

EXAMPLE

X, falsely claiming to have a CPA license, performs an audit for ABC Company. Upon learning the true facts, ABC may legally refuse to pay X any fees or expenses. This is true even if X properly performed the audit in compliance with all regulations.

---

        (2) Revenue-seeking statute—purpose is to raise revenue for government

          (a) Contract is enforceable

EXAMPLE

Y, based on a contract, performed extensive yard work for M. M then finds out that Y failed to obtain a license required by the local government to raise revenue. M is obligated to pay Y the agreed-upon amount.

---

    (4) Usury (contract for greater than legal interest rate)
    (5) Contracts against public policy

      (a) Contracts in restraint of trade such as covenant not to compete after end of an employment contract

(1) Courts must balance need of former employer such as protection of trade secrets or customer base with need of employee to practice his/her line of work

(2) Typically, contract will restrict employee from competing in named areas for stated period of time

(3) Employer must show that covenant not to compete is needed to protect interests of employer and that restraints are reasonable as to geographical area and as to time period

(b) Upon sale of business, seller agrees to not compete with sold type of business in named areas for stated period of time

(1) Courts will look at reasonableness as to geographical area, reasonableness as to time, and whether covenant is unduly restrictive for public's need

(2) Courts are generally more likely to enforce a covenant not to compete in the sale of a business rather than such a covenant in an employment contract because the parties in the sale of a business are viewed as having equal bargaining power.

(c) Exculpatory clauses are clauses found in contracts in which one party tries to avoid liability for own negligence

(1) Generally, such clauses are enforceable if it attempts to excuse merely negligent behavior

(2) If the clause tries to excuse intentional or reckless behavior then the clause is unenforceable

EXAMPLE

Sally decides to go skiing. When she buys her lift ticket, she signs a clause promising to not hold the owners of the mountain liable for any injuries that Sally suffers while skiing. If Sally is injured while skiing as a result of the conduct of the owners of the ski resort, Sally can still recover against the ski resort if she can show that the injuries were due to reckless or intentional conduct on the part of the owners.

NOW REVIEW MULTIPLE-CHOICE QUESTIONS 10 THROUGH 27

D. Written Contracts

1. Generally, an oral contract is as enforceable as a written contract
2. The Statute of Frauds, however, requires that certain types of contracts be evidenced by a writing to be enforceable.

   a. Evidenced by a writing means either

   (1) That the contract, itself, be in writing, or
   (2) That there is sufficient written evidence to prove the existence of a contract

3. Contracts that need to be evidenced by a writing

   a. An agreement to sell or transfer any interest in land (real estate)

   (1) Includes buildings, easements, and contracts to sell real estate
   (2) Part performance typically satisfies Statute of Frauds even though real estate contract was oral, but this requires

   (a) Possession of the land
   (b) Either part payment or making of improvements on real estate
   (c) Many courts require all three

   b. An agreement that cannot be performed within one year from the making of agreement

   (1) Contract that can be performed in exactly one year or less may be oral

EXAMPLE

W agrees to hire X for ten months starting in four months. This contract must be in writing because it cannot be performed until fourteen months after the agreement is made.

(2) Any contract which can conceivably be completed in one year, irrespective of how long the task actually takes, may be oral

---

EXAMPLE

A agrees to paint B's portrait for $400. It actually is not completed until over a year later. This contract did not have to be in writing because it was possible to complete it within one year.

---

(3) If performance is contingent on something which could take place in less than one year, agreement may be oral

---

EXAMPLE

"I will employ you as long as you live." Party could possibly die in less than one year.

---

(4) But if its terms call for more than one year, it must be written even if there is possibility of taking place in less than one year

---

EXAMPLE

"I will employ you for five years." The employee's death could occur before the end of five years, but the terms ("five years") call for the writing requirement under the Statute of Frauds.

---

(5) Generally, if one side of performance is complete but other side cannot be performed within year, it is not within Statute (i.e., may be oral). Especially true if performance has been accepted and all that remains is the payment of money.

EXAMPLE

X orally agrees to pay E $6,000 salary per month and a bonus of $50,000 if he works for at least two years. After two years, X refuses to pay the bonus. The $50,000 is payable and the Statute of Frauds is no defense here.

    (a) An agreement to answer for debt or default of another (contract of guaranty, see suretyship in Module 31)

        (1) A secondary promise is within this section of the Statute of Frauds (i.e., must be in writing)

EXAMPLE

"If Jack doesn't pay, I will."

---

        (2) A primary promise is not within this section of the Statute of Frauds because it is in reality the promisor's own contract

---

EXAMPLE

"Let Jack have it, and I will pay."

---

(3) Promise for benefit of promisor may be oral ("Main Purpose Doctrine")

EXAMPLE

Promisor agrees to answer for default of X, because X is promisor's supplier and he needs X to stay in business to keep himself in business.

---

    (4) Promise of indemnity (will pay based on another's fault, for example, insurance) is not within Statute

c. Agreement for sale of goods for $500 or more is required to be in writing under UCC

EXAMPLE

Oral contract for the sale of fifty calculators for $10 each is not enforceable.

EXAMPLE

Oral contract to perform management consulting services over the next six months for $100,000 is enforceable because the $500 rule does not apply to contracts that are under common law.

EXAMPLE

Same as previous example except that the agreed time was for fourteen months. This one is required to be in writing to be enforceable because of the one-year rule.

---

    (1) Exceptions to writing requirement (these are important)

        (a) Oral contract involving specially manufactured goods (i.e., not saleable in ordinary course of business) if seller has made substantial start in their manufacture (or even made a contract for necessary raw materials) is enforceable

        (b) Oral contract is enforceable against party who admits it in court but not beyond quantity of goods admitted

        (c) Goods that have been paid for (if seller accepts payment) or goods which buyer has accepted are part of enforceable contract even if oral

---

EXAMPLE

B orally agrees to purchase 10,000 parts from S for $1 each. B later gives S $6,000 for a portion of the parts. S accepts the money. In absence of a written agreement, B may enforce a contract for 6,000 parts but not for the full 10,000 parts.

---

    (2) Modifications of written contracts involve two issues under UCC

        (a) New consideration on both sides is not required under UCC although it is required under common law

            (1) Under UCC, modification must be done in good faith

        (b) Modified contract must be in writing if contract, as modified, is within Statute of Frauds (i.e., sale of goods for $500 or more)

> **EXAMPLE**
>
> S agrees orally to sell B 100 widgets for $4.80 each. B later agrees, orally, to pay $5.00 for the 100 widgets due to changed business conditions. The modified contract is not enforceable because it must have been in writing. Therefore, the original contract is enforceable.

> **EXAMPLE**
>
> Same as above except that the modification is in writing. Now the modified contract is enforceable despite the fact that S is giving no new consideration.

> **EXAMPLE**
>
> X and Y have a written contract for the sale of goods for $530. They subsequently both agree orally to a price reduction of $40. The modified contract for $490 is enforceable.

    (3) Parties may exclude future oral agreements in a signed writing
    (4) Agreement for sale of intangibles over $5,000 must be in writing (e.g., patents, copyrights, or contract rights)

4. The Statute of Frauds is a rule of evidence; thus, the Statute only applies to executory contracts

    a. The Statute requires a writing to act as proof of the existence of a contract
    b. If the parties have already executed (performed) the contract, there is no need for written evidence because the parties' performance is evidence that a contract existed.

5. The writing requirement

    a. The Statute of Frauds does not require that the actual contract be in writing, rather that there is a writing, or writings, that prove the existence of a contract.
    b. The writing requirement may be satisfied by one writing or by combining multiple writings
    c. A sufficient writing must

       (1) Identify the parties to the contract,
       (2) Identify the subject matter of the contract, and
       (3) Be signed by the party to be charged (the party we are seeking to hold liable for the contract).

> **EXAMPLE**
>
> On May 1, 2013, Patrick provides a written offer to Rod for Rod to work for Patrick from August 1, 2013 until June 30, 2014. Rod accepts the offer orally on May 3, 2013. On July 15, 2013, Rod receives a better job offer from George and informs Patrick that Rod will not work for Patrick. Patrick sues Rod for breach of contract.
>
>   Analysis: First this contract is covered by the Statute of Frauds since it cannot be performed within 1 year from the date of formation. (May 3, 2013–June 30, 2014) Patrick's written offer to Rod satisfies two of the conditions for a writing: Identifies the parties and the nature of the contract. Patrick's writing, however, is only signed by Patrick, not Rod. Since Rod is the party to be charged, the writing is not sufficient and the Statute of Frauds will prevent Patrick from enforcing the employment contract against Rod.
>
> > **NOTE:** If Rod had responded to Patrick's offer via e-mail, instead of orally, then the contract is binding upon both parties. Patrick's written offer, as discussed above, satisfies two of the conditions for a writing; Rod's e-mail would provide the signature of the party to be charged. Combining the two writings would satisfy the Statute of Frauds.

6. Noncompliance with Statute of Frauds (i.e., failure to make a writing) will make contract unenforceable
7. Parol evidence rule

   a. Applies only if a written contract exists

   b. Provides that any written agreement intended by parties to be final and complete contract (called an integration) may not be contradicted by previous or contemporaneous (written or oral) evidence

      (1) Applies to such written contracts whether Statute of Frauds required writing or not

      (2) Evidence of integration is often shown by a clause such as "This agreement is the complete agreement between the parties; no other representations have been made."

EXAMPLE

A and B enter into a home purchase agreement that is intended as a complete contract. B wishes to introduce oral evidence into court that the price of $150,000 that was in the home purchase agreement was put in to get a larger loan from a bank. B claims that they orally agreed the price would be $130,000. The oral evidence is not allowed to contradict the written contract under the parol evidence rule.

---

      (3) Exceptions (party may present oral proof)

         (a) To prove the existence of a formation defense (e.g., fraud, forgery, duress, mistake, failure of consideration; see part C.3 of this outline above).

         (b) To show terms not inconsistent with writing that parties would not be expected to have included

---

EXAMPLE

Builder promises orally to use reasonable care not to damage nearby trees when building a house.

         (c) To explain intended meaning of an ambiguity (proof cannot contradict terms in contract but can explain them)

         (d) To show condition precedent—proof can be presented to show a fact or event must occur before agreement is valid

         (e) Under UCC, written terms may be supplemented or explained by course of dealing, usage of trade, or course of performance

      (4) Does not apply to subsequent transactions (e.g., promises made after original agreement, or separate and distinct agreement made at same time as written contract)

EXAMPLE

M and N have a complete written employment contract. Later, M and N orally modify the contract with M agreeing to pay more and N agreeing to take on more duties. The oral evidence is allowed because it arose subsequent to the written contract.

---

8. Contracting using faxes

   a. Legal issues arise with use of faxes

      (1) Was an agreement really reached?

         (a) Courts examine faxes to see if "meeting of minds" actually took place under common law principles

      (2) Validity of signatures sent by faxes

         (a) Majority of courts that have examined this issue conclude that signatures sent by fax are valid

9. Contracting online

    a. When individuals make contracts over the Internet, basic rules of contract law still apply; however, this technology has created and will create more additional legal issues—only some of which have been settled

    b. E-SIGN Act—Federal law that makes electronic signatures valid like written ones, also makes electronic documents as valid as ones on paper

        (1) Electronic signatures are also referred to as e-signatures

            (a) Challenge is to verify that one using e-signature is person s/he claims to be

        (2) Electronic document is valid only if it is in form that is retainable and is accurately reproduced

        (3) Some documents are exempt from E-SIGN Act such as wills, court papers, and foreclosures

        (4) Act is considered important to promote use of technology

            (a) Does not provide uniform standard for authenticating e-signatures

                (1) However, recommended methods to authenticate e-signatures include

                    (a) Use devices that recognize iris of user's eye or other portions of eye

                    (b) Use devices that recognize fingerprints

                    (c) Use secret passwords

                    (d) Use cards to identify persons such as "smart cards"

            (b) Various states are adopting statutes that provide for procedures to determine validity of e-signatures

            (c) Many companies enter into written contracts to accept electronic data and e-signatures between them

            (d) Companies and individuals may use exceptions that exist under statute of frauds without need to resort to E-SIGN Act or state statutes

        (5) Federal law has following provisions to protect consumers

            (a) Consumers need to consent to receiving electronic contracts and records

            (b) Businesses required to tell consumers of their right to receive hard-copy documents of electronic transactions

            (c) Consumers must be able to indicate or demonstrate they have access to electronic records for businesses to send them electronic records

10. Computer shrink-wrap licenses and contracts generally enforceable

    a. Sale of shrink-wrap licenses is often conducted over Internet

    b. Individual or company often buys these without seeing or reviewing them first (thus the term shrink-wrap)

        (1) Court cases have held these shrink-wrap licenses or goods purchased online to be enforceable especially if purchaser has time to examine them with right of return

11. Federal antispam law does not prohibit spam but instead allows businesses to spam when they do not lie in spam

12. Internet and online transactions are changing how goods and services are paid for

    a. Some methods have developed for electronic payment

        (1) Person-to-person payment often called PayPal is a system in which buyer authorizes payment of goods or services and seller goes to a site to provide information needed to authorize payment—amount is deducted from buyer's bank account

        (2) Virtual credit card is a system used by ones who doubt security of Internet

            (a) System creates new credit card number for each transaction which cannot be reused

        (3) Digital cash is a method whereby retailers create their own currency on the Internet and customers with the right software can purchase the currency to pay for items with their currency account

            (a) It is good for those who wish not to use credit cards on the web

        (4) Digital Wallets is a one-stop payment location authorized by a buyer so retailers can be paid from the wallet when given access by the buyer

(5) Virtual points allow web users to accumulate points which can be used to make purchases

    (a) These systems must have a sufficient number of retailers to make them work well

(6) Virtual escrow is a method in which a third party handles the Internet transaction and makes sure seller has performed according to the contract before releasing payment from buyer

> **NOW REVIEW MULTIPLE-CHOICE QUESTIONS 28 THROUGH 37**

E. Assignment and Delegation

1. Assignment is the transfer of a right under a contract by one person to another
2. Delegation is the transfer of duties under a contract
3. Generally, a party's rights in a contract are assignable and duties are delegable

   a. No consideration is needed for valid assignment

     (1) Gratuitous assignments are revocable

EXAMPLE

A owes B a debt for services B performed for A, but B has been unable to collect because A has been in financial difficulty. B may gratuitously assign this debt to X if X can collect it. If A's financial position improves, B may revoke the assignment to X and collect the debt himself or assign it to another for consideration.

---

   b. Rights may be assigned without delegating duties, or duties may be delegated without assigning rights
   c. Partial assignments may be made (e.g., only assign part of one's rights such as right to receive money)
   d. An assignment of a contract is generally taken to mean both assignment of rights and delegation of duties unless language or facts indicate otherwise
   e. Exceptions to ability to make assignments and delegations

     (1) Contract involving personal services, trust, or confidence (e.g., an artist cannot delegate his/her duty to paint a portrait)

       (a) With permission, these can be delegated
       (b) Note that a contractor building a house according to a blueprint can delegate his/her duty to someone qualified

     (2) Provision of contract or statute prohibits assignment or delegation

       (a) Trend is to look with disfavor on prohibitions against assignments where only a right to money is concerned
       (b) The UCC makes prohibition against assignment of monetary rights ineffective

     (3) If assignment would materially change risk or burden of obligor

       (a) For example, insurance contracts, requirement and output contracts, and contracts where personal credit is involved

   f. A delegation of duties is not an anticipatory breach

EXAMPLE

X Company contracted to deliver certain goods to Y. If X Company is low on these goods, it may delegate this duty to S Company, its subsidiary. It is not an anticipatory breach because X has not indicated that performance will not occur.

---

4. An assignment generally extinguishes any rights of assignor but a delegation does not relieve delegator of his/her duties

   a. The assignee acquires assignor's rights against obligor and has exclusive right to performance

   b. If obligor has notice of assignment, s/he must pay assignee, not assignor

     (1) If obligor has no notice, s/he may pay assignor and assignee can only recover from assignor

5. Party taking an assignment generally steps into shoes of assignor—s/he gets no better rights than assignor had

   a. Assignee is subject to any defenses obligor could assert against assignor

   b. If assignee releases obligor, then assignor is also released

> **EXAMPLE**
>
> A and B enter into a contract in which B agrees to pay A $300 for a stereo he received. A assigns his right to the $300 to C. C then releases B from the obligation of paying C the $300. This also releases A.

6. Assignor for value makes implied warranties to assignee that

   a. Assignor will do nothing to impair rights of assignee

   b. Assignor has no knowledge of any fact that would impair value of assignment

7. If assignor makes more than one assignment of same right, there are two rules to be applied depending upon the state

   a. First assignment prevails regardless of notice (majority rule)

   b. First assignee to give notice to obligor prevails (minority rule)

NOW REVIEW MULTIPLE-CHOICE QUESTIONS 38 THROUGH 40

F. Third-Party Beneficiary Contracts

1. Contracting parties enter into agreement intended to benefit third party(ies)

   a. Creditor beneficiary—a debtor contracts with a second party to pay the debt owed to creditor (third-party beneficiary)

> **EXAMPLE**
>
> X owes C $100. X contracts with Y to paint Y's house if Y will pay C $100. C is a creditor beneficiary.

> **EXAMPLE**
>
> B buys some real estate from S and agrees to assume S's mortgage that is owed to XYZ bank. XYZ is a creditor beneficiary because B and S made a contract in which B agreed to pay XYZ. If B later defaults, XYZ may recover from either B or S. XYZ may recover from S based on the original contract. XYZ may recover from B because XYZ is a creditor beneficiary.

> **EXAMPLE**
>
> Buyer purchases some property subject to a mortgage that the seller owes a bank. The bank is not a third-party beneficiary because buyer did not agree to pay the mortgage. The seller is still the only debtor on the mortgage.

b. Donee beneficiary—almost the same as creditor beneficiary except promisee's intent is to confer a gift upon third party through promisor's performance

> **EXAMPLE**
>
> X contracts to buy Y's car if Y will deliver it to D, X's son; D is a donee beneficiary.

c. Incidental beneficiary—third party who receives an unintended benefit from a contract. S/he obtains **no** rights under the contract

> **EXAMPLE**
>
> X and Y contract to build an apartment building. A, a nearby store owner, would benefit from increased business and is an incidental beneficiary.

2. Only intended beneficiary (creditor or donee) can maintain an action against contracting parties for nonperformance

a. Intent of the promisee controls
b. Creditor beneficiary can proceed against either contracting party

> **EXAMPLE**
>
> X owes C $100. X contracts with M to paint M's house if M will pay C $100. If X does not paint M's house, C may sue X because X still owes C $100. C may also sue M, because M now owes C $100 under the contract. C is a creditor beneficiary and can sue either party.

c. Donee beneficiary can proceed against the promisor only

> **EXAMPLE**
>
> X contracts to buy Y's car if Y will deliver it to D. If Y does not deliver the car, D may sue Y. However, D may not sue X because it was a gift from X, not an obligation.

3. If the third-party beneficiary contract is executory, the parties may rescind and defeat the third party's rights

> **EXAMPLE**
>
> X owes C $100. X contracts with Y to paint Y's house if Y will pay C $100. X and Y may rescind the contract before Y pays C $100. Then there is no contract for C to enforce; however, C may still sue X for the $100 owed. Or in other words, C has no third-party rights on an executory contract.

4. The promisor can assert any defenses against third-party beneficiary that s/he has against promisee

NOW REVIEW MULTIPLE-CHOICE QUESTIONS 41 THROUGH 45

G. Performance of Contract

1. Duty to perform may depend upon a condition

   a. Condition precedent is condition that must occur before stated promise or duty in contract becomes due

   ---

   EXAMPLE

   B agrees to plant trees on specified land once C removes an old tennis court from the land. Until C removes the tennis court, B has no obligation to plant the trees.

   ---

   b. Condition subsequent is condition that when it occurs it modifies or takes away a duty specified in contract

   ---

   EXAMPLE

   M agrees to rent N a certain home until M finds a buyer.

   ---

   c. Satisfaction as a condition—normally when a contract guarantees satisfaction, this means agreement is performed when a reasonable person would be satisfied. However, if agreement is expressly conditioned upon personal satisfaction of one of contracting parties, then performance does not occur until that party is actually satisfied.

2. Tender of performance is an offer to perform (e.g., offer to pay debt)

   EXAMPLE

   X has contracted to buy goods from Y with delivery and payment to take place concurrently. X must offer the money to Y before Y has breached the contract for failure to deliver.

   ---

3. Under the **doctrine of substantial performance** (very important), performance is satisfied if

   a. There has been substantial performance (i.e., **deviations are minor**), and
   b. There has been **good-faith** effort to comply with contract
   c. Then damages for deviations are deducted from price if above are met
   d. This is often used in relation to construction contracts

4. Payment of less than agreed-upon sum does not fulfill obligation unless both parties compromise based on a bona fide dispute as to amount owed
5. Standards of interpretation of contracts

   a. For ordinary words, courts use normal meaning in dictionary
   b. For technical words, courts use technical meaning supplied by expert testimony if necessary
   c. Any ambiguity in contract is construed against party who drafted contract
   d. Typed words prevail over preprinted words—handwritten words prevail over both preprinted and typed words
   e. When both parties are members of same profession or trade, words are given meaning in that profession or trade unless contract states otherwise

NOW REVIEW MULTIPLE-CHOICE QUESTIONS 46 AND 47

H. Discharge of Contracts

1. By agreement—new consideration is necessary, but often it is supplied by a promise for a promise (e.g., both parties agreeing to release other party of contractual obligation)

   a. Both parties may mutually agree to rescind contract—mutual rescission

      (1) Both parties of a contract may agree to satisfy contract by doing something different called accord and satisfaction

         (a) An accord is an agreement to substitute new performance for the original performance.
         (b) Satisfaction is the performance of the accord.

   b. A novation is an agreement between three parties, the original two parties to the agreement and a new party, where the new party takes the place of one of the original parties to the contract.

      (1) Original party, who has been replaced, has no obligation or rights under the original contract.
      (2) New party has all rights and liabilities of original party.

EXAMPLE

X has agreed to do some accounting work for Y for $2,000. Since X is very busy, X, Y, and Z all agree to let X out of the contract and insert Z in his place. This is a novation. X and Y no longer have any obligations to each other.

EXAMPLE

A party purchases land and assumes a mortgage. The original mortgagor is still liable unless a novation has occurred.

---

2. By performance becoming objectively impossible

   a. But mere fact of performance becoming more costly does not excuse performance

---

EXAMPLE

A agreed to sell a specified quantity of corn to B at specified prices. He had planned to sell his own corn until his crop was destroyed. Even though he may make less profit or even suffer a loss, he can still fulfill the contract by purchasing the corn from others to resell to B under his contract.

---

3. Breach of contract

   a. If party breaches contract s/he will probably have to pay damages (see Section I. Remedies immediately below in this outline).
   b. Courts consider most breaches to be nonmaterial and award money damages as the usual remedy.
   c. If breach is material, the nonbreaching party's performance will be excused.

4. Anticipatory breach (repudiation) is renunciation before performance is due; the nonbreaching party

   a. May sue at once, or
   b. Cancel contract, or
   c. Wait until time performance is due or for a reasonable time and then sue, but nonbreaching party has duty to mitigate damages
   d. If other party has not changed position in reliance upon the repudiation, repudiating party can retract repudiation and perform at appointed time, thereby discharging his/her contractual obligation

> **EXAMPLE**
>
> X agrees to convey and Y agrees to pay for land on April 1. On February 1, Y learns that X has sold the land to Z. Y may sue before April 1, or he may wait and sue on April 1.

> **EXAMPLE**
>
> M agrees to deliver 1,000 widgets to Q by December 1. Three months before that date, M says, he will be unable to deliver on December 1. Q may sue immediately or wait until December 1.

5. Bankruptcy discharges a party's contractual obligations
6. Statute of Limitations requires that most lawsuits, including breach of contract lawsuits, be filed in a timely manner

   a. The time begins from the date of the breach of the contract.
   b. If lawsuit is not filed in the time permitted by the law, then the injured party is barred from filing the lawsuit.
   c. Claim (lawsuit) may be revived if breaching party admits to the breach even after Statute of Limitations has expired.

> **EXAMPLE**
>
> Laurie Yur, an attorney, promised to do some legal work for Carrie Client, who paid Yur $500. Yur never performed the work. Several years later, after the Statute of Limitations had expired, Client wrote Yur a letter stating that Yur needed to return the $500 plus interest or Client would sue Yur for breach of contract. If Yur does nothing, Client will be unsuccessful because the Statute of Limitations bars Client's lawsuit. If, however, Yur responds by stating, "Too bad, while I did breach the contract, it is too late for you," then the Statute of Limitations begins to run again. Thus Client could successfully bring the lawsuit, since Yur admitted her breach. By admitting the breach, Yur has allowed the Statute of Limitations to start over.

NOW REVIEW MULTIPLE-CHOICE QUESTIONS 48 THROUGH 51

I. Remedies

1. Monetary damages

   a. Purpose is to place injured party in as good a position as s/he would have occupied if contract had been performed
   b. Actual or compensatory damages are equal to amount caused by breach

      (1) This is the **most common remedy** under contract law

   c. Consequential damages

      (1) These are damages that arise as a consequence of the breach (e.g., lost profits)
      (2) Only awarded by the court if the consequential damages are foreseeable to the breaching party. Courts rarely find these damages to be foreseeable.

   d. Punitive damages are generally not allowed in contract law
   e. Liquidated damage clause is a provision agreed to in a contract to set the amount of damages in advance if a breach occurs

      (1) These are used instead of awarding actual compensatory damages
      (2) Not enforceable if punitive; therefore, amount set in advance must be reasonably based on what actual damages are expected to be

f. Party injured by breach must use reasonable care to minimize loss because s/he cannot recover costs that could have been avoided—called mitigation of damages

---

EXAMPLE

One who receives perishables which are not the goods bargained for must take reasonable steps to prevent loss from spoilage.

EXAMPLE

X contracts to fix Y's car. After X begins work, Y breaches and says "Stop." X cannot continue to work and incur more costs (i.e., put in more parts and labor).

---

2. Rescission—cancellation of contract whereby parties are placed in position they were in before contract was formed
3. Specific performance—compels performance promised

   a. Used when money damages will not suffice (e.g., when subject matter is unique, or rare, as in contract for sale of land)
   b. Injured party may seek compensatory damages if s/he reasonably chooses them
   c. Not available to compel personal services
   d. Only the party who is to receive the unique item, e.g., land, may demand specific performance as a remedy.

EXAMPLE

Madison entered into a written contract to sell her house to Lucas for $300,000. If Madison breaches the contract, Lucas may demand that Madison still sell Lucas the house (specific performance), or Lucas may take money damages instead. If Lucas breaches the contract, then Madison may only receive money damages as a remedy.

---

4. Restitution—return of consideration to injured party
5. Injunction—compels an act or restrains an act
6. Release—one party relieves other party of part of obligations in contract
7. Waiver—one party voluntarily gives up some right in contract either by express agreement or by consistently not enforcing such right in past
8. Arbitration—resolution of dispute, outside of judicial system, agreed to by disputing parties
9. Reformation—if parties have failed to express true intentions in contract, court may reform it to express true intentions of contract

---

NOW REVIEW MULTIPLE-CHOICE QUESTIONS 52 THROUGH 56

J. Jurisdiction over Defendant for Online Transactions

1. Courts generally grant plaintiffs personal jurisdiction over defendants in foreign state if plaintiff intentionally engaged in commercial activities for use outside of home state
2. Generally, Web sites or advertising by persons or entities seen by others in other jurisdictions do not create personal jurisdiction to allow lawsuits in those other jurisdictions

   a. Minimum contacts such as actively selling products are needed to require defendant to defend self in other state

3. Parties to contracts made online may agree to use law of given jurisdiction just as in other contracts

      a. Often, Web sites put forum selection clause at end of home page in case lawsuit is brought against online company

         (1) Some courts may not enforce these clauses since they are not negotiable and thus lead to adhesion contracts

            (a) Increasing trend is not to enforce these unless they are fair and reasonable

   4. Courts typically invalidate state laws that regulate the Internet when those laws extend to activities outside their state and place a burden on interstate commerce

K. Interference with Contractual Relations

   1. Happens when a party to a contract shows that defendant's interference with other party's performance of such contract wrongfully caused plaintiff to lose benefit of performance of that contract

      a. Typically defendant must have **intended** to cause said breach of contract and defendant's conduct must be improper

         (1) For example, when a contract's performance is stopped by bribery, criminal actions, or threats of violence

KEY TERMS

Suffixes "-or" and "-ee." These suffixes are used frequently in the law, but especially in contract law. The " - or" indicates the person performing the action, for example, the promisor is making a promise, the assignor is making an assignment, the offeror makes an offer, etc. The " - ee" is the receiver of the action, for example, the promisee is a person to whom the promise is made, the assignee is someone who receives the assignment, the offeree is a person to whom an offer is made, etc.

  Acceptance. An unequivocal expression to enter into a contract based on the terms provided in the offer.

  Capacity. The mental ability to understand the nature of the terms of the contract.

  Compensatory damages. The most common remedy for breach of contract. Designed to pay the nonbreaching party for the amount of loss that has been suffered.

  Consideration. Something that has value in the eyes of the law that induces another to enter into a contract

  Contract. Promises that the courts will enforce.

  Counteroffer. When an offeree alters the terms of the original offer, which terminates the original offer. The offeree now becomes the offeror.

  Formation defenses. These actions invalidate what otherwise would be mutual assent. The actions include duress, fraud, mistake, and undue influence. While offer and acceptance appear to be present on the surface, the presence of a formation defense shows a lack of true mutual assent.

  Minor. A person who is younger than the legal age to enter into a binding contract. A minor's contract is voidable by the minor.

  Mirror image rule. An acceptance must precisely reflect (mirror) the offer to be a valid acceptance

  Mitigation of damages. The nonbreaching party has an obligation to keep damages as low as is reasonably possible.

  Mutual assent. Parties have voluntarily come to a common understanding of the terms of the bargain. Mutual assent is the combination of a valid offer and a valid acceptance.

  Offer. An unequivocal expression of party's willingness to enter into a contract.

  Parol evidence rule. Prevents the introduction of any documents, testimony, or any evidence that contradicts the language of a *written* contract. This rule only forbids that evidence that arose prior to, or at the same time, that the written contract was created.

  Promissory estoppel. An implied contract at law, where a court rules that a contract exists even though an element of a contract is missing. Court will possibly use this where a promissee has reasonably relied on a promisor's promise and that reliance has injured the promisee.

  Specific performance. A remedy that is available for unique items, where money damages would not be adequate to compensate the nonbreaching party. Effectively, the court orders the breaching party to perform the original promise under the contract.

  Statute of Frauds. A rule of evidence that requires certain contracts be in writing or have written evidence to support the contracts' existence. These include contracts that transfer interests in real property (real estate); cannot, by the terms of the contract, be possibly performed within one year; answer for the debts of another; or involve the sale of **goods** for $500 or more.

  Void. Contracts that are void are not enforceable by either party.

  Voidable. Contracts that are voidable are valid unless the party, with the option to do so, chooses to make the contract void.

Multiple-Choice Questions (1–56)

C.1. Offer

1. Carson Corp., a retail chain, asked Alto Construction to fix a broken window at one of Carson's stores. Alto offered to make the repairs within three days at a price to be agreed on after the work was completed. A contract based on Alto's offer would fail because of indefiniteness as to the

    a. Price involved.
    b. Nature of the subject matter.
    c. Parties to the contract.
    d. Time for performance.

2. On September 10, Harris, Inc., a new car dealer, placed a newspaper advertisement stating that Harris would sell ten cars at its showroom for a special discount only on September 12, 13, and 14. On September 12, King called Harris and expressed an interest in buying one of the advertised cars. King was told that five of the cars had been sold and to come to the showroom as soon as possible. On September 13, Harris made a televised announcement that the sale would end at 10:00 PM that night. King went to Harris' showroom on September 14 and demanded the right to buy a car at the special discount. Harris had sold the ten cars and refused King's demand. King sued Harris for breach of contract. Harris' **best** defense to King's suit would be that Harris'

    a. Offer was unenforceable.
    b. Advertisement was **not** an offer.
    c. Television announcement revoked the offer.
    d. Offer had **not** been accepted.

3. On June 15, Peters orally offered to sell a used lawn mower to Mason for $125. Peters specified that Mason had until June 20 to accept the offer. On June 16, Peters received an offer to purchase the lawn mower for $150 from Bronson, Mason's neighbor. Peters accepted Bronson's offer. On June 17, Mason saw Bronson using the lawn mower and was told the mower had been sold to Bronson. Mason immediately wrote to Peters to accept the June 15 offer. Which of the following statements is correct?

    a. Mason's acceptance would be effective when received by Peters.
    b. Mason's acceptance would be effective when mailed.
    c. Peters' offer had been revoked and Mason's acceptance was ineffective.
    d. Peters was obligated to keep the June 15 offer open until June 20.

4. Calistoga offers to sell her home to Drake for $300,000. Drake asks her if she would accept $250,000. Which of the following is true?

    a. Drake's response is mere inquiry; therefore, the $300,000 offer by Calistoga is still in force.
    b. Drake's response is a counteroffer effectively terminating the $300,000 offer and instigating an offer for $250,000.
    c. Drake's response is a rejection of the $300,000 offer, and there is no offer for $250,000 because it is too indefinite to be an offer.
    d. Because of ambiguity, both offers are terminated by operation of law.

5. Opal offered, in writing, to sell Larkin a parcel of land for $300,000. If Opal dies, the offer will

    a. Terminate prior to Larkin's acceptance only if Larkin received notice of Opal's death.
    b. Remain open for a reasonable period of time after Opal's death.
    c. Automatically terminate despite Larkin's prior acceptance.
    d. Automatically terminate prior to Larkin's acceptance.

C.2. Acceptance

6. On April 1, Fine Corp. faxed Moss an offer to purchase Moss' warehouse for $500,000. The offer stated that it would remain open only until April 4 and that acceptance must be received to be effective. Moss sent an acceptance on April 4 by overnight mail and Fine received it on April 5. Which of the following statements is correct?

    a. No contract was formed because Moss sent the acceptance by an unauthorized method.
    b. No contract was formed because Fine received Moss' acceptance after April 4.
    c. A contract was formed when Moss sent the acceptance.
    d. A contract was formed when Fine received Moss' acceptance.

7. On February 12, Harris sent Fresno a written offer to purchase Fresno's land. The offer included the following provision: "Acceptance of this offer must be by registered or certified mail, received by Harris no later than February 18 by 5:00 p.m. CST." On February 18, Fresno sent Harris a letter accepting the offer by private overnight delivery service. Harris received the letter on February 19. Which of the following statements is correct?

    a. A contract was formed on February 19.
    b. Fresno's letter constituted a counteroffer.
    c. Fresno's use of the overnight delivery service was an effective form of acceptance.
    d. A contract was formed on February 18 regardless of when Harris actually received Fresno's letter.

8. Kay, an art collector, promised Hammer, an art student, that if Hammer could obtain certain rare artifacts within two weeks, Kay would pay for Hammer's postgraduate education. At considerable effort and expense, Hammer obtained the specified artifacts within the two-week period. When Hammer requested payment, Kay refused. Kay claimed that there was no consideration for the promise. Hammer would prevail against Kay based on

    a. Unilateral contract.
    b. Unjust enrichment.
    c. Public policy.
    d. Quasi contract.

9. On September 27, Summers sent Fox a letter offering to sell Fox a vacation home for $150,000. On October 2, Fox replied by mail agreeing to buy the home for $145,000. Summers did not reply to Fox. Do Fox and Summers have a binding contract?

    a. No, because Fox failed to sign and return Summers' letter.
    b. No, because Fox's letter was a counteroffer.
    c. Yes, because Summers' offer was validly accepted.
    d. Yes, because Summers' silence is an implied acceptance of Fox's letter.

C.3. *Formation Defenses*

10. Wick Company made a contract in writing to hire Zake for five years for $150,000 per year. After two years, Zake asked Wick for a raise of $20,000 per year. Wick at first refused but agreed to pay Zake a $60,000 bonus after Zake completed the fifth year of work. Zake put some pressure on Wick to get Wick to agree to these terms. After the fifth year, Zake left and demanded Wick pay Zake the $60,000 bonus and Wick refused. Zake sued Wick for the $60,000 bonus. Who wins?

    a. Zake, because Wick agreed to the bonus.
    b. Zake, if the bonus was agreed to in writing.
    c. Wick, even though Wick agreed to the bonus.
    d. Wick, because Zake had applied some pressure to get the bonus.

11. Grove is seeking to avoid performing a promise to pay Brook $1,500. Grove is relying on lack of consideration on Brook's part. Grove will prevail if he can establish that

    a. Prior to Grove's promise, Brook had already performed the requested act.
    b. Brooks' only claim of consideration was the relinquishment of a legal right.
    c. Brook's asserted consideration is only worth $400.
    d. The consideration to be performed by Brook will be performed by a third party.

12. Dunne and Cook signed a contract requiring Cook to rebind 500 of Dunne's books at $0.80 per book. Later, Dunne requested, in good faith, that the price be reduced to $.70 per book. Cook agreed orally to reduce the price to $.70. Under the circumstances, the oral agreement is

    a. Enforceable, but proof of it is inadmissible into evidence.
    b. Enforceable, and proof of it is admissible into evidence.
    c. Unenforceable, because Dunne failed to give consideration, but proof of it is otherwise admissible into evidence.
    d. Unenforceable, due to the statute of frauds, and proof of it is inadmissible into evidence.

13. In which of the following situations does the first promise serve as valid consideration for the second promise?

    a. A police officer's promise to catch a thief for a victim's promise to pay a reward.
    b. A builder's promise to complete a contract for a purchaser's promise to extend the time for completion.
    c. A debtor's promise to pay $500 for a creditor's promise to forgive the balance of a $600 liquidated debt.
    d. A debtor's promise to pay $500 for a creditor's promise to forgive the balance of a $600 disputed debt.

14. Which of the following will be legally binding despite lack of consideration?

    a. An employer's promise to make a cash payment to a deceased employee's family in recognition of the employee's many years of service.
    b. A promise to donate money to a charity on which the charity relied in incurring large expenditures.
    c. A modification of a signed contract to purchase a parcel of land.
    d. A merchant's oral promise to keep an offer open for sixty days.

15. Rail, who was sixteen years old, purchased an $800 computer from Elco Electronics. Rail and Elco are located in a state where the age of majority is eighteen. On several occasions Rail returned the computer to Elco for repairs. Rail was very unhappy with the computer. Two days after reaching the age of eighteen, Rail was still frustrated with the computer's reliability, and returned it to Elco, demanding an $800 refund. Elco refused, claiming that Rail no longer had a right to disaffirm the contract. Elco's refusal is

    a. Correct, because Rail's multiple requests for service acted as a ratification of the contract.
    b. Correct, because Rail could have transferred good title to a good-faith purchaser for value.
    c. Incorrect, because Rail disaffirmed the contract within a reasonable period of time after reaching the age of eighteen.
    d. Incorrect, because Rail could disaffirm the contract at any time.

16. Green was adjudicated incompetent by a court having proper jurisdiction. Which of the following statements is correct regarding contracts subsequently entered into by Green?

    a. All contracts are voidable.
    b. All contracts are valid.
    c. All contracts are void.
    d. All contracts are enforceable.

17. All of the following are effective methods of ratifying a contract entered into by a minor **except**

    a. Expressly ratifying the contract after reaching the age of majority.
    b. Failing to disaffirm the contract within a reasonable time after reaching the age of majority.

c. Ratifying the contract before reaching the age of majority.

d. Ratifying the contract by implication after reaching the age of majority.

18. Under a personal services contract, which of the following circumstances will cause the discharge of a party's duties?

a. Death of the party who is to receive the services.

b. Cost of performing the services has doubled.

c. Bankruptcy of the party who is to receive the services.

d. Illegality of the services to be performed.

19. Which of the following would be unenforceable because the subject matter is illegal?

a. A contingent fee charged by an attorney to represent a plaintiff in a negligence action.

b. An arbitration clause in a supply contract.

c. A restrictive covenant in an employment contract prohibiting a former employee from using the employer's trade secrets.

d. An employer's promise **not** to press embezzlement charges against an employee who agrees to make restitution.

20. Which of the following, if intentionally misstated by a seller to a buyer, would be considered a fraudulent inducement to make a contract?

a. Nonexpert opinion.

b. Appraised value.

c. Prediction.

d. Immaterial fact.

21. If a buyer accepts an offer containing an immaterial unilateral mistake, the resulting contract will be

a. Void as a matter of law.

b. Void at the election of the buyer.

c. Valid as to both parties.

d. Voidable at the election of the seller.

22. If a person is induced to enter into a contract by another person because of the close relationship between the parties, the contract may be voidable under which of the following defenses?

a. Fraud in the inducement.

b. Unconscionability.

c. Undue influence.

d. Duress.

23. Long purchased a life insurance policy with Tempo Life Insurance Co. The policy named Long's daughter as beneficiary. Six months after the policy was issued, Long died of a heart attack. Long had failed to disclose on the insurance application a known preexisting heart condition that caused the heart attack. Tempo refused to pay the death benefit to Long's daughter. If Long's daughter sues, Tempo will

a. Win, because Long's daughter is an incidental beneficiary.

b. Win, because of Long's failure to disclose the preexisting heart condition.

c. Lose, because Long's death was from natural causes.

d. Lose, because Long's daughter is a third-party donee beneficiary.

24. Petersen went to Jackson's home to buy a used car advertised in the newspaper. Jackson told Petersen that "it is a great car" and that "the engine had been overhauled a year ago." Shortly after he bought the car, Petersen began experiencing problems with the engine. When Jackson refused to refund his money, Petersen sued for fraud based on it was not a "great car" and also based on the fact, as learned later, the overhaul was done thirteen months ago, not a year. Will Petersen win his case?

a. Yes, Jackson's statement that "it is a great car" is actionable fraud.

b. Yes, Jackson's statement about the overhaul is actionable fraud.

c. Yes, both the statement that "it is a great car" and the statement about the overhaul are actionable fraud.

d. No.

25. A building subcontractor submitted a bid for construction of a portion of a high-rise office building. The bid contained material computational errors. The general contractor accepted the bid with knowledge of the errors. Which of the following statements **best** represents the subcontractor's liability?

a. Not liable because the contractor knew of the errors.

b. Not liable because the errors were a result of gross negligence.

c. Liable because the errors were unilateral.

d. Liable because the errors were material.

26. Maco, Inc. and Kent contracted for Kent to provide Maco certain consulting services at an hourly rate of $20. Kent's normal hourly rate was $90 per hour, the fair market value of the services. Kent agreed to the $20 rate because Kent was having serious financial problems. At the time the agreement was negotiated, Maco was aware of Kent's financial condition and refused to pay more than $20 per hour for Kent's services. Kent has now sued to rescind the contract with Maco, claiming duress by Maco during the negotiations. Under the circumstances, Kent will

a. Win, because Maco refused to pay the fair market value of Kent's services.

b. Win, because Maco was aware of Kent's serious financial problems.

c. Lose, because Maco's actions did **not** constitute duress.

d. Lose, because Maco **cannot** prove that Kent, at the time, had **no** other offers to provide consulting services.

27. To prevail in a common law action for fraud in the inducement, a plaintiff must prove that the

a. Defendant was an expert with regard to the misrepresentations.

b. Defendant made the misrepresentations with knowledge of their falsity and with an intention to deceive.

c. Misrepresentations were in writing.

d. Plaintiff was in a fiduciary relationship with the defendant.

D. *Written Contracts*

28. On June 1, 2013, Decker orally guaranteed the payment of a $5,000 note Decker's cousin owed Baker. Decker's agreement with Baker provided that Decker's guaranty would terminate in eighteen months. On June 3, 2013, Baker wrote Decker confirming Decker's guaranty. Decker did not object to the confirmation. On August 23, 2013, Decker's cousin defaulted on the note and Baker demanded that Decker honor the guaranty. Decker refused. Which of the following statements is correct?

  a. Decker is liable under the oral guaranty because Decker did **not** object to Baker's June 3 letter.
  b. Decker is **not** liable under the oral guaranty because it expired more than one year after June 1.
  c. Decker is liable under the oral guaranty because Baker demanded payment within one year of the date the guaranty was given.
  d. Decker is **not** liable under the oral guaranty because Decker's promise was **not** in writing.

29. Nolan agreed orally with Train to sell Train a house for $100,000. Train sent Nolan a signed agreement and a down payment of $10,000. Nolan did not sign the agreement, but allowed Train to move into the house. Before closing, Nolan refused to go through with the sale. Train sued Nolan to compel specific performance. Under the provisions of the Statute of Frauds

  a. Train will win because Train signed the agreement and Nolan did **not** object.
  b. Train will win because Train made a down payment and took possession.
  c. Nolan will win because Nolan did **not** sign the agreement.
  d. Nolan will win because the house was worth more than $500.

30. Cherry contracted orally to purchase Picks Company for $1,500,000 if it is profitable for one full year after the making of the oral contract. An auditor would be brought in at the end of the year to verify this. Even though the company turns out to be profitable during the upcoming year, Cherry refuses to go through with the contract, claiming that it was unenforceable because it was not in writing. Is Cherry correct?

  a. Yes, because the contract could not be completed within one year.
  b. Yes, because the contract was for $500 or more.
  c. No, because the company was profitable as agreed for one year.
  d. No, because Picks Company relied on Cherry's promise.

31. Which of the following statements is true with regard to the Statute of Frauds?

  a. All contracts involving consideration of more than $500 must be in writing.
  b. The written contract must be signed by all parties.
  c. The Statute of Frauds applies to contracts that can be fully performed within one year from the date they are made.
  d. The contract terms may be stated in more than one document.

32. Carson agreed orally to repair Ives' rare book for $450. Before the work was started, Ives asked Carson to perform additional repairs to the book and agreed to increase the contract price to $650. After Carson completed the work, Ives refused to pay and Carson sued. Ives' defense was based on the Statute of Frauds. What total amount will Carson recover?

  a. $0
  b. $200
  c. $450
  d. $650

33. Landry Company contracted orally with Newell to pay her $50,000 for the completion of an ethics audit of Landry Company. The report is to span a period of time of at least ten months and is due in fourteen months from now. Newell has agreed orally to perform the ethics audit and says that she will begin within three months, noting that even if she delays the full three months, she will have the report ready within the fourteen-month deadline. Does this contract fall under the Statute of Frauds?

  a. Yes, because the contract is for $500 or more.
  b. Yes, because the deadline for the contract is over one year.
  c. No, despite the due date of fourteen months.
  d. No, because both parties waived the Statute of Frauds by their oral agreement.

34. Rogers and Lennon entered into a written computer consulting agreement that required Lennon to provide certain weekly reports to Rogers. The agreement also stated that Lennon would provide the computer equipment necessary to perform the services, and that Rogers' computer would not be used. As the parties were executing the agreement, they orally agreed that Lennon could use Rogers' computer. After executing the agreement, Rogers and Lennon orally agreed that Lennon would report on a monthly, rather than weekly, basis. The parties now disagree on Lennon's right to use Rogers' computer and how often Lennon must report to Rogers. In the event of a lawsuit between the parties, the parol evidence rule will

  a. Not apply to any of the parties' agreements because the consulting agreement did **not** have to be in writing.
  b. Not prevent Lennon from proving the parties' oral agreement that Lennon could use Rogers' computer.
  c. Not prevent the admission into evidence of testimony regarding Lennon's right to report on a monthly basis.
  d. Not apply to the parties' agreement to allow Lennon to use Rogers' computer because it was contemporaneous with the written agreement.

35. Where the parties have entered into a written contract intended as the final expression of their agreement, which of the following agreements will be admitted into evidence because they are **not** prohibited by the parol evidence rule?

	Subsequent oral agreements	Prior written agreements
a.	Yes	Yes
b.	Yes	No
c.	No	Yes
d.	No	No

36. In negotiations with Andrews for the lease of Kemp's warehouse, Kemp orally agreed to pay one-half of the cost of the utilities. The written lease, later prepared by Kemp's attorney, provided that Andrews pay all of the utilities. Andrews failed to carefully read the lease and signed it. When Kemp demanded that Andrews pay all of the utilities, Andrews refused, claiming that the lease did not accurately reflect the oral agreement. Andrews also learned that Kemp intentionally misrepresented the condition of the structure of the warehouse during the negotiations between the parties. Andrews sued to rescind the lease and intends to introduce evidence of the parties' oral agreement about sharing the utilities and the fraudulent statements made by Kemp. The parol evidence rule will prevent the admission of evidence concerning thet

	Oral agreement regarding who pays the utilities	Fraudulent statements by Kemp
a.	Yes	Yes
b.	No	Yes
c.	Yes	No
d.	No	No

37. Joan Silver had viewed some land that she wished to purchase. It was offered for sale by Daniel Tweney over the Internet for $200,000. Silver believes this to be a good deal for her and thus wishes to purchase it. Silver and Tweney have communicated online and wish to make a contract for the land over the Internet. Which of the following statements is (are) correct?

I. Because this contract is covered by the Statute of Frauds, this contract cannot be accomplished over the Internet.
II. Because of the parol evidence rule, this contract cannot be completed over the Internet.
III. Because this contract is covered by the Uniform Commercial Code, it may not be accomplished over the Internet.

    a. Only I is correct.
    b. I and II only are correct.
    c. I and III only are correct.
    d. Neither I, II, nor III is correct.

E. Assignment and Delegation

38. Generally, which of the following contract rights are assignable?

	Option contract rights	Malpractice insurance policy rights
a.	Yes	Yes
b.	Yes	No
c.	No	Yes
d.	No	No

39. One of the criteria for a valid assignment of a sales contract to a third party is that the assignment must

    a. Be supported by adequate consideration from the assignee.
    b. Be in writing and signed by the assignor.

    c. Not materially increase the other party's risk or duty.
    d. Not be revocable by the assignor.

Items 40 and 41 are based on the following:

Egan contracted with Barton to buy Barton's business. The contract provided that Egan would pay the business debts Barton owed Ness and that the balance of the purchase price would be paid to Barton over a ten-year period. The contract also required Egan to take out a decreasing term life insurance policy naming Barton and Ness as beneficiaries to ensure that the amounts owed Barton and Ness would be paid if Egan died.

40. Barton's contract rights were assigned to Vim, and Egan was notified of the assignment. Despite the assignment, Egan continued making payments to Barton. Egan died before completing payment and Vim sued Barton for the insurance proceeds and the other payments on the purchase price received by Barton after the assignment. To which of the following is Vim entitled?

	Payments on purchase price	Insurance proceeds
a.	No	Yes
b.	No	No
c.	Yes	Yes
d.	Yes	No

F. Third-Party Beneficiary Contracts

41. Which of the following would describe Ness' status under the contract and insurance policy?

	Contract	Insurance policy
a.	Donee beneficiary	Donee beneficiary
b.	Donee beneficiary	Creditor beneficiary
c.	Creditor beneficiary	Donee beneficiary
d.	Creditor beneficiary	Creditor beneficiary

42. Your client, Bugle, owns a parking lot near downtown San Francisco. One day Bugle is excited because he learns that Fargo, who owns a parking lot next door, has made a contract with ABC Company to sell her land. ABC Company can then construct a building that will contain several nice professional offices. Bugle figures that he will charge more for his parking. He later discovers that the contract fell through. He says that when he finds out who breached the contract, he will sue that party for lost profits that he would have earned. Which of the following is correct?

    a. If Fargo was the one who breached the contract, Bugle may sue her if ABC had already made some payments on the contract.
    b. If ABC was the party who breached, ABC is liable to Bugle.
    c. Bugle may sue either party, and the nonbreaching party may then recover from the breaching party.
    d. Bugle has no legal rights against either party.

43. Baxter, Inc. and Globe entered into a contract. After receiving valuable consideration from Clay, Baxter assigned its rights under the contract to Clay. In which of the following circumstances would Baxter **not** be liable to Clay?

    a. Clay released Globe.
    b. Globe paid Baxter.
    c. Baxter released Globe.
    d. Baxter breached the contract.

44. Mackay paid Manus $1,000 to deliver a painting to Mackay's friend Mann. When they met and signed the contract, Mackay said she wanted the painting delivered as soon as possible because it was a gift for Mann's birthday. Several months have passed without the delivery. Mann can maintain lawsuits against which parties to get the painting?

    a. Manus only.
    b. Mackay only.
    c. Manus, but only if he also brings suit against Mackay.
    d. Manus or Mackay at Mann's option.

45. Ferco, Inc. claims to be a creditor beneficiary of a contract between Bell and Allied Industries, Inc. Allied is indebted to Ferco. The contract between Bell and Allied provides that Bell is to purchase certain goods from Allied and pay the purchase price directly to Ferco until Allied's obligation is satisfied. Without justification, Bell failed to pay Ferco and Ferco sued Bell. Ferco will

    a. Not prevail, because Ferco lacked privity of contract with either Bell or Allied.
    b. Not prevail, because Ferco did **not** give any consideration to Bell.
    c. Prevail, because Ferco was an intended beneficiary of the contract between Allied and Bell.
    d. Prevail, provided Ferco was aware of the contract between Bell and Allied at the time the contract was entered into.

G. Performance of Contract

46. Parc hired Glaze to remodel and furnish an office suite. Glaze submitted plans that Parc approved. After completing all the necessary construction and painting, Glaze purchased minor accessories that Parc rejected because they did not conform to the plans. Parc refused to allow Glaze to complete the project and refused to pay Glaze any part of the contract price. Glaze sued for the value of the work performed. Which of the following statements is correct?

    a. Glaze will lose because Glaze breached the contract by **not** completing performance.
    b. Glaze will win because Glaze substantially performed and Parc prevented complete performance.
    c. Glaze will lose because Glaze materially breached the contract by buying the accessories.
    d. Glaze will win because Parc committed anticipatory breach.

47. Which of the following types of conditions affecting performance may validly be present in contracts?

	Conditions precedent	Conditions subsequent	Concurrent conditions
a.	Yes	Yes	Yes
b.	Yes	Yes	No
c.	Yes	No	Yes
d.	No	Yes	Yes

H. Discharge of Contracts

48. Which of the following actions if taken by one party to a contract generally will discharge the performance required of the other party to the contract?

    a. Material breach of the contract.
    b. Delay in performance.
    c. Tender.
    d. Assignment of rights.

49. Which of the following actions will result in the discharge of a party to a contract?

	Prevention of performance	Accord and satisfaction
a.	Yes	Yes
b.	Yes	No
c.	No	Yes
d.	No	No

50. To cancel a contract and to restore the parties to their original positions before the contract, the parties should execute a

    a. Novation.
    b. Release.
    c. Rescission.
    d. Revocation.

51. Ordinarily, in an action for breach of a construction contract, the statute of limitations time period would be computed from the date the

    a. Contract is negotiated.
    b. Contract is breached.
    c. Construction is begun.
    d. Contract is signed.

I. Remedies

52. Kaye contracted to sell Hodges a building for $310,000. The contract required Hodges to pay the entire amount at closing. Kaye refused to close the sale of the building. Hodges sued Kaye. To what relief is Hodges entitled?

    a. Punitive damages and compensatory damages.
    b. Specific performance and compensatory damages.
    c. Consequential damages or punitive damages.
    d. Compensatory damages or specific performance.

53. Ames Construction Co. contracted to build a warehouse for White Corp. The construction specifications required Ames to use Ace lighting fixtures. Inadvertently, Ames installed Perfection lighting fixtures which are of slightly lesser quality than Ace fixtures, but in all other respects meet White's needs. Which of the following statements is correct?

- a. White's recovery will be limited to monetary damages because Ames' breach of the construction contract was **not** material.
- b. White will **not** be able to recover any damages from Ames because the breach was inadvertent.
- c. Ames did not breach the construction contract because the Perfection fixtures were substantially as good as the Ace fixtures.
- d. Ames must install Ace fixtures or White will **not** be obligated to accept the warehouse.

54. Master Mfg., Inc. contracted with Accur Computer Repair Corp. to maintain Master's computer system. Master's manufacturing process depends on its computer system operating properly at all times. A liquidated damages clause in the contract provided that Accur pay $1,000 to Master for each day that Accur was late responding to a service request. On January 12, Accur was notified that Master's computer system failed. Accur did not respond to Master's service request until January 15. If Master sues Accur under the liquidated damage provision of the contract, Master will

- a. Win, unless the liquidated damage provision is determined to be a penalty.
- b. Win, because under all circumstances liquidated damage provisions are enforceable.
- c. Lose, because Accur's breach was **not** material.
- d. Lose, because liquidated damage provisions violate public policy.

55. Nagel and Fields entered into a contract in which Nagel was obligated to deliver certain goods to Fields by September 10. On September 3, Nagel told Fields that Nagel had no intention of delivering the goods required by the contract. Prior to September 10, Fields may successfully sue Nagel under the doctrine of

- a. Promissory estoppel.
- b. Accord and satisfaction.
- c. Anticipatory repudiation.
- d. Substantial performance.

56. Maco Corp. contracted to sell 1,500 bushels of potatoes to LBC Chips. The contract did not refer to any specific supply source for the potatoes. Maco intended to deliver potatoes grown on its farms. An insect infestation ruined Maco's crop but not the crops of other growers in the area. Maco failed to deliver the potatoes to LBC. LBC sued Maco for breach of contract. Under the circumstances, Maco will

- a. Lose, because it could have purchased potatoes from other growers to deliver to LBC.
- b. Lose, unless it can show that the purchase of substitute potatoes for delivery to LBC would make the contract unprofitable.
- c. Win, because the infestation was an act of nature that could **not** have been anticipated by Maco.
- d. Win, because both Maco and LBC are assumed to accept the risk of a crop failure.

Multiple-Choice Answers and Explanations

Answers

1. a ___ ___	13. d ___ ___	25. a ___ ___	37. d ___ ___	49. a ___ ___
2. b ___ ___	14. b ___ ___	26. c ___ ___	38. b ___ ___	50. c ___ ___
3. c ___ ___	15. c ___ ___	27. b ___ ___	39. c ___ ___	51. b ___ ___
4. a ___ ___	16. c ___ ___	28. d ___ ___	40. c ___ ___	52. d ___ ___
5. d ___ ___	17. c ___ ___	29. b ___ ___	41. d ___ ___	53. a ___ ___
6. b ___ ___	18. d ___ ___	30. a ___ ___	42. d ___ ___	54. a ___ ___
7. b ___ ___	19. d ___ ___	31. d ___ ___	43. a ___ ___	55. c ___ ___
8. a ___ ___	20. b ___ ___	32. d ___ ___	44. a ___ ___	56. a ___ ___
9. b ___ ___	21. c ___ ___	33. c ___ ___	45. c ___ ___	
10. c ___ ___	22. c ___ ___	34. c ___ ___	46. b ___ ___	
11. a ___ ___	23. b ___ ___	35. b ___ ___	47. a ___ ___	1st: ___/56 = ___%
12. c ___ ___	24. d ___ ___	36. c ___ ___	48. a ___ ___	2nd: ___/56 = ___%

Explanations

1. (a) Under common law, an offer must be definite and certain as to what will be agreed upon in the contract. Essential terms are the parties involved, the price, the time for performance, and the subject matter (quantity and type). The price element of the contract was not present. While it is true that the subject matter must be definite, here the terms of the contract are sufficiently definite: Fix a broken window, thus answer (b) is incorrect. Likewise the parties—Carson and Alto are specified, and the time for performance—3 days is specified; therefore answers(c) and (d) are incorrect.

2. (b) Advertisements in almost all cases are merely invitations for interested parties to make an offer. Thus, Harris has not made an offer, but is seeking offers through the use of the advertisement. Answers (a), (c), and (d) are incorrect since each of the answers assumes that an offer was made, but the advertisement does not constitute an offer.

3. (c) Generally an offeror may revoke an offer at any time prior to acceptance by the offeree. Revocation is effective when it is received by the offeree. Revocation also occurs if the offeree learns by a reliable means that the offeror has already sold the subject of the offer. In this situation, Peters' offer was effectively revoked when Mason learned that the lawn mower had been sold to Bronson. Therefore, Mason's acceptance was ineffective. Answers (a) and (b) are incorrect because the offer had been revoked prior to Mason's acceptance. Answer (d) is incorrect because Peters was not obligated to keep the offer open. Note that if consideration had been paid by Mason to keep the offer open, an option contract would exist and the offer could not be revoked before the stated time.

4. (a) Drake did not intend to reject the $300,000 offer but is simply seeing if Calistoga might consider selling the home for less. Answer (b) is incorrect because a counteroffer takes place when the original offer is rejected and a new offer takes its place. Answer (c) is incorrect because Drake showed no intention of rejecting the offer by his mere inquiry. Answer (d) is incorrect because ambiguity is not one of the grounds to have an offer terminated by operation of law.

5. (d) An offer automatically terminates upon the occurrence of any of the following events: (1) the death or insanity of either the offeror or offeree, (2) bankruptcy or insolvency of either the offeror or offeree, or (3) the destruction of the specific, identified subject matter. Thus the offer automatically terminates at the date of Opal's death. Answer (a) is incorrect because notice is not required when termination occurs automatically by operation of law. Answer (b) is incorrect because termination occurs immediately upon Opal's death. Answer (c) is incorrect because if Larkin accepted the offer prior to Opal's death, a valid contract was formed.

6. (b) Under the mailbox rule, an acceptance is ordinarily effective when sent if transmitted by the means authorized by the offeror, by the same means used to transmit the offer, or by customary means if no means was authorized. However, the offeror may stipulate that acceptance is effective only when received by the offeror; effectively removing the mailbox rule. In this situation, no contract was formed because Moss' acceptance was not received by the date specified in Fine's offer; therefore answers (c) and (d) are incorrect. Answer (a) is incorrect because even if the method is unauthorized, the acceptance would still be valid if it is received in a timely fashion. Here, the acceptance is late, no matter what method was used.

7. (b) Fresno's acceptance by overnight delivery was made by a method other than the methods specified by Harris in the written offer. When acceptance is sent by a method other than the method specified in the offer or different than the method used to transmit the offer, acceptance is considered valid only when actually received by the offeror. Late acceptance is not valid, but instead constitutes a counteroffer. A valid contract would be formed only if the original offeror (Harris) then accepts.

8. (a) A unilateral offer exists when the offeror expects acceptance of an offer by action of the offeree. A unilateral contract is then formed when the offeree accepts the contract through performance of the offeror's required action. In this case, a valid contract is formed when Hammer accepts Kay's unilateral offer by obtaining the artifacts within a two-week period. Answers (b) and (d) are incorrect because a quasi-contract is an implied-in-law rather than express agreement which results when one of the parties has been unjustly enriched at the expense of the other. The law creates such a contract when there is no binding agreement present to keep the unjust enrichment from occurring. Answer (c) is incorrect because public policy causes enforcement of promises despite lack of any other legal enforcement of the contract. For example, public policy would normally allow enforcement of a promise by a debtor to pay a debt barred by the statute of limitations.

9. (b) Common law applies to this contract because it involves real estate. In this situation, Fox's reply on October 2 is a counteroffer and terminates Summers' original offer made on September 27. The acceptance of an offer must conform exactly to the terms of the offer under common law. By agreeing to purchase the vacation home at a price different from the original offer, Fox is rejecting Summers' offer and is making a counteroffer. Answer (a) is incorrect because the fact that Fox failed to return Summers' letter is irrelevant to the formation of a binding contract. Fox's reply constitutes a counteroffer as Fox did not intend to accept Summers' original offer. Answer (c) is incorrect because Summers' offer was rejected by Fox's counteroffer. Answer (d) is incorrect because with rare exceptions, silence does not constitute acceptance.

10. (c) Both Zake and Wick had a contract that was binding for five years. To modify this contract, both of them must give new consideration under common law rules, which apply to employment contracts such as this one. When Wick agreed to the bonus, only Wick gave new consideration in the form of $60,000. Zake did not give new consideration because he would perform in the last three years as originally agreed. Answers (a) and (b) are incorrect because Zake did not give new consideration whether or not the raise was in writing. Answer (d) is incorrect because duress needed to make a contract voidable or void requires more than "some pressure."

11. (a) Consideration is an act, promise, or forbearance which is offered by one party and accepted by another as inducement to enter into an agreement. A party must bind him/herself to do something s/he is not legally obligated to do. Furthermore, the consideration must be bargained for. Past consideration is not sufficient to serve as consideration for a new contract because it is not bargained for. Answer (b) is incorrect because relinquishment of a legal right constitutes consideration. Answer (c) is incorrect because even though the consideration must be adequate, courts generally do not look into the amount of exchange, as long as it is legal consideration and is bargained for. Answer (d) is incorrect as this performance by a third party is still deemed consideration.

12. (c) The rebinding of Dunne's books is considered a service and not a sale of goods, therefore, common law applies. Under common law, modification of an existing contract needs new consideration by both parties to be legally binding. Since Dunne has not given any new consideration for Cook's reduction in price, the contract is unenforceable. Additionally, the parol evidence rule prohibits the presentation of evidence of any prior or contemporaneous oral or written statements for the purpose of modifying or changing a written agreement intended by the payor to be the final and complete expression of their contract. However, it does not bar from evidence any oral or written agreements entered into by the parties subsequent to the written contract. Therefore, the agreement between Dunne and Cook is unenforceable, but evidence of the modification is admissible into evidence.

Note that if the contract had been for the sale of goods (UCC), modification of the contract terms would have been enforceable. Under the UCC, a contract for the sale of goods may be modified orally or in writing without new consideration if such modification is done in good faith.

13. (d) A preexisting legal duty is not sufficient as consideration because no new legal detriment is suffered by performing the prior obligation. Answer (c) is incorrect because when a creditor agrees to accept as full payment an amount less than the full amount of the undisputed (liquidated) debt, the agreement lacks valid consideration to be enforceable. However, when the amount of an obligation is disputed, the creditor's promise to accept a lesser amount as full payment of the debt is enforceable. Answer (a) is incorrect because a police officer has a preexisting legal duty to catch a thief. Preexisting legal duties are not valid as consideration. Answer (b) is incorrect because the builder already has an obligation to complete the contract, so the builder is offering no new consideration to modify the contract.

14. (b) A promise to donate money to a charity which the charity relied upon in incurring large expenditures is a situation involving promissory estoppel. Promissory estoppel acts as a substitute for consideration and renders the promise enforceable. The elements necessary for promissory estoppel are (1) detrimental reliance on a promise, (2) reliance on the promise is reasonable and foreseeable, and (3) damage results (injustice) if the promise is not enforced. Answer (a) is incorrect because the failure to enforce an employer's promise to make a cash payment to a deceased employee's family will not result in damages, and therefore, promissory estoppel will not apply. Answer (c) is incorrect because the modification of a contract requires consideration, unless the contract involves the sale of goods under the UCC. Answer (d) is incorrect because an irrevocable oral promise by a merchant to keep an offer open for sixty days is an option contract that must be supported by consideration. A firm offer under the UCC requires an offer signed by the merchant.

15. (c) A minor may disaffirm a contract at any time during his minority and within a reasonable time after reaching the age of majority. When Rail disaffirmed the contract two days after reaching the age of eighteen, he did so within a reasonable time after reaching majority age. Answer (a) is incorrect because Rail could ratify the contract only after reaching the age of majority. Answer (b) is incorrect because although Rail could have transferred good title to a good-faith purchaser for value, Rail's title was still voidable and subject to disaffirmance. Answer (d) is incorrect because Rail could disaffirm the contract only for a reasonable time after reaching the age of majority. Failure to disaffirm within a reasonable time serves to act as ratification.

16. (c) When a person has previously been adjudicated by a court of law to be incompetent, all of the contracts that s/he makes are void. Answer (a) is incorrect because the contracts are only voidable at the option of Green if there was no formal, previous court determination of incompetence for Green. Answer (b) is incorrect because once the court determines that Green is incompetent, all of the contracts that s/he makes are not valid but are void. Answer (d) is incorrect because the contracts cannot be enforced by either Green or the other contracting party.

17. (c) Ratification of a contract prior to reaching majority age is not effective. A minor **may** ratify a contract expressly or by actions indicating ratification after reaching the age of majority; therefore, answers (a) and (c) are incorrect. Answer (d) is incorrect because failure to disaffirm within a reasonable time after reaching majority age **does** act as ratification.

18. (d) An agreement is unenforceable if it is illegal or violates public policy. Therefore, if the personal services of the contract are illegal, the party will not have to perform them. Answer (a) is incorrect because the death of the party who is to **receive** the benefits does not terminate the duties under the contract. His/her heirs can still receive and pay for the personal services. Answer (b) is incorrect because making less profit or losing money are not grounds for getting out of a contract. Answer (c) is incorrect because bankruptcy of the receiver does not discharge the performer from the contract, although it can allow for forgiveness of all or part of the payment.

19. (d) An employer's promise not to press criminal charges against an employee-embezzler who agrees to return the embezzled money is not legally binding. The promise not to press charges is an illegal bargain, and, even if the employee returns the money, the employer is free to cooperate in prosecution of the criminal. Answer (a) is incorrect because attorneys may take negligence cases on a contingency, which means that the attorney only gets paid if the attorney's client prevails in the negligence lawsuit. Answer (b) is incorrect because arbitration clauses, where the parties agree to submit any contractual disputes to an arbitrator, are permissible. Answer (c) is incorrect because a covenant not to compete is enforceable where it is reasonable and necessary to protect a legitimate employer interest. Trade secrets are an example of a legitimate interest.

20. (b) Fraud is the intentional misrepresentation of a material fact upon which a third party reasonably relies to his or her detriment. An intentionally misstated appraised value would be an example of a fraudulent inducement to make a contract. Answers (a) and (c) are incorrect because a third party cannot reasonably rely on a nonexpert opinion or a prediction. Answer (d) is incorrect because by definition, fraud applies to material facts.

21. (c) An immaterial unilateral mistake generally does not allow either party to void the contract.

22. (c) Undue influence is a defense that makes a contract voidable. Classic situations of this concept involve close relationships in which a dominant person has extreme influence over a weaker person. Answer (a) is incorrect because although fraud in the inducement can make a contract voidable, it typically does not occur between parties that have a close relationship. Answer (b) is incorrect because unconscionability involves an oppressive contract in which one party has taken severe, unfair advantage of another which is often based on the latter's absence of choice or poor education rather than the parties' close relationship. Answer (d) is incorrect because duress involves acts or threats of violence or pressure, which need not result from close relationships.

23. (b) An insurance policy is voidable at the option of the insurer if the insured failed to inform the insurer at the time of application of a fact material to the insurer's risk (e.g., failure to disclose a preexisting heart condition on a life insurance application). The insured's concealment causes the policy to be voidable due to fraud in the inducement. Answer (a) is incorrect because Long's daughter is an intended beneficiary, not an incidental beneficiary; more importantly, the insurance's company's defense of fraud is valid against any type of beneficiary. Answers (c) and (d) are incorrect because the insurance policy was agreed to based on fraudulent statements; therefore the beneficiary will not prevail against the insurance company.

24. (d) One of the elements needed to prove fraud is a misrepresentation of a material fact. That statement that "it is a great car" is sales talk or puffing and does not establish this element. The fact that the overhaul was done thirteen months earlier instead of the stated one year is not a misrepresentation of a **material** fact. How long ago the engine was overhauled is material, but the fact that it was thirteen months rather than twelve months is immaterial.

25. (a) A mistake is an understanding that is not in agreement with a fact. A unilateral mistake (made by one party) generally does not allow the party to void the contract. However, a mistake unknown to the party making it becomes voidable if the other party recognizes it as a mistake. Particularly, this is the case in bid contract computations. The contract is voidable by the party making the mistake if the other party knew of the mistake or if the calculation was far enough off that the other party should have known that a mistake was made.

26. (c) Duress is any wrongful threat or act of violence made toward a person (or his family) which forces a person to enter into a contract against his will. For duress to be present a threat must be made and the threatened party must believe that the other party has the ability to carry out the threat. In this situation, Maco's actions did not constitute duress. Kent's safety and property were in no way threatened by Maco and Kent was able to validly consent to the contract. Answers (a) and (b) are incorrect because regardless of Kent's financial problems and the FMV of Kent's services, duress was not present in that Kent was able to enter into the contract at will. Answer (d) is incorrect because Maco does not need to prove that Kent had no other offers to provide financial services.

27. (b) To establish a common law action for fraud, the following elements must be present: (1) misrepresentation of a material fact, (2) either knowledge of the falsity with intent to mislead or reckless disregard for the truth (scienter), (3) reasonable reliance by third party, and (4) injury resulted from misrepresentation. If the misrepresentation occurs during contract negotiations, fraud in the inducement is present resulting in a contract voidable at the option of the injured party. Answer (a) is incorrect because the defendant need not be an expert with regard to the misrepresentation to establish fraud in the inducement. Answer (c) is incorrect because the misrepresentation may be written or oral. Answer (d) is incorrect because the presence of fraud in the inducement does not require a fiduciary relationship between the parties.

28. (d) The Statute of Frauds requires that a contract to answer the debt or default of another be in writing and signed by the party to be charged. The guarantee that Decker made was only oral. Answer (b) is incorrect, the reason Decker is not liable for the oral guaranty is not because it expires more than one year after June 1, but because a contract of guaranty must be in writing. Decker is not liable regardless of Baker's confirmation letter; thus answer (a) is incorrect. Answer (c) is incorrect because Decker's oral guaranty is not enforceable. The time period between the date of the oral guaranty and the date payment is demanded has no bearing in this situation.

29. (b) Any agreement to sell land or any interest in land falls under the requirements of the Statute of Frauds. Agreements within the Statute of Frauds require contracts to be in writing and signed by the party to be charged (the party being sued). An exception to the above rule is "part performance" by the purchaser. Part performance exists when the purchaser of property takes possession of the property with the landowner's consent. Some states also require either partial payment for the property or permanent improvement of the property by the purchaser. Answer (b) is correct because even though Nolan failed to sign a written agreement, the part performance exception has been satisfied. Answer (a) is incorrect because the fact that Nolan simply failed to object to the agreement does not make the contract valid under the Statute of Frauds. Answer (c) is incorrect because the part performance exception has been met and Train will therefore prevail. Answer (d) is incorrect because no such requirement exists to alleviate Nolan's liability. The part performance rule allows Train to prevail. Note that **all** sales of land are covered under the Statute of Frauds, and not just those greater than $500.

30. (a) Contracts that cannot be performed within one year must be in writing. In this case Cherry agreed to purchase Picks Company if an audit after one year shows that the company has been profitable. This would take longer than a year to perform. Answer (b) is incorrect because the $500 provision is in the Uniform Commercial Code for a sale of goods. Answer (c) is incorrect because despite the actual profitability, the contract could not be completed within one year of the making of the contract. Answer (d) is incorrect because although promissory estoppel may be used in the absence of a writing, there are not the facts sufficient to show promissory estoppel.

31. (d) Contracts which fall within the requirements of the Statute of Frauds are required to be in writing and signed by the party to be charged. It is not required that the contract terms be formalized in a single writing. Two or more documents may be combined to create a writing which satisfies the Statute of Frauds as long as one of the documents refers to the others. Answer (a) is incorrect because the Statute of Frauds requires that agreements for the sale of goods for $500 or more be in writing; however, contracts that come under common law are not included in this requirement. Answer (b) is incorrect because the Statute of Frauds requires that the written contract be signed by the party to be charged, not by all parties to the contract. Answer (c) is incorrect because the Statute of Frauds applies to contracts that **cannot** be performed within one year from the making of the agreement.

32. (d) The Statute of Frauds applies to the following types of contracts: (1) an agreement to sell land or any interest in land, (2) an agreement that cannot be performed within one year from the making of the agreement, (3) an agreement to answer for the debt or default of another, and (4) an agreement for the sale of goods for $500 or more. Since the agreement between Carson and Ives meets none of the above requirements, it is an enforceable oral contract under common law. Furthermore, under common law, modification of an existing contract needs new consideration

by both parties to be legally binding. Since Ives received the benefit of additional repairs to his book, Carson's increase in the contract price is enforceable. Therefore, Carson will recover $650.

33. (c) Under The Statute of Frauds, agreements that can be performed within one year of their making can be oral. In this case the ethics audit need only span ten months and the completion of the report will take less than one additional month for a total of less than one year. We know that the report can be done in less than a month because Newell points out that even if she delays start for three months, she will still complete the ten-month audit before the fourteen-month deadline. The fact that it might take longer than a year does not require it to be in writing since it **possibly could** be completed within one year. Answer (a) is incorrect because the $500 provision is for sales of goods not services. Answer (b) is incorrect because the contract can be completed within one year. Answer (d) is incorrect because there is no such provision involved here for the Statute of Frauds.

34. (c) The parol evidence rule provides that a written agreement intended by contracting parties to be a final and complete contract may not be contradicted by previous or contemporaneous oral evidence. The parol evidence rule does not apply to any subsequent oral promises made after the original agreement. Thus, the subsequent oral agreement between Rogers and Lennon regarding Lennon's right to report on a monthly basis will be allowed as evidence in a lawsuit between the parties. Answer (a) is incorrect because the parol evidence rule applies to all written contracts regardless of the applicability of the Statute of Frauds. Answer (b) is incorrect because the parol evidence rule will prevent the admission into evidence of the contemporaneous oral agreement that Lennon could use Rogers' computer. Answer (d) is incorrect because the parol evidence rule does apply to the contemporaneous oral agreement.

35. (b) The parol evidence rule provides that any written agreement intended by parties to be final and complete contract may not be contradicted by previous or contemporaneous evidence, written or oral. Thus, previous written agreements are prohibited by the rule. Exceptions to the parol evidence rule include proof to invalidate the contract between the parties, to show terms not inconsistent with writing that parties would not be expected to have included, to explain the intended meaning of an ambiguity, or to show a condition precedent. The parol evidence rule does not apply to subsequent transactions, such as oral promises made after the original agreement.

36. (c) The parol evidence rule prohibits the presentation as evidence of any prior or contemporaneous oral statements concerning a written agreement intended by the parties to be the final and complete expression of their contract. Therefore, the evidence related to the oral agreement regarding the payment of utilities would not be allowed. However, the parol evidence rule does **not** bar the admission of evidence which is presented to establish fraud.

37. (d) Even though this contract falls under the Statute of Frauds and, therefore, generally must be written and signed, most states have passed laws allowing contracts to be made over the Internet to facilitate commerce. The statutes encourage technology to overcome concerns over authenticity of such contracts. Therefore, answer (a) is incorrect. Answer

(b) is incorrect because the parol evidence rule does not specify when a contract must be written and signed. Answer (c) is incorrect because a sale of land is governed by common law rules and not the UCC.

38. (b) Assignment is the transfer of a right under a contract by one person to another. Almost all contract rights are assignable as long as the parties agree to it, but there are some exceptions. Contracts involving personal services, trust or confidence are not assignable. If assignment would materially change the risk or burden of the obligor, it is not allowed. For example, a contract for insurance against certain risks is not assignable because they were made upon the character of the contracting party (the insured). Assigning the rights to another party would alter the risk. Therefore, malpractice insurance policy rights are not assignable. A further exception is that future rights are not assignable, with the exception under the UCC that future rights for the sale of goods are assignable, whether based on an existing or nonexisting contract. As the assignment of option contract rights does not fall under any exception, they would be assignable.

39. (c) Assignment is the transfer of a right under a contract by one person to another. Answer (a) is incorrect because no consideration is needed for valid assignment. Normally an assignment is done in writing, but any act, oral or written, is sufficient if it gives clear intent of the assignment; therefore answer (b) is incorrect. Only situations included under the Statute of Frauds are required to be in writing. When consideration is given in exchange for an assignment, it is irrevocable. Also, as a general rule a gratuitous assignment is revocable unless it is evidenced by a writing signed by the assignor, effected by a delivery of a writing used as evidence of the right (i.e., bill of lading), and the assignment is executed; thus, answer (d) is incorrect. A contract right cannot be assigned if it would materially change the risk or burden of the obligor.

40. (c) Assignment is the transfer of a right under a contract by one person to another. If the obligor has notice of the assignment, s/he must pay the assignee, not the assignor. The contract between Barton and Egan provided for both payments on the purchase price and the insurance policy in case of Egan's death. Because Barton assigned his contract rights to Vim, Vim was then entitled to payments on the purchase price and the insurance proceeds. Since Barton received payments on the purchase price and insurance proceeds after the assignment, Vim is entitled to sue Barton for these amounts.

41. (d) When a debtor contracts with a second party to pay the debt owed to a creditor, the creditor becomes a creditor beneficiary. Barton contracted with Egan for Egan to pay Ness the business' debts. The contract also required Egan to provide a life insurance policy to pay Ness if Egan died. In both the contract and the insurance policy, Ness was a creditor beneficiary. Neither the contract nor the insurance policy were entered into to confer a gift to Ness, and therefore he was not a donee beneficiary.

42. (d) Bugle would have received an unintended benefit under the contract between Fargo and ABC Company. Therefore, Bugle is an incidental beneficiary, not an intended beneficiary and, thus, has no legal rights against either Fargo or ABC. No matter who breached the contract, Bugle has no rights against either party. Therefore, answers (a), (b), and (c) are incorrect.

43. (a) In an assignment, the assignee (Clay) acquires the assignor's (Baxter) rights against the obligor (Globe) and has the right to performance. Baxter is still liable to the assignee if Globe does not perform. However, if Clay released Globe from the contract, Baxter would also be released and no longer liable to Clay. Answer (b) is incorrect because if the obligor has no notice of the assignment, s/he may pay the assignor, and the assignee must recover from the assignor. Thus, if Globe was unaware of the assignment and paid Baxter, Clay would have to collect from Baxter. Answers (c) and (d) are incorrect because even if Baxter released Globe or breached the contract, Baxter would still be liable to Clay.

44. (a) Mann is a donee beneficiary and, thus, can bring suit against the promisor, Manus, only. He cannot maintain a suit against Mackay, who was just giving a gift. Mann cannot maintain any action against Mackay either alone or in combination with Manus; therefore none of the other answer choices can be correct.

45. (c) When a debtor contracts with a second party to pay the debt owed to a creditor, the creditor becomes a creditor beneficiary. A creditor beneficiary has the right to enforce the contract which gives him the intended benefits and may commence an action for nonperformance against either of the contracting parties. For this reason, Ferco (creditor beneficiary) will prevail in a lawsuit against Bell because Ferco has an enforceable right to receive payment. Answer (a) is incorrect because Ferco, as a creditor beneficiary, has the right to recover from either Bell or Allied. Answer (b) is incorrect because the creditor beneficiary is not required to give consideration to have an enforceable right. Answer (d) is incorrect because having knowledge of the contract between Bell and Allied at the time the contract was made is not necessary to later enforce this legal action. Ferco must establish that he is a creditor beneficiary to maintain an action for nonperformance.

46. (b) Under the doctrine of substantial performance, a contract obligation may be discharged even though the performance tendered was not in complete conformity with the terms of the agreement. Under this doctrine, if it can be shown that the defect in performance was only minor in nature, that a good-faith effort was made to conform completely with the terms of the agreement, and if the performing party is willing to accept a decrease in compensation equivalent to the amount of the minor defect in performance, the contractual obligation will be discharged. Since the defect in Glaze's performance was only minor in nature, and since Parc refused to allow Glaze to complete the project, Glaze will prevail in its action against Parc; therefore answer (a) is incorrect. Answer (c) is incorrect because the purchase of accessories would be viewed as a minor deviation in the performance of the contract. Anticipatory breach applies only to executory bilateral contracts. An executory contract is a contract wherein both parties have yet to perform. In this instance, Glaze has substantially performed its part of the agreement so there is no anticipatory breach; thus, answer (d) is incorrect.

47. (a) The duty to perform a contract may depend upon a condition. Conditions that could be present include: condition precedent, which is one that must occur before there is duty to perform; condition subsequent, which is one that removes a preexisting duty to perform; or condition concurrent, which is mutually dependent upon performance at nearly the same time.

48. (a) Once one party materially breaches the contract, the other party is discharged from performing his or her obligations under the contract. Answer (b) is incorrect because a reasonable delay in the performance of the contract is not a breach unless time was of the essence. Answer (c) is incorrect because tender or offer to pay or perform obligates the other party to do what s/he promised. Answer (d) is incorrect because assignment of rights typically is allowed under contract law.

49. (a) The discharge of a contract can come about in several ways. The first is by agreement. Accord and satisfaction involves an agreed substitute for performance under the contract (accord) and the actual performance of that substitute (satisfaction). An agreement can also be entered into by three parties whereby the previous agreement is discharged by the creation of a new agreement (a novation). The second method of discharge is by release of the contract or parties from performance. Another method of discharging a contract is by performance of the specified action becoming impossible, such as destruction of the subject matter, or death of a party where personal service is necessary. Lastly, breach of the contract discharges the injured party.

50. (c) Rescission entails canceling a contract and placing the parties in the position they were in before the contract was formed. Answer (a) is incorrect as a novation is an agreement between three parties whereby a previous agreement is discharged by the creation of a new agreement. Answer (b) is incorrect because release is a means of discharging (abandoning) a contract but it does not place the parties in the same position as before the contract. Answer (d) is incorrect because revocation is used by an offeror to terminate an offer.

51. (b) The statute of limitations bars suit if it is not brought within the statutory period. The period varies for different types of cases and from state to state. The statute begins to run from the time the cause of action accrues (e.g., breach).

52. (d) The remedy of specific performance is used when money damages will not sufficiently compensate the afflicted party due to the unique nature of the subject matter of the contract. In a contract for the sale of land, the buyer has the right to enforce the agreement by seeking the remedy of specific performance because real property is considered unique. Another remedy for this breach of contract would be for the buyer to seek compensatory damages. If the buyer desires, s/he may seek this remedy instead of specific performance. Hodges could sue for either specific performance or compensatory damages but would not be entitled to both remedies. Both remedies would provide excessive compensation; therefore, answer (b) is incorrect. Answers (a) and (c) are incorrect because an injured party is generally not allowed to seek punitive damages. Punitive damages are awarded only when the court is seeking to punish a party for their improper actions and are not usually granted in breach of contract actions.

53. (a) Under the doctrine of substantial performance, a contract obligation may be discharged even though the performance tendered was not in complete conformity with the terms of the agreement. If it can be shown that the defect in performance was only minor in nature, that a good-faith effort was made to conform completely with the terms of the agreement, and if the performing party is willing to accept a decrease in compensation equivalent to the amount of the minor defect in performance, the contractual obligation will be discharged. Because Ames' breach of contract was both inadvertent and not material, the doctrine of substantial performance applies and recovery will be limited to monetary damages; therefore, answer (b) is incorrect. The installation of fixtures other than those specified in the contract constitutes a breach, although the breach is considered immaterial; thus, answer (c) is incorrect. The doctrine of substantial performance applies in this situation and the contractual obligation will be discharged; therefore White will have to take delivery of the warehouse and answer (d) is incorrect.

54. (a) A liquidated damage clause is a contractual provision which states the amount of damages that will occur if a party breaches the contract. The liquidated damage clause is enforceable if the amount is reasonable in light of the anticipated or actual harm caused by the breach. Answer (b) is incorrect because excessive liquidated damages will not be enforceable in court even if both parties have agreed in writing. Answer (d) is incorrect because a clause providing for excessive damages is a penalty and the courts will not enforce a penalty. Answer (c) is incorrect because materiality does not impact the enforceability of liquidated damage provisions.

55. (c) The doctrine of anticipatory repudiation allows a party to either sue at once or wait until after performance is due when the other party indicates s/he will not perform. This doctrine is in effect because Nagel told Fields that Nagel had no intention of delivering the goods (i.e., repudiation of the contract) prior to the date of performance. Answer (a) is incorrect because promissory estoppel acts as a substitute for consideration which is an element in the forming of a contract but is not relevant in this fact situation. Answer (b) is incorrect because accord and satisfaction is an agreement wherein a party with an existing duty or performance under a contract promises to do something other than perform the duty originally promised in the contract. Answer (d) is incorrect because the doctrine of substantial performance would allow for a contract obligation to be discharged even though the performance tendered was not in complete conformity with the terms of the agreement. In this case, Fields is suing Nagel for breach of contract.

56. (a) Events occurring after a contract is entered into usually do not affect performance. Some exceptions to this rule include subsequent illegality of the performance, death of a party, or destruction of the subject matter, all of which constitute impossibility of performance. In this case, even though Maco's own potatoes were destroyed, it wasn't specified that Maco's own potato crop be used to fulfill the contract. It was not impossible, therefore, for Maco to perform, because he could have purchased potatoes from another grower to deliver to LBC. If there had been a worldwide infestation of the potato crop, Maco would have reason to not perform on the basis of impossibility. Answer (b) is incorrect because the doctrine of impossibility is not used where a party could have protected itself from potential losses. Answer (c) is incorrect because insects, droughts, blights, and other natural disasters are something a farmer should and does anticipate. Answer(d) is incorrect because courts will usually place the risk of loss upon the party in the best position to prevent the loss; here that is the grower of the crops.

Simulations

Task-Based Simulation 1

Consideration		
	Authoritative Literature	Help

For each of the numbered statements or groups of statements select either A, B, or C.

List

A. Both parties have given consideration legally sufficient to support a contract.
B. One of the parties has **not** given consideration legally sufficient to support a contract. The promise, agreement, or transaction is generally **not** enforceable.
C. One of the parties has **not** given consideration legally sufficient to support a contract. However, the promise, agreement, or transaction **is** generally enforceable.

		(A)	(B)	(C)
1.	Party S feels a moral obligation because Party F let S stay in his place for free when S attended college. S now promises to pay F for the past kindness.	O	O	O
2.	F agrees to deliver all of the sugar that Company S will need in her business for the following year. S agrees to purchase it at the market price.	O	O	O
3.	F does not smoke for one year pursuant to S's agreement to pay F $200 if she does not smoke for one year.	O	O	O
4.	F dies leaving a valid will which gives S $100,000.	O	O	O
5.	F is an auditor of XYZ Company. S is a potential investor of XYZ and offers to pay F $1,000 if F performs a professional, quality audit of XYZ Company. The $1,000 is in addition to the fee F will get from XYZ. F does perform a professional, quality audit.	O	O	O
6.	F had agreed, in writing, to work for S for five years for $100,000 per year. After two years, F asks for a 20% raise. S first agrees then later changes his mind. F, while not agreeing to additional duties or changing his position, wants to enforce the raise in salary.	O	O	O
7.	S promised to pay F $1,000 if he crosses the Golden Gate Bridge on his hands and knees. F does so.	O	O	O
8.	F promised to pay S $200 for a computer worth $2,000. S agreed to the deal.	O	O	O
9.	F agreed to purchase all of the parts from S that S can produce in her business for the next six months. S also agreed.	O	O	O
10.	S agreed to accept $1,000 from F for a $1,500 debt that is not disputed. S now wants the additional $500. Focus on the agreement to accept the lesser amount.	O	O	O
11.	S agreed to accept $1,000 from F for a debt that S claims is $1,500 but F in good faith claims is $800. F agreed to the $1,000 initially, then decides he will pay only $800. Focus on the enforceability of the agreement for $1,000.	O	O	O
12.	S agreed to donate $100 to F, a public charity.	O	O	O

Task-Based Simulation 2

Contractual Relationship		
	Authoritative Literature	Help

Situation

On December 15, Blake Corp. telephoned Reach Consultants, Inc. and offered to hire Reach to design a security system for Blake's research department. The work would require two years to complete. Blake offered to pay a fee of $100,000 but stated that the offer must be accepted in writing, and the acceptance received by Blake no later than December 20.

On December 20, Reach faxed a written acceptance to Blake. Blake's offices were closed on December 20 and Reach's fax was not seen until December 21.

Reach's acceptance contained the following language:

"We accept your $1,000,000 offer. Weaver has been assigned $5,000 of the fee as payment for sums owed Weaver by Reach. Payment of this amount should be made directly to Weaver."

On December 22, Blake sent a signed memo to Reach rejecting Reach's December 20 fax but offering to hire Reach for a $75,000 fee. Reach telephoned Blake on December 23 and orally accepted Blake's December 22 offer.

Items 1 through 7 relate to whether a contractual relationship exists between Blake and Reach. For each item, determine whether the statement is True or False.

	True	False
1. Blake's December 15 offer had to be in writing to be a legitimate offer.	O	O
2. Reach's December 20 fax was an improper method of acceptance.	O	O
3. Reach's December 20 fax was effective when sent.	O	O
4. Reach's acceptance was invalid because it was received after December 20.	O	O
5. Blake's receipt of Reach's acceptance created a voidable contract.	O	O
6. If Reach had rejected the original offer by telephone on December 17, he could not validly accept the offer later.	O	O
7. Reach's December 20 fax was a counteroffer.	O	O

Items 8 through 12 relate to the attempted assignment of part of the fee to Weaver. Assume that a valid contract exists between Blake and Reach. For each item, determine whether the statement is True or False.

	True	False
8. Reach is prohibited from making an assignment of any contract right or duty.	O	O
9. Reach may validly assign part of the fee to Weaver.	O	O
10. Under the terms of Reach's acceptance, Weaver would be considered a third-party creditor beneficiary.	O	O
11. In a breach of contract suit by Weaver, against Blake, Weaver would not collect any punitive damages.	O	O
12. In a breach of contract suit by Weaver, against Reach, Weaver would be able to collect punitive damages.	O	O

Items 13 through 15 relate to Blake's December 22 signed memo. For each item, determine whether the statement is True or False.

	True	False
13. Reach's oral acceptance of Blake's December 22 memo may be enforced by Blake against Reach.	O	O
14. Blake's memo is a valid offer even though it contains no date for acceptance.	O	O
15. Blake's memo may be enforced against Blake by Reach.	O	O

Simulation Solutions

Task-Based Simulation 1

Consideration

Authoritative Literature | **Help**

	(A)	(B)	(C)
1. Party S feels a moral obligation because Party F let S stay in his place for free when S attended college. S now promises to pay F for the past kindness.	○	●	○
2. F agrees to deliver all of the sugar that Company S will need in her business for the following year. S agrees to purchase it at the market price.	●	○	○
3. F does not smoke for one year pursuant to S's agreement to pay F $200 if she does not smoke for one year.	●	○	○
4. F dies leaving a valid will which gives S $100,000.	○	○	●
5. F is an auditor of XYZ Company. S is a potential investor of XYZ and offers to pay F $1,000 if F performs a professional, quality audit of XYZ Company. The $1,000 is in addition to the fee F will get from XYZ. F does perform a professional, quality audit.	○	●	○
6. F had agreed, in writing, to work for S for five years for $100,000 per year. After two years, F asks for a 20% raise. S first agrees then later changes his mind. F, while not agreeing to additional duties or changing his position, wants to enforce the raise in salary.	○	●	○
7. S promised to pay F $1,000 if he crosses the Golden Gate Bridge on his hands and knees. F does so.	●	○	○
8. F promised to pay S $200 for a computer worth $2,000. S agreed to the deal.	●	○	○
9. F agreed to purchase all of the parts from S that S can produce in her business for the next six months. S also agreed.	●	○	○
10. S agreed to accept $1,000 from F for a $1,500 debt that is not disputed. S now wants the additional $500. Focus on the agreement to accept the lesser amount.	○	●	○
11. S agreed to accept $1,000 from F for a debt that S claims is $1,500 but F in good faith claims is $800. F agreed to the $1,000 initially, then decides he will pay only $800. Focus on the enforceability of the agreement for $1,000.	●	○	○
12. S agreed to donate $100 to F, a public charity.	○	○	●

Explanations

1. (B) Party F gave S a gift in the past. S's promise to now pay for the usage is not enforceable because F's action is past consideration, and the contract needs consideration on both sides. Furthermore, S's feeling of a moral obligation does not create consideration.

2. (A) This is an example of a requirements contract. F has given consideration because s/he gave up the right to sell that sugar to someone else.

3. (A) F refrained from doing something which she had a right to do. This constitutes consideration.

4. (C) This is not enforceable under contract law because S does not give any consideration in return. It is enforceable, however, as a will which does not require the elements of a contract such as consideration, but does require other formalities.

5. (B) F already had a preexisting legal duty to do a professional, quality audit of XYZ Company.

6. (B) F had a contract to work for S for five years for $100,000 per year. F is not giving any new consideration for the raise since during that five years, he already is obligated to complete the contract.

7. (A) F did something which he did not have to do in exchange for the agreed $1,000. This is a unilateral contract.

8. (A) F agreed to pay $200 and in exchange S agreed to sell the computer. Both have given consideration that is **legally** sufficient. Legally sufficient refers to the validity of the consideration, not the amount. Consideration does not have to be of equal value as long as it is legal consideration and bargained for.

9. (A) Both parties have given consideration for this output contract. F gave up the right to buy these parts elsewhere and S gave up the right to sell her output to someone else.

10. (B) F has a preexisting legal duty to pay the full $1,500. When S agreed to accept less, F gave up nothing. F still owes the remaining $500.

11. (A) In this case, both parties gave consideration. S, in agreeing to accept the $1,000, gave up the right to collect more of the disputed amount. F gave up the right to pay less of the disputed amount.

12. (C) Although the charity gave no consideration in exchange for the promised donation, the promise to donate to a charity is generally enforceable based on public policy reasons.

Task-Based Simulation 2

Contractual Relationship		
	Authoritative Literature	Help

	True	False
1. Blake's December 15 offer had to be in writing to be a legitimate offer.	○	●
2. Reach's December 20 fax was an improper method of acceptance.	○	●
3. Reach's December 20 fax was effective when sent.	○	●
4. Reach's acceptance was invalid because it was received after December 20.	○	●
5. Blake's receipt of Reach's acceptance created a voidable contract.	○	●
6. If Reach had rejected the original offer by telephone on December 17, he could not validly accept the offer later.	●	○
7. Reach's December 20 fax was a counteroffer.	●	○

Explanations

1. (F) Although the final contract has to be in writing to be enforceable since performance of contract would take longer than a year, the offer itself can be oral.

2. (F) The offer specified that the acceptance must be in writing. Since Reach put the acceptance in writing and faxed it to Blake, this was a proper method of acceptance.

3. (F) Common law applies to this fact pattern since the contract does not involve a sale of goods. Reach's attempted acceptance stated $1,000,000 instead of $100,000 as contained in the offer. Reach's attempted acceptance thus was instead a counteroffer. Under both common law and the Uniform Commercial Code, offers, revocations, rejections and counteroffers are valid when received.

4. (F) Blake's offer specified that the acceptance must be received no later than December 20. Reach's faxed acceptance was received in Blake's office on December 20 on the fax machine. Therefore, Blake did receive the fax on time even though it was not seen until the following day.

5. (F) Reach's attempted acceptance stated $1,000,000 instead of $100,000 as contained in the offer. Since the terms did not match, no contract was formed, voidable or otherwise.

6. (T) Since there is no firm offer or option contract, the rejection terminates the offer.

7. (T) Since the December 20 fax terms did not match the original offer's terms, it serves as a counteroffer which rejects the original offer and creates a new offer.

	True	False
8. Reach is prohibited from making an assignment of any contract right or duty.	○	●
9. Reach may validly assign part of the fee to Weaver.	●	○
10. Under the terms of Reach's acceptance, Weaver would be considered a third-party creditor beneficiary.	●	○
11. In a breach of contract suit by Weaver, against Blake, Weaver would not collect any punitive damages.	●	○
12. In a breach of contract suit by Weaver, against Reach, Weaver would be able to collect punitive damages.	○	●

Explanations

8. (F) Parties may typically assign the contract right to receive money to another party.

9. (T) When parties have a right to receive money, they may validly assign all or a portion of this right to a third party.

10. (T) The terms of Reach's acceptance names Weaver as a third-party beneficiary to receive $5,000. Since the intent was to pay a debt owed by Reach to Weaver, this makes Weaver a creditor beneficiary.

11. (T) Punitive damages are not awarded for mere breach of contract cases such as this suit by Weaver against Blake.

12. (F) In a suit by Weaver against Reach, no punitive damages will be awarded since this would be only a breach of contract case.

	True	False
13. Reach's oral acceptance of Blake's December 22 memo may be enforced by Blake against Reach.	○	●
14. Blake's memo is a valid offer even though it contains no date for acceptance.	●	○
15. Blake's memo may be enforced against Blake by Reach.	●	○

Explanations

13. (F) Since the work would require two years to complete, the contract cannot be performed within one year and, therefore, must be in writing to be enforceable. The party to be charged must have signed the contract and Reach did not do this.

14. (T) An offer does not need to have a date for acceptance, in which case, the offer remains open for a reasonable time.

15. (T) Blake's signed memo sets forth an offer which was later accepted orally by Reach. This can be construed as enough written evidence to satisfy the Statute of Frauds. Because Blake, the party to be charged, signed the memo, it is enforceable against Blake by Reach.

Module 27: Sales

Overview

The law of sales governs contracts for the sale of goods. Since a sale of goods is involved, Article 2 of the Uniform Commercial Code (UCC) applies. A sale of goods under the UCC is the sale of tangible, moveable property. Be sure that when you are faced with a contract question to determine whether the contract involved the sale of goods; if so, then you will apply the UCC rules outlined in this module. If the contract involved something other than goods, then you want to use the common law rules outlined in Module 26.

One of the areas tested in sales is product liability. When studying this area, you should pay particular attention to the different legal theories under which an injured party may recover. Realize that an injured party may recover under the legal theories of breach of warranty, negligence, and strict liability. It is important that you know the circumstances under which these theories may be used. Other areas that are often tested are warranties; disclaimers; risk of loss; and remedies, rights, and duties of the buyer and seller. You should understand that a binding contract may be present under the UCC if the parties intend to be bound, even though certain elements of a contract may be missing. These open terms will be filled by specific provisions of the UCC. The parties to a sale need not be merchants for the UCC to apply; however, some rules vary if merchants are involved in the sales contract.

As you study this area, note that it builds on much of the material under contracts in the previous module. Therefore, as you study this area you should review the contract law rules, especially those in the previous module that apply to the UCC. Before beginning the reading you should review the key terms at the end of the module.

A. Contracts for Sale of Goods

1. Article 2 of the Uniform Commercial Code, in general, controls contracts for the sale of goods for any dollar amount

   a. "Goods" include tangible personal property (whether specially manufactured or not)

      (1) Does not include sales of investment securities, accounts receivable, contract rights, copyrights, or patents

---

EXAMPLE

S sells B a stereo. The UCC applies.

EXAMPLE

S sells a home to B. The common law rules rather than the UCC rules apply to this contract since it involves the sale of real property.

> **EXAMPLE**
>
> F sells to M several bushels of wheat. The UCC applies to fungible goods also (i.e., goods in which one unit is considered the equivalent of the other units).

b. In general, UCC applies to sales and leases of hardware as well as to sales and licensing of software.

   (1) However, if software is heavily customized based on services of consultant, common law applies.

c. Article 2 of UCC has been passed into law by every state (except Louisiana which has adopted only portions of UCC)

   (1) Federal courts also use principles in Article 2 for sales of goods.

d. UCC applies whether sale is between merchants or consumers but some rules change if merchant involved

> **EXAMPLE**
>
> S sells his used refrigerator to B, a neighbor. The UCC applies to this transaction.

e. The UCC, unlike the common law, implies that a contract exists where it is the intent of the parties to create a contract, even though some technical element of contract may be missing

2. General concepts

   a. Merchant—one who deals in the kind of goods being sold, or one who holds self out as having superior knowledge and skills as to the goods involved, or one who employs another who qualifies as a merchant
   b. Good faith

      (1) The UCC assume that parties entering into sales contracts will do so in good faith
      (2) Good faith means that parties will be honest with each other
      (3) Additionally for merchants it also means to observe reasonable commercial standards of fair dealing in the trade

   c. UCC supplies missing terms for contracts

      (1) Under common law if terms are missing there is no contract because the terms are not definite
      (2) UCC fills in missing terms if parties have shown intent to enter into a contract

   d. When terms of a sales contract are unclear the terms can be explained by

      (1) Course of dealing: If parties have had previous dealings, we look to see how the unclear term was interpreted or acted upon by the parties in the past
      (2) Usage of trade: How the term is typically used in the particular trade, business, or industry.

NOW REVIEW MULTIPLE-CHOICE QUESTIONS 1 AND 2

B. Forming the Contract for the Sale of Goods

1. The UCC adopts most of the common law rules for contracts

   a. Assume the common law rule is the same as the UCC rule
   b. What follows are the changes that the UCC makes to the common law rules

2. Offer

   a. Offer under the UCC can be less definite
   b. Generally the UCC permits:

    (1) Open price terms: A reasonable/market price will be supplied if necessary.

    (2) Open quantity terms

        (a) Quantity term does need to be included for contracts over $500, under the Statute of Frauds

        (b) Quantity term does not, however have to be precise

        (c) Output contracts are permissible: Buyer promises to purchase all that a seller can produce

        (d) Requirements contracts are permissible: Seller will provide the quantity of goods that the buyer needs

  c. Firm offer rule

    (1) Promise to hold an offer open, even if not supported by consideration, is irrevocable if the promise is

        (a) In writing, **and,**

        (b) Made by a merchant.

    (2) If firm offer does not state specific time, it will remain open for reasonable time, based on the nature of the subject matter not to exceed three months

> **EXAMPLE**
>
> M, a merchant, agrees in a letter signed by M to sell B 1,000 widgets, with the offer to remain open for five weeks. Even if M tries to revoke this offer before the five-week period, B may still accept.

> **EXAMPLE**
>
> M, a merchant, agrees in signed writing to sell B 1,000 widgets, stating that the offer will remain open for 120 days. B accepts the offer on the 95th day. If nothing has occurred to terminate the offer prior to acceptance, offer and acceptance are present. The irrevocable nature of this offer would end after three months, but the offer would not automatically terminate. The offer would remain in existence for the stated period (120 days) unless terminated by other means.

3. Acceptance

  a. UCC rejects the mirror image rule; instead the UCC focuses on the parties' intent to be bound

  b. The intent to be bound approach creates some problems

> **EXAMPLE**
>
> I offer to sell you 1,000 pens for $100 and ship them via UPS; you accept, but you want them shipped via Federal Express. Under the UCC there is a contract because we both agreed to the sale/purchase of the pens. But how should the goods be shipped: UPS or Federal Express? The answer is contained in the material below entitled Battle of forms.

  c. Battle of forms—between merchants, additional terms included in the acceptance become part of the contract unless

    (1) Original offer precludes such, or

    (2) New terms materially alter the original offer, or

    (3) The original offeror gives notice of his/her objection within a reasonable time

> **EXAMPLE**
>
> In the above example, if we are both merchants, then the additional/changed term you proposed: shipping via Federal Express would become part of the contract unless I make a timely objection.

(4) If the parties are not merchants, then the offeror needs to expressly accept the additional/changed term.

   d. Accommodation

     (1) When a seller ships substitute goods because the seller does not have the goods ordered by the buyer

     (2) If the buyer accepts substituted goods, a contract exists

     (3) If buyer refuses substituted goods, then there is no contract

     (4) If seller provides notice to buyer that shipment is only an accommodation, seller's actions are not viewed as an acceptance

---

EXAMPLE

Value Hardware placed an order with Odin Industries for 800 Thor hammers on June for delivery on August 15. On June 3, Odin sent Value a written acceptance. On August 12, Odin shipped 800 Asgard hammers because Odin was out of Thor hammers. Odin also stated on the invoice that the shipment was an accommodation. The hammers arrived at Value on August 15. Odin has breached the contract. Once a seller has accepted an order, the seller cannot simply substitute goods and call it an accommodation.

EXAMPLE

Assume Value placed the same order, on June 1 and stated, "I need the hammers as soon as possible." Odin responded by shipping the 800 Asgard hammers on June 3 with a note stating that the shipment was an accommodation. If Value accepts, there is a contract. If Value does not accept, then Value can return the hammers and there is no contract.

---

4. a. Under the UCC, a contract may be modified without new consideration if done in good faith

---

EXAMPLE

B agrees in a contract to buy 300 electrical parts for $1.00 each from S. B later points out to S that he can get the same parts from D for $.90 each and asks for a price reduction. S reduces the price to $.90 each. This new contract is enforceable even though B gave no new consideration. Note that if S had required B to pay the $1.00 as originally agreed, B would be in breach of contract if he failed to go through with the original contract.

---

   b. Common law requires new consideration on both sides for any modification

---

EXAMPLE

B agreed, in a written contract, to pay $10,000 to S for certain real estate. Later, B said he was having difficulty getting the $10,000 so S agreed to reduce the price to $9,000. S can still enforce the full $10,000 because B gave no new consideration for the modification.

---

5. Legality and Capacity are the same under the UCC and the common law
6. Under the UCC version of Statute of Frauds, contracts for sale of goods for $500 or more must be in writing or be evidenced by a writing.

   a. A sufficient writing

     (1) Must contain quantity term

     (2) Signature of party to be charged

     (3) Indicate the existence of a contract

b. If the contract is between merchants, then a written confirmation is sufficient to serve as a writing unless objection is made within 10 days of receiving the confirmation

---

EXAMPLE

Pat operates a fish market. Pat phoned Shelley, a fish wholesaler, to see if Shelley could sell Pat 200 pounds of sockeye salmon for $1,000 for delivery in two weeks. Shelley agreed and e-mailed Pat a written confirmation of Pat's order. Pat did not respond to the e-mail. When the fish is delivered two weeks later is Pat obligated to take delivery? Yes, the contract falls under the UCC provision of the Statute of Frauds: Salmon is a good and the contract exceeds $500. Although the signature of the party to be charged, Pat, is not present here; Shelley's written confirmation is sufficient since both parties are merchants.

> **NOTE:** If Pat was not a merchant, then the writing is not sufficient to satisfy the Statute of Frauds and Pat could refuse delivery.

---

c. If contract is modified, must be in writing if after modification it is for $500 or more

---

EXAMPLE

B agrees in a contract to buy widgets from S for $500. Later, S agrees to a reduction in price to $490. The first contract must be in writing (absent any exceptions), but the modified contract may be oral.

---

d. Exceptions to writing requirement (these are important)

   (1) Oral contract involving specially manufactured goods (i.e., not saleable in ordinary course of business) if seller has made substantial start in their manufacture (or even made a contract for necessary raw materials) is enforceable
   (2) Oral contract is enforceable against party who admits it in court, but not beyond quality of goods admitted
   (3) Goods that have been paid for (if seller accepts payment) or goods which buyer has accepted are part of enforceable contract even if oral

---

EXAMPLE

B orally agrees to purchase 10,000 parts from S for $1 each. B later gives S $6,000 for a portion of the parts. S accepts the money. In absence of a written agreement, B may enforce a contract for 6,000 parts but not for the full 10,000 parts.

NOW REVIEW MULTIPLE-CHOICE QUESTIONS 3 THROUGH 12

C. Performance of the Sales Contract

1. Seller's performance

   a. Tender: A party is ready, willing, and able to perform the obligations of the contract.
   b. Place of tender (performance) is the seller's place of business, unless contract provides otherwise

      (1) Parties may choose place of tender by contract
      (2) This is one of the UCC's "gap" filling provisions: It only applies if the parties have not accounted for the place of tender in the contract

   c. Perfect tender rule

      (1) Seller's tender of goods must conform exactly, to the terms of the contract
      (2) If Seller's tender is not perfect, buyer may:

         (a) Reject the whole lot of goods
         (b) Accept the whole lot of goods
         (c) Accept some units and reject the remaining units

---

EXAMPLE

Wonka ordered 5,000 orange gaskets from Acme. The gaskets are used in various machines that Wonka uses to produce candy. Acme timely delivered 5,000 gaskets in five crates of 1,000 gaskets each. When Wonka opened the crates he saw that the gaskets were yellow instead of orange. Even if the color has no effect on how the gaskets work, Wonka may still reject the lot. If Wonka needed 1,500 gaskets immediately, Wonka could accept two crates, or 2,000 gaskets. Wonka cannot, however, split a shipping unit, a crate, so if he needs 1,500 gaskets, he will need to accept two crates.

---

      (3) Exceptions

         (a) Agreement by parties that seller did not need to perfectly tender
         (b) Seller cures (fixes) the defect
         (c) Installment contracts: Buyer may only reject a defective installment, not entire contract

---

EXAMPLE

Wonka orders 5,000 orange gaskets from Acme to be delivered in boxes of 500 each month for the next 10 months. Acme perfectly tendered for the first three months, but in the fourth month Acme sent yellow gaskets instead. Wonka may reject only the shipment in the fourth month.

---

2. Buyer's performance

   a. Payment is due at the time of delivery
   b. Buyer has a right to inspect the goods prior to payment; except for good that were shipped COD (Cash on delivery)
   c. Buyer should inspect goods at time of delivery to preserve buyer's remedies against a seller who has shipped defective or nonconforming goods
   d. Buyer may reject good if goods are defective

      (1) Buyer must disclose nature of the defect to seller. (Gives seller opportunity to cure defect)
      (2) Buyer must either return goods or hold goods with reasonable care

   e. Buyer may accept goods

      (1) Buyer may revoke prior acceptance if

         (a) Seller did not provide promised cure, or
         (b) Goods contained hidden defect: A hidden defect is a defect that the buyer could not perceive with reasonable inspection at the time of delivery

3. Excused performance: Either buyer or seller's obligation to perform may be excused if any of the following occur

   a. Destruction of the goods prior to performance
   b. Commercial impracticality: Performance has become excessively expensive or difficult due to unforeseeable events
   c. Assurance of performance

      (1) If there is a reasonable basis to believe that the other party will not perform as promised, the uncertain party may

         (a) Make a written demand for adequate assurance of performance
         (b) A response assuring performance must be provided within a reasonable time, not exceeding 30 days.
         (c) Failure to respond in a timely fashion is evidence of anticipatory repudiation

d. Anticipatory repudiation: One party clearly indicates that it is unwilling, or unable, to perform the contract as promised

e. Cooperation necessary for performance was not provided

EXAMPLE

Wonka ordered 5,000 orange gaskets from Acme. Wonka promised to provide Acme with a specific orange dye. Despite repeated requests from Acme, Wonka never provided the dye. Acme's performance of coloring the gadgets orange is excused.

---

f. Performance is not excused when substitute performance is possible

---

EXAMPLE

Wonka ordered 5,000 orange gaskets from Acme. Acme agreed to ship the gaskets by truck to Wonka's factory. At the time of delivery there was a trucker's strike. The strike does not excuse Acme's performance. Acme could have the gaskets delivered by train or some other method of transportation.

---

g. Consignment—Arrangement in which agent (consignee) is appointed by consignor to sell goods if all the following conditions are met:

   (1) Consignor keeps title to goods,
   (2) Consignee is not obligated to buy or pay for goods,
   (3) Consignee receives a commission upon sale, and
   (4) Consignor receives proceeds of sale.

h. Document of title—Any document that in the regular course of business is accepted as adequate evidence that the person in possession of the document is entitled to receive, hold, and dispose of the document and the goods it covers

i. Bill of lading—A document of title that is issued by a private or common carrier in exchange for goods delivered to it for shipment. It may be negotiable or nonnegotiable.

j. Warehouse receipt—A document of title issued by a person engaged in the business of storing goods (i.e., a warehouseman). It acknowledges receipt of the goods, describes the goods stored, and contains the terms of the storage contract. It may be negotiable or nonnegotiable.

NOW REVIEW MULTIPLE-CHOICE QUESTIONS 13 AND 14

D. Transfer of Title (Property Rights)

1. Transfer of title to third parties

   a. These are situations where a person acquires the property and then tries to transfer ownership of the acquired property to another person (a third party)

   b. If party having voidable title transfers goods to a good-faith purchaser for value, the latter obtains good title

      (1) Examples in which there is voidable title

         (a) Goods paid for with a check subsequently dishonored
         (b) Goods obtained by fraud, mistake, duress, or undue influence
         (c) Goods obtained from minor
         (d) Thieves and/or finders of property have **void** title

---

EXAMPLE

B buys a stereo from S but the check bounces. P, a good-faith purchaser, pays B for the stereo. S cannot get the stereo from P but must recover money from B.

> **EXAMPLE**
>
> Same as above except that B stole the stereo. P does not obtain title of the stereo. S can recover the stereo from P. This is true even if P was unaware that the stereo was stolen.

    c. If a person entrusts possession of goods to a merchant who deals in those goods, a good-faith purchaser for value obtains title to these goods, unless s/he knew that this merchant did not own the goods.

> **EXAMPLE**
>
> C leaves his watch at a shop for repairs. The shop mistakenly sells the watch to B who is unaware of C's interest. C cannot force B to turn over the watch because B now has title. Of course, C can recover monetary damages from the shop.

  2. Transfer of title from a seller to a buyer

    a. Once goods exist and are identified to the contract, the parties may agree as to when title passes

      (1) Sale cannot take place until goods exist and have been identified to the contract

        (a) Identification—occurs when the goods that are going to be used to perform the contract are shipped, marked or otherwise designated as such

        (b) Identification gives buyer

          [1] An insurable interest in the goods once they are identified to contract

          [2] Right to demand goods upon offering full contract price once other conditions are satisfied

    b. Otherwise, title generally passes when the seller completes his/her performance with respect to physical delivery

      (1) If a destination contract, title passes on tender at destination (i.e., buyer's place of business)

      (2) If a shipping (point) contract, title passes when seller puts goods in the possession of the carrier

    c. If seller has no duty to move the goods

      (1) Title passes upon delivery of documents of title

> **EXAMPLE**
>
> Delivery of negotiable or nonnegotiable warehouse receipt passes title to buyer.

      (2) If no document of title exists, title passes at the time and place of contracting if the goods are identifiable

      (3) If goods not identified, there is only a contract to sell; no title passes

    d. Rejection (justified or not) of goods or a justified revocation of acceptance by buyer reverts title to seller

    e. Taking a security interest is irrelevant to passage of title

NOW REVIEW MULTIPLE-CHOICE QUESTIONS 15 THROUGH 18

E. Risk of Loss

  1. Risk of loss is independent of title under UCC, but rules regarding the transfer of both are similar

  2. General rules when seller ships goods that conform to the contract

    a. Parties may agree as to which party bears risk of loss or has title; otherwise UCC rules below apply

    b. Shipment contract

(1) Risk of loss transfers to buyer when the goods are delivered to the common carrier
(2) Generally designated as "FOB seller's warehouse," but any indication of the seller's place of business is sufficient

---

EXAMPLE

Seller is in San Francisco and buyer is in Chicago: FOB San Francisco: Thus, if the goods are shipped via common carrier from San Francisco and destroyed in transit, the buyer bears the risk of loss.

    (a) Other shipment contract designations

        [1] CIF: Cost, insurance, and freight are included in price
        [2] C & F: Shipping contract in which cost and freight are included in price

c. In international sales shipment contracts under United Nations Convention for the International Sale of Goods, risk of loss passes to buyer upon delivery to first carrier for transmission to buyer.

    (1) This can be modified by agreement.

d. Destination contract

    (1) Risk of loss transfer to buyer when the goods reach their intended destination and are tendered to the buyer
    (2) Usually designated as "FOB buyer's place of business"

e. If no shipping terms are specified, then the presumption is a shipment contract
f. Trial sales: Seller is allowing buyer to try the good prior to the actual sale

    (1) Sale on approval: Goods may be returned even if they conform to the contract

        (a) Goods not considered sold until buyer approves or accepts as sale
        (b) Seller retains title and risk of loss until buyer accepts goods
        (c) Creditors of buyer cannot reach goods until buyer accepts

    (2) Sale or return: Goods may be returned even if they conform to the contract

        (a) Goods bought for use or resale
        (b) Sale is final if goods not returned during period specified
        (c) Buyer obtains risk of loss and title until goods are returned
        (d) Creditors of buyer can reach the goods while in buyer's possession, unless notice of seller's interest is posted or filed as required

g. If risk of loss is not covered by above rules, then

    (1) Merchant sellers transfer the risk of loss when buyer takes physical possession of goods
    (2) Nonmerchant sellers transfer risk of loss to buyer upon tender

---

EXAMPLE

Max agreed to purchase a used drum set from Buddy. Buddy is not in the business of selling musical instruments. Buddy tendered delivery to Max, after receiving Max's check in the mail. Max told Buddy that he would stop by the following week and pick up the drum set. The next night, after a huge storm, Buddy's basement flooded, and ruined the drum set. Who bears the loss of the drum set? Max will bear the loss because the risk transferred to Max upon tender. Note: If Buddy had been a merchant, Buddy would bear the loss.

---

h. If goods are held in warehouse and seller has no right to move them, risk of loss passes to buyer

    (1) Upon proper negotiation of a negotiable document of title
    (2) Within a reasonable time after delivery of a nonnegotiable document of title
    (3) Once warehouseman acknowledges buyer's right to goods if no document of title

3. Sales involving breach of contract

   a. If seller breaches (typically seller has shipped nonconforming goods)

      (1) Risk of loss remains with seller until cure by seller or acceptance by buyer to extent of buyer's deficiency in insurance coverage
      (2) Title passes under original terms despite delivery of nonconforming goods

---

EXAMPLE

Wonka orders 5,000 orange gaskets from Acme. The contract states that the gaskets will be shipped FOB Acme's warehouse. While the gaskets are in transit to Wonka's warehouse, the gaskets are destroyed when the common carrier transporting the gaskets is involved in an accident. A review of the common carrier's bill of lading reveals that Acme had shipped 5,000 yellow gaskets, instead of orange gaskets.

   Analysis: Title to the gaskets passed to Wonka because this is a shipment contract. Normally, the shipment contract would also place the risk of loss upon Wonka as well. However, since Acme shipped nonconforming gaskets (yellow instead of orange), the risk of loss never transferred to Wonka, so Acme bears the loss here.

---

   b. If buyer breaches, risk of loss passes to buyer to extent of seller's deficiency in insurance for a commercially reasonable time.

4. Risk of loss can be covered by insurance. Do not assume that either party has insurance on the CPA Exam. The Examiners will tell you if insurance is involved. In general, party has an insurable interest whenever s/he can suffer damage.

   a. Buyer usually allowed an insurable interest when goods are identified to the contract
   b. Seller usually has an insurable interest so long as s/he has title or a security interest

---

NOW REVIEW MULTIPLE-CHOICE QUESTIONS 19 THROUGH 25

F. **Product Liability**—a manufacturer or seller may be responsible when a product is defective and causes injury or damage to a person or property. There are three theories under which manufacturers and sellers may be held liable. (In each fact pattern, consider all three, although proof of any one creates liability.)

1. Warranty Liability—purchaser of a product may sue based on the warranties made

   a. Warranty of title

      (1) Seller warrants good title, rightful transfer, and freedom from any security interest or lien of which the buyer has no knowledge

---

EXAMPLE

A seller of stolen goods would be liable to a buyer for damages since the seller has no title.

---

      (2) Merchant warrants goods to be free of rightful claim of infringement (e.g., patent or trademark), unless buyer furnished specifications to seller for manufacture of the goods
      (3) Can only be disclaimed by specific language or circumstances that give buyer reason to know s/he is receiving less than full title

         (a) Cannot be disclaimed by language such as "as is"

   b. Express warranties (may be written or oral)

      (1) Any affirmation of fact or promise made by the seller to the buyer that relates to the goods and becomes part of the basis of the bargain creates an express warranty that the goods shall conform to the affirmation or promise

     (a) Sales talk, puffing, or a statement purporting to be merely the seller's opinion does not create a warranty

     (b) Must form part of the basis of bargain

          [1] Would include advertisements read by buyer

          [2] Normally would not include warranties given after the sale or contract was made

     (c) No intent to create warranty is needed on the part of the seller

     (d) Seller or buyer may be merchant or consumer

  (2) Any description of the goods which is made part of the basis of the bargain creates an express warranty that the goods shall conform to the description

  (3) Any sample or model that is made part of the basis of the bargain creates an express warranty that the goods shall conform to the sample or model

  (4) It is not necessary to the creation of an express warranty that the seller use formal words such as "warranty" or "guarantee"

c. Implied warranties

  (1) Warranty of merchantability—goods are fit for ordinary purpose

     (a) This warranty also guarantees that goods are properly packaged and labeled

     (b) This warranty applies if

          [1] Seller must be a merchant with respect to goods of the kind being sold, and

          [2] Warranty is not modified or excluded

          [3] Then if goods not fit for ordinary use, breach of this warranty occurs

  (2) Warranty of fitness for a particular purpose

     (a) Created when the seller knows of the particular use for which the goods are required and further knows that the buyer is relying on skill and judgment of seller to select and furnish suitable goods for this particular use

---

EXAMPLE

A buyer relies upon a paint salesperson to select a particular exterior house paint that will effectively cover existing siding.

     (b) Buyer must actually rely on seller's skill and judgment

     (c) Product is then warranted for the particular expressed purpose and seller may be liable if the product fails to so perform

     (d) Applicable both to merchants and nonmerchants

d. UCC, being consumer oriented, allows these warranties to extend to parties other than the purchaser even without privity of contract (contractual connection between parties)

  (1) Extends to a buyer's family and also to guests who may reasonably be expected to use and/or be affected by the goods and who are injured

---

EXAMPLE

A dinner guest breaks a tooth on a small piece of metal in the food. Note that in food, the substance causing injury normally must be foreign, not something customarily found in it (bone in fish).

---

e. Disclaimers—warranty liability may be escaped or modified by disclaimers (also available at common law without rules defining limits of disclaimers)

  (1) A disclaimer of merchantability can be written or oral but must use the word "merchantability" unless implied warranties are disclaimed as in (3) below

(2) To disclaim the implied warranty of fitness for a particular purpose, the disclaimer must be in writing and conspicuous

(3) Both the warranty of merchantability and fitness for a particular purpose can be disclaimed by oral or written language such as "as is" or "with all faults"

(4) Written disclaimers must be clear and conspicuous

(5) If the buyer has had ample opportunity to inspect the goods or sample, there is no implied warranty as to any defects which ought reasonably to have been discovered

(6) Implied warranties may be excluded or modified by course of dealings, course of performance, or usage of trade

(7) A disclaimer inconsistent with an express warranty is not effective (i.e., a description of a warranty in a contract cannot be disclaimed)

(8) Limitations on consequential damages for personal injuries are presumed to be unconscionable and thus unenforceable if on consumer goods

2. Negligence

  a. Must prove the following elements

    (1) Duty of manufacturer to exercise reasonable (due) care to the injured party

      (a) Consider likelihood of harm, seriousness of harm

      (b) May be based on violation of statute but this is not necessary

    (2) Breach of duty of reasonable care

      (a) Insufficient instructions may cause breach of duty

      (b) Did the manufacturer/seller fail to act as a reasonable manufacturer/seller?

    (3) Manufacturer's failure to exercise reasonable care caused the injury/damages.

      (a) Direct cause: In general, if injury would not have happened without defendant's conduct, there is cause in fact

      (b) Proximate cause: Negligence set into motion an unbroken chain of events which led to injury/ damages

    (4) Injury/damages: The plaintiff must be able to show that s/he has suffered some recognizable loss

  b. Privity of contract is not needed because suit not based on contract

---

EXAMPLE

A car manufacturer is negligent in the manufacture and design of brakes and as a result, a driver is severely injured. The driver may sue the manufacturer even if he bought the car from a retailer.

EXAMPLE

In the example above, even a pedestrian injured because of the brake problem may recover from the manufacturer.

---

  c. Defenses to negligence

    (1) Contributory negligence

      (a) That is, plaintiff helped cause accident

      (b) Complete bar to recovery

      (c) Most states instead use comparative negligence in which damages are allocated between plaintiff and defendant based on relative fault

    (2) Assumption of risk

3. Strict product liability

   a. Manufacturers, sellers, and lessors who normally deal in this type of product are liable to users of products without proof of fault or lack of reasonable care if following other elements are proven

      (1) Product was defective when sold

         (a) Based on poor design, inadequate warnings, improper assembly, or unsafe materials

      (2) Defect is unreasonably dangerous to user

         (a) Based on normal expectations

      (3) Product reaches user without significant changes

      (4) Defect caused the injury

   b. Defense of acting with reasonable care, contributory negligence, comparative negligence, disclaimer or lack of privity is unavailable

      (1) Assumption of risk and misuse are defenses

EXAMPLE

Herb is injured while lifting up his power lawnmower to trim his hedges. Manufacturer would not be liable since product was not being used for intended purpose.

---

4. American Law Institute has published its Restatement (Third) of Torts: Product Liability

   a. This is significant development and many courts now cite it

   b. However, treat it as a minority rule which has not superceded important long-standing rules of negligence

   c. Restatement (Third)'s product liability rule basically states those in business of selling or distributing defective products are liable for harm to individuals or property resulting from such defect

      (1) Rule covers not only manufacturers but other sellers engaged in business of selling such products that caused harm to plaintiffs

      (2) Note that Restatement (Third) does **not** require products to be unreasonably dangerous

   d. Restatement (Third) adds to general rule above by establishing three types of product defects

      (1) Manufacturing defects

         (a) Take place when product does not conform with its intended use when leaves manufacturer

---

EXAMPLE

Flawed products, damaged products, or products assembled incorrectly.

---

      (2) Inadequate warnings and instructions

         (a) Manufacturers and sellers liable for failing to warn or instruct about reasonably foreseeable harms

            [1] Need not warn of generally known or obvious risks

      (3) Design defects

         (a) A product has a design defect if its foreseeable risk of harm could have been avoided or reduced by different design

---

NOW REVIEW MULTIPLE-CHOICE QUESTIONS 26 THROUGH 35

G. Remedies under Sales Law

1. In general, either party may, upon breach by other, cancel the contract and terminate executory obligations

    a. Unlike common law rescission, however, cancellation does not discharge a claim for damages

2. Seller's remedies

    a. Seller has right to cure nonconformity (i.e., tender conforming goods)

        (1) Within original time of contract, or
        (2) Within reasonable time if seller thought nonconforming tender would be acceptable
        (3) Seller must notify buyer of his intention to cure

    b. Seller may resell goods if buyer breaches before acceptance

        (1) May be public or private sale

            (a) If private, must give notice to buyer who breached; otherwise, losses cannot be recovered
            (b) If seller resells in a commercially reasonable manner, s/he may recover any loss on the sale from the buyer who breached, but s/he is not responsible to buyer who breached for profits made on resale
            (c) In any event, good-faith purchasers take free of original buyer's claims

    c. If seller learns that buyer is insolvent and buyer does not have the document of title, seller may stop delivery of goods in carrier's possession unless buyer pays cash
    d. Seller may recover goods received by an insolvent buyer if demand is made within ten days of receipt

        (1) However, if the buyer has made a written misrepresentation of solvency within three months before delivery, this ten-day limitation does not apply
        (2) If buyer is insolvent, seller may demand cash to make delivery

    e. Seller may recover damages

        (1) If buyer repudiates agreement or refuses goods, seller may recover the difference between market price at time of tender and contract price, plus incidental damages, minus expenses saved due to buyer's breach
        (2) If the measure of damages stated above in (1) is inadequate to place the seller in as good a position as performance would have, then the seller can sue for the lost profits, plus incidental damages, less expenses saved due to the buyer's breach

            (a) Loss profits are consequential damages and as such are recoverable when foreseeable by breaching party

        (3) The seller can recover the full contract price when

            (a) The buyer has already accepted the goods
            (b) Conforming goods have been destroyed after the risk of loss had transferred to buyer
            (c) The seller is unable to resell the identified goods

    f. Under Uniform Computer Information Transactions Act (UCITA), licensor of its software has special self-help remedies available to protect its software, the right to be paid for usage, or its trade secrets.

        (1) Licensor may use bugs, etc., that disable that software from further misuse if certain requirements are met

            (a) Licensee must have specifically agreed to that self-help remedy
            (b) Licensor must give licensee at least fifteen days' notice before using that remedy as well as who licensee can contact about any questions
            (c) Licensor is not permitted to use this remedy if there is a significant risk of personal injury or public safety, or if there is a significant risk to information of other parties

3. Buyer's remedies

    a. Buyer may reject nonconforming goods, either in entirety or any commercial unit (e.g., bale, carload, etc.)

        (1) Buyer has right to inspect goods before acceptance or payment

            (a) Must do so in reasonable time and give notice to seller (failure may operate as acceptance)
            (b) Buyer must have reasonable time to inspect

(2) Buyer must care for goods until returned

(3) If buyer is a merchant, s/he must follow reasonable instructions of seller (e.g., ship, sell)

    (a) Right to indemnity for costs

(4) If goods are perishable or threatened with decline in value, buyer must make reasonable effort to sell

(5) Buyer has a security interest in any goods in his/her possession to the extent of any payments made to seller and any expenses incurred

    (a) S/he may sell the goods to recover payments

b. Under Uniform Computer Information Transactions Act (UCITA), consumers who make electronic errors while ordering have special rights, if consumer, upon learning of error, does following

(1) Immediately notifies seller that s/he made error (as soon as s/he learns of error)

(2) Buyer does not use or benefit from information, software or products ordered

(3) Delivers all copies to seller or destroys them at seller's request

(4) Buyer in error pays all costs of processing and shipping to seller

(5) Note that nonconsumer buyer may not use these more favorable provisions of this Act

---

EXAMPLE

Buyer intends to purchase one copy of a DVD from ABC Company. The buyer, who is purchasing this DVD for consumer use, mistakenly orders ten copies from ABC's website. The buyer is protected by following the steps given above.

---

c. Buyer may recover damages measured by the difference between the contract price and the market value of the goods at the time buyer learns of the breach, plus any incidental damages and consequential damages

(1) Consequential damages are damages resulting from buyer's needs that the seller was aware of at the time of contracting

(2) Consequential damages cannot be recovered if buyer could reasonably have prevented these (mitigation of damages)

d. Buyer has the right of cover

(1) Buyer can buy substitute goods from another seller—buyer will still have the right to damages after engaging in "cover"

    (a) Damages are difference between cost of cover and contract price, plus incidental and consequential damages

    (b) Failure to cover does not bar other remedies

e. Once goods to the contract have been identified, buyer obtains rights in those goods

(1) Identification occurs when goods under contract are

    (a) Shipped

    (b) Marked as part of the contract, or

    (c) In some way designated as part of contract

(2) Buyer obtains

    (a) Insurable interest in those goods, and

    (b) Right to obtain goods, called replevin, upon offering contract price

        [1] Replevin (suing for possession of the goods wrongfully held by the seller) is not allowed if buyer can cover

f. Buyer may obtain specific performance if goods are unique or in other proper circumstances even if goods are not identified to the contract

       (1) Proper circumstances may exist when other remedies (such as monetary damages or remedy of cover) are inadequate

---

EXAMPLE

S agrees to sell B an antique car of which only one exists. If S later refuses to go through with the contract, B may require S to sell him the unique car under the remedy of specific performance.

---

   4. Statute of limitations for sale of goods is four years

      a. An action for breach must be commenced within this period
      b. Parties may agree to reduce to not less than one year but may not extend it
      c. Statute of limitations begins running when the contract is breached

---

NOW REVIEW MULTIPLE-CHOICE QUESTIONS 36 THROUGH 45

H. Leases under UCC

   1. Law governing leases has been slow to develop and has been "tacked on" for various other areas of law such as property law and secured transactions
   2. Now Article 2A of the UCC applies to any transaction creating a lease regardless of form
   3. Article 2A is now law in majority of states
   4. Article 2A is quite lengthy, but for purpose of CPA exam, note that its provisions are similar to Article 2 except that Article 2A applies to leases and Article 2 applies to sales of goods
   5. Under Article 2A

      a. Lessor is person who transfers right to possess named goods and to use them in described ways by lessee

   6. Note the following provisions where Article 2A is similar to Article 2:

      a. Statute of frauds except that stated minimum is $1,000 instead of $500 that applies to sales of goods

          (1) There are three exceptions to Statute of Frauds whereby leases need not be in writing even if for $1000 or more (note that these are similar to three exceptions to Statute of Frauds for sales of goods)

             (a) Specially manufactured goods when goods are not suitable for sale or lease in the ordinary course of lessor's business
             (b) Lessor or lessee admits to oral lease in court proceedings

                 [1] Only enforceable up to quantity admitted

             (c) Part acceptance in which lease is enforceable up to amount accepted by lessee

---

EXAMPLE

E leases under an oral agreement 900 personal computers. A, the lessor, ships 400 of the personal computers to E. After accepting the 400, E decides she does not want to lease the other 500. E is liable for the lease of the 400 personal computers under the part acceptance exception even though the agreement was oral. She would be liable for the lease of the full 900 personal computers if the agreement had been for less than $1,000 which is not the case here.

---

      b. Rules on acceptance, revocation of acceptance, and rejection of goods
      c. Remedies are similar to sellers' and buyers' remedies including the important concept of cure
      d. Principles for performance include anticipatory repudiation or breach, (including use of adequate assurance to avoid a breach), and the concept of impracticability

    e. Leases may be assigned

    f. Use general principles of contract and sales law for these

        (1) Warranties

        (2) Parol evidence

        (3) Firm offers

        (4) Risk of loss rules

        (5) Concept of unconscionable agreements

    g. Provision for sublease by lessee

    h. Leased goods may become fixtures

    i. Lessor has right to take possession of leased property after default without requirement of court adjudication

7. Leases under Article 2A of UCC may be in any manner sufficient to show by words or conduct that lessor and lessee intended to form a lease of identified goods

8. Finance lease is three-party transaction in which lessor acquires title or right to possess goods from supplier

    a. Lessor does not manufacture or supply goods for lessee but third-party supplier does according to lease agreement

I. Contracts for the International Sales of Goods (CISG)

1. Contracts for sales of goods between persons or companies of different countries follow the important rules of CISG

2. Many provisions of CISG are similar to UCC provisions but differences are handled under CISG because USA has this treaty with many countries in South America, Central America, North America, and most countries in Europe

    a. By Constitutional Law, CISG has priority over UCC when it applies and when it conflicts with UCC

    b. The following are important areas where CISG and UCC are different

        (1) Price terms

            (a) May be left open under UCC, in which case UCC provides that price is reasonable price at time of delivery

            (b) CISG requires that price term be included for there to be a contract

                [1] CISG allows exception if method to determine price in future is clearly specified in contract

        (2) Time contract formed

            (a) Unlike UCC, CISG specifies that contract is formed only when acceptance is received by offeror

            (b) Also under CISG, acceptance happens at moment requested act is performed, not at the time notice is given of acceptance to offeror

        (3) Acceptances

            (a) CISG provides that there is no contract if terms in acceptance are different from terms in offer

                [1] Acceptance is effective if differences are not material

                    [a] However, almost ever term in contract under CISG is considered material

        (4) Irrevocable offers

            (a) UCC allows offers that are not supported by consideration to be irrevocable if they are written and also meet certain other criteria

            (b) CISG allows offeror to make offer irrevocable by orally stating so

        (5) Written contracts

            (a) UCC has $500 rule for sales of goods

            (b) CISG provides that sales contracts may be oral with no rule regarding amount of money

                [1] Also provides that proof of contract can be by any reasonable means

        (6) Parties are encouraged to have choice-of-language and choice-of-law clauses in contracts to help settle any disputes

KEY TERMS

Destination contract. An agreement that generally transfers title and risk of loss of the goods to the buyer when the goods reach their destination, usually the buyer's place of business.

Firm offer. An offer that is irrevocable despite the lack of consideration from the offeree to hold the offer open. Offer must be in writing and made by a merchant to be firm.

Good faith. Parties will operate honestly in the course of the transaction; think of trying to honor the spirit of the agreement more than the literal agreement.

Goods. Moveable personal property

Implied warranty. A guarantee that automatically exists, unless it is disclaimed by the seller. Some examples include the warranty of title, the implied warranty of merchantability, and the implied warranty of fitness for a particular purpose.

Merchant. A person who regularly buys or sells the goods that are involved in the contract.

Perfect tender rule. The goods that the seller delivers must conform exactly to the terms of the contract.

Risk of loss. Parties to the contract allocate which party will bear the loss if the goods are damaged or destroyed.

Shipment contract. An agreement that generally provides that title and risk of loss pass to the buyer when the seller delivers the goods to the common carrier.

Strict product liability. Sellers are held responsible for injuries that their goods cause, even if the seller exercised due care.

Tender. When a party to the contract is ready, willing, and able to perform the promise of the contract.

Transfer of title. Ownership of goods is transferred from the seller to the buyer.

Warranty. A guarantee concerning the quality, performance, or other characteristic of the good.

Multiple-Choice Questions (1–45)

A. Contracts for Sale of Goods

1. Under the Sales Article of the UCC, which of the following statements is correct?

   a. The obligations of the parties to the contract must be performed in good faith.

   b. Merchants and nonmerchants are treated alike.

   c. The contract must involve the sale of goods for a price of more than $500.

   d. None of the provisions of the UCC may be disclaimed by agreement.

2. Which of the following contracts is handled under common law rules rather than under Article 2 of the Uniform Commercial Code?

   a. Oral contract to have hair styled in which expensive products will be used on the hair.

   b. Oral contract to purchase a textbook for $100.

   c. Written contract to purchase an old handcrafted chair for $600 from a private party.

   d. Written contract to purchase a heater from a dealer to be installed by the buyer in her home.

B. Forming the Contract for the Sale of Goods

3. Under the Sales Article of the UCC, when a written offer has been made without specifying a means of acceptance but providing that the offer will only remain open for ten days, which of the following statements represent(s) a valid acceptance of the offer?

  I. An acceptance sent by regular mail the day before the ten-day period expires that reaches the offeror on the eleventh day.

  II. An acceptance faxed the day before the ten-day period expires that reaches the offeror on the eleventh day, due to a malfunction of the offeror's printer.

   a. I only.

   b. II only.

   c. Both I and II.

   d. Neither I nor II.

4. Under the Sales Article of the UCC, a firm offer will be created only if the

   a. Offer states the time period during which it will remain open.

   b. Offer is made by a merchant in a signed writing.

   c. Offeree gives some form of consideration.

   d. Offeree is a merchant.

5. On May 2, Mason orally contracted with Acme Appliances to buy for $480 a washer and dryer for household use. Mason and the Acme salesperson agreed that delivery would be made on July 2. On May 5, Mason telephoned Acme and requested that the delivery date be moved to June 2. The Acme salesperson agreed with this request. On June 2, Acme failed to deliver the washer and dryer to Mason because of an inventory shortage. Acme advised Mason that it would deliver the appliances on July 2 as originally agreed. Mason believes that Acme has breached its agreement with Mason. Acme contends that its agreement to deliver on June 2 was not binding. Acme's contention is

   a. Correct, because Mason is not a merchant and was buying the appliances for household use.

   b. Correct, because the agreement to change the delivery date was not in writing.

   c. Incorrect, because the agreement to change the delivery date was binding.

   d. Incorrect, because Acme's agreement to change the delivery date is a firm offer that cannot be withdrawn by Acme.

6. Cookie Co. offered to sell Distrib Markets 20,000 pounds of cookies at $1.00 per pound, subject to certain specified terms for delivery. Distrib replied in writing as follows:

> We accept your offer for 20,000 pounds of cookies at $1.00 per pound, weighing scale to have valid city certificate.

Under the UCC

   a. A contract was formed between the parties.

   b. A contract will be formed only if Cookie agrees to the weighing scale requirement.

   c. No contract was formed because Distrib included the weighing scale requirement in its reply.

   d. No contract was formed because Distrib's reply was a counteroffer.

7. EG Door Co., a manufacturer of custom exterior doors, verbally contracted with Art Contractors to design and build a $2,000 custom door for a house that Art was restoring. After EG had completed substantial work on the door, Art advised EG that the house had been destroyed by fire and Art was canceling the contract. EG finished the door and shipped it to Art. Art refused to accept delivery. Art contends that the contract cannot be enforced because it violated the Statute of Frauds by not being in writing. Under the Sales Article of the UCC, is Art's contention correct?

   a. Yes, because the contract was not in writing.

   b. Yes, because the contract cannot be fully performed due to the fire.

   c. No, because the goods were specially manufactured for Art and cannot be resold in EG's regular course of business.

   d. No, because the cancellation of the contract was not made in writing.

8. On May 2, Handy Hardware sent Ram Industries a signed purchase order that stated, in part, as follows:

> Ship for May 8 delivery 300 Model A-X socket sets at current dealer price. Terms 2/10/net 30.

Ram received Handy's purchase order on May 4. On May 5, Ram discovered that it had only 200 Model A-X socket sets and 100 Model W-Z socket sets in stock. Ram shipped the Model A-X and Model W-Z sets to Handy without any explanation concerning the shipment. The socket sets were received by Handy on May 8.

Which of the following statements concerning the shipment is correct?

    a. Ram's shipment is an acceptance of Handy's offer.
    b. Ram's shipment is a counteroffer.
    c. Handy's order must be accepted by Ram in writing before Ram ships the socket sets.
    d. Handy's order can only be accepted by Ram shipping conforming goods.

9. Under the UCC Sales Article, which of the following conditions will prevent the formation of an enforceable sale of goods contract?

    a. Open price.
    b. Open delivery.
    c. Open quantity.
    d. Open acceptance.

10. Webstar Corp. orally agreed to sell Northco, Inc. a computer for $20,000. Northco sent a signed purchase order to Webstar confirming the agreement. Webstar received the purchase order and did not respond. Webstar refused to deliver the computer to Northco, claiming that the purchase order did not satisfy the UCC Statute of Frauds because it was not signed by Webstar. Northco sells computers to the general public and Webstar is a computer wholesaler. Under the UCC Sales Article, Webstar's position is

    a. Incorrect because it failed to object to Northco's purchase order.
    b. Incorrect because only the buyer in a sale-of-goods transaction must sign the contract.
    c. Correct because it was the party against whom enforcement of the contract is being sought.
    d. Correct because the purchase price of the computer exceeded $500.

11. Patch, a frequent shopper at Soon-Shop Stores, received a rain check for an advertised sale item after Soon-Shop's supply of the product ran out. The rain check was in writing and stated that the item would be offered to the customer at the advertised sale price for an unspecified period of time. A Soon-Shop employee signed the rain check. When Patch returned to the store one month later to purchase the item, the store refused to honor the rain check. Under the Sales Article of the UCC, will Patch win a suit to enforce the rain check?

    a. No, because one month is too long a period of time for a rain check to be effective.
    b. No, because the rain check did not state the effective time period necessary to keep the offer open.
    c. Yes, because Soon-Shop is required to have sufficient supplies of the sale item to satisfy all customers.
    d. Yes, because the rain check met the requirements of a merchant's firm offer even though no effective time period was stated.

12. A sheep rancher agreed in writing to sell all the wool shorn during the shearing season to a weaver. The contract failed to establish the price and a minimum quantity of wool. After the shearing season, the rancher refused to deliver the wool. The weaver sued the rancher for breach of contract. Under the Sales Article of the UCC, will the weaver win?

    a. Yes, because this was an output contract.
    b. Yes, because both price and quantity terms were omitted.
    c. No, because quantity cannot be omitted for a contract to be enforceable.
    d. No, because the omission of price and quantity terms prevents the formation of a contract.

C.   *Performance of the Sales Contract*

13. Under the Sales Article of the UCC, and unless otherwise agreed to, the seller's obligation to the buyer is to

    a. Deliver the goods to the buyer's place of business.
    b. Hold conforming goods and give the buyer whatever notification is reasonably necessary to enable the buyer to take delivery.
    c. Deliver all goods called for in the contract to a common carrier.
    d. Set aside conforming goods for inspection by the buyer before delivery.

14. Rowe Corp. purchased goods from Stair Co. that were shipped COD. Under the Sales Article of the UCC, which of the following rights does Rowe have?

    a. The right to inspect the goods before paying.
    b. The right to possession of the goods before paying.
    c. The right to reject nonconforming goods.
    d. The right to delay payment for a reasonable period of time.

D.   *Transfer of Title (Property Rights)*

15. McGraw purchased an antique rocking chair from Tillis by check. The check was dishonored by the bank due to insufficient funds. In the meantime, McGraw sold the rocking chair to Rio who had no knowledge that McGraw's check had been dishonored. Which of the following is correct?

    a. Tillis may repossess the rocking chair from Rio.
    b. Tillis may recover money damages from Rio.
    c. Tillis may recover money damages from McGraw.
    d. Tillis may recover damages from McGraw based on fraud.

16. Yancie took her bike in to Pete's Bike Sales and Repair to have it repaired. Pete said he would need to have her leave it for two days. The next day, one of Pete's employees sold Yancie's bike to Jake. Jake paid for the bike with a credit card, unaware that Pete did not own the bike. Which of the following is correct?

    a. Yancie can repossess the bike from Jake if she pays Jake. Yancie then recovers the price from Pete.
    b. Pete can repossess the bike from Jake and then return it to Yancie.

c. Yancie can sue Jake for monetary damages only.

d. Jake has title to the bike.

17. Under the Sales Article of the UCC, unless a contract provides otherwise, before title to goods can pass from a seller to a buyer, the goods must be

a. Tendered to the buyer.

b. Identified to the contract.

c. Accepted by the buyer.

d. Paid for.

18. On May 2, Lace Corp., an appliance wholesaler, offered to sell appliances worth $3,000 to Parco, Inc., a household appliances retailer. The offer was signed by Lace's president, and provided that it would not be withdrawn before June 1. It also included the shipping terms: "FOB Parco's warehouse." On May 29, Parco mailed an acceptance of Lace's offer. Lace received the acceptance June 2. If Lace inadvertently ships the wrong appliances to Parco and Parco rejects them two days after receipt, title to the goods will

a. Pass to Parco when they are identified to the contract.

b. Pass to Parco when they are shipped.

c. Remain with Parco until the goods are returned to Lace.

d. Revert to Lace when they are rejected by Parco.

E. Risk of Loss

19. Under the Sales Article of the UCC, in an FOB place of shipment contract, the risk of loss passes to the buyer when the goods

a. Are identified to the contract.

b. Are placed on the seller's loading dock.

c. Are delivered to the carrier.

d. Reach the buyer's loading dock.

20. Under the Sales Article of the UCC and the United Nations Convention for the International Sale of Goods (CISG), absent specific terms in an international sales shipment contract, when will risk of loss pass to the buyer?

a. When the goods are delivered to the first carrier for transmission to the buyer.

b. When the goods are tendered to the buyer.

c. At the conclusion of the execution of the contract.

d. At the time the goods are identified to the contract.

21. Which of the following statements applies to a sale on approval under the UCC Sales Article?

a. Both the buyer and seller must be merchants.

b. The buyer must be purchasing the goods for resale.

c. Risk of loss for the goods passes to the buyer when the goods are accepted after the trial period.

d. Title to the goods passes to the buyer on delivery of the goods to the buyer.

22. Under the Sales Article of UCC, which of the following events will result in the risk of loss passing from a merchant seller to a buyer?

	Tender of the goods at the seller's place of business	Use of the seller's truck to deliver the goods
a.	Yes	Yes
b.	Yes	No
c.	No	Yes
d.	No	No

23. Cey Corp. entered into a contract to sell parts to Deck, Ltd. The contract provided that the goods would be shipped "FOB Cey's warehouse." Cey shipped parts different from those specified in the contract. Deck rejected the parts. A few hours after Deck informed Cey that the parts were rejected, they were destroyed by fire in Deck's warehouse. Cey believed that the parts were conforming to the contract. Which of the following statements is correct?

a. Regardless of whether the parts were conforming, Deck will bear the loss because the contract was a shipment contract.

b. If the parts were nonconforming, Deck had the right to reject them, but the risk of loss remains with Deck until Cey takes possession of the parts.

c. If the parts were conforming, risk of loss does **not** pass to Deck until a reasonable period of time after they are delivered to Deck.

d. If the parts were nonconforming, Cey will bear the risk of loss, even though the contract was a shipment contract.

24. Under the Sales Article of the UCC, which of the following factors is most important in determining who bears the risk of loss in a sale of goods contract?

a. The method of shipping the goods.

b. The contract's shipping terms.

c. Title to the goods.

d. How the goods were lost.

25. Bond purchased a painting from Wool, who is not in the business of selling art. Wool tendered delivery of the painting after receiving payment in full from Bond. Bond informed Wool that Bond would be unable to take possession of the painting until later that day. Thieves stole the painting before Bond returned. The risk of loss

a. Passed to Bond at Wool's tender of delivery.

b. Passed to Bond at the time the contract was formed and payment was made.

c. Remained with Wool, because the parties agreed on a later time of delivery.

d. Remained with Wool, because Bond had **not** yet received the painting.

F. Product Liability

26. Under the Sales Article of the UCC, the warranty of title

a. Provides that the seller cannot disclaim the warranty if the sale is made to a bona fide purchaser for value.

b. Provides that the seller deliver the goods free from any lien of which the buyer lacked knowledge when the contract was made.

c. Applies only if it is in writing and assigned by the seller.

d. Applies only if the seller is a merchant.

27. Under the Sales Article of the UCC, most goods sold by merchants are covered by certain warranties. An example of an express warranty would be a warranty of

a. Usage of trade.
b. Fitness for a particular purpose.
c. Merchantability.
d. Conformity of goods to sample.

28. Under the Sales Article of the UCC, which of the following statements is correct regarding the warranty of merchantability arising when there has been a sale of goods by a merchant seller?

a. The warranty must be in writing.
b. The warranty arises when the buyer relies on the seller's skill in selecting the goods purchased.
c. The warranty cannot be disclaimed.
d. The warranty arises as a matter of law when the seller ordinarily sells the goods purchased.

29. On May 2, Handy Hardware sent Ram Industries a signed purchase order that stated, in part, as follows:

Ship for May 8 delivery 300 Model A-X socket sets at current dealer price. Terms 2/10/net 30.

Ram received Handy's purchase order on May 4. On May 5, Ram discovered that it had only 200 Model A-X socket sets and 100 Model W-Z socket sets in stock. Ram shipped the Model A-X and Model W-Z sets to Handy without any explanation concerning the shipment. The socket sets were received by Handy on May 8.

Assuming a contract exists between Handy and Ram, which of the following implied warranties would result?

 I. Implied warranty of merchantability.
 II. Implied warranty of fitness for a particular purpose.
III. Implied warranty of title.

a. I only.
b. III only.
c. I and III only.
d. I, II, and III.

30. Under the UCC Sales Article, an action for breach of the implied warranty of merchantability by a party who sustains personal injuries may be successful against the seller of the product only when

a. The seller is a merchant of the product involved.
b. An action based on negligence can also be successfully maintained.
c. The injured party is in privity of contract with the seller.
d. An action based on strict liability in tort can also be successfully maintained.

31. Which of the following conditions must be met for an implied warranty of fitness for a particular purpose to arise in connection with a sale of goods?

 I. The warranty must be in writing.
 II. The seller must know that the buyer was relying on the seller in selecting the goods.

a. I only.
b. II only.
c. Both I and II.
d. Neither I nor II.

32. Under the UCC Sales Article, the implied warranty of merchantability

a. May be disclaimed by a seller's oral statement that mentions merchantability.
b. Arises only in contracts involving a merchant seller and a merchant buyer.
c. Is breached if the goods are **not** fit for all purposes for which the buyer intends to use the goods.
d. Must be part of the basis of the bargain to be binding on the seller.

33. High sues the manufacturer, wholesaler, and retailer for bodily injuries caused by a power saw High purchased. Which of the following statements is correct under strict liability theory?

a. Contributory negligence on High's part will always be a bar to recovery.
b. The manufacturer will avoid liability if it can show it followed the custom of the industry.
c. Privity will be a bar to recovery insofar as the wholesaler is concerned if the wholesaler did **not** have a reasonable opportunity to inspect.
d. High may recover even if he **cannot** show any negligence was involved.

34. To establish a cause of action based on strict liability in tort for personal injuries that result from the use of a defective product, one of the elements the injured party must prove is that the seller

a. Was aware of the defect in the product.
b. Sold the product to the injured party.
c. Failed to exercise due care.
d. Sold the product in a defective condition.

35. Larch Corp. manufactured and sold Oak a stove. The sale documents included a disclaimer of warranty for personal injury. The stove was defective. It exploded causing serious injuries to Oak's spouse. Larch was notified one week after the explosion. Under the UCC Sales Article, which of the following statements concerning Larch's liability for personal injury to Oak's spouse would be correct?

a. Larch **cannot** be liable because of a lack of privity with Oak's spouse.
b. Larch will **not** be liable because of a failure to give proper notice.
c. Larch will be liable because the disclaimer was **not** a disclaimer of all liability.
d. Larch will be liable because liability for personal injury **cannot** be disclaimed.

G. Remedies under Sales Law

36. Under the Sales Article of the UCC, which of the following statements regarding liquidated damages is (are) correct?

I. The injured party may collect any amount of liquidated damages provided for in the contract.
II. The liquidated damage provision cannot be excessive.

   a. I only.
   b. II only.
   c. Both I and II.
   d. Neither I nor II.

37. Under the Sales Article of the UCC, which of the following rights is (are) available to a seller when a buyer materially breaches a sales contract?

	Right to cancel the contract	Right to recover damages
a.	Yes	Yes
b.	Yes	No
c.	No	Yes
d.	No	No

38. Under the Sales Article of the UCC, the remedies available to a seller when a buyer breaches a contract for the sale of goods may include

	The right to resell goods identified to the contract	The right to stop a carrier from delivering the goods
a.	Yes	Yes
b.	Yes	No
c.	No	Yes
d.	No	No

39. Lazur Corp. entered into a contract with Baker Suppliers, Inc. to purchase a used word processor from Baker. Lazur is engaged in the business of selling new and used word processors to the general public. The contract required Baker to ship the goods to Lazur by common carrier pursuant to the following provision in the contract: "FOB Baker Suppliers, Inc. loading dock." Baker also represented in the contract that the word processor had been used for only ten hours by its previous owner. The contract included the provision that the word processor was being sold "as is" and this provision was in a larger and different type style than the remainder of the contract.

Assume that Lazur refused to accept the word processor even though it was in all respects conforming to the contract and that the contract is otherwise silent. Under the UCC Sales Article,

   a. Baker can successfully sue for specific performance and make Lazur accept and pay for the word processor.
   b. Baker may resell the word processor to another buyer.
   c. Baker must sue for the difference between the market value of the word processor and the contract price plus its incidental damages.

   d. Baker cannot successfully sue for consequential damages unless it attempts to resell the word processor.

40. On February 15, Mazur Corp. contracted to sell 1,000 bushels of wheat to Good Bread, Inc. at $6.00 per bushel with delivery to be made on June 23. On June 1, Good advised Mazur that it would not accept or pay for the wheat. On June 2, Mazur sold the wheat to another customer at the market price of $5.00 per bushel. Mazur had advised Good that it intended to resell the wheat. Which of the following statements is correct?

   a. Mazur can successfully sue Good for the difference between the resale price and the contract price.
   b. Mazur can resell the wheat only after June 23.
   c. Good can retract its anticipatory breach at any time before June 23.
   d. Good can successfully sue Mazur for specific performance.

41. Pickens agreed to sell Crocket 100 cases of napkins with the name of Crocket's restaurant on the napkins. In the enforceable contract, it was specified that delivery will take place on April 15, which is one month after Pickens and Crocket signed the contract. Crocket wanted the napkins by April 15 because the grand opening of the restaurant was scheduled for April 17. On April 11, Pickens tells Crocket that he has too many orders and will not be able to deliver the napkins. What options does Crocket have?

I. Treat it as a present breach of contract and cancel the contract.
II. Wait for a reasonable time to see if Pickens will deliver.

   a. I only.
   b. II only.
   c. Either I or II.
   d. Neither I nor II.

42. Under the Sales Article of the UCC, which of the following rights is (are) available to the buyer when a seller commits an anticipatory breach of contract?

	Recover damages	Cancel the contract	Collect punitive damages
a.	Yes	Yes	Yes
b	Yes	Yes	No
c.	Yes	No	Yes
d.	No	Yes	Yes

43. Under the Sales Article of the UCC, which of the following events will release the buyer from all its obligations under a sales contract?

   a. Destruction of the goods after risk of loss passed to the buyer.
   b. Impracticability of delivery under the terms of the contract.
   c. Anticipatory repudiation by the buyer that is retracted before the seller cancels the contract.
   d. Refusal of the seller to give written assurance of performance when reasonably demanded by the buyer.

44. Under the UCC Sales Article, a plaintiff who proves fraud in the formation of a contract may

    a. Elect to rescind the contract and need **not** return the consideration received from the other party.

    b. Be entitled to rescind the contract and sue for damages resulting from the fraud.

    c. Be entitled to punitive damages, provided physical injuries resulted from the fraud.

    d. Rescind the contract even if there was **no** reliance on the fraudulent statement.

45. Sklar, CPA, purchased from Wiz Corp. two computers. Sklar discovered material defects in the computers ten months after taking delivery. Three years after discovering the defects, Sklar commenced an action for breach of warranty against Wiz. Wiz has raised the statute of limitations as a defense. The original contract between Wiz and Sklar contained a conspicuous clause providing that the statute of limitations for breach of warranty actions would be limited to eighteen months. Under the circumstances, Sklar will

    a. Win because the action was commenced within the four-year period as measured from the date of delivery.

    b. Win because the action was commenced within the four-year period as measured from the time he discovered the breach or should have discovered the breach.

    c. Lose because the clause providing that the statute of limitations would be limited to eighteen months is enforceable.

    d. Lose because the statute of limitations is three years from the date of delivery with respect to written contracts.

Multiple-Choice Answers and Explanations

Answers

1.	a	__ __	11.	d	__ __	21.	c	__ __	31.	b	__ __	41.	c __ __
2.	a	__ __	12.	a	__ __	22.	d	__ __	32.	a	__ __	42.	b __ __
3.	c	__ __	13.	b	__ __	23.	d	__ __	33.	d	__ __	43.	d __ __
4.	b	__ __	14.	c	__ __	24.	b	__ __	34.	d	__ __	44.	b __ __
5.	c	__ __	15.	c	__ __	25.	a	__ __	35.	d	__ __	45.	c __ __
6.	a	__ __	16.	d	__ __	26.	b	__ __	36.	b			
7.	c	__ __	17.	b	__ __	27.	d	__ __	37.	a			
8.	a	__ __	18.	d	__ __	28.	d	__ __	38.	a			
9.	d	__ __	19.	c	__ __	29.	c	__ __	39.	b	__ __	1st:	__/45 = __%
10.	a	__ __	20.	a	__ __	30.	a	__ __	40.	a	__ __	2nd:	__/45 = __%

Explanations

1. (a) Under the Sales Article of the UCC, both the seller and buyer are obligated to perform a contract in good faith. Answer (b) is incorrect because certain provisions, such as the battle of forms provision, only apply to merchants. Answer (c) is incorrect because the Sales Article of the UCC applies to the sale of goods without regard to the price of goods. Answer (d) is incorrect because certain provisions of the UCC may be disclaimed by written or oral agreement, such as warranty liability.

2. (a) Article 2 of the UCC applies to sales of goods. Common law generally applies to contracts for services and real estate. Even though goods are used in this service contract, the predominate feature of this contract is the service. Article 2 of the UCC governs this contract even though it is oral and for a small sum. Answer (b) is incorrect because a textbook is a good and thus the transaction is covered under Article 2 of the UCC. Note that whether the contract is written or oral is irrelevant to determining whether the agreement is covered by the common law or the UCC. Even though the chair at one time involved a lot of labor, it is still a sale of goods. Also, whether the parties are merchants or not is not an issue on whether Article 2 applies; therefore answer (c) is incorrect. Answer (d) is incorrect because the heater which is not yet installed in the home is a sale of goods. Once it is installed in the home, it becomes part of the real estate for any future sale of the home. Common law rules would apply to any such future sale, but that is because the heater is now part of the real estate, which is not the case in this question.

3. (c) Under the Sales Article of the UCC, acceptance is valid when sent if a reasonable method is used; therefore answer (c) is correct as both acceptances were sent prior to the end of the ten-day period.

4. (b) A firm offer is a written, signed offer concerning the sale of goods, by a merchant, giving assurance that it will be held open for a specified time and is irrevocable for that period, not to exceed three months. Answer (a) is incorrect because if the firm offer does not state a period of time, it will remain open for a reasonable period of time, not to exceed three months. Answer (c) is incorrect as consideration is not required for a firm offer, but for an option contract. Answer (d)

is incorrect because under the firm offer rule, only the offeror need be a merchant.

5. (c) Under the UCC, an oral modification of an existing contract for the sale of goods for a price less than $500 is considered binding. Since the washer and dryer Mason contracted to buy cost less than $500, Acme's oral agreement to change the date of delivery would be enforceable; therefore, answer (b) is incorrect. The fact that Mason is not a merchant won't affect whether or not the oral modification is binding; therefore, answer (a) is incorrect. In order to have a firm offer, the offer must be made by a merchant in a signed writing which gives assurance that the offer will be held open. In this situation, the modification of an offer already accepted is being discussed rather than a firm offer; therefore, answer (d) is incorrect.

6. (a) Under common law, an acceptance must be unequivocal and unqualified in agreeing to the precise terms specified by the offer. However, the Uniform Commercial Code alters this general rule as far as the sales of goods is concerned. Under the UCC, an acceptance containing additional terms is a valid acceptance unless the acceptance is expressly conditional upon the offeror's agreement to the additional terms. In this situation, a valid contract has been formed between Cookie Co. and Distrib Markets. Answer (b) is incorrect because Distrib Markets' acceptance was not conditional upon Cookie's agreement to the additional term and, thus, a contract is formed. There is a contract here unless Cookie objects to the additional term, but there is no need for specific approval for additional terms between merchants. This contract was for the sale of goods and is governed by the UCC rather than by common law. Under common law, Distrib Markets' reply would have been a rejection and counteroffer; but under the UCC, a contract was formed; therefore, answers (c) and (d) are incorrect.

7. (c) This exception for specially manufactured goods, even if the contract is for over $500, is one of the important exceptions found in the Statute of Fraud provisions of the Uniform Commercial Code. Answer (a) is incorrect because the exception for specially manufactured goods applies to this fact pattern and thus this contract need not be in writing. Answer (b) is incorrect because the fire did not prevent the custom door contract from being performed. Answer (d) is incorrect because the contract was fully enforceable and Art had no legal right to cancel the contract.

8. (a) Ram may accept the offer by shipping the goods. Under the UCC, shipping nonconforming goods constitutes an acceptance, also unless the seller notifies the buyer that the shipment is given only as an accommodation to the buyer; therefore, answer (d) is incorrect. Answer (b) is incorrect because this shipment counts as an acceptance, not as a counteroffer. Answer (c) is incorrect because an order to buy goods for prompt shipment allows the seller to accept by either a prompt promise to ship or by the actual prompt shipment itself. Answer (d) is incorrect because shipping nonconforming goods constitutes an acceptance under the UCC.

9. (d) In order to have a contract, there must be both an offer and an acceptance. Even though an acceptance can occur in different ways, by speech, by writing, or by action, the actual acceptance is a required element of a contract. Under the UCC Sales Article, a binding contract may be present if the parties had intended to form a contract even though certain elements of the contract are missing. These open terms will be filled by specific provisions of the UCC, including provisions for open price, open delivery, or open quantity; therefore, answers (a), (b), and (c) are incorrect. Note that in the case of quantity, output contracts, requirements contracts, and exclusive dealing's contracts are enforceable though the actual quantity may not be known in advance.

10. (a) The UCC provides that a confirmation satisfies the UCC Statute of Frauds, if an oral contract between merchants is confirmed in writing within a reasonable period of time, and the confirmation is signed by the party sending it and received by the other party. Both parties are bound unless the party receiving the confirmation submits a written objection within ten days of receipt. In this situation, a valid contract has been formed since Webstar did not object to Northco's purchase order. In a sale-of-goods transaction, the contract must be signed by the party to be charged to be enforceable. However, in the case of a written confirmation of an oral agreement between merchants, the confirmation need only be signed by the party sending the confirmation. The use of a signed purchase order satisfies the UCC Statute of Frauds; therefore answers (c) and (d) are incorrect. Answer (b) is incorrect because normally it is the party to be charged that must sign the writing, except as explained above; it is not necessarily the buyer.

11. (d) A firm offer is an offer for the sale of goods that is written and signed by a merchant (or employee of the merchant) that agrees to keep the offer open. This offer is valid without consideration for three months since no time was specified in the fact pattern. Patch will win in a suit to enforce the rain check because Patch tried to use it one month later. Answer (a) is incorrect because the UCC specifies a three-month period when no time is detailed in the firm offer. Answer (b) is incorrect because when no time is specified, the UCC gives Patch three months to accept the offer. Answer (c) is incorrect because there was no offer and acceptance when Patch first tried to purchase the advertised item.

12. (a) An output contract is enforceable under the UCC even though an actual quantity is not mentioned in the contract.

The output contract is supported by consideration because the seller has agreed not to sell that output to any other party. Answer (b) is incorrect because when the price is omitted, the UCC construes it as the reasonable price at the time of delivery. The quantity is construed as the output of the sheep rancher. Answer (c) is incorrect because although quantity is an important term in the contract, the UCC allows the quantity term to be defined by output. Answer (d) is incorrect because the UCC allows price terms to be based on the reasonable price and quantity terms to be defined by output.

13. (b) The seller generally discharges his obligation to the buyer by placing conforming goods at the buyer's disposition and giving the buyer reasonable notice to enable the buyer to take delivery. This is the concept of tender and under the UCC the place of tender is the seller's place of business unless the parties alter the place of tender in their contract; therefore, answer (a) is incorrect. Answer (c) is incorrect because delivery to the common carrier is necessary to shift the risk of loss, but it is not the seller's obligation. Answer (d) is incorrect because there is no obligation to allow the buyer to inspect the goods under the UCC.

14. (c) The Sales Article of the UCC provides that a buyer has the right to reject goods which are not in conformity with the terms of contract between seller and buyer. The buyer also has the option to accept nonconforming goods and recover damages resulting from the nonconformity. The UCC allows the buyer to inspect the goods before payment except when they are shipped COD. When goods are shipped COD, the buyer must pay for the goods before inspection and before taking possession; therefore answers (a) and (b) are incorrect. Answer (d) is incorrect since payment must be made in advance for goods shipped COD.

15. (c) Since Rio was a good-faith purchaser, Rio obtains good title to the rocking chair. Therefore, the remedy that Tillis has left is to sue McGraw for money damages; thus, answers (a) and (b) are incorrect. Answer (d) is incorrect because there are insufficient facts to show fraud, since the facts do not mention whether McGraw knew that the check would be dishonored when he wrote it.

16. (d) If a person entrusts possession of goods to a merchant who normally deals in that type of goods, a goodfaith purchaser obtains title to those goods. Jake purchased the bike as he was unaware that Pete did not own the bike. As a good-faith purchaser, he obtains title to the bike. Answer (a) is incorrect because Yancie cannot repossess the bike from Jake because Jake obtained good title to the bike. Yancie can, however, get the value of the bike from Pete. Answer (b) is incorrect because Jake obtains title to the bike and, thus, Pete cannot repossess it from him. Answer (c) is incorrect because Yancie can recover the value of the bike from Pete, not Jake.

17. (b) A requirement needed for the title of goods to pass to the buyer is that the goods must have been identified to the contract. Answers (a) and (c) are incorrect because the seller can keep possession of goods and identify them to the contract and still have title pass to the buyer. Answer (d) is incorrect because title passes to the buyer based upon the terms of the agreement. Payment can take place before or after.

18. (d) The title of goods generally passes to the buyer when the seller completes performance with respect to the physical delivery of the goods. Because the shipping terms of the contract are FOB Parco's warehouse, the title of goods passes to Parco on tender at the destination. This is true even if the goods are nonconforming. Therefore, answers (a) and (b) are incorrect. Answer (c) is incorrect because Parco's rejection of the appliances will revert the title of the goods back to Lace at the time of the rejection.

19. (c) In an FOB place of shipment contract, the buyer obtains the risk of loss once the goods are delivered to the carrier. Answer (a) is incorrect because when goods are identified allows title to pass, not risk of loss. Answer (b) is incorrect because it does not specify that the good have actually been delivered to the carrier. Answer (d) is incorrect because this is when risk of loss passes pursuant to a destination contract, not a shipment contract.

20. (a) Under the Sales Article of the Uniform Commercial Code and the United Nations Convention for the International Sale of Goods, generally the risk of loss of the goods sold will pass to the buyer when the seller delivers goods to the first carrier for transmission to the buyer. Answers (b), (c), and (d) are incorrect because these would result in risk of loss to the buyer only if the contract specifically stated so, thus changing the general rule.

21. (c) The purchase of goods on a sale on approval allows the buyer to return the goods even if they conform to the contract. Therefore, the seller retains the title and the risk of loss until the buyer accepts the goods; thus, answer (d) is incorrect. Answer (a) is incorrect because there is no requirement that either of the parties is a merchant. Answer (b) is incorrect because there is no requirement concerning the type of goods involved in the transaction.

22. (d) Risk of loss transfers from a merchant seller to a buyer upon the buyer's physical receipt of goods. Therefore, neither tender of the goods at the seller's place of business, nor use of the seller's truck to deliver the goods are events which transfer risk of loss to the buyer as the merchant seller still retains possession of the goods.

23. (d) The UCC places risk of loss on the breaching party. Since Cey shipped nonconforming goods, it breached the contract and would have risk of loss until the nonconforming goods were accepted by the buyer or until the goods were cured by Cey. Since Deck rejected the goods and Cey did not cure the goods, risk of loss remained with Cey. Shipping terms have no bearing on risk of loss in this situation because the goods did not conform to the contract. Answer (a) is incorrect because Deck would only bear risk of loss if the goods conformed to the contract. Answer (b) is incorrect because the risk of loss was never transferred to Deck since the goods were nonconforming. Answer (c) is incorrect because if the goods were conforming, risk of loss would pass to Deck at Cey's warehouse based on the shipping terms "FOB Cey's warehouse."

24. (b) The parties to the contract may agree as to which party bears risk of loss. In the absence of this, under the UCC, the shipping terms determine who bears risk of loss.

25. (a) In this situation, since Wool is not a merchant seller, the risk of loss passed to Bond on Wool's tender of delivery. If Wool had been a merchant seller, then the risk of loss would not have passed until the buyer received the goods. Answers (c) and (d) are incorrect because the risk of loss passed when the nonmerchant seller (Wool) tendered delivery of the painting. Answer (b) is incorrect because the risk of loss would not pass at the time the contract was formed since the seller still had possession of the painting and had not attempted to deliver it to the buyer.

26. (b) Under the warranty of title, the seller warrants good title, rightful transfer and freedom from any security interest or lien of which the buyer has no knowledge at the time of sale. Answer (a) is incorrect because the warranty of title can be disclaimed by specific language or circumstances which give the buyer reason to know s/he is receiving less than full title. Answer (c) is incorrect because the warranty does not have to be in writing. Answer (d) is incorrect because the seller does not have to be a merchant for the seller to give the warranty of title.

27. (d) In the Sales Article of the UCC, express warranties include warranties that the goods will conform to any description used or any sample or model shown. Answer (a) is incorrect because although usage of trade can help interpret terms used in contracts, it is not a warranty. Answers (b) and (c) are incorrect because the warranty of fitness for a particular purpose and the warranty of merchantability are both implied warranties.

28. (d) The implied warranty of merchantability, which guarantees that goods are fit for ordinary purposes, arises as a matter of law when the seller is a merchant who ordinarily sells the goods purchased. Answer (a) is incorrect because the warranty is implied, and therefore need not be in writing. Answer (c) is incorrect because the warranty applies unless specifically disclaimed by the merchant. Answer (b) is incorrect because it describes the implied warranty of fitness for a particular purpose, not the implied warranty of merchantability.

29. (c) The implied warranty of merchantability is always implied if the seller is a merchant with respect to the type of goods being sold. Since Ram is a merchant, this warranty would apply. Also, under the UCC, the seller warrants good title, rightful transfer, and freedom from any security interest or lien of which the buyer has no knowledge when the contract was made. This warranty of title applies unless the merchant specifically disclaims it. In this situation, both the implied warranty of merchantability and the implied warranty of title apply. The implied warranty of fitness for a particular purpose is created only when a seller has reason to know the buyer's particular purpose and knows the buyer is relying on the skill and judgment of the seller selecting the goods, which is not present here.

30. (a) The implied warranty of merchantability applies only when the seller is a merchant with respect to the type of goods being sold. The seller must be a merchant in order for the buyer to successfully sue under this warranty. Answer (b) is incorrect because the buyer does not have to prove negligence to be able to recover under this implied warranty. Answer (c) is incorrect because the implied warranty of merchantability extends to parties other than the purchaser even without privity of contract. Answer (d) is incorrect because an action for a breach based on the warranty of merchantability would not depend on the outcome of an action based on strict liability.

31. (b) The implied warranty of fitness for a particular purpose is created when a seller (merchant or nonmerchant) has reason to know the buyer's particular purpose and knows the buyer is relying on the skill and judgment of the seller selecting the goods. Since the warranty of fitness for a particular purpose is an implied warranty, there is no requirement that it be made in writing.

32. (a) The implied warranty of merchantability may be disclaimed by a seller's oral or written statement. This statement normally must contain some form of the word "merchantability" to be effective. However, goods sold "as is" or "with all faults" are an exception to that rule. Answer (b) is incorrect because the implied warranty of merchantability arises whenever the seller is a merchant with respect to the goods being sold. The status of the buyer is irrelevant. Answer (c) is incorrect because the implied warranty of merchantability guarantees that the goods are of an average fair quality and are fit for ordinary purposes. Under this warranty, the seller does not guarantee that the goods are fit for all purposes for which the buyer intends to use the goods. Answer (d) is incorrect because this warranty is always implied if the seller is a merchant. It does not have to be a part of the basis of the bargain to be binding on the seller.

33. (d) Under the theory of strict liability, the plaintiff must establish the following: (1) the seller was engaged in the business of selling the product, (2) the product was defective, (3) the defect was unreasonably dangerous to the plaintiff, and (4) the defect caused injury to the plaintiff. If the plaintiff can prove these elements, then the seller will be liable regardless of whether the seller was negligent or at fault for the defect. Thus, High can recover even if he cannot show any negligence was involved. Answer (a) is incorrect because contributory negligence is not an available defense in a strict liability case. Answer (b) is incorrect because the manufacturer's only defenses are misuse and assumption of risk by the buyer. The fact that the manufacturer followed the custom of the industry is irrelevant under strict liability. Answer (c) is incorrect because privity of contract is not a defense under strict liability since the suit is not based on contract law.

34. (d) Under the theory of strict liability, the plaintiff must establish the following: (1) the seller was engaged in the business of selling the product, (2) the product was defective when sold, (3) the defect was unreasonably dangerous to the plaintiff, and (4) the defect caused injury to the plaintiff. If the plaintiff can prove these elements, then the seller is liable. Answer (b) is incorrect because a responsible party must only be in the business of selling the product; not selling it directly to the injured party. Answers (a) and (c) are incorrect because each proposes an element of negligence, which is not relevant to strict liability.

35. (d) UCC Section 2-719(3) states that a limitation of damages for personal injury in the **case of consumer goods** is considered to be unconscionable and thus not allowed. Although limitations of damages for personal injury in the case of nonconsumer goods can be allowed, answer (d) is correct since one limits "personal injury" to the stove which was apparently being used for consumer use in this fact pattern. Answer (a) is incorrect because under the UCC, the spouse, being a member of the household expecting to use the stove, may recover for damages. Answer (b) is incorrect because Larch was notified shortly after the explosion. This notice, however, was not required. Answer (c) is incorrect because even though the disclaimer did not disclaim all liability, it did attempt to disclaim personal injury. This disclaimer for personal injuries, however, is not allowed for the reasons mentioned above. Answer (d) is chosen as being more specific than answer (c).

36. (b) Statement I is incorrect because a liquidated damages provision is enforced if it is not punitive but amounts to a reasonable estimate of what the loss will be in the event of a breach of contract. If a reasonable estimate of the loss from a breach of contract cannot be estimated with a reasonable degree of certainty, the parties can agree on an amount, but still the amount cannot be punitive. Statement II is correct because damages that are excessive are viewed as punitive.

37. (a) Under the Sales Article of the UCC, the seller has the following remedies against the buyer upon breach: withhold delivery of the goods; stop delivery of the carrier of the goods; resell the goods; recover compensatory and incidental damages; recover the goods from the buyer upon the buyer's insolvency; cancel the contract. Therefore, answer (a) is correct as the seller has the rights of contract cancellation and damage recovery available to him/her.

38. (a) The UCC gives the seller a choice of many remedies when the buyer breaches the contract involving a sale of goods. These remedies include allowing the seller to resell the goods identified to the contract and to recover the amount that the seller receives that is less than the contract price. Also, once the buyer breaches, the seller may suspend his/her performance and may prevent the carrier from making the delivery of the goods.

39. (b) A seller has the right to resell goods to another if the buyer refuses to accept the goods upon delivery. Answer (a) is incorrect because specific performance is not a remedy available to the seller, since the seller is only receiving money, which is not unique. Baker cannot force Lazur to accept the word processor. Answer (c) is incorrect because Baker has a couple of additional remedies available. Baker can recover the full contract price plus incidental damages if he is unable to resell the identified goods. Alternatively, if the difference between the market value and contract price is inadequate to place Baker in as good a position as performance would have, then Baker can sue for lost profits plus incidental damages. Answer (d) is incorrect because Baker could sue for consequential damages that Lazur had reason to know Baker would incur as a result of Lazur's breach.

40. (a) By advising Mazur on June 1 that it would not accept or pay for the wheat, Good has engaged in anticipatory repudiation. Anticipatory repudiation occurs when a party renounces the duty to perform the contract before the party's obligation to perform arises. Anticipatory repudiation discharges the nonrepudiating party (Mazur) from the contract and allows this party to sue for breach immediately. In this situation, Mazur could successfully sue Good for the difference between the resale price and the contract price on June 2. Answer (b) is incorrect because Mazur was discharged from the contract on June 1 and would not have to wait until after June 23 to resell the wheat. Answer (c) is incorrect because Good would only be allowed to retract its anticipatory breach if Mazur had ignored this breach and awaited performance at the appointed date. Answer (d) is incorrect because specific performance is only allowed for unique goods or for other situations in which monetary damages are not appropriate.

41. (c) Pickens has committed an anticipatory breach of contract. Thus, Crocket, as the aggrieved party, has different options. Crocket may treat it as a present breach of contract with the remedies available for breach of contract. One of these remedies is that the aggrieved party (Crocket) may cancel the contract. Another option is that Crocket may wait for a reasonable time to see if Pickens will change his/her mind and still deliver.

42. (b) The buyer has the following remedies against the seller: upon receipt of nonconforming goods, the buyer may reject the goods, accept the goods, or accept any unit and reject the remainder; the buyer has the right to cover (purchase goods elsewhere upon the seller's breach); the buyer may recover damages (not punitive) for nondelivery of goods or repudiation of the sales contract by the seller; the buyer may recover damages (not punitive) for breach in regard to accepted goods; the buyer may recover goods identified in the contract in possession of the seller upon the seller's insolvency; the buyer may sue for specific performance when the goods are unique; the buyer has the right of replevin (form of legal action to recover specific goods from the seller which are being withheld from the buyer wrongfully); the buyer can cancel the contract; the buyer has a security interest in the goods after the seller's breach; the buyer can recover liquidated damages.

Punitive damages, however, are not an available remedy in either the common law or the UCC.

43. (d) Either party in a sales contract under the Sales Article of the UCC may demand adequate assurance of performance when reasonable grounds for insecurity exist with respect to the performance of the other party. Refusal to give written assurance will release the other party from all obligations from the sales contract. Answer (a) is incorrect because the buyer has assumed the risk of loss. Answer (b) is incorrect because a seller may substitute another reasonable delivery method if the method of delivery specified in the contract has been made impracticable. A seller may recover damages based on a buyer's repudiation of the agreement, but here the repudiation has been retracted and the obligations of buyer and seller remain intact.

44. (b) There are two remedites for fraud under the UCC Sales Article: (1) the plaintiff may affirm the agreement and sue for damages under the tort of deceit, or (2) the plaintiff may rescind the contract and sue for damages resulting from the fraud. Answer (a) is incorrect because the plaintiff must return any consideration received from the other party when the contract is rescinded. Answer (c) is incorrect because although punitive damages are allowed in fraud actions because they are intentional torts, they do not require physical injuries. Answer (d) is incorrect because without reliance by the plaintiff on the misrepresentation, there is no fraud, and therefore, the plaintiff may not rescind the contract.

45. (c) The statute of limitations for the sale of goods is generally four years; however, the parties may agree to reduce the statute to a period of not less than one year. Therefore, Sklar will lose because the clause providing that the statute of limitations would be limited to eighteen months is enforceable, and the action was not brought within the required time period. Answer (b) is incorrect because a breach of warranty occurs upon the tender of delivery, not upon the discovery of the defect, and the statute begins running at the time the breach occurs. Answer (d) is incorrect because the statute is eighteen months as outlined in the contract.

Simulations

Task-Based Simulation 1

Analysis		
	Authoritative Literature	Help

Situation

Angler Corp., a food distributor, is involved in the following disputes:

- On September 8, Angler shipped the wrong grade of tuna to Mason Restaurants, Inc. under a contract that stated as follows: "FOB Angler's loading dock." During shipment, the tuna was destroyed in an accident involving the common carrier's truck. Mason has refused to pay for the tuna, claiming the risk of loss belonged to Angler at the time of the accident.
- On October 3, Angler shipped 100 bushels of peaches to Classic Foods, Inc., a retail grocer. Because of a delay in shipping, the peaches rotted. Classic elected to reject the peaches and notified Angler of this decision. Angler asked Classic to return the peaches at Angler's expense. Classic refused the request, claiming it had no obligation to do so.
- On October 23, Angler orally contracted to sell Regal Fast-Food 1,500 pounds of hamburger meat for $1,500. Delivery was to be made on October 31. On October 29, after Angler had shipped the hamburger meat to Regal, Regal sent Angler the following signed correspondence:

  "We are not going to need the 1,500 pounds of meat we ordered on October 23. Don't ship."

  Regal rejected the shipment and claimed it is not obligated to purchase the hamburger meat because there is no written contract between Angler and Regal.
  Determine whether each of the numbered legal conclusions is Correct or Incorrect.

		Correct	Incorrect
1.	When the accident happened, the risk of loss belonged to Angler.	O	O
2.	If Angler had shipped the correct grade of tuna to Mason, the risk of loss would have been Angler's at time of the accident.	O	O
3.	The contract between Angler and Mason was an FOB destination point contract.	O	O
4.	Angler had title to the tuna at time of the accident since Angler shipped nonconforming goods.	O	O
5.	Classic is required to return the peaches at Angler's expense per Angler's instructions.	O	O
6.	Classic may throw the peaches away because they were rotted.	O	O
7.	Since Classic elected to reject the rotted peaches, Classic may not also sue for damages.	O	O
8.	Regal is not obligated to purchase the hamburger meat because there was no written contract between Angler and Regal.	O	O
9.	The Uniform Commercial Code applies to the contract between Angler and Regal.	O	O
10.	Regal's correspondence to Angler, dated October 29, satisfies the appropriate Statute of Frauds.	O	O
11.	Angler should keep the hamburger until Regal finally accepts it and sue Regal for $1,500.	O	O
12.	Assuming that all of the original facts are the same except that Regal never sent Angler the correspondence dated October 29, then Angler may hold Regal in breach of contract.	O	O
13.	Assuming that all of the original facts are the same except that the contract was for $450, then Angler may hold Regal in breach of contract.	O	O
14.	Assume that all of the original facts are the same except that Regal never sent Angler the correspondence and Angler shipped to Regal 800 pounds of the hamburger on October 29. Regal accepted the 800 pounds. Regal, then, on October 31 orally rejected the shipment for the remaining 700 pounds. Under these facts, the contract is enforceable against Regal for the 800 pounds but not the full 1,500 pounds.	O	O
15.	Under the same facts found in **14.** above, the contract is enforceable against Regal for the full 1,500 pounds.	O	O

Task-Based Simulation 2

Analysis		
	Authoritative Literature	Help

Situation

On February 1, Grand Corp., a manufacturer of custom cabinets, contracted in writing with Axle Co., a kitchen contractor, to sell Axle 100 unique, custom-designed, kitchen cabinets for $250,000. Axle had contracted to install the cabinets in a luxury condominium complex. The contract provided that the cabinets were to be ready for delivery by April 15 and were to be shipped FOB seller's loading dock. On April 15, Grand had eighty-five cabinets complete and delivered them, together with fifteen standard cabinets, to the trucking company for delivery to Axle. Grand faxed Axle a copy of the shipping invoice, listing the fifteen standard cabinets. On May 1, before reaching Axle, the truck was involved in a collision and all the cabinets were damaged beyond repair.

Items 1 through 5 refer to the above fact pattern. For each item, determine whether (A), (B), or (C) is correct.

			(A)	**(B)**	**(C)**
1.	A.	The contract between Grand and Axle was a shipment contract.	○	○	○
	B.	The contract between Grand and Axle was a destination contract.			
	C.	The contract between Grand and Axle was a consignment contract.			
2.	A.	The risk of loss for the eighty-five custom cabinets passed to Axle on April 15.	○	○	○
	B.	The risk of loss for the 100 cabinets passed to Axle on April 15.			
	C.	The risk of loss for the 100 cabinets remained with Grand.			
3.	A.	The contract between Grand and Axle was invalid because **no** delivery date was stated.	○	○	○
	B.	The contract between Grand and Axle was voidable because Grand shipped only eighty-five custom cabinets.			
	C.	The contract between Grand and Axle was void because the goods were destroyed.			
4.	A.	Grand's shipment of the standard cabinets was a breach of the contract with Axle.	○	○	○
	B.	Grand would **not** be considered to have breached the contract until Axle rejected the standard cabinets.			
	C.	Grand made a counteroffer by shipping the standard cabinets.			
5.	A.	Axle is entitled to specific performance from Grand because of the unique nature of the goods.	○	○	○
	B.	Axle is required to purchase substitute goods (cover) and is entitled to the difference in cost from Grand.			
	C.	Axle is entitled to punitive damages because of Grand's intentional shipment of nonconforming goods.			

Simulation Solutions

Task-Based Simulation 1

Analysis		
	Authoritative Literature	Help

	Correct	Incorrect
1. When the accident happened, the risk of loss belonged to Angler.	●	○
2. If Angler had shipped the correct grade of tuna to Mason, the risk of loss would have been Angler's at time of the accident.	○	●
3. The contract between Angler and Mason was an FOB destination point contract.	○	●
4. Angler had title to the tuna at time of the accident since Angler shipped nonconforming goods.	○	●
5. Classic is required to return the peaches at Angler's expense per Angler's instructions.	●	○
6. Classic may throw the peaches away because they were rotted.	○	●
7. Since Classic elected to reject the rotted peaches, Classic may not also sue for damages.	○	●
8. Regal is not obligated to purchase the hamburger meat because there was no written contract between Angler and Regal.	○	●
9. The Uniform Commercial Code applies to the contract between Angler and Regal.	●	○
10. Regal's correspondence to Angler, dated October 29, satisfies the appropriate Statute of Frauds.	●	○
11. Angler should keep the hamburger until Regal finally accepts it and sue Regal for $1,500.	○	●
12. Assuming that all of the original facts are the same except that Regal never sent Angler the correspondence dated October 29, then Angler may hold Regal in breach of contract.	○	●
13. Assuming that all of the original facts are the same except that the contract was for $450, then Angler may hold Regal in breach of contract.	●	○
14. Assume that all of the original facts are the same except that Regal never sent Angler the correspondence and Angler shipped to Regal 800 pounds of the hamburger on October 29. Regal accepted the 800 pounds. Regal, then, on October 31 orally rejected the shipment for the remaining 700 pounds. Under these facts, the contract is enforceable against Regal for the 800 pounds but not the full 1,500 pounds.	●	○
15. Under the same facts found in **14.** above, the contract is enforceable against Regal for the full 1,500 pounds.	○	●

Explanations

1. (C) Angler breached the contract by shipping nonconforming goods to Mason. Therefore, Angler retains the risk of loss until it cures or until Mason accepts the goods despite the nonconformity.

2. (I) This was an FOB shipping point contract so that the risk of loss would have passed over to the buyer upon delivery to the carrier.

3. (I) Because the terms were FOB the seller's loading dock, it was an FOB shipping point contract.

4. (I) Title and risk of loss do not necessarily pass to a buyer at the same time. In this case, risk of loss remained with the seller because of the shipment of nonconforming goods. However, title passed under the original terms despite the breach of contract.

5. (C) Classic is obligated to follow any reasonable instructions of the seller as a merchant who rejects goods, even nonconforming, under a contract.

6. (I) Classic must follow the reasonable instructions given by Angler to return the peaches at Angler's expense.

7. (I) Classic may also sue for any damages that were caused by the delay in shipping.

8. (I) Although the contract must be evidenced by a writing because it involved a sale of goods for more than $500, the correspondence that Regal sent to Angler on October 29 satisfies the writing requirement under the UCC Statute of Frauds. It indicated that a contract had been made. It was signed by Regal, the party to be charged, and it stated the quantity. The price was not needed in the correspondence.

9. (C) The Uniform Commercial Code applies because the contract was for a sale of goods (i.e., hamburger meat).

10. (C) The correspondence satisfies the UCC Statute of Frauds which does not require that all terms be in writing.

11. (I) Angler should resort to an appropriate remedy such as reselling the hamburger to someone else in a commercially reasonable fashion. If Angler gets less than the original contract price, it may recover the difference from Regal.

12. (I) Since there was no writing to evidence the contract for $1,500, it is not enforceable.

13. (C) The contract need not be in writing because it was for less than $500.

14. (C) Since Angler shipped and Regal accepted a portion of the goods, the oral contract is enforceable up to the amount shipped and accepted. This is one of the exceptions in the UCC Statute of Frauds.

15. (I) The exception in the UCC Statute of Frauds allows the oral contract to be enforced up to the amount delivered and accepted or paid for.

Task-Based Simulation 2

Analysis		
	Authoritative Literature	Help

		(A)	(B)	(C)
1.	A. The contract between Grand and Axle was a shipment contract.	●	○	○
	B. The contract between Grand and Axle was a destination contract.			
	C. The contract between Grand and Axle was a consignment contract.			
2.	A. The risk of loss for the eighty-five custom cabinets passed to Axle on April 15.	○	○	●
	B. The risk of loss for the 100 cabinets passed to Axle on April 15.			
	C. The risk of loss for the 100 cabinets remained with Grand.			
3.	A. The contract between Grand and Axle was invalid because **no** delivery date was stated.	○	●	○
	B. The contract between Grand and Axle was voidable because Grand shipped only eighty-five custom cabinets.			
	C. The contract between Grand and Axle was void because the goods were destroyed.			
4.	A. Grand's shipment of the standard cabinets was a breach of the contract with Axle.	●	○	○
	B. Grand would **not** be considered to have breached the contract until Axle rejected the standard cabinets.			
	C. Grand made a counteroffer by shipping the standard cabinets.			
5.	A. Axle is entitled to specific performance from Grand because of the unique nature of the goods.	●	○	○
	B. Axle is required to purchase substitute goods (cover) and is entitled to the difference in cost from Grand.			
	C. Axle is entitled to punitive damages because of Grand's intentional shipment of nonconforming goods.			

Explanations

1. **(A)** The terms of the contract were "FOB seller's loading dock" which is a shipment contract. Answer (B) is incorrect because a destination contract would state terms meaning FOB buyer's location. Answer (C) is incorrect because a consignment is treated as a sale or return. That is, the owner of the goods delivers them to another party to attempt to sell them. If this other party, known as the consignee, does not sell the goods, they are returned. Such is not the case in this fact pattern.

2. **(C)** Risk of loss would normally pass to the buyer, Axle Co., under this shipment contract. However, since the seller, Grand, breached the contract, risk of loss remains with Grand. Since the cabinets are "custom designed, kitchen cabinets" for a luxury condominium complex, they would need to match. Therefore, the 100 units could be construed as a commercial unit and the risk of loss for the entire 100 cabinets remained with Grand. Answer (A) is incorrect because the 100 cabinets were a commercial unit and thus the risk of loss of the entire commercial unit remained with Grand. Answer (B) is incorrect because even though the terms were "FOB seller's loading dock," the risk of loss remained with the seller, Grand, because of Grand's breach of contract.

3. **(B)** The contract between Grand and Axle was voidable because Axle may at its option choose to accept or reject all or part of the cabinets. Answer (C) is incorrect because if the contract were void, neither party would have the option of remaining in the contract. Answer (A) is incorrect because under the UCC, if the delivery date is not stated, the time becomes within a reasonable time.

4. **(A)** Once Grand ships nonconforming goods, a breach of contract has occurred. Answer (B) is incorrect because the breach has occurred even without Axle needing to reject the shipment. Axle then has the right to accept all, part, or none of the shipment. Answer (C) is incorrect because the shipment of nonconforming goods acts as a breach rather than a counteroffer.

5. **(A)** Since the cabinets are unique and custom-designed, specific performance is allowed if Axle so chooses. Answer (B) is incorrect because Axle is not required to cover, especially because the cabinets are unique. Answer (C) is incorrect because punitive damages are generally not allowed for a breach of contract even if the breach is intentional.

Module 28: Negotiable Instruments

Overview

Coverage of negotiable instruments includes the types of negotiable instruments, the requirements of negotiability, negotiation, the holder in due course concept, defenses to a claim of liability, and the rights of parties to a negotiable instrument. The functions of negotiable instruments are to provide a medium of exchange that is readily transferable like money and to provide an extension of credit. Negotiable instruments are easier to transfer than contract rights and are not subject to as many defenses as contracts. To be negotiable, an instrument must

1. Be written
2. Be signed by the maker or drawer
3. Contain an unconditional promise or order to pay
4. State a fixed amount in money
5. Be payable on demand or at definite time
6. Be payable to order or bearer

These requirements must be present on the **face** (front) of the instrument. Instruments that do not comply with these provisions are nonnegotiable and are transferable only by assignment. The assignee of a nonnegotiable instrument takes it subject to all defenses, whereas a holder of a negotiable instrument may avoid certain defenses.

A central theme of exam questions on negotiable instruments is the liability of the primary parties and of the secondarily liable parties under various fact situations. Similar questions in different form emphasize the rights that a holder of a negotiable instrument has against primary and secondary parties. Your review of this area should emphasize the legal liability arising upon execution of negotiable paper, the legal liability arising upon various types of endorsements, and the warranty liabilities of various parties upon transfer or presentment for payment. A solid understanding of the distinction between real and personal defenses is required. Also tested is the relationship between a bank and its customers. Before beginning the reading you should review the key terms at the end of the module.

A. General Concepts of Negotiable Instruments

1. Negotiable instruments have two important functions

   a. Used as a substitute for money

> **EXAMPLE**
>
> One often pays a bill with a check instead of using cash.

b. Used as extension of credit

EXAMPLE

X gives a promissory note to Y for $100 that is due one year later.

---

2. To encourage economic transactions, negotiable instruments were created.

a. If an instrument is negotiable, favorable laws of Article 3 of UCC apply as discussed in this module
b. If an instrument is nonnegotiable, laws of ordinary contract law apply (i.e., assignment of contract rights)

(1) Assignees of contract rights can get only the rights given by the assignor and therefore are burdened by any defenses between prior parties

---

EXAMPLE

C receives a nonnegotiable instrument from B. C now wishes to collect from A, the one who had issued the non-negotiable note to B when he purchased some goods from B. Assume that A would have owed B only two-thirds of the amount stated on the instrument due to defects in the goods. Since C obtained only the rights that B had under an assignment under contract law, C can only collect two-thirds from A on this nonnegotiable instrument.

---

3. It is helpful to get "the big picture" of negotiable instruments before covering details

a. Whether an instrument is negotiable is determined by only looking at its form and content on the face (front) of the instrument

(1) This allows individuals seeing an instrument to determine whether it is negotiable
(2) If a person has a negotiable instrument and is also a holder in due course (discussed later), s/he may collect on the instrument despite simple contract defenses

B. Types of Negotiable Instruments

1. Article 3 of UCC describes two types of negotiable instruments

a. A draft (also called bill of exchange)

(1) Has three parties in which one person or entity (drawer) **orders** another (drawee) to pay a third party (payee) a sum of money

---

EXAMPLE

June 5, 2011

On June 5, 2012, pay to the order of Bob Smith

$1,000 plus 10% annual interest from June 5, 2011

To: ABC Corporation

(Signed) Sue Van Deventer

The above is a draft in which Sue Van Deventer is the drawer, ABC Corporation is the drawee, and Bob Smith is the payee

---

(a) A check

(1) Is a special type of draft that is payable on demand (unless postdated) and drawee must be a bank; banks include savings and loan associations, credit unions, and trust companies
(2) One writing check is drawer (and customer of drawee bank)

b. A note (also called a promissory note)

  (1) Unlike a draft or check, is a two-party instrument

    (a) One party is called the maker—this party **promises** to pay a specified sum of money to another party called the payee

---

EXAMPLE

> I promise to pay to the order of Becky Hoger $5,000 plus 10% annual interest on July 10, 2020.
>
>   (Signed) Bill Jones

The above is a note in which Bill Jones is the maker and Becky Hoger is the payee.

---

  (2) May be payable on demand or at a definite time

    (a) Certificate of deposit (CD): Is an acknowledgement by a financial institution of receipt of money and a promise to repay it. The financial institution is the maker and the customer is the payee.

    (b) Most commonly tested note on the CPA exam is a promissory note; see the example above with Bill Jones as the maker.

NOW REVIEW MULTIPLE-CHOICE QUESTIONS 1 THROUGH 4

C. Requirements of Negotiability

1. All of the following requirements must be on face of instrument for it to be a negotiable instrument (be sure to know these)
2. To be negotiable, the instrument must satisfy all of the following requirements

  a. Be written
  b. Be signed by maker or drawer
  c. Contain an unconditional promise or order to pay
  d. State a fixed amount in money
  e. Be payable on demand or at a definite time
  f. Be payable to order or to bearer, unless it is a check

3. Details of requirements of negotiability

  a. Must be in writing

    (1) Satisfied by printing, typing, handwriting or any other reduction to physical form that is relatively permanent and portable
    (2) The UCC has a very liberal definition of a writing under Article 3; it is easy to satisfy this requirement

  b. Must be signed by maker (of a note or CD) or drawer (of a draft or check)

    (1) Signature includes any symbol used with intent to authenticate instrument

      (a) Rubber stamp, initials, letterhead satisfy signing requirement
      (b) Assumed name or trade name operates as that party's signature
      (c) Signature may be anywhere on face of instrument

    (2) Again, very liberal interpretation.

   c. Must contain an unconditional promise or order to pay

      (1) This is really two requirements

         (a) That the instrument contains an order or a promise to pay, and

         (b) That the promise or order be unconditional

      (2) If payment depends upon (is subject to) another agreement or event, then it is conditional and therefore destroys negotiability

---

EXAMPLE

An instrument that is otherwise negotiable states that it is subject to a particular contract. This condition destroys the negotiability of this instrument.

EXAMPLE

An instrument states: "I, Janice Jones, promise to pay to the order of Richard Riley, $1,000 if the stereo delivered to me is not defective." This instrument is not negotiable. Whether the stereo is defective or not is a conditional promise.

         (a) However, the following are permitted and do not destroy negotiability

            (1) Instrument may state its purpose

EXAMPLE

On a check, the drawer writes "for purchase of textbooks."

---

            (2) Instrument may refer to or state that it arises from another agreement; note here that it is not subject to that agreement. Being "subject to" destroys negotiability.

            (3) Instrument is permitted to show that it is secured by a mortgage or by collateral

            (4) Instrument is permitted to contain promise to provide extra collateral

            (5) Instrument is permitted to limit payment out of particular fund

         (b) The key to determining if the promise/order is conditional. Does the language in the instrument make the actual payment subject to some event?

      (3) Promises

         (a) Are usually contained in a note (as opposed to a draft)

         (b) Must be an affirmative obligation to pay, not a mere acknowledgement of a debt.

EXAMPLE

Deb Tore gives a piece of paper to Lance Lender, which states, "IOU $500," signed Deb Tore. Deb's IOU only acknowledges the debt; she never promised to pay Lance. This instrument is nonnegotiable since it does not contain either a promise or an order to pay money. IOUs are nonnegotiable.

---

(4) Orders

  (a) Are usually contained in a draft
  (b) The order is a command or a direction to the drawee to pay
  (c) On a check this is the word "Pay"

> **NOTE:** The order is not the "order of" language on a check; it is the command, "pay."

d. Must state a fixed amount in money—called sum certain under former law

  (1) Amount of principal, but not interest, must be determinable from instrument without need to refer to other sources

    (a) Stated interest rates are allowed because amount can be calculated

> **EXAMPLE**
>
> A negotiable note states that $1,000 is due one year from October 1 at 14% interest.

> **EXAMPLE**
>
> A note states that $1,000 is payable on demand and bears interest at 14%. This also is negotiable because once payment is demanded, the amount of interest can be calculated.

    (b) Variable interest rates are allowed and do not destroy negotiability even if formula for interest rate or amount requires reference to information outside of negotiable instrument

> **EXAMPLE**
>
> The following does not destroy negotiability in an otherwise negotiable instrument: Interest rates tied to some published key interest rate, consumer index market rate, etc.

    (c) If interest rate based on legal rate or judgment rate (fixed by statute), then negotiability not destroyed
    (d) Stated different rates of interest before and after default or specified dates are allowed
    (e) Stated discounts or additions if instrument paid before or after payment dates do not destroy negotiability
    (f) Clauses allowing collection costs and attorney's fees upon default are allowed because they reduce the risk of holding instruments and promote transferability
    (g) Must be payable only in money; option to be payable in money or something else destroys negotiability because of possibility that payment will not be in money.

> **EXAMPLE**
>
> A note is payable in $1,000 or its equivalent in gold. This note is not negotiable.

  (2) Foreign currency is acceptable even though reference to exchange rates may be needed due to international trade realities

e. Must be payable on demand or at a definite time

   (1) On demand includes

      (a) Payable on sight
      (b) Payable on presentation
      (c) No time for payment stated

   (2) It is a definite time if payable

      (a) On a certain date, or
      (b) A fixed period after sight, or
      (c) Within a certain time, or
      (d) On a certain date subject to acceleration; for example, when a payment is missed, total balance may become due at once
      (e) On a certain date subject to an extension of time if

         (1) At option of holder, or
         (2) At option of maker or drawer only if extension is limited to a definite amount of time

---

EXAMPLE

Promissory note which states, I promise to pay to the order of Will Smith $1000 on May 15, 2020, but if I lose my job, payment will be made on August 1, 2020. This instrument is negotiable, since any party taking the instrument knows that the latest they will be paid is August 1, 2020.

---

   (3) It is not definite if payable on an act or event that is not certain as to time of occurrence

---

EXAMPLE

An instrument contains a clause stating that it is payable ten days after drawer obtains a bank loan. This destroys negotiability because it is unknown when, or even if, the drawer will obtain the loan.

---

f. Must be payable to order or to bearer **(these are critical words of negotiability and are often a central issue on the CPA exam)**

   (1) Instrument is payable to order if made payable to the order of

      (a) Any person, including the maker, drawer, drawee, or payee
      (b) Two persons together or alternatively
      (c) Any entity

   (2) Instrument is also payable to order if it is payable "to A or order"
   (3) Instrument other than a check is not payable to order if it is only payable to a person (e.g., "Pay John Doe")

EXAMPLE

A draft that is otherwise negotiable states: "Pay to XYZ Corporation." This statement destroys negotiability because the draft is not payable "to the order of" XYZ Corporation.

      (a) It is not negotiable
      (b) "Pay to the order of John Doe" would be negotiable

   (4) If a **check** says "pay to A," it is negotiable order paper—this is not true of other instruments
   (5) Instrument is payable to bearer if it is payable to

       (a) "Bearer"

       (b) "Cash"

       (c) "A person or bearer" is bearer paper if "bearer" handwritten; however, "pay to John Doe, the bearer" is not negotiable because it is not payable to order or to bearer but to a person and simply refers to him as the bearer

       (d) "Order of bearer" or "order of cash"

       (e) Pay to the order of (payee left blank) is bearer paper unless holder inserts payee's name

    (6) Instrument cannot be made payable to persons consecutively (i.e., maker cannot specify subsequent holders)

D. Interpretation of Ambiguities in Negotiable Instruments

  1. Contradictory terms

    a. Words control over figures (numerals)

    b. Handwritten terms control over typewritten and printed (typeset) terms

    c. Typewritten terms control over printed (typeset) terms

  2. Omissions

    a. Omission of date does not destroy negotiability unless date necessary to determine when payable

---

EXAMPLE

A check is not dated. It is still negotiable because a check is payable on demand.

EXAMPLE

A draft states that it is payable thirty days after its date. If the date is left off, it is not payable at a definite time and, therefore, it is not negotiable. However, an authorized party may fill in the appropriate date and make the instrument negotiable.

---

    b. Omission of interest rate is allowed because the judgment rate of interest (rate used on a court judgment) is automatically used

    c. Statement of consideration or where instrument is drawn or payable not required

  3. Other issues

    a. Instrument may be postdated or antedated and remain negotiable

      (1) Bank is not liable for damages to customer if it pays on postdated check before date on check unless individual notifies bank not to pay check earlier in a separate written document

      (2) Once customer does this, bank is liable for any damages caused by early payment

    b. Instrument may have a provision that by endorsing or cashing it, the payee acknowledges full satisfaction of debt and remain negotiable

    c. If an instrument is payable to order of more than one person

      (1) Either payee may negotiate or enforce it if payable to him/her in the alternative

---

EXAMPLE

"Pay $100 to the order of X or Y." Either X or Y may endorse it.

---

      (2) All payees must negotiate or enforce it if **not** payable to them in the alternative

   d. If not clear whether instrument is draft or note, holder may treat it as either

   e. UCC requires only that a negotiable instrument need be written, must lend itself to permanence, and must be easily transferable (i.e., movable).

NOW REVIEW MULTIPLE-CHOICE QUESTIONS 5 THROUGH 15

E. Negotiation

1. There are two methods of transferring negotiable instruments

   a. By assignment

      (1) Assignment occurs when transfer does not meet all requirements of negotiation

      (2) Assignee can obtain only same rights that assignor had, and is subject to any defenses that can be asserted against assignor

   b. By negotiation

      (1) One receiving negotiable instrument by negotiation is called a holder

      (2) If holder further qualifies as a holder in due course (as discussed later) s/he can obtain **more rights** than what transferor had

      (3) There are two methods of negotiation, which is dependent on whether the transferor is trying to negotiate order paper or bearer paper

         (a) Order paper is a negotiable instrument that is payable to a specific party (e.g., "Pay to the order of Acme Corp.")

            (1) Transferred by physical delivery of the instrument **and** endorsement

            (2) A holder needs possession of the instrument and any necessary endorsements

         (b) Bearer paper is a negotiable instrument that is payable to any party (e.g., "Pay to cash")

            (1) Transferred by delivery alone

            (2) Holder only needs possession of the instrument

            (3) Subsequent parties may require endorsements (even though UCC does not) for identification

            (4) Holder may, in any event, endorse it if s/he chooses to do so

      (4) Endorsement (Indorsement) refers to signature of payee, drawee, accommodation endorser, or holder

2. Types of endorsements

   a. Blank endorsement

      (1) Does not specify any endorsee

EXAMPLE

A check made payable to the order of M on the front can be endorsed in blank by M writing only his signature on the back.

---

      (2) Converts order paper into bearer paper

      (3) Note that bearer paper may be negotiated by mere delivery; hence a finder, or even a thief, can be a valid holder

---

EXAMPLE

B endorses a check in blank that had been made payable to his order. He lost it and C found it who delivered it to D. D is a valid holder since C's endorsement was not required.

---

b. Special endorsement

   (1) Indicates specific person to whom endorsee wishes to negotiate instrument

---

EXAMPLE

On the back of a check payable to the order of M. Jordan he signs as follows: Pay to L. Smith, (signed) M. Jordan.

     (a) Note that words "pay to the order of" are not required on back as endorsements—the instrument needs to be payable to order or to bearer on front only

     (b) Also, note that if instrument is not payable to order or to bearer on its face, it **cannot** be turned into a negotiable instrument by using these words in an endorsement on the back

---

EXAMPLE

A particular instrument would have been negotiable except that on the front it was payable to A. On the back, A signed it. "Pay to the order of B, (signed) A." This does not convert it into a negotiable instrument.

---

   (2) Bearer paper may be converted into order paper by use of special endorsement

---

EXAMPLE

A check made out to cash is delivered to Carp. Carp writes on the back; Pay to Durn, (signed) Carp. It was bearer paper until this special endorsement.

EXAMPLE

Continuing the previous example, Durn simply endorses it in blank. The check is bearer paper again.

---

   (3) If last (or only) endorsement on instrument is a blank endorsement, any holder may convert that bearer paper into order paper by writing "Pay to X," etc., above that blank endorsement

c. Restrictive endorsement is an attempt by the endorser to restrict further negotiation; some restrictions are enforceable, others are not.

   (1) Valid restrictive endorsements

     (a) Collection endorsements (e.g. "for deposit only" or "pay any bank")

     (b) Endorsements in trust (e.g. "Pay Smith for Jones")

   (2) Invalid restrictive endorsements

     (a) The following endorsements are viewed by the law as saying "Pay to the order of Smith;" the rest of the language in the endorsement is simply ignored or altered by the law.

       (1) Pay to Smith, if Smith washes my car

       (2) Pay to Smith only

     (b) Remember the endorsements cannot affect negotiability, thus order language is not required in an endorsement

     (c) Endorsements cannot prohibit further negotiation; to the extent the endorsement attempts to limit further negotiation, the language is ignored.

d. Qualified endorsement

   (1) Normally, endorser, upon signing, promises automatically to pay holder or any subsequent endorser the amount of instrument if it is later dishonored

   (2) Qualified endorsement disclaims this liability

EXAMPLE

Ann Knolls endorses "Without recourse, (signed) Ann Knolls."

---

   (3) Qualified endorsements, otherwise, have same effects as other endorsements

e. Combinations of endorsements occur

   (1) Special qualified endorsement

EXAMPLE

"Pay to Pete Bell without recourse, (signed) Tom Lack." Tom Lack has limited his liability and also Pete Bell's endorsement is needed to negotiate this instrument further.

---

   (2) Blank qualified endorsement

EXAMPLE

"Without recourse, (signed) D. Hamilton."

---

   (3) Endorsement that is restrictive, qualified, and blank

EXAMPLE

"For deposit only, without recourse, (signed) Bill Coffey."

---

3. If payee's name misspelled, s/he may endorse in proper spelling or misspelling or both; but endorsee may require both

4. If an order instrument is transferred for value without endorsement, transferee may require endorsement from transferor

5. Federal law standardizes endorsements on checks—endorser should turn check over and sign in designated area

   a. Purpose is to avoid interference with bank's endorsements

   b. Endorsements placed outside this area do not destroy negotiability but may delay clearing process.

6. If check has statement that it is nonnegotiable, check is still negotiable

   a. This is not true of other negotiable instruments whereby such statement destroys negotiability

---

NOW REVIEW MULTIPLE-CHOICE QUESTIONS 16 THROUGH 21

F. Holder in Due Course

1. Concept of **holder in due course** (also called **HDC**) is very important for CPA exam purposes. An HDC is entitled to payment on negotiable instrument **despite personal defenses** that maker or drawer of instrument may have

    a. Recall that an assignee of contract rights receives only rights that assignor had (i.e., assignee takes subject to all defenses that could have been asserted against assignor)
    b. Likewise, an ordinary holder of a negotiable instrument has same rights as assignee

2. To be holder in due course, a taker of instrument must

    a. Be a **holder** of a properly negotiated negotiable instrument
    b. Give **value** for instrument

       (1) Holder gives value if s/he

           (a) Pays or performs agreed consideration; be careful, an executory promise (promise to give value in the future is not value. Promise must actually have been performed.

EXAMPLE

DeMaurice gave $3000 to Roger for a $5000 promissory note and promised to pay Roger an additional $1000 in one month. One week after the initial payment, and before making the final payment to Roger, DeMaurice found out that Roger had stolen the note from Jerry. DeMaurice qualifies as a holder in due course for $3,750. Once DeMaurice learns of the theft he cannot further qualify as a holder in due course. When DeMaurice made the initial payment of $3000, he did not know of the theft, so he qualifies as a holder in due course to the extent he has actually provided value. So why does DeMaurice qualify for $3750 and not just $3000? The law recognizes that DeMaurice was never going to pay $5000 for the $5000 instrument. Instead, he purchased the note at a discount. DeMaurice has paid 75% ($3000/$4000) of what he intended to pay, so the law states that he is entitled to 75% of the face value of the instrument: $3750.

       (b) Takes as a satisfaction of a previous existing debt
       (c) Gives another negotiable instrument
       (d) Acquires a security interest in the instrument (e.g., the holder takes possession of the instrument as collateral for another debt)

    (2) A bank takes for value to the extent that credit has been given for a deposit and withdrawn

        (a) FIFO method is used to determine whether it has been withdrawn (money is considered to be withdrawn from an account in the order in which it was deposited)

    (3) Value does not have to be for full amount of instrument

        (a) Purchase at a reasonable discount is value for full face amount of instrument

---

EXAMPLE

Purchase of a $1,000 instrument in good faith for $950 is considered full value, but purchase of the same instrument for $500 is not considered full value when market conditions show that the discount is excessive.

> NOTE: Do not just assume that a large discount is excessive; the Examiners need to provide you with facts that indicate the discount is excessive. Do not forget during the recent financial crisis, there were instruments being sold for pennies on the dollar.

---

c. Take in **good faith**

    (1) Good faith defined as honesty in fact and observance of reasonable commercial standards of fair dealing

d. Take **without notice** that the instrument is overdue, has been dishonored, or that any person has a defense or claim of ownership to the instrument

    (1) Holder has notice when s/he knows or has reason to know (measured by objective "reasonable person" standard)

    (2) Overdue

EXAMPLE

I offer to sell you a $10,000 promissory note for $9,000. The note was payable last week. You should be suspicious since I could go to the maker of the note and collect $10,000 immediately; why would I sell it to you for only $9000, unless there was something wrong with the note? Therefore you cannot qualify as a holder in due course.

        (a) Instrument not overdue if default is on payment of interest only

        (b) Domestic check, although payable on demand, is overdue ninety days after its date

    (3) Defense or claim

        (a) Obvious signs of forgery or alteration so as to call into question its authenticity

        (b) Incomplete instrument or irregular instrument

        (c) If purchaser has notice of any party's claim, or that all parties have been discharged

    (4) There is no notice of a defense or claim if

        (a) It is antedated or postdated

        (b) S/he knows that there has been a default in payment of interest

        (c) The note was purchased at a reasonable discount.

    (5) But if one acquires notice **after** becoming a holder and giving value, s/he may still be an HDC to the extent of the value given (see the above example under value with DeMaurice and Roger)

3. Payee of a negotiable instrument may qualify as an HDC if meets all requirements

---

NOW REVIEW MULTIPLE-CHOICE QUESTIONS 22 THROUGH 25

G. Rights of a Holder in Due Course

1. The general rule is that a transfer of a negotiable instrument to an HDC cuts off all **personal defenses** against an HDC

    a. Personal defenses are assertable against ordinary holders and assignees of contract rights to avoid payment

---

EXAMPLE

Art Dobbs negotiates a note to Mary Price in payment of a stereo. Mary negotiates this note to Finch who qualifies as an HDC. When Finch seeks payment, Dobbs points out that Price breached the contract by never delivering the stereo. Finch, as a HDC, still has the right to collect because breach of contract is a personal defense. Dobbs then has to seek recourse directly against Price.

---

2. Some defenses are assertable against any party including an HDC—these defenses are called **real (or universal) defenses**

3. Types of **personal defenses**

a. Breach of contract, including breach of warranty
b. Lack or failure of consideration
c. Prior payment

> **EXAMPLE**
>
> Maker of a negotiable note pays on the note but does not keep or cancel the note. A subsequent party who qualifies as an HDC seeks to collect on this same note. Maker, having only a personal defense, must pay the HDC even though it was paid previously.

d. Unauthorized completion

> **EXAMPLE**
>
> X signs a check leaving the amount blank. He tells Y to fill in the amount necessary to buy a typewriter. Y fills in $22,000 and negotiates the check to an HDC. The HDC may enforce the full amount of the check against X.

e. Fraud in the inducement

    (1) Occurs when person signs a negotiable instrument and knows what s/he is signing; however, s/he was induced into doing so by intentional misrepresentation

f. Nondelivery

    (1) Occurs when bearer instrument is lost or stolen

> **EXAMPLE**
>
> M issues a note that is bearer paper. It is stolen by T who sells it to an HDC. The HDC wins against M.

g. Ordinary duress or undue influence

    (1) Most types of duress are considered a personal defense unless they become very extreme and thus are considered real defenses

> **EXAMPLE**
>
> Jessica threatened to post some unflattering pictures of Anthony on Facebook. Anthony writes Jessica a check so Jessica will not post the pictures. Anthony would only have a personal defense against paying the check.

h. Mental incapacity

    (1) Personal defense if state law makes transaction voidable
    (2) Real defense if state law makes transaction void

> **EXAMPLE**
>
> Contracts of people who have been adjudicated incompetent are void; those people would have a real defense against enforcement of a negotiable instrument. People who only suffer from some diminished capacity would only have a personal defense.

i. Illegality

    (1) Personal defense if state law makes transaction voidable

    (2) If state law makes it void, then real defense

j. Theft by holder or subsequent holder after theft

4. Real Defenses

  a. Forgery

    (1) Forgery of maker's or drawer's signature does not act as his/her signature

       (a) Does allow forger to be held liable

EXAMPLE

X forges M's name on a note and sells it to P. P cannot collect from M whether she is an HDC or not. Her recourse is against X. The UCC recognizes the forged signature as X's signature, not M's. So even though the instrument states "M," in the eyes of the law it states "X."

---

  b. Bankruptcy

  c. Fraud in the execution

    (1) Occurs when a party is tricked into signing a negotiable instrument believing it to be something else

       (a) This defense will not apply if signer, based on his/her age, experience, etc., should have known what was happening

    (2) Recall that fraud in the inducement is a personal defense

  d. Minority (or infancy)

    (1) When minor may disaffirm contract under state law, then is a real defense for a negotiable instrument

  e. Mental incapacity, illegality, or extreme duress

    (1) Real defenses if transaction is void under state law

  f. Material alteration of instrument

    (1) Is actually only partially a real defense

       (a) If dollar amount was altered, then HDC can collect according to original terms—a non-HDC collects nothing

       (b) If an instrument was incomplete originally and then completed without authorization, HDC can enforce it as completed—a non-HDC collects nothing

    (2) Material alteration exists when terms between any two parties are changed in any way including

       (a) Changes in amount, rate of interest, or days

EXAMPLE

Janice Parks negotiates a $200 negotiable note to Jim Bivins. Bivins deftly changes the amount to $500 and transfers it to E. Melvin for $500 who qualifies as an HDC. The HDC can collect only the original $200 from Janice Parks.

EXAMPLE

Same facts as before except that the material alteration is poorly done by Jim Bivins so that E. Melvin could not qualify as a holder in due course because the change was obvious. E. Melvin cannot collect even the original $200.

    (b) Additions to writing or removal of part of instrument

    (c) Completion of instrument without authorization

    (d) Considered "material" even if small change such as a penny

    (e) But not material alteration if done to correct error on address, math computations, or to place marks on instrument for audit purposes. Alterations that are not material are neither real nor personal defenses so all non-HDCs as well as HDCs can enforce the instrument.

    (f) Not a real defense if maker's or drawer's negligence substantially contributed to the alteration—is a personal defense

5. Holder through a holder in due course ("Shelter Rule")

  a. A party who does not qualify as an HDC but obtains a negotiable instrument from an HDC has the standing of HDC.

  b. Obtains all rights of an HDC

    (1) Based on fact that is an assignee that gets rights of previous party

    (2) Also called shelter provision

  c. An HDC "washes" an instrument so that any holder thereafter can be a holder through a holder in due course

---

EXAMPLE

An HDC transfers a note to H.V. Shelton who knew that the maker of the note has a personal defense. Shelton does not qualify as an HDC but has the same rights because he is a holder through a holder in due course.

EXAMPLE

Extending the example, H.V. Shelton gives the note to B. Evans. B. Evans does not qualify as an HDC (no value given) but is a holder through a holder in due course.

NOTE: Be careful to remember that in the above examples if the Examiners were to ask you if Shelton or Evans is an HDC, the answer is no. If you are asked do Shelton or Evans have the rights of an HDC, the answer is yes.

---

  d. Exceptions

    (1) If a party reacquires an instrument, his/her status remains what it originally was

---

EXAMPLE

P acquires a check from the payee. Neither qualifies in this case as a holder in due course. P delivers the check to Q who qualifies as an HDC. If the check is negotiated back to P, his rights remain those of a non-HDC.

---

    (2) One who was involved in fraud or illegality affecting the instrument may not subsequently become a holder through a holder in due course

6. Federal Trade Commission Rule significantly limits HDC status in consumer credit transactions

  a. This federal law takes precedence over state UCCs

b. Law was passed because it was felt standard HDC rule was causing hardship on consumers who signed notes promising to pay retailers for goods purchased which were defective. Retailer could sell notes to other parties cutting off important remedies against retailer who sold defective goods.
c. FTC rule applies to consumer credit transactions when

(1) Consumer signs installment sales contract containing waiver of defenses
(2) Consumer signs sales contract containing promissory note
(3) Retailer arranges financing with a separate party for consumer financing

d. Lenders and sellers of negotiable instruments must put notice defenses consumers could use against sellers
e. Payments for goods or services using checks are not covered by FTC rule
f. Note that rule does not apply to any nonconsumer transactions and does not apply to any consumer noncredit transactions

---

EXAMPLE

Connie Consumer purchases goods for consumer use and writes out a check. Subsequent holders are governed by ordinary HDC law.

NOW REVIEW MULTIPLE-CHOICE QUESTIONS 26 THROUGH 35

H. **Liability of Parties**—There are two general types of warranties on negotiable instruments: contractual liability and warranty liability. This explains who is responsible to pay the holder/holder in due course.

1. Contractual liability

a. This is the liability for payment of the instrument's face value.
b. Applies to any party who signs negotiable instrument. This could include a maker, drawer, acceptor of a draft, or endorser.
c. Primary liability

(1) The holder/HDC must first seek payment from this party
(2) The primary party on a note is the maker
(3) The primary party on a draft is the acceptor of a draft

(a) This is a drawee who accepts the instrument for payment
(b) If drawee dishonors (refuses to make payment) the draft, then no party has primary liability on the draft

d. Secondary liability

(1) If primary party does not pay, then the holder/HDC may either

(a) Sue the primary party to force the primary party to pay, or
(b) Seek payment from a secondary party

(2) Secondary parties are

(a) Endorsers of any instrument
(b) Drawers on a draft
(c) There is no secondary liability on a draft if the draft was accepted by the drawee

(3) Several conditions must be met to hold a secondary party liable for payment

(a) Presentment (demand for payment) of the instrument to the primary party by the holder/HDC
(b) Dishonor (refusal to pay) of the instrument by the primary party
(c) Timely notice of the dishonor provided to the endorsers (notice is not required for the drawer)

(1) Banks, and similar institutions, must provide notice by midnight of the next banking day
(2) All other parties have 30 days to provide notice of the dishonor

e. Drawers, **except** drawers of a check, and endorsers may avoid secondary liability by signing without recourse
f. Upon certification of check, drawer and all previous endorsers are discharged from liability because bank has accepted check and agreed to pay it
g. A holder/HDC may only seek to collect from prior signatory parties, not subsequent signers

---

EXAMPLE

Assume that first John and then Paul previously endorsed a note that is in George's possession. Later George transfers the instrument, by endorsement, to Ringo. Ringo presents the note to the primary party, Peter, for payment; Peter dishonored the note. Ringo then notified all the endorsers of the dishonor and sought payment from Paul, who paid Ringo. Paul could now proceed against John for secondary liability because John signed the note prior to Paul. Paul cannot, however, collect from George because George endorsed after Paul.

---

2. Warranty liability—two types under which holder can seek payment from secondary parties are transfer warranties and presentment warranties

a. Transfer warranties—transferor gives following transfer warranties whenever negotiable instrument is transferred for consideration

(1) Transferor has good title, which means that there are

(a) No missing endorsements
(b) No unauthorized endorsements

(2) All signatures are genuine or authorized
(3) Instrument has not been materially altered
(4) No defense of any party is good against transferor
(5) Transferor has no notice of insolvency of maker, drawer, or acceptor

---

EXAMPLE

Pat issued a promissory note made payable to Vince. Vince endorsed the note and negotiated it to Tracy for value. Tracy provided a qualified endorsement and gave the note to Andy as a gift. Andy then transferred the note for value, without endorsement, to Shelley. When the instrument was due, Shelley presented the note to Pat for payment. Pat refused payment because he was a minor. Shelley now seeks to collect on the instrument from Tracy and Andy. Neither Tracy nor Andy has contract liability on the note. Tracy is not liable because his endorsement was qualified; Andy did not sign the instrument, so he has no contract liability. Tracy does not have warranty liability either, because Tracy did not receive consideration to transfer the note. Andy does have warranty liability because he breached the warranty that there were no valid defenses against Andy if he sought to enforce the note. Pat's minority is a real defense and would prevent Andy from collecting on the note even if Andy was a holder in due course. Even though Andy did not transfer the note by endorsement, he still gives transferor warranties to his immediate transferee, Shelley.

---

b. These warranties generally allocate the loss to parties that dealt face to face with wrongdoer and thus were in best position to prevent or avoid forged, altered, or stolen instruments

(1) Party bearing loss must then seek payment if possible, from one who forged, altered, or stole instrument

c. Note that transferor, if s/he did not endorse, makes all five warranties only to immediate transferee but if transferor did endorse, makes them to all subsequent holders taking in good faith
d. Presentment warranties—holder/HDC presenting negotiable instrument for payment or acceptance and all prior transferors of the instrument provide presentment warranties to the party who pays on the instrument. The presentment warranties for an unaccepted draft are

(1) The warrantor is entitled to enforce the instrument (i.e. warrantor has good title)
(2) Warrantor has no knowledge that drawer's signature is forged or unauthorized
(3) The instrument was not altered

e. Presentment warranty for all other instruments (other than unaccepted drafts) is only the first warranty listed: Good title.

f. To recover under warranty liabilities (either transfer or presentment warranties), party does not have to meet conditions of proper presentment, dishonor, or timely notice of dishonor that are required under contractual liability against endorsers

g. Recovery under a warranty theory only allows the injured party to receive what they paid for the instrument. The injured party is not entitled to recover the face value, as s/he would be able to under contract liability, unless the injured party actually paid the face value of the instrument.

3. Signatures by authorized agents

a. Drawers or makers at times authorize agents to sign negotiable instruments on behalf of such drawers or makers

(1) Organizations such as corporations often use corporate officers or employees to be agents to sign their negotiable instruments

(a) Drawers or makers are liable and agent is not personally liable on negotiable instrument if agent's signature clearly discloses both agency status and identity of drawer or maker

(2) Individuals may also use agents to sign negotiable instruments and same law applies

> **EXAMPLE**
>
> A negotiable instrument has the following signature, signed entirely by A. Underwood, the authorized agent: Mary Johnson, by A. Underwood, agent.

> **EXAMPLE**
>
> If A. Underwood had simply signed Mary Johnson as she had authorized, this would also bind Mary Johnson.

> **EXAMPLE**
>
> If A. Underwood had signed his name only, he is liable. The principal is not liable even if the agent intended her to be liable because her name is not on the instrument.

4. Accommodation party is liable on the instrument in the capacity in which s/he has signed even if taker knows of his/her accommodation status

> **EXAMPLE**
>
> Accommodating maker is liable as a maker would be.

> **EXAMPLE**
>
> Accommodating endorser is liable as an endorser would be.

a. Accommodation party is one who signs to lend his/her name to other party

> **EXAMPLE**
>
> Father-in-law endorses a note for son-in-law so creditor will accept it.

    (1) Notice of default need not be given to accommodation party

    (2) The accommodation party has right of recourse against accommodated party if accommodation party is held liable

5. Discharge of parties

  a. Once primary party pays, all endorsers are discharged from liability

  b. Cancellation of prior party's endorsement discharges that party from liability

    (1) Oral renunciation or oral attempt to discharge a party is not effective

  c. Intentional destruction of instrument by holder discharges prior parties to instrument

6. Liability on instruments with forged signatures

  a. Person whose signature was forged on instrument is not liable on that instrument

    (1) Unless later ratifies it

  b. Forged signature operates as signature of forger

  c. Therefore, if signature of **maker or drawer** is forged, instrument can still be negotiated between parties and thus a holder can acquire good title

    (1) Recall that forgery is a real defense so that innocent maker or drawer cannot be required to pay even an HDC—forger can be required to pay if found

  d. However, a **forged endorsement** does **not** transfer title; thus, persons receiving it after forgery cannot collect on it

    (1) Three important exceptions to rule that forged endorsements cannot transfer title are imposter rule, fictitious payee rule, and negligence of maker or drawer—these cause maker or drawer to be liable

      (a) **Imposter rule** applies when maker or drawer issues a note or draft to an imposter thinking s/he actually is the real payee—when that imposter forges the real payee's name, this effectively negotiates this note or draft so that a subsequent holder (if not part of scheme) can collect from maker or drawer

        (1) Note that this rule normally places loss on person who was in best position to avoid this scheme (i.e., maker or drawer)

          (a) Of course, upon payment, maker or drawer may try to collect from imposter

> **EXAMPLE**
>
> J. Loux owes Larsen (whom she has not met) $2,000. Sawyer, claiming to be Larsen, gets Loux to issue him a check for $2,000. Sawyer forges Larsen's endorsement and transfers the check to P. Jenkins. Jenkins can collect from Loux because of the imposter rule exception.

> **EXAMPLE**
>
> If in the example above, J. Loux had given the check to the real Larsen and he lost it, the imposter rule would not apply even if someone found the check and forged Larsen's endorsement. No one after the forgery can collect on the check.

  (2) This imposter rule exception also applies if an imposter pretends to be **agent** of the named payee

  (b) **Fictitious payee rule** applies when maker, drawer, or his/her agent (employee) issues a note or a check to a fictitious payee—then maker, drawer, or employee forges the endorsement—subsequent parties can enforce the note or check against the maker or drawer

  (1) Actually payee may be a real person as long as maker, drawer, or other person supplying name never intended for that payee to ever get payment

---

EXAMPLE

R. Stewart submits a time card for a nonexistent employee and the employer issues the payroll check. Stewart forges the endorsement and transfers it to L. Reed. Reed wins against the employer even though the employer was unaware of the scheme at the time.

  (c) If person's negligence substantially contributes to the forgery that person is prevented from raising the defense of forgery and thus holder wins

---

EXAMPLE

D. Wolter has a signature stamp and leaves it lying around. Unauthorized use of the stamp is not a defense against a holder as Wolter's negligence substantially contributed to the forgery. If the forger could be caught, Wolter could sue the forger for losses.

NOW REVIEW MULTIPLE-CHOICE QUESTIONS 36 THROUGH 44

I. Additional Issues

1. Types of drafts—although they follow general rules of drafts, definitions are helpful

 a. Trade acceptance is a draft in which a seller of goods extends credit to buyer by drawing a draft on that buyer directing him/her to pay seller a sum of money on a specified date

  (1) Trade acceptance also requires signature of buyer on face of instrument—called acceptance—buyer is also called acceptor at this point

  (2) Then seller may negotiate trade acceptance at a discount to another party to receive immediate cash

  (3) Seller is normally both drawer and payee of a trade acceptance

 b. Banker's acceptance is a draft in which drawee and drawer are a bank

 c. Sight draft is one payable upon presentment to drawee

 d. Time draft is one payable at a specified date or payable a certain period of time after a specified date

 e. Money order is a draft purchased by one party to pay payee in which the third party is typically post office, a bank, or a company

2. Definitions for certain types of checks are also helpful

 a. Traveler's check is purchased from a bank (or company)—drawer (traveler) must sign twice for purposes of identification (once at the time s/he purchases the check and again at the time s/he uses the check)—drawee is bank or company—payee is one who gets paid

  (1) Technically, drawee must be a bank to be a true "check"—if drawee is not a bank then traveler's check is actually a draft

 b. Cashier's check is a check in which drawer and drawee are the same bank with a separate party being the payee

(1) This is still considered a "three-party" instrument even though drawer and drawee are same bank

   c. Certified check is a check that payor bank has agreed in advance to pay so that bank becomes primarily liable

   d. Teller's check (bank draft) is draft drawn by one bank on another bank

J. Banks

1. Banks include savings and loan associations, credit unions, and trust companies
2. Relationship between bank and depositor is debtor-creditor

   a. Even though the depositor has funds in the bank, a payee cannot force a drawee to make payment

   b. Only drawer has an action against drawee-bank for wrongfully dishonoring a check—based on contract between customer (drawer) and bank

   c. Bank required to report to IRS any transaction or series of related transactions greater than $10,000

      (1) Ordinary checks are exempted but cash and other types of checks such as cashier's checks come under reporting requirement

   d. Bank must report to IRS suspected crimes involving $1,000 or more in funds

   e. It is a crime to structure or assist in structuring transactions to evade these reporting requirements

      (1) May be punishable by money penalties or under criminal law

3. Checks

   a. Banks are not obligated to pay on a check presented more than six months after date

      (1) But they may pay in good faith and charge customer's account

   b. Even if check creates an overdraft, a bank may charge customer's account

   c. Bank is liable to drawer for damages caused by wrongful dishonor of a check

      (1) Wrongful dishonor may occur if the bank in error believes funds are insufficient when they are sufficient

   d. Payment of bad checks (e.g., forgery of drawer or altered checks)

      (1) Bank is liable to drawer for payment on bad checks unless drawer's negligence contributed because bank presumed to know signatures of its drawers

      (2) If drawer fails to notify bank of forgery or alterations within thirty days of bank statement, the drawer is held liable on subsequent forgeries or alterations done in same way by same person

         (a) In any event, drawer must give notice of forgeries or alterations within one year to keep bank liable or else drawer is liable. This applies to nonrepeating cases as well, even when bank was paying in bad faith.

EXAMPLE

G. Wilson forges the name of M. Gibson as a drawer on a check in an artful way. A subsequent HDC cashes this check at the drawee bank. The bank is liable on this check and cannot recover from either the HDC or M. Gibson as long as Gibson notifies the bank of the forgery within one year. The loss falls on the bank because the bank should know its drawer's signature.

         (b) Forgeries of endorsements are treated differently—depositor has three years to notify bank and also bank may charge check back to party that presented check to bank. Recall that one cashing check gave warranty that all signatures are genuine.

EXAMPLE

D issues a check to P. P loses the check which is found by X. X forges the endorsement and transfers it to H. Finally, H cashes the check at the drawee bank. D soon notifies the bank of the forgery. The bank may charge it back to H (whether or not an HDC) but not to D.

---

e. Bank is not liable for early payment of postdated check unless drawer notified bank to not pay check until date on check

f. Oral **stop payment order** is good for fourteen days; written stop payment order is good for six months and is renewable

  (1) Stop payment order must be given so as to give bank reasonable opportunity to act on it

  (2) Bank is liable to drawer if it pays after effective stop payment order only when drawer can prove that the bank's failure to obey the order caused drawer's loss. If drawer has no valid defense to justify dishonoring instrument, then bank has no liability for failure to obey stop payment order.

EXAMPLE

W. Paisley buys a TV set from the Burke Appliance Store and pays for the set with a check. Later in the day Paisley finds a better model for the same price at another store. Paisley telephones his bank and orders the bank to stop payment on the check. If the bank mistakenly pays Paisley's check two days after receiving the stop payment order, the bank will not be liable if Paisley could not rightfully rescind his agreement with the Burke Appliance Store. With these facts, Paisley suffered no damages from the bank's mistake.

---

  (3) If drawer stops payment on the check, s/he is still liable to holder of check unless s/he has a valid defense (e.g., if holder qualifies as a holder in due course then drawer must be able to assert a real defense to free him/herself of liability)

g. Bank is entitled to a depositor's endorsement on checks deposited with the bank

  (1) If missing, bank may supply endorsement to negotiate check

h. Banks may choose which checks are charged to account first when several checks received in same day

NOW REVIEW MULTIPLE-CHOICE QUESTIONS 45 AND 46

K. Electronic Fund Transfer Act and Regulation E

1. Applied to consumer electronic fund transfers
2. For lost or stolen debit cards, customer is liable for

a. Limit of $50 if notifies bank within two days of discovery of loss or theft
b. Limit of $500 if notifies bank after two days, but before sixty days after unauthorized use appears on customer's bank statement
c. Limit of $500 does not apply if fails to notify bank before sixty-day period
d. Note how these rules are very different from those that apply to lost or stolen credit cards

3. Bank is liable for failure to pay electronic fund transfer when customer has sufficient funds in account
4. Unauthorized use of electronic fund transfer is felony under federal law

a. Banks and their officers must comply with strict rules for prevention or be subject to strict fines and/or imprisonment

L. Fund Transfers under UCC Article 4A

1. Applies to commercial electronic fund transfers

a. Adopted by majority of states
b. Does not apply to consumer transfers
c. Applies to any method of transfer including electronic or mail

2. When party gives payment order to bank and that bank or another bank pays too much money or to wrong party, that bank in error is liable for error

a. Then bank has burden of recovery for wrongfully paid amount

M. Transfer of Negotiable Documents of Title

1. Transfer of documents of title is very similar to transfer of negotiable instruments.
2. A document of title symbolizes ownership of the item it describes.
3. Types of documents of title

    a. Bill of lading is a document issued by a common carrier (a person engaged in the business of transporting or forwarding goods) and given to seller evidencing receipt of the goods for shipment

    b. A warehouse receipt is a document issued by a warehouseman (a person engaged in the business of storing goods for hire) and given to seller evidencing receipt of goods for storage

        (1) Warehouse receipt must contain the following terms:

            (a) Location of the warehouse
            (b) Date the receipt was issued
            (c) Statement to whom the goods will or can be delivered
            (d) Rates (charges) for storing the goods
            (e) Description of the goods.
            (f) Signature of the warehouseman

4. Form

    a. Document of title is negotiable if face of the document contains words of negotiability (order or bearer)

        (1) Document of title containing promise to deliver goods to the order of a named person is an order document

            (a) If person is named on face of document or, if there are endorsements, on back of document and last endorsement is a special endorsement, then document is an order document

                (1) Proper negotiation requires delivery of document and endorsement by named individual(s)

        (2) Document of title containing a promise to deliver the goods to bearer is bearer document

            (a) If "bearer" is stated on face of document or, if there are endorsements on back of document and last endorsement is a blank endorsement, it is a bearer document

                (1) Proper negotiation merely requires delivery of document

    b. Nonnegotiable (straight) documents of title are assigned, not negotiated

        (1) Assignee will never receive any better rights than assignor had

5. Due negotiation—document of title is "duly negotiated" when negotiated to a holder who takes it in good faith in the ordinary course of business without notice of a defense and pays value

    a. Value does not include payment of a preexisting (antecedent) debt—this is an important difference from value concept required to create a holder in due course for negotiable instruments

6. Holder by due negotiation acquires rights very similar to those acquired by a holder in due course

    a. These rights include

        (1) Title to document
        (2) Title to goods
        (3) All rights accruing under law of agency or estoppel, including rights to goods delivered after document was issued, and
        (4) The direct obligation of the issuer to hold or deliver the goods according to terms of document

    b. A holder by due negotiation defeats similar defenses to those defeated by a holder in due course for negotiable instruments (personal but not real defenses)

    c. A document of title procured by a thief upon placing stolen goods in a warehouse confers no rights in the underlying goods

        (1) This defense is valid against subsequent holder to whom document of title has been duly negotiated
        (2) Therefore, original owner of goods can assert better title to goods than a holder who has received document through due negotiation

7. Rights acquired in absence of due negotiation

    a. Transferee of a document, whether negotiable or nonnegotiable, to whom document has been delivered, but not duly negotiated, acquires title and rights which his/her transferor had or had actual authority to convey

8. Transferor for value warrants that

    a. Document is genuine
    b. S/he has no knowledge of any fact that would impair its validity or worth, and
    c. His/her negotiation or transfer is rightful and fully effective with respect to document of title and goods it represents

---

NOW REVIEW MULTIPLE-CHOICE QUESTIONS 47 THROUGH 50

N. Agencies Involved in Banking

1. Federal Reserve

    a. Central bank of US which regulates US monetary system and oversees bank holding companies

2. FDIC is US entity which insures customer deposits against bank failure

    a. Also created to help maintain public confidence and encourage stability in our financial system by promoting sound banking practices

3. OCC is arm of Treasury Department established to regulate and supervise national banks and federal branches of foreign banks

    a. Its objective is to promote safety and soundness of banking system
    b. Conducts on-site examination of banks

4. CFTC is US agency established to ensure open and efficient operation of futures markets which have grown from trading agricultural futures to more sophisticated financial products

5. OTS issues and enforces regulation governing nation's savings and loan industry

    a. This bureau is responsible for helping to ensure safety and soundness of deposits in thrift banks

6. Agencies involved in banking could be tested on CPA exam especially because of recent debates among business people and politicians over how to better regulate banks

    a. There is widespread consensus that current regulatory system does not work well enough
    b. Many are recommending merging the SEC and the CFTC, reflecting the blurred lines between securities and commodities

KEY TERMS

Bearer paper. A negotiable instrument that is payable to whomever possesses it.

Contract liability. When a party is responsible to pay the holder/HDC the face value of the instrument.

Draft. A type of negotiable instrument that contains an order to pay money. A draft has three parties: A drawer, a drawee, and the payee.

Drawer. The person who creates the draft and signs the draft on its face.

Drawee. The party that the drawer has instructed to pay the payee; typically this is the drawer's bank.

Endorsement. A signature, usually on the back of a negotiable instrument, by the payee or some other holder. The endorsement is **necessary** to further negotiate the instrument when the instrument is order paper.

Face value. The amount for which the instrument is payable.

Holder. A person who has possession of a negotiable instrument, and the instrument has all necessary endorsements.

Holder in due course (HDC). A holder with enhanced rights in the negotiable instrument. Those rights include the best claim of ownership, and HDC's claims for payment cannot be denied because of a personal defense.

Maker. The person who creates a note and has primary liability for its payment.

Negotiable. A characteristic of an instrument that means the instrument is freely transferable from one party to another.

Negotiation. The actual transfer of ownership of a negotiable instrument from one party to another. Negotiation can be accomplished by delivery alone if the instrument is bearer paper; if the instrument is order paper, then it must be transferred by delivery and the necessary endorsements.

Note. A two-party (the maker and payee) negotiable instrument that contains a promise to pay money.

Order paper. An instrument that is payable to a particular party.

Payee. The party to whom the negotiable instrument was originally payable.

Primary liability. The party from whom the holder/HDC of a negotiable instrument must first seek payment: the maker of a note or the acceptor of a draft.

Secondary liability. Parties who are liable to the holder/HDC if the primary party dishonors the instrument: endorsers and drawers.

Warranty liability. Responsibility to a holder/HDC to return the money actually paid for the negotiable instrument.

Multiple-Choice Questions (1–50)

B. Types of Negotiable Instruments

1.

```
To:       Middlesex National Bank

          Nassau, N.Y.

                                September 15, 2013

Pay to the order of   Robert Silver      $4,000.00

Four Thousand and xx/100              Dollars

On October 1, 2013

                                     Lynn Dexter
                                     _____
                                     Lynn Dexter
```

The above instrument is a

a. Draft.
b. Postdated check.
c. Trade acceptance.
d. Promissory note.

2. Which of the following statements regarding negotiable instruments is **not** correct?

a. A certificate of deposit is a type of note.
b. A check is a type of draft.
c. A promissory note is a type of draft.
d. A certificate of deposit is issued by a bank.

3. Based on the following instrument:

```
                                          May 19

I promise to pay to the order of A. B. Shark $1,000 (one
thousand and one hundred dollars) with interest thereon at
the rate of 12% per annum.

                         T. T. Tile
                         _____
                         T. T. Tile

                         Guaranty

I personally guaranty payment by T. T. Tile.

                         N. A. Abner
                         _____
                         N. A. Abner
```

The instrument is a

a. Promissory demand note.
b. Sight draft.
c. Check.
d. Trade acceptance.

4. Under the Negotiable Instruments Article of the UCC, which of the following documents would be considered an order to pay?

I. Draft
II. Certificate of deposit

a. I only.
b. II only.
c. Both I and II.
d. Neither I nor II.

C. Requirements of Negotiability

5. An instrument that is otherwise negotiable on its face states "Pay to Jenny Larson." Which of the following statements is (are) correct?

I.   It is negotiable if it is a check.
II. It is negotiable if it is a draft drawn on a corporation.
III. It is negotiable if it is a promissory note.

a. I only.
b. I and II only.
c. II and III only.
d. I, II, and III.

6. Under the Negotiable Instruments Article of the UCC, for a note to be negotiable it must

a. Be payable to order or to bearer.
b. Be signed by the payee.
c. Contain references to all agreements between the parties.
d. Contain necessary conditions of payment.

7. On February 15, P.D. Stone obtained the following instrument from Astor Co. for $1,000. Stone was aware that Helco, Inc. disputed liability under the instrument because of an alleged breach by Astor of the referenced computer purchase agreement. On March 1, Willard Bank obtained the instrument from Stone for $3,900. Willard had no knowledge that Helco disputed liability under the instrument.

```
                                       February 12

Helco, Inc. promises to pay to Astor Co. or bearer the
sum of $4,900 (four thousand four hundred and 00/100
dollars) on March 12 (maker may elect to extend due date
to March 31) with interest thereon at the rate of 12% per
annum.

                    HELCO, INC.

         By:  A. J. Help
              _____
              A. J. Help, President

Reference: Computer purchase agreement dated Febru-
ary 12
```

The reverse side of the instrument is endorsed as follows:

> Pay to the order of Willard Bank, without recourse
>
> *P.D. Stone*
> —————————
> P.D. Stone

The instrument is

- a. Nonnegotiable, because of the reference to the computer purchase agreement.
- b. Nonnegotiable, because the numerical amount differs from the written amount.
- c. Negotiable, even though the maker has the right to extend the time for payment.
- d. Negotiable, when held by Astor, but nonnegotiable when held by Willard Bank.

8. A draft made in the United States calls for payment in Canadian dollars.

- a. The draft is nonnegotiable because it calls for payment in money of another country.
- b. The draft is nonnegotiable because the rate of exchange may fluctuate thus violating the sum certain rule.
- c. The instrument is negotiable if it satisfies all of the other elements of negotiability.
- d. The instrument is negotiable only if it has the exchange rate written on the draft.

9. An instrument reads as follows:

> $10,000   Ludlow, Vermont   February 1
>
> I promise to pay to the order of Custer Corp. $10,000 within ten days after the sale of my two-carat diamond ring. I pledge the sale proceeds to secure my obligation hereunder.
>
> *R. Harris*
> —————————
> R. Harris

Which of the following statements correctly describes the above instrument?

- a. The instrument is nonnegotiable because it is **not** payable at a definite time.
- b. The instrument is nonnegotiable because it is secured by the proceeds of the sale of the ring.
- c. The instrument is a negotiable promissory note.
- d. The instrument is a negotiable sight draft payable on demand.

10. Kline is holding a promissory note in which he is the payer and Breck is the promissor. One of the terms of the note states that payment is subject to the terms of the contract dated March 1 of the current year between Breck and Kline. Does this term destroy negotiability?

- a. No, if the contract is readily available.
- b. No, since the note can be enforced without regard to the mentioned contract.
- c. No, as long as the terms in the mentioned contract are commercially reasonable.
- d. Yes, since this term causes the note to have a conditional promise.

11. Based on the following instrument:

> May 19
>
> I promise to pay to the order of A. B. Shark $1,000 (one thousand and one hundred dollars) with interest thereon at the rate of 12% per annum.
>
> *T. T. Tile*
> —————————
> T. T. Tile
>
> **Guaranty**
>
> I personally guaranty payment by T. T. Tile.
>
> *N. A. Abner*
> —————————
> N. A. Abner

The instrument is

- a. Nonnegotiable even though it is payable on demand.
- b. Nonnegotiable because the numeric amount differs from the written amount.
- c. Negotiable even though a payment date is **not** specified.
- d. Negotiable because of Abner's guaranty.

12. A note has an interest rate that varies based on the stated rate of 2% above the prime rate as determined by XYZ Bank in New York City. Under the Revised Article 3 of the Uniform Commercial Code, which of the following is true?

- a. This interest rate provision destroys negotiability since it does not constitute a sum certain.
- b. This note is not negotiable because the holder has to look outside the instrument to determine what the prime rate is.
- c. The interest rate provision destroys negotiability because the prime rate can vary before the time the note comes due.
- d. The interest rate provision is allowed in negotiable notes and does not destroy negotiability.

13. While auditing your client, Corbin Company, you see a check that is postdated and states "Pay to Corbin Company." You also see a note that is due in forty days and also says "Pay to Corbin Company." You note that both instruments contain all of the elements of negotiability except for possibly the ones raised by this fact pattern. Which of the following is(are) negotiable instruments?

- a. The check.
- b. The note.
- c. Both the check and the note.
- d. Neither the check nor the note.

14. Under the Revised Article 3 of the Uniform Code, which of the following is true if the maker of a note provides that payment must come out of a designated fund?

- a. This is allowed even though the maker is not personally obligated to pay.
- b. Since the instrument is not based on the general credit of the maker, the instrument is not negotiable.
- c. The promise to pay is conditional; therefore, the note is not negotiable.
- d. The instrument is not negotiable if the designated fund has insufficient funds.

D.   *Interpretation of Ambiguities in Negotiable Instruments*

15. Wyden holds a check that is written out to him. The check has the amount in words as five hundred dollars. The amount in figures on this check states $200. Which of the following is correct?

   a.   The check is cashable for $500.
   b.   The check is cashable for $200.
   c.   The check is not cashable because the amounts differ.
   d.   The check is not cashable because the amounts differ by more than 10%.
   e.   Negotiation

E.   *Negotiation*

16. Under the Negotiable Instruments Article of the UCC, an endorsement of an instrument "for deposit only" is an example of what type of endorsement?

   a.   Blank.
   b.   Qualified.
   c.   Restrictive.
   d.   Special.

17. Under the Negotiable Instruments Article of the UCC, which of the following requirements must be met for a transferee of order paper to become a holder?

   I.   Possession
   II. Endorsement of transferor

   a.   I only.
   b.   II only.
   c.   Both I and II.
   d.   Neither I nor II.

18. The following endorsements appear on the back of a negotiable promissory note payable to Lake Corp.

> Pay to John Smith only
> *Frank Parker*, President of Lake Corp.
>
> *John Smith*
>
> Pay to the order of Sharp, Inc. without recourse, but only if Sharp delivers computers purchased by Mary Harris by March 15.
>
> *Mary Harris*
>
> *Sarah Sharp,* President of Sharp, Inc.

Which of the following statements is correct?

   a.   The note became nonnegotiable as a result of Parker's endorsement.
   b.   Harris' endorsement was a conditional promise to pay and caused the note to be nonnegotiable.
   c.   Smith's endorsement effectively prevented further negotiation of the note.
   d.   Harris' signature was **not** required to effectively negotiate the note to Sharp.

19. A note is made payable to the order of Ann Jackson on the front. On the back, Ann Jackson signs it in blank and delivers

it to Jerry Lin. Lin puts "Pay to Jerry Lin" above Jackson's endorsement. Which of the following statements is false concerning this note?

   a.   After Lin wrote "Pay to Jerry Lin," the note became order paper.
   b.   After Jackson endorsed the note but before Lin wrote on it, the note was bearer paper.
   c.   Lin needs to endorse this note to negotiate it further, even though he personally wrote "Pay to Jerry Lin" on the back.
   d.   The note is not negotiable because Lin wrote "Pay to Jerry Lin" instead of "Pay to the order of Jerry Lin."

20. You are examining some negotiable instruments for a client. Which of the following endorsements can be classified as a special restrictive endorsement?

   a.   Pay to Alex Ericson if he completes the contracted work within ten days, (signed) Stephanie Sene.
   b.   Pay to Alex Ericson without recourse (signed) Stephanie Sene.
   c.   For deposit only, (signed) Stephanie Sene.
   d.   Pay to Alex Ericson, (signed) Stephanie Sene.

21. On February 15, P.D. Stone obtained the following instrument from Astor Co. for $1,000. Stone was aware that Helco, Inc. disputed liability under the instrument because of an alleged breach by Astor of the referenced computer purchase agreement. On March 1, Willard Bank obtained the instrument from Stone for $3,900. Willard had no knowledge that Helco disputed liability under the instrument.

> February 12
>
> Helco, Inc. promises to pay to Astor Co. or bearer the sum of $4,900 (four thousand four hundred and 00/100 dollars) on March 12 (maker may elect to extend due date to March 31) with interest thereon at the rate of 12% per annum.
>
> HELCO, INC.
>
> By: *A. J. Help*
> _____
> A. J. Help, President
>
> Reference: Computer purchase agreement dated February 12

The reverse side of the instrument is endorsed as follows:

> Pay to the order of Willard Bank, without recourse
>
> *P.D. Stone*
> _____
> P.D. Stone

Which of the following statements is correct?

   a.   Willard Bank **cannot** be a holder in due course because Stone's endorsement was without recourse.
   b.   Willard Bank must endorse the instrument to negotiate it.
   c.   Neither Willard Bank **nor** Stone are holders in due course.
   d.   Stone's endorsement was required for Willard Bank to be a holder in due course.

F. Holder in Due Course

22. Under the Negotiable Instruments Article of the UCC, which of the following circumstances would prevent a person from becoming a holder in due course of an instrument?

   a. The person was notified that payment was refused.
   b. The person was notified that one of the prior endorsers was discharged.
   c. The note was collateral for a loan.
   d. The note was purchased at a discount.

23. One of the requirements needed for a holder of a negotiable instrument to be a holder in due course is the value requirement. Ruper is a holder of a $1,000 check written out to her. Which of the following would **not** satisfy the value requirement?

   a. Ruper received the check from a tax client to pay off a four-month-old debt.
   b. Ruper took the check in exchange for a negotiable note for $1,200 which was due on that day.
   c. Ruper received the check in exchange for a promise to do certain specified services three months later.
   d. Ruper received the check for a tax service debt for a close relative.

24. Larson is claiming to be a holder in due course of two instruments. One is a draft that is drawn on Picket Company and says "Pay to Brunt." The other is a check that says "Pay to Brunt." Both are endorsed by Brunt on the back and made payable to Larson. Larson gave value for and acted in good faith concerning both the draft and the check. Larson also claims to be ignorant of any adverse claims on either instrument which are not overdue or have not been dishonored. Which of the following is (are) true?

   I. Larson is a holder in due course of the draft.
   II. Larson is a holder in due course of the check.

   a. I only.
   b. II only.
   c. Both I and II.
   d. Neither I nor II.

25. In order to be a holder in due course, the holder, among other requirements, must give value. Which of the following will satisfy this value requirement?

   I. An antecedent debt.
   II. A promise to perform services at a future date.

   a. I only.
   b. II only.
   c. Both I and II.
   d. Neither I nor II.

G. Rights of a Holder in Due Course

26. Bond fraudulently induced Teal to make a note payable to Wilk, to whom Bond was indebted. Bond delivered the note to Wilk. Wilk negotiated the instrument to Monk, who purchased it with knowledge of the fraud and after it was overdue. If Wilk qualifies as a holder in due course, which of the following statements is correct?

   a. Monk has the standing of a holder in due course through Wilk.
   b. Teal can successfully assert the defense of fraud in the inducement against Monk.
   c. Monk personally qualifies as a holder in due course.
   d. Teal can successfully assert the defense of fraud in the inducement against Wilk.

27. To the extent that a holder of a negotiable promissory note is a holder in due course, the holder takes the note free of which of the following defenses?

   a. Minority of the maker where it is a defense to enforcement of a contract.
   b. Forgery of the maker's signature.
   c. Discharge of the maker in bankruptcy.
   d. Nonperformance of a condition precedent.

28. Under the Negotiable Instruments Article of the UCC, in a nonconsumer transaction, which of the following are real defenses available against a holder in due course?

	Material alteration	Discharge of bankruptcy	Breach of contract
a.	No	Yes	Yes
b.	Yes	Yes	No
c.	No	No	Yes
d.	Yes	No	No

29. On February 15, P.D. Stone obtained the following instrument from Astor Co. for $1,000. Stone was aware that Helco, Inc. disputed liability under the instrument because of an alleged breach by Astor of the referenced computer purchase agreement. On March 1, Willard Bank obtained the instrument from Stone for $3,900. Willard had no knowledge that Helco disputed liability under the instrument.

February 12

Helco, Inc. promises to pay to Astor Co. or bearer the sum of $4,900 (four thousand four hundred and 00/100 dollars) on March 12, (maker may elect to extend due date to March 31) with interest thereon at the rate of 12% per annum.

HELCO, INC.

By: *A. J. Help*
_____
A. J. Help, President

Reference: Computer purchase agreement dated February 12

The reverse side of the instrument is endorsed as follows:

Pay to the order of Willard Bank, without recourse

P.D. Stone
_____
P.D. Stone

If Willard Bank demands payment from Helco and Helco refuses to pay the instrument because of Astor's breach of the computer purchase agreement, which of the following statements would be correct?

a. Willard Bank is **not** a holder in due course because Stone was **not** a holder in due course.
b. Helco will **not** be liable to Willard Bank because of Astor's breach.
c. Stone will be the only party liable to Willard Bank because he was aware of the dispute between Helco and Astor.
d. Helco will be liable to Willard Bank because Willard Bank is a holder in due course.

30. Northup made out a negotiable promissory note that was payable to the order of Port. This promissory note was meant to purchase some furniture that Port used to own, but he lied to Northup when he claimed he still owned it. Port immediately negotiated the note to Johnson who knew about Port's lie. Johnson negotiated the note to Kenner who was a holder in due course. Kenner then negotiated the note back to Johnson. When Johnson sought to enforce the promissory note against Northup, she refused claiming fraud. Which of the following is correct?

a. Johnson, as a holder through a holder in due course, can enforce the promissory note.
b. Northup wins because Johnson does not have the rights of a holder in due course.
c. Northup wins because she has a real defense on this note.
d. Johnson's knowledge of the lie does not affect his rights on this note.

31. Goran wrote out a check to Ruz to pay for a television set he purchased at a flea market from Ruz. When Goran got home, he found out the box did not have the television set but some weights. Goran immediately gave his bank a stop payment order over the phone. He followed this up with a written stop payment order. In the meantime, Ruz negotiated the check to Schmidt who qualified as a holder in due course. Schmidt gave the check as a gift to Buck. When Buck tried to cash the check, the bank and Goran both refused to pay. Which of the following is correct?

a. Buck cannot collect on the check from the bank because Goran has a real defense.
b. Buck cannot collect on the check from Goran because Goran has a personal defense.
c. Buck can require the bank to pay because Buck is a holder through a holder in due course.
d. Buck can require Goran to pay on the check even though the check was a gift.

32. Under the Negotiable Instruments Article of the UCC, which of the following parties will be a holder but **not** be entitled to the rights of a holder in due course?

a. A party who, knowing of a real defense to payment, received an instrument from a holder in due course.
b. A party who found an instrument payable to bearer.
c. A party who received, as a gift, an instrument from a holder in due course.
d. A party who, in good faith and without notice of any defect, gave value for an instrument.

33. A holder in due course will take free of which of the following defenses?

a. Infancy, to the extent that it is a defense to a simple contract.
b. Discharge of the maker in bankruptcy.
c. A wrongful filling-in of the amount payable that was omitted from the instrument.
d. Duress of a nature that renders the obligation of the party a nullity.

34. Cobb gave Garson a signed check with the amount payable left blank. Garson was to fill in, as the amount, the price of fuel oil Garson was to deliver to Cobb at a later date. Garson estimated the amount at $700, but told Cobb it would be no more than $900. Garson did not deliver the fuel oil, but filled in the amount of $1,000 on the check. Garson then negotiated the check to Josephs in satisfaction of a $500 debt with the $500 balance paid to Garson in cash. Cobb stopped payment and Josephs is seeking to collect $1,000 from Cobb. Cobb's maximum liability to Josephs will be

a. $0
b. $500
c. $900
d. $1,000

35. A maker of a note will have a real defense against a holder in due course as a result of any of the following conditions **except**

a. Discharge in bankruptcy.
b. Forgery.
c. Fraud in the execution.
d. Lack of consideration.

H. Liability of Parties

36. Which of the following parties has (have) **primary** liability on a negotiable instrument?

I. Drawer of a check.
II. Drawee of a time draft before acceptance.
III. Maker of a promissory note.

a. I and II only.
b. II and III only.
c. I and III only.
d. III only.

37. Which of the following actions does **not** discharge a prior party to a commercial instrument?

a. Good faith payment or satisfaction of the instrument.
b. Cancellation of that prior party's endorsement.
c. The holder's oral renunciation of that prior party's liability.
d. The holder's intentional destruction of the instrument.

38. Under the Negotiable Instruments Article of the UCC, when an instrument is endorsed "Pay to John Doe" and signed "Faye Smith," which of the following statements is (are) correct?

	Payment of the instrument is guaranteed	The instrument can be further negotiated
a.	Yes	Yes
b.	Yes	No
c.	No	Yes
d.	No	No

39.

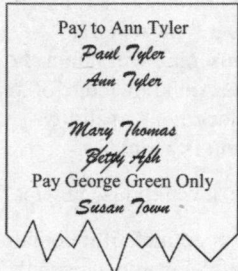

> Pay to Ann Tyler
> *Paul Tyler*
> *Ann Tyler*
>
> *Mary Thomas*
> *Betty Ash*
> Pay George Green Only
> *Susan Town*

Susan Town, on receiving the above instrument, struck Betty Ash's endorsement. Under the Negotiable Instruments Article of the UCC, which of the endorsers of the above instrument will be completely discharged from secondary liability to later endorsers of the instrument?

    a. Ann Tyler.
    b. Mary Thomas.
    c. Betty Ash.
    d. Susan Town.

40. A subsequent holder of a negotiable instrument may cause the discharge of a prior holder of the instrument by any of the following actions **except**

    a. Unexcused delay in presentment of a time draft.
    b. Procuring certification of a check.
    c. Giving notice of dishonor the day after dishonor.
    d. Material alteration of a note.

41. A check has the following endorsements on the back:

> *Paul Folk*
> without recourse
>
> **George Hopkins**
>
> payment guaranteed
>
> *Ann Quarry*
> collection guaranteed
>
> *Rachel Ott*

Which of the following conditions occurring subsequent to the endorsements would discharge all of the endorsers?

    a. Lack of notice of dishonor.
    b. Late presentment.
    c. Insolvency of the maker.
    d. Certification of the check.

42. Robb, a minor, executed a promissory note payable to bearer and delivered it to Dodsen in payment for a stereo system. Dodsen negotiated the note for value to Mellon by delivery alone and without endorsement. Mellon endorsed the note in blank and negotiated it to Bloom for value. Bloom's demand for payment was refused by Robb because the note was executed when Robb was a minor. Bloom gave prompt notice of Robb's default to Dodsen and Mellon. None of the holders of the note were aware of Robb's minority. Which of the following parties will be liable to Bloom?

	Dodsen	Mellon
a.	Yes	Yes
b.	Yes	No
c.	No	No
d.	No	Yes

43. Vex Corp. executed a negotiable promissory note payable to Tamp, Inc. The note was collateralized by some of Vex's business assets. Tamp negotiated the note to Miller for value. Miller endorsed the note in blank and negotiated it to Bilco for value. Before the note became due, Bilco agreed to release Vex's collateral. Vex refused to pay Bilco when the note became due. Bilco promptly notified Miller and Tamp of Vex's default. Which of the following statements is correct?

    a. Bilco will be unable to collect from Miller because Miller's endorsement was in blank.
    b. Bilco will be able to collect from either Tamp or Miller because Bilco was a holder in due course.
    c. Bilco will be unable to collect from either Tamp or Miller because of Bilco's release of the collateral.
    d. Bilco will be able to collect from Tamp because Tamp was the original payee.

44. Under the Negotiable Instruments Article of the UCC, which of the following statements **best** describes the effect of a person endorsing a check "without recourse"?

    a. The person has **no** liability to prior endorsers.
    b. The person makes **no** promise or guarantee of payment on dishonor.
    c. The person gives **no** warranty protection to later transferees.
    d. The person converts the check into order paper.

J. Banks

45. A check is postdated to November 20 even though the check was written out on November 3 of the same year. The drawer provided notice to the bank of the postdated check. Which of the following is correct under the Revised Article 3 of the Uniform Commercial Code?

    a. The check is payable on demand on or after November 3 because part of the definition of a check is that it be payable on demand.
    b. The check ceases to be demand paper and is payable on November 20.
    c. The postdating destroys negotiability.
    d. A bank that pays the check is automatically liable for early payment.

46. Stanley purchased a computer from Comp Electronics with a personal check. Later that day, Stanley saw a better deal on the computer so he orally stopped payment on the check with his bank. The bank, however, still paid Comp Electronics

when the check was presented three days later. Which of the
following is correct?

    a. The bank is liable to Stanley for failure to follow the
oral stop payment order.

    b. The bank is not liable to Stanley because the stop pay-
ment order was not in writing.

    c. The bank is not liable to Stanley if Comp Electronics
qualifies as a holder in due course.

    d. Comp Electronics is liable to Stanley to return the
amount of the check.

M.   *Transfer of Negotiable Documents of Title*

47. A trade acceptance is an instrument drawn by a

    a. Seller obligating the seller or designee to make pay-
ment.

    b. Buyer obligating the buyer or designee to make pay-
ment.

    c. Seller ordering the buyer or designee to make pay-
ment.

    d. Buyer ordering the seller or designee to make pay-
ment.

48. Under the Documents of Title Article of the UCC,
which of the following statements is (are) correct regarding a
common carrier's duty to deliver goods subject to a negotiable
bearer bill of lading?

  I. The carrier may deliver the goods to any party designated
by the holder of the bill of lading.

  II. A carrier who, without court order, delivers goods to a
party claiming the goods under a missing negotiable bill
of lading is liable to any person injured by the misdelivery.

    a. I only.
    b. II only.
    c. Both I and II.
    d. Neither I nor II.

49. Which of the following is **not** a warranty made by the
seller of a negotiable warehouse receipt to the purchaser of the
document?

    a. The document transfer is fully effective with respect
to the goods it represents.

    b. The warehouseman will honor the document.

    c. The seller has **no** knowledge of any facts that would
impair the document's validity.

    d. The document is genuine.

50. Under the UCC, a warehouse receipt

    a. Will **not** be negotiable if it contains a contractual
limitation on the warehouseman's liability.

    b. May qualify as both a negotiable warehouse receipt
and negotiable paper if the instrument is payable
either in cash or by the delivery of goods.

    c. May be issued only by a bonded and licensed ware-
houseman.

    d. Is negotiable if by its terms the goods are to be deliv-
ered to bearer or the order of a named person.

Multiple-Choice Answers and Explanations

Answers

1. a ___ ___	12. d ___ ___	22. c ___ ___	34. d ___ ___	45. b ___ ___
2. c ___ ___	13. a ___ ___	24. b ___ ___	35. d ___ ___	46. c ___ ___
3. a ___ ___	14. a ___ ___	25. a ___ ___	36. d ___ ___	47. c ___ ___
4. a ___ ___	15. a ___ ___	26. a ___ ___	37. c ___ ___	48. c ___ ___
5. a ___ ___	16. c ___ ___	27. d ___ ___	38. a ___ ___	49. b ___ ___
6. a ___ ___	17. c ___ ___	28. b ___ ___	39. c ___ ___	50. d ___ ___
7. c ___ ___	18. d ___ ___	29. d ___ ___	40. c ___ ___	
8. c ___ ___	19. d ___ ___	30. b ___ ___	41. d ___ ___	
9. a ___ ___	20. a ___ ___	31. d ___ ___	42. d ___ ___	
10. d ___ ___	21. b ___ ___	32. b ___ ___	43. c ___ ___	1st: ___/50 = ___%
11. c ___ ___	22. a ___ ___	33. c ___ ___	44. b ___ ___	2nd: ___/50 = ___%

Explanations

1. (a) This instrument is a draft because it is a three-party instrument where a drawer (Dexter) orders a drawee (Middlesex National Bank) to pay a fixed amount in money to the payee (Silver). Answer (b) is incorrect because in order for the instrument to qualify as a check, the instrument must be payable on demand. In this situation, the instrument held by Silver is a time draft which specifies the payment date as October 1, 2013. Answer (d) is incorrect because a promissory note is a two-party instrument in which one party promises to pay a fixed amount in money to the payee. Answer (c) is incorrect because a trade acceptance is a special type of draft in which a seller of goods extends credit to the buyer by drawing a draft on that buyer directing the buyer to pay a fixed amount in money to the seller on a specified date. The seller is therefore both the drawer and payee in a trade acceptance.

2. (c) Under the Revised Article 3 of the UCC, there are two basic categories of negotiable instruments (i.e., promissory notes and drafts). A certificate of deposit is a promissory note issued by a bank; therefore, answers (a) and (d) are incorrect. Answer (b) is incorrect because a check is a draft drawn on a bank and payable on demand unless it is postdated.

3. (a) A promissory demand note is a two-party instrument in which the maker (T. T. Tile) promises to pay to the order of the payee (A. B. Shark) and the payment is made upon demand with no time period stated. N. A. Abner made a guaranty but it is still a two-party note. Answers (b), (c), and (d) are all incorrect because sight drafts, checks, and trade acceptances are all three-party instruments requiring a drawee.

4. (a) Drafts and checks are three-party instruments in which the drawer orders the drawee to pay the payee. Notes and certificates of deposit are two-party instruments in which the maker promises to pay the payee.

5. (a) All negotiable instruments are required to be payable to order or bearer with the exception of checks. This instrument says "Pay to Jenny Larson," therefore, it can only be negotiable if it is a check. All of these instruments in the question would be negotiable if they said "Pay to the order of Jenny Larson," including a check.

6. (a) One of the elements of negotiability is that the note be payable to order or to bearer. Under the revised UCC, this is true for all negotiable instruments except checks that do not need the words "to the order of" or "bearer." Answer (b) is incorrect because signing by the payee is a method of negotiation but is not a requirement to make the instrument negotiable. Answer (c) is incorrect because such references are not required. Answer (d) is incorrect because the elements of negotiability do not require the stating of any conditions of payment. In fact, such conditions can destroy negotiability.

7. (c) This promissory note is negotiable because it meets all of the requirements of negotiability. It is written and signed. It contains an unconditional promise to pay a fixed amount in money. It is payable at a definite time under the UCC even though the maker may extend the due date to March 31, because this option of the maker to extend the time is limited to a definite date. And finally, the instrument is payable to bearer because it states "Pay to Astor Co. or bearer." Answer (a) is incorrect because the reference to the computer purchase agreement does not condition payment on this agreement, it simply refers to it. Answer (b) is incorrect because when the words and numbers are contradictory, the written words control and thus, the instrument still contains a fixed amount. Answer (d) is incorrect because once an instrument is negotiable and remains unaltered, it is negotiable for all parties.

8. (c) The Revised Article 3 of the UCC allows a negotiable instrument to be payable in any medium of exchange of the US or a foreign government. Therefore, answer (a) is incorrect. Answer (b) is incorrect because negotiability is maintained despite the fact that rate of exchange can fluctuate. This is a fact of doing business internationally. Answer (d) is incorrect because the exchange rate can be determined readily.

9. (a) This instrument satisfies all of the requirements for negotiability except for the requirement that it be payable on demand or at a definite time. Since it is payable ten days after the sale of the maker's diamond ring, the time of payment is not certain as to the time of occurrence. It is unknown when, or if, the ring will be sold. Answer (b) is incorrect because a negotiable instrument may contain a promise to provide collateral. Answer (c) is incorrect because although it is a two-party note, it is not negotiable because it is not payable at a definite time. Answer (d) is incorrect because it is not negotiable and is not a draft. A draft requires a drawer ordering a drawee to pay the payee.

10. (d) Since this note is subject to the terms of another document, the promise in the note is conditional, causing negotiability to be destroyed. Answer (a) is incorrect because since one must look to a document outside of the note, this destroys negotiability. Answer (b) is incorrect because the note itself makes its promise conditioned on the contract. Thus, the contract cannot be ignored. Answer (c) is incorrect because the contract, which is outside of the note, must be examined. This destroys the note's negotiability.

11. (c) For a note to be negotiable, it must be written and signed by the maker, contain an unconditional promise to pay a fixed amount in money, be payable at a definite time or on demand, and be payable to order or to bearer. This note fulfills all of these requirements. It is therefore negotiable and does not require that the payment date be specified because it is payable on demand. Answer (a) is incorrect because the note fulfills all the requirements of negotiability. Answer (b) is incorrect because in cases of inconsistencies between words and figures, the words control. Answer (d) is incorrect because although the guaranty may make the note more desirable, it was already negotiable.

12. (d) Under the Revised Article 3 of the UCC, interest rates are allowed to be variable or fluctuate. Negotiability is not destroyed. Answer (a) is incorrect because the sum certain rule allows the interest rate to vary based on such things as the prime rate of interest of a given bank. Answer (b) is incorrect because negotiability is not destroyed by needing to resort to information outside of the negotiable instrument. Answer (c) is incorrect because it is allowed for the interest to vary while the negotiable instrument is still outstanding.

13. (a) Under the Revised Article 3 of the UCC, a check may be postdated and need not be payable to order. The words "Pay to Corbin Company" are allowed for checks. However, all negotiable instruments other than checks need to be payable to order or to bearer.

14. (a) Under the Revised Article 3 of the UCC, unlike under earlier versions, payment on a negotiable instrument may be designated to come from a particular source or fund. The maker or drawer does not have to be personally obligated. Therefore, answer (b) is incorrect. Answer (c) is incorrect because this provision is not deemed to make the instrument not negotiable for reason of a conditional promise. Answer (d) is incorrect because lack of payment due to insufficient funds does not destroy negotiability.

15. (a) When the amount in words differs from the amount in figures on a negotiable instrument, the words control over the figures. Answer (b) is incorrect because the law has settled this ambiguity in favor of the words on negotiable instruments. An-

swer (c) is incorrect because the instrument is still negotiable and can be cashed. Answer (d) is incorrect because there is no such rule involving 10%.

16. (c) This is a very common type of restrictive endorsement. Answer (a) is incorrect because a blank endorsement is one that does not specify any endorsee. Answer (b) is incorrect because a qualified endorsement is one in which the endorser disclaims liability to pay the holder or any subsequent endorser for the instrument if it is later dishonored. An example of this is the endorser putting in the words "without recourse" on the back of the instrument. Answer (d) is incorrect because a special endorsement refers to when the endorser indicates a specific person who needs to subsequently endorse it.

17. (c) Although negotiating bearer paper only requires delivery, negotiating order paper requires both delivery and endorsement by the transferor. Delivery requires that the holder get possession of the instrument.

18. (d) Since John Smith endorsed the instrument in blank (i.e., did not specify any endorsee) it became bearer paper. Since it was bearer paper in Harris's hands, she did not need to endorse it to negotiate it to the next party, Sharp. Answer (a) is incorrect because when Parker endorsed "Pay to John Smith only" he made the instrument require John Smith's signature to negotiate it further. Parker's endorsement will not restrict negotiations beyond John Smith's and it does not destroy negotiability. Answer (b) is incorrect as although conditions on the front generally destroy the negotiability of an instrument, conditions put into an endorsement do not. Answer (c) is incorrect because the wording "Pay to John Smith only" will not restrict further negotiation after John Smith. When John Smith endorsed it in blank, it became bearer paper.

19. (d) The words "Pay to the order of Jerry Lin" are not necessary because the note is already negotiable on its face where it was payable to the order of Ann Jackson. Answer (a) is not chosen because although when Jackson endorsed the note in blank, it became bearer paper, it was converted back to order paper when Lin put "Pay to Jerry Lin" above Jackson's endorsement. Answer (b) should not be chosen because when Jackson endorsed it without specifying any payee, the note became bearer paper. Answer (c) should not be chosen because it became order paper once "Pay to Jerry Lin" was written, whether he personally did it or not.

20. (a) This endorsement is special because it indicates "Pay to Alex Ericson" and it is restrictive because of the phrase "if he completes…." Answer (b) is incorrect because this endorsement is special and qualified. Answer (c) is incorrect because although it is restrictive, it is also a blank endorsement. Answer (d) is incorrect because although it is a special endorsement stating "Pay to Alex Ericson," it is not restrictive.

21. (b) Although the note was originally a bearer instrument, Stone endorsed it with a special endorsement when s/he indicated "Pay to the order of Willard Bank, without recourse" above the endorsement. This means that Willard Bank must endorse the note to negotiate it further. Answer (a) is incorrect because qualified endorsements such as "without recourse" disclaim some liability but do not prevent subsequent parties from becoming a holder in due course. Answer (c) is incorrect because although Stone is not a holder in due course because s/he had notice that the maker disputed liability under the note, Willard Bank is a holder in due course because Willard was unaware that Helco disputed liability on the note. Additionally, Willard meets the other requirements to be a holder in due course, because he was a holder of a negotiable note, gave value ($3,900) for it, took in good faith, and had no notice, not only of the alleged breach by Astor, but of any other relevant problems such as being overdue or having been dishonored. Answer (d) is incorrect because the note was bearer paper when Stone received it and thus did not require an endorsement.

22. (a) To be a holder in due course, the holder must, among other things, take without notice that the instrument is overdue, has been dishonored, or that any person has a defense or claim to it. In this case, the person was notified that payment was refused. Answer (b) is incorrect because a prior endorser being discharged does not mean that person necessarily had a defense to the instrument. Answer (c) is incorrect because the use of a note as collateral does not prevent a holder from becoming a holder in due course. Answer (d) is incorrect because reasonable discounts are allowed and do not indicate bad faith or that a person has a defense or claim to the instrument.

23. (c) An executory promise does not satisfy the value requirement to be a holder in due course until the promise is actually performed. Answer (a) is incorrect because Ruper received the check to pay off a previous debt owed to her. Taking in satisfaction of a previous debt constitutes value to be a holder in due course. Answer (b) is incorrect because she took the check in exchange for another negotiable instrument. The fact that the check was for less than the face value of the negotiable note does not violate the value requirements. Answer (d) is incorrect because taking the check to pay off an antecedent debt constitutes value whether the debtor was a relative or not.

24. (b) In order to be a holder in due course, the individual must be a holder of a negotiable instrument as well as fulfilling the additional requirements referred to in the question. In this case, the draft is not negotiable because it is not payable to order or to bearer. However, the check is negotiable because checks do not have to be payable to order or to bearer to be negotiable.

25. (a) Even though an antecedent debt would not be valid for the consideration requirement under contract law, it is valid for the value requirement under negotiable instruments law. A promise to perform services at a future date is an executory promise and is not value until actually performed.

26. (a) Monk is not personally an HDC because although he was a holder of the negotiable note for which he gave value, he did not take in good faith because he had knowledge of the fraud before he purchased the note. Furthermore, he had notice that the note was overdue. Therefore, answer (c) can be ruled out. Answer (a) however, is correct because even though Monk was not an HDC, he obtained the instrument from Wilk who was an HDC. Therefore, Monk qualifies as a holder through an HDC and thus obtains all of the rights of an HDC. Answers (b) and (d) are incorrect because fraud in

the inducement is a personal defense. Wilk, as an HDC, and Monk, as a holder through an HDC, both take the note free of personal defenses.

27. (d) A holder in due course takes an instrument free of personal defenses but is subject to real defenses. Answer (d) is correct because it involves a breach of contract or nonperformance of a condition precedent which describes a personal defense. Answer (c) is incorrect because bankruptcy is a real defense. Answer (a) is incorrect because when a minor may disaffirm a contract, it is treated as a real defense. Answer (b) is incorrect because a forgery of a maker's or drawer's signature is a real defense.

28. (b) Real defenses include bankruptcy and material alterations of the instrument. Material alterations include a change of any monetary amount. They also include changes in the interest rate, if any, on the instrument or changes in the date if the date affects when it is paid or the amount of interest to be paid. Personal defenses include the more typical defenses such as breach of contract, breach of warranty, and fraud in the inducement.

29. (d) Helco is claiming breach of contract which is a personal defense. The general rule is that transfer of a negotiable instrument to a holder in due course cuts off all personal defenses against the holder in due course. Since Willard Bank is a holder in due course, Helco is liable to Willard Bank. Answer (a) is incorrect because Willard Bank meets all of the requirements to be a holder in due course. That is, Willard is a holder of a negotiable instrument, gave value, took in good faith, and took without notice of certain problems such as Helco's disputed liability. The fact that Stone was not a holder in due course does not change this. Answer (b) is incorrect because Willard Bank as a holder in due course wins against Helco's claim of Astor's breach. The breach of contract would only constitute a personal defense. Answer (c) is incorrect because Helco is liable to Willard Bank.

30. (b) When a negotiable instrument is negotiated from a holder in due course to another holder, this other holder normally obtains the rights of a holder in due course. However, an important exception applies to this case. Since Johnson knew of the lie when he first acquired the note, he was not an HDC and cannot improve his status by reacquiring from an HDC. Answer (a) is incorrect because he did not qualify as an HDC due to his knowledge of the defense. Answer (c) is incorrect because fraud in the inducement is a personal, not real, defense. Answer (d) is incorrect because his knowledge of the lie prevents his becoming an HDC at first and prevents his later becoming a holder through a holder in due course.

31. (d) Even though Buck did not personally qualify as an HDC, he was a holder through a holder in due course and can collect from the drawer despite the drawer's personal defense. Answer (a) is incorrect because Goran's defense is a personal defense. Also, the bank is permitted to follow the customer's stop payment order. Answer (b) is incorrect because Buck as a holder through a holder in due course can collect despite the personal defense. Answer (c) is incorrect because the bank is permitted to refuse payment and then Buck collects from the drawer.

Module 28: Negotiable Instruments

32. (b) A party who found an instrument payable to bearer is a holder but not a holder through a holder in due course. To be the latter, s/he must obtain a negotiable instrument from a holder in due course. If this had been the case, s/he would have obtained the rights of a holder in due course. However, since s/he found the instrument, it cannot be established that the previous holder was a holder in due course. Answer (a) is incorrect because s/he did receive the instrument from a holder in due course. S/he, therefore, does obtain the rights of a holder in due course even though s/he cannot be a holder in due course him/herself because of having notice of the defense on the instrument. Answer (c) is incorrect because the party received the instrument from a holder in due course and thus becomes a holder through a holder in due course. Answer (d) is incorrect because this party personally qualifies as a holder in due course, thereby obtaining those rights.

33. (c) An unauthorized completion of an incomplete instrument is a personal defense, and, as such, will not be valid against an HDC. Infancy (unless the instrument is exchanged for necessaries), bankruptcy of the maker, and extreme duress are all real defenses which are good against an HDC therefore answers (a), (b), and (d) are incorrect.

34. (d) Since Cobb left the amount blank on the signed check and Garson filled it in contrary to Cobb's instructions, this is a case of unauthorized completion which is a personal defense. Garson then negotiated the check to Josephs who is a holder in due course because he gave value for the negotiable instrument and took in good faith without notice of any problems. He gave value for the full $1,000 since cash and taking the check for a previous debt are both value under negotiable instrument law. Therefore, Josephs may collect the full $1,000 and prevail against the personal defense that Cobb has.

35. (d) A maker of a note may use real defenses against a holder in due course but not personal defenses. Lack of consideration is a personal defense. Discharge in bankruptcy, forgery, and fraud in the execution are all real defenses, which create a valid defense against a holder in due course; therefore, answers (a), (b), and (c) are incorrect.

36. (d) The maker of a note has **primary** liability on that note. No one has primary liability on a draft or check unless the drawee accepts it. This is true because although the drawee has been ordered by the drawer to pay, the drawee has not agreed to pay unless it accepts the draft or check.

37. (c) When there are multiple endorsers on a negotiable instrument, each is liable to subsequent endorsers or holders. Oral renunciation of a prior party's liability does not discharge that party's liability. Renunciation must be in writing to discharge liability. Answer (a) is incorrect because once the primary party pays on the instrument, all endorsers are discharged from liability. Answer (b) is incorrect because cancellation of a prior party's endorsement does discharge that party's liability. Answer (d) is incorrect because when a holder intentionally destroys a negotiable instrument, the prior endorsers are discharged.

38. (a) When a negotiable instrument is endorsed and a specific person is indicated, the instrument is order paper and can be further negotiated by that person. Note also that

payment of the instrument is guaranteed. If the primary party to the negotiable instrument does not pay, the endorser(s) are obligated to pay on the instrument when the holder demands payment or acceptance in a timely manner.

39. (c) Striking out the endorsement of a person discharges that person's secondary liability and discharges subsequent endorsers who have already endorsed. This does not, however, discharge any of the prior parties. Therefore, in this case, Betty Ash is discharged from secondary liability to the later endorsers. All of the other endorsers are secondarily liable since their signature were not struck and none of them signed without recourse. Therefore, answer (a), (b), and (d) are incorrect.

40. (c) Various acts or failures of a holder can cause a discharge of prior holders of an instrument. Among these are an unexcused delay in presenting an instrument, cancellation or renunciation of the instrument, fraudulent or material alteration, and certification of a check. Notice of dishonor generally should be given by midnight of the third business day after the dishonor or notice of the dishonor. Banks must give notice by midnight of the next banking day. In either case, answer (c) is correct. Answers (a), (b), and (d) are all incorrect because they are all acts that cause the discharge of prior holders.

41. (d) When a holder procures certification of a check, all prior endorsers are discharged. This is true because when a bank certifies a check, it has accepted the check and agreed to honor it as presented. Answers (a) and (b) are incorrect because although lack of notice of dishonor to other endorsers and late presentment of the instrument will normally discharge all endorsers, this is not true if the lack of notice of dishonor or the late presentment is excused. They can be excused in such cases as the delay is beyond the party's control or the presentment is waived. Furthermore in this fact pattern, Hopkins endorsed the check "payment guaranteed" and Quarry endorsed it "collection guaranteed." When words of guaranty are used, presentment or notice of dishonor are not required to hold the users liable. Answer (c) is incorrect because when the maker is insolvent the endorsers will likely be sought after for payment.

42. (d) Since Dodsen did not endorse the note, s/he gave transfer warranties and presentment warranties only to the immediate transferee (i.e., Mellon). Mellon gave these warranties to Bloom. Therefore although Mellon will be liable to Bloom, Dodsen will not be.

43. (c) Normally, Bilco could seek collection on the defaulted note from the previous endorsers, Tamp and Miller. However, in this case, Bilco agreed to release the collateral underlying this note. Since this materially affects the rights of Tamp and Miller to use this collateral, this act releases them. Answer (a) is incorrect because except for the release of the collateral, Bilco could have collected from his/her immediate transferor even without the endorsement. Answers (b) and (d) are incorrect because the release of the collateral releases Tamp and Miller.

44. (b) When a person endorses a negotiable instrument, s/he is normally secondarily liable to later endorsers. This liability means that the endorser can be required to make good on the instrument. If s/he endorses without recourse, the endorser can avoid this liability. Answer (a) is incorrect because the endorser is not liable to prior endorsers anyway whether or not s/he endorses without recourse. Answer (c) is incorrect because the endorser still gives the transferor's warranties with some modification. Answer (d) is incorrect because a check is converted into order paper only if the endorser also specifies a payee.

45. (b) Under the Revised Article 3, postdating a check does not destroy negotiability, but makes the check properly payable on or after the date written on the check; therefore answers (a) and (c) are incorrect. Although the postdated check is not properly payable before the date on the instrument, if a bank pays it earlier, it is not liable unless the drawer had notified the bank that the check was postdated. The word "automatically" is what makes answer (d) incorrect.

46. (c) If the bank fails to follow a stop payment order, it is liable to the customer only if the customer had a valid defense on the check and therefore suffers a loss. Comp Electronics, the payee, can qualify as an HDC and Stanley would have to pay anyway despite the stop payment order. Answer (a) is incorrect because the bank did not cause Stanley a loss. Answer (b) is incorrect because oral stop payment orders are valid for fourteen days. Answer (d) is incorrect because from the facts given, there is no evidence that Comp Electronics breached the contract.

47. (c) A trade acceptance is a special type of draft in which a seller of goods extends credit to the buyer by drawing the draft on the buyer ordering the buyer to make payment to the seller on a specified date. Since the trade acceptance is drawn by the seller, answers (b) and (d) are incorrect. Answer (a) is incorrect because the buyer not the seller is ordered to make payment.

48. (c) A negotiable bearer bill of lading is a document of title that under the UCC allows the bearer the rights to the goods mentioned including the right to designate who will receive delivery of the goods. The carrier is required to deliver the goods to the holder of negotiable bearer bill of lading or to that holder's designee. The carrier is liable for any misdelivery for any damages caused.

49. (b) A person who negotiates a negotiable document of title for value extends the following warranties to the immediate purchaser: (1) negotiation by the transferor is rightful and fully effective with respect to the goods it represents, (2) the transferor has no knowledge of any facts that would impair the document's validity or worth, and (3) the document is genuine; therefore answers (a), (c), and (d) are incorrect. However, the transferor of a negotiable warehouse receipt does not necessarily warrant that the warehouseman will honor the document.

50. (d) A negotiable warehouse receipt is a document issued as evidence of receipt of goods by a person engaged in the business of storing goods for hire. The warehouse receipt is negotiable if the face of the document contains the words of negotiability (order or bearer). Answer (a) is incorrect because the negotiability of the warehouse receipt is not destroyed by the inclusion of a contractual limitation on the warehouseman's liability. Answer (b) is incorrect because to qualify as negotiable paper, the instrument must be payable only in money. If an instrument is payable in money or by the delivery of goods, it is a nonnegotiable instrument. Answer (c) is incorrect because the UCC does not state that only a bonded and licensed warehouseman can issue a warehouse receipt.

Simulations

Task-Based Simulation 1

Fact Patterns		
	Authoritative Literature	Help

This simulation has four separate fact patterns, each followed by five legal conclusions relating to the fact pattern preceding those five numbered legal conclusions. Determine whether each conclusion is Correct or Incorrect.

An instrument purports to be a negotiable instrument. It otherwise fulfills all the elements of negotiability and it states "Pay to Rich Crane."

	Correct	Incorrect
1. It is negotiable if it is a check and Rich Crane has possession of the check.	○	○
2. It is negotiable if it is a draft drawn on a corporation.	○	○
3. It is negotiable if it is a promissory note due one year later with 5% interest stated on its face.	○	○
4. It is negotiable if it is a certificate of deposit.	○	○
5. It is negotiable even if it is a cashier's check.	○	○

Another instrument fulfills all of the elements of negotiability except possibly one, that is, the instrument does not identify any payee.

	Correct	Incorrect
6. The instrument is **not** negotiable if it is a draft.	○	○
7. The instrument is bearer paper if it is a check.	○	○
8. The instrument is negotiable if it is a promissory note.	○	○
9. The instrument is bearer paper if it is a promissory note.	○	○
10. The instrument is negotiable only if it also states the word "negotiable" on its face.	○	○

A promissory note states that the maker promises to pay to the order of ABC Company $10,000 plus interest at 2% above the prime rate of XYZ Bank in New York City one year from the date on the promissory note.

	Correct	Incorrect
11. The interest rate provision destroys negotiability because the prime rate can fluctuate during the year.	○	○
12. The interest rate provision destroys negotiability because one has to look outside the note to see what the prime rate of XYZ Bank is.	○	○
13. The maker is obligated to pay only the $10,000 because the amount of interest is not a sum certain.	○	○
14. The maker must pay $10,000 plus the judgment rate of interest because the amount of interest cannot be determined without referring to facts outside the instrument.	○	○
15. Any holder of this note could not qualify as a holder in due course because of the interest provision.	○	○

An individual fills out his personal check. He postdates the check for ten days later, notifies his bank of the postdated check, and notes on the face of the check that it is for "Payment for textbooks."

	Correct	Incorrect
16. The instrument is demand paper because it is a check and is thus payable immediately.	○	○
17. The check is not payable before the date on its face.	○	○
18. If a bank pays on this check before its stated date, the bank is liable to the drawer.	○	○
19. The notation "Payment for textbooks" destroys negotiability because it makes payment conditional.	○	○
20. The notation "Payment for textbooks" does **not** destroy negotiability but only if the check was actually used to pay for textbooks.	○	○

Task-Based Simulation 2

Instruments		
	Authoritative Literature	**Help**

During an audit of Trent Realty Corp.'s financial statements, Clark, CPA, reviewed two instruments.

Instrument 1

$300,000   Belle, MD
                                                                             April 1, 2009

For value received, ten years after date, I promise to pay to the order of Dart Finance Co. Three Hundred Thousand and 00/100 dollars with interest at 9% per annum compounded annually until fully paid.

This instrument arises out of the sale of land located in MD.

It is further agreed that

    1. Maker will pay all costs of collection including reasonable attorney fees.
    2. Maker may prepay the amount outstanding on any anniversary date of this instrument.

                                        G. Evans
                                        ‾‾‾‾‾‾‾‾‾
                                        G. Evans

The following transactions relate to Instrument 1.

- On March 15, 2010, Dart endorsed the instrument in blank and sold it to Morton for $275,000.
- On July 10, 2010, Evans informed Morton that Dart had fraudulently induced Evans into signing the instrument.
- On August 15, 2010, Trent, which knew of Evans' claim against Dart, purchased the instrument from Morton for $50,000.

Items 1 through 5 relate to Instrument 1. For each item, select from List I the correct answer. An answer may be selected once, more than once, or not at all.

List I

A.	Draft	E.	Holder in due course	H.	Nonnegotiable
B.	Promissory Note	F.	Holder with rights of a holder in due	I.	Evans, Morton, and Dart
C.	Security Agreement		course under the shelter provision	J.	Morton and Dart
D.	Holder	G.	Negotiable	K.	Only Dart

(A) (B) (C) (D) (E) (F) (G) (H) (I) (J) (K)

	(A)	(B)	(C)	(D)	(E)	(F)	(G)	(H)	(I)	(J)	(K)
1. Instrument 1 is a (type of instrument)	○	○	○	○	○	○	○	○	○	○	○
2. Instrument 1 is (negotiability)	○	○	○	○	○	○	○	○	○	○	○
3. Morton is considered a (type of ownership)	○	○	○	○	○	○	○	○	○	○	○
4. Trent is considered a (type of ownership)	○	○	○	○	○	○	○	○	○	○	○
5. Trent could recover on the instrument from (liable party[ies])	○	○	○	○	○	○	○	○	○	○	○

Instrument 2

<table>
<tr><td align="center">**Front**</td><td align="center">**Back**</td></tr>
<tr>
<td>

To: Pure Bank
         Upton, VT

               April 5, 2013

Pay to the order of M. West $1,500.00
One Thousand Five Hundred and 00/100
Dollars on May 1, 2013

         W. Fields
         ———————
         W. Fields

</td>
<td>

M. West

Pay to C. Larr
T. Keetin

C. Larr
without recourse

</td>
</tr>
</table>

Items 6 through 13 relate to Instrument 2. For each item, select from List II the correct answer. An answer may be selected once, more than once, or not at all.

List II

A. Bearer paper	F. Nonnegotiable
B. Blank	G. Note
C. Check	H. Order paper
D. Draft	I. Qualified
E. Negotiable	J. Special

                                    (A) (B) (C) (D) (E) (F) (G) (H) (I) (J)

6. Instrument 2 is a (type of instrument)   ○ ○ ○ ○ ○ ○ ○ ○ ○ ○

7. Instrument 2 is (negotiability)   ○ ○ ○ ○ ○ ○ ○ ○ ○ ○

8. West's endorsement makes the instrument (type of instrument)   ○ ○ ○ ○ ○ ○ ○ ○ ○ ○

9. Keetin's endorsement makes the instrument (type of instrument)   ○ ○ ○ ○ ○ ○ ○ ○ ○ ○

10. Larr's endorsement makes the instrument (type of instrument)   ○ ○ ○ ○ ○ ○ ○ ○ ○ ○

11. West's endorsement would be considered (type of endorsement)   ○ ○ ○ ○ ○ ○ ○ ○ ○ ○

12. Keetin's endorsement would be considered (type of endorsement)   ○ ○ ○ ○ ○ ○ ○ ○ ○ ○

13. Larr's endorsement would be considered (type of endorsement)   ○ ○ ○ ○ ○ ○ ○ ○ ○ ○

Simulation Solutions

Task-Based Simulation 1

Fact Patterns		
	Authoritative Literature	Help

	Correct	Incorrect
1. It is negotiable if it is a check and Rich Crane has possession of the check.	●	○
2. It is negotiable if it is a draft drawn on a corporation.	○	●
3. It is negotiable if it is a promissory note due one year later with 5% interest stated on its face.	○	●
4. It is negotiable if it is a certificate of deposit.	○	●
5. It is negotiable even if it is a cashier's check.	●	○

Explanations

1. (C) Even though the instrument states "Pay to Rich Crane," it is negotiable because a check does **not** have to be payable to order or bearer.

2. (I) A draft to be negotiable must be payable to order or to bearer, regardless of the drawer of the draft. "Pay to the order of Rich Crane" would have made it negotiable.

3. (I) Promissory notes to be negotiable must be payable to order or to bearer.

4. (I) Certificates of deposit, unlike checks, must be payable to order or to bearer.

5. (C) A cashier's check is an actual check and thus does **not** have to be payable to order or to bearer.

	Correct	Incorrect
6. The instrument is **not** negotiable if it is a draft.	○	●
7. The instrument is bearer paper if it is a check.	●	○
8. The instrument is negotiable if it is a promissory note.	●	○
9. The instrument is bearer paper if it is a promissory note.	●	○
10. The instrument is negotiable only if it also states the word "negotiable" on its face.	○	●

Explanations

6. (I) If an instrument does not name any payee, it is considered to be payable to bearer. Thus, negotiability is not destroyed.

7. (C) If no payee is named, it is bearer paper.

8. (C) Since no payee was named, it is bearer paper and thus negotiability is maintained.

9. (C) Like the cases of drafts, checks, and certificates of deposit, it is bearer paper.

10. (I) There is no such requirement to state "negotiable" on its face.

	Correct	Incorrect
11. The interest rate provision destroys negotiability because the prime rate can fluctuate during the year.	○	●
12. The interest rate provision destroys negotiability because one has to look outside the note to see what the prime rate of XYZ Bank is.	○	●
13. The maker is obligated to pay only the $10,000 because the amount of interest is **not** a sum certain.	○	●
14. The maker must pay $10,000 plus the judgment rate of interest because the amount of interest cannot be determined without referring to facts outside the instrument.	○	●
15. Any holder of this note could **not** qualify as a holder in due course because of the interest provision.	○	●

Explanations

11. (I) The negotiability of an instrument is not destroyed simply because the interest rate used may fluctuate.

12. (I) Negotiability is not destroyed even if one has to look outside of the document to determine what the actual rate is.

13. (I) Even though the interest rate may fluctuate, the maker is still obligated to pay the $10,000 plus the interest.

14. (I) The maker must pay the $10,000 plus the interest described on the promissory note.

15. (I) Since this note is negotiable despite the possible fluctuation of the interest rate, a holder could qualify to be a holder in due course under those applicable rules.

	Correct	Incorrect
16. The instrument is demand paper because it is a check and is thus payable immediately.	○	●
17. The check is **not** payable before the date on its face.	●	○
18. If a bank pays on this check before its stated date, the bank is liable to the drawer.	●	○
19. The notation "Payment for textbooks" destroys negotiability because it makes payment conditional.	○	●
20. The notation "Payment for textbooks" does **not** destroy negotiability but only if the check was actually used to pay for textbooks.	○	●

Explanations

16. (I) Normally a check is demand paper. However, when it is postdated, it is not payable until that date.

17. (C) The postdating overrides the normal characteristic that it is payable on demand.

18. (C) The bank is liable because the drawer has given the bank prior notice of the postdating.

19. (I) Notations on negotiable instruments that note what it is for do not put conditions on the payment and thus do not destroy negotiability.

20. (I) These notations can be ignored because they are not conditions of payment.

Task-Based Simulation 2

Instruments		
	Authoritative Literature	Help

	(A)	(B)	(C)	(D)	(E)	(F)	(G)	(H)	(I)	(J)	(K)
1. Instrument 1 is a (type of instrument)	○	●	○	○	○	○	○	○	○	○	○
2. Instrument 1 is (negotiability)	○	○	○	○	○	○	●	○	○	○	○
3. Morton is considered a (type of ownership)	○	○	○	○	●	○	○	○	○	○	○
4. Trent is considered a (type of ownership)	○	○	○	○	○	●	○	○	○	○	○
5. Trent could recover on the instrument from (liable party[ies])	○	○	○	○	○	○	○	○	●	○	○

Explanations

1. (B) Instrument 1 is a two-party instrument in which Evans promises to pay a fixed amount in money to Dart; therefore it qualifies as a promissory note. A promissory note may be payable on demand or at a specific point in time.

2. (G) Instrument 1 meets the requirements of negotiability. It is written and signed by the maker. It contains an unconditional promise or order to pay a fixed amount in money, at a definite time or on demand. The document is also payable to order. The fact that it is payable on a certain date subject to acceleration does not destroy its negotiability.

3. (E) To qualify as a holder in due course, an individual must be a holder of a properly negotiated negotiable instrument, give value for the instrument, and take the instrument in good faith and without notice that it is overdue, has been dishonored, or that any person has a defense or claim to it.

4. (F) When a negotiable instrument is negotiated from a holder in due course to a second holder, the second holder usually acquires the rights of a holder in due course through the shelter provision. The shelter provision applies to holders who have not previously held the instrument with knowledge of any defenses.

5. (I) A holder with rights of a holder in due course under the shelter provision obtains all the rights of a holder in due course. A holder in due course takes an instrument free of personal defenses, including fraud in the inducement. Therefore, Evans' claim that Dart had fraudulently induced Evans into signing the instrument would not prevent Trent from recovering from Evans. Trent would also be able to recover from Morton and Dart based on his holder in due course status.

	(A)	(B)	(C)	(D)	(E)	(F)	(G)	(H)	(I)	(J)
6. Instrument 2 is a (type of instrument)	○	○	○	●	○	○	○	○	○	○
7. Instrument 2 is (negotiability)	○	○	○	○	●	○	○	○	○	○
8. West's endorsement makes the instrument (type of instrument)	●	○	○	○	○	○	○	○	○	○
9. Keetin's endorsement makes the instrument (type of instrument)	○	○	○	○	○	○	○	●	○	○
10. Larr's endorsement makes the instrument (type of instrument)	●	○	○	○	○	○	○	○	○	○
11. West's endorsement would be considered (type of endorsement)	○	●	○	○	○	○	○	○	○	○
12. Keetin's endorsement would be considered (type of endorsement)	○	○	○	○	○	○	○	○	○	●
13. Larr's endorsement would be considered (type of endorsement)	○	○	○	○	○	○	○	○	●	○

Explanations

6. **(D)** Instrument 2 is a draft because it is a three-party instrument where a drawer (Fields) orders a drawee (Pure Bank) to pay a fixed amount in money to the payee (West). It is not a check because it is not payable on demand.

7. **(E)** The draft qualifies as a negotiable instrument as it meets all of the required elements of negotiability. The draft is written and signed by the drawer. It contains an unconditional order to pay a fixed amount in money. It is made payable to order and is payable at a definite time.

8. **(A)** A blank endorsement which does not specify any endorsee converts order paper to bearer paper.

9. **(H)** An endorsement which indicates the specific person to whom the endorsee wishes to negotiate the instrument is a special endorsement. The use of a special endorsement converts bearer paper into order paper.

10. **(A)** Because Larr's endorsement does not specify any endorsee, the endorsement converts the order paper into bearer paper.

11. **(B)** West's endorsement is a blank endorsement because it does not specify any endorsee.

12. **(J)** Because Keetin's endorsement indicates a specific person to whom the instrument is being negotiated, the endorsement is a special endorsement.

13. **(I)** Larr's endorsement is a qualified endorsement because Larr disclaimed liability by signing without recourse.

Module 29: Secured Transactions

Overview

The concept of secured transactions is important to modern business. A creditor often requires some security from the debtor beyond a mere promise to pay. In general, the creditor may require the debtor to provide some collateral to secure payment on the debt. The creditor then becomes known as a secured party because the debt repayment has additional assurance of collateral rather than just the mere promise to repay. If the debt is not paid, the creditor then can resort to the collateral. Under Revised Article 9 of the UCC, the collateral is generally personal property. You need to understand the concept of attachment as discussed in this module. You also need to understand the important concept of perfection

discussed in this module that allows a secured party to obtain greater rights over many third parties. Be sure to understand the three methods by which perfection can be accomplished. The examination also covers rules of priorities when competing interests exist in the same collateral. Before beginning the reading you should review the key terms at the end of the module.

A. The Elements of Secured Transactions

1. The parties

   a. Secured party is the person/bank that provides credit to the debtor and takes an interest in the debtor's collateral to help assure repayment of the debt

      (1) Debtor is entity (or person) that owes either payment or some specified performance to the secured party
      (2) Security interest is legal interest in collateral that secures either payment or debtor's specified performance of some obligation
      (3) Security agreement is transaction that creates security interest

2. Types of collateral

   a. Goods: Moveable, tangible personal property, which is classified by the initial reason the debtor bought the goods (these classifications are very important)

      (1) Consumer goods are goods that were purchased for personal use
      (2) Equipment is goods that were purchased for use in a business
      (3) Inventory is goods that were purchased for sale or lease to a third party

---

EXAMPLE

Think of a computer. If I purchased a computer for use in my home, it is a consumer good. If I purchased a computer to use for my business, even if it is in my home, then the computer is equipment. If I purchased the computer to resell at my computer store, then it is inventory.

---

    (4) Fixtures are goods that have been attached permanently or relatively permanently to real property

    (5) Farm products are goods produced on a farm such as livestock or crops.

  b. Indispensible paper: Collateral evidenced by a writing

    (1) Instruments, which include negotiable instruments (see Module 28) as well as stock, bonds, and other investment securities.

    (2) Chattel paper is a writing that provides evidence of the monetary obligation and the security interest in the good. Basically, a piece of paper that recites the indebtedness.

    (3) Documents of title, such as bills of lading and warehouse receipts (This is discussed in more detail in Module 28, subsection M.)

  c. Intangibles include

    (1) Account, or account receivable

    (2) Commercial tort claim

    (3) General intangibles, includes anything else that may be considered collateral, such as intellectual property rights or goodwill.

3. The security agreement

  a. This is an agreement between the debtor and the creditor, which gives the creditor a security interest in the debtor's collateral.

  b. Requirements of a valid security agreement

    (1) The agreement must be in writing, unless the creditor has physical possession of the collateral (a pledge)

    (2) Must be signed by the debtor; creditor's signature is not required

    (3) A reasonable description of the collateral

B. Attachment of Security Interests

1. Attachment is a term used to describe the moment when security interest is enforceable against a debtor by the secured party

2. Security interest attaches when all of the following occur in any order (these are important)

  a. Secured party gives value (value is any consideration that supports any contract)

    (1) Preexisting claim (although not consideration) is value

---

EXAMPLE

D already owes S $5,000 on a previous debt. Subsequently, D signs a security agreement giving S an interest in some furniture owned by D. Value has been given by S based on the previous debt.

EXAMPLE

A bank grants a loan to allow B to purchase a washer and dryer. This extension of credit is a typical type of value.

---

  b. Debtor has rights in collateral

    (1) Debtor must have rights in collateral

      (a) Ownership interest suffices or having some right to possession of collateral but debtor is not required to have actual legal title

> **EXAMPLE**
>
> M obtains a loan from a bank to purchase a sofa. She signs a security agreement granting the credit union a security interest in any sofa that she will buy with this loan. Attachment cannot occur until she buys a sofa. Note that the other two elements of attachment have occurred.

   c. A valid security agreement (See A.3. above for requirements of security agreement) unless the secured party has a pledge (physical possession of the collateral)

> **NOW REVIEW MULTIPLE-CHOICE QUESTIONS 1 THROUGH 6**

C. Perfecting a Security Interest

1. Entails steps **in addition to** attachment (with one exception discussed later) to give secured party priority over many other parties that may claim collateral

   a. Attachment focuses primarily on rights between creditor and debtor
   b. Perfection, however, focuses on rights between various **other parties** that may claim an interest in same collateral

      (1) Generally, perfecting a security interest gives (constructive) **notice to other parties** that the perfecting party claims an interest (security interest) in certain collateral
      (2) Only an attached security interest can be perfected

2. There are three primary ways that an attached security interest may be perfected—these are important

   a. Most security interests either can or must be perfected by filing financing statement(s) in the appropriate state office
   b. Secured party takes possession of collateral, or in certain cases takes control
   c. Automatic perfection can occur, but only with a purchase money security interest in consumer goods

3. Depending on the type of collateral there may be only one way or there may be several ways to perfect
4. Perfection by filing financing statement(s)

   a. Financing statement requirements

      (1) Names of the debtor and the secured party
      (2) Indication of collateral covered; descriptions such as "all assets" are sufficient
      (3) Signatures are not required on a financing statement; the debtor's signature, however, is required on the security agreement, see A.3. above.
      (4) Minor errors in financing statement do not invalidate it if they are not seriously misleading
      (5) Law now allows that filing may be done either electronically or in writing

   b. Filings last for five years but can be continued with a continuation statement if filed within six months of expiration
   c. Financing statements can be refiled for each new five-year period

5. Perfection by secured party's possession or control of collateral

   a. Possession means actual physical possession of the collateral

> **EXAMPLE**
>
> Clint needed some cash so he took his saxophone to a pawnbroker. The pawnbroker loaned Clint $100 and took the saxophone as collateral.

b. Control is similar to possession, but control applies to collateral that cannot be physically possessed (e.g., electronic documents of title, deposit accounts, or investment property)

c. Secured party must use reasonable care to preserve collateral and may charge reasonable expenses to do so

6. Automatic perfection

    a. Under the following conditions, perfection is accomplished by completing attachment with no further steps

        (1) **Purchase money security interest in consumer goods**

            (a) Purchase money security interest (PMSI) occurs in two important cases

                1] Seller retains security interest in same item sold on credit to secure payment

                2] Another party, such as bank, provides loan for and retains security interest in same item purchased by debtor

            (b) "In consumer goods" means that goods are bought primarily for personal, family, or household purposes

---

EXAMPLE

B buys a refrigerator for his home from Friendly Appliance Dealer on credit. Friendly has B sign a written security agreement. Because all three elements needed for attachment took place, this is automatic perfection. This is true because the refrigerator is a purchase money security interest in consumer goods.

EXAMPLE

Same as previous example except that Second Intercity Bank provides the loan having B sign a security agreement. This is also a purchase money security interest in consumer goods. Perfection takes place when all three elements of attachment occur.

EXAMPLE

In the two examples above, if B had purchased the refrigerator for use in a restaurant, the collateral would be equipment. Therefore, automatic perfection would not occur. This is still a PMSI; it just does not perfect automatically. The secured party, however, could file a financing statement to perfect the security interest in both cases.

---

        (2) PMSIs may arise in other goods such as equipment and inventory, but there is no automatic perfection in those goods because they are not consumer goods.

        (3) Perfection by attachment does not occur for motor vehicles, trailers, or both. These are perfected by a lien on certificate of title filed with state

            (a) Automatic perfection is not effective against bona fide purchaser for value who buys goods from consumer for consumer use

                1] **Is effective,** however, if secured party had **filed**

EXAMPLE

B purchases a washer and dryer from Dear Appliances for use in his home giving Dear a security interest, then sells the washer and dryer to C for a fair price for C's household use. C is unaware of the security interest that Dear has in the washer and dryer. Dear's PMSI is not effective against C.

> **EXAMPLE**
>
> Same example as above except that Dear had filed a financing statement. Dear wins because filing is effective even against a subsequent bona fide purchaser such as C even if he buys for consumer use.

> **EXAMPLE**
>
> In the two examples above, if C had purchased the items from B for other than consumer use, C is not free of Dear's security interest. This is so because the rule only applies to bona fide purchasers for consumer use.

      2] **Is effective** if subsequent purchaser knows of security interest before buying

> **EXAMPLE**
>
> An appliance dealer sells a freezer to Jack for family use. Assume attachment has occurred. Jack then sells it to Cindy who is aware of the security interest that the dealer still has in the freezer. Even if Cindy is buying this for household use, she takes it subject to the security interest.

  (4) Sale of promissory notes
  (5) Assignment of health care insurance to health care provider
  (6) Temporary automatic perfection for twenty days for instruments, certificated securities, negotiable documents, and proceeds of sale of perfected security interest

D. Other Issues under Secured Transactions

1. Security interests in goods acquired in the future

  a. An after-acquired property clause, sometimes referred to as a floating lien, allows the secured party to acquire a security interest in good that the debtor acquires in the future

    (1) Not permitted to be used on consumer goods
    (2) Typically used for inventory and equipment

> **EXAMPLE**
>
> Fred agreed to buy Billy's furniture store. Billy financed the sale himself and took a security interest in all current inventory and equipment and all after-acquired inventory and equipment. Billy filed a financing statement covering this transaction.
>
> Analysis: Billy has a perfected security interest in all current inventory and equipment. If and when Fred purchases additional furniture for resale or goods, such as a computer, for use in the store, then Fred will have a security interest in those goods as well.

2. Computer software embedded in goods is treated as part of those goods and not as software
3. Field warehousing is used to perfect security interest (analogous to possession or control)

  a. Debtor keeps inventory on his/her premises under control of third party such as bonded warehouseman or secured party's employee
  b. Secured party keeps control over inventory such as use of separate room or fenced-off portion with sign showing secured party's control

4. Consignments

a. Consignment of security interest

(1) If it is a "true consignment," consignee is simply a sales agent who does not own the goods but sells them for consignor

(a) "True consignment" exists when

1] Consignor retains title to goods
2] Consignee has no obligation to buy goods
3] Consignor has right to all proceeds (pays consignee commission)

EXAMPLE

Manufacturer (consignor) gives possession of goods to a marketing representative (consignee) to sell those goods on commission.

(b) To perfect his/her interest, a consignor must

1] File a financing statement under secured transactions law and give notice to the consignee's creditors who have perfected security interests in the same type of goods. Notice must contain description of the goods to be delivered and be given before the consignee receives possession of goods

---

EXAMPLE

P delivers goods to A on consignment. The consignment is a "true consignment" in that P has title to the goods and pays A a commission for selling the goods. Any goods that are unsold are returned by A to P. A does not pay for any unsold goods. Creditors of A can assert claims against the goods that A possesses unless P has given notice to the creditors. The general way to accomplish this is by filing a financial statement under the secured transactions law.

---

(2) If transaction is not a true consignment because it is actually a sale from creditor to debtor in which debtor then owns the goods, look for a security agreement. Attachment and perfection occur as in typical secured transaction

---

NOW REVIEW MULTIPLE-CHOICE QUESTIONS 7 THROUGH 14

E. **Priorities**

1. If more than one party claims a security interest in same collateral, rules of priority should be examined. These rules determine which party has the best rights to the collateral. This is extremely important, both on the exam and in real life, because frequently the value of the collateral is insufficient to pay all creditors and the first creditor gets paid in full before the lower priority creditor receives anything.
2. A secured party will prevail over an unsecured party. Unsecured parties are usually referred to as general creditors.
3. If both parties are secured, then the following rules apply:

a. If neither party is perfected, then the interest that attached first prevails
b. A perfected party will prevail over an unperfected party
c. If both parties are perfected, then generally, the first interest that was perfected prevails

(1) A very important exception may arise if one of the party's perfected interests is a PMSI
(2) A PMSI may take priority over all other security interests, even those security interests perfected prior to the PMSI.

(3) For the PMSI to gain this "super priority" status certain rules must be followed; the rules vary depending on what type of goods the PMSI has perfected in

(4) If the goods are equipment or consumer goods, then the PMSI party has 20 days after the debtor receives possession of the collateral to perfect the PMSI

  (a) If the PMSI party follows this rule, then it will prevail over other perfected security interests in the same collateral.

EXAMPLE

Fred agreed to buy Billy's furniture store. Billy financed the sale himself and took a security interest in all current inventory and equipment and all after-acquired inventory and equipment. Billy filed a financing statement covering this transaction on June 1, 2010. On May 29, 2011, Fred purchased and took delivery of a new computer from Mega for use at his store. Fred purchased the computer on credit and entered into a security agreement with Mega giving Mega a security interest in the computer that Fred had purchased. Mega filed a financing statement covering this transaction on June 10, 2011. If Fred defaults on his payments to Mega and Billy, who has priority to the recently purchased computer?

Analysis: Although Billy's security interest in after-acquired equipment arose first, Mega has a PMSI in the computer and perfected within the 20-day window, so Mega will prevail. If Mega had waited until June 25th to perfect its interest in the computer, Mega would have a PMSI, but would not gain the priority over Billy because Mega did not perfect within the 20-day window.

  (b) Technically the 20-day rule does apply to consumer goods, but the creditor with a PMSI in consumer goods does not need to file a financing statement since perfection occurs automatically.

(5) If the goods are inventory, the PMSI party must perform two tasks to gain priority over earlier perfected interests:

  (a) Perfection must occur prior to or simultaneously to the debtor receiving the inventory

> **NOTE:** There is no 20-day window for inventory.

  (b) Written notice must be given to all holders of prior perfected security interests in the collateral prior to or simultaneously to the debtor receiving the inventory.

EXAMPLE

Fred agreed to buy Billy's furniture store. Billy financed the sale himself and took a security interest in all current inventory and equipment and all after-acquired inventory and equipment. Billy filed a financing statement covering this transaction on June 1, 2010. Fred purchased some furniture to resell in his store from Highpoint Furniture Corp. Highpoint sold the furniture to Fred on credit and took a PMSI in the furniture it sold Fred. If Highpoint wants to get priority over Billy's earlier perfected interest on future inventory, Highpoint must provide written notice to Billy of its PMSI and perfect its interest in the furniture. Both tasks must be performed prior to the furniture being delivered to Fred.

---

4. Secured creditors versus subsequent buyers of collateral

  a. Buyers in the ordinary course of business take free of any security interest whether perfected or not (be sure to know this one)

    (1) In general, buying in the ordinary course of business means buying from inventory of a person or company that normally deals in those goods

    (2) Buyer has priority even if s/he knows that security agreement exists between the seller and a secured party, but buyer must have possession of the collateral

    (3) Purpose is to allow purchasers to buy from merchants without fear of security agreements between merchants and other parties

---

EXAMPLE

S, a dealer in stereos, obtained financing from L by securing the loan with her inventory in stereos. B purchases one of the stereos from that inventory. B takes the stereo free of the security interest that L has in the inventory of S whether it is perfected or not.

---

  b. Distinguish between buyers in the ordinary course of business and the subsequent bona fide purchaser from consumers

    (1) The latter defeats only a purchase money security interest in consumer goods (perfection on attachment) unless filing takes place—applies to sale by consumer to consumer

    (2) The former applies whether buyer is consumer or not but seller is dealer in those goods

---

EXAMPLE

See previous example. The result is the same whether or not B was a consumer when he bought the stereo in the ordinary course of business from S.

EXAMPLE

Refer again to the same example using S, L, and B. Now let's add on one more security interest: B is buying the stereo on credit from S and for his own personal use. Attachment has occurred. There is perfection by attachment because between B and S, it is a purchase money security interest in consumer goods. If B sells the stereo to N, his neighbor, for consumer use, then N takes the stereo free of the perfected security interest (unless S had filed or N had notice of the security interest).

---

5. Secured creditors versus other creditors

  a. Possessor of negotiable document of title has priority over other creditors

  b. Lien creditor (e.g., repairman or contractor)

    (1) Has priority over an unperfected security interest

       (a) Knowledge of security interest is immaterial

    (2) Has priority over a security interest perfected after attachment of the lien unless it is a purchase money security interest perfected within the 20-day grace period

    (3) A security interest perfected before the lien usually has priority

  c. Trustee in bankruptcy as a lien creditor

    (1) Trustee has the rights of a lien creditor from the date of filing of petition in bankruptcy

       (a) So has priority over a security interest perfected after date of filing petition unless it is a purchase money security interest perfected within the 20-day grace period

    (2) Trustee also takes the position of any existing lien creditor

    (3) A security interest perfected before the bankruptcy trustee usually has priority

6. Collateral removed from the state where collateral was perfected.

  a. The perfection of collateral takes place in the state where the collateral is located.

  b. What if debtor removes collateral from the state where perfection occurred, but the secured party was not given notice of this fact?

c. Generally, secured party has a 4-month grace period to perfect in the new jurisdiction (state) where the collateral was moved to.

d. Filing within the grace period allows the secured party to maintain its perfected interest in the new state.

EXAMPLE

First Bank makes a loan to Poor Corp. The loan is secured by Poor's equipment located in Illinois. First Bank properly files a financing statement on January 10, 2013 covering this transaction. On March 1, 2014, Poor Corp. relocates to Indiana taking its equipment with it. First Bank's perfected interest will remain in effect in Indiana until July 1, 2014. If First Bank files a financing statement in Indiana by July 1, 2014, then First Bank's original perfection date of January 10, 2013 will be in effect in Indiana.

NOW REVIEW MULTIPLE-CHOICE QUESTIONS 15 THROUGH 24

F. Rights of Parties upon Default

1. If collateral consists of claims (e.g., receivables), the secured party has the right of collection from third parties

   a. Secured party may notify third party to pay secured party directly
   b. Secured party must account for any surplus and debtor is liable for any deficiency
   c. Secured party may deduct his/her reasonable expenses

2. Secured party may retain collateral already in his/her possession or may take possession or control from debtor

   a. May do so him/herself if s/he can without breach of the peace. Breaching the peace means violating the law. Typically the issue is trespass, in other words, secured party may not trespass to repossess the collateral.
   b. Otherwise, s/he must use judicial process to foreclose on collateral
   c. Secured party has duty to take reasonable care of collateral in his/her possession

      (1) Expenses to protect collateral are responsibility of debtor

3. If secured party proposes to satisfy obligation by retaining the collateral, s/he must

   a. Send written notice to debtor
   b. Must notify other secured parties (who have sent written notice of their interest), unless consumer goods
   c. Can only retain consumer goods if debtor has paid less than 60% of the purchase price or obligation

      (1) If 60% or more has been paid for a PMSI in consumer goods, secured party must sell collateral within ninety days after taking possession or be liable to the debtor unless debtor waives this right to sale **after** the default

4. Secured party may sell collateral

   a. May be a public or a private sale
   b. Must use commercially reasonable practices—this right cannot be waived by debtor
   c. Must sell within a reasonable time
   d. Must notify debtor of time and place of public sale or time after which private sale will occur unless collateral is perishable, threatens to decline in value, or is type sold on a recognized market

      (1) Must also notify other secured parties (who have sent written notice of their interest) unless collateral consists of consumer goods

   e. Secured party may buy at any public sale and also at a private sale if rights of debtor protected
   f. Distribution of the sale proceeds. The following are paid in order, with each level paid in full before any money is distributed to the next level.

      (1) Secured party's expenses
      (2) Secured part's debt
      (3) Junior security interests
      (4) Any remainder to the debtor

5. Debtor has right to redeem collateral before secured party disposes of it by paying

   a. Entire debt, and
   b. Secured party's reasonable expenses

6. Most remedies can be varied by agreement if reasonable

   a. Provision that secured party must account for any surplus to debtor cannot be varied by agreement

7. Good-faith purchaser (i.e., for value and with no knowledge of defects in sale) of collateral takes free of debtor's rights and any secured interest or lien subordinate to it

   a. Receives debtor's title
   b. If sale was improper, remedy of debtor is money damages against secured party who sold collateral, not against good-faith purchaser

---

NOW REVIEW MULTIPLE-CHOICE QUESTIONS 25 THROUGH 30

G. Other Rights of Parties

1. Debtor has right to request that creditor show proof of unpaid debt or request that creditor correct incorrect filings on collateral

   a. Creditor must either show that debt or filing is correct or make correction

2. When debtor pays debt in full, s/he has right to termination statement of creditor which creditor files or in some cases provides to debtor

   a. This provides notice that earlier filing has been satisfied

3. After expenses are paid for repossessing collateral, storage, and reselling collateral, excess proceeds go to secured party, then to other lien holders

KEY TERMS

Attachment. When the secured party's security interest becomes enforceable against the debtor.

Collateral. Property that is subject to a security interest. It is used to help assure a secured party that the debt will be repaid.

Consumer goods. A type of collateral that was purchased for personal use.

Debtor. The party in a secured transaction who owes an obligation to the secured party.

Default. When the debtor fails to make a scheduled payment to a secured party. When this occurs it allows the secured party to take action against the collateral.

Equipment. A type of collateral that was purchased for a business use.

Financing statement. A document filed with the state government that perfects security interest in collateral

Floating lien. A security interest in the future inventory or equipment that the debtor acquires.

Inventory. A type of collateral that was purchased for resale.

Perfection. When the secured party's security interest is enforceable against third parties. Perfection cannot occur before attachment.

Pledge. When the secured party perfects by taking possession of the collateral.

Purchase money security interest (PMSI). Arises when the secured party extends credit to the debtor to purchase a specific good. The secured party takes a security interest in that specific good.

Secured party. A creditor who receives a promise from a debtor to repay a debt and the debtor also provides collateral to assure repayment of the debt.

Security agreement. The contact between the debtor and secured party, which creates a security interest in the collateral.

Security interest. The interest in the collateral that helps to assure repayment of the debt.

B. Attachment of Security Interests

1. Under the Revised UCC Secured Transaction Article, when collateral is in a secured party's possession, which of the following conditions must also be satisfied to have attachment?

- a. There must be a written security agreement.
- b. The public must be notified.
- c. The secured party must receive consideration.
- d. The debtor must have rights to the collateral.

2. Under the Revised UCC Secured Transaction Article, which of the following after-acquired property may be attached to a security agreement given to a secured lender?

	Inventory	Equipment
a.	Yes	Yes
b.	Yes	No
c.	No	Yes
d.	No	No

3. Gardner Bank loaned Holland Company $20,000 to purchase some inventory to resell in its store. Gardner had Holland sign a security agreement that listed as collateral all present and future inventory of Holland as well as the proceeds of any sales of the inventory. Later, Boldon Company, who was aware of Gardner's security interest, extended credit to Holland but Holland failed to pay back either Gardner or Boldon. Boldon has sought to defeat the security interest pointing out that Gardner never filled out a financing statement. Which of the following is correct?

- a. Gardner has an enforceable security interest that is valid against Holland and has priority over Boldon's interests.
- b. Gardner does not have an enforceable security interest valid against Holland or against Boldon.
- c. Gardner does have an enforceable security interest valid against Holland but not valid against Boldon.
- d. Gardner does not have an enforceable security interest valid against Holland but does have one valid against Boldon.

4. Article 9 of the UCC, which governs security interests, has added some items that now are covered by security interests law. Which of the following is true?

- a. Security interests in tort claims already assessed by a court of law are covered.
- b. After-acquired commercial tort claims are covered.
- c. Both a and b.
- d. Neither a nor b.

5. Under the Revised Secured Transactions Article of the UCC, which of the following requirements is necessary to have a security interest attach?

	Debtor had rights in the collateral	Proper filing of a security agreement	Value given by the creditor
a.	Yes	Yes	Yes
b.	Yes	Yes	No
c.	Yes	No	Yes
d.	No	Yes	Yes

6. Under the Revised UCC Secured Transaction Article, which of the following events will always prevent a security interest from attaching?

- a. Failure to have a written security agreement.
- b. Failure of the creditor to have possession of the collateral.
- c. Failure of the debtor to have rights in the collateral.
- d. Failure of the creditor to give present consideration for the security interest.

C. Perfecting a Security Interest

7. Perfection of a security interest permits the secured party to protect its interest by

- a. Avoiding the need to file a financing statement.
- b. Preventing another creditor from obtaining a security interest in the same collateral.
- c. Establishing priority over the claims of most subsequent secured creditors.
- d. Denying the debtor the right to possess the collateral.

8. Under the Revised UCC Secured Transaction Article, what is the effect of perfecting a security interest by filing a financing statement?

- a. The secured party can enforce its security interest against the debtor.
- b. The secured party has permanent priority in the collateral even if the collateral is removed to another state.
- c. The debtor is protected against all other parties who acquire an interest in the collateral after the filing.
- d. The secured party has priority in the collateral over most creditors who acquire a security interest in the same collateral after the filing.

9. A secured creditor wants to file a financing statement to perfect its security interest. Under the Revised UCC Secured Transaction Article, which of the following must be included in the financing statement?

- a. A listing or description of the collateral.
- b. An after-acquired property provision.
- c. The creditor's signature.
- d. The collateral's location.

10. Which of the following transactions would illustrate a secured party perfecting its security interest by taking possession of the collateral?

    a. A bank receiving a mortgage on real property.
    b. A wholesaler borrowing to purchase inventory.
    c. A consumer borrowing to buy a car.
    d. A pawnbroker lending money.

11. Under the Revised UCC Secured Transaction Article, which of the following actions will **best** perfect a security interest in a negotiable instrument against any other party?

    a. Filing a security agreement.
    b. Taking possession of the instrument.
    c. Perfecting by attachment.
    d. Obtaining a duly executed financing statement.

12. Grey Corp. sells computers to the public. Grey sold and delivered a computer to West on credit. West executed and delivered to Grey a promissory note for the purchase price and a security agreement covering the computer. West purchased the computer for personal use. Grey did not file a financing statement. Is Grey's security interest perfected?

    a. Yes, because Grey retained ownership of the computer.
    b. Yes, because it was perfected at the time of attachment.
    c. No, because the computer was a consumer good.
    d. No, because Grey failed to file a financing statement.

13. In which of the following cases does a seller have automatic perfection of a security interest as soon as attachment takes place?

   I. Purchase money security interest in consumer goods.
   II. Purchase money security interest in inventory.
   III. Purchase money security interest in equipment.

    a. I only.
    b. I and II only.
    c. II and III only.
    d. I, II, and III.

14. Mars, Inc. manufactures and sells computers on credit directly to wholesalers, retailers, and consumers. Mars can perfect its security interest in the computers it sells without having to file a financing statement or take possession of the computers if the sale is made to

    a. Retailers.
    b. Wholesalers that sell to distributors for resale.
    c. Consumers.
    d. Wholesalers that sell to buyers in the ordinary course of business.

E. Priorities

15. Under the Revised Secured Transaction Article of the UCC, which of the following purchasers will own consumer goods free of a perfected security interest in the goods?

    a. A merchant who purchases the goods for resale.
    b. A merchant who purchases the goods for use in its business.

    c. A consumer who purchases the goods from a consumer purchaser who gave the security interest.
    d. A consumer who purchases the goods in the ordinary course of business.

16. Under the Revised UCC Secured Transaction Article, what is the order of priority for the following security interests in store equipment?

   I. Security interest perfected by filing on April 15.
   II. Security interest attached on April 1.
   III. Purchase money security interest in noninventory goods attached April 11 and perfected by filing on April 20.

    a. I, III, II.
    b. II, I, III.
    c. III, I, II.
    d. III, II, I.

17. Noninventory goods were purchased and delivered on June 15. Several security interests exist in these goods. Which of the following security interests has priority over the others?

    a. Security interest in future goods attached June 10.
    b. Security interest attached June 15.
    c. Security interest perfected June 20.
    d. Purchase money security interest perfected June 24.

18. Under the Revised Secured Transaction Article of the UCC, what would be the order of priority for the following security interests in consumer goods?

   I. Financing statement filed on April 1.
   II. Possession of the collateral by a creditor on April 10.
   III. Financing statement perfected on April 15.

    a. I, II, III.
    b. II, I, III.
    c. II, III, I.
    d. III, II, I.

19. A party who filed a security interest in inventory on April 1 would have a superior interest to which of the following parties?

    a. A holder of a mechanic's lien whose lien was filed on March 15.
    b. A holder of a purchase money security interest in after-acquired property filed on March 20.
    c. A purchaser in the ordinary course of business who purchased on April 10.
    d. A judgment lien creditor who filed its judgment on April 15.

20. W & B, a wholesaler, sold on credit some furniture to Broadmore Company, a retailer. W & B perfected its security interest by filing a financing statement. Lean purchased some furniture from Broadmore for his home. He was unaware of W & B's perfected security interest. McCoy purchased some furniture from Broadmore for her home. She was aware that Broadmore's inventory was subject to security interests since Broadmore was having financial problems and had to buy the furniture on credit. Norsome purchased some furniture from Broadmore for use in his business. Broadmore defaults on its loans from W & B, who wants to repossess the furniture purchased and delivered to Lean, McCoy, and Norsome. From which parties can W & B legally repossess the furniture?

a. McCoy.
b. Lean and McCoy.
c. Norsome.
d. None of these parties.

21. Rand purchased a sofa from Abby Department Store for use in her home. Abby had her sign a security agreement for the balance Rand owed. Rand did not pay the balance and sold the sofa to her neighbor, Gram, for use in his home. Gram did not realize that Rand had not paid off the balance. Abby filed a financing statement after Rand defaulted. This filing was also after Gram purchased the sofa from Rand. Which of the following is correct?

a. Abby can repossess the sofa from Gram since it has a written security agreement covering the sofa.
b. Abby can repossess the sofa from Gram since it perfected its security agreement by filing.
c. Abby can repossess the sofa from Gram since it obtained automatic perfection.
d. Abby has no right to repossess the sofa from Gram.

22. Wine purchased a computer using the proceeds of a loan from MJC Finance Company. Wine gave MJC a security interest in the computer. Wine executed a security agreement and financing statement, which was filed by MJC. Wine used the computer to monitor Wine's personal investments. Later, Wine sold the computer to Jacobs, for Jacobs' family use. Jacobs was unaware of MJC's security interest. Wine now is in default under the MJC loan. May MJC repossess the computer from Jacobs?

a. No, because Jacobs was unaware of the MJC security interest.
b. No, because Jacobs intended to use the computer for family or household purposes.
c. Yes, because MJC's security interest was perfected before Jacobs' purchase.
d. Yes, because Jacobs' purchase of the computer made Jacobs personally liable to MJC.

23. Rally Co. has purchased some inventory from Kantar Corporation to sell to customers who will use the inventory primarily for consumer use. Which of the following is **not** correct?

a. If Kantar sells the inventory to Rally on credit and takes out a security interest using the inventory as collateral, this a purchase money security interest.
b. If Kantar sells the inventory to Rally on credit and takes out a security interest using the inventory as collateral, this is a purchase money security interest in consumer goods.
c. If Kantar sells the inventory to Rally but Rally pays for it by getting a loan from a bank who takes out a security interest using the inventory as collateral, this is a purchase money security interest.
d. If a customer purchases some inventory on credit from Rally for home use and signs a written security agreement presented by Rally that lists the inventory as collateral for the credit, this is a purchase money security interest in consumer goods.

24. On June 15, Harper purchased equipment for $100,000 from Imperial Corp. for use in its manufacturing process. Harper paid for the equipment with funds borrowed from Eastern Bank. Harper gave Eastern a security agreement and financing statement covering Harper's existing and after-acquired equipment. On June 21, Harper was petitioned involuntarily into bankruptcy under Chapter 7 of the Federal Bankruptcy Code. A bankruptcy trustee was appointed. On June 23, Eastern filed the financing statement. Which of the parties will have a superior security interest in the equipment?

a. The trustee in bankruptcy, because the filing of the financing statement after the commencement of the bankruptcy case would be deemed a preferential transfer.
b. The trustee in bankruptcy, because the trustee became a lien creditor before Eastern perfected its security interest.
c. Eastern, because it had a perfected purchase money security interest without having to file a financing statement.
d. Eastern, because it perfected its security interest within the permissible time limits.

F. Rights of Parties upon Default

Items 25 and 26 are based on the following:

Drew bought a computer for personal use from Hale Corp. for $3,000. Drew paid $2,000 in cash and signed a security agreement for the balance. Hale properly filed the security agreement. Drew defaulted in paying the balance of the purchase price. Hale asked Drew to pay the balance. When Drew refused, Hale peacefully repossessed the computer.

25. Under the Revised UCC Secured Transaction Article, which of the following remedies will Hale have?

a. Obtain a deficiency judgment against Drew for the amount owed.
b. Sell the computer and retain any surplus over the amount owed.
c. Retain the computer over Drew's objection.
d. Sell the computer without notifying Drew.

26. Under the Revised UCC Secured Transaction Article, which of the following rights will Drew have?

a. Redeem the computer after Hale sells it.
b. Recover the sale price from Hale after Hale sells the computer.
c. Force Hale to sell the computer.
d. Prevent Hale from selling the computer.

27. Under the Revised UCC Secured Transaction Article, which of the following statements is correct concerning the disposition of collateral by a secured creditor after a debtor's default?

a. A good-faith purchaser for value and without knowledge of any defects in the sale takes free of any subordinate liens or security interests.
b. The debtor may not redeem the collateral after the default.
c. Secured creditors with subordinate claims retain the right to redeem the collateral after the collateral is sold to a third party.
d. The collateral may only be disposed of at a public sale.

28. Bean defaulted on a promissory note payable to Gray Co. The note was secured by a piece of equipment owned by Bean. Gray perfected its security interest on May 29 Bean had also pledged the same equipment as collateral for another loan from Smith Co. after he had given the security interest to Gray. Smith's security interest was perfected on June 30. Bean is current in his payments to Smith. Subsequently, Gray took possession of the equipment and sold it at a private sale to Walsh, a good-faith purchaser for value. Walsh will take the equipment

    a. Free of Smith's security interest because Bean is current in his payments to Smith.
    b. Free of Smith's security interest because Walsh acted in good faith and gave value.
    c. Subject to Smith's security interest because the equipment was sold at a private sale.
    d. Subject to Smith's security interest because Smith is a purchase money secured creditor.

29. Under the Revised Secured Transactions Article of the UCC, which of the following remedies is available to a secured creditor when a debtor fails to make a payment when due?

	Proceed against the collateral	Obtain a general judgment against the debtor
a.	Yes	Yes
b.	Yes	No
c.	No	Yes
d.	No	No

30. In what order are the following obligations paid after a secured creditor rightfully sells the debtor's collateral after repossession?

  I. Debt owed to any junior security holder.
 II. Secured party's reasonable sale expenses.
III. Debt owed to the secured party.

    a. I, II, III.
    b. II, I, III.
    c. II, III, I.
    d. III, II, I.

Answers

1. d __ __	8. d __ __	15. d __ __	22. c __ __	29. a __ __
2. a __ __	9. a __ __	16. c __ __	23. b __ __	30. c __ __
3. a __ __	10. d __ __	17. d __ __	24. d __ __	
4. a __ __	11. b __ __	18. a __ __	25. a __ __	
5. c __ __	12. b __ __	19. d __ __	26. c __ __	
6. c __ __	13. a __ __	20. d __ __	27. a __ __	1st: __/30 = __%
7. c __ __	14. c __ __	21. d __ __	28. b __ __	2nd: __/30 = __%

Explanations

1. (d) Under the Revised Article 9 on Secured Transactions, attachment of a security interest takes place when the secured party gives value, the debtor has rights in the collateral, and one of the following three is true:

1. The secured party must possess the collateral if the debtor agrees to it
2. The secured party must have control of certain types of collateral, or
3. The secured party must have a signed security agreement (or an authenticated electronic transmission).

Answer (a) is incorrect because a written security agreement is not required when the secured party has physical possession of the collateral. Answer (b) is incorrect because notification of the public is not a requirement of attachment. Answer (c) is incorrect because a requirement of attachment is that the secured party has given value, not received value.

2. (a) An after-acquired property clause in a security agreement allows the secured party's interest in such property to attach once the debtor acquires the property, without the need to make a new security agreement. These clauses are typically used for inventory and accounts receivable, and can also be used for equipment. After-acquired clauses are not valid for consumer goods though.

3. (a) The security interest did attach because there was a signed security agreement, Gardner gave value, and Holland had rights in the collateral. Upon attachment, Gardner's security interest is fully enforceable against Holland; therefore answers (b) and (d) are incorrect. Even though Gardner never perfected the security interest, it still has priority over Boldon's interests because Boldon was aware of the security interest; therefore answer (c) is incorrect.

4. (a) Security interests in tort claims are covered under the Revised UCC Secured Transactions Article; this is not true of after-acquired commercial tort claims.

5. (c) In order for attachment of a security interest to occur, three elements must take place. First, the secured party must give value, second, the debtor must have rights in the collateral, and third, there must be a security agreement. This security agreement may be oral if the secured party has possession or control of the collateral. Otherwise, it must be in writing and signed by the debtor. An exception to the signature requirement is made if it is an authenticated electronic transmission. The filing of a security interest is one method of perfecting a security interest, but it is not necessary for attachment.

6. (c) In order for a security interest to attach, there must be a valid security agreement, the secured party must have given value, and the debtor must have rights in the collateral. If any one of these items is missing, attachment cannot take place. Answer (a) is incorrect because the security interest may be oral if the secured party has possession or control of the collateral. Answer (b) is incorrect because if the security agreement is in writing, the secured party does not need possession of the collateral to achieve attachment. Answer (d) is incorrect because the secured party must give value, not necessarily consideration. A preexisting claim, although not consideration, does count as value.

7. (c) Perfection of a security interest is important in that it establishes for a secured party priority over the claims that may be made by most subsequent secured creditors. Answer (a) is incorrect because there are three methods of obtaining perfection and one of them is filing a financing statement. Answer (b) is incorrect because subsequent creditors may still obtain security interests in the same collateral although they will normally obtain a lower priority. Answer (d) is incorrect because of times the debtor retains possession of the collateral.

8. (d) Perfection by filing a financing statement will not defeat all other parties who acquire an interest in the same collateral; rather, perfection by filing gives the secured party most possible rights in the collateral. Note, purchasers from a merchant in the ordinary course of business take the collateral free from any prior perfected security interest. The only time a purchaser would take the collateral subject to a prior perfected security interest would be when the purchaser knew that the merchant was selling the goods in violation of a financing statement. Answer (a) is incorrect because a creditor need not perfect the security interest in order to enforce it against the debtor. Answer (c) is incorrect because the filing of a financing statement does not protect the debtor's rights but rather the creditor's rights. Answer (b) is incorrect, because if the collateral is removed from the state and the secured party fails to perfect in the new state, then a subsequent secured party in the new state may get priority in the collateral over the original secured party.

9. (a) Filing a financing statement is one method of perfecting a security interest in personal property. Under the Revised UCC Secured Transaction Article, a financing statement must include the following: the names of the debtor and creditor, and a listing or description of the collateral. Answers (b), (c), and (d) are incorrect because neither an after-acquired property provision, the creditor's signature, nor the collateral's location are required to be included in the financing statement.

10. (d) One way to perfect a security interest is for the secured party to take possession of the collateral in addition to attaining attachment. A pawnbroker lending money is such a case. There is a security agreement which may be oral since the secured party has possession of the collateral. The secured party gives value by lending the money. The third step in attachment is that the debtor has rights in the collateral such as ownership. Since these steps constitute attachment, perfection is accomplished by the pawnbroker, the secured party, taking possession of the collateral. Answer (a) is incorrect because the secured transactions laws apply to security interests in personal property, not real property; additionally, the homeowner will have possession of the home, not the bank. Answers (b) and (c) are incorrect because in both cases the purchasers of inventory and the car will have possession of the goods; the secured party will not have possession.

11. (b) In general, the **best** way to perfect a security interest in a negotiable instrument is to take possession of the instrument. This is true because negotiable instruments are easily negotiated to other holders who can become holders in due course. Answer (a) is incorrect because a holder can become a holder in due course even if a security agreement is filed. Answer (c) is incorrect because perfecting by attachment requires a purchase money security interest in consumer goods. Answer (d) is incorrect because this cannot even accomplish perfection until it is filed.

12. (b) Since West purchased the computer for personal use and the computer itself was the collateral for the security agreement, the fact pattern involves a purchase money security interest in consumer goods. Therefore, once attachment took place, perfection was automatic. Answer (c) is incorrect because since the computer was a consumer good, perfection was automatic upon attachment. Answer (d) is incorrect because filing a financing statement is not required for perfecting a purchase money security interest in consumer goods. Answer (a) is incorrect because retaining or obtaining possession, not ownership, by the secured party is a way to perfect. In any event, Grey Corp. did not retain either ownership or possession since they sold and delivered the computer to West.

13. (a) Automatic perfection (perfection by attachment) takes place in the case of a purchase money security interest (PMSI) in consumer goods only. Answers (b), (c), and (d) are incorrect because they include PMSI in inventory or equipment which do not qualify for automatic perfection.

14. (c) Mars holds a purchase money security interest in the goods sold, which allowed the buyers of these goods to secure the credit for their purchase. When a purchase money security interest is in consumer goods, the secured party (Mars) obtains perfection when attachment takes place without the need to file a financing statement or take possession or control of the collateral. Answers (a), (b), and (d) are incorrect because in those cases the goods comprise inventory, not consumer goods.

15. (d) Buyers in the ordinary course of business take goods free of any security interest whether perfected or not. The buyer can be, but need not be, a consumer. Answer (a) is incorrect because a merchant who purchases consumer goods for resale may not be buying in the ordinary course of business. Answer (b) is incorrect because the merchant who buys the consumer goods for use in his/her business may not be buying in the ordinary course of business. Answer (c) is incorrect because although a consumer can take goods free of a security interest when buying from another consumer, this requires certain facts along with a purchase money security interest in consumer goods. There are no facts in the question to show this.

16. (c) In general, a purchase money security interest in noninventory has priority over nonpurchase money security interests if it was perfected within 20 days after the debtor received the collateral. Item III, therefore, has the first priority because the purchase money security interest was perfected on April 20, which was within twenty days of the attachment. Item I has priority over Item II because the security interest in Item I was perfected, while the security interest in Item II was not.

17. (d) A purchase money security interest in noninventory goods has a special rule. Since it was perfected within twenty days after the debtor got possession of the collateral, it has priority over all of the others. Answers (a) and (b) are incorrect because unperfected security interests have a lower priority than perfected security interests. Answer (c) is incorrect because although this security interest was perfected before the purchase money security interest, the latter has priority if perfected within twenty days of the debtor taking possession of the collateral.

18. (a) Since security interest I was perfected first when the financing statement was filed on April 1, it has the first priority. Security interest II was perfected on April 10 when the creditor took possession of the collateral. It has the second priority. Security interest III has the third priority since it was perfected last on April 15.

19. (d) The party perfected by filing a security interest in inventory on April 1. S/he would therefore have priority over a judgment lien creditor who filed later on April 15. Answer (a) is incorrect because the mechanic's lien was filed on March 15 before the perfection of the security interest. Therefore, the mechanic's lien has priority over the perfected security interest. Answer (b) is incorrect because the holder of the purchase money security interest in after-acquired property filed and perfected before April 1. Answer (c) is incorrect because a purchaser in the ordinary course of business is free of other security interests even if they are perfected before s/he purchases the inventory.

20. (d) Lean, McCoy, and Norsome all purchased the furniture in the ordinary course of business. As such, all three parties take free of the security interest even if it was perfected. This is true whether they purchased the furniture for consumer or business use and whether they knew of the security agreement or not.

21. (d) Abby had a perfected security agreement because of the purchase money security interest in consumer goods. This, however, is not effective against a good-faith purchaser for value who buys from a consumer for consumer use as in the case of Gram. Perfection by filing is, however, effective in such a case but only if the filing is done before Gram purchases the sofa. Answer (a) is incorrect because the attachment of the written security interest makes it enforceable against Rand, not Gram. Answer (b) is incorrect because the filing of the financing statement took place after Gram bought the sofa. Answer (c) is incorrect because, although Abby did accomplish automatic perfection by way of the PMSI in consumer goods, this type of perfection was not effective against Gram because he was a good-faith purchaser for value who bought it from a consumer (Rand) for consumer use.

22. (c) MJC obtained a security interest in the computer purchased by Wine and perfected it by filing. Answer (a) is incorrect. Even though when Jacobs later purchased it for consumer use he was unaware of MJC's security interest, MJC still has priority. This is true because the filing is constructive notice to all subsequent parties. MJC has priority and may repossess the computer even if Jacobs was unaware of the filed security interest. Answer (b) is incorrect because the filing of the financing statement gives MJC priority over Jacob despite his intended use for family. Answer (d) is incorrect: Jacobs is not personally liable to MJC because he made no contract and did not agree to take on liability with MJC.

23. (b) Because Kantar has a security interest in the inventory it sold and is also using the same inventory as collateral for the credit, this is a purchase money security interest. However, because the items Rally purchased are inventory, not consumer goods, in **Rally's** hands, this is not a PMSI in consumer goods. Answer (a) is not chosen because this does describe a PMSI since Kantar retained a security interest in the same items sold on credit to secure payment. Answer (c) is not chosen because a PMSI includes a third party giving a loan who retains a security interest in the same items purchased by the loan. Answer (d) is not chosen because this is a PMSI in consumer goods since the customer purchased the items for his/her home use.

24. (d) When a purchase money security interest uses noninventory as collateral, it has priority over prior competing interests as long as it is perfected within twenty days of the debtor obtaining possession of the collateral. Answers (a) and (b) are incorrect since the collateral in this fact pattern was equipment, and Eastern filed within twenty days, Eastern has priority over the trustee in bankruptcy. Answer (c) is incorrect: Perfection was not automatic since it was a purchase money security interest in equipment, not in consumer goods. Furthermore, since the secured party did not have possession of the collateral, the way to perfect this security interest is by filing a financing statement.

25. (a) After Hale repossesses the computer and sells it in a commercially reasonable fashion, Hale may obtain a deficiency judgment for the amount still owed after the proceeds from the sale pay the expenses of repossession and sale and the debt owed to Hale. Hale may not, however, retain any amounts beyond what Hale is owed, thus answer (b) is incorrect. Any remaining proceeds go to the debtor after repossession and sale expenses and secured parties are paid. Answer (c) is incorrect because for consumer goods, such as the personal computer in this fact pattern, the goods must be sold if the debtor has paid more than 60% of the debt secured by the consumer goods. In this fact pattern, Drew paid two-thirds of the debt. Answer (d) is incorrect because Hale must notify Drew in writing of the impending sale unless Drew had agreed otherwise in writing.

26. (c) Since Drew has paid two-thirds of the price, which is over 60% payment on the secured debt for consumer goods, Hale is obligated to sell the computer rather than keep it in satisfaction of the debt. Answer (a) is incorrect because the debtor may redeem before, not after, the sale. Answer (b) is incorrect because Hale, not Drew, may keep the proceeds needed to pay off repossession and sale expenses and the debt owed to Hale. Any excess would go to Drew. Answer (d) is incorrect because Hale has the right to sell the repossessed computer to pay off the secured debt unless Drew properly redeems the interest s/he has in the computer.

27. (a) Upon the debtor's default, the secured party may take possession of the collateral and sell it. A good-faith purchaser for value buys the collateral free of any liens or security interests. Answer (b) is incorrect because the debtor has the right to redeem the collateral before the secured party disposes of it. The debtor does this by paying the debt in full as well as the secured party's reasonable expenses. Answer (c) is incorrect as a good-faith purchaser of the collateral takes it free of the debtor's rights and any secured interest or lien subordinate to it. Answer (d) is incorrect because although the collateral may be disposed of by a public sale, it also may be disposed of by a private sale if the sale uses commercially reasonable practices.

28. (b) A good-faith purchaser for value at a private sale will take the property free from any security interest or subordinate liens in the property, but remains subject to security interests which are senior to that being discharged at the sale. In this case, Smith perfected his security interest later than Gray and has a subordinate interest in the property. Thus, Walsh takes the equipment free from this subordinate security interest. Answer (a) is incorrect because the fact that Bean is current in his payments to Smith would not affect Smith's interest in the property. Answer (c) is incorrect because as long as Walsh is a good-faith purchaser for value, it doesn't matter if the equipment is sold at a public or private sale. Answer (d) is incorrect because Smith is not a purchase money secured creditor since the proceeds of Smith's loan to Bean were not used to purchase the equipment acting as collateral.

29. (a) If the debtor defaults on the debt, the secured party may proceed against the collateral. This extra protection is one of the main reasons for having secured transactions. If the creditor chooses, s/he may obtain a general judgment against the debtor.

30. (c) Under the UCC, after a secured creditor rightfully sells the debtor's collateral after repossession, the secured party's reasonable sale expenses are paid first. Next, the debt owed to the secured party is paid. Any junior security holders then get paid to the extent of any money remaining.

Simulation

Task-Based Simulation 1

Analysis		
	Authoritative Literature	Help

Situation

On January 2, 2013, Gray Interiors Corp., a retailer of sofas, contracted with Shore Furniture Co. to purchase 150 sofas for its inventory. The purchase price was $250,000. Gray paid $50,000 cash and gave Shore a note and security agreement for the balance. On March 1, 2013, the sofas were delivered. On March 10, 2013, Shore filed a financing statement.

On February 1, 2013, Gray negotiated a $1,000,000 line of credit with Float Bank, pledged its present and future inventory as security, and gave Float a security agreement. On February 20, 2013, Gray borrowed $100,000 from the line of credit. On March 5, 2013, Float filed a financing statement.

On April 1, 2013, Dove, a consumer purchaser in the ordinary course of business, purchased a sofa from Gray. Dove was aware of both security interests.

Items 1 through 6 refer to the fact pattern. For each item, determine whether (A), (B), or (C) is correct.

	(A)	(B)	(C)
1. Shore's security interest in the sofas attached on	○	○	○
A. January 2, 2013.			
B. March 1, 2013.			
C. March 10, 2013.			
2. Shore's security interest in the sofas was perfected on	○	○	○
A. January 2, 2013.			
B. March 1, 2013.			
C. March 10, 2013.			
3. Float's security interest in Gray's inventory attached on	○	○	○
A. February 1, 2013.			
B. March 1, 2013.			
C. March 5, 2013.			
4. Float's security interest in Gray's inventory was perfected on	○	○	○
A. February 1, 2013.			
B. February 20, 2013.			
C. March 5, 2013.			
5. A. Shore's security interest has priority because it was a purchase money security interest.	○	○	○
B. Float's security interest has priority because Float's financing statement was filed before Shore's.			
C. Float's security interest has priority because Float's interest attached before Shore's.			
6. A. Dove purchased the sofa subject to Shore's security interest.	○	○	○
B. Dove purchased the sofa subject to both the Shore and Float security interests.			
C. Dove purchased the sofa free of either the Shore or Float security interests.			

Simulation Solution

Task-Based Simulation 1

Analysis		
	Authoritative Literature	Help

	(A)	(B)	(C)
1. Shore's security interest in the sofas attached on	○	●	○

   A. January 2, 2013.
   B. March 1, 2013.
   C. March 10, 2013.

	(A)	(B)	(C)
2. Shore's security interest in the sofas was perfected on	○	○	●

   A. January 2, 2013.
   B. March 1, 2013.
   C. March 10, 2013.

	(A)	(B)	(C)
3. Float's security interest in Gray's inventory attached on	●	○	○

   A. February 1, 2013.
   B. March 1, 2013.
   C. March 5, 2013.

	(A)	(B)	(C)
4. Float's security interest in Gray's inventory was perfected on	○	○	●

   A. February 1, 2013.
   B. February 20, 2013.
   C. March 5, 2013.

	(A)	(B)	(C)
5. A. Shore's security interest has priority because it was a purchase money security interest.	○	●	○

   B. Float's security interest has priority because Float's financing statement was filed before Shore's.
   C. Float's security interest has priority because Float's interest attached before Shore's.

	(A)	(B)	(C)
6. A. Dove purchased the sofa subject to Shore's security interest.	○	○	●

   B. Dove purchased the sofa subject to both the Shore and Float security interests.
   C. Dove purchased the sofa free of either the Shore or Float security interests.

Explanations

1. **(B)** Gray gave Shore a security agreement on January 2. Shore also gave value but Gray did not receive the goods or have rights in them until March 1. Therefore, it was not until March 1 that attachment occurred.

2. **(C)** Perfection took place on March 10, when Shore filed the financing statement, since attachment had already been accomplished. Note that the filing was needed for perfection since this was not a purchase money security interest in consumer goods but in inventory.

3. **(A)** Float gave value by giving the $1,000,000 line of credit on February 1. On this same date, Gray gave Float a security agreement. Since Gray had rights in the collateral it already possessed, attachment took place on February 1 for that inventory possessed.

4. **(C)** Perfection occurred on March 5, when Float filed the financing statement, since attachment had already taken place previously.

5. (B) Generally, when two parties have perfected security interests in the same collateral, the first to either file or perfect has priority. When a purchase money security interest exists in the collateral, however, the general rule may vary, depending on whether the collateral is inventory or noninventory. In this case the collateral is inventory. A purchase money security interest in inventory may obtain priority over previously perfected conflicting security interests if (1) the purchase money security holder perfects his interest in the inventory at the time the debtor receives the inventory, and (2) the purchase money security holder provides written notice of his purchase money security interest and a description of the inventory to all holders of conflicting security interests who have filed financing statements covering the same type of inventory. If the purchase money security holder does not take these steps, the general rule applies. Answer (A) is incorrect because Shore did not take the necessary steps for its purchase money security interest to obtain priority. Answer (B) is correct because the general rule applies, and Float filed first. Answer (C) is incorrect because when both security interests are perfected, priority is not based on the order of attachment.

6. (C) A buyer in the ordinary course of business takes free of any security interests even if perfected and even if the buyer is aware of the security interests. Therefore, answers (A) and (B) are incorrect because Dove purchased the goods in the ordinary course of business.

Module 30: Bankruptcy

Overview

The overall objective of bankruptcy law is to allow honest insolvent debtors to surrender most of their assets and obtain release from their debts.

A secondary purpose is to give creditors fair opportunity to share in the debtor's limited assets in proportion to their claims.

Bankruptcy questions normally emphasize when involuntary and voluntary proceedings can be conducted, the federal exemptions, the role of the trustee in bankruptcy, preferential transfers, priorities of the creditors, and conditions under which debts may be discharged in bankruptcy. Although bankruptcy under Chapter 7 is emphasized on the CPA examination, you should also be familiar with the other portions of this module. Recently, for example, Chapter 11 on business reorganizations has received some increased treatment. Before beginning the reading you should review the key terms at the end of the module.

> NOTE: Various dollar amounts in this module have been increased, so the dollar amounts in various textbooks may be too low under current bankruptcy law.

A. Alternatives to Bankruptcy Proceedings

1. Creditors may choose to do nothing

   a. Expense of collection may exceed what creditors could recover
   b. Creditors may expect debtor to pull through

2. Creditors may rush to satisfy their claims individually through legal proceedings (i.e., legal judgments, garnishing of wages, etc.; these are discussed in more detail in Module 31.)

   a. Bankruptcy proceedings may result anyway, especially if some creditors are dissatisfied

3. Receiverships

   a. This provides for general administration of debtor's assets by a court appointee (a receiver) for benefit of all parties; these are discussed in more detail in Module 31.

4. Agreements can be used to avoid bankruptcy such as composition agreements with creditors whereby creditors agree to accept less; these are discussed in more detail in Module 31.

   a. Creditors who do not agree may force debtor into bankruptcy

B. Bankruptcy in General

1. Bankruptcy is based mostly on federal law
2. Bankruptcy provides a method of protecting creditors' rights and granting the debtor relief from his/her indebtedness

   a. Debtor is permitted to have a fresh start free of previous debt.
   b. Creditors are treated more fairly according to the priorities stated in bankruptcy laws to effect an equitable distribution of debtor's property

C. Types of Bankruptcy

1. Chapter 7

   a. Liquidation: Turning the majority of the debtor's assets into cash to pay debts
   b. Subject to the conditions discussed below; any debtor may file for Chapter 7 **except:**

      (1) Railroads
      (2) Banking institutions
      (3) Insurance companies

2. Chapter 11

   a. Reorganization of debts
   b. Usually businesses who do not want to liquidate choose Chapter 11, but most debtors who qualify for Chapter 7 bankruptcy qualify for Chapter 11

      (1) Railroads may file under Chapter 11
      (2) Stockbrokers and commodity brokers are not eligible for Chapter 11

3. Chapter 13

   a. Reorganization of debts primarily for individuals
   b. Similar to Chapter 11, but more streamlined

D. Filing the Bankruptcy Petition

1. Filing the petition stays most other legal proceedings

   a. This effectively stops creditors, current and future, from pursuing claims against the debtor, except in bankruptcy court.
   b. A stay does not apply to actions concerning paternity, alimony, or child support (i.e., those matters may be pursued outside the bankruptcy court).

2. Educational requirements

   a. Consumer filers must receive credit counseling from an approved agency within 180 days prior to filing the petition.

      (1) Failure to obtain a certificate of completion from counseling agency will result in a dismissal of the bankruptcy petition
      (2) Does not apply to debtors who are incapacitated, disabled, or on active duty in a military zone

   b. Consumers seeking a discharge of their debts, under either Chapter 7 or 13, must also attend an approved financial management course or their discharge will be denied.

E. Chapter 7 Voluntary Bankruptcy Petitions

1. Voluntary bankruptcy petition is a formal request by debtor for an order of relief

   a. Petition is filed with court along with list of debtor's assets and liabilities
   b. Debtor is automatically given an order of relief upon filing of petition
   c. The Bankruptcy Abuse and Protection Act of 2005 imposes criteria that a consumer debtor must meet to prove that the debtor is not abusing the Bankruptcy Code. In other words, the law is trying to assure that debtors with the ability to repay their debts are not declaring bankruptcy.

(1) If the consumer debtor's income falls below the state's median income, then the presumption of abuse is removed and the debtor may continue under Chapter 7.

(2) If the debtor's income exceeds the state's median income, then the law presumes abuse unless the debtor's monthly income falls below certain dollar limits. The law does permit the deduction of monthly living expenses when calculating monthly income.

(3) Other special circumstances such as a medical conditions or service in the armed forces will be considered.

(4) If the debtor's income exceeds the statutory amount and the debtor is unable to remove the presumption of abuse, the debtor may proceed under Chapter 13 instead of Chapter 7.

   d. Petition may be filed by husband and wife jointly

2. There is no minimum number of creditors required to file for bankruptcy

---

NOW REVIEW MULTIPLE-CHOICE QUESTIONS 1 THROUGH 4

F. Chapter 7 Involuntary Bankruptcy Petitions

1. Involuntary bankruptcy petition may be filed with bankruptcy court by creditors requesting an order for relief
2. Requirements to file petition

   a. If there are fewer than twelve creditors, a single creditor may file the petition as long as his/her claim aggregates $15,325 in excess of any security s/he may hold

      (1) Claims must be undisputed

      (2) If necessary, more than one creditor may join together to have combined debts of more than $15,325 of unsecured claims

---

EXAMPLE

Poor-R-Us Company is not paying its debts as they become due. Its creditors are A (owed $17,000), B (owed $8,000), and C (owed $10,000). A alone may file the involuntary petition to force the company into bankruptcy; however, if A does not wish to do so, neither B nor C **separately** may force the company into bankruptcy because of failure to meet the $15,325 test. B and C may join together to file the petition.

EXAMPLE

XYZ Corporation is unable to pay current obligations. XYZ has three creditors: L (owed $17,000 which is secured by personal property), M (owed $35,000 of which one-half is secured), and N (owed $18,000 of which none is secured). L may not file an involuntary bankruptcy petition but can use the personal property to pay off the debt. Either M or N can file the petition.

EXAMPLE

Trump Inc. is not paying its debts as they become due. Trump has two creditors: Hart and Diamond. Hart claims Trump owes him $18,000, while Diamond claims she is owed $6,000. Trump admits to owing Diamond $6,000, but in good faith claims to owe Hart $12,000. Hart cannot force Trump into bankruptcy by himself. The bankruptcy court will only count the $12,000 toward the $15,325 because that amount is not in dispute. If Hart wants to force Trump into bankruptcy Hart must get Diamond to join the petition.

b. If there are twelve or more creditors, then at least three must sign the petition and they must have claims that aggregate $15,325 in excess of any security held by them

(1) Claims must be undisputed
(2) Claims subject to bona fide dispute are not counted in above $15,325 tests

---

EXAMPLE

Poor, Inc. is unable to meet its current obligations as they are becoming due because of severe business difficulties. It owes over $25,000 to a dozen different creditors. One of the unsecured creditors, Green, is owed $18,000. Green may not force Poor, Inc. into Chapter 7 bankruptcy because even though Green is owed more than $15,325, Green must be joined by two other creditors, even if their claims are very small.

EXAMPLE

Same facts as above except that Poor, Inc. has only eleven creditors. Now Green alone may force Poor, Inc. into bankruptcy under Chapter 7.

---

c. Creditors who file petition in bankruptcy may need to post a bond that indemnifies debtor for losses caused by contesting petition to avoid frivolous petitions

(1) Bankruptcy court may award damages including attorneys' fees to debtor who successfully challenges involuntary bankruptcy petition against creditors filing petition
(2) If petition was made in bad faith, punitive damages may also be awarded

3. Exempt from involuntary bankruptcy are

a. Persons (individuals, partnerships, or corporations) owing less than $15,325
b. Farmers
c. Charitable organizations

4. Bankruptcy not available for deceased person's estate, but once bankruptcy has begun, it is not stopped if bankrupt (debtor) dies
5. An order for relief will be granted if the requirements for filing are met, and

a. The petition is uncontested; or
b. The petition is contested; and

(1) The debtor is generally not paying his/her debts as they become due; or
(2) During the 120 days preceding the filing of the petition, a custodian was appointed or took possession of substantially all of the property of the debtor

---

EXAMPLE

Debtor assigns his property for the benefit of his creditor.

---

c. Note that the above rules involve a modified insolvency in the "equity sense" (i.e., debtor not paying debts as they become due). The rest of the Bankruptcy Act uses insolvency in the "bankruptcy sense" (i.e., liabilities exceed fair market value of all nonexempt assets). The use of insolvency in the equity sense for involuntary proceedings is important.

```
NOW REVIEW MULTIPLE-CHOICE QUESTIONS 5 THROUGH 10
```

G. Chapter 7 Bankruptcy Proceedings (also called a liquidation or straight bankruptcy)

1. Take place under federal law

   a. An order of relief is sought
   b. Court appoints interim trustee
   c. Filing petition automatically stays other legal proceedings, except lawsuits involving "family law" (paternity, child support, alimony, etc.), against debtor's estate until bankruptcy case is over or until court orders otherwise
   d. Debtor may regain property in possession of interim trustee by filing court approved bond

---

EXAMPLE

Mortgage foreclosure by savings and loan will be suspended against debtor.

---

2. First creditors' meeting

   a. Debtor furnishes a schedule of assets, their locations, and a list of creditors
   b. Claims of debtors are deemed allowed unless objected to, in which case the court will determine their validity

      (1) Claims must be filed within six months of first creditors' meeting
      (2) Contingent and unliquidated claims are estimated
      (3) Any attorneys' fees above those ruled reasonable by court are disallowed when objected to by creditors

   c. Trustee may be elected by creditors in Chapter 7 proceeding

      (1) If no election requested by creditors, interim trustee appointed by court continues in office

3. Trustee—the representative of the estate

   a. Trustee has right to receive compensation for services rendered based on value of those services (rather than only on size of estate)
   b. Duties—to collect, liquidate, and distribute the estate, keeping accurate records of all transactions
   c. Trustee represents estate of bankrupt (debtor)

4. Property of the estate

   a. Property presently owned by debtor as of the filing date
   b. Property owed to debtor by third parties that can be recovered by trustee
   c. Property acquired by the estate after the filing date of the petition is generally not part of the estate. The following are exceptions to this rule; thus the following are included in the estate:

EXAMPLE

Mitch filed Chapter 7 bankruptcy on April 1. Mitch received a paycheck on April 15; the paycheck is not part of the estate.

---

      (1) Property received by debtor within 180 days after filing of petition by following methods: inheritance, life insurance, property settlement with spouse

> **EXAMPLE**
>
> Mitch filed Chapter 7 bankruptcy on April 1. Mitch received an inheritance of $5,000 on June 1, when his aunt dies unexpectedly. The $5,000 is part of the estate.

    (2) Income from property owned by estate after petition is filed

> **EXAMPLE**
>
> Mitch filed Chapter 7 bankruptcy on April 1. Mitch received a royalty check of $400 from a book he had published the previous January. The $400 is part of the estate.

5. Exempt property: Property that does not go to the estate

    a. Keeps any interests in joint tenancy property if those interests are exempt under other nonbankruptcy law, and

    b. Debtor usually has option of choosing either exemptions under state law or exemptions under the Bankruptcy Code

    c. The Examiners expect you to be familiar with the Bankruptcy Code exemptions; the dollar amounts for the exemptions are generally not tested.

        (1) $22,975 equity in principal residence including co-op or mobile home

        (2) $3,675 equity in one motor vehicle

        (3) $2,300 in books and tools of one's trade

        (4) $575 per item qualifying for personal, family, or home use (has an aggregate ceiling of $12,250)

        (5) $1,550 in jewelry

        (6) Life insurance with accrued dividends and interest to $12,250

        (7) Unmatured life insurance contracts

        (8) Social security benefits

        (9) Unemployment compensation

        (10) Disability, illness, or unemployment benefits

        (11) Alimony and child support

        (12) Veteran's benefits

        (13) Prescribed health aids

        (14) Public assistance

        (15) Pensions and retirement benefits needed for support and ERISA qualified

        (16) Lost earnings payments

        (17) Wrongful death payments that bankrupted party depended on

        (18) Wages up to maximum of specified formula (75% of person's disposable income or 30 times federal minimum wage

        (19) Crime victim's compensation

        (20) Interest in any property not to exceed $1,225 plus $11,500 of any unused portion of the homestead exemption (item [1] above); can be used to protect any type of property including cash

        (21) Specified personal injury awards up to $22,975 (not to include pain and suffering or monetary loss)

    d. Above exemptions doubled for married couples

6. Duties of trustee under Chapter 7 bankruptcy (i.e., a liquidation)

    a. In general, to liquidate and sell assets owned to pay creditors based on priorities discussed later and to examine propriety of claims brought by creditors

        (1) Considers how best to sell, use, or lease property of estate to act in best interest of estate

(2) Acquires all legal assets owed to estate for equitable distribution to creditors
(3) Trustee makes interim reports and presents final accounting of the administration of the estate to the court

7. Powers of trustee

a. Trustee may take any legal action necessary to carry out duties

(1) Trustee may utilize any defense available to the debtor against third parties
(2) Trustee may continue or cease any legal action started by the debtor for the benefit of the estate

b. Trustee, with court approval, may employ professionals (e.g., accountants and lawyers) to assist trustee in carrying out duties that require professional expertise

(1) Employed professional must not hold any interest adverse to that of debtor (i.e., to avoid conflicts of interest)
(2) Employed professional has right to receive compensation for reasonable value of services performed

(a) Reasonable fee is based on amount and complexity of services rendered, not on size of estate

(3) Trustee, with court approval, may act in professional capacity if capable and be compensated separately for professional services rendered

c. Trustee must within sixty days of the order for relief assume or reject any executory contract, including leases, made by the debtor

(1) Any not assumed are deemed rejected
(2) Trustee must perform all obligations on lease of nonresidential property until lease is either assumed or rejected
(3) Rejection of a contract is a breach of contract and injured party may become an unsecured creditor
(4) Trustee may assign or retain leases if good for bankrupt's estate and if allowed under lease and state law
(5) Rejection or assumption of lease is subject to court approval

d. Trustee may set aside liens (those which arise automatically under law) if lien

(1) Becomes effective when bankruptcy petition is filed or when debtor becomes insolvent
(2) Is not enforceable against a bona fide purchaser when the petition is filed
(3) In the case of a security interest, is not perfected before filing of bankruptcy petition

e. Trustee **may set aside transfers made within one year prior** to the filing of the bankruptcy petition if

(1) The transfer was made with intent to hinder, delay, or defraud any creditor. The debtor need not be insolvent at time of transfer.
(2) Debtor received less than a reasonably equivalent value in exchange for such transfer or obligation and the debtor was insolvent at the time, or became insolvent as a result of the transfer

f. Trustee may also set aside preferential transfers of nonexempt property to a creditor made within the **previous ninety days** prior to the filing of the petition

(1) Preferential transfers are those made for **preexisting debts** that enable the creditor to receive more than s/he would have otherwise under a Chapter 7 liquidation proceeding

(a) Includes a security interest given by debtor to secure antecedent debt

---

EXAMPLE

Debtor paid off a loan, before the loan was due, to BB Bank sixty days before Debtor filed a bankruptcy petition. This is a preferential transfer.

EXAMPLE

Debtor gave CC Bank a security interest in some office furniture he owns to secure a previous loan CC Bank had granted him. This is a preferential transfer if Debtor gave the security interest within ninety days of the filing of bankruptcy. The reason for this is that it gives the creditor (bank) greater rights than it had before.

> **EXAMPLE**
>
> Debtor prepaid some installments on an installment loan on equipment. This is also a preferential transfer.

(2) Preferential transfers **made to insiders** within the **previous twelve months** may be set aside

    (a) Insiders are close blood relatives, officers, directors, controlling stockholders of corporations, or general partners of partnerships

> **EXAMPLE**
>
> S is a secured creditor of XYZ Co. that is in Chapter 7 bankruptcy. S is not an insider.

> **EXAMPLE**
>
> One year ago Herb purchased a car on credit from Ike. Thirty days before filing for bankruptcy, Herb, while insolvent, makes a payment to Ike concerning the auto. This is a preferential transfer. If Ike were Herb's brother, this preference could have been set aside if it had occurred, for example, 120 days before the filing of the petition while Herb was insolvent (insider preference).

(3) Exceptions to trustee's power to avoid preferential transfers

    (a) A contemporaneous exchange between creditor and debtor whereby debtor receives new value

> **EXAMPLE**
>
> Herb, while insolvent, purchases a car for cash from Ike within ninety days of filing a petition in bankruptcy. The trustee could not avoid this transaction because Herb, the debtor, received present (i.e., contemporaneous) value (the car) for the cash transferred to Ike, the creditor. This is not a voidable preference.

    (b) Transfer made in the ordinary course of business is not a voidable preference, nor is the perfected security interest that arises from it (if filed within forty-five days of creation of that debt)

> **EXAMPLE**
>
> Debtor pays the utility bill for the business.

    (c) A security interest given by debtor to acquire property that is perfected within ten days after such security interest attaches

    (d) Consumer debts less than $650

    (e) Business debts less than $6,225

g. When the bankruptcy trustee sets aside a transaction, the trustee places the parties back in their original positions.

> **EXAMPLE**
>
> Rhonda "sells" her car to her sister for $200. The car had a fair market value of $10,000. Two weeks later Rhonda declares bankruptcy. The trustee will set the aforementioned transaction aside. As a result, the estate will get the car and Rhonda's sister will get back her $200.

8. Trustee may be sued or sue on behalf of estate

NOW REVIEW MULTIPLE-CHOICE QUESTIONS 11 THROUGH 17

H. Claims

1. Property rights—where claimant has a property right, property is turned over to claimant, because not considered part of debtor's estate

    a. Reclamation is a claim against specific property by a person claiming it to be his/hers

    > **EXAMPLE**
    >
    > A person rented a truck for a week and in the meantime he becomes bankrupt. The lessor will make a reclamation.

    b. Trust claim is made by beneficiary for trust property when the trustee is bankrupt

    > **EXAMPLE**
    >
    > Trustee maintains a trust account for beneficiary under a trust set up in a will. Trustee becomes bankrupt. The trust account is not part of trustee's estate. The beneficiary may claim the trust account as his property.

    c. Secured claim when creditor has a security interest (e.g., mortgage in property or security interest under Article 9 of the UCC)

    (1) As long as trustee does not successfully attack the security—basically, security interest must be without defects to prevail against trustee (i.e., perfected security interests)

    (2) Secured status may be achieved by subrogation (e.g., surety is subrogated to creditor's collateral)

    d. Setoffs are allowed to the extent the bankrupt and creditor have mutual debts whether unsecured or not

2. Filing of claims

    a. All claims must be filed within six months after the first creditors' meeting

3. Proof of claims

    a. Timely claims are deemed allowed unless creditor objects

    (1) Contingent and unliquidated claims may be estimated

    b. Claims below are not allowed if an objection is made

    (1) Unenforceable claims (by law or agreement)

(2) Unmatured interest as of date of filing bankruptcy petition

(3) Claims that may be offset

(4) Property tax claim in excess of the property value

(5) Insider or attorney claims in excess of reasonable value of services as determined by court

(6) Alimony, maintenance, and support claims for amounts due after bankruptcy petition is filed (they are not dischargeable)

(7) Landlord's damages for lease termination in excess of specified amounts

(8) Damages for termination of an employment contract in excess of one year's wages

(9) Certain employment tax claims

I. **Priority of Claims** (be sure to know)

1. Secured creditors

  a. Technically, they are not a part of the priorities because they never become part of the bankrupt estate. Valid security interests though, perfected prior to the filing of the bankruptcy petition, supersede the bankruptcy trustee's interest. Therefore, these secured creditors' claims must be satisfied first to see if there are any assets left over for the bankruptcy estate.

   (1) If the value of the collateral is sufficient to pay off the secured party, then any excess will go to junior secured parties. If there is any money left after all secured parties are paid, then the trustee may use that money as part of the estate to pay the general creditors (discussed below).

   (2) If the value of the collateral is insufficient to satisfy the claim of the secured party, the secured party will receive the money from the collateral and the remaining debt that the secured party is owed will be treated as a general obligation.

   (3) The secured party must have a security interest in the specific collateral or the secured party has no priority to the collateral.

EXAMPLE

Sandy Clause Corp., a toy wholesaler, was petitioned involuntarily into bankruptcy under Chapter 7 of the Federal Bankruptcy Code on July 21. Keebler Inc., has a perfected PMSI in some toys that it has sold to Clause. Clause owes Keebler $30,000 and has not been paying Keebler's or its others creditors' debts as they have become due. When Clause's assets were liquidated the toys were sold for $40,000. Keebler will be paid in full; the extra $10,000 will go to the bankruptcy trustee and be used to pay the general creditors.

EXAMPLE

Same facts as above except the toys are only sold for $25,000. Keebler will receive the $25,000. Keebler will be treated as a nonpriority general creditor for the remaining $5,000 it is owed.

---

2. Unsecured creditors' (general creditors) claims are paid in full at each level of priority before any lower level is paid. If there are insufficient assets to pay any given level, then assets are prorated at that level and the next levels receive nothing.

  a. Priority general creditors

   (1) Domestic support obligations (e.g., child support, alimony)

   (2) Administration costs

    (a) Includes fees to accountants, attorneys, trustees, and appraisers as well as expenses incurred in recovering, preserving, selling, or discovering property that should be included in debtor's estate

> **EXAMPLE**
>
> Bee, Ware, and Watch, a partnership of CPAs, performed professional services for Dee-Funct Company before it was forced into bankruptcy by its creditors. These fees are not put in the first priority but the last because they do not qualify as administration costs.

   (b) Also includes reasonable fees, salary, or wages needed for services such as operating the business after the bankruptcy action begins

(3) Claims arising in ordinary course of debtor's business after involuntary bankruptcy petition is filed but before the order for relief is entered (gap creditors)

(4) Wages, salaries, and commissions, including vacation, severance, and sick leave owing to bankrupt's employees up to $12,475 per employee earned within 180 days before the petition in bankruptcy was filed (or cessation of business, whichever occurred first)

   (a) Any amount earned in excess of $12,475 is treated as a general claim as explained in (11) below
   (b) This priority does not include officers' salaries

(5) Contributions to employee benefit plans within the prior 180 days, limited to $12,475 per employee, reduced by amount received as wage preference

(6) Claims on storage of grain or fish up to $6,150 for each individual

(7) Consumer deposits for undelivered goods or services limited to $2,775 per individual

> **EXAMPLE**
>
> Mary placed a $3,000 deposit for a $10,000 wedding dress at Barb's Bridal Boutique. Before the dress was delivered Barb declared bankruptcy. Mary's claim for $2,775 would fall at this level; the remaining $225 will fall to the nonpriority general creditor group below.

(8) Taxes (federal, state, and local)

(9) Obligations to an insured bank

(10) Debts arising from motor vehicle accidents while under the influence of drugs or alcohol

(11) General (unsecured) creditors that filed timely proofs of claims

   (a) Includes amounts owed to secured creditors in excess of amount for which security sells
   (b) Includes amounts owed to priority general creditors that exceed the priority amount
   (c) Unsecured claims filed late (unless excused) are paid after timely claims

NOW REVIEW MULTIPLE-CHOICE QUESTIONS 18 AND 19

J. Discharge of the Debtor

1. A discharge is the release of a debtor from all his/her debts not paid in bankruptcy; the debtor has no further obligation even for the debts that were not paid at all or partially paid

2. Creditors not paid are prohibited from any further debt collection on the discharged debts.

3. There are, however, some **nondischargeable debts,** which are discussed in detail below

4. Debtor must be an individual to be discharged

   a. Business organizations do not receive a discharge because they no longer exist; all of their assets have been liquidated.

   b. Conversely, individual debtors need to be discharged to get a fresh start.

5. Debtor must be adjudged an "honest debtor" to be discharged
6. Discharge will only be granted once every 8 years
7. Acts that bar discharge of **all** debts

   a. Improper actions during bankruptcy proceeding

     (1) Making false claims against the estate
     (2) Concealing property
     (3) Transfer of property after filing with intent to defeat the law (i.e., fraudulent transfer)
     (4) Making any false entry in or on any document of account relating to bankrupt's affairs
     (5) These acts are also punishable by fines and imprisonment

   b. Failing to satisfactorily explain any loss of assets
   c. Refusing to obey court orders
   d. Removing or destroying property within twelve months prior to filing of petition with intent to hinder, delay, or defraud any creditor
   e. Destroying, falsifying, concealing, or failing to keep books of account or records unless such act is justified under the circumstances
   f. "Substantial abuse" of bankruptcy by individual debtor with primarily consumer debts
   g. A preferential transfer does **not** bar discharge (but can be set aside)

K. Debts Not Discharged by Bankruptcy (even though general discharge allowed)

1. Taxes within three years of filing bankruptcy petition
2. Loans for payment of federal taxes
3. Unscheduled debts unless creditor had actual notice of proceedings (i.e., where bankrupt failed to list creditor and debt)

EXAMPLE

In a petition in bankruptcy, a mistake was made so that a debt owed to ABC Company was listed as owed to XYZ Company. The debt to ABC is not discharged unless ABC somehow was aware of the mistake.

---

4. Alimony, separate maintenance, or child support
5. Liability due to theft or embezzlement
6. Debts arising from debtor's fraud about his/her financial condition or fraud in connection with purchase or sale of securities

---

EXAMPLE

Obtaining credit using false information such as materially fraudulent financial statements that the creditor relied on.

---

7. Willful and/or malicious injuries to a person or property of another (intentional torts)

   a. Unintentional torts (i.e., negligence) and breaches of contract are dischargeable

8. Congress amended Bankruptcy Code making it more difficult for student loans to be discharged in bankruptcy

   a. This was prompted because many students have had large student loans to pay for tuition and living expenses

     (1) Upon graduation some students have few assets and may be inclined to file for bankruptcy trying to get student loans discharged

   b. Student loans are defined by bankruptcy code to include those loans made or guaranteed by units of government

    (1) Recent additions include loans for students made also by nongovernmental commercial institutions such as banks

        (a) Also includes stipends, scholarships or benefits given by educational institutions

  c. Bankruptcy Code now provides that student loans can be discharged in cases of "undue hardship" to debtor and any dependants

    (1) "Undue hardship" is defined very strictly so s/he needs to basically show payment would negate payment of basic necessities of food or shelter

    (2) Cosigners such as parents who guarantee family member's student loan must meet same "undue hardship" test to discharge obligation

  9. Governmental fines or penalties imposed within prior three years

 10. Those from a prior bankruptcy proceeding in which the debtor waived discharge or was denied discharge

 11. Liability incurred by operating any vehicle, vessel or aircraft while legally intoxicated

 12. To avoid the practice of "loading up on luxury goods" before bankruptcy, there is a presumption of nondischargeability for

  a. Consumer debts to a single debtor under specified conditions for luxury goods or services made within 60 days of filing

  b. Certain cash advances based on consumer credit taken within 60 days of filing

 13. Any debt from violation of securities laws including those under Sarbanes-Oxley Act

 14. Sarbanes-Oxley Act makes it criminal for any person to intentionally falsify, destroy, or cover up records intending to influence proper investigation or administration of matters involving bankruptcy cases

 15. Debts owed to pension plans, profit sharing plans or similar employee plans

 16. Homeowner association, condo, or cooperative fees

L. Revocation of Discharge

  1. Discharge may be revoked if

    a. Bankrupt committed fraud during bankruptcy proceedings unknown to creditors seeking revocation

---

EXAMPLE

A bankrupt conceals assets in order to defraud creditors.

---

    (1) Must be applied for within one year of discharge

    b. Bankrupt acquired rights or title to property of estate and fraudulently failed to report this

    c. Bankrupt refused to obey lawful court order or refused to testify when not in violation of his/her constitutional right against self-incrimination

M. Reaffirmation

  1. Debtor promises to pay a debt that will be discharged. The Code makes it difficult to reaffirm dischargeable debt.

    a. To be enforceable, reaffirmation of dischargeable debt must satisfy the following conditions:

      (1) Reaffirmation must take place before discharge granted

      (2) Must be approved by bankruptcy court

      (3) Debtor is allowed sixty days to rescind reaffirmation once agreed to

        (a) Debtor must have received appropriate warnings from the court or attorney on effects of reaffirmation, and

        (b) If also involves consumer debt not secured by real property, court must approve new agreement as being in best interests of debtor and not imposing undue hardship on debtor

NOW REVIEW MULTIPLE-CHOICE QUESTIONS 20 THROUGH 26

N. Business Reorganization—Chapter 11

1. Goal is to keep financially troubled firm in business

   a. It is an alternative to liquidation under Chapter 7 (straight bankruptcy)
   b. In general, allows debtor to keep assets of business

2. Can be initiated by debtor (voluntary) or creditors (involuntary)

   a. Available to individuals, partnerships, or corporations including railroads. Other entities ineligible to be debtors under Chapter 7 are ineligible under Chapter 11.
   b. If involuntary, same requirements must be met as needed to initiate a Chapter 7 involuntary proceeding

3. Creditor's committee is appointed after the order for relief is entered. This committee essentially functions as the bankruptcy trustee.

   a. Investigation of debtor's financial affairs is conducted
   b. Committee is made up of unsecured creditors only
   c. If debtor's management capable of continuing business, no trustee is appointed
   d. If debtor's management is not considered capable of running business, then trustee is appointed to conduct business
   e. Trustee may also be appointed if it is in the best interest of the creditors
   f. Committee will create a reorganization plan; however, the debtor has an exclusive right to file its own plan within 120 days after the order for relief is entered.

4. A reorganization plan

   a. Allows for continued operation of business unless court orders otherwise
   b. Provides for payment of part or all of debts over extended period

      (1) Payment to creditors comes primarily from future income

   c. Must divide claims into classes of similar claims, and claims within a class must be treated equally.

EXAMPLE

A reorganization plan might put employees who are owed back wages in one class, shareholders in another class, and unpaid suppliers in a third class. Assume that the plan calls for the suppliers to be paid 70 cents for each dollar owed. All suppliers must get 70 cents, some cannot get 80 cents, and others only 60 cents on the dollar.

---

   d. Plan may provide for some creditors to receive stock in place of debt

      (1) Preferred shareholders may be converted to common shareholders
      (2) Common shareholders may forfeit shares of stock
      (3) Typically, claimants receive reduced amounts

   e. Approval of reorganization plan needs

      (1) Over 1/2 of creditors in each committee owed at least 2/3 of the total debt in that class, and
      (2) Acceptance of stockholders holding at least 2/3 in amount of the stock
      (3) Complete reorganization plan can still be approved by court if court determines plan is fair even if some committees fail to approve it; called "cram down" power

   f. Priority general creditors must be paid in full (e.g., bankruptcy administrative fees, employee wages up to $12,475 per employee; see Section I.2.a. of this outline for further examples).

5. Fast tracking provides for small businesses (having debt less than $2,490,925) which cuts out much of red tape of bankruptcy proceedings

6. After court confirms plan and issues final decree

   a. Debtor is discharged from debts that arose before confirmation of plan, except

   (1) Those agreed to continue under the recognized plan
   (2) Those exempted by law (e.g., taxes; see part F. of this outline for further examples)

7. Court may convert Chapter 11 reorganization into Chapter 7 straight bankruptcy if fairer
8. SEC has limited power to participate in bankruptcy reorganizations
9. When debtor keeps and operates business, debtor has right to retain employees and professionals it used before reorganization

---

EXAMPLE

Debtor, after a Chapter 11 reorganization, wishes to keep its CPA firm. This is permitted.

O. **Debts Adjustment Plans—Chapter 13**

1. Most individuals are eligible if

   a. Have regular income, and
   b. Owe unsecured debts of less than $383,175, and
   c. Owe secured debts of less than $1,149,525

2. Initiated when debtor files voluntary petition in bankruptcy court

   a. Creditors may not file involuntary petition under Chapter 13
   b. Filing of petition stays all collection and straight bankruptcy proceedings against debtor
   c. Debtor has exclusive right to propose plan

   (1) If debtor does not file plan, creditors may force debtor into involuntary proceeding under Chapter 7

   d. Plan will be confirmed or denied by court without approval of unsecured creditors

   (1) However, unsecured creditors must receive as much as they would get under Chapter 7, and

      (a) Either be paid in full, or
      (b) Have all debtor's disposable income committed to plan
      (c) Plan may put claims in different classifications but may not discriminate unfairly against any of designated classes and each claimant within same classification must receive same treatment

   (2) If debts to unsecured creditors are not paid in full, plan must commit to payments for three years. If debtor's monthly income exceeds the state's average median annual income, plan must make payment for five years.

   e. Court must appoint trustee in Chapter 13 cases
   f. Debtor engaged in business may continue to operate that business subject to limitations imposed by court
   g. Completion of plan discharges debtor from debts dischargeable by law. Nondischargeable debts are similar to those under Chapter 7 of the Bankruptcy Code (see section K. of this outline)

NOW REVIEW MULTIPLE-CHOICE QUESTIONS 27 THROUGH 30

P. **The Bankruptcy Abuse Prevention and Consumer Protection Act of 2005**

1. Amends various parts of US Bankruptcy Code including consumer bankruptcies and business bankruptcies
2. Provisions under new Act allow trade creditors to treat large portions, sometimes most or even all of vendors' claims as being administrative expenses, significantly increasing their priority status.

3. This Act creates a new Bankruptcy Code section that imposes limits on the payment of severance pay or retention bonuses to key employees in a Chapter 11 case

   a. Retention bonuses are permitted only if key employees have good-faith offers from other businesses at the same or greater compensation

4. For consumer cases, the time between discharges has been increased so that Bankruptcy Code will deny discharge to a Chapter 7 debtor if that debtor received either a Chapter 7 or Chapter 11 discharge in a case filed within 8 years of filing of pending case

   a. Prior law said 6 years between such discharges under Chapter 7 or Chapter 11
   b. Under the new act, Chapter 13 debtors have a few different time limitations when combined with the various chapters.

5. This Bankruptcy Abuse Prevention and Consumer Protection Act of 2005 creates a new Chapter 15 of the US Bankruptcy Code on cross-border insolvency cases

   a. Meant to make bankruptcy proceedings across international borders more functional

      (1) Favors and promotes cooperation and communication with both foreign courts and foreign representatives

---

NOW REVIEW MULTIPLE-CHOICE QUESTION 31

Q. Bankruptcy Fees

1. In recent years, bankruptcy specialists have made much larger fees. Rising fees have elicited major objections coming from

   a. Federal watchdogs
   b. Organized labor
   c. Major creditors of bankrupt companies

2. Major complaint is that lawyers and other advisors have been taking too many fees and leaving less money for others in the bankruptcy
3. Thus bankruptcy is more likely testable on CPA Exam because it is now on minds of many

KEY TERMS

Chapter 7 bankruptcy. Debtor liquidates assets, except exempt assets, to pay creditors.

Chapter 11 bankruptcy. Debtor reorganizes debts to pay creditors; primarily used by businesses.

Chapter 13 bankruptcy. Debtor reorganizes debts to pay creditors; primarily used by individuals.

Creditor's committee. A group of unsecured creditors who essentially function as the bankruptcy trustee in Chapter 11 cases.

Discharge. After debtor completes bankruptcy, debtor is relieved of all previous debt except debts that are nondischargeable. This allows debtor to get a financial fresh start.

Estate. The debtor's assets that are used to pay the creditors.

Insider. A party who has a close relationship with the debtor. Relevant in the area of preferential transfers: Transactions with insiders are examined by the trustee for 1 year prior to the filing of the bankruptcy petition.

Involuntary petition. Debtor is sued by creditors and forced into bankruptcy.

Liquidation. The process of turning assets into cash to pay creditors.

Order for relief. Granted, in most cases, to the debtor upon the filing of the bankruptcy petition. Allows debtor to stop paying creditors until the bankruptcy can be finalized.

Preferential transfer. When the debtor provides payment or security to a creditor, which would allow creditor to collect more than the creditor would have under Chapter 7 bankruptcy. If such a transfer took place 90 days prior to the filing of the bankruptcy petition, the trustee may set the transaction aside. This is done to assure all creditors are treated fairly.

Reaffirmation. When a debtor voluntarily chooses to repay a debt that otherwise would be fully discharged under the Bankruptcy Code.

Reorganization (rehabilitation). A debtor retains assets, as opposed to liquidating the assets, and agrees to pay creditors out of future earnings under Chapters 11 or 13 of the Bankruptcy Code.

Set aside. If a bankruptcy trustee discovers a preferential transfer then the trustee will reclaim the asset improperly taken from the estate and return whatever consideration, if any, was given to the creditor. Effectively this action returns the parties back to their original position before the wrongful transfer took place.

Stay. A court order that prevents further collection actions by creditors. The stay is issued upon the filing of the bankruptcy petition, but does not apply to family law issues.

Trustee. The bankruptcy trustee presides over the bankruptcy estate and organizes the estate for the court. The trustee determines what the assets and liabilities of the estate are.

Voluntary petition. A debtor chooses to file bankruptcy, as opposed to being forced into bankruptcy by creditors.

Multiple-Choice Questions (1–31)

E. Chapter 7 Voluntary Bankruptcy Petitions

1. Which of the following statements is correct concerning the voluntary filing of a petition in bankruptcy?

    a. If the debtor has twelve or more creditors, the unsecured claims must total at least $15,325.

    b. The debtor must be insolvent.

    c. If the debtor has less than twelve creditors, the unsecured claims must total at least $15,325.

    d. The petition may be filed jointly by spouses.

2. A voluntary petition filed under the liquidation provisions of Chapter 7 of the Federal Bankruptcy Code

    a. Is **not** available to a corporation unless it has previously filed a petition under the reorganization provisions of Chapter 11 of the Federal Bankruptcy Code.

    b. Automatically stays collection actions against the debtor **except** by secured creditors.

    c. Will be dismissed unless the debtor has twelve or more unsecured creditors whose claims total at least $15,325.

    d. Does **not** require the debtor to show that the debtor's liabilities exceed the fair market value of assets.

3. On February 28, Master, Inc. had total assets with a fair market value of $1,200,000 and total liabilities of $990,000. On January 15, Master made a monthly installment note payment to Acme Distributors Corp., a creditor holding a properly perfected security interest in equipment having a fair market value greater than the balance due on the note. On March 15, Master voluntarily filed a petition in bankruptcy under the liquidation provisions of Chapter 7 of the Federal Bankruptcy Code. One year later, the equipment was sold for less than the balance due on the note to Acme.

If a creditor challenged Master's right to file, the petition would be dismissed

    a. If Master had less than twelve creditors at the time of filing.

    b. Unless Master can show that a reorganization under Chapter 11 of the Federal Bankruptcy Code would have been unsuccessful.

    c. Unless Master can show that it is unable to pay its debts in the ordinary course of business or as they come due.

    d. If Master is an insurance company.

4. Which of the following conditions, if any, must a debtor meet to file a voluntary bankruptcy petition under Chapter 7 of the Federal Bankruptcy Code?

	Insolvency	Three or more creditors
a.	Yes	Yes
b.	Yes	No
c.	No	Yes
d.	No	No

F. Chapter 7 Involuntary Bankruptcy Petitions

5. Brenner Corporation is trying to avoid bankruptcy but its four creditors are trying to force Brenner into bankruptcy. The four creditors are owed the following amounts:

Anteed Corporation	–	$7,000 of unsecured debt
Bounty Corporation	–	$5,000 of unsecured debt and $12,000 of secured debt
Courtney Corporation	–	$3,000 of unsecured debt
Dauntless Corporation	–	$2,000 of unsecured debt

Which of the creditors must sign the petition to force Brenner into bankruptcy?

    a. Bounty is sufficient.

    b. At least Anteed and Bounty are needed.

    c. At least Bounty, Courtney, and Dauntless are needed.

    d. All of these four creditors are needed.

Items 6 through 10 are based on the following:

Dart Inc., a closely held corporation, was petitioned involuntarily into bankruptcy under the liquidation provisions of Chapter 7 of the Federal Bankruptcy Code. Dart contested the petition.

Dart has not been paying its business debts as they became due, has defaulted on its mortgage loan payments, and owes back taxes to the IRS. The total cash value of Dart's bankruptcy estate after the sale of all assets and payment of administration expenses is $100,000.

Dart has the following creditors:

- Fracon Bank is owed $75,000 principal and accrued interest on a mortgage loan secured by Dart's real property. The property was valued at and sold, in bankruptcy, for $70,000.
- The IRS has a $12,000 recorded judgment for unpaid corporate income tax.
- JOG Office Supplies has an unsecured claim of $3,000 that was timely filed.
- Nanstar Electric Co. has an unsecured claim of $1,200 that was not timely filed.
- Decoy Publications has a claim of $14,000, of which $2,000 is secured by Dart's inventory that was valued and sold, in bankruptcy, for $2,000. The claim was timely filed.

6. Which of the following statements would correctly describe the result of Dart's opposing the petition?

    a. Dart will win because the petition should have been filed under Chapter 11.

    b. Dart will win because there are **not** more than 12 creditors.

    c. Dart will lose because it is **not** paying its debts as they become due.

    d. Dart will lose because of its debt to the IRS.

7. Which of the following events will follow the filing of the Chapter 7 involuntary petition?

	A trustee will be appointed	A stay against creditor collection proceedings will go into effect
a.	Yes	Yes
b.	Yes	No
c.	No	Yes
d.	No	No

For **items 8 through 10** assume that the bankruptcy estate was distributed.

8. What dollar amount would Nanstar Electric Co. receive?

   a. $0
   b. $800
   c. $1,000
   d. $1,200

9. What total dollar amount would Fracon Bank receive on its secured and unsecured claims?

   a. $70,000
   b. $72,000
   c. $74,000
   d. $75,000

10. What dollar amount would the IRS receive?

   a. $0
   b. $8,000
   c. $10,000
   d. $12,000

G. Chapter 7 Bankruptcy Proceedings

11. Which of the following is **not** allowed as a federal exemption under the Federal Bankruptcy Code?

   a. Some specified amount of equity in one motor vehicle.
   b. Unemployment compensation.
   c. Some specified amount of value in books and tools of one's trade.
   d. All of the above are allowed.

12. Flax, a sole proprietor, has been petitioned involuntarily into bankruptcy under the Federal Bankruptcy Code's liquidation provisions. Simon & Co., CPAs, has been appointed trustee of the bankruptcy estate. If Simon also wishes to act as the tax return preparer for the estate, which of the following statements is correct?

   a. Simon is prohibited from serving as both trustee and preparer under any circumstances because serving in that dual capacity would be a conflict of interest.
   b. Although Simon may serve as both trustee and preparer, it is entitled to receive a fee only for the services rendered as a preparer.
   c. Simon may employ itself to prepare tax returns if authorized by the court and may receive a separate fee for services rendered in each capacity.
   d. Although Simon may serve as both trustee and preparer, its fees for services rendered in each capacity will be determined solely by the size of the estate.

13. Which of the following transfers by a debtor, within 90 days of filing for bankruptcy, could be set aside as a preferential payment?

   a. Making a gift to charity.
   b. Paying a business utility bill.
   c. Borrowing money from a bank secured by giving a mortgage on business property.
   d. Prepaying an installment loan on inventory.

Items 14 and 15 are based on the following:

   On August 1, Hall filed a voluntary petition under Chapter 7 of the Federal Bankruptcy Code. Hall's assets are sufficient to pay general creditors 40% of their claims.

   The following transactions occurred before the filing:

- On May 15, Hall gave a mortgage on Hall's home to National Bank to secure payment of a loan National had given Hall two years earlier. When the loan was made, Hall's twin was a National employee.
- On June 1, Hall purchased a boat from Olsen for $10,000 cash.
- On July 1, Hall paid off an outstanding credit card balance of $500. The original debt had been $2,500.

14. The National mortgage was

   a. Preferential, because National would be considered an insider.
   b. Preferential, because the mortgage was given to secure an antecedent debt.
   c. Not preferential, because Hall is presumed insolvent when the mortgage was given.
   d. Not preferential, because the mortgage was a security interest.

15. The payment to Olsen was

   a. Preferential, because the payment was made within ninety days of the filing of the petition.
   b. Preferential, because the payment enabled Olsen to receive more than the other general creditors.
   c. Not preferential, because Hall is presumed insolvent when the payment was made.
   d. Not preferential, because the payment was a contemporaneous exchange for new value.

16. Under the liquidation provisions of Chapter 7 of the Federal Bankruptcy Code, a debtor will be denied a discharge in bankruptcy if the debtor

   a. Fails to list a creditor.
   b. Owes alimony and support payments.
   c. Cannot pay administration expenses.
   d. Refuses to satisfactorily explain a loss of assets.

17. On May 1, 2013, two months after becoming insolvent, Quick Corp., an appliance wholesaler, filed a voluntary petition for bankruptcy under the provisions of Chapter 7 of the Federal Bankruptcy Code. On October 15, 2012, Quick's board of directors had authorized and paid Erly $50,000 to repay Erly's April 1, 2012, loan to the corporation. Erly is a sibling of Quick's president. On March 15, 2013, Quick paid Kray $100,000 for inventory delivered that day.

Which of the following is **not** relevant in determining whether the repayment of Erly's loan is a voidable preferential transfer?

   a. Erly is an insider.
   b. Quick's payment to Erly was made on account of an antecedent debt.
   c. Quick's solvency when the loan was made by Erly.
   d. Quick's payment to Erly was made within one year of the filing of the bankruptcy petition.

I. Priority of Claims

18. Brook Corporation has filed for bankruptcy. Of the following debts Brook owes, indicate their priorities from the highest to the lowest.

  I. Federal taxes unpaid for the previous year.
  II. Wages of $3,000 owed to employees.
  III. Balance of $5,000 owed to a creditor that had a security interest. This creditor got paid fully by selling off the collateral except for this $5,000 deficiency.

   a. I, II, III.
   b. I, III, II.
   c. II, I, III.
   d. III, I, II.

19. Kessler Company has filed a voluntary bankruptcy petition. Kessler's debts include administration costs owed to accountants, attorneys, and appraisers. It also owes federal and state taxes. Kessler still owes various employees for the previous month's wages accrued before the petition was filed. None of these wages are owed to the officers and at most total $4,000 per employee. The company also owes several creditors for claims arising in the ordinary course of business. All of these latter claims arose before Kessler filed the bankruptcy petition. What are the priorities from highest to lowest of these listed debts and claims?

   a. The claims arising in the ordinary course of business; the administration costs; the employees' wages; the federal and state taxes.
   b. The administration costs; the employees' wages; the federal and state taxes; the claims arising in the ordinary course of business.
   c. The federal and state taxes; the administration costs; the claims arising in the ordinary course of business; the employees' wages.
   d. The claims arising in the ordinary course of business; the federal and state taxes; the administration costs; the employees' wages.

J. Discharge of the Debtor

20. Which of the following acts will **not** bar a general discharge in bankruptcy?

   a. The debtor tried to hide some property to prevent the estate from getting it.
   b. The debtor intentionally injured a creditor during an argument about the bankruptcy proceedings.

   c. The debtor is unwilling to explain satisfactorily why some assets are missing.
   d. The debtor intentionally destroyed records of his assets.

21. Chapter 7 of the Federal Bankruptcy Code will deny a debtor a discharge when the debtor

   a. Made a preferential transfer to a creditor.
   b. Accidentally destroyed information relevant to the bankruptcy proceeding.
   c. Obtained a Chapter 7 discharge ten years previously.
   d. Is a corporation or a partnership.

22. Eckson was granted an order for relief after having filed a petition in bankruptcy. Which of the following actions would bar a general discharge in bankruptcy?

  I. Ten months before the bankruptcy proceedings, Eckson had obtained credit from Cardinal Corporation by using false information on the credit application.
  II. Six months before he filed the petition, Eckson removed assets from his land with the intent to defraud creditors.
  III. During the bankruptcy proceedings, Eckson made a false entry on some records pertaining to his assets.

   a. I only.
   b. I and II only.
   c. II and III only.
   d. I, II, and III.

23. Which of the following acts by a debtor could result in a bankruptcy court revoking the debtor's discharge?

  I. Failure to list one creditor.
  II. Failure to answer correctly material questions on the bankruptcy petition.

   a. I only.
   b. II only.
   c. Both I and II.
   d. Neither I nor II.

24. Which of the following debts will **not** be discharged by bankruptcy even though a general discharge is allowed?

  I. Debt owed to a corporation because the debtor was caught embezzling from it.
  II. Money owed to a bank because the debtor was found to have committed fraud about her financial condition to get a loan.
  III. Damages owed to a major customer because the debtor intentionally breached an important contract.

   a. I only.
   b. II only.
   c. I and II only.
   d. I, II, and III.

25. Which of the following claims will **not** be discharged in bankruptcy?

   a. A claim that arises from alimony or maintenance.
   b. A claim that arises out of the debtor's breach of contract.

c. A claim brought by a secured creditor that remains unsatisfied after the sale of the collateral.

d. A claim brought by a judgment creditor whose judgment resulted from the debtor's negligent operation of a motor vehicle.

26. By signing a reaffirmation agreement on April 15, a debtor agreed to pay certain debts that would be discharged in bankruptcy. On June 20, the debtor's attorney filed the reaffirmation agreement and an affidavit with the court indicating that the debtor understood the consequences of the reaffirmation agreement. The debtor obtained a discharge on August 25. The reaffirmation agreement would be enforceable only if it was

a. Made after discharge.
b. For debts aggregating less than $5,000.
c. Not for a household purpose debt.
d. Not rescinded before discharge.

N. Business Reorganization—Chapter 11

27. Strong Corp. filed a voluntary petition in bankruptcy under the reorganization provisions of Chapter 11 of the Federal Bankruptcy Code. A reorganization plan was filed and agreed to by all necessary parties. The court confirmed the plan and a final decree was entered.

Which of the following statements **best** describes the effect of the entry of the court's final decree?

a. Strong Corp. will be discharged from all its debts and liabilities.
b. Strong Corp. will be discharged only from the debts owed creditors who agreed to the reorganization plan.
c. Strong Corp. will be discharged from all its debts and liabilities that arose before the date of confirmation of the plan.
d. Strong Corp. will be discharged from all its debts and liabilities that arose before the confirmation of the plan, except as otherwise provided in the plan, the order of confirmation, or the Bankruptcy Code.

28. Which of the following statements is correct with respect to the reorganization provisions of Chapter 11 of the Federal Bankruptcy Code?

a. A trustee must always be appointed.
b. The debtor must be insolvent if the bankruptcy petition was filed voluntarily.
c. A reorganization plan may be filed by a creditor anytime after the petition date.
d. The commencement of a bankruptcy case may be voluntary or involuntary.

29. Under Chapter 11 of the Federal Bankruptcy Code, which of the following would **not** be eligible for reorganization?

a. Retail sole proprietorship.
b. Advertising partnership.
c. CPA professional corporation.
d. Savings and loan corporation.

O. Debts Adjustment Plans—Chapter 13

30. Which of the following is false regarding a Chapter 13 bankruptcy?

a. Individuals in general need not have regular income.
b. Creditors may not file involuntary petitions under this chapter.
c. It is initiated when the debtor files a voluntary petition in a bankruptcy court.
d. All of the above are true.

P. The Bankruptcy Abuse Prevention and Consumer Protection Act of 2005

31. Under the Bankruptcy Abuse Prevention and Consumer Protection Act of 2005, which of the following type(s) of debts is (are) nondischargeable in bankruptcy?

I. Death caused while intoxicated when operating an aircraft.
II. Injury caused while intoxicated when driving any motor vehicle.
III. Debts for Homeowner Association fees.

a. Only I.
b. I and II but not III.
c. I and III but not II.
d. I, II, and III.

Multiple-Choice Answers and Explanations

Answers

1. d	__ __	8. a	__ __	15. d	__ __	22. c	__ __	29. d	__ __
2. d	__ __	9. c	__ __	16. d	__ __	23. b	__ __	30. a	__ __
3. d	__ __	10. d	__ __	17. c	__ __	24. c	__ __	31. d	__ __
4. d	__ __	11. d	__ __	18. c	__ __	25. a	__ __		
5. d	__ __	12. c	__ __	19. b	__ __	26. d	__ __		
6. c	__ __	13. d	__ __	20. b	__ __	27. d	__ __	1st: __/31 = __%
7. a	__ __	14. b	__ __	21. d	__ __	28. d	__ __	2nd: __/31 = __%

Explanations

1. **(d)** Voluntary bankruptcy petition is a formal request by the debtor for an order of relief. This voluntary bankruptcy petition may be filed jointly by a husband and a wife. Answer (b) is incorrect because the debtor in a voluntary bankruptcy petition need not be insolvent but needs to state that s/he has debts and generally, has income below the state's median income. Answers (a) and (c) are incorrect because there is no requirement as to the minimum amount of the debtor's liabilities in a voluntary proceeding.

2. **(d)** Under Chapter 7 of the Federal Bankruptcy Code, a debtor may file a voluntary petition without showing that s/he is insolvent. S/he merely has to state the existence of debts and generally, has income below the state's median income. Therefore, the debtor is not required to show that liabilities exceed the fair market value of assets. Answer (a) is incorrect because a corporation may generally file a voluntary bankruptcy petition and there is not a requirement that it has previously filed under Chapter 11. Answer (b) is incorrect because when the debtor is automatically given an order for relief upon filing the petition, the actions to collect money by creditors are stayed. Secured creditors will resort to the collateral, however. Answer (c) is incorrect because the debtor is voluntarily going into bankruptcy and there is no requirement that twelve or more unsecured creditors be owed at least $15,325. Note that this requirement, as written, does not exist for an involuntary bankruptcy petition either.

3. **(d)** Most debtors may file a voluntary bankruptcy petition. Among those that may not are insurance companies, banks, and saving and loan associations. Answer (a) is incorrect because the number of creditors is not relevant for a voluntary bankruptcy petition. Answer (b) is incorrect because there is no need to show that a Chapter 11 bankruptcy would have been unsuccessful. Answer (c) is incorrect because the inability of the debtor to pay its debts as they become due is not relevant to a voluntary bankruptcy, only for involuntary bankruptcy.

4. **(d)** A debtor may file a voluntary bankruptcy petition without showing that s/he is insolvent. As long as the debtor's income does not exceed the state's median income, then the debtor may merely state that s/he has debts. There is also no requirement as to the number of creditors needed.

5. **(d)** Since there are fewer than twelve creditors, it is true that only one creditor is needed to file the petition. However, no one creditor is owed at least $15,325 of unsecured debt. Therefore, the claims can be aggregated to total at least $15,325 of unsecured debt. The only way this can be accomplished is by aggregating the claims of all four creditors. Note that Bounty Corporation is not enough because the secured debt is not counted in the total.

6. **(c)** When the debtor contests the petition s/he can still be forced into bankruptcy if the debtor is generally not paying his/her debts as they become due. Answer (a) is incorrect because the petition may be filed under either Chapter 7 (straight bankruptcy) or Chapter 11 (business reorganization). When the bankruptcy is involuntary, Chapter 7 and Chapter 11 are alternatives and have the same requirements for filing against business debtors. Answer (b) is incorrect because although the rules are different when there are fewer than twelve creditors versus when there are twelve or more creditors, Dart can be forced into bankruptcy when Decoy Publications files the petition because Decoy is owed over $15,325 of unsecured debt. Answer (d) is incorrect because there is no exception for the IRS.

7. **(a)** Once a valid petition in bankruptcy is filed, this automatically stays other legal proceedings against the debtor's estate. Also, the court appoints an interim trustee.

8. **(a)** The bankruptcy estate contains $100,000 after the sale of all assets and payment of administration expenses. The secured debt of $70,000 to Fracon Bank and the secured debt of $2,000 to Decoy Publications are satisfied first. (This actually takes place as a higher priority over the administrative expenses.) Therefore, after paying this $72,000 there is $28,000 left. The $12,000 of unpaid income tax has the next highest priority of those listed. This leaves $16,000 for the general creditors who filed on time. There are three of these, that is, Fracon who is owed $5,000 in excess of what the sale of the property brought, JOG who is owed $3,000, and Decoy who is still owed $12,000 in excess of the security interest. These three creditors together are owed $20,000 ($5,000 + $3,000 + $12,000). Since this is more than the $16,000 left, these 3 general creditors' debts are prorated. The last priority of unsecured claimants who filed late get nothing. Therefore, Nanstar Electric gets $0.

9. (c) The bankruptcy estate contains $100,000 after the sale of all assets and payment of administration expenses. The secured debt of $70,000 to Fracon Bank and the secured debt of $2,000 to Decoy Publications are satisfied first. (This actually takes place as a higher priority over the administrative expenses.) Therefore, after paying this $72,000 there is $28,000 left. The $12,000 of unpaid income tax has the next highest priority of those listed. This leaves $16,000 for the general creditors who filed on time. There are three of these, that is, Fracon who is owed $5,000 in excess of what the sale of the property brought, JOG who is owed $3,000, and Decoy who is still owed $12,000 in excess of the security interest. These three creditors together are owed $20,000 ($5,000 + $3,000 + $12,000). Since this is more than the $16,000 left, these three general creditors' debts are prorated. Fracon Bank gets money from both the unsecured and secured claims. From the unsecured claim, Fracon receives a prorated share or

$$\frac{16,000}{\$5,000 + \$3,000 + \$12,000} \times \$5,000 = \$4,000$$

Add this prorated share of $4,000 to the $70,000 Fracon received from the sold property to arrive at $74,000.

10. (d) The bankruptcy estate contains $100,000 after the sale of all assets and payment of administration expenses. The secured debt of $70,000 to Fracon Bank and the secured debt of $2,000 to Decoy Publications are satisfied first. (This actually takes place as a higher priority over the administrative expenses.) Therefore, after paying this $72,000 there is $28,000 left. The $12,000 of unpaid income tax has the next highest priority of those listed.

11. (d) Federal exemptions allowed under the Federal Bankruptcy Code include some equity in one motor vehicle and some equity in books and tools of one's trade. They also include various sources of income, among others, unemployment compensation.

12. (c) A trustee in bankruptcy has the power to employ court approved professionals, such as accountants and attorneys, to handle estate matters which require professional expertise. These professionals have the right to reimbursement for services rendered. A trustee is not deemed to have the appropriate expertise required to prepare tax returns; thus, a trustee may employ a CPA to perform this function. Simon, as trustee, has the power to employ himself to prepare tax returns if authorized by the court and may receive a separate fee for services rendered. Answer (a) is incorrect because Simon may serve as both trustee and preparer if authorized to do so by the court. Answer (b) is incorrect because Simon has the right to receive fees for services rendered as both a trustee and a preparer. Answer (d) is incorrect because the fee for services rendered in each capacity is determined on the basis of the value of the services rendered, not solely the size of the estate.

13. (d) Preferential transfers are payments made for antecedent debts which enable the creditor to receive more than s/he would under a Chapter 7 liquidation proceeding. Answer (a) is incorrect because a gift is not payment for an antecedent debt. Answer (b) is incorrect because transfers made in the ordinary course of business are exceptions to the trustee's power to

avoid a preferential transfer. Answer (c) is incorrect because a contemporaneous exchange between a creditor and the debtor whereby the debtor receives new value is not a preferential transfer. Prepaying an existing installment loan on inventory is making a payment on an antecedent debt which enables the creditor to receive more than s/he would in a liquidation proceeding.

14. (b) Under Chapter 7 of the Federal Bankruptcy Code, the trustee may set aside preferential transfers made to a creditor within ninety days prior to the filing of the petition for bankruptcy. Preferential transfers are those made for antecedent debts that allow the creditor to receive more than s/he would have under the bankruptcy law. All of these conditions were met for the National mortgage. Answer (a) is incorrect because National would not be considered an insider. Even though Hall's twin was a National employee, he was not an officer, director, or controlling stockholder of National. Furthermore, the preferential transfer was not made to him personally but to National Bank. Answer (c) is incorrect because to set aside a preferential transfer, the debtor must have made the transfer while he was insolvent in the bankruptcy sense. Therefore, if Hall was presumed insolvent when the mortgage was given, the trustee is able to set aside the preferential transfer. Note that insolvency is irrelevant to whether a transfer is preferential or nonpreferential. Answer (d) is incorrect because when Hall gave National Bank the mortgage to secure payment of the two-year-old loan, this was a preferential transfer because it attempted to give National Bank more priority than it would have had as a general unsecured creditor.

15. (d) An exception to the trustee's powers to avoid preferential transfers is a contemporaneous exchange between the debtor and creditor for new values. When Hall paid the $10,000 cash, he received the boat he had purchased from Olsen. Therefore, this $10,000 payment was a contemporaneous exchange for new value. Answer (a) is incorrect because this fact pattern fits the contemporaneous exchange exception. It does not matter that the exchange occurred within ninety days of the filing. Answer (b) is incorrect because Olsen received the $10,000 cash in exchange for the boat. Olsen therefore has not been put in a better position than other general creditors, as Hall received new value for the cash. Answer (c) is incorrect because the issue of presumption of insolvency is not relevant when determining whether a transfer is preferential or nonpreferential.

16. (d) Improper actions during a bankruptcy that bar a discharge of all of the debts include concealing property and refusing to explain a loss of assets. Answer (a) is incorrect because this action means that this particular creditor's claim will not be discharged but does not bar a general discharge of the other debts. Answer (b) is incorrect because although alimony and support payments are not discharged themselves, their existence does not bar a general discharge. Answer (c) is incorrect because the inability to pay does not bar a general discharge.

17. (c) The trustee in bankruptcy may set aside preferential transfers made within ninety days before the filing of the bankruptcy petition while the debtor is insolvent. The time is extended to the previous twelve months if the preferential transfer was made to an insider. In this question, Quick's solvency when the loan was made by Erly is not relevant because this loan was made thirteen months before the filing of the petition for bankruptcy. Answer (a) is incorrect because since payment to Erly was made more than three months but less than twelve months before the filing, it is important that Erly is an insider. Answer (b) is incorrect because the definition of a preferential transfer incorporates transfers made for an antecedent debt. Answer (d) is incorrect because since Erly is an insider, it is relevant that the payment to Erly was made within one year of the filing of the bankruptcy petition.

18. (c) Of those listed, wages of the bankrupt's employees receive the highest priority for up to a specified formula. Federal taxes have a low priority but are ahead of general creditors. Any deficiency for secured creditors after the collateral is sold is paid along with the general creditors.

19. (b) Administrative costs are one of the highest priorities among the priority general creditors. Only domestic support obligations have a superior claim to the administrative costs and there is no mention of domestic support obligations in this problem. Of those listed, the wages to employees each accrued within 180 days before the petition was filed have the next priority. Federal and state taxes are the next priority general creditor. Finally the claims in the ordinary course of business are a nonpriority general creditor so this claim is last.

20. (b) This is an intentional tort and the liability for these injuries would not be discharged in bankruptcy; however, this does not bar a general discharge of the debts. Answer (a) is incorrect because this is one of the prime acts that the law attempts to prevent. Answer (c) is incorrect because failing to satisfactorily explain a loss of assets can bar a general discharge. Answer (d) is incorrect because this is an act that can bar a general discharge.

21. (d) Corporations and partnerships cannot receive a discharge under Chapter 7 of the Federal Bankruptcy Code. Answer (a) is incorrect because although preferential transfers can be set aside, this would not prevent the discharge in bankruptcy. Answer (b) is incorrect because the rule is that destroying information relevant to the bankruptcy proceeding can bar a general discharge unless the act was justified under the circumstances. The accidental nature of the act in answer (b) is not a good case to bar the discharge. Answer (c) is incorrect because the rule states that the discharge is not allowed if the debtor has been discharged in bankruptcy within the past six years rather than ten years.

22. (c) Actions that bar a general discharge in bankruptcy include removing or destroying property within twelve months prior to filing the petition with intent to hinder, delay, or defraud creditors. Also included is making a false entry in a document related to the bankrupt's affairs. Obtaining credit by fraud involving the debtor's financial condition causes that debt to be nondischargeable. It, however, does not prevent a general discharge of all debts.

23. (b) The bankruptcy court can revoke the debtor's discharge if the debtor committed fraud during the bankruptcy proceedings, refused to obey lawful court orders, or failed to answer correctly material questions on the bankruptcy petition. Failure to list a creditor causes that creditor's debt not to be discharged but does not cause a revocation of the discharge.

24. (c) There is a list of various types of debts that will not be discharged in bankruptcy, even though a general discharge is allowed. Among these are liabilities from theft, embezzlement, and committing fraud about one's financial condition. Note that liabilities from ordinary negligence or from breaches of contract, whether intentional or not, are dischargeable in bankruptcy.

25. (a) Debts that are not discharged in bankruptcy include alimony, separate maintenance, and child support. Answer (b) is incorrect because a claim from a breach of contract is a typical type of claim discharged. Answer (c) is incorrect because any amount unsatisfied after sale of the collateral is paid along with the rest of the general creditors if sufficient funds remain after all of the other creditors are paid. These are discharged in bankruptcy. Answer (d) is incorrect because although intentional torts are not dischargable in bankruptcy, claims based on mere negligence are.

26. (d) To get debtors to reaffirm debts that have been discharged in bankruptcy, creditors must comply with certain procedures. In general, the reaffirmation must take place before the discharge is granted and it must be approved by the bankruptcy court. The debtor is given sixty days to rescind the reaffirmation after s/he agrees to it. Answer (a) is incorrect because it must be agreed to before discharge. Answer (b) is incorrect because there is no such limitation on the dollar amounts. Answer (c) is incorrect because the reaffirmation agreement is valid for almost all debt including household purpose debt.

27. (d) Under the reorganization provisions of Chapter 11 of the Federal Bankruptcy Code, a court supervised rehabilitation plan is adopted. It typically allows for the continued operation of the business and provides for the payment of all or part of the debts over an extended period of time. The payments to the creditors often come largely from future earnings. Answer (a) is incorrect because the court typically does not discharge the debtor from all of its debts under a Chapter 11 bankruptcy but provides for payments of debts out of future earnings. Answer (b) is incorrect because the plans can apply to any creditors whether they were in the portion that agreed to the plan or not. Answer (c) is incorrect because the debtor under Chapter 11 is often required to pay all or part of the debts out of future earnings.

28. (d) The Chapter 11 bankruptcy petition may either be filed voluntarily by the debtor or filed by the creditors to force the debtor into bankruptcy. Answer (a) is incorrect because a trustee need not be appointed. Answer (b) is incorrect because the debtor need not be insolvent to file a voluntary bankruptcy petition. Answer (c) is incorrect because only the debtor has the right to file the reorganization plan during the first 120 days the order for relief occurs.

29. (d) Under Chapter 11 of the Federal Bankruptcy Code, individuals, partnerships, and corporations are eligible for reorganization. Savings and loan companies, banks, and insurance companies are not eligible.

30. (a) It is a false statement and therefore the correct answer to be chosen because under a Chapter 13 bankruptcy—Debts Adjustment Plan—in general individuals need to have regular income along with other specified requirements. Answers (b) and (c) are not correct because they are both accurate statements for a Chapter 13 bankruptcy. Answer (d) is incorrect because response (a) is an accurate statement.

31. (d) Under the Bankruptcy Abuse Prevention and Consumer Protection Act of 2005, all three of the listed types of debts are nondischargeable in bankruptcy. Note that this act causes bankruptcy law to be much less friendly to debtors over previous law. Also note that Statement I is still true even if the situation caused injury rather than death.

Simulations

Task-Based Simulation 1

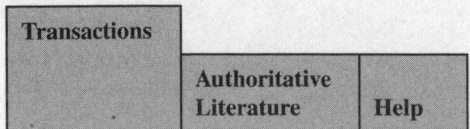

Situation

On May 1, 2013, Able Corp. was petitioned involuntarily into bankruptcy under the provisions of Chapter 7 of the Federal Bankruptcy Code.

When the petition was filed, Able had the following unsecured creditors:

Creditor	Amount owed
Cole	$18,000
Lake	2,000
Young	1,500
Thorn	1,000

The following transactions occurred before the bankruptcy petition was filed:

- On February 15, 2013, Able paid Vista Bank the $1,000 balance due on an unsecured business loan.
- On February 28, 2013, Able paid $1,000 to Owen, an officer of Able, who had lent Able money.
- On March 1, 2013, Able bought a computer for use in its business from Core Computer Co. for $2,000 cash.

Items 1 through 3 refer to the bankruptcy filing. For each item, determine whether the statement is True or False.

	True	False
1. Able can file a voluntary petition for bankruptcy if it is solvent.	○	○
2. Lake, Young, and Thorn can file a valid involuntary petition.	○	○
3. Cole alone can file a valid involuntary petition.	○	○

Items 4 through 6 refer to the transactions that occurred before the filing of the involuntary bankruptcy petition. Assuming the bankruptcy petition was validly filed, for each item determine whether the statement is True or False.

	True	False
4. The payment to Vista Bank would be set aside as a preferential transfer.	○	○
5. The payment to Owen would be set aside as a preferential transfer.	○	○
6. The purchase from Core Computer Co. would be set aside as a preferential transfer.	○	○

Task-Based Simulation 2

On April 25, 2013, Rusk Corporation was petitioned involuntarily into bankruptcy. At the time of the filing, Rusk had the following creditors:

- Safe Bank, for the balance due on the secured note and mortgage on Rusk's warehouse.
- Employee salary claims.
- 2012 federal income taxes due.
- Accountant's fees outstanding.
- Utility bills outstanding.

Prior to the bankruptcy filing, but while insolvent, Rusk engaged in the following transactions:

- On January 15, 2013, Rusk repaid all corporate directors' loans made to the corporation.
- On February 1, 2013, Rusk purchased raw materials for use in its manufacturing business and paid cash to the supplier.

Items 1 through 4 relate to Rusk's creditors and the January 15 and February 1 transactions. For each item, select from List I whether only statement I is correct, whether only statement II is correct, whether both statements I and II are correct, or whether neither statement I nor II is correct.

List I

A. I only.

B. II only.

C. Both I and II.

D. Neither I nor II.

	(A)	(B)	(C)	(D)
1. I. Safe Bank's claim will be the first paid of the listed claims because Safe is a secured creditor. II. Safe Bank will receive the entire amount of the balance of the mortgage due as a secured creditor regardless of the amount received from the sale of the warehouse.	○	○	○	○
2. I. The claim for 2012 federal income taxes due will be paid as a secured creditor claim. II. The claim for 2012 federal income taxes due will be paid prior to the general creditor claims.	○	○	○	○
3. I. The January 15 repayments of the directors' loans were preferential transfers even though the payments were made more than ten days before the filing of the petition. II. The January 15 repayments of the directors' loans were preferential transfers because the payments were made to insiders.	○	○	○	○
4. I. The February 1 purchase and payment was **not** a preferential transfer because it was a transaction in the ordinary course of business. II. The February 1 purchase and payment was a preferential transfer because it occurred within ninety days of the filing of the petition.	○	○	○	○

Simulation Solutions

Task-Based Simulation 1

Analysis		
	Authoritative Literature	Help

	True	False
1. Able can file a voluntary petition for bankruptcy if it is solvent.	●	○
2. Lake, Young, and Thorn can file a valid involuntary petition.	○	●
3. Cole alone can file a valid involuntary petition.	●	○

Explanations

1. (T) A debtor need not be insolvent to file a voluntary petition for bankruptcy. S/he merely needs to state that s/he has debts. Thus, Able could file even if solvent.

2. (F) In order to file a valid involuntary petition when there are fewer than twelve creditors, a single creditor may file the petition as long as s/he is owed at least $15,325 of unsecured debt. More than one creditor may be used to reach the $15,325 requirement. However, Lake, Young, and Thorn may not file a valid involuntary petition because they are collectively owed only $4,500.

3. (T) In order to file a valid involuntary petition when there are fewer than twelve creditors, a single creditor can file the petition as long as s/he is owed at least $15,325 of unsecured debt. Cole may file alone as s/he is owed $18,000.

	True	False
4. The payment to Vista Bank would be set aside as a preferential transfer.	●	○
5. The payment to Owen would be set aside as a preferential transfer.	●	○
6. The purchase from Core Computer Co. would be set aside as a preferential transfer.	○	●

Explanations

4. (T) The trustee may set aside preferential transfers of nonexempt property to a creditor made within the previous ninety days while insolvent. The payment made to Vista Bank is a preferential transfer because it was made less than ninety days before May 1, 2013, the date the involuntary petition was filed.

5. (T) The trustee may set aside preferential transfers of nonexempt property to a creditor made within the previous ninety days while insolvent. If the creditor was an insider, the time period is extended to within one year prior to the filing of the bankruptcy petition. The payment to Owen is a preferential transfer because Owen, an officer of Able Corp., is an insider, and the payment was made within one year prior to the filing of the petition.

6. (F) The payment to Core is not a preferential transfer because contemporaneously, Able received new value; that is, the computer. A contemporaneous exchange between creditor and debtor whereby the debtor receives new value is an exception to the trustee's power to set aside as a preferential transfer.

Task-Based Simulation 2

Transactions		
	Authoritative Literature	Help

	(A)	(B)	(C)	(D)

1. I. Safe Bank's claim will be the first paid of the listed claims because Safe is a secured creditor.

II. Safe Bank will receive the entire amount of the balance of the mortgage due as a secured creditor regardless of the amount received from the sale of the warehouse.

    ● (A)   ○ (B)   ○ (C)   ○ (D)

2. I. The claim for 2012 federal income taxes due will be paid as a secured creditor claim.

II. The claim for 2012 federal income taxes due will be paid prior to the general creditor claims.

    ○ (A)   ● (B)   ○ (C)   ○ (D)

3. I. The January 15 repayments of the directors' loans were preferential transfers even though the payments were made more than ten days before the filing of the petition.

II. The January 15 repayments of the directors' loans were preferential transfers because the payments were made to insiders.

    ○ (A)   ○ (B)   ● (C)   ○ (D)

4. I. The February 1 purchase and payment was **not** a preferential transfer because it was a transaction in the ordinary course of business.

II. The February 1 purchase and payment was a preferential transfer because it occurred within ninety days of the filing of the petition.

    ● (A)   ○ (B)   ○ (C)   ○ (D)

Explanations

1. (A) Statement I is correct since secured creditors receive payments before unsecured creditors (up to the value of the collateral) or receive the collateral itself. Statement II is incorrect because a secured creditor gets paid first only up to the value of the security. Any debt above the value of the security is given the lowest priority along with the general creditors.

2. (B) Statement I is incorrect because there is no collateral backing the 2012 federal income tax claim. It will thus not be paid as a secured creditor. Statement II is correct because taxes (federal, state, or local) have a higher priority than the general creditors.

3. (C) Statement I is correct because preferential transfers to insiders may be set aside when made within the previous **twelve** months. Thus, the January 15 repayment of corporate directors' loans are preferential transfers. Statement II is correct because the preferential transfer rule of ninety days is extended to twelve months in the case of insiders.

4. (A) Both transfers in the ordinary course of business and contemporaneous exchanges between creditors and debtors (whereby the debtors receive new value) are exceptions to the trustee's power to avoid preferential transfers. In this case, Rusk had purchased raw materials for use in its manufacturing business and paid cash to the supplier. These facts constitute an exception to the trustee's power to avoid a preferential transfer. Statement II is incorrect because the purchase and payment constitute an exception to the preferential transfer avoiding powers.

Module 31: Debtor-Creditor Relationships

Overview

The first part of this module discusses the rights and duties of debtors and creditors. One of the important areas is the idea of a lien. Note the different types of liens and their effect on debtors and creditors. Also covered are the concepts of composition agreements with creditors and assignments for the benefit of creditors. These can be used as alternatives to bankruptcy.

This module also discusses the concepts of guaranty and suretyship. These two are nearly the same concept. The main difference is that the guarantor is typically secondarily liable to the creditor, whereas the surety is normally primarily liable to the creditor. The rights and duties are otherwise almost the same for both the guarantors and the sureties. Before beginning the reading you should review the key terms at the end of the module.

A. Rights and Duties of Debtors and Creditors

1. Liens are creditors' claims on real or personal property to secure payment of debt or performance of obligations
2. Mechanic's lien or materialman's lien

    a. Statutory lien on real property (real estate) to secure payment of debts for services or materials to improve real property

> **EXAMPLE**
>
> Worker puts a new roof on an owner's building. Since the owner has not paid, the worker puts a lien on the building to secure payment. The worker may, after giving notice to the owner, foreclose on the property.

3. Artisan's lien

    a. Occurs when one repairs or improves personal property for another and retains possession of that personal property

> **EXAMPLE**
>
> A has a mechanic repair his car. Upon completion of the repairs, the mechanic retains possession of the car until A pays for the repairs.

    b. Artisan's lien terminates when creditor receives or is offered payment or when s/he gives up possession of property
    c. Artisan's lien generally has priority over other liens or interests as long as creditor retains possession of the personal property

    d. If debtor does not pay, most statutes allow lienholder to give notice to owner and then to sell property

4. Innkeeper's lien allows hotel to keep possession of guest's baggage until hotel charges are paid
5. Tax lien is imposed by federal, state, or local governments to secure the payment of taxes
6. Attachment is a court-ordered seizure of property due to lack of payment **prior** to court judgment for past-due debt

    a. If creditor wins at trial, property is sold to pay off debt
    b. There are certain constitutional requirements to protect debtors because property is seized based on word of creditors
    c. Writ of attachment allows creditor to take possession of personal property to satisfy debt pursuant to successful legal action

7. Writ of execution is remedy in which court order directs sheriff to seize debtor's property which can then be sold at judicial sale to pay off creditor

    a. Any excess over debt owed is paid to debtor
    b. Some property is exempt from seizure

8. Garnishment allows creditor to seize property, usually money, owed to debtor by third party

    a. Garnishment involves seizing debtor's property possessed by third parties such as banks (debtor's bank account) or employers (debtor's wages)

EXAMPLE

Creditor obtains a writ of garnishment from the court to collect from a bank $5,000 in the debtor's bank account.

---

    b. State and federal laws limit amount of wages that can be garnished

9. Judgment lien

    a. Occurs when a party is awarded damages by a court and the party files a lien against property to secure payment
    b. Debtor sometimes fraudulently tries to prevent creditor from satisfying a judgment (fraudulent conveyance)

        (1) Evidence of fraud includes one or more of the following:

            (a) Transfer of all assets
            (b) Debtor maintains use or possession of property after the alleged transfer
            (c) Secret transfer
            (d) Transfer made to a family member
            (e) Transfer made for inadequate consideration
            (f) Transfer done in anticipation of litigation

        (2) Conveyance is usually set aside

EXAMPLE

Debtor appears to sell all interest in some property but in fact names herself as the beneficiary as she conveys the legal title to the trustee.

---

10. Composition agreement with creditors (also called composition of creditors' agreement)

   a. Occurs by two or more creditors' agreement with debtor to accept less than full amount of debt as full satisfaction of debt
   b. Based on contract law so needs new consideration to be enforceable

      (1) New consideration is construed as two or more creditors each agreeing to accept less than full amount

         (a) Note that all creditors need not be part of agreement
         (b) Creditors need not be treated equally but treatment must be disclosed and agreed to by affected parties

      (2) Once debtor pays creditors at agreed rates, those debts are discharged

         (a) If debtor does not perform as agreed in composition agreement, creditors may choose to enforce either original debts or reduced debts under composition agreement.
         (b) Creditors not part of agreement are not bound by agreement and thus may resort to bankruptcy law or settle debt by own method

11. Assignment for the benefit of creditors

   a. Debtor voluntarily transfers all of his/her assets to an assignee (or trustee) to be sold for the benefit of creditors
   b. Assignee takes legal title

      (1) Debtor must convey all control of assets

   c. No agreement between creditors is necessary

      (1) Creditors who accept assignment receive pro rata share of debt they are owed
      (2) Dissatisfied creditors may file a petition in bankruptcy and assignments may be set aside

   d. Debts are not discharged unless they are paid in full by assignee

12. Homestead exemption

   a. In addition to providing exemptions against execution on debtor's assets, also provides exception for debtor's home so that unsecured creditors and trustees in bankruptcy may not satisfy debts from equity in debtor's home

      (1) However, mortgage liens and IRS tax liens take priority over homestead exemption

13. Fair Debt Collection Practices Act restricts how creditors may collect debts

   a. Collection agencies are prevented from contacting debtor-consumer at inconvenient hours, inconvenient places, or at work if employer objects

      (1) Also generally prevented from directly contacting debtor represented by an attorney

   b. Collection agencies may not use methods that are abusive or misleading
   c. Debt collector must provide debtor written notice of amount of debt and to whom the debt is owed within five days of first communication
   d. When debtor contests validity of debt, collection attempts must cease until collector sends debtor verification
   e. Debt collectors must bring suit in court near debtor's residence or in jurisdiction where contract signed
   f. If debt collector violates Act, that person is liable for actual damages plus other damages such as court costs and attorneys' fees
   g. Federal Trade Commission enforces this Act

      (1) May use cease and desist orders against debt collector
      (2) Civil lawsuits for damages are also allowed

   h. Act applies to collection agent collecting debt for another—does not apply if creditor collects own debt

14. Truth-in-Lending Act requires lenders and sellers to disclose credit terms on loans to consumer-debtors

    a. Disclosures include finance charges and annual percentage rate of interest charged

    b. Consumer has right to rescind credit within three days

    c. The Bankruptcy Abuse Prevention and Consumer Protection Act of 2005 not only has far-reaching effects on the US Bankruptcy Code (see Module 30), but also affects the Truth-in-Lending Act

        (1) The following are important provisions that are testable on the CPA exam:

            (a) Consumer lenders required to make additional disclosures in credit card statements relating to minimum payments, late fees, and introductory rates

                1] Also required to disclose toll-free number that consumer may call for estimate of time required to repay balance by making only minimum payments

            (b) Consumer lenders required to make more disclosures on tax consequences of home equity loans, and Internet-based credit card solicitations

            (c) Preserves defenses and claims of consumers against predatory loans sold by bankruptcy trustees that are covered by Truth-in-Lending Act

15. Equal Credit Opportunity Act prohibits discrimination in consumer credit transactions based on marital status, sex, race, color, religion, national origin, age, or receipt of welfare, or because applicant has exercised legal rights

    a. If creditor denies or revokes credit or worsens credit terms, must provide notice to debtor of specific reasons for adverse action

    b. Provides for civil and criminal penalties

16. Fair Credit Reporting Act prohibits consumer reporting agencies from including in consumer reports any inaccurate or obsolete information

    a. Information includes creditworthiness, mode of living, character, reputation in general

    b. Consumer is allowed access to credit reports

    c. If consumer disagrees with information in report, agency must investigate and correct if appropriate

        (1) If dispute remains, consumer may file statement of his/her version that becomes part of permanent consumer's credit record

17. Fair Credit Billing Act allows consumer to complain of billing errors and requires creditor to either explain or correct them

    a. If dispute remains, debtor may use lawsuit.

18. Fair Credit and Charge Card Disclosure Act requires disclosure of annual percentage rate, membership fee, etc. for credit or charge card solicitations or applications

    a. Credit card holder's liability is limited to $50 per credit card for unauthorized charges due to lost or stolen credit cards

        (1) Additional limitation—not liable for any charges after holder notifies issuer

---

EXAMPLE

Abel carelessly lost his credit card. He quickly notified the issuer. The person who found the card charged $100 on the card. All of this was after the issuer was notified that the card was lost. Abel is not liable for any of the unauthorized charges.

---

19. Bank debit cards

    a. Banks are liable for wrongful dishonor for failure to pay electronic fund transfer when customer has sufficient funds in account

> **NOW REVIEW MULTIPLE-CHOICE QUESTIONS 1 THROUGH 6**

B. Nature of Suretyship and Guaranty

1. In both suretyship and guaranty, third party promises to pay debt owed by debtor if debtor does not pay

   a. Third party's credit acts as security for debt to creditor
   b. Purpose of a suretyship agreement is to protect creditor by providing creditor with added security for obligation and to reduce creditor's risk of loss

---

EXAMPLE

In order for D to obtain a loan from C, S (who has a good credit standing) promises to C that S will pay debt if D does not.

---

2. Suretyship and guaranty agreements involve three parties

   a. Creditor (C in above example)

      (1) Obligee of principal debtor

   b. Principal debtor (D in above example)

      (1) Has liability for debt owed to creditor

   c. Surety (S in above example) or guarantor

      (1) Promises to perform or pay debt of principal debtor

3. Suretyship and guaranty contracts are similar, but many courts distinguish them as such

   a. In strict suretyship, the surety promises to be responsible for the debt and is **primarily** liable for debt

      (1) Creditor can demand payment from surety when debt is due
      (2) Unconditional guaranty is the standard suretyship relationship in which there are no further conditions required for guarantor to be asked to pay if debtor does not

---

EXAMPLE

G agreed in writing to act as surety when D took out a loan with C, the lender. If D does not pay, C may proceed directly against G. C need not try to collect from D first.

        (a) Creditor need not attempt collection from debtor first
        (b) Creditor need not give notice of debtor's default

   b. In contrast to suretyship, in guaranty contract, guarantor is normally **secondarily liable**

      (1) Guarantor can be required to pay debt only after debtor defaults and creditor demands payment from debtor
      (2) Sometimes guaranty contract requires creditor to both seek payment from debtor and bring suit if necessary, but do not assume that the creditor must sue the debtor first unless the Examiners specifically state that a lawsuit is required against the debtor before proceeding against the guarantor under the terms of the suretyship agreement

         (a) Called guarantor of collection

> **NOTE:** With those few exceptions noted in this outline, the rights and duties of both guarantors and sureties are essentially the same and the remainder of this outline will generally use surety and guarantor interchangeably.

4. Examples of typical suretyship and guaranty arrangements

   a. Seller of goods on credit requires buyer to obtain a surety to guarantee payment for goods purchased
   b. Bank requires owners or directors of closely held corporation to act as sureties for loan to corporation
   c. Endorser of negotiable instrument agrees to pay if instrument not paid
   d. In order to transfer a check or note, transferor may be required to obtain a surety (accommodation endorser) to guarantee payment
   e. Purchaser of real property expressly assumes seller's mortgage on property (i.e., promises to pay mortgage debt)

      (1) Seller then has become surety

5. Suretyship and guaranty contracts should satisfy elements of contracts in general

   a. If surety's or guarantor's agreement arises at same time as the contract between creditor and debtor, no separate consideration is needed

      (1) If creditor gave loan or credit before surety's promise, separate consideration is necessary to support surety's new promise

---

EXAMPLE

C loaned $200,000 to D. Terms provided that the loan is callable by C with one month notice to D. C gave the agreed notice and exercised her right to call the loan. D requested a sixty-day extension. C agreed to the extension when S agreed to be a surety on this loan. There is consideration for the new surety agreement since C gave up the right to call the loan sooner.

      (a) Consideration need not be received by surety—often it is principal debtor that benefits

   b. Surety's agreement to answer for debt or default of another must be in writing

      (1) Recall that under the Statute of Frauds under contract law, this is one of the types of contracts that must be in writing
      (2) However, if guarantor's promise is primarily for his/her own benefit, ("Main Purpose Doctrine") it need not be in writing

---

EXAMPLE

S agrees to pay D's debt to D's creditor if he defaults. The main motive of S is to keep D in business to assure a steady supply of an essential component. S's agreement need not be in writing.

EXAMPLE

A del credere agent is one who sells goods on credit to purchasers for the principal and agrees to pay the principal if the customers do not. Since his promise is primarily for his own benefit, it need not be in writing.

---

6. Third-party beneficiary contract is not a suretyship contract

   a. Third-party beneficiary contract is one in which third party receives benefits from agreement made between promisor and promisee, although third person is not party to contract

> **EXAMPLE**
>
> Father says: "Ship goods to my son and I will pay for them." This describes a third-party beneficiary contract, not a suretyship arrangement. Father is not promising to pay the debt of another, but rather engaging in an original promise to pay for goods that creditor delivers to son.

7. Indemnity contract is not a suretyship contract

   a. An indemnity contract is between two parties (rather than three) whereby indemnitor makes a promise to a potential debtor, indemnitee, (not to creditor as in suretyship arrangement), to indemnify and reimburse debtor for payment of debt or for loss that may arise in future. Indemnitor pays because it has assumed risk of loss, not because of any default by principal debtor as in suretyship arrangement.

> **EXAMPLE**
>
> Under terms of standard automobile collision insurance policy, insurance company agrees to indemnify automobile owner against damage to his/her car caused by collision.

8. Warranty (sometimes called guaranty) is not same as the type of guaranty under suretyship law

   a. Warranties arise under, for example, real property law or sales law

      (1) Involve making representations as to facts, title, quality, etc. of property

9. Capacity to act as surety or guarantor

   a. In general, individuals that have capacity to contract
   b. Partnerships may act as sureties unless partnership agreement expressly prohibits it from entering into suretyship contracts
   c. Individual partner normally has no authority to bind partnership as surety
   d. Modern trend is that corporations may act as sureties

NOW REVIEW MULTIPLE-CHOICE QUESTION 7

C. Creditor's Rights and Remedies

1. Against principal debtor

   a. Creditor has right to receive payment or performance specified in contract
   b. Creditor may proceed immediately against debtor upon default, unless contract states otherwise
   c. When a debtor has more than one debt outstanding with same creditor and makes a part payment, debtor may give instructions as to which debt the payment is to apply

      (1) If debtor gives no instructions, creditor is free to apply part payment to whichever debt s/he chooses; if one debt is guaranteed by surety and other is not makes no difference in absence of instructions by debtor

2. Against surety

   a. Creditor may proceed immediately against surety upon principal debtor's default

        (1) Unless contract requires it, it is not necessary to give surety notice of debtor's default

        (2) Since surety is primarily liable, s/he can be sued without creditor first attempting to collect from debtor

3. Against guarantor of collection

   a. A guarantor of collection's liability is conditioned on creditor notifying guarantor of debtor's default and creditor first attempting to collect from debtor

   b. Creditor must exhaust remedies by going against debtor before guarantor of collection's liability arises, even by lawsuit if necessary

   c. The specific language "guarantor of collection" must be used on the CPA Exam for these rules to apply; normally the Examiners are testing the ordinary surety.

   d. **Note that a guarantor of collection is different than a mere guarantor.** A creditor only needs to request payment from the debtor before proceeding against a guarantor, whereas the creditor must exhaust all legal remedies against the debtor before proceeding against a guarantor of collection.

4. Against security (collateral) held by surety or creditor

   a. Upon principal debtor's default, creditor may resort to collateral to satisfy debt

        (1) If creditor does resort to collateral, any excess collateral or amount realized by its disposal over debt amount must be returned to principal debtor

        (2) If collateral is insufficient to pay debt, creditor may proceed against surety or debtor for balance due (deficiency)

   b. Creditor is not required to use collateral; creditor may instead proceed immediately against surety or principal debtor

> ### NOW REVIEW MULTIPLE-CHOICE QUESTIONS 8 THROUGH 12

D. Surety's/Guarantor's Rights and Remedies

1. When the debt or obligation for which surety has given promise is due

   a. Exoneration

        (1) Surety may require (by lawsuit if necessary) debtor to pay obligation if debtor is able before surety has paid

        (2) Exoneration is not available if creditor demands prompt performance from surety

   b. Surety may request creditor to resort first to collateral if surety can show collateral is seriously depreciating in value, or if surety can show undue hardship will otherwise result

2. When surety pays debt or obligation

   a. S/he is entitled to right of reimbursement from debtor

        (1) May recover only actual payments to creditor

        (2) Surety is entitled to resort to collateral as satisfaction of right of reimbursement

        (3) Surety's payment after having received notice of principal debtor's valid defense against creditor causes surety to lose right of reimbursement

   b. S/he has right of subrogation

        (1) Upon payment, surety obtains same rights against principal debtor that creditor had

            (a) That is, surety steps into creditor's shoes

            (b) If debtor is bankrupt, surety is subrogated to rights of creditor's priority in bankruptcy proceeding

> **EXAMPLE**
>
> C, the creditor, required D, the debtor, to put up personal property as collateral on a loan and to also use S as a surety on the same loan. Upon D's default, C chooses to resort to S for payment. Upon payment, S may now sell the collateral under the right of subrogation because the creditor could have used the same right of sale of the collateral.

3. Creditor owes duty to surety to disclose, before surety agrees to contract, any information about material risks that are greater than surety aware of

   a. Creditor must also disclose facts inquired by surety

E. Surety's/Guarantor's Defenses

1. Surety may generally exercise defenses on contract that would be available **to debtor**

   a. Breach or failure of performance by **creditor**
   b. Impossibility or illegality of performance
   c. Creditor obtains debtor's promise by fraud, duress, or misrepresentation
   d. Statute of limitations
   e. Except that surety may **not use** debtor's **personal** defenses as discussed later

2. Surety may take advantage of **own** contractual defenses

   a. Fraud or duress

      (1) If creditor obtains surety's promise by fraud or duress, contract is voidable at surety's option

> **EXAMPLE**
>
> Creditor forces X to sign suretyship agreement at threat of great bodily harm.

   (2) If creditor gets principal debtor's promise using fraud or duress, then surety not liable

      (a) Exception: surety is liable if was aware of fraud or duress before s/he became surety

   (3) Fraud by principal debtor on surety to induce a suretyship agreement will **not** release surety if creditor has extended credit in good faith

      (a) But if creditor had knowledge of debtor's fraudulent representations, then surety may avoid liability

> **EXAMPLE**
>
> Y asked Ace to act as surety on a loan from Bank. In order to induce Ace to act as surety, Y made fraudulent representations concerning its financial position to Ace. This fraud by Y will not release surety, Ace, if the creditor, Bank, had no knowledge of the fraud and extended credit in good faith. But if Bank had knowledge of Y's fraudulent representations, then Ace has a good defense and can avoid liability. Note that if Bank finds out about Y's fraudulent representations after Bank has extended credit, Ace has no defense.

   b. Suretyship contract itself is void due to illegality
   c. Incapacity of surety (e.g., surety is a minor)
   d. Failure of consideration for suretyship contract

(1) However, when surety's and principal debtor's obligations are incurred at same time, there is no need for any separate consideration beyond that supporting principal debtor's contract; if surety's undertaking is entered into subsequent to debtor's contract, it must be supported by separate consideration (see section B.5.a. of this outline)

e. Suretyship agreement is **not** in writing as required under Statute of Frauds
f. Creditor fails to notify surety of any material facts within creditor's knowledge concerning debtor's ability to perform

---

EXAMPLE

Creditor's failure to report to surety that debtor has defaulted on several previous occasions.

EXAMPLE

Creditor's failure to report to surety that debtor submitted fraudulent financial statements to surety to induce suretyship agreement.

---

g. Surety, in general, may use any obligations owed by creditor to surety as a setoff against any payments owed to creditor

(1) True even if setoff arises from separate transaction

3. Acts of creditor or debtor materially affecting surety's obligations

a. Tender of performance by debtor or surety and refusal by creditor will discharge surety

(1) However, tender of performance for obligation to pay money does not normally release principal debtor but stops accrual of interest on debt

b. Release of principal debtor from liability by creditor without consent of surety will also discharge surety's liability

(1) But surety is not released if creditor specifically reserves his/her rights against surety

(a) However, surety upon paying may then seek recovery from debtor

NOTE: If the Examiners test this issue of the creditor releasing the debtor, they usually have the creditor reserve its rights against the surety; thus the surety is still liable to the creditor. The reason the release of the debtor does not materially affect the surety's obligation is that the surety is primarily liable to the creditor. Thus, the creditor already had the right to pursue the debt directly from the surety.

c. Release of surety by creditor

(1) Does **not** release principal debtor because debtor is liable whether or not surety is liable

d. Proper performance by debtor or satisfaction of creditor through collateral will discharge surety
e. Variance in terms and conditions of contract subsequent to surety's undertaking

(1) Accommodation (noncompensated) surety is completely discharged for any change in contract made by creditor on terms required of principal debtor

(2) Commercial (compensated) surety is completely released if modification in principal debtor's contract materially increases risk to surety

    (a) If risk not increased materially, then surety not released but his/her obligation is reduced by amount of loss due to modification

(3) Surety may consent to modifications so that they are not defenses

(4) Surety is not released if creditor modifies principal debtor's duties to be beneficial to surety (i.e., decreases surety's risk)

EXAMPLE

Creditor reduces interest rate on loan to principal debtor from 12% to 10%.

---

(5) Modifications that affect rights of sureties based on above principles

    (a) Extension of time on principal debtor's obligation, but only to the extent that the extension causes a loss to the surety and only that additional loss will be discharged.

    (b) Change in amount, place, or manner of principal debtor's obligations

    (c) Modification of duties of principal debtor

    (d) Substitution of debtor's or delegation of debtor's obligation to another

        1] Note how this may result in change in risk to the surety

    (e) Release, surrender, destruction, or impairment of collateral by creditor before or after debtor's default releases surety by amount decreased

---

EXAMPLE

S is a surety on a $10,000 loan between Creditor and Debtor. Creditor is also holding $1,000 of Debtor's personal property as collateral on the $10,000 loan. Before the loan is paid, Creditor returns the collateral to Debtor. This action releases S from $1,000 of the $10,000 loan.

EXAMPLE

S is a compensated surety for a loan between Debtor and Creditor. The loan had also been secured by collateral. Upon default, Creditor took possession of the collateral but let it get damaged by rain. The collateral was impaired by $500. Creditor also sought payment from S, the compensated surety. S may reduce his payment to Creditor by $500.

---

(6) In order to release surety, there must be an actual alteration or variance in terms of contract and not an option or election that principal debtor can exercise under express terms of original agreement which surety has guaranteed

---

EXAMPLE

Tenant and landlord entered into a two-year leasing agreement which expressly contained an option for an additional year which could be exercised by tenant, with X acting as surety on lease contract. If tenant exercises this option, X still remains bound as surety.

4. Following are **not** defenses of surety/guarantor

a. Personal defenses of principal debtor

(1) Death of debtor or debtor's lack of capacity (e.g., debtor is a minor or was legally insane when contract was made)

(2) Insolvency (or discharge in bankruptcy) of debtor

(a) Possibility of debtor's insolvency is a primary reason for engaging in a surety arrangement

(3) Personal debtor's setoffs

(a) Unless debtor assigns them to surety

b. Creditor did not give notice to surety of debtor's default or creditor did not first proceed against principal debtor

(1) Unless a conditional guarantor and creditor violated condition

c. Creditor does not resort to collateral

d. Creditor delays in proceeding against debtor unless delay exceeds statute of limitations

e. When creditor is owed multiple debts by same debtor, creditor may choose to apply payment to any of the debts unless debtor directs otherwise—surety cannot direct which debt payment applies to

---

EXAMPLE

Debtor owes two debts to Creditor. S is acting as a surety on one of these debts. When Debtor makes a payment, Creditor applies it to the debt on which S is not a surety since Debtor did not indicate which one. The surety has no defense from these facts and is not released.

NOW REVIEW MULTIPLE-CHOICE QUESTIONS 13 THROUGH 20

F. Cosureties

1. Cosureties exist when there is more than one surety for same obligation of principal debtor to same creditor

a. Not relevant whether cosureties are aware of each other or became cosureties at different times

(1) Must be sureties for same debtor for same obligation

b. Cosureties need not be bound for same amount; they can guarantee equal or unequal amounts of debt

(1) Collateral, if any, need not be held equally

c. Cosureties need not sign same document

2. Cosureties are jointly and severally liable to creditor

a. That is, creditor can proceed against any of the sureties jointly or against each one individually to extent surety has assumed liability

b. If creditor sues multiple sureties, s/he may recover in any proportion from each, but may not recover more than debtor's total obligation

c. Proceeding against one or more sureties does not release remaining surety or sureties

3. Right of contribution exists among cosureties

a. Right of contribution arises when cosurety, in performance of debtor's obligation, pays more than his/her proportionate share of total liability, and thereby entitles cosurety to compel other cosureties to compensate him/her for excess amount paid (i.e., contribution from other cosureties for their pro rata share of liability)

4. Cosureties are only liable in contribution for their proportionate share

a. Cosurety's pro rata share is proportion that each surety's risk (i.e., amount each has personally guaranteed) bears to total amount of risk assumed by all sureties by using the following formula:

$$\frac{\text{Dollar amount individual cosurety personally guaranteed}}{\text{Total dollar amount of risk assumed by all cosureties}}$$

> **EXAMPLE**
>
> X and Y are cosureties for $5,000 and $10,000, respectively, of a $10,000 debt. Each is liable in proportion to amount each has personally guaranteed. Since X guaranteed $5,000 of debt and Y guaranteed $10,000 of debt, then X is individually liable for 1/3 ($5,000/$15,000) of debt and Y is individually liable for 2/3 ($10,000/$15,000) of debt. If debtor defaults on only $3,000 of debt, X is liable for $1,000 (1/3 × $3,000) and Y is liable for $2,000 (2/3 × $3,000). Although creditor may recover $3,000 from either, each cosurety has right of contribution from other cosurety.

> **EXAMPLE**
>
> Refer to the preceding example. If the creditor recovers all of the $3,000 debt from Y, then Y, under the right of contribution, can recover $1,000 from X so that each will end up paying his/her proportionate amount.

5. Each cosurety is entitled to share in any collateral pledged (either held by creditor or other cosurety) in proportion to cosurety's liability for debtor's default

> **EXAMPLE**
>
> If in above illustration, cosurety Y held collateral pledged by debtor worth $900, both cosureties X and Y would be entitled to share in collateral in proportion to their respective liabilities. X would be entitled to 1/3 ($5,000/$15,000) of $900 collateral, or $300; and Y would be entitled to 2/3 ($10,000/$15,000) of $900 collateral, or $600.

6. Discharge or release of one cosurety by creditor results in a reduction of liability of remaining cosurety

 a. Remaining cosurety is released only to extent of released cosurety's pro rata share of debt liability (unless there is a reservation of rights by creditor against remaining cosurety)

> **EXAMPLE**
>
> A and B are cosureties for $4,000 and $12,000, respectively, on a $12,000 debt. If creditor releases cosurety A, cosurety B is released to extent of cosurety A's liability. Each is liable in proportion to amount each has personally guaranteed. Since A guaranteed $4,000 of debt and B guaranteed $12,000 of debt, then A is individually liable for 1/4 ($4,000/$16,000) of debt and B is individually liable for 3/4 ($12,000/$16,000) of debt, that is, $9,000. Therefore, cosurety B is released of A's pro rata liability of $3,000 (1/4 × $12,000), and only remains a surety for $9,000 ($12,000 − $3,000) of debt.

7. A cosurety is not released from obligation to perform merely because another cosurety refuses to perform

    a. However, upon payment of full obligation, cosurety can demand a pro rata contribution from his/her non-performing cosurety

    b. Cosurety is not released if other cosureties are **unable** to pay (i.e., dead, bankrupt)

       (1) In which case, modify the formula found at Section F.4.a. by taking those cosureties that cannot pay completely out of formula and use it with all remaining cosureties

8. Cosureties have rights of exoneration, reimbursement, and subrogation like any surety

> **NOW REVIEW MULTIPLE-CHOICE QUESTIONS 21 THROUGH 27**

G. Surety Bonds

1. An acknowledgment of an obligation to make good the performance by another of some act or responsibility

    a. Usually issued by companies which for a stated fee assume risk of performance by bonded party

    b. Performance of act or responsibility by bonded party discharges surety's obligation

2. Performance bonds are used to have surety guarantee completion of terms of contracts

    a. Construction bond guarantees builder's obligation to complete construction

       (1) If builder breaches contract, surety can be held liable for damages but not for specific performance (i.e., cannot be required to complete construction)

          (a) Surety may complete construction if chooses to

3. Fidelity bonds are forms of insurance that protects an employer against losses sustained due to acts of dishonest employees.
4. Official bond is guaranteeing that public officials will faithfully execute their duties.
5. Surety bonding company retains right of subrogation against bonded party

KEY TERMS

Assignment for the benefit of creditors. A possible alternative to bankruptcy. This occurs where a debtor assigns assets to a third party who uses those assets to pay the debtor's creditors. It is important to remember that an assignment for the benefit of creditors does *not* release the debtor from the debt, unless the debts are paid in full.

Bond. A contract involving a compensated surety.

Composition. A possible alternative to bankruptcy; compare and contrast to the assignment for the benefit of creditors (above). This is an agreement between a debtor and its creditors where the debtor will repay a portion of the debt owed. This agreement releases the debtor from its obligations only to the creditors who are part of the composition.

Contribution. When a cosurety pays more than its proportionate share of the debt it can demand payment from other cosureties so that each surety is paying its proportionate share of the debt.

Cosurety. Two or more sureties are guaranteeing the same debt.

Guarantor. Similar to a surety, but a guarantor is secondarily liable to the creditor. Thus, in the event that the debtor defaults the creditor must at least ask the debtor to pay, but it the event the debtor says no, then the creditor may seek payment from the guarantor.

Reimbursement. If the surety pays the debt, the surety is entitled to receive whatever it paid to the creditor from the debtor.

Subrogation. After the surety has paid the debt it acquires the rights of the creditor and may now exercise those rights against the debtor. Thus, if the debtor had given the creditor collateral, the surety would have rights against the collateral.

Surety. A party who promises to pay the debts of another party. Sureties are primarily liable to the creditor.

Multiple-Choice Questions (1–27)

A. Rights and Duties of Debtors and Creditors

1. A debtor may attempt to conceal or transfer property to prevent a creditor from satisfying a judgment. Which of the following actions will be considered an indication of fraudulent conveyance?

	Debtor remaining in possession after conveyance	Secret conveyance	Debtor retains an equitable benefit in the property conveyed
a.	Yes	Yes	Yes
b.	No	Yes	Yes
c.	Yes	Yes	No
d.	Yes	No	Yes

2. A homestead exemption ordinarily could exempt a debtor's equity in certain property from postjudgment collection by a creditor. To which of the following creditors will this exemption apply?

	Valid home mortgage lien	Valid IRS tax lien
a.	Yes	Yes
b.	Yes	No
c.	No	Yes
d.	No	No

3. Which of the following statements is (are) correct regarding debtors' rights?

I. State exemption statutes prevent all of a debtor's personal property from being sold to pay a federal tax lien.
II. Federal social security benefits received by a debtor are exempt from garnishment by creditors.

a. I only.
b. II only.
c. Both I and II.
d. Neither I nor II.

4. Under the Federal Fair Debt Collection Practices Act, which of the following would a collection service using improper debt collection practices be subject to?

a. Abolishment of the debt.
b. Reduction of the debt.
c. Civil lawsuit for damages for violating the Act.
d. Criminal prosecution for violating the Act.

5. Which of the following liens generally require(s) the lienholder to give notice of legal action before selling the debtor's property to satisfy the debt?

	Mechanic's lien	Artisan's lien
a.	Yes	Yes
b.	Yes	No
c.	No	Yes
d.	No	No

6. Which of the following prejudgment remedies would be available to a creditor when a debtor owns no real property?

	Writ of attachment	Garnishment
a.	Yes	Yes
b.	Yes	No
c.	No	Yes
d.	No	No

B. Nature of Suretyship and Guaranty

7. Which of the following involve(s) a suretyship relationship?

I. Transferee of a note requires transferor to obtain an accommodation endorser to guarantee payment.
II. The purchaser of goods agrees to pay for the goods but to have them shipped to another party.
III. The shareholders of a small, new corporation agree in writing to be personally liable on a corporate loan if the corporation defaults.

a. I only.
b. II only.
c. I and II only.
d. I and III only.

C. Creditor's Rights and Remedies

8. Which of the following events will reduce a surety's liability to the creditor?

a. The principal debtor was involuntarily petitioned into bankruptcy.
b. The creditor failed to notify the surety of a partial surrender of the principal debtor's collateral.
c. The creditor was adjudicated incompetent after the debt arose.
d. The principal debtor exerted duress to obtain the surety agreement.

9. Reuter Bank loaned Sabean Corporation $500,000 in writing. As part of the agreement, Reuter required that the three owners of Sabean act as sureties on the loan. The corporation also required that some real estate owned by Sabean Corporation be used as collateral for 40% of the loan. The collateral and suretyship agreements were put in writing and signed by all relevant parties. When the $500,000 loan became due, which of the following rights does Reuter Bank have?

I. May demand payment of the full amount immediately from the sureties when the corporation defaults on the loan.
II. May demand payment of the full amount immediately from the sureties even if Reuter does not attempt to recover any amount from the collateral.
III. May attempt to recover up to $200,000 from the collateral and the remainder from the sureties, even if the remainder is more than $300,000.
IV. Must first attempt to collect the debt from Sabean Corporation before it can resort to the sureties or the collateral.

a. I and III only.
b. II only.

c. I, II, and III only.
d. IV only.

10. Belmont acts as a surety for a loan to Diablo from Chaffin. In which of the following cases would Belmont be released from liability?

  I. Diablo dies.
 II. Diablo files bankruptcy.
III. Chaffin modifies Diablo's contract, increasing Diablo's risk of nonpayment.

    a. I only.
    b. III only.
    c. I and III only.
    d. I, II, and III.

11. A party contracts to guaranty the collection of the debts of another. As a result of the guaranty, which of the following statements is correct?

    a. The creditor may proceed against the guarantor without attempting to collect from the debtor.
    b. The guaranty must be in writing.
    c. The guarantor may use any defenses available to the debtor.
    d. The creditor must be notified of the debtor's default by the guarantor.

12. Sorus and Ace have agreed, in writing, to act as guarantors of collection on a debt owed by Pepper to Towns, Inc. The debt is evidenced by a promissory note. If Pepper defaults, Towns will be entitled to recover from Sorus and Ace unless

    a. Sorus and Ace are in the process of exercising their rights against Pepper.
    b. Sorus and Ace prove that Pepper was insolvent at the time the note was signed.
    c. Pepper dies before the note is due.
    d. Towns has **not** attempted to enforce the promissory note against Pepper.

D.   Surety's/Guarantor's Rights and Remedies

13. Which of the following rights does a surety have?

	Right to compel the creditor to collect from the principal debtor	Right to compel the creditor to proceed against the principal debtor's collateral
a.	Yes	Yes
b.	Yes	No
c.	No	Yes
d.	No	No

14. Under the law of suretyship, which are generally among the rights that the surety may use?

    I. Subrogation.
  II. Exoneration.
III. Reimbursement from debtor.

    a. I only.
    b. III only.

c. I and II only.
d. I, II, and III.

E.   Surety's/Guarantor's Defenses

15. Which of the following defenses would a surety be able to assert successfully to limit the surety's liability to a creditor?

    a. A discharge in bankruptcy of the principal debtor.
    b. A personal defense the principal debtor has against the creditor.
    c. The incapacity of the surety.
    d. The incapacity of the principal debtor.

16. Which of the following events will release a noncompensated surety from liability?

    a. Release of the principal debtor's obligation by the creditor but with the reservation of the creditor's rights against the surety.
    b. Modification by the principal debtor and creditor of their contract that materially increases the surety's risk of loss.
    c. Filing of an involuntary petition in bankruptcy against the principal debtor.
    d. Insanity of the principal debtor at the time the contract was entered into with the creditor.

17. Which of the following is **not** a defense that a surety may use to avoid payment of a debtor's obligation to a creditor?

    a. The creditor had committed fraud against the debtor to induce the debtor to take on the debt with this creditor.
    b. The creditor had committed fraud against the surety to induce the surety to guarantee the debtor's payment of a loan.
    c. The statute of limitations has run on the debtor's obligation.
    d. The debtor took out bankruptcy.

18. Which of the following acts always will result in the total release of a compensated surety?

    a. The creditor changes the manner of the principal debtor's payment.
    b. The creditor extends the principal debtor's time to pay.
    c. The principal debtor's obligation is partially released.
    d. The principal debtor's performance is tendered.

19. Green was unable to repay a loan from State Bank when due. State refused to renew the loan unless Green provided an acceptable surety. Green asked Royal, a friend, to act as surety on the loan. To induce Royal to agree to become a surety, Green fraudulently represented Green's financial condition and promised Royal discounts on merchandise sold at Green's store. Royal agreed to act as surety and the loan was renewed. Later, Green's obligation to State was discharged in Green's bankruptcy. State wants to hold Royal liable. Royal may avoid liability

    a. If Royal can show that State was aware of the fraudulent representations.
    b. If Royal was an uncompensated surety.

c. Because the discharge in bankruptcy will prevent Royal from having a right of reimbursement.

d. Because the arrangement was void at the inception.

20. Wright agreed to assure King's loan from Ace Bank. Which of the following events would release Wright from the obligation to pay the loan?

a. Ace seeking payment of the loan only from Wright.
b. King is granted a discharge in bankruptcy.
c. Ace is paid in full by King's spouse.
d. King is adjudicated mentally incompetent.

F. Cosureties

21. A distinction between a surety and a cosurety is that only a cosurety is entitled to

a. Reimbursement (Indemnification).
b. Subrogation.
c. Contribution.
d. Exoneration.

22. Ivor borrowed $420,000 from Lear Bank. At Lear's request, Ivor entered into an agreement with Ash, Kane, and Queen for them to act as cosureties on the loan. The agreement between Ivor and the cosureties provided that the maximum liability of each cosurety was: Ash, $84,000; Kane, $126,000; and Queen, $210,000. After making several payments, Ivor defaulted on the loan. The balance was $280,000. If Queen pays $210,000 and Ivor subsequently pays $70,000, what amounts may Queen recover from Ash and Kane?

a. $0 from Ash and $0 from Kane.
b. $42,000 from Ash and $63,000 from Kane.
c. $70,000 from Ash and $70,000 from Kane.
d. $56,000 from Ash and $84,000 from Kane.

23. Nash, Owen, and Polk are cosureties with maximum liabilities of $40,000, $60,000, and $80,000, respectively. The amount of the loan on which they have agreed to act as cosureties is $180,000. The debtor defaulted at a time when the loan balance was $180,000. Nash paid the lender $36,000 in full settlement of all claims against Nash, Owen, and Polk. The total amount that Nash may recover from Owen and Polk is

a. $0
b. $24,000
c. $28,000
d. $140,000

24. Ingot Corp. lent Flange $50,000. At Ingot's request, Flange entered into an agreement with Quill and West for them to act as compensated cosureties on the loan in the amount of $100,000 each. Ingot released West without Quill's or Flange's consent, and Flange later defaulted on the loan. Which of the following statements is correct?

a. Quill will be liable for 50% of the loan balance.
b. Quill will be liable for the entire loan balance.
c. Ingot's release of West will have **no** effect on Flange's and Quill's liability to Ingot.
d. Flange will be released for 50% of the loan balance.

25. Mane Bank lent Eller $120,000 and received securities valued at $30,000 as collateral. At Mane's request, Salem and Rey agreed to act as uncompensated cosureties on the loan. The agreement provided that Salem's and Rey's maximum liability would be $120,000 each.

Mane released Rey without Salem's consent. Eller later defaulted when the collateral held by Mane was worthless and the loan balance was $90,000. Salem's maximum liability is

a. $30,000
b. $45,000
c. $60,000
d. $90,000

26. Lane promised to lend Turner $240,000 if Turner obtained sureties to secure the loan. Turner agreed with Rivers, Clark, and Zane for them to act as cosureties on the loan from Lane. The agreement between Turner and the cosureties provided that compensation be paid to each of the cosureties. It further indicated that the maximum liability of each cosurety would be as follows: Rivers $240,000, Clark $80,000, and Zane $160,000. Lane accepted the commitments of the sureties and made the loan to Turner. After paying ten installments totaling $100,000, Turner defaulted. Clark's debts, including the surety obligation to Lane on the Turner loan, were discharged in bankruptcy. Later, Rivers properly paid the entire outstanding debt of $140,000. What amount may Rivers recover from Zane?

a. $0
b. $56,000
c. $70,000
d. $84,000

27. Which of the following rights does one cosurety generally have against another cosurety?

a. Exoneration.
b. Subrogation.
c. Reimbursement.
d. Contribution.

Multiple-Choice Answers and Explanations

Answers

1.	a	__ __	7.	d	__ __	13.	d	__ __	19.	a	__ __	25.	b	__ __
2.	d	__ __	8.	b	__ __	14.	d	__ __	20.	c	__ __	26.	b	__ __
3.	b	__ __	9.	c	__ __	15.	c	__ __	21.	c	__ __	27.	d	__ __
4.	c	__ __	10.	b	__ __	16.	b	__ __	22.	b	__ __			
5.	a	__ __	11.	b	__ __	17.	d	__ __	23.	c	__ __	1st: __/27 = __%
6.	a	__ __	12.	d	__ __	18.	d	__ __	24.	a	__ __	2nd: __/27 = __%

Explanations

1. (a) Fraudulent conveyance of property is done with the intent to defraud a creditor, hinder or delay him/her, or put the property out of his/her reach. If the debtor maintains possession of the property, secretly transfers or hides the property, or retains an equitable interest in the property, then a fraudulent conveyance has occurred as all of the three actions prevent the creditor from receiving the full property.

2. (d) Although a homestead exemption can exempt a debtor's equity in certain property from postjudgment collection by a creditor, the exemption applies to general creditors and the bankruptcy trustee, not secured creditors or lien holders.

3. (b) Under garnishment procedures, creditors may attach a portion of the debtor's wages to pay off a debt. There are legal limits as to how much of the wages can be garnished. Likewise, federal social security benefits are protected from garnishment by creditors. Therefore, statement II is correct. Statement I, however, is incorrect because federal tax liens can be used to sell a debtor's personal property to pay taxes.

4. (c) The Federal Fair Debt Collection Practices Act was passed to prevent debt collectors from using unfair or abusive collection methods. The Federal Trade Commission is charged with enforcement of this Act but aggrieved parties may also use a civil lawsuit against the debt collector who violates this Act. Answers (a) and (b) are incorrect because the remedy is a suit for damages or a suit for up to $1,000 for violation of the Act if damages are not proven. The remedy is not a reduction or abolishment of the debt. Answer (d) is incorrect because this Act does not provide for criminal prosecution.

5. (a) Liens are used by creditors to secure payment for services or materials, in the case of a mechanic's lien, or for repairs, in the case of an artisan's lien. They require that notice be given to the debtor before the creditor can sell the property to satisfy the debt. Generally, a debtor is entitled to notice prior to the disposition of his/her property for any type of lien.

6. (a) When a creditor wishes to collect a past-due debt from the debtor, s/he may use a writ of attachment. This is a prejudgment remedy in which the creditor is allowed to take into possession some personal property of the debtor prior to getting a judgment in a lawsuit for the past-due debt. The

debtor may also wish to collect the debt by use of garnishment. This allows the creditor to obtain property of the debtor that is held by a third party. Typical examples include garnishing wages owed by the employer to the employee-debtor or garnishing the debtor's bank account. To avoid abuses, there are limitations on both of these remedies.

7. (d) Statement I illustrates a suretyship relationship in which the endorser of the note is the surety. Statement II illustrates a third-party beneficiary contract, not a suretyship relationship. The purchaser has agreed to pay for the goods as his/her own debt. The party to receive the goods is the third-party beneficiary. Statement III illustrates a suretyship relationship in which the shareholders are sureties.

8. (b) The release or impairment of collateral injures a surety's interest since a surety would acquire rights against the collateral upon paying the off the debt. Accordingly if collateral is released or impaired, then the surety's obligation is reduced by the value of the collateral or by the amount of the impairment. Answer (a) is incorrect—bankruptcy is a personal defense of the debtor and is not a defense for the surety. Answer (c) is incorrect because this is a debt that is voidable at the option of the creditor. Answer (d) is incorrect because there is a possible wrong against the debtor but this does not release the surety.

9. (c) The creditor, Reuter Bank, has a lot of flexibility in remedies. Although Reuter may attempt to collect from Sabean when the loan is due, it is not required to but instead may resort to the sureties or to the collateral up to the 40% agreed upon, or both.

10. (b) When the creditor modifies the debtor's contract, increasing the surety's risk, the surety is released. Note that death of the principal debtor or the debtor's filing bankruptcy are personal defenses of the debtor that the surety cannot use. Such risks are some of the reasons creditors prefer sureties.

11. (b) Under the Statute of Frauds under contract law, a surety's (guarantor's) agreement to answer for the debt or default of another must be in writing. Answer (a) is incorrect, as a guarantor of collection's liability is conditioned on the creditor notifying the guarantor of the debtor's default and the creditor first attempting to collect from the debtor. Answer (c) is incorrect as the guarantor may not use the debtor's personal defenses, such as death or insolvency. Answer (d) is incorrect because it is the creditor that must notify the guarantor of the debtor's default, not vice versa.

12. (d) A guarantor's liability is conditioned on the creditor notifying the guarantor of the debtor's default and the creditor first attempting to collect from the debtor. In this case, if Towns has not attempted to collect against Pepper, then Towns would not yet be able to collect against Sorus and Ace. Answer (a) is incorrect because Sorus' and Ace's performance of the right of reimbursement from Pepper does not preclude Towns' recovery from Sorus and Ace. Answers (b) and (c) are incorrect because insolvency of the debtor and death of the debtor are not valid defenses of the guarantor against the creditor.

13. (d) The surety is primarily liable on the debt of the principal debtor. Therefore, the creditor can seek payment directly from the surety as soon as the debt is due. For this reason, the surety cannot require the creditor to collect from the debtor nor can s/he compel the creditor to proceed against any collateral the principal debtor may have.

14. (d) Upon payment, the surety obtains the right of subrogation which is the ability to use the same rights the creditor had. Also, the surety may resort to the right of exoneration by requiring the debtor to pay when s/he is able if the creditor has not demanded immediate payment directly from the surety. If the surety has paid the debtor's obligation, the surety may attempt reimbursement from the debtor.

15. (c) The surety may use his/her own defenses of incapacity of the **surety** or bankruptcy of the **surety** to limit his/her own liability. Although the surety may use most defenses that the **debtor** has to limit his/her (surety's) liability, the surety may not use the **personal** defenses of the debtor. These include the debtor's bankruptcy and the debtor's incapacity; therefore answers (a), (b), and (d) are incorrect.

16. (b) A modification by the principal debtor and creditor in the terms and conditions of their original contract without the surety's consent will automatically release the surety if the surety's risk of loss is thereby materially increased. Note that a noncompensated surety is discharged even if the creditor does not change the surety's risk. However, a compensated surety is discharged only if the modification causes a material increase in risk. Answers (c) and (d) are incorrect because a surety may not exercise the principal debtor's personal defenses (i.e., insolvency and insanity). Answer (a) is incorrect because although a release of the principal debtor without the surety's consent will usually discharge the surety, there is no discharge if the creditor expressly reserves rights against the surety.

17. (d) Personal defenses that the debtor has such as bankruptcy or death of the debtor cannot be used by the surety to avoid payment of the debtor's obligation to the creditor. Answer (a) is incorrect because the surety may generally exercise the defenses on the contract that the debtor has against the creditor. Answer (b) is incorrect because the surety may take advantage of his/her own personal defenses such as fraud by the creditor against the surety. Answer (c) is incorrect because the surety generally may exercise the defenses on the contract that would be available to the debtor such as the running of the statute of limitations.

18. (d) A compensated surety will be released from an obligation to the creditor upon tender of performance by either the principal debtor or the surety. A compensated surety will also be completely released if modifications are made to the principal debtor's contract which materially increase risk to the surety. However, if the risk is not materially increased, the surety is not completely released but rather his/her obligation is reduced by the amount of loss due to modification. The surety also is not released if the modifications are beneficial to the surety. Answers (a) and (b) are incorrect because these modifications will not necessarily result in a material increase in the surety's risk or could even be beneficial to the surety. Answer (c) is incorrect because partial release of the principal debtor's obligation will result in partial release of the surety.

19. (a) Normally, fraud by the debtor on the surety to induce him/her to act as a surety will not release the surety. However, when the creditor is aware of the debtor's fraudulent misrepresentation, then the surety can avoid liability. Answer (b) is incorrect because the above principle is true whether the surety is compensated or not. Answer (c) is incorrect because the risk of bankruptcy is one of the reasons that the creditor desires a surety. Answer (d) is incorrect because fraudulent misrepresentations do not make a contract void but can make it voidable.

20. (c) Once the debt is paid by someone, both the principal debtor and the cosigner are released from obligations to pay the loan. Answer (a) is incorrect because the creditor may proceed against the cosigner without needing to proceed against the principal debtor. Answer (b) is incorrect because the possibility that the principal debtor may qualify for bankruptcy is one of the reasons that the creditor may desire a cosigner. Answer (d) is incorrect because even if the main debtor is adjudicated mentally incompetent, this can allow the main debtor to escape liability but not the cosigner.

21. (c) A suretyship relationship exists when one party agrees to answer for the obligations of another. Cosureties exist when there is more than one surety guaranteeing the same obligation of the principal debtor. Answer (a) is incorrect because both sureties and cosureties are entitled to reimbursement from the debtor if the surety pays the obligation. Answer (b) is incorrect because sureties and cosureties both have the right of subrogation in that upon making payment, the surety has the same rights against the principal debtor that the creditor had. Answer (d) is incorrect because both are also entitled to exoneration. Sureties and cosureties both may require the debtor to pay the obligation for which they have given promise if the debtor is able to do so. The right of contribution, however, exists only among cosureties. If a cosurety pays more than his/her proportionate share of the total liability, he/she is entitled to be compensated by the other cosureties for the excess amount paid.

22. (b) The right of contribution arises when one cosurety, in performance of the principal debtor's obligation, pays more than his/her proportionate share of the total liability. The right of contribution allows the performing cosurety to receive reimbursement from the other cosureties for their pro rata shares of the liability. The pro rata shares of the cosureties are determined as follows:

	Surety's pro rata share		Remaining liability		Surety's liability
Queen	(210,000/420,000)	×	210,000	=	105,000
Ash	(84,000/420,000)	×	210,000	=	42,000
Kane	(126,000/420,000)	×	210,000	=	63,000

Thus, Queen is entitled to receive $42,000 from Ash and $63,000 from Kane.

23. (c) A surety relationship is present when one party agrees to answer for the obligation of another. When there is more than one surety guaranteeing the same obligation of the principal debtor, the sureties become cosureties jointly and severally liable to the claims of the creditor. A right of contribution arises when one cosurety, in performance of the debtor's obligation, pays more than his proportionate share of the total liability. The right of contribution entitles the performing cosurety to reimbursement from the other cosureties for their pro rata shares of the liability. The pro rata shares of the cosureties are determined as follows:

	Surety's pro rata share		Remaining liability		Surety's liability
Nash	(40,000/180,000)	×	36,000	=	8,000
Owen	(60,000/180,000)	×	36,000	=	12,000
Polk	(80,000/180,000)	×	36,000	=	16,000

Thus, Nash is entitled to recover $12,000 from Owen and $16,000 from Polk for a total of $28,000.

24. (a) A discharge or release of one cosurety by a creditor results in a reduction of liability of the remaining cosurety. The remaining cosurety is released to the extent of the released cosurety's pro rata share of debt liability, unless there is a reservation of rights by the creditor against the remaining cosurety. Quill and West each had maximum liability of $100,000. Thus, Ingot's release of West will result in Quill's liability being reduced by West's pro rata share of the total debt liability, which was one-half. Therefore, Quill's liability has been reduced to $25,000 (i.e., 50% of the loan balance) due to the release of West as a cosurety. Answer (c) is therefore incorrect. Answer (d) is incorrect because the release of the cosurety does not release the principal debtor since the debtor's obligation is not affected in any way by Ingot's release of West. Answer (b) is incorrect because as discussed above, Quill's liability has been reduced due to Ingot's release of West.

25. (b) The discharge or release of one cosurety by the creditor results in a reduction of liability of the remaining cosurety. This reduction of liability is limited to the released cosurety's pro rata share of debt liability (unless there is a reservation of rights by the creditor against the remaining cosurety). Since Mane released Rey without reserving rights against Salem, Salem is released to the extent of Rey's pro rata share of the $90,000 liability. Salem's maximum liability can be calculated as follows:

Rey's %	$\dfrac{\$120,000}{\$240,000} = .50$

Loan balance	$90,000
× Rey's %	× .50
	$45,000
Loan balance	$90,000
Rey's pro rata share	(45,000)
Salem's maximum liability	$45,000

26. (b) The right of contribution arises when one cosurety, in performance of debtor's obligation, pays more than his proportionate share of the total liability. The right of contribution entitles the performing cosurety to reimbursement from the other cosureties for their pro rata shares of the liability. Since Clark's debts have been discharged in bankruptcy, River may only exercise his right of contribution against Zane, and may recover nothing from Clark. Zane's pro rata share of the remaining $140,000 would be determined as follows:

$$\frac{\text{Dollar amount guaranteed by Zane}}{\substack{\text{Total amount of risk assumed by} \\ \text{remaining cosureties}}} \times \text{Remaining obligation}$$

$$\frac{160,000}{160,000 + 240,000} \times 140,000 = 56,000$$

27. (d) Cosureties are jointly and severally liable to the creditor up to the amount of liability each agreed to. If a cosurety pays more than his/her proportionate share of the debt, s/he may seek contribution from the other cosureties for the excess. Answer (a) is incorrect because the right of exoneration refers to the surety requiring the debtor to pay the debt when able. Answer (b) is incorrect because subrogation refers to the right of the surety to obtain the same rights against the debtor that the creditor had, once the surety pays the creditor. Answer (c) is incorrect because the right of reimbursement allows the surety to recover payments from the debtor that the surety has made to the creditor.

Simulation

Task-Based Simulation 1

Consideration		
	Authoritative Literature	Help

For each of the numbered words or phrases, select the one best phrase or sentence from the list A through J. Each response may be used only once.

A. Relationship whereby one person agrees to answer for the debt or default of another.
B. Requires certain contracts to be in writing to be enforceable.
C. Jointly and severally liable to creditor.
D. Promises to pay debt on default of principal debtor.
E. One party promises to reimburse debtor for payment of debt or loss if it arises.
F. Receives intended benefits of a contract.
G. Right of surety to require the debtor to pay before surety pays.
H. Upon payment of more than his/her proportionate share, each cosurety may compel other cosureties to pay their shares.
I. Upon payment of debt, surety may recover payment from debtor.
J. Upon payment, surety obtains same rights against debtor that creditor had.

		(A)	(B)	(C)	(D)	(E)	(F)	(G)	(H)	(I)	(J)
1.	Indemnity contract	O	O	O	O	O	O	O	O	O	O
2.	Suretyship contract	O	O	O	O	O	O	O	O	O	O
3.	Surety	O	O	O	O	O	O	O	O	O	O
4.	Third-party beneficiary	O	O	O	O	O	O	O	O	O	O
5.	Cosurety	O	O	O	O	O	O	O	O	O	O
6.	Statute of Frauds	O	O	O	O	O	O	O	O	O	O
7.	Right of contribution	O	O	O	O	O	O	O	O	O	O
8.	Reimbursement	O	O	O	O	O	O	O	O	O	O
9.	Subrogation	O	O	O	O	O	O	O	O	O	O
10.	Exoneration	O	O	O	O	O	O	O	O	O	O

Simulation Solution

Task-Based Simulation 1

Consideration		
	Authoritative Literature	Help

	(A)	(B)	(C)	(D)	(E)	(F)	(G)	(H)	(I)	(J)
1. Indemnity contract	○	○	○	○	●	○	○	○	○	○
2. Suretyship contract	●	○	○	○	○	○	○	○	○	○
3. Surety	○	○	○	●	○	○	○	○	○	○
4. Third-party beneficiary	○	○	○	○	○	●	○	○	○	○
5. Cosurety	○	○	●	○	○	○	○	○	○	○
6. Statute of Frauds	○	●	○	○	○	○	○	○	○	○
7. Right of contribution	○	○	○	○	○	○	○	●	○	○
8. Reimbursement	○	○	○	○	○	○	○	○	●	○
9. Subrogation	○	○	○	○	○	○	○	○	○	●
10. Exoneration	○	○	○	○	○	○	●	○	○	○

Explanations

1. (E) An indemnity contract is not a suretyship contract. Instead it is a contract involving two parties in which the first party agrees to indemnify and reimburse the second party for covered debts or losses should they take place.

2. (A) The suretyship contract involves three parties. The surety agrees with the creditor to pay for the debt or default if the debtor does not.

3. (D) The surety is the party that agrees to pay the creditor if the debtor defaults.

4. (F) When two parties make a contract that intends to benefit a third party, that party is a third-party beneficiary.

5. (C) When two or more sureties agree to be sureties for the same obligation to the same creditor, they are known as cosureties. They have joint and several liability.

6. (B) The Statute of Frauds sets out rules that require certain contracts to be in writing, such as those in which a surety agrees to answer for the debt or default of another.

7. (H) Cosureties are liable in contribution for their proportionate shares of the debt. If a cosurety pays more than this amount, s/he may seek contribution for the excess from the other cosureties.

8. (I) The right of reimbursement is against the debtor to collect any amounts paid by the surety.

9. (J) When the surety pays the creditor, it "steps into the shoes of the creditor" and obtains the same rights against the debtor that the creditor had.

10. (G) If the debtor is able to pay, the surety may require the debtor to pay before the surety pays. This is called exoneration.

Module 32: Agency

Overview

Agency is a relationship in which one party (agent) is authorized to act on behalf of another party (principal). The law of agency is concerned with the rights, duties, and liabilities of the parties in an agency relationship. Important to this relationship is the fact that the agent has a fiduciary duty to act in the best interest of the principal. A good understanding of this module is important because business structures (Module 25) apply the concepts of agency frequently.

The CPA exam emphasizes the creation and termination of the agency relationship, the fiduciary duties that the agent owes to the principal, the undisclosed as well as the disclosed principal relationship, unauthorized acts or torts committed by the agent within the course and scope of the agency relationship and principal's liability for agent's unauthorized contracts. Before beginning the reading you should review the key terms at the end of the module.

A. Characteristics

1. Agency is a relationship between two parties, whereby one party (agent) agrees to act on behalf of the other party (principal) with respect to third parties. A contract is not required but is frequently present.

   a. Agent is subject to control of principal
   b. Agent is a fiduciary and must act for the benefit of principal
   c. Agent's specific authority is determined by the principal but generally agent has authority to bind the principal contractually with third parties

---

NOW REVIEW MULTIPLE-CHOICE QUESTIONS 1 AND 2

B. Examples of Principals and Agents

1. Employer (principal) and Employee (agent)

   a. Employee is a type of agent in which employee's physical conduct is subject to control by employer
   b. Business structures (e.g., corporations, partnerships, limited partnerships) are principals; their various employees are agents.

      (1) Employees include corporate officers, but not directors, general partners, and other employees such as professional support staff.

   c. Some older CPA questions may use the terms master (principal) and servant (agent)
   d. The employer/employee relationship is the most commonly tested principal-agent relationship on the CPA Exam

2. Independent contractor distinguished from employee/agent

   a. Not subject to control of employer as to methods of work
   b. Not subject to regular supervision as an employee
   c. Employer controls results only (independent contractor controls the methods)

d. Typically an independent contractor is paid by the job, while an employee is paid a salary or an hourly wage on a continuous basis.

e. Often independent contractors provide their own tools/supplies for a job, while an employee usually has tools/supplies provided by the principal.

f. The distinction is important because generally employer is not liable for torts committed by independent contractor, but the employer can be held liable for the torts of an agent (see Section B.3. of this outline)

(1) Unless independent contractor is employed to do something inherently dangerous (e.g., blasting)

(2) Unless employer was negligent in hiring independent contractor

g. Independent contractor may also be an agent in certain cases

---

EXAMPLE

An attorney represents a client in tax court.

---

3. Special agency situations

a. Power of attorney: A person authorizes another person to act as his/her representative.

EXAMPLE

Catherine recognizes that she is not as mentally sharp as she once was and is fearful that she may one day lack capacity to manager her own affairs. Catherine executes a power of attorney giving James, her adult son, power of attorney.

---

(1) Principal, in writing, grants authority to agent

(a) Only principal need sign because the principal is the only party relinquishing a legal right, and the law needs evidence of the principal's intent to do so.

(b) This is similar to the idea of needing the signature of the party to be charged from contract law.

(2) Agent need not be an attorney but anyone with capacity to be agent

(3) Power of attorney may grant general authority or restricted authority

b. Broker—special agent acting for either buyer or seller in business transactions (e.g., real estate broker)

c. Exclusive—only agent the principal may deal with for a certain purpose during life of the contract (e.g., real estate broker who has sole right to sell property except for personal sale by principal)

d. Del credere—a sales agent who, prior to the creation and as a condition of the agency, guarantees the accounts of the customers to his/her principal (if the customers fail to pay)

(1) Guarantee is not within the Statute of Frauds (i.e., it is not required to be in writing)

e. E-agent is computer program or electronic method to take some action without specific human review

---

EXAMPLE

P authorizes an online search to find the lowest price of a certain product found through online stores.

---

f. A general agent is an agent with a broad range of powers; a special agent is one that engages in only one specific type of transaction for the principal.

EXAMPLE

Cathy hires Nancy, a licensed real estate agent, to sell Cathy's house. Nancy is a special agent.

---

g. Subagent: An agent who is hired by another agent.

   (1) Generally, agents have no authority to hire subagents unless principal so authorizes

h. Relationship resembling agency

   (1) Agency coupled with an interest—agent has an interest in subject matter through a security interest

      (a) For example, mortgagee with right to sell property on default of mortgagor

         1] Agreement stipulating agent is to receive profits or proceeds does not by itself create an agency coupled with an interest

      (b) Principal does not have the power to terminate agency coupled with an interest

      (c) Actually not an agency relationship because one who creates this relationship surrenders power—fact patterns may still use terms of principal and agent

---

NOW REVIEW MULTIPLE-CHOICE QUESTIONS 3 THROUGH 6

C. Methods of Creation

1. Contract

   a. Generally the agency contract need not be in writing in situations where the agent enters into agreements which themselves fall under the Statute of Frauds

> **EXAMPLE**
>
> A, in his capacity as agent of P, signs a contract for the sale of goods costing $600. Even though the sales contract must normally be in writing under the UCC version of the Statute of Frauds, the agency agreement between A and P need not be expressed in writing.

      (1) But if agency contract cannot be completed within one year, it must be in writing

> **EXAMPLE**
>
> P agrees to pay A as his agent and to keep him as his agent for two years; this agreement needs to be in writing under the Statute of Frauds.

      (2) In some states, agency contract needs to be written if agent is to buy or sell a specific piece of real estate named in agency contract

   b. Capacity

      (1) Principal must be able to give legal consent

         (a) Minors (person under age of majority, that is, 18 or 21) can, in most jurisdictions, appoint an agent, but minor may disaffirm agency

         (b) If act requires some legal capacity (e.g., legal age to sell land), then principal must meet this requirement or agent cannot legally perform even if s/he has capacity. Capacity cannot be increased by appointment of an agent.

      (2) An agent must merely have sufficient mental and physical ability to carry out instructions of his/her principal

         (a) Can bind principal even if agent is a minor or legally unable to act for self

         (b) Principal will be responsible for contract that the minor agent entered into on principal's behalf. Principal cannot use minor's lack of capacity as a defense.

   c. Consideration is not required to enter into a valid principal-agency relationship. When consideration is missing, this is known as a gratuitous agency.

2. Agency can also be implied by the conduct or lack of conduct by either the principal or agent that allows third parties to reasonably believe an agency exists; this is agency by estoppel.

EXAMPLE

Marcus put up a sign outside of Paula's restaurant that says, "Valet parking for Paula's $10.00." Paula's never hired Marcus or asked Marcus to do this, but Paula knew that parking was a problem, so she decided not to say anything. Third parties (customers in this case) can reasonably believe that Marcus is Paula's agent, creating agency by estoppel.

---

3. An agent must merely have sufficient mental and physical ability to carry out instructions of his/her principal

   a. Can bind principal even if agent is a minor or legally unable to act for self

   b. Corporations, unincorporated associations, and partnerships may act as agents

   c. A mental incompetent or an infant of tender years may not be an agent

---

NOW REVIEW MULTIPLE-CHOICE QUESTIONS 7 THROUGH 9

D. Duties (Obligations) and Rights

1. Principal's duties (obligations) to agent

   a. Most of the principal's duties to the agent are determined by the employment agreement (principal/agent) contract that the principal and agent enter into.

   b. Compensate agent as per agreement, or, in the absence of an agreement, pay a reasonable amount for the agent's service

   c. Reimburse agent for reasonable expenses, unless their agreement states otherwise, and indemnify agent against loss or liability for duties performed at the principal's direction which are not illegal

   d. Duty to cooperate with agent and assist him/her perform duties as agreed to between principal and agent

   e. Inform agent of risks (e.g., physical harm, pecuniary loss)

   f. May have remedies of discharging agent, restitution, damages, and accounting, or an injunction

   g. Principal does not owe agent any fiduciary duties; only the agent is a fiduciary in the principal-agent relationship.

2. Agent's duties (obligations) to principal

   a. Agent is a fiduciary and must act in the best interest of the principal and with loyalty

   b. Carry out instructions of principal exercising reasonable care and skill

   c. Account to the principal for profits and property that rightfully belong to the principal and not commingle funds

---

EXAMPLE

Agent makes authorized purchase order from Mega Corp. As a token of its appreciation, Mega provides two tickets to a sporting event for agent. The gift of tickets needs to be disclosed to the principal, otherwise the agent is breaching a fiduciary duty.

---

   d. Duty not to compete or act adversely to principal

     (1) Includes not acting for oneself unless principal knows and agrees

   e. Give any information to principal that s/he would want or need to know

   f. After termination, must cease acting as agent

NOW REVIEW MULTIPLE-CHOICE QUESTION 10

E. Liability to Third Parties

1. When a third party (typically a customer, client, or business associate) suffers a loss as a result of the principal's and/or agent's actions, who is responsible for the loss?

2. Before determining liability, ask why the third party is suing. Was the third party's loss due to breach of contract or the commission of a tort?

3. Contract liability is based on two issues:

   a. What authority did the agent have to enter into the contract with the third party?
   b. Was the principal disclosed to the third party?

4. The authority that the agent has depends on from whom the agent received the authority

   a. **Actual authority** comes from the principal

      (1) Express actual authority is explicit power that the principal gives to the agent to enter into a contract.
      (2) Implied actual authority arises from express authority.

EXAMPLE

King owns several hardware stores and hires Smith to manage one of the stores. King tells Smith that Smith is in charge of the personnel at his store, but that King is the exclusive purchaser of inventory for sale.

Analysis: Smith has express authority to hire/fire employees for the store he manages. Smith has implied authority to enter into contracts that a manager would normally have in this situation, such as selling merchandise. That is an example of implied authority. Smith has no actual authority to buy inventory for the store.

---

   b. **Apparent authority** comes from a third party's **reasonable**, but mistaken, belief that the agent has actual authority to enter into the contract.

      (1) Apparent authority occurs where the principal's words, actions, lack of words, or lack of action allows a **reasonable** third party to believe that the agent has actual authority to enter into a contract for the principal.
      (2) Focus on whether the third party's belief is reasonable.

EXAMPLE

King owns several hardware stores and hires Smith to manage one of the stores. King gives Smith authority to purchase up to $500 of inventory for the store. King never informed the companies that sold to the store of the dollar limit on Smith's authority. Over several years Smith has made several purchases of Abbot deck stain to resell at the store. While the purchases were always for several hundred dollars, none of the purchases exceeded $500. King always paid Abbot when he was billed. Recently, Smith made a purchase for $600 of Abbot deck stain.

Analysis: Even though Smith did not have actual authority to purchase more than $500 of deck stain, Smith is cloaked with apparent authority. King's failure to inform Abbot of the limitation and the fact that King has approved of similar past purchases allows Abbot to reasonably believe that Smith has authority.

EXAMPLE

Marcus put up a sign outside of Paula's restaurant that says, "Valet parking for Paula's $10.00." Paula's never hired Marcus or asked Marcus to do this, but Paula knew that parking was a problem, so she decided not to say anything. Third parties (customers in this case) can reasonably believe that Marcus is Paula's agent, creating agency by estoppel.

Analysis: Even though Marcus is not an agent, third parties can reasonably assume that Marcus is an agent and therefore has authority to park cars as well; this is apparent authority.

---

   c. No authority occurs where the agent has neither actual nor apparent authority

5. Disclosure of the principal to the third party

   a. Disclosed principal occurs when the third party knows of the existence of the principal **and** knows the identity of the principal

b. Partially disclosed principal occurs when the third party knows of the existence of the principal, but does not know the identity of the principal

c. Undisclosed principal is when the third party does not know of the existence of the principal.

6. Principal's contract liability to third parties

a. If agent acts with authority, either actual or apparent, the principal is liable, regardless of disclosure status.

b. If agent acts with no authority, then the principal is not liable, **unless the principal ratifies the contract**

   (1) Ratification occurs when a principal chooses to be bound by the terms of an unauthorized contract. Ratification is valid when all of the following are true:

      (a) Third party knew of the principal's existence at the time the contract was entered into
      (b) The principal has knowledge of all the material facts of the contract
      (c) Third party does not withdraw from contract prior to ratification

   (2) Ratification must be for the entire contract (i.e., the principal cannot choose to be bound by just part of the contract). Therefore ratification cannot occur when the principal is undisclosed since the third party was unaware of the existence of the principal.

   (3) Ratification can be explicit or implied from the principal's actions

7. Agent's contract liability to third parties

a. If the principal is disclosed and agent has authority, either actual or apparent, agent has no liability.

b. If the principal is partially disclosed or undisclosed, the principal is personally liable, regardless of authority.

c. If the agent acts without authority, then the agent is personally liable.

   (1) Exception: If the principal ratifies the contract, the agent is relieved of personal liability

8. Tort liability arises when the conduct of the agent creates a loss for third party.

9. Torts can arise from

a. Careless conduct or negligence, or

b. Purposeful conduct: Intentional tort

10. The agent is always personally liable for the tort

11. The principal's liability for the agent's tort depends upon whether the agent's tort was committed in the **scope of employment**.

12. If the agent's tort occurred in the scope of employment, then the principal is liable for the tort under the doctrine of *respondeat superior*

13. Scope of employment means that the agent is engaged in the performance of the agency relationship

a. Generally, if the tort occurs during working hours, at the workplace, while doing the tasks that the agent is employed to perform, then the tort is in the scope of employment.

b. Torts that occur slightly outside the work environment are still considered in the scope of employment; these are known as detours.

c. Torts that occur substantially outside the work environment are still considered outside the scope of employment; these are known as frolics.

EXAMPLE

Valdez, an employee of Cocoa Corp., is having a cup of coffee at work. Juan accidently spills some coffee on a client during a business meeting. Juan's tort is clearly in the scope of employment. Therefore, Juan and/or Cocoa Corp. may be held liable for the damages the client suffered.

EXAMPLE

Juan Valdez is having a business meeting at Cocoa Corp.'s, his employer's, office with a client who is from a foreign country. After the meeting concludes, the client expresses concern about being able to tell the cab driver his next destination. Juan grabs a cup of coffee and escorts the client out of the building to hail a cab and assist the client with the cab driver. While hailing the cab, Juan inadvertently spills coffee on the client. This is a mere detour and Juan's tort would be in the scope of employment. Juan and/or Cocoa Corp. may be held liable for the damages the client suffered.

> **EXAMPLE**
>
> After work, Juan Valdez, stops in the Beanery Café to grab a cup of coffee. Juan happens to see a client sitting at another table and goes over to say hello. Juan then accidently spills the coffee on the client. This is a frolic. Juan has left the workplace and he is on personal time. This was not a business meeting, just a casual or social occurrence. Juan is outside the scope of employment. Only Juan is liable for the damages the client suffered.

d. The issue is not whether the principal authorized the particular activity that the employee engaged in; rather does the agent's activity fall within the scope of employment.

> **EXAMPLE**
>
> Assume in the previous example, where Juan escorted the client out of the building, that the employer has a policy that employees cannot leave the office building without permission during working hours. Juan will still be considered in the scope of employment because his actions were related to work and Juan is furthering the interests of the principal by assisting a client.

14. Intentional torts are normally outside the scope of employment.

> **EXAMPLE**
>
> If, in any of the previous examples, Juan purposefully dumped coffee on the client, then Juan's tort is outside the scope of employment. Only Juan would be liable for the damages.

a. Most intentional torts are also crimes.
b. Intentional torts which are foreseeable and relate to the job are normally in the scope of employment.

> **EXAMPLE**
>
> A bouncer at a bar pushes an unruly patron in an attempt to get the patron off the premises. This intentional tort, battery, is in the scope of employment. The bouncer and/or the bar can be held liable for any damages

c. Intentional torts committed to primarily benefit the principal are usually in the scope of employment.

15. If an agent commits a tort in the scope of employment, then the principal and agent are jointly and severally liable.

a. Joint liability means that the injured third party can sue both the principal and the agent in the same lawsuit
b. Several liability means to separate liability; thus the injured third party could choose just to sue the principal or just to sue the agent.

NOW REVIEW MULTIPLE-CHOICE QUESTIONS 11 THROUGH 24

F. Termination of Principal-Agent Relationship

1. Termination occurs either by the actions of the parties (principal and/or agent) or by operation of law.
2. Acts of the parties

a. By agreement

(1) Time specified in original agreement (e.g., agency for one year)
(2) Mutual consent to terminate
(3) Accomplishment of objective (e.g., agency to buy a piece of land)

b. Principal or agent may terminate agency

(1) Party that terminates is liable for breach of contract if termination is before specified period of time

    (a) One still has power to terminate relationship even though s/he has no right to terminate (i.e., results in breach of contract)

EXAMPLE

A and P agree to be agent and principal for six months. P terminates A after two months. P is liable to A for breach of contract for the damages that this wrongful termination causes A. However, P does have the power to remove A's authority to act on behalf of P.

---

    (2) If either party breaches duties owed, other party may terminate agency without liability

    (3) If no time is specified in agency, then either party may terminate without liability

c. Agency coupled with an interest is irrevocable

    (1) Refers to cases in which agent has actual interest in property involved in this agency, see Section B.3.h. of this outline.

3. Termination by operation of law: The law automatically ends the principal-agent relationship

  a. If subject of agreement becomes illegal or impossible

  b. Death, insanity, or court determined incompetence of either party

    (1) Exception is an agency coupled with an interest

  c. Bankruptcy of principal terminates the relationship

    (1) Bankruptcy of agent does not affect unless agent's solvency is needed for performance

  d. If subject matter necessary for the performance of the relationship is destroyed

4. Notice of termination to third parties

  a. Termination eliminates any actual authority that the agent had.

  b. Apparent authority could still exist, if third parties are unaware that the principal-agent relationship was terminated.

  c. To eliminate apparent authority, notice of the termination must be provided to third parties.

    (1) Constructive notice (e.g., publishing in a newspaper or a trade journal) is sufficient to third parties who have not previously dealt with agent

---

EXAMPLE

P fired A, who had been P's agent for a few years. P published in the newspaper that A was no longer his agent. A subsequently made a contract with X purporting to bind P to the contract. X had never dealt with P and A before but was aware that A had been P's agent. X was not aware that A had been fired because he had not read the notice. X cannot hold P to the contract because of the constructive notice. X does not have to read it for the constructive notice to be valid.

---

    (2) Actual notice (e.g., orally informing or sending a letter, etc.) must be given to third parties who have previously dealt with agent unless third party learns of termination from another source

---

EXAMPLE

A, while acting as an agent of P, had previous dealings with T. P fires A but A makes a contract with T purporting to act as P's agent. T can still hold P liable unless he received actual notice of termination.

EXAMPLE

Same as above except that the principal gave constructive notice. T may hold P liable.

EXAMPLE

Same as above except that although P only gave constructive notice through a trade journal, T happened to read it. This qualifies as actual notice. Therefore, unlike above, T may not hold P liable.

---

d. Notice is not required when termination occurs due to operation of law

---

EXAMPLE

A, while acting as an agent of P, had previous dealings with T. P is declared incompetent in a judicial proceeding and T is unaware of P's incapacity. No notice was given of P's incapacity. T may not hold P liable on the contract. The moment P was declared incompetent the agency terminated due to operation of law. At that moment, A lost all authority, including apparent authority.

NOW REVIEW MULTIPLE-CHOICE QUESTIONS 25 THROUGH 27

KEY TERMS

Actual authority. The power given by a principal to an agent that allows the agent to enter into contracts upon the principal's behalf.

Agent. A party who works on behalf of another party known as the principal.

Apparent authority. When a third party reasonably believes that an agent has actual authority even though the agent lacks actual authority.

Disclosed principal. A principal who is known by the third party.

Fiduciary duties. The obligations that an agent owes to a principal that require the agent to act in the best interests of the principal.

Independent contractor. A party who works for another party, but is not subject to the control of the other party; therefore an independent contractor generally does not create liability for the other party.

Joint and several liability. When a principal and agent can both be held liable by the third party or the third party may choose to sever liability and only hold either the principal or the agent liable.

Partially disclosed principal. When the third party knows of the existence of the principal, but does not know the principal's identity.

Principal. The party for whom the agent acts.

Ratification. When a principal approves of a contract that was entered into by an agent lacking authority. Ratification means that the principal is now liable for the contract.

Respondeat superior (Latin). Literally means that the superior should be held responsible. When an agent commits a tort in the scope of employment, then the principal is liable for the agent's tort.

Scope of employment. Agent's actions that occur substantially in the work environment.

Third party. Term in principal/agent law that applies to a party who is interacting with either the principal or the agent. The principal and agent are the first two parties.

Undisclosed principal. When the third party to a contract does not know that a principal exists.

Multiple-Choice Questions (1–27)

A.   Characteristics

1. Young Corp. hired Wilson as a sales representative for six months at a salary of $5,000 per month plus 6% of sales. Which of the following statements is correct?

    a. Young does **not** have the power to dismiss Wilson during the six-month period without cause.
    b. Wilson is obligated to act solely in Young's interest in matters concerning Young's business.
    c. The agreement between Young and Wilson is **not** enforceable unless it is in writing and signed by Wilson.
    d. The agreement between Young and Wilson formed an agency coupled with an interest.

2. Which of the following statement(s) concerning agency law is (are) true?

   I. A contract is needed to have an agency relationship.
   II. The agent owes a fiduciary duty to the principal.
   III. The principal owes a fiduciary duty to the agent.

    a. I and II only.
    b. I and III only.
    c. II only.
    d. I, II, and III.

B.   Examples of Principles and Agents

3. Noll gives Carr a written power of attorney. Which of the following statements is correct regarding this power of attorney?

    a. It must be signed by both Noll and Carr.
    b. It must be for a definite period of time.
    c. It may continue in existence after Noll's death.
    d. It may limit Carr's authority to specific transactions.

4. Lee repairs high-speed looms for Sew Corp., a clothing manufacturer. Which of the following circumstances best indicates that Lee is an employee of Sew and **not** an independent contractor?

    a. Lee's work is not supervised by Sew personnel.
    b. Lee's tools are owned by Lee.
    c. Lee is paid weekly by Sew.
    d. Lee's work requires a high degree of technical skill.

5. Generally, a disclosed principal will be liable to third parties for its agent's unauthorized misrepresentations if the agent is an

	Employee	Independent Contractor
a.	Yes	Yes
b.	Yes	No
c.	No	Yes
d.	No	No

6. Which of the following terms **best** describes the relationship between a corporation and the CPA it hires to audit corporate books?

    a. Employer and employee.
    b. Employer and independent contractor.
    c. Master and servant.
    d. Employer and principal.

C.   Methods of Creation

7. A principal and agent relationship requires a

    a. Written agreement.
    b. Power of attorney.
    c. Meeting of the minds and consent to act.
    d. Specified consideration.

8. Trent was retained, in writing, to act as Post's agent for the sale of Post's memorabilia collection. Which of the following statements is correct?

   I. To be an agent, Trent must be at least twenty-one years of age.
   II. Post would be liable to Trent if the collection was destroyed before Trent found a purchaser.

    a. I only.
    b. II only.
    c. Both I and II.
    d. Neither I nor II.

9. Which of the following actions requires an agent for a corporation to have a written agency agreement?

    a. Purchasing office supplies for the principal's business.
    b. Purchasing an interest in undeveloped land for the principal.
    c. Hiring an independent general contractor to renovate the principal's office building.
    d. Retaining an attorney to collect a business debt owed the principal.

D.   Duties (Obligations) and Rights

10. Blue, a used car dealer, appointed Gage as an agent to sell Blue's cars. Gage was authorized by Blue to appoint subagents to assist in the sale of the cars. Vond was appointed as a subagent. To whom does Vond owe a fiduciary duty?

    a. Gage only.
    b. Blue only.
    c. Both Blue and Gage.
    d. Neither Blue nor Gage.

E.   Liability to Third Parties

11. Harris, while delivering parts to a customer for his employer, negligently ran into and injured Wolfe. Harris had been asked by his employer to make these deliveries even though Harris was using his personal pickup truck. Neither Harris nor the employer had insurance to cover this injury. Which of the following is correct?

    a. Wolfe can hold Harris liable but not the employer because Harris was driving his own vehicle.

    b. Wolfe can hold the employer liable but not Harris because the employer had asked Harris to make the deliveries.

    c. Wolfe can hold either Harris or the employer or both liable.

    d. Wolfe can hold either Harris or the employer liable but not both.

12. Chiron employed Sherwin as a mechanic. Chiron has various rules that all employed mechanics must follow. One day a customer was injured severely when her car's brakes failed. It was shown that her car's brakes failed because Sherwin did not follow one of the specific rules of Chiron. Which of the following is correct?

    a. Sherwin is liable to the customer but Chiron is not because the accident was caused by Sherwin breaking one of Chiron's specific rules.

    b. The customer should sue Sherwin for fraud, not negligence, because Sherwin broke a rule of the employer.

    c. The customer can hold Chiron liable but not Sherwin, because her contract to get the car repaired was with Chiron.

    d. The customer may choose to recover damages from both Chiron and Sherwin.

13. Pine, an employee of Global Messenger Co., was hired to deliver highly secret corporate documents for Global's clients throughout the world. Unknown to Global, Pine carried a concealed pistol. While Pine was making a delivery, he suspected an attempt was being made to steal the package, drew his gun and shot Kent, an innocent passerby. Kent will **not** recover damages from Global if

    a. Global discovered that Pine carried a weapon and did nothing about it.

    b. Global instructed its messengers **not** to carry weapons.

    c. Pine was correct and an attempt was being made to steal the package.

    d. Pine's weapon was unlicensed and illegal.

14. When an agent acts for an undisclosed principal, the principal will **not** be liable to third parties if the

    a. Principal ratifies a contract entered into by the agent.

    b. Agent acts within an implied grant of authority.

    c. Agent acts outside the grant of actual authority.

    d. Principal seeks to conceal the agency relationship.

15. Which of the following under agency law is **not** a type of authority that an agent might have?

    a. Actual express.

    b. Actual implied.

    c. Resulting.

    d. Apparent.

16. Frost's accountant and business manager has the authority to

    a. Mortgage Frost's business property.

    b. Obtain bank loans for Frost.

    c. Insure Frost's property against fire loss.

    d. Sell Frost's business.

17. Ames, claiming to be an agent of Clar Corporation, makes a contract with Trimon in the name of Clar Corporation. Later, Clar Corporation, for the first time, learns what Ames has done and notifies Trimon of the truth that Ames was not an agent of Clar Corporation. Which of the following statements is incorrect?

    a. Clar Corporation may ratify this contract if it does so with the entire contract.

    b. Trimon may withdraw from the contract before Clar attempts to ratify it.

    c. Clar Corporation may ratify this contract by performing under the contract without stating that it is ratifying.

    d. Trimon may enforce this contract even if Clar Corporation does not wish to be bound.

18. Which of the following generally may ratify a contract that was agreed to by his/her agent without authority from the principal?

	Fully disclosed principal	Partially disclosed principal	Undisclosed principal
a.	Yes	Yes	Yes
b.	Yes	Yes	No
c.	Yes	No	No
d.	No	No	Yes

19. Beele authorized McDonald to be his agent to go to Denver and purchase some real estate that would be suitable to open up a branch office for Beele's business. He tells McDonald not to pay more than $125,000 for the real estate. McDonald contacts York to buy some real estate she owns. York calls Beele and Beele tells York that McDonald is his agent to buy the real estate. Nothing is mentioned about the $125,000 limitation. After negotiations between McDonald and York, McDonald signs a contract purchasing the real estate for $140,000. McDonald signed it indicating on the contract that he was signing as agent for Beele. Further facts show that the real estate is worth $140,000. Which of the following is correct?

    a. There is a fully enforceable contract between Beele and York for $140,000.

    b. Beele may enforce the contract with York for $125,000.

    c. There is no contract between Beele and York because McDonald did not have authority to purchase the real estate for $140,000.

    d. York may require that Beele pay $140,000 because the real estate was worth $140,000 not $125,000.

20. Easy Corp. is a real estate developer and regularly engages real estate brokers to act on its behalf in acquiring parcels of land. The brokers are authorized to enter into such contracts, but are instructed to do so in their own names without disclosing Easy's identity or relationship to the transaction. If a broker enters into a contract with a seller on Easy's behalf,

    a. The broker will have the same actual authority as if Easy's identity has been disclosed.
    b. Easy will be bound by the contract because of the broker's apparent authority.
    c. Easy will **not** be liable for any negligent acts committed by the broker while acting on Easy's behalf.
    d. The broker will **not** be personally bound by the contract because the broker has express authority to act.

21. An agent will usually be liable under a contract made with a third party when the agent is acting on behalf of a(n)

	Disclosed principal	Undisclosed principal
a.	Yes	Yes
b.	Yes	No
c.	No	Yes
d.	No	No

22. When a valid contract is entered into by an agent on the principal's behalf, in a nondisclosed principal situation, which of the following statements concerning the principal's liability is correct?

	The principal may be held liable once disclosed	The principal must ratify the contract to be held liable
a.	Yes	Yes
b.	Yes	No
c.	No	Yes
d.	No	No

23. Which of the following rights will a third party be entitled to after validly contracting with an agent representing an undisclosed principal?

    a. Disclosure of the principal by the agent.
    b. Ratification of the contract by the principal.
    c. Performance of the contract by the agent.
    d. Election to void the contract after disclosure of the principal.

24. Able, as agent for Baker, an undisclosed principal, contracted with Safe to purchase an antique car. In payment, Able issued his personal check to Safe. Able could not cover the check but expected Baker to give him cash to deposit before the check was presented for payment. Baker did not do so and the check was dishonored. Baker's identity became known to Safe. Safe may not recover from

    a. Baker individually on the contract.
    b. Able individually on the contract.
    c. Baker individually on the check.
    d. Able individually on the check.

F.   *Termination of Principal-Agent Relationship*

25. Thorp was a purchasing agent for Ogden, a sole proprietor, and had the express authority to place purchase orders with Ogden's suppliers. Thorp placed an order with Datz, Inc. on Ogden's behalf after Ogden was declared incompetent in a judicial proceeding. Thorp was aware of Ogden's incapacity. Which of the following statements is correct concerning Ogden's liability to Datz?

    a. Ogden will be liable because Datz was **not** informed of Ogden's incapacity.
    b. Ogden will be liable because Thorp acted with express authority.
    c. Ogden will **not** be liable because Thorp's agency ended when Ogden was declared incompetent.
    d. Ogden will **not** be liable because Ogden was a nondisclosed principal.

26. Generally, an agency relationship is terminated by operation of law in all of the following situations **except** the

    a. Principal's death.
    b. Principal's incapacity.
    c. Agent's renunciation of the agency.
    d. Agent's failure to acquire a necessary business license.

27. Bolt Corp. dismissed Ace as its general sales agent and notified all of Ace's known customers by letter. Young Corp., a retail outlet located outside of Ace's previously assigned sales territory, had never dealt with Ace. Young knew of Ace as a result of various business contacts. After his dismissal, Ace sold Young goods, to be delivered by Bolt, and received from Young a cash deposit for 20% of the purchase price. It was not unusual for an agent in Ace's previous position to receive cash deposits. In an action by Young against Bolt on the sales contract, Young will

    a. Lose, because Ace lacked any implied authority to make the contract.
    b. Lose, because Ace lacked any express authority to make the contract.
    c. Win, because Bolt's notice was inadequate to terminate Ace's apparent authority.
    d. Win, because a principal is an insurer of an agent's acts.

Multiple-Choice Answers and Explanations

Answers

1.	b	__ __	7.	c	__ __	13.	d	__ __	19.	a	__ __	25.	c	__ __
2.	c	__ __	8.	d	__ __	14.	c	__ __	20.	a	__ __	26.	c	__ __
3.	d	__ __	9.	b	__ __	15.	c	__ __	21.	c	__ __	27.	c	__ __
4.	c	__ __	10.	c	__ __	16.	c	__ __	22.	b	__ __			
5.	b	__ __	11.	c	__ __	17.	d	__ __	23.	c	__ __	1st:	__/27 = __%
6.	b	__ __	12.	d	__ __	18.	b	__ __	24.	c	__ __	2nd:	__/27 = __%

Explanations

1. (b) As a fiduciary to the principal, an agent must act in the best interest of the principal. Therefore, the agent has an obligation to refrain from competing with or acting adversely to the principal, unless the principal knows and approves of such activity. Answer (c) is incorrect because the Statute of Frauds would not require that the described agency relationship be contained in a signed writing since it is possible for the contract to be performed within one year. Answer (d) is incorrect because the mere right of the agent to receive a percentage of proceeds is not sufficient to constitute an agency coupled with an interest. In order to have an agency coupled with an interest, the agent must have either a property interest or a security interest in the subject matter of the agency relationship. Answer (a) is incorrect because in all agency relationships, except agencies coupled with an interest, the principal always has the power to dismiss the agent. However, the principal does not necessarily have the right to terminate the relationship. In certain situations the dismissed agent could sue for breach of contract.

2. (c) In an agency relationship, the agent owes a fiduciary duty to the principal but the principal does not owe a fiduciary duty to the agent. Also, even though there is often a contract between the principal and agent, this is not a requirement, for example, when the agent consents to act for the principal as a friend.

3. (d) A power of attorney is written authority conferred to an agent. It is conferred in a formal writing. A power of attorney can be general or it can grant the agent only restricted authority. Answer (a) is incorrect because the power of attorney must be signed only by the person granting such authority. Answer (b) is incorrect because the power of attorney does not have to be for a definite, specified time period. Answer (c) is incorrect because the death of the principal constitutes the termination of an agency relationship by operation of law.

4. (c) An employee is generally subject to control as to the methods used to complete the work. An independent contractor is typically paid for the completion of the project rather than on an hourly, weekly, or monthly basis. Answer (a) is incorrect because supervision by Sew Corp. personnel shows an employment relationship. Answer (b) is incorrect because independent contractors typically provide their own tools. Answer (d) is incorrect because the work of both employees and independent contractors can require a high degree of skill.

5. (b) Generally, principals are liable for the unauthorized misrepresentations of employees because the employees are subject to the control or supervision of the principal. Principals are not responsible for the misrepresentations of an independent contractor since the principal does not control the independent contractor's actions.

6. (b) The main factors that are used to determine whether a party is an independent contractor or an agents are the amount of control that the principal exercises over the party; an auditor is not subject to the control of the corporation. The auditor is probably paid by the job; this is another characteristic of an independent contractor relationship. Besides the legal reasoning provided above, answers (a) and (c) are virtually the same, and they cannot both be correct. Answer (d) does not make sense since an employer and a principal are the same entity.

7. (c) The relationship between a principal and agent is based upon the consent of both parties, also involving a meeting of the minds. Answer (d) is incorrect because specified consideration is not needed to create an agency relationship; the relationship between the principal and the agent need not be contractual. Answer (a) is incorrect because although the principal and agent relationship may be written, a written agreement is not required. Answer (b) is incorrect because power of attorney is not needed to create an agency relationship.

8. (d) An agent must merely have sufficient mental and physical ability to carry out instructions of his/her principal. An agent can bind the principal even if the agent is a minor. If the memorabilia collection was destroyed before Trent found a purchaser, Post would not be liable to Trent. Upon the loss or destruction of the subject matter on which the agency relationship is based, the agency relationship is terminated.

9. (b) An agency agreement normally does not need to be in writing. Exceptions to this general rule include agency contracts that cannot be completed within one year and agreements whereby the agent is to buy specific real estate for the principal. This question incorporates the latter. Typical agency agreements need not be in writing; these would include purchasing office supplies, retaining an independent contractor to do renovation work, or hiring an attorney to collect a business debt; therefore answers (a), (c), and (d) are incorrect.

10. (c) The fiduciary duty is an important duty owed by agents to their principals. Gage as Blue's agent was authorized by Blue to appoint subagents to assist in the sales transactions. Since Gage did appoint Vond as a subagent, legally Bond is an agent both of Blue and Gage. Therefore, Vond owes a fiduciary duty to both Blue and Gage making (a), (b), and (d) all incorrect.

11. (c) Since Harris was acting within the scope of his employment when he negligently injured Wolfe, both Harris and his employer are liable. Wolfe can recover from either one or both. Answer (a) is incorrect because both are liable since Harris was acting within the scope of the employment. The ownership of the vehicle does not change this. Answer (b) is incorrect because Harris is liable for his own tort even though the employer can also be held liable. Answer (d) is incorrect because Wolfe may recover the full damages from either or may recover a portion of the damages from both.

12. (d) Because the repairs Sherwin did were within the scope of the employment, the employer is also liable. This is true even if the employer was diligent in creating excellent rules that were not followed by an employee. Answer (a) is incorrect because the failure to properly repair the vehicle is a negligent act that was in the scope of employment. In such situations, both the principal and agent can be held liable. Answer (b) is incorrect because there was no fraud present here. Fraud requires an intentional misrepresentation of material facts. There is no evidence of such conduct present here. Answer (c) is incorrect because the customer may recover from both under tort law. Additionally, the contract has no bearing on a matter involving a tort.

13. (d) In general, the employer is not responsible for the crimes of the employee unless the employer aided or permitted the illegal activity, even if the activity was within the scope of the employment. Answer (a) is incorrect because if the employer did nothing to instruct the employee about the use of the weapon, this could help establish negligence on the part of the employer and would not prevent the use of the doctrine of *respondeat superior*, which makes employers liable for the tortious acts of their employees within the scope of the employment. Answer (b) is incorrect because the employer is liable for torts of the employee committed within the course and scope of the employment even if the employee was violating the employer's instructions. Answer (c) is incorrect because even if the employee's suspicions were correct, the shooting of an innocent passerby should establish at least negligence for which the employer and the employee are liable.

14. (c) A principal, whether disclosed, partially disclosed, or undisclosed is liable on contracts where the agent has actual or apparent authority, or where the principal ratifies an agent's contract. Actual authority includes express or implied authority projected by the principal to the agent. Apparent authority of an agent is authority perceived by a third party based on the principal's representations. Therefore, apparent authority can exist only where there is a disclosed or a partially disclosed principal. It follows, then, that an undisclosed principal will **not** be liable to third parties if the agent acts outside the grant of **actual** authority. Answer (a) is incorrect because when a principal ratifies a contract it is liable for the terms of the contract. Answer (b) is incorrect because when agents act with

any type of authority, then the principal is liable. Answer (d) is incorrect because whether the principal tried to hide the agency relationship is irrelevant to determine the principal's liability. The critical issue is did the agent act with some type of authority.

15. (c) Resulting authority is not one of the types of authority that an agent might have. Answer (a) is not chosen because actual express authority is a common type of authority and consists of all authority expressly given by the principal to his/her agent. Answer (b) includes the authority that can be reasonably implied from the express authority and the conduct of the principal. Answer (d) is not chosen because even though a party was never authorized by a principal to be an agent, if the principal leads a third party to believe that the party did have authority, this is apparent agency.

16. (c) An agent has implied authority to do what is customary for agents of that type to do under the circumstances. It would be customary for one who is a principal's accountant and business manager to have authority to insure the principal's property against fire loss. Answers (a), (b), and (d) are incorrect because they involve authority that is beyond customary, ordinary authority.

17. (d) Since Ames had no express, implied, or actual authority, Trimon cannot enforce the contract. Apparent authority is not present either; there are no facts present to show that Trimon was reasonable to believe Ames' unsubstantiated claim. Answer (a) is not chosen because ratifications under agency law require that the contract be ratified in its entirety or not at all. Answer (b) is not chosen because until Clar ratifies the contract in its entirety, Trimon may withdraw from the contract since Ames had no authority to make the contract. Answer (c) is not chosen because ratification can be accomplished by actions as well as words.

18. (b) When the third party is aware that there is a principal, that principal, fully disclosed or partially disclosed, may generally ratify the contract when he or she is aware of all material facts and if ratification of the entire contract takes place. Since a third party would not know of the existence of an undisclosed principal, ratification is not possible in that circumstance.

19. (a) Since Beele authorized McDonald to be his agent, the secret limitation has no effect on York. York may enforce the contract for the full $140,000. Answer (b) is incorrect because Beele authorized McDonald to be his agent. Even though his agent was instructed to pay at most $125,000 in the contract, this was a secret limitation that did not limit York who was unaware of it. Answer (c) is incorrect because McDonald was given authority to purchase real estate on Beele's behalf. The limitation on the dollar amount was not known by York and therefore does not limit her. Answer (d) is incorrect because although York can enforce the contract against Beele, it is because Beele gave authority to McDonald rather than how much the real estate is worth.

20. (a) When the principal is undisclosed in an agency relationship, the agent generally has the same authority as if the principal were disclosed. The main difference is in the liability of the agent to third parties. Answer (b) is incorrect because the principal is liable on the contract because of the express authority given to the agent to make the contract on behalf of the principal. Apparent authority exists when the principal represents the agent to third parties to be his/her agent. In this case, the principal wished to be undisclosed. Answer (c) is incorrect because principal can be held liable for negligence committed by the agent within the course and scope of the agency. Answer (d) is incorrect because the agent can be held liable on the contract by third parties when the principal is undisclosed.

21. (c) An agent is liable to a third party on a contract when the principal is undisclosed or partially disclosed. If the principal is fully disclosed, the agent is not liable.

22. (b) When an agent enters into a contract with a third person on behalf of an undisclosed principal, the agent is personally liable, unless the third person discovers the existence and identity of the principal and chooses to hold the principal to the contract instead of the agent. Ratification is the approval after the fact of an unauthorized act done by an agent or of an act done by someone who is not yet an agent. Undisclosed principals cannot ratify unauthorized acts of the agent.

23. (c) When a third party contracts with an agent representing an undisclosed principal, the agent is liable for performance of the contract. The third party is not entitled to disclosure of the principal. Answer (b) is incorrect because ratification of a contract by the principal is the approval required after the fact related to an unauthorized act by the agent or one not yet an agent. Answer (d) is incorrect because the third party generally is not allowed the option of voiding the contract after disclosure of the principal.

24. (c) One who issues a personal check is liable on it; however, any party or principal who is not disclosed on the check is not liable on the negotiable instrument. Answers (a) and (b) are incorrect because the third party can elect to hold either the agent or the principal liable when the agent makes a contract for an undisclosed principal. Answer (d) is incorrect because the party who signs a check is liable on it.

25. (c) The declaration of Ogden's incapacity constitutes the termination of the agency relationship by operation of law. When an agency relationship is terminated by operation of law, the agent's authority to enter into a binding agreement on behalf of the principal ceases. There is no requirement that notice be given to third parties when the agency relationship is terminated by operation of law. In this case, Ogden will not be liable to Datz because Thorp was without authority to enter into the contract. Answer (a) is incorrect because insanity of the principal terminates the agency relationship even though the third parties are unaware of the principal's insanity. Answer (b) is incorrect because Thorp's authority terminated upon the declaration of Ogden's incapacity. Answer (d) is incorrect because an undisclosed principal is liable unless the third party holds the agent responsible, the agent has fully performed the contract, the undisclosed principal is expressly excluded by contract or the contract is a negotiable instrument. However, Ogden will not be liable as Thorp was without authority to enter into the agreement.

26. (c) An agency relationship is terminated by operation of law if the subject of the agreement becomes illegal or impossible, the principal or the agent dies or becomes insane, or the principal becomes bankrupt. Answers (a), (b), and (d) are incorrect because they will cause the termination of an agency relationship by operation of law. Answer (c), agent's renunciation of the agency, will not cause the termination of an agency relationship by operation of law; instead it terminates the relationship by the actions of one of the parties, the agent.

27. (c) When the agency relationship is terminated by an act of the principal and/or agent, third parties are entitled to notice of the termination from the principal. Failure of the principal to give the required notice gives the agent apparent authority to act on behalf of the principal. Specifically, the principal must give actual notice to all parties who had prior dealings with the agent or principal. Constructive or public notice must be given to parties who knew of the existence of the agency relationship, but did not actually have business dealings with the agent or principal. Since Bolt Corp. did not give proper constructive notice to Young Corp., Ace had apparent authority to bind the principal and, therefore, Young Corp. will win. Accordingly, answer (a) is incorrect. Answer (b) is incorrect because although Ace lacked express authority, apparent authority was present due to the inadequacy of Bolt's notice. Answer (d) is incorrect because a principal is not an absolute insurer of his agent's acts. A principal is liable for his agent's torts only if the principal expressly authorizes the conduct or the tort is committed within the scope of the agent's employment.

Simulation

Task-Based Simulation 1

Relationships		
	Authoritative Literature	Help

Situation

Lace Computer Sales Corp. orally contracted with Banks, an independent consultant, for Banks to work part time as Lace's agent to perform Lace's customers' service calls. Banks, a computer programmer and software designer, was authorized to customize Lace's software to the customers' needs, on a commission basis, but was specifically told not to sell Lace's computers.

On March 15, Banks made a service call on Clear Co. to repair Clear's computer. Banks had previously called on Clear, customized Lace's software for Clear, and collected cash payments for the work performed. During the call, Banks convinced Clear to buy an upgraded Lace computer for a price much lower than Lace would normally charge. Clear had previously purchased computers from other Lace agents and had made substantial cash down payments to the agents. Clear had no knowledge that the price was lower than normal. Banks received a $1,000 cash down payment and promised to deliver the computer the next week. Banks never turned in the down payment and left town. When Clear called the following week to have the computer delivered, Lace refused to honor Clear's order.

Items 1 through 5 relate to the relationships between the parties. For each item, select from List I whether only statement I is correct, whether only statement II is correct, whether both statements I and II are correct, or whether neither statement I nor II is correct.

List I

A.   I only
B.   II only
C.   Both I and II
D.   Neither I nor II

		(A)	(B)	(C)	(D)
1.	I. Lace's agreement with Banks had to be in writing for it to be a valid agency agreement.	○	○	○	○
	II. Lace's agreement with Banks empowered Banks to act as Lace's agent.				
2.	I. Clear was entitled to rely on Banks' implied authority to customize Lace's software.	○	○	○	○
	II. Clear was entitled to rely on Banks' express authority when buying the computer.				
3.	I. Lace's agreement with Banks was automatically terminated by Banks' sale of the computer.	○	○	○	○
	II. Lace must notify Clear before Banks' apparent authority to bind Lace will cease.				
4.	I. Lace is **not** bound by the agreement made by Banks with Clear.	○	○	○	○
	II. Lace may unilaterally amend the agreement made by Banks to prevent a loss on the sale of the computer to Clear.				
5.	I. Lace, as a disclosed principal, is solely contractually liable to Clear.	○	○	○	○
	II. Both Lace and Banks are contractually liable to Clear.				

Simulation Solution

Task-Based Simulation 1

Relationships		
	Authoritative Literature	Help

	(A)	(B)	(C)	(D)
1. I. Lace's agreement with Banks had to be in writing for it to be a valid agency agreement. II. Lace's agreement with Banks empowered Banks to act as Lace's agent.	○	●	○	○
2. I. Clear was entitled to rely on Banks' implied authority to customize Lace's software. II. Clear was entitled to rely on Banks' express authority when buying the computer.	●	○	○	○
3. I. Lace's agreement with Banks was automatically terminated by Banks' sale of the computer. II. Lace must notify Clear before Banks' apparent authority to bind Lace will cease.	○	●	○	○
4. I. Lace is **not** bound by the agreement made by Banks with Clear. II. Lace may unilaterally amend the agreement made by Banks to prevent a loss on the sale of the computer to Clear.	○	○	○	●
5. I. Lace, as a disclosed principal, is solely contractually liable to Clear. II. Both Lace and Banks are contractually liable to Clear.	●	○	○	○

Explanations

1. **(B)** Statement I is incorrect because normally an agency agreement need not be in writing unless the agency contract cannot be completed in one year. Statement II is correct because Lace authorized Banks to be Lace's agent.

2. **(A)** Statement I is correct because Banks was given actual, express authority by Lace to perform Lace's customers' service calls and to customize Lace's software to the customer's needs. As an extension to this actual, express authority, Clear can also rely on what is customary and ordinary for such an agent to be able to do under implied authority. Statement II is incorrect because Banks did not have express authority to sell the computer. In fact, Banks was told **not** to sell Lace's computers.

3. **(B)** Banks breached his/her fiduciary duty to Lace and breached his/her duty to follow instructions when s/he sold the computer. This, however, does not automatically terminate their agreement. Statement II is correct because Banks had dealt with Clear before as Lace's agent. Therefore, Clear must receive actual notice to terminate the apparent authority.

4. **(D)** Statement I is incorrect because Banks had apparent authority to sell the computer even though Banks did not have actual authority to do so. Statement II is incorrect because Lace is bound by the contract with Clear. Any modification of the contract must be made by both parties to the contract, not just one.

5. **(A)** Statement I is correct because since Lace was a disclosed principal, only Lace, the principal, is liable under the contract to Clear, the third party. Banks, the agent, is not. For the same reason, statement II is incorrect.

Module 33: Regulation of Business Employment, Environment, and Antitrust

Overview

Issues on this topic are based on the Workers' Compensation Laws and Federal Social Security Rules including the Federal Insurance Contributions Act (FICA) and the Federal Unemployment Tax Act (FUTA). These laws supplement the law of agency. In this area, emphasis is placed on the impact that state and federal laws have on the regulation of employment.

To adequately understand these materials, you should emphasize the theory and purpose underlying the Workers' Compensation Laws. You should also focus on the effect that these laws have on employers and employees. Notice the changes these laws have made on common law.

For Federal Social Security Laws, emphasize the coverage and benefits of the respective programs.

Also, focus on the various discrimination laws.

Be familiar with the various environmental laws; you do not need to know them in great detail, but you must be familiar with the purpose and the basics of each provision.

Candidates should also understand the important parts of the Sherman Act, the Clayton Act, the Robinson-Patman Act, and the Federal Trade Commission Act which, as amended, form the basis for antitrust law, as well as key money laundering statutes. These laws and regulations are now testable on the CPA exam. Before beginning the reading you should review the key terms at the end of the module.

A. Federal Social Security Act

1. Main purpose of Act is as name implies (i.e., attainment of the social security of people in our society)

   a. Basic programs include

      (1) Old age insurance
      (2) Survivor's and disability insurance
      (3) Hospital insurance (Medicare)
      (4) Unemployment insurance

   b. Sources of financing for these programs

      (1) Old-age, survivor's, disability, and hospital insurance programs are financed out of taxes paid by employers, employees, and self-employed under provisions of Federal Insurance Contributions Act and Self-Employment Contributions Act

      (2) Unemployment insurance programs are financed out of taxes paid by employers under the Federal Unemployment Tax Act and various state unemployment insurance laws

2. Federal Insurance Contributions Act (FICA)

  a. Imposes social security tax on employees, self-employed, and employers

  b. Social security tax applies to compensation received that is considered to be wages

  c. In general, tax rates are same for both employer and employee

  d. Taxes are paid only up to base amount that is also changed frequently

      (1) If employee pays FICA tax on more than base amount, s/he has right to refund for excess

         (a) May happen when employee works for two or more employers; these two or more employers, however, do not get refunds

  e. FICA is also used to fund Medicare, **not Medicaid**

      (1) There is no earnings cap for the Medicare portion, thus employees pay the Medicare portion of the tax on all earned wages.

  f. It is employer's duty to withhold employee's share of FICA from employee's wages and remit both employee's amount and employer's equal share to government

      (1) Employer subject to fines for failure to make timely FICA deposits

         (a) Also, employer subject to fine for failure to supply taxpayer identification number

      (2) Employer is required to match FICA contributions of employees on dollar-for-dollar basis

      (3) If employer neglects to withhold, employer may be liable for both employee's and employer's share of taxes (i.e., to pay double tax)

         (a) Once employer pays, s/he has right to collect employee's share from employee

         (b) Employer may voluntarily pay not only its share but also employee's share

            1] Employee's share is deductible by employer as additional compensation and is taxable to the employee as compensation

      (4) Employer is required to furnish employee with written statement of wages paid and FICA contributions withheld during calendar year

  g. Taxes paid by employer are deducted on tax return of employer

      (1) But employee may not deduct taxes paid on his/her tax return

  h. Neither pension plans nor any other programs may be substituted for FICA coverage

      (1) Individuals receiving payments from private pension plans may also receive social security payments

3. Self-Employment Contributions Act

  a. Self-employed persons are required to report their own taxable earnings and pay required social security tax

  b. Self-employment income is net earnings from self-employment

  c. Tax rates paid on self-employment income up to base amount

      (1) Since self-employed does not have employer to match the rate, tax rate is that of employer and employee combined

      (2) Base amount and tax rate are subject to amendment

      (3) Base rate is reduced by any wages earned from another employer during year because wages are subject to FICA

      (4) Self-employed can deduct half of FICA tax paid on his/her income tax form

4. Unemployment Insurance (Federal Unemployment Tax Act—FUTA)

    a. Tax is used to provide unemployment compensation benefits to workers who lose jobs and cannot find replacement work

    b. Federal unemployment tax must be paid by employer if employer employs one or more persons covered by Act

        (1) Deductible as business expense on employer's federal income tax return

        (2) Not deductible by employee because not paid by employee

    c. Employer must also pay a state unemployment tax

        (1) An employer is entitled to credit against his/her federal unemployment tax for state unemployment taxes paid

        (2) State unemployment tax may be raised or lowered according to number of claims against employer

        (3) If employer pays a low state unemployment tax because of good employment record, then employer is entitled to additional credit against federal unemployment tax

5. Coverage under Social Security Act is mandatory for qualifying employees

    a. Person may not elect to avoid coverage

    b. Part-time and full-time employees are covered

    c. Compensation received must be "wages"

6. Definitions

    a. Wages—all compensation for employment

        (1) Include

            (a) Money wages

            (b) Contingent fees

            (c) Compensation in general even though not in cash

            (d) Base pay of those in the service

            (e) Bonuses and commissions

            (f) Most tips

            (g) Vacation and dismissal allowances

        (2) Exclude

            (a) Wages greater than base amount

            (b) Reimbursed travel expenses

            (c) Employee medical and hospital expenses paid by employer

            (d) Employee insurance premiums paid by employer

            (e) Payment to employee retirement plan by employer

    b. Employee—person whose performance is subject to physical control by employer not only as to results but also as to methods of accomplishing those results

        (1) Partners, self-employed persons, directors of corporations, and independent contractors are not covered by unemployment compensation provisions since they are not "employees"

            (a) Are covered as self-employed persons for old-age, survivor's, and disability insurance program purposes

        (2) Independent contractor distinguished from an employee

            (a) Independent contractor not subject to control of employer or regular supervision as employee

            (b) That is, employer seeks results only and contractor controls method

---

EXAMPLE

A builder of homes has only to produce the results.

---

(3) Officers and directors of corporations are "employees" if they perform services and receive remuneration for these services from corporation

c. Employment—all service performed by employee for person employing him/her

   (1) Must be continuing or recurring work

   (2) Services from following are exempt from coverage

      (a) Student nurses

      (b) Certain public employees

      (c) Nonresident aliens

   (3) Services covered if performed by employee for employer without regard to residence or citizenship

      (a) Unless employer not connected with US

   (4) Domestic workers, agricultural workers, government employees, and casual workers are governed by special rules

d. Self-employment—carrying on trade or business either as individual or in partnership

   (1) Wages greater than base amount are excluded

   (2) Can be both employed (in one job) and self-employed (another business), but must meet requirements of trade or business (i.e., not a hobby, occasional investment, etc.)

   (3) Includes director fees if director is not otherwise employed by the corporation

e. Employer

   (1) For Federal Unemployment Tax Act (FUTA) need only employ one person or more for some portion of a day for twenty weeks, or pays $1,500 or more in total wages in any calendar quarter

   (2) In general, may be individual, corporation, partnership, trust, or other entity

7. Old-age, survivor's, and disability insurance benefits

a. Availability of benefits depends upon attainment by individual of "insured status"

   (1) Certain lengths of working time are required to obtain insured status

b. An individual who is "fully insured" is eligible for following benefits

   (1) Survivor benefits for widow or widower and dependents

   (2) Benefits for disabled worker and his/her dependents

   (3) Old-age retirement benefits payable to retired worker and dependents

      (a) Reduced benefits for retirement at age sixty-two

   (4) Lump-sum death benefits

c. Individual who is "currently insured" is eligible for following benefits

   (1) Limited survivor benefits

      (a) In general, limited to dependent minors or those caring for dependent minors

   (2) Benefits for disabled worker and his/her dependents

   (3) Lump-sum death benefits

   (4) Survivors or dependents need not have paid in program to receive benefits

   (5) Divorced spouses may receive benefits

d. Amount of benefits defined by statute which changes from time to time and depends upon

   (1) Average monthly earnings, and

   (2) Relationship of beneficiary to retired, deceased, or disabled worker

      (a) For example, husband, wife, child, grandchild—may be entitled to different benefits

   (3) Benefits increased based on cost of living

   (4) Benefits increased for delayed retirement

8. Reduction of social security benefits

   a. Early retirement results in reduced benefits

     (1) Retirement age is increasing in steps

   b. Returning to work after retirement can affect social security benefits

     (1) Income from private pension plans, savings, investments, or insurance does not affect benefits because not earned income

     (2) Income from limited partnership is considered investment income rather than self-employment income

9. Unemployment benefits

   a. Eligibility for and amount of unemployment benefits governed by state laws

   b. Does not include self-employed

   c. Generally available only to persons unemployed through no fault of their own; however, not available to seasonal workers if paid on yearly basis (e.g., professional sports player in off-season)

   d. One must have worked for specified period of time and/or earned specified amount of wages

---

NOW REVIEW MULTIPLE-CHOICE QUESTIONS 1 THROUGH 9

B. Workers' Compensation Act

1. Workers' compensation is a form of strict liability whereby employer is liable to employee for injuries or diseases sustained by employee which arise out of and in course of employment

   a. Also may include those injuries or diseases only partially sustained in course of employment

   b. Employee is worker subject to control and supervision of employer

   c. Distinguish from independent contractor (see Module 32, section B.2.)

   d. Course of employment includes work-related activities, such as a company picnic

2. Purpose

   a. To give employees and their dependents benefits for job-related injuries or diseases with little difficulty

     (1) Previously, employee had to sue employer for negligence to receive any benefits in form of damages

     (2) Employee usually cannot waive his/her right to benefits

   b. Cost is passed on as an expense of production

   c. **No fault need be shown;** payment is automatic upon satisfaction of requirements

     (1) Removes employer's common law defenses of

       (a) Assumption of risk

       (b) Negligence of a fellow employee—employer formerly could avoid liability by proving it was another employee's fault

       (c) Contributory negligence—injured employee was also negligent

3. Regulated by states

   a. Except that federal government employees are covered by federal statute

   b. Each state has its own statute

4. Generally, there are two types of statutes

   a. Elective statutes

     (1) If employer rejects, s/he loses the three common law defenses against employee's common law suit for damages so most accept

   b. Compulsory statutes

        (1) Require that all employers within coverage of statute provide benefits

        (2) Majority of states have compulsory coverage

5. Insurance used to provide benefits

  a. In lieu of insurance policy, employer may assume liability for workers' compensation claims but must show proof of financial responsibility to carry own risk

6. Legislative scope

  a. Workers' compensation coverage extends to all employees who are injured on the job or in the course of the employment (i.e., while acting in furtherance of employer's business purpose)

  b. Coverage also extends to occupational diseases and preexisting diseases that are aggravated by employment

  c. Coverage does not extend to employee while traveling to or from work

  d. Out-of-state work may be covered if it meets above mentioned criteria

  e. All states have workers' compensation law; most employees covered

  f. Must be employee; coverage does not extend to independent contractors

  g. Public employees are often covered

7. Legal action for damages

  a. Employers covered by workers' compensation insurance are generally exempt from lawsuits by employees

        (1) If employee does not receive benefits covered under workers' compensation, s/he may sue insurance company that agreed to cover workers

  b. Benefits under workers' compensation laws received by employee are in lieu of action for damages against employer and such a suit is barred

        (1) Employer assumes liability in exchange for employee giving up his/her common law rights to sue employer for damages caused by the job (e.g., suit based on negligence)

        (2) When employee is covered by workers' compensation law, his/her sole remedy against employer is that which is provided for under appropriate workers' compensation act

        (3) However, if employer **intentionally** injures employee, employee may proceed against employer based on intentional tort in addition to recovering under workers' compensation benefits

  c. Employee is entitled to workers' compensation benefits **without regard to fault**

        (1) Negligence or even gross negligence of injured employee is not a bar to recovery

        (2) Employee's negligence plays no role in determination of amount of benefits awarded

        (3) Failure of employee to follow employer's rules is not a bar to recovery

        (4) However, injuries caused by intentional self-infliction, or intoxication of employee, can bar recovery

  d. When employer fails to provide workers' compensation insurance or when employer's coverage is inadequate, injured employee may sue in common law for damages, and employer cannot resort to usual common law defenses

        (1) When employer uninsured, many states have a fund to pay employee for job-related injuries

            (a) State then proceeds against uninsured company

            (b) Penalties imposed

8. Actions against third parties

  a. Employee's acceptance of workers' compensation benefits does not bar suit against third party whose negligence or unreasonably dangerous product caused injury

        (1) If employee sues and recovers from third party, employer (or its insurance carrier) is entitled to compensation for workers' compensation benefits paid to employee

            (a) Any recovery in excess of workers' compensation benefits received belongs to injured employee

            (b) To the extent that recovery duplicates benefits already obtained from employer (or carrier), that employer (or carrier) is entitled to reimbursement from employee

EXAMPLE

Kraig, an employee of Badger Corporation, was injured in an auto accident while on the job. The accident was due to the negligence of Todd. Kraig can recover under workers' compensation and also fully recover from Todd in a civil court case. However, Kraig must reimburse the workers' compensation carrier to the extent the recovery from Todd duplicates benefits already obtained under workers' compensation laws.

    b. If employee accepts workers' compensation benefits, employer (or its insurance carrier) is subrogated to rights of employee against third party who caused injury

      (1) Therefore, if employee elects not to sue third party, employer (or its insurance carrier) obtains employee's right of action against third person

9. Claims

    a. Employees are required to file claim forms on timely basis

10. Benefits

    a. Medical

      (1) Provides for medical care to injured or diseased employee

    b. Disability

      (1) This is partial wage continuation plan

    c. Death

      (1) Various plans and schedules provide payments to widow(er) and minor children

    d. Special provisions

      (1) Normally, statutes call for specific scheduled payments for loss of limb or eye
      (2) Also, if employee's injury is of a nature that prevents his/her returning to his/her occupation, plan may pay cost of retraining

    e. Normally not subject to waiver by employee

NOW REVIEW MULTIPLE-CHOICE QUESTIONS 10 THROUGH 16

C. Employee Safety

1. Occupational Safety and Health Act (OSHA)

    a. OSHA applies to almost all employers except federal government, state governments, and certain industries subject to other safety regulations
    b. Purpose of OSHA is to promote safety standards and job safety
    c. Occupational Safety and Health Administration (OSHA) administers this law

      (1) OSHA develops and enforces standards in work place on health and safety
      (2) OSHA investigates complaints and makes inspections of workplace

        (a) Employers can require OSHA to get search warrant for inspection

          1] Search warrant issued based on probable cause

            a] High employee complaint rate can form basis for probable cause

      (3) Employers required to keep records of job-related injuries and report serious accidents to OSHA

    (4) Employers required to comply with regulations set by OSHA

    (5) Employers are prohibited from discriminating against or discharging employees for exercising his/her rights under OSHA

    (6) OSHA may assess civil penalties for violations

    (7) Employers may be criminally liable if willful violation results in death of employee

        (a) Possible fine, imprisonment, or both

NOW REVIEW MULTIPLE-CHOICE QUESTION 17

D. Employment Discrimination

1. Title VII of the 1964 Civil Rights Act forbids discrimination in employment on the basis of race, color, religion, sex, or national origin

   a. Applies to employers and labor unions having fifteen or more employees whose business affects interstate commerce; also applies to government employers and employment agencies

   b. Job discrimination applies to discrimination in hiring, promotion, transfers, firing, compensation, etc.

   c. Enforced by Equal Employment Opportunity Commission (EEOC) which is a federal government administrative agency, or by lawsuits of private individuals

   d. Not necessarily illegal to treat employees differently, but

      (1) Illegal discrimination occurs when employee treated differently because of his/her race, color, religion, sex, or national origin; this is referred to as disparate treatment.

      (2) Illegal discrimination may occur when employer adopts seemingly neutral rules that adversely affect a member of a protected class

---

EXAMPLE

Rules requiring certain minimum standards on weight and/or height have historically discriminated against women as a class since generally men are taller and weigh more.

---

      (3) Illegal discrimination may be proven statistically to show pattern of discrimination

      (4) Defendant may have defenses to Title VII violations

         (a) In those certain instances where sex, religion, or national origin is a bona fide (Latin—good faith) occupational qualification (BFOQ) reasonably necessary to the normal operation of that particular enterprise

           1] Courts construe this defense narrowly

         (b) Bona fide seniority or merit system

         (c) Professionally developed employment testing and education requirements

           1] Employers must be able to show that the test/educational requirements are job related and/or related to job performance if the test is adversely affecting a protected class.

         (d) National security reasons

         (e) Employer only needs to make reasonable accommodations for discrimination based on religion

         (f) No BFOQs exist for discrimination on the basis of race or color

   e. Sexual harassment

      (1) Quid pro quo (Latin—this for that) is intentional harassment involving promotions, job offers, job benefits, in exchange for sexual relations. It also includes sex in exchange for not being fired, demoted, etc.

      (2) Hostile work environment involves harassment that creates an offensive or intimidating work environment. This can include jokes, lewd comments, graphic pictures, etc.

  f. Remedies for a successful claimant under Title VII

      (1) Back pay
      (2) Job or promotion
      (3) Retroactive seniority
      (4) Compensatory damages, and in extreme cases punitive damages, for cases involving intentional discrimination

2. Age Discrimination in Employment Act

  a. Discrimination by employers with 20 or more employees, unions, employment agencies, and federal government
  b. Generally applies to individuals at least forty years old
  c. Very similar in application to Title VII except discrimination is based on age.

3. Vocational Rehabilitation Act of 1973 applies to employers with federal contracts over $2,500

  a. Employers required to take affirmative action to employ and advance qualified handicapped individuals

4. Americans with Disabilities Act (ADA)

  a. Forbids companies and most other entities from discriminating against qualified persons with a disability in various employment decisions including hiring, firing, promotion, and pay

      (1) Qualified individual with disability means person who can perform essential functions of job either with or without reasonable accommodation

         (a) Reasonable accommodation may include acquiring new equipment, modifying facilities, restructuring jobs, modifying work schedules, etc. unless employer can show undue hardship based on significant expense or hardship
         (b) ADA does not protect person using illegal drugs unless rehabilitated and no longer using drugs

      (2) Disabilities include physical impairments, mental impairments, medical conditions, and/or perceived impairments

  b. ADA protects disabled persons from discrimination and guarantees them equal access to, among others,

      (1) Public services including public transportation and public accommodations
      (2) Public services operated by private entities

  c. Enforcement may be by attorney general or by private legal action

5. Pregnancy Discrimination Act

  a. Actually a 1978 amendment to Title VII
  b. Employers prohibited from discriminating against employees becoming pregnant or giving birth

      (1) Unmarried and married woman are covered
      (2) Employers' health and disability insurance must cover pregnancy the same as any other medical condition

6. Vietnam Era Veterans Readjustment Assistance Act

  a. Employers with federal contracts of $10,000 or more must take affirmative action in hiring and promoting qualified veterans of the Vietnam War or qualified disabled veterans

7. Equal Pay Act

  a. Requires equal pay for equal work for both sexes
  b. Differences in pay may be based on merit, quality of work, seniority, or shift differentials
  c. Enforced by Equal Employment Opportunity Commission (EEOC)
  d. To remedy violations, back pay may be required and wages of wronged employees must be raised to eliminate disparity

      (1) Other employees' wages may not be reduced instead

8. Family and Medical Leave Act

    a. Covers employees employed for at least twelve months for at least 1250 hours by employers having at least fifty employees
    b. Employees have the right to up to twelve work weeks of leave during a twelve-month period for any of following reasons

        (1) Employee's own serious health problem
        (2) To care for serious health problem of parent, spouse, or child
        (3) Birth and care of baby
        (4) Child placed with employee for adoption or foster care

    c. Leave of twelve weeks may be done intermittently for cases of serious health problems of employee or his/her covered relatives
    d. Typically, leave is without pay
    e. When employee returns, s/he must get back same or equivalent position
    f. Returning employee cannot lose benefits due to leave
    g. Employers who deny these rights to employee are civilly liable for damages

9. Health Insurance Portability and Accountability Act

    a. Restricts using exclusions for preexisting conditions in employer sponsored group health insurance policies

10. Whistle-Blower Protection Act

    a. Federal law that protects federal employees from retaliation by employers for reporting employer legal violations
    b. Majority of states also have laws that protect whistle-blowers from employers' retaliation

> **NOW REVIEW MULTIPLE-CHOICE QUESTIONS 18 THROUGH 25**

E. Federal Fair Labor Standards Act

1. Applies to all businesses that affect interstate commerce
2. All covered employees must be paid at least "the minimum wage"

    a. Employees younger than twenty may be hired for a somewhat lower "opportunity wage" for ninety calendar days

3. Covered workers who work more than forty hours per week must be paid time and a half
4. Some employees are not covered under some or all of the minimum wage and time-and-a-half provisions

    a. For example, professionals, executives, outside salespersons

5. Some employees must get at least minimum wage but are not covered by the overtime rules

    a. For example, taxi drivers, railroad employees

6. Employees may be paid based on various time bases such as hourly, weekly, monthly, etc.
7. Enforced by Department of Labor and may include fines and/or prison

F. National Labor Relations Act (NLRA)

1. Provides that employees have right to join, assist, or form labor organizations
2. Enforced by the National Labor Relations Board (NLRB)
3. NLRB runs and supervises union elections
4. If union is elected, then management and union must collectively bargain

    a. Mandatory bargaining subjects are topics that both sides **must** negotiate about in good faith. These subjects are

        (1) Wages
        (2) Hours, and
        (3) Other conditions of employment (e.g., benefits, safety conditions, seniority rules, etc.)

b. Illegal bargaining subjects are topics that neither side may bring up (e.g., anything that would violate the NLRA such as an unfair labor practice [UFLP]). Examples include

   (1) Featherbedding, which requires employers to pay employees for work not actually performed
   (2) Involving other parties not directly involved in the labor dispute

c. Permissive bargaining subjects are topics that either side **may** negotiate about. If a subject is not mandatory or illegal, then it is permissive.

5. Strikes, employees refusing to work, are generally legal, but a strike can only be about a mandatory bargaining subject.
6. Certain employees are **not covered** by the NLRA. This does not mean these employees cannot create unions, but they are not protected by the provisions of the NLRA

  a. Government employees
  b. Agricultural employees
  c. Management level employees
  d. Railroad employees

7. The Landrum-Griffin Act amended the NLRA to regulate union abuses against its own members

  a. Requires extensive financial reporting involving unions
  b. Provides for civil and criminal action against misdeeds of union officers
  c. Provides for bill of rights for union members in conducting meetings and elections

NOW REVIEW MULTIPLE-CHOICE QUESTIONS 26 THROUGH 28

G. Federal Consolidated Omnibus Budget Reconciliation Act (COBRA)

1. Provides that when employee quits, s/he may keep same group health insurance coverage for eighteen months for that former employee and spouse

  a. Former employee pays for it
  b. Trade Act increases election period to keep same coverage

2. Applies to employers with 20 or more employees

H. Pensions

1. Employee Retirement Income Security Act (ERISA)

  a. Does not require employer to set up pension plan
  b. If employer does set up plan, it must meet certain standards

    (1) Generally, employee contributions to pension plan vest immediately
    (2) In general, employee's rights to employer's contributions to pension plan vest from five to seven years after beginning employment based on formulas in law
    (3) Standards on investment of funds are set up to avoid mismanagement
    (4) Employers cannot delay employee's participation in pension plan
    (5) Covered plans must give annual reports to employees in plan
    (6) Plan must be in writing
    (7) Plan manager must be named. Manager is a fiduciary.

2. In noncontributory pension plan, employee does not pay but employer pays for all
3. Maximum punishments for violations of Act by individuals increased to imprisonment of ten years and fine of $100,000—by entities, maximum fine is increased to $500,000
4. Sarbanes-Oxley Act requires administrators of employee benefit and profit sharing plans to provide participants and beneficiaries thirty-day advance notice of blackout periods when their rights are temporarily suspended to make changes in plan

    a. Criminal penalties increased by significantly greater fines and longer imprisonment terms

      (1) Based on intent of reducing excesses of some corporations and holding officers and directors more accountable

    b. Prohibits officers and directors from acquiring or transferring stock for services to corporation during blackout periods

---

NOW REVIEW MULTIPLE-CHOICE QUESTIONS 29 THROUGH 31

I. Worker Adjustment and Retraining Notification Act

1. Provides that employers before they close a plant or have mass layoffs must give sixty days notice to employees as well as to state and local officials
2. Act allows shorter notice period in case of emergencies or failing companies
3. Applies to businesses with 100 or more employees

J. Federal Employee Polygraph Protection Act and Drug Testing

1. Private employers may not require employees or prospective employees to take lie detector test or make adverse employment decisions based on such tests or refusals to take them

    a. Act allows polygraph tests to be used by

      (1) Security services hiring employees to protect public health and safety
      (2) Employers that deal with national defense issues
      (3) Drug manufacturers and distributors

    b. Government employers exempted
    c. Private employer may use lie detector tests as part of investigation of economic loss when employer has reason to suspect individual

      (1) Employer is limited in topics of questions that violate privacy especially in topics not directly related to investigation of economic loss

2. Drug testing by public employers and private employers of prospective employees has increased very significantly in the past few years

    a. Employees and job applicants frequently view this as an invasion of privacy
    b. Employers see drug testing as a way to decrease possible liability and also as a way to increase productivity
    c. Generally courts rule preemployment drug screening is legal because job applicants have a lower expectation of privacy than current employees

      (1) Courts generally hold current employees can be tested if either employer has reasonable suspicion employee is drug-impaired or all employees who have had accidents are tested for drugs

K. Employer Rights to E-mail

1. Courts consistently rule employees have no expectation of privacy using employer's e-mail systems

    a. Most employers warn employees about this limitation on privacy at work

      (1) Lack of this warning does not affect employer's rights to review employees' e-mail

2. Unsolicited bulk e-mail or spam has caused problems for both employers and employees

    a. Lawyers have creatively used the traditional tort of trespass to stop some of these problems in cyberspace

L. Environmental Regulation

1. Under common law

    a. Parties may be liable under doctrine of nuisance

(1) Based on party using property in manner that unreasonably interferes with another's right to use and enjoy property

(2) Typically, monetary damages is remedy rather than injunction

(3) Often, plaintiffs need to show their injury is distinct from harm of public in general

b. Businesses may be liable for negligence

(1) Plaintiff shows that his/her harm was caused by business polluter who failed to use reasonable care to prevent foreseeable harm

c. Businesses may be liable under strict liability if involved in ultrahazardous activities

---

EXAMPLE

B is in the business of transporting radioactive materials. Strict liability may be used which makes B liable for all damages it causes without the need to prove negligence.

---

2. Under federal statutory laws

a. Environmental Protection Agency (EPA)

(1) Administrative agency set up to ensure compliance with environmental protection laws

(2) EPA may enforce federal environmental laws by use of administrative orders and/or civil penalties

(a) May also refer criminal or civil actions to Department of Justice

(3) EPA also adopts regulations and conducts research on environment and effects of pollution

(4) Most environmental statutes provide for criminal liability

(a) Generally, corporate officers must be "blameworthy," based on ability to prevent or correct, to be criminally liable

(5) EPA generally uses civil suits more than criminal prosecutions because civil suits require preponderance of evidence to win but criminal convictions require proof beyond a reasonable doubt

(6) Private citizens may also sue violators or may sue EPA to enforce compliance with laws

(7) States may also sue violators

b. National Environmental Policy Act

(1) Requires all federal agencies consider environmental factors in all major decisions

(a) Requires preparation of environmental impact statement (EIS) when federal action or proposed laws significantly affect environment

1] Shows expected impact on environment

2] Describes adverse consequences of action that are unavoidable

3] Must examine alternatives to achieve goals

4] For EIS, environment means more than natural environment—can include aesthetic, cultural, and national heritage interests, etc.

(b) Federal agency must consider environmental impact prior to project

(c) If federal government needs to grant a permit to a private party, then typically private party will need to submit EIS

(d) If agency finds no EIS is warranted, it must prepare and make available to public document called "Finding of No Significant Impact" with reasons for no action needed

c. Clean Air Act

(1) EPA is required to create national ambient air quality standards (NAAQS)

(a) Primary standards are created to protect the public health

(b) Secondary standards are created to protect public welfare (e.g., crops, animals, structures)

(2) States must then submit a state implementation plan (SIP) detailing how the state will achieve the NAAQS

(3) Provides that EPA set air quality standards for mobile sources, such as autos, and stationary sources, such as factories

    (a) Recent amendments now require more, including some smaller businesses to be regulated by Clean Air Act such as many paint shops, bakeries, and dry cleaners

    (b) Recent amendments have also encouraged cities and counties to impose residential regulations such as no-burn days for fireplaces, regulations on reducing numbers of fireplaces in certain areas, or restrictions on charcoal barbeques

    (c) EPA notes air in some buildings is more polluted than outside air

(4) New stationary sources constructed after a NAAQS must show that they are using the best technological system of emissions reduction

(5) Regulates various toxic pollutants, including those that affect acid rain and ozone layer

(6) Act allows private citizens to sue violators of Act and also state or federal officials who fail to take action under the law

    (a) Those winning successful citizens' lawsuits can get attorneys' fees and court costs and punitive damages

    (b) Court may also order EPA to perform its duties and impose civil penalties

(7) Encourages and requires use of alternative fuels to help meet pollution goals

(8) Federal government may force recall of automobiles violating emission regulations

(9) EPA can assess stated civil penalties per violation

    (a) When company finds it cost effective to violate Clean Air Act, EPA may wage penalty equal to benefit company received by not complying

    (b) Criminal fines and imprisonment for intentional violations have recently been made harsher

        1] Most violations under Act are now felonies rather than misdemeanors

        2] Act allows that any responsible corporate officers can be criminally liable

(10) Amendments to Clean Air Act allow companies to trade some rights to pollute

(11) Recent Supreme Court case says that Clean Air Act does not require EPA to consider cost in making air clean

    (a) EPA required to strictly reduce certain toxic pollutants such as mercury

(12) Areas that have already met or exceeded clean air requirements are prohibited from any significant deterioration of their current air quality

d. Clean Water Act

(1) EPA sets standards to reduce, eliminate, or prevent pollution of rivers, seas, ponds, wetlands, streams, etc.

    (a) For example, controls dredging or filling of rivers and wetlands

    (b) Also by amendments, requires acid rain control program

(2) Implemented similar to Clean Air Act: EPA creates framework of clean water standards and states are responsible for making sure that the federal standards are met

(3) Owners of point sources such as floating vessels, pipes, ditches, and animal feeding operations must obtain permits which control water pollution

    (a) Nonpoint sources such as farms, forest lands, and mining are exempt

(4) Broad in scope—includes regulation of discharge of heated water (e.g., by nuclear power plant or electric utilities)

    (a) EPA awards grants for programs to notify public of potential exposure to disease-causing organisms in coastal recreation waters

        1] Many states are now directed to increase monitoring programs for recreational water for such things as E. coli

2] Applies to coastal regions on oceans and Great Lakes

(5) Provides for fines and prison for neglect or knowing violations or endangerment (i.e., knowingly putting person in imminent danger of death or serious bodily harm)

e. Safe Drinking Water Act

(1) Regulates safety of water supplied to homes by public water systems

(a) EPA required to prepare new list every three years that identifies contaminants that EPA is considering for future regulation and for drinking water research, monitoring, and health advisory guidance
(b) Recently identified threat to water systems is from terrorism

1] Recent law requires activities at local, state, and national levels to help public health community to respond to threat of terrorism

(2) Prohibits discharge of waste into wells for drinking water

f. Oil Pollution Act

(1) Requires establishment of oil pollution cleanup contingency plans by tanker owners and operators to handle worst case spills under adverse weather conditions
(2) Requires that new tankers have double hulls
(3) Requires phase-in of double hulls on existing oil tankers and barges

g. Noise Control Act

(1) Regulates noise pollution and encourages research on its effects
(2) EPA establishes noise standards for products sold in US
(3) Violations may result in fines, imprisonment, or injunctions

h. Resource Conservation and Recovery Act

(1) Creates permit system to regulate businesses that store, use, or transport hazardous waste
(2) Requires companies to keep strict records of hazardous waste from "cradle to grave" transport
(3) Producers required to label and package correctly hazardous materials that are to be transported
(4) Generators of hazardous waste must implement waste minimization program that reduces toxicity and quantity of hazardous waste.
(5) Fines and prison for violators

(a) Can be doubled for certain violations

(6) Also, household waste regulated

i. Toxic Substances Control Act

(1) Mandates testing and regulation of chemicals that pose unreasonable risk to health or environment

(a) Requires testing before marketing allowed

(2) Requires special labeling of toxic substances

j. Federal Insecticide, Fungicide, and Rodenticide Act

(1) Provides that pesticides and herbicides must be registered with EPA before sale
(2) EPA can

(a) Deny registration
(b) Certify them for general or restricted use
(c) Suspend registration if emergency or imminent danger
(d) Grant conditional registration when useful until effects known

(3) Limits set for amount of pesticide residue permitted on crops for human or animal consumption
(4) Act has labeling requirements
(5) Violators subject to fine and imprisonment

(6) Private party may petition EPA to suspend or cancel registration

k. Federal Environmental Pesticide Control Act

    (1) All who distribute pesticides must register them with EPA

    (2) EPA uses cost-benefit analysis to decide to register pesticides rather than deciding if they will pose health hazard

l. Comprehensive Environmental, Compensation, and Liability Act (CERCLA)

    (1) Often known as the Superfund legislation

    (2) Levies taxes on manufacturers of certain dangerous chemicals

    (3) Identifies hazardous waste sites needed to be cleaned up

    (4) Regulates generation and transportation of hazardous substances

        (a) Does not regulate petroleum or natural gas

    (5) Government can impose broad liability for cleanup costs and environmental damages

        (a) Parties have **joint and several liability** and include

            1] **Current owners and operators** of site

            2] **Past owners and operators** of site

            3] Persons who **transported** waste to site

            4] Persons who arranged to have waste transported

        (b) With limited exceptions, the standard is based on **strict liability** for all cleanup costs

        (c) One who is responsible for portion of waste can be liable for all cleanup costs

        (d) Liability is retroactive under this statute

        (e) CERCLA lender liability—one important issue is when a lender has responsibility for cleanup when it takes possession of real property due to a foreclosure sale or a deed in lieu of foreclosure

            1] Recent statute specifically excludes lender from CERCLA liability in most situations when it takes possession of real estate due to foreclosure

            2] Lender is still liable under CERCLA if it participates in management or operational affairs of the facility foreclosed on

            3] Lender can do any of following and NOT be liable under CERCLA

                a] Lease the property

                b] Sell the property

                c] Monitor or enforce terms of security agreement involved

                d] Provide financial advice

                e] Restructure loan terms

                f] Mandate debtor to take action on hazardous materials

        (f) CERCLA does **not** make polluters liable to private parties; they generally use private suits under common law

m. Emergency Planning and Community Right-to-Know Act

    (1) Companies having specified amounts of extremely hazardous substances must notify state and local agencies and also must issue annual reports of releases of specified toxic chemicals that result from operations

        (a) This information is available to public

n. International protection of ozone layer

    (1) Many countries, including US, have agreed to reduce or eliminate certain chemicals believed to harm ozone layer

o. Nuclear Waste Policy Act

    (1) Creates national plan to dispose of highly radioactive nuclear waste

    (2) State may regulate emissions of radioactive particles under Clean Air Act

  p. Energy Independence and Security Act

    (1) Purpose of Act is to move US toward greater energy independence, to increase production of clean renewable fuels, to increase efficiency of products, vehicles, and buildings, among others

    (2) Automakers required to increase fleet-wide gas mileage to specified standards

      (a) Applies to all passenger vehicles including light trucks

    (3) Requires vehicle technology and transportation electrification

      (a) Incentives given for development of plug-in hybrids

    (4) Requires specified standards for greater efficiency for lightbulb or similar energy savings

    (5) New initiatives to improve efficiency of highway, sea, and railroad infrastructure

    (6) Creation of Office of Climate Change and Environment in Department of Transportation

    (7) Modernization of electricity grid to improve efficiency

    (8) Small business loans toward improving energy efficiency

    (9) Creation of training program for green jobs (i.e., energy efficiency and renewable energy workers)

    (10) Taxpayer funding for increased funding of biofuels added to gasoline

  q. Marine Protection, Research, and Sanctuaries Act

    (1) Regulates dumping into oceans

    (2) Establishing marine sanctuaries

  r. Endangered Species Act

    (1) Enforced by both EPA and Department of Commerce

    (2) Protects both endangered as well as threatened species

  s. Pollution Prevention Act

    (1) Provides incentives to industry to prevent some pollution from initially being formed

    (2) Facilities must minimize or eliminate pollutants whenever feasible.

  t. SEC requires that companies report in financial statements their environmental liabilities

3. Environmental Compliance Audits

  a. These are systematic, objective reviews designed to evaluate compliance with federal and state regulations and laws on environment

    (1) Some states have environmental audit privilege laws. In these states, businesses' environmental audits are exempt from discovery in a lawsuit.

    (2) EPA will substantially reduce or, in some circumstances, waive fines if companies disclose and correct wrongdoing.

  b. Purposes of audit

    (1) To discover violations or questionable practices to allow company to avoid litigation

    (2) Voluntary discovery allows companies to avoid criminal sanctions

    (3) To meet disclosure requirements under securities laws

---

NOW REVIEW MULTIPLE-CHOICE QUESTIONS 32 THROUGH 44

M. Telephone Consumer Protection Act

1. Restricts use of prerecorded messages
2. Act requires that in order to use prerecorded messages, a live person must introduce prerecorded message and receive from telephoned person permission to play that message

   a. Act exempts calls by nonprofit organizations, calls made for emergencies, and calls to businesses
   b. Act does not cover personal phone calls

N. Federal Telecommunications Act

1. Prevents local or state governments from preventing entry of the growing telecommunications industry

O. Identity Theft

1. Hackers can collect much information on individuals to piece together information on them to, in many cases, obtain credit or make purchases or obtain government benefits
2. Increased penalties for identity theft to help reduce it
3. FTC is appointed to help victims of identity theft to restore credit and minimize impacts of identity theft
4. All banks, savings associations, and credit unions are required to have an identity theft prevention program

P. Antitrust Law

1. The main purpose of federal antitrust laws is to promote the production and distribution of goods and services in the most economical and efficient manner by preserving free, competitive markets

   a. Also promotes fairness and gives consumer a wider choice

2. Regulation (for the CPA Exam) is by federal law, so interstate commerce must be affected before the activity is regulated

   a. If there is a substantial economic effect on interstate commerce, then federal law governs

   (1) Even if a business is only carried on within a state, it may substantially affect interstate commerce if it

   (a) Competes or deals with businesses that do business among several states, or
   (b) Purchases or sells a substantial amount of products that come from or wind up in interstate commerce

---

EXAMPLE

Wholesale dealers in a state agree to divide the state market among them. This agreement is intrastate but it reduces the chances for out-of-state dealers to enter the local market and therefore the agreement affects interstate commerce.

---

3. If the contract in restraint of trade is illegal, it is unenforceable by the parties, in addition to possible criminal or civil penalties and injunctions

   a. Vertical restraints are agreements between parties from different levels of the distribution chain (i.e., between manufacturer and retailer)
   b. Horizontal restraints are agreements between parties of the same level of the distribution chain (i.e., between two retailers or two manufacturers)

4. Some contracts in restraint of trade **are** legal and enforceable

   a. Seller of a business agrees not to compete with the buyer

   (1) Only valid if for a reasonable time and a reasonable geographic area and if a proper business interest is sought to be protected

   (a) Reasonable time is what is fair under the circumstances to protect buyer (e.g., one year)
   (b) Reasonable area would be where the business is conducted (e.g., neighborhood). If business is statewide, then restriction can be for whole state

---

EXAMPLE

Seller of a bakery covenants not to compete in the immediate locality for one year. This is a reasonable area and also a reasonable length of time.

---

    b. Similarly, partners and employees can covenant not to compete with partnership or employer while relationship lasts and for a reasonable time thereafter and within a reasonable area

    c. Buyer or lessee of property may covenant not to use it in competition with, or to the injury of the seller or lessor

       (1) Same standards of reasonableness apply

5. Exceptions to the antitrust laws

    a. Labor unions unless they join with nonlabor group and act in violation

    b. Patents are a twenty-year monopoly; fourteen years for design patents

    c. Copyrights are a monopoly for the author's life plus seventy years

       (1) For publishers, 95 years after publication or 120 years after creation

    d. Trademarks are a monopoly with an indefinite number of renewals if still used

    e. Insurance business that is covered by state regulations

    f. US exporters may cooperate to compete with foreign entities

    g. State allowed to have quotas on oil marketed for interstate commerce

    h. Agricultural cooperatives

    i. State government actions

       (1) These are industries comprehensively regulated by the state

       (2) Utilities, insurance are examples of industries where this is true

    j. Legislative activities such as lobbying

    k. Professional baseball, no other sports, just baseball

6. Enforcement of the Antitrust Laws

    a. Justice Department

       (1) Enforces Sherman Act and Clayton Act

       (2) Only enforcement entity that may seek criminal penalties

    b. Federal Trade Commission (FTC)

       (1) Enforces Clayton Act and Federal Trade Commission Act

       (2) May only pursue civil enforcement

    c. Private parties

       (1) Entitled to treble (triple) actual damages and reasonable attorney fees if successful.

       (2) May only pursue civil enforcement

Q. Sherman Act of 1890

1. Contracts, combinations, conspiracies, or agreements in restraint of trade are illegal under Section 1 of the Sherman Act.

    a. The agreement must be between separate economic entities

---

EXAMPLE

McDonald's can decide that all of its stores will sell Quarter Pounders for $1.99. McDonald's cannot agree with Burger King that if Burger King will charge at least $3.50 for a Whopper, McDonald's will sell Quarter Pounders for $3.50.

---

b. Only unreasonable restraints are illegal

c. There are two approaches that courts use to determine whether the restraint is unreasonable:

    (1) The per se rule

    (2) The rule of reason

d. The per se rule means that the restraint is automatically illegal

    (1) Certain activities are viewed as so inherently anticompetitive that there can be no valid justification to engage is such activities

    (2) Generally, the per se rule applies to horizontal restraints of trade. (See section 2. of this outline below)

    (3) Activities that do not fall under the per se rule are analyzed under the rule of reason

e. The rule of reason balances the procompetitive effects of the agreement versus the anticompetitive effects of the agreement

    (1) If on balance, the agreement is more procompetitive than anticompetitive, the agreement is legal

    (2) Conversely, if the agreement is more anticompetitive than procompetitive, the agreement is illegal

2. Horizontal restraints of trade involve agreements between competitors

---

EXAMPLE

An agreement between McDonald's and Burger King.

---

a. Many horizontal restraints are analyzed under the per se rule because they tend to directly reduce competition

b. Per se horizontal restraints include

    (1) Price fixing (agreement)

        (a) Whether it actually affects prices or not

        (b) Whether the fixed price is fair or not (presumed unfair)

        (c) Dollar volume is unimportant; existence of any price fixing agreement is illegal

        (d) An actual agreement is not necessary if the parties have a tacit understanding and adhere to it

        (e) Includes quantity limitations and minimum, maximum, buying, and selling prices

    (2) Joint boycotts (i.e., group agreements not to deal with another) are per se violations

    (3) Horizontal territorial limitation is a per se violation

---

EXAMPLE

Two competitors agree not to sell in each other's section of the city.

---

c. Not all horizontal agreements are illegal per se

    (1) A joint venture is analyzed under the rule of reason because most anticompetitive effects are temporary

    (2) Trade and professional organization agreements are examined under the rule of reason

3. Vertical restraints of trade involve agreements between businesses at different levels in the distribution chain

---

EXAMPLE

McDonald's entering into an agreement with Coke to use only Coca Cola products in McDonald's restaurants

---

a. All vertical restraints are subject to a rule of reason analysis (i.e. there are no per se violations for vertical restraints)

b. Resale price maintenance (Vertical price fixing)

(1) Manufacturers may suggest a retail price; this is legal because there is no agreement.

(2) Manufacturers may refuse to sell to retailers who promise to sell at suggested price. This is a unilateral decision by the manufacturer, so there is no agreement. This activity is also legal.

EXAMPLE

Colgate toothpaste tells Mega Mart that it must resell Colgate at a price of no less than $2 a tube. Mega Mart refuses and Colgate does not sell toothpaste to Mega Mart. Since there is no agreement between Colgate and Mega, there cannot be a violation of Section 1 of the Sherman Act.

---

c. Rule of reason analysis for vertical restraints usually focuses on interbrand and intrabrand competition.

(1) Interbrand competition is the competition between different brands of the same product.

EXAMPLE

Campbell's soup and Progresso soup.

---

(2) Intrabrand competition is between the same brands at different places.

EXAMPLE

The price of Campbell's soup at different competing supermarkets.

---

(3) Generally interbrand competition is viewed as more beneficial to consumers

(4) Thus, many vertical restraints which injure or limit intrabrand competition, but enhance or promote interbrand competition, are usually legal under the rule of reason

d. Vertical territorial limitations, often contained in franchising agreements, where franchisee receives an exclusive right to sell in a specific territory but is precluded from selling in any area are only illegal if unreasonable (Rule of Reason)

EXAMPLE

A distributor requires dealer to sell only in X suburban area.

---

4. Monopolization violates Section 2 of the Sherman Act

a. Section 2 makes it illegal for a firm to obtain or maintain a monopoly; it is not illegal to actually have a monopoly

b. Unlike Section 1 of the Sherman Act, there is no agreement necessary to violate Section 2 of the Sherman Act

c. Monopoly is the power to exclude competition and/or to control prices; a firm does not need 100% of the market to have a monopoly under the antitrust laws

(1) Percentage share of the relevant market is a determining factor

    (a) Generally, 70% of the relevant market is a presumption of monopoly power

    (b) Less than 50% of the relevant market there is a presumption of no monopoly power

    (c) A much lower percentage will suffice if the charge is attempting to monopolize rather than holding monopoly power

(2) The relevant market consists of the product market and the geographic market

    (a) Product market consists of commodities reasonably interchangeable by consumers

---

EXAMPLE

In a case involving a cellophane wrapping manufacturer, the product market was flexible wrapping material.

    (b) Geographic market is the area in which the defendant and competitors sell the product

---

EXAMPLE

A geographic market for a major beer brewer is national while for a taxi company it is very local.

---

d. Intent is also required to violate Section 2

(1) Therefore, to engage in illegal monopolization there needs to be monopoly power and intent

(2) If no intent, or monopoly is thrust on defendant, then not illegal

    (a) Growth resulting from superior product, quality of management, or historical accident is not illegal

    (b) There must not be any predatory or coercive conduct

EXAMPLE

There are several hotels in a town. Business drops and all but one close. The remaining hotel has taken no action to get the others to close. Although the remaining hotel has a monopoly, it was thrust upon the hotel and is therefore not illegal.

---

5. Sanctions (not mutually exclusive, both civil and governmental prosecution available)

a. Injunctions, forced divisions, forced divestiture (by individuals, corporations, or government)

(1) Government may seize property shipped in interstate commerce and violating party forfeits it

b. Criminal penalties (by government)

c. Treble damages (by individuals and corporations)

(1) That is, actual damages (e.g., loss of profits, multiplied by three)

(2) Plus attorney fees and court costs

(3) Instituted to encourage private parties to enforce the antitrust laws

R. Clayton Act of 1914

1. Supplemented the Sherman Act to prohibit a corporation from acquiring the stock of a competing corporation (merger) where the effect **might** substantially lessen competition or tend to create a monopoly

   a. Acquisitions tending to create a monopoly are violations

      (1) No actual monopoly need be created
      (2) To stop monopolistic trends in their incipiency
      (3) Applies where there is a reasonable likelihood the merger or acquisition will substantially lessen competition
      (4) As under the Sherman Act, use the percentage of market (product and geographic) test

   b. Amendment of 1950 added the prohibition of the acquisition of assets of another corporation where the effect might lessen competition

      (1) Thus both asset and stock acquisitions are covered
      (2) Includes vertical mergers (sellers-buyers) and conglomerate mergers (e.g., not in same industry) as well as horizontal mergers (competitors)

EXAMPLE

A shoe manufacturer buys out one of its retailers. This is a vertical merger.

EXAMPLE

A shoe retailer buys out another shoe retailer. This is a horizontal merger.

EXAMPLE

A pen manufacturer buys out a clothing retailer. This is a conglomerate merger.

---

   c. Suit may be brought either before or after completion of the merger

      (1) For example, preliminary injunction to prevent violation
      (2) For example, forced divestiture any time after completion of a merger if competition is threatened

   d. Under "failing company doctrine," a merger that is anticompetitive may be allowed if

      (1) The acquired company is failing, and
      (2) There is no other willing purchaser whose acquisition of the company would reduce competition less

   e. Factors to determine whether a merger will result in a substantial lessening of competition include

      (1) Market concentration

         (a) If the market is controlled by just a few firms, then it is more likely that the merger will result in a substantial lessening of competition.
         (b) If the market is controlled by many firms, then it is less likely that the merger will result in a substantial lessening of competition.

      (2) Entry barriers to the market are how difficult or how easy it is for new firms to enter the market. If entry barriers are high, it is more likely a merger will result in a substantial lessening of competition.

(3) Generally, horizontal mergers are the most likely to result in a substantial lessening of competition, and conglomerate mergers are the least likely to do so.

2. Interlocking directorates are prohibited under the Clayton Act

   a. Applies to a director sitting on boards of two or more competing corporations that are "large"
   b. No proof required that this will lessen competition
   c. Remedy typically is to required offending director to resign one of the director positions

3. Tying arrangements

   a. Occurs where seller forces buyer to take one or more other products as a condition to acquiring the desired product

---

EXAMPLE

A manufacturer of a very popular line of jeans requires its retailers to also stock the manufacturer's line of shirts in order to obtain the jeans.

---

   b. Elements of a tying arrangement

      (1) Two separate products

         (a) Tying product is the product that is actually desired. In the example above, the tying products are the jeans.
         (b) Tied product is the product that the buyer is being "forced" to purchase. In the above example, the tied products are the shirts.

      (2) There must be economic power in the tying market. Economic power can be shown by either

         (a) A market share of 30% or more in the tying market, or
         (b) The product is unique. Uniqueness can often be demonstrated by an intellectual property right such as a patent or a copyright.

EXAMPLE

When the movie Gone with the Wind was released, movie theaters were told that they would also have to take a movie called Getting Gertie's Garter. While Gone with the Wind did not have a 30% market share, it was a unique production, and thus qualifies as economic power.

---

      (3) Substantial commerce in the tied market

   c. Generally, all three elements must be met for the tying arrangement to be considered illegal

S. Robinson-Patman Act of 1936

1. Prohibits price discrimination
2. Price discrimination is when a seller charges different prices to different buyers of the same good.

EXAMPLE

Thor's Hammers Inc. charges Home Depot $3.00 per hammer, but it charges Mom and Pop Hardware $3.50 per hammer.

---

3. Price differences are permitted, however, if there is a cost justification

---

EXAMPLE

Home Depot buys an entire truckload of hammers: Mom and Pop Hardware buys 1/20 of a truckload of hammers. The lower transportation costs for Home Depot can be passed on to Home Depot in the form of a lower price without violating the law.

---

4. Sellers may also temporarily reduce prices in one region to meet the price of a lower-priced competitor

T. Federal Trade Commission Act of 1914

1. Created the Federal Trade Commission (FTC)

   a. FTC has authority to enforce most of the antitrust laws, but not criminal violations
   b. FTC has exclusive authority to enforce this Act's prohibitions (i.e., individuals may not enforce)
   c. FTC has authority to determine what practices are unfair or undesirable

2. Prohibits unfair methods of competition and deceptive practices involving advertising, telemarketing, electronic advertising

   a. FTC has exclusive authority under this Act and can determine what is unfair
   b. FTC may stop unfair and deceptive practices in their incipiency (i.e., before an actual violation occurs) as well as after a violation occurs

---

EXAMPLE

An oil company agreed with a tire company that the oil company would promote the sale of the tire company's accessories to the oil company's independent dealers. There was no tying or overt coercion in these promotions to the independent dealers, but the dominant position of the oil company over its dealers created strong potential for stifling competition. The agreement was therefore an unfair method of competition.

---

   c. Unfairness standards

      (1) Cause of substantial injury to competitors or consumers
      (2) Offends public policy
      (3) Oppressive or unscrupulous practices

3. Sanctions

   a. Cease and desist orders

      (1) Civil penalty for each violation
      (2) Each day of continued violation is separate offense
      (3) FTC may also use cease and desist orders for the Sherman Act and Clayton Act

U. Money Laundering

1. Money laundering is a process by which one conceals the existence, illegal source, or illegal application of income, and disguises that income to make it appear legitimate.

   a. Money laundering statutes originally targeted primarily drug activity by organized crime, but now aim at a wider range of illicit activities ranging from terrorism to income tax evasion.

2. Key Statutes

   a. The Bank Secrecy Act of 1970, 31 U.S.C. 5313

(1) Requires record keeping and reporting by banks and other financial institutions to trace the movement of currency into and out of the U.S. or deposited into banks.

    (a) Reporting of cash transactions over $10,000

    (b) Identifying persons conducting all transactions

    (c) Maintenance of a traceable paper trail

b. 31 U.S.C. 5324

(1) Helps prevent evasion of the Bank Secrecy Act by making it illegal to break large transactions down into denominations smaller than $10,000 each in order to evade these reporting requirements.

c. Money Laundering Control Act of 1986

(1) Key statute in the criminal area, consisting of primarily two provisions: Section 1956 and 1957 of Title 18 of the United States Code.

    (a) Section 1956 contains two primary prohibitions

        1] Prohibits *transaction money laundering* where the prohibited act is the financial transaction itself. Examples include financial transactions conducted with intent to: promote unlawful activity, engage in violations of Sections 7201 or 7206 of the Tax Code, attempt to conceal the nature, location, source, ownership, or control of proceeds from specified unlawful activity, and attempt to avoid state or federal reporting requirements

        2] Prohibits *transportation money laundering*, the transportation of criminally derived funds into or out of the U.S. with the intent to: promote illegal activity, transport illegal proceeds in an attempt to hide those proceeds, or transport illegal proceeds to avoid reporting requirements

        3] Carries a $10,000 maximum civil penalty and a maximum criminal penalty of 20 years in jail and a $500,000 fine or twice the value of the laundered money (whichever is greater)

    (b) Section 1957 addresses monetary transactions in criminally derived property over $10,000

        1] Property must be derived from unlawful activities such as drug dealing, gambling, mail fraud, wire fraud, or some other related offense.

        2] To be liable the recipient must "knowingly" engage in a transaction involving criminally derived property.

NOW REVIEW MULTIPLE-CHOICE QUESTIONS 45 THROUGH 48

KEY TERMS

Employment Law

Age Discrimination in Employment Act (ADEA). Law that prohibits discrimination against people who are 40 and older.

Americans with Disabilities Act (ADA). Prohibits discrimination against differently abled persons. Includes both physical and mental disabilities.

Bona fide occupational qualification (BFOQ). An employer's defense to a claim of employment discrimination based on Title VII. The employer is claiming to have a legitimate reason, usually related to job qualifications, for what appears to be discrimination.

Consolidated Omnibus Budget Reconciliation Act (COBRA). Allows former employees, at their own expense, to continue coverage of their group health plan for up to 18 months after losing their job.

Employee Retirement Income Security Act (ERISA). Regulates pension plans for companies that choose to have pensions.

Fair Labor Standards Act (FLSA). Federal law that regulates minimum wage, employment hours, and child labor.

Family and Medical Leave Act. Allows employees to take up to 12 weeks of unpaid leave to deal with family and medical issues.

Federal Insurance Contributions Act (FICA). Law that requires employers and employees to each pay half of the social security tax. Self-employed individuals must pay the entire tax.

Federal Unemployment Tax Act (FUTA). Provides temporary payments to workers who have lost their jobs through no fault of their own.

National Labor Relations Act (NLRA). Legislation that regulates the union/management relationship.

Occupational Safety and Health Act (OSHA). Creates workplace standards of health and safety.

Social Security Act. Provides income/benefits to retirees, disabled workers, and dependents of deceased workers.

Title VII of the 1964 Civil Rights Act. Prohibits discrimination on the basis of race, color, religion, national origin, or gender in all aspects of employment.

Worker's compensation. Provides payments to workers for injuries that are sustained at work or that arise out of work. This is a no-fault system.

Environmental Law

Clean Air Act. Establishes air quality standards that states enforce.

Clean Water Act. Establishes water quality standards that states enforce.

Comprehensive Environmental Response, Compensation, and Liability Act (CERCLA). Creates a strict liability system for the cleanup of hazardous waste sites and spills.

Environmental compliance audit. A voluntary review by a company to ensure that it is in compliance with the various environmental laws.

Environmental impact statement. A report required for any federal action that will significantly impact the environment.

Environmental Protection Agency (EPA). Primary enforcer and administrator of environmental laws and regulations.

State implementation plan. Plan submitted by a state to show the EPA how the state will achieve the environmental standards set by the EPA.

Antitrust

Horizontal restraint. An agreement among competing economic entities that limits competition.

Merger. Two separate economic entities that combine into one company. Only mergers that will result in a substantial lessening of competition violate the antitrust laws.

Monopolization. When a firm has monopoly power in the relevant market and keeps others out of the market through methods other than legitimate competition.

Monopoly power. A firm has the ability to exclude competitors and control prices in the relevant market.

Per se rule. Applies to inherently anticompetitive activities that are automatically illegal.

Price discrimination. Sellers charging different buyers different prices for the same product.

Relevant market. Refers to the meaningful areas of competition both geographically and by product.

Restraint of trade. An agreement that limits competition.

Rule of reason. If a restraint of trade does not fall under the per se rule, then it is analyzed under the rule of reason, which balances the procompetitive effects of the agreement versus the anticompetitive effects.

Treble damages. One of the remedies for a private party who successfully proves an antitrust violation; the private party receives three times its actual damages.

Tying arrangement. Seller of a desired product forces a buyer to purchase an additional product if the buyer wants the desired product.

Vertical restraint of trade. An agreement between separate economic entities in the chain of distribution that limits competition.

A. Federal Social Security Act

1. Taxes payable under the Federal Unemployment Tax Act (FUTA) are

    a. Calculated as a fixed percentage of all compensation paid to an employee.

    b. Deductible by the employer as a business expense for federal income tax purposes.

    c. Payable by employers for all employees.

    d. Withheld from the wages of all covered employees.

2. An unemployed CPA generally would receive unemployment compensation benefits if the CPA

    a. Was fired as a result of the employer's business reversals.

    b. Refused to accept a job as an accountant while receiving extended benefits.

    c. Was fired for embezzling from a client.

    d. Left work voluntarily without good cause.

3. After serving as an active director of Lee Corp. for twenty years, Ryan was appointed an honorary director with the obligation to attend directors' meetings with no voting power. Last year, Ryan received an honorary director's fee of $5,000. This fee is

    a. Reportable by Lee as employee compensation subject to social security tax.

    b. Reportable by Ryan as self-employment income subject to social security self-employment tax.

    c. Taxable as "other income" by Ryan, **not** subject to any social security tax.

    d. Considered to be a gift **not** subject to social security self-employment or income tax.

4. Syl Corp. does **not** withhold FICA taxes from its employees' compensation. Syl voluntarily pays the entire FICA tax for its share and the amounts that it could have withheld from the employees. The employees' share of FICA taxes paid by Syl to the IRS is

    a. Deductible by Syl as additional compensation that is includible in the employees' taxable income.

    b. Not deductible by Syl because it does **not** meet the deductibility requirement as an ordinary and necessary business expense.

    c. A nontaxable gift to each employee, provided that the amount is less than $1,000 annually to each employee.

    d. Subject to prescribed penalties imposed on Syl for its failure to withhold required payroll taxes.

5. Social security benefits may include all of the following **except**

    a. Payments to divorced spouses.

    b. Payments to disabled children.

    c. Medicare payments.

    d. Medicaid payments.

6. Which of the following forms of income, if in excess of the annual exempt amount, will cause a reduction in a retired person's social security benefits?

    a. Annual proceeds from an annuity.

    b. Director's fees.

    c. Pension payments.

    d. Closely held corporation stock dividends.

7. Which of the following payments are deducted from an employee's salary?

	Unemployment compensation insurance	Worker's compensation insurance
a.	Yes	Yes
b.	Yes	No
c.	No	Yes
d.	No	No

8. Which of the following types of income is subject to taxation under the provisions of the Federal Insurance Contributions Act (FICA)?

    a. Interest earned on municipal bonds.

    b. Capital gains of $3,000.

    c. Car received as a productivity award.

    d. Dividends of $2,500.

9. Under the Federal Insurance Contributions Act (FICA), which of the following acts will cause an employer to be liable for penalties?

	Failure to supply taxpayer identification numbers	Failure to make timely FICA deposits
a.	Yes	Yes
b.	Yes	No
c.	No	Yes
d.	No	No

B. Workers' Compensation Act

10. Which of the following parties generally is ineligible to collect workers' compensation benefits?

    a. Minors.

    b. Truck drivers.

    c. Union employees.

    d. Temporary office workers.

11. Kroll, an employee of Acorn, Inc., was injured in the course of employment while operating a forklift manufactured and sold to Acorn by Trell Corp. The forklift was defectively designed by Trell. Under the state's mandatory workers' compensation statute, Kroll will be successful in

	Obtaining workers' compensation benefits	A negligence action against Acorn
a.	Yes	Yes
b.	Yes	No
c.	No	Yes
d.	No	No

12. Which of the following provisions is basic to all workers' compensation systems?

a. The injured employee must prove the employer's negligence.
b. The employer may invoke the traditional defense of contributory negligence.
c. The employer's liability may be ameliorated by a coemployee's negligence under the fellow-servant rule.
d. The injured employee is allowed to recover on strict liability theory.

13. Workers' Compensation Acts require an employer to

a. Provide coverage for all eligible employees.
b. Withhold employee contributions from the wages of eligible employees.
c. Pay an employee the difference between disability payments and full salary.
d. Contribute to a federal insurance fund.

14. Generally, which of the following statements concerning workers' compensation laws is correct?

a. The amount of damages recoverable is based on comparative negligence.
b. Employers are strictly liable without regard to whether or **not** they are at fault.
c. Workers' compensation benefits are **not** available if the employee is negligent.
d. Workers' compensation awards are payable for life.

15. Workers' compensation laws provide for all of the following benefits **except**

a. Burial expenses.
b. Full pay during disability.
c. The cost of prosthetic devices.
d. Monthly payments to surviving dependent children.

16. Which of the following claims is (are) generally covered under workers' compensation statutes?

	Occupational disease	Employment aggravated preexisting disease
a.	Yes	Yes
b.	Yes	No
c.	No	Yes
d.	No	No

C. Employee Safety

17. Under which of the following conditions is an on-site inspection of a workplace by an investigator from the Occupational Safety and Health Administration (OSHA) permissible?

a. Only if OSHA obtains a search warrant after showing probable cause.
b. Only if the inspection is conducted after working hours.
c. At the request of employees.
d. After OSHA provides the employer with at least twenty-four hours' notice of the prospective inspection.

D. Employment Discrimination

18. Which of the following Acts prohibit(s) an employer from discriminating among employees based on sex?

	Equal Pay Act	Title VII of the Civil Rights Act
a.	Yes	Yes
b.	Yes	No
c.	No	Yes
d.	No	No

19. Under the Age Discrimination in Employment Act, which of the following remedies is (are) available to a covered employee?

	Early retirement	Back pay
a.	Yes	Yes
b.	Yes	No
c.	No	Yes
d.	No	No

20. Which of the following company policies would violate the Age Discrimination in Employment Act?

a. The company will not hire any accountant below twenty-five years of age.
b. The office staff must retire at age sixty-five or younger.
c. Both of the above.
d. None of the above.

21. Under the provisions of the Americans With Disabilities Act of 1990, in which of the following areas is a disabled person protected from discrimination?

	Public transportation	Privately operated public accommodations
a.	Yes	Yes
b.	Yes	No
c.	No	Yes
d.	No	No

22. Under the Americans With Disabilities Act, which is (are) true?

I. The Act requires that companies with at least ten employees set up a specified plan to hire people with disabilities.
II. The Act requires companies to make reasonable accommodations for disabled persons unless this results in undue hardship on the operations of the company.

a. I only.
b. II only.
c. Both I and II.
d. Neither I nor II.

23. The Americans With Disabilities Act has as a purpose to give remedies for discrimination to individuals with disabilities. Which of the following is (are) true of this Act?

I. It protects most individuals with disabilities working for companies but only if the companies do not need to incur any expenses to modify the work environment to accommodate the disability.
II. It may require a company to modify work schedules to accommodate persons with disabilities.
III. It may require a company to purchase equipment at company expense to accommodate persons with disabilities.

　　a. I only.
　　b. I and II only.
　　c. II and III only.
　　d. III only.

D.8.　Family and Medical Leave Act

24. Which of the following is **not** true under the Family and Medical Leave Act?

　　a. An employee has a right to take a leave from work for the birth and care of her child for one month at half of her regular pay.
　　b. An employee has a right to take a leave from work for twelve workweeks to care for his/her seriously ill parent.
　　c. An employee, upon returning under the provisions of the Act, must get back the same or equivalent position in the company.
　　d. This Act does not cover all employees.

25. The Family Medical Leave Act provides for

I. Unpaid leave for the employee to care for a newborn baby.
II. Unpaid leave for the employee to care for the serious health problem of his or her parent.
III. Paid leave for the employee to care for a serious health problem of his or her spouse.

　　a. I only.
　　b. II only.
　　c. I and II but not III.
　　d. III but not I or II.

E.　Federal Fair Labor Standards Act

26. Under the Fair Labor Standards Act, which of the following pay bases may be used to pay covered, nonexempt employees who earn, on average, the minimum hourly wage?

	Hourly	Weekly	Monthly
a.	Yes	Yes	Yes
b.	Yes	Yes	No
c.	Yes	No	Yes
d.	No	Yes	Yes

27. Under the Fair Labor Standards Act, if a covered, nonexempt employee works consecutive weeks of forty-five, forty-two, thirty-eight, and thirty-three hours, how many hours of overtime must be paid to the employee?

　　a. 0
　　b. 7
　　c. 18
　　d. 20

F.　National Labor Relations Act (NLRA)

28. Which of the following employee benefits is (are) exempt from the provisions of the National Labor Relations Act?

	Sick pay	Vacation pay
a.	Yes	Yes
b.	Yes	No
c.	No	Yes
d.	No	No

G.　Federal Consolidated Budget Reconciliation Act (COBRA)

29. Under the Federal Consolidated Budget Reconciliation Act of 1985 (COBRA), when an employee voluntarily resigns from a job, the former employee's group health insurance coverage that was in effect during the period of employment with the company

　　a. Automatically ceases for the former employee and spouse, if the resignation occurred before normal retirement age.
　　b. Automatically ceases for the former employee's spouse, but continues for the former employee for an eighteen-month period at the former employer's expense.
　　c. May be retained by the former employee at the former employee's expense for at least eighteen months after leaving the company, but must be terminated for the former employee's spouse.
　　d. May be retained for the former employee and spouse at the former employee's expense for at least eighteen months after leaving the company.

H.　Pensions

30. Under the Employee Retirement Income Security Act of 1974 (ERISA), which of the following areas of private employer pension plans is (are) regulated?

	Employee vesting	Plan funding
a.	Yes	Yes
b.	Yes	No
c.	No	Yes
d.	No	No

31. Under the provisions of the Employee Retirement Income Security Act of 1974 (ERISA), which of the following statements is correct?

　　a. Employees are entitled to have an employer established pension plan.

    b. Employers are prevented from unduly delaying an employee's participation in a pension plan.

    c. Employers are prevented from managing retirement plans.

    d. Employees are entitled to make investment decisions.

L. Environmental Regulation

32. Under the Comprehensive Environmental Response, Compensation, and Liability Act (CERCLA), commonly known as Superfund, which of the following parties would be liable to the Environmental Protection Agency (EPA) for the expense of cleaning up a hazardous waste disposal site?

I. The current owner or operator of the site.

II. The person who transported the wastes to the site.

III. The person who owned or operated the site at the time of the disposal.

    a. I and II.

    b. I and III.

    c. II and III.

    d. I, II, and III.

33. Which of the following activities is (are) regulated under the Federal Water Pollution Control Act (Clean Water Act)?

	Discharge of heated water by nuclear power plants	Dredging of wetlands
a.	Yes	Yes
b.	Yes	No
c.	No	Yes
d.	No	No

34. Environmental Compliance Audits are used for which of the following purpose(s)?

I. To voluntarily discover violations to avoid criminal sanctions.

II. To discover violations to avoid civil litigation.

III. To meet disclosure requirements to the SEC under the securities laws.

    a. I only.

    b. I and II only.

    c. II only.

    d. I, II, and III.

35. Which of the following is (are) true under the Federal Insecticide, Fungicide, and Rodenticide Act?

I. Herbicides and pesticides must be certified and can be used only for applications that are approved.

II. Herbicides and pesticides must be registered under the Act before companies can sell them.

III. Pesticides, when used on food crops, can only be used in quantities that are limited under the Act.

    a. I only.

    b. I and II only.

    c. II and III only.

    d. I, II, and III.

36. Under the Comprehensive Environmental Response, Compensation and Liability Act as amended by the Superfund Amendments, which of the following is (are) true?

I. The present owner of land can be held liable for cleanup of hazardous chemicals placed on the land by a previous owner.

II. An employee of a company that had control over the disposal of hazardous substances on the company's land can be held personally liable for cleanup costs.

    a. I only.

    b. II only.

    c. Both I and II.

    d. Neither I nor II.

37. The National Environmental Policy Act was passed to enhance and preserve the environment. Which of the following is **not** true?

    a. The Act applies to all federal agencies.

    b. The Act requires that an environmental impact statement be provided if any proposed federal legislation may significantly affect the environment.

    c. Enforcement of the Act is primarily accomplished by litigation of persons who decide to challenge federal government decisions.

    d. The Act provides generous tax breaks to those companies that help accomplish national environmental policy.

38. Under the federal statutes governing water pollution, which of the following areas is (are) regulated?

	Dredging of coastal or freshwater wetlands	Drinking water standards
a.	Yes	Yes
b.	Yes	No
c.	No	Yes
d.	No	No

39. The Clean Air Act provides for the enforcement of standards for

I. The emissions of radioactive particles from private nuclear power plants.

II. The emissions of pollution from privately owned automobiles.

III. The emissions of air pollution from factories.

    a. I and II only.

    b. I and III only.

    c. II and III only.

    d. I, II and III.

40. Under the Clean Air Act, which of the following statements is (are) correct regarding actions that may be taken against parties who violate emission standards?

I. The federal government may require an automobile manufacturer to recall vehicles that violate emission standards.

II. A citizens' group may sue to force a coal burning power plant to comply with emission standards.

a. I only.
b. II only.
c. Both I and II.
d. Neither I nor II.

41. The Environmental Protection Agency is an administrative agency in the federal government that aids in the protection of the environment. Which of the following is **not** a purpose or function of this agency?

   a. It adopts regulations to protect the quality of water.
   b. It aids private citizens to make cases for private civil litigation.
   c. It may refer criminal matters to the Department of Justice.
   d. It may refer civil cases to the Department of Justice.

42. Whenever a federal agency recommends actions or legislation that may affect the environment, the agency must prepare an environmental impact statement. Which of the following is **not** required in the environmental impact statement?

   a. A description of the source of funds to accomplish the action without harming the environment.
   b. An examination of alternate methods of achieving the goals of the proposed actions or legislation.
   c. A description in detail of the proposed actions or legislation on the environment.
   d. A description of any unavoidable adverse consequences.

43. Which of the following is (are) possible when a company violates the Clean Air Act?

  I. The company can be assessed a criminal fine.
  II. Officers of the company can be imprisoned.
  III. The Environmental Protection Agency may assess a civil penalty equal to the savings of costs by the company for noncompliance.

   a. I only.
   b. I or II only.
   c. III only.
   d. I, II or III.

44. Green, a former owner of Circle Plant, caused hazardous waste pollution at the Circle Plant site two years ago. Sason purchased the plant and caused more hazardous waste pollution. It can be shown that 20% of the problem was caused by Green and that 80% of the problem was caused by Sason. Sason went bankrupt recently. The government wishes to clean up the site and hold Green liable. Which of the following is true?

   a. The most Green can be held liable for is 20%.
   b. Green is not liable for any of the cleanup costs since the site was sold.
   c. Green is not liable for any of the cleanup costs because Green was responsible for less than half of the problem.
   d. Green can be held liable for all the cleanup costs even if Sason has some funds.

P.   Antitrust Law

45. Which of the following would be a horizontal agreement to fix prices and thus be illegal per se under Section 1 of the Sherman Act?

  I. An agreement between several sellers of lumber to no longer sell on credit to purchasers.
  II. An agreement between two sellers of lumber to set a maximum price for what they will charge for lumber.
  III. An agreement between a lumber wholesaler and a lumber retailer that the retailer will charge at least $8.00 for a particular piece of lumber.

   a. I only.
   b. I and II only.
   c. I, II, and III.
   d. None of these agreements is illegal per se.

46. Loop Corp. has made a major breakthrough in the development of a micropencil. Loop has patented the product and is seeking to maximize the profit potential. In this effort, Loop can legally

   a. Require its retailers to sell only Loop's products, including the micropencils, and **not** sell similar competing products.
   b. Require its retailers to take stipulated quantities of its other products in addition to the micropencils.
   c. Sell the product at whatever price the traffic will bear even though Loop has a monopoly.
   d. Cut the price Loop is charging to retailers below its cost anytime a competitor attempts to compete against Loop's micropencil.

S.   Robinson-Patman Act of 1936

47. Robinson's pricing policies have come under attack by several of its retailers. In fact, one of those retailers, Patman, has instigated legal action against Robinson alleging that Robinson charges other favored retailers prices for its products which are lower than those charged to it. Patman's legal action against Robinson

   a. Will fail unless Patman can show that there has been an injury to competition.
   b. Will be sufficient if the complaint alleges that Robinson charged different prices to different customers and there is a reasonable possibility that competition may be adversely affected.
   c. Is groundless since one has the legal right to sell at whatever price one wishes as long as the price is determined unilaterally.
   d. Is to be tested under the Rule of Reason and if the different prices charged are found to be reasonable, the complaint will be dismissed.

U.   Money Laundering

48. The Money Laundering Control Act of 1986 prohibits which of the following?

  I. Transaction money laundering.
  II. Transportation money laundering.
  III. Monetary transactions in criminally derived property.

   a. I only.
   b. I and II only.
   c. III only.
   d. I, II, and III.

Multiple-Choice Answers and Explanations

Answers

1. b	__	__	11. b	__	__	21. a	__	__	31. b	__	__	41. b	__ __
2. a	__	__	12. d	__	__	22. b	__	__	32. d	__	__	42. a	__ __
3. b	__	__	13. a	__	__	23. c	__	__	33. a	__	__	43. d	__ __
4. a	__	__	14. b	__	__	24. a	__	__	34. d	__	__	44. d	__ __
5. d	__	__	15. b	__	__	25. c	__	__	35. d	__	__	45. b	__ __
6. b	__	__	16. a	__	__	26. a	__	__	36. c	__	__	46. c	__ __
7. d	__	__	17. c	__	__	27. b	__	__	37. d	__	__	47. b	__ __
8. c	__	__	18. a	__	__	28. d	__	__	38. a	__	__	48. d	__ __
9. a	__	__	19. c	__	__	29. d	__	__	39. d	__	__	1st: __/48 = __%
10. d	__	__	20. b	__	__	30. a	__	__	40. c	__	__	2nd: __/48 = __%

Explanations

1. (b) Taxes payable under the Federal Unemployment Tax Act (FUTA) are used to provide unemployment compensation benefits to workers who lose jobs and cannot find replacement work. These taxes paid are deductible by the employer as a business expense for federal income tax purposes. Therefore, answer (b) is correct. Answer (c) is incorrect because only those employers who paid wages of $1,500 or more during any calendar quarter or who employed at least one employee for at least one day a week for twenty weeks must pay FUTA taxes. Answer (d) is incorrect because it is the employer, not the employee, who pays the taxes. Answer (a) is incorrect because the taxes payable under the FUTA are calculated as a fixed percentage of only the first $7,000 of wages of each employee.

2. (a) Unemployment compensation is intended for workers who lose jobs through no fault of their own and cannot find replacement work. Answer (a) is correct because a CPA fired as a result of the employer's business reversals is entitled to receive unemployment compensation. Answer (b) is incorrect because an accountant who refuses to accept replacement work offered him/her would not receive unemployment compensation. Answers (c) and (d) are incorrect because unemployment compensation is not intended for an employee whose actions led to his/her loss of a job.

3. (b) Directors' fees are generally treated as self-employment income and thus are subject to social security self-employment tax. Answer (a) is incorrect because directors' fees are not usually viewed as employee compensation; rather it is treated as self-employment income. Answers (c) and (d) are incorrect because director's fees are treated as self-employment income.

4. (a) Answer (a) is correct since the nondeduction of the FICA tax **and** the payment of it by the employer effectively raises the income of the employee. Answer (d) is not correct because although the employer is required to withhold tax on wages and is liable for payment of such tax whether or not it is collected, the employer's liability can be relieved after showing the employee's related income tax liability has been paid. Therefore, since the employer has paid the taxes, the employer is not subject to penalty. Answer (c) is not correct since no mention is made of a gift. Answer (b) is not correct

since no reference is made to wages not being an ordinary and necessary business expense.

5. (d) Social security benefits may include payments to spouses, including divorced spouses in some cases, and to children. It may also include Medicare payments but not Medicaid payments.

6. (b) **Earned** income in excess of the annual limitation will cause a reduction in a retired person's social security benefits. Answer (b) is therefore correct, since "director's fees" are considered earned income. Answers (a), (c), and (d) are incorrect because proceeds from an annuity, pension payments, and stock dividends are not considered earned income.

7. (d) Unemployment insurance tax must be paid by the employer if the employer employs one or more persons covered by the act. Payments for unemployment insurance are not deducted from employees' salaries. Workers' compensation is a form of strict liability whereby the employer is liable to the employee for injuries or diseases sustained by the employee which arise out of and in the course of employment. The insurance is paid by the employer and the cost is passed on as an expense of doing business. Thus, worker's compensation insurance also is not paid by the employee.

8. (c) Social security tax applies to wages, defined as all compensation for employment. Employment compensation does not have to be in the form of cash to be included in wages taxed under the Federal Insurance Contributions Act (FICA). Therefore, a car received as a productivity award is considered employment compensation subject to the social security tax and answers (a), (b), and (d) are incorrect, because these are not wages.

9. (a) Both a failure to supply taxpayer identification numbers and a failure to make timely FICA deposits would be violations of the Act. As all employees are required to participate in Social Security, their identification numbers must be supplied in order to track employment and cumulative FICA tax paid to the government. The Act also explicitly states that an employer's failure to collect and deposit taxes in a timely manner subjects him/her to penalties and interest.

10. (d) Workers' compensation benefits arise out of a type of strict liability whereby employers are liable for injuries or diseases sustained by employees which arise from the scope of the employment. Temporary office workers are usually either independent contractors or are employees of a separate employment agency. Answer (a) is incorrect because the employment laws are especially meant to protect minors. Answer (b) is incorrect because truck drivers are not exempted. Answer (c) is incorrect because union affiliation does not create an exemption.

11. (b) Under workers' compensation laws, any employee injured during the course of employment is entitled to workers' compensation benefits regardless of fault, as long as the injury is not self-inflicted, and not the result of a fight or intoxication. However, acceptance of benefits under workers' compensation laws precludes an employee from suing the employer for damages in a civil court.

12. (d) Workers' compensation is a form of strict liability in which an employer is liable to employees for injuries or diseases sustained in the course of employment, without regard to fault. Answer (a) is incorrect because the injured employee is not required to establish employer negligence to recover a workers' compensation action. Answer (b) is incorrect because contributory negligence of the employee is not a valid defense in workers' compensation cases. The workers' compensation act removes the employer's common law defense of negligence of a fellow employee, therefore answer (c) is incorrect.

13. (a) Workers' Compensation Acts require an employer to provide coverage for all eligible employees. Furthermore, the employer is required to cover the cost of injuries to employees, and no amount is deducted from the employees' wages. Therefore, answer (b) is incorrect. Answer (c) is incorrect because under workers' compensation, the disability benefit payments are usually a percentage of weekly earnings. The employer does not have to make up the difference between the benefit payments and the employee's salary. Answer (d) is incorrect because a business covered under workers' compensation laws may be self-insured but it must show proof of financial responsibility to carry this risk.

14. (b) Most workers' compensation laws provide that the employer is strictly liable to an employee without regard to negligence of the employer or employee. Therefore, answers (a) and (c) are incorrect. Answer (d) is incorrect because worker's compensation awards may or may not be payable for life; it depends on the type of injury suffered.

15. (b) Normally workers are paid wages under workers' compensation, but the payment is **partial** wages, not full wages. The following are some examples of workers' compensation benefits: burial expenses, the cost of prosthetic devices, monthly payments to surviving dependent children; therefore answers (a), (c) and (d) are incorrect.

16. (a) Both occupational disease and employment aggravated preexisting disease are covered by the statutes in that all consequences of an injury on the job, regardless of whether such injury was actually caused by an accident, are deemed to be "accidental" injuries resulting from employment. If any conditions in the workplace could have possibly contributed to or aggravated consequences, the doctrine of strict employer liability applies.

17. (c) OSHA investigates complaints and makes inspections of the workplace. Employers can require that OSHA obtain a search warrant in most cases to conduct the search. Probable cause is needed to obtain a search warrant and complaints by employees can provide the needed probable cause. Answer (a) is incorrect because the employer can allow the search or give permission, in which cases, search warrants are not needed. Answer (b) is incorrect because inspections can be made during working hours. In fact, this may be the only or most effective time to conduct the inspection. Answer (d) is incorrect because there is no requirement that OSHA give the employers advance notice of the inspections. Such a requirement would make many inspections less effective.

18. (a) Under the Equal Pay Act, employers cannot pay some employees less money than that paid to employees of the opposite sex when equal work is performed. Under Title VII of the Civil Rights Act, employers cannot discriminate against a prospective employee on the basis of race, color, national origin, religion, or sex.

19. (c) The Age Discrimination in Employment Act does not specifically use the term "back pay" but the Act provides equitable relief as deemed appropriate and otherwise authorizes back pay. The Act does provide for employment reinstatement or promotion, but does not provide for early retirement.

20. (b) The Age Discrimination in Employment Act generally prohibits mandatory retirement under age seventy. Answers (a) and (c) are incorrect because the Act generally applies to individuals over forty years old. Answer (d) is incorrect because forced retirement under the age of seventy is generally prohibited under the Act.

21. (a) The Americans With Disabilities Act of 1990 prohibits all businesses with fifteen employees or more from considering a person's handicap when making a hiring decision. Also, the act requires businesses to make special accommodations available to handicapped employees and customers, unless the cost is too burdensome. Therefore, answer (a) is correct as the act covers both public transportation and privately operated public accommodations.

22. (b) The Americans With Disabilities Act provides the disabled with better access to employment, public accommodations, and transportation. The Act requires companies to make reasonable accommodations for the disabled unless this would cause undue hardship for the business. The Act does not require companies to set up a hiring plan. Additionally, the ADA only applies to businesses with 15 or more employees.

23. (c) The Americans With Disabilities Act requires most companies and entities to not discriminate against qualified individuals with disabilities who can perform the essential functions of the job either with or without reasonable accommodation, unless the company can show undue hardship. Reasonable accommodation may include purchasing new equipment, modifying facilities, or modifying work schedules.

24. (a) A covered employee has the right to a leave from work for specified reasons for twelve workweeks in a twelve-month period but typically receives leave without pay. Answer (b) is incorrect because it mentions one of the specified reasons allowed for a leave. Answer (c) is incorrect because an important right under the Act is to get back the same or similar position upon returning. Answer (d) is an incorrect response because not all employees are covered. To be covered employees must have worked for twelve months, for at least 1,250 hours in those twelve months, and be one of at least fifty employees.

25. (c) The Act provides for up to twelve workweeks of unpaid leave for the employee to care for serious health problems of his or her parent, spouse, or child. It also provides the same right to care for his or her newborn baby. Note that (d) is incorrect because it provides for paid leave to care for his or her spouse who is seriously ill.

26. (a) The Fair Labor Standards Act allows employees to be paid on a piecework basis or salary. Workers must receive at least the equivalent of the minimum hourly rate, but the basis on which the workers are paid can be hourly, weekly, or monthly.

27. (b) The Fair Labor Standards Act requires overtime pay to be paid when hours worked in any given week exceed forty hours. Therefore, the additional five hours and two hours worked in the first two weeks constitute overtime.

28. (d) Among other fringe benefits, sick pay and vacation pay are subjects for collective bargaining. Therefore, sick pay and vacation pay are not exempt from the provisions of the National Labor Relations Act.

29. (d) Under the Federal Consolidated Budget Reconciliation Act of 1985 (COBRA), a former employee may retain group health coverage under the employer for him/herself and his/her spouse at the former employee's expense for at least eighteen months after leaving the company. Answer (a) is incorrect because the former employee and spouse may retain the coverage for at least eighteen months. Answers (b) and (c) are incorrect because not only the former employee but also the spouse may retain the coverage for eighteen months at the former employee's expense.

30. (a) If a pension plan is established, employee contributions to the pension plan vest immediately. In addition, standards on investment of funds are set up to avoid mismanagement.

31. (b) The Employee Retirement Income Security Act of 1974 (ERISA) does not require an employer to establish a pension plan. Therefore, answer (a) is incorrect. If the employer does set up a plan, it must meet certain standards. These standards prevent employers from unduly delaying an employee's participation in a pension plan. Therefore, answer (b) is correct. Standards are also set up for the investment of funds to avoid mismanagement. However, employers are able to manage the retirement plans. Therefore, answer (c) is incorrect. Answer (d) is incorrect because ERISA provisions do not require that the employees make the investment decisions. This is a function of the particular company's plan.

32. (d) CERCLA imposes environmental liability on a broad group of potentially responsible parties. The courts have included the following classes: (1) current owners and operators, (2) owners and operators at the time of waste disposal, (3) generators of hazardous waste, (4) transporters of hazardous waste, and (5) lenders who finance borrowers' hazardous waste sites.

33. (a) The Clean Water Act regulates the dredging or filling of wetlands. Without a permit, these are generally prohibited. The discharging of heated water by nuclear power plants is also regulated.

34. (d) All of the purposes listed are reasons to have an Environmental Compliance Audit. Since the environmental laws and regulations can be complex and may result in both criminal violations and civil liability, both statements I and II are correct. Statement III is also correct because problems with the environmental laws can be significant under the federal securities laws.

35. (d) The Federal Insecticide, Fungicide, and Rodenticide Act does have all three of the provisions. Herbicides and pesticides are required to be registered before they can be sold. Furthermore, they need to be used only for the purposes certified. Also, when used on food crops, the amount that can be used is limited.

36. (c) The provisions of the Comprehensive Environmental Response, Compensation, and Liability Act (CERCLA) as amended is very broad in scope. If the EPA cleans up the hazardous chemicals, it can recover the costs from any responsible party including present owners of the facility and any person who arranged for the disposal of the hazardous substance.

37. (d) The National Environmental Policy Act is centered around requiring the federal government and its agencies to consider the effects of its actions on the environment. It does not provide tax breaks to companies to accomplish environmental goals. Answer (a) is not chosen because it correctly states that the Act applies to all federal agencies. Answer (b) is not chosen because it is also correct. The Act does require an environmental impact statement if the environment may be significantly hurt. Answer (c) is not chosen because private litigation is the main way this Act is enforced.

38. (a) The Clean Water Act regulates the dredging of both coastal and freshwater wetlands. The Safe Drinking Water act regulates the safety of water supplied by public water systems to homes.

39. (d) The Clean Air Act regulates emissions into the air from automobiles, factories, and nuclear power plants. Note that emissions from the nuclear power plant are handled by the Clean Air Act rather than the Nuclear Waste Policy Act. The latter creates a national plan to dispose of highly radioactive nuclear waste.

40. (c) The Clean Air Act sets air quality standards for mobile sources such as autos, and for stationary sources such as power plants. The federal government has ways to encourage and require compliance, such as requiring manufacturers to recall vehicles that violate emission standards. The Act also allows private citizens to sue violators to enforce compliance.

41. (b) The Environmental Protection Agency (EPA) is an administrative agency designed to aid the federal government in national environmental policy. When citizens have private lawsuits about the environment, they would typically seek remedies by resorting to common law or statutory remedies. The Environmental Protection Agency was not set up to help in this manner. This agency does, however, adopt regulations on the environment. Therefore answer (a) is not chosen. Answers (c) and (d) are not chosen because the EPA does refer both criminal and civil cases over to the Department of Justice.

42. (a) The environmental impact statement is not designed to show the cost or source of the funds for the actions or legislation being proposed. Answers (b), (c), and (d) are all not chosen because these are all required as part of the environmental impact statement.

43. (d) The Clean Air Act provides for both criminal and civil penalties against violators. For criminal violations, both fines and prison are possible. Civil penalties can also be assessed by the EPA including an amount equal to any benefits in costs for not complying.

44. (d) Green as a part owner is one of the parties that has joint and several liability for the cleanup costs. Even though Sason also has joint and several liability, Green can be held liable for any portion or all of the cleanup costs without regard to percent of responsibility. Answer (a) is incorrect because Green, having joint and several liability, can be held liable for all of the cleanup costs. Answer (b) is incorrect because past as well as present owners have potential liability. Answer (c) is incorrect because there is no such defense as having less than half of the responsibility.

45. (b) A horizontal agreement is an agreement between competitors. I and II satisfy that requirement; III is a vertical agreement between a wholesaler and a retailer. Additionally, vertical price fixing is not illegal per se. Agreements to fix prices include agreements that directly affect price, such as a refusal to provide credit. Horizontal price fixing is illegal per se, regardless of whether the agreement is to set a minimum price or a maximum price.

46. (c) Government creation of monopoly status through a patent is permissible under the antitrust laws as long as no other anticompetitive conduct is involved. Loop Corporation is, therefore, entitled to sell the micropencil at a price determined by the normal competitive forces of supply and demand. A patent grants the holder a twenty-year exclusive

right to market the product. The twenty years starts at the application date. For design patents, the period is fourteen years. Answer (a) is incorrect because prohibiting the retailers from selling competing products is an exclusive dealing agreement which is illegal where the effect is to substantially lessen competition in that market. By not allowing retailers to sell competing products, Loop is effectively raising barriers to entry into the market and that illegally maintains a monopoly. (The fact that Loop has a patent is evidence of monopoly power.) Answer (b) is incorrect because tying agreements involving patented products are illegal per se if a substantial amount of business is involved. Answer (d) is incorrect because below cost pricing to keep competitors out of the market is known as predatory pricing and is evidence of trying to maintain a monopoly.

47. (b) The Robinson-Patman Act prohibits price discrimination in interstate commerce of commodities of like grade and quality. A violation of the Act exists if the effect of the price discrimination may be to substantially lessen competition or tend to create a monopoly. Therefore, all that Patman must do to maintain a sufficient legal action is to allege that due to Robinson's pricing activities there is a reasonable possibility that competition may be adversely affected. Answer (a) is incorrect because Patman does not have to show actual injury to competition; Patman must show that such discrimination may substantially lessen competition. Answer (c) is incorrect because Congress purposely adopted the Robinson-Patman Act to prevent unilateral price determination which has the resultant effect of lessening competition or tending to create a monopoly. Answer (d) is incorrect because the reasonableness of the prices charged is irrelevant. The issue is whether the price discrimination may substantially lessen competition or tend to create a monopoly.

48. (d) Section 1956 of the Monetary Laundering Control Act of 1986 prohibits both transaction money laundering and transportation money laundering. Section 1957 of the Act addresses the prohibition of monetary transactions in criminally derived property over $10,000. Answer (a) is incorrect because Section 1956 of the Monetary Control Act of 1986 prohibits transportation money laundering and Section 1957 of the Act prohibits monetary transactions in criminally derived property. Answer (b) is incorrect because Section 1957 of the Monetary Control Act of 1986 also addresses the prohibition of monetary transactions in criminally derived property. Answer (c) is incorrect because Section 1956 of the Monetary Control Act of 1986 prohibits both transaction and transportation money laundering.

Simulation

Task-Based Simulation 1

Consideration		
	Authoritative Literature	Help

For each of the numbered items, indicate: Yes, this item is considered to be wages under the Social Security Act, or No, this item is **not** considered to be wages under the Social Security Act.

		Yes	No
1.	Wages, paid in money, to a construction worker.	○	○
2.	Reimbursed normal travel expenses of a salesperson.	○	○
3.	Compensation not paid in cash.	○	○
4.	Commissions of a salesperson.	○	○
5.	Bonuses paid to employees.	○	○
6.	Employee insurance premiums paid by the employer.	○	○
7.	Wages paid to a secretary who is working part-time.	○	○
8.	Vacation allowance pay given to employees who are working full-time.	○	○
9.	Wages paid to a full-time secretary who wishes to elect not to be covered under the Social Security Act.	○	○
10.	Tips of a waitress.	○	○

Simulation Solution

Task-Based Simulation 1

Consideration		
	Authoritative Literature	Help

		Yes	No
1.	Wages, paid in money, to a construction worker.	●	○
2.	Reimbursed normal travel expenses of a salesperson.	○	●
3.	Compensation not paid in cash.	●	○
4.	Commissions of a salesperson.	●	○
5.	Bonuses paid to employees.	●	○
6.	Employee insurance premiums paid by the employer.	○	●
7.	Wages paid to a secretary who is working part-time.	●	○
8.	Vacation allowance pay given to employees who are working full-time.	●	○
9.	Wages paid to a full-time secretary who wishes to elect not to be covered under the Social Security Act.	●	○
10.	Tips of a waitress.	●	○

Explanations

1. **(Y)** Under the Social Security Act, money wages are considered wages.

2. **(N)** Reimbursed travel expenses are generally excluded from wages.

3. **(Y)** Compensation whether in cash or not is generally considered to be wages.

4. **(Y)** Commissions are a method of compensation.

5. **(Y)** Bonuses are a method of compensation.

6. **(N)** Insurance premiums paid by employers for employees generally are excluded from wages.

7. **(Y)** Part-time employees are covered under this law.

8. **(Y)** Vacation allowance pay is another form of compensation.

9. **(Y)** Qualifying employees may not elect to avoid the Social Security Act.

10. **(Y)** Tips are another form of wages.

Module 34: Property

Overview

Property entails items capable of being owned (i.e., the rights related to the ownership of things that society will recognize and enforce). Property is classified as real or personal, and as tangible or intangible. Protection of property and settlement of disputes concerning property is a major function of the legal system.

The candidate should be able to distinguish between personal and real property and between tenancies in common, joint tenancies, and tenancies by the entirety. The candidate also should understand that an instrument given primarily as security for real property is a mortgage and be able to distinguish between the legal results arising from "assumption" of a mortgage and taking "subject to" a mortgage. Other questions concerning mortgages require basic knowledge of the concepts of novation, suretyship, subrogation, and redemption.

Questions on deeds may distinguish between the legal implication of warranty deeds, quitclaim deeds, and special warranty deeds. Both mortgages and deeds should be publicly recorded, and the questions may require the candidate to identify a priority and constructive notice. The most important topics under lessor-lessee law are the Statute of Frauds, the effect of a sale of leased property, assignment, and subleasing. Before beginning the reading you should review the key terms at the end of the module.

A. Distinctions between Real and Personal Property

1. Real property (realty)—includes land and things attached to land in a relatively permanent manner

> **EXAMPLE**
>
> A building is erected on a parcel of land. Both the land and the building are real property.

    a. Crops harvested are not real property because they are separate from land
    b. Growing crops are generally part of land and therefore realty

        (1) Growing crops can be sold separately from land in which case they are considered personal property

            (a) True whether buyer or seller will sever growing crops from land

2. Personal property (personalty)—property not classified as real property or a fixture

    a. May be either

        (1) Tangible—subject to physical possession

> **EXAMPLE**
>
> Automobiles and books are tangible personal property.

        (2) Intangible—not subject to physical possession but subject to legal ownership

> **EXAMPLE**
>
> Contractual rights to receive payment for automobiles sold and intellectual property, such as copyrights, are intangible personal property.

3. Fixture—item that was originally personal property but which is affixed to real property in relatively permanent fashion such that it is considered to be part of real property

    a. Several factors are applied in determining whether personal property that has been attached to real property is a fixture

        (1) Affixer's objective intent as to whether property is to be regarded as personalty or realty
        (2) Method and permanence of physical attachment to real property

            (a) If item cannot be removed without material injury to real property, it is generally held that item has become part of realty (i.e., a fixture)

        (3) Adaptability of use of personal property for purpose for which real property is used

            (a) If personal property is necessary or beneficial to use of real property, more likely that item is fixture
            (b) But if use or purpose of item is unusual for type of realty involved, it normally would be personal property

    b. Trade fixture is a fixture installed by tenant in connection with business on leased premises

> **EXAMPLE**
>
> A tenant who is leasing premises for use as grocery store installs refrigeration unit on property. Refrigeration unit is integral to conducting of business for which tenant occupies premises and therefore qualifies as trade fixture.

        (1) Trade fixtures remain personal property, giving tenant right to remove these items upon expiration of lease

            (a) If item is so affixed to real property that removing it would cause substantial damage, then it is considered part of realty

B. Personal Property can be acquired by

1. Gift—a present, voluntary transfer of property without consideration

    a. Necessary elements

        (1) Donative intent by donor
        (2) Delivery
        (3) Acceptance by donee (usually presumed)

b. Promise to make a gift is unenforceable because it is not a contract due to lack of consideration given by donee

c. Inter vivos gift is made while donor is living and is irrevocable once completed

d. Gift causa mortis is a conditional gift in contemplation of death and is automatically revoked if the donor does not die of impending illness or crisis causing gift

2. Will or intestate succession

a. Property passes under terms of will that is valid at death (i.e., dies testate)

b. If deceased has no valid will (i.e., dies intestate) then property passes under laws of state

3. Finding personal property

a. Mislaid property

(1) Happens when owner **voluntarily** puts the property somewhere but forgets to take it

(2) Finder does **not** obtain title to mislaid property

(a) Owner of premises becomes caretaker in case true owner of mislaid property comes back

b. Lost property

(1) Happens when owner **involuntarily** leaves property somewhere

(2) Finder has title to lost property which is valid against all parties except the true owner

---

EXAMPLE

A loses his watch. B finds it but C attempts to take it from B even though both know it is not C's watch. B has the right to keep it from C.

---

c. Abandoned property

(1) Generally, finder has title valid against all parties including owner that abandoned property

---

NOW REVIEW MULTIPLE-CHOICE QUESTIONS 1 THROUGH 5

C. Bailments

1. Bailment exists when owner of personal property gives possession without giving title to another (bailee)—for example, dry cleaners or valet at restaurant—bailee has duty to either return personal property to bailor or to dispose of it as directed by owner

2. Requirements for creation

a. Delivery of personal property to bailee

b. Possession by bailee

c. Bailee has duty to return property or dispose of property as directed by owner

3. Types of bailments

a. For benefit of bailor (i.e., bailee takes care of bailor's property)

b. For mutual benefit (i.e., bailee takes care of bailor's property for a fee)

c. For benefit of bailee (i.e., bailor gratuitously allows bailee use of his/her property)

4. Bailee's duty of care

a. Older view depended on the type of bailment (i.e., slight care if for benefit of bailor, ordinary care if for mutual benefit, extreme care if for benefit of bailee)

b. Now general rule is bailee must take reasonable care in light of the facts and circumstances

(1) Type of bailment is determined by given facts and the facts are used to determine what is reasonable care

    (a) Bailee is absolutely liable for delivery to improper person

        [1] But a receipt or ticket that is for identification of bailor entitles bailee to deliver bailed goods to holder of ticket without liability

  c. Bailee has absolute liability for unauthorized use of property
  d. Bailee usually cannot limit liability with exculpatory clauses

---

EXAMPLE

A coat check ticket often limits liability on its back side. If the ticket is to be just a means of identification, then the bailee's liability is not limited. If the bailor is aware of the liability limitations statement, liability may be limited if reasonable.

---

5. Bailee has duty to use property as directed to fulfill purpose of bailment only

  a. Liable to bailor for misuse
  b. In cases of theft, destruction of property, or failing to return property, this constitutes tort of conversion
  c. Bailee may normally limit liability for his/her negligence but not for intentional conduct

6. Bailee is not an agent of bailor, so bailor is not responsible for bailee's actions
7. Bailments normally terminated by

  a. Fulfillment of purpose of bailment
  b. Agreement to terminate by both bailor and bailee
  c. Bailee using property inappropriately

8. Common carriers are licensed to provide transportation for public

  a. Liability is based on strict liability, so common carriers are liable for damage to goods being transported even if loss caused by third parties or by accidents

    (1) Exceptions—common carrier not liable for

        (a) Acts of shipper, such as improperly packing goods to be shipped
        (b) Acts of God, such as earthquakes
        (c) Acts of public enemies
        (d) Loss because of inherent nature of goods

    (2) Common carriers allowed to limit liability to dollar amount specified in contract

NOW REVIEW MULTIPLE CHOICE QUESTIONS 6 THROUGH 9

D. Intellectual Property and Computer Technology Rights

1. Two general but competing goals

  a. Incentives to create products and services

    (1) By granting property rights so creators have incentive to create and market

  b. Provide public access to intellectual property and computer ideas and uses

    (1) By limiting intellectual and computer technology rights so that public has access to this

2. Copyright law

  a. Protects original works (e.g., literary, musical, or artistic works)

    (1) Expressions of ideas are generally copyrightable—ideas may not by themselves be copyrighted
    (2) Amendments to Copyright Act give added protection to computer hardware and computer software

  b. Copyrights created after January 1, 1978, are valid for life of author plus seventy years

    (1) Are valid for 95 years from publication date when owned by publishing house, or 120 years from creation date, whichever expires first

   c. Registration of copyright not required because copyright begins when author puts expression in tangible form

      (1) Registration, however, gives copyright owner, in case of infringement, rights to statutory damages and attorneys' fees

   d. Works published after March 1, 1989, no longer need copyright notice on them

   e. Fair use doctrine allows use for limited purposes without violating copyright

      (1) Examples include portions for comment, news reporting, research, or teaching

---

EXAMPLE

Professor hands out copies of a portion of copyrighted work to each member of the class. Note that the professor is allowed to share a portion of the copyrighted work, not the entire copyrighted work.

---

      (2) Accessing a digital work is not protected by fair use doctrine

   f. Consumer Software Copyright Act amends copyright law to include computer programs as creative works protected by federal copyright law

      (1) Covers not only portions of computer program readable by humans but also binary language portions normally read by computer

      (2) Covers general items in program such as its basic structure and organizations

   g. Remedies include stated statutory damages or actual damages including profits attributed to infringement of copyright—injunctions also allowed

      (1) Higher damages can be statutorily assessed for willful infringement

   h. Criminal penalties of fines and imprisonment are allowed for willful infringement

   i. No Electronic Theft Act (NET Act)

      (1) Act criminalizes copyright infringement over Internet regardless of financial gain where retail value of copyrighted works exceeds $1,000

      (2) Provides for imprisonment and fines

3. Patent Law

   a. Covers machines, processes, art, methods, composition of matter, new and useful improvements including genetically engineered plants or animals

   b. Mere ideas are not covered

      (1) But practical applications may be

      (2) Cyber business plans can be patented when they use a practical application of formulas, calculations, or algorithms because they produce results that are useful, tangible, and concrete even though some have argued these cyber plans are intangible.

   c. Invention must be novel, useful, and not obvious

   d. Patents administered by US Patent and Trademark Office

      (1) Inventor may not obtain patent if invention was on sale or in public use in US at least one year before attempt to obtain patent

   e. Generally, patents are valid for twenty years from when patent application was filed

      (1) By treaties, patents generally receive international protection for twenty years

      (2) Design patents are valid for fourteen years from date of issuance of patent

   f. Owner of patent must mark it using word patent to give notice to others

      (1) May also use "Pat" abbreviation

   g. US gives patent protection to first inventor to invent rather than first to file for that patent

      (1) Most countries give protection to the first to file the patent

   h. Earlier views of computer software often categorized it as based on ideas and thus not patentable—more recent authority and court decisions protect software and Internet business methods as patentable

(1) Financial and business models used over the Internet can also be patented

---

EXAMPLE

Pratt Company patented a computer program that used mathematical formulas to constantly improve a curing process for synthetic rubber upon receiving feedback in the process. This computer program was patentable because Pratt did not attempt to patent the mathematical formula to exclude others from using the formula but patented the process.

EXAMPLE

River.com Inc. receives a patent for the company storing customers' shipping (and billing information) with a one-click ordering system to reduce customers' need to reenter data on future orders.

EXAMPLE

Dual Softie, Inc. receives a patent that allows purchasers of automobiles over Internet to select options they want on the auto.

EXAMPLE

Silvernet, Inc. patents a system that pays individuals who respond to online surveys.

---

i. Even when patent issued by US Patent Trade Office (PTO), PTO may reexamine and reject patent

(1) Patent may be overturned or narrowed in case brought to court
(2) Unlike earlier, computer-related patents focus now on whether they are novel and nonobvious rather than on whether they can be patented at all

j. Patent law is exclusively federal law

(1) There is no state patent law

k. Remedies include injunctions, damages including lost profits traceable to infringement, or assessment of reasonable royalties

(1) If infringement is willful, inventor may be awarded treble damages and require infringer to also pay attorney's fees

l. US Supreme Court recently affirmed important part of patent law providing that one cannot escape liability for patent infringement by making only insubstantial changes to a patent and attempting to claim it to be a new patent

m. Paris convention—allows patent protection in many foreign countries

(1) Most comprehensive agreement between nations involving intellectual property
(2) Signed by nearly all industrialized countries and by many developing countries
(3) Generally, allows a one-year grace period for inventors to file in other countries once inventor files for patent protection in first country

4. Trade Secrets Law

a. Economic Espionage Act makes it federal crime to use trade secrets

(1) Trade secrets include such information as financial, engineering, scientific, technical, software programs, or codes

(a) Also protects processes used by company

(2) Federal law helps protect against computer hackers who steal trade secrets such as data bases and computer lists.

b. Alternative to protection by copyright or patent
c. Protects formulas, patterns, devices, or compilations of information that give business an advantage over competitors

(1) Must be secret that others have difficulty in acquiring except by improper means
(2) Owner must take reasonable steps to guard trade secret
(3) Can cover computer hardware and software

d. Remedies for violations include breach of contract, breach of fiduciary duties, wrongful appropriation of trade secret, injunction, theft, and espionage

(1) Civil law as well as criminal law may be used

e. Trade secret protection by law may be lost if

(1) Owner of trade secret fails to take extraordinary measures to keep it secret, or
(2) Other person independently discovers what was subject of trade secret

f. Methods to help protect trade secret include

(1) Licensing of software

(a) Prohibit copying except for backup copies

(2) Provide in license that it is terminated for any breach of confidentiality
(3) Sell software in object code instead of source code
(4) Have employees and buyers sign confidentiality agreements

5. Semiconductor Chip Protection Act

a. Amends copyright laws
b. Prohibits taking apart chips to copy them

(1) Allows such act if used to create new chip rather than copy
(2) Not prohibiting copying if design embodies the unoriginal or commonplace

c. Protection is for ten years from time of registration or first commercial application, whichever is first
d. Permits civil recovery and penalties up to $250,000 for chip piracy
e. Reverse engineering of chips allowed if it creates some new innovation

6. Federal Counterfeit Access Device and Computer Fraud and Abuse Act has criminalized many intentional, unauthorized uses of computer to

a. Obtain classified information to hurt US
b. Collect credit or financial information protected by privacy laws

---

EXAMPLE

Obtaining credit card limits and credit card numbers by accessing credit card accounts.

---

c. Modify material financial data in computers
d. Destroy or alter computer data to hurt rightful users

EXAMPLE

A person intentionally transfers a computer virus to a company computer.

---

7. Trademarks under Lanham Act

    a. Purposes

        (1) To provide identification symbol for company's product
        (2) To guarantee consistent quality of all goods from same source
        (3) Advertising

    b. Protection for trademark for distinctive graphics, words, shapes, packaging, or sounds

---

EXAMPLE

Coca-Cola has a trademark for its distinctive bottle.

---

        (1) Colors may be trademarked now if they are associated with particular goods such that those colors are identified with that brand

    c. Marks normally need to be distinctive to be protected

        (1) Secondary meaning of things not inherently distinctive can develop to make them protectable

---

EXAMPLE

Microsoft registered "Windows" as a trademark when "Windows" acquired its secondary meaning.

EXAMPLE

Windows store cannot be used as a trademark because it sells windows to put on homes and is thus generic rather than distinctive.

---

    d. Generic words like software cannot be protected

        (1) Many words that were once trademarks have become generic so are no longer protectable

---

EXAMPLE

Escalator was originally a brand name but is no longer protectable due to its generic use. Other examples are Yo-Yo and Dry Ice.

EXAMPLE

Xerox takes out advertisements explaining that Xerox is not a verb, but instead say "copy" the document. Xerox is trying to protect its trademark by trying not to let the name grow into common usage.

---

    e. Trademark rights in US are obtained initially by its use in commerce

        (1) For distinctive marks, generally first seller to use trademark owns it
        (2) Company can register trademark

            (a) Although this is not required, provides constructive notice to others of claim of trademark

(3) Online company may register domain name as trademark with US Patent and Trademark Office

    (a) Various companies may use same trademark for different types of goods or services but only one company may register the domain name

---

EXAMPLE

Both Star Fences Inc. and Star Insurance Company wish to use Star.com. Only one may do so.

    (b) Cybersquatting is registering sites and domain names that are confusingly or deceptively similar to other existing trademarks

       [1] Congress passed the Federal Anticybersquatting Consumer Protection Act to help stop cyber-squatting and to provide clearer standards of proof and remedies for this activity such as injunctions to stop the activity as well as money damages

f. Loss of trademark rights

  (1) Actual abandonment when not used in ordinary course of business

    (a) Presumption of abandonment if not used for three years unless owner can prove intent to use trademark

  (2) Constructive abandonment—Company allows trademark to lose its distinctiveness by frequent and common usage

g. Trademark infringement

  (1) Can infringe on trademark whether registered or not
  (2) Proof of infringement

    (a) Establish trademark is valid—federally registered mark is prima facie valid
    (b) Priority of usage
    (c) Violation against trademark if similarities will likely cause confusion in minds of prospective or actual purchasers

  (3) 1995 Trademark Dilution Act expands the Lanham Act to protect a weakening of a famous mark's ability to distinguish goods. Prior law required the infringing trademark to cause confusion as to the source of the product.

h. Remedies for infringement

  (1) Injunction against use
  (2) Lost profits caused by confusion
  (3) Attorneys' fees in some situations

8. Other symbols under Lanham Act

a. Certification mark

  (1) Used to certify characteristics such as origin by geographical location, origin by organization, mode of manufacture.

EXAMPLE

Product XYZ receives the Good Housekeeping Seal of Approval.

---

b. Collective mark

  (1) Used to identify that product or service is provided by certain collective group, union, or fraternal society.

c. Service mark

    (1) Used to identify that services come from certain company or person

---

EXAMPLE

All of the shops of a group of shops called The Green Roof Plaza have similar style of roofs painted in the same shade of green.

---

d. Similar to trademarks, these additional three types of trade symbols need to be distinctive and not deceptive so that prospective customers do not confuse these products or services with others

    (1) Registration is not required but advisable because it provides federal protection for ten years

        (a) Renewable for as many additional ten-year periods as desired

9. Invasion of Privacy—Increased computer use puts on more pressure

a. Computer Matching and Privacy Act

    (1) Regulates computer systems used to determine eligibility for various government programs such as student financial aid

b. Right to Financial Privacy Act

    (1) Restricts government access to financial institution records without customer approval

c. Family Educational Rights and Privacy Act

    (1) Grants adult students and parents of minors access and right to correct records at institutions of higher learning

10. Palming off results when one company sells its product by confusing buyers and leading them to believe they are purchasing another company's product

a. Proof of palming off requires that there is likely to be confusion due to the appearance or name of the competing product

11. Counterfeit Access Device and Computer Fraud and Abuse Act

a. Crime to obtain financial institution's financial records
b. Crime to use cards, codes, counterfeit devices, etc. to obtain valuable items or to transfer funds without authorization

12. Information Infrastructure Protection Act

a. Helps protect individuals or companies from another's unauthorized use of or access to computer's data

    (1) Law encompasses computer hackers, transmitting computer viruses or worms, etc.

13. Identity Theft and Assumption Deterrence Act is federal law that makes identity theft and identify fraud felonies

a. Act also helps victims of identity theft by having Federal Trade Commission aid them to erase effects of identity theft and to aid them to restore their credit

14. Digital Millennium Copyright Act

a. Federal law based on treaties with other countries to minimize pirating and distribution of copyrighted works
b. Provides civil and criminal penalties against those that circumvent antipiracy protections or manufacture or sell such equipment to allow circumvention

    (1) Also provides civil and criminal penalties for unauthorized access to copyrighted digital works by circumventing technology that protects such intellectual property

      (a) It is not required that accessed information be misused

      (b) Mere access is sufficient under this Act

  (2) This Act also modifies fair use doctrine of copyright law for digital protected works so that it is now illegal to merely access these works by circumventing the encryption technology that protects these

      (a) Fair use doctrine is unchanged for nondigital works so that misuse, not mere access of copyrighted works is required

  c. Internet Service Provider (ISP) is generally not liable for customers' copyright infringement unless ISP became aware of infringement and failed to correct problem

15. Uniform Computer Information Transactions Act (UCITA) requires that the following be in writing:

  a. Contracts for licensing of information rights for over $5,000

  b. Contracts for licensing of information services that cannot be performed within one year

  c. User agrees to contract by clicking, for example, on "I agree prompt button"

16. Federal Telecommunications Act passed

  a. To increase competition in telecommunications market

  b. Preempts any state or local government laws that have effect of minimizing or eliminating competition in telecommunications market

    (1) Such as county laws that prohibit ability of company to provide telecommunications service

17. Online dispute resolution is becoming increasingly used to resolve disputes

  a. Advantages include low cost, fast communication, and often no need to bring in third parties

  b. Disadvantage includes hard to enforce settlement because no court or sheriff involved

18. Internet Treaties

  a. Grants between many signing nations providing copyright protection for computer programs, producers' rights, performers' rights over the Internet

    (1) Includes rental copies, transmissions over satellite, encrypted signals, and any type of media

---

NOW REVIEW MULTIPLE-CHOICE QUESTIONS 10 THROUGH 16

E. Interests in Real Property

1. Present interests

  a. Fee simple absolute

    (1) Highest estate in law (has the most ownership rights)

    (2) May be transferred inter vivos (while living), by intestate succession (without will), or by will (testate at death)

    (3) May be subject to mortgages, state laws, etc.

> **EXAMPLE**
>
> Most private residences are fee simple absolute estates although they are commonly subject to mortgage.

  b. Fee simple defeasible

    (1) Fee simple determinable—upon the happening of the stated event the estate automatically reverts to the grantor

> **EXAMPLE**
>
> Conveyance to the holder of an interest was, "to A as long as A uses it for church purposes." The interest will revert back to the grantor or his heirs if the property is not used for church purposes.

(2) Fee simple subject to condition subsequent—upon the happening of the stated event the grantor must take affirmative action to divest the grantee of the estate

> **EXAMPLE**
>
> Conveyance to the holder of the interest was "to A, but if liquor is ever served on the premises, the grantor has right to enter the premises." The grantor has power of termination so as to repossess the premises.

c. Life interest (life estate)—an interest whose duration is usually measured by the life of the holder but may be measured by lives of others

> **EXAMPLE**
>
> Conveyance of land, "to A so long as she shall live."

(1) Upon termination (death), property reverts to grantor or grantor's heirs, or to a named remainderman
(2) Usual life interest can be transferred by deed only (i.e., not by a will because it ends on death)
(3) Holder of a life interest (life tenant) is entitled to ordinary use and profits of land but may not commit waste (injure interests of remainderman)

    (a) Must maintain property (in reasonable state of repair)
    (b) May not misuse property

d. Leaseholds—see Lessor-Lessee at end of this module, section N.

2. Future interest (holder of this interest has right to or possibility of possession in the future)

a. Reversion—future interest reverts back to transferor (or his/her heirs) at end of transferee's estate

(1) Usually kept when conveying a life interest or an interest for a definite period of time

> **EXAMPLE**
>
> X conveys, "to Y for life" or "to Y for ten years." X has a reversion.

b. Remainder—future interest is in a third party at the end of transferee's estate

> **EXAMPLE**
>
> X conveys, "to Y for life, upon Y's death to Z and her heirs." Z has a remainder.

3. Concurrent interest—two or more persons (cotenants) have undivided interests and concurrent possessory rights in real or personal property—each has a nonexclusive right to possess whole property

a. Tenancy in common

  (1) A concurrent interest with no right of survivorship (interest passes to heirs, donee, or purchaser)

EXAMPLE

A and B each own 1/2 of Greenacre as tenants in common. If B dies, then A still owns 1/2 and B's heirs own the other half.

---

  (2) Unless stated otherwise, multiple grantees are presumed to be tenants in common

  (3) Tenant in common may convey individual interest in the whole but cannot convey a specific portion of property

    (a) Unless there is a judicial partition to split up ownership

      [1] Creditors may sue to compel a partition to satisfy individual's debts

b. Joint tenancy

  (1) A concurrent interest with all rights of ownership going to the surviving joint tenants (i.e., have rights of survivorship)

    (a) To create a joint tenancy, all of following unities are required: time, title, interest, and possession

    (b) Cannot be transferred by will because upon death, other cotenants own it

    (c) Corporation may not be joint tenant

EXAMPLE

A and B each own 1/2 of Redacre as joint tenants. If B dies, A owns all of Redacre because of her right of survivorship. B's heirs do not receive any interest.

---

  (2) If rights in property are conveyed, the new owner becomes a tenant in common rather than joint tenant; remaining cotenants are still joint tenants

---

EXAMPLE

A, B, and C are joint tenants of Greenacre. A sells his interest to D. D is a tenant in common with a one-third interest in the whole. B and C are still joint tenants (with the right of survivorship) each having a one-third undivided interest.

---

c. Tenancy by the entirety

  (1) Joint interest held by husband and wife; must be legally married to qualify for tenancy by the entirety.

  (2) To transfer, both must convey

  (3) Each spouse has a right of survivorship

  (4) Divorce creates a tenancy in common

  (5) Creditors of one spouse cannot place a lien or satisfy a judgment against property held in this manner. The creditor must be a creditor of both spouses.

4. Nonpossessory interests in land

a. Easement is right to enter another's land and use it in limited way. Very common for utility companies, for example, to have easements on private property for the benefit of all; usually provided for when the property is divided.

> **EXAMPLE**
>
> A is granted an easement to drive over a certain segment of B's land.

(1) Methods of creation

   (a) Express grant in deed
   (b) Express reservation in deed

> **EXAMPLE**
>
> S sells B some land whereby in the deed S reserves an easement to walk across the land.

   (c) By necessity

> **EXAMPLE**
>
> A owns a piece of land that blocks B's access to any public road. B has the right to use A's land for access to the public road.

b. Profit is right to enter another's land and remove items such as trees, grass, or gravel

   (1) Profits may be created by grant or by reservation

> ## NOW REVIEW MULTIPLE-CHOICE QUESTIONS 17 THROUGH 24

F. Contracts for Sale of Land

1. Generally precede transfers of land. Often includes escrows.

> **EXAMPLE**
>
> An earnest money agreement. The purchaser puts the money down to show his seriousness while he investigates the title and arranges for a mortgage.

a. Generally, agreement must

   (1) Be in writing and signed by party to be bound

      (a) To satisfy Statute of Frauds under contract law

   (2) Identify land and parties
   (3) Identify purpose
   (4) Contain terms or promises
   (5) Contain purchase price

b. Assignable unless prohibited in contract

2. If not expressed, there is an implied promise that seller will provide a marketable title (implied warranty of marketability)

    a. A marketable title is one reasonably free from doubt. Does not contain such defects as breaks in chain of title, outstanding liens, or defective instruments in past (chain of title).

        (1) Zoning restrictions do not make a title unmarketable

    b. Agreement may provide for marketable or "insurable" title

        (1) Insurable title is one that a title insurance company will insure against defects, liens, and invalidity

    c. If title is not marketable, purchaser may

        (1) Rescind and recover any down payment
        (2) Sue for damages
        (3) Sue for specific performance with a reduction in price

3. Risk of loss before deed is conveyed (e.g., if house burns down, who bears the burden?)

    a. General rule is purchaser bears the risk of loss, subject to terms of the contract
    b. Courts may look to who has the most ownership rights and benefits (normally buyer)
    c. Either party can insure against risk of loss

G. Types of Deeds

1. Warranty deeds contain the following covenants (unconditional promises) by grantor

    a. Grantor has title and right to convey it
    b. Free from encumbrances except as disclosed in the deed

---

EXAMPLE

O conveys by warranty deed Blackacre to P. There is a mortgage still unpaid on Blackacre. Unless O discloses this mortgage to P, O has violated the covenant that the deed be free from encumbrances.

---

    c. Quiet enjoyment—neither grantor nor third party with rightful claim will disturb grantee's possession

2. Bargain and sale deed (grant deeds)

    a. Generally, only covenants that grantor has done nothing to impair title (e.g., s/he has not created any encumbrances)
    b. Does not warrant against prior (before grantor's ownership) impairments

3. Quitclaim deed conveys only whatever interest in land the grantor has. No warranty of title is made by grantor.

    a. It is insurable, recordable, and mortgagable as with any other deed

H. Executing a Deed

1. Deed must have description of the real estate

    a. Purchase price generally not necessary in deed

2. There must be delivery for deed to be effective; there must be an intent on part of grantor to pass title (convey) to grantee

    a. Possession of the deed by grantee raises a presumption (rebuttable) of delivery
    b. A recorded deed raises a presumption (rebuttable) of delivery
    c. A deed given to a third party to give to grantee upon performance of a condition is a delivery in escrow

        (1) Escrow agent—intermediary between the two parties who holds deed until grantee pays, then gives deed to grantee and money to grantor

    d. Destruction of deed does not destroy title

3. Deed must identify the buyer and seller
4. Must have the seller's signature; buyers signature is not required

I. Recording a Deed

    1. Gives constructive notice to the world of grantee's ownership (this is important)

        a. Protects grantee (new owner) against subsequent purchasers

> **EXAMPLE**
>
> X sells land to Y. Y records his deed. Later X sells land to Z. Z loses against Y because Y recorded the deed giving constructive notice of the prior sale.

           (1) However, deed is valid between immediate parties without recording

        b. Most recording statutes provide that subsequent purchaser (bona fide) who takes without notice of the first sale has priority

           (1) Under a notice-type statute, a subsequent bona fide (good-faith) purchaser, whether s/he records or not, wins over previous purchaser who did not record before that subsequent purchase

> **EXAMPLE**
>
> A sells the same piece of property in a state having a notice-type statute to B and C in that order. B did not record the purchase. C is unaware of the sale to B and is thus a bona fide purchaser. C defeats B. Note that C should record the purchase or run the risk of another bona fide purchaser (i.e., D defeating C's claim).

           (2) Under a race-notice type (notice-race) statute, the subsequent bona fide purchaser wins over a previous purchaser only if s/he also records first (i.e., a "race" to file first) (Historically the Examiners have tested the notice-race statute most frequently)

> **EXAMPLE**
>
> X sells some property to Y and then to Z, a good-faith purchaser. After the sale to Z, Y records the purchase and then Z records the purchase. Although Y wins in a state having a race-notice statute, Z wins in a state having a notice-type statute.

> **EXAMPLE**
>
> Same as above except that Z does not record, both results above are not affected.

           (3) Under a race statute, the first to record deed wins

        c. Notice refers to actual knowledge of prior sale or constructive knowledge (i.e., one is deemed to be aware of what is filed in records)

        d. To be a purchaser, one must give value that does not include antecedent debts

J. Title Insurance

    1. Generally used to insure that title is good and to cover the warranties by seller

        a. Not required if contract does not require it

    2. Without title insurance, purchaser's only recourse is against grantor and s/he may not be able to satisfy the damages

    a. Standard insurance policies generally insure against all defects of record and defects grantee may be aware of, but not defects disclosed by survey and physical inspection of premises

    b. Title insurance company is liable for any damages or expenses if there is a title defect or encumbrance that is insured against

      (1) Certain defects are not insured by the title policy

        (a) These exceptions must be shown on face of policy

    c. Title insurance does not pass to subsequent purchasers

K. Adverse Possession

1. Possessor of land who was not owner may acquire title if s/he holds it for the statutory period

    a. The statutory period is the running of the statute of limitations. Varies by state from five to twenty years.

    b. The statute begins to run upon the taking of possession

    c. True owner must commence legal action before statute runs or adverse possessor obtains title

    d. Successive possessors may tack (cumulate required time together)

      (1) Each possessor must transfer to the other. One cannot abandon or statute begins over again for the next possessor.

    e. True owner of a future interest (e.g., a remainder, is not affected by adverse possession)

EXAMPLE

X dies and leaves his property to A for life, remainder to B. A pays little attention to the property and a third party acquires it by adverse possession. When A dies, B is entitled to the property regardless of the adverse possession but the statute starts running against B.

---

2. Necessary elements

    a. Open and notorious possession

      (1) Means type of possession that would give reasonable notice to owner

    b. Hostile possession

      (1) Must indicate intentions of ownership

        (a) Does not occur when possession started permissively or as cotenants

        (b) Not satisfied if possessor acknowledges other's ownership

      (2) Color of title satisfies this requirement. When possession is taken under good-faith belief in a defective instrument or deed purporting to convey the land.

    c. Actual possession

      (1) Possession of land consistent with its normal use (e.g., farm land is being farmed)

    d. Continuous possession

      (1) Need not be constant, but possession as normally used

    e. Exclusive possession

      (1) Possession to exclusion of all others

L. Easement by Prescription

1. Person obtains right to use another's land (i.e., easement) in way similar to adverse possession

2. Same elements are used as for adverse possession except for exclusive possession—state laws require several years to obtain this

---

EXAMPLE

X cuts across Y's land for several years in such a way that she meets all of the same requirements as those needed for adverse possession except for exclusive possession. X obtains an easement to use the path even if Y later tries to stop X.

NOW REVIEW MULTIPLE-CHOICE QUESTIONS 25 THROUGH 34

M. Mortgages

1. Lien on real property to secure payment of loan

   a. Mortgage is an interest in real property and thus must satisfy Statute of Frauds

      (1) Must be in writing and signed by party to be charged

         (a) Party to be charged in this case is mortgagor (i.e., party taking out mortgage, the borrower)

      (2) Must include description of property and debt to be incurred

   b. Debt is usually evidenced by a promissory note
   c. Mortgage must be delivered to mortgagee (i.e., lender)
   d. Mortgage may be given to secure future advances
   e. Purchase-money mortgage is created when seller takes a mortgage from buyer at time of sale

      (1) Or lender furnishes money with which property is purchased

2. Mortgage may be recorded and receives the same benefits as recording a deed or recording an assignment of contract

   a. Gives constructive notice of the mortgage

      (1) But mortgage **is effective** between mortgagor and mortgagee and third parties, who have actual notice, even without recording

   b. Protects mortgagee against subsequent mortgagees, purchasers, or other takers
   c. Recording statutes for mortgages are like those used for recording deeds

      (1) Under a notice-type statute, a subsequent good-faith mortgagee has priority over previous mortgagee who did not file

         (a) This is true whether subsequent mortgagee files or not; but of course if s/he does not file, a subsequent good-faith mortgagee will have priority.

EXAMPLE

Banks A, B, and C, in that order, grant a mortgage to a property owner. None of these record the mortgage and none knows of the others. Between A and B, B has priority. However, C has priority over B.

EXAMPLE

Same facts as before, however, B does record before C grants the mortgage. B has priority over A again. B also has priority over C because now C has constructive notice of B and thus has lower priority.

         (b) Notice is either actual notice or constructive notice based on recording

    (2) Under a race-notice type (notice-race) statute, the subsequent good-faith mortgagee wins over a previous mortgagee only if s/he also records first

    (3) Under a race statute, the first mortgagee to record mortgage wins

    (4) First mortgage to have priority is satisfied in full (upon default) before next mortgage to have priority is satisfied

        (a) Second mortgagee can require first mortgagee to resort to other property for payment if first mortgagee has other property available as security

3. When mortgaged property is sold the buyer may

  a. Assume the mortgage (if the mortgagee allows)

    (1) If "assumed," the buyer becomes personally liable (mortgage holder is third-party beneficiary)

    (2) Seller remains liable (unless released by mortgagee by a novation)

        (a) Mortgagee may hold either seller or buyer liable on mortgage

    (3) Normally the mortgagee's consent is needed due to "due on sale clauses"

        (a) Terms of mortgage may permit acceleration of principal or renegotiation of interest rate upon transfer of the property

  b. Take subject to the mortgage

    (1) If buyer takes "subject to" then buyer accepts **no** liability for mortgage and seller is still primarily liable

    (2) Mortgagee may still foreclose on the property even in the hands of buyer

        (a) Buyer may pay mortgage if s/he chooses to avoid foreclosure

    (3) Mortgagee's consent to allow buyer to take subject to the mortgage is not needed unless stipulated in mortgage

  c. Novation—occurs when purchaser assumes mortgage and mortgagee (lender) releases in writing the seller from the mortgage

---

EXAMPLE

O has mortgaged Redacre. He sells Redacre to T. T agrees to assume mortgage and mortgagee bank agrees in writing to substitute T as the only liable party in place of O. Because of this novation, O is no longer liable on the mortgage.

---

4. Rights of parties

  a. Mortgagor (owner, debtor) retains possession and right to use land

    (1) May transfer land encumbered by mortgage

  b. Mortgagee (creditor) has a lien on the land

    (1) Even if mortgagor transfers land, it is still subject to the mortgage if it has been properly recorded

  c. Mortgagee has right to assign mortgage to third party without mortgagors' consent

  d. Upon mortgagor's default, mortgagee may assign mortgage to third parties or mortgagee may foreclose on the land

    (1) Foreclosure requires judicial action that directs foreclosure sale

        (a) Court will refuse to confirm sale if price is so low as to raise a presumption of unfairness

        (b) However, court will not refuse to confirm sale merely because higher price might have been received at a later time

    (2) Mortgagor usually can save real estate (redeem the property) by use of equity of redemption

        (a) Pays interest, debt, and expenses

        (b) Exists until foreclosure sale

        (c) Cannot be curtailed by prior agreement

      (3) After foreclosure sale debtor has right of redemption if state law grants statutory right of redemption (Examiners will tell you if it is a "right of redemption" jurisdiction)

          (a) Affords mortgagor one last chance to redeem property
          (b) Pays off loan within statutory period

      (4) If mortgagee forecloses and sells property and mortgagor does not use equity of redemption or right of redemption

          (a) Mortgagee must return any excess proceeds from sale to mortgagor

             1] Equity above balance due does not give right to mortgagor to retain possession of property

          (b) If proceeds from sale are insufficient to pay note, mortgagor is still indebted to the mortgagee for deficiency

             1] Grantee of the mortgagor who **assumed** mortgage would also be liable for deficiency, but one who took **subject to** the mortgage would not be personally liable

5. Mortgage lenders are regulated by Real Estate Settlement Procedures Act (RESPA)

    a. Provides home buyers with extensive information about settlement process and helps protect them from high settlement fees

6. Deed of trust—also a nonpossessory lien on real property to secure a debt

    a. Like a mortgage, debtor retains possession of land and creditor has a lien on it
    b. Legal title is given to a trustee to hold

      (1) Upon default, trustee may sell the land for the benefit of creditor

7. Sale on contract

    a. Unlike a mortgage or a deed of trust, the seller retains title to property
    b. Purchaser takes possession and makes payments on the contract
    c. Purchaser gets title when debt fully paid

8. When mortgaged property is sold or destroyed, the proceeds from sale or insurance go to mortgagee with highest priority until it is completely paid, then the proceeds, if any, go to any mortgagees or other interest holders, with the next highest priority, etc.

NOW REVIEW MULTIPLE-CHOICE QUESTIONS 35 THROUGH 42

N. Lessor-Lessee

1. A lease is a contract and a conveyance

    a. Contract is the primary source of rights and duties
    b. Contract must contain essential terms including description of leased premises
    c. May be oral if less than one year; the Statute of Frauds applies under the one year rule not the real estate provision.

2. Types of leaseholds

    a. Periodic tenancy

      (1) Lease is for a fixed time such as a month or year but it continues from period to period until proper notice of termination
      (2) Notice of termination normally must be given in the same amount of time as rent or tenancy period (i.e., if tenancy is from month to month then the landlord or tenant usually must give at least one month's notice)

    b. Tenancy for a term (also called tenancy for years)

      (1) Lease is for a fixed amount of time (e.g., lease of two years or six months)

      (2) Ends automatically at date of termination

  c. Tenancy at sufferance

      (1) Created when tenant remains in property after lease expires

      (2) Landlord has option of treating tenant as trespasser and ejecting him/her or treating him/her as tenant and collecting rent

  d. Tenancy at will

      (1) Property is leased for indefinite period of time

      (2) Either party may terminate lease at will

3. Lessor covenants (promises) and tenant's rights

  a. Generally, lessor's covenants are independent of lessee's rights; therefore, lessor's breach does not give lessee right to breach

  b. Right to possession—lessor makes premises available to lessee

      (1) Residential lease for real estate entitles tenant to exclusive possession of property during period of lease unless otherwise agreed in lease

  c. Quiet enjoyment—neither lessor nor a third party with a valid claim will evict lessee unless tenant has breached lease contract

  d. Fitness for use—premises are fit for human occupation (i.e., warranty of habitability)

  e. In general, if premises are destroyed through no fault of either party, then contract is terminated

---

EXAMPLE

Landlord's building is destroyed by a sudden flood. Tenant cannot hold landlord liable for loss of use of building.

---

  f. Lessee may assign or sublease unless prohibited or restricted in lease

      (1) Assignment is transfer by lessee of his/her entire interest reserving no rights

         (a) Assignee is in privity of contract with lessor and lessor may proceed against him/her for rent and breaches under lease agreement

         (b) Assignor (lessee) is still liable to lessor unless there is a novation or release

         (c) Lease may have clause that requires consent of lessor for subleases

            [1] In which case, consent to each individual sublease is required

            [2] Lack of consent makes sublease voidable

         (d) Clause prohibiting sublease does not prohibit assignment

      (2) A sublease is the transfer by lessee of less than his/her entire interest (e.g., for three months during summer, then lessee returns to it in the fall)

         (a) Lessee (sublessor) is still liable on lease

         (b) Lessor has no privity with sublessee and can take no action against him/her for rent, but certain restrictions of original lease run with the land and are enforceable against sublessee

         (c) Sublessee can assume obligations in sublease and be liable to pay landlord

         (d) Clause prohibiting assignment does not prohibit sublease

  g. Subject to lease terms, trade fixtures attached by lessee may be removed if can be removed without substantial damage to premises

  h. Tenant can use premises for any legal purpose unless lease restricts

4. Lessee's duties and lessor's rights

   a. Rent—due at end of term or period of tenancy unless otherwise agreed in lease

     (1) No right to withhold rent even if lessor is in breach (unless so provided by lease or by statute)

     (2) Nonpayment gives lessor right to sue for it or to bring an eviction suit or both

   b. Lessee has obligation to make ordinary repairs. Lease or statute may make lessor liable.

     (1) Structural repairs are lessor's duty

   c. If tenant wrongfully retains possession after termination, lessor may

     (1) Evict lessee, or

     (2) Treat as holdover tenant and charge with fair rental value, or

     (3) Tenancy becomes one of period-to-period, and lessee is liable for rent the same as in expired lease

5. Termination

   a. Expiration of lease
   b. Proper notice in a tenancy from period-to-period
   c. Surrender by lessee and acceptance by lessor
   d. Death of lessee terminates lease except for a lease for a period of years

     (1) Death of lessor generally does not terminate lease

   e. Eviction

     (1) Actual eviction—ousting directly

     (2) Constructive eviction—allowing conditions which make property unusable if lessor is liable for condition of premises

   f. Transfer of property does not affect tenancy

     (1) New owner cannot rightfully terminate lease unless old owner could have (e.g., breach by tenant)

        (a) However, if tenant purchases property then lease terminates

NOW REVIEW MULTIPLE-CHOICE QUESTIONS 43 THROUGH 46

KEY TERMS

Bailee. A party who is entrusted to hold the goods of another person.

Bailment. When a party entrusts goods to another party.

Bailor. The party who gives his/her own goods to another to hold.

Common carrier. A party who transports goods for hire and is strictly liable for any damage to those goods. Damages are generally limited by statute though.

Copyright. Intellectual property right that provides protection for the original expression of an idea.

Deed. A written instrument that transfers ownership of real property.

Easement. A legal right to use another's property in a specific manner.

Fair use doctrine. Allows copyrighted material to be used without paying royalties. Use is generally limited to educational, news and other not-for-profit purposes.

Joint tenancy. A type of co-ownership of real property with the right of survivorship.

Landlord. The owner of the leased premises.

Lease. A contract used to rent real property for a period of time.

Mortgage. A security interest in real property.

Mortgagee. The party with the security interest in the real property (the lender).

Mortgagor. The party who uses his/her real property as collateral to secure a loan (the borrower).

Notice statute. A law that applies to the recording of interests in real property. Notice states allow parties who take an interest in real property without notice to have a superior interest than a party who had an earlier interest.

Notice-race statute. A law that applies to the recording of interests in real property. Notice-race states allow parties who take an interest in real property without notice to have a superior interest than a party who had an earlier interest if the subsequent party records before the party with the earlier interest.

Patent. An intellectual property right that gives an inventor the exclusive right to use the invention.

Race statute. A law that applies to the recording of interests in real property. Race statutes give the superior interest to whichever party records its interest first.

Real estate contract. A written instrument that contains the terms of the bargain to transfer real property.

Real property. Land, the interests in land, and the permanent structures attached to the land.

Recording. The filing of property interests with the appropriate local government that allows the party who records to protect its interest against subsequent parties.

Tenancy by the entirety. A type of co-ownership of real property that is only available to married couples. Helps to protect the property from claims of individual creditors.

Tenant. The party who rents the rental property and acquires a right to use the premises.

Tenants in common. A type of co-ownership of real property that does not include the right of survivorship.

Title insurance. Insures against defects of title of the real property.

Trademark. A distinctive mark, word, symbol, design, etc. that a manufacturer/seller uses to identify its goods.

Trade secrets. Information that a business does not want disclosed to the public. Business must take extraordinary measures to keep the information private.

Multiple-Choice Questions (1–46)

A. Distinctions between Real and Personal Property

1. Which of the following items is tangible personal property?

   a. Share of stock.
   b. Trademark.
   c. Promissory note.
   d. Oil painting.

2. What is an example of property that can be considered either personal property or real property?

   a. Air rights.
   b. Mineral rights.
   c. Harvested crops.
   d. Growing crops.

B. Personal Property

3. Which of the following factors help determine whether an item of personal property is a fixture?

  I. Degree of the item's attachment to the property.
  II. Intent of the person who had the item installed.

   a. I only.
   b. II only.
   c. Both I and II.
   d. Neither I nor II.

4. Getty owned some personal property which was later found by Morris. Both Getty and Morris are claiming title to this personal property. In which of the following cases will Getty win over Morris?

  I. Getty had mislaid the property and had forgotten to take it with him.
  II. Getty had lost the property out of his van while driving down a road.
  III. Getty had abandoned the property but later changed his mind after Morris found it.

   a. I only.
   b. II only.
   c. I and II only.
   d. I, II, and III.

5. Rand discarded an old rocking chair. Stone found the rocking chair and, realizing that it was valuable, took it home. Later, Rand learned that Stone had the rocking chair and wanted it back. Rand subsequently put a provision in his will that his married daughter Walters will get the rocking chair. Who has the actual title to the rocking chair?

	Stone has title	Rand, while living, has title	Walters obtains title upon Rand's death
a.	No	Yes	Yes
b.	No	Yes	No
c.	Yes	Yes	Yes
d.	Yes	No	No

C. Bailments

6. Which of the following standards of liability **best** characterizes the obligation of a common carrier in a bailment relationship?

   a. Reasonable care.
   b. Gross negligence.
   c. Shared liability.
   d. Strict liability.

7. Cook Company, a common carrier trucking company, made a contract to transport some video equipment for Jackson Company. Cook is trying to limit its liability in the contract. In which of the following situations can Cook not avoid liability?

  I. In transit, the driver of Cook's truck damages the video equipment when the driver causes an accident.
  II. An unknown thief steals the video equipment while in transit. Cook committed no negligence in this theft.
  III. The video equipment is destroyed when a bridge under the truck collapses because of an earthquake.

   a. I only.
   b. I and II only.
   c. I, II, and III.
   d. I and III only.

8. A common carrier bailee generally would avoid liability for loss of goods entrusted to its care if the goods are

   a. Stolen by an unknown person.
   b. Negligently destroyed by an employee.
   c. Destroyed by the derailment of the train carrying them due to railroad employee negligence.
   d. Improperly packed by the party shipping them.

9. Funston, a retailer, shipped goods worth $600 to a customer by using a common carrier. The contract used by the common carrier, and agreed to by Funston, limited liability to $100 unless a higher fee is paid. Funston did not pay the higher fee. The goods were shipped FOB destination point and were destroyed in transit due to a flash flood. Which of the following is correct?

   a. Funston will suffer a loss of $500.
   b. Funston will suffer a loss of $600.
   c. Funston's customer will suffer a loss of $500.
   d. Funston's customer will suffer a loss of $600.

D. Intellectual Property and Computer Technology Rights

10. Multicomp Company wishes to protect software it has developed. It is concerned about others copying this software and taking away some of its profits. Which of the following is true concerning the current state of the law?

   a. Computer software is generally copyrightable.
   b. To receive protection, the software must have a conspicuous copyright notice.

c. Software in human readable source code is copyrightable but in machine language object code is not.

d. Software can be copyrighted for a period not to exceed twenty years.

11. Which of the following is **not** correct concerning computer software purchased by Gultch Company from Softtouch Company? Softtouch originally created this software.

a. Gultch can make backup copies in case of machine failure.

b. Softtouch can typically copyright its software for at least seventy-five years.

c. If the software consists of compiled computer databases it cannot be copyrighted.

d. Computer programs are generally copyrightable.

12. Which of the following statements is correct?

a. Patent law is largely based on state law.

b. Accessing a digital work is protected by the fair use doctrine.

c. Financial and business models used over the Internet can be patented.

d. All of the above statements are incorrect.

13. Professor Bell runs off fifteen copies to distribute to his accounting class using his computer from a database in some software he had purchased for his personal research. The creator of this software is claiming a copyright. Which of the following is correct?

a. This is an infringement of a copyright since he bought the software for personal use.

b. This is not an infringement of a copyright since databases cannot be copyrighted.

c. This is not an infringement of a copyright because the copies were made using a computer.

d. This is not an infringement of a copyright because of the fair use doctrine.

14. Intellectual property rights included in software may be protected under which of the following?

a. Patent law.

b. Copyright law.

c. Both of the above.

d. None of the above.

15. Which of the following statements is **not** true of the law of trademarks in the United States?

a. Trademark law may protect distinctive shapes as well as distinctive packaging.

b. Trademark protection can be lost if the trademark becomes so popular that its use becomes commonplace.

c. Trademarks to receive protection need not be registered.

d. Trademarks are valid for twenty years after their formation.

16. Diane Trucco recently wrote a novel which is an excellent work of art. She wishes to copyright and publish this novel. Which of the following is correct?

a. Her copyright is valid for her life plus seventy years.

b. She must register her copyright to receive protection under the law.

c. She is required to put on a copyright notice to obtain a copyright.

d. All of the above are correct.

E. Interests in Real Property

17. Long, Fall, and Pear own a building as joint tenants with the right of survivorship. Long gave Long's interest in the building to Green by executing and delivering a deed to Green. Neither Fall nor Pear consented to this transfer. Fall and Pear subsequently died. After their deaths, Green's interest in the building would consist of

a. A 1/3 interest as a joint tenant.

b. A 1/3 interest as a tenant in common.

c. No interest because Fall and Pear did not consent to the transfer.

d. Total ownership due to the deaths of Fall and Pear.

18. What interest in real property generally gives the holder of that interest the right to sell the property?

a. Easement.

b. Leasehold.

c. License.

d. Fee simple.

19. Which of the following unities (elements) are required to establish a joint tenancy?

	Time	Title	Interest	Possession
a.	Yes	Yes	Yes	Yes
b.	Yes	Yes	No	No
c.	No	No	Yes	Yes
d.	Yes	No	Yes	No

20. Which of the following is **not** an interest that a person can have in real property?

a. Fee simple absolute.

b. Tenancy by default.

c. Life interest.

d. Remainder.

21. On July 1, Quick, Onyx, and Nash were deeded a piece of land as tenants in common. The deed provided that Quick owned 1/2 the property and Onyx and Nash owned 1/4 each. If Nash dies, the property will be owned as follows:

a. Quick 1/2, Onyx 1/2.

b. Quick 5/8, Onyx 3/8.

c. Quick 1/3, Onyx 1/3, Nash's heirs 1/3.

d. Quick 1/2, Onyx 1/4, Nash's heirs 1/4.

22. Brett conveys his real property by deed to his sister, Jan, for life with the remainder to go to his friend, Randy, for his life. Brett is still living. Randy died first and Jan died second. Who has title to this real property?

a. Brett.

b. Brett's heirs.

c. Jan's heirs.

d. Randy's heirs.

23. Court, Fell, and Miles own a parcel of land as joint tenants with right of survivorship. Court's interest was sold to Plank. As a result of the sale from Court to Plank

a. Fell, Miles, and Plank each own one-third of the land as joint tenants.

b. Fell and Miles each own one-third of the land as tenants in common.

c. Plank owns one third of the land as a tenant in common.

d. Plank owns one-third of the land as a joint tenant.

24. The following contains three fact patterns involving land. In which of the following is an easement involved?

I. O sells land to B in which O retains in the deed the right to use a roadway on B's newly purchased property.

II. O sells land to B in which O in the deed has the right to cut and keep ten specified trees on the land sold.

III. O sells land to B. O continues that year to use a roadway on B's newly purchased property when B is not looking.

a. I only.

b. I and II only.

c. II and III only.

d. I, II, and III.

G. Types of Deeds

25. A method of transferring ownership of real property that **most** likely would be considered an arm's-length transaction is transfer by

a. Inheritance.

b. Eminent domain.

c. Adverse possession.

d. Sale.

26. Which of the following elements must be contained in a valid deed?

	Purchase price	Description of the land
a.	Yes	Yes
b.	Yes	No
c.	No	Yes
d.	No	No

27. Which of the following warranties is (are) contained in a general warranty deed?

I. The grantor has the right to convey the property.

II. The grantee will **not** be disturbed in possession of the property by the grantor or some third party's lawful claim of ownership.

a. I only.

b. II only.

c. Both I and II.

d. Neither I nor II.

H. Executing a Deed

28. For a deed to be effective between the purchaser and seller of real estate, one of the conditions is that the deed must

a. Contain the signatures of the seller and purchaser.

b. Contain the actual sales price.

c. Be delivered by the seller with an intent to transfer title.

d. Be recorded within the permissible statutory time limits.

I. Recording a Deed

Items 29 and 30 are based on the following:

On February 1, Frost bought a building from Elgin, Inc. for $250,000. To complete the purchase, Frost borrowed $200,000 from Independent Bank and gave Independent a mortgage for that amount; gave Elgin a second mortgage for $25,000; and paid $25,000 in cash. Independent recorded its mortgage on February 2 and Elgin recorded its mortgage on March 12.

The following transactions also took place:

• On March 1, Frost gave Scott a $20,000 mortgage on the building to secure a personal loan Scott had previously made to Frost.

• On March 10, Scott recorded this mortgage.

• On March 15, Scott learned about both prior mortgages.

• On June 1, Frost stopped making payments on all the mortgages.

• On August 1, the mortgages were foreclosed. Frost, on that date, owed Independent, $195,000; Elgin, $24,000; and Scott, $19,000.

A judicial sale of the building resulted in proceeds of $220,000 after expenses were deducted. The above transactions took place in a notice-race jurisdiction.

29. What amount of the proceeds will Scott receive?

a. $0

b. $1,000

c. $12,500

d. $19,000

30. Why would Scott receive this amount?

a. Scott knew of the Elgin mortgage.

b. Scott's mortgage was recorded before Elgin's and before Scott knew of Elgin's mortgage.

c. Elgin's mortgage was first in time.

d. After Independent is fully paid, Elgin and Scott share the remaining proceeds equally.

J. Title Insurance

31. A purchaser who obtains real estate title insurance will

a. Have coverage for the title exceptions listed in the policy.

b. Be insured against all defects of record other than those excepted in the policy.

c. Have coverage for title defects that result from events that happen after the effective date of the policy.

d. Be entitled to transfer the policy to subsequent owners.

32. Which of the following is a defect in marketable title to real property?

    a. Recorded zoning restrictions.
    b. Recorded easements referred to in the contract of sale.
    c. Unrecorded lawsuit for negligence against the seller.
    d. Unrecorded easement.

K. Adverse Possession

33. Which of the following is **not** a necessary element for an individual to obtain title of a piece of real estate by adverse possession?

    a. Continuous possession.
    b. Possession that is to the exclusion of others.
    c. Possession permitted by the actual owner.
    d. Open and notorious possession.

34. Rake, twenty-five years ago, put a fence around a piece of land. At the time, Rake knew that fence not only surrounded his land but also a sizable piece of Howe's land. Every summer Rake planted a garden on this land surrounded by the fence. Howe recently sold all of his land to Cross. Cross has found out about the fence line and has asked Rake to either move the fence or pay Cross for the land in question. What is the result?

    a. Rake does not have to move the fence but must pay Cross for the land in question.
    b. Rake does not have to move the fence but must pay Howe for the land in question.
    c. Rake must move the fence.
    d. Rake must neither move the fence nor pay either party for the land in question.

M. Mortgages

35. Generally, which of the following federal acts regulate mortgage lenders?

	Real Estate Settlement Procedures Act (RESPA)	Federal Trade Commission Act
a.	Yes	Yes
b.	Yes	No
c.	No	Yes
d.	No	No

36. Gilmore borrowed $60,000 from Dix Bank. The loan was used to remodel a building owned by Gilmore as investment property and was secured by a second mortgage that Dix did not record. FCA Loan Company has a recorded first mortgage on the building. If Gilmore defaults on both mortgages, Dix

    a. Will not be entitled to any mortgage foreclosure sale proceeds, even if such proceeds are in excess of the amount owed to FCA.
    b. Will be unable to successfully claim any security interest in the building.
    c. Will be entitled to share in any foreclosure sale proceeds pro rata with FCA.
    d. Will be able to successfully claim a security interest that is subordinate to FCA's security interest.

37. Wilk bought an apartment building from Dix Corp. There was a mortgage on the building securing Dix's promissory note to Xeon Finance Co. Wilk took title subject to Xeon's mortgage. Wilk did not make the payments on the note due Xeon and the building was sold at a foreclosure sale. If the proceeds of the foreclosure sale are less than the balance due on the note, which of the following statements is correct regarding the deficiency?

    a. Xeon must attempt to collect the deficiency from Wilk before suing Dix.
    b. Dix will not be liable for any of the deficiency because Wilk assumed the note and mortgage.
    c. Xeon may collect the deficiency from either Dix or Wilk.
    d. Dix alone would be liable for the entire deficiency.

38. On April 6, Ford purchased a warehouse from Atwood for $150,000. Atwood had executed two mortgages on the property: a purchase money mortgage given to Lang on March 2, which was not recorded; and a mortgage given to Young on March 9, which was recorded the same day. Ford was unaware of the mortgage to Lang. Under the circumstances

    a. Ford will take title to the warehouse subject only to Lang's mortgage.
    b. Ford will take title to the warehouse free of Lang's mortgage.
    c. Lang's mortgage is superior to Young's mortgage because Lang's mortgage is a purchase money mortgage.
    d. Lang's mortgage is superior to Young's mortgage because Lang's mortgage was given first in time.

39. Which of the following conditions must be met to have an enforceable mortgage?

    a. An accurate description of the property must be included in the mortgage.
    b. A negotiable promissory note must accompany the mortgage.
    c. Present consideration must be given in exchange for the mortgage.
    d. The amount of the debt and the interest rate must be stated in the mortgage.

40. On February 1, Frost bought a building from Elgin, Inc. for $250,000. To complete the purchase, Frost borrowed $200,000 from Independent Bank and gave Independent a mortgage for that amount; gave Elgin a second mortgage for $25,000; and paid $25,000 in cash. Independent recorded its mortgage on February 2 and Elgin recorded its mortgage on March 12.

The following transactions also took place:

- On March 1, Frost gave Scott a $20,000 mortgage on the building to secure a personal loan Scott had previously made to Frost.
- On March 10, Scott recorded this mortgage.
- On March 15, Scott learned about both prior mortgages.
- On June 1, Frost stopped making payments on all the mortgages.

- On August 1, the mortgages were foreclosed. Frost, on that date, owed Independent, $195,000; Elgin, $24,000; and Scott, $19,000.

A judicial sale of the building resulted in proceeds of $220,000 after expenses were deducted. The above transactions took place in a notice-race jurisdiction.

Frost may redeem the property before the judicial sale only if

    a. There is a statutory right of redemption.
    b. It is probable that the sale price will result in a deficiency.
    c. All mortgages are paid in full.
    d. All mortgagees are paid a penalty fee.

41. A mortgagor's opportunity to redeem will be terminated by a judicial foreclosure sale unless

    a. The proceeds from the sale are not sufficient to fully satisfy the mortgage debt.
    b. The mortgage instrument does not provide for a default sale.
    c. The mortgagee purchases the property for market value.
    d. The jurisdiction has enacted a statutory right of redemption.

42. Rich purchased property from Sklar for $200,000. Rich obtained a $150,000 loan from Marsh Bank to finance the purchase, executing a promissory note and a mortgage. By recording the mortgage, Marsh protects its

    a. Rights against Rich under the promissory note.
    b. Rights against the claims of subsequent bona fide purchasers for value.
    c. Priority against a previously filed real estate tax lien on the property.
    d. Priority against all parties having earlier claims to the property.

N. Lessor-Lessee

43. Which of the following provisions must be included to have an enforceable written residential lease?

	A description of the leased premises	A due date for the payment of rent
a.	Yes	Yes
b.	Yes	No
c.	No	Yes
d.	No	No

44. Which of the following rights is (are) generally given to a lessee of residual property?

  I. A covenant of quiet enjoyment.
  II. An implied warranty of habitability.

    a. I only.
    b. II only.
    c. Both I and II.
    d. Neither I nor II.

45. Which of the following methods of obtaining personal property will give the recipient ownership of the property?

	Lease	Finding abandoned property
a.	Yes	Yes
b.	Yes	No
c.	No	Yes
d.	No	No

46. Which of the following forms of tenancy will be created if a tenant stays in possession of the leased premises without the landlord's consent, after the tenant's one-year written lease expires?

    a. Tenancy at will.
    b. Tenancy for years.
    c. Tenancy from period to period.
    d. Tenancy at sufferance.

Multiple-Choice Answers and Explanations

Answers

1.	d	__ __	11.	c	__ __	21.	d	__ __	31.	b	__ __	41.	d	__ __
2.	d	__ __	12.	c	__ __	22.	a	__ __	32.	d	__ __	42.	b	__ __
3.	c	__ __	13.	d	__ __	23.	c	__ __	33.	c	__ __	43.	b	__ __
4.	c	__ __	14.	c	__ __	24.	a	__ __	34.	d	__ __	44.	c	__ __
5.	d	__ __	15.	d	__ __	25.	d	__ __	35.	b	__ __	45.	c	__ __
6.	d	__ __	16.	a	__ __	26.	c	__ __	36.	d	__ __	46.	d	__ __
7.	b	__ __	17.	b	__ __	27.	c	__ __	37.	d	__ __			
8.	d	__ __	18.	d	__ __	28.	c	__ __	38.	b	__ __			
9.	b	__ __	19.	a	__ __	29.	d	__ __	39.	a	__ __	1st:	__/46= __%	
10.	a	__ __	20.	b	__ __	30.	b	__ __	40.	c	__ __	2nd:	__/46= __%	

Explanations

1. (d) Real property is land and objects attached to land in a relatively permanent manner; personal property is property not classified as real. Tangible property is subject to physical possession; intangible property cannot be physically possessed, but can be legally owned. Ownership of intangible property is often represented by a piece of paper, but the property itself is intangible; thus answers (a), (b), and (c) are incorrect. A share of stock is part ownership of a company; a trademark is ownership of the use of a particular mark, design, word, or picture, and a promissory note is ownership of the right to receive payment of a debt at a future date. These are all usually represented by a piece of paper, but are intangible. An oil painting is personal property subject to physical possession.

2. (d) Growing crops generally are part of the land and therefore considered real property. However, the crops can be sold separately from the land, in which case they are considered personal property under the UCC, whether the buyer or the seller will sever the growing crops later from the land. Answer (a) is incorrect because air rights are not discussed in the UCC as one of those that can be either. Answer (b) is incorrect because mineral rights are associated with land or realty. Answer (c) is incorrect because unlike growing crops that may be realty until sold in a contract, harvested crops are personal property separate from the realty.

3. (c) The factors used to determine whether an item of personal property is considered a fixture are (1) the affixer's intent, (2) the method and permanence of attachment, and (3) whether the personal property is customarily necessary to use the real property.

4. (c) When the owner mislays personal property and forgets to take it with him or her, the finder does not obtain title but the owner of the premise acts as caretaker in case the true owner comes back. In the case of lost property (involuntarily left), the finder obtains title; however, the true owner, Getty, wins over this title. In the case of abandoned property, the finder gets valid title that is even valid against Getty.

5. (d) When property is discarded with no intention of keeping ownership over it, it is considered abandoned property. In such cases, the one who finds and keeps the abandoned property becomes the owner with title that is good against all other parties, even the owner who abandoned it. Note that Walters cannot obtain title from Rand because Rand no longer owns the rocking chair.

6. (d) The general rule for a bailee is to exercise reasonable care in light of the particular facts and circumstances. However, a common carrier holds itself out as a public delivery service, and is held to a very high standard for property placed in its care; therefore answer (a) is incorrect, and answer (d) is correct. Answer (b) is incorrect because gross negligence is reckless conduct and any bailee owes a duty of at least reasonable care. Answer (c) is incorrect because the common carrier does not share liability for losses.

7. (b) Common carriers' liability is based on strict liability. As such, the common carrier is liable for losses to property whether or not the common carrier was negligent. Common law exceptions to strict liability include natural disasters which are responsible for damages.

8. (d) The standard of care required for a common carrier bailee is based on strict liability rather than reasonable care. Common carrier bailees, however, are not liable for acts of God, acts of the shipper, or acts of a public enemy. In this case, the improper packing was done by the party doing the shipping. Answer (a) is incorrect because acts or theft by other parties make the common carrier liable. Answer (b) is incorrect because acts such as negligence, by others, still leave the common carrier liable. Answer (c) is incorrect because acts of a railroad employee cause the common carrier to be liable.

9. (b) Common carriers are not liable for losses due to causes deemed acts of God. Although a common carrier may limit its damages to a dollar amount specified in the contract, it is not liable at all in this case; therefore answer (a) is incorrect. Answers (c) and (d) are incorrect because Funston, not the customer, had the risk of loss due to the FOB terms.

10. (a) Computer software is covered under the general copyright laws and is therefore usually copyrightable as an

(b) is incorrect because the remaining cotenants are still joint tenants. Thus, after the sale of land from Court to Plank without the consent of the others, Plank owns one third of the land as a tenant in common. Both Fell and Miles will continue to each own 1/3 of the land as joint tenants.

24. (a) Fact pattern I involves an easement in which O reserves the right to use B's land in the deed to B. O does not any longer own the roadway but retains the right to use it. Fact pattern II is a profit rather than an easement in which O has the right to enter B's land to cut and keep the ten trees. Fact pattern III is not an easement because O has not retained nor has s/he been given the right to use the roadway. Note that this is not an easement by prescription in that the use is not open and notorious nor has it occurred for several years.

25. (d) An arm's-length transaction is a negotiation between unrelated parties acting in his/her interest. A way to test an arm's-length transaction is to consider what a disinterested third party would pay for the property. Answer (d) is correct because a sale involves the transfer of property for consideration in which a third party would generally negotiate and act in his/her interest. Answer (a) is incorrect because the property passes to a party as the decedent directs, subject to certain state limitations. Answer (b) is incorrect because eminent domain is the power of the government to take, with just compensation, private property for public use. Answer (c) is incorrect because adverse possession allows a person to gain title to real property if the person has continuously and openly occupied the land of another for a statutory period of time.

26. (c) In order for a deed to be valid, a description of the land must be included. The purchase price of the land need not be present to form a valid deed. The purchase price is part of the terms of the bargain and needs to be included in the real estate contract, not the deed.

27. (c) A general warranty deed warrants that (1) the seller has title and the power to convey the property described in the deed, (2) the property is free from any encumbrances, except as disclosed in the deed, and (3) the grantee (purchaser) will not be disturbed in his/her possession of the property by the grantor (seller) or some third party's lawful claim of ownership. Thus, a general warranty deed would contain both of the warranties listed and answers (a), (b), and (d) are incorrect.

28. (c) In order for a deed to be effective between the purchaser and seller of real estate, the deed must be delivered by the seller with an intent to transfer title. Even though a deed may be executed it does not become effective until delivery is made with the proper intent. Answer (d) is incorrect because a deed need not be recorded in order for it to be valid between the seller and purchaser. Recordation of a deed is important because it gives constructive notice to all third parties of the grantee's ownership; however, it does not affect the resolution of any disputes between the grantor and the grantee. Answer (a) is incorrect since a deed need be signed by only the seller in order for it to be effective; it does not have to be signed by the purchaser. Answer (b) is incorrect since the form of a deed is very different from a contract for the sale of real property. There is no requirement that the deed must contain the actual sales price.

29. (d) Under a notice-race statute, if a mortgagee fails to record its mortgage, a subsequent mortgagee who records will have a superior security interest if s/he did not have notice of the prior mortgage. In this situation, Independent Bank was the first to record its mortgage and would receive the $195,000 owed it. Scott would then receive $19,000 because Scott recorded his/her mortgage before Elgin. Since Scott did not have knowledge of Elgin's mortgage until after Scott had recorded his/her mortgage, Scott would have priority over Elgin.

30. (b) Under a notice-race statute, a subsequent mortgagee (lender) who loans money without notice of a previous mortgage and records the mortgage first has priority over that previous mortgage. Thus, since Scott recorded his/her mortgage before Elgin and without knowledge of Elgin's mortgage, Scott would have priority in a notice-race jurisdiction. Answer (a) is incorrect because Scott did not know of Elgin's mortgage at the time Scott recorded his/her mortgage. Although Scott later learned about both prior mortgages, this would not affect Scott's priority over Elgin's mortgage. Answer (c) is incorrect because Elgin's mortgage would have priority only if it had been recorded before Scott's. Answer (d) is incorrect because Scott's mortgage had priority over Elgin's. Therefore, Scott would be entitled to receive the full $19,000 before Elgin received any of the proceeds from the judicial sale.

31. (b) Title insurance insures against all defects of record and defects the grantee may be aware of. Any exceptions not insured by the title policy must be shown on the face of the policy. Answer (a) is incorrect because title exceptions are not insured by the title policy. Answer (c) is incorrect because title insurance covers only defects of record. Answer (d) is incorrect because title insurance does not pass to subsequent purchasers.

32. (d) Marketable title means that the title to real property is free from encumbrances, such as mortgages, easements, and liens and defects in the chain of title. However, there is an exception. Most courts hold that the seller's obligation to convey marketable title does not require the seller to convey the title free from recorded zoning restrictions, visible public rights-of-way or recorded easements; therefore answers (a) and (b) are incorrect. An unrecorded easement, however, would be a defect in marketable title. Therefore, answer (d) is correct. Answer (c) is incorrect because a lawsuit concerning negligence would generally not affect marketable title.

33. (c) One of the elements to obtain title to property by adverse possession is that the possession be hostile to the ownership interests of the actual owner. This does not occur when possession is permitted by the actual owner. Answers (a), (b), and (d) are all necessary elements to obtain ownership by adverse possession and are therefore incorrect.

34. (d) Rake has fulfilled the elements necessary to gain title to this land in question by adverse possession. These are: (1) open and notorious possession, (2) hostile possession shown by the fence, (3) actual possession, (4) continuous possession, and (5) exclusive possession for twenty-five years. Note that it is considered continuous possession even though the gardening is only during the summer, because the fence is constantly there. Answers (a), (b), and (c) are incorrect because since Rake obtained title to the land in question, he does not have to move the fence or pay for the land.

35. (b) Congress enacted the Real Estate Settlement Procedures Act (RESPA) in 1974 to provide home buyers with more extensive information about the settlement process and to protect them from unnecessarily high settlement fees. The act applies to all federally related mortgage loans, and nearly all first mortgage loans. Therefore, the general purpose of this act is to regulate mortgage lenders.

The purpose of the Federal Trade Commission Act is to prevent unfair methods of competition and unfair or deceptive practices in commerce. It is a general consumer protection act, and regulates compliance with antitrust laws. Although it may apply to mortgage lenders, its general purpose is not to regulate mortgage lenders.

36. (d) Dix's second mortgage on Gilmore's property will allow Dix to claim a security interest subordinate to FCA's first mortgage security interest. Dix's failure to record the second mortgage will not affect their right to successfully enforce the mortgage against Gilmore. Therefore, answer (b) is incorrect. Answer (a) is incorrect because Dix would be entitled to receive mortgage foreclosure sale proceeds if such proceeds were in excess of the amount owed to FCA. Answer (c) is incorrect because FCA's first mortgage must be fully satisfied before any payments can be made to Dix.

37. (d) If a buyer takes a mortgage "subject to," then the buyer accepts no liability for the mortgage and the seller is still primarily liable. The mortgagor does not have to attempt to collect from the buyer first; he can go directly against the seller. Therefore, answer (d) is correct, and answers (a) and (c) are incorrect. Answer (b) is incorrect because Wilk did not **assume** the mortgage but bought the building **subject to** the mortgage.

38. (b) A purchaser of real estate takes title subject to any mortgage he was aware of or any mortgage that was recorded before the purchase. Ford, therefore, takes title to the warehouse subject to Young's mortgage, but free of Lang's mortgage. Therefore, answer (b) is correct and answer (a) is incorrect. Answer (c) is incorrect because there is no such provision. Answer (d) is incorrect because the recording statutes change the first in time concept to encourage the recording of mortgages.

39. (a) To have an enforceable mortgage it must be in writing and must include a description of the property and debt to be incurred. Therefore, answer (a) is correct. Answer (b) is incorrect, because although debt is usually evidenced by a promissory note, this is not required to be. Answer (c) is incorrect because the promise to pay is adequate consideration. Answer (d) is incorrect because the amount of the debt and the interest rate are not required to be stated in the mortgage.

40. (c) A mortgagor has the right to redeem the mortgaged property after default and before a judicial sale by payment of all principal and interest due on the mortgage note. Thus, Frost may redeem the property only if all mortgages are paid in full prior to the judicial sale. Answer (a) is incorrect because the right of redemption is a right that occurs **after** the judicial sale. Most states allow a mortgagor a period of time, usually one year after the foreclosure sale, to reinstate the debt and mortgage by paying to the purchaser at the judicial sale the amount of the purchase price plus the statutory interest rate. Answer (b) is incorrect because Frost may redeem the property prior to the judicial sale by paying all mortgages in full without regard to the probable sale price of the property. Answer (d) is incorrect because Frost would not have to pay penalty fees to the mortgagees.

41. (d) After foreclosure of the mortgage, the mortgagor may redeem the property by payment of all principal and interest due on the mortgage note. However, the right of redemption will terminate at the time of the judicial foreclosure sale unless the jurisdiction has enacted a statutory right of redemption. Answers (a), (b), and (c) are incorrect because they do not affect when the mortgagor's right of redemption terminates.

42. (b) Recording a mortgage protects the mortgagee against **subsequent** mortgagees, purchasers, or other takers. Therefore, answers (a), (c), and (d) are incorrect because those answers involve parties with existing claims on the property.

43. (b) A residential lease agreement must contain the following essential elements: the parties involved, lease payment amount, lease term, and a description of the leased property. The omission of any of these terms will cause the agreement to fail for indefiniteness. The other terms of payment due date, liability insurance requirements, and responsibility for repairs are optional, but not required. They will not cause the contract to fail for indefiniteness.

44. (c) The lessee of residential property, although not the owner, generally has the right to possession of the property and the right to quiet enjoyment of the property. The right to quiet enjoyment means that neither the lessor nor a third party with a valid claim will evict the lessee unless the lessee has breached the lease contract. The lessee also has the implied warranty of habitability which means that s/he has the right to inhabit premises that are fit for human occupation.

45. (c) A lease is not a sale and does not involve a transfer of title. A lessee may have possession and control of the property but will not have ownership. When property is abandoned, the owner relinquishes possession and title of the property. Subsequent parties who acquire abandoned property with the intent to own it acquire title.

46. (d) A tenancy at sufferance is created when a tenant stays in possession of the leased property after the expiration of the lease without the landlord's consent. A tenant at sufferance is a trespasser and the landlord may evict the tenant by instituting legal proceedings. Answer (a) is incorrect because a tenancy at will is an agreement that is not for a fixed period but is terminable at the will of the landlord or tenant. In this situation, the tenant does not have the consent of the landlord to stay in possession of the property and a tenancy at will is not created. Answer (b) is incorrect because a tenancy for years is a tenancy that has a fixed beginning and end at the time of creation of the tenancy. Answer (c) is incorrect because a tenancy from period to period would only be created if the landlord allowed the tenant to remain in possession of the property.

Simulation

Task-Based Simulation 1

Legal Issues		
	Authoritative Literature	Help

Situation

On June 10, 2010, Bond sold real property to Edwards for $100,000. Edwards assumed the $80,000 recorded mortgage Bond had previously given to Fair Bank and gave a $20,000 purchase money mortgage to Heath Finance. Heath did not record this mortgage. On December 15, 2011, Edwards sold the property to Ivor for $115,000. Ivor bought the property subject to the Fair mortgage but did not know about the Heath mortgage. Ivor borrowed $50,000 from Knox Bank and gave Knox a mortgage on the property. Knox knew of the unrecorded Heath mortgage when its mortgage was recorded. Ivor, Edwards, and Bond defaulted on the mortgages. Fair, Heath, and Knox foreclosed and the property was sold at a judicial foreclosure sale for $60,000. At the time of the sale, the outstanding balance of principal and accrued interest on the Fair mortgage was $75,000. The Heath mortgage balance was $18,000 and the Knox mortgage was $47,500.

Fair, Heath, and Knox all claim that their mortgages have priority and should be satisfied first from the sale proceeds. Bond, Edwards, and Ivor all claim that they are not liable for any deficiency resulting from the sale.

The above transactions took place in a jurisdiction that has a notice-race recording statute and allows foreclosure deficiency judgments.

Items 1 through 3. For each mortgage, select from List A the priority of that mortgage. A priority should be selected only once.

List A

A. First Priority
B. Second Priority
C. Third Priority

	(A)	(B)	(C)
1. Knox Bank	○	○	○
2. Heath Finance	○	○	○
3. Fair Bank	○	○	○

Items 4 through 6. For each mortgage, select from List B the reason for its priority. A reason may be selected once, more than once, or not at all.

List B

A. An unrecorded mortgage has priority over any subsequently recorded mortgage.
B. A recorded mortgage has priority over any unrecorded mortgage.
C. The first recorded mortgage has priority over all subsequent mortgages.
D. An unrecorded mortgage has priority over a subsequently recorded mortgage if the subsequent mortgagee knew of the unrecorded mortgage.
E. A purchase money mortgage has priority over a previously recorded mortgage.

	(A)	(B)	(C)	(D)	(E)
4. Knox Bank	○	○	○	○	○
5. Heath Finance	○	○	○	○	○
6. Fair Bank	○	○	○	○	○

Items 7 through 9. For each mortgage, select from List C the amount of the sale proceeds that each mortgagee would be entitled to receive. An amount may be selected once, more than once, or not at all.

List C

A.	$0	E.	$42,000
B.	$12,500	F.	$47,500
C.	$18,000	G.	$60,000
D.	$20,000		

	(A)	(B)	(C)	(D)	(E)	(F)	(G)
7. Knox Bank	O	O	O	O	O	O	O
8. Heath Finance	O	O	O	O	O	O	O
9. Fair Bank	O	O	O	O	O	O	O

Items 10 through 12. Determine whether each party would be liable to pay a mortgage foreclosure deficiency judgment on the Fair Bank mortgage. If the party would be held liable, select from List D the reason for that party's liability. A reason may be selected once, more than once, or not at all.

List D

A.	Original mortgagor.	C.	Took subject to the mortgage.
B.	Assumed the mortgage.	D.	Not liable.

	(A)	(B)	(C)	(D)
10. Edwards	O	O	O	O
11. Bond	O	O	O	O
12. Ivor	O	O	O	O

For **items 13 through 15,** determine whether each party would be liable to pay a mortgage foreclosure deficiency judgment on the Heath Finance mortgage. If the party would be held liable, select from List E the reason for that party's liability. A reason may be selected once, more than once, or not at all.

List E

A.	Original mortgagor.	C.	Took subject to the mortgage.
B.	Assumed the mortgage.	D.	Not liable.

	(A)	(B)	(C)	(D)
13. Edwards	O	O	O	O
14. Bond	O	O	O	O
15. Ivor	O	O	O	O

For **items 16 through 18,** determine whether each party would be liable to pay a mortgage foreclosure deficiency judgment on the Knox Bank mortgage. If the party would be held liable, select from List F the reason for that party's liability. A reason may be selected once, more than once, or not at all.

List F

A.	Original mortgagor.	C.	Took subject to the mortgage.
B.	Assumed the mortgage.	D.	Not liable.

	(A)	(B)	(C)	(D)
16. Edwards	O	O	O	O
17. Bond	O	O	O	O
18. Ivor	O	O	O	O

Simulation Solution

Task-Based Simulation 1

Legal Issues

	Authoritative Literature	Help

	(A)	(B)	(C)
1. Knox Bank	○	○	●
2. Heath Finance	○	●	○
3. Fair Bank	●	○	○

Explanations

1. (C) 2. (B) 3. (A) Under a notice-race recording statute, a subsequent mortgagee (lender) who loans money without notice of the previous mortgagee and records the mortgage first has priority over that previous mortgagee. Once a mortgagee records, this gives constructive notice to any subsequent parties who then cannot obtain priority over the one who recorded. In this fact pattern, Fair Bank was the first mortgagee. Since Fair Bank also recorded this mortgage first, Fair Bank has the first priority over the subsequent mortgagees. Therefore, the answer to number 3 is (A). Of the two remaining mortgagees, Heath Finance was next in time but did not record the mortgage. Knox Bank was third in time and did record. However, Knox is unable to gain priority over Heath because Knox, when it recorded, knew of the Heath mortgage. Therefore, Knox does not meet all of the rules necessary to have priority over Heath. Thus Heath has the second priority after Fair Bank and Knox has the third priority. Therefore, the answer to number 2 is (B) and number 1 is (C).

	(A)	(B)	(C)	(D)	(E)
4. Knox Bank	○	○	○	●	○
5. Heath Finance	○	○	○	●	○
6. Fair Bank	○	○	●	○	○

4. (D) 5. (D) 6. (C) This part covers the reason for the priority that applies to each of the mortgagees. Reason (A) states that "an unrecorded mortgage has priority over any subsequently recorded mortgage." This is incorrect for all mortgagees and goes against the policy behind the recording statutes to encourage recording to warn subsequent parties of the previous mortgages. Reason (B) is not a correct statement. It states that "A recorded mortgage has priority over any unrecorded mortgage." In this fact pattern, Knox recorded but Heath did not; however, Knox still has a lower priority because Knox knew of the Heath mortgage when its mortgage was recorded. Reason (C) is the correct answer for Fair Bank. It states that "The first recorded mortgage has priority over all subsequent mortgages." This is true because once Fair Bank recorded, subsequent mortgagees had constructive notice of the Fair Bank mortgage and thus could not obtain priority. The correct answer to number 6 is therefore (C). Reason (D) states that "An unrecorded mortgage has priority over a subsequently recorded mortgage if the subsequent mortgagee knew of the unrecorded mortgage." In this fact pattern, the Heath mortgage was the unrecorded mortgage that still had a higher priority than the recorded Knox mortgage because Knox Bank knew of the Heath mortgage when its mortgage was recorded. Thus Knox never fulfilled the rule which would allow it as the subsequent mortgagee, to gain a higher priority. Therefore, reason (D) is the correct answer for both Knox Bank, number 4, and Heath Finance, number 5, because the same rule determines the relative priority of these two parties. Note that reason (E) is not a correct statement for any of the mortgagees because there is no rule that gives purchase money mortgages priority over previously recorded mortgages.

	(A)	(B)	(C)	(D)	(E)	(F)	(G)
7. Knox Bank	●	○	○	○	○	○	○
8. Heath Finance	●	○	○	○	○	○	○
9. Fair Bank	○	○	○	○	○	○	●

7. (**A**) **8.** (**A**) **9.** (**G**) Since Fair Bank has the highest priority, its mortgage will be satisfied first. Since the outstanding balance of the Fair Bank **mortgage** was greater than the $60,000 received at the judicial foreclosure, Fair Bank receives all of the $60,000 and Knox Bank and Heath Finance each receive nothing.

	(A)	(B)	(C)	(D)
10. Edwards	○	●	○	○
11. Bond	●	○	○	○
12. Ivor	○	○	○	●

10. (**B**) **11.** (**A**) **12.** (**D**) When a foreclosure sale does not provide enough money to pay off the mortgages, the mortgagee, in states that allow foreclosure deficiency judgments, will attempt to collect any deficiency from the parties involved. In this fact pattern, Bond is liable because s/he was the original mortgagor on the property and as such agreed to pay the mortgage. Thus, (A) is the correct answer for number 11. When Edwards later bought the property from Bond, s/he assumed the Fair Bank mortgage. Edwards, thus, became personally liable on the mortgage even though the seller, Bond, also remained liable. Therefore, (B) is the correct answer for number 10. When Ivor subsequently purchased the property from Edwards, Ivor purchased the property subject to the Fair Bank mortgage. In so doing, s/he did not accept any liability on the mortgage. Note that although reason (C) states "Took subject to the mortgage," the correct answer for number 12 is (D) "Not liable." This is true because the directions to part d. indicate that reasons (A), (B), or (C) are to be chosen as reasons **for liability** and (D) is to be chosen if the party is **not** liable.

	(A)	(B)	(C)	(D)
13. Edwards	●	○	○	○
14. Bond	○	○	○	●
15. Ivor	○	○	○	●

13. (**A**) **14.** (**D**) **15.** (**D**) When Edwards purchased the property, s/he gave a mortgage to Heath Finance. Therefore, (A) is the correct answer for number 13 because as the original mortgagor on the Heath mortgage, s/he agreed to be liable on it. Bond is not liable on the Heath mortgage because s/he having owned the property earlier, never agreed to be liable on this mortgage. Therefore, the correct answer to number 14 is (D). Ivor is not liable on the Heath mortgage because s/he never had actual notice or constructive notice of the unrecorded mortgage, and never agreed to be liable on it. Therefore, the correct answer to number 15 is (D).

	(A)	(B)	(C)	(D)
16. Edwards	○	○	○	●
17. Bond	○	○	○	●
18. Ivor	●	○	○	○

16. (**D**) **17.** (**D**) **18.** (**A**) Since Ivor borrowed from Knox Bank and gave Knox a mortgage on the property, Ivor is liable as the original mortgagor, making (A) the correct reason for number 18. Both Edwards and Bond owned the property prior to the Knox mortgage and never agreed to be liable on it. Therefore, the correct answer to numbers 16 and 17 is (D).

FEDERAL TAXATION

As indicated previously, this section consists of five modules designed to facilitate your study for the Federal Taxation portion of the Regulation section of the Uniform CPA Examination. The table of contents at the right describes the content of each module.

Module 35: Individual Taxation

This section outlines (1) gross income in general, (2) exclusions from gross income, (3) items to be included in gross income, (4) tax accounting methods, and (5) items to be included in gross income net of deductions (e.g., business income, sales, and exchanges).

I. GROSS INCOME ON INDIVIDUAL RETURNS

A. In General

1. **Gross income** includes all income from whatever source derived, unless specifically excluded

   a. Does not include a return of capital (e.g., if a taxpayer loans $6,000 to another and is repaid $6,500 at a later date, only the $500 difference is included in gross income)

   b. The income must be **realized** (i.e., there must be a transaction which gives rise to the income)

      (1) A mere appreciation in the value of property is not income (e.g., value of one's home increases $2,000 during year. Only if the house is sold will the increase in value be realized)

      (2) A transaction may be in the form of actual receipt of cash or property, accrual of a receivable, or sale or exchange

   c. The income must also be **recognized** (i.e., the transaction must be a taxable event, and not a transaction for which non recognition is provided in the Internal Revenue Code)

   d. An **assignment of income** will not be recognized for tax purposes

      (1) If income from property is assigned, it is still taxable to the owner of the property.

EXAMPLE

X owns a building and assigns the rents to Y. The rents remain taxable to X, even though the rents are received by Y.

---

      (2) If income from services is assigned, it is still taxable to the person who earns it.

EXAMPLE

X earns $200 per week. To pay off a debt owed to Y, he assigns half of it to Y. $200 per week remains taxable to X.

---

2. Distinction between exclusions, deductions, and credits

   a. **Exclusions**—income items which are not included in gross income

      (1) Exclusions must be specified by law. Remember, gross income includes all income except that specifically excluded.

      (2) Although exclusions are exempt from income tax, they may still be taxed under other tax rules (e.g., gifts may be subject to the gift tax).

   b. **Deductions**—amounts that are subtracted from income to arrive at adjusted gross income or taxable income

      (1) Deductions for adjusted gross income (above the line deductions)—amounts deducted from gross income to arrive at adjusted gross income

      (2) Itemized deductions (below the line deductions)—amounts deducted from adjusted gross income to arrive at taxable income

   c. **Credits**—amounts subtracted from the computed tax to arrive at taxes payable

B. Exclusions from Gross Income (not reported)

1. Payments received for **support** of minor children

   a. Must be children of the parent making the payments

   b. Decree of divorce or separate maintenance generally must specify the amount to be treated as child support, otherwise payments may be treated as alimony

2. **Property settlement** (division of capital) received in a divorce
3. **Annuities** and pensions are excluded to the extent they represent a return of capital

    a. Excluded portion of each payment is

$$\frac{\text{Net cost of annuity}}{\text{Expected total annuity payments}} = \text{Payment received}$$

    b. "Expected total annuity payments" is calculated by multiplying the annual return by

      (1) The number of years receivable if it is an annuity for a definite period
      (2) A life expectancy multiple (from IRS tables) if it is an annuity for life

    c. Once this exclusion ratio is determined, it remains constant until the cost of the annuity is completely recovered. Any additional payments will be fully taxable.

EXAMPLE

Mr. Jones purchased an annuity contract for $3,600 that will pay him $1,500 per year beginning in 2015. His expected return under the contract is $10,800. Mr. Jones' exclusion ratio is $3,600 ÷ $10,800 = 1/3. For 2015, Mr. Jones will exclude $1,500 × 1/3 = $500; and will include the remaining $1,000 in gross income.

---

    d. If the taxpayer dies before total cost is recovered, unrecovered cost is allowed as a miscellaneous itemized deduction on the taxpayer's final tax return.

4. **Life insurance proceeds** (face amount of policy) are generally excluded if paid by reason of death

    a. If proceeds are received in **installments,** amounts received in excess of pro rata part of face amount are taxable as interest.
    b. **Dividends** on unmatured insurance policies are excluded to the extent not in excess of cumulative premiums paid.
    c. **Accelerated death benefits** received under a life insurance policy by a *terminally or chronically ill* individual are generally excluded from gross income

      (1) Similarly, if a portion of a life insurance contract on the life of a terminally or chronically ill individual is assigned or sold to a viatical settlement provider, proceeds received from the provider are excluded.
      (2) For a chronically ill individual, the exclusion is limited to the amount paid by the individual for unreimbursed long-term care costs. Payments made on a per diem basis, up to $330 per day for 2014, are excludable regardless of actual long-term care costs incurred.

    d. All interest is taxable if proceeds are left with insurance company under agreement to pay only interest.
    e. If insurance proceeds are paid for reasons other than death or under c. above, or if the policy was obtained by the beneficiary in exchange for valuable consideration from a person other than the insurance company, all proceeds in excess of cost are taxable. Annuity rules apply to installment payments.

EXAMPLE

Able was the owner and beneficiary of a $30,000 life insurance policy on Baker. Able sold the policy for $10,000 to Carr who subsequently paid $6,000 of premiums. If Baker dies, Carr's gross income from the proceeds of the life insurance policy would total $30,000 – ($10,000 + $6,000) = $14,000.

---

    f. **Company-owned life insurance.** In the case of an *employer-owned* life insurance contract, the amount of insurance proceeds that can be excluded from gross income by the employer (or related person) is generally *limited* to the sum of the premiums and other amounts paid by the policyholder for the contract. However, the full amount of proceeds paid at death can be excluded if specified notice and consent requirements as well as additional requirements are met.

(1) The notice and consent requirements specify that the employee must (a) be notified in writing of the intent to insure the employee's life and the maximum amount for which the employee could be insured, (b) provide written consent to being insured and acknowledge that coverage may continue after the employee terminates employment, and (c) be informed in writing that the employer (or related person) will be the beneficiary of proceeds payable upon the death of the employee.

(2) Additionally, the insured must have been an employee at any time during the 12-month period before the insured's death, or at the time the contract was issued was a director or highly compensated employee. Alternatively, the proceeds must be paid to a member of the insured's family or designated beneficiary of the insured, or the proceeds are used to buy an equity (or capital or profits) interest in the employer from insured's heir.

5. Certain **employee benefits** are excluded

a. **Group-term life insurance** premiums paid by employer (the **cost of up to $50,000** of insurance coverage is excluded). Exclusion not limited if beneficiary is the employer or a qualified charity.

b. Insurance premiums employer pays to fund an accident or health plan for employees are excluded.

c. **Accident and health benefits** provided by employer are excluded if benefits are for

(1) Permanent injury or loss of bodily function

(2) Reimbursement for medical care of employee, spouse, or dependents

(a) Employee cannot take itemized deduction for reimbursed medical expenses

(b) Exclusion may not apply to highly compensated individuals if reimbursed under a discriminatory self-insured medical plan

d. Employees of small businesses (50 or fewer employees) and self-employed individuals may qualify for a **medical savings account** (MSA) if covered under a high-deductible health insurance plan. An MSA is similar to an IRA, except used for health care.

(1) Employer contributions to an employee's MSA are excluded from gross income (except if made through a cafeteria plan), and employee contributions are deductible for AGI.

(2) Contributions are limited to 65% (75% for family coverage) of the annual health insurance deductible amount.

(3) Earnings of an MSA are not subject to tax; distributions from an MSA used to pay qualified medical expenses are excluded from gross income.

e. **Meals or lodging** furnished for the convenience of the employer on the employer's premises are excluded.

(1) For the convenience of the employer means there must be a non compensatory reason such as the employee is required to be on duty during this period.

(2) In the case of lodging, it also must be a condition of employment.

f. Employer-provided educational assistance (e.g., payment of tuition, books, fees) derived from an employer's qualified **educational assistance program** is excluded up to maximum of **$5,250** per year. The exclusion applies to both undergraduate as well as graduate-level courses, but does not apply to assistance payments for courses involving sports, games, or hobbies, unless they involve the employer's business or are required as part of a degree program. Excludable assistance does not include tools or supplies that the employee retains after completion of the course, nor the cost of meals, lodging, or transportation.

g. Employer payments to an employee for **dependent care assistance** are excluded from an employee's income if made under a written, nondiscriminatory plan. Maximum exclusion is **$5,000** per year ($2,500 for a married person filing a separate return).

h. **Qualified adoption expenses** paid or incurred by an employer in connection with an employee's adoption of a child are excluded from the employee's gross income. For 2014, the maximum exclusion is **$13,400** per eligible child (including special needs children) and the exclusion is ratably phased out for modified AGI between $201,010 and $241,010.

i. **Employee fringe benefits** are generally excluded if

(1) **No additional-cost services**—for example, airline pass

(2) **Employee discount** that is nondiscriminatory

(3) **Working condition fringes**—excluded to the extent that if the amount had been paid by the employee, the amount would be deductible as an employee business expense

(4) **De minimis fringes**—small value, impracticable to account for (e.g., coffee, personal use of copying machine)

(5) **Qualified transportation fringes**

    (a) Up to $130 per month for 2015 can be excluded for employer-provided transit passes and transportation in a commuter highway vehicle if the transportation is between the employee's home and work place.

    (b) Up to $250 per month for 2015 can be excluded for employer-provided parking on or near the employer's place of business.

(6) **Qualified moving expense reimbursement**—an individual can exclude any amount received from an employer as payment for (or reimbursement of) expenses which would be deductible as moving expenses if directly paid or incurred by the individual. The exclusion does not apply to any payment (or reimbursement of) an expense actually deducted by the individual in a prior taxable year.

  j. **Workers' compensation** is fully excluded if received for an occupational sickness or injury and is paid under a workers' compensation act or statute.

6. Accident and health insurance benefits derived from policies **purchased by the taxpayer** are excluded, but not if the medical expenses were deducted in a prior year and the tax benefit rule applies.

7. **Damages for physical injury or physical sickness** are excluded.

  a. If an action has its origin in a physical injury or physical sickness, then all damages therefrom (other than punitive damages) are excluded (e.g., damages received by an individual on account of a claim for loss due to a physical injury to such individual's spouse are excludible from gross income).

  b. Damages (other than punitive damages) received on account of a claim of wrongful death, and damages that are compensation for amounts paid for medical care (including medical care for emotional distress) are excluded.

  c. Emotional distress is not considered a physical injury or physical sickness. No exclusion applies to damages received from a claim of employment discrimination, age discrimination, or injury to reputation (even if accompanied by a claim of emotional distress).

  d. Punitive damages generally must be included in gross income, even if related to a physical injury or physical sickness.

8. **Gifts, bequests, devises, or inheritances** are excluded.

  a. Income subsequently derived from property so acquired is not excluded (e.g., interest or rent).

  b. "Gifts" from employer except for noncash holiday presents are generally not excluded.

9. The receipt of **stock dividends** (or stock rights) is generally excluded from income, but the FMV of the stock received will be included in income if the distribution

  a. Is on preferred stock

  b. Is payable, at the election of any shareholder, in stock or property

  c. Results in the receipt of preferred stock by some common shareholders, and the receipt of common stock by other common shareholders

  d. Results in the receipt of property by some shareholders, and an increase in the proportionate interests of other shareholders in earnings or assets of the corporation

> **NOW REVIEW MULTIPLE-CHOICE QUESTIONS 1 THROUGH 14**

10. Certain **interest income** is excluded.

  a. Interest on obligations of a **state** or one of its political subdivisions (e.g., **municipal** bonds), the District of Columbia, and US possessions is generally **excluded** from income if the bond proceeds are used to finance traditional governmental operations.

b. Other state and local government-issued obligations (private activity bonds) are generally fully taxable. An obligation is a private activity bond if (1) more than 10% of the bond proceeds are used (directly or indirectly) in a private trade or business and more than 10% of the principal or interest on the bonds is derived from, or secured by, money or property used in the trade or business, or (2) the lesser of 5% or $5 million of the bond proceeds is used (directly or indirectly) to make or finance loans to private persons or entities.

c. The following bonds are **excluded from the private activity bond category** even though their proceeds are not used in traditional government operations. The interest from these bonds is excluded from income.

   (1) Qualified bonds issued for the benefit of schools, hospitals, and other charitable organizations
   (2) Bonds used to finance certain exempt facilities, such as airports, docks, wharves, mass commuting facilities, etc.
   (3) Qualified redevelopment bonds, small-issue bonds (i.e., bonds not exceeding $1 million), and student loan bonds
   (4) Qualified mortgage and veterans' mortgage bonds

d. Interest on **US obligations** is **included** in income.

11. **Savings bonds for higher education**

a. The accrued interest on Series EE US savings bonds that are redeemed by the taxpayer is excluded from gross income to the extent that the aggregate redemption proceeds (principal plus interest) are used to finance the higher education of the taxpayer, taxpayer's spouse, or dependents.

   (1) The bonds must be issued after December 31, 1989, to an individual age twenty-four or older at the bond's issue date.
   (2) The purchaser of the bonds must be the sole owner of the bonds (or joint owner with his or her spouse). Married taxpayers must file a joint return to qualify for the exclusion.
   (3) The redemption proceeds must be used to pay qualified higher education expenses (i.e., tuition and required fees less scholarships, fellowships, and employer-provided educational assistance) at an accredited university, college, junior college, or other institution providing postsecondary education, or at an area vocational education school.
   (4) If the redemption proceeds exceed the qualified higher education expenses, only a pro rata amount of interest can be excluded.

EXAMPLE

During 2015, a married taxpayer redeems Series EE bonds receiving $6,000 of principal and $4,000 of accrued interest. Assuming qualified higher education expenses total $9,000, accrued interest of $3,600 ($9,000/$10,000 × $4,000) can be excluded from gross income.

---

b. If the taxpayer's modified AGI exceeds a specified level, the exclusion is subject to phase-out as follows:

Filing status	2015 AGI phase-out range
Married filing jointly	$115,750–$145,750
Single (including head of household)	$77,200–$92,200

   (1) The reduction of the exclusion is computed as

$$\left(\frac{\text{Excess AGI}}{\$15,000 \ (\$30,000 \text{ for joint returns})}\right) \times \left(\begin{array}{c}\text{Otherwise}\\ \text{excludable}\\ \text{interest}\end{array}\right) = \text{Reduction}$$

   (2) If the taxpayer's modified AGI exceeds the applicable phase-out range, no exclusion is available.

EXAMPLE

Assume the joint return of the married taxpayer in the above example has modified AGI of $135,750 for 2015. The reduction would be ($20,000/$30,000) × $3,600 = $2,400. Thus, of the $4,000 of interest received, a total of $1,200 could be excluded from gross income.

NOW REVIEW MULTIPLE-CHOICE QUESTIONS 15 THROUGH 22

12. **Scholarships and Fellowships**

   a. A **degree candidate** can exclude the amount of a scholarship or fellowship that is used for tuition and course-related fees, books, supplies, and equipment. Amounts used for other purposes including room and board are included in income.
   b. Amounts received as a grant or a tuition reduction that represent payment for teaching, research, or other services are generally not excludable.
   c. Non degree students may not exclude any part of a scholarship or fellowship grant.
   d. The exclusion from gross income also applies to scholarships with obligatory service requirements received by degree candidates at qualified educational organizations from the National Health Service Corps Scholarship Program and the F. Edward Hebert Armed Forces Health Professions Scholarship Program.

13. Political contributions received by candidates' campaign funds are excluded from income, but included if put to personal use.
14. Rental value of parsonage or cash rental allowance for a parsonage is excluded by a minister.
15. **Discharge of indebtedness** normally results in income to debtor, but may be **excluded** if

   a. A discharge of certain student loans pursuant to a loan provision providing for discharge if the individual works in a certain profession for a specified period of time
   b. A discharge of a corporation's debt by a shareholder (treated as a contribution to capital)
   c. The discharge is a gift
   d. The discharge is a purchase money debt reduction (treat as a reduction of purchase price)
   e. The discharge is a cancellation of up to $2 million ($1 million for married filing separately) of acquisition indebtedness on a principal residence before January 1, 2015. The amount excluded from income reduces the taxpayer's basis for the principal residence (but not below zero).
   f. Debt is discharged in a bankruptcy proceeding, or debtor is insolvent both before and after discharge

      (1) If debtor is insolvent before but solvent after discharge of debt, income is recognized to the extent that the FMV of assets exceeds liabilities after discharge
      (2) The amount excluded from income in e. above must be applied to reduce tax attributes in the following order

         (a) Net operating loss (NOL) for taxable year and loss carryovers to taxable year
         (b) General business credit
         (c) Minimum tax credit
         (d) Capital loss of taxable year and carryovers to taxable year
         (e) Reduction of the basis of property
         (f) Passive activity loss and credit carryovers
         (g) Foreign tax credit carryovers to or from taxable year

      (3) Instead of reducing tax attributes in the above order, taxpayer may elect to first reduce the basis of depreciable property

16. **Lease improvements.** Increase in value of property due to improvements made by lessee is excluded from lessor's income unless improvements are made in lieu of fair value rent.

17. **Foreign earned income exclusion.** An individual meeting either a bona fide residence test or a physical presence test may elect to exclude up to $100,800 of income earned in a foreign country for 2015. Qualifying taxpayers also may elect to exclude additional amounts based on foreign housing costs.

   a. To qualify, an individual must be a (1) US citizen who is a foreign resident for an uninterrupted period that includes an entire taxable year (bona fide residence test), or (2) US citizen or resident present in a foreign country for at least 330 full days in any twelve-month period (physical presence test).

   b. An individual who elects to exclude the housing cost amount can exclude only the lesser of (1) the housing cost amount attributable to employer-provided amounts, or (2) the individual's foreign earned income for the year.

   c. Housing cost amounts not provided by an employer can be deducted for AGI, but deduction is limited to the excess of the taxpayer's foreign earned income over the applicable foreign earned income exclusion.

NOW REVIEW MULTIPLE-CHOICE QUESTIONS 23 THROUGH 25

C. Items to Be Included in Gross Income

Gross income includes all income from any source except those specifically excluded. The more common items of gross income are listed below. Those items requiring a detailed explanation are discussed on the following pages.

1. Compensation for services, including wages, salaries, bonuses, commissions, fees, and tips

   a. Property received as compensation is included in income at FMV on date of receipt.

   b. Bargain purchases by an employee from an employer are included in income at FMV less amount paid.

   c. Life insurance premiums paid by employer must be included in an employee's gross income except for group-term life insurance coverage of $50,000 or less.

   d. Employee expenses paid or reimbursed by the employer unless the employee has to account to the employer for these expenses and they would qualify as deductible business expenses for employee.

   e. **Tips** must be included in gross income

      (1) If an individual receives less than $20 in tips while working for one employer during one month, the tips do not have to be reported to the employer, but the tips must be included in the individual's gross income when received.

      (2) If an individual receives $20 or more in tips while working for one employer during one month, the individual must report the total amount of tips to the employer by the tenth day of the following month for purposes of withholding of income tax and social security tax. Then the total amount of tips must be included in the individual's gross income for the month in which reported to the employer.

2. Gross income derived from business or profession
3. Distributive share of partnership or S corporation income
4. Gain from the sale or exchange of real estate, securities, or other property
5. Rents and royalties
6. Dividends
7. **Interest** including

   a. Earnings from savings and loan associations, mutual savings banks, credit unions, etc.

   b. Interest on bank deposits, corporate or US government bonds, and Treasury bills

      (1) Interest from US obligations is included, while interest on state and local obligations is generally excluded.

      (2) If a taxpayer elects to amortize the bond premium on taxable bonds acquired after 1987, any bond premium amortization is treated as an offset against the interest earned on the bond. The amortization of bond premium reduces taxable income (by offsetting interest income) as well as the bond's basis.

   c. **Interest on tax refunds**

   d. Imputed interest from interest-free and low-interest loans

(1) Borrower is treated as making imputed interest payments (subject to the same deduction restrictions as actual interest payments) which the lender reports as interest income.

(2) Lender is treated as making gifts (for personal loans) or paying salary or dividends (for business-related loans or corporation-shareholder loans) to the borrower.

(3) Rate used to impute interest is tied to average yield on certain federal securities and is compounded semiannually; if the federal rate is greater than the interest rate charged on a loan (e.g., a low-interest loan), impute interest only for the excess.

    (a) For demand loans, the deemed transfers are generally treated as occurring at the end of each year, and will fluctuate with interest rates.

    (b) For term loans, the interest payments are determined at the date of the loan and then allocated over the term of the loan; lender's payments are treated as made on date of loan.

(4) No interest is imputed to either the borrower or the lender for any day on which the aggregate amount of loans between such individuals (and their spouses) does not exceed $10,000.

(5) For any day that the aggregate amount of loans between borrower and lender (and their spouses) does not exceed $100,000, imputed interest is limited to borrower's "net investment income;" no interest is imputed if borrower's net investment income does not exceed $1,000.

EXAMPLE

Parents make a $200,000 interest-free demand loan to their unmarried daughter on January 1, 2015. Assume the average federal short-term rate is 3% for 2015. If the loan is outstanding for the entire year, under Step 1, the daughter is treated as making a ($200,000 × 3% × 1/2) + ($203,000 × 3% × 1/2) = $6,045 interest payment on 12/31/15, which is included as interest income on the parents' 2015 tax return. Under Step 2, the parents are treated as making a $6,045 gift to their daughter on 12/31/15. (Note that the gift will be offset by annual exclusions totaling $28,000 (for 2015) for gift tax purposes as discussed in Module 39.)

---

8. **Alimony** and separate maintenance payments

  a. Alimony is included in the recipient's gross income and is deductible toward AGI by the payor. In order for a payment to be considered as alimony, the payment must

    (1) Be made **pursuant to a decree** of divorce or written separation instrument
    (2) Be made in **cash** and received **by or on behalf** of the payee's spouse
    (3) **Terminate upon death** of the recipient
    (4) Not be made to a member of the same household at the time the payments are made
    (5) Not be made to a person with whom the taxpayer is filing a joint return
    (6) Not be characterized in the decree or written instrument as other than alimony

  b. **Alimony recapture** may occur if payments sharply decline in the second or third years. This is accomplished by making the payor report the recaptured alimony from the first and second years as income (and allowing the payee to deduct the same amount) in the third year.

    (1) Recapture for the second year occurs to the extent that the alimony paid in the second year exceeds the third-year alimony by more than $15,000.

    (2) Recapture for the first year occurs to the extent that the alimony paid in the first year exceeds the average alimony paid in the second year (reduced by the recapture for that year) and third year by more than $15,000.

(3) Recapture will not apply to any year in which payments terminate as a result of the death of either spouse or the remarriage of the payee.

(4) Recapture does not apply to payments that may fluctuate over three years or more and are not within the control of the payor spouse (e.g., 20% of the net income from a business).

EXAMPLE

If a payor makes alimony payments of $50,000 in 2013 and no payments in 2014 or 2015, $50,000 − $15,000 = $35,000 will be recaptured in 2015 (assuming none of the exceptions apply).

EXAMPLE

If a payor makes alimony payments of $50,000 in 2013, $20,000 in 2014, and nothing in 2015, the recapture amount for 2014 is $20,000 − $15,000 = $5,000. The recapture amount for 2013 is $50,000 − ($15,000 + $7,500) = $27,500. The $7,500 is the average payments for 2014 and 2015 after reducing the $20,000 year 2014 payment by the $5,000 of recapture for 2014. The recapture amounts for 2013 and 2014 total $32,500 and are reported in 2015.

---

c. Any amounts specified as **child support** are not treated as alimony.

(1) Child support is not gross income to the payee and is not deductible by the payor.

(2) If the decree or instrument specifies both alimony and child support, but **less is paid than required,** then amounts are first allocated to child support, with any remainder allocated to alimony.

(3) If a specified amount of alimony is to be reduced upon the happening of some **contingency relating to a child,** then an amount equal to the specified reduction will be treated as child support rather than alimony.

EXAMPLE

A divorce decree provides that payments of $1,000 per month will be reduced by $400 per month when a child reaches age twenty-one. Here, $400 of each $1,000 monthly payment will be treated as child support.

---

9. **Social security,** pensions, annuities (other than excluded recovery of capital)

a. Up to 50% of social security retirement benefits may be included in gross income if the taxpayer's provisional income (AGI + tax-exempt income + 50% of the social security benefits) exceeds a threshold that is $32,000 for a joint return, $0 for married taxpayers filing separately, and $25,000 for all other taxpayers. The amount to be included in gross income is the lesser of

(1) 50% of the social security benefits, or

(2) 50% of the excess of the taxpayer's provisional income over the base amount.

EXAMPLE

A single taxpayer with AGI of $20,000 received tax-exempt interest of $2,000 and social security benefits of $7,000. The social security to be included in gross income is the lesser of

$$1/2 \ (\$7,000) = \$3,500; \text{ or}$$

$$1/2 \ (\$25,500 - \$25,000) = \$250.$$

---

b. **Up to 85%** of social security retirement benefits may be included in gross income for taxpayers with provisional income above a higher second threshold that is $44,000 for a joint return, $0 for married taxpayers filing separately, and $34,000 for all other taxpayers. The amount to be included in gross income is the lesser of

    (1) 85% of the taxpayer's social security benefits, or

    (2) The sum of (a) 85% of the excess of the taxpayer's provisional income above the applicable higher threshold amount plus (b) the smaller of (i) the amount of benefits included under a. above, or (ii) $4,500 for single taxpayers or $6,000 for married taxpayers filing jointly.

c. **Rule of thumb:** Social security retirement benefits are fully excluded by low-income taxpayers (i.e., provisional income less than $25,000); 85% of benefits must be included in gross income by high-income taxpayers (i.e., provisional income greater than $60,000).

d. **Lump-sum distributions** from qualified pension, profit-sharing, stock bonus, and Keogh plans (but not IRAs) may be eligible for special tax treatment.

    (1) The portion of the distribution allocable to pre-1974 years is eligible for long-term capital gain treatment.

    (2) If the employee was born before 1936, the employee may elect ten-year averaging.

    (3) Alternatively, the distribution may be rolled over tax-free (within sixty days) to a traditional IRA, but subsequent distributions from the IRA will be treated as ordinary income.

10. **Income in respect of a decedent** is income that would have been income of the decedent before death but was not includible in income under the decedent's method of accounting (e.g., installment payments that are paid to a decedent's estate after his/her death). Such income has the same character as it would have had if the decedent had lived and must be included in gross income by the person who receives it.

11. Employer supplemental unemployment benefits or strike benefits from union funds

12. Fees, including those received by an executor, administrator, director, or for jury duty, or precinct election board duty

13. Income from discharge of indebtedness unless specifically excluded

14. **Stock options**

a. An **incentive stock option** receives favorable tax treatment.

    (1) The option must meet certain technical requirements to qualify.

    (2) No income is recognized by employee when option is granted or exercised.

    (3) If employee holds the stock acquired through exercise of the option at least two years from the date the option was granted, and holds the stock itself at least one year, the

        (a) Employee's realized gain will be long-term capital gain

        (b) Employer receives no deduction

    (4) If the holding period requirements above are not met, the employee has ordinary income to the extent that the FMV at date of exercise exceeds the option price.

        (a) Remainder of gain is short-term or long-term capital gain.

        (b) Employer receives a deduction equal to the amount employee reports as ordinary income.

    (5) An incentive stock option may be treated as a nonqualified stock option if a corporation so elects at the time the option is issued.

b. A **nonqualified stock option** is included in income when received if option has a determinable FMV.

    (1) If option has no ascertainable FV when received, then income arises when option is exercised; to the extent of the difference between the FV when exercised and the option price.

    (2) Amount recognized (at receipt or when exercised) is treated as ordinary income to employee; employer is allowed a deduction equal to amount included in employee's income.

c. An **employee stock purchase plan** that does not discriminate against rank and file employees

    (1) No income when employee receives or exercises option

    (2) If the employee holds the stock at least two years after the option is granted and at least one year after exercise, then

        (a) Employee has ordinary income to the extent of the lesser of

        [1] FMV at time option granted over option price, or
        [2] FMV at disposition over option price

    (b) Capital gain to the extent realized gain exceeds ordinary income

  (3) If the stock is not held for the required time, then

    (a) Employee has ordinary income at the time of sale for the difference between FV when exercised and the option price. This amount also increases basis.
    (b) Capital gain or loss for the difference between selling price and increased basis

15. **Prizes and awards** are generally taxable.

  a. Prizes and awards received for religious, charitable, scientific, educational, artistic, literary, or civic achievement can be excluded only if the recipient

    (1) Was selected without any action on his/her part,
    (2) Is not required to render substantial future services, and
    (3) Designates that the prize or award is to be transferred by the payor to a governmental unit or a tax-exempt charitable, educational, or religious organization
    (4) The prize or award is excluded from the recipient's income, but no charitable deduction is allowed for the transferred amount.

  b. **Employee achievement awards** are excluded from an employee's income if the cost to the employer of the award does not exceed the amount allowable as a deduction (generally from $400 to $1,600).

    (1) The award must be for length of service or safety achievement and must be in the form of tangible personal property (cash does not qualify).
    (2) If the cost of the award exceeds the amount allowable as a deduction to the employer, the employee must include in gross income the greater of

      (a) The portion of cost not allowable as a deduction to the employer, or
      (b) The excess of the award's FMV over the amount allowable as a deduction.

16. **Tax benefit rule.** A recovery of an item deducted in an earlier year must be included in gross income to the extent that a tax benefit was derived from the prior deduction of the recovered item.

  a. A tax benefit was derived if the previous deduction reduced the taxpayer's income tax.
  b. A recovery is excluded from gross income to the extent that the previous deduction did not reduce the taxpayer's income tax.

    (1) A deduction would not reduce a taxpayer's income tax if the taxpayer was subject to the alternative minimum tax in the earlier year and the deduction was not allowed in computing AMTI (e.g., state income taxes).
    (2) A recovery of state income taxes, medical expenses, or other items deductible on Schedule A (Form 1040) will be excluded from gross income if an individual did not itemize deductions for the year the item was paid.

EXAMPLE

Individual X, a single taxpayer, did not itemize deductions but instead used the standard deduction of $6,200 for 2014. In 2015, a refund of $300 of 2014 state income taxes is received. X would exclude the $300 refund from income in 2015.

EXAMPLE

Individual Y, a single taxpayer, had total itemized deductions of $6,300 for 2014, including $800 of state income taxes. In 2015, a refund of $300 of 2014 state income taxes is received. Since Y's total itemized deductions of $6,300 exceeded his available standard deduction of $6,200 by $100, Y must include $100 of the refund in gross income for 2015.

17. Embezzled or other illegal income
18. **Gambling winnings**
19. **Unemployment compensation** must generally be included in gross income.

> **NOW REVIEW MULTIPLE-CHOICE QUESTIONS 26 THROUGH 49**

D. Accounting Periods

1. The term **taxable year** refers to a taxpayer's annual accounting period. Annual accounting period means the annual period that the taxpayer uses to compute income in keeping his books.

   a. **Calendar year** is a period of 12 months ending on December 31.
   b. **Fiscal year** is a period of 12 months ending on the last day of a month other than December.
   c. **52–53 week year** is an annual period always ending on the same day of the week (e.g., last Sunday of a month, or the Sunday closest to the end of a month).

2. Taxpayer establishes an accounting period by filing first tax return. A taxpayer who does not keep books (e.g., an employee with wage income) must use a calendar year.
3. Rules for adoption of taxable year.

   a. **Corporation** that is a "C" corporation (other than a personal service corporation) may adopt any taxable year that it chooses. A **personal service corporation** generally must adopt a calendar year.
   b. **Sole proprietor** must use same taxable year for business as is used for personal return.
   c. **Partnership** is a pass-through entity and generally must use the same tax year as that used by its partners owning more than 50% of partnership income and capital. A different taxable year may be permitted if there is a substantial business purpose.
   d. **S corporation** is a pass-through entity and generally must adopt a calendar year. A different taxable year may be permitted if there is a substantial business purpose.
   e. **Estate** may adopt any taxable year for its income tax return that it chooses.
   f. **Trust** (other than charitable and tax-exempt trusts) must adopt a calendar year.

4. Substantial business purpose and IRS approval are generally required to **change a taxable year**. Taxpayers can request permission to change a year by filing Form 1128, Application for Change in Accounting Period, by the 15th day of the second month after the close of a short period.

   a. The business purpose requirement may be satisfied if the taxpayer is requesting a change to a natural business year. The business purpose test will be met if the taxpayer receives at least 25% of its gross receipts in the last two months of the selected year, and this 25% test has been satisfied for three consecutive years.
   b. The IRS may require that certain conditions be met before it approves a request for change (e.g., the IRS may require partners to switch to the same year as is being requested by the partnership).

5. Some changes in tax years require *no* approval.

   a. Newly married individuals may adopt the taxable year of the other spouse without prior approval.
   b. A corporation (other than an S Corporation) may change its year if its taxable year has not changed within the past 10 years ending with the calendar year of change; the resulting short period does not have an NOL; the corporation's annualized taxable income for the short period is at least 90% of its taxable income for the preceding year; and the corporation's status (e.g., personal holding company) for the short period is the same as the preceding year.
   c. A newly acquired subsidiary that will be included in a consolidated return must change its taxable year to the same year as used by its parent.

6. Taxable periods of less than 12 months

   a. If due to beginning or ending of taxpayer's existence, tax is computed in normal way (e.g., corporation is formed, or individual dies). The taxpayer's exemptions and credits are not prorated. In the case of a decedent, the income tax return can be filed as if the decedent lived throughout the entire tax year.

b. If the short period is due to a *change in taxable year*, taxable income generally must be **annualized**. However, a new subsidiary that has a short year because of being included in a consolidated return is not required to annualize.

   (1) When annualizing, an individual cannot use the tax tables and must itemize deductions. Personal exemptions must be prorated.
   (2) Taxable income is multiplied by 12 and divided by the number of months in short period.
   (3) The tax is computed and multiplied by the number of months in the short period, then divided by 12.

EXAMPLE

Pearl Corp. is a C Corporation that has been using a fiscal year ending June 30. It changes to a fiscal year ending September 30 for 2015. Pearl must file a tax return for its fiscal year ending June 30, 2015, as well as a tax return for its short period beginning July 1, 2015, and ending September 30, 2015. Pearl determines that its taxable income for the short period ending September 30 is $30,000. Because Pearl's short period is the result of a change in taxable year, Pearl must annualize its taxable income for the short period and determine its tax as follows:

Taxable income $30,000 × 12/3	=	$120,000
Tax on $120,000	=	$30,050
Tax for short period $30,050 × 3/12	=	$7,513

E. Tax Accounting Methods

Tax accounting methods often affect the period in which an item of income or deduction is recognized. Note that the classification of an item is not changed, only the time for its inclusion in the tax computation.

1. Cash method or accrual method is commonly used.

   a. **Cash method** recognizes income when first received or constructively received; expenses are deductible when paid.

      (1) **Constructive receipt** means that an item is unqualifiedly available without restriction (e.g., interest on bank deposit is income when credited to account).
      (2) Not all receipts are income (e.g., loan proceeds, return of investment); not all payments are deductible (e.g., loan repayment, expenditures benefiting future years generally must be capitalized and deducted over cost recovery period).

   b. Under the cash method, expenses are generally deductible when paid. Payment by check is considered payment so long as the check is honored by the bank. A payment by credit card is considered a payment at the time of the charge.

      (1) Generally, a capital expenditure or prepayment that results in a benefit that extends substantially beyond the end of the tax year does not result in an immediate deduction. However, a cash method taxpayer is not required to capitalize a payment so long as (1) the benefit does not extend beyond 12 months after the first date that the benefit is received, and (2) the benefit does not extend beyond the end of the taxable year following the taxable year in which payment is made.

EXAMPLE

On December 1, 2014, a calendar-year taxpayer pays a $10,000 property insurance premium with a 1-year term that begins on February 1, 2015. The amount paid must be capitalized and is not deductible for 2014 because the benefit attributable to the $10,000 payment extends beyond the end of the taxable year following the taxable year in which the payment is made. The premium will be deductible over the period to which it relates.

EXAMPLE

Assume the same facts as in the example above, except that the policy has a term beginning on December 15, 2014. The 12-month rule applies to the $10,000 payment because the benefit attributable to the payment extends neither more than 12 months beyond December 15, 2014, nor beyond the end of the taxable year following the taxable year in which the payment is made. Thus, the taxpayer is not required to capitalize the payment, and may deduct the $10,000 payment in 2014.

   (2) The 12-month rule in (1) above does not apply to prepaid interest, which generally must be deducted over the loan period to which it is allocated.

  c. The cash method cannot generally be used if inventories are necessary to clearly reflect income, and cannot generally be used by C corporations, partnerships that have a C corporation as a partner, tax shelters, and certain tax-exempt trusts. However, the following may use the cash method:

   (1) A qualified personal service corporation (e.g., corporation performing services in health, law, engineering, accounting, actuarial science, performing arts, or consulting) if at least 95% of stock is owned by specified shareholders including employees.

   (2) An entity (other than a tax shelter) if for every year it has average annual gross receipts of **$5 million or less** for any prior three-year period and provided it does not have inventories for sale to customers.

   (3) A **small business taxpayer** with average annual gross receipts of **$1 million or less** for any prior three-year period can use the cash method and is excepted from the requirements to account for inventories and use the accrual method for purchases and sales of merchandise.

   (4) A **small business taxpayer** is eligible to use the cash method of accounting if, in addition to having average gross receipts of more than $1 million and less than $10 million, the business meets any one of three requirements.

    (a) The principal business activity is **not** retailing, wholesaling, manufacturing, mining, publishing, or sound recording;

    (b) The principal business activity is the provision of services, or custom manufacturing; or

    (c) Regardless of the principal business activity, a taxpayer may use the cash method with respect to any separate business that satisfies (a) or (b) above.

   (5) A taxpayer using the accrual method who meets the requirements in (3) or (4) can change to the cash method but must treat merchandise inventory as a material or supply that is not incidental (i.e., only deductible in the year actually consumed or used in the taxpayer's business).

  d. **Accrual method** must be used by taxpayers (other than small business taxpayers) for purchases and sales when inventories are required to clearly reflect income.

   (1) **Income** is recognized when "all events" have occurred that fix the taxpayer's right to receive the item of income and the amount can be determined with reasonable accuracy.

   (2) An **expense** is deductible when "all events" have occurred that establish the fact of the liability and the amount can be determined with reasonable accuracy. The all-events test is not satisfied until **economic performance** has taken place.

    (a) For property or services to be provided **to the taxpayer,** economic performance occurs when the property or services are actually provided by the other party.

    (b) For property or services to be provided **by the taxpayer,** economic performance occurs when the property or services are physically provided by the taxpayer.

   (3) An exception to the economic performance rule treats certain **recurring items of expense** as incurred in advance of economic performance provided

    (a) The all-events test, without regard to economic performance, is satisfied during the tax year;

    (b) Economic performance occurs within a reasonable period (but in no event more than 8.5 months after the close of the tax year);

    (c) The item is recurring in nature and the taxpayer consistently treats items of the same type as incurred in the tax year in which the all-events test is met; and

    (d) Either the amount is not material or the accrual of the item in the year the all-events test is met results in a better matching against the income to which it relates.

2. **Special rules** regarding methods of accounting

    a. **Rents and royalties received in advance** are included in gross income in the year received under both the cash and accrual methods.

        (1) A **security deposit** is included in income when not returned to tenant.
        (2) An amount called a "security deposit" that may be used as final payment of rent is considered to be advance rent and included in income when received.

EXAMPLE

In 2015, a landlord signed a five-year lease. During 2015, the landlord received $5,000 for that year's rent, and $5,000 as advance rent for the last year (2019) of the lease. All $10,000 will be included in income for 2015.

---

    b. Dividends are included in gross income in the year received under both the cash and accrual methods.
    c. No advance deduction is generally allowed for accrual method taxpayers for estimated or contingent expenses; the obligation must be "fixed and determinable."

3. The **installment method** applies to gains (not losses) from the disposition of property where at least one payment is to be received after the year of sale. The installment method does not change the character of the gain to be reported (e.g., ordinary, capital, etc.), and is required unless the taxpayer makes a negative election to report the full amount of gain in year of sale.

    a. The installment method **cannot be used** for property held for sale in the ordinary course of business (except time-share units, residential lots, and property used or produced in farming), and cannot be used for sales of stock or securities traded on an established securities market.
    b. The amount to be reported in each year is determined by the formula

$$\frac{\text{Gross profit}}{\text{Total contract price}} \times \text{Amount received in year}$$

        (1) **Contract price** is the selling price reduced by the seller's liabilities that are assumed by the buyer, to the extent not in excess of the seller's basis in the property.

EXAMPLE

Taxpayer sells property with a basis of $80,000 to buyer for a selling price of $150,000. As part of the purchase price, buyer agrees to assume a $50,000 mortgage on the property and pay the remaining $100,000 in 10 equal annual installments together with adequate interest.

  The contract price is $100,000 ($150,000 – $50,000); the gross profit is $70,000 ($150,000 – $80,000); and the gross profit ratio is 70% ($70,000 ÷ $100,000). Thus, $7,000 of each $10,000 payment is reported as gain from the sale.

EXAMPLE

Assume the same facts as above except that the seller's basis is $30,000. The contract price is $120,000 ($150,000 – mortgage assumed but only to extent of seller's basis of $30,000); the gross profit is $120,000 ($150,000 – $30,000); and the gross profit ratio is 100% ($120,000 ÷ $120,000). Thus, 100% of each $10,000 payment is reported as gain from the sale. In addition, the amount by which the assumed mortgage exceeds the seller's basis ($20,000) is deemed to be a payment in year of sale. Since the gross profit ratio is 100%, all $20,000 is reported as gain in the year the mortgage is assumed.

---

(2) Any depreciation recapture under Sections 1245, 1250, and 291 must be included in income in the year of sale. Amount of recapture included in income is treated as an increase in the basis of the property for purposes of determining the gross profit ratio. Remainder of gain is spread over installment payments.

EXAMPLE

Baxter sells equipment with an adjusted basis of $50,000 to a buyer for $50,000 cash plus a $50,000 interest-bearing note to be paid next year. The equipment had originally cost $90,000, and Baxter had deducted depreciation of $40,000 on the equipment. Baxter realizes a gain of $100,000 – $50,000 = $50,000 on the installment sale, and must immediately recognize gain to the extent of Sec. 1245 depreciation recapture of $40,000, which is not eligible for installment reporting. The gross profit ratio is determined after adding the $40,000 of recapture to the $50,000 of adjusted basis, resulting in a gross profit ratio of 10% [$100,000 – $90,000)/$100,000]. As a result, the $40,000 of depreciation recapture plus 10% × $50,000 cash payment = $5,000 must be recognized this year, while the remaining 10% × $50,000 = $5,000 of gain will be recognized next year when payment on the note is received.

---

(3) The receipt of readily tradable debt or debt that is payable on demand is considered the receipt of a payment for purposes of the installment method. Additionally, if installment obligations are pledged as security for a loan, the net proceeds of the loan are treated as payments received on the installment obligations.

(4) Installment obligations arising from non dealer sales of property used in the taxpayer's trade or business or held for the production of rental income (e.g., factory building, warehouse, office building, apartment building) are subject to an interest charge on the tax that is deferred on such sales to the extent that the amount of deferred payments arising from all dispositions of such property during a taxable year and outstanding as of the close of the taxable year exceeds $5,000,000. This provision does not apply to installment sales of property if the sales price does not exceed $150,000, to sales of personal use property, and to sales of farm property.

4. **Percentage-of-completion** method can be used for contracts that are not completed within the year they are started.

   a. Percentage-of-completion method recognizes income each year based on the percentage of the contract completed that year.
   b. Taxpayer may elect not to recognize income or account for costs from a contract for a tax year if less than 10% of the estimated total contract costs have been incurred as of the end of the year.

NOW REVIEW MULTIPLE-CHOICE QUESTIONS 50 THROUGH 59

F. Business Income and Deductions

1. **Gross income** for a business includes sales less cost of goods sold plus other income. In computing cost of goods sold

   a. Inventory is generally valued at (1) cost, or (2) market, whichever is lower
   b. Specific identification, FIFO, and LIFO are allowed
   c. If LIFO is used for taxes, it must also be used on books
   d. Lower of cost or market cannot be used with LIFO

2. All **ordinary** (customary and not a capital expenditure) and **necessary** (appropriate and helpful) **expenses** incurred in a trade or business are deductible.

   a. Business expenses that violate public policy (fines or illegal kickbacks) are not deductible.
   b. No deduction or credit is allowed for any amount paid or incurred in carrying on a trade or business that consists of trafficking in controlled substances. However, this limitation does not alter the definition of gross income (i.e., sales less cost of goods sold).
   c. Business expenses must be reasonable.

      (1) If salaries are excessive (unreasonable compensation), they may be disallowed as a deduction to the extent unreasonable.

(2) Reasonableness of compensation issue generally arises only when the relationship between the employer and employee exceeds that of the normal employer-employee relationship (e.g., employee is also a shareholder).

(3) Use test of what another enterprise would pay under similar circumstances to an unrelated employee.

d. In the case of an individual, any charge (including taxes) for basic local telephone service with respect to the **first telephone line** provided to any residence of the taxpayer shall be treated as a nondeductible personal expense. Disallowance does not apply to charges for long-distance calls, charges for equipment rental, and optional services provided by a telephone company, or charges attributable to additional telephone lines to a taxpayer's residence other than the first telephone line.

e. **Uniform capitalization rules** (UNICAP) generally require that all costs incurred (both direct and indirect) in manufacturing or constructing real or personal property, or in purchasing or holding property for sale, must be capitalized as part of the cost of the property.

   (1) These costs become part of the basis of the property and are recovered through depreciation or amortization, or are included in inventory and recovered through cost of goods sold as an offset to selling price.

   (2) The rules apply to inventory, property other than inventory produced or held for sale to customers, and to assets or improvements to assets constructed by a taxpayer for the taxpayer's own use in a trade or business or in an activity engaged in for profit.

   (3) Taxpayers subject to the rules are required to capitalize not only direct costs, but also most indirect costs that benefit the assets produced or acquired for resale, including general, administrative, and overhead costs.

   (4) Retailers and wholesalers must include in inventory all costs incident to purchasing and storing inventory such as wages of employees responsible for purchasing inventory, handling, processing, repackaging and assembly of goods, and off-site storage costs. These rules do not apply to "small retailers and wholesalers" (i.e., a taxpayer who acquires personal property for resale if the taxpayer's average annual gross receipts for the three preceding taxable years do not exceed $10,000,000).

   (5) Interest must be capitalized if the debt is incurred or continued to finance the construction or production of real property, property with a recovery period of twenty years, property that takes more than two years to produce, or property with a production period exceeding one year and a cost exceeding $1 million.

   (6) The UNICAP rules do not apply to advertising, selling, and research and experimentation expenditures, mine development and exploration costs, property held for personal use, and to freelance authors, photographers, and artists whose personal efforts create the product.

f. **Business meals, entertainment, and travel**

   (1) Receipts must be maintained for all lodging expenditures and for other expenditures of **$75** or more except transportation expenditures where receipts are not readily available.

   (2) Adequate contemporaneous records must be maintained for business meals and entertainment to substantiate the amount of expense, for example, who, when, where, and why (the 4 W's).

   (3) Business meals and entertainment must be directly related or associated with the active conduct of a trade or business to be deductible. The taxpayer or a representative must be present to satisfy this requirement.

   (4) The amount of the otherwise allowable deduction for business meals or entertainment must be reduced by 50%. This **50% reduction rule** applies to all food, beverage, and entertainment costs (even though incurred in the course of travel away from home) after determining the amount otherwise deductible. The 50% reduction rule will not apply if

      (a) The full value of the meal or entertainment is included in the recipient's income or excluded as a fringe benefit.

      (b) An employee is reimbursed for the cost of a meal or entertainment (the 50% reduction rule applies to the party making the reimbursement).

      (c) The cost is for a traditional employer-paid employee recreation expense (e.g., a company Christmas party).

      (d) The cost is for samples and other promotional activities made available to the public.

      (e) The expense is for a sports event that qualifies as a charitable fund-raising event.

      (f) The cost is for meals or entertainment sold for full consideration.

   (5) The cost of a ticket to any entertainment activity is limited (prior to the 50% reduction rule) to its face value.

   (6) No deduction is generally allowed for expenses with respect to an entertainment, recreational, or amusement facility.

(a) Entertainment facilities include yachts, hunting lodges, fishing camps, swimming pools, etc.

(b) If the facility or club is used for a business purpose, the related out-of-pocket expenditures are deductible even though depreciation, etc. of the facility is not deductible.

(7) No deduction is allowed for dues paid to country clubs, golf and athletic clubs, airline clubs, hotel clubs, and luncheon clubs. Dues are generally deductible if paid to professional organizations (accounting, medical, and legal associations), business leagues, trade associations, chambers of commerce, boards of trade, and civic and public service organizations (Kiwanis, Lions, Elks).

(8) **Transportation and travel expenses** are deductible if incurred in the active conduct of a trade or business.

    (a) Deductible transportation expenses include local transportation between two job locations, but excludes commuting expenses between residence and job.

    (b) Deductible travel expenses are those incurred while temporarily "away from tax home" overnight including meals, lodging, transportation, and expenses incident to travel (clothing care, etc.).

        [1] Travel expenses to and from domestic destination are fully deductible if business is the primary purpose of trip.

        [2] Actual automobile expenses can be deducted, or taxpayers can use standard mileage rate of 57.5¢ per mile beginning January 1, 2015, for all business miles (plus parking and tolls).

        [3] No deduction is allowed for travel as a form of education. This rule applies when a travel expense would otherwise be deductible only on the ground that the travel itself serves educational purposes.

        [4] No deduction is allowed for expenses incurred in attending a convention, seminar, or similar meeting for investment purposes.

g. Deductions for **business gifts** are limited to **$25** per recipient each year.

(1) Advertising and promotional gifts costing $4 or less are not limited.

(2) Gifts of tangible personal property costing $400 or less are deductible if awarded as an employee achievement award for length of service or safety achievement.

(3) Gifts of tangible personal property costing $1,600 or less are deductible if awarded as an employee achievement award under a qualified plan for length of service or safety achievement.

    (a) Plan must be written and nondiscriminatory.

    (b) Average cost of all items awarded under the plan during the tax year must not exceed $400.

h. **Bad debts** are generally deducted in the year they become worthless.

(1) There must have been a valid "debtor-creditor" relationship.

(2) A **business bad debt** is one that is incurred in the trade or business of the lender.

    (a) Deductible against ordinary income (toward AGI)

    (b) Deduction allowed for partial worthlessness

(3) Business bad debts must be deducted under the specific charge-off method (the reserve method generally cannot be used).

    (a) A deduction is allowed when a specific debt becomes partially or totally worthless.

    (b) A bad debt deduction is available for accounts or notes receivable only if the amount owed has already been included in gross income for the current or a prior taxable year. Since receivables for services rendered of a **cash method** taxpayer have not yet been included in gross income, the receivables cannot be deducted when they become uncollectible.

(4) A **nonbusiness bad debt** (not incurred in trade or business) can only be deducted

    (a) If totally worthless

    (b) As a short-term capital loss

(5) Guarantor of debt who has to pay takes same deduction as if the loss were from a direct loan

    (a) Business bad debt if guarantee related to trade, business, or employment

    (b) Nonbusiness bad debt if guarantee entered into for profit but not related to trade or business

i. A **hobby** is an activity not engaged in for profit (e.g., stamp or card collecting engaged in for recreation and personal pleasure).

(1) Special rules generally limit the deduction of hobby expenses to the amount of hobby gross income. No net loss can generally be deducted for hobby activities.
(2) Hobby expenses are deductible as itemized deductions in the following order:

    (a) First deduct taxes, interest, and casualty losses pertaining to the hobby.
    (b) Then other hobby operating expenses are deductible to the extent they do not exceed hobby gross income reduced by the amounts deducted in (a). Out-of-pocket expenses are deducted before depreciation. These hobby expenses are aggregated with other miscellaneous itemized deductions that are subject to the 2% of AGI floor.

EXAMPLE

Glenn is an engineer who races a Formula Three car as a hobby. This year Glenn received a salary of $97,000 from his employer and won $3,000 in various car races, while incurring $9,000 of out-of-pocket expenses in his racing hobby. Glenn must include the $3,000 of prizes in his gross income, raising his AGI to $100,000. His $9,000 of hobby expenses are only deductible to the extent of $3,000. Assuming that Glenn itemizes his deductions but has no other miscellaneous itemized deductions, his hobby expenses would result in a deduction of $3,000 – (2% × $100,000) = $1,000.

---

(3) An activity is presumed to be for profit (not a hobby) if it produces a net profit in at least three out of five consecutive years (two out of seven years for horses).

NOW REVIEW MULTIPLE-CHOICE QUESTIONS 60 THROUGH 69

---

3. **Net operating loss**

a. An NOL is generally a business loss but may occur even if an individual is not engaged in a separate trade or business (e.g., an NOL created by a personal casualty loss).
b. An NOL may be carried **back two years** and carried **forward twenty years** to offset taxable income in those years.

    (1) Carryback is first made to the second preceding year.
    (2) Taxpayer may elect not to carry back and only carry forward twenty years.
    (3) A three-year carryback period is permitted for the portion of the NOL that relates to casualty and theft losses of individual taxpayers, and to NOLs that are attributable to presidentially declared disasters and are incurred by taxpayers engaged in farming or by a small business.
    (4) A *small business* is any trade or business (including one conducted by a corporation, partnership, or sole proprietorship) with average annual gross receipts of $5 million or less for the three-year tax period preceding the loss year.

c. The following cannot be included in the computation of an NOL:

    (1) Any NOL carryforward or carryback from another year
    (2) Excess of capital losses over capital gains. Excess of nonbusiness capital losses over nonbusiness capital gains even if overall gains exceed losses
    (3) Personal and dependency exemptions
    (4) Excess of nonbusiness deductions (usually itemized deductions) over nonbusiness income

        (a) The standard deduction is treated as a nonbusiness deduction.
        (b) Contributions to a self-employed retirement plan are considered nonbusiness deductions.
        (c) Casualty losses (even if personal) are considered business deductions.
        (d) Dividends and interest are nonbusiness income; salary and rent are business income.

    (5) The domestic production activities deduction (DPAD).
    (6) Any remaining loss is an NOL and must be carried back first, unless election is made to carry forward only.

EXAMPLE

George, single with no dependents, started his own delivery business and incurred a loss from the business for 2014. In addition, he earned interest on personal bank deposits of $1,800. After deducting his itemized deductions for interest and taxes of $9,000, and his personal exemption of $3,950, the loss shown on George's Form 1040 was $20,850. George's net operating loss would be computed as follows:

Taxable income		$(20,850)
Nonbusiness deductions	$9,000	
Nonbusiness income	−1,800	7,200
Personal exemption		3,950
Net operating loss		$(9,700)

NOW REVIEW MULTIPLE-CHOICE QUESTIONS 70 THROUGH 72

---

4. Limitation on deductions for **business use of home**. To be deductible

   a. A portion of the home must be used exclusively and regularly as the *principal place of business,* or as a meeting place for patients, clients, or customers.

      (1) Exclusive use rule does not apply to the portion of the home used as a day care center and to a place of regular storage of business inventory or product samples if the home is the sole fixed location of a trade or business selling products at retail or wholesale.
      (2) If an employee, the exclusive use must be for the convenience of the employer.
      (3) A home office qualifies as a taxpayer's *principal place of business* if

         (a) It is the place where the primary income-generating functions of the trade or business are performed; or
         (b) The office is used to conduct administrative or management activities of the taxpayer's business, and there is no other fixed location of the business where substantial administrative or management activities are performed. Activities that are administrative or managerial in nature include billing customers, clients, or patients; keeping books and records; ordering supplies; setting up appointments; and forwarding orders or writing reports.

   b. Deduction is limited to the excess of gross income derived from the business use of the home over deductions otherwise allowable for taxes, interest, and casualty losses.
   c. Any business expenses not allocable to the use of the home (e.g., wages, transportation, supplies) must be deducted before home use expenses.
   d. Any business use of home expenses that are disallowed due to the gross income limitation can be carried forward and deducted in future years subject to the same restrictions.

EXAMPLE

Taxpayer uses 10% of his home exclusively for business purposes. Gross income from his business totaled $750, and he incurred the following expenses:

	Total	10% Business
Interest	4,000	$400
Taxes	2,500	250
Utilities, insurance	1,500	150
Depreciation	2,000	200

Since total deductions for business use of the home are limited to business gross income, the taxpayer can deduct the following for business use of his home: $400 interest; $250 taxes; $100 utilities and insurance; and $0 depreciation (operating expenses such as utilities and insurance must be deducted before depreciation). The remaining $50 of utilities and insurance, and $200 of depreciation can be carried forward and deducted in future years subject to the same restrictions.

e. For tax years beginning after 2012, a taxpayer may elect to use an *optional safe harbor method* for deducting business use of home expenses. Under this method, a prescribed rate of $5 is multiplied by the square footage devoted to business use (limited to 300 square feet). The business use of home deduction (maximum of $1,500) is then limited to business gross income less business expenses not allocable to the use of the home. No depreciation deduction for the business use of the home is allowed for a year in which the safe harbor method is used.

5. Loss deductions incurred in a trade or business, or in the production of income, are limited to the amount a taxpayer has "**at risk**."

   a. Applies to all activities except the leasing of personal property by a closely held corporation (5 or fewer individuals own more than 50% of stock)
   b. Applies to individuals and closely held regular corporations
   c. Amount "at risk" includes

      (1) The cash and adjusted basis of property contributed by the taxpayer, and
      (2) Liabilities for which the taxpayer is personally liable; excludes nonrecourse debt.

   d. For real estate activities, a taxpayer's amount at risk includes "qualified" nonrecourse financing secured by the real property used in the activity.

      (1) Nonrecourse financing is qualified if it is borrowed from a lender engaged in the business of making loans (e.g., bank, savings and loan) provided that the lender is not the promoter or seller of the property or a party related to either; or is borrowed from or guaranteed by any federal, state, or local government or instrumentality thereof.
      (2) Nonrecourse financing obtained from a qualified lender who has an equity interest in the venture is treated as an amount at risk, as long as the terms of the financing are commercially reasonable.
      (3) The nonrecourse financing must not be convertible, and no person can be personally liable for repayment.

   e. Excess losses can be carried over to subsequent years (no time limit) and deducted when the "at risk" amount has been increased.
   f. Previously allowed losses will be recaptured as income if the amount at risk is reduced below zero.

6. **Losses and credits from passive activities** may generally only be used to offset income from (or tax allocable to) passive activities. Passive losses may not be used to offset active income (e.g., wages, salaries, professional fees, etc.) or portfolio income (e.g., interest, dividends, annuities, royalties, etc.).

EXAMPLE

Ken has salary income, a loss from a partnership in whose business Ken does not materially participate, and income from a limited partnership. Ken may offset the partnership loss against the income from the limited partnership, but not against his salary income.

EXAMPLE

Robin has dividend and interest income of $40,000 and a passive activity loss of $30,000. The passive activity loss cannot be offset against the dividend and interest income.

---

   a. Applies to individuals, estates, trusts, closely held C corporations, and personal service corporations

      (1) A closely held C corporation is one with five or fewer shareholders owning more than 50% of stock.
      (2) Personal service corporation is an incorporated service business with more than 10% of its stock owned by shareholder-employees.

   b. **Passive activity** is any activity that involves the conduct of a trade or business in which the taxpayer does "not materially participate," any rental activity, and any limited partnership interest.

(1) Material participation is the taxpayer's involvement in an activity on a regular, continuous, and substantial basis considering such factors as time devoted, physical duties performed, and knowledge of or experience in the business.

(2) Passive activity does not include (1) a working interest in any oil or gas property that a taxpayer owns directly or through an entity that does not limit the taxpayer's liability, (2) operating a hotel or transient lodging if significant services are provided, or (3) operating a short-term equipment rental business.

c. **Losses** from passive activities may be deducted only against income from passive activities.

(1) If there is insufficient passive activity income to absorb passive activity losses, the excess losses are carried forward indefinitely to future years.

(2) If there is insufficient passive activity income in subsequent years to fully absorb the loss carryforwards, the unused losses from a passive activity may be deducted when the taxpayer's entire interest in the activity that gave rise to the unused losses is finally disposed of in a fully taxable transaction.

(3) Other dispositions

(a) A transfer of a taxpayer's interest in a passive activity by reason of the taxpayer's death results in suspended losses being allowed (to the decedent) to the extent they exceed the amount of the step-up in basis allowed.

(b) If the disposition is by gift, the suspended losses are added to the basis of the gift property. If less than 100% of an interest is transferred by gift, an allocable portion of the suspended losses is added to the basis of the gift.

(c) An installment sale of a passive interest triggers the recognition of suspended losses in the ratio that the gain recognized in each year bears to the total gain on sale.

(d) If a formerly passive activity becomes an active one, suspended losses are allowed against income from the now active business (if the activity remains the same).

d. **Credits** from passive activities can only be used to offset the tax liability attributable to passive activity income.

(1) Excess credits are carried forward indefinitely (subject to limited carryback during the phase-in period).

(2) Excess credits (unlike losses) cannot be used in full in the year in which the taxpayer's entire passive activity interest is disposed of. Instead, excess credits continue to be carried forward.

(3) Credits allowable under the passive activity limitation rules are also subject to the general business credit limitation.

e. Although a **rental activity** is defined as a passive activity regardless of the property owner's participation in the operation of the rental property, a special rule permits an individual to offset up to $25,000 of income that is **not** from passive activities by losses or credits from rental real estate if the individual **actively participates** in the rental real estate activity.

(1) "Active participation" is less stringent than "material participation" and is met if the taxpayer personally operates the rental property; or, if a rental agent operates the property, the taxpayer participates in management decisions or arranges for others to provide services.

(2) An individual is not considered to actively participate in a rental real estate activity unless the individual's interest in the activity (including any interest owned by the individual's spouse) was at least 10% of the value of all interests in the activity throughout the year.

(3) The active participation requirement must be met in both the year that the loss arises and the year in which the loss is allowed.

(4) For losses, the $25,000 amount is reduced by 50% of AGI in excess of $100,000 and fully phased out when AGI exceeds $150,000. For this purpose, AGI is computed before including taxable social security, before deducting IRA contributions, and before the exclusion of interest from Series EE bonds used for higher education.

(5) For low-income housing and rehabilitation credits, the $25,000 amount is reduced by 50% of AGI in excess of $200,000 and fully phased out when AGI exceeds $250,000.

f. If a taxpayer meets certain eligibility requirements, losses and credits from rental real estate activities in which the taxpayer materially participates are not subject to the passive loss limitations. This provision applies to individuals and closely held C corporations.

(1) Individuals are eligible if (a) more than half of all the personal services they perform during the year are for real property trades or businesses in which they materially participate, and (b) they perform more than 750 hours of service per year in those real estate activities. On a joint return, this relief is available if either spouse separately satisfies the requirements.

(2) Closely held C corporations are eligible if more than 50% of their gross receipts for the taxable year are derived from real property trades or businesses in which the corporation materially participated.

(3) Suspended losses from any rental real property that is not treated as passive by the above provision are treated as losses from a former passive activity. The deductibility of these suspended losses is limited to income from the activity; they are not allowed to offset other income.

g. The passive activity limitation rules do not apply to losses disallowed under the at risk rules.

> **NOW REVIEW MULTIPLE-CHOICE QUESTIONS 73 THROUGH 77**

G. Depreciation, Depletion, and Amortization

Depreciation is an allowance for the exhaustion, wear and tear of property used in a trade or business, or of property held for the production of income. The depreciation class of property is generally determined by reference to its Asset Depreciation Range (ADR) guideline class. Taxpayers must determine annual deductions based on the applicable property class, depreciation method, and averaging convention.

1. For property placed in service prior to 1981, the basis of property reduced by salvage value was recovered over its useful life using the straight-line, declining balance, or sum-of-the-years' digits method. Whether an accelerated method of depreciation could be used depended on the classification and useful life of the property, and whether it was new or used when acquired. The Accelerated Cost Recovery System (ACRS) was used to recover the basis of depreciable property placed in service after 1980 and before 1987.

2. **Modified Accelerated Cost Recovery System (MACRS)**

   a. MACRS is **mandatory** for most depreciable property placed in service **after 1986**.

   b. Salvage value is completely ignored under MACRS; the method of cost recovery and the recovery period are the same for both new and used property.

   c. **Recovery property** includes all property other than land, intangible assets, and property the taxpayer elects to depreciate under a method not expressed in terms of years (e.g., units of production or income forecast methods). Recovery property placed in service after 1986 is divided into six classes of personal property based on ADR midpoint life and into two classes of real property. Each class is assigned a recovery period and a depreciation method. Recovery deductions for the first six classes are based on the declining balance method, switching to the straight-line method to maximize deductions.

      (1) **3-year, 200% class.** Includes property with an ADR midpoint of four years or less (except for autos and light trucks) and certain horses

      (2) **5-year, 200% class.** Includes property with an ADR midpoint of more than four and less than ten years. Also included are autos and light trucks, computers and peripheral equipment, office machinery (typewriters, calculators, copiers, etc.)

      (3) **7-year, 200% class.** Includes property with an ADR midpoint of at least ten and less than sixteen years. Also included are property having no ADR midpoint and not classified elsewhere, and office furniture and fixtures (desks, files, etc.)

      (4) **10-year, 200% class.** Includes property with an ADR midpoint of at least sixteen and less than twenty years

      (5) **15-year, 150% class.** Includes property with an ADR midpoint of at least twenty years and less than twenty-five years

      (6) **20-year, 150% class.** Includes property with an ADR midpoint of twenty-five years or more, other than real property with an ADR midpoint of 27.5 years or more

      (7) **27 1/2-year, straight-line class.** Includes residential rental property (i.e., a building or structure with 80% or more of its rental income from dwelling units)

      (8) **39-year, straight-line class.** Includes any property that is neither residential real property nor property with a class life of less than 27.5 years

d. Instead of using the declining balance method for three-year through twenty-year property, taxpayers can elect to use the straight-line method over the MACRS class life. This is an annual class-by-class election.

e. Instead of using the 200% declining balance method for three-year through ten-year property, taxpayers can elect to use the 150% declining balance method. This is an annual class-by-class election.

f. An **alternative depreciation system** (ADS) provides for straight-line depreciation over the property's ADS class life (twelve years for personal property with no ADS class life, and forty years for real property).

   (1) A taxpayer may elect to use the alternative system for any class of property placed in service during a taxable year. For real property, the election is made on a property-by-property basis.

   (2) Once made, the election is irrevocable and continues to apply to that property for succeeding years, but does not apply to similar property placed in service in a subsequent year, unless a new election is made.

   (3) The alternative system must be used for foreign use property, property used 50% or more for personal use, and for purposes of computing earnings and profits.

g. An **averaging convention** is used to compute depreciation for the taxable year in which property is placed in service or disposed of under both the regular MACRS and alternative depreciation system.

   (1) **Personal property** is treated as placed in service or disposed of at the midpoint of the taxable year, resulting in a **half-year** of depreciation for the year in which the property is placed in service or disposed of. However, no depreciation is allowed for personal property disposed of in the same taxable year in which it was placed in service.

EXAMPLE

A calendar-year taxpayer purchased machinery (5-year, 200% class) for $10,000 in January 2015. Because of the averaging convention, the MACRS depreciation for 2015 will be ($10,000 × 40% × 1/2) = $2,000.

---

   (2) A **midquarter** convention must be used if more than 40% of all personal property is placed in service during the last quarter of the taxpayer's taxable year. Under this convention, property is treated as placed in service (or disposed of) in the middle of the quarter in which placed in service (or disposed of).

EXAMPLE

In January 2015 a calendar-year taxpayer purchased used machinery for $10,000. In December 2015 the taxpayer purchased additional used machinery for $30,000. All machinery was assigned to the 5-year, 200% class. No other depreciable assets were purchased during the year.

   Since the machinery placed in service during the last three months of the year exceeded 40% of the depreciable basis of all personal property placed in service during the taxable year, all machinery must be depreciated using the mid-quarter convention. The taxpayer may claim 3 1/2 quarters depreciation on the machinery acquired in January ($10,000 × 40% × 3.5/4 = $3,500), and only 1/2 quarter of depreciation for the machinery acquired in December ($30,000 × 40% × .5/4 = $1,500).

---

   (3) **Real property** is treated as placed in service or disposed of in the middle of a month, resulting in a **half-month** of depreciation for the month disposed of or placed in service.

EXAMPLE

A calendar-year taxpayer purchased a warehouse (39-year property) for $150,000 and placed it in service on March 26, 2015. Because of the mid-month convention, the depreciation for 2015 will be ($150,000 × 9.5/468 months) = $3,045.

---

h. **Bonus (additional first-year) depreciation** equal to **50%** of the adjusted basis of qualified property is available for qualifying property acquired after December 31, 2007, and placed in service before January, 1, 2015.

(1) *Qualified property* includes new MACRS property with a recovery period of 20 years or less (most tangible personal property), off-the-shelf computer software, and qualified leasehold property. Original use of the property must begin with the taxpayer, and the property's business use must exceed 50%. Property with a long production period is property that has a production period exceeding one year and a cost exceeding $1 million.

(2) Bonus depreciation is computed before regular MACRS depreciation, but after any amount expensed under Sec. 179.

(3) There is no annual dollar limit on the amount of bonus depreciation that can be taken, nor is it affected by a short tax year, or the date during the year that the property was placed in service.

(4) The bonus depreciation deduction and regular MACRS depreciation on bonus depreciation property are allowed in full for AMT purposes (i.e., there is no AMT depreciation adjustment).

(5) A taxpayer may elect not to take bonus depreciation for any class of property (e.g., 5-year, 7-year) for a tax year.

EXAMPLE

During August 2014, a taxpayer purchases new 5-year MACRS property for $2,000. The additional first-year depreciation would be $2,000 × 50% = $1,000. Regular MACRS deprecation for 2014 using the 200% declining balance and the half-year convention would be ($2,000 – $1,000) × 2/5 × 1/2 = $200. As a result, the total deduction for this property for 2014 would be $1,000 + $200 = $1,200.

EXAMPLE

A taxpayer purchases $500,000 of new 5-year MACRS property during March 2014 and elects to expense $100,000 of its cost under Sec. 179. Bonus depreciation would be ($500,000 – $100,000) × 50%= $200,000. MACRS depreciation using the 200% declining balance method and the half-year convention would be [$500,000 – ($100,000 + $200,000)] × 2/5 ×1/2= $40,000. Thus, the total deduction for this property for 2014 would be $100,000 +$200,000 + $40,000 = $340,000.

---

i. The cost of **leasehold improvements** made by a lessee generally must be recovered over the MACRS recovery period of the underlying property without regard to the lease term. For *qualified leasehold improvement property* (i.e., an improvement to the interior portion of nonresidential real property), *qualified restaurant property, and qualified retail improvement property* generally placed in service after October 22, 2004, and before January 1, 2015, cost is recovered over a 15-year recovery period using the straight-line method and half-year convention (unless the mid-quarter convention applies). Upon the expiration of the lease, any unrecovered adjusted basis in abandoned leasehold improvements is treated as a loss.

j. **Sec. 179 expense election.** A taxpayer (other than a trust or estate) may annually elect to treat the cost of qualifying depreciable property as an expense rather than a capital expenditure.

(1) Qualifying property is generally recovery property that is new or used tangible personal property acquired by purchase from an unrelated party for use in the active conduct of a trade or business. Off-the-shelf computer software with a useful life of more than one year is treated as qualifying property that may be expensed.

(2) For tax years beginning in 2010 through 2014, a taxpayer can elect to treat qualified real property as Sec. 179 property. Qualified real property generally consists of qualified leasehold improvements, qualified restaurant property, and qualified retail improvement property.

(3) The maximum cost that can be annually expensed is **$500,000** for a tax year beginning in 2014 ($25,000 for 2015), but is reduced dollar-for-dollar by the cost of qualifying property that is placed in service during the taxable year that exceeds $2 million ($200,000 for 2015).

(4) The amount of expense deduction is further limited to the taxable income derived from the active conduct by the taxpayer of any trade or business. Any expense deduction disallowed by this limitation is carried forward to the succeeding taxable year.

(5) If property is converted to nonbusiness use at any time, the excess of the amount expensed over the MACRS deductions that would have been allowed must be recaptured as ordinary income in the year of conversion.

(6) The amount of cost that can be expensed under Sec. 179 for a sport utility vehicle (SUV) is limited to $25,000. This limitation applies to an SUV that is exempt from the limitations in k., below, because its gross vehicle weight exceeds 6,000 pounds.

k. Special restriction apply to the depreciation and expensing of passenger automobiles with a gross vehicle weight (GVW) of 6,000 pounds or less. For a passenger automobile first placed in service during 2014, the amount of MACRS (including expensing) deductions is limited to $3,160 in the year placed in service, $5,100 for the second year, $3,050 for the third year, and $1,875 for each year thereafter. These amounts are indexed for inflation.

(1) These limits are reduced to reflect personal use (e.g., if auto is used 30% for personal use and 70% for business use, limits are [70% × $3,160] = $2,212 for the year of acquisition, [70% × $5,100] = $3,570 for the second year, etc.).

(2) If automobile is not used more than 50% for business use, MACRS is limited to straight-line depreciation over five years.

(a) Use of the automobile for income-producing purposes is not counted in determining whether the more than 50% test is met, but is considered in determining the amount of allowable depreciation.

> **EXAMPLE**
>
> An automobile is used 40% in a business, 35% for production of income, and 25% for personal use. The 200% declining balance method cannot be used because business use is not more than 50%. However, depreciation limited to the straight-line method is allowed based on 75% of use.

(b) If the more than 50% test is met in year of acquisition, but business use subsequently falls to 50% or less, MACRS deductions in excess of five-year straight-line method are recaptured.

(3) For passenger automobiles with a GVW of 6,000 pounds or less that qualify for bonus depreciation, the first year depreciation limit is increased by $8,000, to $11,160. To qualify, the auto must be new and its original use must begin with the taxpayer after December 31, 2007, and before January 1, 2015, and the auto must be predominantly used for business. The $8,000 increase applies for qualifying automobiles unless the taxpayer elects not to use bonus depreciation.

> **EXAMPLE**
>
> An individual purchased a new automobile and places it in service during 2014. If the first year depreciation limit otherwise would be $3,160, it is increased by $8,000 so that the maximum depreciation for 2014 would be $11,160.

> **EXAMPLE**
>
> Assume the same facts as in the preceding example except that the individual uses the auto 70% for business and 30% for personal use. The maximum depreciation for 2014 would be $11,160 × 70% = $7,812.

l. Transportation property other than automobiles (e.g., airplanes, trucks, boats, etc.), entertainment property (including real property), and any computer or peripheral equipment not used exclusively at a regular business establishment are subject to the same more than 50% business use requirement and consequent restrictions on depreciation as are applicable to automobiles.

(1) Failure to use these assets more than 50% for business purposes will limit the deductions to the straight-line method.

(2) If the more than 50% test is met in year of acquisition, but business use subsequently falls to 50% or less, MACRS deductions in excess of the applicable straight-line method are recaptured.

3. **Depletion**

a. Depletion is allowed on timber, minerals, oil, and gas, and other exhaustible natural resources or wasting assets.

b. There are two basic methods to compute depletion for the year.

(1) **Cost** method divides the adjusted basis by the total number of recoverable units and multiplies by the number of units sold (or payment received for, if cash basis) during the year.

   (a) Adjusted basis is cost less accumulated depletion (not below zero).

EXAMPLE

Land cost $10,050,000 of which $50,000 is the residual value of the land. There are 1,000,000 barrels of oil recoverable. If 10,000 barrels were sold, cost depletion would be ($10,000,000 ÷ 1,000,000 barrels) × 10,000 = $100,000.

---

(2) **Percentage** method uses a specified percentage of gross income from the property during the year.

   (a) Deduction may not exceed 50% of the taxable income (before depletion) from the property.
   (b) May be taken even after costs have been recovered and there is no basis
   (c) May be used for domestic oil and gas wells by "independent producer" or royalty owner; cannot be used for timber
   (d) The percentage is a statutory amount and generally ranges from 5% to 20% depending on the mineral.

4. **Amortization** is allowed for several special types of capital expenditures

a. **Business start-up costs** (e.g., survey of potential markets, expenses of securing prospective distributors or suppliers, advertising, employee training) are deductible in the year paid or incurred if the taxpayer is currently in a similar line of business as the start-up business. If not in a similar line of business and the new business is

(1) Not acquired by the taxpayer, then start-up costs are not deductible.

(2) Acquired by the taxpayer, start-up costs must be capitalized. However, a taxpayer may elect to deduct up to $5,000 of start-up costs for the tax year in which business begins. The $5,000 amount must be reduced (but not below zero) by the amount by which start-up costs exceed $50,000. Remaining expenditures are deducted ratably over the 180-month period beginning with the month in which business begins.

b. Pollution control facilities can be amortized over sixty months if installed on property that was placed in operation prior to 1976. The pollution control investment must not increase output, capacity, or the useful life of the asset.

c. Patents and copyrights may be amortized over their useful life.

(1) Seventeen years for patents; life of author plus fifty years for copyrights
(2) If become obsolete early, deduct in that year

d. Research and experimental expenses may be amortized over sixty months or more. Alternatively, may be expensed at election of taxpayer if done so for year in which such expenses are first incurred or paid.

e. Intangible assets for which the Code does not specifically provide for amortization are amortizable over their useful lives.

5. **Sec. 197 intangibles**

a. Most **acquired intangible assets** are to be amortized over a fifteen-year period, beginning with the month in which the intangible is acquired (the treatment of self-created intangible assets is not affected). Sec. 197 applies to most intangibles acquired either in stand-alone transactions or as part of the acquisition of a trade or business.

b. An amortizable Sec. 197 intangible is any qualifying intangible asset which is acquired by the taxpayer, and which is held in connection with the conduct of a trade or business. Qualifying intangibles include goodwill, going concern value, workforce, information base, know-how, customer-based intangibles, government licenses and permits, franchises, trademarks, and trade names.

   c. Certain assets qualify as Sec. 197 intangibles only if acquired in connection with the acquisition of a trade or business or substantial portion thereof. These include covenants not to compete, computer software, film, sound recordings, videotape, patents, and copyrights.

   d. Certain intangible assets are expressly excluded from the definition of Sec. 197 intangibles including many types of financial interests, instruments, and contracts; interests in a corporation, partnership, trust, or estate; interests in land; professional sports franchises; and leases of tangible personal property.

   e. No loss can be recognized on the disposition of a Sec. 197 intangible if the taxpayer retains other Sec. 197 intangibles acquired in the same transaction or a series of transactions. Any disallowed loss is added to the basis of remaining Sec. 197 intangibles and recovered through amortization.

H. Domestic Production Activities Deduction (DPAD)

1. The deduction is available to all taxpayers including C corporations, farming cooperatives, estates, trusts, and their beneficiaries, and partners and shareholders of S corporations (not to partnerships or S corporations themselves).

2. The DPAD equals 9% of the *lesser of* the taxpayer's (1) qualified production activities income (QPAI), or (2) taxable income (or in the case of an individual, trust, or estate, adjusted gross income) computed before this deduction. The amount of the allowable deduction for any taxable year is limited to 50% of the W-2 wages paid by the taxpayer for the taxable year allocable to the taxpayer's domestic production gross receipts (DPGR). W-2 wages include wages, tips and other compensation as well as elective deferrals to 401(k) and certain other plans.

EXAMPLE

Assume unrelated manufacturing corporations A, B, and C incurred the following amounts for the current taxable year. Their Sec. 199 DPAD would be computed as follows:

	A	B	C
Qualified production activities income	$200,000	$200,000	$200,000
Taxable income	$100,000	$300,000	$300,000
Lesser of above	$100,000	$200,000	$200,000
Tentative deduction (9% × lesser amount)	$9,000	$18,000	$18,000
W-2 wages paid	$30,000	$40,000	$30,000
Wage limitation (50% × wages)	$15,000	$20,000	$15,000
Sec. 199 DPAD deduction	$9,000	$18,000	$15,000

Corporation A's deduction equals 9% of its taxable income of $100,000 or $9,000. Corporation B's deduction equals 9% of its QPAI of $200,000, or $18,000. Corporation C's tentative deduction of 9% of its QPAI of $200,000, or $18,000, is limited to 50% of the $30,000 of W-2 wages that it paid, or $15,000.

---

   a. QPAI is equal to the excess of DPGR over the sum of the cost of goods sold allocable to such receipts, and other expenses and deductions allocable to such receipts.

   b. If a manufacturer produces some of its finished products at an overseas facility and some of its products at a US plant, only income from the products produced in the US will qualify for the deduction. As a result, the taxpayer must segregate qualifying gross receipts from non qualifying gross receipts, and must apportion the cost of goods sold and other expenses and deductions accordingly. A taxpayer can treat all gross receipts as DPGR if less than 5% of the taxpayer's gross receipts are non-DPRG.

3. Qualified production activities eligible for the deduction *include* (1) the manufacture, production, growth or extraction of tangible personal property such as goods, clothing, or food, as well as computer software and music recordings within the US; (2) film production if at least 50% of the total compensation relating to the production is for services performed within the US; and (3) construction or substantial renovation of residential and nonresidential buildings, and infrastructure such as roads, power lines, water systems, and communication facilities, as well as engineering and architectural services performed in the US relating to such property. Qualified production activities *do not include* the sale of food and beverages prepared by the taxpayer at a retail establishment, and the transmission or distribution of electricity, natural gas, or potable water.

NOW REVIEW MULTIPLE-CHOICE QUESTIONS 78 THROUGH 85

II. "ABOVE THE LINE" DEDUCTIONS

"Above the line" deductions are taken from gross income to determine adjusted gross income. Adjusted gross income is important, because it may affect the amount of allowable charitable contributions, medical expenses, casualty losses, and miscellaneous itemized deductions. The deductions that reduce gross income to arrive at adjusted gross income are

1. Business deductions of a self-employed person (see Business Income and Deductions in Section F of part I of this outline.)
2. Losses from sale or exchange of property (discussed in Module 36: Transactions in Property)
3. Deductions attributable to rents and royalties
4. One-half of self-employment tax
5. Moving expenses
6. Contributions to self-employed retirement plans and IRAs
7. Deduction for interest on education loans
8. Penalties for premature withdrawals from time deposits
9. Alimony payments
10. Jury duty pay remitted to employer
11. Costs involving discrimination suits
12. Expenses of elementary and secondary teachers

A. The treatment of **reimbursed employee business expenses** depends on whether the employee makes an adequate accounting to the employer and returns amounts in excess of substantiated expenses.

1. Per diem reimbursements at a rate not in excess of the federal per diem rate and 57.5¢ per mile are deemed to satisfy the substantiation requirement if employee provides time, place, and business purpose of expenses.
2. If the employee **makes an adequate accounting** to employer and reimbursements equal expenses, or if the employee substantiates expenses and returns any excess reimbursement, the reimbursements are excluded from gross income and the expenses are not deductible.
3. If the employee **does not make an adequate accounting** to the employer or does not return excess reimbursements, the total amount of reimbursement is included in the employee's gross income and the related employee expenses are deductible as miscellaneous itemized deductions subject to the 50% limitation for business meals and entertainment and the 2% of AGI floor (same as for unreimbursed employee business expenses).

B. **Expenses attributable to property held for the production of rents or royalties** are deductible "above the line."

1. **Rental of vacation home**

a. If there is any personal use, the **amount deductible** is

$$(1) \quad \frac{\text{No. of days rented}}{\text{Total days used}} \times \text{Total expenses} = \text{Amount deductible}$$

(2) Personal use is by taxpayer or any other person to whom a fair rent is not charged.

b. **If used as a residence,** amount deductible is further limited to rental income less deductions otherwise allowable for interest, taxes, and casualty losses.

(1) Used as a residence if personal use exceeds greater of fourteen days or 10% of number of days rented
(2) These limitations do not apply if rented or held for rental for a continuous twelve-month period with no personal use.

> **EXAMPLE**
>
> Use house as a principal residence and then begin to rent in June. As long as rental continues for twelve consecutive months, limitations do not apply in year converted to rental.

  c. If used as a residence (above) and **rented for less than fifteen days** per year, then income therefrom is not reported and rental expense deductions are not allowed.

> **EXAMPLE**
>
> Taxpayer rents his condominium for 120 days for $2,000 and uses it himself for 60 days. The rest of the year it is vacant. His expenses are
>
> | | |
> |---|---|
> | Mortgage interest | $1,800 |
> | Real estate taxes | 600 |
> | Utilities | 300 |
> | Maintenance | 300 |
> | Depreciation | 2,000 |
> | | $5,000 |
>
> Taxpayer may deduct the following expenses:
>
> | | Rental expense | Itemized deduction |
> |---|---|---|
> | Mortgage interest | $1,200 | $600 |
> | Real estate taxes | 400 | 200 |
> | Utilities | 200 | -- |
> | Maintenance | 200 | -- |
> | Depreciation | -- | -- |
> | | $2,000 | $800 |
>
> Taxpayer may not deduct any depreciation because his rental expense deductions are limited to rental income when he has made personal use of the condominium in excess of the fourteen-day or 10% rule.

C. A self-employed individual can deduct **50% of self-employment taxes** in arriving at AGI.

D. A **self-employed** individual can **deduct 100%** of the **premiums for medical insurance** for the individual, spouse, dependents, and any child of the taxpayer under age 27 as of the close of the tax year in arriving at AGI.

  1. This deduction cannot exceed the individual's net earnings from the trade or business with respect to which the plan providing for health insurance was established. For purposes of this limitation, an S corporation more-than-two-percent shareholder's earned income is determined exclusively by reference to the shareholder's wages received from the S corporation.

  2. No deduction is allowed if the self-employed individual or spouse is eligible to participate in an employer's subsidized health plan. The determination of whether self-employed individuals or their spouses are eligible for employer-paid health benefits is to be made on a calendar month basis.

  3. Any medical insurance premiums not deductible under the above rules are deductible as an itemized medical expense deduction from AGI.

  4. The deduction for medical insurance premiums can also be subtracted in computing an individual's self-employment tax.

E. Moving Expenses

  1. The distance between the former residence and new job (d2) must be **at least fifty miles** farther than from the former residence to the former job (d1) (i.e., d2 – d1 > 50 miles). If no former job, new job must be at least fifty miles from former residence.

  2. Employee must be **employed** at least thirty-nine weeks out of the twelve months following the move. Self-employed individual must be employed seventy-eight weeks out of the twenty-four months following the move

(in addition to thirty-nine weeks out of first twelve months). Time test does not have to be met in case of death, taxpayer's job at new location ends because of disability, or taxpayer is laid off for other than willful misconduct.

3. **Deductible** moving expenses include the costs of moving household goods and personal effects from the old to the new residence, and the costs of traveling (including lodging) from the old residence to the new residence. Actual auto expenses can be deducted, or taxpayer can use standard rate of 23¢ per mile beginning January 1, 2015.

4. **Nondeductible** moving expenses include the costs of meals, house-hunting trips, temporary lodging in the general location of the new work site, expenses incurred in selling an old house or buying a new house, and expenses in settling a lease on an old residence or acquiring a lease on a new residence.

NOW REVIEW MULTIPLE-CHOICE QUESTIONS 86 THROUGH 91

F. Contributions to Certain Retirement Plans

1. Contributions to an **Individual Retirement Account** (IRA)

   a. If neither the taxpayer nor the taxpayer's spouse is an active participant in an employer-sponsored retirement plan or a Keogh plan, there is no phase-out of IRA deductions.

      (1) The maximum deduction for an individual's contributions to an IRA is generally the lesser of

         (a) **$5,500** (for 2015) or
         (b) 100% of compensation (including alimony)

      (2) For married taxpayers filing a joint return, up to $5,500 can be deducted for contributions to the IRA of each spouse (even if one spouse is not working), provided that the combined earned income of both spouses is at least equal to the amounts contributed to the IRAs.

   b. For 2015, the IRA deduction for individuals who are active participants in an employer retirement plan or a Keogh plan is proportionately phased out for married individuals filing jointly with AGI between $98,000 and $118,000, and for single individuals with AGI between $61,000 and $71,000.

      (1) An individual will not be considered an active participant in an employer plan merely because the individual's spouse is an active participant for any part of the plan year.

      (2) The maximum deductible IRA contribution for an individual who is not an active participant, but whose spouse is, will be proportionately phased out at a combined AGI between $183,000 and $193,000.

   c. Under the **phase-out rule,** the $5,500 maximum deduction is reduced by a percentage equal to adjusted gross income in excess of the lower AGI amount (above) divided by $10,000 ($20,000 for married filing jointly). The deduction limit is rounded to the next lowest multiple of $10.

      (1) A taxpayer whose AGI is not above the applicable phase-out range can make a $200 deductible contribution regardless of the proportional phase-out rule. This $200 minimum applies separately to taxpayer and taxpayer's spouse.

      (2) A taxpayer who is partially or totally prevented from making deductible IRA contributions can make **nondeductible IRA contributions**.

      (3) Total IRA contributions (whether deductible or not) are subject to the $5,500 or 100% of compensation limit.

EXAMPLE

For 2015, a single individual who has compensation income (and AGI) of $67,000 and who is an active participant in an employer-sponsored retirement plan would be subject to a limit reduction of $3,300 computed as follows: $5,500 × [($67,000 − $61,000) ÷ $10,000)] = $3,300. Thus, the individual's deductible IRA contribution would be limited to $5,500 − $3,300 = $2,200. However, the individual could make nondeductible IRA contributions of up to $3,300 more.

> **EXAMPLE**
>
> For 2015, a single individual who has compensation income (and AGI) of $70,800 and who is an active participant in an employer-sponsored retirement plan would normally be limited to an IRA deduction of $5,500 − [($70,800 − $61,000) ÷ $10,000] × $5,500 = $110. However, because of the special rule in (2) above, a $200 IRA contribution deduction is allowable.

    d. An individual at least age 50 before the close of the taxable year can make an additional "catch-up" contribution of $1,000 to an IRA. Thus, for 2015, the maximum IRA contribution and deduction for an individual at least age 50 is $5,500 + $1,000 = $6,500.

    e. The 10% penalty tax on early withdrawals (pre-age 59 1/2) does not apply to amounts withdrawn for "qualified higher education expenses" and "first-time homebuyer expenses" ($10,000 lifetime cap), nor to distributions made to unemployed individuals for health insurance premiums, and distributions to the extent that deductible medical expenses exceed 7.5% of AGI.

       (1) Qualified higher education expenses include tuition, fees, books, supplies, and equipment for postsecondary education for the taxpayer, taxpayer's spouse, or any child or grandchild of the taxpayer or the taxpayer's spouse.

       (2) Qualified first-time homebuyer distributions must be used in 120 days to buy, build, or rebuild a first home that is a principal residence for the taxpayer or taxpayer's spouse. Acquisition costs include reasonable financing or other closing costs.

2. Contributions to a **Roth IRA** are not deductible, but qualified distributions of earnings are tax-free. Individuals making contributions to a Roth IRA can still make contributions to a deductible or nondeductible IRA, but maximum contributions to all IRAs is limited to $5,500 for 2015. ($6,500 if the individual is at least age 50).

    a. For 2015, eligibility for a Roth IRA is phased out for single taxpayers with AGI between $116,000 and $131,000, and for joint filers with AGI between $183,000 and $193,000.

    b. Unlike traditional IRAs contributions may be made to Roth IRAs even after the individual reaches age 70 1/2.

    c. Qualified distributions from a Roth IRA are not included in gross income and are not subject to the 10% early withdrawal penalty. A qualified distribution is a distribution that is made after the five-year period beginning with the first tax year for which a contribution was made and the distribution is made (1) after the individual reaches age 59 1/2, (2) to a beneficiary (or the individual's estate) after the individual's death, (3) after the individual becomes disabled, or (4) for the first-time homebuyer expenses of the individual, individual's spouse, children, grandchildren, or ancestors ($10,000 lifetime cap).

    d. Nonqualified distributions are includible in income to the extent attributable to earnings and generally subject to the 10% early withdrawal penalty. Distributions are deemed to be made from contributed amounts first.

    e. For tax years beginning before 2010, taxpayers (other than individuals filing separately) with AGI of less than $100,000 could convert assets in traditional IRAs to a Roth IRA at any time without paying the 10% tax on early withdrawals, although the deemed distributions of IRA assets is included in income. For tax years beginning after December 31, 2009, the AGI and filing status limitations are eliminated, allowing higher-income taxpayers to convert traditional IRAs to Roth accounts.

3. Contributions can be made to a **Coverdell Education Savings Account** of up to $2,000 per beneficiary (until the beneficiary reaches age eighteen), to pay the costs of the beneficiary's elementary, secondary, or postsecondary education.

    a. Contributions are not deductible, but withdrawals to pay the cost of a beneficiary's education expenses are tax-free.

    b. Any earnings of an education IRA that are distributed but are not used to pay a beneficiary's education expenses must be included in the distributee's gross income and are subject to a 10% penalty tax.

    c. Under a special rollover provision, the amount left in an education IRA before the beneficiary reaches age 30 can be rolled over to another family member's education IRA without triggering income taxes or penalties.

    d. Eligibility is phased out for single taxpayers with modified AGI between $95,000 and $110,000, and for married taxpayers with modified AGI between $190,000 and $220,000.

e. Expenses that may be paid tax-free from an education IRA include expenses for enrollment (including room and board, uniforms, transportation, computers, and Internet access services) in elementary or secondary schools, whether public, private, or religious. Furthermore, taxpayers may take advantage of the exclusion for distributions from education IRAs, the Hope and lifetime learning credits, and the qualified tuition program in the same year.

4. **Self-employed** individuals (sole proprietors and partners) may contribute to a qualified retirement plan (called H.R.-10 or Keogh Plan).

   a. The maximum contribution and deduction to a defined-contribution self-employed retirement plan is the lesser of

      (1) $53,000 ($52,000 for 2014), or 100% of earned income for 2015.
      (2) The definition of "earned income" includes the retirement plan and self-employment tax deductions (i.e., earnings from self-employment must be reduced by the retirement plan contribution and the self-employment tax deduction for purposes of determining the maximum deduction).

   b. A taxpayer may elect to treat contributions made up until the due date of the tax return (including extensions) as made for the taxable year for which the tax return is being filed, if the retirement plan was established by the end of that year.

5. An employer's contributions to an employee's **simplified employee pension (SEP) plan** are deductible by the employer, limited to the lesser of 25% of compensation (up to a compensation ceiling of $265,000 for 2015) or $52,000.

   a. The employer's SEP contributions are excluded from the employee's gross income.
   b. In addition, the employee may make deductible IRA contributions subject to the IRA phase-out rules (discussed in 2.c. above).

6. A **savings incentive match plan for employees (SIMPLE)** is not subject to the nondiscrimination rules (including top-heavy provisions) and certain other complex requirements generally applicable to qualified plans, and may be structured as an IRA or as a 401(k) plan.

   a. Limited to employers with 100 or fewer employees who received at least $5,000 in compensation from the employer in the preceding year.

      (1) Plan allows employees to make elective contributions of up to $12,500 of their pretax salaries (expressed as a percentage of compensation, not a fixed dollar amount) and requires employers to match a portion of the contributions.
      (2) Eligible employees are those who earned at least $5,000 in any two prior years and who may be expected to earn at least $5,000 in the current year.

   b. Employers must satisfy one of two contribution formulas.

      (1) Matching contribution formula generally requires an employer to match the employee contribution dollar-for-dollar up to 3% of the employee's compensation for the year.
      (2) Alternatively, an employer can make a non elective contribution of 2% of compensation for each eligible employee who has at least $5,000 of compensation from the employer during the year.

   c. Contributions to the plan are immediately vested, but a 25% penalty applies to employee withdrawals made within two years of the date the employee began participating in the plan.

G. Deduction for Interest on Education Loans

1. An individual is allowed to deduct **up to $2,500** for interest on qualified education loans. However, the deduction is not available if the individual is claimed as a dependent on another taxpayer's return.
2. A *qualified education loan* is any debt incurred to pay the qualified higher education expenses of the taxpayer, taxpayer's spouse, or dependents (as of the time the debt was incurred), and the education expenses must relate to a period when the student was enrolled on at least a half-time basis. However, any debt owed to a related party is not a qualified educational loan (e.g., education debt owed to family member).
3. Qualified education expenses include such costs as tuition, fees, room, board, and related expenses.
4. For 2015, the deduction is phased out for single taxpayers with modified AGI between $65,000 and $80,000, and for married taxpayers with modified AGI between $130,000 and $160,000.

H. Deduction for Qualified Tuition and Related Expenses

1. For 2007 through 2014, individuals are allowed to deduct qualified higher education expenses in arriving at AGI. The deduction is limited to $4,000 for individuals with AGI at or below $65,000 ($130,000 for joint filers). The deduction is limited to $2,000 for individuals with AGI above $65,000, but equal to or less than $80,000 ($130,000 and $160,000 respectively for joint filers).
2. Taxpayers with AGI above these levels, married individuals filing separately, and an individual who can be claimed as a dependent are not entitled to any deduction.
3. *Qualified tuition and related expenses* means tuition and fees required for enrollment of the taxpayer, taxpayer's spouse, or dependent at a postsecondary educational institution. Such term does not include expenses with respect to any course involving sports, games, or hobbies, or any noncredit course, unless such course is part of the individual's degree program. Also excluded are nonacademic fees such as student activity fees, athletic fees, and insurance expenses.
4. The deduction is allowed for expenses paid during the tax year, in connection with enrollment during the year or in connection with an academic term beginning during the year or the first three months of the following year.
5. If a taxpayer takes an American Opportunity credit or lifetime learning credit with respect to a student, the qualified higher education expenses of that student for the year are not deductible under this provision.

I. Penalties for Premature Withdrawals from Time Deposits

1. Full amount of interest is included in gross income.
2. Forfeited interest is then subtracted "above the line."

J. Alimony or Separate Maintenance Payments Are Deducted "Above the Line."
K. Jury Duty Pay Remitted to Employer

1. An employee is allowed to deduct the amount of jury duty pay that was surrendered to an employer in return for the employer's payment of compensation during the employee's jury service period.
2. Both regular compensation and jury duty pay must be included in gross income.

L. Costs Involving Discrimination Suits

1. Attorneys' fees and court costs incurred by, or on behalf of, an individual in connection with any action involving a claim for unlawful discrimination (e.g., age, sex, or race discrimination) are allowable as a deduction from gross income in arriving at AGI.
2. The amount of deduction is limited to the amount of judgment or settlement included in the individual's gross income for the tax year.

M. Expenses of Elementary and Secondary Teachers

1. For tax years beginning before 2015, eligible educators are allowed an above-the-line deduction for up to $250 for unreimbursed expenses for books, supplies, computer equipment (including related software and services) and supplementary materials used in the classroom.
2. An eligible educator is a kindergarten through grade 12 teacher, instructor, counselor, principal, or aide working in a school for at least 900 hours during the school year.
3. For joint filers, if both spouses are eligible, the maximum deduction is $500, but neither spouse can deduct more than $250 of expenses.

NOW REVIEW MULTIPLE-CHOICE QUESTIONS 92 THROUGH 103

III. ITEMIZED DEDUCTIONS FROM ADJUSTED GROSS INCOME

Itemized deductions reduce adjusted gross income, and are sometimes referred to as "below the line" deductions because they are deducted from adjusted gross income. Itemized deductions (or a standard deduction) along with personal exemptions are subtracted from adjusted gross income to arrive at taxable income.

A taxpayer will itemize deductions only if the taxpayer's total itemized deductions exceed the applicable standard deduction that is available to the taxpayer. The amount of the standard deduction is based on the filing status of the taxpayer, whether the taxpayer is a dependent, and is indexed for inflation. Additional standard deductions are allowed for age and blindness.

Filing status	Basic standard deduction 2015
a) Married, filing jointly; or surviving spouse	$12,600
b) Married, filing separately	6,300
c) Head of household	9,250
d) Single	6,300

A dependent's basic standard deduction is limited to the lesser of (1) the basic standard deduction for single taxpayers of $6,300 or (2) the greater of (a) $1,050, or (b) the dependent's earned income plus $350. For example, a dependent who receives wages (earned income) of $1,200 would have a basic standard deduction of $1,200 + $350 = $1,550.

An unmarried individual who is not a surviving spouse, and is either age sixty-five or older or blind, receives an additional standard deduction of $1,550 for 2015. The standard deduction is increased by $3,100 if the individual is both elderly and blind. The increase is $1,250 for 2015 for each married individual who is age sixty-five or older or blind. The increase for a married individual who is both elderly and blind is $2,500. An elderly or blind individual who may be claimed as a dependent on another taxpayer's return may claim the basic standard deduction plus the additional standard deduction(s). For example, an unmarried dependent, age sixty-five, with only unearned income would have a standard deduction of $1,050 + $1,550 = $2,600.

The major itemized deductions are outlined below. It should be remembered that some may be deducted in arriving at AGI if they are incurred by a self-employed taxpayer in a trade or business, or for the production of rents or royalties.

A. Medical and Dental Expenses

1. Medical and dental expenses paid by taxpayer for himself, spouse, or dependent (relationship, support, and citizenship tests are met) are deductible in year of payment, if not reimbursed by insurance, employer, etc. A child of divorced or separated parents is treated as a dependent of both parents for this purpose.
2. Computation—for tax years beginning after 2012, unreimbursed medical expenses (including *prescribed* medicine and insulin, and medical insurance premiums) are deducted to the extent **in excess of 10%** of adjusted gross income. However for tax years 2013 through 2016 the lower 7.5% of AGI threshold continues to apply for taxpayers or their spouses who are age 65 or older before the close of the tax year.

EXAMPLE

Ralph and Alice Jones, both age 37, who have adjusted gross income of $60,000, paid the following medical expenses: $3,900 for hospital and doctor bills (above reimbursement), $1,250 for prescription medicine, and $1,600 for medical insurance. The Joneses would compute their medical expense deduction as follows:

Prescribed medicine	$1,250
Hospital, doctors	3,900
Medical insurance	1,600
	$6,750
Less 10% of AGI	−6,000
Medical expense deduction	$750

---

3. Deductible medical care does not include **cosmetic surgery** or other procedures, unless the surgery or procedure is necessary to ameliorate a deformity arising from, or directly related to, a congenital abnormality, a personal injury resulting from an accident or trauma, or a disfiguring disease. In addition, to be deductible, the procedure must promote proper body function or prevent or treat illness or disease (e.g., LASIK and radial keratotomy are deductible; teeth whitening is not deductible).

    a. Cosmetic surgery is defined as any procedure directed at improving the patient's appearance and does not meaningfully promote the proper function of the body or prevent or treat illness or disease.
    b. If expenses for cosmetic surgery are not deductible under this provision, then amounts paid for insurance coverage for such expenses are not deductible, and an employer's reimbursement of such expenses under a health plan is not excludable from the employee's gross income.

4. Expenses incurred by physically handicapped individuals for **removal of structural barriers** in their residences to accommodate their handicapped condition are fully deductible as medical expenses. Qualifying expenses include constructing entrance or exit ramps, widening doorways and hallways, the installation of railings and support bars, and other modifications.

5. **Capital expenditures** for special equipment (other than in 4. above) installed for medical reasons in a home or automobile are deductible as medical expenses to the extent the expenditures exceed the increase in value of the property.

6. **Deductible** medical expenses include

   a. Fees for doctors, surgeons, dentists, osteopaths, ophthalmologists, optometrists, chiropractors, chiropodists, podiatrists, psychiatrists, psychologists, and Christian Science practitioners

   b. Fees for hospital services, therapy, nursing services (including nurses' meals you pay for), ambulance hire, and laboratory, surgical, obstetrical, diagnostic, dental, and X-ray services

   c. Meals and lodging provided by a hospital during medical treatment, and meals and lodging provided by a center during treatment for alcoholism or drug addiction

   d. Amounts paid for lodging (but not meals) while away from home primarily for medical care provided by a physician in a licensed hospital or equivalent medical care facility. Limit is $50 per night for each individual.

   e. Medical and hospital insurance premiums

   f. *Prescribed* medicines and insulin

   g. Transportation for needed medical care. Actual auto expenses can be deducted, or taxpayer can use standard rate of 23¢ per mile beginning January 1, 2015 (plus parking and tolls).

   h. Special items and equipment, including false teeth, artificial limbs, eyeglasses, hearing aids, crutches, guide dogs, motorized wheelchairs, hand controls on a car, and special telephones for deaf

   i. The cost of stop-smoking programs and the cost of participation in a weight-loss program as a treatment for the disease of obesity qualify. However, the costs of reduced-calorie diet foods are not deductible if these foods merely substitute for food the individual would normally consume.

7. Items **not deductible** as medical expenses include

   a. Bottled water, maternity clothes, and diaper service

   b. Household help, and care of a normal and healthy baby by a nurse (but a portion may qualify for child or dependent care tax credit)

   c. Toothpaste, toiletries, cosmetics, etc.

   d. Weight-loss expenses that are not for the treatment of obesity or other disease

   e. Trip, social activities, or health club dues for general improvement of health

   f. Non prescribed medicines and drugs (e.g., over-the-counter medicines)

   g. Illegal operation or treatment

   h. Funeral and burial expenses

8. Reimbursement of expenses deducted in an earlier year may have to be included in gross income in the period received under the tax benefit rule.

9. Reimbursement in excess of expenses is includible in income to the extent the excess reimbursement was paid by policies provided by employer.

NOW REVIEW MULTIPLE-CHOICE QUESTIONS 104 THROUGH 115

B. Taxes

1. The following taxes are **deductible as a tax** in year paid if they are imposed on the taxpayer:

   a. **Income tax** (state, local, or foreign)

      (1) The deduction for state and local taxes includes amounts withheld from salary, estimated payments made during the year, and payments made during the year on a tax for a prior year.

      (2) A refund of a prior year's taxes is not offset against the current year's deduction, but is generally included in income under the tax benefit rule.

   b. For tax years beginning before January 1, 2015, an individual may elect to deduct state and local general sales taxes in lieu of state and local income taxes. The amount that can be deducted is either the total of actual general sales taxes paid as substantiated by receipts, or an amount from IRS-provided tables, plus the amount of general sales taxes paid with regard to the purchase of a motor vehicle, boat, or other items prescribed in Pub. 600.

(1) The sales taxes imposed on food, clothing, medical supplies, and motor vehicles may be deducted even if imposed at a rate lower than the general rate.

(2) In the case of sales taxes on motor vehicles that are higher than the general rate, only an amount up to the general rate is allowed. The sales tax on boats is deductible only if imposed at the general sales tax rate.

c. **Real property taxes** (state, local, or foreign) are deductible by the person on whom the taxes are imposed.

(1) When real property is sold, the deduction is apportioned between buyer and seller on a daily basis within the real property tax year, even if parties do not apportion the taxes at the closing. Real property taxes are allocated to the buyer beginning with the date of sale.

(2) **Assessments** for improvements (e.g., special assessments for streets, sewers, sidewalks, curbing) are generally not deductible, but instead must be added to the basis of the property. However, the portion of an assessment that is attributable to repairs or maintenance, or to meeting interest charges on the improvements, is deductible as taxes.

d. **Personal property taxes** (state or local, not foreign) are deductible if ad valorem (i.e., assessed in relation to the value of property). A motor vehicle tax based on horsepower, weight, or model year is not deductible.

2. The following taxes are **deductible only as an expense** incurred in a trade or business or in the production of income (above the line):

a. Social security and other employment taxes paid by employer
b. Federal excise taxes on automobiles, tires, telephone service, and air transportation
c. Customs duties and gasoline taxes
d. State and local taxes not deductible as such (stamp or cigarette taxes) or charges of a primarily regulatory nature (licenses, etc.)

3. The following taxes are **not deductible**:

a. Federal income taxes
b. Federal, state, or local estate or gift taxes
c. Social security and other federal employment taxes paid by employee (including self-employment taxes)
d. Social security and other employment taxes paid by an employer on the wages of an employee who only performed domestic services (i.e., maid, etc.)

NOW REVIEW MULTIPLE-CHOICE QUESTIONS 116 THROUGH 124

C. Interest Expense

1. The classification of interest expense is generally determined by tracing the use of the borrowed funds. Interest expense is not deductible if loan proceeds were used to produce tax-exempt income (e.g., purchase municipal bonds).

2. No deduction is allowed for prepaid interest; it must be capitalized and deducted in the future period(s) to which it relates. However, an individual may elect to deduct *mortgage points* when paid if the points represent interest and mortgage proceeds were used to buy, build, or substantially improve a principal residence. Otherwise points must be capitalized and deducted over the term of the mortgage.

3. **Personal interest.** No deduction is allowed for personal interest.

a. Personal interest **includes** interest paid or incurred to purchase an asset for personal use, credit card interest for personal purchases, interest incurred as an employee, and interest on income tax underpayments.

b. Personal interest **excludes** qualified residence interest, investment interest, interest allocable to a trade or business (other than as an employee), interest incurred in a passive activity, and interest on deferred estate taxes.

EXAMPLE

X, a **self-employed** consultant, finances a new automobile used 80% for business and 20% for personal use. X would treat 80% of the interest as deductible business interest expense (toward AGI), and 20% as nondeductible personal interest.

> **EXAMPLE**
>
> Y, an **employee**, finances a new automobile used 80% in her employer's business and 20% for personal use. All of the interest expense on the auto loan would be considered nondeductible personal interest.

4. **Qualified residence interest.** The disallowance of personal interest above does not apply to interest paid or accrued on acquisition indebtedness or home equity indebtedness secured by a security interest perfected under local law on the taxpayer's principal residence or a second residence owned by the taxpayer.

   a. **Acquisition indebtedness.** Interest is deductible on up to $1,000,000 ($500,000 if married filing separately) of loans secured by the residence if such loans were used to acquire, construct, or substantially improve the home.

      (1) Acquisition indebtedness is reduced as principal payments are made and cannot be restored or increased by refinancing the home.
      (2) If the home is refinanced, the amount qualifying as acquisition indebtedness is limited to the amount of acquisition debt existing at the time of refinancing plus any amount of the new loan that is used to substantially improve the home.

   b. **Home equity indebtedness.** Interest is deductible on up to $100,000 ($50,000 if married filing separately) of loans secured by the residence (other than acquisition indebtedness) regardless of how the loan proceeds are used (e.g., automobile, education expenses, medical expenses, etc.). The amount of home equity indebtedness cannot exceed the FV of the home as reduced by any acquisition indebtedness.

> **EXAMPLE**
>
> Allan purchased a home for $380,000, borrowing $250,000 of the purchase price that was secured by a fifteen-year mortgage. In 2015, when the home was worth $400,000 and the balance of the first mortgage was $230,000, Allan obtained a second mortgage on the home in the amount of $120,000, using the proceeds to purchase a car and to pay off personal loans. Allan may deduct the interest on the balance of the first mortgage acquisition indebtedness of $230,000. However, Allan can deduct interest on only $100,000 of the second mortgage as qualified residence interest because it is considered home equity indebtedness (i.e., the loan proceeds were not used to acquire, construct, or substantially improve a home). The interest on the remaining $20,000 of the second mortgage is nondeductible personal interest.

   c. The term "residence" includes houses, condominiums, cooperative housing units, and any other property that the taxpayer uses as a dwelling unit (e.g., mobile home, motor home, boat, etc.).
   d. In the case of a residence used partly for rental purposes, the interest can only be qualified residence interest if the taxpayer's personal use during the year exceeds the greater of fourteen days or 10% of the number of days of rental use (unless the residence was not rented at any time during the year).
   e. Qualified residence interest does not include interest on unsecured home improvement loans, but does include mortgage prepayment penalties.
   f. Qualified *mortgage insurance premiums* paid or accrued before January 1, 2015, in connection with acquisition indebtedness are deductible as qualified residence interest. However, for every $1,000 ($500 if married filing separately) by which the taxpayer's AGI exceeds $100,000 the amount of premiums treated as interest is reduced by 10%. The deduction does not apply to mortgage insurance contracts issued before January 1, 2007, nor to premiums allocable to any period after December 31, 2014.

5. **Investment interest.** The deduction for investment interest expense for non-corporate taxpayers is limited to the amount of net investment income. Interest disallowed is carried forward indefinitely and is allowed only to the extent of net investment income in a subsequent year.

> **EXAMPLE**
>
> For 2015, a single taxpayer has investment interest expense of $40,000 and net investment income of $24,000. The deductible investment interest expense for 2015 is limited to $24,000, with the remaining $16,000 carried forward and allowed as a deduction to the extent of net investment income in subsequent years.

a. Investment interest expense is interest paid or accrued on indebtedness properly allocable to property held for investment, including

　(1) Interest expense allocable to portfolio income, and
　(2) Interest expense allocable to a trade or business in which the taxpayer does not materially participate, if that activity is not treated as a passive activity

b. Investment interest expense excludes interest expense taken into account in determining income or loss from a passive activity, interest allocable to rental real estate in which the taxpayer actively participates, qualified residence interest, and personal interest.

c. Net investment income includes

　(1) Interest, rents, dividends (other than qualified dividends), and royalties in excess of any related expenses, and
　(2) The net gain (all gains minus all losses) on the sale of investment property, but only to the extent that the net gain exceeds the net capital gain (i.e., net LTCG in excess of net STCL).

d. A taxpayer may elect to treat **qualified dividends** and **net capital gain** (i.e., an excess of net LTCG over net STCL) as investment income. However, if this election is made, a taxpayer must reduce the amount of qualified dividends income and net capital gain otherwise eligible for reduced maximum tax rates by the amount included as investment income.

EXAMPLE

Assume a taxpayer has the following items of income and expense for 2015:

Interest income	$15,000
Net long-term capital gain	18,000
Investment interest expense	25,000

The taxpayer's deduction for investment interest expense is generally limited to $15,000 for 2015 unless the taxpayer elects to include a portion of the net LTCG in the determination of the investment interest expense limitation. If the taxpayer elects to treat $10,000 of the net LTCG as investment income, all of the taxpayer's investment interest expense will be deductible. But by doing this, $10,000 of the net LTCG will be taxed at ordinary tax rates, leaving only the remaining $8,000 of net LTCG to be taxed at preferential rates.

---

e. Only investment expenses (e.g., rental fees for safety-deposit box rental, investment counseling fees, subscriptions to investment periodicals) remaining after the 2% of AGI limitation are used in computing net investment income.

f. Income and expenses taken into account in computing the income or loss from a passive activity are excluded from net investment income.

NOW REVIEW MULTIPLE-CHOICE QUESTIONS 125 THROUGH 131

D. Charitable Contributions

Contributions to qualified domestic charitable organizations are deductible in the year actually paid or donated (for both accrual- and cash-basis taxpayers) with some carryover allowed. A "pledge" is *not* a payment. Charging the contribution on your credit card *does constitute payment*.

1. **Qualified organizations** include

a. A state, a US possession or political subdivision, or the District of Columbia if made exclusively for public purposes
b. A community chest, corporation, foundation, etc., operated exclusively for charitable, religious, educational, scientific, or literary purposes, or for the prevention of cruelty to children or animals, or for fostering national or international amateur sports competition (unless they provide facilities or equipment)

      (1) No part of the earnings may inure to any individual's benefit

      (2) May not attempt to influence legislation or intervene in any political campaign

    c. Church, synagogue, or other religious organizations

    d. War veterans' organizations

    e. Domestic fraternal societies operating under the lodge system (only if contribution used exclusively for the charitable purposes listed in b. above)

    f. Nonprofit cemetery companies if the funds are irrevocably dedicated to the perpetual care of the cemetery as a whole, and not a particular lot or mausoleum crypt

2. Dues, fees, or assessments paid to qualified organizations are deductible to the extent that payments exceed benefits received. Dues, fees, or assessments are not deductible if paid to veterans' organizations, lodges, fraternal organizations, and country clubs

3. Out-of-pocket expenses to maintain a **student** (domestic or foreign) in a taxpayer's home are deductible (limited to $50/month for each month the individual is a full-time student) if

    a. Student is in 12th or lower grade and not a dependent or relative

    b. Based on written agreement between taxpayer and qualified organization

    c. Taxpayer receives no reimbursement

4. Payments to qualified organizations for goods or services are deductible to the extent the amount paid exceeds the fair market value of benefits received.

5. A taxpayer who makes a payment to or for the benefit of a college or university and is thereby entitled to purchase tickets to athletic events is allowed to deduct 80% of the payment as a charitable contribution. Any payment that is attributable to the actual cost of tickets is not deductible as a charitable contribution.

6. Unreimbursed out-of-pocket expenses incurred while rendering services to a charitable organization without compensation are deductible, including actual auto expenses or a standard rate of 14¢ per mile.

7. No deduction will be allowed for **contributions of cash**, checks, or other monetary gifts unless the donor maintains a canceled check, a receipt, or letter or other written communication from the donee, indicating the donee's name, contribution date, and the amount.

8. No charitable deduction is allowed for any **contribution of $250 or more** unless the donor obtains written acknowledgment of the contribution from the donee organization including a good-faith estimate of the value of any goods or services provided to the donor in exchange for the contribution. The acknowledgement must be received by the earlier of the date the taxpayer's return is filed, or the due date (including extensions) for filing the taxpayer's return. A canceled check is not sufficient substantiation for a contribution of $250 or more.

9. For any noncash property donation **exceeding $500 in value,** the taxpayer must maintain a written record containing (1) the approximate date and manner of acquisition of the property, and (2) the cost or other basis of the property if it was held less than twelve months. Additionally, a description of the donated property must be included with the return for the tax year in which the contribution was made. If the donated item exceeds **$5,000** in value, the taxpayer is required to obtain a qualified appraisal and attach a summary of the appraisal to the return. If the donated item exceeds **$500,000** in value, a qualified appraisal must be attached to the return. Similar noncash items, whether donated to a single donee or multiple donees, must be aggregated for purposes of determining whether the above dollar thresholds are exceeded.

10. **Nondeductible** contributions include contributions to/for/of

    a. Civic leagues, social clubs, and foreign organizations

    b. Communist organizations, chambers of commerce, labor unions

    c. The value of the taxpayer's time or services

    d. The use of property, or less than an entire interest in property

    e. Blood donated

    f. Tuition or amounts in place of tuition

    g. Payments to a hospital for care of particular patients

    h. "Sustainer's gift" to retirement home

    i. Raffles, bingo, etc. (but may qualify as gambling loss)

    j. Fraternal societies if the contributions are used to defray sickness or burial expenses of members

    k. Political organizations

    l. Travel, including meals and lodging (e.g., trip to serve at charity's national meeting), if there is any significant element of personal pleasure, recreation, or vacation involved

11. Contributions of property to qualified organizations are **deductible**

    a. At fair market value when FMV is below basis
    b. At basis when fair market value exceeds basis and property would result in short-term capital gain or ordinary income if sold (e.g., gain would be ordinary because of depreciation recapture or if property is inventory)
    c. If contributed property is *capital gain property* that would result in LTCG if sold (i.e., generally investment property and personal-use property held more than one year), the amount of contribution is the property's FMV. However, if the contributed property is *tangible personal capital gain property* and its use is unrelated to the charity's activity, the amount of contribution is restricted to the property's basis.
    d. Appraisal fees on donated property are a miscellaneous itemized deduction.

12. For contributions of **vehicles** (automobiles, boats, and airplanes) with a claimed value exceeding $500, the charitable deduction is limited to the gross proceeds received by the charitable organization upon subsequent sale of the vehicle. Additionally, the donee organization must provide the donor with a written acknowledgement within 30 days of (1) the contribution of the qualified vehicle, or (2) the date of sale of the qualified vehicle. If the vehicle is not sold, the donee must provide certification of the intended use of the vehicle and the intended duration of use.

13. For contributions of **patents** and other **intellectual property**, the amount of deduction is limited to the lesser of (1) the taxpayer's basis for the property, or (2) the property's FMV. A donor is also allowed an additional charitable deduction for certain amounts in the year of contribution and in later years based on a specified percentage of qualified donee income received or accrued by the charity from the donated property.

14. The overall limitation for contribution deductions is **50%** of adjusted gross income (before any net operating loss carryback). A second limitation is that contributions of long-term capital gain property to charities in Section 14.a. below (where gain is not reduced) are limited to **30%** of AGI. A third limitation is that some contributions to certain charities are limited to **20%** of AGI or a lesser amount.

    a. Contributions to the following are taken first and may be taken up to **50%** of AGI limitation

        (1) Public charities

            (a) Churches
            (b) Educational organizations
            (c) Tax-exempt hospitals
            (d) Medical research
            (e) States or political subdivisions
            (f) US or District of Columbia

        (2) All private operating foundations, that is, foundations that spend their income directly for the active conduct of their exempt activities (e.g., public museums)
        (3) Certain private non operating foundations that distribute proceeds to public and private operating charities

    b. Deductions for contributions of **long-term capital gain property** (when the gain is not to be reduced) to organizations in Section 14.a. above are limited to **30%** of adjusted gross income; but, taxpayer may elect to reduce all appreciated long-term capital gain property by the potential gain and not be subject to this 30% limitation.

    c. Deductions for contributions to charities that do not qualify in Section 14.a. above (generally private non operating foundations) are subject to special limitations.

        (1) The deduction limitation for gifts of

            (a) Ordinary income property is the lesser of (1) 30% of AGI, or (2) (50% × AGI) – gifts to charities in Section 14.a. above
            (b) Capital gain property is lesser of (1) 20% of AGI, or (2) (30% × AGI) – gifts of long-term capital gain property to charities in Section 14.a. above where no reduction is made for appreciation

        (2) These deductions are taken after deductions to organizations in Section 14.a. above without the 30% limitation on capital gain property in Section 14.b. above.

A CHARITABLE CONTRIBUTION FLOWCHART FOR INDIVIDUALS

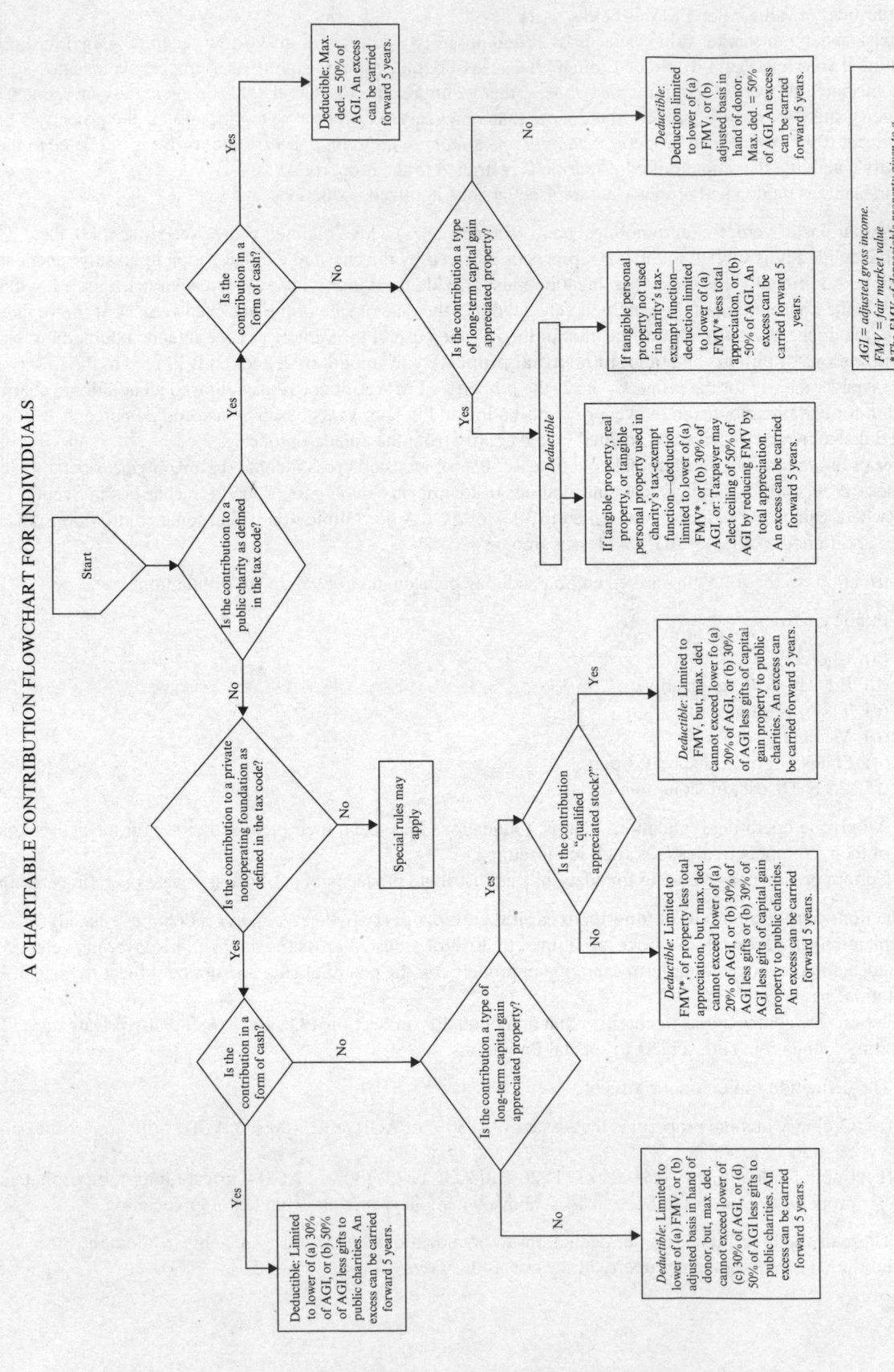

> **EXAMPLE**
>
> An individual with AGI of $9,000 made a contribution of capital gain appreciated property with an FMV of $5,000 to a church, and gave $2,000 cash to a private non operating foundation. Since the contribution to the church (before the 30% limit) exceeds 50% of AGI, no part of the contribution to the foundation is deductible this year. Assuming no election is made to reduce the contribution of the capital gain property by the amount of its appreciation, the current deduction for the contribution to the church is limited to 30% × $9,000 = $2,700.

15. Contributions in excess of the 50%, 30%, or 20% limitation can be carried forward for **five years** and remain subject to the 50%, 30%, or 20% limitation in the carryforward years.

> **EXAMPLE**
>
> Ben's adjusted gross income is $50,000. During the year he gave his church $2,000 cash and land (held for investment more than one year) having a fair market value of $30,000 and a basis of $22,000. Ben also gave $5,000 cash to a private foundation to which a 30% limitation applies.
>
> Since Ben's contributions to an organization to which the 50% limitation applies (disregarding the 30% limitation for capital gain property) exceed $25,000 (50% of $50,000), his contribution to the private foundation is not deductible this year. The $2,000 cash donated to the church is deducted first. The donation for the gift of land is not required to be reduced by the appreciation in value, but is limited to $15,000 (30% × $50,000). Thus, Ben may deduct only $17,000 ($2,000 + $15,000). The unused portion of the land contribution ($15,000) and the gift to the private foundation ($5,000) are carried over to the next year, still subject to their respective 30% limitations.
>
> Alternatively, Ben may elect to reduce the value of the land by its appreciation of $8,000 and not be subject to the 30% limitation for capital gain property. In such case, his current deduction would be $25,000 ($2,000 cash + $22,000 land + $1,000 cash to private foundation), but only the remaining $4,000 cash to the private foundation would be carried over to the next year.

> **NOW REVIEW MULTIPLE-CHOICE QUESTIONS 132 THROUGH 141**

E. Personal Casualty and Theft Gains and Losses

Gains and losses from casualties and thefts of **property held for personal use** are not subject to the Sec. 1231 netting process. Instead, personal casualty and theft gains and losses are **separately netted,** without regard to the holding period of the converted property.

1. A **casualty loss** must be identifiable, damaging to property, and sudden, unexpected, or unusual. Casualty losses **include**

   a. Damage from a fire, storm, accident, mine cave-in, sonic boom, or loss from vandalism
   b. Damage to trees and shrubs if there is a decrease in the total value of the real estate
   c. A loss on personal residence that has been rendered unsafe by reason of a disaster declared by the President and has been ordered demolished or relocated by a state or local government

2. Losses **not deductible** as casualties include

   a. Losses from the breakage of china or glassware through handling or by a family pet
   b. Disease, termite, or moth damage
   c. Expenses incident to casualty (temporary quarters, etc.)
   d. Progressive deterioration through a steadily operating cause and damage from normal process. Thus, the steady weakening of a building caused by normal or usual wind and weather conditions is not a casualty loss.
   e. Losses from nearby disaster (property value reduced due to location near a disaster area)
   f. Loss of future profits from, for example, ice storm damage to standing timber that reduces the rate of growth or the quality of future timber. To qualify as a casualty, the damage must actually result in existing timber being rendered unfit for use.

3. Casualty loss is deductible in the year the loss occurs.

   a. Theft loss is deductible in the year the loss is discovered.
   b. Loss in a federally declared disaster area is deductible either in the year loss occurs or the preceding year (by filing an amended return).

4. The **amount of loss** is the lesser of (1) the decrease in the FMV of the property resulting from the casualty, or (2) the adjusted basis of the property. The amount of loss must be reduced by

   a. Any insurance or reimbursement, and
   b. $100 floor for each separate nonbusiness casualty

5. An individual is not permitted to deduct a casualty loss for damage to **insured property** not used in a trade or business or in a transaction entered into for profit unless the individual files a timely insurance claim with respect to the loss. Casualty insurance premiums are considered a personal expense and are not deductible.

6. If personal casualty and theft **gains exceed losses** (after the $100 floor for each loss), then all gains and losses are treated as capital gains and losses.

EXAMPLE

An individual incurred a $5,000 personal casualty gain, and a $1,000 personal casualty loss (after the $100 floor) during the current taxable year. Since there was a net gain, the individual will report the gain and loss as a $5,000 capital gain and a $1,000 capital loss.

---

7. If losses **(after the $100 floor for each loss) exceed gains,** the losses (1) offset gains, and (2) are an ordinary deduction from AGI to the extent **in excess of 10% of AGI.**

EXAMPLE

An individual had AGI of $40,000 (before casualty gains and losses), and also had a personal casualty loss of $12,000 (after the $100 floor) and a personal casualty gain of $3,000. Since there was a personal casualty net loss, the net loss will be deductible as an itemized deduction of [$12,000 – $3,000 – (10% × $40,000)] = $5,000.

EXAMPLE

Frank Jones' lakeside cottage, which cost him $13,600 (including $1,600 for the land) on April 30, 1991, was partially destroyed by fire on July 12, 2015. The value of the property immediately before the fire was $46,000 ($24,000 for the building and $22,000 for the land), and the value immediately after the fire was $36,000. He collected $7,000 from the insurance company. It was Jones' only casualty for 2015 and his AGI was $20,000. Jones' casualty loss deduction from the fire would be $900, computed as follows:

Value of entire property before fire	$46,000
Value of entire property after fire	−36,000
Decrease in fair market value of entire property	$10,000
Adjusted basis (cost in this case)	$13,600
Loss sustained (lesser of decrease in FMV or adjusted basis)	$10,000
Less insurance recovery	−7,000
Casualty loss	$3,000
Less $100 floor	– 100
Loss after $100 floor	$2,900
Less 10% of AGI	−2,000
Casualty loss deduction	$900

NOW REVIEW MULTIPLE-CHOICE QUESTIONS 142 THROUGH 146

F. Miscellaneous Deductions

1. The following miscellaneous expenses are only deductible to the extent they (in the aggregate) **exceed 2% of AGI**.

   a. **Outside salesman expenses** include all business expenses of an employee who principally solicits business for his/her employer while away from the employer's place of business.

   b. All **unreimbursed employee expenses** including

      (1) Employee **education** expenses if

         (a) Incurred to maintain or improve skills required in employee's present job, or to meet requirements to keep job

         (b) Deductible expenses include unreimbursed transportation, travel, tuition, books, supplies, etc.

         (c) Education expenses are not deductible if required to meet minimum educational requirements in employee's job, or the education qualifies the employee for a new job (e.g., CPA review course) even if a new job is not sought

         (d) Travel as a form of education is not deductible

      (2) **Other deductible unreimbursed employee expenses** include

         (a) Transportation and travel (including 50% of meals and entertainment)

         (b) Uniforms not adaptable to general use

         (c) Employment agency fees to secure employment in same occupation

         (d) Subscription to professional journals

         (e) Dues to professional societies, union dues, and initiation fees

         (f) Physical examinations required by employer

         (g) A college professor's research, lecturing, and writing expenses

         (h) Amounts teacher pays to a substitute

         (i) Surety bond premiums

         (j) Malpractice insurance premiums

         (k) A research chemist's laboratory breakage fees

         (l) Small tools and supplies

   c. Tax counsel, assistance, and tax return preparation fees

   d. Expenses for the production of income other than those incurred in a trade or business or for production of rents and royalties (e.g., investment counsel fees, clerical help, safe-deposit box rent, legal fees to collect alimony, etc.)

2. The following miscellaneous expenses are **not subject to the 2% floor,** but instead are **deductible in full**.

   a. Gambling losses to the extent of gambling winnings

   b. Impairment-related work expenses for handicapped employees

   c. Estate tax related to income in respect of a decedent

   d. Deduction for repayment of amounts under a claim of rights if over $3,000.

   e. Amortizable bond premium on bonds acquired before October 23, 1986

   f. Casualty and theft losses of income-producing property

   g. The balance of an employee's investment in an annuity contract where the employee dies before recovering the entire investment

3. Examples of **nondeductible expenses** include

   a. Fees and licenses, such as auto licenses, marriage licenses, and dog tags

   b. Home repairs, insurance, rent

   c. Personal legal expenses

   d. Life insurance

   e. Burial expenses

   f. Capital expenditures

    g. Illegal bribes and kickbacks

    h. Fines and tax penalties

    i. Collateral

    j. Commuting to and from work

    k. Professional accreditation fees

    l. Bar examination fees and incidental expenses in securing admission to the bar

    m. Medical and dental license fees paid to obtain initial licensing

    n. Campaign expenses of a candidate for any office are not deductible, nor are registration fees for primary elections, even if taxpayer is the incumbent of the office to be contested.

    o. Cost of midday meals while working late (except while traveling away from home)

    p. Political contributions

G. Reduction of Total Itemized Deductions

1. High income taxpayers whose AGI exceeds a threshold must reduce certain itemized deductions by 3% of the excess of AGI over the threshold amount. For 2015, the threshold amounts are: $309,900 for married couples and surviving spouses; $284,050 for heads of households; $258,250 for unmarried taxpayers; and $154,950 for married taxpayers filing separately.

    a. Itemized deductions **subject to reduction** include taxes, qualified residence interest, charitable contributions, and miscellaneous itemized deductions, (other than gambling).

    b. Itemized deductions **not subject to reduction** include medical, investment interest, casualty and theft losses, and gambling losses.

2. The **reduction can't exceed 80%** of allowable itemized deductions not counting itemized deductions not subject to reduction (i.e., medical, investment interest, casualty and theft, and gambling losses).

EXAMPLE:

Married taxpayers filing jointly have AGI of $340,000 for 2015. Their itemized deductions consist of taxes and charitable contributions totaling $20,000 and investment interest expense of $5,000. Their reduction is the lesser of: (1) 3% × ($340,000 − $309,900) = $903, or, (2) 80% × $20,000 = $16,000. As a result, their reduction is $903, and their deduction for itemized deductions will total $24,097 (i.e., $20,000 − $903 reduction, plus $5,000 investment interest expense).

> **NOW REVIEW MULTIPLE-CHOICE QUESTIONS 147 THROUGH 152**

IV. EXEMPTIONS

Personal exemptions are similar to itemized deductions in that they are deducted from adjusted gross income. Personal exemptions are allowed for the taxpayer, spouse, and dependent if the dependent is a US citizen or resident.

1. The personal exemption amount is **$4,000** for 2015 ($3,950 for 2014).

2. Personal exemption for **taxpayer**

    a. Full exemption even if birth or death occurred during the year

    b. No personal exemption for taxpayer if eligible to be claimed as a dependent on another taxpayer's return

3. Exemption for **spouse**

    a. Exemption on joint return

    b. Not allowed if divorced or legally separated at end of year

    c. If a separate return is filed, taxpayer may claim spouse exemption only if the spouse had no gross income and was not the dependent of another taxpayer.

4. Exemption for a **dependent** who is either a *qualifying child* or a *qualifying relative*. A full exemption is allowed even if birth or death occurred during the year. To be a dependent, an individual must be a citizen, national, or resident of the US, or a resident of Canada or Mexico.

a. An individual must satisfy additional tests relating to relationship, age, abode, and support to be classified as a qualifying child. A **qualifying child**

(1) Must be the taxpayer's child or a descendant of the taxpayer's child, or the taxpayer's sibling (including half and step siblings) or a descendant of the taxpayer's sibling. *Taxpayer's child* includes son, daughter, stepson, or stepdaughter, or eligible foster child. A legally adopted child or an individual placed with the taxpayer for legal adoption is treated as a child of the taxpayer by blood.

(2) Must be younger than the taxpayer and must be under age nineteen, or must be a full-time student for at least five months during year and under age twenty-four as of the close of the year. The age test does not apply to a child who is permanently and totally disabled.

(3) Must have the same principal place of abode as the taxpayer for more than half of the taxpayer's tax year.

(4) Must not have provided more than one-half of his or her own support during the calendar year in which the taxpayer's tax year begins. If the child is the taxpayer's child and is a full-time student, amounts received as scholarships are not considered support.

(5) Must not file a joint return with his or her spouse, unless filed solely for refund of tax withheld.

(6) Cannot be claimed as a dependent on more than one return, even though the child satisfies the qualifying child tests for two or more taxpayers. If none of the taxpayers is the child's parent, the child is a qualifying child for the taxpayer with the highest AGI. If only one of the taxpayers is the child's parent, the child is a qualifying child for that parent. If two of the taxpayers are the child's parents and they do not file a joint return together, the child is a dependent of the parent with whom the child resided for the longest period during the year. If equal time spent with each parent, the parent with the highest AGI is entitled to the exemption.

b. An individual must satisfy five additional tests to be classified as a qualifying relative. A **qualifying relative**

(1) Must *not* be a qualifying child (as defined above).

(2) **Joint return.** Dependent cannot file a joint return, unless filed solely for refund of tax withheld.

(3) **Member of household or related.** Dependent must either live with the taxpayer for the entire year or be a relative (closer than cousin).

(a) *Relatives* includes ancestors, descendants, brothers and sisters, uncles and aunts, nephews and nieces, half and step relationships, and in-laws.

(b) Relationships established by marriage are not ended by death or divorce.

(c) A person temporarily absent for vacation, school, or sickness, or indefinitely confined in a nursing home meets the member of household test.

(d) A person who died during the year but was a member of household until death, and a child who is born during the year and is a member of household for the rest of year, meet the member of household requirement.

(4) **Gross income.** Dependent had gross income less than $4,000 ($3,950 for 2014). Gross income does not include tax-exempt income (e.g., nontaxable social security).

(5) **Support.** Taxpayer must furnish over one-half of support.

(a) Includes food, clothing, FV of lodging, medical, education, recreation, and certain capital expenses.

(b) Excludes life insurance premiums, funeral expenses, nontaxable scholarships, income and social security taxes paid from a dependent's own income.

c. A **multiple support agreement** may be used if no one person furnishes more than 50% of the support of a dependent. Then a person can be treated as having provided more than half of a dependent's support if (1) over half of the support was received from persons who each would have been entitled to claim the exemption had they contributed more than half of the support, (2) **more than 10%** of the support was provided by the person claiming the exemption, and (3) each other person who contributed more than 10% of the support signs a written declaration stating that he or she will not claim the exemption.

    d. A special rule applies to a child who receives over one-half of the child's support from the **child's parents who are divorced** or legally separated, or who lived apart at all times during the last six months of the year, if the child was in the custody of one or both parents for more than one-half of the year.

        (1) The child will be treated as the qualifying child or qualifying relative of the noncustodial parent if any of the following requirements are satisfied:

            (a) The parents' divorce or separation instrument provides that the noncustodial parent is entitled to the dependency exemption.
            (b) The custodial parent provides the IRS with a signed, written declaration waiving the child's dependency exemption.
            (c) A pre-1985 divorce decree or written separation agreement entitles the noncustodial parent to the exemption and that parent provides at least $600 for the child's support.

        (2) These special rules do not apply if over one-half of the support of the child is treated as having been received from a taxpayer under a multiple support agreement.

    e. If an individual is a dependent of another taxpayer for any taxable year, the individual will be treated as having no dependents for such taxable year.

5. Reduction of personal exemptions. The deduction for personal exemptions is reduced by 2% for each $2,500 ($1,250 for married filing separately) or fraction thereof by which AGI exceeds a threshold amount.

    a. For 2015, the threshold amounts are: $309,900 for married couples and surviving spouses; $284,050 for heads of households: $258,250 for unmarried taxpayers; and $154,950 for married taxpayers filing separately.
    b. All personal exemptions are completely eliminated when AGI exceeds the thresholds by more than $122,500.

EXAMPLE:

An unmarried individual with one exemption has AGI of $333,250 for 2015. Her AGI exceeds the applicable threshold by $75,000 ($333,250 − $258,250). Dividing the $75,000 excess by $2,500 equals 30. Thus, the reduction of her exemption will be 30 × 2% = 60% × $4,000 = $2,400, and her allowable personal exemption amount will be $4,000 − $2,400 = $1,600.

NOW REVIEW MULTIPLE-CHOICE QUESTIONS 153 THROUGH 165

V. TAX COMPUTATION

A. Tax Tables

1. Tax tables contain pre-computed tax liability based on taxable income.

    a. AGI less itemized deductions and exemptions
    b. Filing status

        (1) Single
        (2) Head of household
        (3) Married filing separately
        (4) Married filing joint return (even if only one had income)
        (5) Surviving spouse (qualifying widow[er] with dependent child)

2. Tax tables must be used by taxpayers unless taxable income is $100,000 or more.

B. Tax Rate Schedules

1. For 2015 the tax rates for individuals are as follows:

Tax rate	Joint return surviving spouse			Married filing separately		
10%	$0	–	$18,450	$0	–	$9,225
15%	$18,451	–	$74,900	$9,226	–	$37,450
25%	$74,901	–	$151,200	$37,451	–	$75,600
28%	$151,201	–	$230,450	$75,601	–	$115,225
33%	$230,451	–	$411,500	$115,226	–	$205,750
35%	$411,501	–	$464,850	$205,751	–	$232,425
39.6%	Over $464,850			Over $232,425		

Tax rate	Head of household			Single		
10%	$0	–	$13,150	$0	–	$9,225
15%	$13,151	–	$50,200	$9,226	–	$37,450
25%	$50,201	–	$129,600	$37,451	–	$90,750
28%	$129,601	–	$209,850	$90,751	–	$189,300
33%	$209,851	–	$411,500	$189,301	–	$411,500
35%	$411,501	–	$439,000	$411,501	–	$413,200
39.6%	Over $439,000			Over $413,200		

2. **Kiddie tax on unearned income.** The earned income of a child of any age and the unearned income of a child 24 years or older as of the end of the taxable year is taxed at the child's own marginal rate. However, the **unearned income in excess of $2,100** of a child under age eighteen is generally taxed at the rates of the child's parents.

   a. This rule also applies to 18-year-old children, as well as 19 to 23-year-old children who are full-time students, if they do not provide at least half of their support with earned income.
   b. Unearned income will be taxed at the parents' rates regardless of the source of the assets creating the child's unearned income so long as the child has at least one living parent as of the close of the tax year and does not file a joint return.
   c. The amount taxed at the parents' rates equals the child's unearned income less the sum of (1) any penalty for early withdrawal of savings, (2) $1,050, and (3) the greater of $1,050 or the child's itemized deductions directly connected with the production of unearned income.

      (1) Directly connected itemized deductions are those expenses incurred to produce or collect income, or maintain property that produces unearned income, including custodian fees, service fees to collect interest and dividends, and investment advisory fees. These are deductible as miscellaneous itemized deductions subject to a 2% of AGI limitation.
      (2) The amount taxed at the parents' rates cannot exceed the child's taxable income.

EXAMPLE

Janie (age 11) is claimed as a dependent on her parents' return and in 2015 receives interest income of $10,000, and has no itemized deductions. Janie's taxable income would be $8,950 ($10,000 – $1,050 basic standard deduction). The amount of Janie's income taxed at her parents' tax rates would be $7,900 [$10,000 – ($1,050 + $1,050)], with the remaining $1,050 of taxable income taxed at Janie's tax rate.

EXAMPLE

Brian (age 12) is claimed as a dependent on his parents' return and in 2015 receives interest income of $15,000 and has itemized deductions of $1,200 that are directly connected to the production of the interest income. The amount of Brian's income taxed at his parents' tax rates is $12,750 [$15,000 – ($1,050 + $1,200)].

EXAMPLE

Kerry (age 10) is claimed as a dependent on her parents' return and in 2015 receives interest income of $12,000, has an early withdrawal penalty of $350, and itemized deductions of $400 that are directly connected to the production of the interest income. The amount of Kerry's income taxed at her parents' tax rates is $9,550 [$12,000 – ($350 + $1,050 + $1,050)].

---

    d. A child's tax liability on unearned income taxed at the parents' rates is the child's share of the increase in tax (including alternative minimum tax) that would result from adding to the parents' taxable income the unearned income of their children subject to this rule.

    e. If the child's parents are divorced, the custodial parent's taxable income will be used in determining the child's tax liability.

    f. If child's parents are divorced and both parents have custody, the taxable income of the parent having custody for the greater portion of the calendar year will be used in determining the child's tax liability.

3. **Reporting unearned income of a child on parent's return.** For 2015, parents may elect to include on their return the unearned income of their child under age eighteen whose income consists solely of interest and dividends and is between $1,050 and $10,500.

    a. The child is treated as having no gross income and does not have to file a tax return for the year the election is made.

    b. The electing parents must include the child's gross income in excess of $2,100 on their return for the tax year, resulting in the taxation of that income at the parents' highest marginal rate. Also, the parents must report additional tax liability equal to 10% of the child's income between $1,050 and $2,100.

    c. The election cannot be made if estimated tax payments were made for the tax year in the child's name and social security number, or if the child is subject to backup withholding.

C. Filing Status

1. Married persons (married at year-end or at time of death of spouse) can file joint return or separate returns.
2. **Qualifying widow(er) with dependent child** (i.e., surviving spouse) may use joint tax rates for the two years following the year in which the spouse died.

    a. Surviving spouse must have been eligible to file a joint return in the year of the spouse's death.

    b. Dependent son, stepson, daughter, or stepdaughter must live in household with surviving spouse.

    c. Surviving spouse must provide more than 50% of costs of maintaining a household that was the main home of the child for the entire year.

3. **Head of household** status applies to an unmarried person (other than a qualifying widow(er) with dependent child) who provides more than 50% of costs of maintaining a household which, for more than one-half of the year, is the principal place of abode for

    a. A *qualifying child* of the taxpayer (e.g., taxpayer's children, siblings, step-siblings, and their descendants under age nineteen, or under age twenty-four and a student), but not if such qualifying child is married at the end of the taxable year and is not a dependent of the taxpayer because of filing a joint return, or was not a citizen, resident, or national of the US, nor a resident of Canada or Mexico.

    b. Relative (closer than cousin) for whom the taxpayer is entitled to a dependency exemption for the taxable year.

    c. Parents need not live with head of household, but parents' household must be maintained by taxpayer (e.g., nursing home) and parents must qualify as taxpayer's dependents.

    d. Cannot qualify for head of household status through use of multiple support agreement, or if taxpayer was a nonresident alien at any time during taxable year.

    e. Unmarried requirement is satisfied if legally separated from spouse under a decree of separate maintenance, or if spouse was a nonresident alien at any time during taxable year.

4. **Cost of maintaining household**

    a. *Includes* rent, mortgage interest, taxes, insurance on home, repairs, utilities, and food eaten in the home.

    b. *Excludes* the cost of clothing, education, medical expenses, vacations, life insurance, transportation, rental value of home, value of taxpayer's services.

NOW REVIEW MULTIPLE-CHOICE QUESTIONS 166 THROUGH 172

D. Alternative Minimum Tax (AMT)

1. The alternative minimum tax for non corporate taxpayers is computed by applying a two-tiered rate schedule to a taxpayer's alternative minimum tax base. A rate of 26% generally applies to the first $185,400 of a taxpayer's alternative minimum taxable income (AMTI) in excess of the exemption amount. A 28% rate generally applies to AMTI greater than $185,400 ($92,700) for married taxpayers filing separately) above the exemption amount. The AMT treatment of net capital gain and qualified dividends is the same as for regular tax purposes, including the netting of capital gains and losses into separate tax-rate groups. Thus, net capital gain and qualified dividends are taxed at the same reduced rates for AMT as they are for regular tax purposes (generally 15%).

2. A taxpayer's AMT is generally the amount by which the applicable percentage (26% or 28%) of AMTI as reduced by an exemption amount and reduced by the AMT foreign tax credit exceeds the amount of a taxpayer's regular tax as reduced by the regular tax foreign tax credit.

3. AMT computation formula

           Regular taxable income
        + (–)   Adjustments
        +   Tax preferences

  = Alternative minimum taxable income
     –   Exemption amount

  = Alternative minimum tax base
     ×   26% or 28% (but reduced rates for qualified dividends and net capital gain)

  = Tentative before foreign tax credit
     –   AMT foreign tax credit

  = Tentative minimum tax
     –   Regular tax liability (reduced by regular tax foreign tax credit)

  = AMT (if positive)

4. **Exemption.** AMTI is offset by an exemption. However, the AMT exemption amount is phased out at the rate of 25% of AMTI between certain specified levels. For 2015, the exemption and phase-out ranges are

Filing status	AMT exemption	Phase-out range
Married filing jointly;		
Surviving Spouse	$83,400	$158,900 – $492,500
Single; Head of Household	$53,600	$119,200 – $333,600
Married filing separately	$41,700	$79,450 – $246,250

In the case of a child under the age of eighteen, the AMT exemption (normally $53,600) is limited to the child's earned income plus $7,400 (for 2015).

5. **Adjustments.** In determining AMTI, taxable income must be computed with various adjustments. Example of adjustments include

a. For real property placed in service after 1986 and before 1999, the difference between regular tax depreciation and straight-line depreciation over forty years.

b. For personal property placed in service after 1986, the difference between regular tax depreciation using the 200% declining balance method and depreciation using the 150% declining balance method (switching to straight-line when necessary to maximize the deduction).

c. Excess of stock's FMV over amount paid upon exercise of incentive stock options.

d. The medical expense deduction is computed using a 10% floor (instead of the 7.5% floor that may have been used for regular tax).

e. No deduction is allowed for home mortgage interest if the loan proceeds were not used to buy, build, or improve the home.

f. No deduction is allowed for personal, state, and local taxes, and for miscellaneous itemized deductions subject to the 2% floor for regular tax purposes.

g. No deduction is allowed for personal exemptions and the standard deduction.

h. For long-term contracts, the excess of income under the percentage-of-completion method over the amount reported using the completed-contract method.

i. The installment method cannot be used for sales of dealer property.

6. **Preference items.** The following are examples of preference items added to taxable income (as adjusted above) in computing AMTI:

a. Tax-exempt interest on certain private activity bonds reduced by related interest expense that is disallowed for regular tax purposes. Tax-exempt interest on private activity bonds issued in 2009 and 2010 is not an item of tax preference.

b. Accelerated depreciation on real property and leased personal property placed in service before 1987—excess of accelerated depreciation over straight-line

c. The excess of percentage depletion over the property's adjusted basis

d. 7% of the amount of excluded gain from the sale of Sec. 1202 qualified small business stock (QSBS). However, there is no preference for QSBS gains qualifying for the 100% exclusion through 2014.

7. **Tax credits.** Generally, an individual's tax credits are allowed to reduce regular tax liability, but only to the extent that regular income tax liability exceeds tentative minimum tax liability.

a. All nonrefundable personal credits are allowed to offset both regular tax liability and the alternative minimum tax.

b. An individual's AMT is also reduced by the alternative minimum tax foreign tax credit, the alcohol fuels credit, the renewable electricity production credit, and several other specified credits.

8. **Minimum tax credit.** The amount of AMT paid (net of exclusion preferences) is allowed as a credit against regular tax liability in future years.

a. The amount of the AMT credit to be carried forward is the excess of the AMT paid over the AMT that would be paid if AMTI included only exclusion preferences (e.g., disallowed itemized deductions and the preferences for excess percentage depletion, and tax-exempt interest).

b. The credit can be carried forward indefinitely, but not carried back.

c. The AMT credit can only be used to reduce regular tax liability, **not** future AMT liability.

NOW REVIEW MULTIPLE-CHOICE QUESTIONS 173 THROUGH 179

E. Other Taxes

1. **Social security** (FICA) tax is imposed on both employers and employees (withheld from wages). The FICA tax has two components: old age, survivor, and disability insurance (OASDI) and Medicare hospital insurance (HI). For 2015, the OASDI rate is 6.2% and the HI rate is 1.45%, resulting in a combined rate of 7.65% that applies to both employees and employers. For 2015, the OASDI portion is capped at $118,500, while the HI portion (1.45%) applies to all wages.

a. Beginning in 2013, the employee portion of the Medicare tax is increased by 0.9% (to 2.35%) for wages in excess of $200,000 ($250,000 on a joint return, $125,000 for a married individual filing separately).

b. In the case of a joint return, the additional 0.9% Medicare tax is imposed on the combined income of both spouses.

c. The employer is required to withhold on the employee's wages in excess of $200,000 per year, and may disregard the wages of the employee's spouse for this purpose. The amount of tax not withheld by an employer must be paid by the employee and is subject to estimated tax requirements.

2. **Federal unemployment** (FUTA) tax is imposed only on employers at a rate of 6.2% of the first $7,000 of wages paid to each employee. A credit of up to 5.4% is available for unemployment taxes paid to a state, leaving a net federal tax of 0.8%.

3. **Self-employment** tax is imposed on individuals who work for themselves (e.g., sole proprietor, independent contractor, partner). The combined self-employment tax rate 15.3%, of which the Medicare portion is 2.9%.

   a. The full self-employment tax is capped at $118,500 for 2015, while the Medicare portion (2.9%) applies to all self-employment earnings.

   b. Beginning in 2013, the Medicare tax rate is increased by 0.9% (to 3.8%) for net earnings from self-employment in excess of $200,000 ($250,000 on a joint return, $125,000 for a married individual filing separately). On a joint return, the additional 0.9% Medicare tax is imposed on the combined income of both spouses. The deductions that usually apply for self-employment and income tax purposes for a portion of the self-employment tax do not apply to this additional tax.

   c. Income from self-employment generally includes all items of business income less business deductions. Self-employment income does *not* include personal interest, dividends, rents, capital gains and losses, and gains and losses on the disposition of business property.

   d. Wages subject to FICA tax are deducted from $118,500 for 2015 in determining the amount of income subject to self-employment tax.

   e. No tax if net earnings from self-employment are less than $400.

   f. A deduction equal to one-half of the self-employment tax rate (7.65%) multiplied by the taxpayer's self-employment income (without regard to this deduction) is allowed in computing the taxpayer's net earnings from self-employment. The purpose of this deduction is to allow the amount on which the self-employment tax is based to be adjusted downward to reflect the fact that employees do not pay FICA tax on the amount of the FICA tax that is paid by their employers.

   g. Individuals normally deduct one-half of their total self-employment tax for AGI.

EXAMPLE

A taxpayer has self-employment income of $50,000 before the deemed deduction for 2015. The deemed deduction is $50,000 × 7.65% = $3,825, resulting in *net earnings from self-employment* of $50,000 – $3,825 = $46,175, and a self-employment tax of $46,175 × 15.3% = $7,065. In computing AGI, the taxpayer is allowed to deduct 50% × $7,065 = $3,533.

EXAMPLE

A taxpayer has self-employment income of $130,000 before the deemed deduction for 2015. The deemed deduction is $130,000 × 7.65% = $9,945, resulting in *net earnings from self-employment* of $130,000 – $9,945 = $120,055. The taxpayer's self-employment tax will be ($118,500 × 15.3%) + [($120,055 – $118,500) × 2.9%] = $18,176. In computing AGI, the taxpayer is allowed to deduct 50% × $18,176 = $9,088.

---

4. **Net Investment Income Tax (NIIT)** also known as the Medicare Contribution Tax is imposed on individuals for tax years beginning after December 31, 2012 at a rate of 3.8% on the *lesser of* (a) net investment income, or (b) the excess of modified AGI over a threshold amount. The threshold amount for an individual is $200,000 ($250,000 on a joint return, $125,000 for a married individual filing separately). Modified AGI is the taxpayer's AGI increased by any foreign earned income exclusion reduced by any allocable deductions and credits. The tax applies to all individuals subject to US taxation other than nonresident aliens.

   a. Investment income is composed of three categories: (1) traditional portfolio income such as dividends, interest, royalties, nonqualified annuity income, and income from certain types of rental activities; (2) trade or business income from passive investments and income from trading in financial instruments; and, (3) gains from the sale of stocks, bonds, and mutual funds, capital gain distributions from mutual funds, gains from the sale of investment real estate, gains from the sale of interests in partnerships and S corporations (to the extent the taxpayer was a passive owner), and gains (after exclusion) from the sale of a primary or secondary residence. Losses in one category are not allowed to offset income or gain in another category.

   b. Investment income is reduced by expenses properly allocable to investment income such as investment interest expense, investment advisory and brokerage fees, expenses related to rental and royalty income, and state and local income taxes allocable to net investment income.

> **EXAMPLE**
>
> Mary is single and has wage income of $190,000 and dividend income of $30,000. Her modified AGI is $220,000, and she has no investment expenses. Mary is subject to the NIIT on $20,000, which is the lesser of her net investment income of $30,000, or her $20,000 of income in excess of the $200,000 threshold.

> **EXAMPLE**
>
> Melissa is single and has wage income of $270,000 and interest income of $30,000. Her modified AGI is $300,000, and she has no investment expenses. Melissa is subject to the NIIT on $30,000, which is the lesser of her net investment income of $30,000, or her $100,000 of income is excess of the $200,000 threshold.

NOW REVIEW MULTIPLE-CHOICE QUESTIONS 180 THROUGH 186

VI.   TAX CREDITS/ESTIMATED TAX PAYMENTS

Tax credits directly reduce tax liability. The tax liability less tax credits equals taxes payable. Taxes that have already been withheld on wages and estimated tax payments are credited against tax liability without limitation, even if the result is a refund due to the taxpayer.

A.   General Business Credit

1. It is comprised of numerous credits such as the (1) investment credit (energy and rehabilitation), (2) work opportunity credit, (3) alcohol fuels credit, (4) research credit, (5) low-income housing credit, (6) disabled access credit, (7) renewable resources electricity production credit, (8) empowerment zone employment credit, (9) Indian employment credit, (10) employer social security credit, (11) orphan drug credit, (12) new markets tax credit, (13) small-employer pension plan startup cost credit, and (14) the employer-provided child care credit.
2. The general business credit is allowed to the extent of "net income tax" less the greater of (1) the tentative minimum tax or (2) 25% of "net regular tax liability" above $25,000.

   a. "Net income tax" means the amount of the regular income tax plus the alternative minimum tax, and minus nonrefundable tax credits (except the alternative minimum tax credit).
   b. "Net regular tax liability" is the taxpayer's regular tax liability reduced by nonrefundable tax credits (except the alternative minimum tax credit).

> **EXAMPLE**
>
> An individual (not subject to the alternative minimum tax) has a net income tax of $65,000. The individual's general business credit cannot exceed $65,000 − [25% × ($65,000 − $25,000)] = $55,000.

3. A general business credit in excess of the limitation amount is carried back one year and forward twenty years.

B.   Business Energy Credit

1. The business energy credit is 10% to 30% for qualified investment in property that uses solar, geothermal, or ocean thermal energy. The property must be constructed by the taxpayer, or if acquired, the taxpayer must be the first person to use the property.
2. The recoverable basis of energy property must be reduced by 50% of the amount of business energy credit.

C. Credit for Rehabilitation Expenditures

1. Special investment credit (in lieu of regular income tax credits and energy credits) for qualified expenditures incurred to substantially rehabilitate old buildings. Credit percentages are (1) 10% for nonresidential buildings placed in service before 1936 (other than certified historic structures), and (2) 20% for residential and nonresidential certified historic structures.
2. **To qualify** for credit on other than certified historic structures

   a. 75% of external walls must remain in place as external or internal walls
   b. 50% or more of existing external walls must be retained in place as external walls
   c. 75% or more of existing internal structural framework must be retained in place

3. A building's recoverable basis must be reduced by 100% of the amount of rehabilitation credit.

D. Work Opportunity Credit

1. Credit is generally 40% of the first $6,000 of qualified first year wages paid to each qualified new employee who begins work before January 1, 2015. For qualified summer youth employees, the credit is 40% of the first $3,000 of wages for services performed during any ninety-day period between May 1 and September 15.
2. Qualified new employees include a (1) qualified IV-A recipient, (2) qualified veteran, (3) qualified ex-felon, (4) designated community resident, (5) vocational rehabilitation referral, (6) qualified summer youth employee, (7) qualified food stamp recipient, (8) qualified SSI recipient, (9) long-term family assistance recipients, (10) unemployed veterans, and (11) disconnected youth.
3. Employer's deduction for wages is reduced by the amount of credit.
4. Taxpayer may elect not to claim credit (to avoid reducing wage deduction).

E. Alcohol Fuels Credit

1. A ten cents per gallon tax credit is allowed for the production of up to fifteen million gallons per year of ethanol by an eligible small ethanol producer (i.e., one having a production capacity of up to sixty million gallons of alcohol per year).
2. The tax credit for ethanol blenders is sixty cents per gallon for 190 or greater proof ethanol and forty-five cents per gallon for 150 to 190 proof ethanol.

F. Research Credit

1. The research credit applies to amounts paid or incurred through December 31, 2014, and is the sum of (a) 20% of the excess of qualified research expenses for the current year over a base period amount, (b) 20% of the basic research payments made to a qualified organization, and (c) 20% of the amounts paid to an energy research consortium for qualified energy research.
2. Taxpayers may elect an alternative method to calculate the increased research activities credit amount using an alternative simplified credit computation.

G. Low-Income Housing Credit

1. The amount of credit for owners of low-income housing projects depends upon (1) whether the taxpayer acquires existing housing or whether the housing is newly constructed or rehabilitated, and (2) whether or not the housing project is financed by tax-exempt bonds or other federally subsidized financing. The applicable credit rates are the appropriate percentages issued by the IRS for the month in which the building is placed in service.
2. The amount on which the credit is computed is the portion of the total depreciable basis of a qualified housing project that reflects the portion of the housing units within the project that are occupied by qualified low-income individuals.
3. The credit is claimed each year (for a ten-year period) beginning with the year that the property is placed in service. The first-year credit is prorated to reflect the date placed in service.

H. Disabled Access Credit

1. A tax credit is available to an eligible small business for expenditures incurred to make the business accessible to disabled individuals. The amount of this credit is equal to 50% of the amount of the eligible access expenditures for a year that exceed $250 but do not exceed $10,250.
2. An eligible small business is one that either (1) had gross receipts for the preceding tax year that did not exceed $1 million, or (2) had no more than 30 full-time employees during the preceding tax year, and (3) elects to have this credit apply.

3. Eligible access expenditures are amounts incurred to comply with the requirements of the Americans with Disabilities Act of 1990 and include amounts incurred for the purpose of removing architectural, communication, physical, or transportation barriers that prevent a business from being accessible to, or usable by, disabled individuals; amounts incurred to provide qualified readers to visually impaired individuals, and amounts incurred to acquire or modify equipment or devices for disabled individuals. Expenses incurred in connection with new construction are not eligible for the credit.

4. This credit is included as part of the general business credit; no deduction or credit is allowed under any other Code provision for any amount for which a disabled access credit is allowed.

I. Empowerment Zone Employment Credit

1. The credit is generally equal to 20% of the first $15,000 of wages paid to each employee who is a resident of a designated empowerment zone and performs substantially all services within the zone in an employer's trade or business.

2. The deduction for wages must be reduced by the amount of credit.

J. Employer Social Security Credit

1. Credit allowed to food and beverage establishments for the employer's portion of FICA tax (7.65%) attributable to reported tips in excess of those tips treated as wages for purposes of satisfying the minimum wage provisions of the Fair Labor Standards Act.

2. No deduction is allowed for any amount taken into account in determining the credit.

K. Employer-Provided Child Care Credit

1. Employers who provide child care facilities to their employees during normal working hours are eligible for a credit equal to 25% of qualified child care expenditures, and 10% of qualified child care resource and referral expenditures. The maximum credit is $150,000 per year, and is subject to a ten-year recapture rule.

2. *Qualified child care expenditures* include amounts paid to acquire, construct, and rehabilitate property which is to be used as a qualified child care facility (e.g., training costs of employees, scholarship programs, compensation for employees with high levels of child care training).

3. To prevent a double benefit, the basis of qualifying property is reduced by the amount of credit, and the amount of qualifying expenditures that would otherwise be deductible must be reduced by the amount of credit.

L. Credit for the Elderly and the Disabled

1. Eligible taxpayers are those who are either (1) 65 or older or (2) permanently and totally disabled.

   a. Permanent and total disability is the inability to engage in substantial gainful activity for a period that is expected to last for a continuous twelve-month period.
   b. Married individuals must file a joint return to claim the credit unless they have not lived together at all during the year.
   c. Credit cannot be claimed if Form 1040A or 1040EZ is filed.

2. Credit is **15%** of an initial amount reduced by certain amounts excluded from gross income and AGI in excess of certain levels. The amount of credit is limited to the amount of tax liability.

   a. Initial amount varies with filing status.

      (1) $5,000 for single or joint return where only one spouse is 65 or older
      (2) $7,500 for joint return where both spouses are 65 or older
      (3) $3,750 for married filing a separate return
      (4) Limited to disability income for taxpayers under age 65

   b. Reduced by annuities, pensions, social security, or disability income that is excluded from gross income
   c. Also reduced by 50% of the excess of AGI over

      (1) $7,500 if single
      (2) $10,000 if joint return
      (3) $5,000 for married individual filing separate return

---

EXAMPLE

H, age 67, and his wife, W, age 65, file a joint return and have adjusted gross income of $12,000. H received social security benefits of $2,000 during the year. The computation of their credit would be as follows:

Initial amount		$7,500
Less: social security	$2,000	
50% of AGI over $10,000	1,000	3,000
Balance		4,500
		× 15%
Amount of credit (limited to tax liability)		$675

M. Child and Dependent Care Credit

1. The credit may vary from **20% to 35%** of the amount paid for qualifying household and dependent care expenses incurred to enable taxpayer to be gainfully employed or look for work. Credit is 35% if AGI is $15,000 or less, but is reduced by 1 percentage point for each $2,000 (or portion thereof) of AGI in excess of $15,000 (but not reduced below 20%).

EXAMPLE

Able, Baker, and Charlie have AGIs of $10,000, $20,000, and $50,000 respectively, and each incurs child care expenses of $2,000. Able's child care credit is $700 (35% × $2,000); Baker's credit is $640 (32% × $2,000); and Charlie's credit is $400 (20% × $2,000).

---

2. **Eligibility** requirements include

   a. Expenses must be incurred on behalf of a qualifying individual and must enable taxpayer to be gainfully employed or look for work
   b. Married taxpayer must file joint return. If divorced or separated, credit available to parent having custody longer time during year
   c. A **qualifying individual** must have the same principal place of abode as the taxpayer for more than one-half of the tax year. A qualifying individual includes

      (1) The taxpayer's qualifying child (e.g., taxpayer's child, stepchild, sibling, stepsibling, or descendant of any of these) under age thirteen, or
      (2) Dependent or spouse who is physically or mentally incapable of self-care

   d. **Qualifying expenses** are those incurred for care of qualifying individual and for household services that were partly for care of qualifying individual to enable taxpayer to work or look for work

      (1) Expenses incurred outside taxpayer's household qualify only if incurred for a qualifying individual who regularly spends at least eight hours each day in taxpayer's household
      (2) Payments to taxpayer's child under age nineteen do not qualify
      (3) Payments to a relative do not qualify if taxpayer is entitled to a dependency exemption for that relative

3. **Maximum amount of expenses** that qualify for credit is the least of

   a. Actual expenses incurred, or
   b. **$3,000** for one, **$6,000** for two or more qualifying individuals, or
   c. Taxpayer's earned income (or spouse's earned income if smaller)
   d. If spouse is a student or incapable of self-care and thus has little or no earned income, spouse is treated as being gainfully employed and having earnings of not less than $250 per month for one, $500 per month for two or more qualifying individuals

---

EXAMPLE

Husband and wife have earned income of $15,000 each, resulting in AGI of $30,000. They have one child, age 3. They incurred qualifying household service expenses of $1,500 and child care expenses at a nursery school of $2,200.

Household expenses	$1,500
Add child care outside home	2,200
Total employment-related expenses	$3,700
Maximum allowable expenses	$3,000
Credit = 27% × $3,000	$810

N. Foreign Tax Credit

1. Foreign income taxes on US taxpayers can either be deducted or used as a credit at the option of the taxpayer each year.
2. The credit is limited to the overall limitation of

$$\frac{\text{TI from all foreign countries}}{\text{Taxable income + Exemptions}} \times \quad (\text{US tax} - \text{Credit for elderly})$$

3. The foreign tax credit limitation must be computed separately for general category income and passive category income (i.e., dividends, interest, royalties, rents, and annuities).
4. Foreign tax credit in excess of the overall limitation is subject to a one-year carryback and a ten-year carryforward.
5. There is no limitation if foreign taxes are used as a deduction.

> **NOW REVIEW MULTIPLE-CHOICE QUESTIONS 187 THROUGH 195**

O. Earned Income Credit

1. The earned income credit is a **refundable** tax credit for eligible low-income workers. Earned income includes wages, salaries, and other employee compensation (including union strike benefits), plus earnings from self-employment (after the deduction for one-half self-employment taxes). Earned income excludes income from pensions and annuities, and investment income such as interest and dividends.
2. For 2015, the earned income credit is allowed at a rate of 34% of the first $9,880 of earned income for taxpayers with one qualifying child, is allowed at a rate of 40% on the first $13,870 of earned income for taxpayers with two qualifying children, and is allowed at a rate of 45% of the first $13,870 of earned income for an individual with three or more qualifying children. The maximum credit is reduced by 15.98% (21.06% for two or more qualifying children) of the amount by which earned income (or AGI if greater) exceeds $18,110 ($23,630 for married taxpayers filing jointly).
3. To be eligible for the credit an individual must

   a. Have earned income and a return that covers a twelve-month period
   b. Maintain a household for more than half the year for a qualifying child in the US
   c. Have a filing status other than married filing a separate return
   d. Not be a qualifying child of another person
   e. Not claim the exclusion for foreign earned income
   f. Not have disqualified income in excess of $3,400

4. **A qualifying child** must be

   a. The taxpayer's child, adopted child, eligible foster child, stepchild, sibling, stepsibling, or descendant of any of these who has the same principal place of abode as the taxpayer for more than one-half of the tax year, and is
   b. Under age nineteen, or a full-time student under age twenty-four, or permanently and totally disabled.
   c. If a custodial parent would be entitled to a child's dependency exemption but for having released it to the noncustodial parent for purposes of the earned income credit.

5. **Disqualified income** includes both taxable and tax-exempt interest, dividends, net rental and royalty income, net capital gain income, and net passive income.
6. A **reduced earned income credit** is available to an individual who does not have qualifying children if (1) the individual's principal place of abode for more than half the tax year is in the US, (2) the individual (or spouse) is at least age twenty-five (but under sixty-five) at the end of the tax year, and (3) the individual does not qualify as a dependency exemption on another taxpayer's return. For 2015, the maximum credit is 7.65% of the first $6,580 of earned income, and is reduced by 7.65% of earned income (or AGI if greater) in excess of $8,240 ($13,750 for married taxpayers filing jointly).
7. The earned income credit is refundable if the amount of credit exceeds the taxpayer's tax liability.

P. Credit for Adoption Expenses

1. A nonrefundable credit of up to $13,400 (for 2015) for qualified adoption expenses incurred for each eligible child (including a child with special needs).

    a. An *eligible child* is an individual who has not attained the age of 18 as of the time of the adoption, or who is physically or mentally incapable of self-care.
    b. Married taxpayers generally must file a joint return to claim the credit.
    c. The credit is phased out ratably for modified AGI between $201,010 and $241,010.
    d. The amount of credit that can be claimed is subject to tax liability limitations, but any unused credit can be carried forward for up to five tax years.

2. *Qualified adoption expenses* incurred or paid during a tax year prior to the year in which the adoption is finalized may be claimed as a credit in the tax year following the year the expense was incurred. Adoption expenses incurred during the year the adoption becomes final or in the year following the finalization of the adoption are claimed in the year they were incurred. Qualified adoption expenses are taken into account in the year the adoption becomes final and include all reasonable and necessary adoption fees, court costs, attorney fees, and other expenses that are directly related to the legal adoption by the taxpayer of an eligible child. However, expenses incurred in carrying out a surrogate parenting arrangement or in adopting a spouse's child do not qualify for the credit.

Q. Child Tax Credit (CTC)

1. The amount of the credit is $1,000 per qualifying child.
2. A *qualifying child* is a US citizen or resident who is the taxpayer's child, adopted child, eligible foster child, stepchild, step-sibling, or descendant of any of these who is less than seventeen years old as of the close of the calendar year in which the tax year of the taxpayer begins.
3. The child tax credit begins to phase out when modified adjusted gross income reaches $110,000 for joint filers, $55,000 for married taxpayers filing separately, and $75,000 for single taxpayers and heads of households. The credit is reduced by $50 for each $1,000, or fraction thereof, of modified AGI above the thresholds.
4. The CTC is refundable to the extent of 15% of the taxpayer's earned income in excess of $3,000 (for 2010 through 2017), up to the per child credit amount of $1,000 per child. Taxpayers with more than two children may calculate the refundable portion of the credit using the excess of their social security taxes (i.e., taxpayer's share of FICA taxes and one-half of self-employment taxes) over their earned income credit, if it results in a larger amount. The amount of refundable CTC reduces the amount of nonrefundable CTC.

R. American Opportunity Credit (AOC)

1. For the *first four years* of a postsecondary school program, qualifying taxpayers may elect to take a tax credit of 100% for the first $2,000 of qualified tuition, fees, books and course materials (not room and board), and a 25% credit for the next $2,000 of such expenses, for a total credit of up to $2,500 a year per student.
2. The credit is available on a *per student basis* and covers tuition payments for the taxpayer as well as the taxpayer's spouse and dependents.

    a. To be eligible for the credit, the student must be enrolled on at least a half-time basis for one academic period during the year.
    b. If a student is claimed as a dependent of another taxpayer, only that taxpayer may claim the education credit for the student's qualified tuition and related expenses. However, if the taxpayer is eligible to, but does **not** claim the student as a dependent, only the student may claim the education credit for the student's qualified tuition and related expenses.

3. The credit is phased out ratably for single taxpayers with modified AGI between $80,000 and $90,000, and for joint filers with a modified AGI between $160,000 and $180,000.

4. 40% of the credit is refundable.
5. The nonrefundable portion of the credit can be claimed against a taxpayer's AMT as well as regular tax liability.
6. For a tax year, a taxpayer may elect only one of the following with respect to one student: (1) the AOC credit, or (2) the lifetime learning credit.

S. Lifetime Learning Credit

1. A nonrefundable 20% tax credit is available for up to $10,000 of qualified tuition and related expenses per year for graduate and undergraduate courses at an eligible educational institution.
2. The credit may be claimed for an unlimited number of years, is available on a *per taxpayer basis*, and applies to tuition payments for the taxpayer, spouse, and dependents.
3. Similar to the AOC credit, if a student is claimed as a dependent of another taxpayer, only that taxpayer may claim the education credit for the student's qualified tuition and related expenses. However, if the taxpayer is eligible to, but does **not** claim the student as a dependent, only the student may claim the education credit for the student's qualified tuition and related expenses.
4. The credit is phased out for single taxpayers with a modified AGI between $55,000 and $65,000, and for joint filers with modified AGI between $110,000 and $130,000.
5. For a tax year, a taxpayer may elect only one of the following with respect to one student: (1) the AOC credit, or (2) the lifetime learning credit.

EXAMPLE

Alan paid qualified tuition and related expenses for his dependent, Betty, to attend college. Assuming all other relevant requirements are met, Alan may claim either an American Opportunity credit or lifetime learning credit with respect to his dependent, Betty, but not both.

EXAMPLE

Cathy paid $2,000 in qualified tuition and related expenses for her dependent, Doug, to attend college. Also during the year, Cathy paid $600 in qualified tuition to attend a continuing education course to improve her job skills. Assuming all relevant requirements are met, Cathy may claim the American Opportunity credit for the $2,000 paid for her dependent, Doug, and a lifetime learning credit for the $600 of qualified tuition that she paid for the continuing education course to improve her job skills.

EXAMPLE

The facts are the same as in the preceding example, except that Cathy paid $4,500 in qualified tuition and related expenses for her dependent, Doug, to attend college. Although an American Opportunity credit is available only with respect to the first $4,000 of qualified tuition and related expenses paid with respect to Doug, Cathy **cannot** add the $500 of excess expenses to her $600 of qualified tuition in computing the amount of her lifetime learning credit.

EXAMPLE

Ernie has one dependent, Frank. During the current year, Ernie paid qualified tuition and related expenses for Frank to attend college. Although Ernie is eligible to claim Frank as a dependent on Ernie's federal income tax return, Ernie does **not** do so. Therefore, assuming all other relevant requirements are met, Frank is allowed an education credit on Frank's federal income tax return for his qualified tuition and related expenses paid by Ernie, and Ernie is not allowed an education credit with respect to Frank's education expenses. The result would be the same if Frank had paid his qualified tuition expenses himself.

T. Credit for Qualified Retirement Savings

1. The amount of nonrefundable credit is from 10% to 50% of up to $2,000 of elective contributions to IRAs and most retirement plans. The credit rate (10% to 50%) is based on AGI, and the credit is in addition to any deduction or exclusion that would otherwise apply to the contributions.
2. For 2015, only individuals filing joint returns with AGI of $61,000 or less, filing as a head of household with AGI of $45,750 or less, and filing other returns with AGI of $30,500 or less qualify for the credit.
3. The credit is available to an individual taxpayer at least eighteen years old at the close of the tax year who is not a full-time student nor claimed as a dependent on another taxpayer's return.

U. Estimated Tax Payments

1. An individual whose regular and alternative minimum tax liability is not sufficiently covered by withholding on wages must pay estimated tax in quarterly installments or be subject to penalty.
2. Quarterly payments of estimated tax are due by the 15th day of the 4th, 6th, and 9th month of the taxable year, and by the 15th day of the 1st month of the following year.
3. For 2015, individuals (other than high-income individuals) will incur no penalty if the amount of tax withheld plus estimated payments are at least equal to the lesser of

   a. 90% of the current year's tax,
   b. 90% of the tax determined by annualizing current-year taxable income through each quarter, or
   c. 100% of the prior year's tax.

4. For 2015, high-income individuals must use 110% (instead of 100%) if they base their estimates on their prior year's tax. A person is a high-income individual if the AGI shown on the individual's return for the preceding tax year exceeds $150,000 ($75,000 for a married individual filing separately).
5. The penalty is based on the difference between the required annual payment (i.e., lesser of a., b., or c. above) and the amount paid.
6. Generally no penalty if

   a. Total tax due was less than $1,000;
   b. Taxpayer had no tax liability for prior year (i.e., total tax was zero), prior year was a twelve-month period, and taxpayer was a US citizen or resident for entire year; or
   c. IRS waives penalty because failure to pay was the result of casualty, disaster, or other unusual circumstances.

> **NOW REVIEW MULTIPLE-CHOICE QUESTIONS 196 THROUGH 205**

VII. FILING REQUIREMENTS

A. Form 1040 must generally be filed if gross income at least equals the sum of the taxpayer's standard deduction plus personal exemptions allowable (e.g., generally $6,300 + $4,000 = $10,300 for single taxpayer for 2015).

1. The $1,550 (or $1,250) additional standard deduction for age is included in determining an individual's filing requirement; the additional standard deduction for blindness and dependency exemptions are *not* included.

> **EXAMPLE**
>
> A single individual age 65 and blind who *cannot* be claimed as a dependency exemption by another taxpayer must file a return for 2015 if the individual's gross income is at least $6,500 + $4,000 + $1,550 = $11,850

2. An individual who can be claimed as a dependency exemption by another taxpayer must file a return if the individual either has (1) unearned income in excess of the sum of $1,050 plus any additional standard deductions allowed for age and blindness, or (2) total gross income in excess of the individual's standard deduction (i.e., earned income plus $300 up to the normal amount of the basic standard deduction—$6,300 for single taxpayer—plus additional standard deductions for age and blindness).

> **EXAMPLE**
>
> A single individual age 65 who can be claimed as a dependency exemption by another taxpayer must file a return for 2014 if the individual has unearned income (e.g., interest and dividends) in excess of $1,050 + $1,550 = $2,600.

3. Self-employed individual must file if *net earnings from self-employment* are **$400** or more.
4. A married individual filing separately must file if gross income is $4,000 or more for 2015.

B. Return must be filed by 15th day of 4th calendar month following close of taxable year.
C. An automatic six-month extension of time for filing the return can be obtained by filing Form 4868 by the due date of the return, and paying any estimated tax due.

> **NOW REVIEW MULTIPLE-CHOICE QUESTIONS 206 AND 207**

VIII. FARMING INCOME AND EXPENSES

A. A farming business involves the cultivating of land or raising or harvesting of any agricultural or horticultural commodity. It does not include contract harvesting, or the buying or reselling of plants or animals grown or raised by another person.
B. An individual engaged in farming must file Schedule F (Form 1040), Farm Income and Expenses. Additionally, a farmer must also file Schedule SE in order to compute self-employment tax on farm earnings. Completing Schedule F for farming is similar to completing a Schedule C which is used by sole proprietors. Partnerships engaged in farming must file Form 1065, while corporations engaged in farming must file the appropriate Form 1120.
C. The income and expenses from farming are generally treated in the same manner as the income and expenses from any other business. Similarly, the general rules that apply to all cash and accrual taxpayers also apply to farming businesses.

1. A cash-basis farmer who receives insurance proceeds as a result of the destruction or damage to crops may elect to include the proceeds in income for the year after the year of damage if the farmer can show that the income from the crops would normally have been reported in the following year.
2. Income from the sale of a crop is normally reported in the year of sale. However, if the farmer has pledged all of part of the crop production to secure a Commodity Credit Corporation loan, the farmer may elect to report the loan proceeds as income in the year received rather than reporting income in the year the crop is sold. The amount reported as income becomes the farmer's basis for the crop and is used to determine gain or loss upon the sale of the crop.
3. A farmer may generally deduct soil and water conservation expenditures that are consistent with a conservation plan approved by a federal or state agency. However, the deduction is annually limited to 25% of the farmer's gross income from farming. Excess expenses can be carried over for an unlimited number of years subject to the 25 % limitation in each carryover year.

    a. Expenses related to the draining of wetlands or to land preparation for the installation of center pivot irrigation systems may not be deducted under this provision.
    b. Land clearing expenses must be capitalized and added to the farmer's basis in the land.

> **EXAMPLE**
>
> A farmer had gross income from Farm A of $25,000 and gross income from Farm B of $19,000 for the current year. During the year the farmer spent $16,000 on Farm B for soil and water conservation expenditures under a plan approved by a state agency. For the current year, the farmer's deduction of the $16,000 of soil and water conservation expenditures would be limited to ($25,000 + $19,000) × 25% =$11,000.

4. Cash-basis farmers can generally deduct prepaid feed costs in the year of payment if the deduction does not materially distort income. However, no deduction is allowed for advance payments for feed, seed, fertilizer, or other supplies to the extent such prepayments exceed 50% of total deductible farming expenses (excluding the prepaid items).

EXAMPLE

During December 2014, a calendar-year farmer purchased a 6-month supply of feed for $6,000 and also purchased $2,000 of seed to be used in the subsequent spring planting season. The farmer's other farm expenses totaled $9,000. In this case the farmer's 2014 deduction for prepaid feed and seed would be limited to 50% × $9,000 = $4,500.

---

5. The cost of most tangible personal property used in a farming business cannot be depreciated under the 200% declining balance method, but instead is generally recovered using the MACRS 150% declining balance method over a 5-year recovery period.
6. An individual engaged in farming can elect to determine current year tax liability by averaging, over the previous three years, all or part of his/her current year income from farming.

IX. TAX PROCEDURES

A. Audit and Appeal Procedures

1. Taxpayer makes determination of tax when return is filed.
2. Examination of questionable returns may be conducted by correspondence, in an IRS office (i.e., office audit), or at taxpayer's place of business (i.e., field audit).
3. If taxpayer does not agree with the changes proposed by the examiner and the examination was made in an IRS office or by correspondence, the taxpayer may request a meeting with the examiner's supervisor.
4. If no agreement is reached, or if the examination was conducted in the field, the IRS will send the taxpayer a copy of the examination report and a letter stating the proposed changes (**thirty-day letter**).
5. A taxpayer has thirty days to (1) accept deficiency, (2) appeal the examiner's findings, or (3) may disregard the thirty-day letter and wait for a statutory notice of deficiency (**ninety-day letter**).
6. If taxpayer has appealed and agreement is not reached at appellate level of IRS, a ninety-day letter is sent.
7. Taxpayer has ninety days to file a petition in the Tax Court.

   a. Assessment and collection are prohibited so long as the taxpayer can petition the Tax Court. Payment of deficiency is not required before going to Tax Court.
   b. If a petition is not filed within ninety days, the tax deficiency is assessed and the amount is subject to collection if not paid within ten days.

B. Choice of Courts

1. A taxpayer may begin tax litigation in any of three courts: the US Tax Court; US district courts; or US Court of Federal Claims.
2. **Tax Court** is a court of national jurisdiction that hears only tax cases. It is composed of 19 judges who are specialists in the tax area that travel to approximately 100 cities throughout the US to hear tax cases. Although a jury trial is not available, a major advantage of the Tax Court is that the tax does not have to be paid before the taxpayer goes to Court. The Tax Court issues regular and memorandum decisions, both of which can be used as precedent.

   a. The IRS has adopted an *acquiescence policy* for regular Tax Court decisions that it loses. *Acquiescence* indicates that the IRS will follow the decision in future situations, involving similar facts and issues. *Non acquiescence* indicates that the IRS will not follow the decision and can be expected to litigate in situations involving similar facts and issues.
   b. Decisions of the Tax Court are appealed to US Court of Appeals. As a matter of policy known as the *Golsen Rule*, the Tax Court will follow the law of the circuit to which a case is appealable.
   c. A taxpayer may take a case to the Small Tax Case Division if the disputed amount does not exceed $50,000. Procedures are simplified and taxpayers can represent themselves without an attorney. Cases are heard by special commissioners instead of a Tax Court judge, and a possible disadvantage is that a decision is binding and cannot be appealed.

3. Each state has at least one **US district court** which is independent of other district courts. District courts adjudicate all types of cases, not just tax cases.

    a. A district court is the only court in which a jury trial is available, which may be advantageous to the taxpayer if the case involves a sympathetic issue.
    b. Unlike a proceeding in the Tax Court, taxpayers must first pay the tax and then file suit in district court for refund.
    c. Decisions of a district court are appealed to the US Court of Appeals.

4. **US Court of Federal Claims** is a court of national jurisdiction. A jury trial is not available and taxpayers must first pay tax and then file suit for refund. Decisions are appealed to US Court of Appeals for the Federal Circuit.

5. There are 11 geographical **Circuit Courts of Appeals** plus one for the District of Columbia and one for the Federal Circuit. Lower court decisions are generally appealable to the court of appeals for an individual's place of residence, or in the case of a corporation, its principal place of business. Decisions of the Appellate Courts have more authority than lower court decisions. The losing party may appeal to the US Supreme Court.

6. **US Supreme Court** normally hears tax cases only if they involve a conflict regarding the treatment of an item between circuits of the Appeals courts. Decisions of the Supreme Court are the law of the land and take precedence over all other court decisions.

C. Assessments

1. The normal period for assessment of a tax deficiency is **three years** after the due date of the return or three years after the return is filed, whichever is later.
2. The assessment period is extended to **six years** if gross income omissions exceed 25% of the gross income stated on the return.
3. There is no time limit for assessment if no return is filed, if the return is fraudulent, or if there is a willful attempt to evade taxes.
4. If a taxpayer fails to include any required information on a tax return or statement relating to a listed transaction, the statute of limitations with respect to that listed transaction will not expire until one year after the date the information is provided to the IRS.
5. Assessment period (normally three years) is suspended for 150 days after timely mailing of deficiency notice (90-day letter) to taxpayer.
6. Within sixty days after making the assessment, the IRS is required to provide a notice and demand for payment. If tax is not paid, the tax may be collected by levy or by court proceedings started within ten years of assessment.

D. Collection from Transferees and Fiduciaries

1. Transferee provisions are a method of collecting a predetermined tax that the transferor taxpayer cannot pay.
2. Generally transferor must be insolvent, or no longer in existence (e.g., corporation was dissolved).
3. Generally transferees are liable only to the extent of property received from the transferor taxpayer.

E. Closing Agreement and Compromise

1. A closing agreement is a final determination of tax liability that is binding on both the IRS and taxpayer.
2. A compromise is a writing-down of the tax liability. The IRS has broad authority to compromise in the event that doubt exists as to the existence of actual tax liability or because of the taxpayer's inability to pay.

F. Claims for Refund

1. An income tax refund claim is made on Form 1040X. Form 843 should be used to file a refund claim for taxes other than income taxes. Form 1045 may be used to file for a tentative adjustment or refund of taxes when an overpayment of taxes for a prior year results from the carryback of a current year's net operating loss.
2. Period for filing refund claims

    a. Refund claim must be filed within **three years** from date return was filed, or **two years** from payment of tax, whichever is later. If return filed before due date, the return is treated as filed on due date.
    b. Three-year period is extended to seven years for claims resulting from bad debts or worthless securities.
    c. If refund claim results from a carryback (e.g., NOL), the three-year period begins with the return for the year in which the carryback arose.

3. Suit for refund

    a. Only recourse from IRS's disallowance of refund claim is to begin suit in court within two years of notice of disallowance.

    b. If IRS fails to act on refund claim within six months, the taxpayer may treat it as disallowed.

G. Interest

1. Interest is allowed on overpayments from date of overpayment to thirty days before date of refund check.

    a. If an overpayment, amounts of tax withheld and estimated payments are deemed paid on due date of return.

    b. No interest is allowed if refund is made within forty-five days of later of (1) return due date or (2) actual filing of return.

2. For underpayments of tax, the interest rate is equal to the three-month Treasury bill rate plus three percentage points. For overpayments, the interest rate is equal to the federal short-term rate plus two percentage points.

H. Taxpayer Penalties

1. Penalties may be imposed for late filing or failure to file, and late payment of tax.

    a. **Late filing** or failure to file penalty is 5% of the net tax due per month (up to 25%).

    b. **Late payment** of tax penalty is 0.5% of the net tax due per month (up to 25%).

        (1) For any month to which both of the above apply, the late filing penalty is reduced by the late payment penalty so that the maximum is 5% per month (up to 25%).

        (2) For returns not filed within sixty days of due date (including extensions), the IRS may assess a minimum late filing penalty which is the lesser of $100 or the amount of net tax due.

2. An **accuracy-related penalty of 20%** of the underpayment applies if the underpayment of tax is attributable to one or more of the following: (1) negligence or disregard of rules and regulations, (2) any substantial understatement of income tax, (3) any substantial valuation overstatement, (4) any substantial overstatement of pension liabilities, or (5) any substantial gift or estate tax valuation understatement.

    a. Accuracy-related penalty does not apply if the underpayment is due to reasonable cause, or there is adequate disclosure and the position has a reasonable basis for being sustained.

    b. **Negligence penalty** applies to any careless, reckless, or intentional disregard of rules or regulations, and any failure to make a reasonable attempt to comply with the provisions of the tax law. Penalty is imposed only on the portion of tax liability due to negligence, and can be avoided by adequate disclosure of a position that has a reasonable basis.

    c. **Substantial understatement of income tax penalty** applies if the understatement exceeds the greater of (1) 10% of the tax due, or (2) $5,000 ($10,000 for most corporations). Penalty can be avoided by adequate disclosure of a position that has a reasonable basis, or if there is substantial authority for the position taken.

    d. **Substantial valuation misstatement penalty** may be imposed if the value (or adjusted basis) of property stated on the return is 150% or more of the amount determined to be correct.

        (1) Penalty applies to the extent resulting income tax underpayment exceeds $5,000 ($10,000 for most corporations).

        (2) Penalty is applied at a 40% rate if gross overvaluation is 200% or more of the amount determined to be correct.

    e. **Substantial overstatement of pension liabilities penalty** applies if the amount of stated pension liabilities is 200% or more of the amount determined to be correct. Penalty is 40% if misstatement is 400% or more, but penalty is not applicable if resulting underpayment is $1,000 or less.

    f. **Gift or estate tax valuation misstatement penalty** applies if the value of property on a gift or estate return is 50% or less of the amount determined to be correct.

        (1) Penalty is 40% if valuation used is 25% or less of amount determined to be correct.

        (2) No penalty if resulting understatement of tax is $5,000 or less.

3. A separate accuracy-related penalty applies to **tax shelter transactions**. The penalty is 30% of the tax understatement if the taxpayer fails to disclose a listed transaction or other reportable transaction with a significant tax-avoidance purpose. A lower penalty of 20% of the tax understatement applies if there is disclosure.

    a. The penalty may be waived for reasonable cause if the taxpayer made adequate disclosure, the position is (or was) supported by substantial authority, and the taxpayer reasonably believed the position was more-likely-than-not correct.

    b. Even if a taxpayer reasonably believed that its position was correct, the penalty cannot be waived if there was no disclosure.

   4. **Civil fraud penalty** is 75% of the portion of underpayment attributable to fraud. The accuracy-related penalty does not apply to the portion of underpayment subject to the fraud penalty.

NOW REVIEW MULTIPLE-CHOICE QUESTIONS 208 THROUGH 217

KEY TERMS

Accounting method. The rules used to determine the tax year in which income and expenses are reported for tax purposes. Two major overall methods of accounting are the cash method and the accrual method.

Accounting period. The period of time, usually 12 months, used by a taxpayer for the determination of taxable income. Taxpayers who do not keep records must use a calendar year, while taxpayers who do keep books and records generally may choose between a calendar year and a fiscal year. A fiscal year is a tax year that ends on the last day of a month other than December.

Adjusted gross income (AGI). Unique to individual taxpayers, it generally represents an individual's gross income less business expenses, expenses attributable to the production of rents and royalty income, the capital loss deduction, and certain personal expenses (deductions for AGI).

Amount realized. The amount received by a taxpayer from the sale or other disposition of property. The amount realized includes the sum of cash and the fair market value of any other property or services received, plus any debt of the taxpayer assumed by the buyer. Determining the amount realized is the starting point for arriving at the taxpayer's realized gain or loss.

At-risk limitation. Under the at-risk rules, a taxpayer's deductible loss from an activity is limited to the amount the taxpayer has at risk in the activity at the end of the taxable year. The initial amount at risk is generally the sum of the amount of cash and the adjusted basis of property contributed to the activity, plus amounts borrowed for use in the activity for which the taxpayer is personally liable.

Cash method. A method of accounting under which the taxpayer generally reports income for the taxable year in which payments are actually or constructively received. Expenses are deductible when paid.

Gross income. All income from whatever source derived including (but not limited to) compensation for services, gains from property, interest, rents, royalties, dividends, alimony, and income from discharge of indebtedness.

Material participation. The level of participation by a taxpayer in an activity that determines whether the activity is a passive activity or an active trade or business. Material participation can be achieved by meeting any one of the seven tests provided in Regulations.

Passive loss. A loss generated from a passive activity. Generally, passive losses are not allowed to offset trade or business income or portfolio (investment) income.

Realized gain or loss. The gain or loss determined by taking the amount realized from the sale or exchange of property and subtracting the property's adjusted basis.

Statute of limitations. The period of time after which a taxpayer's return is no longer subject to assessment, and the taxpayer can no longer file a claim for refund. The normal stature of limitations is generally three years from the alter of the date the tax return is filed, or its due date.

Stock redemption. The acquisition by a corporation of its own stock from a shareholder in exchange for property. A shareholder's redemption of stock may be treated as an exchange if it meets specified requirements, or otherwise will be treated as a dividend.

Tax benefit rule. The recovery of an item that was deducted in a prior year (e.g., state income tax refund) must be included in gross income for the year of recovery to the extent that the deduction of the item in the prior year produced a tax benefit by reducing the taxpayer's tax.

I.B.3. Annuities

1. Richard Brown, who retired on May 31, 2014, receives a monthly pension benefit of $700 payable for life. His life expectancy at the date of retirement is ten years. The first pension check was received on June 15, 2014. During his years of employment, Brown contributed $12,000 to the cost of his company's pension plan. How much of the pension amounts received may Brown exclude from taxable income for the years 2014, 2015, and 2016?

	2014	2015	2016
a.	$0	$0	$0
b.	$4,900	$4,900	$4,900
c.	$700	$1,200	$1,200
d.	$4,900	$8,400	$8,400

I.B.4. Life Insurance Proceeds

2. Fuller was the owner and beneficiary of a $200,000 life insurance policy on a parent. Fuller sold the policy to Decker, for $25,000. Decker paid a total of $40,000 in premiums. Upon the death of the parent, what amount must Decker include in gross income?

a. $0
b. $135,000
c. $160,000
d. $200,000

3. Seymour Thomas named his wife, Penelope, the beneficiary of a $100,000 (face amount) insurance policy on his life. The policy provided that upon his death, the proceeds would be paid to Penelope with interest over her present life expectancy, which was calculated at twenty-five years. Seymour died during 2015, and Penelope received a payment of $5,200 from the insurance company. What amount should she include in her gross income for 2015?

a. $200
b. $1,200
c. $4,200
d. $5,200

I.B.5. Employee Benefits

4. Under a "cafeteria plan" maintained by an employer,

a. Participation must be restricted to employees, and their spouses and minor children.
b. At least three years of service are required before an employee can participate in the plan.
c. Participants may select their own menu of benefits.
d. Provision may be made for deferred compensation other than 401(k) plans.

5. David Autrey was covered by an $80,000 group-term life insurance policy of which his wife was the beneficiary. Autrey's employer paid the entire cost of the policy, for which the uniform annual premium was $8 per $1,000 of coverage. Autrey died during 2015, and his wife was paid the $80,000 proceeds of the insurance policy. What amount of group-term life insurance proceeds must be included in gross income by Autrey's widow?

a. $0
b. $30,000
c. $50,000
d. $80,000

6. Howard O'Brien, an employee of Ogden Corporation, died on June 30, 2015. During July, Ogden made employee death payments (which do not represent the proceeds of life insurance) of $10,000 to his widow, and $10,000 to his fifteen-year-old son. What amounts should be included in gross income by the widow and son in their respective tax returns for 2015?

	Widow	Son
a.	$5,000	$5,000
b.	$5,000	$10,000
c.	$7,500	$7,500
d.	$10,000	$10,000

7. John Budd files a joint return with his wife. Budd's employer pays 100% of the cost of all employees' group-term life insurance under a qualified plan. Under this plan, the maximum amount of tax-free coverage that may be provided for Budd by his employer is

a. $100,000
b. $50,000
c. $10,000
d. $5,000

8. During the current year Hal Leff sustained a serious injury in the course of his employment. As a result of this injury, Hal received the following payments during the year:

Workers' compensation	$2,400
Reimbursement from his employer's accident and health plan for medical expenses paid by Hal and not deducted by him	1,800
Damages for physical injuries	8,000

The amount to be included in Hal's gross income for the current year should be

a. $12,200
b. $8,000
c. $1,800
d. $0

9. James Martin received the following compensation and fringe benefits from his employer during the current year:

Salary	$50,000
Year-end bonus	10,000
Medical insurance premiums paid by employer	1,000
Reimbursement of qualified moving expenses	5,000

What amount of the preceding payments should be included in Martin's current year gross income?

a. $60,000
b. $61,000
c. $65,000
d. $66,000

I.B.8. Gifts and Inheritances

10. On February 1, 2015, Hall learned that he was bequeathed 500 shares of common stock under his father's will. Hall's father had paid $2,500 for the stock in 2010. Fair market value of the stock on February 1, 2015, the date of his father's death, was $4,000 and had increased to $5,500 six months later. The executor of the estate elected the alternate valuation date for estate tax purposes. Hall sold the stock for $4,500 on June 1, 2015, the date that the executor distributed the stock to him. How much income should Hall include in his 2015 individual income tax return for the inheritance of the 500 shares of stock that he received from his father's estate?

a. $5,500
b. $4,000
c. $2,500
d. $0

I.B.9. Stock Dividends

11. During the current year, Gail Judd received the following dividends from

Benefit Life Insurance Co., on Gail's life insurance policy (Total dividends received have not yet exceeded accumulated premiums paid)	$100
Safe National Bank, on bank's common stock	300
Roe Mfg. Corp., a Delaware corporation, on preferred stock	500

What amount of dividend income should Gail report in her current year income tax return?

a. $900
b. $800
c. $500
d. $300

12. Amy Finch had the following cash receipts during 2015:

Dividend from a mutual insurance company on a life insurance policy	$500
Dividend on listed corporation stock; payment date by corporation was 12/30/14, but Amy received the dividend in the mail on 1/2/15	875

Total dividends received to date on the life insurance policy do not exceed the aggregated premiums paid by Amy. How much should Amy report for dividend income for 2015?

a. $1,375
b. $875
c. $500
d. $0

13. Jack and Joan Mitchell, married taxpayers and residents of a separate property state, elect to file a joint return for 2015 during which they received the following dividends:

	Received by	
	Jack	Joan
Alert Corporation (a qualified, domestic corporation)	$400	$50
Canadian Mines, Inc. (a Canadian company)		300
Eternal Life Mutual Insurance Company (dividends on life insurance policy)	200	

Total dividends received to date on the life insurance policy do not exceed cumulative premiums paid. For 2015, what amount should the Mitchells report on their joint return as dividend income?

a. $550
b. $600
c. $750
d. $800

14. During 2012, Karen purchased 100 shares of preferred stock of Boling Corp. for $5,500. During 2015, Karen received a stock dividend of ten additional shares of Boling Corp. preferred stock. On the date the preferred stock was distributed, it had a fair market value of $60 per share. What is Karen's basis in the ten shares of preferred stock that she received as a dividend?

a. $0
b. $500
c. $550
d. $600

I.B.10. Interest Income

15. Micro Corp., a calendar-year accrual-basis corporation, purchased a five-year, 8%, $100,000 taxable corporate bond for $108,530 on July 1, 2015, the date the bond was issued. The bond paid interest semiannually. Micro elected to amortize the bond premium. For Micro's 2015 tax return, the bond premium amortization for 2015 should be

I. Computed under the constant yield to maturity method.
II. Treated as an offset to the interest income on the bond.

a. I only.
b. II only.
c. Both I and II.
d. Neither I nor II.

16. In a tax year where the taxpayer pays qualified education expenses, interest income on the redemption of qualified US Series EE Bonds may be excluded from gross income. The exclusion is subject to a modified gross income limitation and a limit of aggregate bond proceeds in excess of qualified higher education expenses. Which of the following is (are) true?

 I. The exclusion applies for education expenses incurred by the taxpayer, the taxpayer's spouse, or any person whom the taxpayer may claim as a dependent for the year.
 II. "Otherwise qualified higher education expenses" must be reduced by qualified scholarships not includible in gross income.

    a. I only.
    b. II only.
    c. Both I and II.
    d. Neither I nor II.

17. During 2015 Kay received interest income as follows:

On US Treasury certificates	$4,000
On refund of 2012 federal income tax	500

The total amount of interest subject to tax in Kay's 2015 tax return is

    a. $4,500
    b. $4,000
    c. $500
    d. $0

18. Charles and Marcia are married cash-basis taxpayers. In 2015, they had interest income as follows:

- $500 interest on federal income tax refund.
- $600 interest on state income tax refund.
- $800 interest on federal government obligations.
- $1,000 interest on state government obligations.

What amount of interest income is taxable on Charles and Marcia's 2015 joint income tax return?

    a. $500
    b. $1,100
    c. $1,900
    d. $2,900

19. Clark bought Series EE US Savings Bonds in the current year. Redemption proceeds will be used for payment of college tuition for Clark's dependent child. One of the conditions that must be met for tax exemption of accumulated interest on these bonds is that the

    a. Purchaser of the bonds must be the sole owner of the bonds (or joint owner with his or her spouse).
    b. Bonds must be bought by a parent (or both parents) and put in the name of the dependent child.
    c. Bonds must be bought by the owner of the bonds before the owner reaches the age of twenty-four.
    d. Bonds must be transferred to the college for redemption by the college rather than by the owner of the bonds.

20. Daniel Kelly received interest income from the following sources during the current year.

New York Port Authority bonds	$1,000
Puerto Rico Commonwealth bonds	1,800

What portion of such interest is tax exempt?

    a. $0
    b. $1,000
    c. $1,800
    d. $2,800

21. In 2015 Uriah Stone received the following interest payments:

- Interest of $400 on refund of federal income tax for 2013.
- Interest of $300 on award for personal injuries sustained in an automobile accident during 2012.
- Interest of $1,500 on municipal bonds.
- Interest of $1,000 on United States savings bonds (Series HH).

What amount, if any, should Stone report as interest income on his 2015 tax return?

    a. $0
    b. $700
    c. $1,700
    d. $3,200

22. For the year ended December 31, 2014, Don Raff earned $1,000 interest at Ridge Savings Bank on a certificate of deposit scheduled to mature in 2015. In January 2015, before filing his 2014 income tax return, Raff incurred a forfeiture penalty of $500 for premature withdrawal of the funds. Raff should treat this $500 forfeiture penalty as a

    a. Reduction of interest earned in 2014, so that only $500 of such interest is taxable on Raff's 2014 return.
    b. Deduction from 2015 adjusted gross income, deductible only if Raff itemizes his deductions for 2015.
    c. Penalty **not** deductible for tax purposes.
    d. Deduction from gross income in arriving at 2015 adjusted gross income.

I.B.12. *Scholarships and Fellowships*

23. Which payment(s) is (are) included in a recipient's gross income?

 I. Payment to a graduate assistant for a part-time teaching assignment at a university. Teaching is not a requirement toward obtaining the degree.
 II. A grant to a Ph.D. candidate for his participation in a university-sponsored research project for the benefit of the university.

    a. I only.
    b. II only.
    c. Both I and II.
    d. Neither I nor II.

24. Majors, a candidate for a graduate degree, received the following scholarship awards from the university during the current year:

- $10,000 for tuition, fees, books, and supplies required for courses.
- $2,000 stipend for research services required by the scholarship.

What amount of the scholarship awards should Majors include as taxable income for the current year?

a. $12,000
b. $10,000
c. $2,000
d. $0

I.B.16.   Lease Improvements

25. In July 1996, Dan Farley leased a building to Robert Shelter for a period of fifteen years at a monthly rental of $1,000 with no option to renew. At that time the building had a remaining estimated useful life of twenty years.

Prior to taking possession of the building, Shelter made improvements at a cost of $18,000. These improvements had an estimated useful life of twenty years at the commencement of the lease period. The lease expired on June 30, 2015, at which point the improvements had a fair market value of $2,000. The amount that Farley, the landlord, should include in his gross income for 2015 is

a. $6,000
b. $8,000
c. $10,000
d. $18,500

I.C.   Items to Be Included in Gross Income

26. Bob and Sue Stewart were divorced in 2013. Under the terms of their divorce decree, Bob paid alimony to Sue at the rate of $50,000 in 2013, $20,000 in 2014, and nothing in 2015. What amount of alimony recapture must be included in Bob's gross income for 2015?

a. $0
b. $23,283
c. $30,000
d. $32,500

27. Which of the following conditions must be present in a divorce agreement for a payment to qualify as deductible alimony?

I. Payments must be in cash.
II. The payment must end at the recipient's death

a. I only.
b. II only.
c. Both I and II.
d. Neither I nor II.

28. Darr, an employee of Sorce C corporation, is not a shareholder. Which of the following would be included in a taxpayer's gross income?

a. Employer-provided medical insurance coverage under a health plan.
b. A $10,000 gift from the taxpayer's grandparents.
c. The fair market value of land that the taxpayer inherited from an uncle.
d. The dividend income on shares of stock that the taxpayer received for services rendered.

29. With regard to the inclusion of social security benefits in gross income for the 2015 tax year, which of the following statements is correct?

a. The social security benefits in excess of modified adjusted gross income are included in gross income.
b. The social security benefits in excess of one half the modified adjusted gross income are included in gross income.
c. Eighty-five percent of the social security benefits is the maximum amount of benefits to be included in gross income.
d. The social security benefits in excess of the modified adjusted gross income over $32,000 are included in gross income.

30. Perle, a dentist, billed Wood $600 for dental services. Wood paid Perle $200 cash and built a bookcase for Perle's office in full settlement of the bill. Wood sells comparable bookcases for $350. What amount should Perle include in taxable income as a result of this transaction?

a. $0
b. $200
c. $550
d. $600

31. John and Mary were divorced in 2014. The divorce decree provides that John pay alimony of $10,000 per year, to be reduced by 20% on their child's 18th birthday. During 2015, John paid $7,000 directly to Mary and $3,000 to Spring College for Mary's tuition. What amount of these payments should be reported as income in Mary's 2015 income tax return?

a. $5,600
b. $8,000
c. $8,600
d. $10,000

32. Clark filed Form 1040EZ for the 2014 taxable year. In July 2015, Clark received a state income tax refund of $900, plus interest of $10, for overpayment of 2014 state income tax. What amount of the state tax refund and interest is taxable in Clark's 2015 federal income tax return?

a. $0
b. $10
c. $900
d. $910

33. Hall, a divorced person and custodian of her twelve-year-old child, submitted the following information to the CPA who prepared her 2014 return:

The divorce agreement, executed in 2011, provides for Hall to receive $3,000 per month, of which

$600 is designated as child support. After the child reaches age eighteen, the monthly payments are to be reduced to $2,400 and are to continue until remarriage or death. However, for the year 2014, Hall received a total of only $5,000 from her former husband. Hall paid an attorney $2,000 in 2014 in a suit to collect the alimony owed.

What amount should have been reported in Hall's 2014 return as alimony income?

    a. $28,800
    b. $5,000
    c. $3,000
    d. $0

34. Lee, an attorney, uses the cash receipts and disbursements method of reporting. In 2014, a client gave Lee 500 shares of a listed corporation's stock in full satisfaction of a $10,000 legal fee the client owed to Lee. This stock had a fair market value of $8,000 on the date it was given to Lee. The client's basis for this stock was $6,000. Lee sold the stock for cash in January 2015. In Lee's 2014 income tax return, what amount of income should be reported in connection with the receipt of the stock?

    a. $10,000
    b. $8,000
    c. $6,000
    d. $0

35. In 2010, Ross was granted an incentive stock option (ISO) by her employer as part of an executive compensation package. Ross exercised the ISO in 2013 and sold the stock in 2015 at a gain. Ross was subject to regular tax for the year in which the

    a. ISO was granted.
    b. ISO was exercised.
    c. Stock was sold.
    d. Employer claimed a compensation deduction for the ISO.

36. Ed and Ann Ross were divorced in January of the current year. In accordance with the divorce decree, Ed transferred the title in their home to Ann. The home, which had a fair market value of $150,000, was subject to a $50,000 mortgage that had twenty more years to run. Monthly mortgage payments amount to $1,000. Under the terms of settlement, Ed is obligated to make the mortgage payments on the home for the full remaining twenty-year term of the indebtedness, regardless of how long Ann lives. Ed made twelve mortgage payments during the current year. What amount is taxable as alimony in Ann's current year return?

    a. $0
    b. $12,000
    c. $100,000
    d. $112,000

37. Income in respect of a cash-basis decedent

    a. Covers income earned and collected after a decedent's death.
    b. Receives a stepped-up basis in the decedent's estate.

    c. Includes a bonus earned before the taxpayer's death but not collected until after death.
    d. Must be included in the decedent's final income tax return.

38. The following information is available for Ann Drury for the current year:

Salary	$36,000
Premiums paid by employer on group-term life insurance in excess of $50,000	500
Proceeds from state lottery	5,000

How much should Drury report as gross income on her current year tax return?

    a. $36,000
    b. $36,500
    c. $41,000
    d. $41,500

39. Mr. and Mrs. Alvin Charak took a foster child, Robert, into their home in 2015. A state welfare agency paid the Charaks $3,900 during the year for related expenses. Actual expenses incurred by the Charaks during 2015 in caring for Robert amounted to $3,000. The remaining $900 was spent by the Charaks in 2015 towards their own personal expenses. How much of the foster child payments is taxable income to the Charaks in 2015?

    a. $0
    b. $900
    c. $2,900
    d. $3,900

40. Pierre, a headwaiter, received tips totaling $2,000 in December 2014. On January 5, 2015, Pierre reported this tip income to his employer in the required written statement. At what amount, and in which year, should this tip income be included in Pierre's gross income?

    a. $2,000 in 2014.
    b. $2,000 in 2015.
    c. $1,000 in 2014, and $1,000 in 2015.
    d. $167 in 2014, and $1,833 in 2015.

41. With regard to the alimony deduction in connection with a divorce, which one of the following statements is correct?

    a. Alimony is deductible by the payor spouse, and includible by the payee spouse, to the extent that payment is contingent on the status of the divorced couple's children.
    b. The divorced couple may be members of the same household at the time alimony is paid, provided that the persons do not live as husband and wife.
    c. Alimony payments must terminate on the death of the payee spouse.
    d. Alimony may be paid either in cash or in property.

42. In 2015, Joan accepted and received a $10,000 award for outstanding civic achievement. Joan was selected without any action on her part, and no future services are expected of her as a condition of receiving the award. What amount should Joan include in her 2015 adjusted gross income in connection with this award?

    a. $0
    b. $4,000
    c. $5,000
    d. $10,000

43. In 2015, Emil Gow won $5,000 in a state lottery. Also in 2015, Emil spent $400 for the purchase of lottery tickets. Emil elected the standard deduction on his 2015 income tax return. The amount of lottery winnings that should be included in Emil's 2015 taxable income is

    a. $0
    b. $2,000
    c. $4,600
    d. $5,000

I.C.5.   *Rents and Royalties*

44. Lake Corp., an accrual-basis calendar-year corporation, had the following 2015 receipts:

Advanced rental payments where the lease ends in 2017	$125,000
Lease cancellation payment from a five-year lease tenant	50,000

Lake had no restrictions on the use of the advanced rental payments and renders no services. What amount of income should Lake report on its 2015 tax return?

    a. $0
    b. $50,000
    c. $125,000
    d. $175,000

45. Paul Bristol, a cash-basis taxpayer, owns an apartment building. The following information was available for 2014:

- An analysis of the 2014 bank deposit slips showed recurring monthly rents received totaling $50,000.
- On March 1, 2014, the tenant in apartment 2B paid Bristol $2,000 to cancel the lease expiring on December 31, 2014.
- The lease of the tenant in apartment 3A expired on December 31, 2014, and the tenant left improvements valued at $1,000. The improvements were not in lieu of any rent required to have been paid.

In computing net income from that apartment building for 2014, Bristol should report gross income of

    a. $50,000
    b. $51,000
    c. $52,000
    d. $53,000

46. Emil Gow owns a two-family house that has two identical apartments. Gow lives in one apartment and rents out the other.

In 2015, the rental apartment was fully occupied and Gow received $7,200 in rent. During the year ended December 31, 2015, Gow paid the following:

Real estate taxes	$6,400
Painting of rental apartment	800
Annual fire insurance premium	600

In 2015, depreciation for the entire house was determined to be $5,000. What amount should Gow include in his adjusted gross income for 2015?

    a. $2,900
    b. $800
    c. $400
    d. $100

47. Amy Finch had the following cash receipts during 2015:

Net rent on vacant lot used by a car dealer (lessee pays all taxes, insurance, and other expenses on the lot)	$6,000
Advance rent from lessee of above vacant lot, such advance to be applied against rent for the last two months of the five-year lease in 2019	1,000

How much should Amy include in her 2015 taxable income for rent?

    a. $7,000
    b. $6,800
    c. $6,200
    d. $6,000

48. Royce Rentals, Inc., an accrual-basis taxpayer, reported rent receivable of $25,000 and $35,000 in its 2015 and 2014 balance sheets, respectively. During 2015, Royce received $50,000 in rent payments and $5,000 in nonrefundable rent deposits. In Royce's 2015 corporate income tax return, what amount should Royce include as rent revenue?

    a. $45,000
    b. $50,000
    c. $55,000
    d. $65,000

I.C.19.   *Unemployment Compensation*

49. John Budd is single, with no dependents. During 2015, John received wages of $11,000 and state unemployment compensation benefits of $2,000. He had no other source of income. The amount of state unemployment compensation benefits that should be included in John's 2015 adjusted gross income is

    a. $2,000
    b. $1,000
    c. $500
    d. $0

I.E.   Tax Accounting Methods

50. A cash-basis taxpayer should report gross income

   a. Only for the year in which income is actually received in cash.
   b. Only for the year in which income is actually received whether in cash or in property.
   c. For the year in which income is either actually or constructively received in cash only.
   d. For the year in which income is either actually or constructively received, whether in cash or in property.

51. Which of the following taxpayers may use the cash method of accounting?

   a. A tax shelter.
   b. A qualified personal service corporation.
   c. A C corporation with annual gross receipts of $50,000,000.
   d. A manufacturer with annual gross receipts of $3,000,000.

52. In 2014, Stewart Corp. properly accrued $5,000 for an income item on the basis of a reasonable estimate. In 2015, after filing its 2014 federal income tax return, Stewart determined that the exact amount was $6,000. Which of the following statements is correct?

   a. No further inclusion of income is required as the difference is less than 25% of the original amount reported and the estimate had been made in good faith.
   b. The $1,000 difference is includible in Stewart's 2015 income tax return.
   c. Stewart is required to notify the IRS within 30 days of the determination of the exact amount of the item.
   d. Stewart is required to file an amended return to report the additional $1,000 of income.

53. Axis Corp. is an accrual-basis calendar-year corporation. On December 13, 2014, the Board of Directors declared a 2% of profits bonus to all employees for services rendered during 2014 and notified them in writing. None of the employees own stock in Axis. The amount represents reasonable compensation for services rendered and was paid on March 13, 2015. Axis' bonus expense may

   a. Not be deducted on Axis' 2014 tax return because the per share employee amount **cannot** be determined with reasonable accuracy at the time of the declaration of the bonus.
   b. Be deducted on Axis' 2014 tax return.
   c. Be deducted on Axis' 2015 tax return.
   d. Not be deducted on Axis' tax return because payment is a disguised dividend.

54. On December 1, 2014, Michaels, a self-employed cash-basis calendar-year taxpayer, borrowed $100,000 to use in her business. The loan was to be repaid on November 30, 2015. Michaels paid the entire interest of $12,000 on December 1, 2014. What amount of interest is deductible on Michaels' 2015 income tax return?

   a. $12,000
   b. $11,000
   c. $1,000
   d. $0

55. Blair, CPA, uses the cash receipts and disbursements method of reporting. In 2014, a client gave Blair 100 shares of a listed corporation's stock in full satisfaction of a $5,000 accounting fee the client owed Blair. This stock had a fair market value of $4,000 on the date it was given to Blair. The client's basis for this stock was $3,000. Blair sold the stock for cash in January 2015. In Blair's 2014 return, what amount of income should be reported in connection with the receipt of the stock?

   a. $0
   b. $3,000
   c. $4,000
   d. $5,000

56. Unless the Internal Revenue Service consents to a change of method, the accrual method of tax reporting is generally mandatory for a sole proprietor when there are

	Accounts receivable for services rendered	Year-end merchandise inventories
a.	Yes	Yes
b.	Yes	No
c.	No	No
d.	No	Yes

57. Alex Burg, a cash-basis taxpayer, earned an annual salary of $80,000 at Ace Corp. in 2014, but elected to take only $50,000. Ace, which was financially able to pay Burg's full salary, credited the unpaid balance of $30,000 to Burg's account on the corporate books in 2014, and actually paid this $30,000 to Burg on January 30, 2015. How much of the salary is taxable to Burg in 2014?

   a. $50,000
   b. $60,000
   c. $65,000
   d. $80,000

58. Dr. Berger, a physician, reports on the cash basis. The following items pertain to Dr. Berger's medical practice in 2014:

Cash received from patients in 2014	$200,000
Cash received in 2014 from third-party reimbursers for services provided by Dr. Berger in 2013	30,000
Salaries paid to employees in 2014	20,000
Year-end 2014 bonuses paid to employees in 2015	1,000
Other expenses paid in 2014	24,000

What is Dr. Berger's net income for 2014 from his medical practice?

   a. $155,000
   b. $156,000

c. $185,000
d. $186,000

59. Which of the following taxpayers may use the cash method of accounting for tax purposes?

   a. Partnership that is designated as a tax shelter.
   b. Retail store with $2 million inventory, and $9 million average annual gross receipts.
   c. An international accounting firm.
   d. C corporation manufacturing exercise equipment with average annual gross receipts of $8 million.

I.F. Business Income and Deductions

60. The uniform capitalization method must be used by

   I. Manufacturers of tangible personal property.
   II. Retailers of personal property with $2 million dollars in average annual gross receipts for the three preceding years.

   a. I only.
   b. II only.
   c. Both I and II.
   d. Neither I nor II.

61. Mock operates a retail business selling illegal narcotic substances. Which of the following item(s) may Mock deduct in calculating business income?

   I. Cost of merchandise.
   II. Business expenses other than the cost of merchandise.

   a. I only.
   b. II only.
   c. Both I and II.
   d. Neither I nor II.

62. Banks Corp., a calendar-year corporation, reimburses employees for properly substantiated qualifying business meal expenses. The employees are present at the meals, which are neither lavish nor extravagant, and the reimbursement is not treated as wages subject to withholdings. For 2015, what percentage of the meal expense may Banks deduct?

   a. 0%
   b. 50%
   c. 80%
   d. 100%

63. Which of the following costs is **not** included in inventory under the Uniform Capitalization rules for goods manufactured by the taxpayer?

   a. Research.
   b. Warehousing costs.
   c. Quality control.
   d. Taxes excluding income taxes.

64. Under the uniform capitalization rules applicable to property acquired for resale, which of the following costs should be capitalized with respect to inventory if **no** exceptions are met?

	Marketing costs	Off-site storage costs
a.	Yes	Yes
b.	Yes	No
c.	No	No
d.	No	Yes

65. In the case of a corporation that is **not** a financial institution, which of the following statements is correct with regard to the deduction for bad debts?

   a. Either the reserve method or the direct charge-off method may be used, if the election is made in the corporation's first taxable year.
   b. On approval from the IRS, a corporation may change its method from direct charge-off to reserve.
   c. If the reserve method was consistently used in prior years, the corporation may take a deduction for a reasonable addition to the reserve for bad debts.
   d. A corporation is required to use the direct charge-off method rather than the reserve method.

66. Ram Corp.'s operating income for the current year amounted to $100,000. Included in Ram's current year operating expenses is a $6,000 insurance premium on a policy insuring the life of Ram's president. Ram is beneficiary of this policy. In Ram's current year tax return, what amount should be deducted for the $6,000 life insurance premium?

   a. $6,000
   b. $5,000
   c. $1,000
   d. $0

67. Jason Budd, CPA, reports on the cash basis. In April 2014, Budd billed a client $3,500 for the following professional services:

Personal estate planning	$2,000
Personal tax return preparation	1,000
Compilation of business financial statements	500

No part of the $3,500 was ever paid. In April 2015, the client declared bankruptcy, and the $3,500 obligation became totally uncollectible. What loss can Budd deduct on his 2015 tax return for this bad debt?

   a. $0
   b. $500
   c. $1,500
   d. $3,500

68. Earl Cook, who worked as a machinist for Precision Corp., loaned Precision $1,000 in 2012. Cook did not own any of Precision's stock, and the loan was not a condition of Cook's employment by Precision. In 2015, Precision declared bankruptcy, and Cook's note receivable from Precision became worthless. What loss can Cook claim on his 2015 income tax return?

   a. $0
   b. $500 long-term capital loss.
   c. $1,000 short-term capital loss.
   d. $1,000 business bad debt.

69. During the current year holiday season, Palo Corp. gave business gifts to seventeen customers. These gifts, which were not of an advertising nature, had the following fair market values:

4	at	$10
4	at	25
4	at	50
5	at	100

How much of these gifts was deductible as a business expense for the current year?

a. $840
b. $365
c. $140
d. $0

I.F.3. Net Operating Loss (NOL)

70. Jennifer, who is single, has the following items of income and deduction for 2015:

Salary	$30,000
Itemized deductions (all attributable to a personal casualty loss when a hurricane destroyed her residence)	45,000
Personal exemption	4,000

What is the amount of Jennifer's net operating loss for 2015?

a. $0
b. $15,000
c. $19,000
d. $45,000

71. Robin Moore, a self-employed taxpayer, reported the following information for 2015:

Income:	Dividends from investments	$500
	Net short-term capital gain on sale of investment	1,000
Deductions:	Net loss from business	(6,000)
	Personal exemption	(4,000)
	Standard deduction	(6,300)

What is the amount of Moore's net operating loss for 2015?

a. $4,500
b. $5,000
c. $6,000
d. $10,700

72. Destry, a single taxpayer, reported the following on his US Individual Income Tax Return Form 1040:

Income

Wages	$5,000
Interest on savings account	1,000
Net rental income	4,000

Deductions

Personal exemption	$4,000
Standard deduction	6,300
Net business loss	16,000
Net short-term capital loss	2,000

What is Destry's net operating loss that is available for carryback or carryforward?

a. $7,000
b. $9,000
c. $13,000
d. $16,000

I.F.6. Losses and Credits from Passive Activities

73. Cobb, an unmarried individual, had an adjusted gross income of $200,000 in 2015 before any IRA deduction, taxable social security benefits, or passive activity losses. Cobb incurred a loss of $30,000 in 2015 from rental real estate in which he actively participated. What amount of loss attributable to this rental real estate can be used in 2015 as an offset against income from non passive sources?

a. $0
b. $12,500
c. $25,000
d. $30,000

74. The rule limiting the deductibility of passive activity losses and credits applies to

a. Partnerships.
b. S corporations.
c. Personal service corporations.
d. Widely held C corporations.

75. Don Wolf became a general partner in Gata Associates on January 1, 2015, with a 5% interest in Gata's profits, losses, and capital. Gata is a distributor of auto parts. Wolf does not materially participate in the partnership business. For the year ended December 31, 2015, Gata had an operating loss of $100,000. In addition, Gata earned interest of $20,000 on a temporary investment. Gata has kept the principal temporarily invested while awaiting delivery of equipment that is presently on order. The principal will be used to pay for this equipment. Wolf's passive loss for 2015 is

a. $0
b. $4,000
c. $5,000
d. $6,000

76. With regard to the passive loss rules involving rental real estate activities, which one of the following statements is correct?

a. The term "passive activity" includes any rental activity without regard as to whether or not the taxpayer materially participates in the activity.

b. Gross investment income from interest and dividends **not** derived in the ordinary course of a trade or business is treated as passive activity income that can be offset by passive rental activity losses when the "active participation" requirement is **not** met.

c. Passive rental activity losses may be deducted only against passive income, but passive rental activity credits may be used against tax attributable to non passive activities.

d. The passive activity rules do **not** apply to taxpayers whose adjusted gross income is $300,000 or less.

77. If an individual taxpayer's passive losses relating to rental real estate activities cannot be used in the current year, then they may be carried

a. Back two years, but they cannot be carried forward.
b. Forward up to a maximum period of twenty years, but they cannot be carried back.
c. Back two years or forward up to twenty years, at the taxpayer's election.
d. Forward indefinitely or until the property is disposed of in a taxable transaction.

I.G. Depreciation, Depletion, and Amortization

78. Aviation Corp. manufactures model airplanes for children. During 2014, Aviation purchased $570,000 of production machinery to be used in its business. For 2014, Aviation's taxable income before any Sec. 179 expense deduction was $405,000. What is the maximum amount of Sec. 179 expense election Aviation will be allowed to deduct for 2014 and the maximum amount of Sec. 179 expense election that can carryover to 2015?

	Expense	Carryover
a.	$405,000	$0
b.	$405,000	$95,000
c.	$500,000	$0
d.	$570,000	$0

79. Which of the following conditions must be satisfied for a taxpayer to expense, in the year of purchase, under Internal Revenue Code Section 179, the cost of new or used tangible depreciable personal property?

I. The property must be purchased for use in the taxpayer's active trade or business.
II. The property must be purchased from an unrelated party.

a. I only.
b. II only.
c. Both I and II.
d. Neither I nor II.

80. Krol Corp., a calendar-year taxpayer, purchased used furniture and fixtures for use in its business and placed the property in service on November 1, 2014. The furniture and fixtures cost $56,000 and represented Krol's only acquisition of depreciable property during the year. Krol did **not** elect to expense any part of the cost of the property under Sec. 179.

What is the amount of Krol Corp.'s depreciation deduction for the furniture and fixtures under the Modified Accelerated Cost Recovery System (MACRS) for 2014?

a. $2,000
b. $2,667
c. $8,000
d. $16,000

81. On June 29, 2015, Sullivan purchased and placed into service an apartment building costing $360,000 including $30,000 for the land. What was Sullivan's MACRS deduction for the apartment building in 2015?

a. $7,091
b. $6,500
c. $6,000
d. $4,583

82. Data Corp., a calendar-year corporation, purchased and placed into service used office equipment during October 2014. No other equipment was placed into service during 2014. Under the general MACRS depreciation system, what convention must Data use?

a. Full-year.
b. Half-year.
c. Mid-quarter.
d. Mid-month.

83. Under the modified accelerated cost recovery system (MACRS) of depreciation for property placed in service after 1986,

a. Used tangible depreciable property is excluded from the computation.
b. Salvage value is ignored for purposes of computing the MACRS deduction.
c. No type of straight-line depreciation is allowable.
d. The recovery period for depreciable realty must be at least 27.5 years.

84. With regard to depreciation computations made under the general MACRS method, the half-year convention provides that

a. One-half of the first year's depreciation is allowed in the year in which the property is placed in service, regardless of when the property is placed in service during the year, and a half-year's depreciation is allowed for the year in which the property is disposed of.
b. The deduction will be based on the number of months the property was in service, so that one-half month's depreciation is allowed for the month in which the property is placed in service and for the month in which it is disposed of.
c. Depreciation will be allowed in the first year of acquisition of the property only if the property is placed in service **no** later than June 30 for calendar-year corporations.
d. Depreciation will be allowed in the last year of the property's economic life only if the property is

disposed of after June 30 of the year of disposition for calendar-year corporations.

85. During August 2014, Roe Corp. purchased and placed in service a machine to be used in its manufacturing operations. This machine cost $600,000. What portion of the cost may Roe elect to treat as a Sec. 179 expense deduction rather than as a capital expenditure?

    a. $99,000
    b. $139,000
    c. $500,000
    d. $600,000

II. "Above the Line" Deductions

86. Easel Co. has elected to reimburse employees for business expenses under a nonaccountable plan. Easel does not require employees to provide proof of expenses and allows employees to keep any amount not spent. Under the plan, Mel, an Easel employee for a full year, gets $400 per month for business automobile expenses. At the end of the year Mel informs Easel that the only business expense incurred was for business mileage of 8,000 at a rate of 56.5 cents per mile, the IRS standard mileage rate at the time. Mel encloses a check for $280 to refund the overpayment to Easel. What amount should be reported in Mel's gross income for the year?

    a. $0
    b. $280
    c. $4,520
    d. $4,800

87. Adams owns a second residence that is used for both personal and rental purposes. During the current year, Adams used the second residence for 50 days and rented the residence for 200 days. Which of the following statements is correct?

    a. Depreciation may not be deducted on the property under any circumstances.
    b. A rental loss may be deducted if rental-related expenses exceed rental income.
    c. Utilities and maintenance on the property must be divided between personal and rental use.
    d. All mortgage interest and taxes on the property will be deducted to determine the property's net income or loss

88. Charles Gilbert, a corporate executive, incurred business-related unreimbursed expenses for the current year as follows:

Entertainment	$900
Travel	700
Education	400

Assuming that Gilbert does not itemize deductions, how much of these expenses should he deduct on his current year tax return?

    a. $0
    b. $700
    c. $1,300
    d. $1,600

II.E. Moving Expenses

89. James, a calendar-year taxpayer, was employed and resided in Boston. On February 4, 2015, James was permanently transferred to Florida by his employer. James worked full-time for the entire year. In 2015, James incurred and paid the following unreimbursed expenses in relocating.

Lodging and travel expenses while moving	$1,000
Meals while in route to Florida	300
Cost of insuring household goods and personal effects during move	200
Cost of shipping household pets to new home	100
Costs of moving household furnishings and personal effects	3,000

What amount was deductible as moving expenses on James' 2015 tax return?

    a. $4,600
    b. $4,500
    c. $4,300
    d. $4,000

90. Martin Dawson, who resided in Detroit, was unemployed for the last six months of 2014. In January 2015, he moved to Houston to seek employment, and obtained a full-time job there in February. He kept this job for the balance of the year. Martin paid the following expenses in 2015 in connection with his move:

Rental of truck to move his personal belongings to Houston	$800
Penalty for breaking the lease on his Detroit apartment	300
Total	$1,100

How much can Martin deduct in 2015 for moving expenses?

    a. $0
    b. $300
    c. $800
    d. $1,100

91. Richard Putney, who lived in Idaho for five years, moved to Texas during the current year to accept a new position. His employer reimbursed him in full for all direct moving costs, but did not pay for any part of the following indirect moving expenses incurred by Putney:

Househunting trips to Texas	$800
Temporary housing in Texas	900

How much of the indirect expenses can be deducted by Putney as moving expenses?

    a. $0
    b. $900
    c. $1,500
    d. $1,700

II.F. *Contributions to Certain Retirement Plans*

92. Which one of the following statements concerning Roth IRAs is **not** correct?

   a. The maximum annual contribution to a Roth IRA is reduced if adjusted gross income exceeds certain thresholds.
   b. Contributions to a Roth IRA are not deductible.
   c. An individual is allowed to make contributions to a Roth IRA even after age 70½.
   d. A contribution to a Roth IRA must be made by the due date for filing the individual's tax return for the year (including extensions).

93. What is the maximum amount of adjusted gross income that a taxpayer may have for 2015 and still qualify to roll over the balance from a traditional individual retirement account (IRA) into a Roth IRA?

   a. $50,000
   b. $80,000
   c. $100,000
   d. There is no maximum AGI limitation.

94. Which one of the following statements concerning an education IRA (Coverdell Education Savings Account) is **not** correct?

   a. Contributions to an education IRA are not deductible.
   b. A taxpayer may contribute up to $2,000 in 2015 to an education IRA to pay the costs of the designated beneficiary's higher education.
   c. Eligibility for an education IRA is phased out if adjusted gross income exceeds certain threshold levels.
   d. Contributions can be made to an education IRA on behalf of a beneficiary until the beneficiary reaches age twenty-one.

95. For 2015, Val and Pat White (both age 40) filed a joint return. Val earned $55,000 in wages and was covered by his employer's qualified pension plan. Pat was unemployed and received $4,000 in alimony payments for the first four months of the year before remarrying. The couple had no other income. Each contributed $5,500 to an IRA account. The allowable IRA deduction on their 2015 joint tax return is

   a. $11,000
   b. $10,000
   c. $9,000
   d. $5,500

96. Davis, a sole proprietor with no employees, has a Keogh profit-sharing plan to which he may contribute 15% of his annual earned income. For this purpose, "earned income" is defined as net self-employment earnings reduced by the

   a. Deductible Keogh contribution.
   b. Self-employment tax.
   c. Self-employment tax and one-half of the deductible Keogh contribution.
   d. Deductible Keogh contribution and one-half of the self-employment tax.

97. Ronald Birch, who is single and age 28, earned a salary of $80,000 in 2015 as a plumber employed by Lupo Company. Birch was covered for the entire year 2015 under Lupo's qualified pension plan for employees. In addition, Birch had a net income of $15,000 from self-employment in 2015. What is the maximum amount that Birch can deduct in 2015 for contributions to an individual retirement account (IRA)?

   a. $5,500
   b. $4,000
   c. $3,000
   d. $0

98. Sol and Julia Crane (both age 43) are married and will file a joint return for 2015. Sol earned a salary of $140,000 in 2015 from his job at Troy Corp., where Sol is covered by his employer's pension plan. In addition, Sol and Julia earned interest of $3,000 in 2015 on their joint savings account. Julia is not employed, and the couple had no other income. On July 15, 2015, Sol contributed $5,500 to an IRA for himself, and $5,500 to an IRA for his spouse. The allowable IRA deduction in the Cranes' 2015 joint return is

   a. $0
   b. $3,000
   c. $5,500
   d. $11,000

99. Paul and Lois Lee, both age fifty-three, are married and will file a joint return for 2015. Their 2015 adjusted gross income is expected to be $85,000, including Paul's $75,000 salary. Lois has no income of her own. Neither spouse is covered by an employer-sponsored pension plan. What amount can the Lees contribute to IRAs for 2015 to take advantage of their maximum allowable IRA deduction in their 2015 return?

   a. $5,000
   b. $11,000
   c. $12,000
   d. $13,000

100. In 2015, contributions to a defined contribution qualified retirement plan on behalf of a self-employed individual whose income from self-employment is $55,000 are limited to

   a. $5,500
   b. $52,000
   c. $53,000
   d. $55,000

101. Which allowable deduction can be claimed in arriving at an individual's 2015 adjusted gross income?

   a. Charitable contribution.
   b. Foreign income taxes.
   c. Tax return preparation fees.
   d. Self-employed health insurance deduction.

II.G. *Deduction for Interest on Education Loans*

102. Which one of the following statements concerning the deduction for interest on qualified education loans is **not** correct?

a. The deduction is available even if the taxpayer does not itemize deductions.

b. The deduction only applies to the first sixty months of interest payments.

c. Qualified education expenses include tuition fees, room, and board.

d. The educational expenses must relate to a period when the student was enrolled on at least a half-time basis.

103. Dale received $1,000 during the current year for jury duty. In exchange for regular compensation from her employer during the period of jury service, Dale was required to remit the entire $1,000 to her employer in the current year. In Dale's current year income tax return, the $1,000 jury duty fee should be

a. Claimed in full as an itemized deduction.

b. Claimed as an itemized deduction to the extent exceeding 2% of adjusted gross income.

c. Deducted from gross income in arriving at adjusted gross income.

d. Included in taxable income without a corresponding offset against other income.

III. Itemized Deductions from Adjusted Gross Income

104. During 2015, George (age nine and claimed as a dependency exemption by his parents) received dividend income of $3,700, and had wages from an after-school job of $1,700. What is the amount that will be reported as George's taxable income for 2015?

a. $250
b. $3,350
c. $3,450
d. $5,400

105. Which of the following requirements must be met in order for a single individual to qualify for the additional standard deduction?

	Must be age 65 or older or blind	Must support dependent child or aged parent
a.	Yes	Yes
b.	No	No
c.	Yes	No
d.	No	Yes

III.A. Medical and Dental Expenses

106. Carroll, an unmarried taxpayer age 41 with an adjusted gross income of $100,000, incurred and paid the following unreimbursed medical expenses for 2015:

Doctor bills resulting from a serious fall	$5,000
Cosmetic surgery that was necessary to correct a congenital deformity	15,000

Carroll had no medical insurance. For regular income tax purposes, what was Carroll's maximum allowable medical

expense deduction, after the applicable threshold limitation, for the year?

a. $0
b. $10,000
c. $12,500
d. $20,000

107. Charlene and Gene Blair, age 51, are married and filed a joint return for 2015. Their medical related expenditures for 2015 included the following:

Medical insurance premiums	$1,550
Medicines prescribed by doctors	450
Aspirin and over-the-counter cold capsules	80
Unreimbursed doctor fees	1,000
Transportation to and from doctors	150
Emergency room fee	500

The emergency room fee related to an injury incurred by the Blairs' adult son, Eric, during a visit to their home. The Blairs graciously paid the bill; however, they provided no other support for Eric during the year. For 2015, Eric earned $18,000 as a self-employed house painter. Assuming the Blairs' adjusted gross income was $30,000, what amount of medical expenses can the Blairs deduct as an itemized deduction for 2015?

a. $0
b. $150
c. $650
d. $1,750

108. Tom and Sally White, married and filing joint income tax returns, derive their entire income from the operation of their retail stationery shop. Their 2015 adjusted gross income was $100,000. The Whites itemized their deductions on Schedule A for 2015. The following unreimbursed cash expenditures were among those made by the Whites during 2015:

Repair and maintenance of motorized wheelchair for physically handicapped dependent child	$600
Tuition, meals, lodging at special school for physically handicapped dependent child in an institution primarily for the availability of medical care, with meals and lodging furnished as necessary incidents to that care	8,000

Without regard to the adjusted gross income percentage threshold, what amount may the Whites claim in their 2015 return as qualifying medical expenses?

a. $8,600
b. $8,000
c. $600
d. $0

109. In 2015, Wells paid the following expenses:

Premiums on an insurance policy against loss of earnings due to sickness or accident	$3,000

Physical therapy after spinal surgery	2,000
Premium on an insurance policy that covers reimbursement for the cost of prescription drugs	500

In 2015, Wells recovered $1,500 of the $2,000 that she paid for physical therapy through insurance reimbursement from a group medical policy paid for by her employer. Disregarding the adjusted gross income percentage threshold, what amount could be claimed on Wells' 2015 income tax return for medical expenses?

a. $4,000
b. $3,500
c. $1,000
d. $500

110. Mr. and Mrs. Sloan incurred the following expenses during the current year when they adopted a child:

Child's medical expenses	$5,000
Legal expenses	9,000
Agency fee	4,000

Before consideration of any "floor" or other limitation on deductibility, what amount of the above expenses may the Sloans deduct on their current year joint income tax return?

a. $18,000
b. $14,000
c. $13,000
d. $5,000

111. Ruth and Mark Cline are married and plan to file a joint 2015 income tax return. Among their expenditures during 2015 were the following discretionary costs that they incurred for the sole purpose of improving their physical appearance and self-esteem:

Face-lift for Ruth, performed by a licensed surgeon	$5,000
Hair transplant for Mark, performed by a licensed surgeon	3,600

Disregarding the adjusted gross income percentage threshold, what total amount of the aforementioned doctors' bills may be claimed by the Clines in their 2015 return as qualifying medical expenses?

a. $0
b. $3,600
c. $5,000
d. $8,600

112. During 2014, Scott charged $4,000 on his credit card for his dependent son's medical expenses. Payment to the credit card company had not been made by the time Scott filed his income tax return in 2015. However, in 2014, Scott paid a physician $2,800 for the medical expenses of his wife, who died in 2013. Disregarding the adjusted gross income percentage threshold, what amount could Scott claim in his 2014 income tax return for medical expenses?

a. $0
b. $2,800
c. $4,000
d. $6,800

113. Which one of the following expenditures qualifies as a deductible medical expense for tax purposes?

a. Diaper service.
b. Funeral expenses.
c. Nursing care for a healthy baby.
d. Premiums paid for Medicare B supplemental medical insurance.

114. Jon Stenger, a cash-method taxpayer, age 32, had adjusted gross income of $35,000 in 2015. During the year he incurred and paid the following medical expenses:

Drugs and medicines prescribed by doctors	$300
Health insurance premiums	1,750
Doctors' fees	2,550
Eyeglasses	75
	$4,675

Stenger received $900 in 2015 as reimbursement for a portion of the doctors' fees. If Stenger were to itemize his deductions, what would be his allowable net medical expense deduction?

a. $0
b. $275
c. $1,050
d. $2,475

115. During 2015, Mr. and Mrs. Benson provided substantially all the support, in their own home, for their son John, age twenty-six, and for Mrs. Benson's cousin Nancy, age seventeen. John had $4,100 of income for 2015, and Nancy's income was $2,500. The Bensons paid the following medical expenses during the year:

Medicines and drugs:	
For themselves	$400
For John	500
For Nancy	100
Doctors:	
For themselves	600
For John	900
For Nancy	200

What is the total amount of medical expenses (before application of any limitation rules), that would enter into the calculation of itemized deductions on the Bensons' 2015 tax return?

a. $1,000
b. $1,300
c. $2,400
d. $2,700

III.B. Taxes

116. All of the following taxes are deductible as itemized deductions by a self-employed taxpayer **except**

    a. Foreign real estate taxes.
    b. Foreign income taxes.
    c. Personal property taxes.
    d. One-half of self-employment taxes.

117. Matthews was a cash-basis taxpayer whose records showed the following:

2014 state and local income taxes withheld	$1,500
2014 state estimated income taxes paid December 30, 2014	400
2014 federal income taxes withheld	2,500
2014 state and local income taxes paid April 17, 2015	300

What total amount was Matthews entitled to claim for taxes on her 2014 Schedule A of Form 1040?

    a. $4,700
    b. $2,200
    c. $1,900
    d. $1,500

118. In 2014, Farb, a cash-basis individual taxpayer, received an $8,000 invoice for personal property taxes. Believing the amount to be overstated by $5,000, Farb paid the invoiced amount under protest and immediately started legal action to recover the overstatement. In June 2015, the matter was resolved in Farb's favor, and he received a $5,000 refund. Farb itemizes his deductions on his tax returns. Which of the following statements is correct regarding the deductibility of the property taxes?

    a. Farb should deduct $8,000 in his 2014 income tax return and should report the $5,000 refund as income in his 2015 income tax return.
    b. Farb should **not** deduct any amount in his 2014 income tax return and should deduct $3,000 in his 2015 income tax return.
    c. Farb should deduct $3,000 in his 2014 income tax return.
    d. Farb should **not** deduct any amount in his 2014 income tax return when originally filed, and should file an amended 2014 income tax return in 2015.

119. In 2015, Burg paid $8,000 to the tax collector of Sun City for realty taxes on a two-family house owned in joint tenancy between Burg and his mother. Of this amount, $3,800 covered back taxes for 2014, and $4,200 covered 2015 taxes. Burg resides on the second floor of the house, and his mother resides on the first floor. In Burg's itemized deductions on his 2015 return, what amount was Burg entitled to claim for realty taxes?

    a. $0
    b. $4,000
    c. $4,200
    d. $8,000

120. Sara Harding is a cash-basis taxpayer who itemized her deductions. The following information pertains to Sara's state income taxes for the taxable year 2014:

Withheld by employer in 2014		$2,000
Payments on 2014 estimate:		
4/15/14	$300	
6/15/14	300	
9/15/14	300	
1/15/15	300	1,200
Total paid and withheld		$3,200
Actual tax, per state return		3,000
Overpayment		$200

There was no balance of tax or refund due on Sara's 2013 state tax return. How much is deductible for state income taxes on Sara's 2014 federal income tax return?

    a. $2,800
    b. $2,900
    c. $3,000
    d. $3,200

121. During 2015, Jack and Mary Bronson paid the following taxes:

Taxes on residence (for period January 1 to December 31, 2015)	$2,700
State motor vehicle tax on value of the car	360

The Bronsons sold their house on June 30, 2015, under an agreement in which the real estate taxes were not prorated between the buyer and sellers. What amount should the Bronsons deduct as taxes in calculating itemized deductions for 2015?

    a. $1,350
    b. $1,692
    c. $2,160
    d. $3,060

122. George Granger sold a plot of land to Albert King on July 1, 2015. Granger had not paid any realty taxes on the land since 2013. Delinquent 2014 taxes amounted to $600, and 2015 taxes amounted to $700. King paid the 2014 and 2015 taxes in full in 2015, when he bought the land. What portion of the $1,300 is deductible by King in 2015?

    a. $353
    b. $700
    c. $952
    d. $1,300

123. During the current year Mr. and Mrs. West paid the following taxes:

Property taxes on residence	$1,800
Special assessment for installation of a sewer system in their town	1,000
State personal property tax on their automobile	600
Property taxes on land held for long-term appreciation	300

What amount can the Wests deduct as property taxes in calculating itemized deductions for the current year?

 a. $2,100
 b. $2,700
 c. $3,100
 d. $3,700

124. Alex and Myra Burg, married and filing joint income tax returns, derive their entire income from the operation of their retail candy shop. Their 2015 adjusted gross income was $54,142. The Burgs itemized their deductions on Schedule A for 2015. The following unreimbursed cash expenditures were among those made by the Burgs during 2015:

State income tax	$1,200
Self-employment tax	7,650

What amount should the Burgs deduct for taxes in their itemized deductions on Schedule A for 2015?

 a. $1,200
 b. $3,825
 c. $5,025
 d. $7,650

III.C. *Interest Expense*

125. The 2015 deduction by an individual taxpayer for interest on investment indebtedness is

 a. Limited to the investment interest paid in 2015.
 b. Limited to the taxpayer's 2015 interest income.
 c. Limited to the taxpayer's 2015 net investment income.
 d. Not limited.

126. The Browns borrowed $20,000, secured by their home, to purchase a new automobile. At the time of the loan, the fair market value of their home was $400,000, and it was unencumbered by other debt. The interest on the loan qualifies as

 a. Deductible personal interest.
 b. Deductible qualified residence interest.
 c. Nondeductible interest.
 d. Investment interest expense.

127. On January 2, 2011, the Philips paid $50,000 cash and obtained a $200,000 mortgage to purchase a home. In 2015 they borrowed $15,000 secured by their home, and used the cash to add a new room to their residence. That same year they took out a $5,000 auto loan.

The following information pertains to interest paid in 2015:

Mortgage interest	$17,000
Interest on room construction loan	1,500
Auto loan interest	500

For 2015, how much interest is deductible, prior to any itemized deduction limitations?

 a. $17,000
 b. $17,500

 c. $18,500
 d. $19,000

128. Jackson owns two residences. The second residence, which has never been used for rental purposes, is the only residence that is subject to a mortgage. The following expenses were incurred for the second residence during the current year:

Mortgage interest	$5,000
Utilities	1,200
Insurance	6,000

For regular income tax purposes, what is the maximum amount allowable as a deduction for Jackson's second residence for the current year?

 a. $6,200 in determining adjusted gross income.
 b. $11,000 in determining adjusted gross income.
 c. $5,000 as an itemized deduction.
 d. $12,200 as an itemized deduction.

129. Robert and Judy Parker made the following payments during 2015:

Interest on a life insurance policy loan (the loan proceeds were used for personal use)	$1,200
Interest on home mortgage for period January 1 to October 4, 2015	3,600
Penalty payment for prepayment of home mortgage on October 4, 2015	900

How much can the Parkers utilize as interest expense in calculating itemized deductions for 2015?

 a. $5,700
 b. $4,620
 c. $4,500
 d. $3,600

130. Charles Wolfe purchased the following long-term investments at par during the current year:

 • $20,000 general obligation bonds of Burlington County (wholly tax-exempt)
 • $10,000 debentures of Arrow Corporation

Wolfe financed these purchases by obtaining a $30,000 loan from the Union National Bank. For the current year, Wolfe made the following interest payments:

Union National Bank	$3,600
Interest on home mortgage	3,000
Interest on credit card charges (items purchased for personal use)	500

What amount can Wolfe utilize as interest expense in calculating itemized deductions for the current year?

 a. $3,000
 b. $4,200
 c. $5,400
 d. $7,100

131. During 2015, William Clark was assessed a deficiency on his 2013 federal income tax return. As a result of this assessment he was required to pay $1,120 determined as follows:

Additional tax	$900
Late filing penalty	60
Negligence penalty	90
Interest	70

What portion of the $1,120 would qualify as itemized deductions for 2015?

a. $0
b. $14
c. $150
d. $220

III.D. Charitable Contributions

132. Smith, a single individual, made the following charitable contributions during the current year. Smith's adjusted gross income is $60,000.

Donation to Smith's church	$5,000
Artwork donated to the local art museum. Smith purchased it for $2,000 four months ago. A local art dealer appraised it for	3,000
Contribution to a needy family	1,000

What amount should Smith deduct as a charitable contribution?

a. $5,000
b. $7,000
c. $8,000
d. $9,000

133. Stein, an unmarried taxpayer, had adjusted gross income of $80,000 for the year and qualified to itemize deductions. Stein had no charitable contribution carryovers and only made one contribution during the year. Stein donated stock, purchased seven years earlier for $17,000, to a tax-exempt educational organization. The stock was valued at $25,000 when it was contributed. What is the amount of charitable contributions deductible on Stein's current year income tax return?

a. $17,000
b. $21,000
c. $24,000
d. $25,000

134. Moore, a single taxpayer, had $50,000 in adjusted gross income for 2015. During 2015 she contributed $18,000 to her church. She had a $10,000 charitable contribution carryover from her 2014 church contributions. What was the maximum amount of properly substantiated charitable contributions that Moore could claim as an itemized deduction for 2015?

a. $10,000
b. $18,000

c. $25,000
d. $28,000

135. Spencer, who itemizes deductions, had adjusted gross income of $60,000 for the current year. The following additional information is available for the current year:

Cash contribution to church	$4,000
Purchase of art object at church bazaar (with a fair market value of $800 on the date of purchase)	1,200
Donation of used clothing to Salvation Army (fair value evidenced by receipt received)	600

What is the maximum amount Spencer can claim as a deduction for charitable contributions for the current year?

a. $5,400
b. $5,200
c. $5,000
d. $4,400

136. Ruth Lewis has adjusted gross income of $100,000 for 2015 and itemizes her deductions. On September 1, 2015, she made a contribution to her church of stock held for investment for two years that cost $10,000 and had a fair market value of $70,000. The church sold the stock for $70,000 on the same date. Assume that Lewis made no other contributions during 2015 and made no special election in regard to this contribution on her 2015 tax return. How much should Lewis claim as a charitable contribution deduction for 2015?

a. $50,000
b. $30,000
c. $20,000
d. $10,000

137. On December 15, 2014, Donald Calder made a contribution of $500 to a qualified charitable organization, by charging the contribution on his bank credit card. Calder paid the $500 on January 20, 2015, upon receipt of the bill from the bank. In addition, Calder issued and delivered a promissory note for $1,000 to another qualified charitable organization on November 1, 2014, which he paid upon maturity four months later. If Calder itemizes his deductions, what portion of these contributions is deductible in 2014?

a. $0
b. $500
c. $1,000
d. $1,500

138. Under a written agreement between Mrs. Norma Lowe and an approved religious exempt organization, a ten-year-old girl from Vietnam came to live in Mrs. Lowe's home on August 1, 2015, in order to be able to start school in the US on September 3, 2015. Mrs. Lowe actually spent $500 for food, clothing, and school supplies for the student during 2015, without receiving any compensation or reimbursement of costs. What portion of the $500 may Mrs. Lowe deduct on her 2015 income tax return as a charitable contribution?

a. $0
b. $200
c. $250
d. $500

139. During the current year, Vincent Tally gave to the municipal art museum title to his private collection of rare books that was assessed and valued at $60,000. However, he reserved the right to the collection's use and possession during his lifetime. For the current year, he reported an adjusted gross income of $100,000. Assuming that this was his only contribution during the year, and that there were no carryovers from prior years, what amount can he deduct as contributions for the current year?

a. $0
b. $30,000
c. $50,000
d. $60,000

140. Jimet, an unmarried taxpayer, qualified to itemize 2015 deductions. Jimet's 2015 adjusted gross income was $30,000 and he made a $2,000 cash donation directly to a needy family. In 2015, Jimet also donated stock, valued at $3,000, to his church. Jimet had purchased the stock four months earlier for $1,500. What was the maximum amount of the charitable contribution allowable as an itemized deduction on Jimet's 2015 income tax return?

a. $0
b. $1,500
c. $2,000
d. $5,000

141. Taylor, an unmarried taxpayer, had $90,000 in adjusted gross income for 2015. During 2015, Taylor donated land to a church and made no other contributions. Taylor purchased the land in 2001 as an investment for $14,000. The land's fair market value was $25,000 on the day of the donation. What is the maximum amount of charitable contribution that Taylor may deduct as an itemized deduction for the land donation for 2015?

a. $25,000
b. $14,000
c. $11,000
d. $0

III.E. *Personal Casualty and Theft Gains and Losses*

142. In 2015, Joan Frazer's residence was totally destroyed by fire. The property had an adjusted basis and a fair market value of $130,000 before the fire. During 2015, Frazer received insurance reimbursement of $120,000 for the destruction of her home. Frazer's 2015 adjusted gross income was $70,000. Frazer had no casualty gains during the year. What amount of the fire loss was Frazer entitled to claim as an itemized deduction on her 2015 tax return?

a. $2,900
b. $8,500
c. $8,600
d. $10,000

143. Alex and Myra Burg, married and filing joint income tax returns, derive their entire income from the operation of their retail candy shop. Their 2015 adjusted gross income was $50,000. The Burgs itemized their deductions on Schedule A for 2015. The following unreimbursed cash expenditures were among those made by the Burgs during 2015:

Repair of glass vase accidentally broken in home
  by dog; vase cost $500 in 2011; fair value $600
  before accident and $200 after accident $90

Without regard to the $100 "floor" and the adjusted gross income percentage threshold, what amount should the Burgs deduct for the casualty loss in their itemized deductions on Schedule A for 2015?

a. $0
b. $90
c. $300
d. $400

144. Hall, a divorced person and custodian of her twelve-year-old child, filed her 2015 federal income tax return as head of a household. During 2015 Hall paid a $490 casualty insurance premium on her personal residence. Hall does not rent out any portion of the home, nor use it for business.
    The casualty insurance premium of $490 is

a. Allowed as an itemized deduction subject to the $100 floor and the 10% of adjusted gross income floor.
b. Allowed as an itemized deduction subject to the 2% of adjusted gross income floor.
c. Deductible in arriving at adjusted gross income.
d. Not deductible in 2015.

Items 145 and 146 are based on the following selected 2015 information pertaining to Sam and Ann Hoyt, who filed a joint federal income tax return for the calendar year 2015. The Hoyts had adjusted gross income of $34,000 and itemized their deductions for 2015. Among the Hoyts' cash expenditures during 2015 were the following:

- $2,500 repairs in connection with 2015 fire damage to the Hoyt residence. This property has a basis of $50,000. Fair market value was $60,000 before the fire and $55,000 after the fire. Insurance on the property had lapsed in 2014 for nonpayment of premium.
- $800 appraisal fee to determine amount of fire loss.

145. What amount of fire loss were the Hoyts entitled to deduct as an itemized deduction on their 2015 return?

a. $5,000
b. $2,500
c. $1,600
d. $1,500

146. The appraisal fee to determine the amount of the Hoyts' fire loss was

a. Deductible from gross income in arriving at adjusted gross income.

b. Subject to the 2% of adjusted gross income floor for miscellaneous itemized deductions.
c. Deductible after reducing the amount by $100.
d. Not deductible.

III.F. Miscellaneous Deductions

147. Which of the following is **not** a miscellaneous itemized deduction?

a. Legal fee for tax advice related to a divorce.
b. IRA trustee's fees that are separately billed and paid.
c. Appraisal fee for a charitable contribution.
d. Check-writing fees for a personal checking account.

148. Hall, a divorced person and custodian of her twelve-year-old child, submitted the following information to the CPA who prepared her 2014 return:

The divorce agreement, executed in 2011, provides for Hall to receive $3,000 per month, of which $600 is designated as child support. After the child reaches eighteen, the monthly payments are to be reduced to $2,400 and are to continue until remarriage or death. However, for the year 2014, Hall received a total of only $5,000 from her former husband. Hall paid an attorney $2,000 in 2014 in a suit to collect the alimony owed.

The $2,000 legal fee that Hall paid to collect alimony should be treated as

a. A deduction in arriving at adjusted gross income.
b. An itemized deduction subject to the 2% of adjusted gross income floor.
c. An itemized deduction **not** subject to the 2% of adjusted gross income floor.
d. A nondeductible personal expense.

149. Hall, a divorced person and custodian of her twelve-year-old child, submitted the following information to the CPA who prepared her 2014 return:

During 2014, Hall spent a total of $1,000 for state lottery tickets. Her lottery winnings in 2014 totaled $200.

Hall's lottery transactions should be reported as follows:

Schedule A—itemized deductions
Other miscellaneous deductions

	Other income on page 1	Subject to 2% AGI floor	Not subject to 2% AGI floor
a.	$0	$0	$0
b.	$200	$0	$200
c.	$200	$200	$0
d.	$200	$0	$0

150. Joel Rich is an outside salesman, deriving his income solely from commissions, and personally bearing all expenses without reimbursement of any kind. During the current year, Joel paid the following expenses pertaining directly to his activities as an outside salesman:

Travel	$10,000
Secretarial	7,000
Telephone	1,000

How should these expenses be deducted in Joel's current year return?

	From gross income, in arriving at adjusted gross income	As itemized deductions
a.	$18,000	$0
b.	$11,000	$7,000
c.	$10,000	$8,000
d.	$0	$18,000

151. Magda Micale, a public school teacher with adjusted gross income of $10,000, paid the following items in 2015 for which she received no reimbursement:

Initiation fee for membership in teachers' union	$100
Dues to teachers' union	180
Voluntary unemployment benefit fund contributions to union-established fund	72

How much can Magda claim in 2015 as allowable miscellaneous deductions on Schedule A of Form 1040?

a. $80
b. $280
c. $252
d. $352

152. Harold Brodsky is an electrician employed by a contracting firm. His adjusted gross income is $25,000. During the current year he incurred and paid the following expenses:

Use of personal auto for company business (reimbursed under an accountable plan by employer for $200)	$300
Specialized work clothes	550
Union dues	600
Cost of income tax preparation	150
Preparation of will	100

If Brodsky were to itemize his personal deductions, what amount should he claim as miscellaneous deductible expenses?

a. $800
b. $900
c. $1,500
d. $1,700

IV. Exemptions

153. Which one of the following is **not** included in determining the total support of a dependent?

a. Fair rental value of dependent's lodging.
b. Medical insurance premiums paid on behalf of the dependent.
c. Birthday presents given to the dependent.
d. Nontaxable scholarship received by the dependent.

154. In 2015, Smith, a divorced person, provided over one-half the support for his widowed mother, Ruth, and his son, Clay, both of whom are US citizens. During 2015, Ruth did not live with Smith. She received $9,000 in social security benefits. Clay, a full-time graduate student, and his wife lived with Smith. Clay had no income but filed a joint return for 2015, owing an additional $500 in taxes on his wife's income. How many exemptions was Smith entitled to claim on his 2015 tax return?

    a. 4
    b. 3
    c. 2
    d. 1

155. Jim and Kay Ross contributed to the support of their two children, Dale and Kim, and Jim's widowed parent, Grant. For 2015, Dale, a twenty-year-old full-time college student, earned $4,500 from a part-time job. Kim, a twenty-three-year-old bank teller, earned $18,000. Grant received $5,000 in dividend income and $4,000 in nontaxable social security benefits. Grant, Dale, and Kim are US citizens and were over one-half supported by Jim and Kay. How many exemptions can Jim and Kay claim on their 2015 joint income tax return?

    a. Two
    b. Three
    c. Four
    d. Five

156. Joe and Barb are married, but Barb refuses to sign a 2015 joint return. On Joe's separate 2015 return, an exemption may be claimed for Barb if

    a. Barb was a full-time student for the entire 2015 school year.
    b. Barb attaches a written statement to Joe's income tax return, agreeing to be claimed as an exemption by Joe for 2015.
    c. Barb was under the age of nineteen.
    d. Barb had **no** gross income and was **not** claimed as another person's dependent in 2015.

157. Al and Mary Lew are married and filed a joint 2015 income tax return in which they validly claimed the $4,000 personal exemption for their dependent seventeen-year-old daughter, Doris. Since Doris earned $5,400 in 2015 from a part-time job at the college she attended full-time, Doris was also required to file a 2015 income tax return. What amount was Doris entitled to claim as a personal exemption in her 2015 individual income tax return?

    a. $0
    b. $1,000
    c. $3,900
    d. $5,400

158. During 2015 Robert Moore, who is fifty years old and unmarried, maintained his home in which he and his widower father, age seventy-five, resided. His father had $4,700 interest income from a savings account and also received $2,400 from social security during 2015. Robert provided 60% of his father's total support for 2015. What is Robert's filing status

for 2015, and how many exemptions should he claim on his tax return?

    a. Head of household and two exemptions.
    b. Single and two exemptions.
    c. Head of household and one exemption.
    d. Single and one exemption.

159. John and Mary Arnold are a childless married couple who lived apart (alone in homes maintained by each) the entire year 2015. On December 31, 2015, they were legally separated under a decree of separate maintenance. Which of the following is the only filing status choice available to them when filing for 2015?

    a. Single.
    b. Head of household.
    c. Married filing separate return.
    d. Married filing joint return.

160. Albert and Lois Stoner, age sixty-six and sixty-four, respectively, filed a joint tax return for 2015. They provided all of the support for their blind nineteen-year-old son, who has no gross income. Their twenty-three-year-old daughter, a full-time student until her graduation on June 14, 2015, earned $4,900, which was 40% of her total support during 2015. Her parents provided the remaining support. The Stoners also provided the total support of Lois' father, who is a citizen and lifelong resident of Peru. How many exemptions can the Stoners claim on their 2015 income tax return?

    a. 4
    b. 5
    c. 6
    d. 7

161. Jim Planter, who reached age sixty-five on January 1, 2015, filed a joint return for 2015 with his wife Rita, age fifty. Mary, their twenty-one-year-old daughter, was a full-time student at a college until her graduation on June 2, 2015. The daughter had $6,500 of income and provided 25% of her own support during 2015. In addition, during 2015 the Planters were the sole support for Rita's niece, age 27, who had no income. How many exemptions should the Planters claim on their 2015 tax return?

    a. 2
    b. 3
    c. 4
    d. 5

162. In 2015, Sam Dunn provided more than half the support for his wife, his father's brother, and his cousin. Sam's wife was the only relative who was a member of Sam's household. None of the relatives had any income, nor did any of them file an individual or a joint return. All of these relatives are US citizens. Which of these relatives should be claimed as a dependent or dependents on Sam's 2015 return?

    a. Only his wife.
    b. Only his father's brother.
    c. Only his cousin.
    d. His wife, his father's brother, and his cousin.

163. In 2015, Alan Kott provided more than half the support for his following relatives, none of whom qualified as a member of Alan's household:

Cousin
Niece
Foster parent

None of these relatives had any income, nor did any of these relatives file an individual or joint return. All of these relatives are US citizens. Which of these relatives could be claimed as a dependent on Alan's 2015 return?

a. No one.
b. Niece.
c. Cousin.
d. Foster parent.

164. Sara Hance, who is single and lives alone in Idaho, has no income of her own and is supported in full by the following persons:

	Amount of support	Percent of total
Alma (an unrelated friend)	$2,400	48
Ben (Sara's brother)	2,150	43
Carl (Sara's son)	450	9
	$5,000	100

Under a multiple support agreement, Sara's dependency exemption can be claimed by

a. No one.
b. Alma.
c. Ben.
d. Carl.

165. Mr. and Mrs. Vonce, both age sixty-two, filed a joint return for 2015. They provided all the support for their daughter, who is nineteen, legally blind, and who has no income. Their son, age twenty-one and a full-time student at a university, had $6,200 of income and provided 70% of his own support during 2015. How many exemptions should Mr. and Mrs. Vonce have claimed on their 2015 joint income tax return?

a. 2
b. 3
c. 4
d. 5

V.C.   Filing Status

166. Which of the following is(are) among the requirements to enable a taxpayer to be classified as a "qualifying widow(er)"?

I. A dependent has lived with the taxpayer for six months.
II. The taxpayer has maintained the cost of the principal residence for six months.

a. I only.
b. II only.
c. Both I and II.
d. Neither I nor II.

167. For head of household filing status, which of the following costs are considered in determining whether the taxpayer has contributed more than one-half the cost of maintaining the household?

	Insurance on the home	Rental value of home
a.	Yes	Yes
b.	No	No
c.	Yes	No
d.	No	Yes

168. A husband and wife can file a joint return even if

a. The spouses have different tax years, provided that both spouses are alive at the end of the year.
b. The spouses have different accounting methods.
c. Either spouse was a nonresident alien at any time during the tax year, provided that at least one spouse makes the proper election.
d. They were divorced before the end of the tax year.

169. Emil Gow's wife died in 2013. Emil did not remarry, and he continued to maintain a home for himself and his dependent infant child during 2014 and 2015, providing full support for himself and his child during these years. For 2012, Emil properly filed a joint return. For 2015, Emil's filing status is

a. Single.
b. Head of household.
c. Qualifying widower with dependent child.
d. Married filing joint return.

170. Nell Brown's husband died in 2012. Nell did not remarry, and continued to maintain a home for herself and her dependent infant child during 2013, 2014, and 2015, providing full support for herself and her child during these three years. For 2011, Nell properly filed a joint return. For 2015, Nell's filing status is

a. Single.
b. Married filing joint return.
c. Head of household.
d. Qualifying widow with dependent child.

171. Mrs. Irma Felton, by herself, maintains her home in which she and her unmarried twenty-six-year-old son reside. Her son, however, does not qualify as her dependent. Mrs. Felton's husband died in 2014. What is Mrs. Felton's filing status for 2015?

a. Single.
b. Qualifying widow with dependent child.
c. Head of household.
d. Married filing jointly.

172. Poole, forty-five years old and unmarried, is in the 15% tax bracket. He had 2015 adjusted gross income of $20,000. The following information applies to Poole:

Medical expenses	$7,500
Standard deduction	6,300
Personal exemption	4,000

Poole wishes to minimize his income tax. What is Poole's 2015 total income tax?

    a. $3,000
    b. $1,508
    c. $1,478
    d. $1,455

V.D.   Alternative Minimum Tax (AMT)

173. Which of the following itemized deductions are deductible when computing the alternative minimum tax for individuals?

    a. State income taxes.
    b. Home equity mortgage interest when the loan proceeds were used to purchase an auto.
    c. Unreimbursed employee expenses in excess of 2% of adjusted gross income.
    d. Gambling losses.

174. Randy Lowe reported the following items in computing his regular federal income tax for 2015:

Personal exemption	$4,000
Itemized deduction for state taxes	1,500
Cash charitable contributions	1,250
Net long-term capital gain	700
Tax-exempt interest from private activity bonds issued in 2008	1,000

What are the amounts of tax preference items and adjustments that must be added to or subtracted from regular taxable income in order to compute Lowe's alternative minimum taxable income for 2015?

	Preferences	Adjustments
a.	$1,000	$5,500
b.	$1,000	$5,900
c.	$1,700	$6,150
d.	$2,250	$5,400

175. In 2014, Karen Miller had an alternative minimum tax liability of $20,000. This was the first year that she paid an alternative minimum tax. When she recomputed her 2014 alternative minimum tax using only exclusion preferences and adjustments, her alternative minimum tax was $9,000. For 2015, Karen had a regular tax liability of $50,000 and a tentative minimum tax of $45,000. What is the amount of Karen's unused minimum tax credit from 2015 that will carry over to 2016?

    a. $0
    b. $4,000
    c. $5,000
    d. $6,000

176. In 2015, Don Mills, a single taxpayer, had $70,000 in taxable income before personal exemptions. Mills had no tax preferences. His itemized deductions were as follows:

State and local income taxes	$5,000
Home mortgage interest on loan to acquire residence	6,000
Miscellaneous deductions that exceed 2% of adjusted gross income	2,000

What amount did Mills report as alternative minimum taxable income before the AMT exemption?

    a. $72,000
    b. $75,000
    c. $77,000
    d. $83,000

177. An individual's alternative minimum tax adjustments include

	Net long-term capital gain in excess of net short-term capital loss	Home equity interest expense where loan proceeds not used to buy, build, or improve home
a.	Yes	Yes
b.	Yes	No
c.	No	Yes
d.	No	No

178. The credit for prior year alternative minimum tax liability may be carried

    a. Forward for a maximum of five years.
    b. Back to the three preceding years or carried forward for a maximum of five years.
    c. Back to the three preceding years.
    d. Forward indefinitely.

179. The alternative minimum tax (AMT) is computed as the

    a. Excess of the regular tax over the tentative AMT.
    b. Excess of the tentative AMT over the regular tax.
    c. The tentative AMT plus the regular tax.
    d. Lesser of the tentative AMT or the regular tax.

V.E.   Other Taxes

180. The following information pertains to Joe Diamond, a cash-method sole proprietor for the current year:

Gross receipts from business	$150,000
Interest income from personal investments	10,000
Cost of goods sold	80,000
Other business operating expenses	40,000

What amount of net earnings from self-employment would be multiplied by the applicable self-employment tax rate to compute Diamond's self-employment tax for the current year?

    a. $25,410
    b. $27,705
    c. $30,000
    d. $40,000

181. Freeman, a single individual, reported the following income in the current year:

Guaranteed payment from services rendered to a partnership	$50,000
Ordinary income from an S corporation	20,000

What amount of Freeman's income is subject to self-employment tax?

a. $0
b. $20,000
c. $50,000
d. $70,000

182. Rich is a cash-basis self-employed air-conditioning repairman with current year gross business receipts of $20,000. Rich's cash disbursements were as follows:

Air conditioning parts	$2,500
Yellow Pages listing	2,000
Estimated federal income taxes on self-employment income	1,000
Business long-distance telephone calls	400
Charitable contributions	200

What amount should Rich report as net self-employment income?

a. $15,100
b. $14,900
c. $14,100
d. $13,900

183. The self-employment tax is

a. Fully deductible as an itemized deduction.
b. Fully deductible in determining net income from self-employment.
c. Partially deductible from gross income in arriving at adjusted gross income.
d. Not deductible.

184. An employee who has had social security tax withheld in an amount greater than the maximum for a particular year, may claim

a. Such excess as either a credit or an itemized deduction, at the election of the employee, if that excess resulted from correct withholding by two or more employers.
b. Reimbursement of such excess from his employers, if that excess resulted from correct withholding by two or more employers.
c. The excess as a credit against income tax, if that excess resulted from correct withholding by two or more employers.
d. The excess as a credit against income tax, if that excess was withheld by one employer.

185. Alex Berger, a retired building contractor, earned the following income during the current year:

Director's fee received from Keith Realty Corp.	$600
Executor's fee received from the estate of his deceased sister	7,000

Berger's gross income from self-employment for the current year is

a. $0
b. $600
c. $7,000
d. $7,600

186. Smith, a retired corporate executive, earned consulting fees of $8,000 and director's fees of $2,000 during the current year. Smith's gross income from self-employment for the current year is

a. $0
b. $2,000
c. $8,000
d. $10,000

VI.A. General Business Credit

187. Which one of the following credits is **not** a component of the general business credit?

a. Disabled access credit.
b. Employer social security credit.
c. Foreign tax credit.
d. Work opportunity credit.

188. Which of the following credits is a combination of several tax credits to provide uniform rules for the current and carryback-carryover years?

a. General business credit.
b. Foreign tax credit.
c. Minimum tax credit.
d. Enhanced oil recovery credit.

VI.L. Credit for the Elderly and the Disabled

189. Melvin Crane is sixty-six years old, and his wife, Matilda, is sixty-five. They filed a joint income tax return for 2015, reporting an adjusted gross income of $22,200, on which they owed a tax of $61. They received $3,000 from social security benefits in 2015. How much can they claim on Form 1040 in 2015, as a credit for the elderly?

a. $0
b. $61
c. $255
d. $675

VI.M. Child and Dependent Care Credit

190. Nora Hayes, a widow, maintains a home for herself and her two dependent preschool children. In 2015, Nora's earned income and adjusted gross income was $44,000. During 2015,

Nora paid work-related expenses of $6,000 for a housekeeper to care for her children. How much can Nora claim for child care credit in 2015?

a. $0
b. $960
c. $1,200
d. $2,100

191. Robert and Mary Jason, filing a joint tax return for 2015, had a tax liability of $9,000 based on their tax table income and three exemptions. Robert and Mary had earned income of $30,000 and $22,000, respectively, during 2015. In order for Mary to be gainfully employed, the Jasons incurred the following employment-related expenses for their four-year-old son John in 2015:

Payee	Amount
Union Day Care Center	$2,500
Acme Home Cleaning Service	500
Wilma Jason, babysitter (Robert Jason's mother)	1,000

Assuming that the Jasons do not claim any other credits against their tax, what is the amount of the child care tax credit they should report on their tax return for 2015?

a. $500
b. $600
c. $700
d. $1,050

192. To qualify for the child care credit on a joint return, at least one spouse must

	Have an adjusted gross income of $10,000 or less	Be gainfully employed when related expenses are incurred
a.	Yes	Yes
b.	No	No
c.	Yes	No
d.	No	Yes

VI.N. Foreign Tax Credit

193. Sunex Co., an accrual-basis, calendar-year domestic C corporation, is taxed on its worldwide income. In the current year, Sunex's US tax liability on its domestic and foreign-source income is $60,000 and no prior year foreign income taxes have been carried forward. Which factor(s) may affect the amount of Sunex's foreign tax credit available in its current year corporate income tax return?

	Income source	The foreign tax rate
a.	Yes	Yes
b.	Yes	No
c.	No	Yes
d.	No	No

194. The following information pertains to Wald Corp.'s operations for the current year:

Worldwide taxable income	$300,000
US source taxable income	180,000
US income tax before foreign tax credit	96,000
Foreign nonbusiness-related interest earned	30,000
Foreign income taxes paid on nonbusiness-related interest earned	12,000
Other foreign source taxable income	90,000
Foreign income taxes paid on other foreign source taxable income	27,000

What amount of foreign tax credit may Wald claim for the current year?

a. $28,800
b. $36,600
c. $38,400
d. $39,000

195. Foreign income taxes paid by a corporation

a. May be claimed either as a deduction or as a credit, at the option of the corporation.
b. May be claimed only as a deduction.
c. May be claimed only as a credit.
d. Do **not** qualify either as a deduction or as a credit.

VI.O. Earned Income Credit

196. Which of the following credits can result in a refund even if the individual had **no** income tax liability?

a. Lifetime learning credit.
b. Credit for the elderly or the disabled.
c. Earned income credit.
d. Child and dependent care credit.

197. Kent qualified for the earned income credit. This credit could result in a

a. Refund even if Kent had no tax withheld from wages.
b. Refund only if Kent had tax withheld from wages.
c. Carryback or carryforward for any unused portion.
d. Subtraction from adjusted gross income to arrive at taxable income.

198. Which one of the following statements is correct with regard to the earned income credit?

a. The credit is available only to those individuals whose earned income is equal to adjusted gross income.
b. For purposes of the earned income test, "earned income" includes workers' compensation benefits.
c. The credit can result in a refund even if the individual had **no** tax withheld from wages.
d. The credit is available on a tax return that covers less than twelve months.

199. Which of the following tax credits **cannot** be claimed by a corporation?

a. Foreign tax credit.

b. Earned income credit.
c. Alternative fuel production credit.
d. General business credit.

VI.P. Credit for Adoption Expenses

200. Which one of the following statements is correct regarding the credit for adoption expenses?

a. The credit for adoption expenses is a nonrefundable credit.
b. The maximum credit is $5,000 for the adoption of a child with special needs.
c. Qualified adoption expenses are always taken into account in the year that the adoption becomes final.
d. An eligible child is an individual who has not attained the age of twenty-one as of the time of adoption.

VI.Q. Child Tax Credit

201. Which one of the following statements is **not** correct with regard to the child tax credit?

a. The credit is $1,000 per qualifying child for tax years that begin in 2015.
b. The amount of credit is reduced if modified adjusted gross income exceeds certain thresholds.
c. To qualify for the credit, a dependent child must be less than sixteen years old.
d. A qualifying child must be a US citizen or resident.

VI.R. American Opportunity Credit

202. Which one of the following statements concerning the American Opportunity credit is **not** correct?

a. The credit is available for the first four years of postsecondary education program.
b. The credit is available on a per student basis.
c. To be eligible for the credit, the student must be enrolled full-time for at least one academic period during the year.
d. If a parent claims a child as a dependent, any qualified expenses paid by the child are deemed to be paid by the parent.

VI.S. Lifetime Learning Credit

203. Which one of the following statements concerning the lifetime learning credit is **not** correct?

a. The credit is 20% of the first $10,000 of qualified tuition and related expenses.
b. Qualifying expenses include the cost of tuition for graduate courses at an eligible educational institution.
c. The credit may be claimed for an unlimited number of years.
d. The credit is available on a per student basis.

VI.T. Estimated Tax Payments

204. Chris Baker's adjusted gross income on her 2014 tax return was $160,000. The amount covered a twelve-month period. For the 2015 tax year, Baker may avoid the penalty for the underpayment of estimated tax if the timely estimated tax payments equal the required annual amount of

I. 90% of the tax on the return for the current year, paid in four equal installments.
II. 100% of prior year's tax liability, paid in four equal installments.

a. I only.
b. II only.
c. Both I and II.
d. Neither I nor II.

205. Krete, an unmarried taxpayer, had income exclusively from wages. By December 31, 2014, Krete's employer had withheld $16,000 in federal income taxes and Krete had made no estimated tax payments. On April 15, 2015, Krete timely filed an extension request to file her individual tax return and paid $300 of additional taxes. Krete's 2014 income tax liability was $16,500 when she timely filed her return on April 30, 2015, and paid the remaining income tax liability balance. What amount would be subject to the penalty for the underpayment of estimated taxes?

a. $0
b. $200
c. $500
d. $16,500

VII. Filing Requirements

206. John Smith is the executor of his father's estate. His father, a calendar-year taxpayer, died on July 15, 2015. As executor of his father's estate, John is required to file a final income tax return Form 1040 for his father's 2015 tax year. What is the due date of his father's 2015 federal income tax return assuming John does not file for an extension?

a. November 1, 2015.
b. November 15, 2015.
c. March 15, 2016.
d. April 15, 2016.

207. Ray Birch, age sixty, is single with no dependents. Birch's only income is from his occupation as a self-employed plumber. Birch must file a return for 2014 if his net earnings from self-employment are at least

a. $400
b. $950
c. $3,900
d. $6,100

IX.C Assessments

208. Jackson Corp., a calendar-year corporation, mailed its 2014 tax return to the Internal Revenue Service by certified mail on Friday, March 8, 2015. The return, postmarked

March 8, 2015, was delivered to the Internal Revenue Service on March 12, 2015. The statute of limitations on Jackson's corporate tax return begins on

    a. December 31, 2014.
    b. March 12, 2015.
    c. March 16, 2015.
    d. March 17, 2015.

209. A calendar-year taxpayer files an individual tax return for 2014 on March 20, 2015. The taxpayer neither committed fraud nor omitted amounts in excess of 25% of gross income on the tax return. What is the latest date that the Internal Revenue Service can assess tax and assert a notice of deficiency?

    a. March 20, 2018.
    b. March 20, 2017.
    c. April 15, 2018.
    d. April 15, 2019.

210. Harold Thompson, a self-employed individual, had income transactions for 2014 (duly reported on his return filed in April 2015) as follows:

Gross receipts	$400,000
Less cost of goods sold and deductions	320,000
Net business income	$80,000
Capital gains	36,000
Gross income	$116,000

In November 2015, Thompson discovers that he had inadvertently omitted some income on his 2014 return and retains Mann, CPA, to determine his position under the statute of limitations. Mann should advise Thompson that the six-year statute of limitations would apply to his 2014 return only if he omitted from gross income an amount in excess of

    a. $20,000
    b. $29,000
    c. $100,000
    d. $109,000

211. If a taxpayer omits from his or her income tax return an amount that exceeds 25% of the gross income reported on the return, the Internal Revenue Service can issue a notice of deficiency within a maximum period of

    a. Three years from the date the return was filed, if filed before the due date.
    b. Three years from the date the return was due, if filed by the due date.
    c. Six years from the date the return was filed, if filed before the due date.
    d. Six years from the date the return was due, if filed by the due date.

IX.F. Claims for Refund

212. A claim for refund of erroneously paid income taxes, filed by an individual before the statute of limitations expires, must be submitted on Form

    a. 1139
    b. 1045
    c. 1040X
    d. 843

213. If an individual paid income tax in 2014 but did **not** file a 2014 return because his income was insufficient to require the filing of a return, the deadline for filing a refund claim is

    a. Two years from the date the tax was paid.
    b. Two years from the date a return would have been due.
    c. Three years from the date the tax was paid.
    d. Three years from the date a return would have been due.

214. A married couple filed their joint 2013 calendar-year return on March 15, 2014, and attached a check for the balance of tax due as shown on the return. On June 15, 2015, the couple discovered that they had failed to include $2,000 of home mortgage interest in their itemized deductions. In order for the couple to recover the tax that they would have saved by using the $2,000 deduction, they must file an amended return no later than

    a. December 31, 2016.
    b. March 15, 2017.
    c. April 15, 2017.
    d. June 15, 2017.

215. Richard Baker filed his 2014 individual income tax return on April 15, 2015. On December 31, 2015, he learned that 100 shares of stock that he owned had become worthless in 2014. Since he did not deduct this loss on his 2014 return, Baker intends to file a claim for refund. This refund claim must be filed not later than April 15,

    a. 2016
    b. 2018
    c. 2021
    d. 2022

IX.H. Taxpayer Penalties

216. A taxpayer filed his income tax return after the due date but neglected to file an extension form. The return indicated a tax liability of $50,000 and taxes withheld of $45,000. On what amount would the penalties for late filing and late payment be computed?

    a. $0
    b. $5,000
    c. $45,000
    d. $50,000

217. An accuracy-related penalty applies to the portion of tax underpayment attributable to

    I. Any substantial gift or estate tax valuation understatement
    II. Any substantial income tax valuation overstatement.

    a. I only.
    b. II only.
    c. Both I and II.
    d. Neither I nor II.

Multiple-Choice Answers and Explanations

Answers

1. c	__ __	46. c	__ __	91. a	__ __	136. b	__ __	181. c	__ __
2. b	__ __	47. a	__ __	92. d	__ __	137. b	__ __	182. a	__ __
3. b	__ __	48. a	__ __	93. d	__ __	138. b	__ __	183. c	__ __
4. c	__ __	49. a	__ __	94. d	__ __	139. a	__ __	184. c	__ __
5. a	__ __	50. d	__ __	95. a	__ __	140. b	__ __	185. b	__ __
6. d	__ __	51. b	__ __	96. d	__ __	141. a	__ __	186. d	__ __
7. b	__ __	52. b	__ __	97. d	__ __	142. a	__ __	187. c	__ __
8. d	__ __	53. b	__ __	98. c	__ __	143. a	__ __	188. a	__ __
9. a	__ __	54. b	__ __	99. d	__ __	144. d	__ __	189. a	__ __
10. d	__ __	55. c	__ __	100. c	__ __	145. d	__ __	190. c	__ __
11. b	__ __	56. d	__ __	101. d	__ __	146. b	__ __	191. b	__ __
12. b	__ __	57. d	__ __	102. b	__ __	147. d	__ __	192. b	__ __
13. c	__ __	58. d	__ __	103. c	__ __	148. b	__ __	193. a	__ __
14. d	__ __	59. c	__ __	104. b	__ __	149. b	__ __	194. b	__ __
15. c	__ __	60. a	__ __	105. c	__ __	150. d	__ __	195. a	__ __
16. c	__ __	61. a	__ __	106. b	__ __	151. a	__ __	196. c	__ __
17. a	__ __	62. b	__ __	107. b	__ __	152. b	__ __	197. a	__ __
18. c	__ __	63. a	__ __	108. a	__ __	153. d	__ __	198. c	__ __
19. a	__ __	64. d	__ __	109. c	__ __	154. c	__ __	199. b	__ __
20. d	__ __	65. d	__ __	110. d	__ __	155. b	__ __	200. a	__ __
21. c	__ __	66. d	__ __	111. a	__ __	156. d	__ __	201. c	__ __
22. d	__ __	67. a	__ __	112. d	__ __	157. a	__ __	202. c	__ __
23. c	__ __	68. c	__ __	113. d	__ __	158. d	__ __	203. d	__ __
24. c	__ __	69. b	__ __	114. b	__ __	159. a	__ __	204. a	__ __
25. a	__ __	70. b	__ __	115. d	__ __	160. a	__ __	205. a	__ __
26. d	__ __	71. c	__ __	116. d	__ __	161. c	__ __	206. d	__ __
27. c	__ __	72. a	__ __	117. c	__ __	162. b	__ __	207. a	__ __
28. d	__ __	73. a	__ __	118. a	__ __	163. b	__ __	208. c	__ __
29. c	__ __	74. c	__ __	119. d	__ __	164. c	__ __	209. c	__ __
30. c	__ __	75. c	__ __	120. b	__ __	165. b	__ __	210. d	__ __
31. b	__ __	76. a	__ __	121. b	__ __	166. d	__ __	211. d	__ __
32. b	__ __	77. d	__ __	122. a	__ __	167. c	__ __	212. c	__ __
33. d	__ __	78. b	__ __	123. b	__ __	168. b	__ __	213. a	__ __
34. b	__ __	79. c	__ __	124. a	__ __	169. c	__ __	214. c	__ __
35. c	__ __	80. a	__ __	125. c	__ __	170. c	__ __	215. d	__ __
36. a	__ __	81. b	__ __	126. b	__ __	171. a	__ __	216. b	__ __
37. c	__ __	82. c	__ __	127. c	__ __	172. d	__ __	217. c	__ __
38. d	__ __	83. b	__ __	128. c	__ __	173. d	__ __		
39. a	__ __	84. a	__ __	129. c	__ __	174. a	__ __		
40. b	__ __	85. c	__ __	130. a	__ __	175. d	__ __		
41. c	__ __	86. d	__ __	131. a	__ __	176. c	__ __		
42. d	__ __	87. c	__ __	132. b	__ __	177. c	__ __		
43. d	__ __	88. a	__ __	133. c	__ __	178. d	__ __		
44. d	__ __	89. c	__ __	134. c	__ __	179. b	__ __	1st: __/217 = __%
45. c	__ __	90. c	__ __	135. c	__ __	180. b	__ __	2nd: __/217 = __%

Explanations

1. (c) The requirement is to determine the pension (annuity) amounts excluded from income for 2014, 2015, and 2016. Brown's contribution of $12,000 will be recovered pro rata over the life of the annuity. Under this rule, $100 per month ($12,000 ÷ 120 months) is excluded from income.

	Received	Excluded	Included
2014	$4,900	$700	$4,200
2015	8,400	1,200	7,200
2016	8,400	1,200	7,200

2. (b) The requirement is to determine the amount of life insurance proceeds that must be included in gross income by Decker, on the death of Fuller's parent. Life insurance proceeds paid because of the insured person's death are generally excluded from gross income. However, the exclusion generally does not apply if the insurance policy was obtained by the beneficiary in exchange for valuable consideration from a person other than the insurance company. Here, Decker purchased the policy from Fuller for $25,000 and paid an additional $40,000 in premiums, so Decker must include in gross income the excess of insurance proceeds over his investment in the policy [$200,000 − ($25,000 + $40,000) = $135,000.

3. (b) The requirement is to determine the amount of life insurance payments to be included in a widow's gross income. Life insurance proceeds paid by reason of death are excluded from income if paid in a lump sum or in installments. If the payments are received in installments, the principal amount of the policy divided by the number of annual payments is excluded each year. Therefore, $1,200 of the $5,200 insurance payment is included in Penelope's gross income.

Annual installment	$5,200
Principal amount ($100,000 ÷ 25)	− 4,000
Gross income	$1,200

4. (c) The requirement is to determine the correct statement regarding a "cafeteria plan" maintained by an employer. Cafeteria plans are employer-sponsored benefit packages that offer employees a choice between taking cash and receiving qualified benefits (e.g., accident and health insurance, group-term life insurance, coverage under a dependent care or group legal services program). Thus, employees "may select their own menu of benefits." If an employee chooses qualified benefits, they are excluded from the employee's gross income to the extent allowed by law. If an employee chooses cash, it is includible in the employee's gross income as compensation. Answer (a) is incorrect because participation is restricted to employees only. Answer (b) is incorrect because there is no minimum service requirement that must be met before an employee can participate in a plan. Answer (d) is incorrect because deferred compensation plans other than 401(k) plans are not included in the definition of a cafeteria plan.

5. (a) The requirement is to determine the amount of group-term life insurance proceeds that must be included in gross

income by Autrey's widow. Life insurance proceeds paid by reason of death are generally excluded from gross income. Note that although only the cost of the first $50,000 of group-term insurance coverage can be excluded from gross income during the employee's life, the entire amount of insurance proceeds paid by reason of death will be excluded from the beneficiary's income.

6. (d) The requirement is to determine the amount of employee death payments to be included in gross income by the widow and the son. The $5,000 employee death benefit exclusion was repealed for decedents dying after August 20, 1996.

7. (b) The requirement is to determine the maximum amount of tax-free group-term life insurance coverage that can be provided to an employee by an employer. The cost of the first $50,000 of group-term life insurance coverage provided by an employer will be excluded from an employee's income.

8. (d) The requirement is to determine the amount to be included in Hal's gross income for the current year. All three amounts that Hal received as a result of his injury are excluded from gross income. Benefits received as workers' compensation and compensation for damages for physical injuries are always excluded from gross income. Amounts received from an employer's accident and health plan as reimbursement for medical expenses are excluded so long as the medical expenses are not deducted as itemized deductions.

9. (a) James Martin's gross income consists of

Salary	$50,000
Bonus	10,000
	$60,000

Medical insurance premiums paid by an employer are excluded from an employee's gross income. Additionally, qualified moving expense reimbursements are an employee fringe benefit and can be excluded from gross income. This means that an employee can exclude an amount paid by an employer as payment for (or reimbursement of) expenses that would be deductible as moving expenses if directly paid or incurred by the employee.

10. (d) The requirement is to determine how much income Hall should include in his 2015 tax return for the inheritance of stock which he received from his father's estate. Since the definition of gross income excludes property received as a gift, bequest, devise, or inheritance, Hall recognizes no income upon receipt of the stock. Since the executor of his father's estate elected the alternate valuation date (August 1), and the stock was distributed to Hall before that date (June 1), Hall's basis for the stock would be its $4,500 FMV on June 1. Since Hall also sold the stock on June 1 for $4,500, Hall would have no gain or loss resulting from the sale.

11. (b) The requirement is to determine the amount of dividend income that should be reported by Gail Judd. The $100 dividend on Gail's life insurance policy is treated as a reduction of the cost of insurance (because total dividends have not yet exceeded accumulated premiums paid) and is excluded from gross income. Thus, Gail will report the $300 dividend on common stock and the $500 dividend on preferred stock, a total of $800 as dividend income.

12. (b) The requirement is to determine the amount of dividend income to be reported on Amy's 2015 return. Dividends are included in income at earlier of actual or constructive receipt. When corporate dividends are paid by mail, they are included in income for the year in which received. Thus, the $875 dividend received 1/2/15 is included in income for 2015. The $500 dividend on a life insurance policy from a mutual insurance company is treated as a reduction of the cost of insurance and is excluded from gross income.

13. (c) The requirement is to determine the amount of dividends to be reported by the Mitchells on a joint return. The amount of dividends would be ($400 + $50 + $300) = $750. The $200 dividend on the life insurance policy is not gross income, but is considered a reduction of the cost of the policy.

14. (d) The requirement is to determine Karen's basis in the 10 shares of preferred stock received as a stock dividend. Generally, stock dividends are nontaxable, and a taxpayer's basis for original stock is allocated to the dividend stock in proportion to fair market values. However, any stock that is distributed **on** preferred stock results in a taxable stock dividend. The amount to be included in the shareholder's income is the stock's fair market value on date of distribution. Similarly, the shareholder's basis for the dividend shares will be equal to their fair market value on date of distribution (10 × $60 = $600).

15. (c) The requirement is to determine the correct statement(s) regarding the amortization of bond premium on a taxable bond. The amount of premium amortization on taxable bonds acquired by the taxpayer after 1987 is treated as an offset to the amount of interest income reported on the bond. The method of calculating the annual amortization is determined by the date the bond was issued, as opposed to the acquisition date. If the bond was issued after September 27, 1985, the amortization must be calculated under the constant yield to maturity method. Otherwise, the amortization must be made ratably over the life of the bond. Under the constant yield to maturity method, the amortizable bond premium is computed on the basis of the taxpayer's yield to maturity, using the taxpayer's basis for the bond, and compounding at the close of each accrual period.

16. (c) The requirement is to determine whether two statements are true concerning the exclusion of interest income on US Series EE Bonds that are redeemed to pay for higher education. The accrued interest on US Series EE savings bonds that are redeemed by a taxpayer is excluded from gross income to the extent that the aggregate redemption proceeds (principal plus interest) are used to finance the higher education of the taxpayer, taxpayer's spouse, or dependents. Qualified higher educational expenses include tuition and fees, but not room and board or the cost of courses involving sports, games, or hobbies that are not part of a degree program. In determining the amount of available exclusion, qualified educational expenses must be reduced by qualified scholarships that are exempt from tax, and any other nontaxable payments such as veteran's educational assistance and employer-provided educational assistance.

17. (a) The requirement is to determine the amount of interest subject to tax in Kay's 2015 tax return. Interest must generally be included in gross income, unless a specific statutory provision provides for its exclusion (e.g., interest on municipal bonds). Interest on US Treasury certificates and on a refund of federal income tax would be subject to tax on Kay's 2015 tax return.

18. (c) The requirement is to determine the amount of interest income taxable on Charles and Marcia's joint income tax return. A taxpayer's income includes interest on state and federal income tax refunds and interest on federal obligations, but excludes interest on state obligations. Here, their joint taxable income must include the $500 interest on federal income tax refund, $600 interest on state income tax refund, and $800 interest on federal government obligations, but will exclude the $1,000 tax-exempt interest on state government obligations. Although a refund of federal income tax would be excluded from gross income, any interest on a refund must be included in gross income.

19. (a) The requirement is to determine the condition that must be met for tax exemption of accumulated interest on Series EE US Savings Bonds. An individual may be able to exclude from income all or a part of the interest received on the redemption of Series EE US Savings Bonds. To qualify, the bonds must be issued after December 31, 1989, the purchaser of the bonds must be the sole owner of the bonds (or joint owner with his or her spouse), and the owner(s) must be at least twenty-four years old before the bond's issue date. To exclude the interest the redemption proceeds must be used to pay the tuition and fees incurred by the taxpayer, spouse, or dependents to attend a college or university or certain vocational schools.

20. (d) The requirement is to determine the amount of tax-exempt interest. Interest on obligations of a state or one of its political subdivisions (e.g., New York Port Authority bonds), or a possession of the US (e.g., Puerto Rico Commonwealth bonds) is tax-exempt.

21. (c) Stone will report $1,700 of interest income. Interest on FIT refunds, personal injury awards, US savings bonds, and most other sources is fully taxable. However, interest on state or municipal bonds is generally not taxable.

22. (d) The requirement is to determine how Don Raff's $500 interest forfeiture penalty should be reported. An interest forfeiture penalty for making a premature withdrawal from a certificate of deposit should be deducted from gross income in arriving at adjusted gross income in the year in which the penalty is incurred, which in this case is 2015.

23. (c) The requirement is to determine which payment(s) must be included in a recipient's gross income. A candidate for a degree can exclude amounts received as a scholarship or fellowship if, according to the conditions of the grant, the amounts are used for the payment of tuition and fees, books, supplies, and equipment required for courses at an educational institution. All payments received for services must be included in income, even if the services are a condition of receiving the grant or are required of all candidates for the degree. Here, the payment to a graduate assistant for a part-time teaching assignment and the grant to a Ph.D. candidate for participation in research are payments for services and must be included in income.

24. (c) The requirement is to determine the amount of scholarship awards that Majors should include as taxable income. Only a candidate for a degree can exclude amounts received as a scholarship award. The exclusion available to degree candidates is limited to amounts received for the payment of tuition and fees, books, supplies, and equipment required for courses at the educational institution. Since Majors is a candidate for a graduate degree, Majors can exclude the $10,000 received for tuition, fees, books, and supplies required for courses. However, the $2,000 stipend for research services required by the scholarship must be included in taxable income.

25. (a) The requirement is to determine a lessor's 2015 gross income. A lessor excludes from income any increase in the value of property caused by improvements made by the lessee, unless the improvements were made in lieu of rent. In this case, there is no indication that the improvements were made in lieu of rent. Therefore, for 2015, Farley should only include the six rent payments in income: 6 × $1,000 = $6,000.

26. (d) The requirement is to determine the amount of alimony recapture that must be included in Bob's gross income for 2015. Alimony recapture may occur if alimony payments sharply decline in the second and third years that payments are made. The payor must report the recaptured alimony as gross income in the third year, and the payee is allowed a deduction for the same amount. Recapture for the second year (2014) occurs to the extent that the alimony paid in the second year ($20,000) exceeds the alimony paid in the third year ($0) by more than $15,000 [i.e., $20,000 − ($0 + $15,000) = $5,000 of recapture].

Recapture for the first year (2013) occurs to the extent that the alimony paid in the first year ($50,000) exceeds the *average alimony* paid in the second and third years by more than $15,000. For this purpose, the alimony paid in the second year ($20,000) must be reduced by the amount of recapture for that year ($5,000).

First year (2013) payment		$50,000
Second year (2014) payment ($20,000 − $5,000)	$15,000	
Third year (2015) payment	+ 0	
Total	$15,000	
	÷ 2	(7,500)
		(15,000)
Recapture for first year (2013)		$27,500

Thus, the total recapture to be included in Bob's gross income for 2015 is $5,000 + $27,500 = $32,500.

27. (c) The requirement is to determine which conditions must be present in a divorce agreement for a payment to qualify as deductible alimony. In order for a payment to be deductible by the payor as alimony, the payment must be made in cash or its equivalent, the payment must be received by or on behalf of a spouse under a divorce or separation instrument, the payments must terminate at the recipient's death, and must not be designated as other than alimony (e.g., child support).

28. (d) The requirement is to determine which of the following would be included in gross income by Darr who is an employee of Sorce C corporation. The definition of gross income includes income from whatever source derived and would include the dividend income on shares of stock that Darr received for services rendered. However, items specifically excluded from gross income include amounts received as a gift or inheritance, as well as employer-provided medical insurance coverage under a health plan.

29. (c) The requirement is to determine the correct statement regarding the inclusion of social security benefits in gross income for 2015. A maximum of 85% of social security benefits may be included in gross income for high-income taxpayers. Thus, no matter how high a taxpayer's income, 85% of the social security benefits is the maximum amount of benefits to be included in gross income.

30. (c) The requirement is to determine the amount that Perle should include in taxable income as a result of performing dental services for Wood. An exchange of services for property or services is sometimes called bartering. A taxpayer must include in income the amount of cash and the fair market value of property or services received in exchange for the performance of services. Here, Perle's taxable income should include the $200 cash and the bookcase with a comparable value of $350, a total of $550.

31. (b) The requirement is to determine the amount of payments to be included in Mary's income tax return for 2015. Alimony must be included in gross income by the payee and is deductible by the payor. In order to be treated as alimony, a payment must be made in cash and be received by or paid on behalf of the former spouse. Amounts treated as child support are not alimony; they are neither deductible by the payor, nor taxable to the payee. Payments will be treated as child support to the extent that payments will be reduced upon the happening of a contingency relating to a child (e.g., the child attaining a specified age, marrying, becoming employed). Here, since future payments will be reduced by 20% on their child's 18th birthday, the total cash payments of $10,000 ($7,000 paid directly to Mary plus the $3,000 of tuition paid on Mary's behalf) must be reduced by 20% and result in $8,000 of alimony income for Mary. The remaining $2,000 is treated as child support and is not taxable.

32. (b) The requirement is to determine the amount of interest for overpayment of 2014 state income tax and state income tax refund that is taxable in Clark's 2015 federal income tax return. The $10 of interest income on the tax refund is taxable and must be included in gross income. On the other hand, a state income tax refund is included in gross income under the "tax benefit rule" only if the refunded amount was deducted in a prior year and the deduction provided a benefit because it reduced the taxpayer's federal income tax. The payment of state income taxes will not result in a "benefit" if an individual does not itemize deductions, or is subject to the alternative minimum tax for the year the taxes are paid. Individuals who file Form 1040EZ are not allowed to itemize deductions and must use the standard deduction. Since state income taxes are only allowed as an itemized deduction and Clark did not itemize for 2014 (he used Form 1040EZ), his $900 state income tax refund is nontaxable and is excluded from gross income.

33. (d) The requirement is to determine the amount to be reported in Hall's 2014 return as alimony income. If a divorce agreement specifies both alimony and child support, but less is paid than required, then payments are first allocated to child support, with only the remainder in excess of required child support to be treated as alimony. Pursuant to Hall's divorce agreement, $3,000 was to be paid each month, of which $600 was designated as child support, leaving a balance of $2,400 per month to be treated as alimony. However, during 2014, only $5,000 was paid to Hall by her former husband which was less than the $36,000 required by the divorce agreement. Since required child support payments totaled $600 × 12 = $7,200 for 2014, all $5,000 of the payments actually received by Hall during 2014 is treated as child support, with nothing remaining to be reported as alimony.

34. (b) The requirement is to determine the amount of income to be reported by Lee in connection with the receipt of stock for services rendered. Compensation for services rendered that is received by a cash method taxpayer must be included in income at its fair market value on the date of receipt.

35. (c) The requirement is to determine when Ross was subject to "regular tax" with regard to stock that was acquired through the exercise of an incentive stock option. There are no tax consequences when an incentive stock option is granted to an employee. When the option is exercised, any excess of the stock's FMV over the option price is a tax preference item for purposes of the employee's alternative minimum tax. However, an employee is not subject to regular tax until the stock acquired through exercise of the option is sold.

If the employee holds the stock acquired through exercise of the option at least two years from the date the option was granted (and holds the stock itself at least one year), the employee's realized gain is treated as long-term capital gain in the year of sale, and the employer receives no compensation deduction. If the preceding holding period rules are not met at the time the stock is sold, the employee must report ordinary income to the extent that the stock's FMV at date of exercise exceeded the option price, with any remaining gain reported as long-term or short-term capital gain. As a result, the employer receives a compensation deduction equal to the amount of ordinary income reported by the employee.

36. (a) The requirement is to determine the amount that is taxable as alimony in Ann's return. In order to be treated as alimony, a payment must be made in cash and be received by or on behalf of the payee spouse. Furthermore, cash payments must be required to terminate upon the death of the payee spouse to be

treated as alimony. In this case, the transfer of title in the home to Ann is not a cash payment and cannot be treated as alimony. Although the mortgage payments are cash payments made on behalf of Ann, the payments are not treated as alimony because they will be made throughout the full twenty-year mortgage period and will not terminate in the event of Ann's death.

37. (c) The requirement is to determine the correct statement with regard to income in respect of a cash basis decedent. Income in respect of a decedent is income earned by a decedent before death that was not includible in the decedent's final income tax return because of the decedent's method of accounting (e.g., receivables of a cash basis decedent). Such income must be included in gross income by the person who receives it and has the same character (e.g., ordinary or capital) as it would have had if the decedent had lived.

38. (d) The requirement is to determine the amount of gross income. Drury's gross income includes the $36,000 salary, the $500 of premiums paid by her employer for group-term life insurance coverage in excess of $50,000, and the $5,000 proceeds received from a state lottery.

39. (a) The requirement is to determine the amount of foster child payments to be included in income by the Charaks. Amounts received by a foster care provider as qualified foster care payments are excluded from gross income. Record keeping to establish the extent to which payments reimburse actual foster care expenses is not required. As a result, the foster care payments of $3,900 are fully excluded from the Charaks' gross income.

40. (b) The requirement is to determine the amount and the year in which the tip income should be included in Pierre's gross income. If an individual receives less than $20 in tips during one month while working for one employer, the tips do not have to be reported to the employer and the tips are included in the individual's gross income when received. However, if an individual receives $20 or more in tips during one month while working for one employer, the individual must report the total amount of tips to that employer by the tenth day of the next month. Then the tips are included in gross income for the month in which they are reported to the employer. Here, Pierre received $2,000 in tips during December 2014 that he reported to his employer in January 2015. Thus, the $2,000 of tips will be included in Pierre's gross income for 2015.

41. (c) The requirement is to determine the correct statement regarding the alimony deduction in connection with a divorce. To be considered alimony, cash payments must terminate on the death of the payee spouse. Answer (a) is incorrect because alimony payments cannot be contingent on the status of the divorced couple's children. Answer (b) is incorrect because the divorced couple cannot be members of the same household at the time the alimony is paid. Answer (d) is incorrect because only cash payments can be considered alimony.

42. (d) The requirement is to determine the amount of a $10,000 award for outstanding civic achievement that Joan should include in her 2015 adjusted gross income. An award for civic achievement can be excluded from gross income only if the recipient was selected without any action on his/her part, is not required to render substantial future services as a condition of receiving the award, and designates that the award is to be directly transferred by the payor to a governmental unit or a tax-exempt charitable, educational, or religious organization. Here, since Joan accepted and actually received the award, the $10,000 must be included in her adjusted gross income.

43. (d) The requirement is to determine the amount of lottery winnings that should be included in Gow's taxable income. Lottery winnings are gambling winnings and must be included in gross income. Gambling losses are deductible from AGI as a miscellaneous deduction (to the extent of winnings) not subject to the 2% of AGI floor if a taxpayer itemizes deductions. Since Gow elected the standard deduction for 2015, the $400 spent on lottery tickets is not deductible. Thus, all $5,000 of Gow's lottery winnings are included in his taxable income.

44. (d) The requirement is to determine the amount of advance rents and lease cancellation payments that should be reported on Lake Corp.'s 2015 tax return. Advance rental payments must be included in gross income when received, regardless of the period covered or whether the taxpayer uses the cash or accrual method. Similarly, lease cancellation payments are treated as rent and must be included in income when received, regardless of the taxpayer's method of accounting.

45. (c) The requirement is to determine the amount to be reported as gross income. Gross income includes the $50,000 of recurring rents plus the $2,000 lease cancellation payment. The $1,000 of lease improvements are excluded from income since they were **not** required in lieu of rent.

46. (c) The requirement is to determine the amount of net rental income that Gow should include in his adjusted gross income. Since Gow lives in one of two identical apartments, only 50% of the expenses relating to both apartments can be allocated to the rental unit.

Rent	$7,200
Less:	
Real estate taxes (50% × $6,400)	(3,200)
Painting of rental apartment	(800)
Fire insurance (50% × $600)	(300)
Depreciation (50% × $5,000)	(2,500)
Net rental income	$400

47. (a) The requirement is to determine the amount of rent income to be reported on Amy's 2015 return. Both the $6,000 of rent received for 2015, as well as the $1,000 of advance rent received in 2015 for the last two months of the lease must be included in income for 2015. Advance rent must be included in income in the year received regardless of the period covered or the accounting method used.

48. (a) The requirement is to determine the amount to be reported as rent revenue in an accrual-basis taxpayer's tax return for 2015. An accrual-basis taxpayer's rent revenue would consist of the amount of rent earned during the taxable year plus any advance rent received. Advance rents must be

included in gross income when received under both the cash and accrual methods, even though they have not yet been earned. In this case, Royce's rent revenue would be determined as follows:

Rent receivable 12/31/14	$35,000
Rent receivable 12/31/15	25,000
Decrease in receivables	(10,000)
Rent collections during 2015	50,000
Rent deposits	5,000
Rent revenue for 2015	$45,000

The rent deposits must be included in gross income for 2015 because they are nonrefundable deposits.

49. (a) The requirement is to determine the amount of state unemployment benefits that should be included in adjusted gross income for 2015. Unemployment compensation benefits received must generally be included in gross income.

50. (d) The requirement is to determine the correct statement regarding the reporting of income by a cash-basis taxpayer. A cash-basis taxpayer should report gross income for the year in which income is either actually or constructively received, whether in cash or in property. Constructive receipt means that an item of income is unqualifiedly avail-able to the taxpayer without restriction (e.g., interest on bank deposit is income when credited to account).

51. (b) The requirement is to determine which taxpayer may use the cash method of accounting. The cash method cannot generally be used if inventories are necessary to clearly reflect income, and cannot generally be used by C corporations, partnerships that have a C corporation as a partner, tax shelters, and certain tax-exempt trusts. Taxpayers permitted to use the cash method include a qualified personal service corporation, an entity (other than a tax shelter) if for every year it has average gross receipts of $5 million or less for any prior three-year period (and provided it does not have inventories), and a small taxpayer with average annual gross receipts of $1 million or less for any prior three-year period may use the cash method and is excepted from the requirement to account for inventories.

52. (b) The requirement is to select the correct statement regarding the $1,000 of additional income determined by Stewart, an accrual method corporation. Under the accrual method, income generally is reported in the year earned. If an amount is included in gross income on the basis of a reasonable estimate, and it is later determined that the exact amount is more, then the additional amount is included in income in the tax year in which the determination of the exact amount is made. Here, Stewart properly accrued $5,000 of income for 2014 on the basis of a reasonable estimate and discovered that the exact amount was $6,000 in 2015. Therefore, the additional $1,000 of income is properly includible in Stewart's 2015 income tax return.

53. (b) The requirement is to determine the correct statement regarding Axis Corp.'s deduction for its employees bonus expense. An accrual-method taxpayer can deduct compensation (including a bonus) when there is an obligation to make payment, the services have been performed, and the amount can be determined with reasonable accuracy. It is not required that the exact amount of compensation be determined during the taxable year. As long as the computation is known and the liability is fixed, accrual is proper even though the profits upon which the compensation are based is not determined until after the end of the year.

Although compensation is generally deductible only for the year in which the compensation is paid, an exception is made for accrual method taxpayers so long as payment is made within 2 1/2 months after the end of the year. Here, since the services were performed, the method of computation was known, the amount was reasonable, and payment was made by March 15, 2015, the bonus expense may be deducted on Axis Corp.'s 2014 tax return. Note that the bonus could not be a disguised dividend because none of the employees were shareholders.

54. (b) The requirement is to determine the amount of the 2014 interest payment of $12,000 that was deductible on Michaels' 2015 income tax return. Generally, there is no deduction for prepaid interest. When a taxpayer pays interest for a period that extends beyond the end of the tax year, the interest paid in advance must be spread over the period to which it applies. Michaels paid $12,000 of interest during 2014 that relates to the period beginning December 1, 2014, and ending November 30, 2015. Therefore, 1/12 × $12,000 = $1,000 of interest was deductible for 2014, and 11/12 × $12,000 = $11,000 is deductible for 2015.

55. (c) The requirement is to determine the amount of income to be reported in Blair's 2014 return for the stock received in satisfaction of a client fee owed to Blair. Since Blair is a cash method taxpayer, the amount of income to be recognized equals the $4,000 fair market value of the stock on date of receipt. Note that the $4,000 of income is reported by Blair in 2014 when the stock is received; not in 2015 when the stock is sold.

56. (d) The requirement is to determine whether the accrual method of tax reporting is mandatory for a sole proprietor when there are accounts receivable for services rendered, or year-end merchandise inventories. A taxpayer's taxable income should be computed using the method of accounting by which the taxpayer regularly computes income in keeping the taxpayer's books. Either the cash or the accrual method generally can be used so long as the method is consistently applied and clearly reflects income. However, when the production, purchase, or sale of merchandise is an income producing factor, inventories must be maintained to clearly reflect income. If merchandise inventories are necessary to clearly determine income, only the accrual method of tax reporting can be used for purchases and sales.

57. (d) The requirement is to determine the amount of salary taxable to Burg in 2014. Since Burg is a cash-basis taxpayer, salary is taxable to Burg when actually or constructively received, whichever is earlier. Since the $30,000 of unpaid salary was unqualifiedly available to Burg during 2014, Burg is considered to have constructively received it. Thus, Burg

must report a total of $80,000 of salary for 2014; the $50,000 actually received plus $30,000 constructively received.

58. (d) The requirement is to determine the 2014 medical practice net income for a cash basis physician. Dr. Berger's income consists of the $200,000 received from patients and the $30,000 received from third-party reimbursers during 2014. His 2014 deductions include the $20,000 of salaries and $24,000 of other expenses paid in 2014. The year-end bonuses will be deductible for 2015.

59. (c) The requirement is to determine which taxpayer may use the cash method of accounting for tax purposes. The cash method generally cannot be used (and the accrual method must be used to measure sales and cost of goods sold) if inventories are necessary to clearly determine income. Additionally, the cash method generally cannot generally be used by (1) a corporation (other than an S corporation), (2) a partnership with a corporation as a partner, and (3) a tax shelter. However, this prohibition against the use of the cash method in the preceding sentence does not apply to a farming business, a qualified personal service corporation (e.g., a corporation performing services in health, law, engineering, architecture, accounting, actuarial science, performing arts, or consulting), and a corporation or partnership (that is not a tax shelter) that does not have inventories and whose average annual gross receipts for the most recent three-year period do not exceed $5 million.

60. (a) Uniform capitalization rules generally require that all costs incurred (both direct and indirect) in manufacturing or constructing real or personal property, or in purchasing or holding property for sale, must be capitalized as part of the cost of the property. However, these rules do not apply to a "small retailer or wholesaler" who acquires personal property for resale if the retailer's or wholesaler's average annual gross receipts for the three preceding taxable years do not exceed $10 million.

61. (a) The requirement is to determine whether the cost of merchandise, and business expenses other than the cost of merchandise, can be deducted in calculating Mock's business income from a retail business selling illegal narcotic substances. Generally, business expenses that are incurred in an illegal activity are deductible if they are ordinary and necessary, and reasonable in amount. Under a special exception, no deduction or credit is allowed for any amount that is paid or incurred in carrying on a trade or business which consists of trafficking in controlled substances. However, this limitation that applies to expenditures in connection with the illegal sale of drugs does not alter the normal definition of gross income (i.e., sales minus cost of goods sold). As a result, in arriving at gross income from the business, Mock may reduce total sales by the cost of goods sold, and thus is allowed to deduct the cost of merchandise in calculating business income.

62. (b) The requirement is to determine the percentage of business meals expense that Banks Corp. can deduct for 2015. Generally, only 50% of business meals and entertainment is deductible. When an employer reimburses its employees' substantiated qualifying business meal expenses, the 50% limitation on deductibility applies to the employer.

63. (a) The requirement is to determine which of the costs is **not** included in inventory under the Uniform Capitalization (UNICAP) rules for goods manufactured by a taxpayer. UNICAP rules require that specified overhead items must be included in inventory including factory repairs and maintenance, factory administration and officers' salaries related to production, taxes (other than income taxes), the costs of quality control and inspection, current and past service costs of pension and profit-sharing plans, and service support such as purchasing, payroll, and warehousing costs. Nonmanufacturing costs such as selling, advertising, and research and experimental costs are not required to be included in inventory.

64. (d) If no exceptions are met, the uniform capitalization rules generally require that all costs incurred in purchasing or holding inventory for resale must be capitalized as part of the cost of the inventory. Costs that must be capitalized with respect to inventory include the costs of purchasing, handling, processing, repackaging and assembly, and off-site storage. An off-site storage facility is one that is not physically attached to, and an integral part of, a retail sales facility. Service costs such as marketing, selling, advertising, and general management are immediately deductible and need not be capitalized as part of the cost of inventory.

65. (d) The requirement is to determine the correct statement regarding the deduction for bad debts in the case of a corporation that is not a financial institution. Except for certain small banks that can use the experience method of accounting for bad debts, all taxpayers (including those that previously used the reserve method) are required to use the direct charge-off method of accounting for bad debts.

66. (d) The requirement is to determine the amount of life insurance premium that can be deducted in Ram Corp.'s income tax return. Generally, no deduction is allowed for expenditures that produce tax-exempt income. Here, no deduction is allowed for the $6,000 life insurance premium because Ram is the beneficiary of the policy, and the proceeds of the policy will be excluded from Ram's income when the officer dies.

67. (a) The requirement is to determine the amount of bad debt deduction for a cash-basis taxpayer. Accounts receivable resulting from services rendered by a cash-basis taxpayer have a zero tax basis, because the income has not yet been reported. Thus, failure to collect the receivable results in a nondeductible loss.

68. (c) The requirement is to determine the loss that Cook can claim as a result of the worthless note receivable in 2015. Cook's $1,000 loss will be treated as a nonbusiness bad debt, deductible as a short-term capital loss. The loss is **not** a business bad debt because Cook was not in the business of lending money, nor was the loan required as a condition of Cook's employment. Since Cook owned no stock in Precision, the loss could **not** be deemed to be a loss from worthless stock, deductible as a long-term capital loss.

69. (b) The requirement is to determine the amount of gifts deductible as a business expense. The deduction for business gifts is limited to $25 per recipient each year. Thus, Palo Corporation's deduction for business gifts would be [(4 × $10) + (13 × $25)] = $365.

70. (b) The requirement is to determine Jennifer's net operating loss (NOL) for 2015. Jennifer's personal casualty loss of $45,000 incurred as a result of the destruction of her personal residence is allowed as a deduction in the computation of her NOL and is subtracted from her salary income of $30,000, to arrive at an NOL of $15,000. No deduction is allowed for personal and dependency exemptions in the computation of an NOL.

71. (c) The requirement is to determine the amount of net operating loss (NOL) for a self-employed taxpayer for 2015. An NOL generally represents a loss from the conduct of a trade or business and can generally be carried back two years and forward twenty years to offset income in the carryback and carryforward years. Since an NOL generally represents a business loss, an individual taxpayer's personal and dependency exemptions and an excess of nonbusiness deductions over nonbusiness income cannot be subtracted in computing the NOL. Nonbusiness deductions generally include itemized deductions as well as the standard deduction if the taxpayer does not itemize. In this case, the $6,300 standard deduction offsets the $1,500 of nonbusiness income received in the form of dividends and short-term capital gain, but the excess ($4,800) cannot be included in the NOL computation. Thus, the taxpayer's NOL simply consists of the $6,000 business loss.

72. (a) The requirement is to determine Destry's net operating loss (NOL). A net operating loss generally represents a loss from the conduct of a trade or business and can generally be carried back two years and forward twenty years to offset income in the carryback and carryforward years. Since an NOL generally represents a business loss, an individual taxpayer's personal and dependency exemptions and an excess of nonbusiness deductions (e.g., standard deduction) over nonbusiness income (e.g., interest from savings account) cannot be subtracted in computing the NOL. Similarly, no deduction is allowed for a net capital loss. As a result, Destry's NOL consists of his net business loss of $16,000 reduced by his business income of $5,000 from wages and $4,000 of net rental income, resulting in an NOL of $7,000.

73. (a) The requirement is to determine the amount of Cobb's rental real estate loss that can be used as an offset against income from non passive sources. Losses from passive activities may generally only be used to offset income from other passive activities. Although a rental activity is defined as a passive activity regardless of the owner's participation in the operation of the rental property, a special rule permits an individual to offset up to $25,000 of income that is not from passive activities by losses from a rental real estate activity if the individual actively participates in the rental real estate activity. However, this special $25,000 allowance is reduced by 50% of the taxpayer's AGI in excess of $100,000, and is fully phased out when AGI exceeds $150,000. Since Cobb's AGI is $200,000, the special $25,000 allowance is fully phased out and no rental loss can be offset against income from non passive sources.

74. (c) The requirement is to determine the entity to which the rules limiting the deductibility of passive activity losses and credits applies. The passive activity limitations apply to individuals, estates, trusts, closely held C corporations, and personal service corporations. Application of the passive activity loss limitations to personal service corporations is intended to prevent taxpayers from sheltering personal service income by creating personal service corporations and acquiring passive activity losses at the corporate level. A personal service corporation is a corporation (1) whose principal activity is the performance of personal services, and (2) such services are substantially performed by owner-employees. Since passive activity income, losses, and credits from partnerships and S corporations flow through to be reported on the tax returns of the owners of such entities, the passive activity limitations are applied at the partner and shareholder level, rather than to partnerships and S corporations themselves.

75. (c) The requirement is to determine Wolf's passive loss resulting from his 5% general partnership interest in Gata Associates. A partnership is a pass-through entity and its items of income and loss pass through to partners to be included on their tax returns. Since Wolf does not materially participate in the partnership's auto parts business, Wolf's distributable share of the loss from the partnership's auto parts business is classified as a passive activity loss. Portfolio income or loss must be excluded from the computation of the income or loss resulting from a passive activity, and must be separately passed through to partners.

Portfolio income includes all interest income, other than interest income derived in the ordinary course of a trade or business. Interest income derived in the ordinary course of a trade or business includes only interest income on loans and investments made in the ordinary course of a trade or business of lending money, and interest income on accounts receivable arising in the ordinary course of a trade or business. Since the $20,000 of interest income derived by the partnership resulted from a temporary investment, the interest income must be classified as portfolio income and cannot be netted against the $100,000 operating loss from the auto parts business. Thus, Wolf will report a passive activity loss of $100,000 × 5% = $5,000; and will report portfolio income of $20,000 × 5% = $1,000.

76. (a) The requirement is to determine the correct statement regarding the passive loss rules involving rental real estate activities. By definition, any rental activity is a passive activity without regard as to whether or not the taxpayer materially participates in the activity. Answer (b) is incorrect because interest and dividend income not derived in the ordinary course of business is treated as **portfolio** income, and **cannot** be offset by passive rental activity losses when the "active participation" requirement is **not** met. Answer (c) is incorrect because passive rental activity credits **cannot** be used to offset the tax attributable to **non passive** activities. Answer (d) is incorrect because the passive activity rules contain no

provision that excludes taxpayers below a certain income level from the limitations imposed by the passive activity rules.

77. (d) The requirement is to determine the correct statement regarding an individual taxpayer's passive losses relating to rental real estate activities that cannot be currently deducted. Generally, losses from passive activities can only be used to offset income from passive activities. If there is insufficient passive activity income to absorb passive activity losses, the unused losses are carried forward indefinitely or until the property is disposed of in a taxable transaction. Answers (a) and (c) are incorrect because unused passive losses are never carried back to prior taxable years. Answer (b) is incorrect because there is no maximum carryforward period.

78. (b) The requirement is to determine the maximum amount of Sec. 179 expense election that Aviation Corp. will be allowed to deduct for 2014, and the maximum amount of expense election that it can carry over to 2015. Sec. 179 permits a taxpayer to elect to treat up to $500,000 (for 2014) of the cost of qualifying depreciable personal property as an expense rather than as a capital expenditure. The $500,000 maximum is reduced dollar-for-dollar by the cost of qualifying property placed in service during the taxable year that exceeds $2 million. Here, since the production machinery cost $570,000, the maximum amount that can be expensed is $500,000. However, this amount is further limited as a deduction for 2014 to Aviation's taxable income of $405,000 before the Sec. 179 expense deduction. The remainder ($500,000 – $405,000 = $95,000) that is not currently deductible because of the taxable income limitation can be carried over and will be deductible subject to the taxable income limitation in 2015.

79. (c) The requirement is to determine which conditions must be satisfied to enable a taxpayer to expense the cost of new or used tangible depreciable personal property under Sec. 179. For 2013, a taxpayer may elect to expense up to $500,000 of the cost of new or used tangible depreciable personal property placed in service during the taxable year. To qualify, the property must be acquired by purchase from an unrelated party for use in the taxpayer's active trade or business. The maximum cost that can be expensed of $500,000 is reduced dollar-for-dollar by the cost of qualifying property that is placed in service during the year that exceeds $2 million. Additionally, the amount that can be expensed is further limited to the aggregate taxable income derived from the active conduct of any trade or business of the taxpayer.

80. (a) The requirement is to determine the MACRS deduction for the used furniture and fixtures placed in service during 2014. The furniture and fixtures qualify as seven-year property and under MACRS will be depreciated using the 200% declining balance method. Normally, a half-year convention applies to the year of acquisition. However, the mid-quarter convention must be used if more than 40% of all personal property is placed in service during the last quarter of the taxpayer's taxable year. Since this was Krol's only acquisition of personal property and the property was placed in service during the last quarter of Krol's calendar year, the mid-quarter convention must be used. Under this convention, property is treated as placed in service during the middle of the quarter in which placed in service. Since the furniture and fixtures were placed in service in November, the amount of allowable MACRS depreciation is limited to $56,000 × 2/7 × 1/8 = $2,000.

81. (b) The requirement is to determine Sullivan's MACRS deduction for the apartment building in 2015. The MACRS deduction for residential real property placed in service during 2015 must be determined using the mid-month convention (i.e., property is treated as placed in service at the midpoint of the month placed in service) and the straight-line method of depreciation over a 27.5-year recovery period. Here, the $360,000 cost must first be reduced by the $30,000 allocated to the land, to arrive at a basis for depreciation of $330,000. Since the building was placed in service on June 29, the mid-month convention results in 6.5 months of depreciation for 2015. The MACRS deduction for 2015 is [$330,000 × (6.5 months)/(27.5 × 12 months)] = $6,500.

82. (c) The requirement is to determine the depreciation convention that must be used when a calendar-year taxpayer's only acquisition of equipment during the year occurs during November. Generally, a half-year convention applies to depreciable personal property, and a mid-month convention applies to depreciable real property. Under the half-year convention, a half-year of depreciation is allowed for the year in which property is placed in service, regardless of when the property is placed in service during the year, and a half-year of depreciation is allowed for the year in which the property is disposed of. However, a taxpayer must instead use a mid-quarter convention if more than 40% of all depreciable personal property acquired during the year is placed in service during the last quarter of the taxable year. Under this convention, property is treated as placed in service (or disposed of) in the middle of the quarter in which placed in service (or disposed of). Since Data Corp. is a calendar-year taxpayer and its only acquisition of depreciable personal property was placed in service during October (i.e., the last quarter of its taxable year), it must use the mid-quarter convention, and will only be allowed a half-quarter of depreciation of its office equipment for the current year.

83. (b) The requirement is to determine the correct statement regarding the modified accelerated cost recovery system (MACRS) of depreciation for property placed in service after 1986. Under MACRS, salvage value is completely ignored for purposes of computing the depreciation deduction, which results in the recovery of the entire cost of depreciable property. Answer (a) is incorrect because used tangible depreciable property is depreciated under MACRS. Answer (c) is incorrect because the cost of some depreciable realty must be depreciated using the straight-line method. Answer (d) is incorrect because the cost of some depreciable realty is included in the ten-year (e.g., single purpose agricultural and horticultural structures) and twenty-year (e.g., farm buildings) classes.

84. (a) The requirement is to determine the correct statement regarding the half-year convention under the general MACRS method. Under the half-year convention that generally applies to depreciable personal property, one-half of the first year's depreciation is allowed in the year in which the property is

placed in service, regardless of when the property is placed in service during the year, and a half-year's depreciation is allowed for the year in which the property is disposed of, regardless of when the property is disposed of during the year. Answer (b) is incorrect because allowing one-half month's depreciation for the month that property is placed in service or disposed of is known as the "midmonth convention."

85. (c) The requirement is to determine the portion of the $600,000 cost of the machine that can be treated as a Sec. 179 expense deduction for 2014. Sec. 179 permits a taxpayer to elect to treat up to $500,000 (for 2014) of the cost of qualifying depreciable personal property as an expense rather than as a capital expenditure. However, the $500,000 maximum is reduced dollar-for-dollar by the cost of qualifying property placed in service during the taxable year that exceeds $2 million.

86. (d) The requirement is to determine the amount to be reported in Mel's gross income for the $400 per month received for business automobile expenses under a nonaccountable plan from Easel Co. Reimbursements and expense allowances paid to an employee under a nonaccountable plan must be included in the employee's gross income and are reported on the employee's W-2. The employee must then complete Form 2106 and itemize to deduct business-related expenses such as the use of an automobile.

87. (c) The requirement is to determine the correct statement regarding a second residence that is rented for 200 days and used 50 days for personal use. Deductions for expenses related to a dwelling that is also used as a residence by the taxpayer may be limited. If the taxpayer's personal use exceeds the greater of 14 days, or 10% of the number of days rented, deductions allocable to rental use are limited to rental income. Here, since Adams used the second residence for 50 days and rented the residence for 200 days, no rental loss can be deducted. All expenses related to the property, including utilities and maintenance, must be allocated between personal use and rental use. Answer (d) is incorrect because only the mortgage interest and taxes allocable to rental use would be deducted in determining the property's net rental income or loss. Answer (a) is incorrect, since depreciation on the property could be deducted if Adams' gross rental income exceeds allocable out-of-pocket rental expenses.

88. (a) The requirement is to determine the amount of unreimbursed employee expenses that can be deducted by Gilbert if he does not itemize deductions. Gilbert cannot deduct any of the expenses listed if he does not itemize deductions. The unreimbursed employee business expenses are deductible only as itemized deductions, subsequent to the 2% of AGI floor.

89. (c) The requirement is to determine the amount of moving expense that James can deduct for 2015. Direct moving expenses are deductible if closely related to the start of work at a new location and a distance test (i.e., distance from new job to former residence is at least fifty miles further than distance from old job to former residence) and a time test (i.e., employed at least thirty-nine weeks out of twelve months following move) are met. Since both tests are met, James' unreimbursed lodging and travel expenses ($1,000), cost of insuring household goods and personal effects during move ($200), cost of shipping household pets ($100), and cost of moving household furnishings and personal effects ($3,000) are deductible. Indirect moving expenses such as pre-move house-hunting, temporary living expenses, and meals while moving are not deductible.

90. (c) The requirement is to determine Martin's deductible moving expenses. Moving expenses are deductible if closely related to the start of work at a new location and a distance (i.e., new job must be at least fifty miles from former residence) and time (i.e., employed at least thirty-nine weeks out of twelve months following move) tests are met. Here, both tests are met and Martin's $800 cost of moving his personal belongings is deductible. However, the $300 penalty for breaking his lease is not deductible.

91. (a) Only the direct costs incurred for transporting a taxpayer, his or her family, and their household goods and personal effects from their former residence to their new residence can qualify as deductible moving expenses. The indirect moving expense costs incurred for meals while in transit, house hunting, temporary lodging, to sell or purchase a home, and to break or acquire a lease are not deductible.

92. (d) The requirement is to determine the incorrect statement concerning a Roth IRA. The maximum annual contribution to a Roth IRA is subject to reduction if the taxpayer's adjusted gross income exceeds certain thresholds. Unlike a traditional IRA, contributions are not deductible and can be made even after the taxpayer reaches age 70½. The contribution must be made by the due date of the taxpayer's tax return (**not** including extensions).

93. (d) The requirement is to determine the maximum amount of adjusted gross income that a taxpayer may have and still qualify to roll over a traditional IRA into a Roth IRA for 2015. For tax years beginning before 2010, a conversion or rollover of a traditional IRA to a Roth IRA could occur if the taxpayer's AGI did not exceed $100,000 and the taxpayer was not married filing a separate return. The IRA conversion or rollover amount was not taken into account in determining the $100,000 AGI ceiling. However, both the AGI limit and the joint filing requirement have been eliminated for tax years beginning after 2009.

94. (d) The requirement is to determine which statement concerning an education IRA is not correct. Contributions to an education IRA are not deductible, but withdrawals of earnings will be tax-free if used to pay the qualified higher education expenses of the designated beneficiary. The maximum amount that can be contributed to an education IRA is limited to $2,000, but the annual contribution is phased out by adjusted gross income in excess of certain thresholds. Contributions generally cannot be made to an education IRA if the designated beneficiary is age eighteen or older.

95. (a) The requirement is to determine the Whites' allowable IRA deduction on their 2015 joint return. For married taxpayers filing a joint return for 2015, up to $5,500 can be deducted for contributions to the IRA of each spouse (even

if one spouse is not working), provided that the combined earned income of both spouses is at least equal to the amounts contributed to the IRAs. Even though Val is covered by his employer's qualified pension plan, the Whites are eligible for the maximum deduction because their gross income of $55,000 + $4,000 = $59,000 does not exceed the base amount ($96,000) at which the maximum $5,500 deduction would be reduced. Also note that Pat's $4,000 of taxable alimony payments is treated as compensation for purposes of qualifying for an IRA deduction. Since they each contributed $5,500 to an IRA account, the allowable deduction on their joint return is $11,000.

96. (d) The requirement is to determine the definition of "earned income" for purposes of computing the annual contribution to a Keogh profit-sharing plan by Davis, a sole proprietor. A self-employed individual may contribute to a qualified retirement plan called a Keogh plan. For 2013, the maximum contribution to a Keogh profit-sharing plan is the lesser of $51,000 or 25% of earned income. For this purpose, "earned income" is defined as net earnings from self-employment (i.e., business gross income minus allowable business deductions) reduced by the deduction for one-half of the self-employment tax, and the deductible Keogh contribution itself.

97. (d) A single individual with AGI over $71,000 for 2015 would only be entitled to an IRA deduction if the taxpayer is not covered by a qualified employee pension plan.

98. (c) The requirement is to determine the allowable IRA deduction on the Cranes' 2015 joint return. Since Sol is covered by his employer's pension plan, Sol's contribution of $5,500 is proportionately phased out as a deduction by AGI between $98,000 and $118,000. Since the Cranes' AGI exceeded $118,000, no deduction is allowed for Sol's contribution. Although Julia is not employed, $5,500 can be contributed to her IRA because the combined earned income on the Cranes' return is at least $11,000. The maximum IRA deduction for an individual who is not covered by an employer plan, but whose spouse is, is proportionately phased out for AGI between $183,000 and $193,000 for 2015. Since Julia is not covered by an employer plan and the Cranes' AGI is below $183,000, the $5,500 contribution to Julia's IRA is fully deductible for 2015.

99. (d) The requirement is to determine the Lees' maximum IRA contribution and deduction on a joint return for 2015. Since neither taxpayer is covered by an employer-sponsored pension plan, there is no phase-out of the maximum deduction due to the level of their adjusted gross income. For married taxpayers filing a joint return, up to $5,500 can be deducted for contributions to the IRA of each spouse (even if one spouse is not working), provided that the combined earned income of both spouses is at least equal to the amounts contributed to the IRAs. Additionally, an individual at least age 50 can make a special catch-up contribution of $1,000 for 2015, resulting in an increased maximum contribution and deduction of $6,500 for 2015. Thus, the Lees may contribute and deduct a maximum of $13,000 to their individual retirement accounts for 2015, with a maximum of $6,500 placed into each account.

100. (c) The maximum amount of contributions to a defined contribution self-employed retirement plan is limited to the lesser of $53,000, or 100% of self-employment income for 2015.

101. (d) The requirement is to determine which allowable deduction can be claimed in arriving at an individual's adjusted gross income. One hundred percent of a self-employed individual's health insurance premiums are deductible in arriving at an individual's adjusted gross income for 2015. Charitable contributions, foreign income taxes (if not used as a credit), and tax return preparation fees can be deducted only from adjusted gross income if an individual itemizes deductions.

102. (b) The requirement is to determine the incorrect statement concerning the deduction for interest on qualified education loans. For 2013, an individual is allowed to deduct up to $2,500 for interest on qualified education loans in arriving at AGI. The deduction is subject to an income phaseout and the loan proceeds must have been used to pay for the qualified higher education expenses (e.g., tuition, fees, room, board) of the taxpayer, spouse, or a dependent (at the time the debt was incurred). The education expenses must relate to a period when the student was enrolled on at least a half-time basis. The sixty-month limitation was repealed for tax years beginning after 2002.

103. (c) The requirement is to determine how Dale should treat her $1,000 jury duty fee that she remitted to her employer. Fees received for serving on a jury must be included in gross income. If the recipient is required to remit the jury duty fees to an employer in exchange for regular compensation, the remitted jury duty fees are allowed as a deduction from gross income in arriving at adjusted gross income.

104. (b) The requirement is to determine George's taxable income. George's adjusted gross income consists of $3,700 of dividends and $1,700 of wages. Since George is eligible to be claimed as a dependency exemption by his parents, there will be no personal exemption on George's return and his basic standard deduction is limited to the greater of $1,050, or George's earned income of $1,700, plus $350. Thus, George's taxable income would be computed as follows:

Dividends	$3,700
Wages	1,700
AGI	$5,400
Exemption	0
Std. deduction	(2,050)
Taxable income	$3,350

105. (c) The item asks you to determine the requirements that must be met in order for a single individual to qualify for the additional standard deduction. A single individual who is age sixty-five or older or blind is eligible for an additional standard deduction ($1,500 for 2013). Two additional standard deductions are allowed for an individual who is age sixty-five or older **and** blind. It is not required that an individual support a dependent child or aged parent in order to qualify for an additional standard deduction.

106. (b) The requirement is to determine Carroll's maximum medical expense deduction after the applicable threshold limitation 2015. An individual taxpayer's unreimbursed medical expenses are deductible to the extent in excess of 10% of the taxpayer's adjusted gross income. Although the cost of cosmetic surgery is generally not deductible, the cost is deductible if the cosmetic surgery or procedure is necessary to ameliorate a deformity related to a congenital abnormality or personal injury resulting from an accident, trauma, or disfiguring disease. Here, Carroll's deduction is ($5,000 + $15,000) − ($100,000 × 10%) = $10,000.

107. (b) The requirement is to determine the Blairs' itemized deduction for medical expenses for 2015. A taxpayer can deduct the amounts paid for the medical care of himself, spouse, or dependents. The Blairs' qualifying medical expenses include the $1,550 of medical insurance premiums, $450 of prescribed medicines, $1,000 of unreimbursed doctor's fees, and $150 of transportation related to medical care. These expenses, which total $3,150, are deductible to the extent they exceed 10% of adjusted gross income, and result in a deduction of $150. Note that nonprescription medicines, including aspirin and over-the-counter cold capsules, are not deductible. Additionally, the Blairs cannot deduct the emergency room fee they paid for their son because they did not provide more than half of his support and he therefore does not qualify as their dependent.

108. (a) The requirement is to determine the amount the Whites may deduct as qualifying medical expenses without regard to the adjusted gross income percentage threshold. The Whites' deductible medical expenses include the $600 spent on repair and maintenance of the motorized wheelchair and the $8,000 spent for tuition, meals, and lodging at the special school for their physically handicapped dependent child. Payment for meals and lodging provided by an institution as a necessary part of medical care is deductible as a medical expense if the main reason for being in the institution is to receive medical care. Here, the item indicates that the Whites' physically handicapped dependent child was in the institution primarily for the availability of medical care, and that meals and lodging were furnished as necessary incidents to that care.

109. (c) The requirement is to determine the amount Wells can deduct as qualifying medical expenses without regard to the adjusted gross income percentage threshold. Wells' deductible medical expenses include the $500 premium on the prescription drug insurance policy and the $500 unreimbursed payment for physical therapy. The earnings protection policy is not considered medical insurance because payments are not based on the amount of medical expenses incurred. As a result, the $3,000 premium is a nondeductible personal expense.

110. (d) The requirement is to determine the amount of expenses incurred in connection with the adoption of a child that can be deducted by the Sloans on their joint return. A taxpayer can deduct the medical expenses paid for a child at the time of adoption if the child qualifies as the taxpayer's dependent when the medical expenses are paid. Additionally, if a taxpayer pays an adoption agency for medical expenses the adoption agency already paid, the taxpayer is treated as having paid those expenses. Here, the Sloans can deduct the child's medical expenses of $5,000 that they paid. On the other hand, the legal expenses of $9,000 and agency fee of $4,000 incurred in connection with the adoption are treated as nondeductible personal expenses. However, the Sloans will qualify to claim a nonrefundable tax credit of up to $13,400 (for 2015) for these qualified adoption expenses.

111. (a) The requirement is to determine the amount that can be claimed by the Clines in their 2015 return as qualifying medical expenses. No medical expense deduction is allowed for cosmetic surgery or similar procedures, unless the surgery or procedure is necessary to ameliorate a deformity related to a congenital abnormality or personal injury resulting from an accident, trauma, or disfiguring disease. Cosmetic surgery is defined as any procedure that is directed at improving a patient's appearance and does not meaningfully promote the proper function of the body or prevent or treat illness or disease. Thus, Ruth's face-lift and Mark's hair transplant do not qualify as deductible medical expenses in 2014.

112. (d) The requirement is to determine the amount that Scott can claim as deductible medical expenses. The medical expenses incurred by a taxpayer for himself, spouse, or a dependent are deductible when paid or charged to a credit card. The $4,000 of medical expenses for his dependent son are deductible by Scott in 2014 when charged on Scott's credit card. It does not matter that payment to the credit card issuer had not been made when Scott filed his return. Expenses paid for the medical care of a decedent by the decedent's spouse are deductible as medical expenses in the year they are paid, whether the expenses are paid before or after the decedent's death. Thus, the $2,800 of medical expenses for his deceased spouse are deductible by Scott when paid in 2014, even though his spouse died in 2013.

113. (d) The requirement is to determine which expenditure qualifies as a deductible medical expense. Premiums paid for Medicare B supplemental medical insurance qualify as a deductible expense. Diaper service, funeral expenses, and nursing care for a healthy baby are not deductible as medical expenses.

114. (b) The requirement is to determine Stenger's net medical expense deduction for 2015. It would be computed as follows:

Prescription drugs	$300
Medical insurance premiums	1,750
Doctors ($2,550 – $900)	1,650
Eyeglasses	75
	$3,775
Less 10% of AGI ($35,000)	3,500
Medical expense deduction for 2015	$275

115. (d) The requirement is to determine the total amount of deductible medical expenses for the Bensons before the application of any limitation rules. Deductible medical expenses include those incurred by a taxpayer, taxpayer's spouse, dependents of the taxpayer, or any person for whom the taxpayer could claim a dependency exemption except that the person had gross income of $4,000 or more, or filed a joint return. Thus, the Bensons may deduct medical expenses incurred for themselves, for John (i.e., no dependency exemption only because his gross income is $4,000 or more), and for Nancy (i.e., a dependent of the Bensons).

116. (d) The requirement is to determine the tax that is not deductible as an itemized deduction. One-half of a self-employed taxpayer's self-employment tax is deductible from gross income in arriving at adjusted gross income. Foreign real estate taxes, foreign income taxes, and personal property taxes can be deducted as itemized deductions from adjusted gross income.

117. (c) The requirement is to determine the amount that Matthews can deduct as taxes on her 2014 Schedule A of Form 1040. An individual's state and local income taxes are deductible as an itemized deduction, while federal income taxes are not deductible. For a cash-basis taxpayer, state and local taxes are deductible for the year in which paid or withheld. As a result, Matthew's deduction for 2014 consists of her state and local taxes withheld of $1,500 and the December 30 estimated payment of $400. The state and local income taxes that Matthews paid in April 2015 will be deductible for 2015.

118. (a) The requirement is to determine the correct statement regarding Farb, a cash-basis individual taxpayer who paid an $8,000 invoice for personal property taxes under protest in 2014, and received a $5,000 refund of the taxes in 2015. If a taxpayer receives a refund or rebate of taxes deducted in an earlier year, the taxpayer must generally include the refund or rebate in income for the year in which received. Here, Farb should deduct $8,000 in his 2014 income tax return and should report the $5,000 refund as income in his 2015 income tax return.

119. (d) The requirement is to determine the amount of itemized deduction for realty taxes that can be deducted by Burg. Generally, an individual's payment of state, local, or foreign real estate taxes is deductible as an itemized deduction if the individual is the owner of the property on which the taxes are imposed. Because the property is jointly owned by Burg, he is individually liable for the entire amount of realty taxes and may deduct the entire payment on his return. Even back taxes can be deducted by Burg as long as he was the owner of the property during the period of time to which the back taxes are related.

120. (b) The requirement is to determine Sara's deduction for state income taxes in 2014. Sara's deduction would consist of the $2,000 withheld by her employer in 2014, plus the three estimated payments (3 × $300 = $900) actually paid during 2014, a total of $2,900. Note that the 1/15/15 estimated payment would be deductible for 2015.

121. (b) The requirement is to determine the amount of **taxes** deductible as an itemized deduction. The $360 vehicle tax based on value is deductible as a personal property tax. The real property tax of $2,700 must be apportioned between the Bronsons and the buyer for tax purposes according to the number of days in the real property tax year that each owns the property even though they did not actually make an apportionment. Taxes are apportioned to the seller up to, but not including, the date of the sale, and apportioned to the buyer beginning with the date of sale. Since the house was sold June 30, the Bronson's deduction for real estate taxes would be $2,700 × 180/365 = $1,332. The buyer would deduct the remaining $1,368.

122. (a) The requirement is to determine what portion of the $1,300 of realty taxes is deductible by King in 2015. The $600 of delinquent taxes charged to the seller and paid by King are not deductible, but are added to the cost of the property. The $700 of taxes for 2015 are apportioned between the seller and King according to the number of days that each held the property during the year. King's deduction would be

$$\frac{184}{365} \times \$700 = \$353$$

123. (b) The requirement is to determine the amount of property taxes deductible as itemized deductions. The property taxes on the residence and the land held for appreciation, together with the personal property taxes on the auto are deductible. The special assessment is not deductible, but would be added to the basis of the residence.

124. (a) The requirement is to determine the amount the Burgs should deduct for taxes in their itemized deductions. The $1,200 of state income tax paid by the Burgs is deductible as an itemized deduction. However, the $7,650 of self-employment tax is not deductible as an itemized deduction. Instead, a portion of the self-employment tax is deductible from gross income in arriving at the Burgs' adjusted gross income.

125. (c) The requirement is to determine the correct statement regarding an individual taxpayer's deduction for interest on investment indebtedness. The deduction for interest expense on investment indebtedness is limited to the taxpayer's net investment income. Net investment income includes such income as interest, dividends, and short-term capital gains, less any related expenses.

126. (b) The requirement is to determine the correct statement regarding the interest on the Browns' $20,000 loan that was secured by their home and used to purchase an automobile. Qualified residence interest consists of interest on acquisition indebtedness and home equity indebtedness. Interest on home equity indebtedness loans of up to $100,000 is deductible as qualified residence interest if the loans are secured by a taxpayer's principal or second residence regardless of how the loan proceeds are used. The amount of home equity indebtedness cannot exceed the fair market value of a home as reduced by any acquisition indebtedness. Since the Browns' home had an FMV of $400,000 and was unencumbered by other debt, the interest on the $20,000 home equity loan is deductible as qualified residence interest.

127. (c) The requirement is to determine how much interest is deductible by the Philips for 2015. Qualified residence interest includes the interest on acquisition indebtedness. Such interest is deductible on up to $1 million of loans secured by a principal or second residence if the loans were used to purchase, construct, or substantially improve a home. Here, the Philips' original mortgage of $200,000 as well as the additional loan of $15,000 qualify as acquisition indebtedness, and the resulting $17,000 + $1,500 = $18,500 of interest is deductible. On the other hand, the $500 of interest on the auto loan is considered personal interest and not deductible.

128. (c) The requirement is to determine the maximum amount allowable as a deduction for Jackson's second residence. Qualified residence interest includes acquisition indebtedness and home equity indebtedness on the taxpayer's principal residence and a second residence. Here, the $5,000 of mortgage interest on the second residence is qualified residence interest and is deductible as an itemized deduction. In contrast, the $1,200 of utilities expense and $6,000 of insurance expense are nondeductible personal expenses.

129. (c) The requirement is to determine the amount of interest expense deductible as an itemized deduction. The $3,600 of home mortgage interest, and the $900 mortgage prepayment penalty are fully deductible as interest expense in computing itemized deductions. The $1,200 interest on the life insurance policy is not deductible since it is classified as personal interest.

130. (a) The requirement is to determine the amount of interest deductible as an itemized deduction. Since 2/3 of the loan proceeds were used to purchase tax-exempt bonds, 2/3 of the bank interest is nondeductible. The remaining 1/3 of the bank interest ($1,200) is related to the purchase of the Arrow debentures and is classified as investment interest deductible to the extent of net investment income ($0). The $3,000 of home mortgage interest is fully deductible as qualified residence interest. The interest on credit card charges is personal interest and is not deductible.

131. (a) None of the items listed relating to the tax deficiency for 2013 are deductible. The interest on the tax deficiency is considered personal interest and is not deductible. The additional federal income tax, the late filing penalty, and the negligence penalty are also not deductible.

132. (b) The requirement is to determine the amount that Smith should deduct as a charitable contribution. If appreciated property is contributed, the amount of contribution is generally the property's FMV if a sale of the property would result in a long-term capital gain. Here, the art object worth $3,000 was purchased for $2,000 just four months earlier. Since its holding period did not exceed twelve months, a sale of the art object would result in only a short-term capital gain, and the amount of allowable contribution deduction is limited to its $2,000 cost basis. Additionally, the donation of $5,000 cash to Smith's church is deductible but no deduction is available for the $1,000 contribution to a needy family. To be deductible, a contribution must be made to a qualifying organization.

133. (c) The requirement is to determine the amount of charitable contributions deductible on Stein's current year income tax return. The donation of appreciated stock held more than twelve months is a contribution of intangible, long-term capital gain appreciated property. The amount of contribution is the stock's FMV of $25,000, but is limited in deductibility for the current year to 30% of AGI. Thus, the current year deduction is limited to 30% × $80,000 = $24,000. The remaining $1,000 of contributions can be carried forward for up to five years, subject to the 30% limitation in the carryforward years.

134. (c) The requirement is to determine the maximum amount of properly substantiated charitable contributions that Moore could claim as an itemized deduction for 2015. Moore gave $18,000 to her church during 2015 and had a $10,000 charitable contribution carryover from 2014, resulting in a total of $28,000 of contributions. Since an individual's deduction for charitable contributions cannot exceed an overall limitation of 50% of adjusted gross income, Moore's charitable contribution deduction for 2015 is limited to ($50,000 AGI × 50%) = $25,000. Since Moore's 2015 contributions will be deducted before her carryforward from 2014, Moore will carry over $3,000 of her 2014 contributions to 2016.

135. (c) The requirement is to determine the maximum amount that Spencer can claim as a deduction for charitable contributions for the current year. The cash contribution of $4,000 to church and the $600 fair market value of the used clothing donated to Salvation Army are fully deductible. However, the deduction for the art object is limited to the $400 excess of its cost ($1,200) over its fair market value ($800).

136. (b) The requirement is to determine Lewis' charitable contribution deduction. The donation of appreciated stock held more than twelve months is a contribution of intangible, long-term capital gain appreciated property. The amount of contribution is the stock's FMV of $70,000, but is limited in deductibility for 2015 to 30% of AGI. Thus, the 2015 deduction is $100,000 × 30% = $30,000. The amount of contribution in excess of the 30% limitation ($70,000 − $30,000 = $40,000) can be carried forward for up to five years, subject to the 30% limitation in the carryforward years.

137. (b) The requirement is to determine the amount of contributions deductible in 2014. Charitable contributions are generally deductible in the year actually paid. The $500 charge to his bank credit card made on December 15, 2014, is considered a payment, and is deductible for 2014. The $1,000 promissory note delivered on November 1, 2014, is not considered a contribution until payment of the note upon maturity in 2015.

138. (b) The requirement is to determine the amount of student expenses deductible as a charitable contribution. A taxpayer may deduct as a charitable contribution up to $50 per **school month** of unreimbursed expenses incurred to maintain a student (in the 12th or lower grade) in the taxpayer's home pursuant to a written agreement with a qualified organization. Since the student started school in September, the amount deductible as a charitable contribution is $50 × 4 = $200.

139. (a) Vincent Tally is not entitled to a charitable deduction for the current year because he did not give up his entire interest in the book collection. By reserving the right to use and possess the book collection for his lifetime, Vincent Tally has not made a completed gift. Therefore, no deduction is available. The contribution will be deductible when his entire interest in the books is transferred to the art museum.

140. (b) The requirement is to determine the maximum amount of charitable contribution allowable as an itemized deduction on Jimet's 2015 income tax return. If appreciated property is contributed, the amount of contribution is generally the property's FMV if the property would result in a long-term capital gain if sold. If not, the amount of contribution for appreciated property is generally limited to the property's basis. Here, the stock worth $3,000 was purchased for $1,500 just four months earlier. Since its holding period did not exceed twelve months, a sale of the stock would result in a short-term capital gain, and the amount of allowable contribution deduction is limited to the stock's basis of $1,500. Additionally, to be deductible, a contribution must be made to a qualifying **organization**. As a result, the $2,000 cash given directly to a needy family is not deductible.

141. (a) The requirement is to determine the maximum amount of charitable contribution deductible as an itemized deduction on Taylor's tax return for 2015. The donation of appreciated land purchased for investment and held for more than twelve months is a contribution of real capital gain property (property that would result in long-term capital gain if sold). The amount of contribution is the land's FMV of $25,000, limited in deductibility for the current year to 30% of AGI. In this case, since 30% of AGI would be 30% × $90,000 = $27,000, the full amount of the land contribution ($25,000) is deductible for 2015.

142. (a) The requirement is to determine the amount of the fire loss to her personal residence that Frazer can claim as an itemized deduction. The amount of a personal casualty loss is computed as the lesser of (1) the adjusted basis of the property ($130,000), or (2) the decline in the property's fair market value resulting from the casualty ($130,000 − $0 = $130,000); reduced by any insurance recovery ($120,000), and a $100 floor. Since Frazer had no casualty gains during the year, the net casualty loss is then deductible as an itemized deduction to the extent that it exceeds 10% of adjusted gross income.

Fire loss	$130,000
Insurance proceeds	(120,000)
$100 floor	(100)
10% of $70,000 AGI	(7,000)
Casualty loss itemized deduction	$2,900

143. (a) The requirement is to determine the amount the Burgs should deduct for the casualty loss (repair of glass vase accidentally broken by their dog) in their itemized deductions. A casualty is the damage, destruction, or loss of property resulting from an identifiable event that is sudden, unexpected, or unusual. Deductible casualty losses may result from earthquakes, tornadoes, floods, fires, vandalism, auto accidents, etc. However, a loss due to the accidental breakage of household articles such as glassware or china under normal conditions is not a casualty loss. Neither is a loss due to damage caused by a family pet.

144. (d) The requirement is to determine the proper treatment of the $490 casualty insurance premium. Casualty insurance premiums on an individual's personal residence are considered nondeductible personal expenses. Even though a casualty is actually incurred during the year, no deduction is available for personal casualty insurance premiums.

145. (d) The requirement is to determine the amount of the fire loss damage to their personal residence that the Hoyts can deduct as an itemized deduction. The amount of a nonbusiness casualty loss is computed as the lesser of (1) the adjusted basis of the property, or (2) the property's decline in FMV; reduced by any insurance recovery, and a $100 floor. If an individual has a net casualty loss for the year, it is then deductible as an itemized deduction to the extent that it exceeds 10% of adjusted gross income.

Lesser of:		
Adjusted basis	= $50,000	
Decline in FMV		
($60,000 – $55,000)	= $5,000	$5,000
Reduce by:		
Insurance recovery		(0)
$100 floor		(100)
10% of $34,000 AGI		(3,400)
Casualty loss itemized deduction		$1,500

Note that the $2,500 spent for repairs is not included in the computation of the loss.

146. (b) The requirement is to determine the proper treatment for the $800 appraisal fee that was incurred to determine the amount of the Hoyts' fire loss. The appraisal fee is considered an expense of determining the Hoyts' tax liability; it is not a part of the casualty loss itself. Thus, the appraisal fee is deductible as a miscellaneous itemized deduction subject to a 2% of adjusted gross income floor.

147. (d) The requirement is to determine which item is **not** a miscellaneous itemized deduction. A legal fee for tax advice related to a divorce, IRA trustee's fees that are separately billed and paid, and an appraisal fee for valuing a charitable contribution qualify as miscellaneous itemized deductions subject to the 2% of AGI floor. On the other hand, the check writing fees for a personal checking account are a personal expense and not deductible.

148. (b) The requirement is to determine the proper treatment of the $2,000 legal fee that was incurred by Hall in a suit to collect the alimony owed her. The $2,000 legal fee is considered an expenditure incurred in the production of income. Expenses incurred in the production of income are deductible as miscellaneous itemized deductions subject to the 2% of adjusted gross income floor.

149. (b) The requirement is to determine the proper reporting of Hall's lottery transactions. Hall's lottery winnings of $200 must be reported as other income on page 1 of Hall's Form 1040. Hall's $1,000 expenditure for state lottery tickets is deductible as a miscellaneous itemized deduction not subject to the 2% of AGI floor, but is limited in amount to the $200 of lottery winnings included in Hall's gross income.

150. (d) The requirement is to determine how expenses pertaining to business activities should be deducted by an outside salesman. An outside salesman is an employee who principally solicits business for his employer while away from the employer's place of business. All unreimbursed business expenses of an outside salesman are deducted as miscellaneous itemized deductions, subject to a 2% of AGI floor. Deductible expenses include business travel, secretarial help, and telephone expenses.

151. (a) The requirement is to determine the amount that can be claimed as miscellaneous itemized deductions. Both the initiation fee and the union dues are fully deductible. The voluntary benefit fund contribution is not deductible. Miscellaneous itemized deductions are generally deductible only to the extent they exceed 2% of AGI. In this case the deductible amount is $80 [$280 – (.02 × $10,000)].

152. (b) The requirement is to compute the amount of miscellaneous itemized deductions. The cost of uniforms not adaptable to general use (specialized work clothes), union dues, unreimbursed auto expenses, and the cost of income tax preparation are all miscellaneous itemized deductions. The preparation of a will is personal in nature, and is not deductible. Thus, the computation of Brodsky's miscellaneous itemized deductions in excess of the 2% of AGI floor is as follows:

Unreimbursed auto expenses	$100
Specialized work clothes	550
Union dues	600
Cost of income tax preparation	150
	$1,400
Less (2% × $25,000)	(500)
Deduction allowed	$900

153. (d) The requirement is to determine which item is not included in determining the total support of a dependent. Support includes food, clothing, FMV of lodging, medical, recreational, educational, and certain capital expenditures made on behalf of a dependent. Excluded from support is life insurance premiums, funeral expenses, nontaxable scholarships, and income and social security taxes paid from a dependent's own income.

154. (c) The requirement is to determine the number of exemptions that Smith was entitled to claim on his 2015 tax return. Smith will be allowed one exemption for himself and one exemption for his dependent mother. Smith is entitled to an exemption for his mother because he provided over half of her support, and her gross income ($0) was less than $4,000.

Note that her $9,000 of social security benefits is excluded from her gross income, and that she did not have to live with Smith because she is related to him. No exemption is available to Smith for his son, Clay, because his son filed a joint return on which there was a tax liability.

155. (b) The requirement is to determine how many exemptions Jim and Kay can claim on their 2015 joint income tax return. Jim and Kay are entitled to one personal exemption each on their joint return. They also are entitled to one exemption for their son, Dale, since he is a *qualifying child* (i.e., Dale did not provide more than half of his own support, and Dale is a full-time student under age twenty-four). However, no dependency exemptions are available for Kim and Grant. Kim is not a qualifying child because she is at least age 19 and not a full-time student, and she is not a qualifying relative because her gross income was at least $4,000. Similarly, Grant is not a qualifying relative because his gross income was at least $4,000.

156. (d) The requirement is to determine the requirements which must be satisfied in order for Joe to claim an exemption for his spouse on Joe's separate return for 2015. An exemption can be claimed for Joe's spouse on Joe's separate 2015 return only if the spouse had **no** gross income and was **not** claimed as another person's dependent in 2015.

157. (a) The requirement is to determine the amount of personal exemption on a dependent's tax return. No personal exemption is allowed on an individual's tax return if the individual can be claimed as a dependency exemption by another taxpayer.

158. (d) The requirement is to determine Robert's filing status and the number of exemptions that he should claim. Robert's father does not qualify as Robert's dependent because his father's gross income (interest income of $4,700) was not less than $4,000. Social security is not included in the gross income test. Since his father does not qualify as his dependent, Robert does not qualify for head-of-household filing status. Thus, Robert will file as single with one exemption.

159. (a) The requirement is to determine the filing status of the Arnolds. Since they were legally separated under a decree of separate maintenance on the last day of the taxable year and do not qualify for head-of-household status, they must each file as single.

160. (a) Mr. and Mrs. Stoner are entitled to one exemption each. They are entitled to one exemption for their daughter since she is a qualifying child (i.e., she did not provide more than half of her own support, and she is a full-time student under age twenty-four). An exemption can be claimed for their son because he is a qualifying relative (i.e., they provided more than half of his support, and his gross income was less than $4,000). No exemption is allowable for Mrs. Stoner's father since he was neither a US citizen nor resident of the US, Canada, or Mexico. There is no additional exemption for being age sixty-five or older.

161. (c) The requirement is to determine the number of exemptions the Planters may claim on their joint tax return. There is one exemption for Mr. Planter, and one exemption for his spouse. In addition there is one dependency exemption

for their daughter who is a qualifying child (i.e., she did not provide more than half of her own support, and she is a full-time student under age twenty-four). There is also one dependency exemption for their niece who is a qualifying relative (i.e., they provided more than half of her support, and her gross income was less than $4,000). However, there is no additional exemption for being age sixty-five or older.

162. (b) The requirement is to determine which of the relatives can be claimed as a dependent (or dependents) on Sam's 2015 return. A taxpayer's own spouse is never a dependent of the taxpayer. Although a personal exemption is generally available for a taxpayer's spouse on the taxpayer's return, it is not a "dependency exemption." Generally, a dependency exemption is available for a qualifying relative if (1) the taxpayer furnishes more than 50% of the dependent's support, (2) the dependent's gross income is less than $4,000, (3) the dependent is of specified relationship to the taxpayer or lives in the taxpayer's household for the entire year, (4) the dependent is a US citizen or resident of the US, Canada, or Mexico, and (5) the dependent does not file a joint return. Here, the support, gross income, US citizen, and joint return tests are met with respect to both Sam's cousin and his father's brother (i.e., Sam's uncle). However, Sam's cousin is not of specified relationship to Sam as defined in the IRC, and could only be claimed as a dependent if the cousin lived in Sam's household for the entire year. Since Sam's cousin did not live in Sam's household, Sam cannot claim a dependency exemption for his cousin. On the other hand, Sam's uncle is of specified relationship to Sam as defined in the IRC and can be claimed as a dependency exemption by Sam.

163. (b) The requirement is to determine which relative could be claimed as a dependent. One of the requirements that must be satisfied to claim a dependency exemption for a person as a qualifying relative is that the person must be (1) of specified relationship to the taxpayer, or (2) a member of the taxpayer's household. Cousins and foster parents are not of specified relationship and only qualify if a member of the taxpayer's household. Since Alan's cousin and foster parent do not qualify as members of Alan's household, only Alan's niece can be claimed as a dependent.

164. (c) The requirement is to determine who can claim Sara's dependency exemption under a multiple support agreement. A multiple support agreement can be used if (1) no single taxpayer furnishes more than 50% of a dependent's support, and (2) two or more persons, each of whom would be able to take the exemption but for the support test, together provide more than 50% of the dependent's support. Then, any taxpayer who provides more than 10% of the dependent's support can claim the dependent if (1) the other persons furnishing more than 10% agree not to claim the dependent as an exemption, and (2) the other requirements for a dependency exemption are met. One of the other requirements that must be met is that the dependent be related to the taxpayer or live in the taxpayer's household. Alma is not eligible for the exemption because Sara is unrelated to Alma and did not live in Alma's household. Carl is not eligible for the exemption because he provided only 9% of Sara's support. Ben is eligible to claim the exemption for Sara under a multiple support agreement because Ben is related to Sara and has provided more than 10% of her support.

165. (b) The requirement is to determine the number of exemptions allowable in 2015. Mr. and Mrs. Vonce are entitled to one exemption each. They are also entitled to one exemption for their dependent daughter since they provided over one half of her support and she had less than $4,000 of gross income. An exemption is not available for their son because he provided over one-half of his own support.

166. (d) The requirement is to determine which statements (if any) are among the requirements to enable a taxpayer to be classified as a "qualifying widow(er)." Qualifying widow(er) filing status is available for the two years following the year of a spouse's death if (1) the surviving spouse was eligible to file a joint return in the year of the spouse's death, (2) does not remarry before the end of the current year, and (3) the surviving spouse pays **over 50%** of the cost of maintaining a household that is the principal home for the **entire year** of the surviving spouse's dependent child.

167. (c) The requirement is to determine which items are considered in determining whether an individual has contributed more than one half the cost of maintaining the household for purposes of head of household filing status. The cost of maintaining a household includes such costs as rent, mortgage interest, taxes, insurance on the home, repairs, utilities, and food eaten in the home. The cost of maintaining a household does **not** include the cost of clothing, education, medical treatment, vacations, life insurance, transportation, the rental value of a home an individual owns, or the value of an individual's services or those of any member of the household.

168. (b) The requirement is to determine the correct statement regarding the filing of a joint tax return. A husband and wife can file a joint return even if they have different accounting methods. Answer (a) is incorrect because spouses must have the same tax year to file a joint return. Answer (c) is incorrect because if either spouse was a nonresident alien at any time during the tax year, **both** spouses must elect to be taxed as US citizens or residents for the entire tax year. Answer (d) is incorrect because taxpayers cannot file a joint return if divorced before the end of the year.

169. (c) The requirement is to determine Emil Gow's filing status for 2015. Emil should file as a "Qualifying widower with dependent child" (i.e., surviving spouse) which will entitle him to use the joint return tax rates. This filing status is available for the two taxable years following the year of a spouse's death if (1) the surviving spouse was eligible to file a joint return in the year of the spouse's death, (2) does not remarry before the end of the current tax year, and (3) the surviving spouse pays over 50% of the cost of maintaining a household that is the principal home for the entire year of the surviving spouse's dependent child.

170. (c) The requirement is to determine Nell's filing status for 2015. Nell qualifies as a head of household because she is unmarried and maintains a household for her infant child. Answer (a) is incorrect because although Nell is single, head of household filing status provides for lower tax rates. Answer (b) is incorrect because Nell is unmarried at the end of

2015. Since Nell's spouse died in 2012, answer (d) is incorrect because the filing status of a "qualifying widow" is only available for the two years following the year of the spouse's death.

171. (a) Mrs. Felton must file as a single taxpayer. Even though she is unmarried, Mrs. Felton does not qualify as a head of household because her son is neither a qualifying child (because of his age) nor a qualifying relative (because he is not her dependent). Answer (b) is incorrect because in order for Mrs. Felton to qualify, her son must qualify as a dependent, which he does not. Although Mrs. Felton would have qualified as married filing jointly, answer (d), in 2014 (the year of her husband's death), the problem requirement is her 2015 filing status.

172. (d) The requirement is to determine the 2015 income tax for Poole, an unmarried taxpayer in the 15% bracket with $20,000 of adjusted gross income. To determine Poole's taxable income, his adjusted gross income must be reduced by the greater of his itemized deductions or a standard deduction, and a personal exemption. Since Poole's medical expenses of $7,500 are subject to a 10% of AGI limitation, his itemized deductions of $5,500 are less than his available standard deduction of $6,300. Poole's tax computation is as follows:

Adjusted gross income		$20,000
Less:		
Standard deduction	$6,300	
Personal exemption	4,000	10,300
Taxable income		$9,700
Tax rate		× 15%
Income tax		$1,455

173. (d) The requirement is to determine the itemized deduction that is deductible when computing an individual's alternative minimum tax (AMT). For purposes of computing an individual's AMT, no deduction is allowed for personal, state, and local income taxes, and miscellaneous itemized deductions subject to the 2% of adjusted gross income threshold. Similarly, no deduction is allowed for home mortgage interest if the loan proceeds were not used to buy, build, or substantially improve the home.

174. (a) The requirement is to determine the amount of tax preferences and adjustments that must be included in the computation of Randy's 2015 alternative minimum tax. Tax preferences include the $1,000 of tax-exempt interest on private activity bonds. It must be added to regular taxable income in arriving at alternative minimum taxable income (AMTI). The adjustments include the $4,000 personal exemption and $1,500 of state income taxes that are deductible in computing regular taxable income but are not deductible in computing AMTI. Note that tax-exempt interest on private activity bonds issued in 2009 and 2010 is not an item of tax preference.

175. (d) The requirement is to determine the amount of Karen's unused alternative minimum tax credit that will carry over to 2016. The amount of alternative minimum tax paid by an individual that is attributable to timing preferences and adjustments is allowed as a tax credit (i.e., minimum tax credit) that can be applied against regular tax liability in future years. The minimum tax credit is computed as the excess of the AMT actually paid over the AMT that would have been paid if AMTI included only exclusion preferences and adjustments (e.g., disallowed itemized deductions, excess percentage depletion, tax-exempt private activity bond interest). Since the minimum tax credit can only be used to reduce future regular tax liability, the credit can only reduce regular tax liability to the point at which it equals the taxpayer's tentative minimum tax. In this case, Karen's payment of $20,000 of alternative minimum tax in 2014 generates a minimum tax credit of $20,000 – $9,000 = $11,000 which is carried forward to 2015. Since Karen's 2015 regular tax liability of $50,000 exceeded her tentative minimum tax of $45,000, $5,000 of Karen's minimum tax credit would be used to reduce her 2015 tax liability to $45,000. Therefore, $11,000 – $5,000 = $6,000 of unused minimum tax credit would carry over to 2016.

176. (c) The requirement is to determine the amount that Mills should report as alternative minimum taxable income (AMTI) before the AMT exemption. Certain itemized deductions, although allowed for regular tax purposes, are not deductible in computing an individual's AMTI. As a result, no AMT deduction is allowed for state, local, and foreign income taxes, real and personal property taxes, and miscellaneous itemized deductions subject to the 2% of AGI floor. Also, no deduction is allowed for qualified residence interest if the mortgage proceeds were **not** used to buy, build, or substantially improve the taxpayer's principal residence or a second home. Additionally, no AMT deduction is allowed for personal exemptions and the standard deduction.

Here, Mills' $5,000 of state and local income taxes and $2,000 of miscellaneous itemized deductions that were deducted for regular tax purposes must be added back to his $70,000 of regular taxable income before personal exemption to arrive at Mills' AMTI before AMT exemption of ($70,000 + $5,000 + $2,000)= $77,000. Note that no adjustment was necessary for the mortgage interest because the mortgage loan was used to acquire his residence.

177. (c) The requirement is to determine whether a net capital gain and home equity interest expense are adjustments for purposes of computing the alternative minimum tax. Although an excess of net long-term capital gain over net short-term capital loss may be subject to a reduced maximum tax rate, the excess is neither a tax preference nor an adjustment in computing the alternative minimum tax. On the other hand, home equity interest expense where the home equity loan proceeds were not used to buy, build, or improve the home is an adjustment because the interest expense, although deductible for regular tax purposes, is not deductible for purposes of computing an individual's alternative minimum tax.

178. (d) The requirement is to determine the proper treatment for the credit for prior year alternative minimum tax (AMT). The amount of AMT paid by an individual taxpayer that is attributable to timing differences can be carried forward

indefinitely as a minimum tax credit to offset the individual's future regular tax liability (not future AMT liability). The amount of AMT credit to be carried forward is the excess of the AMT actually paid over the AMT that would have been paid if AMTI included only exclusion preferences (e.g., disallowed itemized deductions, preferences for excess percentage depletion, and tax-exempt private activity bond interest).

179. (b) The requirement is to determine the correct statement regarding the computation of the alternative minimum tax (AMT). A taxpayer is subject to the AMT only if the taxpayer's tentative AMT exceeds the taxpayer's regular tax. Thus, the alternative minimum tax is computed as the excess of the tentative AMT over the regular tax.

180. (b) The requirement is to determine the amount of net earnings from self-employment that would be multiplied by the self-employment tax rate to compute Diamond's self-employment tax. Since self-employment earnings generally represent earnings derived from a trade or business carried on as a sole proprietor, the $10,000 of interest income from personal investments would be excluded from the computation. On the other hand, a self-employed taxpayer is allowed a deemed deduction equal to 7.65% of self-employment earnings in computing the amount of net earnings upon which the tax is based. The purpose of this deemed deduction is to reflect the fact that employees do not pay FICA tax on the corresponding 7.65% FICA tax paid by their employers.

Gross receipts from business	$150,000
Cost of goods sold	(80,000)
Operating expenses	(40,000)
Self-employment earnings	$30,000
Less deemed deduction (100% – 7.65%)	× 92.35%
Net earnings to be multiplied by self-employment tax rate	$27,705

181. (c) The requirement is to determine the amount of Freeman's income that is subject to self-employment tax. The self-employment tax is imposed on self-employment income to provide Social Security and Medicare benefits for self-employed individuals. Self-employment income includes an individual's net earnings from a trade or business carried on as sole proprietor or as an independent contractor. The term also includes a partner's distributive share of partnership ordinary income or loss from trade or business activities, as well as guaranteed payments received by a partner for services rendered to a partnership. Self-employment income excludes gains and losses from the disposition of property used in a trade or business, as well as a shareholder's share of ordinary income from an S corporation.

182. (a) The requirement is to determine the amount of Rich's net self-employment income. Income from self-employment generally includes all items of business income less business deductions. Excluded from the computation would be estimated income taxes on self-employment income, charitable contributions, investment income, and gains and losses on the disposition of property used in a trade or business. An individual's charitable contributions can only be deducted as an itemized deduction. Rich's net self-employment income would be

Business receipts	$20,000
Air conditioning parts	(2,500)
Yellow Pages listing	(2,000)
Business telephone calls	(400)
	$15,100

183. (c) The requirement is to determine the correct statement regarding the self-employment tax. The self-employment tax is imposed at a rate of 15.3% on individuals who work for themselves (e.g., sole proprietor, independent contractor, partner). Generally, one-half of an individual's self-employment tax is deductible from gross income in arriving at adjusted gross income.

184. (c) The requirement is to determine the correct statement with regard to social security tax (FICA) withheld in an amount greater than the maximum for a particular year. If an individual works for more than one employer, and combined wages exceed the maximum used for FICA purposes, too much FICA tax will be withheld. In such case, since the excess results from correct withholding by two or more employers, the excess should be claimed as a credit against income tax. Answer (a) is incorrect because the excess cannot be used as an itemized deduction. Answer (b) is incorrect because if employers withhold correctly, no reimbursement can be obtained from the employers. Answer (d) is incorrect because if the excess FICA tax withheld results from incorrect withholding by any one employer, the employer must reimburse the excess and it cannot be claimed as a credit against tax.

185. (b) The requirement is to determine Berger's gross income from self-employment for the current year. Self-employment income represents the net earnings of an individual from a trade or business carried on as a proprietor or partner, or from rendering services as an independent contractor. The director's fee is self-employment income since it is related to a trade or business, and Berger is not an employee. Fees received by a fiduciary (e.g., executor) are generally not related to a trade or business and not self-employment income. However, executor's fees may constitute self-employment income if the executor is a professional fiduciary or carries on a trade or business in the administration of an estate.

186. (d) The requirement is to determine Smith's gross income from self-employment. Self-employment income represents the net earnings of an individual from a trade or business carried on as a sole proprietor or partner, or from rendering services as an independent contractor (i.e., not an employee). The $8,000 consulting fee and the $2,000 of director's fees are self-employment income because they are related to a trade or business and Smith is not an employee.

187. (c) The requirement is to determine which credit is not a component of the general business credit. The general business credit is a combination of several credits that provide

uniform rules for current and carryback-carryover years. The general business credit is composed of the investment credit, work opportunity credit, alcohol fuels credit, research credit, low-income housing credit, enhanced oil recovery credit, disabled access credit, renewable electricity production credit, empowerment zone employment credit, Indian employment credit, employer social security credit, orphan drug credit, the new markets credit, the small employer pension plan start-up costs credit, and the employer-provided child care facilities credit. A general business credit in excess of the limitation amount is carried back one year and forward twenty years to offset tax liability in those years.

188. (a) The requirement is to determine which tax credit is a combination of credits to provide for uniform rules for the current and carryback-carryover years. The general business credit is composed of the investment credit, work opportunity credit, welfare-to-work credit, alcohol fuels credit, research credit, low-income housing credit, enhanced oil recovery credit, disabled access credit, renewable electricity production credit, empowerment zone employment credit, Indian employment credit, employer social security credit, orphan drug credit, the new markets credit, the small employer pension plan start-up costs credit, and the employer-provided child care facilities credit. A general business credit in excess of the limitation amount is carried back one year and forward twenty years to offset tax liability in those years.

189. (a) The requirement is to determine the amount that can be claimed as a credit for the elderly. The amount of credit (limited to tax liability) is 15% of an initial amount reduced by social security and 50% of AGI in excess of $10,000. Here, the credit is the lesser of (1) the taxpayers' tax liability of $61, or (2) 15% [$7,500 – $3,000 – (.50)($22,200 – $10,000)] = $0.

190. (c) The requirement is to compute Nora's child care credit for 2015. Since she has two dependent preschool children, all $6,000 paid for child care qualifies for the credit. The credit is 35% of qualified expenses, but is reduced by one percentage point for each $2,000 (or fraction thereof) of AGI over $15,000 down to a minimum of 20%. Since Nora's AGI is $44,000, her credit is 20% × $6,000 = $1,200.

191. (b) The requirement is to determine the amount of the child care credit allowable to the Jasons. The credit is from 20% to 35% of certain dependent care expenses limited to the lesser of (1) $3,000 for one qualifying individual, $6,000 for two or more; (2) taxpayer's earned income, or spouse's if smaller; or (3) actual expenses. The $2,500 paid to the Union Day Care Center qualifies, as does the $1,000 paid to Wilma Jason. Payments to relatives qualify if the relative is not a dependent of the taxpayer. Since Robert and Mary Jason only claimed three exemptions, Wilma was not their dependent. The $500 paid to Acme Home Cleaning Service does not qualify since it is *completely* unrelated to the care of their child. To qualify, expenses must be at least partly for the care of a qualifying individual. Since qualifying expenses exceed $3,000, the Jasons' credit is 20% × $3,000 = $600.

192. (b) The requirement is to determine the qualifications for the child care credit that at least one spouse must satisfy on a joint return. The child care credit is a percentage of the amount paid for qualifying household and dependent care expenses incurred to enable an individual to be gainfully employed or look for work. To qualify for the child care credit on a joint return, at least one spouse must be gainfully employed or be looking for work when the related expenses are incurred. Note that it is not required that at least one spouse be gainfully employed, but only needs to be looking for work when the expenses are incurred. Additionally, at least one spouse must have earned income during the year. However, there is no limit as to the maximum amount of earned income or adjusted gross income reported on the joint return.

193. (a) The requirement is to determine which factor(s) may affect the amount of Sunex's foreign tax credit available in its current year corporate income tax return. Since US taxpayers are subject to US income tax on their worldwide income, they are allowed a credit for the income taxes paid to foreign countries. The applicable foreign tax rate will affect the amount of foreign taxes paid, and thereby affect the amount available as a foreign tax credit. Additionally, since the amount of credit that can be currently used cannot exceed the amount of US tax attributable to the foreign-source income, the income source will affect the amount of available foreign tax credit for the current year if the limitation based on the amount of US tax is applicable.

194. (b) The requirement is to determine the amount of foreign tax credit that Wald Corp. may claim. Since US taxpayers are subject to US income tax on their worldwide income, they are allowed a credit for the income taxes paid to foreign countries. However, the amount of credit that can be currently used cannot exceed the amount of US tax that is attributable to the foreign income. This foreign tax credit limitation can be expressed as follows:

$$\frac{\text{Foreign TI}}{\text{Worldwide TI}} \times (\text{US tax}) = \text{Foreign tax credit limitation}$$

One limitation must be computed for foreign source passive income (e.g., interest, dividends, royalties, rents, annuities), with a separate limitation computed for all other foreign source taxable income.

In this case, the foreign income taxes paid on other foreign source taxable income of $27,000 is fully usable as a credit in 2013 because it is less than the applicable limitation amount (i.e., the amount of US tax attributable to the income).

$$\frac{\$90,000}{\$300,000} \times (\$96,000) = \$28,800$$

On the other hand, the credit for the $12,000 of foreign income taxes paid on non-business-related interest is limited to the amount of US tax attributable to the foreign interest income, $9,600.

$$\frac{\$30,000}{\$300,000} \times (\$96,000) = \$9,600$$

Thus, Wald Corp.'s foreign tax credit totals $27,000 + $9,600 = $36,600. The $12,000 – $9,600 = $2,400 of unused foreign tax credit resulting from the application of the limitation on foreign taxes attributable to foreign source interest income can be carried back one year and forward ten years to offset US income tax in those years.

195. (a) The requirement is to determine the correct statement regarding a corporation's foreign income taxes. Foreign income taxes paid by a corporation may be claimed either as a credit or as a deduction, at the option of the corporation.

196. (c) The requirement is to determine the credit that can result in a refund even if an individual had no income tax liability. The earned income credit is a refundable credit and can result in a refund even if the individual had no tax withheld from wages.

197. (a) The requirement is to choose the correct statement regarding Kent's earned income credit. The earned income credit could result in a refund even if Kent had no tax withheld from wages. Since the credit is refundable, answer (c) is incorrect because there will never be any unused credit to carry back or forward. Answer (d) is incorrect because the credit is a direct subtraction from the computed tax.

198. (c) The requirement is to determine the correct statement regarding the earned income credit. The earned income credit is a refundable credit and can result in a refund even if the individual had no tax withheld from wages. To qualify, an individual must have earned income, but the amount of earned income does not have to equal adjusted gross income. For purposes of the credit, earned income excludes workers' compensation benefits. Additionally, the credit is available only if the tax return covers a full twelve-month period.

199. (b) The requirement is to determine the tax credit that cannot be claimed by a corporation. The foreign tax credit, alternative fuel production credit, and general business credit may be claimed by a corporation. The earned income credit cannot be claimed by a corporation; it is available only to individuals.

200. (a) The requirement is to determine the correct statement regarding the credit for adoption expenses. The adoption expenses credit is a nonrefundable credit for up to $13,190 (for 2014) of expenses (including special needs children) incurred to adopt an eligible child. An eligible child is one who is under eighteen years of age at time of adoption, or physically or mentally incapable of self-care. Generally, adoption expenses incurred or paid during a tax year prior to the year in which the adoption is finalized may be claimed as a credit in the tax year following the year the expense was incurred. Adoption expenses incurred during the year the adoption becomes final or in the year following the finalization of the adoption are claimed in the year they were incurred.

201. (c) The requirement is to determine the incorrect statement concerning the child tax credit. Individual taxpayers are permitted to take a tax credit based solely on the number of their dependent children under age seventeen. The amount of the credit is $1,000 per qualifying child, but is subject to reduction if adjusted gross income exceeds certain income levels. A qualifying child must be a US citizen or resident.

202. (c) The requirement is to determine the incorrect statement concerning the American Opportunity credit. The American Opportunity credit provides for a maximum credit of $2,500 per year (100% of the first $2,000, plus 25% of the next $2,000 of tuition, fees, and course materials) for the first four years of postsecondary education. The credit is available on a per student basis and covers tuition paid for the taxpayer, spouse, and dependents. To be eligible, the student must be enrolled on at least a half-time basis for one academic period during the year. If a parent claims a child as a dependent, only the parent can claim the credit and any qualified expenses paid by the child are deemed paid by the parent.

203. (d) The requirement is to determine the incorrect statement concerning the lifetime learning credit. The lifetime learning credit provides a credit of 20% of up to $10,000 of tuition and fees paid by a taxpayer for one or more students for graduate and undergraduate courses at an eligible educational institution. The credit may be claimed for an unlimited number of years, is available on a per taxpayer basis, and covers tuition paid for the taxpayer, spouse, and dependents.

204. (a) The requirement is to determine which statement(s) describe how Baker may avoid the penalty for the underpayment of estimated tax for the 2015 tax year. An individual whose regular and alternative minimum tax liability is not sufficiently covered by withholding from wages must pay estimated tax in quarterly installments or be subject to penalty. Individuals will incur no underpayment penalty for 2015 if the amount of tax withheld plus estimated payments are at least equal to the lesser of (1) 90% of the current year's tax; (2) 100% of the prior year's tax; or (3) 90% of the tax determined by annualizing current year taxable income through each quarter. However, note that high-income individuals (i.e., individuals whose adjusted gross income for the preceding year exceeds $150,000) must use 110% (instead of 100%) if they wish to base their estimated tax payments on their prior year's tax liability.

205. (a) The requirement is to determine what amount would be subject to penalty for the underpayment of estimated taxes. A taxpayer will be subject to an underpayment of estimated tax penalty if the taxpayer did not pay enough tax either through withholding or by estimated tax payments. For 2014, there will be no penalty if the total tax shown on the return less the amount paid through withholding (including excess social security tax withholding) is less than $1,000. Additionally, individuals will incur no penalty if the amount of tax withheld plus estimated payments are at least equal to the lesser of (1) 90% of the current year's tax (determined on the basis of actual income or annualized income), or (2) 100% of the prior year's tax. In this case, since the tax shown on Krete's return ($16,500) less the tax paid through withholding ($16,000) was less than $1,000, there will be no penalty for the underpayment of estimated taxes.

206. (d) The requirement is to determine the original due date for a decedent's federal income tax return. The final return of a decedent is due on the same date the decedent's return would have been due had death not occurred. An individual's federal income tax return is due on the 15th day of the fourth calendar month following the close of the tax year (e.g., April 15 for a calendar-year taxpayer).

207. (a) The requirement is to determine Birch's filing requirement. A self-employed individual must file an income tax return if net earnings from self-employment are $400 or more.

208. (c) The requirement is to determine the date on which the statute of limitations begins for Jackson Corp.'s 2014 tax return. Generally, any tax that is imposed must be assessed within three years of the filing of the return, or if later, the due date of the return. Since Jackson Corp.'s 2014 return was filed on March 8, 2015, and the return was due on March 15, 2015, the statute of limitations expires on March 15, 2018. This means that the statute of limitations begins on March 16, 2015.

209. (c) The requirement is to determine the latest date that the IRS can assert a notice of deficiency for a 2014 calendar-year return if the taxpayer neither committed fraud nor omitted amounts in excess of 25% of gross income. The normal period for assessment is the later of three years after a return is filed, or three years after the due date of the return. Since the 2014 calendar-year return was filed on March 20, 2015, and was due on April 15, 2015, the IRS must assert a deficiency no later than April 15, 2018.

210. (d) A six-year statute of limitations applies if gross income omitted from the return exceeds 25% of the gross income reported on the return. For this purpose, gross income of a business includes total gross receipts before subtracting cost of goods sold and deductions. Thus, a six-year statute of limitations will apply to Thompson if he omitted from gross income an amount in excess of ($400,000 + $36,000) × 25% = $109,000.

211. (d) The requirement is to determine the maximum period during which the IRS can issue a notice of deficiency if the gross income omitted from a taxpayer's return exceeds 25% of the gross income reported on the return. A **six-year** statute of limitations applies if gross income omitted from the return exceeds 25% of the gross income reported on the return. Additionally, a tax return filed **before** its due date is treated as filed **on** its due date. Thus, if a return is filed before its due date, and the gross income omitted from the return exceeds 25% of the gross income reported on the return, the IRS has **six** years from the due date of the return to issue a notice of deficiency.

212. (c) The requirement is to determine the form that must be filed by an individual to claim a refund of erroneously paid income taxes. Form 1040X, Amended US Individual Income Tax Return, should be used to claim a refund of erroneously paid income taxes. Form 843 should be used to file a refund claim for taxes other than income taxes. Form 1139 may be used by a corporation to file for a tentative adjustment or refund of taxes when an overpayment of taxes for a prior year results from the carryback of a current year's net operating loss or net capital loss. Form 1045 may be used by taxpayers other than corporations to apply for similar adjustments.

213. (a) The requirement is to determine the date by which a refund claim must be filed if an individual paid income tax during 2014 but did not file a tax return. An individual must file a claim for refund within three years from the date a return was filed, or two years from the date of payment of tax, whichever is later. If no return was filed, the claim for refund must be filed within two years from the date that the tax was paid.

214. (c) The requirement is to determine the date by which a taxpayer must file an amended return to claim a refund of tax paid on a calendar-year 2014 return. A taxpayer must file an amended return to claim a refund within three years from the date a return was filed, or two years from the date of payment of tax, whichever is later. If a return is filed before its due date, it is treated as filed on its due date. Thus, the taxpayer's 2014 calendar-year return that was filed on March 15, 2015, is treated as filed on April 15, 2015. Therefore, an amended return to claim a refund must be filed not later than April 15, 2018.

215. (d) The requirement is to determine the date by which a refund claim due to worthless security must be filed. The normal three-year statute of limitations is extended to seven years for refund claims resulting from bad debts or worthless securities. Since the securities became worthless during 2014, and Baker's 2014 return was filed on April 15, 2015, Baker's refund claim must be filed no later than April 15, 2022.

216. (b) The requirement is to determine the amount on which the penalties for late filing and late payment would be computed. The late filing and late payment penalties are based on the amount of net tax due. If a taxpayer's tax return indicated a tax liability of $50,000, and $45,000 of taxes were withheld, the late filing and late payment penalties would be based on the $5,000 of tax that is owed.

217. (c) An accuracy-related penalty equal to 20% of the underpayment of tax may be imposed if the underpayment of tax is attributable to one or more of the following: (1) negligence or disregard of the tax rules and regulations; (2) any substantial understatement of income tax; (3) any substantial valuation overstatement; (4) any substantial overstatement of pension liabilities; or (5) any substantial gift or estate tax valuation understatement. The penalty for gift or estate tax valuation understatement may apply if the value of property on a gift or estate tax return is 50% or less of the amount determined to be correct. The penalty for a substantial income tax valuation overstatement may apply if the value (or adjusted basis) of property is 200% or more of the amount determined to be correct.

Simulations

Task-Based Simulation 1

Tax Treatment		
	Authoritative Literature	Help

Cole, a newly licensed CPA, opened an office in 2015 as a sole practitioner engaged in the practice of public accountancy. Cole reports on the cash basis for income tax purposes and is 46 years old.

Listed below are Cole's 2015 business and nonbusiness transactions, as well as possible tax treatments. For each of Cole's transactions (**Items 1 through 20**), select the appropriate tax treatment. A tax treatment may be selected once, more than once, or not at all.

Tax treatments

A. Taxable as interest income in Schedule B—Interest and Dividend Income.

B. Taxable as other income on page 1 of Form 1040.

C. Not taxable.

D. Deductible on page 1 of Form 1040 to arrive at adjusted gross income.

E. Deductible in Schedule A—Itemized Deductions, subject to threshold of 10% of adjusted gross income.

F. Deductible in Schedule A—Itemized Deductions, subject to threshold of 10% of adjusted gross income and additional threshold of $100.

G. Deductible in full in Schedule A—Itemized Deductions (cannot be claimed as a credit).

H. Deductible in Schedule B—Interest and Dividend Income.

I. Deductible in Schedule C—Profit or Loss from Business.

J. Deductible in Schedule D—Capital Gains or Losses.

K. Deductible in Schedule E—Supplemental Income and Loss.

L. Deductible in Form 4797—Sales of Business Property.

M. Claimed in Form 1116—Foreign Tax Credit, or in Schedule A—Itemized Deductions, at taxpayer's option.

N. Based on gross self-employment income.

O. Based on net earnings from self-employment.

P. Not deductible.

Transactions	(A)	(B)	(C)	(D)	(E)	(F)	(G)	(H)	(I)	(J)	(K)	(L)	(M)	(N)	(O)	(P)
1. Fees received for jury duty.	○	○	○	○	○	○	○	○	○	○	○	○	○	○	○	○
2. Interest income on mortgage loan receivable.	○	○	○	○	○	○	○	○	○	○	○	○	○	○	○	○
3. Penalty paid to bank on early withdrawal of savings.	○	○	○	○	○	○	○	○	○	○	○	○	○	○	○	○
4. Write-offs of uncollectible accounts receivable from accounting practice.	○	○	○	○	○	○	○	○	○	○	○	○	○	○	○	○
5. Cost of attending review course in preparation for the Uniform CPA Examination.	○	○	○	○	○	○	○	○	○	○	○	○	○	○	○	○
6. Fee for the biennial permit to practice as a CPA.	○	○	○	○	○	○	○	○	○	○	○	○	○	○	○	○
7. Costs of attending CPE courses in fulfillment of state board requirements.	○	○	○	○	○	○	○	○	○	○	○	○	○	○	○	○
8. Contribution to a qualified Keogh retirement plan.	○	○	○	○	○	○	○	○	○	○	○	○	○	○	○	○
9. Loss sustained from nonbusiness bad debt.	○	○	○	○	○	○	○	○	○	○	○	○	○	○	○	○
10. Loss sustained on sale of "Small Business Corporation" (Section 1244) stock.	○	○	○	○	○	○	○	○	○	○	○	○	○	○	○	○

Transactions	(A)	(B)	(C)	(D)	(E)	(F)	(G)	(H)	(I)	(J)	(K)	(L)	(M)	(N)	(O)	(P)
11. Taxes paid on land owned by Cole and rented out as a parking lot.	O	O	O	O	O	O	O	O	O	O	O	O	O	O	O	O
12. Interest paid on installment purchases of household furniture.	O	O	O	O	O	O	O	O	O	O	O	O	O	O	O	O
13. Alimony paid to former spouse who reports the alimony as taxable income.	O	O	O	O	O	O	O	O	O	O	O	O	O	O	O	O
14. Personal medical expenses charged on credit card in December 2015 but not paid until January 2016.	O	O	O	O	O	O	O	O	O	O	O	O	O	O	O	O
15. Personal casualty loss sustained.	O	O	O	O	O	O	O	O	O	O	O	O	O	O	O	O
16. State inheritance tax paid on bequest received.	O	O	O	O	O	O	O	O	O	O	O	O	O	O	O	O
17. Foreign income tax withheld at source on dividend received.	O	O	O	O	O	O	O	O	O	O	O	O	O	O	O	O
18. Computation of self-employment tax.	O	O	O	O	O	O	O	O	O	O	O	O	O	O	O	O
19. One-half of self-employment tax paid with 2015 return filed in April 2016.	O	O	O	O	O	O	O	O	O	O	O	O	O	O	O	O
20. Insurance premiums paid on Cole's life.	O	O	O	O	O	O	O	O	O	O	O	O	O	O	O	O

Task-Based Simulation 2

Mr. Cole is considering purchasing a new principal residence for $1,500,000, and intends to finance the purchase with a mortgage in the amount of $1,150,000. Which code section, subsection, and paragraph provide the maximum amount of mortgage indebtedness on which the interest expense will be deductible? Indicate the reference to that citation in the shaded boxes below.

Task-Based Simulation 3

Green is self-employed as a human resources consultant and reports on the cash basis for income tax purposes. Green is an unmarried custodial parent with one dependent child.

Listed below are Green's 2015 business and nonbusiness transactions, as well as possible tax treatments. For each of Green's transactions (**Items 1 through 25**), select the appropriate tax treatment. A tax treatment may be selected once, more than once, or not at all.

Tax treatments

A. Taxable as other income on Form 1040.
B. Reported in Schedule B—Interest and Dividend Income.
C. Reported in Schedule C as trade or business income.
D. Reported in Schedule E—Supplemental Income and Loss.
E. Not taxable.
F. Fully deductible on Form 1040 to arrive at adjusted gross income.
G. Fifty percent deductible on Form 1040 to arrive at adjusted gross income.
H. Reported in Schedule A—Itemized Deductions (deductibility subject to threshold of 10% of adjusted gross income).
I. Reported in Schedule A—Itemized Deductions (deductibility subject to threshold of 2% of adjusted gross income).

J. Reported in Form 4562—Depreciation and Amortization and deductible in Schedule A—Itemized Deductions (deductibility subject to threshold of 2% of adjusted gross income).
K. Reported in Form 4562—Depreciation and Amortization, and deductible in Schedule C—Profit or Loss from Business.
L. Fully deductible in Schedule C—Profit or Loss from Business.
M. Partially deductible in Schedule C—Profit or Loss from Business.
N. Reported in Form 2119—Sale of Your Home, and deductible in Schedule D—Capital Gains and Losses.
O. Not deductible.

Transactions	(A)	(B)	(C)	(D)	(E)	(F)	(G)	(H)	(I)	(J)	(K)	(L)	(M)	(N)	(O)
1. Retainer fees received from clients.	○	○	○	○	○	○	○	○	○	○	○	○	○	○	○
2. Oil royalties received.	○	○	○	○	○	○	○	○	○	○	○	○	○	○	○
3. Interest income on general obligation state and local government bonds.	○	○	○	○	○	○	○	○	○	○	○	○	○	○	○
4. Interest on refund of federal taxes.	○	○	○	○	○	○	○	○	○	○	○	○	○	○	○
5. Death benefits from term life insurance policy on parent.	○	○	○	○	○	○	○	○	○	○	○	○	○	○	○
6. Interest income on US Treasury bonds.	○	○	○	○	○	○	○	○	○	○	○	○	○	○	○
7. Share of ordinary income from an investment in a limited partnership reported in Form 1065, Schedule K-1.	○	○	○	○	○	○	○	○	○	○	○	○	○	○	○
8. Taxable income from rental of a townhouse owned by Green.	○	○	○	○	○	○	○	○	○	○	○	○	○	○	○
9. Prize won as a contestant on a TV quiz show.	○	○	○	○	○	○	○	○	○	○	○	○	○	○	○
10. Payment received for jury service.	○	○	○	○	○	○	○	○	○	○	○	○	○	○	○
11. Dividends received from mutual funds that invest in tax-free government obligations.	○	○	○	○	○	○	○	○	○	○	○	○	○	○	○
12. Qualifying medical expenses not reimbursed by insurance.	○	○	○	○	○	○	○	○	○	○	○	○	○	○	○
13. Personal life insurance premiums paid by Green.	○	○	○	○	○	○	○	○	○	○	○	○	○	○	○
14. Expenses for business-related meals where clients were present.	○	○	○	○	○	○	○	○	○	○	○	○	○	○	○
15. Depreciation on personal computer purchased in 2014 used for business.	○	○	○	○	○	○	○	○	○	○	○	○	○	○	○
16. Business lodging expenses, while out of town.	○	○	○	○	○	○	○	○	○	○	○	○	○	○	○
17. Subscriptions to professional journals used for business.	○	○	○	○	○	○	○	○	○	○	○	○	○	○	○
18. Self-employment taxes paid.	○	○	○	○	○	○	○	○	○	○	○	○	○	○	○
19. Qualifying contributions to a simplified employee pension plan.	○	○	○	○	○	○	○	○	○	○	○	○	○	○	○

Transactions	(A) (B) (C) (D) (E) (F) (G) (H) (I) (J) (K) (L) (M) (N) (O)
20. Election to expense business equipment purchased in 2015.	O O O O O O O O O O O O O O O
21. Qualifying alimony payments made by Green.	O O O O O O O O O O O O O O O
22. Subscriptions for investment-related publications.	O O O O O O O O O O O O O O O
23. Interest expense on a home-equity line of credit for an amount borrowed to finance Green's business.	O O O O O O O O O O O O O O O
24. Interest expense on a loan for an auto used 75% for business.	O O O O O O O O O O O O O O O
25. Loss on sale of residence.	O O O O O O O O O O O O O O O

Task-Based Simulation 4

Tax Treatment		
	Authoritative Literature	Help

For 2015, Green, who had adjusted gross income of $40,000, qualified to itemize deductions and was subject to federal income tax liability. For **items 1 through 9,** select from the following list of tax treatments the appropriate tax treatment. A tax treatment may be selected once, more than once, or not at all.

Selections

A. Not deductible on Form 1040.
B. Deductible in full on Schedule A—Itemized Deductions.
C. Deductible in Schedule A—Itemized Deductions subject to a limitation of 50% of adjusted gross income.
D. Deductible in Schedule A—Itemized Deductions as miscellaneous deductions subject to a threshold of 2% of adjusted gross income.

E. Deductible in Schedule A—Itemized Deductions as miscellaneous deductions not subject to a threshold of 2% adjusted gross income.
F. Deductible on Schedule E—Supplemental Income and Loss.
G. A credit is allowable.

	(A) (B) (C) (D) (E) (F) (G)
1. In 2015, Green paid $2,000 interest on the $25,000 home equity mortgage on his vacation home, which he used exclusively for personal use. The mortgage is secured by Green's vacation home, and the loan proceeds were used to purchase an automobile.	O O O O O O O
2. For 2015, Green had a $30,000 cash charitable contribution carryover from his 2014 cash donation to the American Red Cross. Green made no additional charitable contributions in 2015.	O O O O O O O
3. During 2015, Green had investment interest expense that did **not** exceed his net investment income.	O O O O O O O
4. Green's 2015 lottery ticket losses were $450. He had no gambling winnings.	O O O O O O O
5. During 2015, Green paid $2,500 in real property taxes on his vacation home, which he used exclusively for personal use.	O O O O O O O
6. In 2015, Green paid a $500 premium for a homeowner's insurance policy on his principal residence.	O O O O O O O
7. For 2015, Green paid $2,000 to an unrelated babysitter to care for his child while he worked.	O O O O O O O
8. In 2015, Green paid $4,000 interest on the $60,000 acquisition mortgage on his principal residence. The mortgage is secured by Green's home.	O O O O O O
9. During 2015, Green paid $3,600 real property taxes on residential rental property in which he actively participates. There was no personal use of the rental property.	O O O O O O O

Task-Based Simulation 5

Research		
	Authoritative Literature	Help

Mr. Green paid $5,000 during 2015 to an unrelated babysitter for the care of his child while he worked. Which code section and subsection provide the maximum amount of employment-related child care expenses that qualify for a tax credit? Indicate the reference to that citation in the shaded boxes below.

Section	Subsection
§ ▨	(▨)

Task-Based Simulation 6

Deductibility		
	Authoritative Literature	Help

Mark Smith is an employee of Patton Corporation. Additionally, Smith operates a consulting business as a sole proprietor and owns an apartment building. Smith made the expenditures listed below during 2015.

For each of the following items, indicate whether each expenditure is deductible for AGI, from AGI (not subject to 2% limitation), from AGI (subject to 2% limitation), or not deductible. Assume Smith plans to itemize deductions for 2015.

	For AGI (A)	From AGI (No 2%) (B)	From AGI (2% Floor) (C)	Not ded. (D)
1. Smith paid the medical expenses of his mother-in-law. Although Smith provided more than half of her support, she does not qualify as Smith's dependent because she had gross income of $5,000.	O	O	O	O
2. Smith paid the real estate taxes on his rental apartment building.	O	O	O	O
3. Smith paid state sales taxes of $1,500 on a used automobile that he purchased for personal use.	O	O	O	O
4. Smith paid the real estate taxes on his mother-in-law's home. She is the owner of the home.	O	O	O	O
5. Smith paid $1,500 of interest on credit card charges. The charges were for items purchased for personal use.	O	O	O	O
6. Smith paid an attorney $500 to prepare Smith's will.	O	O	O	O
7. Smith incurred $750 of expenses for business meals and entertainment in his position as an employee of Patton Corporation. Smith's expenses were not reimbursed.	O	O	O	O
8. Smith paid self-employment taxes of $3,000 as a result of earnings from the consulting business that he conducts as a sole proprietor.	O	O	O	O
9. Smith made a contribution to his self-employed retirement plan (Keogh Plan).	O	O	O	O
10. Smith had gambling losses totaling $2,500 for the year. He is including a lottery prize of $5,000 in his gross income this year.	O	O	O	O

Task-Based Simulation 7

Research		
	Authoritative Literature	Help

In January of 2015, Mark Smith had to have heart surgery. The total cost of the surgery was $100,000, and his insurance covered a total of $82,000. Smith paid the remaining $18,000 in February of 2015. Which code section and subsection determine the extent to which Smith's unreimbursed medical expenses will be deductible? Indicate the reference to that citation in the shaded boxes below.

Section	Subsection
§ [ ]	([ ])

Task-Based Simulation 8

Adjusted Gross Income		
	Authoritative Literature	Help

Situation

Frank and Dale Cumack are married and filing a joint 2015 income tax return. During 2015, Frank, age sixty-three, was retired from government service and Dale, fifty-five, was employed as a university instructor. In 2015, the Cumacks contributed all of the support to Dale's father, Jacques, an unmarried French citizen and French resident who had no gross income.

For **items 1 through 10,** select the correct amount of income, loss, or adjustment to income that should be reported on page 1 of the Cumacks' 2015 Form 1040—Individual Income Tax Return to arrive at the adjusted gross income for each separate transaction. A tax treatment may be selected once, more than once, or not at all.

Any information contained in an item is unique to that item and is not to be incorporated in your calculations when answering other items.

Selections

A. $0	D. $3,000	F. $4,000	I. $10,000	K. $30,000
B. $1,000	E. $3,500	G. $5,000	J. $25,000	L. $125,000
C. $2,000		H. $9,000		M. $150,000

(A) (B) (C) (D) (E) (F) (G) (H) (I) (J) (K) (L) (M)

1. During 2015, Dale received a $30,000 cash gift from her aunt. ○ ○ ○ ○ ○ ○ ○ ○ ○ ○ ○ ○ ○

2. Dale contributed $3,500 to her traditional Individual Retirement Account (IRA) on January 15, 2015. In 2015, she earned $60,000 as a university instructor. During 2015 the Cumacks were not active participants in an employer's qualified pension or annuity plan. ○ ○ ○ ○ ○ ○ ○ ○ ○ ○ ○ ○ ○

3. In 2015, the Cumacks received a $1,000 federal income tax refund. ○ ○ ○ ○ ○ ○ ○ ○ ○ ○ ○ ○ ○

4. During 2015, Frank, a 50% partner in Diske General Partnership, received a $4,000 guaranteed payment from Diske for services that he rendered to the partnership that year. ○ ○ ○ ○ ○ ○ ○ ○ ○ ○ ○ ○ ○

	(A)	(B)	(C)	(D)	(E)	(F)	(G)	(H)	(I)	(J)	(K)	(L)	(M)
5. In 2015, Frank received $10,000 as beneficiary of his deceased brother's life insurance policy.	○	○	○	○	○	○	○	○	○	○	○	○	○
6. Dale's employer pays 100% of the cost of all employees' group-term life insurance under a qualified plan. Policy cost is $5 per $1,000 of coverage. Dale's group-term life insurance coverage equals $450,000.	○	○	○	○	○	○	○	○	○	○	○	○	○
7. In 2015, Frank won $5,000 at a casino and had $2,000 in gambling losses.	○	○	○	○	○	○	O	U	○	○	○	○	○
8. During 2015, the Cumacks received $1,000 interest income associated with a refund of their prior years' federal income tax.	○	○	○	○	○	○	○	○	○	○	○	○	○
9. In 2015, the Cumacks sold their first and only residence for $400,000. They purchased their home in 1996 for $50,000 and have lived there since then. There were no other capital gains, losses, or capital loss carryovers. The Cumacks do not intend to buy another residence.	○	○	○	○	○	○	○	○	○	○	○	○	○
10. In 2015, Zeno Corp. declared a stock dividend and Dale received one additional share of Zeno common stock for three shares of Zeno common stock that she held. The stock that Dale received had a fair market value of $9,000. There was no provision to receive cash instead of stock.	○	○	○	○	○	○	○	○	○	○	○	○	○

Task-Based Simulation 9

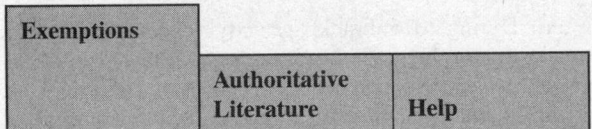

Frank and Dale Cumack are married and filing a joint 2015 income tax return. During 2015, Frank, age sixty-three, was retired from government service and Dale, fifty-five, was employed as a university instructor. In 2015, the Cumacks contributed all of the support to Dale's father, Jacques, an unmarried French citizen and French resident who had no gross income.
Determine whether the Cumacks overstated, understated, or correctly determined the number of both personal and dependency exemptions.

Selections

O. Overstated the number of both personal and dependency exemptions.
U. Understated the number of both personal and dependency exemptions.
C. Correctly determined the number of both personal and dependency exemptions.

	(O)	(U)	(C)
The Cumacks claimed three exemptions on their 2015 joint income tax return.	○	○	○

Task-Based Simulation 10

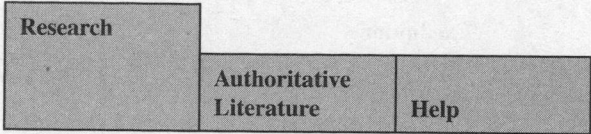

Assume that the Cumacks' automobile was stolen during 2015. The automobile was uninsured for theft and had a fair market value of $7,000, and an adjusted basis of $10,000. Which code section and subsection provide the limitations that apply to the deductibility of the Cumacks' uninsured theft loss? Indicate the reference to that citation in the shaded boxes below.

Task-Based Simulation 11

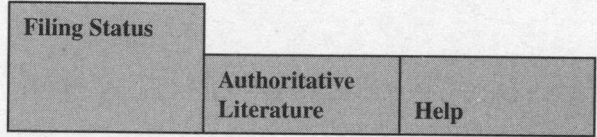

Situation

Mrs. Vick, a forty-year-old cash-basis taxpayer, earned $45,000 as a teacher and $5,000 as a part-time real estate agent in 2014. Mr. Vick, who died on July 1, 2014, had been permanently disabled on his job and collected state disability benefits until his death. For all of 2014 and 2015, the Vicks' residence was the principal home of both their eleven-year-old daughter Joan and Mrs. Vick's unmarried cousin, Fran Phillips, who had no income in either year. During 2014 Joan received $200 a month in survivor social security benefits that began on August 1, 2014, and will continue at least until her eighteenth birthday. In 2014 and 2015, Mrs. Vick provided over one-half the support for Joan and Fran, both of whom were US citizens. Mrs. Vick did not remarry. Mr. and Mrs. Vick received the following in 2014:

Earned income	$50,000
State disability benefits	1,500
Interest on:	
Refund from amended tax return	50
Savings account and certificates of deposit	350
Municipal bonds	100
Gift	3,000
Pension benefits	900
Jury duty pay	200
Gambling winnings	450
Life insurance proceeds	5,000

Additional information:

- Mrs. Vick received the $3,000 cash gift from her uncle.
- Mrs. Vick received the pension distributions from a qualified pension plan, paid for exclusively by her husband's employer.
- Mrs. Vick had $100 in gambling losses in 2014.
- Mrs. Vick was the beneficiary of the life insurance policy on her husband's life. She received a lump-sum distribution. The Vicks had paid $500 in premiums.
- Mrs. Vick received Mr. Vick's accrued vacation pay of $500 in 2015.

For **items 1 and 2,** determine and select from the choices below, **BOTH** the filing status and the number of exemptions for each item.

	Filing Status	Exemptions
S.	Single	1
M.	Married filing joint	2
H.	Head of household	3
Q.	Qualifying widow with dependent child	4

	Filing Status	Exemptions
	(S) (M) (H) (Q)	(1) (2) (3) (4)
1. Determine the filing status and the number of exemptions that Mrs. Vick can claim on the 2014 federal income tax return, to get the most favorable tax results.	○ ○ ○ ○	○ ○ ○ ○
2. Determine the filing status and the number of exemptions that Mrs. Vick can claim on the 2015 federal income tax return to get the most favorable tax results, if she solely maintains the costs of her home.	○ ○ ○ ○	○ ○ ○ ○

For **items 3 through 9,** determine the amount, if any, that is taxable and should be included in Adjusted Gross Income (AGI) on the 2014 federal income tax return filed by Mrs. Vick.

3. State disability benefits
4. Interest income
5. Pension benefits
6. Gift
7. Life insurance proceeds
8. Jury duty pay
9. Gambling winnings

Task-Based Simulation 12

Tax Treatment		
	Authoritative Literature	Help

During 2014 the following payments were made or losses were incurred. For **items 1 through 14,** select the appropriate tax treatment. A tax treatment may be selected once, more than once, or not at all.

Tax treatment

A. Not deductible.
B. Deductible in Schedule A—Itemized Deductions, subject to threshold of 10% of adjusted gross income.
C. Deductible in Schedule A—Itemized Deductions, subject to threshold of 2% of adjusted gross income.

D. Deductible on page 1 of Form 1040 to arrive at adjusted gross income.
E. Deductible in full in Schedule A—Itemized Deductions.
F. Deductible in Schedule A—Itemized Deductions, subject to maximum of 50% of adjusted gross income.

	(A) (B) (C) (D) (E) (F)
1. Premiums on Mr. Vick's personal life insurance policy.	○ ○ ○ ○ ○ ○
2. Penalty on Mrs. Vick's early withdrawal of funds from a certificate of deposit.	○ ○ ○ ○ ○ ○
3. Mrs. Vick's substantiated cash donation to the American Red Cross.	○ ○ ○ ○ ○ ○

(A) (B) (C) (D) (E) (F)

4. Payment of estimated state income taxes.   ○ ○ ○ ○ ○ ○

5. Payment of real estate taxes on the Vick home.   ○ ○ ○ ○ ○ ○

6. Loss on the sale of the family car.   ○ ○ ○ ○ ○ ○

7. Cost in excess of the increase in value of residence, for the installation of a stairlift in   ○ ○ ○ ○ ○ ○
January 2014, related directly to the medical care of Mr. Vick.

8. The Vicks' health insurance premiums for hospitalization coverage.   ○ ○ ○ ○ ○ ○

9. CPA fees to prepare the 2013 tax return.   ○ ○ ○ ○ ○ ○

10. Amortization over the life of the loan of points paid to refinance the mortgage at a   ○ ○ ○ ○ ○ ○
lower rate on the Vick home.

11. One-half the self-employment tax paid by Mrs. Vick.   ○ ○ ○ ○ ○ ○

12. Mrs. Vick's $100 in gambling losses. She had $450 of gambling winnings.   ○ ○ ○ ○ ○ ○

13. Mrs. Vick's union dues.   ○ ○ ○ ○ ○ ○

14. 2013 federal income tax paid with the Vicks' tax return on April 15, 2014.   ○ ○ ○ ○ ○ ○

Task-Based Simulation 13

Research		
	Authoritative Literature	**Help**

Mrs. Vick is considering making contributions to a qualified tuition program to provide savings for her daughter's college education. However, Mrs. Vick is concerned that the contributions will be considered a gift of a future interest and result in a taxable gift. Which code section and subsection provide the gift tax treatment for contributions to a qualified tuition program? Indicate the reference to that citation in the shaded boxes below.

Section	Subsection
§ ▇▇▇▇	(▇▇▇▇)

Task-Based Simulation 14

Income and Loss		
	Authoritative Literature	**Help**

Tom and Joan Moore, both CPAs filed a joint 2015 federal income tax return showing $70,000 in taxable income. During 2015, Tom's daughter Laura, age 16, resided with Tom's former spouse. Laura had no income of her own and was not Tom's dependent. For **items 1 through 10,** determine the amount of income or loss, if any, that should be included on page one of the Moore's 2015 Form 1040.

1. The Moores had no capital loss carryovers from prior years. During 2014 the Moores had the following stock transactions that resulted in a net capital loss:

	Date acquired	Date sold	Sales price	Cost
Revco	2/1/15	3/17/15	$15,000	$25,000
Abbco	2/18/14	4/1/15	8,000	4,000

2. In 2012, Joan received an acre of land as an inter vivos gift from her grandfather. At the time of the gift, the land had a fair market value of $50,000. The grandfather's adjusted basis was $60,000. Joan sold the land in 2015 to an unrelated third party for $56,000.

3. The Moores received a $500 security deposit on their rental property in 2015. They are required to return the amount to the tenant.

4. Tom's 2015 wages were $53,000. In addition, Tom's employer provided group-term life insurance on Tom's life in excess of $50,000. The value of such excess coverage was $2,000.

5. During 2015, the Moores received a $2,500 federal tax refund and a $1,250 state tax refund for 2014 overpayments. In 2014, the Moores were not subject to the alternative minimum tax and were not entitled to any credit against income tax. The Moores' 2014 adjusted gross income was $80,000 and itemized deductions were $1,450 in excess of the standard deduction. The state tax deduction for 2014 was $2,000.

6. In 2015, Joan received $1,300 in unemployment compensation benefits. Her employer made a $100 contribution to the unemployment insurance fund on her behalf.

7. The Moores received $8,400 in gross receipts from their rental property during 2015. The expenses for the residential rental property were

Bank mortgage interest	$1,200
Real estate taxes	700
Insurance	500
MACRS depreciation	3,500

8. The Moores received a stock dividend in 2015 from Ace Corp. They had the option to receive either cash or Ace stock with a fair market value of $900 as of the date of distribution. The par value of the stock was $500.

9. In 2015, Joan received $3,500 as beneficiary of the death benefit that was provided by her brother's employer. Joan's brother did not have a nonforfeitable right to receive the money while living, and the death benefit does not represent the proceeds of life insurance.

10. Tom received $10,000, consisting of $5,000 each of principal and interest, when he redeemed a Series EE savings bond in 2015. The bond was issued in his name in 2005 and the proceeds were used to pay for Laura's college tuition. Tom had not elected to report the yearly increases in the value of the bond.

Task-Based Simulation 15

Tax Treatment		
	Authoritative Literature	Help

Tom and Joan Moore are married filing a joint return. During 2015, the following events took place. For **items 1 through 12,** select the appropriate tax treatment. A tax treatment may be selected once, more than once, or not at all.

Tax treatment

A. Not deductible on Form 1040.
B. Deductible in full in Schedule A—Itemized Deductions.
C. Deductible in Schedule A—Itemized Deductions, subject to a threshold of 10% of adjusted gross income.
D. Deductible in Schedule A—Itemized Deductions, subject to a limitation of 50% of adjusted gross income.

E. Deductible in Schedule A—Itemized Deductions, subject to a $100 floor and a threshold of 10% of adjusted gross income.
F. Deductible in Schedule A—Itemized Deductions, subject to a threshold of 2% of adjusted gross income.

(A) (B) (C) (D) (E) (F)

1. On March 23, 2015, Tom sold fifty shares of Zip stock at a $1,200 loss. He repurchased fifty shares of Zip on April 15, 2015. O O O O O O

2. Payment of a personal property tax based on the value of the Moores' car. O O O O O O

3. Used clothes were donated to church organizations. O O O O O O

	(A)	(B)	(C)	(D)	(E)	(F)
4. Premiums were paid covering insurance against Tom's loss of earnings.	○	○	○	○	○	○
5. Tom paid for subscriptions to accounting journals.	○	○	○	○	○	○
6. Interest was paid on a $10,000 home-equity line of credit secured by the Moores' residence. The fair market value of the home exceeded the mortgage by $50,000. Tom used the proceeds to purchase a sailboat.	○	○	○	○	○	○
7. Amounts were paid in excess of insurance reimbursement for prescription drugs.	○	○	○	○	○	○
8. Funeral expenses were paid by the Moores for Joan's brother.	○	○	○	○	○	○
9. Theft loss was incurred on Joan's jewelry in excess of insurance reimbursement. There were no 2015 personal casualty gains.	○	○	○	○	○	○
10. Loss on the sale of the family's sailboat.	○	○	○	○	○	○
11. Interest was paid on the $300,000 acquisition mortgage on the Moores' home. The mortgage is secured by their home.	○	○	○	○	○	○
12. Joan performed free accounting services for the Red Cross. The estimated value of the services was $500.	○	○	○	○	○	○

Task-Based Simulation 16

Adjustments must be made to regular taxable income in order to compute an individual's alternative minimum taxable income (AMTI). Which code section and subsection provide the adjustments that only apply to individuals when computing the alternative minimum tax? Indicate the reference to that citation in the shaded boxes below.

Task-Based Simulation 17

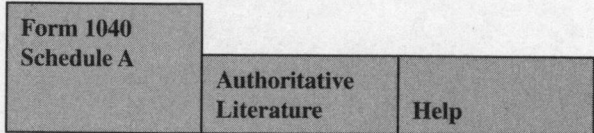

Situation

Fred (social security number 123-67-5489) and Laura Shaw, both age 56, provided you with the following tax return data. The amount from Form 1040, line 38 is $80,000.

Medical and dental expenses	
Medical insurance premiums	$5,600
Disability income insurance premiums	800
Prescription drugs	825
Nonprescription medicine	280
Dr. Jones—neurologist	2,250
Dentist	750

Dr. Smith—LASIK surgery	900
Insurance reimbursement for medical bills	2,000
Transportation to and from doctors	80

Taxes

Balance of state income taxes due for 2013 paid on April 15, 2014	$225
State income taxes withheld for 2014	975
Real estate taxes on principal residence	7,000
Real estate taxes on summer residence	3,000
County personal property tax	410
Registration fee for automobiles	160

Interest

Mortgage interest on principal residence	$5,500
Mortgage interest on summer residence	2,200
Interest paid on automobile loan	800
Interest paid on personal use credit cards	500

Contributions

Cash donated to church	$2,500
Stock donated to church. (The Shaws purchased it for $3,000 18 months ago)	4,000

Miscellaneous payments

Legal fee for preparation of a will	$350
Rent for safety-deposit box containing stocks and bonds	120
Union dues	600
Subscriptions to investment publications	300
Life insurance premiums	2,800
Transportation to and from work	2,400
Fee paid for tax return preparation	400
Unreimbursed business travel away from home overnight	900
Contribution to a national political party	200
Repairs to principal residence	2,000

Complete the following 2014 Form 1040 Schedule A—Itemized Deductions for Fred and Laura Shaw.

SCHEDULE A
(Form 1040)

Department of the Treasury
Internal Revenue Service (99)

Itemized Deductions

▶ Information about Schedule A and its separate instructions is at *www.irs.gov/schedulea.*
▶ Attach to Form 1040.

OMB No. 1545-0074

2014

Attachment
Sequence No. **07**

Name(s) shown on Form 1040

Your social security number

Medical and Dental Expenses	**Caution.** Do not include expenses reimbursed or paid by others.		
	1 Medical and dental expenses (see instructions) **1**		
	2 Enter amount from Form 1040, line 38 **2**		
	3 Multiply line 2 by 10% (.10). But if either you or your spouse was born before January 2, 1950, multiply line 2 by 7.5% (.075) instead **3**		
	4 Subtract line 3 from line 1. If line 3 is more than line 1, enter -0-	**4**	
Taxes You Paid	5 State and local (**check only one box**):		
	a ☐ Income taxes, **or**		
	b ☐ General sales taxes **5**		
	6 Real estate taxes (see instructions) **6**		
	7 Personal property taxes **7**		
	8 Other taxes. List type and amount ▶ -------------------------		
	------------------------- **8**		
	9 Add lines 5 through 8	**9**	
Interest You Paid **Note.** Your mortgage interest deduction may be limited (see instructions).	10 Home mortgage interest and points reported to you on Form 1098 **10**		
	11 Home mortgage interest not reported to you on Form 1098. If paid to the person from whom you bought the home, see instructions and show that person's name, identifying no., and address ▶		

	------------------------- **11**		
	12 Points not reported to you on Form 1098. See instructions for special rules **12**		
	13 Mortgage insurance premiums (see instructions) **13**		
	14 Investment interest. Attach Form 4952 if required. (See instructions.) **14**		
	15 Add lines 10 through 14	**15**	
Gifts to Charity If you made a gift and got a benefit for it, see instructions.	16 Gifts by cash or check. If you made any gift of $250 or more, see instructions **16**		
	17 Other than by cash or check. If any gift of $250 or more, see instructions. You **must** attach Form 8283 if over $500 . . . **17**		
	18 Carryover from prior year **18**		
	19 Add lines 16 through 18	**19**	
Casualty and Theft Losses	20 Casualty or theft loss(es). Attach Form 4684. (See instructions.)	**20**	
Job Expenses and Certain Miscellaneous Deductions	21 Unreimbursed employee expenses—job travel, union dues, job education, etc. Attach Form 2106 or 2106-EZ if required. (See instructions.) ▶ ------------- **21**		
	22 Tax preparation fees **22**		
	23 Other expenses—investment, safe deposit box, etc. List type and amount ▶ -------------		
	------------- **23**		
	24 Add lines 21 through 23 . . . . . . **24**		
	25 Enter amount from Form 1040, line 38 **25**		
	26 Multiply line 25 by 2% (.02) **26**		
	27 Subtract line 26 from line 24. If line 26 is more than line 24, enter -0-	**27**	
Other Miscellaneous Deductions	28 Other—from list in instructions. List type and amount ▶ -------------		
	-------------	**28**	
Total Itemized Deductions	29 Is Form 1040, line 38, over $152,525?		
	☐ **No.** Your deduction is not limited. Add the amounts in the far right column for lines 4 through 28. Also, enter this amount on Form 1040, line 40.	**29**	
	☐ **Yes.** Your deduction may be limited. See the Itemized Deductions Worksheet in the instructions to figure the amount to enter.		
	30 If you elect to itemize deductions even though they are less than your standard deduction, check here . . . . ▶ ☐		

For Paperwork Reduction Act Notice, see Form 1040 instructions.

Cat. No. 17145C

Schedule A (Form 1040) 2014

Task-Based Simulation 18

    The Shaws are considering donating a painting to a state university for display in the university's library. The Shaws acquired the painting six months ago for $90,000 and believe that the painting is now worth $105,000. Which code section and subsection determine the amount of charitable contribution to which the Shaws will be entitled if they donate the painting at the present time? Indicate the reference to that citation in the shaded boxes below.

Section	Subsection
§ ⬛	(⬛)

Simulation Solutions

Task-Based Simulation 1

Tax Treatment		
	Authoritative Literature	Help

Transactions	(A)	(B)	(C)	(D)	(E)	(F)	(G)	(H)	(I)	(J)	(K)	(L)	(M)	(N)	(O)	(P)
1. Fees received for jury duty.	○	●	○	○	○	○	○	○	○	○	○	○	○	○	○	○
2. Interest income on mortgage loan receivable.	●	○	○	○	○	○	○	○	○	○	○	○	○	○	○	○
3. Penalty paid to bank on early withdrawal of savings.	○	○	○	●	○	○	○	○	○	○	○	○	○	○	○	○
4. Write-offs of uncollectible accounts receivable from accounting practice.	○	○	○	○	○	○	○	○	○	○	○	○	○	○	○	●
5. Cost of attending review course in preparation for the Uniform CPA Examination.	○	○	○	○	○	○	○	○	○	○	○	○	○	○	○	●
6. Fee for the biennial permit to practice as a CPA.	○	○	○	○	○	○	○	○	●	○	○	○	○	○	○	○
7. Costs of attending CPE courses in fulfillment of state board requirements.	○	○	○	○	○	○	○	○	●	○	○	○	○	○	○	○
8. Contribution to a qualified Keogh retirement plan.	○	○	○	●	○	○	○	○	○	○	○	○	○	○	○	○
9. Loss sustained from nonbusiness bad debt.	○	○	○	○	○	○	○	○	○	●	○	○	○	○	○	○
10. Loss sustained on sale of "Small Business Corporation" (Section 1244) stock.	○	○	○	○	○	○	○	○	○	○	●	○	○	○	○	○
11. Taxes paid on land owned by Cole and rented out as a parking lot.	○	○	○	○	○	○	○	○	○	○	●	○	○	○	○	○
12. Interest paid on installment purchases of household furniture.	○	○	○	○	○	○	○	○	○	○	○	○	○	○	○	●
13. Alimony paid to former spouse who reports the alimony as taxable income.	○	○	○	●	○	○	○	○	○	○	○	○	○	○	○	○
14. Personal medical expenses charged on credit card in December 2015 but not paid until January 2016.	○	○	○	○	●	○	○	○	○	○	○	○	○	○	○	○
15. Personal casualty loss sustained.	○	○	○	○	○	●	○	○	○	○	○	○	○	○	○	○
16. State inheritance tax paid on bequest received.	○	○	○	○	○	○	○	○	○	○	○	○	○	○	○	●
17. Foreign income tax withheld at source on dividend received.	○	○	○	○	○	○	○	○	○	○	○	○	●	○	○	○
18. Computation of self-employment tax.	○	○	○	○	○	○	○	○	○	○	○	○	○	○	●	○
19. One-half of self-employment tax paid with 2015 return filed in April 2016.	○	○	○	●	○	○	○	○	○	○	○	○	○	○	○	○
20. Insurance premiums paid on Cole's life.	○	○	○	○	○	○	○	○	○	○	○	○	○	○	○	●

Explanations

1. **(B)** Fees received for jury duty represent compensation for services and must be included in gross income. Since there is no separate line for jury duty fees, they are taxable as other income on page 1 of Form 1040.

2. **(A)** Interest income on a mortgage loan receivable must be included in gross income and is taxable as interest income in Schedule B—Interest and Dividend Income.

3. **(D)** An interest forfeiture penalty for making an early withdrawal from a certificate of deposit is deductible on page 1 of Form 1040 to arrive at adjusted gross income.

4. **(P)** The problem indicates that Cole is a CPA reporting on the cash basis. Accounts receivable resulting from services rendered by a cash-basis taxpayer have a zero tax basis, because the income has not yet been reported. Therefore, the write-offs of zero basis uncollectible accounts receivable from Cole's accounting practice are not deductible.

5. **(P)** An educational expense that is part of a program of study that can qualify an individual for a new trade or business is not deductible. This is true even if the individual is not seeking a new job. In this case, the cost of attending a review course in preparation for the CPA examination is a nondeductible personal expense since it qualifies Cole for a new profession.

6. **(I)** Licensing and regulatory fees paid to state or local governments are an ordinary and necessary trade or business expense and are deductible by a sole proprietor on Schedule C—Profit or Loss from Business. Since Cole is a cash method taxpayer, he can deduct the fee for the biennial permit to practice when paid in 2015.

7. **(I)** All trade or business expenses of a self-employed individual are deductible on Schedule C—Profit or Loss from Business. Education must meet certain requirements before the related expenses can be deducted. Generally, deductible education expenses must not be a part of a program that will qualify the individual for a new trade or business and must (1) be required by an employer or by law to keep the individual's present position, or (2) maintain or improve skills required in the individual's present work. In this case, Cole already is a CPA and is fulfilling state CPE requirements, so his education costs of attending CPE courses are deductible in Schedule C—Profit or Loss from Business.

8. **(D)** Contributions to a self-employed individual's qualified Keogh retirement plan are deductible on page 1 of Form 1040 to arrive at adjusted gross income. The maximum deduction for contributions to a defined contribution Keogh retirement plan is limited to the lesser of $53,000 (for 2015), or 25% of self-employment income.

9. **(J)** A loss sustained from a nonbusiness bad debt is always classified as a short-term capital loss. Therefore, Cole's nonbusiness bad debt is deductible in Schedule D—Capital Gains or Losses.

10. **(L)** A loss sustained on the sale of Sec. 1244 stock is generally deductible as an ordinary loss, with the amount of ordinary loss deduction limited to $50,000. On a joint return, the limit is increased to $100,000, even if the stock was owned by only one spouse. The ordinary loss resulting from the sale of Sec. 1244 stock is deductible in Form 4797—Sales of Business Property. To the extent that a loss on Sec. 1244 stock exceeds the applicable $50,000 or $100,000 limit, the loss is deductible as a capital loss in Schedule D—Capital Gains or Losses. Similarly, if Sec. 1244 stock is sold at a gain, the gain would be reported as a capital gain in Schedule D if the stock is a capital asset.

11. **(K)** Rental income and expenses related to rental property are generally reported in Schedule E. Here, the taxes paid on land owned by Cole and rented out as a parking lot are deductible in Schedule E—Supplemental Income and Loss. Schedule E also is used to report the income or loss from royalties, partnerships, S corporations, estates, and trusts.

12. **(P)** The interest paid on installment purchases of household furniture is considered personal interest and is not deductible. Personal interest is any interest that is not qualified residence interest, investment interest, passive activity interest, or business interest. Personal interest generally includes interest on car loans, interest on income tax, underpayments, installment plan interest, credit card finance charges, and late payment charges by a utility.

13. **(D)** Alimony paid to a former spouse who reports the alimony as taxable income is deductible on page 1 of Form 1040 to arrive at adjusted gross income.

14. **(E)** Personal medical expenses are generally deductible as an itemized deduction subject to a 10% of AGI threshold for the year in which they are paid. Additionally, an individual can deduct medical expenses charged to a credit card in the year the charge is made. It makes no difference when the amount charged is actually paid. Here, Cole's personal medical expenses charged on a credit card in December 2015 but not paid until January 2016 are deductible for 2015 in Schedule A—Itemized Deductions, subject to a threshold of 10% of adjusted gross income.

15. **(F)** If an individual sustains a personal casualty loss, it is deductible in Schedule A—Itemized Deductions subject to a threshold of $100 and an additional threshold of 10% of adjusted gross income.

16. (P) State inheritance taxes paid on a bequest that was received are not deductible. Other taxes not deductible in computing an individual's federal income tax include federal estate and gift taxes, federal income taxes, and social security and other employment taxes paid by an employee.

17. (M) An individual can deduct foreign income taxes as an itemized deduction or can deduct foreign income taxes as a tax credit. Cole's foreign income tax withheld at source on foreign dividends received can be claimed in Form 1116—Foreign Tax Credit, or in Schedule A—Itemized Deductions, at Cole's option.

18. (O) A self-employed individual is subject to a self-employment tax if the individual's net earnings from self-employment are at least $400.

19. (D) An individual's self-employment tax is computed in Schedule SE and is added as an additional tax in arriving at the individual's total tax. A portion of the computed self-employment tax is allowed as a deduction in arriving at adjusted gross income. Here, one-half of Cole's self-employment tax for 2015 is deductible for 2015 on page 1 of Form 1040 to arrive at adjusted gross income, even though the tax was not paid until the return was filed in April 2016.

20. (P) Insurance premiums paid on Cole's life are classified as a personal expense and are not deductible.

Task-Based Simulation 2

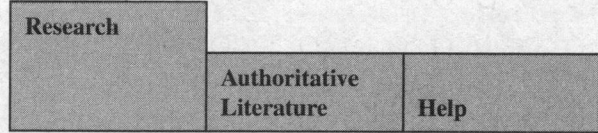

Internal Revenue Code Section 163, subsection (h), paragraph (3) provides that interest is deductible on up to $1,000,000 of acquisition indebtedness, and also is deductible on up to $100,000 of home equity indebtedness.

Section	Subsection	Paragraph
§ 163	(h)	(3)

Task-Based Simulation 3

Transactions	(A)	(B)	(C)	(D)	(E)	(F)	(G)	(H)	(I)	(J)	(K)	(L)	(M)	(N)	(O)
1. Retainer fees received from clients.	○	○	●	○	○	○	○	○	○	○	○	○	○	○	○
2. Oil royalties received.	○	○	○	●	○	○	○	○	○	○	○	○	○	○	○
3. Interest income on general obligation state and local government bonds.	○	○	○	○	●	○	○	○	○	○	○	○	○	○	○
4. Interest on refund of federal taxes.	○	●	○	○	○	○	○	○	○	○	○	○	○	○	○
5. Death benefits from term life insurance policy on parent.	○	○	○	○	●	○	○	○	○	○	○	○	○	○	○
6. Interest income on US Treasury bonds.	○	●	○	○	○	○	○	○	○	○	○	○	○	○	○
7. Share of ordinary income from an investment in a limited partnership reported in Form 1065, Schedule K-1.	○	○	○	●	○	○	○	○	○	○	○	○	○	○	○

	(A)	(B)	(C)	(D)	(E)	(F)	(G)	(H)	(I)	(J)	(K)	(L)	(M)	(N)	(O)
8. Taxable income from rental of a townhouse owned by Green.	○	○	○	●	○	○	○	○	○	○	○	○	○	○	○
9. Prize won as a contestant on a TV quiz show.	●	○	○	○	○	○	○	○	○	○	○	○	○	○	○
10. Payment received for jury service.	●	○	○	○	○	○	○	○	○	○	○	○	○	○	○
11. Dividends received from mutual funds that invest in tax-free government obligations.	○	○	○	○	●	○	○	○	○	○	○	○	○	○	○
12. Qualifying medical expenses not reimbursed by insurance.	○	○	○	○	○	○	○	●	○	○	○	○	○	○	○
13. Personal life insurance premiums paid by Green.	○	○	○	○	○	○	○	○	○	○	○	○	○	○	●
14. Expenses for business-related meals where clients were present.	○	○	○	○	○	○	○	○	○	○	○	○	●	○	○
15. Depreciation on personal computer purchased in 2015 used for business.	○	○	○	○	○	○	○	○	○	○	●	○	○	○	○
16. Business lodging expenses, while out of town.	○	○	○	○	○	○	○	○	○	○	○	●	○	○	○
17. Subscriptions to professional journals used for business.	○	○	○	○	○	○	○	○	○	○	○	●	○	○	○
18. Self-employment taxes paid.	○	○	○	○	○	○	●	○	○	○	○	○	○	○	○
19. Qualifying contributions to a simplified employee pension plan.	○	○	○	○	○	●	○	○	○	○	○	○	○	○	○
20. Election to expense business equipment purchased in 2015.	○	○	○	○	○	○	○	○	○	○	●	○	○	○	○
21. Qualifying alimony payments made by Green.	○	○	○	○	○	●	○	○	○	○	○	○	○	○	○
22. Subscriptions for investment-related publications.	○	○	○	○	○	○	○	○	●	○	○	○	○	○	○
23. Interest expense on a home-equity line of credit for an amount borrowed to finance Green's business.	○	○	○	○	○	○	○	○	○	○	○	●	○	○	○
24. Interest expense on a loan for an auto used 75% for business.	○	○	○	○	○	○	○	○	○	○	○	○	●	○	○
25. Loss on sale of residence.	○	○	○	○	○	○	○	○	○	○	○	○	○	○	●

Explanations

1. (C) All trade or business income and deductions of a self-employed individual are reported on Schedule C—Profit or Loss from Business. Retainer fees received from clients is reported in Schedule C as trade or business income.

2. (D) Income derived from royalties is reported in Schedule E—Supplemental Income and Loss. Schedule E also is used to report the income or loss from rental real estate, partnerships, S corporations, estates, and trusts.

3. (E) Interest from general obligation state and local government bonds is tax-exempt and is excluded from gross income.

4. (B) The interest income on a refund of federal income taxes must be included in gross income and is reported in Schedule B—Interest and Dividend Income. The actual refund of federal income taxes itself is excluded from gross income.

5. (E) Life insurance proceeds paid by reason of death are generally excluded from gross income. Here, the death benefits received by Green from a term life insurance policy on the life of Green's parent are not taxable.

6. (B) Interest income from US Treasury bonds and treasury bills must be included in gross income and is reported in Schedule B—Interest and Dividend Income.

7. (D) A partner's share of a partnership's ordinary income that is reported to the partner on Form 1065, Schedule K-1 must be included in the partner's gross income and is reported in Schedule E—Supplemental Income and Loss.

8. **(D)** The taxable income from the rental of a townhouse owned by Green must be included in gross income and is reported in Schedule E—Supplemental Income and Loss.

9. **(A)** A prize won as a contestant on a TV quiz show must be included in gross income. Since there is no separate line on Form 1040 for prizes, they are taxable as other income on Form 1040.

10. **(A)** Fees received for jury duty represent compensation for services and must be included in gross income. Since there is no separate line for jury duty fees, they are taxable as other income on Form 1040.

11. **(E)** An investor in a mutual fund may receive several different kinds of distributions including ordinary dividends, capital gain distributions, tax-exempt interest dividends, and return of capital distributions. A mutual fund may pay tax-exempt interest dividends to its shareholders if it meets certain requirements. These dividends are paid from the tax-exempt state and local obligation interest earned by the fund and retain their tax-exempt character when reported by the shareholder. Thus, Green's dividends received from mutual funds that invest in tax-free government obligations are not taxable.

12. **(H)** Qualifying medical expenses not reimbursed by insurance are deductible in Schedule A as an itemized deduction to the extent in excess of 10% of adjusted gross income.

13. **(O)** Personal life insurance premiums paid on Green's life are classified as a personal expense and not deductible.

14. **(M)** All trade or business expenses of a self-employed individual are deductible on Schedule C—Profit or Loss from Business. However, only 50% of the cost of business meals and entertainment is deductible. Therefore, Green's expenses for business-related meals where clients were present are partially deductible in Schedule C.

15. **(K)** The deduction for depreciation on listed property (e.g., automobiles, computers, and property used for entertainment etc.) is computed on Form 4562—Depreciation and Amortization. Since Green's personal computer was used in his business as a self-employed consultant, the amount of depreciation computed on Form 4562 is then deductible in Schedule C—Profit or Loss from Business.

16. **(L)** Lodging expenses while out of town on business are an ordinary and necessary business expense and are fully deductible by a self-employed individual in Schedule C—Profit or Loss from Business.

17. **(L)** The cost of subscriptions to professional journals used for business are an ordinary and necessary business expense and are fully deductible by a self-employed individual in Schedule C—Profit or Loss from Business.

18. **(G)** An individual's self-employment tax is computed in Schedule SE and is added as an additional tax in arriving at the individual's total tax liability. A portion of the computed self-employment tax is then allowed as a deduction on Form 1040 in arriving at adjusted gross income.

19. **(F)** Qualifying contributions to a self-employed individual's simplified employee pension plan are deductible on page 1 of Form 1040 to arrive at adjusted gross income.

20. **(K)** Sec. 179 permits a taxpayer to elect to treat the cost of qualifying depreciable personal business property as an expense rather than as a capital expenditure. In this case, Green's election to expense business equipment would be computed on Form 4562—Depreciation and Amortization, and then would be deductible in Schedule C—Profit or Loss from Business.

21. **(F)** Qualifying alimony payments made by Green to a former spouse are fully deductible on Form 1040 to arrive at adjusted gross income.

22. **(I)** The costs of subscriptions for investment publications are not related to Green's trade or business, but instead are considered expenses incurred in the production of portfolio income and are reported as miscellaneous itemized deductions in Schedule A—Itemized Deductions. These investment expenses are deductible to the extent that the aggregate of expenses in this category exceed 2% of adjusted gross income.

23. **(L)** The nature of interest expense is determined by using a tracing approach (i.e., the nature depends upon how the loan proceeds were used). Since the interest expense on Green's home-equity line of credit was for a loan to finance Green's business, the best answer is to treat the interest as a business expense fully deductible in Schedule C—Profit or Loss from Business.

24. **(M)** The interest expense on a loan for an auto used by a self-employed individual in a trade or business is deductible as a business expense. Since Green's auto was used 75% for business, only 75% of the interest expense is deductible in Schedule C—Profit or Loss from Business. The remaining 25% is considered personal interest expense and is not deductible.

25. **(O)** The loss resulting from the sale of Green's personal residence is not deductible because the property was held for personal use. Only losses due to casualty or theft are deductible for personal use property.

Task-Based Simulation 4

Tax Treatment		
	Authoritative Literature	Help

                                                       (A) (B) (C) (D) (E) (F) (G)

1. In 2015, Green paid $2,000 interest on the $25,000 home equity mortgage on his vacation home, which he used exclusively for personal use. The mortgage is secured by Green's vacation home, and the loan proceeds were used to purchase an automobile.   ○ ● ○ ○ ○ ○ ○

2. For 2015, Green had a $30,000 cash charitable contribution carryover from his 2014 cash donation to the American Red Cross. Green made no additional charitable contributions in 2015.   ○ ○ ● ○ ○ ○ ○

3. During 2015, Green had investment interest expense that did not exceed his net investment income.   ○ ● ○ ○ ○ ○ ○

4. Green's 2015 lottery ticket losses were $450. He had no gambling winnings.   ● ○ ○ ○ ○ ○ ○

5. During 2015, Green paid $2,500 in real property taxes on his vacation home, which he used exclusively for personal use.   ○ ● ○ ○ ○ ○ ○

6. In 2015, Green paid a $500 premium for a homeowner's insurance policy on his principal residence.   ● ○ ○ ○ ○ ○ ○

7. For 2015, Green paid $2,000 to an unrelated babysitter to care for his child while he worked.   ○ ○ ○ ○ ○ ○ ●

8. In 2015, Green paid $4,000 interest on the $60,000 acquisition mortgage on his principal residence. The mortgage is secured by Green's home.   ○ ● ○ ○ ○ ○ ○

9. During 2015, Green paid $3,600 real property taxes on residential rental property in which he actively participates. There was no personal use of the rental property.   ○ ○ ○ ○ ○ ● ○

Explanations

1. **(B)** Interest expense on home equity indebtedness is deductible on up to $100,000 of home equity loans secured by a first or second residence regardless of how the loan proceeds were used.

2. **(C)** Contributions in excess of applicable percentage limitations can be carried forward for up to five tax years. Here, the $30,000 of charitable contribution carryover from 2014 is deductible as an itemized deduction for 2015 subject to a limitation of 50% of AGI.

3. **(B)** Investment interest expense is deductible as an itemized deduction to the extent of net investment income. Since Green's investment interest expense did not exceed his net investment income, it is deductible in full.

4. **(A)** Gambling losses (including lottery ticket losses) are deductible as an itemized deduction to the extent of the gambling winnings included in gross income. Since Green had no gambling winnings, the losses are not deductible.

5. **(B)** State, local, or foreign real estate taxes imposed on the taxpayer for property held for personal use are fully deductible as an itemized deduction.

6. **(A)** A premium for a homeowner's insurance policy on a principal residence is a nondeductible personal expense.

7. **(G)** Payments to an unrelated babysitter to care for his child while Green worked would qualify for the child and dependent care credit. For 2015, the credit may vary from 20% to 35% of up to $3,000 ($6,000 for two or more qualifying individuals) of qualifying household and dependent care expenses incurred to enable the taxpayer to be gainfully employed or look for work.

8. **(B)** Interest expense on acquisition indebtedness is deductible on up to $1 million of loans secured by the residence if such loans were used to acquire, construct, or substantially improve a principal residence or a second residence.

9. **(F)** Expenses incurred in the production of rental income (e.g., interest, taxes, depreciation, insurance, utilities) are deductible on Schedule E and are included in the computation of net rental income or loss.

Task-Based Simulation 5

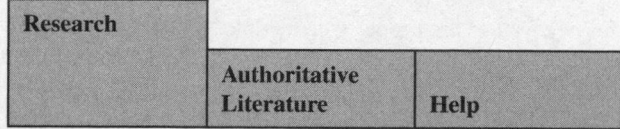

Internal Revenue Code Section 21, subsection (c) provides that the maximum amount of employment-related expenses that qualify for a credit is limited to $3,000 for one qualifying individual.

	Section	Subsection
§	21	(c)

Task-Based Simulation 6

Deductibility		
	Authoritative Literature	Help

	For AGI (A)	From AGI (No 2%) (B)	From AGI (2% Floor) (C)	Not ded. (D)
1. Smith paid the medical expenses of his mother-in-law. Although Smith provided more than half of her support, she does not qualify as Smith's dependent because she had gross income of $5,000.	○	●	○	○
2. Smith paid the real estate taxes on his rental apartment building.	●	○	○	○
3. Smith paid state sales taxes of $1,500 on a used automobile that he purchased for personal use.	○	●	○	○
4. Smith paid the real estate taxes on his mother-in-law's home. She is the owner of the home.	○	○	○	●
5. Smith paid $1,500 of interest on credit card charges. The charges were for items purchased for personal use.	○	○	○	●
6. Smith paid an attorney $500 to prepare Smith's will.	○	○	○	●
7. Smith incurred $750 of expenses for business meals and entertainment in his position as an employee of Patton Corporation. Smith's expenses were not reimbursed.	○	○	●	○
8. Smith paid self-employment taxes of $3,000 as a result of earnings from the consulting business that he conducts as a sole proprietor.	●	○	○	○
9. Smith made a contribution to his self-employed retirement plan (Keogh Plan).	●	○	○	○
10. Smith had gambling losses totaling $2,500 for the year. He is including a lottery prize of $5,000 in his gross income this year.	○	●	○	○

Explanations

1. **(B)** Deductible medical expenses include amounts paid for the diagnosis, cure, relief, treatment or prevention of disease of the taxpayer, spouse, and dependents. The term **dependent** includes any person who qualifies as a dependency exemption, or would otherwise qualify as a dependency exemption except that the gross income and joint return tests are not met. Therefore, the medical expenses of Smith's mother-in-law are properly deductible from Smith's AGI and are not subject to the 2% limitation.

2. **(A)** Expenses attributable to property held for the production of rents or royalties are properly deductible "above the line." "Above the line" deductions are subtracted from gross income to determine adjusted gross income. Therefore, expenses incurred from a passive activity such as Smith's rental apartment building are deductible for AGI.

3. **(B)** For 2015, an individual may elect to deduct state and local general sales taxes in lieu of state and local income taxes. The amount that can be deducted is either the total of actual general sales taxes paid as substantiated by receipts, or an amount from IRS-provided tables, plus the amount of general sales taxes paid with regard to the purchase of a motor vehicle, boat, and specified other items.

4. **(D)** Real estate (real property) taxes are deductible only if imposed on property owned by the taxpayer. Since Smith's mother-in-law is the legal owner of the house, Smith cannot deduct his payment of those real estate taxes.

5. **(D)** No deduction is allowed for personal interest.

6. **(D)** Personal legal expenses are not a deductible expense. Only legal counsel obtained for advice concerning tax matters or incurred in the production of income are deductible. Therefore, Smith cannot deduct the $500 incurred to prepare his will.

7. **(C)** Unreimbursed employee expenses including business meals and entertainment (subject to the 50% rule) are deductible to the extent they exceed 2% of AGI. Therefore, $375 ($750 × 50%) is deductible from AGI, subject to the 2% floor.

8. **(A)** An individual is allowed to deduct a portion of the self-employment tax paid for the taxable year in the computation of AGI. Normally, 50% of the self-employment tax paid is deductible for AGI.

9. **(A)** Contributions by self-employed individuals to a qualified retirement plan (Keogh Plan) are a deduction for AGI.

10. **(B)** Gambling losses to the extent of gambling winnings are categorized as miscellaneous deductions not subject to the 2% floor. Therefore, the $2,500 of Smith's gambling losses would be deductible in full since he properly included his $5,000 winnings in his gross income for 2015.

Task-Based Simulation 7

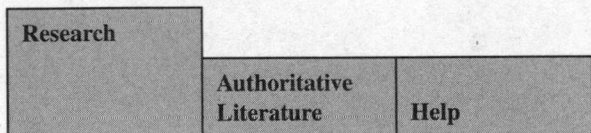

Internal Revenue Code Section 213, subsection (a) provides that the unreimbursed medical expenses of a taxpayer, spouse, and dependents are deductible to the extent in excess of 10% of adjusted gross income.

Task-Based Simulation 8

Adjusted Gross Income		
	Authoritative Literature	**Help**

	(A)	(B)	(C)	(D)	(E)	(F)	(G)	(H)	(I)	(J)	(K)	(L)	(M)
1. During 2015, Dale received a $30,000 cash gift from her aunt.	●	○	○	○	○	○	○	○	○	○	○	○	○
2. Dale contributed $3,500 to her traditional Individual Retirement Account (IRA) on January 15, 2015. In 2015, she earned $60,000 as a university instructor. During 2015 the Cumacks were not active participants in an employer's qualified pension or annuity plan.	○	○	○	○	●	○	○	○	○	○	○	○	○
3. In 2015, the Cumacks received a $1,000 federal income tax refund.	●	○	○	○	○	○	○	○	○	○	○	○	○
4. During 2015, Frank, a 50% partner in Diske General Partnership, received a $4,000 guaranteed payment from Diske for services that he rendered to the partnership that year.	○	○	○	○	○	●	○	○	○	○	○	○	○
5. In 2015, Frank received $10,000 as beneficiary of his deceased brother's life insurance policy.	●	○	○	○	○	○	○	○	○	○	○	○	○
6. Dale's employer pays 100% of the cost of all employees' group-term life insurance under a qualified plan. Policy cost is $5 per $1,000 of coverage. Dale's group-term life insurance coverage equals $450,000.	○	○	●	○	○	○	○	○	○	○	○	○	○
7. In 2015, Frank won $5,000 at a casino and had $2,000 in gambling losses.	○	○	○	○	○	○	●	○	○	○	○	○	○
8. During 2015, the Cumacks received $1,000 interest income associated with a refund of their prior years' federal income tax.	○	●	○	○	○	○	○	○	○	○	○	○	○
9. In 2015, the Cumacks sold their first and only residence for $400,000. They purchased their home in 1996 for $50,000 and have lived there since then. There were no other capital gains, losses, or capital loss carryovers. The Cumacks do not intend to buy another residence.	●	○	○	○	○	○	○	○	○	○	○	○	○
10. In 2015, Zeno Corp. declared a stock dividend and Dale received one additional share of Zeno common stock for three shares of Zeno common stock that she held. The stock that Dale received had a fair market value of $9,000. There was no provision to receive cash instead of stock.	●	○	○	○	○	○	○	○	○	○	○	○	○

Explanations

1. (A) Amounts received as a gift are fully excluded from gross income.

2. (E) The maximum deduction for contributions to a traditional IRA by an individual at least age 50 is the lesser of $6,500, or 100% of compensation for 2015. Since the Cumacks were not active participants in an employer's qualified pension or annuity plan, there is no phase-out of the deduction based on AGI.

3. (A) Since federal income taxes are not deductible in computing a taxpayer's federal income tax liability, a refund of federal income taxes is excluded from gross income.

4. (F) Guaranteed payments are partnership payments to partners for services rendered or for the use of capital without regard to partnership income. A guaranteed payment is deductible by the partnership, and the receipt of a guaranteed payment must be included in the partner's gross income, and is reported as self-employment income in the computation of the partner's self-employment tax.

5. (A) The proceeds of life insurance policies paid by reason of death of the insured are generally excluded from the beneficiary's gross income.

6. (C) An employer's payment of the cost of the first $50,000 of coverage for group-term life insurance can be excluded from an employee's gross income. Since Dale's employer provided group-term insurance of $450,000, and the cost of coverage was $5 per $1,000 of coverage, $5 × 400 = $2,000, must be included in Dale's gross income.

7. (G) Gambling winnings must be included in gross income. Gambling losses cannot be offset against gambling winnings, but instead are deducted from AGI as a miscellaneous itemized deduction limited in amount to the gambling winnings included in gross income.

8. (B) Although a federal income tax refund can be excluded from gross income, interest on the refund must be included in gross income.

9. (A) Up to $250,000 of gain can be excluded from gross income if an individual owned and occupied a residence as a principal residence for an aggregate of at least two of the five years preceding sale. The excludable gain is increased to $500,000 for married individuals filing jointly if either spouse meets the ownership requirement, and both spouses meet the use requirement.

10. (A) Stock dividends are generally excluded from gross income because a shareholder's relative interest in earnings and assets is unaffected.

Task-Based Simulation 9

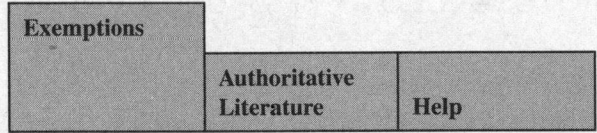

(O) (U) (C)

The Cumacks claimed three exemptions on their 2015 joint income tax return.   ● ○ ○

Explanation

(O) To qualify as a dependency exemption, a dependent must be a US citizen or resident of the US, Canada, or Mexico. Since Dale's father, Jacques, is both a French citizen and French resident, he does not qualify as a dependency exemption even though the Cumacks provided all of his support.

Task-Based Simulation 10

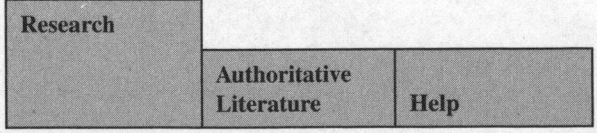

Internal Revenue Code Section 165, subsection (h) provides that an individual's personal casualty loss is allowable to the extent that it exceeds $100 and that a net personal casualty loss is deductible to the extent that it exceeds 10% of adjusted gross income.

Task-Based Simulation 11

Filing Status		
	Authoritative Literature	Help

For **items 1 and 2,** candidates were asked to determine the filing status and number of exemptions for Mrs. Vick.

1. **(M, 4)** Since Mr. Vick died during the year, Mrs. Vick is considered married for the entire year for filing status purposes. There would be four exemptions on the Vicks' joint return—one each for Mr. and Mrs. Vick, one for their 11-year-old daughter Joan, and one for Mrs. Vick's unmarried cousin Fran Phillips. Although Fran is treated as unrelated to the Vicks for dependency exemption purposes, Fran qualifies as a dependency exemption because the Vicks' residence was Fran's principal home for 2014.

2. **(Q, 3)** Mrs. Vick will file as a "qualifying widow with dependent child" which will entitle her to use the joint return rates for 2015. This filing status is available for the two years following the year of the spouse's death if (1) the surviving spouse was eligible to file a joint return in the year of the spouse's death, (2) does not remarry before the end of the taxable year, and (3) the surviving spouse pays over 50% of the cost of maintaining a household that is the principal home for the entire year of the surviving spouse's dependent child. There will be three exemptions on the return—one for Mrs. Vick, a dependency exemption for her daughter Joan, and a dependency exemption for her cousin Fran.

For **items 3 through 9,** candidates were asked to determine the amount that is taxable and should be included in Adjusted Gross Income (AGI) on the 2014 federal income tax return filed by Mrs. Vick.

3. **($0)** State disability benefits are excluded from gross income.

4. **($400)** The $50 interest on the tax refund and $350 interest from a savings account and certificates of deposit are taxable; the $100 interest on municipal bonds is excluded from gross income.

5. **($900)** The pension benefits are fully taxable because they were paid for exclusively by Mr. Vick's employer.

6. **($0)** Property received as a gift is always excluded from gross income.

7. **($0)** The proceeds of life insurance paid because of Mr. Vick's death are excluded from gross income, without regard to the amount of premiums paid.

8. **($200)** Jury duty pay represents compensation for services and must be included in gross income.

9. **($450)** The $450 of gambling winnings must be included in gross income. Mrs. Vick's $100 of gambling losses are deductible only from AGI as a miscellaneous itemized deduction.

Task-Based Simulation 12

Tax Treatment		
	Authoritative Literature	Help

For **items 1 through 14,** candidates were asked to select the appropriate tax treatment for the payments made or losses incurred by Mrs. Vick for 2014.

	(A)	(B)	(C)	(D)	(E)	(F)
1. Premiums on Mr. Vick's personal life insurance policy.	●	○	○	○	○	○
2. Penalty on Mrs. Vick's early withdrawal of funds from a certificate of deposit.	○	○	○	●	○	○
3. Mrs. Vick's substantiated cash donation to the American Red Cross.	○	○	○	○	○	●
4. Payment of estimated state income taxes.	○	○	○	○	●	○
5. Payment of real estate taxes on the Vick home.	○	○	○	○	●	○
6. Loss on the sale of the family car.	●	○	○	○	○	○

	(A)	(B)	(C)	(D)	(E)	(F)
7. Cost in excess of the increase in value of residence, for the installation of a stair lift in January 2014, related directly to the medical care of Mr. Vick.	○	●	○	○	○	○
8. The Vicks' health insurance premiums for hospitalization coverage.	○	●	○	○	○	○
9. CPA fees to prepare the 2013 tax return.	○	○	●	○	○	○
10. Amortization over the life of the loan of points paid to refinance the mortgage at a lower rate on the Vick home.	○	○	○	○	●	○
11. One-half the self-employment tax paid by Mrs. Vick.	○	○	○	●	○	○
12. Mrs. Vick's $100 in gambling losses.	○	○	○	○	●	○
13. Mrs. Vick's union dues.	○	○	●	○	○	○
14. 2013 federal income tax paid with the Vicks' tax return on April 15, 2014.	●	○	○	○	○	○

Explanations

1. (**A**) Life insurance premiums are considered a personal expense and are not deductible.

2. (**D**) An interest forfeiture penalty for making an early withdrawal from a certificate of deposit is deductible on page 1 of Form 1040 to arrive at adjusted gross income.

3. (**F**) Charitable contributions are generally deductible as an itemized deduction up to a **maximum of 50% of AGI**.

4. (**E**) Estimated state income tax payments are deductible in full as an itemized deduction on Schedule A.

5. (**E**) Real estate taxes on a principal residence are deductible in full as an itemized deduction on Schedule A.

6. (**A**) A family car is a personal use asset and a loss from its sale is not deductible. The only type of loss that can be deducted on a personal use asset is a casualty or theft loss.

7. (**B**) A capital expenditure made for medical reasons that improves a residence is deductible as a medical expense to the extent that the expenditure exceeds the increase in value of the residence. As a medical expense, the excess expenditure is deductible as an itemized deduction on Schedule A subject to a 10% of AGI threshold.

8. (**B**) Health insurance premiums qualify as a medical expense and are deductible as an itemized deduction on Schedule A subject to a 10% of AGI threshold.

9. (**C**) Tax return preparation fees are deductible as an itemized deduction on Schedule A subject to a 2% of AGI threshold.

10. (**E**) Points paid to refinance a mortgage are deductible as interest expense over the term of the loan. Interest expense on a personal residence is deductible as an itemized deduction on Schedule A.

11. (**D**) Normally, one-half of a self-employed taxpayer's self-employment tax is deductible on page 1 of Form 1040 to arrive at AGI.

12. (**E**) Gambling losses are deductible as a miscellaneous itemized deduction on Schedule A to the extent that the taxpayer's gambling winnings are included in gross income. Since Mrs. Vick reported $450 of gambling winnings, her $100 of gambling losses are deductible.

13. (**C**) Unreimbursed employee expenses (including union dues) are generally deductible as miscellaneous itemized deductions on Schedule A subject to a 2% of AGI threshold.

14. (**A**) A payment of federal income tax is not deductible in computing a taxpayer's taxable income.

Task-Based Simulation 13

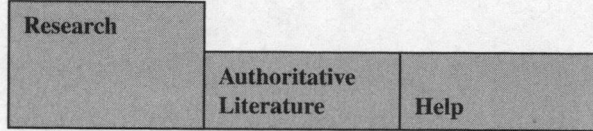

Internal Revenue Code Section 529, subsection (c) provides that any contribution to a qualified tuition program on behalf of a beneficiary shall be treated as a completed gift and not a gift of a future interest in property.

Task-Based Simulation 14

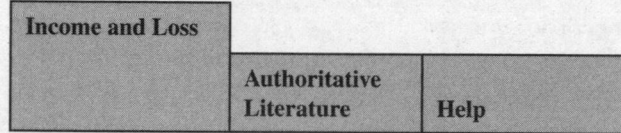

1. **($3,000)** The Moores have a net capital loss of $6,000, of which $3,000 can be currently deducted, with the remaining $3,000 carried forward as a STCL.

2. **($0)** Joan received the land as a gift, and her basis for gain is the land's adjusted basis of $60,000, while her basis for loss is the land's $50,000 fair market value on date of gift. Joan recognizes no gain or loss on the sale because she sold the land for $56,000 and the use of her basis for gain ($60,000) does not result in a gain, and the use of her basis for loss ($50,000) does not result in a loss.

3. **($0)** The security deposit is not treated as rent and only will be included in gross income when not returned to the tenant.

4. **($55,000)** Tom's compensation consists of the wages of $53,000 plus the $2,000 value of group-term life insurance coverage in excess of $50,000.

5. **($1,250)** Since the Moores' itemized deductions exceeded their available standard deduction by $1,450, all $1,250 of the state income tax refund must be included in gross income for 2015 because its deduction in 2014 reduced the Moores' federal income tax.

6. **($1,300)** Unemployment compensation is generally taxable.

7. **($2,500)** The net rental income is computed on Schedule E and reported on page 1 of Form 1040.

8. **($900)** Although generally nontaxable, a stock dividend will be taxable if any shareholder can elect to receive the distribution in either stock or in property. The amount of dividend is equal to the stock's $900 fair market value on date of distribution.

9. **($3,500)** The $5,000 employee death benefit exclusion was repealed for decedents dying after August 20, 1996.

10. **($5,000)** The accrued interest on redeemed Series EE US savings bonds can be excluded from gross income to the extent that the aggregate redemption proceeds (principal plus interest) are used to finance the higher education expenses (tuition and fees) of the taxpayer, taxpayer's spouse, or dependents. Here, there is no interest exclusion available for Tom because the proceeds were used to pay for Laura's tuition, and Laura does not qualify as Tom's dependent.

Task-Based Simulation 15

Tax Treatment		
	Authoritative Literature	**Help**

(A) (B) (C) (D) (E) (F)

1. On March 23, 2015, Tom sold fifty shares of Zip stock at a $1,200 loss. He repurchased fifty shares of Zip on April 15, 2015.
● ○ ○ ○ ○ ○

2. Payment of a personal property tax based on the value of the Moores' car.
○ ● ○ ○ ○ ○

3. Used clothes were donated to church organizations.
○ ○ ○ ● ○ ○

4. Premiums were paid covering insurance against Tom's loss of earnings.
● ○ ○ ○ ○ ○

5. Tom paid for subscriptions to accounting journals.
○ ○ ○ ○ ○ ●

6. Interest was paid on a $10,000 home-equity line of credit secured by the Moores' residence. The fair market value of the home exceeded the mortgage by $50,000. Tom used the proceeds to purchase a sailboat.
○ ● ○ ○ ○ ○

7. Amounts were paid in excess of insurance reimbursement for prescription drugs.
○ ○ ● ○ ○ ○

8. Funeral expenses were paid by the Moores for Joan's brother.
● ○ ○ ○ ○ ○

9. Theft loss was incurred on Joan's jewelry in excess of insurance reimbursement. There were no 2015 personal casualty gains.
○ ○ ○ ○ ● ○

10. Loss on the sale of the family's sailboat.
● ○ ○ ○ ○ ○

11. Interest was paid on the $300,000 acquisition mortgage on the Moores' home. The mortgage is secured by their home.
○ ● ○ ○ ○ ○

12. Joan performed free accounting services for the Red Cross. The estimated value of the services was $500.
● ○ ○ ○ ○ ○

Explanations

1. (A) No loss is deductible if stock is sold at a loss and within thirty days before or after the sale, substantially identical stock in the same corporation is purchased. Here, the loss on the March 23 sale of 50 shares of Zip stock cannot be recognized because Tom repurchased fifty shares of Zip stock on April 15. The $1,200 loss not recognized is added to the basis of the newly acquired stock.

2. (B) Personal property taxes based on value are fully deductible as an itemized deduction.

3. (D) The fair market value of used clothing donated to a qualified charitable organization is deductible as an itemized deduction subject to a 50% of AGI limitation.

4. (A) Premiums on insurance against the loss of earnings in the event of disability are a nondeductible personal expense.

5. (F) Since Tom is a CPA working as an employee, the unreimbursed cost of subscriptions to accounting journals is deductible as an itemized deduction subject to a threshold of 2% of AGI.

6. (B) Interest on home-equity indebtedness of up to $100,000 is fully deductible as an itemized deduction regardless of how the proceeds of the loan were used.

7. (C) The unreimbursed cost of prescriptions qualify as a medical expense deductible as an itemized deduction subject to a threshold of 10% of AGI.

8. (A) Funeral expenses are a nondeductible personal expense.

9. (E) A theft loss on personal use property is deductible as an itemized deduction subject to a $100 floor and a threshold of 10% of AGI.

10. (A) A loss resulting from the sale of personal use property is not deductible.

11. (B) Interest on acquisition indebtedness of up to $1 million is fully deductible as an itemized deduction if the mortgage is secured by the taxpayer's principal or second residence.

12. (A) No charitable deduction is allowable for the value of a taxpayer's services performed for a charitable organization.

Task-Based Simulation 16

Internal Revenue Code Section 56, subsection (b) provides the adjustments to regular taxable income that are applicable only to individuals when computing the alternative minimum tax.

Task-Based Simulation 17

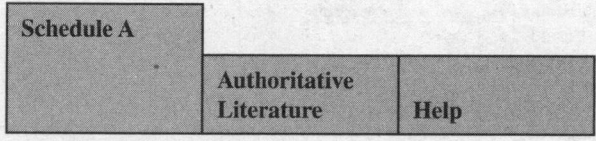

(See Schedule A on the next page)

Medical and Dental Expenses

The disability income insurance premiums do not represent medical insurance and are not deductible. Similarly, although prescription drugs are deductible, nonprescription medicine is not deductible.

Taxes

The automobile registration fee is not deductible.

Interest

Only home mortgage interest and investment interest expense can be deducted as an itemized deduction. The interest on the automobile loan and the credit card interest are considered personal interest and are not deductible.

Contributions

The stock was appreciated and held for more than one year so it qualifies as capital gain property. As a result, the amount of contribution is the stock's fair market value of $4,000.

Miscellaneous

The legal fee for preparation of a will and life insurance premiums are nondeductible personal expenses. Similarly, no deduction is available for transportation to and from work (commuting), political contributions, and repairs to a principal residence.

SCHEDULE A (Form 1040) Department of the Treasury Internal Revenue Service (99)	Itemized Deductions ► Information about Schedule A and its separate instructions is at *www.irs.gov/schedulea*. ► Attach to Form 1040.	OMB No. 1545-0074 2014 Attachment Sequence No. 07

Name(s) shown on Form 1040   Fred & Laura Shaw   Your social security number   123-67-5489

Medical and Dental Expenses		**Caution.** Do not include expenses reimbursed or paid by others.			
	1	Medical and dental expenses (see instructions)	1	8,405	
	2	Enter amount from Form 1040, line 38 **2** 80,000			
	3	Multiply line 2 by 10% (.10). But if either you or your spouse was born before January 2, 1950, multiply line 2 by 7.5% (.075) instead	3	8,000	
	4	Subtract line 3 from line 1. If line 3 is more than line 1, enter -0-		**4**	405
Taxes You Paid	5	State and local (**check only one box**): a ☑ Income taxes, **or** ⎫ b ☐ General sales taxes ⎭	5	1,200	
	6	Real estate taxes (see instructions)	6	10,000	
	7	Personal property taxes	7		
	8	Other taxes. List type and amount ► _____ Personal property taxes _____	8	410	
	9	Add lines 5 through 8		**9**	11,610
Interest You Paid **Note.** Your mortgage interest deduction may be limited (see instructions).	10	Home mortgage interest and points reported to you on Form 1098	10	7,700	
	11	Home mortgage interest not reported to you on Form 1098. If paid to the person from whom you bought the home, see instructions and show that person's name, identifying no., and address ► _____ _____	11		
	12	Points not reported to you on Form 1098. See instructions for special rules	12		
	13	Mortgage insurance premiums (see instructions)	13		
	14	Investment interest. Attach Form 4952 if required. (See instructions.)	14		
	15	Add lines 10 through 14		**15**	7,700
Gifts to Charity If you made a gift and got a benefit for it, see instructions.	16	Gifts by cash or check. If you made any gift of $250 or more, see instructions	16	2,500	
	17	Other than by cash or check. If any gift of $250 or more, see instructions. You **must** attach Form 8283 if over $500 . . .	17	4,000	
	18	Carryover from prior year	18		
	19	Add lines 16 through 18		**19**	6,500
Casualty and Theft Losses	20	Casualty or theft loss(es). Attach Form 4684. (See instructions.)		**20**	
Job Expenses and Certain Miscellaneous Deductions	21	Unreimbursed employee expenses—job travel, union dues, job education, etc. Attach Form 2106 or 2106-EZ if required. (See instructions.) ► _____	21	1,500	
	22	Tax preparation fees	22	400	
	23	Other expenses—investment, safe deposit box, etc. List type and amount ► Subscriptions $300; safe deposit box $120 ____	23	420	
	24	Add lines 21 through 23	24	2,320	
	25	Enter amount from Form 1040, line 38 **25** 80,000			
	26	Multiply line 25 by 2% (.02)	26	1,600	
	27	Subtract line 26 from line 24. If line 26 is more than line 24, enter -0-		**27**	720
Other Miscellaneous Deductions	28	Other—from list in instructions. List type and amount ► _____ _____		**28**	
Total Itemized Deductions	29	Is Form 1040, line 38, over $152,525? ☑ **No.** Your deduction is not limited. Add the amounts in the far right column for lines 4 through 28. Also, enter this amount on Form 1040, line 40. ⎫ ☐ **Yes.** Your deduction may be limited. See the Itemized Deductions Worksheet in the instructions to figure the amount to enter. ⎭		**29**	26,935
	30	If you elect to itemize deductions even though they are less than your standard deduction, check here . . . . ► ☐			

Task-Based Simulation 18

Internal Revenue Code Section 170, subsection (e) provides that the amount of the Shaws' charitable contribution will be limited to the painting's cost of $90,000, since the painting would not result in long-term capital gain if sold (i.e., it has not been held for more than 12 months).

Section	Subsection
§ 170	(e)

Module 36: Transactions in Property

Overview

This module presents the income tax consequences of property transactions including the sale, exchange, or other disposition of property. Basis is covered first with a review of the basis of property acquired by purchase, gift, and from a decedent. Tax-deferred transactions are covered next with a review of like-kind exchanges, involuntary conversions, and the sale of a principal residence. Next, sales and exchanges of securities are reviewed as well as the treatment of losses and expenses incurred in transactions with related taxpayers. Finally, capital gains and losses, as well as gains and losses from business property including Sec. 1231

and depreciation recapture are reviewed. Not only is it important to determine the extent of gain or loss recognition, but it is also important to be able to determine whether the character of the recognized gain or loss is capital, Sec. 1231, or ordinary.

A. Sales and Other Dispositions

A sale or other disposition is a transaction that generally gives rise to the recognition of gain or loss. Gains or losses may be categorized as ordinary or capital. If an exchange is nontaxable, the recognition of gain or loss is generally deferred until a later sale of the newly acquired property. This is accomplished by giving the property received the basis of the old property exchanged.

1. The **basis of property** to determine gain or loss is generally its cost or purchase price.

   a. The **cost** of property is the amount paid for it in cash or the FMV of other property, plus expenses connected with the purchase such as abstract of title fees, installation of utility services, legal fees (including title search, contract, and deed fees), recording fees, surveys, transfer taxes, owner's title insurance, and any amounts the seller owes that the buyer agrees to pay (e.g., back taxes and interest, recording or mortgage fees, charges for improvements or repairs, sales commissions).

   b. If property is acquired subject to a debt, or the purchaser assumes a debt, this debt is also included in cost.

EXAMPLE

Susan purchased a parcel of land by paying cash of $30,000 and assuming a mortgage of $60,000. She also paid $400 for a title insurance policy on the land. Susan's basis for the land is $90,400.

---

   c. If **acquired by gift,** the basis for gain is the basis of the donor (transferred basis) increased by any gift tax paid attributable to the net appreciation in the value of the gift.

   (1) Basis for loss is lesser of gain basis (above), or FMV on date of gift.

   (2) Because of this rule, no gain or loss is recognized when use of the basis for computing loss results in a gain, and use of the basis for computing gain results in a loss.

> **EXAMPLE**
>
> Jill received a boat from her father as a gift. Father's adjusted basis was $10,000 and FMV was $8,000 at date of gift. Jill's basis for gain is $10,000, while her basis for loss is $8,000. If Jill later sells the boat for $9,200, no gain or loss will be recognized.

(3) The increase in basis for gift tax paid is limited to the amount (not to exceed the gift tax paid) that bears the same ratio to the amount of gift tax paid as the net appreciation in value of the gift bears to the amount of the gift.

    (a) The amount of gift is reduced by any portion of the $14,000 annual exclusion allowable with respect to the gift.

    (b) Where more than one gift of a present interest is made to the same donee during a calendar year, the $14,000 exclusion is applied to gifts in chronological order.

> **EXAMPLE**
>
> Tom received a gift of property with an FMV of $104,000 and an adjusted basis of $74,000. The donor paid a gift tax of $18,000 on the transfer. Tom's basis for the property would be $80,000 determined as follows:
>
> $$\$74{,}000 \text{ basis} + \left[\$18{,}000 \text{ gift tax} \times \frac{(\$104{,}000 \text{ FMV} - \$74{,}000 \text{ basis})}{(\$104{,}000 \text{ FMV} - \$14{,}000 \text{ exclusion})} \right] = \$80{,}000$$

d. If **acquired from decedent,** basis is property's FMV on date of decedent's death, or alternate valuation date (generally six months after death).

    (1) Use FMV on date of disposition if alternate valuation is elected and property is distributed, sold, or otherwise disposed of during six-month period following death.

> **EXAMPLE**
>
> Ann received 100 shares of stock as an inheritance from her uncle Henry, who died January 20, 2015. The stock had an FMV of $40,000 on January 20, and an FMV of $30,000 on July 20, 2015. The stock's FMV was $34,000 on June 15, 2015, the date the stock was distributed to Ann.
>
> If the alternate valuation is not elected, or no estate tax return is filed, Ann's basis for the stock is its FMV of $40,000 on the date of Henry's death. If the alternate valuation is elected, Ann's basis will be the stock's $34,000 FMV on June 15 (the date of distribution) since the stock was distributed to Ann within six months after the decedent's death.

    (2) FMV rule not applicable to appreciated property acquired by the decedent by gift within one year before death if such property then passes from the donee-decedent to the original donor or donor's spouse. The basis of such property to the original donor (or spouse) will be the adjusted basis of the property to the decedent immediately before death.

    (3) The portion of jointly held property that is included in a decedent's estate is considered to be acquired from the decedent (i.e., its basis is FMV on date of death, or the alternate valuation). The basis for the portion of jointly held property not included in a decedent's estate is its cost or other basis.

NOW REVIEW MULTIPLE-CHOICE QUESTIONS 1 THROUGH 13

e. The basis of **stock received as a dividend** depends upon whether it was included in income when received.

   (1) If included in income, basis is its FMV at date of distribution.

   (2) If nontaxable when received, the basis of shareholder's original stock is allocated between the dividend stock and the original stock in proportion to their relative FMVs. The holding period of the dividend stock includes the holding period of the original stock.

EXAMPLE

T owns 100 shares of XYZ Corp. common stock that was acquired in 2010 for $12,000. In 2015, T received a nontaxable distribution of 10 XYZ Corp. preferred shares. At date of distribution the FMV of the 100 common shares was $15,000, and the FMV of the 10 preferred shares was $5,000. The portion of the $12,000 basis allocated to the preferred and common shares would be

$$\text{Preferred} = \frac{\$5,000}{\$20,000} \ (\$12,000) = \$3,000$$

$$\text{Common} = \frac{\$15,000}{\$20,000} \ (\$12,000) = \$9,000$$

---

f. The basis of **stock rights** depends upon whether they were included in income when received.

   (1) If rights were nontaxable and allowed to expire, they are deemed to have no basis and no loss can be deducted.

   (2) If rights were nontaxable and exercised or sold

      (a) Basis is zero if FMV of rights is less than 15% of FMV of stock, unless taxpayer elects to allocate basis

      (b) If FMV of rights at date of receipt is at least 15% of FMV of stock, or if taxpayer elects, basis is

$$\frac{\text{FMV of rights}}{\text{FMV of rights} + \text{FMV stock}} \times (\text{Basis in stock})$$

   (3) If rights were taxable and included in income, basis is their FMV at date of distribution.

g. Detailed rules for basis are included in following discussions of exchanges and involuntary conversions.

2. In a sale, the gain or loss is generally the difference between

a. The cash or fair market value received, and the adjusted basis of the property sold

b. If the property sold is mortgaged (or encumbered by any other debt) and the buyer assumes or takes the property subject to the debt

   (1) Include the amount of the debt in the amount realized because the seller is relieved of the obligation

---

EXAMPLE

Property with a $10,000 mortgage, and a basis of $15,000, is sold for $10,000 cash and buyer assumes the mortgage. The amount realized is $20,000, and the gain is $5,000.

---

   (2) If the amount of the mortgage exceeds basis, use the same rules.

EXAMPLE

Property with a $15,000 mortgage, and a basis of $10,000, is given away subject to the mortgage. The amount realized is $15,000, and the gain is $5,000.

c. Casual sellers of property (as opposed to dealers) reduce selling price by any selling expenses.

> **NOW REVIEW MULTIPLE-CHOICE QUESTIONS 14 THROUGH 16**

3. In a **taxable exchange,** the gain or loss is the difference between the adjusted basis of the property exchanged and the FMV of the property received. The basis of property received in a taxable exchange is its FMV.
4. **Nontaxable exchanges** generally are not taxed in the current period. Questions concerning nontaxable exchanges often require a determination of the basis of property received, and the effect of boot on the recognition of gain.

   a. **Like-kind exchange**—an exchange of business or investment property for property of a like-kind

      (1) Does not apply to property held for personal use, inventory, stocks, bonds, notes, intangible evidences of ownership, and interests in a partnership
      (2) Property held for business use may be exchanged for investment property or vice versa.
      (3) Like-kind means "same class of property."

         (a) Real property must be exchanged for real property; personal property must be exchanged for personal property within the same General Asset Class or within the same Product Class. For example

            [1] Land held for investment exchanged for apartment building
            [2] Real estate exchanged for a lease on real estate to run thirty years or more
            [3] Truck exchanged for a truck

         (b) Exchange of personal property for real property does not qualify.
         (c) Exchange of US real property for foreign real property does not qualify.

      (4) To qualify as a like-kind exchange (1) the property to be received must be identified within 45 days after the date on which the old property is relinquished, and (2) the exchange must be completed within 180 days after the date on which the old property is relinquished, but not later than the due date of the tax return (including extensions) for the year that the old property is relinquished.
      (5) The **basis of like-kind property received** is the basis of like-kind property given.

         (a) + Gain recognized
         (b) + Basis of boot given (money or property not of a like-kind)
         (c) – Loss recognized
         (d) – FMV of boot received

      (6) If unlike property (i.e., boot) is received, its basis will be its FMV on the date of the exchange.
      (7) If property is exchanged solely for other like-kind property, no gain or loss is recognized. The basis of the property received is the same as the basis of the property transferred.
      (8) If boot (money or property not of a like-kind) is given, no gain or loss is generally recognized. However, gain or loss is recognized if the boot given consists of property with an FMV different from its basis.

EXAMPLE

Land held for investment plus shares of stock are exchanged for investment real estate with an FMV of $13,000. The land transferred had an adjusted basis of $10,000 and FMV of $11,000; the stock had an adjusted basis of $5,000 and FMV of $2,000. A $3,000 loss is recognized on the transfer of stock. The basis of the acquired real estate is $12,000 ($10,000 + $5,000 basis of boot given – $3,000 loss recognized).

---

   (9) **If boot is received**

      (a) Any realized gain is recognized to the extent of the lesser of (1) the realized gain, or (2) the FMV of the boot received
      (b) No loss is recognized due to the receipt of boot

EXAMPLE

Land held for investment with a basis of $10,000 was exchanged for other investment real estate with an FMV of $9,000, an automobile with an FMV of $2,000, and $1,500 in cash. The realized gain is $2,500. Even though $3,500 of "boot" was received, the recognized gain is only $2,500 (limited to the realized gain). The basis of the automobile (unlike property) is its FMV $2,000; while the basis of the real estate acquired is $9,000 ($10,000 + $2,500 gain recognized – $3,500 boot received).

---

(10) **Liabilities** assumed (or liabilities to which property exchanged is subject) on either or both sides of the exchange are treated as boot.

    (a) Boot received—if the liability was assumed by the other party

    (b) Boot given—if the taxpayer assumed a liability on the property acquired

    (c) If liabilities are assumed on both sides of the exchange, they are offset to determine the net amount of boot given or received.

EXAMPLE

A owns investment land with an adjusted basis of $50,000, FMV of $70,000, but which is subject to a mortgage of $15,000. B owns investment land with an adjusted basis of $60,000, FMV of $65,000, but which is subject to a mortgage of $10,000. A and B exchange real estate investments with A assuming B's $10,000 mortgage, and B assuming A's $15,000 mortgage. The computation of realized gain, recognized gain, and basis for the acquired real estate for both A and B is as follows:

	A		B
FMV of real estate received	$65,000		$70,000
+ Liability on old real estate assumed by other party (boot received)	15,000	(1)	10,000
Amount realized on the exchange	$80,000		$80,000
– Adjusted basis of old real estate transferred	–50,000		– 60,000
– Liability assumed by taxpayer on new real estate (boot given)	–10,000	(2)	– 15,000
Gain realized	$20,000		$5,000
Gain recognized (1) minus (2)	$5,000		$--
Basis of old real estate transferred	$50,000		$60,000
+ Liability assumed by taxpayer on new real estate (boot given)	10,000		15,000
+ Gain recognized	5,000		--
– Liability on old real estate assumed by other party (boot received)	–15,000		– 10,000
Basis of new real estate acquired	$50,000		$65,000

    (d) Boot given in the form of an assumption of a liability does **not** offset boot received in the form of cash or unlike property; however, boot given in the form of cash or unlike property does offset boot received in the form of a liability assumed by the other party.

EXAMPLE

Assume the same facts as above except that the mortgage on B's old real estate was $6,000, and that A paid B cash of $4,000 to make up the difference. The tax effects to A remain unchanged. However, since the $4,000 cash cannot be offset by the liability assumed by B, B must recognize a gain of $4,000, and will have a basis of $69,000 for the new real estate.

---

(11) If within two years after a like-kind exchange between related persons [as defined in Sec. 267(b)] either person disposes of the property received in the exchange, any gain or loss that was not recognized on the exchange must be recognized (subject to the loss limitation rules for related persons) as of the date that the property was disposed of. This gain recognition rule does not apply if the subsequent disposition was the result of the death of one of the persons, an involuntary conversion, or where neither the exchange nor the disposition had tax avoidance as one of its principal purposes.

NOW REVIEW MULTIPLE-CHOICE QUESTIONS 17 THROUGH 22

---

b. **Involuntary conversions**

   (1) Occur when money or other property is received for property that has been destroyed, damaged, stolen, or condemned (even if property is transferred only under threat or imminence of condemnation).
   (2) If payment is received and gain is realized, taxpayer may **elect not to recognize gain** if converted property is replaced with property of similar or related use.

      (a) Gain is recognized only to the extent that the amount realized exceeds the cost of the replacement.
      (b) The **replacement** must be purchased within a **period** beginning with the earlier of the date of disposition or the date of threat of condemnation, and ending two years after the close of the taxable year in which gain is first **realized** (three years for condemned business or investment real property, other than inventory or property held primarily for resale).
      (c) **Basis of replacement property** is the cost of the replacement decreased by any gain not recognized.

EXAMPLE

Taxpayer had unimproved real estate (with an adjusted basis of $20,000) which was condemned by the county. The county paid him $24,000 and he reinvested $21,000 in unimproved real estate. $1,000 of the $4,000 realized gain would not be recognized. His tax basis in the new real estate would be $20,000 ($21,000 cost – $1,000 deferred gain).

EXAMPLE

Assume the same facts as above except the taxpayer reinvested $25,000 in unimproved real estate. None of the $4,000 realized gain would be recognized. His basis in the new real estate would be $21,000 ($25,000 cost – $4,000 deferred gain).

---

   (3) If property is converted directly into property similar or related in service or use, complete non recognition of gain is mandatory. The basis of replacement property is the same as the property converted.
   (4) The meaning of **property similar or related in service or use** is more restrictive than "like-kind."

      (a) For an owner-user—property must be functionally the same and have same end use (business vehicle must be replaced by business vehicle that performs same function).
      (b) For a lessor—property must perform same services for **lessor** (lessor could replace a rental manufacturing plant with a rental-wholesale grocery warehouse even though tenant's functional use differs).
      (c) A purchase of at least 80% of the stock of a corporation whose property is similar or related in service or use also qualifies.
      (d) More liberal "like-kind" test applies to real property held for business or investment (other than inventory or property held primarily for sale) that is converted by seizure, condemnation, or threat of condemnation (e.g., improved real estate could be replaced with unimproved real estate).

   (5) If property is not replaced within the time limit, an amended return is filed to recognize gain in the year realized.

(6) Losses on involuntary conversions are recognized whether the property is replaced or not. However, a loss on condemnation of property held for personal use (e.g., personal residence) is not deductible.

c. **Sale or exchange of principal residence**

(1) An individual may **exclude** from income up to **$250,000** of gain that is realized on the sale or exchange of a residence, if the individual owned and occupied the residence as a principal residence for an aggregate of *at least two of the five years* preceding the sale or exchange. The amount of excludable gain is increased to **$500,000** for married individuals filing jointly if either spouse meets the ownership requirement, and both spouses meet the use requirement.

   (a) The sale of a residence that had been jointly owned and occupied by the surviving and deceased spouse is entitled to the $500,000 gain exclusion provided the sale occurs no later than 2 years after the date of death of the individual's spouse.

   (b) The exclusion does not apply to property acquired in a like-kind exchange of the property occurs during the five-year period beginning with the date of acquisition of the property.

   (c) Gain in excess of the $250,000 (or $500,000) exclusion must be included in income even though the sale proceeds are reinvested in another principal residence.

(2) The exclusion is determined on an individual basis.

   (a) A single individual who otherwise qualifies for the exclusion is entitled to exclude up to $250,000 of gain even though the individual marries someone who has used the exclusion within two years before the marriage.

   (b) In the case of married taxpayers who do not share a principal residence but file joint returns, a $250,000 exclusion is available for a qualifying sale or exchange of each spouse's principal residence.

(3) Special rules apply to divorced taxpayers.

   (a) If a residence is transferred to a taxpayer incident to a divorce, the time during which the taxpayer's spouse or former spouse owned the residence is added to the taxpayer's period of ownership.

   (b) A taxpayer who owns a residence is deemed to use it as a principal residence while the taxpayer's spouse or former spouse is given use of the residence under the terms of a divorce or separation.

(4) A taxpayer's period of ownership of a residence includes the period during which the taxpayer's deceased spouse owned the residence so long as the taxpayer does not remarry before date of sale.

(5) Tenant-stockholders in a cooperative housing corporation can qualify to exclude gain from the sale of the stock.

(6) If the taxpayer does not meet the two-year ownership or use requirements, a pro rata amount of the $250,000 or $500,000 exclusion applies if the sale or exchange is due to a change in place of employment, health, or unforeseen circumstances. A taxpayer is deemed to satisfy the change in employment condition if the taxpayer moves at least fifty miles from his former place of employment, or if previously unemployed at least fifty miles from his former residence. To satisfy the change of health condition, the taxpayer must be instructed to relocate by a physician for health reasons (e.g., advanced age-related infirmities, severe allergies, emotional problems). Unforeseen circumstances include natural or man-made disasters such as war or acts of terrorism, cessation of employment, death, divorce or legal separation, and multiple births from the same pregnancy.

EXAMPLE

Harold, an unmarried taxpayer, purchased a home in a suburb of Chicago on October, 2013. Eighteen months later his employer transferred him to St. Louis and Harold sold his home for a gain of $200,000. Since Harold sold his home because of a change in place of employment and had owned and used the home as a principal residence for eighteen months, the exclusion of his gain is limited to $250,000 × 18/24 = $187,500.

---

(7) If a taxpayer was entitled to take depreciation deductions because the residence was used for business purposes or as rental property, the taxpayer cannot exclude gain to the extent of any depreciation allowed or allowable as a deduction after May 6, 1997.

> **EXAMPLE**
>
> Ron sold his principal residence during 2015 for a gain of $20,000. He used one room of the residence for business and deducted $1,000 of depreciation in 2014. Although Ron meets the ownership and use tests to exclude residence sale gain from income, he can exclude only $20,000 – $1,000 = $19,000 from income. The remaining $1,000 of gain is taxable and must be included in gross income.

(8) For sales and exchanges of a principal residence after 2008, the exclusion does not apply to the amount of gain allocated to periods of nonqualified use after December 31, 2008. *Nonqualified use* is generally any use other than as a principal residence.

    (a) Nonqualified use does not include (1) any portion of the 5-year period ending on the date of sale or exchange after the last use of the property as a principal residence; (2) any period of 10 years or less when the taxpayer or spouse is serving on extended duty in the military; and, (3) any period of two years or less for temporary absence due to a change of employment, health, or unforeseen circumstances.

    (b) To determine the amount of gain allocated to nonqualified use, multiply the gain by the following fraction:

$$\frac{\text{Total nonqualified use during period of ownership after 2008}}{\text{Total period of ownership}}$$

    (c) Any gain recognized because of post-May 6, 1997 depreciation [see (7) above] is not taken into account in determining the amount of gain allocated to nonqualified use.

> **EXAMPLE**
>
> On January 2, 2010, Diane buys a residence for $400,000 and uses it as rental property for two years, claiming $30,000 of depreciation deductions. On January 2, 2012, Diane converts the property to her principal residence. She moves out on January 11, 2014, and sells the property for $700,000 on January 2, 2015, resulting in a gain of $700,000 – $370,000 = $330,000.
>
> The $30,000 of gain that is attributable to depreciation deductions must be included in income. Of the remaining $300,000 of gain, 2 years/5 years × $300,000 = $120,000 of gain is allocated to nonqualified use and is not eligible for exclusion. Since the remaining gain of $300,000 – $120,000 = $180,000 does not exceed the maximum exclusion ($250,000), Diane can exclude a total of $180,000 of gain from gross income. As a result, Diane must include $330,000 – $180,000 = $150,000 in gross income. Finally, note that the period from January 11, 2014, to January 2, 2015, is after she last used the home as her principal residence so it is not a period of nonqualified use.

(9) Gain from the sale of a principal residence generally cannot be excluded from gross income if, during the two-year period ending on the date of the sale, the taxpayer sold another residence at a gain and excluded all or part of that gain from income. However, part of the gain may be excluded if the sale is due to a change in employment, health, or unforeseen circumstances. If the taxpayer cannot exclude the gain, it must be included in gross income.

> **EXAMPLE**
>
> In September 2012, Anna purchased a new principal residence. In November 2012, Anna sold her old residence for a gain of $50,000. Since she met the ownership and use tests, Anna excluded the $50,000 gain from gross income for 2012. On October 1, 2014, Anna sold the residence she had purchased in September 2012 for a gain of $30,000. The sale was not due to a change in place of employment, health, or unforeseen circumstances. Because Anna had excluded gain from the sale of another residence within the two-year period ending on October 1, 2014, she cannot exclude the gain on this sale.

(10) A loss from the sale of personal residence is not deductible.

d. **Exchange of insurance policies.** No gain or loss is recognized on an exchange of certain life, endowment, and annuity contracts to allow taxpayers to obtain better insurance.

> ## NOW REVIEW MULTIPLE-CHOICE QUESTIONS 23 THROUGH 26

---

5. **Sales and exchanges of securities**

   a. Stocks and bonds are not included under like-kind exchanges
   b. Exchange of stock of same corporation

      (1) Common for common, or preferred for preferred is nontaxable
      (2) Common for preferred, or preferred for common is taxable, unless exchange qualifies as a recapitalization

   c. Exercise of conversion privilege in convertible stock or bond is generally nontaxable.
   d. The first-in, first-out (FIFO) method is used to determine the basis of securities sold unless the taxpayer can specifically identify the securities sold and uses specific identification.
   e. **Capital gains exclusion for small business stock**

      (1) A noncorporate taxpayer can exclude 50% of capital gains resulting from the sale of qualified small business stock (QSBS) held for more than five years. The exclusion is increased to 75% if the QSBS was acquired after February 17, 2009, and before September 28, 2010, and 100% for QSBS acquired after September 27, 2010, and before January 1, 2015.
      (2) To qualify, the stock must be acquired directly (or indirectly through a pass-through entity) at its original issuance.
      (3) A qualified small business is a C corporation with $50 million or less of capitalization. Generally, personal service, banking, leasing, investing, real estate, farming, mineral extraction, and hospitality businesses do not qualify as eligible small businesses.
      (4) Gains eligible for exclusion are limited to the greater of $10 million, or 10 times the investor's stock basis.

         (a) 7% of the excluded gain is generally treated as a tax preference for AMT purposes. However, there is no tax preference for gains qualifying for the 100% exclusion.
         (b) Only gains net of exclusion are included in determining the investment interest expense and capital loss limitations.

   f. **Rollover of capital gain from publicly traded securities**

      (1) An individual or C corporation may elect to roll over an otherwise currently taxable capital gain from the sale of publicly traded securities if the sale proceeds are used to purchase common stock or a partnership interest in a specialized small business investment company (SSBIC) within sixty days of the sale of the securities.
      (2) An SSBIC is a partnership or corporation licensed by the Small Business Administration under the Small Business Investment Act of 1958 as in effect on May 13, 1993.
      (3) The amount of gain eligible for rollover is limited to $50,000 per year for individuals (lifetime cap of $500,000) and $250,000 per year for corporations (lifetime cap of $1 million).
      (4) The taxpayer's basis in the SSBIC stock or partnership interest must be reduced by the gain that is rolled over.

   g. **Market discount bonds**

      (1) Gain on the disposition of a bond (including a tax-exempt bond) that was acquired for a price that was less than the principal amount of the bond is treated as taxable interest income to the extent of the accrued market discount for bonds purchased after April 30, 1993.
      (2) Accrued market discount is the difference between the bond's cost basis and its redemption value at maturity amortized over the remaining life of the bond.

h. **Wash sales**

(1) Wash sale occurs when stock or securities (or options to acquire stock or securities) are sold at a loss and within **thirty days before or after the sale,** substantially identical stock or securities (or options to acquire them) in the same corporation are purchased.

(2) Wash sale loss is not deductible, but is added to the basis of the new stock.

(3) Wash sale rules do not apply to gains.

EXAMPLE

C purchased 100 shares of XYZ Corporation stock for $1,000. C later sold the stock for $700, and within thirty days acquired 100 shares of XYZ Corporation stock for $800. The loss of $300 on the sale of stock is not recognized. However, the unrecognized loss of $300 is added to the $800 cost of the new stock to arrive at the basis for the new stock of $1,100. The holding period of the new stock includes the period of time the old stock was held.

---

(4) Does not apply to dealers in stock and securities where loss is sustained in ordinary course of business.

i. **Worthless stock and securities**

(1) Treated as a capital loss as if sold on the last day of the taxable year they become worthless.

(2) Treated as an ordinary loss if stock and securities are those of an **80% or more owned corporate subsidiary** that derived more than 90% of its gross receipts from active-type sources.

6. **Losses on deposits in insolvent financial institutions**

a. Loss resulting from a nonbusiness deposit in an insolvent financial institution is generally treated as a nonbusiness bad debt deductible as a short-term capital loss (STCL) in the year in which a final determination of the amount of loss can be made.

b. As an alternative, if a reasonable estimate of the amount of loss can be made, an individual may elect to

(1) Treat the loss as a personal casualty loss subject to the $100 floor and 10% of AGI limitation. Then no bad debt deduction can be claimed.

(2) In lieu of (1) above, treat up to $20,000 as a miscellaneous itemized deduction subject to the 2% of AGI floor if the deposit was not federally insured. Then remainder of loss is treated as a STCL.

EXAMPLE

An individual with no capital gains and an AGI of $70,000, incurred a loss on a federally insured deposit in a financial institution of $30,000. The individual may treat the loss as a $30,000 STCL subject to the $3,000 net capital loss deduction limitation, with the remaining $27,000 carried forward as a STCL; or, may treat the loss as a personal casualty loss and an itemized deduction of [($30,000 − $100) − (10% × $70,000)] = $22,900. If the deposit had not been federally insured, the individual could also have taken a miscellaneous itemized deduction of [$20,000 − (2% × $70,000)] = $18,600, with the remaining $10,000 treated as a STCL (i.e., $3,000 net capital loss deduction and a $7,000 STCL carryover).

NOW REVIEW MULTIPLE-CHOICE QUESTIONS 27 THROUGH 30

7. **Losses, expenses, and interest between related taxpayers**

a. **Loss is disallowed** on the sale or exchange of property to a related taxpayer.

(1) Transferee's basis is cost; holding period begins when transferee acquires property.

(2) On a later resale, any gain recognized by the transferee is reduced by the disallowed loss (unless the transferor's loss was from a wash sale, in which case no reduction is allowed).

(3) **Related taxpayers** include

    (a) Members of a family, including spouse, brothers, sisters, ancestors, and lineal descendants

    (b) A corporation and a more than 50% shareholder

    (c) Two corporations which are members of the same controlled group

    (d) A person and an exempt organization controlled by that person

    (e) Certain related individuals in a trust, including the grantor or beneficiary and the fiduciary

    (f) A C corporation and a partnership if the same persons own more than 50% of the corporation, and more than 50% of the capital and profits interest in the partnership

    (g) Two S corporations if the same persons own more than 50% of each

    (h) An S corporation and a C corporation if the same persons own more than 50% of each

---

EXAMPLE

During August 2014, Bob sold stock with a basis of $4,000 to his brother Ray for $3,000, its FMV. During June 2015, Ray sold the stock to an unrelated taxpayer for $4,500. Bob's loss of $1,000 is disallowed; Ray recognizes a STCG of ($4,500 – $3,000) – $1,000 disallowed loss = $500.

---

(4) **Constructive stock ownership rules** apply in determining if taxpayers are related. For purposes of determining stock ownership

    (a) Stock owned, directly or indirectly, by a corporation, partnership, estate, or trust is considered as being owned proportionately by its shareholders, partners, or beneficiaries.

    (b) An individual is considered as owning the stock owned, directly or indirectly, by his brothers and sisters (whole or half blood), spouse, ancestors, and lineal descendants.

    (c) An individual owning stock in a corporation [other than by (b) above] is considered as owning the stock owned, directly or indirectly, by his partner.

b. The disallowed loss rule in a. above does not apply to transfers between spouses, or former spouses incident to divorce, as discussed below.

c. Any loss from the sale or exchange of property between corporations that are members of the same **controlled group** is deferred (instead of disallowed) until the property is sold outside the group. Use controlled group definition found in Module 38, D.2., but substitute "more than 50%" for "at least 80%."

EXAMPLE

Mr. Gudjob is the sole shareholder of X Corp. and Y Corp. During 2014, X Corp. sold non depreciable property with a basis of $8,000 to Y Corp. for $6,000, its FMV. During 2015, Y Corp. sold the property to an unrelated taxpayer for $6,500. X Corp.'s loss in 2014 is deferred. In 2015, X Corp. recognizes the $2,000 of deferred loss, and Y Corp. recognizes a gain of $500.

---

d. An accrual-basis payor is effectively placed on the cash method of accounting for purposes of deducting accrued interest and other expenses owed to a related cash-basis payee.

    (1) No deduction is allowable until the year the amount is actually paid.

    (2) This rule applies to pass-through entities (e.g., a partnership and **any** partner; two partnerships if the same persons own more than 50% of each; an S corporation and **any** shareholder) in addition to the related taxpayers described in a.(3) above, but does not apply to guaranteed payments to partners. This rule also applies to a personal service corporation and **any** employee-owner.

> **EXAMPLE**
>
> A calendar-year S corporation accrued a $500 bonus owed to an employee-shareholder in 2014 but did not pay the bonus until February 2015. The $500 bonus will be deductible by the S corporation in 2015, when the employee-shareholder reports the $500 as income.

8. **Transfers in part a sale and in part a gift**

    a. If a transfer of property is in part a sale and in part a gift, the transferor recognizes gain to the extent that the amount realized exceeds the transferor's adjusted basis for the property transferred. However, no loss can be recognized by the transferor.

    b. The basis of the property to the transferee is generally the greater of (1) the amount paid by the transferee for the property, or (2) the transferor's basis for the property at the time of the transfer. However, for purposes of determining a loss, the basis of the property in the hands of the transferee shall not be greater than the fair market value of the property at the time of the transfer.

> **EXAMPLE**
>
> Brett transfers property to his sister, Brianna, for $60,000. The property has a basis of $40,000 and an FMV of $90,000 at date of transfer. Brett must recognize a gain of $60,000 – $40,000 = $20,000, and has made a gift to Brianna of $90,000 – $60,000 = $30,000. Brianna's basis for the property is $60,000.

> **EXAMPLE**
>
> Brian transfers property to his brother, Carl, for $30,000. The transferred property has a basis of $40,000 and an FMV of $90,000 at date of transfer. Brian's realized loss of $40,000 – $30,000 = $10,000 cannot be recognized, and he has made a gift to Carl of $90,000 – $30,000 = $60,000. Carl's basis for the property is $40,000.

> **EXAMPLE**
>
> Henry transfers property to his son, Edan, for $30,000. The property has a basis of $90,000 and an FMV of $60,000 at date of transfer. Henry's realized loss of $90,000 – $30,000 = $60,000 cannot be recognized, and he has made a gift to Edan of $60,000 – $30,000 = 30,000. Edan's basis for the property is $90,000. However, for purposes of determining a loss on a later sale or other disposition of the property by Edan, the property's basis is limited to its FMV at date of transfer of $60,000.

9. **Transfer between spouses**

    a. No gain or loss is generally recognized on the transfer of property from an individual to (or in trust for the benefit of)

    (1) A spouse (other than a nonresident alien spouse), or
    (2) A former spouse (other than a nonresident alien former spouse), if the transfer is related to the cessation of marriage, or occurs within one year after marriage ceases

    b. Transfer is treated as if it were a gift from one spouse to the other.
    c. Transferee's basis in the property received will be the transferor's basis (even if FMV is less than the property's basis).

EXAMPLE

H sells property with a basis of $6,000 to his spouse, W, for $8,000. No gain is recognized to H, and W's basis for the property is $6,000. W's holding period includes the period that H held the property.

---

   d. If property is transferred to a **trust** for the benefit of a spouse or former spouse (incident to divorce)

     (1) Gain is recognized to the extent that the amount of liabilities assumed exceeds the total adjusted basis of property transferred.

     (2) Gain or loss is recognized on the transfer of installment obligations.

10. Gain from the sale or exchange of property will be entirely ordinary gain (no capital gain) if the property is depreciable in hands of transferee and the sale or exchange is between

   a. A person and a more than 50% owned corporation or partnership

   b. A taxpayer and any trust in which such taxpayer or spouse is a beneficiary, unless such beneficiary's interest is a remote contingent interest

   c. Constructive ownership rules apply; use rules in Section 7.a.(4)(a) and (b) above

---

NOW REVIEW MULTIPLE-CHOICE QUESTIONS 31 THROUGH 36

B. Capital Gains and Losses

1. Capital gains and losses result from the "sale or exchange of capital assets." The term **capital assets** includes investment property and property held for personal use. The term specifically **excludes**

   a. Stock in trade, inventory, or goods held primarily for sale to customers in the normal course of business

   b. Depreciable or real property used in a trade or business

   c. Copyrights or artistic, literary, etc., compositions created by the taxpayer

     (1) They are capital assets only if purchased by the taxpayer.

     (2) Patents are generally capital assets in the hands of the inventor.

   d. Accounts or notes receivable arising from normal business activities

   e. US government publications acquired other than by purchase at regular price

   f. Supplies of a type regularly used or consumed by a taxpayer in the ordinary course of the taxpayer's trade or business

2. Whether short-term or long-term depends upon the **holding period**

   a. Long-term if held more than one year

   b. The day property was acquired is excluded and the day it is disposed of is included.

   c. Use calendar months (e.g., if held from January 4 to January 4 it is held exactly one year)

   d. If stock or securities which are traded on an established securities market (or other property regularly traded on an established market) are sold, any resulting gain or loss is recognized on the date the trade is executed (transaction date) by both cash and accrual taxpayers.

   e. The holding period of property received in a nontaxable exchange (e.g., like-kind exchange, involuntary conversion) includes the holding period of the property exchanged, if the property that was exchanged was a capital asset or Sec. 1231 asset.

   f. If the basis of property to a prior owner carries over to the present owner (e.g., gift), the holding period of the prior owner "tacks on" to the present owner's holding period.

   g. If using the lower FMV on date of gift to determine loss, then holding period begins when the gift is received.

> **EXAMPLE**
>
> X purchased property on July 14, 2014, for $10,000. X made a gift of the property to Z on June 10, 2015, when its FMV was $8,000. Since Z's basis for gain is $10,000, Z's holding period for a disposition at a gain extends back to July 14, 2014. Since Z's $8,000 basis for loss is determined by reference to FMV at June 10, 2015, Z's holding period for a disposition at a loss begins on June 11.

h. Property acquired from a decedent is generally given long-term treatment, regardless of how long the property was held by the decedent or beneficiary, and is treated as property held more than twelve months.

3. Computation of capital gains and losses for **all taxpayers**

a. First net STCG with STCL and net LTCG with LTCL to determine

   (1) Net short-term capital gain or loss (NSTCG or NSTCL)
   (2) Net long-term capital gain or loss (NLTCG or NLTCL)

b. Then net these two together to determine whether there is a net capital gain or loss (NCG or NCL)

4. The following rules apply to individuals:

a. Capital gains offset capital losses, with any remaining net capital gains included in gross income.
b. Net capital gains are subject to tax at various rates, depending on the type of assets sold or exchanged and length of time the assets were held.

   (1) Capital gain from assets held one year or less is taxed at the taxpayer's regular tax rates (up to 39.6%).
   (2) Capital gain from the sale of collectibles held more than twelve months (e.g., antiques, art, metals, gems, rugs, stamps, coins, alcoholic beverages) is taxed at a maximum rate of 28%.
   (3) Capital gain attributable to unrecaptured depreciation on Sec. 1250 property held more than twelve months is taxed at a maximum rate of 25%.
   (4) Capital gain from assets held more than twelve months (other than from collectibles and unrecaptured depreciation on Sec. 1250 property) is taxed (for tax years beginning after December 31, 2012) at a rate of 0% for individuals in the 10% or 15% tax brackets, 15% for most taxpayers, and 20% for certain higher-income taxpayers.

   The 15% rate applies to the extent that a taxpayer's taxable income is less than the threshold set for the 39.6% rate ($413,200 for single filers, $464,850 for joint filers for 2015). Long-term capital gains (and qualified dividends) over those thresholds are taxed at a rate of 20%.

   EXAMPLE: If a married couple already has $464,850 of taxable income and an additional $100,000 in long-term capital gains and qualified dividends, the entire $100,000 would be subject to the 20% rate. If, however, they only had $400,000 of other taxable income, then $64,850 of the additional amount would be taxed at 15% and $35,150 would be taxed at 20%.

   (5) For installment sales of assets held more than twelve months, the date an installment payment is received (not the date the asset was sold) determines the capital gains rate that should be applied

c. Gains and losses (including carryovers) within each of the rate groups are netted to arrive at a net gain or loss. A net loss in any rate group is applied to reduce the net gain in the highest rate group first (e.g., a net short-term capital loss is applied to reduce any net gain from the 28% group, then the 25% group, then the 20% group, and finally to reduce gain from the 15% group).

> **EXAMPLE**
>
> Kim, who is in the 35% tax bracket, had the following capital gains and losses for calendar-year 2015:
>
> | | |
> |---|---:|
> | Net short-term capital loss | $(1,500) |
> | 28% group—collectibles net gain | 900 |
> | 25% group—unrecaptured Sec. 1250 net gain | 2,000 |
> | 15% group—net gain | 5,000 |
> | Net capital gain | $6,400 |
>
> In this case, the NSTCL of $1,500 first offsets the $900 of collectibles gain, and then offsets $600 of the unrecaptured Sec. 1250 gain. As a result of this netting procedure, Kim has $1,400 of unrecaptured Sec. 1250 gain that will be taxed at a rate of 25%, and $5,000 of capital gain that will be taxed at a rate of 15%.

d. If there is a **net capital loss** the following rules apply:

(1) A net capital loss is a deduction in arriving at AGI, but limited to the lesser of

    (a) $3,000 ($1,500 if married filing separately), or
    (b) The excess of capital losses over capital gains

(2) Both a NSTCL and a NLTCL are used dollar-for-dollar in computing the capital loss deduction.

EXAMPLE

An individual had $2,000 of NLTCL and $500 of NSTCL for 2015. The capital losses are combined and the entire net capital loss of $2,500 is deductible in computing the individual's AGI.

---

(3) Short-term losses are used before long-term losses. The amount of net capital loss that exceeds the allowable deduction may be carried over for an unlimited period of time. Capital loss carryovers retain their identity; short-term losses carry over as short-term losses, and long-term losses carry over as long-term losses in the 28% group. Losses remaining unused on a decedent's final return are extinguished and provide no tax benefit.

EXAMPLE

An individual has a $4,000 STCL and a $5,000 LTCL for 2014. The $9,000 net capital loss results in a capital loss deduction of $3,000 for 2014, while the remainder is a carryover to 2015. Since $3,000 of the STCL would be used to create the capital loss deduction, there is a $1,000 STCL carryover and a $5,000 LTCL carryover to 2015. The $5,000 LTCL carryover would first offset gains in the 28% group.

---

(4) For purposes of determining the amount of excess net capital loss that can be carried over to future years, the taxpayer's net capital loss for the year is reduced by the lesser of (1) $3,000 ($1,500 if married filing separately), or (2) adjusted taxable income.

    (a) Adjusted taxable income is taxable income increased by $3,000 ($1,500 if married filing separately) and the amount allowed for personal exemptions.
    (b) An excess of deductions allowed over gross income is taken into account as negative taxable income.

EXAMPLE

For 2014, a single individual with no dependents had a net capital loss of $8,000, and had allowable deductions that exceeded gross income by $4,000. For 2014, the individual is entitled to a net capital loss deduction of $3,000, and will carry over a net capital loss of $5,050 to 2015. This amount represents the 2014 net capital loss of $8,000 reduced by the lesser of (1) $3,000, or (2) – $4,000 + $3,000 + $3,950 personal exemption = $2,950.

---

5. **Corporations** have special capital gain and loss rules.

    a. Capital losses are only allowed to offset capital gains, not ordinary income.
    b. A **net capital loss** is carried back three years, and forward five years to offset capital gains in those years. All capital loss carrybacks and carryovers are treated as **short-term** capital losses.

> **EXAMPLE**
>
> A corporation has a NLTCL of $8,000 and a NSTCG of $2,000, resulting in a net capital loss of $6,000 for 2014. The $6,000 NLTCL is not deductible for 2014, but is first carried back as a STCL to 2011 to offset capital gains. If not used up in 2011, the STCL is carried to 2012 and 2013, and then forward to 2015, 2016, 2017, 2018, and 2019 to offset capital gains in those years.

    c. Although an alternative tax computation still exists for a corporation with a net capital gain, the alternative tax computation applies the highest corporate rate (35%) to a net capital gain and thus provides no benefit.

> **NOW REVIEW MULTIPLE-CHOICE QUESTIONS 37 THROUGH 52**

C. Personal Casualty and Theft Gains and Losses

Gains and losses from casualties and thefts of property held for personal use are separately netted, without regard to the holding period of the converted property.

1. If gains exceed losses (after the $100 floor for each loss), then all gains and losses are treated as capital gains and losses, short-term or long-term depending upon holding period.

> **EXAMPLE**
>
> An individual incurred a $25,000 personal casualty gain, and a $15,000 personal casualty loss (after the $100 floor) during the current taxable year. Since there was a net gain, the individual will report the gain and loss as a $25,000 capital gain and a $15,000 capital loss.

2. If losses (after the $100 floor for each loss) exceed gains, the losses (1) offset gains, and (2) are an ordinary deduction from AGI to the extent in excess of 10% of AGI.

> **EXAMPLE**
>
> An individual had AGI of $40,000 (before casualty gains or losses), and also had a personal casualty loss of $25,000 (after the $100 floor) and a personal casualty gain of $15,000. Since there was a net personal casualty loss, the net loss will be deductible as an itemized deduction of [$25,000 – $15,000 – (10% × $40,000)] = $6,000.

D. Gains and Losses on Business Property

Although property used in a business is excluded from the definition of "capital assets," Sec. 1231 extends capital gain and loss treatment to business assets if the gains from these assets exceed losses. However, before Sec. 1231 becomes operative, Sections 1245, 1250, and 291 provide for recapture of depreciation (i.e., gain is taxed as ordinary income to the extent of certain depreciation previously deducted).

1. All gains and losses are **ordinary** on business property **held one year or less**.
2. **Section 1231**

    a. All property included must have been held for **more than one year**.

       (1) Section 1231 gains and losses include those from

    (a) Sale or exchange of property used in trade or business (or held for production of rents or royalties) and which is not

        [1] Inventory
        [2] A copyright or artistic composition

    (b) Casualty, theft, or condemnation of

        [1] Property used in trade or business
        [2] Capital assets held in connection with a trade or business, or a transaction entered into for profit

    (c) Infrequently encountered items such as cut timber, coal and domestic iron ore, livestock, and unharvested crop

b. The combining of Sec. 1231 gains and losses is accomplished in **two steps. First,** net all casualty and theft gains and losses on property held for more than one year.

    (1) If the losses exceed gains, treat them all as ordinary losses and gains and do not net them with other Sec. 1231 gains and losses.
    (2) If the gains exceed losses, the net gain is combined with other Sec. 1231 gains and losses.

c. **Second,** net all other Sec. 1231 gains and losses (except casualty and theft net loss per above).

    (1) Include casualty and theft net gain
    (2) Include gains and losses from condemnations (other than condemnations on nonbusiness, non-income-producing property)
    (3) Include gains and losses from the sale or exchange of property used in trade or business

d. If losses exceed gains, treat all gains and losses as ordinary.
e. If gains exceed losses, treat the Sec. 1231 net gain as a long-term capital gain.

EXAMPLE

Taxpayer has a gain of $10,000 from the sale of land used in his business, a loss of $4,000 on the sale of depreciable property used in his business, and a $2,000 (noninsured) loss when a car used in his business was involved in a collision.

    The net gain or loss from casualty or theft is the $2,000 loss. The net casualty loss of $2,000 is treated as an ordinary loss and not netted with other Sec. 1231 gains and losses.

    The $10,000 gain is netted with the $4,000 loss resulting in a net Sec. 1231 gain of $6,000, which is then treated as a long-term capital gain.

---

f. Net Sec. 1231 gain will be treated as ordinary income (instead of LTCG) to the extent of nonrecaptured net Sec. 1231 losses for the five most recent taxable years.

    (1) Losses are deemed recaptured in the chronological order in which they arose
    (2) Any Sec. 1231 gain recharacterized as ordinary income consists first of gain in the 28% group, then gain in the 25% group, and finally gain in the 20% or 15% group

---

EXAMPLE

Corp. X, on a calendar year, has a net Sec. 1231 gain of $10,000 for 2015. For the years 2010 through 2014, Corp. X had net Sec. 1231 losses totaling $8,000. Of the $10,000 net Sec. 1231 gain for 2015, the first $8,000 will be treated as ordinary income, with only the remaining $2,000 treated as long-term capital gain.

---

3. **Section 1245 Recapture**

   a. Requires the recapture as **ordinary income** of all gain attributable to

      (1) **Post-1961 depreciation** on the disposition of Sec. 1245 property
      (2) **Post-1980 recovery deductions** on the disposition of Sec. 1245 recovery property (including amount expensed under Sec. 179 expense election)

   b. Sec. 1245 property generally includes depreciable tangible and intangible personal property, for example

      (1) Desks, machines, equipment, cars, and trucks
      (2) Special-purpose structures, storage facilities, and other property (but not buildings and structural components); for example, oil and gas storage tanks, grain storage bins and silos, and escalators and elevators

   c. Sec. 1245 recovery property means all ACRS recovery property placed in service after 1980 and before 1987 other than nineteen-year real property that is classified as real residential rental property, real property used outside the US, subsidized low-income housing, and real property for which a straight-line election was made.

> **NOTE:** If the cost of nineteen-year nonresidential real property placed in service before 1987 was recovered using the prescribed percentages of ACRS, the gain on disposition is ordinary income to extent of all ACRS deductions. Such recapture is not limited to the excess of accelerated depreciation over straight-line. However, if the straight-line method was elected for nineteen-year real property, there is no recapture and all gain is Sec. 1231 gain.

   d. Sec. 1245 does not apply to real residential rental property and nonresidential real property placed in service after 1986 because only straight-line depreciation is allowable.
   e. Upon the disposition of property subject to Sec. 1245, any recognized gain will be ordinary income to the extent of all depreciation or post-1980 cost recovery deductions.

      (1) Any remaining gain after recapture will be Sec. 1231 gain if property held more than one year.

EXAMPLE

Megan sold equipment used in her business for $11,000. The equipment had cost $10,000 and $6,000 of depreciation had been taken, resulting in an adjusted basis of $4,000. Megan's recognized gain is $11,000 – $4,000 = $7,000. Since the equipment was Sec. 1245 property, the gain must be recognized as Sec. 1245 ordinary income to the extent of the $6,000 of depreciation deducted. The remaining $1,000 gain ($7,000 gain – $6,000 ordinary income) is recognized as Sec. 1231 gain.

EXAMPLE

Assume the same facts as in the preceding example, except the equipment was sold for $9,000. Megan's recognized gain would be $9,000 – $4,000 = $5,000. Now, since the $6,000 of depreciation deducted exceeds the recognized gain of $5,000, the amount of Sec. 1245 ordinary income would be limited to the recognized gain of $5,000. There would be no Sec. 1231 gain.

EXAMPLE

Assume the same facts as in the first example, except the equipment was sold for only $3,500. Megan's sale of the equipment now results in a recognized loss of $3,500 – $4,000 = ($500). Since there is a loss, there would be no Sec. 1245 depreciation recapture and the $500 loss would be classified as a Sec. 1231 loss.

(2) If the disposition is not by sale, use FMV of property (instead of selling price) to determine gain.

    (a) When boot is received in a like-kind exchange, Sec. 1245 will apply to the recognized gain.

EXAMPLE

Taxpayer exchanged his old machine (adjusted basis of $2,500) for a smaller new machine worth $5,000 and received $1,000 cash. Depreciation of $7,500 had been taken on the old machine. The realized gain of $3,500 ($6,000 – $2,500) will be recognized to the extent of the $1,000 boot, and will be treated as ordinary income as the result of Sec. 1245.

    (b) Sec. 1245 recapture does not apply to transfers by gift (including charitable contributions) or transfers at death.

4. **Section 1250 Recapture**

  a. Applies to all real property (e.g., buildings and structural components) that is not Sec. 1245 recovery property.

    (1) If Sec. 1250 property was held twelve months or less, gain on disposition is recaptured as ordinary income to extent of all depreciation (including straight-line).

EXAMPLE

Alan, who is in the 35% tax bracket, owned an office building purchased for $900,000 during March 2014. The building was sold for $890,000 during February 2015, when its adjusted basis was $880,000. Since the building was not held for more than one year, the $10,000 gain is treated as ordinary income and is subject to tax at Alan's 35% rate.

---

    (2) If Sec. 1250 property was held more than twelve months, gain is recaptured as ordinary income to the extent of post-1969 **additional depreciation** (generally depreciation in excess of straight-line).

EXAMPLE

Baker, who is in the 35% tax bracket, owned an office building purchased for $900,000 during March 2014. Baker deducted $30,000 of straight-line depreciation, and sold the building for $890,000 during May 2015. Since the building was held for more than one year and only straight-line depreciation was deducted, there is no Sec. 1250 recapture. However, the $890,000 – $870,000 = $20,000 of Sec. 1231 gain represents unrecaptured Sec. 1250 depreciation and will be subject to tax at a maximum rate of 25% if treated as LTCG.

EXAMPLE

Curt, who is in the 35% tax bracket, sold an office building with an adjusted basis of $40,000 for $350,000. The building had been purchased for $400,000 in 1980 and $360,000 of accelerated depreciation had been deducted. Straight-line depreciation would have totaled $330,000.

Total gain ($350,000 – $40,000)	$310,000
Sec. 1250 ordinary income ($360,000 – $330,000)	(30,000)
Sec. 1231 gain	$280,000

The $30,000 of ordinary income will be taxed at 35%, while the $280,000 of Sec. 1231 gain represents unrecaptured Sec. 1250 depreciation and is subject to tax at a maximum rate of 25% if treated as LTCG.

---

5. **Section 291 Recapture**

    a. The ordinary income element on the disposition of Sec. 1250 property by **corporations** is increased by 20% of the additional amount that would have been ordinary income if the property had instead been Sec. 1245 property or Sec. 1245 recovery property.

EXAMPLE

Assuming the same facts as in the above example except that the building was owned and sold by Ajax Corporation, the computation of gain would be

Total gain ($350,000 – $40,000)	$310,000
Sec. 1250 ordinary income ($360,000 – $330,000)	(30,000)*
Additional ordinary income—20% of $280,000 (the additional amount that would have been ordinary income if the property were Sec. 1245 property)	(56,000)*
Sec. 1231 gain	$224,000

*All $86,000 ($30,000 + $56,000) of recapture is referred to as Sec. 1250 ordinary income.

---

6. **Summary of Gains and Losses on Business Property.** The treatment of gains and losses (other than personal casualty and theft) on property held for **more than one year** is summarized in the following **four steps** (also enumerated on flowchart at end of this section):

    a. Separate all recognized gains and losses into four categories

        (1) Ordinary gain and loss
        (2) Sec. 1231 casualty and theft gains and losses
        (3) Sec. 1231 gains and losses other than by casualty or theft
        (4) Gains and losses on capital assets (other than by casualty or theft)

> **NOTE:** (2) and (3) are only temporary classifications and all gains and losses will ultimately receive ordinary or capital treatment.

    b. Any gain (casualty or other) on Sec. 1231 property is treated as ordinary income to extent of Sec. 1245, 1250, and 291 depreciation recapture.

    c. After depreciation recapture, any remaining Sec. 1231 casualty and theft gains and losses on business property are netted.

        (1) If losses exceed gains—the losses and gains receive ordinary treatment
        (2) If gains exceed losses—the net gain is combined with other Sec. 1231 gains and losses in d. below

    d. After recapture, any remaining Sec. 1231 gains and losses (other than by casualty or theft), are combined with any net casualty or theft gain from c. above.

        (1) If losses exceed gains—the losses and gains receive ordinary treatment
        (2) If gains exceed losses—the net gain receives LTCG treatment (except ordinary income treatment to extent of nonrecaptured net Sec. 1231 losses for the five most recent tax years)

TAX TREATMENT OF GAINS AND LOSSES (OTHER THAN PERSONAL CASUALTY AND THEFT) ON PROPERTY HELD MORE THAN ONE YEAR

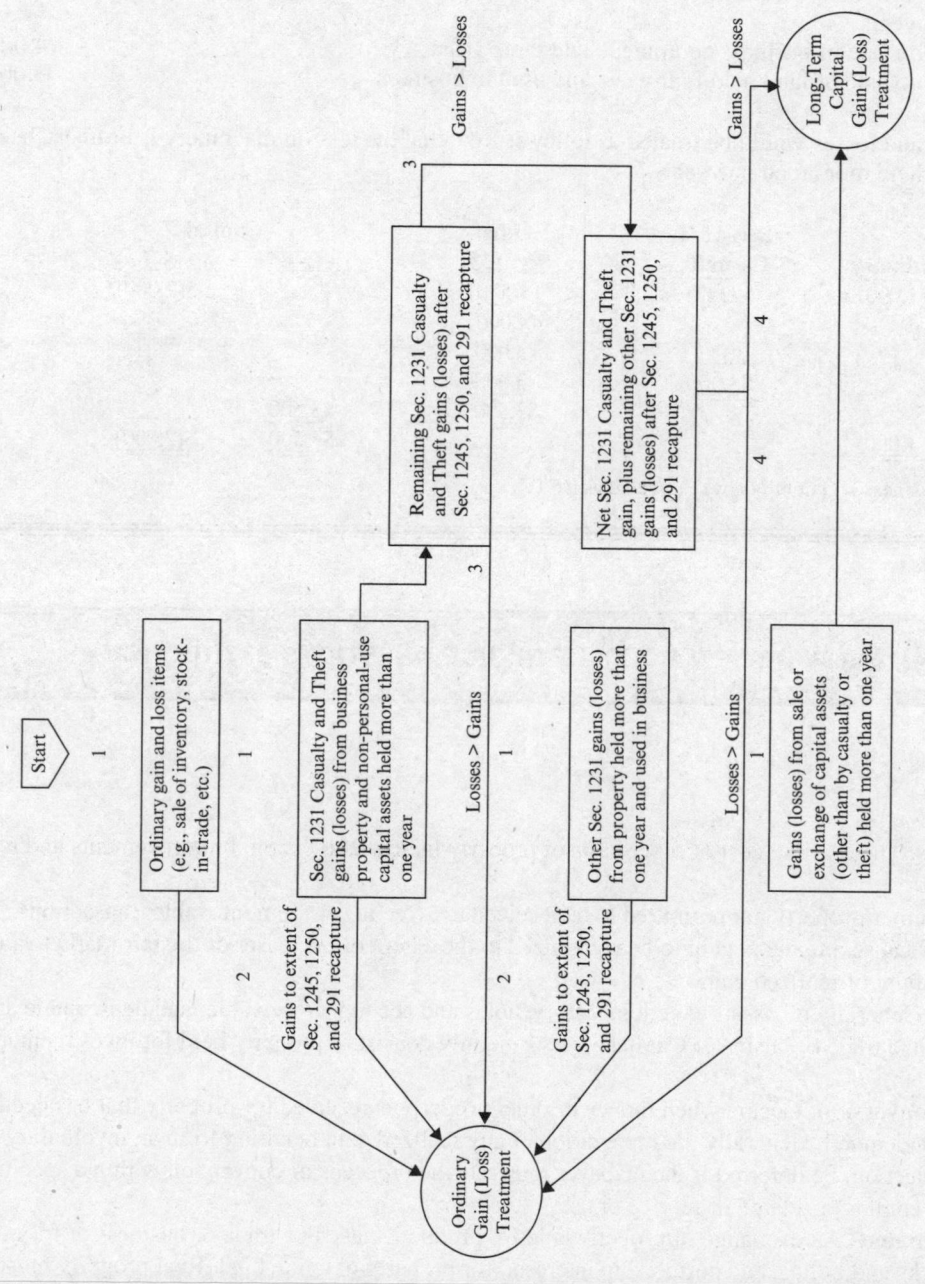

EXAMPLE

Taxpayer incurred the following transactions during the current taxable year:

Loss on condemnation of land used in business held fifteen months	$(500)
Loss on sale of machinery used in business held two months	(1,000)
Bad debt loss on loan made three years ago to friend	(2,000)
Gain from insurance reimbursement for tornado damage to business property held ten years	3,000
Loss on sale of business equipment held three years	(4,000)
Gain on sale of land held four years and used in business	5,000

The gains and losses would be treated as follows: Note that the loss on machinery is ordinary because it was not held more than one year.

	Sec. 1231	Other	Capital	
Ordinary	**Casualty**	**Sec. 1231**	**L-T**	**S-T**
$(1,000)	$3,000	$(500)		$(2,000)*
		(4,000)		
		5,000		
	$3,000	3,000		
		$3,500	$3,500	
$(1,000)			$3,500	$(2,000)

*A nonbusiness bad debt is always treated as a STCL.

NOW REVIEW MULTIPLE-CHOICE QUESTIONS 53 THROUGH 61

KEY TERMS

Adjusted basis. The original cost or other basis of property increased by capital improvements and reduced by depreciation and losses.

Boot. Cash or other property not permitted to be received tax-free in certain nontaxable transactions. The receipt of boot will generally cause a realized gain to be recognized to the extent of the lesser of the fair market value of such boot received or the amount of realized gain.

Capital asset. Generally all assets except inventory, notes and accounts receivable, and depreciable and non depreciable property used in a trade or business. Capital assets generally consist of property held for investment and property held for personal use.

Involuntary conversion. Occurs when money or other property is received for property that has been destroyed, damaged, stolen, or condemned. Generally the recognition of any realized gain resulting from an involuntary conversion can, at the taxpayer's election, be deferred if the taxpayer reinvests the proceeds of conversion within a specified period of time in property that is similar or related in service or use.

Like-kind exchange. An exchange of property held for productive use in a trade or business or for investment (excluding inventory, stocks and bonds, and partnership interests) for property of a like kind. Real property must be exchanged for real property, personal property must be exchanged for personal property within the same general asset class. Generally no gain is recognized unless unlike property (boot) is received.

Long-term capital gain or loss. Gain or loss realized from the sale or exchange of a capital asset held for more than one year.

Related-taxpayer transactions. Generally no loss can be recognized from the sale or exchange of property between related taxpayers. Related taxpayers included members of a family (spouse, brothers, sisters, ancestors, and lineal descendants), and an individual and a more than 50% owned entity. Additionally, gains resulting from transactions between related taxpayers that might otherwise be classified as capital or Sec. 1231 gains may instead be taxed as ordinary income.

Section 1231 property. Depreciable and nondepreciable property used in a trade or business and held for more than one year. Inventory, accounts and notes receivable, US government publications, copyrights, literary, musical, or artistic compositions in the hands of their creator are excluded from the definition.

Section 1245 property. Generally depreciable personal property used in a trade or business or held for the production of income (e.g., machinery, equipment, trucks, autos).

Section 1245 recapture. The gain from the sale or exchange of Sec. 1245 property must be reported as ordinary income to the extent of the lesser of (1) all depreciation (including straight-line), or the recognized gain.

Section 1250 property. Any real property (e.g., building) that (1) is not Sec. 1245 property and (2) is subject to the allowance of depreciation.

Section 1250 recapture. The gain from the sale or exchange of Sec. 1250 property must be reported as ordinary income to the extent that actual depreciation deductions exceeded what straight-line would have been. If Sec. 1250 property was held twelve months or less, gain on disposition is recaptured as ordinary income to the extent of all depreciation (including straight-line).

Wash sale. A loss from the sale of stock or securities is disallowed because the taxpayer, within 30 days before or after the sale, has acquired stock or securities that are substantially identical to those sold.

Multiple-Choice Questions (1–61)

A.1.   Basis of Property

1. Ralph Birch purchased land and a building which will be used in connection with Birch's business. The costs associated with this purchase are as follows:

Cash down payment	$40,000
Mortgage on property	350,000
Survey costs	2,000
Title and transfer taxes	2,500
Charges for hookup of gas, water, and sewer lines	3,000
Back property taxes owed by the seller that were paid by Birch	5,000

What is Birch's tax basis for the land and building?

- a. $44,500
- b. $394,500
- c. $397,500
- d. $402,500

2. Fred Berk bought a plot of land with a cash payment of $40,000 and a purchase money mortgage of $50,000. In addition, Berk paid $200 for a title insurance policy. Berk's basis in this land is

- a. $40,000
- b. $40,200
- c. $90,000
- d. $90,200

A.1.c.   Acquired by Gift

3. Smith made a gift of property to Thompson. Smith's basis in the property was $1,200. The fair market value at the time of the gift was $1,400. Thompson sold the property for $2,500. What was the amount of Thompson's gain on the disposition?

- a. $0
- b. $1,100
- c. $1,300
- d. $2,500

4. Julie received a parcel of land as a gift from her Aunt Agnes. At the time of the gift, the land had a fair market value of $84,000 and an adjusted basis of $24,000. This was the only gift that Julie received from Agnes during 2015. If Agnes paid a gift tax of $14,000 on the transfer of the gift to Julie, what tax basis will Julie have for the land?

- a. $23,000
- b. $35,000
- c. $36,000
- d. $84,000

Items 5 and 6 are based on the following data:

In 2011 Iris King bought shares of stock as an investment, at a cost of $10,000. During 2014, when the fair market value was $8,000, Iris gave the stock to her daughter, Ruth.

5. If Ruth sells the shares of stock in 2015 for $7,000, Ruth's recognized loss would be

- a. $3,000
- b. $2,000
- c. $1,000
- d. $0

6. Ruth's holding period of the stock for purposes of determining her loss

- a. Started in 2011.
- b. Started in 2014.
- c. Started in 2015.
- d. Is irrelevant because Ruth received the stock for no consideration of money or money's worth.

Items 7 through 9 are based on the following data:

Laura's father, Albert, gave Laura a gift of 500 shares of Liba Corporation common stock in 2014. Albert's basis for the Liba stock was $4,000. At the date of this gift, the fair market value of the Liba stock was $3,000.

7. If Laura sells the 500 shares of Liba stock in 2015 for $5,000, her basis is

- a. $5,000
- b. $4,000
- c. $3,000
- d. $0

8. If Laura sells the 500 shares of Liba stock in 2015 for $2,000, her basis is

- a. $4,000
- b. $3,000
- c. $2,000
- d. $0

9. If Laura sells the 500 shares of Liba stock in 2015 for $3,500, what is the reportable gain or loss in 2015?

- a. $3,500 gain.
- b. $500 gain.
- c. $500 loss.
- d. $0.

A.1.d.   Acquired from Decedent

10. On June 1, 2015, Ben Rork sold 500 shares of Kul Corp. stock. Rork had received this stock on May 1, 2015, as a bequest from the estate of his uncle, who died on February 1, 2015. Rork's basis was determined by reference to the stock's fair market value on February 1, 2015. Rork's holding period for this stock was

- a. Short-term.
- b. Long-term.
- c. Short-term if sold at a gain; long-term if sold at a loss.
- d. Long-term if sold at a gain; short-term if sold at a loss.

11. Fred Zorn died on June 5, 2015, bequeathing his entire $6,000,000 estate to his sister, Ida. The alternate valuation date was validly elected by the executor of Fred's estate. Fred's estate included 2,000 shares of listed stock for which Fred's basis was $380,000. This stock was distributed to Ida nine months after Fred's death. Fair market values of this stock were

At the date of Fred's death	$400,000
Six months after Fred's death	450,000
Nine months after Fred's death	480,000

Ida's basis for this stock is

a. $380,000
b. $400,000
c. $450,000
d. $480,000

Items 12 and 13 are based on the following data:

On October 1, 2014, Lois Rice learned that she was bequeathed 1,000 shares of Elin Corp. common stock under the will of her uncle, Pat Prevor. Pat had paid $5,000 for the Elin stock in 2009. Fair market value of the Elin stock on October 1, 2014, the date of Pat's death, was $8,000 and had increased to $11,000 six months later. The executor of Pat's estate elected the alternative valuation for estate tax purposes. Lois sold the Elin stock for $9,000 on December 1, 2014, the date that the executor distributed the stock to her.

12. Lois' basis for gain or loss on sale of the 1,000 shares of Elin stock is

a. $5,000
b. $8,000
c. $9,000
d. $11,000

13. Lois should treat the 1,000 shares of Elin stock as a

a. Short-term Section 1231 asset.
b. Long-term Section 1231 asset.
c. Short-term capital asset.
d. Long-term capital asset.

A.1.e. Stock Received as a Dividend

Items 14 and 15 are based on the following data:

In January 2015, Joan Hill bought one share of Orban Corp. stock for $300. On March 1, 2015, Orban distributed one share of preferred stock for each share of common stock held. This distribution was nontaxable. On March 1, 2015, Joan's one share of common stock had a fair market value of $450, while the preferred stock had a fair market value of $150.

14. After the distribution of the preferred stock, Joan's bases for her Orban stocks are

	Common	Preferred
a.	$300	$0
b.	$225	$75
c.	$200	$100
d.	$150	$150

15. The holding period for the preferred stock starts in

a. January 2015.
b. March 2015.
c. September 2015.
d. December 2015.

16. On July 1, 2009, Lila Perl paid $90,000 for 450 shares of Janis Corp. common stock. Lila received a nontaxable stock dividend of 50 new common shares in August 2014. On December 20, 2014, Lila sold the 50 new shares for $11,000. How much should Lila report in her 2014 return as long-term capital gain?

a. $0
b. $1,000
c. $2,000
d. $11,000

A.4.a. Like-Kind Exchange

17. Tom Gow owned a parcel of investment real estate that had an adjusted basis of $25,000 and a fair market value of $40,000. During the current year, Gow exchanged his investment real estate for the items of property listed below.

Land to be held for investment (fair market value)	$35,000
A small sailboat to be held for personal use (fair market value)	3,000
Cash	2,000

What is Tom Gow's recognized gain and basis in his new investment real estate?

	Gain recognized	Basis for real estate
a.	$2,000	$22,000
b.	$2,000	$25,000
c.	$5,000	$25,000
d.	$5,000	$35,000

18. In a "like-kind" exchange of an investment asset for a similar asset that will also be held as an investment, no taxable gain or loss will be recognized on the transaction if both assets consist of

a. Convertible debentures.
b. Convertible preferred stock.
c. Partnership interests.
d. Rental real estate located in different states.

19. Pat Leif owned an apartment house that he bought in 2001. Depreciation was taken on a straight-line basis. In 2015, when Pat's adjusted basis for this property was $200,000, he traded it for an office building having a fair market value of $600,000. The apartment house has 100 dwelling units, while the office building has 40 units rented to business enterprises. The properties are **not** located in the same city. What is Pat's reportable gain on this exchange?

a. $400,000 Section 1250 gain.
b. $400,000 Section 1231 gain.
c. $400,000 long-term capital gain.
d. $0.

20. Riley exchanged investment real property, with an adjusted basis of $160,000 and subject to a mortgage of $70,000, and received from Wilson $30,000 cash and other investment real property having a fair market value of $250,000. Wilson assumed the mortgage. What is Riley's recognized gain on the exchange?

     a. $30,000
     b. $70,000
     c. $90,000
     d. $100,000

21. During the current year, Donald Anderson exchanged an apartment building having an adjusted basis of $375,000 and subject to a mortgage of $100,000 for $25,000 cash and another apartment building with a fair market value of $550,000 and subject to a mortgage of $125,000. The property transfers were made subject to the outstanding mortgages. What amount of gain should Anderson recognize in his tax return for the current year?

     a. $0
     b. $25,000
     c. $125,000
     d. $175,000

22. The following information pertains to the acquisition of a six-wheel truck by Sol Barr, a self-employed contractor:

Cost of original truck traded in	$20,000
Book value of original truck at trade-in date	4,000
List price of new truck	25,000
Trade-in allowance for old truck	6,000
Business use of both trucks	100%

The basis of the new truck is

     a. $27,000
     b. $25,000
     c. $23,000
     d. $19,000

A.4.b.   Involuntary Conversions

23. An office building owned by Elmer Bass was condemned by the state on January 2, 2013. Bass received the condemnation award on March 1, 2014. In order to qualify for nonrecognition of gain on this involuntary conversion, what is the last date for Bass to acquire qualified replacement property?

     a. August 1, 2015.
     b. January 2, 2016.
     c. March 1, 2017.
     d. December 31, 2017.

A.4.c.   Sale or Exchange of Principle Residence

24. In March 2015, Davis, who is single, purchased a new residence for $200,000. During that same month he sold his former residence for $380,000 and paid the realtor a $20,000 commission. The former residence, his first home, had cost

$65,000 in 1996. Davis added a bathroom for $5,000 in 2011. What amount of gain is recognized from the sale of the former residence on Davis' 2015 tax return?

     a. $160,000
     b. $90,000
     c. $40,000
     d. $0

25. The following information pertains to the sale of Al and Beth Oran's principal residence:

Date of sale	February 2015
Date of purchase	October 1998
Net sales price	$760,000
Adjusted basis	$170,000

Al and Beth owned their home jointly and had occupied it as their principal residence since acquiring the home in 1998. In June 2015, the Orans bought a condo for $190,000 to be used as their principal residence. What amount of gain must the Orans recognize on their 2015 joint return from the sale of their residence?

     a. $90,000
     b. $150,000
     c. $340,000
     d. $400,000

26. Ryan, age fifty-seven, is single with no dependents. In January 2015, Ryan's principal residence was sold for the net amount of $400,000 after all selling expenses. Ryan bought the house in 2002 and occupied it until sold. On the date of sale, the house had a basis of $180,000. Ryan does not intend to buy another residence. What is the maximum exclusion of gain on sale of the residence that may be claimed in Ryan's 2015 income tax return?

     a. $250,000
     b. $220,000
     c. $125,000
     d. $0

A.5.   Sales and Exchanges of Securities

27. Miller, an individual calendar-year taxpayer, purchased 100 shares of Maples Inc. common stock for $10,000 on July 10, 2014, and an additional fifty shares of Maples Inc. common stock for $4,000 on December 24, 2014. On January 8, 2015, Miller sold the 100 shares purchased on July 10, 2014, for $7,000. What is the amount of Miller's recognized loss for 2015 and what is the basis for her remaining fifty shares of Maples Inc. stock?

     a. $3,000 recognized loss; $4,000 basis for her remaining stock.
     b. $1,500 recognized loss; $5,500 basis for her remaining stock.
     c. $1,500 recognized loss; $4,000 basis for her remaining stock.
     d. $0 recognized loss; $7,000 basis for her remaining stock.

28. Smith, an individual calendar-year taxpayer, purchased 100 shares of Core Co. common stock for $15,000 on December 15, 2014, and an additional 100 shares for $13,000 on December 30, 2014. On January 3, 2015, Smith sold the shares purchased on December 15, 2014, for $13,000. What amount of loss from the sale of Core stock is deductible on Smith's 2014 and 2015 income tax returns?

	2014	2015
a.	$0	$0
b.	$0	$2,000
c.	$1,000	$1,000
d.	$2,000	$0

29. On March 10, 2015, James Rogers sold 300 shares of Red Company common stock for $4,200. Rogers acquired the stock in 2012 at a cost of $5,000.

On April 4, 2015, he repurchased 300 shares of Red Company common stock for $3,600 and held them until July 18, 2015, when he sold them for $6,000.

How should Rogers report the above transactions for 2015?

a. A long-term capital loss of $800.
b. A long-term capital gain of $1,000.
c. A long-term capital gain of $1,600.
d. A long-term capital loss of $800 and a short-term capital gain of $2,400.

30. Murd Corporation, a domestic corporation, acquired a 90% interest in the Drum Company in 2011 for $30,000. During 2015, the stock of Drum was declared worthless. What type and amount of deduction should Murd take for 2015?

a. Long-term capital loss of $1,000.
b. Long-term capital loss of $15,000.
c. Ordinary loss of $30,000.
d. Long-term capital loss of $30,000.

A.7. Losses, Expenses, and Interest between Related Taxpayers

Items 32 and 33 are based on the following:

Conner purchased 300 shares of Zinco stock for $30,000 in 2011. On May 23, 2015, Conner sold all the stock to his daughter Alice for $20,000, its then fair market value. Conner realized no other gain or loss during 2015. On July 26, 2015, Alice sold the 300 shares of Zinco for $25,000.

31. What amount of the loss from the sale of Zinco stock can Conner deduct in 2015?

a. $0
b. $3,000
c. $5,000
d. $10,000

32. What was Alice's recognized gain or loss on her sale?

a. $0.
b. $5,000 long-term gain.

c. $5,000 short-term loss.
d. $5,000 long-term loss.

33. In 2015, Fay sold 100 shares of Gym Co. stock to her son, Martin, for $11,000. Fay had paid $15,000 for the stock in 2011. Subsequently in 2015, Martin sold the stock to an unrelated third party for $16,000. What amount of gain from the sale of the stock to the third party should Martin report on his 2015 income tax return?

a. $0
b. $1,000
c. $4,000
d. $5,000

34. Among which of the following related parties are losses from sales and exchanges **not** recognized for tax purposes?

a. Mother-in-law and daughter-in-law.
b. Uncle and nephew.
c. Brother and sister.
d. Ancestors, lineal descendants, and all in-laws.

35. On May 1, 2015, Daniel Wright owned stock (held for investment) purchased two years earlier at a cost of $10,000 and having a fair market value of $7,000. On this date he sold the stock to his son, William, for $7,000. William sold the stock for $6,000 to an unrelated person on July 1, 2015. How should William report the stock sale on his 2015 tax return?

a. As a short-term capital loss of $1,000.
b. As a long-term capital loss of $1,000.
c. As a short-term capital loss of $4,000.
d. As a long-term capital loss of $4,000.

36. Al Eng owns 50% of the outstanding stock of Rego Corp. During 2015, Rego sold a trailer to Eng for $10,000, the trailer's fair value. The trailer had an adjusted tax basis of $12,000, and had been owned by Rego and used in its business for three years. In its 2015 income tax return, what is the allowable loss that Rego can claim on the sale of this trailer?

a. $0
b. $2,000 capital loss.
c. $2,000 Section 1231 loss.
d. $2,000 Section 1245 loss.

B. Capital Gains and Losses

37. For a cash basis taxpayer, gain or loss on a year-end sale of listed stock arises on the

a. Trade date.
b. Settlement date.
c. Date of receipt of cash proceeds.
d. Date of delivery of stock certificate.

38. Lee qualified as head of a household for 2015 tax purposes. Lee's 2015 taxable income was $100,000, exclusive of capital gains and losses. Lee had a net long-term capital loss of $8,000 in 2015. What amount of this capital loss can Lee offset against 2015 ordinary income?

- a. $0
- b. $3,000
- c. $4,000
- d. $8,000

39. For the year ended December 31, 2014, Sol Corp. had an operating income of $20,000. In addition, Sol had capital gains and losses resulting in a net short-term capital gain of $2,000 and a net long-term capital loss of $7,000. How much of the excess of net long-term capital loss over net short-term capital gain could Sol offset against ordinary income for 2014?

- a. $5,000
- b. $3,000
- c. $1,500
- d. $0

40. In 2015, Nam Corp., which is not a dealer in securities, realized taxable income of $160,000 from its business operations. Also, in 2015, Nam sustained a long-term capital loss of $24,000 from the sale of marketable securities. Nam did not realize any other capital gains or losses since it began operations. In Nam's income tax returns, what is the proper treatment for the $24,000 long-term capital loss?

- a. Use $3,000 of the loss to reduce 2015 taxable income, and carry $21,000 of the long-term capital loss forward for five years.
- b. Use $6,000 of the loss to reduce 2015 taxable income by $3,000, and carry $18,000 of the long-term capital loss forward for five years.
- c. Use $24,000 of the long-term capital loss to reduce 2015 taxable income by $12,000.
- d. Carry the $24,000 long-term capital loss forward for five years, treating it as a short-term capital loss.

41. For assets acquired in 2015, the holding period for determining long-term capital gains and losses is more than

- a. 18 months.
- b. 12 months.
- c. 9 months.
- d. 6 months.

42. On July 1, 2015, Kim Wald sold an antique for $12,000 that she had bought for her personal use in 2013 at a cost of $15,000. In her 2015 return, Kim should treat the sale of the antique as a transaction resulting in

- a. A nondeductible loss.
- b. Ordinary loss.
- c. Short-term capital loss.
- d. Long-term capital loss.

43. Paul Beyer, who is unmarried, has taxable income of $30,000 exclusive of capital gains and losses and his personal exemption. In 2015, Paul incurred a $1,000 net short-term

capital loss and a $5,000 net long-term capital loss. His capital loss carryover to 2016 is

- a. $0
- b. $1,000
- c. $3,000
- d. $5,000

B.1. Capital Assets

44. Capital assets include

- a. A corporation's accounts receivable from the sale of its inventory.
- b. Seven-year MACRS property used in a corporation's trade or business.
- c. A manufacturing company's investment in US Treasury bonds.
- d. A corporate real estate developer's unimproved land that is to be subdivided to build homes, which will be sold to customers.

45. Joe Hall owns a limousine for use in his personal service business of transporting passengers to airports. The limousine's adjusted basis is $40,000. In addition, Hall owns his personal residence and furnishings, that together cost him $280,000. Hall's capital assets amount to

- a. $320,000
- b. $280,000
- c. $40,000
- d. $0

46. During the current year, Ruth Lee sold a painting for $25,000 that she had bought for her personal use in 2009 at a cost of $10,000. In her current year return, Lee should treat the sale of the painting as a transaction resulting in

- a. Ordinary income.
- b. Long-term capital gain.
- c. Section 1231 gain.
- d. No taxable gain.

47. In 2015, a capital loss incurred by a married couple filing a joint return

- a. Will be allowed only to the extent of capital gains.
- b. Will be allowed to the extent of capital gains, plus up to $3,000 of ordinary income.
- c. Will be allowed to the extent of capital gains, plus up to $6,000 of ordinary income.
- d. Is **not** an allowable loss.

48. Platt owns land that is operated as a parking lot. A shed was erected on the lot for the related transactions with customers. With regard to capital assets and Section 1231 assets, how should these assets be classified?

	Land	Shed
a.	Capital	Capital
b.	Section 1231	Capital
c.	Capital	Section 1231
d.	Section 1231	Section 1231

49. In 2010, Iris King bought a diamond necklace for her own use, at a cost of $10,000. In 2015, when the fair market value was $12,000, Iris gave this necklace to her daughter, Ruth. No gift tax was due. This diamond necklace is a

  a. Capital asset.
  b. Section 1231 asset.
  c. Section 1245 asset.
  d. Section 1250 asset.

50. Which of the following is a capital asset?

  a. Delivery truck.
  b. Personal-use recreation equipment.
  c. Land used as a parking lot for customers.
  d. Treasury stock, at cost.

51. Don Mott was the sole proprietor of a high-volume drug store which he owned for fifteen years before he sold it to Dale Drug Stores, Inc. in 2015. Besides the $900,000 selling price for the store's tangible assets and goodwill, Mott received a lump sum of $30,000 in 2015 for his agreement not to operate a competing enterprise within ten miles of the store's location for a period of six years. The $30,000 will be taxed to Mott as

  a. $30,000 ordinary income in 2015.
  b. $30,000 short-term capital gain in 2015.
  c. $30,000 long-term capital gain in 2015.
  d. Ordinary income of $5,000 a year for six years.

52. During the current year, Olive Bell bought a house for use partially as a residence and partially for operation of a retail gift shop. In addition, Olive bought the following furniture:

Kitchen set and living room pieces for the residential portion	$8,000
Showcases and tables for the business portion	12,000

How much of this furniture comprises capital assets?

  a. $0
  b. $8,000
  c. $12,000
  d. $20,000

C. Personal Casualty and Theft Gains and Losses

53. An individual's losses on transactions entered into for personal purposes are deductible only if

  a. The losses qualify as casualty or theft losses.
  b. The losses can be characterized as hobby losses.
  c. The losses do not exceed $3,000 ($6,000 on a joint return).
  d. No part of the transactions was entered into for profit.

D. Gains and Losses on Business Property

54. Evon Corporation, which was formed in 2011, had $50,000 of net Sec. 1231 gain for its 2014 calendar year. Its net Sec. 1231 gains and losses for its three preceding tax years were as follows:

Year	Sec. 1231 results
2011	Gain of $10,000
2012	Loss of $15,000
2013	Loss of $20,000

As a result, Evon Corporation's 2014 net Sec. 1231 gain would be characterized as

  a. A net long-term capital gain of $50,000.
  b. A net long-term capital gain of $35,000 and ordinary income of $15,000.
  c. A net long-term capital gain of $25,000 and ordinary income of $25,000.
  d. A net long-term capital gain of $15,000 and ordinary income of $35,000.

55. Which one of the following would **not** be Sec. 1231 property even though held for more than twelve months?

  a. Business inventory.
  b. Unimproved land used for business.
  c. Depreciable equipment used in a business.
  d. Depreciable real property used in a business.

56. Vermont Corporation distributed packaging equipment that it no longer needed to Michael Jason who owns 20% of Vermont's stock. The equipment, which was acquired in 2010, had an adjusted basis of $2,000 and a fair market value of $9,000 at the date of distribution. Vermont had properly deducted $6,000 of straight-line depreciation on the equipment while it was used in Vermont's manufacturing activities. What amount of ordinary income must Vermont recognize as a result of the distribution of the equipment?

  a. $0
  b. $3,000
  c. $6,000
  d. $7,000

57. Tally Corporation sold machinery that had been used in its business for a loss of $22,000 during 2015. The machinery had been purchased and placed in service sixteen months earlier. For 2015, the $22,000 loss will be treated as a

  a. Capital loss.
  b. Sec. 1245 loss.
  c. Sec. 1231 loss.
  d. Casualty loss because the machinery was held less than two years.

58. On January 2, 2013, Bates Corp. purchased and placed into service seven-year MACRS tangible property costing $100,000. On July 31, 2015, Bates sold the property for $102,000, after having taken $47,525 in MACRS depreciation deductions. What amount of the gain should Bates recapture as ordinary income?

  a. $0
  b. $2,000
  c. $47,525
  d. $49,525

59. Thayer Corporation purchased an apartment building on January 1, 2011, for $200,000. The building was depreciated using the straight-line method. On December 31, 2014, the building was sold for $220,000, when the asset balance net of accumulated depreciation was $170,000. On its 2014 tax return, Thayer should report

    a. Section 1231 gain of $42,500 and ordinary income of $7,500.
    b. Section 1231 gain of $44,000 and ordinary income of $6,000.
    c. Ordinary income of $50,000.
    d. Section 1231 gain of $50,000.

60. For the year ended December 31, 2014, McEwing Corporation, a calendar-year corporation, reported book income before income taxes of $120,000. Included in the determination of this amount were the following gain and losses from property that had been held for more than one year:

Loss on sale of building depreciated on the straight-line method	$(7,000)
Gain on sale of land used in McEwing's business	16,000
Loss on sale of investments in marketable securities	(8,000)

For the year ended December 31, 2014, McEwing's taxable income was

    a. $113,000
    b. $120,000
    c. $125,000
    d. $128,000

61. David Price owned machinery which he had acquired in 2014 at a cost of $100,000. During 2015, the machinery was destroyed by fire. At that time it had an adjusted basis of $86,000. The insurance proceeds awarded to Price amounted to $125,000, and he immediately acquired a similar machine for $110,000.

What should Price report as ordinary income resulting from the involuntary conversion for 2015?

    a. $14,000
    b. $15,000
    c. $25,000
    d. $39,000

Multiple-Choice Answers and Explanations

Answers

1. d		15. a		29. c		43. c		57. c	
2. d		16. c		30. c		44. c		58. c	
3. c		17. c		31. a		45. b		59. b	
4. c		18. d		32. a		46. b		60. b	
5. c		19. d		33. b		47. b		61. a	
6. b		20. d		34. c		48. d			
7. b		21. b		35. a		49. a			
8. b		22. c		36. c		50. b			
9. d		23. d		37. a		51. a			
10. b		24. c		38. b		52. b			
11. c		25. a		39. d		53. a			
12. c		26. b		40. d		54. d			
13. d		27. b		41. b		55. a		1st: __/61 = __%	
14. b		28. a		42. a		56. c		2nd: __/61 = __%	

Explanations

1. (d) The requirement is to determine Birch's tax basis for the purchased land and building. The basis of property acquired by purchase is a cost basis and includes not only the cash paid and liabilities incurred, but also includes certain settlement fees and closing costs such as abstract of title fees, installation of utility services, legal fees (including title search, contract, and deed fees), recording fees, surveys, transfer taxes, owner's title insurance, and any amounts the seller owes that the buyer agrees to pay, such as back taxes and interest, recording or mortgage fees, charges for improvements or repairs, and sales commissions.

2. (d) The requirement is to determine the basis for the purchased land. The basis of the land consists of the cash paid ($40,000), the purchase money mortgage ($50,000), and the cost of the title insurance policy ($200), a total of $90,200.

3. (c) The requirement is to determine the amount of gain recognized by Thompson resulting from the sale of appreciated property received as a gift. A donee's basis for appreciated property received as a gift is generally the same as the donor's basis. Since Smith had a basis for the property of $1,200 and Thompson sold the property for $2,500, Thompson must recognize a gain of $1,300.

4. (c) The requirement is to determine Julie's basis for the land received as a gift. A donee's basis for gift property is generally the same as the donor's basis, increased by any gift tax paid that is attributable to the property's net appreciation in value. That is, the amount of gift tax that can be added is limited to the amount that bears the same ratio as the property's net appreciation bears to the amount of taxable gift. For this purpose, the amount of gift is reduced by any portion of the $14,000 annual exclusion that is allowable with respect to the gift. Thus, Julie's basis is $24,000 + [$14,000 ($84,000 − 24,000) / ($84,000 − $14,000)] = $36,000.

5. (c) The requirement is to determine Ruth's recognized loss if she sells the stock received as a gift for $7,000. Since the stock's FMV ($8,000) was less than its basis ($10,000) at date of gift, Ruth's basis for computing a loss is the stock's FMV of $8,000 at date of gift. As a result, Ruth's recognized loss is $8,000 − $7,000 = $1,000.

6. (b) The requirement is to determine Ruth's holding period for stock received as a gift. If property is received as a gift, and the property's FMV on date of gift is used to determine a loss, the donee's holding period begins when the gift was received. Thus, Ruth's holding period started.

7. (b) The requirement is to determine the basis of the Liba stock if it is sold for $5,000. If property acquired by gift is sold at a gain, its basis is the donor's basis ($4,000), increased by any gift tax paid attributable to the net appreciation in value of the gift ($0).

8. (b) The requirement is to determine the basis of the Liba stock if it is sold for $2,000. If property acquired by gift is sold at a loss, its basis is the lesser of (1) its gain basis ($4,000 above), or (2) its FMV at date of gift ($3,000).

9. (d) The requirement is to determine the amount of reportable gain or loss if the Liba stock is sold for $3,500. No gain or loss is recognized on the sale of property acquired by gift if the basis for loss ($3,000) results in a gain and the basis for gain ($4,000) results in a loss.

10. (b) The requirement is to determine the holding period for stock received as a bequest from the estate of a deceased uncle. Property received from a decedent is deemed to be held long-term regardless of the actual period of time that the decedent or beneficiary actually held the property and is treated as held for more than twelve months.

11. (c) The requirement is to determine Ida's basis for stock inherited from a decedent. The basis of property received from a decedent is generally the property's FMV at date of the decedent's death, or FMV on the alternate valuation date (six months after death). Since the executor of Zorn's estate elected to use the alternate valuation for estate tax purposes, the stock's basis to Ida is its $450,000 FMV six months after Zorn's death. Note, if the stock had been distributed to Ida within six months of Zorn's death, the stock's basis would be its FMV on date of distribution.

12. (c) The requirement is to determine Lois' basis for gain or loss on the sale of Elin stock acquired from a decedent. Since the alternate valuation was elected for Prevor's estate, but the stock was distributed to Lois within six months of date of death, Lois' basis is the $9,000 FMV of the stock on date of distribution (12/1/14).

13. (d) The requirement is to determine how Lois should treat the shares of Elin stock that she inherited from her uncle who died during 2014. The stock should be treated as a capital asset held long-term since (1) property acquired from a decedent is considered to be held for more than twelve months regardless of its actual holding period, and (2) the stock is an investment asset in Lois' hands. The stock is not a Sec. 1231 asset because it was not held for use in Lois' trade or business.

14. (b) The requirement is to determine the basis for the common stock and the preferred stock after the receipt of a nontaxable preferred stock dividend. Joan's original common stock basis must be allocated between the common stock and the preferred stock according to their relative fair market value.

Common stock (FMV)	$450
Preferred stock (FMV)	150
Total value	$600

The ratio of the common stock to total value is $450/$600 or 3/4. This ratio multiplied by the original common stock basis of $300 results in a basis for the common stock of $225. The basis of the preferred stock would be ($150/$600 × $300) = $75.

15. (a) The requirement is to determine the holding period for preferred stock that was received in a nontaxable distribution on common stock. Since the tax basis of the preferred stock is determined in part by the basis of the common stock, the holding period of the preferred stock includes the holding period of the common stock (i.e., the holding period of the common stock tacks on to the preferred stock). Thus, the holding period of the preferred stock starts when the common stock was acquired, January 2015.

16. (c) The requirement is to determine the amount of long-term capital gain to be reported on the sale of fifty shares of stock received as a nontaxable stock dividend. After the stock dividend, the basis of each share would be determined as follows:

$$\frac{\$90,000}{450 + 50} = \$180 \text{ per share}$$

Since the holding period of the new shares includes the holding period of the old shares, the sale of the fifty new

shares for $11,000 results in a LTCG of $2,000 [$11,000 – (50 shares × $180)].

17. (c) The requirement is to determine Gow's recognized gain and basis for the investment real estate acquired in a like-kind exchange. In a like-kind exchange of property held for investment, a realized gain ($15,000 in this case) will be recognized only to the extent of unlike property (i.e., boot) received. Here the unlike property consists of the $2,000 cash and $3,000 FMV of the sailboat received, resulting in the recognition of $5,000 of gain. The basis of the acquired like-kind property reflects the deferred gain resulting from the like-kind exchange, and is equal to the basis of the property transferred ($25,000), increased by the amount of gain recognized ($5,000), and decreased by the amount of boot received ($2,000 +$3,000), or $25,000.

18. (d) The requirement is to determine which exchange qualifies for nonrecognition of gain or loss as a like-kind exchange. The exchange of business or investment property solely for like-kind business or investment property is treated as a nontaxable exchange. Like-kind means "the same class of property." Real property must be exchanged for real property, and personal property must be exchanged for personal property. Here, the exchange of rental real estate is an exchange of like-kind property, even though the real estate is located in different states. The like-kind exchange provisions do not apply to exchanges of stocks, bonds, notes, convertible securities, the exchange of partnership interests, and property held for personal use.

19. (d) The requirement is to determine the reportable gain resulting from the exchange of an apartment building for an office building. No gain or loss is recognized on the exchange of business or investment property for property of a like-kind. The term "like-kind" means the same class of property (i.e., real estate must be exchanged for real estate, personal property exchanged for personal property). Thus, the exchange of an apartment building for an office building qualifies as a like-kind exchange. Since no boot (money or unlike property) was received, the realized gain of $600,000 – $200,000 = $400,000 is not recognized.

20. (d) The requirement is to determine the amount of recognized gain resulting from a like-kind exchange of investment property. In a like-kind exchange, gain is recognized to the extent of the lesser of (1) "boot" received, or (2) gain realized.

FMV of property received	$250,000
Cash received	30,000
Mortgage assumed	70,000
Amount realized	$350,000
Basis of property exchanged	(160,000)
Gain realized	$190,000

Since the "boot" received includes both the cash and the assumption of the mortgage, gain is recognized to the extent of the $100,000 of "boot" received.

21. (b) The requirement is to determine the amount of gain recognized to Anderson on the like-kind exchange of apartment buildings. Anderson's realized gain is computed as follows:

FMV of building received		$550,000
Mortgage on old building		100,000
Cash received		25,000
Amount realized		$675,000
Less:		
Basis of old building	$375,000	
Mortgage on new building	125,000	500,000
Realized gain		$175,000

Since the boot received in the form of cash cannot be offset against boot given in the form of an assumption of a mortgage, the realized gain is recognized to the extent of the $25,000 cash received.

22. (c) The requirement is to determine the basis of a new truck acquired in a like-kind exchange. The basis of the new truck is the book value (i.e., adjusted basis) of the old truck of $4,000 plus the additional cash paid of $19,000 (i.e., the list price of the new truck of $25,000 less the trade-in allowance of $6,000).

23. (d) The requirement is to determine the end of the replacement period for nonrecognition of gain following the condemnation of real property. For a condemnation of real property held for productive use in a trade or business or for investment, the replacement period ends three years after the close of the taxable year in which the gain is first realized. Since the gain was realized in 2014, the replacement period ends December 31, 2017. .

24. (c) The requirement is to determine the amount of gain from the sale of the former residence that is recognized on Davis' 2015 return. An individual may exclude from income up to $250,000 of gain that is realized on the sale or exchange of a residence, if the individual owned and occupied the residence as a principal residence for an aggregate of at least two of the five years preceding the sale or exchange. Davis' former residence cost $65,000 and he had made improvements costing $5,000, resulting in a basis of $70,000. Since Davis sold his former residence for $380,000 and paid a realtor commission of $20,000, the net amount realized from the sale was $360,000. Thus, Davis realized a gain of $360,000 – $70,000 = $290,000. Since Davis qualifies to exclude $250,000 of the gain from income, the remaining $40,000 of gain is recognized and included in Davis' income for 2015.

25. (a) The requirement is to determine the amount of gain to be recognized on the Orans' 2015 joint return from the sale of their residence. An individual may exclude from income up to $250,000 of gain that is realized on the sale or exchange of a residence, if the individual owned and occupied the residence as a principal residence for an aggregate of at least two of the five years preceding the sale or exchange. The amount of excludable gain is increased to $500,000 for married individuals filing jointly if either spouse meets the ownership requirement, and both spouses meet the use requirement. Here, the Orans realized a gain of $760,000 – $170,000 = $590,000, and qualify to exclude $500,000 of the gain from income.

The remaining $90,000 of gain is recognized and taxed to the Orans for 2015.

26. (b) The requirement is to determine the maximum exclusion of gain on the sale of Ryan's principal residence. An individual may exclude from income up to $250,000 of gain that is realized on the sale or exchange of a residence, if the individual owned and occupied the residence as a principal residence for an aggregate of at least two of the five years preceding the sale or exchange. Since Ryan meets the ownership and use requirements, and realized a gain of $400,000 – $180,000 = $220,000, all of Ryan's gain will be excluded from his gross income.

27. (b) The requirement is to determine Miller's recognized loss and the basis for her remaining fifty shares of Maples Inc. stock. No loss can be deducted on the sale of stock if substantially identical stock is purchased within thirty days before or after the sale. Any loss that is not deductible because of this rule is added to the basis of the new stock. If the taxpayer acquires less than the number of shares sold, the amount of loss that cannot be recognized is determined by the ratio of the number of shares acquired to the number of shares sold. Miller purchased 100 shares of Maples stock for $10,000 and sold the stock on January 8, 2015, for $7,000, resulting in a loss of $3,000. However, only half of the loss can be deducted by Miller because on December 24, 2014 (within thirty days before the January 8, 2015 sale), Miller purchased an additional 50 shares of Maples stock. Since only $1,500 of the loss can be recognized, the $1,500 of loss not recognized is added to the basis of Miller's remaining 50 shares resulting in a basis of $4,000 + $1,500 = $5,500.

28. (a) The requirement is to determine the amount of loss from the sale of Core stock that is deductible on Smith's 2014 and 2015 income tax returns. No loss can be deducted on the sale of stock if substantially identical stock is purchased within thirty days before or after the sale. Any loss that is not deductible because of this rule is added to the basis of the new stock. In this case, Smith purchased 100 shares of Core stock for $15,000 and sold the stock on January 3, 2015, for $13,000, resulting in a loss of $2,000. However, the loss cannot be deducted by Smith because on December 30, 2014 (within thirty days prior to the January 3, 2015 sale), Smith purchased an additional 100 shares of Core stock. Smith's disallowed loss of $2,000 is added to the $13,000 cost of the 100 Core shares acquired on December 30 resulting in a tax basis of $15,000 for those shares.

29. (c) The purchase of substantially identical stock within thirty days of the sale of stock at a loss is known as a wash sale. The $800 loss incurred in the wash sale ($5,000 basis less $4,200 amount realized) is disallowed. The basis of the replacement (substantially identical) stock is its cost ($3,600) plus the disallowed wash sale loss ($800). The holding period of the replacement stock includes the holding period of the wash sale stock. The amount realized ($6,000) less the basis ($4,400) results in a long-term gain of $1,600.

30. (c) Worthless securities generally receive capital loss treatment. However, if the loss is incurred by a corporation on its investment in an affiliated corporation (80% or more ownership), the loss is generally treated as an ordinary loss.

31. (a) The requirement is to determine the amount of the $10,000 loss that Conner can deduct from the sale of stock to his daughter, Alice. Losses are disallowed on sales or exchanges of property between related taxpayers, including members of a family. For this purpose, the term *family* includes an individual's spouse, brothers, sisters, ancestors, and lineal descendants (e.g., children, grandchildren, etc.). Since Conner sold the stock to his daughter, no loss can be deducted.

32. (a) The requirement is to determine the recognized gain or loss on Alice's sale of the stock that she had purchased from her father. Losses are disallowed on sales or exchanges of property between related taxpayers, including family members. Any gain later realized by the related transferee on the subsequent disposition of the property is not recognized to the extent of the transferor's disallowed loss. Here, her father's realized loss of $30,000 – $20,000 = $10,000 was disallowed because he sold the stock to his daughter, Alice. Her basis for the stock is her cost of $20,000. On the subsequent sale of the stock, Alice realizes a gain of $25,000 – $20,000 = $5,000. However, this realized gain of $5,000 is not recognized because of her father's disallowed loss of $10,000.

33. (b) The requirement is to determine the amount of gain from the sale of stock to a third party that Martin should report on his 2015 income tax return. Losses are disallowed on sales of property between related taxpayers, including family members. Any gain later realized by the transferee on the disposition of the property is not recognized to the extent of the transferor's disallowed loss. Here, Fay's realized loss of $15,000 – $11,000 = $4,000 is disallowed because she sold the stock to her son, Martin. Martin's basis for the stock is his cost of $11,000. On the subsequent sale of the stock to an unrelated third party, Martin realizes a gain of $16,000 – $11,000 = $5,000. However, this realized gain of $5,000 is recognized only to the extent that it exceeds Fay's $4,000 disallowed loss, or $1,000.

34. (c) The requirement is to determine among which of the related individuals are losses from sales and exchanges not recognized for tax purposes. No loss deduction is allowed on the sale or exchange of property between members of a family. For this purpose, an individual's *family* includes only brothers, sisters, half-brothers and half-sisters, spouse, ancestors (parents, grandparents, etc.), and lineal descendants (children, grandchildren, etc.). Since in-laws and uncles are excluded from this definition of a family, a loss resulting from a sale or exchange with an uncle or between in-laws would be recognized.

35. (a) Losses are disallowed on sales between related taxpayers, including family members. Thus, Daniel's loss of $3,000 is disallowed on the sale of stock to his son, William. William's basis for the stock is his $7,000 cost. Since William's stock basis is determined by his cost (not by reference to Daniel's cost), there is no "tack-on" of Daniel's holding period. Thus, a later sale of the stock for $6,000 on July 1 generates a $1,000 STCL for William.

36. (c) The requirement is to determine the amount of loss that Rego Corp. can deduct on a sale of its trailer to a 50% shareholder. Losses are disallowed on transactions between related taxpayers, including a corporation and a shareholder owning more than 50% of its stock. Since Al Eng owns only 50% (not more than 50%), the loss is recognized by Rego. Since the trailer was held for more than one year and used in Rego's business, the $2,000 loss is a Sec. 1231 loss. Answer (d) is incorrect because Sec. 1245 only applies to gains.

37. (a) The requirement is to determine when gain or loss on a year-end sale of listed stock arises for a cash basis taxpayer. If stock or securities that are traded on an established securities market are sold, any resulting gain or loss is recognized on the trade date (i.e., the date on which the trade is executed) by both cash and accrual method taxpayers.

38. (b) The requirement is to determine the amount of an $8,000 net long-term capital loss that can be offset against Lee's taxable income of $100,000. An individual's net capital loss can be offset against ordinary income up to a maximum of $3,000 ($1,500 if married filing separately). Since a net capital loss offsets ordinary income dollar for dollar, Lee has a $3,000 net capital loss deduction for 2015 and a long-term capital loss carryover of $5,000 to 2016.

39. (d) The requirement is to determine the amount of excess of net long-term capital loss over net short-term capital gain that Sol Corp. can offset against ordinary income. A corporation's net capital loss cannot be offset against ordinary income. Instead, a net capital loss is generally carried back three years and forward five years as a STCL to offset capital gains in those years.

40. (d) The requirement is to determine the proper treatment for a $24,000 NLTCL for Nam Corp. A corporation's capital losses can only be used to offset capital gains. If a corporation has a net capital loss, the net capital loss cannot be currently deducted, but must be carried back three years and forward five years as a STCL to offset capital gains in those years. Since Nam had not realized any capital gains since it began operations, the $24,000 LTCL can only be carried forward for five years as a STCL.

41. (b) The requirement is to determine the holding period for determining long-term capital gains and losses. Long-term capital gains and losses result if capital assets are held more than twelve months.

42. (a) The requirement is to determine the treatment for the sale of the antique by Wald. Since the antique was held for personal use, the sale of the antique at a loss is not deductible.

43. (c) The requirement is to determine the capital loss carryover to 2016. The NSTCL and the NLTCL result in a net capital loss of $6,000. LTCLs are deductible dollar for dollar, the same as STCLs. Since an individual can deduct a net capital loss up to a maximum of $3,000, the net capital loss of $6,000 results in a capital loss deduction of $3,000 for 2015, and a long-term capital loss carryover to 2016 of $3,000.

44. (c) The requirement is to determine the item that is included in the definition of capital assets. The definition of capital assets includes property held as an investment and would include a manufacturing company's investment in

US Treasury bonds. In contrast, the definition specifically excludes accounts receivable arising from the sale of inventory, depreciable property used in a trade or business, and property held primarily for sale to customers in the ordinary course of a trade or business.

45. (b) The requirement is to determine the amount of Hall's capital assets. The definition of capital assets includes investment property and property held for personal use (e.g., personal residence and furnishings), but excludes property used in a trade or business (e.g., limousine).

46. (b) The requirement is to determine the proper treatment for the gain recognized on the sale of a painting that was purchased in 2009 and held for personal use. The definition of "capital assets" includes investment property and property held for personal use (if sold at a gain). Because the painting was held for more than one year, the gain from the sale of the painting must be reported as a long-term capital gain. Note that if personal-use property is sold at a loss, the loss is not deductible.

47. (b) The requirement is to determine the correct treatment for a capital loss incurred by a married couple filing a joint return for 2015. Capital losses first offset capital gains, and then are allowed as a deduction of up to $3,000 against ordinary income, with any unused capital loss carried forward indefinitely. Note that a married taxpayer filing separately can only offset up to $1,500 of net capital loss against ordinary income.

48. (d) The requirement is to determine the proper classification of land used as a parking lot and a shed erected on the lot for customer transactions. The definition of capital assets includes investment property and property held for personal use, but excludes any property used in a trade or business. The definition of Sec. 1231 assets generally includes business assets held more than one year. Since the land and shed were used in conjunction with a parking lot business, they are properly classified as Sec. 1231 assets.

49. (a) The requirement is to determine the classification of Ruth's diamond necklace. The diamond necklace is classified as a capital asset because the definition of "capital asset" includes investment property and *property held for personal use*. Answers (b), (c), and (d) are incorrect because Sec. 1231 generally includes only assets used in a trade or business, while Sections 1245 and 1250 only include depreciable assets.

50. (b) The requirement is to determine which asset is a capital asset. The definition of capital assets includes personal-use property, but excludes property used in a trade or business (e.g., delivery truck, land used as a parking lot). Treasury stock is not considered an asset, but instead is treated as a reduction of stockholders' equity.

51. (a) The requirement is to determine how a lump sum of $30,000 received in 2015, for an agreement not to operate a competing enterprise, should be treated. A covenant not to compete is not a capital asset. Thus, the $30,000 received as consideration for such an agreement must be reported as ordinary income in the year received.

52. (b) The requirement is to determine the amount of furniture classified as capital assets. The definition of capital assets includes investment property and property held for personal use (e.g., kitchen and living room pieces), but excludes property used in a trade or business (e.g., showcases and tables).

53. (a) The requirement is to determine the correct statement regarding the deductibility of an individual's losses on transactions entered into for personal purposes. An individual's losses on transactions entered into for personal purposes are deductible only if the losses qualify as casualty or theft losses. Answer (b) is incorrect because hobby losses are not deductible. Answers (c) and (d) are incorrect because losses (other than by casualty or theft) on transactions entered into for personal purposes are not deductible.

54. (d) The requirement is to determine the characterization of Evon Corporation's $50,000 of net Sec. 1231 gain for its 2014 tax year. Although a net Sec. 1231 gain is generally treated as a long-term capital gain, it instead must be treated as ordinary income to the extent of the taxpayer's nonrecaptured net Sec. 1231 losses for its five preceding taxable years. Here, since the nonrecaptured net Sec. 1231 losses for 2012 and 2013 total $35,000, only $15,000 of the $50,000 net Sec. 1231 gain will be treated as a long-term capital gain.

55. (a) The requirement is to determine which item would not be characterized as Sec. 1231 property. Sec. 1231 property generally includes both depreciable and nondepreciable property used in a trade or business or held for the production of income if held for more than twelve months. Specifically excluded from Sec. 1231 is inventory and property held for sale to customers, as well as accounts and notes receivable arising in the ordinary course of a trade or business.

56. (c) The requirement is to determine the amount of ordinary income that must be recognized by Vermont Corporation from the distribution of the equipment to a shareholder. When a corporation distributes appreciated property, it must recognize gain just as if it had sold the property for its fair market value. As a result Vermont must recognize a gain of $9,000 – $2,000 = $7,000 on the distribution of the equipment. Since the distributed property is depreciable personal property, the gain is subject to Sec. 1245 recapture as ordinary income to the extent of the $6,000 of straight-line depreciation deducted by Vermont. The remaining $1,000 of gain would be treated as Sec. 1231 gain.

57. (c) The requirement is to determine the nature of a loss resulting from the sale of business machinery that had been held sixteen months. Property held for use in a trade or business is specifically excluded from the definition of capital assets, and if held for more than one year is considered Sec. 1231 property. Answer (b) is incorrect because Sec. 1245 only applies to gains.

58. (c) The requirement is to determine the amount of gain from the sale of property that must be recaptured as ordinary income. A gain from the disposition of seven-year tangible property is subject to recapture under Sec. 1245 which recaptures gain to the extent of all depreciation previously

644   **Module 36: Transactions in Property**

deducted. Here, Bates' gain from the sale of the property is determined as follows:

Selling price		$102,000
Cost	$100,000	
Depreciation	– 47,525	
Adjusted basis		– 52,475
Gain		$49,525

Under Sec. 1245, Bates Corp's gain is recaptured as ordinary income to the extent of the $47,525 deducted as depreciation. The remaining $2,000 of gain would be classified as Sec. 1231 gain.

59. (b) The requirement is to determine the proper treatment of the $50,000 gain on the sale of the building, which is Sec. 1250 property. Sec. 1250 recaptures gain as ordinary income to the extent of "excess" depreciation (i.e., depreciation deducted in excess of straight-line). The total gain less any depreciation recapture is Sec. 1231 gain. Since straight-line depreciation was used, there is no recapture under Sec. 1250. However, Sec. 291 requires that the amount of ordinary income on the disposition of Sec. 1250 property by corporations be increased by 20% of the additional amount that would have been ordinary income if the property had instead been Sec.

1245 property. If the building had been Sec. 1245 property the amount of recapture would have been $30,000 ($200,000 – $170,000). Thus, the Sec. 291 ordinary income is $30,000 × 20% = $6,000. The remaining $44,000 is Sec. 1231 gain.

60. (b) The requirement is to determine McEwing Corporation's taxable income given book income plus additional information regarding items that were included in book income. The loss on sale of the building ($7,000) and gain on sale of the land ($16,000) are Sec. 1231 gains and losses. The resulting Sec. 1231 net gain of $9,000 is then treated as LTCG and will be offset against the LTCL of $8,000 resulting from the sale of investments. Since these items have already been included in book income, McEwing's taxable income is the same as its book income, $120,000.

61. (a) The realized gain resulting from the involuntary conversion ($125,000 insurance proceeds – $86,000 adjusted basis = $39,000) is recognized only to the extent that the insurance proceeds are not reinvested in similar property ($125,000 – $110,000 = $15,000). Since the machinery was Sec. 1245 property, the recognized gain of $15,000 is recaptured as ordinary income to the extent of the $14,000 of depreciation previously deducted. The remaining $1,000 is Sec. 1231 gain.

Simulations

Task-Based Simulation 1

Form 8949 Schedule D		
	Authoritative Literature	Help

Situation

Lou Thomas (social security #123-45-6789) reported the following transactions for calendar-year 2014:

- Lou sold 100 shares of Copperleaf Industries on October 20, 2014, for $4,200. Lou had acquired the stock for $2,500 on March 1, 2013.
- Lou sold 200 shares of King Corporation stock for $5,000 on November 15, 2014. He had purchased the stock on February 24, 2014, for $4,000.
- Thomas had a net short-term capital loss carryforward from 2013 of $7,300, and during December 2014 received a $1,500 capital gain distribution from the Brooks Mutual fund.
- Thomas did not receive any qualified dividends during this year.

Use the above information to complete the following 2014 Form 1040 Schedule D for Thomas.

SCHEDULE D **(Form 1040)**	**Capital Gains and Losses**	OMB No. 1545-0074
Department of the Treasury Internal Revenue Service (99)	▶ Attach to Form 1040 or Form 1040NR. ▶ Information about Schedule D and its separate instructions is at *www.irs.gov/scheduled*. ▶ Use Form 8949 to list your transactions for lines 1b, 2, 3, 8b, 9, and 10.	20**14** Attachment Sequence No. **12**

Name(s) shown on return	Your social security number

Part I Short-Term Capital Gains and Losses—Assets Held One Year or Less

See instructions for how to figure the amounts to enter on the lines below. This form may be easier to complete if you round off cents to whole dollars.	**(d)** Proceeds (sales price)	**(e)** Cost (or other basis)	**(g)** Adjustments to gain or loss from Form(s) 8949, Part I, line 2, column (g)	**(h) Gain or (loss)** Subtract column (e) from column (d) and combine the result with column (g)
1a Totals for all short-term transactions reported on Form 1099-B for which basis was reported to the IRS and for which you have no adjustments (see instructions). However, if you choose to report all these transactions on Form 8949, leave this line blank and go to line 1b .				
1b Totals for all transactions reported on Form(s) 8949 with **Box A** checked				
2 Totals for all transactions reported on Form(s) 8949 with **Box B** checked				
3 Totals for all transactions reported on Form(s) 8949 with **Box C** checked				

4 Short-term gain from Form 6252 and short-term gain or (loss) from Forms 4684, 6781, and 8824 .	**4**	
5 Net short-term gain or (loss) from partnerships, S corporations, estates, and trusts from Schedule(s) K-1	**5**	
6 Short-term capital loss carryover. Enter the amount, if any, from line 8 of your **Capital Loss Carryover Worksheet** in the instructions	**6** ( )
7 **Net short-term capital gain or (loss).** Combine lines 1a through 6 in column (h). If you have any long-term capital gains or losses, go to Part II below. Otherwise, go to Part III on the back	**7**	

Part II Long-Term Capital Gains and Losses—Assets Held More Than One Year

See instructions for how to figure the amounts to enter on the lines below. This form may be easier to complete if you round off cents to whole dollars.	**(d)** Proceeds (sales price)	**(e)** Cost (or other basis)	**(g)** Adjustments to gain or loss from Form(s) 8949, Part II, line 2, column (g)	**(h) Gain or (loss)** Subtract column (e) from column (d) and combine the result with column (g)
8a Totals for all long-term transactions reported on Form 1099-B for which basis was reported to the IRS and for which you have no adjustments (see instructions). However, if you choose to report all these transactions on Form 8949, leave this line blank and go to line 8b .				
8b Totals for all transactions reported on Form(s) 8949 with **Box D** checked				
9 Totals for all transactions reported on Form(s) 8949 with **Box E** checked				
10 Totals for all transactions reported on Form(s) 8949 with **Box F** checked				

11 Gain from Form 4797, Part I; long-term gain from Forms 2439 and 6252; and long-term gain or (loss) from Forms 4684, 6781, and 8824	**11**	
12 Net long-term gain or (loss) from partnerships, S corporations, estates, and trusts from Schedule(s) K-1	**12**	
13 Capital gain distributions. See the instructions	**13**	
14 Long-term capital loss carryover. Enter the amount, if any, from line 13 of your **Capital Loss Carryover Worksheet** in the instructions	**14** ( )
15 **Net long-term capital gain or (loss).** Combine lines 8a through 14 in column (h). Then go to Part III on the back	**15**	

For Paperwork Reduction Act Notice, see your tax return instructions.   Cat. No. 11338H   **Schedule D (Form 1040) 2014**

Part III   **Summary**

16   Combine lines 7 and 15 and enter the result **16**

    • If line 16 is a **gain,** enter the amount from line 16 on Form 1040, line 13, or Form 1040NR, line 14. Then go to line 17 below.

    • If line 16 is a **loss,** skip lines 17 through 20 below. Then go to line 21. Also be sure to complete line 22.

    • If line 16 is **zero,** skip lines 17 through 21 below and enter -0- on Form 1040, line 13, or Form 1040NR, line 14. Then go to line 22.

17   Are lines 15 and 16 **both** gains?
    ☐ **Yes.** Go to line 18.
    ☐ **No.** Skip lines 18 through 21, and go to line 22.

18   Enter the amount, if any, from line 7 of the **28% Rate Gain Worksheet** in the instructions . . ▶   **18**

19   Enter the amount, if any, from line 18 of the **Unrecaptured Section 1250 Gain Worksheet** in the instructions . . . . ▶   **19**

20   Are lines 18 and 19 **both** zero or blank?
    ☐ **Yes.** Complete the **Qualified Dividends and Capital Gain Tax Worksheet** in the instructions for Form 1040, line 44 (or in the instructions for Form 1040NR, line 42). **Do not** complete lines 21 and 22 below.

    ☐ **No.** Complete the **Schedule D Tax Worksheet** in the instructions. **Do not** complete lines 21 and 22 below.

21   If line 16 is a loss, enter here and on Form 1040, line 13, or Form 1040NR, line 14, the **smaller** of:

    • The loss on line 16 or
    • ($3,000), or if married filing separately, ($1,500)   . . . .   **21** (   )

    Note. When figuring which amount is smaller, treat both amounts as positive numbers.

22   Do you have qualified dividends on Form 1040, line 9b, or Form 1040NR, line 10b?

    ☐ **Yes.** Complete the **Qualified Dividends and Capital Gain Tax Worksheet** in the instructions for Form 1040, line 44 (or in the instructions for Form 1040NR, line 42).

    ☐ **No.** Complete the rest of Form 1040 or Form 1040NR.

Task-Based Simulation 2

Research		
	Authoritative Literature	Help

Thomas contacts you and indicates that he expects to incur a substantial net capital loss for calendar-year 2015 and wonders what the treatment of the carryforwards will be in future years. Which code section and subsection provides for the treatment of an individual's capital loss carryforward? Indicate the reference to that citation in the shaded boxes below.

Section		Subsection	
§		(	)

Simulation Solutions

Task-Based Simulation 1

Form 1040 Schedule D

| Authoritative Literature | Help |

SCHEDULE D (Form 1040)

Department of the Treasury
Internal Revenue Service (99)

Capital Gains and Losses

► Attach to Form 1040 or Form 1040NR.
► Information about Schedule D and its separate instructions is at *www.irs.gov/scheduled*.
► Use Form 8949 to list your transactions for lines 1b, 2, 3, 8b, 9, and 10.

OMB No. 1545-0074

2014
Attachment Sequence No. **12**

Name(s) shown on return: Lou Thomas

Your social security number: 123-45-6789

Part I — Short-Term Capital Gains and Losses—Assets Held One Year or Less

See instructions for how to figure the amounts to enter on the lines below.

This form may be easier to complete if you round off cents to whole dollars.

	(d) Proceeds (sales price)	(e) Cost (or other basis)	(g) Adjustments to gain or loss from Form(s) 8949, Part I, line 2, column (g)	(h) Gain or (loss) Subtract column (e) from column (d) and combine the result with column (g)
1a Totals for all short-term transactions reported on Form 1099-B for which basis was reported to the IRS and for which you have no adjustments (see instructions). However, if you choose to report all these transactions on Form 8949, leave this line blank and go to line 1b .	5,000	4,000		1,000
1b Totals for all transactions reported on Form(s) 8949 with **Box A** checked				
2 Totals for all transactions reported on Form(s) 8949 with **Box B** checked				
3 Totals for all transactions reported on Form(s) 8949 with **Box C** checked				

4 Short-term gain from Form 6252 and short-term gain or (loss) from Forms 4684, 6781, and 8824 .	**4**	
5 Net short-term gain or (loss) from partnerships, S corporations, estates, and trusts from Schedule(s) K-1	**5**	
6 Short-term capital loss carryover. Enter the amount, if any, from line 8 of your **Capital Loss Carryover Worksheet** in the instructions . .	**6** (	7,300)
7 **Net short-term capital gain or (loss).** Combine lines 1a through 6 in column (h). If you have any long-term capital gains or losses, go to Part II below. Otherwise, go to Part III on the back	**7**	(6,300)

Part II — Long-Term Capital Gains and Losses—Assets Held More Than One Year

See instructions for how to figure the amounts to enter on the lines below.

This form may be easier to complete if you round off cents to whole dollars.

	(d) Proceeds (sales price)	(e) Cost (or other basis)	(g) Adjustments to gain or loss from Form(s) 8949, Part II, line 2, column (g)	(h) Gain or (loss) Subtract column (e) from column (d) and combine the result with column (g)
8a Totals for all long-term transactions reported on Form 1099-B for which basis was reported to the IRS and for which you have no adjustments (see instructions). However, if you choose to report all these transactions on Form 8949, leave this line blank and go to line 8b .	4,200	2,500		1,700
8b Totals for all transactions reported on Form(s) 8949 with **Box D** checked				
9 Totals for all transactions reported on Form(s) 8949 with **Box E** checked				
10 Totals for all transactions reported on Form(s) 8949 with **Box F** checked				

11 Gain from Form 4797, Part I; long-term gain from Forms 2439 and 6252; and long-term gain or (loss) from Forms 4684, 6781, and 8824	**11**	
12 Net long-term gain or (loss) from partnerships, S corporations, estates, and trusts from Schedule(s) K-1	**12**	
13 Capital gain distributions. See the instructions	**13**	1,500
14 Long-term capital loss carryover. Enter the amount, if any, from line 13 of your **Capital Loss Carryover Worksheet** in the instructions . .	**14** (	)
15 **Net long-term capital gain or (loss).** Combine lines 8a through 14 in column (h). Then go to Part III on the back	**15**	3,200

For Paperwork Reduction Act Notice, see your tax return instructions. Cat. No. 11338H Schedule D (Form 1040) 2014

Part III	**Summary**

16   Combine lines 7 and 15 and enter the result **16**   (3,100)

     • If line 16 is a **gain,** enter the amount from line 16 on Form 1040, line 13, or Form 1040NR, line 14. Then go to line 17 below.

     • If line 16 is a **loss,** skip lines 17 through 20 below. Then go to line 21. Also be sure to complete line 22.

     • If line 16 is **zero,** skip lines 17 through 21 below and enter -0- on Form 1040, line 13, or Form 1040NR, line 14. Then go to line 22.

17   Are lines 15 and 16 **both** gains?
     ☐ **Yes.** Go to line 18.
     ☑ **No.** Skip lines 18 through 21, and go to line 22.

18   Enter the amount, if any, from line 7 of the **28% Rate Gain Worksheet** in the instructions . . ▶   **18**

19   Enter the amount, if any, from line 18 of the **Unrecaptured Section 1250 Gain Worksheet** in the instructions . . . . ▶   **19**

20   Are lines 18 and 19 **both** zero or blank?
     ☐ **Yes.** Complete the **Qualified Dividends and Capital Gain Tax Worksheet** in the instructions for Form 1040, line 44 (or in the instructions for Form 1040NR, line 42). **Do not** complete lines 21 and 22 below.

     ☐ **No.** Complete the **Schedule D Tax Worksheet** in the instructions. **Do not** complete lines 21 and 22 below.

21   If line 16 is a loss, enter here and on Form 1040, line 13, or Form 1040NR, line 14, the **smaller** of:

     • The loss on line 16 or
     • ($3,000), or if married filing separately, ($1,500)   } **21** (3,000)

     Note. When figuring which amount is smaller, treat both amounts as positive numbers.

22   Do you have qualified dividends on Form 1040, line 9b, or Form 1040NR, line 10b?

     ☐ **Yes.** Complete the **Qualified Dividends and Capital Gain Tax Worksheet** in the instructions for Form 1040, line 44 (or in the instructions for Form 1040NR, line 42).

     ☑ **No.** Complete the rest of Form 1040 or Form 1040NR.

Schedule D (Form 1040) 2014

Task-Based Simulation 2

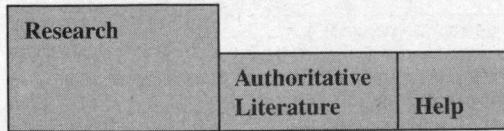

Internal Revenue Code Section 1212, subsection (b) provides that for taxpayers other than corporations, an excess of net short-term capital loss over net long-term capital gain for a taxable year shall be treated as a short-term capital loss in the succeeding taxable year. Similarly, an excess of net long-term capital loss over net short-term capital gain for a taxable year shall be treated as a long-term capital loss in the succeeding taxable year.

Section		**Subsection**	
§	1212	(	b	)

Module 37: Partnership Taxation

Overview

This module presents the federal tax treatment of partnerships and partners. The tax consequences of partnership formation are covered first, followed by a review of the pass-through of partnership income and loss to partners. A partner's basis for a partnership interest is covered next, with emphasis on the effect of partnership liabilities on a partner's basis. Next reviewed are the special rules that apply to transactions with controlled partnerships, as well as the limitations that apply to a partnership's adoption of a tax year. The module continues with a review of the tax effects of a partner's sale of a partnership interest, and concludes with a review of the rules that apply to a partnership's distribution of property to partners in both current and liquidating distributions. It is important to be able to determine a partner's basis for distributed property, as well as the effect of the distribution on the partner's basis for the partnership interest.

Partnerships are organizations of two or more persons to carry on business activities for profit. For tax purposes, partnerships also include a syndicate, joint venture, or other unincorporated business through which any business or financial operation is conducted. Partnerships do not pay any income tax, but instead act as a conduit to pass through tax items to the partners. Partnerships file an informational return (Form 1065), and partners report their share of partnership ordinary income

or loss and other items on their individual returns. The nature or character (e.g., capital, ordinary, Sec. 1231) of income or deductions is not changed by the pass-through nature of the partnership.

A. Entity Classification

1. Eligible business entities (a business entity other than an entity automatically classified as a corporation) may choose how they will be classified for federal tax purposes by filing Form 8832. A business entity with at least two members can choose to be classified as either an association taxable as a corporation or as a partnership. A business entity with a single member can choose to be classified as either an association taxable as a corporation or disregarded as an entity separate from its owner.

    a. An eligible business entity that does not file Form 8832 will be classified under default rules. Under default rules, an eligible business entity will be classified as a partnership if it has two or more members, or disregarded as an entity separate from its owner if it has a single owner.

    b. Once an entity makes an election, a different election cannot be made for sixty months unless there is more than a 50% ownership change and the IRS consents.

2. **General partnerships** exist when two or more partners join together and do not specifically provide that one or more partners is a limited partner. Since each general partner has unlimited liability, creditors can reach the personal assets of a general partner to satisfy partnership debts, including a malpractice judgment against the partnership even though the partner was not personally involved in the malpractice.

3. **Limited partnerships** have two classes of partners, with at least one general partner (who has the same rights and responsibilities as a partner in a general partnership) and at least one limited partner. A limited partner generally cannot participate in the active management of the partnership, and in the event of losses, generally can lose no more than his or her own capital contribution. A limited partnership is often the preferred entity of choice for real estate ventures requiring significant capital contributions.

4. **Limited liability partnerships** differ from general partnerships in that with an LLP, a partner is not liable for damages resulting from the negligence, malpractice, or fraud committed by other partners. However, each partner is personally liable for his or her own negligence, malpractice, or fraud. LLPs are often used by service providers such as architects, accountants, attorneys, and physicians.

5. **Limited liability companies** that do not elect to be treated as an association taxable as a corporation are subject to the rules applicable to partnerships (a single-member LLC would be disregarded as an entity separate from its owner). An LLC combines the nontax advantage of limited liability for each and every owner of the entity, with the tax advantage of pass-through treatment, and the flexibility of partnership taxation. The LLC structure is generally available to both nonprofessional service providers as well as capital-intensive companies.

6. **Electing large partnerships** are partnerships that have elected to be taxed under a simplified reporting system that does not require as much separate reporting to partners as does a regular partnership. For example, charitable contributions are deductible by the partnership (subject to a 10% of taxable income limitation), and the Sec. 179 expense election is deducted in computing partnership ordinary income and not separately passed through to partners. To qualify, the partnership must not be a service partnership nor engaged in commodity trading, must have at least 100 partners, and must file an election to be taxed as an electing large partnership. A partnership will cease to be an electing large partnership if it has fewer than 100 partners for a taxable year.

7. **Publicly traded partnerships** are partnerships whose interests are traded on an established securities exchange or in a secondary market and are generally taxed as C corporations.

B. Partnership Formation

1. As a general rule, **no gain or loss** is recognized by a partner when there is a contribution of property to the partnership in exchange for an interest in the partnership. There are three situations where gain must be recognized.

   a. A partner must recognize gain when property is contributed which is subject to a liability, and the resulting decrease in the partner's individual liability exceeds the partner's partnership basis.

      (1) The excess of liability over adjusted basis is generally treated as a capital gain from the sale or exchange of a partnership interest.
      (2) The gain will be treated as ordinary income to the extent the property transferred was subject to depreciation recapture under Sec. 1245 or 1250.

EXAMPLE

A partner acquires a 20% interest in a partnership by contributing property worth $10,000 but with an adjusted basis of $4,000. There is a mortgage of $6,000 that is assumed by the partnership. The partner must recognize a gain of $800, and has a zero basis for the partnership interest, calculated as follows:

Adjusted basis of contributed property	$4,000
Less: portion of mortgage allocated to other partners (80% × $6,000)	(4,800)
Partner's basis (not reduced below 0)	$0

---

   b. Gain will be recognized on a contribution of property to a partnership in exchange for an interest therein if the partnership would be an investment company if incorporated.
   c. Partner must recognize compensation income when an interest in partnership capital is received in exchange for **services rendered**.

EXAMPLE

X received a 10% capital interest in the ABC Partnership in exchange for services rendered. On the date X was admitted to the partnership, ABC's net assets had a basis of $30,000 and a FMV of $50,000. X must recognize compensation income of $5,000, and would have a basis of $5,000 for the partnership interest.

---

2. Property contributed to the partnership has the same **basis** as it had in the contributing partner's hands (a transferred basis).

    a. The basis for the partner's partnership interest is increased by the adjusted basis of property contributed.
    b. No gain or loss is generally recognized by the partnership upon the contribution.

3. The **partnership's holding period** for contributed property includes the period of time the property was held by the partner.

4. A **partner's holding period** for a partnership interest includes the holding period of property contributed, if the contributed property was a capital asset or Sec. 1231 asset in the contributing partner's hands.

5. Although not a separate taxpaying entity, the partnership must make most elections as to the tax treatment of partnership items. For example, the partnership must select a taxable year and various accounting methods which can differ from the methods used by its partners. Partnership elections include an overall method of accounting, inventory method, the method used to compute depreciation, and the election to expense depreciable assets under Sec. 179.

6. A partnership may elect to deduct up to $5,000 of organizational expenditures for the tax year in which the partnership begins business. The $5,000 amount must be reduced (but not below zero) by the amount by which **organizational expenditures** exceed $50,000. Remaining expenditures can be deducted ratably over the 180-month period beginning with the month in which the partnership begins business.

    a. A partnership is deemed to have made the election to amortize costs and does not have to attach a statement to its return. Alternatively, the partnership may elect to capitalize its costs on a timely filed return (including extensions) for the taxable year in which the partnership begins business.
    b. Similar rules apply to partnership start-up expenditures.
    c. Partnership syndication fees (expenses of selling partnership interests) are neither deductible nor amortizable.

> **NOW REVIEW MULTIPLE-CHOICE QUESTIONS 1 THROUGH 9**

C. Partnership Income and Loss

1. Since a partnership is not a separate taxpaying entity, but instead acts as a conduit to pass-through items of income and deduction to individual partners, the partnership's reporting of income and deductions requires a two-step approach.

    a. **First,** all items having special tax characteristics (i.e., subject to partial or full exclusion, % or dollar limitation, etc.) must be segregated and taken into account separately by each partner so that any special tax characteristics are preserved.

        (1) These special items are listed separately on Schedule K of the partnership return and include

            (a) Capital gains and losses
            (b) Sec. 1231 gains and losses
            (c) Charitable contributions
            (d) Foreign income taxes
            (e) Sec. 179 expense deduction
            (f) Interest, dividend, and royalty income
            (g) Interest expense on investment indebtedness
            (h) Net income (loss) from rental real estate activity
            (i) Net income (loss) from other rental activity

    b. **Second,** all remaining items (since they have no special tax characteristics) are ordinary in nature and are netted in the computation of partnership ordinary income or loss from trade or business activities

    (1) Frequently encountered ordinary income and deductions include

        (a) Sales less cost of goods sold

        (b) Business expenses such as wages, rents, bad debts, and repairs

        (c) Guaranteed payments to partners

        (d) Depreciation

        (e) Amortization (over 180 months) of partnership organization and start-up expenditures

        (f) Sec. 1245, 1250, etc., recapture

        (g) See Form 1065 description at the beginning of this module for more detail

2. The **character** of any gain or loss recognized on the disposition of property is generally determined by the nature of the property in the hands of the partnership. However, for contributed property, the character may be based on the nature of the property to the contributing partner before contribution.

    a. If a partner contributes **unrealized receivables,** the partnership will recognize ordinary income or loss on the subsequent disposition of the unrealized receivables.

    b. If the property contributed was **inventory** property to the contributing partner, any gain or loss recognized by the partnership on the disposition of the property within five years will be treated as ordinary income or loss.

    c. If the contributed property was a **capital asset,** any loss later recognized by the partnership on the disposition of the property within five years will be treated as a capital loss to the extent of the contributing partner's unrecognized capital loss at the time of contribution. This rule applies to losses only, not to gains.

3. A person sitting for the examination should be able to calculate a partnership's ordinary income by adjusting partnership book income (or partnership book income by adjusting ordinary income).

EXAMPLE

A partnership's accounting income statement discloses net income of $75,000 (i.e., book income). The three partners share profit and losses equally. Supplemental data indicate the following information has been included in the computation of net income:

	DR.	CR.
Net sales		$160,000
Cost of goods sold	$88,000	
Tax-exempt income		1,500
Sec. 1231 casualty gain		9,000
Section 1231 gain (other than casualty)		6,000
Section 1250 gain		20,000
Long-term capital gain		7,500
Short-term capital loss	6,000	
Guaranteed payments ($8,000 per partner)	24,000	
Charitable contributions	9,000	
Advertising expense	2,000	
	$129,000	$204,000

Partnership ordinary income is $66,000, computed as follows:

Book income		$75,000
Add:		
Charitable contributions	$9,000	
Short-term capital loss	6,000	15,000
		$90,000
Deduct:		
Tax-exempt income	$1,500	
Sec. 1231 casualty gain	9,000	
Section 1231 gain (other than casualty)	6,000	
Long-term capital gain	7,500	24,000
Partnership ordinary income		$66,000

Each partner's share of partnership ordinary income is $22,000.

---

4. Three sets of rules may limit the amount of partnership loss that a partner can deduct.

a. A partner's distributive share of partnership ordinary loss and special loss items is deductible by the partner only to the extent of the **partner's basis** for the partnership interest at the end of the taxable year [Sec. 704(d)].

    (1) The pass-through of loss is considered to be the last event during the partnership's taxable year; all positive basis adjustments are made prior to determining the amount of deductible loss.

    (2) Unused losses are carried forward and can be deducted when the partner obtains additional basis for the partnership interest.

EXAMPLE

A partner who materially participates in the partnership's business has a distributive share of partnership capital gain of $200 and partnership ordinary loss of $3,000, but the partner's basis in the partnership is only $2,400 before consideration of these items. The partner can deduct $2,600 of the ordinary loss ($2,400 of beginning basis + $200 net capital gain). The remaining $400 of ordinary loss must be carried forward.

---

b. The deductibility of partnership losses is also limited to the amount of the partner's **at-risk basis** [Sec. 465].

    (1) A partner's at-risk basis is generally the same as the partner's regular partnership basis with the exception that liabilities are included in at-risk basis only if the partner is personally liable for such amounts.

    (2) Nonrecourse liabilities are generally excluded from at-risk basis.

    (3) Qualified nonrecourse real estate financing is included in at-risk basis.

c. The deductibility of partnership losses may also be subject to the **passive activity loss limitations** [Sec. 469]. Passive activity losses are deductible only to the extent of the partner's income from other passive activities (see Module 35).

    (1) Passive activities include (a) any partnership trade or business in which the partner does not materially participate, and (b) any rental activity.

    (2) A limited partnership interest generally fails the material participation test.

    (3) To qualify for the $25,000 exception for active participation in a rental real estate activity, a partner (together with spouse) must own at least 10% of the value of the partnership interests.

NOW REVIEW MULTIPLE-CHOICE QUESTIONS 10 THROUGH 15

D. Partnership Agreements

1. A partner's distributive share of income or loss is generally determined by the partnership agreement. Such agreement can have different ratios for income or loss, and may agree to allocate other items (e.g., credits and deductions) in varying ratios.

    a. Special allocations must have **substantial economic effect**.

       (1) Economic effect is measured by an analysis of the allocation on the partners' capital accounts. The special allocation (a) must be reflected in the partners' capital accounts, (b) liquidation distributions must be based upon the positive capital account balances of partners, and (c) there must be a deficit payback agreement wherein partners agree to restore any deficit capital account balances.

       (2) An allocation's economic effect will **not** be substantial if the net change recorded in the partners' capital accounts does not differ substantially from what would have been recorded without the special allocation, and the total tax liability of all partners is less.

    b. If no allocation is provided, or if the allocation of an item does not have substantial economic effect, the partners' distributive shares of that item shall be determined by the ratio in which the partners generally divide the income or loss of the partnership.

    c. **If property is contributed** by a partner to a partnership, related items of income, deduction, gain, or loss must be allocated among partners in a manner that reflects the difference between the property's tax basis and its fair market value at the time of contribution.

> **EXAMPLE**
>
> Partner X contributes property with a tax basis of $1,000 and a fair market value of $10,000 to the XYZ Partnership. If the partnership subsequently sells the property for $12,000, the first $9,000 of gain must be allocated to X, with the remaining $2,000 of gain allocated among partners according to their ratio for sharing gains.

(1) If contributed property has a built-in loss, the built-in loss is taken into account only for determining the amount of partnership items allocated to the contributing partner. For purposes of determining the amount of partnership items allocated to other partners, the basis of contributed property is treated as being equal to FMV at date of contribution. If the contributing partner's interest is transferred or liquidated, the partnership's basis in the property for all future allocations will be based on its FMV at date of contribution, and the built-in loss will be eliminated.

(2) If property contributed to a partnership is distributed within seven years to a partner other than the partner who contributed such property, the contributing partner must recognize the pre-contribution gain or loss to the extent that the pre-contribution gain or loss would be recognized if the partnership had sold the property for its fair market value at the time of distribution.

(3) The above recognition rule will not generally apply if other property of a like-kind to the contributed property is distributed to the contributing partner no later than the earlier of (1) the 180th day after the date on which the originally contributed property was distributed to another partner, or (2) the due date (without extension) for the contributing partner's return for the tax year in which the original distribution of property occurred.

d. If there was any change in the ownership of partnership interests during the year, distributive shares of partnership interest, taxes, and payments for services or for the use of property must be allocated among partners by assigning an appropriate share of each item to each day of the partnership's taxable year.

> **EXAMPLE**
>
> Z becomes a 40% partner in calendar-year Partnership XY on December 1. Previously, X and Y each had a 50% interest. Partnership XY uses the cash method of accounting and on December 31 pays $10,000 of interest expense that relates to its entire calendar year. Z's distributive share of the interest expense will be ($10,000 ÷ 365 days) × 31 days × 40% = $340.

2. **Distributable shares** of income and guaranteed payments are reported by partners for their taxable year during which the end of the partnership fiscal year occurs. All items, including guaranteed payments, are deemed to pass through on the last day of the partnership's tax year.

a. **Guaranteed payments** are payments to a partner determined without regard to income of the partnership. Guaranteed payments are deductible by the partnership and reported as income by the partners.

> **EXAMPLE**
>
> Z (on a calendar-year) has a 20% interest in a partnership that has a fiscal year ending May 31. Z received a guaranteed payment for services rendered of $1,000 a month from 6/1/14 to 12/31/14 and $1,500 a month from 1/1/15 to 5/31/15. After deducting the guaranteed payment, the partnership had ordinary income of $50,000 for its fiscal year ended 5/31/15. Z must include $24,500 in income on Z's calendar-year 2015 return ($50,000 × 20%) + ($1,000 × 7) + ($1,500 × 5).

b. Partners are generally not considered to be employees for purposes of employee fringe benefits (e.g., cost of $50,000 of group-term life insurance, exclusion of premiums or benefits under an employer accident or health plan, etc.). A partner's fringe benefits are deductible by the partnership as guaranteed payments and must be included in a partner's gross income.

3. **Family partnerships** are subject to special rules because of their potential use for tax avoidance.

   a. If the business is primarily service oriented (capital is not a material income-producing factor), a family member will be considered a partner only if the family member shares in the management or performs needed services.

   b. Capital is not a material income-producing factor if substantially all of the gross income of the business consists of fees, commissions, or other compensation for personal services (e.g., accountants, architects, lawyers).

   c. A family member is generally considered a partner if the family member actually owns a capital interest in a business in which capital is a material income-producing factor.

   d. Where a capital interest in a partnership in which capital is a material income-producing factor is treated as created by gift, the distributive shares of partnership income of the donor and donee are determined by first making a reasonable allowance for services rendered to the partnership, and then allocating the remainder according to the relative capital interests of the donor and donee.

NOW REVIEW MULTIPLE-CHOICE QUESTIONS 16 THROUGH 30

E. Partner's Basis in Partnership

1. A partner's **original basis** is generally determined by the manner in which the partnership interest was acquired (e.g., contribution of property, compensation for services, purchase, gift, received from decedent).

2. As the partnership operates, the partner's basis for the partnership interest increases or decreases.

   a. A partner's basis is increased by the adjusted basis of any subsequent capital contributions.

   b. Also, a partner's basis is **increased** by any distributive share of

      (1) Partnership ordinary income
      (2) Capital gains and other special income items
      (3) Tax-exempt income of the partnership
      (4) The excess of the deduction for depletion over the partnership's basis of the property subject to depletion

   c. A partner's basis is **decreased** (but not below zero) by

      (1) The amount of money and the adjusted basis of other property distributed to the partner
      (2) The partner's distributive share of partnership ordinary loss and special expense items, as well as nondeductible items not properly chargeable to capital
      (3) The amount of the partner's deduction for depletion on oil and gas wells

---

EXAMPLE

In the example in Section C. 3, one partner's tax basis (who had a $15,000 tax basis at the beginning of the year) would be $40,000 at the end of the year, calculated as shown below.

Beginning partnership basis		$15,000
Add:		
Distributive share of partnership ordinary income	22,000	
Tax-exempt income	500	
Sec. 1231 casualty gain	3,000	
Section 1231 gain (other than casualty)	2,000	
Long-term capital gain	2,500	30,000
		$45,000
Less:		
Short-term capital loss	$2,000	
Charitable contributions	3,000	5,000
Ending partnership basis		$40,000

d. Changes in liabilities affect a partner's basis.

(1) An **increase** in the **partnership's liabilities** (e.g., loan from a bank, increase in accounts payable) increases each partner's basis in the partnership by each partner's share of the increase.

(2) Any **decrease** in the **partnership's liabilities** is considered to be a distribution of money to each partner and reduces each partner's basis in the partnership by each partner's share of the decrease.

(3) Any **decrease** in a partner's **individual liability** by reason of the assumption by the partnership of such individual liabilities is considered to be a distribution of money to the partner by the partnership (i.e., partner's basis is reduced).

(4) Any **increase** in a partner's **individual liability** by reason of the assumption by the partner of partnership liabilities is considered to be a contribution of money to the partnership by the partner. Thus, the partner's basis is increased.

EXAMPLE

The XYZ partnership owns a warehouse with an adjusted basis of $120,000 subject to a mortgage of $90,000. Partner X (one of three equal partners) has a basis for his partnership interest of $75,000. If the partnership transfers the warehouse and mortgage to Partner X as a current distribution, X's basis for his partnership interest immediately following the distribution would be $15,000, calculated as follows:

Beginning basis	$75,000
Individual assumption of mortgage	+ 90,000
	$165,000
Distribution of warehouse	−120,000
Partner's share of decrease in partnership's liabilities	− 30,000
Basis after distribution	$15,000

EXAMPLE

Assume in the example above that one of the other one-third partners had a basis of $75,000 immediately before the distribution. What would the partner's basis be immediately after the distribution to Partner X? The partner's basis would be $45,000 (i.e., $75,000 less 1/3 of the $90,000 decrease in partnership liabilities).

---

e. A partner's basis for the partnership is adjusted in the following order: (1) increased for all income items (including tax-exempt income); (2) decreased for distributions; and (3) decreased by deductions and losses (including nondeductible items not charged to capital).

EXAMPLE

A partner with a basis of $50 for his partnership interest at the beginning of the partnership year receives a $30 cash distribution during the year and is allocated a $60 distributive share of partnership ordinary loss, and an $8 distributive share of capital gain. In determining the extent to which the ordinary loss is deductible by the partner, the partner's partnership basis of $50 is first increased by the $8 of capital gain and reduced by the $30 cash distribution to $28, so that his deductible ordinary loss is limited to his remaining basis of $28.

NOW REVIEW MULTIPLE-CHOICE QUESTIONS 31 THROUGH 37

F. Transactions with Controlled Partnerships

1. If a person engages in a transaction with a partnership other than as a member of such partnership, any resulting gain or loss is generally recognized. However, if the transaction involves a **more than 50% owned partnership,** one of three special rules may apply. Constructive ownership rules apply in determining whether a transaction involves a more than 50% owned partnership. For this purpose, an individual's family includes brothers and sisters, spouse, ancestors, and lineal descendants.

   a. **No losses** are deductible from sales or exchanges of property between a partnership and a person owning (directly or indirectly) more than 50% of the capital or profits interests in such partnership, or between two partnerships in which the same persons own (directly or indirectly) more than 50% of the capital or profits interests. A gain later realized on a subsequent sale by the transferee will not be recognized to the extent of the disallowed loss.

   > **EXAMPLE**
   >
   > Partnership X is owned by three **equal** partners, A, B, and C, who are brothers. Partnership X sells property at a loss of $5,000 to C. Since C owns a more than 50% interest in the partnership (i.e., C constructively owns his brothers' partnership interests), the $5,000 loss is disallowed to Partnership X.

   > **EXAMPLE**
   >
   > Assume the same facts as in the above example. C later resells the property to Z, an unrelated taxpayer, at a gain of $6,000. C's realized gain of $6,000 will not be recognized to the extent of the $5,000 disallowed loss to the Partnership X.

   b. If a person related to a partner does not indirectly own a more than 50% partnership interest, a transaction between the related person and the partnership is treated as occurring between the related person and the partners individually.

   > **EXAMPLE**
   >
   > X owns 100% of X Corp. and also owns a 25% interest in WXYZ Partnership. X Corp. sells property at a $1,200 loss to the WXYZ Partnership. Since X Corp. is related to partner X (i.e., X owns more than 50% of X Corp.), the transaction is treated as if it occurred between X Corp. and partners W, X, Y, and Z individually. Therefore, the loss disallowed to X Corp. is $1,200 × 25% = $300.

   c. A **gain** recognized on a sale or exchange of property between a partnership and a person owning (directly or indirectly) more than 50% of the capital or profits interests in such partnership, or between two partnerships in which the same persons own (directly or indirectly) more than 50% of the capital or profits interests, will be treated as **ordinary income** if the property is **not a capital asset** in the hands of the transferee.

   > **EXAMPLE**
   >
   > Assume the same facts as in the preceding example. Further assume that F is the father of W, Y, and Z. F sells investment property to Partnership WXYZ at a gain of $10,000. If the property will not be a capital asset to Partnership WXYZ, F must report the $10,000 gain as ordinary income because F constructively owns a more than 50% partnership interest (i.e., F constructively owns his children's partnership interests).

d. A **gain** recognized on a sale or exchange of property between a partnership and a person owning (directly or indirectly) more than 50% of the capital or profits interests in such partnership will be treated as **ordinary income** if the property is **depreciable property** in the hands of the transferee.

> **NOW REVIEW MULTIPLE-CHOICE QUESTIONS 38 THROUGH 41**

G. Taxable Year of Partnership

1. When a partnership adopts (or attempts to change) its taxable year, it is subject to the following restrictions:

    a. A partnership must adopt the taxable year used by one or more of its partners owning an aggregate interest of more than 50% in profits and capital (but only if the taxable year used by such partners has been the same for the lesser of three taxable years or the period the partnership has existed).

    > **EXAMPLE**
    >
    > A partnership is formed by a corporation (which receives a 55% partnership interest) and five individuals (who each receive a 9% partnership interest). The corporation has a fiscal year ending June 30, while the individuals have a calendar year. The partnership must adopt a fiscal year ending June 30.

    b. If partners owning a more than 50% interest in partnership profits and capital do not have the same year-end, the partnership must adopt the same taxable year as used by all of its principal partners (i.e., a partner with a 5% or more interest in capital or profits).

    c. If its principal partners have different taxable years, the partnership must adopt the taxable year that results in the least aggregate deferral of income to partners.

2. A different taxable year than the year determined above can be used by a partnership if a **valid business purpose** can be established and IRS permission is received. The business purpose test will be met if a partnership receives at least 25% of its gross receipts in the last two months of a twelve-month period, and this "25% test" has been satisfied for three consecutive years.

    > **EXAMPLE**
    >
    > Partnership X is owned by three equal partners—A, B, and C, who use a calendar year. Partnership X has received at least 25% of its gross receipts during the months of June and July for each of the last three years. Partnership X may be allowed to change to a fiscal year ending July 31.

3. A partnership that otherwise would be required to adopt or change its tax year (normally to the calendar year) may **elect to use a fiscal year if the election does not result in a deferral period longer than three months,** or, if less, the deferral period of the year currently in use.

    a. The "deferral period" is the number of months between the close of the fiscal year elected and the close of the required year (e.g., if a partnership elects a tax year ending September 30 and a tax year ending December 31 is required, the deferral period of the year ending September 30 is three months).

    b. A partnership that elects a tax year other than a required year must make a "required payment" which is in the nature of a refundable, noninterest-bearing deposit that is intended to compensate the government for the revenue lost as a result of tax deferral. The required payment is due on May 15 each year and is recomputed for each subsequent year.

4. The **taxable year** of a partnership ordinarily **will not close** as a result of the death or entry of a partner, or the liquidation or sale of a partner's interest. But the partnership's taxable year closes as to **the partner** whose **entire interest** is sold or liquidated. Additionally, the partnership tax year closes with respect to a deceased partner as of date of death.

EXAMPLE

A partner sells his entire interest in a calendar-year partnership on March 31. His pro rata share of partnership income up to March 31 is $15,000. Since the partnership year closes with respect to him at the time of sale, the $15,000 is includible in his income and increases the basis of his partnership interest for purposes of computing gain or loss on the sale. However, the partnership's taxable year does not close as to its remaining partners.

EXAMPLE

X (on a calendar year) is a partner in the XYZ Partnership that uses a June 30 fiscal year. X died on April 30, 2015. Since the partnership year closes with respect to X at his death, X's final return for the period January 1 through April 30 will include his share of partnership income for the period beginning July 1, 2014, and ending April 30, 2015. His share of partnership income for May and June 2015 will be reported by his estate or other successor in interest.

> **NOW REVIEW MULTIPLE-CHOICE QUESTIONS 42 THROUGH 45**

H. Partnership's Use of Cash Method

1. The cash method cannot generally be used if inventories are necessary to clearly reflect income and cannot generally be used by tax shelters and partnerships that have a C corporation as a partner.
2. Any partnership (other than a tax shelter) can use the cash method if for every year it has average gross receipts of **$5 million or less** for any prior three-year period and does not have inventories for sale to customers.
3. A small partnership with average annual gross receipts of **$1 million or less** for any prior three-year period can use the cash method and is excepted from the requirements to account for inventories and use the accrual method for purchases and sales of merchandise.

I. Termination or Continuation of Partnership

1. A partnership will terminate when it no longer has at least two partners.
2. A partnership and its taxable year will terminate for all partners if there is a sale or exchange of 50% or more of the **total interests** in partnership capital and profits within a twelve-month period.

   a. Sales or exchanges of at least 50% during any twelve-month period cause a termination.

EXAMPLE

The calendar-year ABC Partnership has three equal partners, A, B, and C. B sold his interest to D on November 1, 2014, and C sold his interest to E on April 1, 2015. The ABC Partnership is considered terminated on April 1 because at least 50% of the total interests have been sold within a twelve-month period.

---

   b. If the same partnership interest is sold more than once during a twelve-month period, the sale is counted only once.

> **EXAMPLE**
>
> The calendar-year RST Partnership has three equal partners, R, S, and T. T sold his interest to X on December 1, 2014, and X sold his interest to Y on May 1, 2015. The RST Partnership is not terminated because multiple sales of the same partnership interest are counted only once.

3. In a **merger** of partnerships, the resulting partnership is a continuation of the merging partnership whose partners have a more than 50% interest in the resulting partnership.

> **EXAMPLE**
>
> Partnerships AB and CD merge on April 1, forming the ABCD Partnership in which the partners' interests are as follows: Partner A, 30%; B, 30%; C, 20%; and D, 20%. Partnership ABCD is a continuation of the AB Partnership. The CD Partnership is considered terminated and its taxable year closed on April 1.

4. In a **division** of a partnership, a resulting partnership is a continuation of the prior partnership if the resulting partnership's partners had a more than 50% interest in the prior partnership.

> **EXAMPLE**
>
> Partnership ABCD is owned as follows: A, 40%; and B, C, and D each own a 20% interest. The partners agree to separate and form two partnerships—AC and BD. Partnership AC is a continuation of ABCD. BD is considered a new partnership and must adopt a taxable year, as well as make any other necessary tax accounting elections.

NOW REVIEW MULTIPLE-CHOICE QUESTIONS 46 THROUGH 51

J. Sale of a Partnership Interest

1. Since a partnership interest is usually a capital asset, the sale of a partnership interest generally results in **capital gain or loss**.

   a. Gain is excess of amount realized over the adjusted basis for the partnership interest.
   b. Include the selling partner's share of partnership liabilities in the amount realized because the selling partner is relieved of them.

> **EXAMPLE**
>
> Miller sold her partnership interest to Carter for $150,000 cash, plus Carter's assumption of Miller's $60,000 share of partnership liabilities. The amount realized by Miller on the sale of her partnership interest is $150,000 + $60,000 = $210,000.

2. **Gain is ordinary** (instead of capital) to extent attributable to unrealized receivables or appreciated inventory (Sec. 751 items).

   a. The term **unrealized receivables** generally refers to the accounts receivable of a cash method taxpayer, but for this purpose also includes any potential recapture under Secs. 1245, 1250, and 1252.

b. The term **inventory** includes all assets except capital assets and Section 1231 assets.

EXAMPLE

X has a 40% interest in the XY Partnership. Partner X sells his 40% interest to Z for $50,000. X's basis in his partnership is $22,000 and the cash-method partnership had the following receivables and inventory:

	Adjusted basis	Fair market value
Accounts receivable	0	$10,000
Inventory	4,000	10,000
Potential Sec. 1250 recapture	0	10,000
	$4,000	$30,000

X's total gain is $28,000 (i.e., $50,000 – $22,000). Since the Sec. 1250 recapture is treated as "unrealized receivables" and the inventory is appreciated, X will recognize ordinary income to the extent that his selling price attributable to Sec. 751 items ($30,000 × 40% = $12,000) exceeds his basis in those items ($4,000 × 40% = $1,600), that is, $10,400. The remainder of X's gain ($28,000 – $10,400 = $17,600) will be treated as capital gain.

NOW REVIEW MULTIPLE-CHOICE QUESTIONS 52 THROUGH 56

K. Pro Rata Distributions from Partnership

1. Partnership recognizes no gain or loss on a distribution.
2. If a single distribution consists of **multiple items of property,** the distributed property reduces the partner's basis for the partnership interest in the **following order:**

   a. Money,
   b. Adjusted basis of unrealized receivables and inventory, and
   c. Adjusted basis of other property.

3. Partner recognizes **gain** only to the extent **money received exceeds the partner's partnership basis.**

   a. Relief from liabilities is deemed a distribution of money.
   b. Gain is capital except for gain attributable to unrealized receivables and substantially appreciated inventory.
   c. The receipt of property (other than money) will not cause the recognition of gain.

EXAMPLE

Casey had a basis of $9,000 for his partnership interest at the time that he received a non liquidating partnership distribution consisting of $5,000 cash and other property with a basis of $3,000 and an FMV of $8,000. No gain is recognized by Casey since the cash received did not exceed his partnership basis. Casey's $9,000 basis for his partnership interest is first reduced by the $5,000 cash, and then reduced by the $3,000 basis of other property, to $1,000. Casey will have a basis for the other property received of $3,000.

---

4. Partner recognizes **loss** only upon **complete liquidation** of a partnership interest through receipt of only money, unrealized receivables, or inventory.

   a. The amount of loss is the basis for the partner's partnership interest less the money and the partnership's basis in the unrealized receivables and inventory received by the partner.
   b. The loss is generally treated as a capital loss.

c. If property other than money, unrealized receivables, or inventory is distributed in complete liquidation of a partner's interest, no loss can be recognized.

EXAMPLE

Day had a basis of $20,000 for his partnership interest before receiving a distribution in complete liquidation of his interest. The liquidating distribution consisted of $6,000 cash and inventory with a basis of $11,000. Since Day's liquidating distribution consisted of only money and inventory, Day will recognize a loss on the liquidation of his partnership interest. The amount of loss is the $3,000 difference between the $20,000 basis for his partnership interest, and the $6,000 cash and the $11,000 basis for the inventory received. Day will have an $11,000 basis for the inventory.

EXAMPLE

Assume the same facts as in the preceding example except that Day's liquidating distribution consists of $6,000 cash and a parcel of land with a basis of $11,000. Since the liquidating distribution now includes property other than money, receivables, and inventory, no loss can be recognized on the liquidation of Day's partnership interest. The basis for Day's partnership interest is first reduced by the $6,000 cash to $14,000. Since no loss can be recognized, the parcel of land must absorb all of Day's unrecovered partnership basis. As a result, the land will have a basis of $14,000.

---

5. In **non liquidating (current) distributions,** a partner's basis in distributed property is generally the same as the partnership's former basis in the property; but is **limited** to the basis for the partner's partnership interest less any money received.

EXAMPLE

Sara receives a current distribution from her partnership at a time when the basis for her partnership interest is $10,000. The distribution consists of $7,000 cash and Sec. 1231 property with an adjusted basis of $5,000 and a FMV of $9,000. No gain is recognized by Sara since the cash received did not exceed her basis. After being reduced by the cash, her partnership basis of $3,000 is reduced by the basis of the property (but not below zero). Her basis for the property is limited to $3,000.

---

6. **If multiple properties are distributed** in a liquidating distribution, or if the partnership's basis for distributed properties exceeds the partner's basis for the partnership interest, the partner's basis for the partnership interest is allocated in the following order:

a. Basis is first allocated to unrealized receivables and inventory items in an amount equal to their adjusted basis to the partnership. If the basis for the partner's interest to be allocated to the assets is less than the total basis of these properties to the partnership, a **basis decrease** is required and is determined under (1) below.

b. To the extent a partner's basis is not allocated to assets under a. above, basis is allocated to other distributed properties by assigning to each property its adjusted basis in the hands of the partnership, and then increasing or decreasing the basis to the extent required in order for the adjusted basis of the distributed properties to equal the remaining basis for the partner's partnership interest.

    (1) A **basis decrease** is allocated

        (a) First to properties with unrealized depreciation in proportion to their respective amounts of unrealized depreciation (but only to the extent of each property's unrealized depreciation), and

        (b) Then in proportion to the respective adjusted basis of the distributed properties.

EXAMPLE

A partnership distributes two items of property (A and B) that are neither unrealized receivables nor inventory to Baker in liquidation of his partnership interest that has a basis of $20.

	Partnership basis	FMV
Property A	$15	$15
Property B	15	5
Total	$30	$20

Basis is first allocated $15 to A and $15 to B (their adjusted bases to the partnership). A $10 basis decrease is required because the assets' bases of $30 exceeds Baker's basis for his partnership interest of $20. The $10 decrease is allocated to B to the extent of its unrealized depreciation. Thus, Baker has a basis of $15 for property A and a basis of $5 for property B.

(2) A **basis increase** is allocated

(a) First to properties with unrealized appreciation in proportion to their respective amounts of unrealized appreciation (but only to the extent of each property's unrealized appreciation), and

(b) Then in proportion to the relative FMVs of the distributed properties.

EXAMPLE

A partnership distributes two items of property (C and D) that are neither unrealized receivables nor inventory to Alan in liquidation of his partnership interest that has a basis of $55.

	Partnership basis	FMV
Property C	$5	$40
Property D	10	10
Total	$15	$50

Basis is first allocated $5 to C and $10 to D (their adjusted bases to the partnership). The $40 basis increase (Alan's $55 basis less the partnership's basis for the assets $15) is then allocated to C to the extent of its unrealized appreciation of $35, with the remaining $5 of basis adjustment allocated according to the relative FMV of C and D [i.e., $4 to C (for a total basis of $44) and $1 to D (for a total basis of $11)]

7. Payments made in liquidation of the interest of a retiring or deceased partner are generally treated as partnership distributions made in exchange for the partner's interest in partnership property. Such payments generally result in capital gain or loss to the retiring or deceased partner.

a. However, payments made to a retiring or deceased general partner in a partnership in which capital is **not** a material income-producing factor must be reported as ordinary income by the partner to the extent such payments are for the partner's share of unrealized receivables or goodwill (unless the partnership agreement provides for a payment with respect to goodwill).

b. Amounts treated as ordinary income by the retiring or deceased partner are either deductible by the partnership (treated as guaranteed payments), or reduce the income allocated to remaining partners (treated as a distributive share of partnership income).

c. Capital is **not** a material income-producing factor if substantially all of the gross income of the business consists of fees, commissions, or other compensation for personal services (e.g., accountants, doctors, dentists, lawyers).

NOW REVIEW MULTIPLE-CHOICE QUESTIONS 57 THROUGH 69

L. Non–Pro Rata Distributions from Partnership

1. A non–pro rata (disproportionate) distribution occurs when

   a. A distribution is disproportionate as to a partner's share of unrealized receivables or substantially appreciated inventory. Inventory is **substantially appreciated** if its FMV exceeds 120% of its basis.

      (1) Partner may receive more than the partner's share of these assets, or
      (2) Partner may receive more than the partner's share of other assets, in effect giving up a share of unrealized receivables or substantially appreciated inventory

   b. The partner may recognize gain or loss.

      (1) The gain or loss is the difference between the FMV of what is received and the basis of what is given up.
      (2) The gain or loss is limited to the disproportionate amount of unrealized receivables or substantially appreciated inventory that is received or given up.
      (3) The character of the gain or loss depends upon the character of the property given up.

   c. The partnership may similarly recognize gain or loss when there is a disproportionate distribution with respect to substantially appreciated inventory or unrealized receivables.

EXAMPLE

A, B, and C each own a one-third interest in a partnership. The partnership has the following assets:

	Adjusted basis	**FMV**
Cash	$6,000	$6,000
Inventory	6,000	12,000
Land	9,000	18,000
	$21,000	$36,000

Assume that A has a $7,000 basis for his partnership interest and that all inventory is distributed to A in liquidation of his partnership interest. He is treated as having exchanged his 1/3 interest in the cash and the land for a 2/3 increased interest in the substantially appreciated inventory. He has a gain of $3,000. He received $8,000 (2/3 × $12,000) of inventory for his basis of $2,000 (1/3 × $6,000) in cash and $3,000 (1/3 × $9,000) of land. The gain is capital if the land was a capital asset. The partnership is treated as having received $8,000 (FMV of A's 1/3 share of cash and land) in exchange for inventory with a basis of $4,000 (basis of inventory distributed in excess of A's 1/3 share). Thus, the partnership will recognize ordinary income of $4,000.

M. Optional Sec. 754 Adjustment to Basis of Partnership Property

1. On a distribution of property to a partner, or on a sale by a partner of a partnership interest, the partnership may elect to adjust the basis of its assets to **prevent any inequities** that otherwise might occur. Once an election is made, it applies to all similar transactions unless IRS approves revocation of the election.

2. Upon the **distribution of partnership property,** the basis of remaining partnership property will be adjusted for **all** partners.

   a. Increased by

      (1) The amount of gain recognized to a distributee partner, and
      (2) The excess of the partnership's basis in the property distributed over the basis of that property in the hands of distributee partner

---

EXAMPLE

If the election were made under the facts used in K.5, the $2,000 of basis that otherwise would be lost will be allocated to remaining partnership Sec. 1231 property.

---

   b. Decreased by

      (1) The amount of loss recognized to a distributee partner, and

      (2) The excess of basis of property in hands of distributee over the prior basis of that property in the partnership

  3. Upon the **sale or exchange of a partnership interest,** the basis of partnership property to the **transferee** (not other partners) will be

    a. Increased by the excess of the basis of the transferee's partnership interest over the transferee's share of the adjusted basis of partnership property

    b. Decreased by the excess of transferee's share of adjusted basis of partnership property over the basis for the transferee's partnership interest

---

EXAMPLE

Assume X sells his 40% interest to Z for $80,000 when the partnership balance sheet reflects the following:

XY Partnership

	Basis	FMV
Assets		
Accounts Receivable	$0	$100,000
Real Property	30,000	100,000
Capital		
X (40%)		$80,000
Y (60%)		120,000

Z will have a basis for his partnership interest of $80,000, while his share of the adjusted basis of partnership property will only be $12,000. If the partnership elects to adjust the basis of partnership property, it will increase the basis of its assets by $68,000 ($80,000 – $12,000) solely for the benefit of Z. The basis of the receivables will increase from 0 to $40,000 with the full adjustment allocated to Z. When the receivables are collected, Y will have $60,000 of income and Z will have none. The basis of the real property will increase by $28,000 to $58,000, so that Z's share of the basis will be $40,000 (i.e., $12,000 + $28,000).

N. Mandatory Adjustments to Basis of Partnership Property

  1. A partnership is required to make a Sec. 743 adjustment to the basis of partnership property upon a transfer of a partnership interest by sale or exchange or on the death of a partner if the partnership has a substantial built-in loss immediately after such transfer. For this purpose, a partnership has a substantial built-in loss if the partnership's adjusted basis for partnership property exceeds the FMV of such property by more than $250,000.

  2. A partnership is required to make a Sec. 734 downward basis adjustment to partnership property in the event of a partnership distribution with respect to which there is a substantial basis reduction. For this purpose, a substantial basis reduction means a downward adjustment of more than $250,000 that would be made to the basis of partnership property if a Sec. 754 election were in effect with respect to the distribution.

KEY TERMS

Current distribution. A nonliquidating partnership distribution made to a partner (i.e., the distribution does not terminate the partner's partnership interest.

Limited liability partnership. Differs from general partnerships in that with an LLP, a partner is not liable for damages resulting from the negligence, malpractice, or fraud committed by other partners. However, each partner is personally liable for his or her own negligence, malpractice, or fraud.

Limited partnership. A partnership with two classes of partners, with at least one general partner and at least one limited partner. A limited partner generally cannot participate in the active management of the partnership, and in the event of losses, generally can lose no more than his or her capital contribution.

Liquidating distribution. A single distribution, or one of a planned series of distributions, that completely terminates a partner's interest in the partnership.

Partnership ordinary income or loss. All partnership items that do not have to be separately stated (because they have no special tax characteristics) and can be combined and just the net amount is passed through to partners.

Sec. 751 property. A partnership's unrealized receivables (including the recapture potential in depreciable assets) and appreciated inventory. The gain on sale of a partnership interest generally must be recognized as ordinary income to the extent of the selling partner's share of unrealized receivables and appreciated inventory. These assets are sometimes referred to as *hot assets*.

Sec. 754 election. An optional election that can be made by a partnership to adjust the basis of its assets to prevent any inequities that might occur as a result of the partnership's distribution of property or the sale by a partner of a partnership interest.

B. Partnership Formation

1. At partnership inception, Black acquires a 50% interest in Decorators Partnership by contributing property with an adjusted basis of $250,000. Black recognizes a gain if

   I. The fair market value of the contributed property exceeds its adjusted basis.

   II. The property is encumbered by a mortgage with a balance of $100,000.

     a. I only.
     b. II only.
     c. Both I and II.
     d. Neither I nor II.

2. On June 1, 2015, Kelly received a 10% interest in Rock Co., a partnership, for services contributed to the partnership. Rock's net assets at that date had a basis of $70,000 and a fair market value of $100,000. In Kelly's 2015 income tax return, what amount must Kelly include as income from transfer of the partnership interest?

     a. $7,000 ordinary income.
     b. $7,000 capital gain.
     c. $10,000 ordinary income.
     d. $10,000 capital gain.

3. Ola Associates is a limited partnership engaged in real estate development. Hoff, a civil engineer, billed Ola $40,000 in 2015 for consulting services rendered. In full settlement of this invoice, Hoff accepted a $15,000 cash payment plus the following:

	Fair market value	Carrying amount on Ola's books
3% limited partnership interest in Ola	$10,000	N/A
Surveying equipment	7,000	$3,000

What amount should Hoff, a cash-basis taxpayer, report in his 2015 return as income for the services rendered to Ola?

     a. $15,000
     b. $28,000
     c. $32,000
     d. $40,000

4. The following information pertains to property contributed by Gray on July 1, 2015, for a 40% interest in the capital and profits of Kag & Gray, a partnership:

As of June 30, 2015	
Adjusted basis	**Fair market value**
$24,000	$30,000

After Gray's contribution, Kag & Gray's capital totaled $150,000. What amount of gain was reportable in Gray's 2015 return on the contribution of property to the partnership?

     a. $0
     b. $6,000
     c. $30,000
     d. $36,000

5. The holding period of a partnership interest acquired in exchange for a contributed capital asset begins on the date

     a. The partner is admitted to the partnership.
     b. The partner transfers the asset to the partnership.
     c. The partner's holding period of the capital asset began.
     d. The partner is first credited with the proportionate share of partnership capital.

6. The following information pertains to Carr's admission to the Smith & Jones partnership on July 1, 2015:

- Carr's contribution of capital: 800 shares of Ed Corp. stock bought in 2003 for $30,000; fair market value $150,000 on July 1, 2015.
- Carr's interest in capital and profits of Smith & Jones: 25%.
- Fair market value of net assets of Smith & Jones on July 1, 2015, after Carr's admission: $600,000.

Carr's gain in 2015 on the exchange of the Ed Corp. stock for Carr's partnership interest was

     a. $120,000 ordinary income.
     b. $120,000 long-term capital gain.
     c. $120,000 Section 1231 gain.
     d. $0.

7. The holding period of property acquired by a partnership as a contribution to the contributing partner's capital account

     a. Begins with the date of contribution to the partnership.
     b. Includes the period during which the property was held by the contributing partner.
     c. Is equal to the contributing partner's holding period prior to contribution to the partnership.
     d. Depends on the character of the property transferred.

8. During the current year, James Elton received a 25% capital interest in Bredbo Associates, a partnership, in return for services rendered plus a contribution of assets with a basis to Elton of $25,000 and a fair market value of $40,000. The fair market value of Elton's 25% interest was $50,000. How much is Elton's basis for his interest in Bredbo?

     a. $25,000
     b. $35,000
     c. $40,000
     d. $50,000

9. Basic Partnership, a cash-basis calendar-year entity, began business on February 1, 2015. Basic incurred and paid the following during 2015:

Filing fees incident to the creation of the partnership	$3,600
Accounting fees to prepare the representations in offering materials	12,000

If Basic wishes to deduct organizational costs, what is the maximum amount that Basic can deduct on the 2015 partnership return?

a. $15,600
b. $3,600
c. $660
d. $220

C. Partnership Income and Loss

10. Thompson's basis in Starlight Partnership was $60,000 at the beginning of the year. Thompson materially participates in the partnership's business. Thompson received $20,000 in cash distributions during the year. Thompson's share of Starlight's current operations was a $65,000 ordinary loss and a $15,000 net long-term capital gain. What is the amount of Thompson's deductible loss for the period?

a. $15,000
b. $40,000
c. $55,000
d. $65,000

11. In computing the ordinary income of a partnership, a deduction is allowed for

a. Contributions to recognized charities.
b. The first $100 of dividends received from qualifying domestic corporations.
c. Short-term capital losses.
d. Guaranteed payments to partners.

12. Which of the following limitations will apply in determining a partner's deduction for that partner's share of partnership losses?

	At-risk	Passive loss
a.	Yes	No
b.	No	Yes
c.	Yes	Yes
d.	No	No

13. Dunn and Shaw are partners who share profits and losses equally. In the computation of the partnership's 2015 book income of $100,000, guaranteed payments to partners totaling $60,000 and charitable contributions totaling $1,000 were treated as expenses. What amount should be reported as ordinary income on the partnership's 2015 return?

a. $100,000
b. $101,000
c. $160,000
d. $161,000

14. The partnership of Martin & Clark sustained an ordinary loss of $84,000 in 2014. The partnership, as well as the two partners, are on a calendar-year basis. The partners share profits and losses equally. At December 31, 2014, Clark, who materially participates in the partnership's business, had an adjusted basis of $36,000 for his partnership interest, before consideration of the 2014 loss. On his individual income tax return for 2014, Clark should deduct a(n)

a. Ordinary loss of $36,000.
b. Ordinary loss of $42,000.
c. Ordinary loss of $36,000 and a capital loss of $6,000.
d. Capital loss of $42,000.

15. The partnership of Felix and Oscar had the following items of income during the taxable year ended December 31, 2015.

Income from operations	$156,000
Tax-exempt interest income	8,000
Dividends from foreign corporations	6,000
Net rental income	12,000

What is the total ordinary income of the partnership for 2015?

a. $156,000
b. $174,000
c. $176,000
d. $182,000

D. Partnership Agreements

16. A guaranteed payment by a partnership to a partner for services rendered, may include an agreement to pay

I. A salary of $5,000 monthly without regard to partnership income.
II. A 25% interest in partnership profits.

a. I only.
b. II only.
c. Both I and II.
d. Neither I nor II.

17. Chris, a 25% partner in Vista partnership, received a $20,000 guaranteed payment in 2014 for deductible services rendered to the partnership. Guaranteed payments were not made to any other partner. Vista's 2014 partnership income consisted of

Net business income before guaranteed payments	$80,000
Net long-term capital gains	10,000

What amount of income should Chris report from Vista Partnership on her 2014 tax return?

a. $37,500
b. $27,500
c. $22,500
d. $20,000

18. On January 2, 2014, Arch and Bean contribute cash equally to form the JK Partnership. Arch and Bean share profits and losses in a ratio of 75% to 25%, respectively. For 2014, the partnership's ordinary income was $40,000. A distribution of $5,000 was made to Arch during 2014. What amount of ordinary income should Arch report from the JK Partnership for 2014?

   a. $5,000
   b. $10,000
   c. $20,000
   d. $30,000

19. Guaranteed payments made by a partnership to partners for services rendered to the partnership, that are deductible business expenses under the Internal Revenue Code, are

   I. Deductible expenses on the US Partnership Return of Income, Form 1065, in order to arrive at partnership income (loss).
   II. Included on Schedule K-1 to be taxed as ordinary income to the partners.

     a. I only.
     b. II only.
     c. Both I and II.
     d. Neither I nor II.

20. The method used to depreciate partnership property is an election made by

   a. The partnership and must be the same method used by the "principal partner."
   b. The partnership and may be any method approved by the IRS.
   c. The "principal partner."
   d. Each individual partner.

21. Under the Internal Revenue Code sections pertaining to partnerships, guaranteed payments are payments to partners for

   a. Payments of principal on secured notes honored at maturity.
   b. Timely payments of periodic interest on bona fide loans that are **not** treated as partners' capital.
   c. Services or the use of capital without regard to partnership income.
   d. Sales of partners' assets to the partnership at guaranteed amounts regardless of market values.

22. Dale's distributive share of income from the calendar-year partnership of Dale & Eck was $50,000 in 2014. On December 15, 2014, Dale, who is a cash-basis taxpayer, received a $27,000 distribution of the partnership's 2014 income, with the $23,000 balance paid to Dale in February 2015. In addition, Dale received a $10,000 interest-free loan from the partnership in 2014. This $10,000 is to be offset against Dale's share of 2015 partnership income. What total amount of partnership income is taxable to Dale in 2014?

   a. $27,000
   b. $37,000
   c. $50,000
   d. $60,000

23. At December 31, 2014, Alan and Baker were equal partners in a partnership with net assets having a tax basis and fair market value of $100,000. On January 2, 2015, Carr contributed securities with a fair market value of $50,000 (purchased in 2013 at a cost of $35,000) to become an equal partner in the new firm of Alan, Baker, and Carr. The securities were sold on December 15, 2015, for $47,000. How much of the partnership's capital gain from the sale of these securities should be allocated to Carr?

   a. $0
   b. $3,000
   c. $6,000
   d. $12,000

24. Gilroy, a calendar-year taxpayer, is a partner in the firm of Adams and Company which has a fiscal year ending June 30. The partnership agreement provides for Gilroy to receive 25% of the ordinary income of the partnership. Gilroy also receives a guaranteed payment of $1,000 monthly which is deductible by the partnership. The partnership reported ordinary income of $88,000 for the year ended June 30, 2014, and $132,000 for the year ended June 30, 2015. How much should Gilroy report on his 2014 return as total income from the partnership?

   a. $25,000
   b. $30,500
   c. $34,000
   d. $39,000

25. On December 31, 2013, Edward Baker gave his son, Allan, a gift of a 50% interest in a partnership in which capital is a material income-producing factor. For the year ended December 31, 2014, the partnership's ordinary income was $100,000. Edward and Allan were the only partners in 2014. There were no guaranteed payments to partners. Edward's services performed for the partnership were worth a reasonable compensation of $40,000 for 2014. Allan has never performed any services for the partnership. What is Allan's distributive share of partnership income for 2014?

   a. $20,000
   b. $30,000
   c. $40,000
   d. $50,000

Items 26 and 27 are based on the following:

Jones and Curry formed Major Partnership as equal partners by contributing the assets below.

	Asset	Adjusted basis	Fair market value
Jones	Cash	$45,000	$45,000
Curry	Land	30,000	57,000

The land was held by Curry as a capital asset, subject to a $12,000 mortgage, that was assumed by Major.

26. What was Curry's initial basis in the partnership interest?

   a. $45,000
   b. $30,000
   c. $24,000
   d. $18,000

27. What was Jones' initial basis in the partnership interest?

    a. $51,000
    b. $45,000
    c. $39,000
    d. $33,000

Items 28 and 29 are based on the following:

    Flagg and Miles are each 50% partners in Decor Partnership. Each partner had a $200,000 tax basis in the partnership on January 1, 2014. Decor's 2014 net business income before guaranteed payments was $45,000. During 2014, Decor made a $7,500 guaranteed payment to Miles for deductible services rendered.

28. What total amount from Decor is includible in Flagg's 2014 tax return?

    a. $15,000
    b. $18,750
    c. $22,500
    d. $37,500

29. What is Miles's tax basis in Decor on December 31, 2014?

    a. $211,250
    b. $215,000
    c. $218,750
    d. $222,500

30. Peters has a one-third interest in the Spano Partnership. During 2014, Peters received a $16,000 guaranteed payment, which was deductible by the partnership, for services rendered to Spano. Spano reported a 2014 operating loss of $70,000 before the guaranteed payment. What is (are) the net effect(s) of the guaranteed payment?

    I. The guaranteed payment decreases Peters' tax basis in Spano by $16,000.
    II. The guaranteed payment increases Peters' ordinary income by $16,000.

    a. I only.
    b. II only.
    c. Both I and II.
    d. Neither I nor II.

E. Partner's Basis in Partnership

31. Dean is a 25% partner in Target Partnership. Dean's tax basis in Target on January 1, 2014, was $20,000. At the end of 2014, Dean received a nonliquidating cash distribution of $8,000 from Target. Target's 2014 accounts recorded the following items:

Municipal bond interest income	$12,000
Ordinary income	40,000

What was Dean's tax basis in Target on December 31, 2014?

    a. $15,000
    b. $23,000
    c. $25,000
    d. $30,000

32. On January 4, 2015, Smith and White contributed $4,000 and $6,000 in cash, respectively, and formed the Macro General Partnership. The partnership agreement allocated profits and losses 40% to Smith and 60% to White. In 2015, Macro purchased property from an unrelated seller for $10,000 cash and a $40,000 mortgage note that was the general liability of the partnership. Macro's liability

    a. Increases Smith's partnership basis by $16,000.
    b. Increases Smith's partnership basis by $20,000.
    c. Increases Smith's partnership basis by $24,000.
    d. Has **no** effect on Smith's partnership basis.

33. Gray is a 50% partner in Fabco Partnership. Gray's tax basis in Fabco on January 1, 2015, was $5,000. Fabco made no distributions to the partners during 2015, and recorded the following:

Ordinary income	$20,000
Tax exempt income	8,000
Portfolio income	4,000

What is Gray's tax basis in Fabco on December 31, 2015?

    a. $21,000
    b. $16,000
    c. $12,000
    d. $10,000

34. On January 1, 2015, Kane was a 25% equal partner in Maze General Partnership, which had partnership liabilities of $300,000. On January 2, 2015, a new partner was admitted and Kane's interest was reduced to 20%. On April 1, 2015, Maze repaid a $100,000 general partnership loan. Ignoring any income, loss, or distributions for 2015, what was the **net** effect of the two transactions for Kane's tax basis in Maze partnership interest?

    a. Has **no** effect.
    b. Decrease of $35,000.
    c. Increase of $15,000.
    d. Decrease of $75,000.

35. Lee inherited a partnership interest from Dale during 2015. The adjusted basis of Dale's partnership interest was $50,000, and its fair market value on the date of Dale's death (the estate valuation date) was $70,000. What was Lee's original basis for the partnership interest?

    a. $70,000
    b. $50,000
    c. $20,000
    d. $0

36. Which of the following should be used in computing the basis of a partner's interest acquired from another partner?

	Cash paid by transferee to transferor	Transferee's share of partnership liabilities
a.	No	Yes
b.	Yes	No
c.	No	No
d.	Yes	Yes

37. Hall and Haig are equal partners in the firm of Arosa Associates. On January 1, 2014, each partner's adjusted basis in Arosa was $40,000. During 2014 Arosa borrowed $60,000, for which Hall and Haig are personally liable. Arosa sustained an operating loss of $10,000 for the year ended December 31, 2014. The basis of each partner's interest in Arosa at December 31, 2014, was

- a. $35,000
- b. $40,000
- c. $65,000
- d. $70,000

F. Transactions with Controlled Partnerships

38. Doris and Lydia are sisters and also are equal partners in the capital and profits of Agee & Nolan. The following information pertains to 300 shares of Mast Corp. stock sold by Lydia to Agee & Nolan.

Year of purchase	2007
Year of sale	2015
Basis (cost)	$9,000
Sales price (equal to fair market value)	$4,000

The amount of long-term capital loss that Lydia recognized in 2015 on the sale of this stock was

- a. $5,000
- b. $3,000
- c. $2,500
- d. $0

39. In March 2015, Lou Cole bought 100 shares of a listed stock for $10,000. In May 2015, Cole sold this stock for its fair market value of $16,000 to the partnership of Rook, Cole & Clive. Cole owned a one-third interest in this partnership. In Cole's 2015 tax return, what amount should be reported as short-term capital gain as a result of this transaction?

- a. $6,000
- b. $4,000
- c. $2,000
- d. $0

40. Kay Shea owns a 55% interest in the capital and profits of Dexter Communications, a partnership. In 2015, Kay sold an oriental lamp to Dexter for $5,000. Kay bought this lamp in 2008 for her personal use at a cost of $1,000 and had used the lamp continuously in her home until the lamp was sold to Dexter. Dexter purchased the lamp as an investment. What is Kay's reportable gain in 2015 on the sale of the lamp to Dexter?

- a. $4,000 ordinary income.
- b. $4,000 long-term capital gain.
- c. $2,200 ordinary income.
- d. $1,800 long-term capital gain.

41. Gladys Peel owns a 50% interest in the capital and profits of the partnership of Peel and Poe. On July 1, 2014, Peel bought land the partnership had used in its business for its fair market value of $10,000. The partnership had acquired the land five years ago for $16,000. For the year ended December 31, 2014, the partnership's net income was $94,000 after recording the $6,000 loss on the sale of land. Peel's distributive share of ordinary income from the partnership for 2014 was

- a. $47,000
- b. $48,500
- c. $49,000
- d. $50,000

G. Taxable Year of Partnership

42. Under Section 444 of the Internal Revenue Code, certain partnerships can elect to use a tax year different from their required tax year. One of the conditions for eligibility to make a Section 444 election is that the partnership must

- a. Be a limited partnership.
- b. Be a member of a tiered structure.
- c. Choose a tax year where the deferral period is **not** longer than three months.
- d. Have less than seventy-five partners.

43. Which one of the following statements regarding a partnership's tax year is correct?

- a. A partnership formed on July 1 is required to adopt a tax year ending on June 30.
- b. A partnership may elect to have a tax year other than the generally required tax year if the deferral period for the tax year elected does **not** exceed three months.
- c. A "valid business purpose" can **no** longer be claimed as a reason for adoption of a tax year other than the generally required tax year.
- d. Within thirty days after a partnership has established a tax year, a form must be filed with the IRS as notification of the tax year adopted.

44. Without obtaining prior approval from the IRS, a newly formed partnership may adopt

- a. A taxable year which is the same as that used by one or more of its partners owning an aggregate interest of more than 50% in profits and capital.
- b. A calendar year, only if it comprises a twelve-month period.
- c. A January 31 year-end if it is a retail enterprise, and all of its principal partners are on a calendar year.
- d. Any taxable year that it deems advisable to select.

45. Irving Aster, Dennis Brill, and Robert Clark were partners who shared profits and losses equally. On February 28, 2015, Aster sold his interest to Phil Dexter. On March 31, 2015,

Brill died, and his estate held his interest for the remainder of the year. The partnership continued to operate and for the fiscal year ending June 30, 2015, it had a profit of $45,000. Assuming that partnership income was earned on a pro rata monthly basis and that all partners were calendar-year taxpayers, the distributive shares to be included in 2015 gross income should be

    a. Aster $10,000, Brill $0, Estate of Brill $15,000, Clark $15,000, and Dexter $5,000.

    b. Aster $10,000, Brill $11,250, Estate of Brill $3,750, Clark $15,000, and Dexter $5,000.

    c. Aster $0, Brill $11,250, Estate of Brill $3,750, Clark $15,000, and Dexter $15,000.

    d. Aster $0, Brill $0, Estate of Brill $15,000, Clark $15,000, and Dexter $15,000.

I. Termination or Continuation of Partnership

46. On January 3, 2014, the partners' interests in the capital, profits, and losses of Able Partnership were

	% of capital profits and losses
Dean	25%
Poe	30%
Ritt	45%

On February 4, 2014, Poe sold her entire interest to an unrelated person. Dean sold his 25% interest in Able to another unrelated person on December 20, 2014. No other transactions took place in 2014. For tax purposes, which of the following statements is correct with respect to Able?

    a. Able terminated as of February 4, 2014.

    b. Able terminated as of December 20, 2014.

    c. Able terminated as of December 31, 2014.

    d. Able did **not** terminate.

47. Curry's sale of her partnership interest causes a partnership termination. The partnership's business and financial operations are continued by the other members. What is (are) the effect(s) of the termination?

    I. There is a deemed distribution of assets to the remaining partners and the purchaser.

    II. There is a hypothetical recontribution of assets to a new partnership.

        a. I only.

        b. II only.

        c. Both I and II.

        d. Neither I nor II.

48. Cobb, Danver, and Evans each owned a one-third interest in the capital and profits of their calendar-year partnership. On September 18, 2014, Cobb and Danver sold their partnership interests to Frank, and immediately withdrew from all participation in the partnership. On March 15, 2015, Cobb and Danver received full payment from Frank for the sale of their partnership interests. For tax purposes, the partnership

    a. Terminated on September 18, 2014.

    b. Terminated on December 31, 2014.

    c. Terminated on March 15, 2015.

    d. Did **not** terminate.

49. Partnership Abel, Benz, Clark & Day is in the real estate and insurance business. Abel owns a 40% interest in the capital and profits of the partnership, while Benz, Clark, and Day each owns a 20% interest. All use a calendar year. At November 1, 2014, the real estate and insurance business is separated, and two partnerships are formed: Partnership Abel & Benz takes over the real estate business, and Partnership Clark & Day takes over the insurance business. Which one of the following statements is correct for tax purposes?

    a. Partnership Abel & Benz is considered to be a continuation of Partnership Abel, Benz, Clark & Day.

    b. In forming Partnership Clark & Day, partners Clark and Day are subject to a penalty surtax if they contribute their entire distributions from Partnership Abel, Benz, Clark & Day.

    c. Before separating the two businesses into two distinct entities, the partners must obtain approval from the IRS.

    d. Before separating the two businesses into two distinct entities, Partnership Abel, Benz, Clark & Day must file a formal dissolution with the IRS on the prescribed form.

50. Under which of the following circumstances is a partnership that is not an electing large partnership considered terminated for income tax purposes?

    I. Fifty-five percent of the total interest in partnership capital and profits is sold within a twelve-month period.

    II. The partnership's business and financial operations are discontinued.

        a. I only.

        b. II only.

        c. Both I and II.

        d. Neither I nor II.

51. David Beck and Walter Crocker were equal partners in the calendar-year partnership of Beck & Crocker. On July 1, 2014, Beck died. Beck's estate became the successor in interest and continued to share in Beck & Crocker's profits until Beck's entire partnership interest was liquidated on April 30, 2015. At what date was the partnership considered terminated for tax purposes?

    a. April 30, 2015.

    b. December 31, 2015.

    c. July 31, 2014.

    d. July 1, 2014.

J. Sale of a Partnership Interest

52. On December 31, 2014, after receipt of his share of partnership income, Clark sold his interest in a limited partnership for $30,000 cash and relief of all liabilities. On that date, the adjusted basis of Clark's partnership interest was $40,000, consisting of his capital account of $15,000 and his share of the partnership liabilities of $25,000. The partnership has no unrealized receivables or appreciated inventory. What is Clark's gain or loss on the sale of his partnership interest?

a. Ordinary loss of $10,000.
b. Ordinary gain of $15,000.
c. Capital loss of $10,000.
d. Capital gain of $15,000.

Items 53 and 54 are based on the following:

The personal service partnership of Allen, Baker & Carr had the following cash basis balance sheet at December 31, 2014:

Assets	Adjusted basis per books	Market value
Cash	$102,000	$102,000
Unrealized accounts receivable	--	420,000
Totals	$102,000	$522,000
Liability and Capital		
Note payable	$60,000	$60,000
Capital accounts:		
Allen	14,000	154,000
Baker	14,000	154,000
Carr	14,000	154,000
Totals	$102,000	$522,000

Carr, an equal partner, sold his partnership interest to Dole, an outsider, for $154,000 cash on January 1, 2015. In addition, Dole assumed Carr's share of the partnership's liability.

53. What was the total amount realized by Carr on the sale of his partnership interest?

a. $174,000
b. $154,000
c. $140,000
d. $134,000

54. What amount of ordinary income should Carr report in his 2015 income tax return on the sale of his partnership interest?

a. $0
b. $20,000
c. $34,000
d. $140,000

55. On April 1, 2014, George Hart, Jr. acquired a 25% interest in the Wilson, Hart, and Company partnership by gift from his father. The partnership interest had been acquired by a $50,000 cash investment by Hart, Sr. on July 1, 2008. The tax basis of Hart, Sr.'s partnership interest was $60,000 at the time of the gift. Hart, Jr. sold the 25% partnership interest for $85,000 on December 17, 2014. What type and amount of capital gain should Hart, Jr. report on his 2014 tax return?

a. A long-term capital gain of $25,000.
b. A short-term capital gain of $25,000.
c. A long-term capital gain of $35,000.
d. A short-term capital gain of $35,000.

56. On June 30, 2015, James Roe sold his interest in the calendar-year partnership of Roe & Doe for $30,000. Roe's adjusted basis in Roe & Doe at June 30, 2015, was $7,500

before apportionment of any 2015 partnership income. Roe's distributive share of partnership income up to June 30, 2015, was $22,500. Roe acquired his interest in the partnership in 2010. How much long-term capital gain should Roe report in 2015 on the sale of his partnership interest?

a. $0
b. $15,000
c. $22,500
d. $30,000

K. Pro Rata Distributions from Partnership

57. Stone and Frazier decided to terminate the Woodwest Partnership as of December 31. On that date, Woodwest's balance sheet was as follows:

Cash	$2,000
Land (adjusted basis)	2,000
Capital—Stone	3,000
Capital—Frazier	1,000

The fair market value of the land was $3,000. Frazier's outside basis in the partnership was $1,200. Upon liquidation, Frazier received $1,500 in cash. What gain should Frazier recognize?

a. $0
b. $250
c. $300
d. $500

58. Curry's adjusted basis in Vantage Partnership was $5,000 at the time he received a nonliquidating distribution of land. The land had an adjusted basis of $6,000 and a fair market value of $9,000 to Vantage. What was the amount of Curry's basis in the land?

a. $9,000
b. $6,000
c. $5,000
d. $1,000

59. Hart's adjusted basis in Best Partnership was $9,000 at the time he received the following nonliquidating distribution of partnership property:

Cash	$5,000
Land	
Adjusted basis	7,000
Fair market value	10,000

What was the amount of Hart's basis in the land?

a. $0
b. $4,000
c. $7,000
d. $10,000

60. Day's adjusted basis in LMN Partnership interest is $50,000. During the year Day received a nonliquidating distribution of $25,000 cash plus land with an adjusted basis of $15,000 to LMN, and a fair market value of $20,000. How much is Day's basis in the land?

a. $10,000
b. $15,000
c. $20,000
d. $25,000

Items 61 and 62 are based on the following:

The adjusted basis of Jody's partnership interest was $50,000 immediately before Jody received a current distribution of $20,000 cash and property with an adjusted basis to the partnership of $40,000 and a fair market value of $35,000.

61. What amount of taxable gain must Jody report as a result of this distribution?

a. $0
b. $5,000
c. $10,000
d. $20,000

62. What is Jody's basis in the distributed property?

a. $0
b. $30,000
c. $35,000
d. $40,000

63. On June 30, 2015, Berk, a calendar-year taxpayer, retired from his partnership. At that time, his capital account was $50,000 and his share of the partnership's liabilities was $30,000. Berk's retirement payments consisted of being relieved of his share of the partnership liabilities and receipt of cash payments of $5,000 per month for eighteen months, commencing July 1, 2015. Assuming Berk makes no election with regard to the recognition of gain from the retirement payments, he should report income of

		2015	2016
a.		$13,333	$26,667
b.		20,000	20,000
c.		40,000	--
d.		--	40,000

64. The basis to a partner of property distributed in complete liquidation of the partner's interest is the

a. Adjusted basis of the partner's interest increased by any cash distributed to the partner in the same transaction.
b. Adjusted basis of the partner's interest reduced by any cash distributed to the partner in the same transaction.
c. Adjusted basis of the property to the partnership.
d. Fair market value of the property.

Items 65 and 66 are based on the following data:

Mike Reed, a partner in Post Co., received the following distribution from Post:

	Post's basis	Fair market value
Cash	$11,000	$11,000
Inventory	5,000	12,500

Before this distribution, Reed's basis in Post was $25,000.

65. If this distribution were nonliquidating, Reed's basis for the inventory would be

a. $14,000
b. $12,500
c. $5,000
d. $1,500

66. If this distribution were in complete liquidation of Reed's interest in Post, Reed's recognized gain or loss resulting from the distribution would be

a. $7,500 gain.
b. $9,000 loss
c. $1,500 loss.
d. $0.

67. In 2010, Lisa Bara acquired a one-third interest in Dee Associates, a partnership. In 2015, when Lisa's entire interest in the partnership was liquidated, Dee's assets consisted of the following: cash, $20,000 and tangible property with a basis of $46,000 and a fair market value of $40,000. Dee has no liabilities. Lisa's adjusted basis for her one-third interest was $22,000. Lisa received cash of $20,000 in liquidation of her entire interest. What was Lisa's recognized loss in 2015 on the liquidation of her interest in Dee?

a. $0.
b. $2,000 short-term capital loss.
c. $2,000 long-term capital loss.
d. $2,000 ordinary loss.

68. For tax purposes, a retiring partner who receives retirement payments ceases to be regarded as a partner

a. On the last day of the taxable year in which the partner retires.
b. On the last day of the particular month in which the partner retires.
c. The day on which the partner retires.
d. Only after the partner's entire interest in the partnership is liquidated.

69. John Albin is a retired partner of Brill & Crum, a personal service partnership. Albin has not rendered any services to Brill & Crum since his retirement in 2012. Under the provisions of Albin's retirement agreement, Brill & Crum is obligated to pay Albin 10% of the partnership's net income each year. In compliance with this agreement, Brill & Crum paid Albin $25,000 in 2014. How should Albin treat this $25,000?

a. Not taxable.
b. Ordinary income.
c. Short-term capital gain.
d. Long-term capital gain.

Multiple-Choice Answers and Explanations

Answers

1.	d	__ __	16	a	__ __	31.	c	__ __	46.	b	__ __	61.	a	__ __
2.	c	__ __	17.	a	__ __	32.	a	__ __	47.	c	__ __	62.	b	__ __
3.	c	__ __	18.	d	__ __	33.	a	__ __	48.	a	__ __	63.	d	__ __
4.	a	__ __	19.	c	__ __	34.	b	__ __	49.	a	__ __	64.	b	__ __
5.	c	__ __	20.	b	__ __	35.	a	__ __	50.	c	__ __	65.	c	__ __
6.	d	__ __	21.	c	__ __	36.	d	__ __	51.	a	__ __	66.	b	__ __
7.	b	__ __	22.	c	__ __	37.	c	__ __	52.	d	__ __	67.	c	__ __
8.	b	__ __	23.	d	__ __	38.	d	__ __	53.	a	__ __	68.	d	__ __
9.	b	__ __	24.	c	__ __	39.	a	__ __	54.	d	__ __	69.	b	__ __
10.	c	__ __	25.	b	__ __	40.	b	__ __	55.	a	__ __			
11.	d	__ __	26.	c	__ __	41.	d	__ __	56.	a	__ __			
12.	c	__ __	27.	a	__ __	42.	c	__ __	57.	c	__ __			
13.	b	__ __	28.	b	__ __	43.	b	__ __	58.	c	__ __			
14.	a	__ __	29.	c	__ __	44.	a	__ __	59.	b	__ __	1st:	__/69= __%	
15.	a	__ __	30.	b	__ __	45.	b	__ __	60.	b	__ __	2nd:	__/69= __%	

Explanations

1. (d) The requirement is to determine which statements are correct regarding Black's recognition of gain on transferring property with an adjusted basis of $250,000 in exchange for a 50% partnership interest. Generally, no gain is recognized when appreciated property is transferred to a partnership in exchange for a partnership interest. However, gain will be recognized if the transferred property is encumbered by a mortgage, and the partnership's assumption of the mortgage results in a decrease in the transferor's individual liabilities that exceeds the basis of the property transferred. Here, the basis of the property transferred is $250,000, and the net decrease in Black's individual liabilities is $50,000 (i.e., $100,000 × 50%), so no gain is recognized.

2. (c) The requirement is to determine the amount that must be included on Kelly's 2015 income tax return as the result of the receipt of a 10% partnership interest in exchange for services. A taxpayer must recognize ordinary income when a capital interest in a partnership is received as compensation for services rendered. The amount of ordinary income to be included on Kelly's 2015 return is the fair market value of the partnership interest received ($100,000 × 10% = $10,000).

3. (c) The requirement is to determine the amount that Hoff, a cash-basis taxpayer, should report as income for the services rendered to Ola Associates. A cash-basis taxpayer generally reports income when received, unless constructively received at an earlier date. The amount of income to be reported is the amount of money, plus the fair market value of other property received. In this case, Hoff must report a total of $32,000, which includes the $15,000 cash, the $10,000 FMV of the limited partnership interest, and the $7,000 FMV of the surveying equipment received. Note that since Hoff is a cash-basis taxpayer, he would not report income at the time that he billed Ola $40,000, nor would he be entitled to a bad debt

deduction when he accepts $32,000 of consideration in full settlement of his $40,000 invoice.

4. (a) The requirement is to determine the amount of gain reportable in Gray's return as a result of Gray's contribution of property in exchange for a 40% partnership interest. Generally, no gain or loss is recognized on the contribution of property in exchange for a partnership interest. Note that this nonrecognition rule applies even though the value of the partnership capital interest received (40% × $150,000 = $60,000) exceeds the fair market value of the property contributed ($30,000).

5. (c) The requirement is to determine the correct statement regarding the holding period for a partnership interest acquired in exchange for a contributed capital asset. The holding period for a partnership interest that is acquired through a contribution of property depends upon the nature of the contributed property. If the contributed property was a capital asset or Sec. 1231 asset to the contributing partner, the holding period of the acquired partnership interest includes the period of time that the capital asset or Sec. 1231 asset was held by the partner. For all other contributed property, a partner's holding period for a partnership interest begins when the partnership interest is acquired.

6. (d) The requirement is to determine the amount of gain recognized on the exchange of stock for a partnership interest. Generally no gain or loss is recognized on the transfer of property to a partnership in exchange for a partnership interest. Since Carr's gain is not recognized, there will be a carryover basis of $30,000 for the stock to the partnership, and Carr will have a $30,000 basis for the 25% partnership interest received.

7. (b) The requirement is to determine the holding period for property acquired by a partnership as a contribution to the contributing partner's capital account. Generally no gain or loss is recognized on the contribution of property to a partnership in exchange for a capital interest. Since the partnership's basis for the contributed property is determined by reference to the contributing partner's former basis for the property (i.e., a transferred basis), the partnership's holding period includes the period during which the property was held by the contributing partner.

8. (b) The requirement is to determine Elton's basis for his 25% interest in the Bredbo partnership. Since Elton received a capital interest with an FMV of $50,000 in exchange for property worth $40,000 and services, Elton must recognize compensation income of $10,000 ($50,000 – $40,000) on the transfer of services for a capital interest. Thus, Elton's basis for his partnership interest consists of the $25,000 basis of assets transferred plus the $10,000 of income recognized on the transfer of services, a total of $35,000.

9. (b) The requirement is to determine the maximum amount of filing fees and accounting fees that Basic could deduct on the 2015 partnership return. The filing fees incident to the creation of the partnership are organizational expenditures. A partnership may deduct up to $5,000 of organizational expenditures for the tax year in which the partnership begins business, with any remaining expenditures deducted ratably over the 180-month period beginning with the month in which the partnership begins business. Here, since the organizational expenditures total only $3,600, they can be fully deducted for 2015.

The accounting fees to prepare the representations in offering materials are considered syndication fees. *Syndication fees* include the costs connected with the issuing and marketing of partnership interests such as commissions, professional fees, and printing costs. These costs must be capitalized and can neither be amortized nor depreciated.

10. (c) The requirement is to determine the amount of loss that Thompson can deduct as a result of his interest in the Starlight Partnership. A partner's distributive share of partnership losses is generally deductible to the extent of the tax basis for the partner's partnership interest at the end of the year. All positive basis adjustments and all reductions for distributions must be taken into account before determining the amount of deductible loss. Here, Thompson's basis of $60,000 at the beginning of the year would be increased by the $15,000 of net long-term capital gain, reduced by the $20,000 cash distribution, to $55,000. As a result, Thompson's deduction of the ordinary loss for the current year is limited to $55,000 which reduces the basis for his partnership interest to zero. He cannot deduct the remaining $10,000 of ordinary loss currently, but will carry it forward and deduct it when he has sufficient basis for his partnership interest.

11. (d) The requirement is to determine the item that is deductible in the computation of the ordinary income of a partnership. Guaranteed payments to partners are always deductible in computing a partnership's ordinary income. Contributions to recognized charities and short-term capital losses cannot be deducted in computing a partnership's ordinary income because they are subject to special limitations and must be separately passed through so that any applicable limitations can be applied at the partner level. Similarly, dividends are an item of portfolio income and must be

separately passed through to partners in order to retain its character as portfolio income when reported on partners' returns.

12. (c) The requirement is to determine whether the at-risk and passive activity loss limitations apply in determining a partner's deduction for that partner's share of partnership losses. A partner's distributive share of partnership losses is generally deductible by the partner to the extent of the partner's basis in the partnership at the end of the taxable year. Additionally, the deductibility of partnership losses is limited to the amount of the partner's at-risk basis, and will also be subject to the passive activity loss limitations if they are applicable. Note that the at-risk and passive activity loss limitations apply at the partner level, rather than at the partnership level.

13. (b) The requirement is to determine the amount to be reported as ordinary income on the partnership's return given partnership book income of $100,000. The $60,000 of guaranteed payments to partners were deducted in computing partnership book income and are also deductible in computing partnership ordinary income. However, the $1,000 charitable contribution deducted in arriving at partnership book income must be separately passed through to partners on Schedule K-1 and cannot be deducted in computing partnership ordinary income. Thus, the partnership's ordinary income is $100,000 + $1,000 = $101,000.

14. (a) The requirement is to determine the amount and type of partnership loss to be deducted on Clark's individual return. Since a partnership functions as a pass-through entity, the nature of a loss as an ordinary loss is maintained when passed through to partners. However, the amount of partnership loss that can be deducted by a partner is limited to a partner's tax basis in the partnership at the end of the partnership taxable year. Thus, Clark's distributive share of the ordinary loss ($42,000) is only deductible to the extent of $36,000. The remaining $6,000 of loss would be carried forward by Clark and could be deducted after his partnership basis has been increased.

15. (a) The requirement is to determine the ordinary income of the partnership. Income from operations is considered ordinary income. The net rental income and the dividends from foreign corporations are separately allocated to partners and must be excluded from the computation of the partnership's ordinary income. Tax-exempt income remains tax-exempt and must also be excluded from the computation of ordinary income. Thus, ordinary income only consists of the income from operations of $156,000.

16. (a) The requirement is to determine the correct statement(s) concerning agreements for guaranteed payments. Guaranteed payments are payments made to a partner for services or for the use of capital if the payments are determined *without regard to the amount of partnership income*. Guaranteed payments are deductible by a partnership in computing its ordinary income or loss from trade or business activities, and must be reported as self-employment income by the partner receiving payment. A payment that represents a 25% interest in partnership profits could not be classified as a guaranteed payment because the payment is conditioned on the partnership having profits.

17. (a) The requirement is to determine the amount of income that Chris should report as a result of her 25% partnership interest. A partnership is a pass-through entity and its items of income and deduction pass through to be reported on partners' returns even though not distributed. The amount to be reported by Chris consists of her guaranteed payment, plus her 25% share of the partnership's business income and capital gains. Since Chris's $20,000 guaranteed payment is for deductible services rendered to the partnership, it must be subtracted from the partnership's net business income before guaranteed payments of $80,000 to determine the amount of net business income to be allocated among partners. Chris's reportable income from the partnership includes

Guaranteed payment	$20,000
Business income [($80,000 − $20,000) × 25%]	15,000
Net long-term capital gain ($10,000 × 25%)	2,500
	$37,500

18. (d) The requirement is to determine Arch's share of the JK Partnership's ordinary income for 2014. A partnership functions as a pass-through entity and its items of income and deduction are passed through to partners according to their profit and loss sharing ratios, which may differ from the ratios used to divide capital. Here, Arch's distributive share of the partnership's ordinary income is $40,000 × 75% = $30,000. Note that Arch will be taxed on his $30,000 distributive share of ordinary income even though only $5,000 was distributed to him.

19. (c) The requirement is to determine whether the statements regarding partners' guaranteed payments are correct. Guaranteed payments made by a partnership to partners for services rendered are an ordinary deduction in computing a partnership's ordinary income or loss from trade or business activities on page 1 of Form 1065. Partners must report the receipt of guaranteed payments as ordinary income (self-employment income) and that is why the payments also must be separately listed on Schedule K and Schedule K-1.

20. (b) The requirement is to determine the correct statement regarding a partnership's election of a depreciation method. The method used to depreciate partnership property is an election made by the partnership and may be any method approved by the IRS. The partnership is not restricted to using the same method as used by its "principal partner." Since the election is made at the partnership level, and not by each individual partner, partners are bound by whatever depreciation method that the partnership elects to use.

21. (c) The requirement is to determine the correct statement regarding guaranteed payments to partners. Guaranteed payments are payments made to partners for their services or for the use of capital without regard to the amount of the partnership's income. Guaranteed payments are deductible by the partnership in computing its ordinary income or loss from trade of business activities, and must be reported as self-employment income by the partners receiving payment.

22. (c) The requirement is to determine the total amount of partnership income that is taxable to Dale in 2014. A partnership functions as a pass-through entity and its items of income and deduction are passed through to partners on the last day of the partnership's taxable year. Income and deduction items pass through to be reported by partners even though not actually distributed during the year. Here, Dale is taxed on his $50,000 distributive share of partnership income for 2014, even though $23,000 was not received until 2015. The $10,000 interest-free loan does not affect the pass-through of income for 2014, and the $10,000 offset against Dale's distributive share of partnership income for 2015 will not affect the pass-through of that income in 2015.

23. (d) The requirement is to determine the amount of the partnership's capital gain from the sale of securities to be allocated to Carr. Normally, the entire amount of pre-contribution gain would be allocated to Carr. However, in this case the allocation to Carr is limited to the partnership's recognized gain resulting from the sale, $47,000 selling price − $35,000 basis = $12,000.

24. (c) The requirement is to determine the amount that Gilroy should report for 2014 as total income from the partnership. Gilroy's income will consist of his share of the partnership's ordinary income for the fiscal year ending June 30, 2014 (the partnership year that ends within his year), plus the twelve monthly guaranteed payments that he received for that period of time.

25% × $88,000	=	$22,000
12 × $1,000	=	12,000
Total income	=	$34,000

25. (b) The requirement is to determine Allan's distributive share of the partnership income. In a family partnership, services performed by family members must first be reasonably compensated before income is allocated according to the capital interests of the partners. Since Edward's services were worth $40,000, Allan's distributive share of partnership income is ($100,000 − $40,000) × 50% = $30,000.

26. (c) The requirement is to determine Curry's initial basis for the 50% partnership interest received in exchange for a contribution of property subject to a $12,000 mortgage that was assumed by the partnership. Generally, no gain or loss is recognized on the contribution of property in exchange for a partnership interest. As a result, Curry's initial basis for the partnership interest received consists of the $30,000 adjusted basis of the land contributed to the partnership, less the net reduction in Curry's individual liability resulting from the partnership's assumption of the $12,000 mortgage. Since Curry received a 50% partnership interest, the net reduction in Curry's individual liability is $12,000 × 50% = $6,000. As a result, Curry's basis for the partnership interest is $30,000 − $6,000 = $24,000.

27. (a) The requirement is to determine Jones' initial basis for the 50% partnership interest received in exchange for a contribution of cash of $45,000. Since partners are individually liable for their share of partnership liabilities, an increase in partnership liabilities increases a partner's basis in the partnership by the partner's share of the increase. Jones' initial basis consists of the $45,000 of cash contributed, increased by the increase in Jones' individual liability resulting from the partnership's assumption of Curry's mortgage ($12,000 × 50% = $6,000). Thus, Jones' initial basis for the partnership interest is $45,000 + $6,000 = $51,000.

28. (b) The requirement is to determine the total amount includible in Flagg's 2014 tax return as a result of Flagg's 50% interest in the Decor Partnership. Decor's net business income of $45,000 would be reduced by the guaranteed payment of $7,500, resulting in $37,500 of ordinary income that would pass through to be reported on partners' returns. Here, Flagg's share of the includible income would be $37,500 × 50% = $18,750.

29. (c) The requirement is to determine Miles's tax basis for his 50% interest in the Decor Partnership on December 31, 2014. The basis for a partner's partnership interest is increased by the partner's distributive share of partnership income that is taxed to the partner. Here, Decor's net business income of $45,000 would be reduced by the guaranteed payment of $7,500, resulting in $37,500 of ordinary income that would pass through to be reported on partners' returns and increase the basis of their partnership interests. Here, Miles's beginning tax basis for the partnership interest of $200,000 would be increased by Miles's distributive share of ordinary income ($37,500 × 50% = $18,750), to $218,750.

30. (b) The requirement is to determine the net effect(s) of the $16,000 guaranteed payment made to Peters by the Spano Partnership who reported an operating loss of $70,000 before deducting the guaranteed payment. A guaranteed payment is a partnership payment made to a partner for services or for the use of capital if the payment is determined without regard to the amount of partnership income. A guaranteed payment is deductible by a partnership in computing its ordinary income or loss from trade or business activities and must be reported as self-employment income by the partner receiving the payment, thereby increasing Peters' ordinary income by $16,000. However, since Peters has only a one-third interest in the Spano Partnership, the $16,000 of guaranteed payment deducted by Spano would have the effect of reducing Peters' tax basis in Spano by only one-third of $16,000.

31. (c) The requirement is to determine the basis for Dean's 25% partnership interest at December 31, 2014. A partner's basis for a partnership interest is increased or decreased by the partner's distributive share of all partnership items. Basis is increased by the partner's distributive share of all income items (including tax-exempt income) and is decreased by all loss and deduction items (including nondeductible items) and distributions received from the partnership. In this case, Dean's beginning basis of $20,000 would be increased by the pass-through of his distributive share of the partnership's ordinary income ($40,000 × 25% = $10,000) and municipal bond interest income ($12,000 × 25% = $3,000), and would be decreased by the $8,000 cash nonliquidating distribution that he received.

32. (a) The requirement is to determine the effect of a $40,000 increase in partnership liabilities on the basis for Smith's 40% partnership interest. Since partners are individually liable for their share of partnership liabilities, a change in the amount of partnership liabilities affects a partner's basis for a partnership interest. When partnership liabilities increase, it is effectively treated as if each partner individually borrowed money and then made a capital contribution of the borrowed amount. As a result, an increase in partnership liabilities increases each partner's basis in the partnership by each partner's share of the increase. Here, Smith's basis is increased by his 40% share of the mortgage (40% × $40,000 = $16,000).

33. (a) The requirement is to determine Gray's tax basis for a 50% interest in the Fabco Partnership. The basis for a partner's partnership interest is increased by the partner's distributive share of all partnership items of income and is decreased by the partner's distributive share of all loss and deduction items. Here, Gray's beginning basis of $5,000 would be increased by Gray's 50% distributive share of ordinary income ($10,000), tax-exempt income ($4,000), and portfolio income ($2,000), resulting in an ending basis of $21,000 for Gray's Fabco partnership interest.

34. (b) The requirement is to determine the net effect of the two transactions on Kane's tax basis for his Maze partnership interest. A partner's basis for a partnership interest consists of the partner's capital account plus the partner's share of partnership liabilities. A decrease in a partner's share of partnership liabilities is considered to be a deemed distribution of money and reduces a partner's basis for the partnership interest. Here, Kane's partnership interest was reduced from 25% to 20% on January 2, resulting in a reduction in Kane's share of liabilities of 5% × $300,000 = $15,000. Subsequently, on April 1, when there was a $100,000 repayment of partnership loans, there was a further reduction in Kane's share of partnership liabilities of 20% × $100,000 = $20,000. Thus, the net effect of the reduction of Kane's partnership interest to 20% from 25%, and the repayment of $100,000 of partnership liabilities would be to reduce Kane's basis for the partnership interest by $15,000 + $20,000 = $35,000.

35. (a) The requirement is to determine the original basis of Lee's partnership interest that was received as an inheritance from Dale. The basis of property received from a decedent dying during 2015 is generally its fair market value as of date of death. Since fair market value on the date of Dale's death was used for estate tax purposes, Lee's original basis is $70,000.

36. (d) The requirement is to determine whether cash paid by a transferee, and the transferee's share of partnership liabilities are to be included in computing the basis of a partner's interest acquired from another partner. When an existing partner sells a partnership interest, the consideration received by the transferor partner, and the basis of the transferee's partnership interest includes both the cash actually paid by the transferee to the transferor, as well as the transferee's assumption of the transferor's share of partnership liabilities.

37. (c) The requirement is to determine the basis of each partner's interest in Arosa at December 31, 2014. Since there are two equal partners, each partner's adjusted basis in Arosa of $40,000 on January 1, 2014, would be increased by 50% of the $60,000 loan and would be decreased by 50% of the $10,000 operating loss. Thus, each partner's basis in Arosa at December 31, 2014, would be $40,000 + $30,000 liability – $5,000 loss = $65,000.

38. (d) The requirement is to determine the amount of long-term capital loss recognized by Lydia from the sale of stock to Agee & Nolan. A loss is disallowed if incurred in a transaction between a partnership and a person owning (directly or constructively) more than a 50% capital or profits interest. Although Lydia directly owns only a 50% partnership interest, she constructively owns her sister's 50% partnership interest. Since Lydia directly and constructively has a 100% partnership interest, her $5,000 loss is disallowed.

39. (a) The requirement is to determine the amount to be reported as short-term capital gain on Cole's sale of stock to the partnership. If a person engages in a transaction with a partnership other than as a partner of such partnership, any resulting gain is generally recognized just as if the transaction had occurred with a nonpartner. Here, Cole's gain of $16,000 – $10,000 = $6,000 is fully recognized. Since the stock was not held for more than twelve months, Cole's $6,000 gain is treated as a short-term capital gain.

40. (b) The requirement is to determine the amount and nature of Kay's gain from the sale of the lamp to Admor. A gain that is recognized on a sale of property between a partnership and a person owning a more than 50% partnership interest will be treated as ordinary income if the property is not a capital asset in the hands of the transferee. Although Kay has a 55% partnership interest, the partnership purchased the lamp as an investment (i.e., a capital asset), and Kay's gain will solely depend on how she held the lamp. Since she used the lamp for personal use, Kay has a $5,000 – $1,000 = $4,000 long-term capital gain.

41. (d) The requirement is to determine Peel's distributive share of ordinary income from the partnership. Although the $6,000 loss that was deducted in arriving at the partnership's net income would also be deductible for tax purposes, it must be separately passed through to partners because it is a Sec. 1231 loss. Thus, the $6,000 loss must be added back to the $94,000 of partnership net income and results in partnership ordinary income of $100,000. Peel's share is $100,000 × 50% = $50,000.

42. (c) The requirement is to determine the correct statement regarding a partnership's eligibility to make a Sec. 444 election. A partnership must generally adopt the same taxable year as used by its one or more partners owning an aggregate interest of more than 50% in partnership profits and capital. However, under Sec. 444, a partnership can instead elect to adopt a fiscal year that does not result in a deferral period of longer than three months. The deferral period is the number of months between the end of its selected year and the year that it generally would be required to adopt. For example,

a partnership that otherwise would be required to adopt a taxable year ending December 31, could elect to adopt a fiscal year ending September 30. The deferral period would be the months of October, November, and December. The partnership is not required to be a limited partnership, be a member of tiered structure, or have less than seventy-five partners.

43. (b) The requirement is to determine the correct statement regarding a partnership's tax year. A partnership must generally determine its taxable year in the following order: (1) it must adopt the taxable year used by its one or more partners owning an aggregate interest of more than 50% in profits and capital; (2) if partners owning a more than 50% interest in profits and capital do not have the same year-end, the partnership must adopt the same taxable year as used by all of its principal partners; and (3) if principal partners have different taxable years, the partnership must adopt the taxable year that results in the least aggregate deferral of income to partners.

A different taxable year other than the year determined above can be used by a partnership if a valid business purpose can be established and IRS permission is received. Alternatively, a partnership can elect to use a tax year (other than one required under the general rules in the first paragraph), if the election does not result in a deferral of income of more than three months. The deferral period is the number of months between the close of the elected tax year and the close of the year that would otherwise be required under the general rules. Thus, a partnership that would otherwise be required to adopt a tax year ending December 31 could elect to adopt a fiscal year ending September 30 (three-month deferral), October 31 (two-month deferral), or November 30 (one-month deferral). Note that a partnership that makes this election must make "required payments" which are in the nature of refundable, noninterest-bearing deposits that are intended to compensate the Treasury for the revenue lost as a result of the deferral period.

44. (a) A newly formed partnership must adopt the same taxable year as is used by its partners owning a more than 50% interest in profits and capital. If partners owning more than 50% do not have the same taxable year, a partnership must adopt the same taxable year as used by all of its principal partners (i.e., partners with a 5% or more interest in capital and profits). If its principal partners have different taxable years, a partnership must adopt the tax year that results in the least aggregate deferral of income to partners.

45. (b) The requirement is to determine the distributive shares of partnership income for the partnership fiscal year ended June 30, 2015, to be included in gross income by Aster, Brill, Estate of Brill, Clark, and Dexter. Clark was a partner for the entire year and is taxed on his distributive 1/3 share ($45,000 × 1/3 = $15,000). Since Aster sold his entire partnership interest to Dexter, the partnership tax year closes with respect to Aster on February 28. As a result, Aster's distributive share is $45,000 × 1/3 × 8/12 = $10,000. Dexter's distributive share is $45,000 × 1/3 / 4/12 = $5,000.

Additionally, a partnership tax year closes with respect to a deceased partner as of date of death. Since Brill died on March

31, the distributive share to be included in Brill's 2015 Form 1040 would be $45,000 × 1/3 × 9/12 = $11,250. Since Brill's estate held his partnership interest for the remainder of the year, the estate's distributive share of income is $45,000 × 1/3 × 3/12 = $3,750.

46. (b) The requirement is to determine the correct statement regarding the termination of the Able Partnership. A partnership is terminated for tax purposes when there is a sale or exchange of 50% or more of the total interests in partnership capital and profits within any twelve-month period. Since Poe sold her 30% interest on February 4, 2014, and Dean sold his 25% partnership interest on December 20, 2014, there has been a sale of 55% of the total interests within a twelve-month period and the Able Partnership is terminated on December 20, 2014.

47. (c) The requirement is to determine which statements are correct concerning the termination of a partnership. A partnership will terminate when there is a sale of 50% or more of the total interests in partnership capital and profits within any twelve-month period. When this occurs, there is a deemed distribution of assets to the remaining partners and the purchaser, and a hypothetical recontribution of these same assets to a new partnership.

48. (a) The requirement is to determine the date on which the partnership terminated for tax purposes. The partnership was terminated on September 18, 2014, the date on which Cobb and Danver sold their partnership interests to Frank, since on that date there was a sale of 50% or more of the total interests in partnership capital and profit.

49. (a) The requirement is to determine the correct statement concerning the division of Partnership Abel, Benz, Clark, & Day into two partnerships. Following the division of a partnership, a resulting partnership is deemed to be a continuation of the prior partnership if the resulting partnership's partners had a more than 50% interest in the prior partnership. Here, as a result of the division, Partnership Abel & Benz is considered to be a continuation of the prior partnership because its partners (Abel and Benz) owned more than 50% of the interests in the prior partnership (i.e., Abel 40% and Benz 20%).

50. (c) The requirement is to determine under which circumstances a partnership, other than an electing large partnership, is considered terminated for income tax purposes. A partnership will be terminated when (1) there are no longer at least two partners, (2) no part of any business, financial operation, or venture of the partnership continues to be carried on by any of its partners in a partnership, or (3) within a twelve-month period there is a sale or exchange of 50% or more of the total interest in partnership capital and profits.

51. (a) The requirement is to determine the date on which the partnership was terminated. A partnership generally does not terminate for tax purposes upon the death of a partner, since the deceased partner's estate or successor in interest continues to share in partnership profits and losses. However, the Beck and Crocker Partnership was terminated when Beck's entire partnership interest was liquidated on April 30,

2015, since there no longer were at least two partners and the business ceased to exist as a partnership.

52. (d) The requirement is to determine the amount and character of gain or loss recognized on the sale of Clark's partnership interest. A partnership interest is a capital asset and a sale generally results in capital gain or loss, except that ordinary income must be reported to the extent of the selling partner's share of unrealized receivables and appreciated inventory. Here, Clark realized $55,000 from the sale of his partnership interest ($30,000 cash + relief from his $25,000 share of partnership liabilities). Since the partnership had no unrealized receivables or appreciated inventory and the basis of Clark's interest was $40,000, Clark realized a capital gain of $55,000 – $40,000 = $15,000 from the sale.

53. (a) The requirement is to determine the total amount realized by Carr on the sale of his partnership interest. The total amount realized consists of the amount of cash received plus the buyer's assumption of Carr's share of partnership liabilities. Thus, the total amount realized is $154,000 + ($60,000 × 1/3) = $174,000.

54. (d) The requirement is to determine the amount of ordinary income that Carr should report on the sale of his partnership interest. Although the sale of a partnership interest generally results in capital gain or loss, ordinary income must be recognized to the extent of the selling partner's share of unrealized receivables and appreciated inventory. Here, Carr must report ordinary income to the extent of his 1/3 share of the unrealized accounts receivable of $420,000, or $140,000.

55. (a) The requirement is to determine the amount and type of capital gain to be reported by Hart, Jr. from the sale of his partnership interest. Since the partnership interest was acquired by gift from Hart, Sr., Jr.'s basis would be the same as Sr.'s basis at date of gift, $60,000. Since Jr.'s basis is determined from Sr.'s basis, Jr.'s holding period includes the period the partnership interest was held by Sr. Thus, Hart, Jr. will report a LTCG of $85,000 – $60,000 = $25,000.

56. (a) The requirement is to determine the amount of LTCG to be reported by Roe on the sale of his partnership interest. Roe's basis for his partnership interest of $7,500 must first be increased by his $22,500 distributive share of partnership income, to $30,000. Since the selling price also was $30,000, Roe will report no gain or loss on the sale of his partnership interest.

57. (c) The requirement is to determine Frazier's recognized gain resulting from the cash received in liquidation of his partnership interest. A distributee partner will recognize any realized gain or loss resulting from the complete liquidation of the partner's interest if only cash is received. Since Frazier's basis for his partnership interest was $1,200 and he received $1,500 cash, Frazier must recognize a $300 capital gain.

58. (c) The requirement is to determine the basis for land acquired in a nonliquidating partnership distribution. Generally, no gain or loss is recognized on the distribution of partnership property to a partner. As a result, the partner's basis for distributed property is generally the same as the partnership's former basis for the property (a transferred basis). However, since the distribution cannot reduce the basis for the partner's partnership interest below zero, the distributed property's basis to the partner is limited to the partner's basis for the partnership interest before the distribution. In this case, Curry's basis for the land will be limited to the $5,000 basis for his partnership interest before the distribution.

59. (b) The requirement is to determine Hart's basis for the land received in a nonliquidating partnership distribution. If both cash and noncash property are received in a single distribution, the basis for the partner's partnership interest is first reduced by the cash, before being reduced by noncash property. Although a partner's basis for noncash property is generally the same as the partnership's basis for the property ($7,000 in this case), the partner's basis for distributed property will be limited to the partner's basis for the partnership interest reduced by any cash received in the same distribution. Here, the $9,000 basis of Hart's partnership interest is first reduced by the $5,000 cash received, with the remaining basis of $4,000 allocated as basis for the land received.

60. (b) The requirement is to determine Day's basis in the land received in a nonliquidating distribution. If both cash and noncash property are received in a single distribution, the basis for the partner's partnership interest is first reduced by the cash, before the noncash property. Since partnership distributions are generally nontaxable, a distributee partner's basis for distributed property is generally the same as the partnership's former basis for the property (a transferred basis). Here, the basis of Day's partnership interest of $50,000 is first reduced by the $25,000 of cash received, and then reduced by the $15,000 adjusted basis of the land, to $10,000. Day's basis for the land received is $15,000.

61. (a) The requirement is to determine the amount of taxable gain that Jody must report as the result of a current distribution of cash and property from her partnership. No loss can be recognized as a result of a proportionate current (nonliquidating) distribution, and gain will be recognized only if the amount of cash received exceeds the basis for the partner's partnership interest. If both cash and noncash property are received in a single distribution, the basis for the partner's interest is first reduced by the cash, before noncash property. Since the $20,000 cash received does not exceed the $50,000 basis of Jody's partnership interest immediately before the distribution, no gain is recognized.

62. (b) The requirement is to determine the basis of property received in a current distribution. If both cash and noncash property are received in a single distribution, the basis for the partner's partnership interest is first reduced by the cash, before being reduced by noncash property. Although a partner's basis for distributed property is generally the same as the partnership's basis for the property ($40,000 in this case), the partner's basis for distributed property will be limited to the partner's basis for the partnership interest reduced by any money received in the same distribution. Here, the $50,000 basis of Jody's partnership interest is first reduced by the $20,000 of cash received, with the remaining basis of $30,000 allocated as the basis for the property received.

63. (d) The requirement is to determine the amount of income from the receipt of retirement payments to be reported by Berk in 2015 and 2016. Payments to a retiring partner are generally treated as received in exchange for the partner's interest in partnership property. As such, they are generally treated under the rules that apply to liquidating distributions. Retirement payments are not deductible by the partnership as guaranteed payments and are not treated as distributive shares of income. Under the rules for liquidating distributions, the $5,000 per month cash payments are treated as a reduction of the basis for Berk's partnership interest, and result in gain to the extent in excess of basis. Berk's $80,000 basis for his partnership interest ($50,000 capital + $30,000 share of liabilities) would first be reduced by the relief from $30,000 of liabilities to $50,000. Next, the $30,000 of cash payments received during 2015 (6 × $5,000) would reduce Berk's basis to $20,000 and result in no gain to be reported for 2015. Finally, the $60,000 of payments for 2016 (12 × $5,000) would exceed his remaining basis and result in Berk's reporting of $40,000 of capital gain for 2016.

64. (b) The requirement is to determine the correct statement regarding the basis of property to a partner that is distributed in complete liquidation of the partner's interest. In a complete liquidation of a partner's interest in a partnership, the property distributed will have a basis equal to the adjusted basis of the partner's partnership interest reduced by any money received in the same distribution. Generally, in a liquidating distribution, the basis for a partnership interest is (1) first reduced by the amount of money received, (2) then reduced by the partnership's basis for any unrealized receivables and inventory received, (3) with any remaining basis for the partnership interest allocated to other property received in proportion to their adjusted bases (not FV) to the partnership.

65. (c) The requirement is to determine the basis of the inventory received in a nonliquidating partnership distribution of cash and inventory. Here, the $25,000 basis of Reed's partnership interest would first be reduced by the $11,000 of cash received, and then reduced by the $5,000 basis of the inventory to $9,000. Reed's basis for the inventory received is $5,000.

66. (b) The requirement is to determine Reed's recognized gain or loss resulting from the cash and inventory received in complete liquidation of Reed's partnership interest. A distributee partner can recognize loss only upon the complete liquidation of the partner's interest through the receipt of only money, unrealized receivables, or inventory. Since Reed received only money and inventory, the amount of recognized loss is the $9,000 difference between the $25,000 basis of his partnership interest and the $11,000 of cash and $5,000 basis for the inventory received.

67. (c) The requirement is to determine the amount of loss recognized by Lisa on the complete liquidation of her one-third partnership interest. A distributee partner can recognize loss only upon the complete liquidation of the partner's interest through receipt of only money, unrealized receivables, or inventory. Since Lisa only received cash, the amount of recognized loss is the $2,000 difference between the $22,000 adjusted basis of her partnership interest and the $20,000 of cash received. Since a partnership interest is a capital asset and Lisa acquired her one-third interest in 2009, Lisa has a $2,000 long-term capital loss.

68. (d) The requirement is to determine when a retiring partner who receives retirement payments ceases to be regarded as a partner. A retiring partner continues to be a partner for income tax purposes until the partner's entire interest has been completely liquidated through distributions or payments.

69. (b) The requirement is to determine the treatment for the payments received by Albin. Payments made by a personal service partnership to a retired partner that are determined by partnership income are distributive shares of partnership income, regardless of the period over which they are paid. Thus, they are taxable to Albin as ordinary income.

Simulations

Task-Based Simulation 1

Partner's Basis		
	Authoritative Literature	Help

Situation

During 2014, Adams, a general contractor, Brinks, an architect, and Carson, an interior decorator, formed the Dex Home Improvement General Partnership by contributing the assets below.

	Asset	Adjusted basis	Fair market value	% of partner share in capital, profits & losses
Adams	Cash	$40,000	$40,000	50%
Brinks	Land	$12,000	$21,000	20%
Carson	Inventory	$24,000	$24,000	30%

The land was a capital asset to Brinks, subject to a $5,000 mortgage, which was assumed by the partnership.
For items 1 and 2, determine and select the initial basis of the partner's interest in Dex.

	(A)	(B)	(C)
1. Brinks' initial basis in Dex is	○	○	○

    A. $21,000

    B. $12,000

    C. $8,000

	(A)	(B)	(C)
2. Carson's initial basis in Dex is	○	○	○

    A. $25,500

    B. $24,000

    C. $19,000

Task-Based Simulation 2

Concepts		
	Authoritative Literature	Help

During 2014, the Dex Partnership breaks even but decides to make distributions to each partner.

For items 1 through 6, determine whether the statement is True or False.

	True	False
1.	A nonliquidating cash distribution may reduce the recipient partner's basis in his partnership interest below zero.	○	○
2.	A nonliquidating distribution of unappreciated inventory reduces the recipient partner's basis in his partnership interest.	○	○
3.	In a liquidating distribution of property other than money, where the partnership's basis of the distributed property exceeds the basis of the partner's interest, the partner's basis in the distributed property is limited to his pre-distribution basis in the partnership interest.	○	○
4.	Gain is recognized by the partner who receives a nonliquidating distribution of property, where the adjusted basis of the property exceeds his basis in the partnership interest before the distribution.	○	○
5.	In a nonliquidating distribution of inventory, where the partnership has no unrealized receivables or appreciated inventory, the basis of inventory that is distributed to a partner cannot exceed the inventory's adjusted basis to the partnership.	○	○
6.	The partnership's nonliquidating distribution of encumbered property to a partner who assumes the mortgage, does not affect the other partners' bases in their partnership interests.	○	○

Task-Based Simulation 3

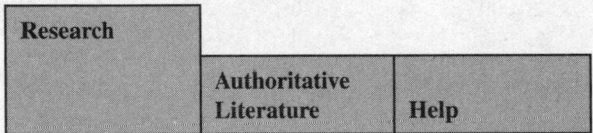

The Dex Home Improvement General Partnership is planning to adopt a fiscal year ending September 30, while Brinks (a 20% partner) uses the calendar year as his taxable year. Research the Internal Revenue Code to determine how Brinks should determine the amount of income and other partnership items from the fiscal-year partnership that must be reported on Brinks' 2014 calendar-year tax return. Indicate the section and subsection from the IRC in the shaded boxes below.

Task-Based Simulation 4

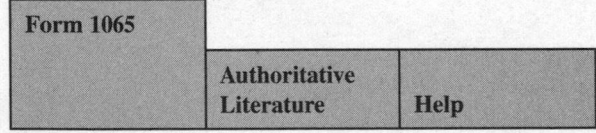

The Madison Restaurant (identification number 11-1111111) was formed as a cash method general partnership to operate the Madison Restaurant, which is located at 321 Anywhere Road, Davie, Florida 33314. Bob Buran (social security number 123-45-6789) manages the restaurant and has a 60% capital and profits interest. His address is 900 Nowhere Road, Plantation, Florida 33324. Ray Hughes owns the remaining 40% partnership interest but is not active in the restaurant business. The partnership made cash distributions of $66,000 and $44,000 to Buran and Hughes respectively, on December 31, 2013, but made no other property distributions. Madison's income statement for the year, ended December 31, 2013, is presented below.

Sales	$980,000
Cost of sales	460,000
Gross profit	520,000

Operating expenses		
Salaries and wages (excluding partners)	$190,000	
Guaranteed payment to Bob Buran	70,000	
Repairs and maintenance	10,000	
Rent expense	24,000	
Amortization of permanent liquor license	2,000	
Annual liquor license fee	1,000	
Depreciation	49,000	
Advertising	20,000	
Charitable contributions (cash)	8,000	
Total expenses		$374,000
Operating profit		$146,000
Other income and losses		
Gain on sale of ABE stock held 13 months	$12,000	
Loss on sale of TED stock held 7 months	(7,000)	
Sec. 1231 gain on sale of land	8,500	
Interest from US Treasury bills	3,000	
Dividends from ABE stock	1,500	
Interest from City of Ft. Lauderdale general obligation bonds	1,000	
Net other income		19,000
Net income		$165,000

Additional information

- Madison Restaurant began business on July 14, 2001, and its applicable business code number is 722110. It files its tax return with the Ogden, Utah IRS Service Center. The partnership had recourse liabilities at the end of the year of $25,000, and total assets of $282,000.
- The guaranteed payment to Bob Buran was for services rendered and was determined without regard to partnership profits. Buran's capital account at the beginning of 2013 totaled $135,000.
- The permanent liquor license was purchased for $10,000 from a café that had gone out of business. This license, which is renewable for an indefinite period, is being amortized per books over the five-year term of Madison's lease.
- The cost of depreciable personal property used in the restaurant operations was $200,000. Madison elected to expense $24,000 of the cost for these Sec. 179 assets. The $49,000 depreciation includes the Sec. 179 expense deduction.
- The gain on the sale of land resulted from the sale of a parking lot that the restaurant no longer needed.

Required:

Prepare Madison Restaurant's income and deductions on page 1 of Form 1065, Partnership Return.

Form **1065**		**U.S. Return of Partnership Income**		OMB No. 1545-0099
Department of the Treasury Internal Revenue Service		For calendar year 2013, or tax year beginning _____, 2013, ending _____, 20 ___. ► Information about Form 1065 and its separate instructions is at *www.irs.gov/form1065*.		**2013**

A Principal business activity	**Type or Print**	Name of partnership	**D** Employer identification number
B Principal product or service		Number, street, and room or suite no. If a P.O. box, see the instructions.	**E** Date business started
C Business code number		City or town, state or province, country, and ZIP or foreign postal code	**F** Total assets (see the instructions) $

G Check applicable boxes: **(1)** ☐ Initial return **(2)** ☐ Final return **(3)** ☐ Name change **(4)** ☐ Address change **(5)** ☐ Amended return
(6) ☐ Technical termination - also check (1) or (2)
H Check accounting method: **(1)** ☐ Cash **(2)** ☐ Accrual **(3)** ☐ Other (specify) ► _____
I Number of Schedules K-1. Attach one for each person who was a partner at any time during the tax year ► _____
J Check if Schedules C and M-3 are attached . . . . ☐

Caution. *Include **only** trade or business income and expenses on lines 1a through 22 below. See the instructions for more information.*

Income	**1a** Gross receipts or sales	**1a**		
	b Returns and allowances	**1b**		
	c Balance. Subtract line 1b from line 1a		**1c**	
	2 Cost of goods sold (attach Form 1125-A)		**2**	
	3 Gross profit. Subtract line 2 from line 1c		**3**	
	4 Ordinary income (loss) from other partnerships, estates, and trusts (attach statement) . .		**4**	
	5 Net farm profit (loss) (attach Schedule F (Form 1040))		**5**	
	6 Net gain (loss) from Form 4797, Part II, line 17 (attach Form 4797)		**6**	
	7 Other income (loss) (attach statement)		**7**	
	8 **Total income (loss).** Combine lines 3 through 7		**8**	
Deductions (see the instructions for limitations)	**9** Salaries and wages (other than to partners) (less employment credits)		**9**	
	10 Guaranteed payments to partners		**10**	
	11 Repairs and maintenance		**11**	
	12 Bad debts		**12**	
	13 Rent		**13**	
	14 Taxes and licenses		**14**	
	15 Interest		**15**	
	16a Depreciation (if required, attach Form 4562)	**16a**		
	b Less depreciation reported on Form 1125-A and elsewhere on return	**16b**	**16c**	
	17 Depletion **(Do not deduct oil and gas depletion.)**		**17**	
	18 Retirement plans, etc.		**18**	
	19 Employee benefit programs		**19**	
	20 Other deductions (attach statement)		**20**	
	21 **Total deductions.** Add the amounts shown in the far right column for lines 9 through 20 .		**21**	
	22 **Ordinary business income (loss).** Subtract line 21 from line 8		**22**	

Sign Here	Under penalties of perjury, I declare that I have examined this return, including accompanying schedules and statements, and to the best of my knowledge and belief, it is true, correct, and complete. Declaration of preparer (other than general partner or limited liability company member manager) is based on all information of which preparer has any knowledge.	May the IRS discuss this return with the preparer shown below (see instructions)? ☐ **Yes** ☐ **No**
	► _____ Signature of general partner or limited liability company member manager　► _____ Date	

Paid Preparer Use Only	Print/Type preparer's name	Preparer's signature	Date	Check ☐ if self-employed	PTIN
	Firm's name ►			Firm's EIN ►	
	Firm's address ►			Phone no.	

For Paperwork Reduction Act Notice, see separate instructions.　　Cat. No. 11390Z　　Form **1065** (2013)

Required:

Prepare Madison Restaurant's Schedule K, Partners' Shares of Income, Credits, Deductions, etc.

Form 1065 (2013)   Page **4**

Schedule K		Partners' Distributive Share Items			Total amount	

	1	Ordinary business income (loss) (page 1, line 22)			1	
	2	Net rental real estate income (loss) (attach Form 8825)			2	
	3a	Other gross rental income (loss)	3a			
	b	Expenses from other rental activities (attach statement)	3b			
	c	Other net rental income (loss). Subtract line 3b from line 3a			3c	
	4	Guaranteed payments			4	
	5	Interest income			5	
	6	Dividends: a Ordinary dividends			6a	
		b Qualified dividends	6b			
	7	Royalties			7	
	8	Net short-term capital gain (loss) (attach Schedule D (Form 1065)) . .			8	
	9a	Net long-term capital gain (loss) (attach Schedule D (Form 1065)) . .			9a	
	b	Collectibles (28%) gain (loss)	9b			
	c	Unrecaptured section 1250 gain (attach statement) . .	9c			
	10	Net section 1231 gain (loss) (attach Form 4797)			10	
	11	Other income (loss) (see instructions) Type ▶			11	
	12	Section 179 deduction (attach Form 4562)			12	
	13a	Contributions			13a	
	b	Investment interest expense			13b	
	c	Section 59(e)(2) expenditures: (1) Type ▶ _____ (2) Amount ▶			13c(2)	
	d	Other deductions (see instructions) Type ▶			13d	
	14a	Net earnings (loss) from self-employment			14a	
	b	Gross farming or fishing income			14b	
	c	Gross nonfarm income			14c	
	15a	Low-income housing credit (section 42(j)(5))			15a	
	b	Low-income housing credit (other)			15b	
	c	Qualified rehabilitation expenditures (rental real estate) (attach Form 3468)			15c	
	d	Other rental real estate credits (see instructions) Type ▶ _____			15d	
	e	Other rental credits (see instructions) Type ▶ _____			15e	
	f	Other credits (see instructions) Type ▶ _____			15f	
	16a	Name of country or U.S. possession ▶ _____				
	b	Gross income from all sources			16b	
	c	Gross income sourced at partner level			16c	
		Foreign gross income sourced at partnership level				
	d	Passive category ▶ _____ e General category ▶ _____ f Other ▶			16f	
		Deductions allocated and apportioned at partner level				
	g	Interest expense ▶ _____ h Other . . . . ▶			16h	
		Deductions allocated and apportioned at partnership level to foreign source income				
	i	Passive category ▶ _____ j General category ▶ _____ k Other ▶			16k	
	l	Total foreign taxes (check one): ▶ Paid ☐ Accrued ☐			16l	
	m	Reduction in taxes available for credit (attach statement)			16m	
	n	Other foreign tax information (attach statement)				
	17a	Post-1986 depreciation adjustment			17a	
	b	Adjusted gain or loss			17b	
	c	Depletion (other than oil and gas)			17c	
	d	Oil, gas, and geothermal properties—gross income			17d	
	e	Oil, gas, and geothermal properties—deductions			17e	
	f	Other AMT items (attach statement)			17f	
	18a	Tax-exempt interest income			18a	
	b	Other tax-exempt income			18b	
	c	Nondeductible expenses			18c	
	19a	Distributions of cash and marketable securities			19a	
	b	Distributions of other property			19b	
	20a	Investment income			20a	
	b	Investment expenses			20b	
	c	Other items and amounts (attach statement)				

Side labels: Income (Loss); Deductions; Self-Employment; Credits; Foreign Transactions; Alternative Minimum Tax (AMT) Items; Other Information

Form **1065** (2013)

Required:

Prepare Bob Buran's Schedule K-1, Partner's Share of Income, Credits, Deductions, etc. (Do **not** prepare a Schedule K-1 for Ray Hughes.)

651113

| ☐ Final K-1 | ☐ Amended K-1 | OMB No. 1545-0099 |

Schedule K-1
(Form 1065)

20**13**

Department of the Treasury
Internal Revenue Service

For calendar year 2013, or tax
year beginning _____, 2013
ending _____, 20 _____

**Partner's Share of Income, Deductions,
Credits, etc.** ▶ See back of form and separate instructions.

| **Part I** | **Information About the Partnership** |

A Partnership's employer identification number

B Partnership's name, address, city, state, and ZIP code

C IRS Center where partnership filed return

D ☐ Check if this is a publicly traded partnership (PTP)

| **Part II** | **Information About the Partner** |

E Partner's identifying number

F Partner's name, address, city, state, and ZIP code

G ☐ General partner or LLC   ☐ Limited partner or other LLC
member-manager   member

H ☐ Domestic partner   ☐ Foreign partner

I1 What type of entity is this partner? _____

I2 If this partner is a retirement plan (IRA/SEP/Keogh/etc.), check here
(see instructions) . . . . ☐

J Partner's share of profit, loss, and capital (see instructions):

	Beginning	**Ending**
Profit	%	%
Loss	%	%
Capital	%	%

K Partner's share of liabilities at year end:

Nonrecourse	$ _____
Qualified nonrecourse financing	$ _____
Recourse	$ _____

L Partner's capital account analysis:

Beginning capital account . . .	$ _____
Capital contributed during the year	$ _____
Current year increase (decrease) .	$ _____
Withdrawals & distributions . .	$ (_____)
Ending capital account	$ _____

☐ Tax basis   ☐ GAAP   ☐ Section 704(b) book
☐ Other (explain)

M Did the partner contribute property with a built-in gain or loss?
☐ Yes   ☐ No
If "Yes," attach statement (see instructions)

| **Part III** | **Partner's Share of Current Year Income,
Deductions, Credits, and Other Items** |

1	Ordinary business income (loss)	15	Credits
2	Net rental real estate income (loss)		
3	Other net rental income (loss)	16	Foreign transactions
4	Guaranteed payments		
5	Interest income		
6a	Ordinary dividends		
6b	Qualified dividends		
7	Royalties		
8	Net short-term capital gain (loss)		
9a	Net long-term capital gain (loss)	17	Alternative minimum tax (AMT) items
9b	Collectibles (28%) gain (loss)		
9c	Unrecaptured section 1250 gain		
10	Net section 1231 gain (loss)	18	Tax-exempt income and nondeductible expenses
11	Other income (loss)		
		19	Distributions
12	Section 179 deduction		
13	Other deductions	20	Other information
14	Self-employment earnings (loss)		

*See attached statement for additional information.

For IRS Use Only

For Paperwork Reduction Act Notice, see Instructions for Form 1065.   IRS.gov/form1065   Cat. No. 11394R   **Schedule K-1 (Form 1065) 2013**

Task-Based Simulation 5

In 2014, Madison is considering making a proportionate nonliquidating distribution of shares of stock that it owns in CDE Corporation to its partners. Research the Internal Revenue Code to determine the basis that the partners will have for the CDE stock that they receive. Indicate the section and subsection from the IRC in the shaded boxes below.

Section	Subsection
§ [ ]	([ ])

Simulation Solutions

Task-Based Simulation 1

Partner's Basis		
	Authoritative Literature	Help

	(A)	(B)	(C)
1. Brinks' initial basis in Dex is	○	○	●
A. $21,000			
B. $12,000			
C. $8,000			
2. Carson's initial basis in Dex is	●	○	○
A. $25,500			
B. $24,000			
C. $19,000			

Explanations

1. **(C)** The requirement is to determine Brinks' initial basis for his 20% partnership interest received in exchange for a contribution of property subject to a $5,000 mortgage. Generally, no gain or loss is recognized on the contribution of property in exchange for a partnership interest. As a result, Brinks' initial basis for the partnership interest received consists of the $12,000 basis of the land contributed to the partnership, less the net reduction in Brinks' individual liability resulting from the partnership's assumption of the mortgage. Since Brinks received a 20% partnership interest, the net reduction in Brinks' individual liability equals $5,000 × 80% = $4,000. As a result, Brinks' basis for the partnership interest is $12,000 – $4,000 = $8,000.

2. **(A)** The requirement is to determine Carson's initial basis for his 30% partnership interest received in exchange for a contribution of inventory. Since partners are individually liable for their share of partnership liabilities, an increase in partnership liabilities increases a partner's basis in the partnership by the partner's share of the increase. Carson's initial basis is the $24,000 adjusted basis of the inventory contributed, increased by the increase in his individual liability resulting from the partnership's assumption of Brinks' mortgage ($5,000 × 30% = $1,500). Thus, Carson's initial basis for the partnership interest is $24,000 + $1,500 = $25,500.

Task-Based Simulation 2

Concepts		
	Authoritative Literature	**Help**

		True	False
1.	A nonliquidating cash distribution may reduce the recipient partner's basis in his partnership interest below zero.	○	●
2.	A nonliquidating distribution of unappreciated inventory reduces the recipient partner's basis in his partnership interest.	●	○
3.	In a liquidating distribution of property other than money, where the partnership's basis of the distributed property exceeds the basis of the partner's interest, the partner's basis in the distributed property is limited to his pre-distribution basis in the partnership interest.	●	○
4.	Gain is recognized by the partner who receives a nonliquidating distribution of property, where the adjusted basis of the property exceeds his basis in the partnership interest before the distribution.	○	●
5.	In a nonliquidating distribution of inventory, where the partnership has no unrealized receivables or appreciated inventory, the basis of inventory that is distributed to a partner cannot exceed the inventory's adjusted basis to the partnership.	●	○
6.	The partnership's nonliquidating distribution of encumbered property to a partner who assumes the mortgage, does not affect the other partners' bases in their partnership interests.	○	●

Explanations

1. **(F)** A partner can never have a negative basis for a partnership interest. Partnership distributions can only reduce a partner's basis to zero.

2. **(T)** Partnership distributions are generally nontaxable and reduce the recipient partner's basis by the adjusted basis of the property distributed.

3. **(T)** A liquidating distribution of property other than money generally does not cause the distributee partner to recognize gain. As a result, the distributee partner's basis in the distributed property is limited to the partner's predistribution basis for the partnership interest.

4. **(F)** Gain is recognized by a distributee partner only if the amount of money distributed exceeds the partner's predistribution basis for the partnership interest. Distributions of property other than money never result in the recognition of gain by the distributee partner.

5. **(T)** Generally, a nonliquidating distribution of inventory is not taxable, and the adjusted basis for the inventory carries over to the distributee partner. As a result, the distributee partner's basis for the inventory cannot exceed the inventory's adjusted basis to the partnership.

6. **(F)** Since partners are individually liable for partnership liabilities, a decrease in partnership liabilities will decrease the basis for a partner's partnership interest by the partner's share of the decrease. Thus, if a distributee partner assumes a mortgage on encumbered property, the other partners' bases in their partnership interests will be decreased by their share of the decrease in partnership liabilities.

Task-Based Simulation 3

Research		
	Authoritative Literature	**Help**

Internal Revenue Code Section 706, subsection (a), provides that in computing the taxable income of a partner for a taxable year, the partnership items of income, gain, loss, deduction, or credit that should be included should be based on the taxable year of the partnership that ends with or within the taxable year of the partner. Therefore, Brinks' calendar year 2014 tax return ending December 31 should reflect only Brinks' distributive share of partnership items for the Dex Partnership fiscal year ended September 30, 2014.

Section	Subsection
§ ☐ 706	(☐ a)

Task-Based Simulation 4

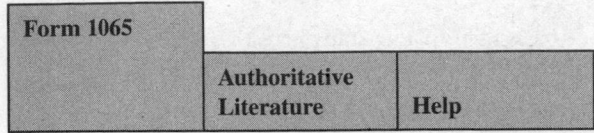

A partnership is a pass-through entity acting as a conduit to pass through items of income, deduction, and credit to be reported on the tax returns of its partners. Partnership items having special tax characteristics (e.g., passive activity losses, deductions subject to dollar or percentage limitations, etc.) must be separately listed and shown on Schedules K and K-1 so that their special characteristics are preserved when reported on partners' tax returns. In contrast, partnership ordinary income and deduction items having no special tax characteristics can be netted together in the computation of a partnership's ordinary income and deductions from trade or business activities on page 1 of Form 1065.

The solutions approach is to determine whether each item listed in the problem should be included in the computation of Madison's ordinary income and deductions on page 1 of Form 1065, or should be separately shown on Madison's Schedule K and Bob Buran's Schedule K-1 to retain any special tax characteristics that the item may have.

Schedule K is a summary schedule, listing the total of all partners' shares of income, deductions, and credits, including the net amount of a partnership's ordinary income (loss) from trade or business activities that is computed on page 1 of Form 1065. A Schedule K-1 is prepared for each partner listing only that particular partner's share of partnership income, deductions, credits, etc. Since Bob Buran has a 60% partnership interest, Buran's Schedule K-1 will generally reflect a 60% share of the amounts reported on Madison's Schedule K.

Specific Items

- Guaranteed payments made to a partner for services or for the use of capital are determined without regard to the income of the partnership. The $70,000 of guaranteed payments made to Bob Buran are deductible by the partnership in computing its ordinary income on page 1 of Form 1065, and must also be separately reported on line 4 of Schedules K and K-1 since the receipt of the guaranteed payments by Buran must be reported as ordinary income.
- No amortization of the permanent liquor license is allowed for tax purposes because the license is renewable for an indefinite period.
- The cost of qualifying property did not exceed $2 million for 2013, so the Sec. 179 expense deduction of $24,000 is available on Madison's return. Since the Sec. 179 expense deduction is subject to a dollar limitation at both the partnership and partner levels, the Sec. 179 expense deduction must be separately reported on Schedules K and K-1. Since the depreciation deducted in the income statement includes the $24,000 of expense deduction, the income statement depreciation of $49,000 must be reduced by $24,000, which results in the $25,000 of depreciation that is deductible in computing Madison's ordinary income. The $24,000 Sec. 179 expense deduction must be separately shown on line 12 of Madison's Schedule K. $24,000 × 60% = $14,400 of Sec. 179 expense deduction reported on Bob Buran's Schedule K-1.
- The $8,000 of charitable contributions are not deductible in computing the partnership's ordinary income. Instead, charitable contributions are separately reported on line 13a of Madison's Schedule K and each partner's Schedule K-1 so the appropriate percentage limitation can be applied on partners' returns.
- The $12,000 of long-term capital gain, $7,000 of short-term capital loss, $3,000 of interest income from Treasury bills, and $1,500 of dividends are items of portfolio income and must be separately reported on Madison's Schedule K, with 60% of each item reported on Buran's Schedule K-1. Similarly, the $8,500 of Sec. 1231 gain must be separately reported on Madison's Schedule K and partners' Schedules K-1 so that the Sec. 1231 netting process can take place at the partner level.
- The $1,000 of interest from City of Ft. Lauderdale bonds is tax-exempt and is reported on line 18a of Schedules K and K-1, while the $110,000 of cash distributions to partners is reported on line 19a of Schedules K and K-1.
- Partners are not employees but instead are treated as self-employed individuals. A partner's share of a partnership's ordinary income plus any guaranteed payments received by the partner must be reported as self-employment income and is subject to self-employment tax. On Schedule K, the ordinary income from trade or business activities of $180,000 (line 1) is added to the $70,000 of guaranteed payments (line 5), with the total of $250,000 reported on lines 14a and 14c as net earnings from self-employment. On Schedule K-1, Buran's 60% share of the ordinary income ($180,000 × 60% = $108,000) is added to the $70,000 of guaranteed payments received by Buran with the total of $178,000 reported as Buran's net earnings from self-employment in box 14.

Form **1065**		**U.S. Return of Partnership Income**	OMB No. 1545-0099

Form **1065**
Department of the Treasury
Internal Revenue Service

U.S. Return of Partnership Income

For calendar year 2013, or tax year beginning _____ , 2013, ending _____ , 20 ____

► Information about Form 1065 and its separate instructions is at *www.irs.gov/form1065*.

OMB No. 1545-0099

2013

A Principal business activity		Name of partnership	**D** Employer identification number
Food Service	**Type or Print**	Madison Restaurant	86-0806200
B Principal product or service		Number, street, and room or suite no. If a P.O. box, see the instructions.	**E** Date business started
Food & Drinks		6001 Palm Trace Landing	7-14-01
C Business code number		City or town, state or province, country, and ZIP or foreign postal code	**F** Total assets (see the instructions)
722110		Davie, FL 33314	$ 282,000

G Check applicable boxes: **(1)** ☐ Initial return **(2)** ☐ Final return **(3)** ☐ Name change **(4)** ☐ Address change **(5)** ☐ Amended return
(6) ☐ Technical termination - also check (1) or (2)

H Check accounting method: **(1)** ☑ Cash **(2)** ☐ Accrual **(3)** ☐ Other (specify) ► _____

I Number of Schedules K-1. Attach one for each person who was a partner at any time during the tax year ► 2

J Check if Schedules C and M-3 are attached . . . . ☐

Caution. *Include **only** trade or business income and expenses on lines 1a through 22 below. See the instructions for more information.*

Income	**1a**	Gross receipts or sales	**1a**	980,000		
	b	Returns and allowances	**1b**			
	c	Balance. Subtract line 1b from line 1a			**1c**	980,000
	2	Cost of goods sold (attach Form 1125-A)			**2**	460,000
	3	Gross profit. Subtract line 2 from line 1c			**3**	520,000
	4	Ordinary income (loss) from other partnerships, estates, and trusts (attach statement) . .			**4**	
	5	Net farm profit (loss) (attach Schedule F (Form 1040))			**5**	
	6	Net gain (loss) from Form 4797, Part II, line 17 (attach Form 4797)			**6**	
	7	Other income (loss) (attach statement)			**7**	
	8	**Total income (loss).** Combine lines 3 through 7			**8**	520,000
Deductions (see the instructions for limitations)	**9**	Salaries and wages (other than to partners) (less employment credits)			**9**	190,000
	10	Guaranteed payments to partners			**10**	70,000
	11	Repairs and maintenance			**11**	10,000
	12	Bad debts			**12**	
	13	Rent			**13**	24,000
	14	Taxes and licenses			**14**	1,000
	15	Interest			**15**	
	16a	Depreciation (if required, attach Form 4562)	**16a**	25,000		
	b	Less depreciation reported on Form 1125-A and elsewhere on return	**16b**		**16c**	25,000
	17	Depletion **(Do not deduct oil and gas depletion.)**			**17**	
	18	Retirement plans, etc.			**18**	
	19	Employee benefit programs			**19**	
	20	Other deductions (attach statement)			**20**	20,000
	21	**Total deductions.** Add the amounts shown in the far right column for lines 9 through 20 .			**21**	340,000
	22	**Ordinary business income (loss).** Subtract line 21 from line 8			**22**	180,000

Sign Here	Under penalties of perjury, I declare that I have examined this return, including accompanying schedules and statements, and to the best of my knowledge and belief, it is true, correct, and complete. Declaration of preparer (other than general partner or limited liability company member manager) is based on all information of which preparer has any knowledge.		
	► _____ Signature of general partner or limited liability company member manager	► _____ Date	May the IRS discuss this return with the preparer shown below (see instructions)? ☐ Yes ☐ No

Paid Preparer Use Only	Print/Type preparer's name	Preparer's signature	Date	Check ☐ if self-employed	PTIN
	Firm's name ►			Firm's EIN ►	
	Firm's address ►			Phone no.	

For Paperwork Reduction Act Notice, see separate instructions.   Cat. No. 11390Z   Form **1065** (2013)

Form 1065 (2013)   Page **4**

		Schedule K **Partners' Distributive Share Items**		**Total amount**
Income (Loss)	1	Ordinary business income (loss) (page 1, line 22)	1	180,000
	2	Net rental real estate income (loss) (attach Form 8825)	2	
	3a	Other gross rental income (loss) 3a		
	b	Expenses from other rental activities (attach statement) 3b		
	c	Other net rental income (loss). Subtract line 3b from line 3a	3c	
	4	Guaranteed payments	4	70,000
	5	Interest income	5	3,000
	6	Dividends: a Ordinary dividends	6a	1,500
		b Qualified dividends 6b 1,500		
	7	Royalties	7	
	8	Net short-term capital gain (loss) (attach Schedule D (Form 1065))	8	(7,000)
	9a	Net long-term capital gain (loss) (attach Schedule D (Form 1065))	9a	12,000
	b	Collectibles (28%) gain (loss) 9b		
	c	Unrecaptured section 1250 gain (attach statement) 9c		
	10	Net section 1231 gain (loss) (attach Form 4797)	10	8,500
	11	Other income (loss) (see instructions) Type ▶	11	
Deductions	12	Section 179 deduction (attach Form 4562)	12	24,000
	13a	Contributions	13a	8,000
	b	Investment interest expense	13b	
	c	Section 59(e)(2) expenditures: **(1)** Type ▶ _____ **(2)** Amount ▶	13c(2)	
	d	Other deductions (see instructions) Type ▶	13d	
Self-Employ-ment	14a	Net earnings (loss) from self-employment	14a	250,000
	b	Gross farming or fishing income	14b	
	c	Gross nonfarm income	14c	520,000
Credits	15a	Low-income housing credit (section 42(j)(5))	15a	
	b	Low-income housing credit (other)	15b	
	c	Qualified rehabilitation expenditures (rental real estate) (attach Form 3468)	15c	
	d	Other rental real estate credits (see instructions) Type ▶	15d	
	e	Other rental credits (see instructions) Type ▶	15e	
	f	Other credits (see instructions) Type ▶	15f	
Foreign Transactions	16a	Name of country or U.S. possession ▶		
	b	Gross income from all sources	16b	
	c	Gross income sourced at partner level	16c	
		Foreign gross income sourced at partnership level		
	d	Passive category ▶ _____ e General category ▶ _____ f Other ▶	16f	
		Deductions allocated and apportioned at partner level		
	g	Interest expense ▶ _____ h Other	16h	
		Deductions allocated and apportioned at partnership level to foreign source income		
	i	Passive category ▶ _____ j General category ▶ _____ k Other ▶	16k	
	l	Total foreign taxes (check one): ▶ Paid ☐ Accrued ☐	16l	
	m	Reduction in taxes available for credit (attach statement)	16m	
	n	Other foreign tax information (attach statement)		
Alternative Minimum Tax (AMT) Items	17a	Post-1986 depreciation adjustment	17a	
	b	Adjusted gain or loss	17b	
	c	Depletion (other than oil and gas)	17c	
	d	Oil, gas, and geothermal properties—gross income	17d	
	e	Oil, gas, and geothermal properties—deductions	17e	
	f	Other AMT items (attach statement)	17f	
Other Information	18a	Tax-exempt interest income	18a	1,000
	b	Other tax-exempt income	18b	
	c	Nondeductible expenses	18c	
	19a	Distributions of cash and marketable securities	19a	110,000
	b	Distributions of other property	19b	
	20a	Investment income	20a	
	b	Investment expenses	20b	
	c	Other items and amounts (attach statement)		

Form **1065** (2013)

651113

☐ Final K-1   ☐ Amended K-1
                                                    OMB No. 1545-0099

Schedule K-1 (Form 1065)	20**13**	**Part III**	**Partner's Share of Current Year Income, Deductions, Credits, and Other Items**

Department of the Treasury
Internal Revenue Service

For calendar year 2013, or tax
year beginning _____ , 2013
         ending _____ , 20 ____

**Partner's Share of Income, Deductions,
Credits, etc.**   ▶ See back of form and separate instructions.

Part I	**Information About the Partnership**

A Partnership's employer identification number
      86-0806200

B Partnership's name, address, city, state, and ZIP code
      Madison Restaurant
      6001 Palm Trace Landing
      Davie, FL. 33314

C IRS Center where partnership filed return
      Ogden, Utah

D ☐ Check if this is a publicly traded partnership (PTP)

Part II	**Information About the Partner**

E Partner's identifying number
      347-54-1212

F Partner's name, address, city, state, and ZIP code
      Bob Buran
      1104 North 8th Court
      Plantation, FL. 33324

G ☒ General partner or LLC   ☐ Limited partner or other LLC
      member-manager   member

H ☒ Domestic partner   ☐ Foreign partner

I1 What type of entity is this partner?   Individual

I2 If this partner is a retirement plan (IRA/SEP/Keogh/etc.), check here
      (see instructions) . . . . ☐

J Partner's share of profit, loss, and capital (see instructions):

	Beginning	Ending
Profit	%	60 %
Loss	%	60 %
Capital	%	60 %

K Partner's share of liabilities at year end:

Nonrecourse	$	
Qualified nonrecourse financing .	$	
Recourse	$	15,000

L Partner's capital account analysis:

Beginning capital account . . .	$	135,000
Capital contributed during the year	$	
Current year increase (decrease) .	$	100,200
Withdrawals & distributions . .	$ (	66,000)
Ending capital account	$	169,200

☒ Tax basis   ☐ GAAP   ☐ Section 704(b) book
☐ Other (explain)

M Did the partner contribute property with a built-in gain or loss?
      ☐ Yes   ☒ No
      If "Yes," attach statement (see instructions)

#		Amount	#	
1	Ordinary business income (loss)	108,000	15	Credits
2	Net rental real estate income (loss)			
3	Other net rental income (loss)		16	Foreign transactions
4	Guaranteed payments	70,000		
5	Interest income	1,800		
6a	Ordinary dividends	900		
6b	Qualified dividends	900		
7	Royalties			
8	Net short-term capital gain (loss)	(4,200)		
9a	Net long-term capital gain (loss)	7,200	17	Alternative minimum tax (AMT) items
9b	Collectibles (28%) gain (loss)			
9c	Unrecaptured section 1250 gain			
10	Net section 1231 gain (loss)	5,100	18	Tax-exempt income and nondeductible expenses
11	Other income (loss)		A	600
12	Section 179 deduction	14,400	19	Distributions
			A	66,000
13	Other deductions	4,800	20	Other information
14	Self-employment earnings (loss)			
A		178,000		
C		340,000		

*See attached statement for additional information.

For IRS Use Only

For Paperwork Reduction Act Notice, see Instructions for Form 1065.   IRS.gov/form1065   Cat. No. 11394R   Schedule K-1 (Form 1065) 2013

Explanation of Schedule K-1, Line L current year increase:

The tax basis for the partner's capital account is increased by all income items and reduced by all loss and deduction items.

The basis for the capital account is increased by the ordinary income of $108,000, interest of $1,800, dividends of $900, net long-term capital gain of $7,200, net Sec. 1231 gain of $5,100, and tax-exempt income of $600.

The basis for the capital account is decreased by the net short-term capital loss of $4,200, Sec. 179 deduction of $14,400, and other deductions of $4,800. The resulting net change is an increase of $100,200.

Note that the guaranteed payments of $70,000 were already deducted in the computation of ordinary income and are not separately taken into account. Also note that there is only $900 of dividends even though that amount is reported on two lines.

Explanation of Schedule K-1, Line 14C self-employment earnings:

Under the nonfarm optional method, the partner's share of gross income consists of the guaranteed payments received by the partner ($70,000) plus the partner's distributive share of the partnership's gross income after it is reduced by all guaranteed payments. In this case, $70,000 + ($520,000 – $70,000) (60%) = $340,000.

Task-Based Simulation 5

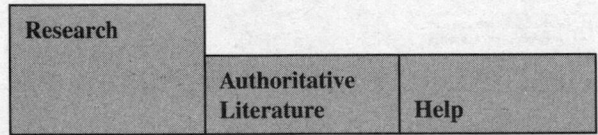

Internal Revenue Code Section 732, subsection (a) provides that the basis of distributed property to a partner is generally the same as the adjusted basis of the property to the partnership immediately before the distribution.

Module 38: Corporate Taxation

Overview

This module covers corporate taxation and reviews the rules that apply throughout the life cycle of a corporation. The tax consequences of corporate formation are covered first, followed by a review of some of the special rules that apply to the income and deductions of a corporation, including the charitable contributions deduction and the dividends received deduction. The Schedule M-1 reconciliation of book income to taxable income, and the tax concepts of affiliated and controlled groups are next reviewed. This is followed by a review of the tax treatment of corporate distributions to shareholders and their taxability as dividends. Next reviewed are the tax consequences of a complete liquidation, as well as the accumulated earnings and personal holding company penalty taxes. The module then continues with a review of the special rules that apply to S corporations and their shareholders, and the tax effects of corporate reorganizations. The module concludes with a comparison of C corporations, S corporations, and partnerships.

I. CORPORATIONS

Corporations are separate taxable entities, organized under state law. Although corporations may have many of the same income and deduction items as individuals, corporations are taxed at different rates and some tax rules are applied differently. There also are special provisions applicable to transfers of property to a corporation, and issuance of stock.

A. Transfers to a Controlled Corporation (Sec. 351)

1. **No gain or loss** is recognized if property is transferred to a corporation solely in exchange for stock and immediately after the exchange those persons transferring property control the corporation.

   a. **Property** includes everything but services.
   b. **Control** means ownership of at least 80% of the total combined voting power and 80% of each class of nonvoting stock.
   c. **Receipt of boot** (e.g., cash, short-term notes, securities, etc.) will cause recognition of gain (but not loss).

      (1) Corporation's assumption of liabilities is treated as boot only if there is a tax avoidance purpose, or no business purpose.
      (2) Shareholder recognizes gain if liabilities assumed by corporation exceed the total basis of property transferred by the shareholder.

2. **Shareholder's basis for stock** = Adjusted basis of property transferred

   a. +Gain recognized
   b. −Boot received (assumption of liability always treated as boot for purposes of determining stock basis)

3. **Corporation's basis for property** = Transferor's adjusted basis + Gain recognized to transferor.

EXAMPLE

Individuals A, B, & C form ABC Corp. and make the following transfer to their corporation:

Item transferred	A	B	C
Property – FMV	$10,000	$8,000	$--
– Adjusted basis	1,500	3,000	--
Liability assumed by ABC Corp.	2,000	--	--
Services	--	--	1,000
Consideration received			
Stock (FMV)	$8,000	$7,600	$1,000
Two-year note (FMV)	--	400	--
Gain recognized to shareholder	$500[a]	$400[b]	$1,000[c]
Basis of stock received	--	3,000	1,000
Basis of property to corp.	2,000	3,400	1,000[d]

[a] Liability in excess of basis: $2,000 – $1,500 = $500
[b] Assumes B elects out of the installment method
[c] Ordinary compensation income
[d] Expense or asset depending on nature of services rendered

---

  a. If the aggregate adjusted basis of transferred property exceeds its aggregate FMV, the corporate transferee's aggregate basis for the property is generally limited to its aggregate FMV immediately after the transaction. Any required basis reduction is allocated among the transferred properties in proportion to their built-in loss immediately before the transaction.

  b. Alternatively, the transferor and the corporate transferee are allowed to make an irrevocable election to limit the basis in the stock received by the transferor to the aggregate FMV of the transferred property.

EXAMPLE

Amy transferred Lossacre with a basis of $6,000 (FMV of $2,000) and Gainacre with a basis of $4,000 (FMV of $5,000) to ABE Corp. in exchange for stock in a Sec. 351 transaction. Since the aggregate adjusted basis of the transferred property ($10,000) exceeds its aggregate FMV ($7,000), ABE's aggregate basis for the property is limited to $7,000. The required basis reduction of $3,000 would reduce ABE's basis for Lossacre to $3,000 ($6,000 – $3,000). Amy's basis for her stock would equal the total basis of the transferred property, $10,000.

    Alternatively, if Amy and ABE elect, ABE's basis for the transferred property will be $6,000 for Lossacre and $4,000 for Gainacre, and Amy's basis for her stock will be limited to its FMV of $7,000.

NOW REVIEW MULTIPLE-CHOICE QUESTIONS 1 THROUGH 7

B. Section 1244—Small Business Corporation (SBC) Stock

  1. Sec. 1244 stock permits shareholders to deduct an **ordinary loss** on sale or worthlessness of stock.

    a. Shareholder must be the original holder of stock, and an individual or partnership.

    b. Stock can be common or preferred, voting or nonvoting, and must have been issued for money or property (other than stock or securities)

    c. Ordinary loss limited to **$50,000 ($100,000** on joint return); any excess is treated as a capital loss.

    d. The corporation during the five-year period before the year of loss, received less than 50% of its total gross receipts from royalties, rents, dividends, interest, annuities, and gains from sales or exchanges of stock or securities.

EXAMPLE

Jim (married and filing a joint return) incurred a loss of $120,000 from the sale of Sec. 1244 stock during 2014. $100,000 of Jim's loss is deductible as an ordinary loss, with the remaining $20,000 treated as a capital loss.

---

2. If Sec. 1244 stock is received in exchange for property whose FMV is less than its adjusted basis, the stock's basis is reduced to the FMV of the property to determine the amount of ordinary loss.

EXAMPLE

Joe made a Sec. 351 transfer of property with an adjusted basis of $20,000 and an FMV of $16,000 in exchange for Sec. 1244 stock. The basis of Joe's stock is $20,000, but solely for purposes of Sec. 1244 the stock's basis is reduced to $16,000. If Joe subsequently sold his stock for $15,000, $1,000 of his loss would be treated as an ordinary loss under Sec. 1244, with the remaining $4,000 treated as a capital loss.

---

3. For purposes of determining the amount of ordinary loss, increases in basis through capital contributions or otherwise are treated as allocable to stock which is not Sec. 1244 stock.

EXAMPLE

Jill acquired 100 shares of Sec. 1244 stock for $10,000. Jill later made a $2,000 contribution to the capital of the corporation, increasing her stock basis to $12,000. Jill subsequently sold the 100 shares for $9,000. Of Jill's $3,000 loss, ($10,000 ÷ $12,000) × $3,000 = $2,500 qualifies as an ordinary loss under Sec. 1244, with the remaining ($2,000 ÷ $12,000) × $3,000 = $500 treated as a capital loss.

---

4. SBC is any domestic corporation whose aggregate amount of money and adjusted basis of other property received for stock, as a contribution to capital, and as paid-in surplus, does not exceed $1,000,000. If more than $1 million of stock is issued, up to $1 million of qualifying stock can be designated as Sec. 1244 stock.

> **NOW REVIEW MULTIPLE-CHOICE QUESTIONS 8 THROUGH 11**

C. Variations from Individual Taxation

1. Filing and payment of tax

   a. A corporation generally must file a Form 1120 every year even though it has no taxable income. A short-form Form 1120-A may be filed if gross receipts, total income, and total assets are each less than $500,000.
   b. The return must be filed by the fifteenth day of the third month following the close of its taxable year (e.g., March 15 for calendar-year corporation).

      (1) An automatic six-month extension may be obtained by filing Form 7004.
      (2) Any balance due on the corporation's tax liability must be paid with the request for extension.

   c. Estimated tax payments must be made by every corporation whose estimated tax is expected to be $500 or more. A corporation's estimated tax is its expected tax liability (including alternative minimum tax) less its allowable tax credits.

      (1) Quarterly payments are due on the fifteenth day of the fourth, sixth, ninth, and twelfth months of its taxable year (April 15, June 15, September 15, and December 15 for a calendar-year corporation). Any balance due must be paid by the due date of the return.
      (2) No penalty for underpayment of estimated tax will be imposed if payments at least equal the lesser of

(a) 100% of the current year's tax (determined on the basis of actual income or annualized income), or

(b) 100% of the preceding year's tax (if the preceding year was a full twelve months and showed a tax liability).

(3) A corporation with $1 million or more of taxable income in any of its three preceding tax years (i.e., **large corporation**) can use its preceding year's tax only for its first installment and must base its estimated payments on 100% of its current year's tax to avoid penalty.

(4) If any amount of tax is not paid by the original due date, interest must be paid from the due date until the tax is paid.

(5) A failure-to-pay tax delinquency penalty will be owed if the amount of tax paid by the original due date of the return is less than 90% of the tax shown on the return. The failure-to-pay penalty is imposed at a rate of 0.5% per month (or fraction thereof), with a maximum penalty of 25%.

2. Corporations are subject to

   a. **Regular tax rates**

	Taxable income	Rate
(1)	$0–$50,000	15%
(2)	$50,001–$75,000	25
(3)	$75,001–$10 million	34
(4)	Over $10 million	35

     (5) The less-than-34% brackets are phased out by adding an additional tax of 5% of the excess of taxable income over $100,000, up to a maximum additional tax of $11,750.

     (6) The 34% bracket is phased out for corporations with taxable income in excess of $15 million by adding an additional 3% of the excess of taxable income over $15 million, up to a maximum additional tax of $100,000.

   b. Certain personal service corporations are not eligible to use the less-than-35% brackets and their taxable income is taxed at a flat 35% rate.

NOW REVIEW MULTIPLE-CHOICE QUESTIONS 12 THROUGH 20

---

   c. **Alternative minimum tax (AMT)**

     (1) **Computation.** The AMT is generally the amount by which 20% of alternative minimum taxable income (AMTI) as reduced by an exemption and the alternative minimum tax foreign tax credit, exceeds the regular tax (i.e., regular tax liability reduced by the regular tax foreign tax credit). AMTI is equal to taxable income computed with specified adjustments and increased by tax preferences.

     (2) **Exemption.** AMTI is offset by a $40,000 exemption. However, the exemption is reduced by 25% of AMTI over $150,000, and completely phased out once AMTI reaches $310,000.

     (3) **AMT formula**

	Regular taxable income before Net Operation Loss (NOL) deduction
+	Tax preference items
+(−)	Adjustments other than Adjusted Current Earnings (ACE) and NOL deduction
	Pre-ACE AMTI
+(−)	ACE adjustment (75% of difference between pre-ACE AMTI and ACE)
−	AMT NOL deduction (limited to 90% of pre-NOL AMTI)
	AMTI
−	Exemption ($40,000 less 25% of AMTI over $150,000)
	Alternative minimum tax base
×	20% rate

Tentative AMT before foreign tax credit
− AMT foreign tax credit
Tentative minimum tax (TMT)
− Regular income tax (less regular tax foreign tax credit)
Alternative minimum tax (if positive)

(4) **Preference items.** The following are examples of items added to regular taxable income in computing pre-ACE AMTI:

    (a) Tax-exempt interest on private activity bonds (net of related expenses). However, tax-exempt interest on private activity bonds issued in 2009 and 2010 is not an item of tax preference.
    (b) Excess of accelerated over straight-line depreciation on real property and leased personal property placed in service before 1987
    (c) The excess of percentage depletion deduction over the property's adjusted basis
    (d) The excess of intangible drilling costs using a ten-year amortization over 65% of net oil and gas income

(5) **Adjustments.** The following are examples of adjustments to regular taxable income in computing pre-ACE AMTI:

    (a) For real property placed in service after 1986 and before 1999, the difference between regular tax depreciation and straight-line depreciation over forty years
    (b) For personal property placed in service after 1986, the difference between regular tax depreciation using the 200% declining balance method and depreciation using the 150% declining balance method
    (c) The installment method cannot be used for sales of inventory-type items
    (d) Income from long-term contracts must be determined using the percentage of completion method

(6) **Adjusted Current Earnings (ACE).** ACE is a concept based on a corporation's earnings and profits, and is calculated by making adjustments to pre-ACE AMTI.

AMTI before ACE adjustment and NOL deduction

    Add: Tax-exempt interest on municipal bonds (less expenses); except not interest on tax-exempt bonds issued in 2009 or 2010.
    Tax-exempt life insurance death benefits (less expenses)
    70% dividends-received deduction

    Deduct: Depletion using cost depletion method
    Depreciation using ADS straight-line for all property (this adjustment eliminated for property placed in service after 1993)

    Other: Capitalize organizational expenditures and circulation expenses
    Add increase (subtract decrease) in LIFO recapture amount (i.e., excess of FIFO value over LIFO basis)
    Installment method cannot be used for non dealer sales of property
    Amortize intangible drilling costs over five years

ACE (Adjusted Current Earnings)
− Pre-ACE AMTI
Balance (positive or negative)
× 75%
ACE adjustment (positive or negative)

EXAMPLE

Acme, Inc. has adjusted current earnings (ACE) of $100,000 and alternative minimum taxable income (before this adjustment) of $60,000. Since adjusted current earnings exceeds pre-ACE AMTI by $40,000, 75% of this amount must be added to Acme's AMTI. Thus, Acme's AMTI before exemption for the year is [$60,000 + ($40,000 × 75%)] = $90,000.

    (a) The ACE adjustment can be positive or negative, but a negative ACE adjustment is limited in amount to prior years' net positive ACE adjustments.

    (b) The computation of ACE is *not* the same as the computation of a corporation's E&P. For example, federal income taxes, penalties and fines, and the disallowed portion of business meals and entertainment would be deductible in computing E&P, but are not deductible in computing ACE.

(7) **Minimum tax credit.** The amount of AMT paid is allowed as a credit against regular tax liability in future years.

    (a) The credit can be carried forward indefinitely, but not carried back.

    (b) The AMT credit can only be used to reduce regular tax liability, not future AMT liability.

(8) **Small corporation exemption.** A corporation is exempt from the corporate AMT for its first tax year (regardless of income levels). After the first year, it is exempt from AMT if it passes a gross receipts test. It is exempt for its second year if its first year's gross receipts do not exceed $5 million. To be exempt for its third year, the corporation's average gross receipts for the first two years must not exceed $7.5 million. To be exempt for the fourth year (and subsequent years), the corporation's average gross receipts for all prior three-year periods must not exceed $7.5 million.

EXAMPLE

Zero Corp., a calendar-year corporation, was formed on January 2, 2011, and had gross receipts for its first four taxable years as follows:

Year	Gross receipts
2011	$4,500,000
2012	9,000,000
2013	8,000,000
2014	6,500,000

Zero is automatically exempt from AMT for 2011. It is exempt for 2012 because its gross receipts for 2011 do not exceed $5 million. Zero also is exempt for 2013 because its average gross receipts for 2011–2012 do not exceed $7.5 million. Similarly, it is exempt for 2014 because its average gross receipts for 2011–2013 do not exceed $7.5 million. However, Zero will lose its exemption from AMT for 2015 and all subsequent years because its average gross receipts for 2012–2014 exceed $7.5 million.

NOW REVIEW MULTIPLE-CHOICE QUESTIONS 21 THROUGH 28

3. **Gross income** for a corporation is computed much the same as for individual taxpayers. However, there are a few differences.

    a. A corporation does not recognize gain or loss on the **issuance of its own stock** (including treasury stock), or on the lapse or acquisition of an option to buy or sell its stock (including treasury stock).

       (1) It generally recognizes gain (but not loss) if it distributes appreciated property to its shareholders.

(2) **Contributions to capital** are excluded from a corporation's gross income, whether received from shareholders or non shareholders.

    (a) If property is received from a shareholder, the shareholder recognizes no gain or loss, the shareholder's basis for the contributed property transfers to the corporation, and the shareholder's stock basis is increased by the basis of the contributed property.

    (b) If property is received as a capital contribution from a non shareholder, the corporation's basis for the contributed property is zero.

        1] If money is received, the basis of property purchased within one year afterwards is reduced by the money contributed.

        2] Any money not used reduces the basis of the corporation's existing property beginning with depreciable property.

b. No gain or loss is recognized on the **issuance of debt**.

    (1) Premium or discount on bonds payable is amortized as income or expense over the life of bonds.

    (2) Ordinary income/loss is recognized by a corporation on the repurchase of its bonds, determined by the relationship of the repurchase price to the net carrying value of the bonds (issue price plus or minus the discount or premium amortized).

    (3) Interest earned and gains recognized in a bond sinking fund are income to the corporation.

c. Gains are treated as ordinary income on sales of property to or from a more than 50% shareholder, or between corporations which are more than 50% owned by the same individual, if the property is subject to depreciation in the hands of the buyer.

NOW REVIEW MULTIPLE-CHOICE QUESTIONS 29 THROUGH 33

---

4. Deductions for a corporation are much the same as for individuals. However, there are some major differences.

a. Adjusted gross income is not applicable to corporations.

b. A corporation may elect to deduct up to $5,000 of **organizational expenditures** for the tax year in which the corporation begins business. The $5,000 amount must be reduced (but not below zero) by the amount by which organizational expenditures exceed $50,000. Remaining expenditures can be deducted ratably over the 180-month period beginning with the month in which the corporation begins business.

> **EXAMPLE**
>
> A calendar-year corporation was organized and began business during 2015 incurring $4,800 or organizational expenditures. The corporation may deduct the $4,800 of organizational expenditures for 2015.

> **EXAMPLE**
>
> A calendar-year corporation was organized during February 2015 incurring organizational expenditures of $6,000. Assuming the corporation begins business during April 2015, its maximum deduction for organizational expenditures for 2015 would be $5,000 + [($6,000 − $5,000) × 9/180] = $5,050.

> **EXAMPLE**
>
> A calendar-year corporation was organized during February 2015 incurring organizational expenditures of $60,000. Assuming the corporation begins business during April 2015, its maximum deduction for organizational expenditures for 2015 would be $60,000 × 9/180 = $3,000.

(1) For amounts paid or incurred after September 8, 2008, the corporation is deemed to have made the election, but instead may choose to forgo the deemed election by clearly electing to capitalize its costs on a timely filed return (including extensions) for the taxable year in which the corporation begins business.

(2) Organizational expenditures include expenses of temporary directors and organizational meetings, state fees for incorporation, accounting and legal service costs incident to incorporation (e.g., drafting bylaws, minutes of organizational meetings, and terms of original stock certificates).

(3) Expenditures connected with issuing or selling shares of stock, or listing stock on an exchange are neither deductible nor amortizable. Expenditures connected with the transfer of an asset to the corporation must be capitalized as part of the cost of the asset.

NOW REVIEW MULTIPLE-CHOICE QUESTIONS 34 THROUGH 37

---

c. The deduction for **charitable contributions is limited to 10% of taxable income** before the contributions deduction, the dividends received deduction, a NOL carryback (but after carryover), a capital loss carryback (but after carryover), and before the domestic production activities deductions (DPAD).

(1) Generally the same rules apply for valuation of contributed property as for individuals except

   (a) Deduction for donations of inventory and other appreciated ordinary income-producing property is the donor's basis plus one-half of the unrealized appreciation but limited to twice the basis, provided

      1] Donor is a corporation (but not an S corporation)
      2] Donee must use property for care of ill, needy, or infants
      3] Donor must obtain a written statement from the donee that the use requirement has been met
      4] No deduction allowed for unrealized appreciation that would be ordinary income under recapture rules

   (b) Deduction for donation of appreciated scientific personal property to a college or university is the donor's basis plus one-half the unrealized appreciation but limited to twice the basis, provided

      1] Donor is a corporation (but not an S corporation, personal holding company, or service organization)
      2] Property was constructed by donor and contributed within two years of substantial completion, and donee is original user of property
      3] Donee must use property for research or experimentation
      4] Donor must obtain a written statement from the donee that the use requirement has been met
      5] No deduction allowed for unrealized appreciation that would be ordinary income under recapture rules

(2) Contributions are deductible in period paid (subject to 10% limitation) unless corporation is an accrual method taxpayer and then deductible (subject to 10% limitation) when authorized by board of directors if payment is made within 2 1/2 months after tax year end, and corporation elects to deduct contributions when authorized.

(3) Excess contributions over the 10% limitation may be carried forward for up to five years.

EXAMPLE

The books of a calendar-year, accrual method corporation for 2014 disclose net income of $350,000 after deducting a charitable contribution of $50,000. The contribution was authorized by the Board of Directors on December 24, 2014, and was actually paid on January 31, 2015. The allowable charitable contribution deduction for 2014 (if the corporation elects to deduct it when accrued) is $40,000, calculated as follows: ($350,000 + $50,000) × .10 = $40,000. The remaining $10,000 is carried forward for up to five years.

NOW REVIEW MULTIPLE-CHOICE QUESTIONS 38 THROUGH 44

d. A **100% Dividends Received Deduction (DRD)** for dividends received from affiliated (i.e., at least 80% owned) corporations if a consolidated tax return is not filed.

    (1) If a consolidated tax return is filed, intercompany dividends are eliminated in the consolidation process and not included in consolidated gross income.

    (2) See Section D. for discussion of affiliated corporations

e. An **80% DRD** is allowed for qualified dividends from taxable domestic unaffiliated corporations that are **at least 20% owned** (but less than 80% owned).

    (1) DRD may be **limited to 80% of taxable income** before the 80% dividends received deduction, the net operating loss deduction, a capital loss carryback, and the domestic production activities deduction (DPAD).

EXAMPLE

A corporation has income from sales of $20,000, dividend income of $10,000, and business expenses of $22,000, resulting in taxable income before the DRD of $8,000. Since taxable income before the DRD ($8,000) is less than dividend income ($10,000), the DRD is limited to $8,000 × 80% = $6,400. As a result, taxable income would be $8,000 – $6,400 = $1,600.

---

    (2) Exception: The 80% of **taxable income limitation does not apply** if the full 80% DRD creates or increases a net operating loss.

EXAMPLE

In the example above, assume the same facts except that business expenses are $22,001, resulting in taxable income before the DRD of $7,999. Since the full DRD ($8,000) would create a $1 net operating loss ($7,999 – $8,000), the taxable income limitation does not apply and the full DRD ($8,000) would be allowed.

---

f. Only a **70% dividends received deduction** (instead of 80%) is allowed for qualified dividends from taxable domestic unaffiliated corporations that are **less than 20% owned**.

    (1) A 70% of taxable income limitation (instead of 80%) and a limitation exception for a net operating loss apply as in e.(1) and (2) above.

    (2) If dividends are received from both 20% owned corporations and corporations that are less than 20% owned, the 80% DRD and 80% DRD limitation for dividends received from 20% owned corporations is computed first. Then the 70% DRD and 70% DRD limitation is computed for dividends received from less than 20% owned corporations. For purposes of computing the 70% DRD limitation, taxable income is reduced by the total amount of dividends received from 20% owned corporations.

EXAMPLE

A corporation has taxable income before the dividends received deduction of $100,000. Included in taxable income are $65,000 of dividends from a 20% owned corporation and $40,000 of dividends from a less than 20% owned corporation. First, the 80% DRD for dividends received from the 20% owned corporation is computed. That deduction equals $52,000 [i.e., the lesser of 80% of the dividends received (80% × $65,000), or 80% of taxable income (80% × $100,000)].

    Second, the 70% DRD for the dividends received from the less than 20% owned corporation is computed. That deduction is $24,500 [i.e., the lesser of 70% of the dividends received (70% × $40,000), or 70% of taxable income after deducting the amount of dividends from the 20% owned corporation (70% × [$100,000 – $65,000])].

    Thus, the total dividends received deduction is $52,000 + $24,500 = $76,500.

---

g. A portion of a corporation's 80% (or 70%) DRD will be disallowed if the dividends are directly attributable to **debt-financed portfolio stock**.

   (1) "Portfolio stock" is any stock (except stock of a corporation if the taxpayer owns at least 50% of the voting power and at least 50% of the total value of such corporation).
   (2) The DRD percentage for debt-financed portfolio stock = [80% (or 70%) × (100% – average % of indebtedness on the stock)].

EXAMPLE

P, Inc. purchased 25% of T, Inc. for $100,000, paying with $50,000 of its own funds and $50,000 borrowed from its bank. During the year P received $9,000 in dividends from T, and paid $5,000 in interest expense on the bank loan. No principal payments were made on the loan during the year. If the stock were not debt financed, P's DRD would be $9,000 × 80% = $7,200. However, because half of the stock investment was debt financed, P's DRD is $9,000 × [80% × (100% – 50%)] = $3,600.

---

   (3) The reduction in the DRD cannot exceed the interest deduction allocable to the portfolio stock indebtedness.

EXAMPLE

Assume the same facts as above except that the interest expense on the bank loan was only $3,000. The reduction in the DRD would be limited to the $3,000 interest deduction on the loan. The DRD would be ($9,000 × 80%) – $3,000 = $4,200.

---

h. **No DRD** is allowed if the dividend paying stock is held **less than 46 days** during the 91-day period that begins 45 days before the stock becomes ex-dividend. In the case of preferred stock, no DRD is allowed if the dividends received are for a period or periods in excess of 366 days and the stock has been held for less than 91 days during the 181-day period that begins 90 days before the stock becomes ex-dividend.

i. The **basis of stock** held by a corporation must be reduced by the nontaxed portion of a non liquidating **extraordinary dividend** received with respect to the stock, unless the corporation has held the stock for more than two years before the dividend is announced. To the extent the nontaxed portion of an extraordinary dividend exceeds the adjusted basis of the stock, the excess is recognized as gain for the taxable year in which the extraordinary dividend is received.

   (1) The nontaxed portion of a dividend is generally the amount that is offset by the DRD.
   (2) A dividend is considered "extraordinary" when it equals or exceeds 10% (5% for preferred stock) of the stock's adjusted basis (or FMV if greater on the day preceding the ex-dividend date).
   (3) Aggregation of dividends

      (a) All dividends received that have ex-dividend dates that occur within a period of 85 consecutive days are treated as one dividend.
      (b) All dividends received within 365 consecutive days are treated as extraordinary dividends if they in total exceed 20% of the stock's adjusted basis.

   (4) This provision is not applicable to dividends received from an affiliated corporation, and does not apply if the stock was held during the entire period the paying corporation (and any predecessor) was in existence.

EXAMPLE

Corporation X purchased 30% of the stock of Corporation Y for $10,000 during June 2014. During December 2014 X received a $20,000 dividend from Y. X sold its Y stock for $5,000 in February 2015.

   Because the dividend from Y is an extraordinary dividend, the nontaxed portion (equal to the DRD allowed to X) $20,000 × 80% = $16,000 has the effect of reducing the Y stock basis from $10,000 to $0, with the remaining $6,000 recognized as gain for 2014. When the stock is sold in 2015 the excess of sale proceeds over the reduced stock basis $5,000 – $0 = $5,000 is also recognized as gain.

> **NOW REVIEW MULTIPLE-CHOICE QUESTIONS 45 THROUGH 50**

j. **Losses** in the ordinary course of business are deductible.

(1) Loss is **disallowed** if the sale or exchange of property is between--

(a) A corporation and a more than 50% shareholder.

(b) A C corporation and an S corporation if the same persons own more than 50% of each.

(c) A corporation and a partnership if the same persons own more than 50% of the corporation, and more than 50% of the capital and profits interest in the partnership.

(d) Constructive ownership rules apply for purposes of determining stock ownership. Family constructive ownership includes an individual's brothers and sisters, spouse, ancestors, and lineal descendants.

(e) In the event of a disallowed loss, the transferee on a subsequent disposition only recognizes gain to the extent it exceeds the disallowed loss.

(2) Any loss from the sale or exchange of property between corporations that are members of the same **controlled group** is **deferred** (instead of disallowed) until the property is sold outside the group. See controlled group definition in Section D.2., except substitute "more than 50%" for "at least 80%."

(3) An accrual method C corporation is effectively placed on the cash method of accounting for purposes of deducting accrued interest and other expenses owed to a related cash method payee. No deduction is allowable until the year the amount is actually paid.

> **EXAMPLE**
>
> A calendar-year corporation accrues $10,000 of salary to an employee (a 60% shareholder) during 2014 but does not make payment until February 2015. The $10,000 will be deductible by the corporation and reported as income by the employee-shareholder in 2015.

(4) **Capital losses** are deductible only to the extent of capital gains (i.e., may not offset ordinary income).

(a) Unused capital losses are carried back three years and then carried forward five years to offset capital gains.

(b) All corporate capital loss carrybacks and carry forwards are treated as **short-term**.

(5) Bad debt losses are treated as ordinary deductions.

(6) Casualty losses are treated the same as for an individual except

(a) There is no $100 floor

(b) If property is completely destroyed, the amount of loss is the property's adjusted basis

(c) A partial loss is measured the same as for an individual's nonbusiness loss (i.e., the lesser of the decrease in FMV, or the property's adjusted basis)

(7) A corporation's **NOL** is computed the same way as its taxable income.

(a) The dividends received deduction is allowed without limitation.

(b) No deduction is allowed for a NOL carryback or carryover from other years, and no deduction is allowed for the domestic production activities deduction (DPAD).

(c) A NOL is generally carried back two years and forward twenty years to offset taxable income in those years. However, a three-year carryback is permitted for the portion of a NOL that is attributable to a presidentially declared disaster and is incurred by a small business corporation (i.e., a corporation whose average annual gross receipts are $5 million or less for the three-tax-year period preceding the loss year). A corporation may elect to forego carryback and only carry forward twenty years.

k. Depreciation and depletion computations are same as for individuals.

l. Research and development expenditures of a corporation (or individual) may be treated under one of three alternatives

(1) Currently expensed in year paid or incurred
(2) Amortized over a period of sixty months or more if life not determinable
(3) Capitalized and depreciated over determinable life

m. Contributions to a pension or profit-sharing plan

(1) Defined benefit plans

(a) Maximum deductible contribution is actuarially determined.
(b) There also are minimum funding standards.

(2) Defined contribution plans

(a) **Maximum deduction** for contributions to qualified profit-sharing or stock bonus plans is generally limited to 25% of the compensation paid or accrued during the year to covered employees.
(b) If more than 25% is paid, the excess can be carried forward as part of the contributions of succeeding years to the extent needed to bring the deduction up to 25%.

5. In working a corporate problem, certain calculations must be made in a specific order [e.g., charitable contributions (CC) must be computed before the DRD]. The following memory device is quite helpful:
Gross income

–	Deductions (except CC , DRD, and DPAD)	
	Taxable income before CC, DRD, and DPAD	
–	CC (limited to 10% of TI before CC, DRD, capital loss and NOL carrybacks, and DPAD)	
	Taxable income before DRD and DPAD	
–	DRD (may be limited* to 80% or 70%) of TI before DRD, capital loss carryback, NOL carryover or carryback, and the DPAD)	
	Taxable income before DPAD ·	
–	DPAD (limited to 9% of TI before DPAD)	
×	Taxable income Applicable rates	
=	Tax liability before tax credits	
–	Tax credits	
	Tax liability	

* Limitation not applicable if full 80% (or 70%) of dividends received creates or increases an NOL.

NOW REVIEW MULTIPLE-CHOICE QUESTIONS 51 THROUGH 57

---

6. A person sitting for the CPA examination should be able to **reconcile book and taxable income**.

a. If you begin with book income to calculate taxable income, make the following adjustments:

(1) **Increase book income** by

(a) Federal income tax expense
(b) Excess of capital losses over capital gains because a net capital loss is not deductible
(c) Income items in the tax return not included in book income (e.g., prepaid rents, royalties, interest)
(d) Charitable contributions in excess of the 10% limitation
(e) Expenses deducted on the books but not on the tax return (e.g., amount of business gifts in excess of $25, nondeductible life insurance premiums paid, 50% of business meals and entertainment)

(2) **Deduct from book income**

    (a) Income reported on the books but not on the tax return (e.g., tax-exempt interest, life insurance proceeds)

    (b) Expenses deducted on the tax return but not on the books (e.g., MACRS depreciation above straight-line, charitable contribution carryover)

    (c) The dividends received deduction

    (d) The domestic production activities deduction

b. When going from taxable income to book income, the above adjustments would be reversed.

c. **Schedule M-1** of Form 1120 provides a reconciliation of income per books with taxable income before the NOL deduction and DRD, and must be completed by corporations with less than *$10 million* of total assets. Schedule M-1 items are either *permanent* book-to-tax differences (e.g., tax-exempt interest) or *temporary* differences (e.g., accelerated depreciation used on tax return while straight-line used per books). The starting point on Schedule M-1 is net income (or loss) per books. Additions and subtractions are then made to reflect the differences between financial and tax accounting. The end result is the amount of taxable income before the NOL deduction and DRD that is reported on the current year return.

    (1) Items added to book income include

        (a) Federal income tax expense that was deducted per books

        (b) Excess of capital losses over capital gains deducted per books but not deductible for tax purposes

        (c) Income subject to tax in the current year but not included in current year book income (e.g., receipt of prepaid rent)

        (d) Expenses deducted per books but not allowed in computing taxable income (e.g., 50% of business meals and entertainment, expenses incurred in the production of tax-exempt income, charitable contributions in excess of the 10% of taxable income limitation).

    (2) Items subtracted from book income include

        (a) Income reported on books this year not included in the tax return (e.g., tax-exempt interest, nontaxable life insurance proceeds)

        (b) Deductions on the return not charged against book income this year (e.g., tax depreciation in excess of book depreciation, domestic production activities deduction)

EXAMPLE

A corporation discloses that it had net income after taxes of $36,000 per books. Included in the computation were deductions for charitable contributions of $10,000, a net capital loss of $5,000, and federal income taxes paid of $9,000. What is the corporation's TI?

Net income per books after tax	$36,000
Nondeductible net capital loss	+ 5,000
Federal income tax expense	+ 9,000
Charitable contributions	+10,000
Taxable income before CC	$60,000
CC (limited to 10% × 60,000)	− 6,000
Taxable income	$54,000

---

d. **Schedule M-2** of Form 1120 analyzes changes in a corporation's Unappropriated Retained Earnings per books between the beginning and end of the year.

Balance at beginning of year

Add: Net income per books
        Other increases
Less: Dividends to shareholders
Other decreases (e.g., addition to reserve for contingencies)
Balance at end of year

e. **Schedule M-3** Net Income (Loss) Reconciliation must be completed and attached to a corporation's Form 1120 if the corporation's total assets at the end of the tax year equal or exceed **$10 million**. A corporation filing Schedule M-3 must not complete Schedule M-1. A corporation with total assets less than $10 million can elect to complete Schedule M-3 instead of completing Schedule M-1.

(1) Total assets at the end of the year must be determined using the same method as used for financial statement purposes. If a corporation uses the accrual method for financial statement purposes and the cash method for tax purposes, the corporation's total assets must be determined using the accrual method.

  (a) In the case of a US consolidated tax group, total assets at the end of the tax year must be determined based on the total year-end assets of all includible corporations, net of eliminations for intercompany transactions and balances between the includible corporations.

  (b) A corporation is not required to file Schedule M-3 if total assets at the end of the current year are less than $10 million, even though the corporation was required to file Schedule M-3 for the preceding tax year.

  (c) No schedule M-3 is required for taxpayers filing Form 1120-REIT (Real Estate Investment Trusts); Form 1120-RIC (Regulated Investment Companies); Form 1120-H (Homeowners Associations); and Form 1120-SF (Settlement Funds).

(2) Schedule M-3 consists of three parts: Part I adjusts worldwide income per books to worldwide book income for only those corporations includible on the tax return; Part II reconciles income and loss items for includible corporations; and Part III reconciles expense and deduction items. The total of items for Part III carry over to Part II for the overall reconciliation.

  (a) Schedule M-3 requires much greater detail (Parts II and III contain a total of 66 line items) than Schedule M-1 (10 line items) because it requires taxpayers to separately list each type of transaction that gives rise to a book-tax difference and to identify whether each difference is permanent or temporary.

  (b) Parts II and III each contain four columns: (a) income statement items; (b) temporary differences; (c) permanent differences; and, (d) tax return items. Part III requires a corporation to separate its book federal income tax expense between its current income tax expense and its deferred income tax expense. If its financial statements do not separately report current and deferred income tax expense, all income tax expense should be reported as current income tax expense in Part III.

  (c) A US consolidated tax group required to file Schedule M-3 must file multiple Schedules M-3. It must file one Schedule M-3, Parts I, II, and III to reflect the activity of the entire US consolidated tax group. Additionally, a separate Schedule M-3 Parts II and III must be completed for the parent corporation and each subsidiary to reflect each corporation's separate activity. Lastly, it generally is necessary to complete Parts II and III of a separate Schedule M-3 to eliminate differences related to intercompany transactions, and to include limitations on deductions (e.g., charitable contributions and capital loss limitations) and carryover amounts. As a result, a US consolidated group consisting of a parent corporation and three subsidiary corporations would have to complete a total of six Schedules M-3.

  (d) A corporation or group of corporations that files a Form 1120 and is required to file Schedule M-3, must also file Schedule B (Form 1120), Additional Information for Schedule M-3 Filers. In the case of a consolidated group, a parent corporation files only one Schedule B (Form 1120) for the entire consolidated group.

  (e) **Schedule UTP** (Uncertain Tax Positions) must be completed and attached to Form 1120 if the corporation (1) has total assets of at least $100 million, and (2) the corporation has taken a tax position on its return and the corporation or a related party has either recorded a reserve with respect to that position in audited financial statements, or did not record a reserve because the corporation expects to litigate the position.

1] A tax position taken on a tax return is a tax position that would result in an adjustment to a line item on that return if the position is not sustained.

2] Schedule UTP requires a concise description of each uncertain tax position. Additionally, the corporation must rank each listed tax position by size, must indicate whether each position is temporary or permanent, and must disclose whether a tax position is greater than 10% of the aggregate amount of reserves for all tax positions.

3] If the corporation or a related party determined that, under applicable accounting standards, either no reserve was required for a tax position taken on a return because the amount was immaterial for audited financial statement purposes, or that a tax position was sufficiently certain so that no reserve was required, then the tax position is not required to be reported on Schedule UTP.

NOW REVIEW MULTIPLE-CHOICE QUESTIONS 58 THROUGH 71

D. Affiliated and Controlled Corporations

1. An **affiliated group** is a parent-subsidiary chain of corporations in which **at least 80%** of the combined voting power and total value of all stock (except nonvoting preferred) are owned by includible corporations.

   a. They may elect to file a consolidated return. Election is binding on all future returns.

   b. If affiliated corporations file a consolidated return, intercompany dividends are eliminated in the consolidation process. If separate tax returns are filed, dividends from affiliated corporations are eligible for a 100% dividends received deduction.

   c. Possible advantages of a consolidated return include the deferral of gain on intercompany transactions and offsetting operating/capital losses of one corporation against the profits/capital gains of another.

> **EXAMPLE**
>
> P Corp. owns 80% of the stock of A Corp., 40% of the stock of B Corp., and 45% of the stock of C Corp. A Corp. owns 40% of the stock of B Corp. A consolidated tax return could be filed by P, A, and B.

> **EXAMPLE**
>
> Parent and Subsidiary file consolidated tax returns using a calendar year. During 2014, Subsidiary paid a $10,000 dividend to Parent. Also during 2014, Subsidiary sold land with a basis of $20,000 to Parent for its FMV of $50,000. During 2015, Parent sold the land to an unrelated taxpayer for $55,000.
>
> The intercompany dividend is eliminated in the consolidation process and is excluded from consolidated taxable income. Additionally, Subsidiary's $30,000 of gain from the sale of land to Parent is deferred for 2014. The $30,000 will be included in consolidated taxable income for 2015 when Parent reports $5,000 of income from the sale of that land to the unrelated taxpayer.

2. A **controlled group** of corporations is limited to an aggregate of $75,000 of taxable income taxed at less than 35%, one $250,000 accumulated earnings credit, one Sec. 179 expense election, and one $40,000 AMT exemption. There are three basic types of controlled groups.

   a. **Parent-subsidiary**—Basically same as P-S group eligible to file consolidated return, except ownership requirement is 80% of combined voting power **or** total value of stock. Affiliated corporations are subject to the controlled group limitations if the corporations file separate tax returns.

   b. **Brother-sister**—Two or more corporations if 5 or fewer persons who are individuals, estates, or trusts own stock possessing more than 50% of the total combined voting power, or more than 50% of the total combined voting power, or more than 50% of the total value of all shares of stock of each corporation, taking into account the stock ownership of each person only to the extent such stock ownership is identical with respect to each corporation.

EXAMPLE

Individual shareholder	Corporations		Stock considered for 50% test
	W	**X**	
A	30%	20%	20%
B	5	40	5%
C	30	35	30%
D	15	5	5%
E	20	–	–
	100%	100%	60%

Corporations W and X are a controlled group since five or fewer individuals own more than 50% of each corporation when counting only identical ownership.

EXAMPLE

Individual shareholder	Corporations		Stock considered for 50% test
	Y	**Z**	
F	80%	5%	5%
G	10	90	10
H	10	5	5
	100%	100%	20%

Corporations Y and Z are not a controlled group since shareholders F, G, and H do not own more than 50% of Y and Z when counting only identical stock ownership.

---

c. **Combined**—The parent in a P-S group is also a member of a brother-sister group of corporations.

EXAMPLE

Individual H owns 100% of the stock of Corporations P and Q. Corporation P owns 100% of the stock of Corporation S. P, S, and Q are members of one controlled group.

NOW REVIEW MULTIPLE-CHOICE QUESTIONS 72 THROUGH 78

E. Dividends and Distributions

1. **Ordinary corporate distributions**

   a. Corporate distributions of property to shareholders on their stock are subject to a **three-step** treatment.

      (1) Dividend—to be included in gross income
      (2) Return of stock basis—nontaxable and reduces shareholder's basis for stock
      (3) Gain—to extent distribution exceeds shareholder's stock basis

b. The **amount** of distribution to a shareholder is the cash plus the FMV of other property received, reduced by liabilities assumed.

c. A shareholder's tax **basis** for distributed property is the property's FMV at date of distribution (not reduced by liabilities).

d. A **dividend** is a distribution of property by a corporation to its shareholders out of

    (1) Earnings and profits of the current taxable year (CEP), computed at the end of the year, without regard to the amount of earnings and profits at the date of distribution; or,

    (2) Earnings and profits accumulated after February 28, 1913 (AEP).

EXAMPLE

Corporation X has earnings and profits of $6,000 and makes a $10,000 distribution to its sole shareholder, A, who has a stock basis of $3,000. The $10,000 distribution to A will be treated as a dividend of $6,000, a nontaxable return of stock basis of $3,000, and a capital gain of $1,000.

    (a) CEP are first allocated to distributions on preferred stock, then to common stock.

    (b) CEP are allocated pro rata to multiple distributions on the same class of stock if distributions exceed CEP.

    (c) AEP are allocated to distributions in the order in which the distributions are made.

EXAMPLE

A corporation has both preferred and common stock outstanding and no accumulated earnings and profits. For the current year, it has current earnings and profits of $15,000, and during the year distributes cash of $10,000 to its preferred shareholders, and $10,000 to its common shareholders. The $15,000 of CEP is first allocated to the distribution to the preferred shareholders, making all $10,000 taxable as a dividend. The remaining $5,000 of CEP is then allocated to the $10,000 distribution to common shareholders, making only $5,000 taxable as a dividend.

EXAMPLE

A corporation has accumulated earnings and profits of $4,000 and current earnings and profits of $20,000. During the current year it distributes $15,000 to its common shareholders in March, and another $15,000 to its common shareholders in October. The $20,000 of CEP are allocated pro rata to the two distributions, making $10,000 of the March distribution and $10,000 of the October distribution taxable as a dividend. The AEP of $4,000 are then allocated to the March distribution. As a result, $14,000 of the March distribution and $10,000 of the October distribution are taxable as a dividend.

---

e. The **distributing corporation recognizes gain** on the distribution of appreciated property as if such property were sold for its FMV. However, no loss can be recognized on the non liquidating distribution of property to shareholders.

EXAMPLE

A corporation distributes property with an FMV of $10,000 and a basis of $3,000 to a shareholder. The corporation recognizes a gain of $10,000 − $3,000 = $7,000.

---

(1) If the distributed property is subject to a liability (or if the distributee assumes a liability) and the FMV of the distributed property is less than the amount of liability, then the gain is the difference between the amount of liability and the property's basis.

EXAMPLE

A corporation distributes property with an FMV of $10,000 and a basis of $3,000 to a shareholder, who assumes a liability of $12,000 on the property. The corporation recognizes a gain of $12,000 – $3,000 = $9,000.

---

(2) The type of gain recognized (e.g., ordinary, Sec. 1231, capital) depends on the nature of the property distributed (e.g., recapture rules may apply).

2. **Earnings and profits**

   a. **Current earnings and profits** (CEP) are **similar to book income,** but are computed by making adjustments to taxable income.

      (1) Add—tax-exempt income, dividends received deduction, excess of MACRS depreciation over depreciation computed under ADS, etc.
      (2) Deduct—federal income taxes, net capital loss, excess charitable contributions, expenses relating to tax-exempt income, penalties, etc.

   b. **Accumulated earnings and profits** (AEP) represent the sum of prior years' CEP, reduced by distributions and net operating loss of prior years.
   c. CEP is increased by the gain recognized on a distribution of appreciated property (excess of FMV over basis).
   d. Distributions reduce earnings and profits (but not below zero) by

      (1) The amount of money
      (2) The face amount (or issue price if less) of obligations of the distributing corporation, and
      (3) The adjusted basis (or FMV if greater) of other property distributed
      (4) Above reductions must be adjusted for any liability assumed by the shareholder, or the amount of liability to which the property distributed is subject.

EXAMPLE

Z Corp. has two 50% shareholders, Alan and Baker. Z Corp. distributes a parcel of land (held for investment) to each shareholder. Gainacre with an FMV of $12,000 and an adjusted basis of $8,000 is distributed to Alan, while Lossacre with an FMV of $12,000 and an adjusted basis of $15,000 is distributed to Baker. Each shareholder assumes a liability of $3,000 on the property received. Z Corp. must recognize a gain of $4,000 on the distribution of property to Alan, but cannot recognize the loss on the distribution to Baker.

	Alan	Baker
Dividend ($12,000 – $3,000)	$9,000	$9,000
Tax basis for property received	12,000	12,000
Effect (before tax) on Z's earnings & profits:		
	Alan	**Baker**
Increased by gain (FMV-basis)	4,000	0
Increased by liabilities distributed	3,000	3,000
Decreased by greater of FMV or adjusted basis of property distributed	(12,000)	(15,000)

NOW REVIEW MULTIPLE-CHOICE QUESTIONS 79 THROUGH 90

3. **Stock redemptions**

   a. A stock redemption is **treated as an exchange,** generally resulting in capital gain or loss treatment to the shareholder if at least one of the following five tests is met. Constructive stock ownership rules of Sec. 318 generally apply in determining whether the exchange tests are met. For this purpose, an individual's family consists of only spouse, children, grandchildren, and parents. A stock redemption will receive exchange treatment if:

      (1) The redemption is not essentially equivalent to a dividend (this has been interpreted by Revenue Rulings to mean that a redemption must reduce a shareholder's right to vote, share in earnings, and share in assets upon liquidation; and after the redemption the shareholder's stock ownership [both direct and constructive] must not exceed 50%), or

      (2) The redemption is substantially disproportionate (i.e., after redemption, shareholder's percentage ownership is less than 80% of shareholder's percentage ownership prior to redemption, and less than 50% of shares outstanding), or

      (3) All of the shareholder's stock is redeemed, or

      (4) The redemption is from a non corporate shareholder in a partial liquidation, or

      (5) The distribution is a redemption of stock to pay death taxes under Sec. 303.

   b. If none of the above tests are met, the redemption proceeds are treated as an ordinary Sec. 301 distribution, **taxable as a dividend** to the extent of the distributing corporation's earnings and profits.

   c. A corporation cannot deduct amounts paid or incurred in connection with a redemption of its stock (except for interest expense on loans used to purchase stock).

NOW REVIEW MULTIPLE-CHOICE QUESTIONS 91 THROUGH 93

---

4. **Complete liquidations**

   a. Amounts received by **shareholders** in liquidation of a corporation are treated as received in exchange for stock, generally resulting in capital gain or loss. Property received will have a basis equal to FMV.

   b. A **liquidating corporation** generally recognizes gain or loss on the sale or distribution of its assets in complete liquidation.

      (1) If a distribution, gain or loss is computed as if the distributed property were sold to the distributee for FMV.

      (2) If distributed property is subject to a liability (or a shareholder assumes a liability) in excess of the basis of the distributed property, FMV is deemed to be not less than the amount of liability.

   c. **Distributions to related persons**

      (1) No loss is generally recognized to a liquidating corporation on the distribution of property to a related person if

         (a) The distribution is not pro rata, *or*

         (b) The property was acquired by the liquidating corporation during the five-year period ending on the date of distribution in a Sec. 351 transaction or as a contribution to capital. This includes any property whose basis is determined by reference to the adjusted basis of property described in the preceding sentence.

      (2) Related person is a shareholder who owns (directly or constructively) more than 50% of the corporation's stock. The constructive ownership rules of Sec. 267 apply to determine whether a person owns more than 50%. For this purpose, an individual's family includes spouse, brothers and sisters, ancestors, and lineal descendants.

   d. **Carryover basis property**

      (1) If a corporation acquires property in a Sec. 351 transaction or as a contribution to capital at any time after the date that is two years before the date of the adoption of the plan of complete liquidation, any loss resulting from the property's sale, exchange, or distribution can be recognized only to the extent of the decline in value that occurred subsequent to the date that the corporation acquired the property.

(2) The above rule applies only where the loss is not already completely disallowed by c.(1) above, and is intended to apply where there is no clear and substantial relationship between the contributed property and the conduct of the corporation's business. If the contributed property is actually used in the corporation's business, the above rule should not apply if there is a business purpose for placing the property in the corporation.

EXAMPLE

During September 2014, a shareholder makes a capital contribution which includes property unrelated to the corporation's business with a basis of $15,000 and an FMV of $10,000 on the contribution date. Within two years the corporation adopts a plan of liquidation and sells the property for $8,000. The liquidating corporation's recognized loss will be limited to $10,000 – $8,000 = $2,000.

---

e. **Liquidation of subsidiary**

(1) **No gain or loss** is recognized to a **parent corporation** under Sec. 332 on the receipt of property in complete liquidation of an **80% or more owned subsidiary**. The subsidiary's basis for its assets along with all tax accounting attributes (e.g., earnings and profits, NOL, and charitable contribution carry forwards) will transfer to the parent corporation.

(2) **No gain or loss** is recognized to a **subsidiary corporation** on the distribution of property to its parent if Sec. 332 applies to the parent corporation.

(a) If the subsidiary has debt outstanding to the parent, non recognition also applies to property distributed in satisfaction of the debt.

(b) Gain (but not loss) is recognized on the distribution of property to minority (20% or less) shareholders.

(3) Non recognition does not extend to minority shareholders. A minority shareholder's gain or loss will be recognized under the general rule at 4.a. above.

EXAMPLE

Parent Corp. owns 80% of Subsidiary Corp., with the remaining 20% of Subsidiary stock owned by Alex. Parent's basis in its Subsidiary stock is $100,000, while Alex has a basis for her Subsidiary stock of $15,000. Subsidiary Corp. is to be liquidated and will distribute to Parent Corp. assets with an FMV of $200,000 and a basis of $150,000, and will distribute to Alex assets with an FMV of $50,000 and a basis of $30,000. Subsidiary has an unused capital loss carryover of $10,000. The tax effects of the liquidation will be as follows:

　Parent Corp. will not recognize gain on the receipt of Subsidiary's assets in complete liquidation, since Subsidiary is an at least 80%-owned corporation. The basis of Subsidiary's assets to Parent will be their transferred basis of $150,000, and Parent will inherit Subsidiary's unused capital loss carryover of $10,000.

　Alex will recognize a gain of $35,000 ($50,000 FMV – $15,000 stock basis) from the liquidation. Alex's tax basis for Subsidiary's assets received in the liquidation will be their FMV of $50,000.

　Subsidiary Corp. will not recognize gain on the distribution of its assets to Parent Corp., but will recognize a gain of $20,000 ($50,000 FMV – $30,000 basis) on the distribution of its assets to Alex.

---

5. **Stock purchases treated as asset acquisitions**

a. An acquiring corporation that has purchased at least 80% of a target corporation's stock within a 12-month period may elect under Sec. 338 to have the purchase of stock treated as an acquisition of assets.

b. Old target corporation is deemed to have sold all its assets on the acquisition date, and is treated as a new corporation that has purchased those assets on the day after the acquisition date.

(1) Acquisition date is the date on which at least 80% of the target's stock has been acquired by purchase within a 12-month period.

(2) Gain or loss is generally recognized to old target corporation on deemed sale of assets.

(3) The deemed sales price for the target corporation's assets is generally the FMV of the target's assets as of the close of the acquisition date.

> **NOW REVIEW MULTIPLE-CHOICE QUESTIONS 94 THROUGH 102**

F. Personal Holding Company and Accumulated Earnings Taxes

1. Personal holding companies (PHC) are subject to a penalty tax on undistributed PHC income to discourage taxpayers from accumulating their investment income in a corporation taxed at lower than individual rates.

   a. A **PHC** is any corporation (except certain banks, financial institutions, and similar corporations) that meets two requirements.

      (1) During anytime in the last half of the tax year, five or fewer individuals own more than 50% of the value of the outstanding **stock** directly or indirectly, **and**

      (2) The corporation receives at least 60% of its adjusted ordinary gross **income** as "PHC income" (e.g., dividends, interest, rents, royalties, and other passive income)

   b. Taxed at ordinary corporate rates on taxable income, plus 20% tax rate on undistributed PHC income

   c. The PHC tax

      (1) Is **self-assessing** (i.e., computed on Sch. PH and attached to Form 1120); a six-year statute of limitations applies if no Sch. PH is filed

      (2) May be avoided by dividend payments sufficient in amount to reduce undistributed PHC income to zero

   d. The PHC tax is computed as follows:

	Taxable Income
+	Dividends-received deduction
+	Net operating loss deduction (except NOL of immediately preceding year allowed without a dividends-received deduction)
−	Federal and foreign income taxes
−	Charitable contributions in excess of 10% limit
−	Net capital loss
−	Net LTCG over NSTCL (net of tax)
	Adjusted Taxable Income
−	Dividends paid during taxable year
−	Dividends paid within 2 1/2 months after close of year (limited to 20% of dividends actually paid during year)
−	Dividend carryover
−	Consent dividends
	Undistributed PHC Income
×	20%
	Personal Holding Company Tax

   e. **Consent dividends** are hypothetical dividends that are treated as if they were paid on the last day of the corporation's taxable year. Since they are not actually distributed, shareholders increase their stock basis by the amount of consent dividends included in their gross income.

   f. PHC tax liability for a previous year (but not interest and penalties) may be avoided by payment of a deficiency dividend within ninety days of a "determination" by the IRS that the corporation was a PHC for a previous year.

2. Corporations may be subject to an **accumulated earnings tax** (AET), in addition to regular income tax, if they accumulate earnings beyond reasonable business needs in order to avoid a shareholder tax on dividend distributions.

   a. The tax is not self-assessing, but is based on the IRS' determination of the existence of tax avoidance intent.

   b. AET may be imposed without regard to the number of shareholders of the corporation, but does not apply to personal holding companies.

  c. **Accumulated earnings credit** is allowed for greater of

    (1) $250,000 ($150,000 for personal service corporations) minus the accumulated earnings and profits at end of prior year, or

    (2) Reasonable needs of the business (e.g., expansion, working capital, to retire debt, etc.).

  d. Balance of accumulated taxable income is taxed at 20% tax rate.

  e. The AET may be avoided by dividend payments sufficient in amount to reduce accumulated taxable income to zero.

  f. The accumulated earnings tax is computed as follows:

	Taxable Income
+	Dividends-received deduction
+	NOL deduction
−	Federal and foreign income taxes
−	Excess charitable contributions (over 10% limit)
−	Net capital loss
−	Net LTCG over net STCL (net of tax)
	Adjusted Taxable Income
−	Dividends paid last 9 1/2 months of tax year and 2 1/2 months after close
−	Consent dividends
−	Accumulated earnings credit
	Accumulated Taxable Income
×	20%
	Accumulated Earnings Tax

NOW REVIEW MULTIPLE-CHOICE QUESTIONS 103 THROUGH 121

G. S Corporations

An S corporation generally pays no corporate income taxes. Instead, it functions as a pass-through entity (much like a partnership) with its items of income, gain, loss, deduction, and credit passed through and directly included in the tax computations of its shareholders. Electing small business corporations are designated as S corporations; all other corporations are referred to as C corporations.

1. **Eligibility** requirements for S corporation status

  a. Must be a domestic corporation.

  b. An S corporation may own any percent of the stock of a C corporation, and 100% of the stock of a qualified subchapter S subsidiary.

    (1) An S corporation cannot file a consolidated return with an affiliated C corporation.

    (2) A *qualified subchapter S subsidiary* (QSSS) is any domestic corporation that qualifies as an S corporation and is 100% owned by an S corporation parent, which elects to treat it as a QSSS. A QSSS is not treated as a separate corporation and all of its assets, liabilities, and items of income, deduction, and credit are treated as belonging to the parent S corporation.

  c. Only **one class of stock** issued and outstanding. A corporation will not be treated as having more than one class of stock solely because of differences in voting rights among the shares of common stock (i.e., both voting and nonvoting common stock may be outstanding).

d. **Shareholders** must be individuals, estates, or trusts created by will (only for a two-year period), voting trusts, an Electing Small Business Trust (ESBT), a Qualified Subchapter S Trust (QSST), or a trust all of which is treated as owned by an individual who is a citizen or resident of the US (i.e., Subpart E trust).

   (1) A QSST and a Subpart E trust may continue to be a shareholder for two years beginning with the date of death of the deemed owner.
   (2) Code Sec. 401(a) qualified retirement plan trusts and Code Sec. 501(c) charitable organizations that are exempt from tax under Code Sec. 501(a) are eligible to be shareholders of an S corporation. The S corporation's items of income and deduction will flow through to the tax-exempt shareholder as unrelated business taxable income (UBIT).

e. No nonresident alien shareholders
f. The number of shareholders is limited to 100.

   (1) Husband and wife (and their estates) are counted as one shareholder.
   (2) Each beneficiary of a voting trust is considered a shareholder.
   (3) If a trust is treated as owned by an individual, that individual (not the trust) is treated as the shareholder.
   (4) All members of a family can elect to be treated as one shareholder. The election may be made by any family member and will remain in effect until terminated. Members of a family include the common ancestor, the lineal descendants of the common ancestor, and the spouses (or former spouses) of the common ancestor and lineal descendants. The common ancestor cannot be more than six generations removed from the youngest generation of shareholders at the time the S election is made.

2. An **election must be filed** anytime in the preceding taxable year or on or before the fifteenth day of the third month of the year for which effective.

   a. All shareholders on date of election, plus any shareholders who held stock during the taxable year but before the date of election, must consent to the election.

      (1) If an election is made on or before the fifteenth day of the third month of taxable year, but either (1) a shareholder who held stock during the taxable year and before the date of election does not consent to the election, or (2) the corporation did not meet the eligibility requirements during the part of the year before the date of election, then the election is treated as made for the following taxable year.
      (2) An election made after the fifteenth day of the third month of the taxable year is treated as made for the following year.

   b. A newly formed corporation's election will be timely if made within two and one-half months of the first day of its taxable year (e.g., a calendar-year corporation formed on April 6, 2015, could make an S corporation election that would be effective for its 2015 calendar year if the election is filed on or before June 20, 2015).
   c. A valid election is effective for all succeeding years until terminated.
   d. The IRS has the authority to waive the effect of an invalid election caused by a corporation's inadvertent failure to qualify as a small business corporation or to obtain required shareholder consents (including elections regarding qualified subchapter S trusts), or both. Additionally, the IRS may treat late-filed subchapter S elections as timely filed if there is reasonable cause justifying the late filing.

3. **LIFO recapture.** A C corporation using LIFO that converts to S status must recapture the excess of the inventory's value using a FIFO cost flow assumption over its LIFO tax basis as of the close of its last tax year as a C corporation.

   a. The LIFO recapture is included in the C corporation's gross income and the tax attributable to its inclusion is payable in four equal installments.
   b. The first installment must be paid by the due date of the tax return for the last C corporation year, with the three remaining installments due by the due dates of the tax returns for the three succeeding taxable years.

4. A corporation making an S election is generally required to **adopt or change to (1) a year ending December 31,** or (2) a fiscal year that is the same as the fiscal year used by shareholders owning more than 50% of the corporation's stock.

   a. An S corporation may use a different fiscal year if a valid business purpose can be established (i.e., natural business year) and IRS permission is received. The business purpose test will be met if an S corporation receives at least 25% of its gross receipts in the last two months of the selected fiscal year, and this 25% test has been satisfied for three consecutive years.

> **EXAMPLE**
>
> An S corporation, on a calendar year, has received at least 25% of its gross receipts during the months of May and June for each of the last three years. The S corporation may be allowed to change to a fiscal year ending June 30.

b. An S corporation that otherwise would be required to adopt or change its tax year (normally to the calendar year) may elect to use a fiscal year if the election does not result in a deferral period longer than three months, or, if less, the deferral period of the year currently in use.

   (1) The "deferral period" is the number of months between the close of the fiscal year elected and the close of the required year (e.g., if an S corporation elects a tax year ending September 30 and a tax year ending December 31 is required, the deferral period of the year ending September 30 is three months).

   (2) An S corporation that elects a tax year other than a required year must make a "required payment" which is in the nature of a refundable, noninterest-bearing deposit that is intended to compensate the government for the revenue lost as a result of tax deferral. The required payment is due on May 15 each year and is recomputed for each subsequent year.

5. An S corporation must **file Form 1120S** by the fifteenth day of the third month following the close of its taxable year (e.g., March 15 for a calendar-year S corporation).

   a. An automatic six-month extension may be obtained by filing Form 7004.

   b. Estimated tax payments must be made if estimated tax liability (e.g., built-in gains tax, excess net passive income tax) is expected to be $500 or more.

6. **Termination** of S corporation status may be caused by

   a. Shareholders owning **more than 50%** of the shares of stock of the corporation consent to **revocation** of the election.

      (1) A revocation made on or before the fifteenth day of the third month of the taxable year is generally effective on the first day of such taxable year.

      (2) A revocation made after the fifteenth day of the third month of the taxable year is generally effective as of the first day of the following taxable year.

      (3) Instead of the dates mentioned above, a revocation may specify an effective date on or after the date on which the revocation is filed.

> **EXAMPLE**
>
> For a calendar-year S corporation, a revocation not specifying a revocation date that is made on or before 3/15/15 is effective as of 1/1/15. A revocation not specifying a revocation date that is made after 3/15/15 is effective as of 1/1/16. If a revocation is filed 3/11/15 and specifies a revocation date of 7/1/15, the corporation ceases to be an S corporation on 7/1/15.

b. The corporation's **failing to satisfy any of the eligibility requirements** listed in 1. Termination is effective on the date an eligibility requirement is failed.

> **EXAMPLE**
>
> A calendar-year S corporation with common stock outstanding issues preferred stock on April 1, 2015. Since its S corporation status terminates on April 1, it must file an S corporation tax return (Form 1120S) for the period January 1 through March 31, and a C corporation tax return (Form 1120) for the period April 1 through December 31, 2015. Both tax returns would be due by March 15, 2016.

c. Passive investment income exceeding 25% of gross receipts for three consecutive taxable years if the corporation has subchapter C earnings and profits at the end of each of those years.

   (1) Subchapter C earnings and profits are earnings and profits accumulated during a taxable year for which the corporation was a C corporation.
   (2) Termination is effective as of the first day of the taxable year beginning after the third consecutive year of passive investment income in excess of 25% of gross receipts.

> **EXAMPLE**
>
> An S corporation with subchapter C earnings and profits had passive investment income in excess of 25% of its gross receipts for its calendar years 2013, 2014, and 2015. Its S corporation status would terminate 1/1/16.

d. Generally once terminated, S corporation status can be reelected only after five non–S corporation years.

   (1) The corporation can request IRS for an earlier reelection.
   (2) IRS may treat an inadvertent termination as if it never occurred.

7. An **S corporation** generally pays no federal income taxes, but may have to pay a tax on its built-in gain, or on its excess passive investment income if certain conditions are met.

   a. The S corporation is treated as a **pass-through entity;** the character of any item of income, expense, gain, loss, or credit is determined at the corporate level, and passes through to shareholders, retaining its identity.
   b. An S corporation must recognize gain on the distribution of appreciated property (other than its own obligations) to its shareholders. Gain is recognized in the same manner as if the property had been sold to the distributee at its FMV.

> **EXAMPLE**
>
> An S corporation distributes property with an FMV of $900 and an adjusted basis of $100 to its sole shareholder. Gain of $800 will be recognized by the corporation. The character of the gain will be determined at the corporate level, and passed through and reported by its shareholder. The shareholder is treated as receiving a $900 distribution, subject to the distribution rules discussed in Section G.11.

   c. Expenses and interest owed to any cash-method shareholder are deductible by an accrual-method S corporation only when paid.

> **EXAMPLE**
>
> An accrual-method calendar-year S corporation accrues $2,000 of salary to a cash-method employee (a 1% shareholder) during 2014, but does not make payment until February 2015. The $2,000 will be deductible by the corporation in 2015, and reported by the shareholder-employee as income in 2015.

   d. An S corporation will not generate any earnings and profits. All items are reflected in adjustments to the basis of shareholders' stock and/or debt.
   e. S corporations must make estimated tax payments for the tax liability attributable to the built-in gains tax, excess passive investment income tax, and the tax due to investment credit recapture.
   f. The provisions of subchapter C apply to an S corporation, except where inconsistent with subchapter S. For example, an S corporation can use Secs. 332 and 337 to liquidate an acquired subsidiary, and can make a Sec. 338 election if otherwise qualified.

8. A **shareholder** of an S corporation must separately take into account (for the shareholder's taxable year in which the taxable year of the S corporation ends) (1) the shareholder's pro rata share of the corporation's items of income (including tax-exempt income), loss, deduction, or credit the separate treatment of which could affect the tax liability of **any** shareholder, plus (2) the shareholder's pro rata share of all remaining items which are netted together into "ordinary income (loss) from trade or business activity."

   a. Some of the **items which must be separately passed through** to retain their identity include

      (1) Net long-term capital gain (loss)
      (2) Net short-term capital gain (loss)
      (3) Net gain (loss) from Sec. 1231 casualty or theft
      (4) Net gain (loss) from other Sec. 1231 transactions
      (5) Tax-exempt interest
      (6) Charitable contributions
      (7) Foreign income taxes
      (8) Depletion
      (9) Investment interest expense
     (10) Dividend, interest, and royalty income
     (11) Net income (loss) from real estate activity
     (12) Net income (loss) from other rental activity
     (13) Sec. 179 expense deduction

   b. All separately stated items plus the ordinary income or loss are allocated on a **per-share, per-day basis** to anyone who was a shareholder during the year. Items are allocated to shareholders' stock (both voting and nonvoting) but not to debt.

      (1) A shareholder who disposes of stock in an S corporation is treated as the shareholder for the day of disposition. A shareholder who dies is treated as the shareholder for the day of the shareholder's death.

EXAMPLE

Alan owned 100% of a calendar-year S corporation's stock on January 1, 2015. Alan sold all his stock to Betty on January 31. Assuming the S corporation had $365,000 of ordinary income for the entire 2015 calendar year, the amount allocated to Alan would be $31,000 (31 days × $1,000 per day), and the amount allocated to Betty would be $334,000 (334 days × $1,000 per day).

---

      (2) The per-share, per-day rule will not apply if

        (a) A shareholder's interest is completely terminated and all affected shareholders consent to allocate items as if the corporation's taxable year consisted of two years, the first of which ends on the date the shareholder's interest was terminated. The closing of the books method applies only to the affected shareholders. *Affected shareholders* include the shareholder whose interest was terminated and shareholders to whom the terminating shareholder transferred shares during the year.

EXAMPLE

Assume in the above example that the S corporation had net income of $40,000 for the month of January. If both Alan and Betty consent, $40,000 would be allocated to Alan, and $325,000 would be allocated to Betty.

        (b) An S corporation's election is terminated on other than the first day of the taxable year, and all shareholders during the S short year and all persons who were shareholders on the first day of the C short year consent to allocate items using the corporation's financial accounting records.

> **EXAMPLE**
>
> Bartec Corporation, with ordinary income of $365,000 for calendar year 2015, had its S status terminated on February 1, 2015, when the Post Partnership became a shareholder. Assuming Bartec's shareholders do not elect to allocate items using Bartec's financial accounting records, the ordinary income for calendar year 2015 of $365,000 would be allocated on a daily basis between Bartec's S short year and its C short year. Thus, the amount of income to be reported on Bartec's S return would be $365,000/365 days (31 days) = $31,000. The remaining $365,000 – $31,000 = $334,000 of ordinary income would be reported on Bartec's C return for 2015.

  (3) The per share, per day rule **cannot** be used if

   (a) There is a sale or exchange of 50% or more of the stock of the corporation during an S termination year. Financial accounting records must be used to allocate items.
   (b) A Sec. 338 election is made. Then the gains and losses resulting from the Sec. 338 election must be reported on a C corporation return.

9. Three sets of rules may limit the amount of S corporation loss that a shareholder can deduct.

  a. A shareholder's allocation of the aggregate **losses and deductions** of an S corporation can be deducted by the shareholder to the extent of the **shareholder's basis for stock plus basis of any debt** owed the shareholder by the corporation [Sec. 1366 (d)]. A shareholder receives basis for the bona fide debt of an S corporation that runs directly to the shareholder. Whether indebtedness is bona fide debt is based on all of the facts and circumstances. A shareholder does not obtain debt basis by merely guaranteeing an S corporation's debt to a third party. However, a shareholder will receive basis for debt when the shareholder makes a payment on an S corporation's debt for which the shareholder has acted as guarantor.

   (1) An excess of loss over combined basis for stock and debt can be carried forward indefinitely and deducted when there is basis to absorb it.

> **EXAMPLE**
>
> An S corporation incurred losses totaling $50,000. Its sole shareholder (who materially participates in the business and is at-risk) had a stock basis of $30,000 and debt with a basis of $15,000. The shareholder's loss deduction is limited to $45,000. The losses first reduce stock basis to zero, then debt basis is reduced to zero. The excess loss of $5,000 can be carried forward and deducted when there is basis to absorb it.

   (2) Once reduced, the basis of debt is later increased (but not above its original basis) by *net undistributed income*.

> **EXAMPLE**
>
> An S corporation incurred a loss of $20,000 for 2014. Its sole shareholder (who materially participates in the business and is at-risk) had a stock basis of $10,000 and debt with a basis of $15,000. The pass-through of the $20,000 loss would first reduce stock basis to zero, and then reduce debt basis to $5,000.
>
>   Assume that for 2015, the same S corporation had ordinary income of $10,000, and made a $4,000 cash distribution to its shareholder during the year. The first $4,000 of basis increase resulting from the pass-through of income would be allocated to stock in order to permit the $4,000 distribution to be nontaxable. The remaining basis increase (net undistributed income of $6,000) would restore debt basis to $11,000 (from $5,000).

  b. The deductibility of S corporation losses is also limited to the amount of the shareholder's **at-risk basis** at the end of the taxable year [Sec. 465].

   (1) A shareholder's amount at-risk includes amounts borrowed and re-loaned to the S corporation if the shareholder is personally liable for repayment of the borrowed amount, or has pledged property not used in the activity as security for the borrowed amount.
   (2) A shareholder's amount at-risk does not include any debt of the S corporation to any person other than the shareholder, even if the shareholder guarantees the debt.

c. The deductibility of S corporation losses may also be subject to the **passive activity loss limitations** [Sec. 469]. Passive activity losses are deductible only to the extent of the shareholder's income from other passive activities (See Module 35).

   (1) Passive activities include (a) any S corporation trade or business in which the shareholder does not materially participate, and (b) any rental activity.

   (2) If a shareholder "actively participates" in a rental activity and owns (together with spouse) at least 10% of the value of an S corporation's stock, up to $25,000 of rental losses may be deductible against earned income and portfolio income.

10. A shareholder's S corporation **stock basis** is **increased** by all income items (including tax-exempt income), plus depletion in excess of the basis of the property subject to depletion; **decreased** by all loss and deduction items, nondeductible expenses not charged to capital, and the shareholder's deduction for depletion on oil and gas wells; and **decreased** by distributions that are excluded from gross income. Stock basis is **adjusted in the following order:**

   a. Increased for all income items
   b. Decreased for distributions that are excluded from gross income
   c. Decreased for nondeductible, noncapital items
   d. Decreased for deductible expenses and losses

EXAMPLE

An S corporation has tax-exempt income of $5,000, and an ordinary loss from business activity of $6,000 for calendar year 2015. Its sole shareholder had a stock basis of $2,000 on January 1, 2015. The $5,000 of tax-exempt income would pass through to the shareholder, increasing the shareholder's stock basis to $7,000, and would permit the pass-through and deduction of the $6,000 of ordinary loss, reducing the shareholder's stock basis to $1,000.

EXAMPLE

An S corporation had an ordinary loss from business activity of $6,000 and made a $7,000 cash distribution to its sole shareholder during calendar year 2015. The sole shareholder had a stock basis of $8,000 on January 1, 2015. The $7,000 cash distribution would be nontaxable and would reduce stock basis to $1,000. As a result, only $1,000 of the $6,000 ordinary loss would be allowable as a deduction to the shareholder for 2015. The remaining $5,000 of ordinary loss would be carried forward and deducted by the shareholder when there is stock or debt basis to absorb it.

---

11. The **treatment of distributions** (Cash + FMV of other property) to shareholders is determined as follows:

   a. Distributions are **nontaxable** to the extent of the Accumulated Adjustments Account (AAA) and are applied to **reduce the AAA and the shareholder's stock basis**.

      (1) The AAA represents the cumulative total of undistributed net income items for S corporation taxable years beginning after 1982.

      (2) If there is more than one distribution during the year, a pro rata portion of each distribution is treated as made from the AAA.

      (3) The AAA can have a negative balance if expenses and losses exceed income.

      (4) No adjustment is made to the AAA for tax-exempt income and related expenses, and Federal taxes attributable to a year in which the corporation was a C corporation. Tax-exempt income and related expenses are reflected in the corporation's Other Adjustments Account (OAA).

      (5) For purposes of determining the treatment of a distribution, the amount in the AAA at the close of any taxable year is determined without regard to any **net negative adjustment** (i.e., the excess of reductions over increases to the AAA for the taxable year) for such taxable year.

   b. Distributions in excess of the AAA are treated as **ordinary dividends** to the extent of the corporation's **accumulated earnings and profits (AEP).** These amounts represent earnings and profits that were accumulated (and never taxed to shareholders) during C corporation taxable years.

   c. Distributions are **next nontaxable** to the extent of **remaining stock basis** and are applied to reduce the OAA and paid-in capital.

   d. Distributions **in excess of stock basis** are treated as **gain** from the sale of stock.

EXAMPLE

A calendar year S corporation had subchapter C accumulated earnings and profits of $10,000 at December 31, 2014. During calendar year 2015, the corporation had net income of $20,000, and distributed $38,000 to its sole shareholder on June 20, 2015. Its shareholder had a stock basis of $15,000 at January 1, 2015.

    The $20,000 of net income passes through and is includible in gross income by the shareholder for 2015. The shareholder's stock basis is increased by the $20,000 of income (to $35,000), as is the AAA which is increased to $20,000. Of the $38,000 distribution, the first $20,000 is nontaxable and (1) reduces stock basis to $15,000, and (2) the AAA to zero; the next $10,000 of distribution is reported as dividend income (no effect on stock basis); while the remaining $8,000 of distribution is nontaxable and reduces stock basis to $7,000.

---

12. Health and accident insurance premiums and other **fringe benefits** paid by an S corporation on behalf of a more than 2% shareholder-employee are deductible by the S corporation as compensation and includible in the shareholder-employee's gross income on Form W-2.

13. An S corporation (that previously was a C corporation) is taxed on its **net recognized built-in gain** if the gain is (1) attributable to an excess of the FMV of its assets over their aggregate adjusted basis as of the beginning of its first taxable year as an S corporation, and (2) is recognized within **ten years** after the effective date of its S corporation election.

   a. This provision generally applies to C corporations that make an S corporation election after December 31, 1986.

   b. For S corporation taxable years beginning in 2012 through 2014, the recognition period is reduced to five years (e.g., the recognition period will end at the beginning of 2014 if the S election was made for the 2009 tax year).

   c. To determine the tax, (1) take the lesser of (a) the net recognized built-in gain for the taxable year, or (b) taxable income determined as if the corporation were a C corporation (except the NOL and dividends-received deductions are not allowed); (2) subtract any NOL and capital loss carry forwards from C corporation years; (3) multiply the resulting amount by the highest corporate tax rate (currently 35%); and (4) subtract any general business credit carryovers from C corporation years and the special fuels tax credit.

   d. Any net recognized built-in gain that escapes the built-in gains tax because of the taxable income limitation is carried forward and is subject to the built-in gains tax to the extent the corporation subsequently has other taxable income (that is not already subject to the built-in gains tax) for any taxable year within the ten-year recognition period.

   e. Recognized built-in gain **does not include** gain from the disposition of an asset if

     (1) The asset was not held by the corporation when its S election became effective (e.g., an asset was purchased after the first day of its S election), or

     (2) The gain is attributable to appreciation that occurred after the S election became effective (e.g., an asset is sold for a gain of $1,000, but $600 of its appreciation occurred after the first day of its S election; the corporation would be taxed on only $400 of gain).

   f. The total amount of net recognized built-in gain that will be taxed to an S corporation is limited to the aggregate net unrealized built-in gain when the S election became effective.

   g. The **built-in gains tax** that is paid by an S corporation is **treated as a loss** sustained by the S corporation during the taxable year. The character of the loss is determined by allocating the loss proportionately among the recognized built-in gains giving rise to such tax.

EXAMPLE

For 2015, an S corporation has taxable income of $100,000, which includes a $40,000 long-term capital gain that is also a recognized built-in gain. Since its recognized built-in gain of $40,000 is less than its taxable income, its built-in gains tax for 2015 is $40,000 × 35% = $14,000. Since the built-in gain was a long-term capital gain, the built-in gains tax paid of $14,000 is treated as a long-term capital loss. As a result, a net long-term capital gain of $26,000 ($40,000 LTCG – $14,000 LTCL) passes through to shareholders for 2015.

EXAMPLE

For 2014, an S corporation has taxable income of $10,000, which includes a $40,000 long-term capital gain that is also a recognized built-in gain. Since its taxable income of $10,000 is less than its recognized built-in gain of $40,000, its built-in gains tax for 2014 is limited to $10,000 × 35% = $3,500. As a result, a net long-term capital gain of $40,000 − $3,500 = $36,500 passes through to shareholders for 2014.

    The remaining $30,000 of untaxed recognized built-in gain would be suspended and carried forward to 2015, where it would again be treated as a recognized built-in gain. If the S corporation has at least $30,000 of taxable income in 2015 that is not already subject to the built-in gains tax, the suspended gain from 2014 will be taxed. As a result, the amount of built-in gains tax paid by the S corporation for 2015 will be $30,000 × 35% = $10,500, and will pass through to shareholders as a long-term capital loss, since the original gain in 2014 was a long-term capital gain.

---

14. If an S corporation has subchapter C accumulated earnings and profits, and its **passive investment income exceeds 25% of gross receipts,** a tax is imposed at the highest corporate rate on the lesser of (1) excess net passive income (ENPI), or (2) taxable income.

    a. $$\text{ENPI} = \left(\begin{array}{c}\text{Net passive} \\ \text{income}\end{array}\right) \times \left(\frac{\text{(Passive investment income} - \text{25\% of Gross receipts)}}{\text{Passive investment income}}\right)$$

    b. **Passive investment income** means gross receipts derived from dividends, interest, royalties, rents, annuities, and gains from the sale or exchange of stock or securities. However, dividends from an affiliated C corporation subsidiary are not treated as passive investment income to the extent the dividends are attributable to the earnings and profits derived from the active conduct of a trade or business by the C corporation.

    c. The tax paid reduces the amount of passive investment income passed through to shareholders.

EXAMPLE

An S corporation has gross receipts of $80,000, of which $50,000 is interest income. Expenses incurred in the production of this passive income total $10,000. The ENPI is $24,000.

$$\text{ENPI} = \left(\$50,000 - \$10,000\right) \times \left(\frac{\$50,000 - (25\% \times \$80,000)}{\$50,000}\right) = \$24,000$$

NOW REVIEW MULTIPLE-CHOICE QUESTIONS 122 THROUGH 151

H. Corporate Reorganizations

Certain exchanges, usually involving the exchange of one corporation's stock for the stock or property of another, result in deferral of gain or loss.

1. There are seven different **types** of reorganizations which generally result in nonrecognition treatment.

    a. Type A—statutory mergers or consolidations

       (1) Merger is one corporation absorbing another by operation of law

       (2) Consolidation is two corporations combining in a new corporation, the former ones dissolving

    b. Type B—the use of solely voting stock of the acquiring corporation (or its parent) to acquire at least 80% of the voting power and 80% of each class of nonvoting stock of the target corporation

(1) No boot can be used by the acquiring corporation to acquire the target's stock
(2) Results in the acquisition of a controlled subsidiary

c. Type C—the use of solely voting stock of the acquiring corporation (or its parent) to acquire substantially all of the target's properties

(1) In determining whether the acquisition is made for solely voting stock, the assumption by the acquiring corporation of a liability of the target corporation, or the fact that the property acquired is subject to a liability is disregarded.
(2) "Substantially all" means at least 90% of the FMV of the target's net assets, and at least 70% of its gross assets.
(3) The target (acquired) corporation must distribute the consideration it receives, as well as all of its other properties, in pursuance of the plan of reorganization.

d. Type D—a transfer by a corporation of part or all of its assets to another if immediately after the transfer the transferor corporation, or its shareholders, control the transferee corporation (i.e., own at least 80% of the voting power and at least 80% of each class of nonvoting stock)

(1) Although it may be acquisitive, this type of reorganization is generally used to divide a corporation.
(2) Generally results in a spin-off, split-off, or split-up

e. Type E—a recapitalization to change the capital structure of a single corporation (e.g., bondholders exchange old bonds for new bonds or stock)
f. Type F—a mere change in identity, form, or place of organization (e.g., name change, change of state of incorporation)
g. Type G—a transfer of assets by an insolvent corporation or pursuant to bankruptcy proceedings, with the result that former creditors often become the owners of the corporation

2. For the reorganization to be tax free, it must meet one of the above definitions and the exchange must be made under a plan of reorganization involving the affected corporations as parties to the reorganization. It generally must satisfy the judicial doctrines of continuity of shareholder interest, business purpose, and continuity of business enterprise.

a. **Continuity of shareholder interest**—The shareholders of the transferor (acquired) corporation must receive stock in the transferee (acquiring) corporation at least equal in value to 40% of the value of all of the transferor's formerly outstanding stock. This requirement does not apply to Type E and Type F reorganizations.
b. **Continuity of business enterprise**—The transferor's historic business must be continued, or a significant portion (e.g., 1/3) of the transferor's historic assets must be used in a business. This requirement does not apply to Type E and Type F reorganizations.

3. **No gain or loss** is generally recognized to a **transferor corporation** on the transfer of its property pursuant to a plan of reorganization.

a. The **transferee corporation's basis for property** received equals the transferor's basis plus gain recognized (if any) to the transferor.
b. Gain is recognized on the distribution to shareholders of any property other than stock or securities of a party to the reorganization (e.g., property the transferor retained and did not transfer to the acquiring corporation), as if such property were sold for its FMV.

4. No gain or loss is recognized by a corporation on the disposition of stock or securities in another corporation that is a party to the reorganization.

a. No gain or loss is generally recognized on the distribution of stock or securities of a controlled subsidiary in a qualifying spin-off, split-off, or split-up. However, the distributing corporation must recognize gain on the distribution of its subsidiary's stock if immediately after the distribution, any person holds a 50% or greater interest in the distributing corporation or a distributed subsidiary that is attributable to stock acquired by purchase during the five-year period ending on date of distribution.
b. Gain is recognized on the distribution of appreciated boot property.

5. If a **shareholder receives boot** in a reorganization, gain is recognized (but not loss).

a. Boot includes the FMV of an excess of principal (i.e., face) amount of securities received over the principal amount of securities surrendered.

EXAMPLE

In a recapitalization, a bondholder exchanges a bond with a face amount and basis of $1,000, for a new bond with a face amount of $1,500 and a fair market value of $1,575. Since an excess face amount of security ($500) has been received, the bondholder's realized gain of $575 will be recognized to the extent of the fair market value of the excess [($500/$1,500) × $1,575] = $525.

---

   b. Recognized gain will be treated as a dividend to the extent of the shareholder's ratable share of earnings and profits of the acquired corporation if the receipt of boot has the effect of the distribution of a dividend.

     (1) Whether the receipt of boot has the effect of a dividend is determined by applying the Sec. 302(b) redemption tests based on the shareholder's stock interest in the acquiring corporation (i.e., as if only stock had been received, and then the boot was used to redeem the stock that was not received).

     (2) The receipt of boot will generally not have the effect of a dividend, and will thus result in capital gain.

6. A shareholder's **basis for stock and securities received** equals the basis of stock and securities surrendered, plus gain recognized, and minus boot received.

EXAMPLE

Pursuant to a merger of Corporation T into Corporation P, Smith exchanged 100 shares of T that he had purchased for $1,000, for 80 shares of P having an FMV of $1,500 and also received $200 cash. Smith's realized gain of $700 is recognized to the extent of the cash received of $200, and is treated as a capital gain. Smith's basis for his P stock is $1,000 ($1,000 + $200 recognized gain – $200 cash received).

---

7. **Carryover of tax attributes**

   a. The tax attributes of the acquired corporation (e.g., NOL carryovers, earnings and profits, accounting methods, etc.) generally carry over to the acquiring corporation in an acquisitive reorganization.

   b. The amount of an **acquired corporation's NOL** carryovers that can be utilized by the acquiring corporation for its first taxable year ending after the date of acquisition is **limited by Sec. 381** to

$$\text{Acquiring corporation's TI before NOL deduction} \times \frac{\text{Days after acquisition date}}{\text{Total days in taxable year}}$$

EXAMPLE

Corporation P (on a calendar year) acquired Corporation T in a statutory merger on October 19, 2014, with the former T shareholders receiving 60% of P's stock. If T had an NOL carryover of $70,000, and P has taxable income (before an NOL deduction) of $91,500, the amount of T's $70,000 NOL carryover that can be deducted by P for 2014 would be limited to

$$\$91,500 \times \frac{73}{365} = \$18,300$$

---

   c. If there is a **more than 50% change in ownership** of a loss corporation, the taxable income for any year of the new loss (or surviving) corporation may be reduced by an NOL carryover from the old loss corporation only to the extent of the value of the old loss corporation's stock on the date of the ownership change multiplied by the "long-term tax-exempt rate" (**Sec. 382 limitation**).

(1) An ownership change has occurred when the percentage of stock owned by an entity's 5% or more shareholders has increased by more than 50 percentage points relative to the lowest percentage owned by such shareholders at any time during the preceding 3-year testing period.

(2) For the year of acquisition, the Sec. 382 limitation amount is available only to the extent allocable to days after the acquisition date.

$$\text{Section 382 limitation} \times \frac{\text{Days after acquisition date}}{\text{Total days in taxable year}}$$

EXAMPLE

If T's former shareholders received only 30% of P's stock in the preceding example, there would be a more than 50 percentage point change in ownership of T Corporation, and T's NOL carryover would be subject to a Sec. 382 limitation. If the FMV of T's stock on October 19, 2014, was $500,000 and the long-term tax-exempt rate were 3%, the Sec. 382 limitation for 2014 would be ($500,000 × 3%) × (73/365 days) = $3,000.

Thus, only $3,000 of T's NOL carryover could be deducted by P for 2014. The remaining $70,000 – $3,000 = $67,000 of T's NOL would be carried forward by P and can be used to offset P's taxable income for 2015 to the extent of the Sec. 382 annual limitation (i.e., $500,000 × 3% = $15,000).

NOW REVIEW MULTIPLE-CHOICE QUESTIONS 152 THROUGH 161

II. COMPARISON OF C CORPORATIONS, S CORPORATIONS, AND PARTNERSHIPS

	C Corporations	**S Corporations**	**Partnerships**
Formation	Generally can be formed tax free. No gain or loss for transferors if requirements of Sec. 351 are satisfied (i.e., transferors of property must own at least 80% of stock immediately after transfer). No gain or loss to corporation when issuing stock. Corporation will have a transferred basis for property received; shareholders will have basis for stock equal to basis of property transferred.	Same as for C corporation.	Generally can be formed tax free. Unlike corporations, there is no 80% control test. Property will have a transferred basis to partnership; partners will have a basis for partnership interest equal to basis of property transferred.
Operation	Separate taxpaying entity. Corporate taxable income taxed at corporate rates. Corporate earnings taxed to shareholders as dividends if distributed.	Pass-through entity. Generally pays no corporate income tax. Income, deduction, loss, and credit items retain their characteristics when passed through to be reported on shareholder returns.	Pass-through entity. Pays no entity level income taxes. Income, deduction, loss, and credit items retain their characteristics when passed through to be reported on partner returns.

	C Corporations	S Corporations	Partnerships
Non-liquidating Distributions			
Effect on owner	Taxable as dividends to shareholders to extent made out current or accumulated E&P. Distributions in excess of E&P treated as a nontaxable reduction of stock basis, and will result in capital gain to the extent in excess of stock basis.	Generally treated as nontaxable return of stock basis, and will result in capital gain to the extent in excess of stock basis. Taxable as dividend income to the extent made out of accumulated E&P from C years.	Generally nontaxable to partners, but gain recognized if money or FMV of securities received by partner exceed the partner's basis for partnership interest.
	Noncash property distributions measured by FMV; property received will have FMV basis to distributee.	Same as for C corporation shareholders.	Noncash property distributions generally measured by partnership's basis for the distributed property; property will generally have a transferred basis to the distributee partner.
Effect on entity	Gain (but not loss) recognized on distributions to shareholders as if corporation had sold property for FMV.	Same as for C corporation.	Generally no gain or loss recognized by partnership unless distribution is disproportionate and Sec. 751 applies.
Liquidating Distributions			
Effect on owner	Shareholder treats distributions as received in exchange for stock, generally resulting in capital gain or loss. Noncash property received will have an FMV basis to distributee.	Same as for C corporation shareholders.	Partner generally recognizes *no* gain or loss on receipt of liquidating distributions unless distribution is disproportionate and Sec. 751 applies. Partner can recognize loss if liquidating distribution consists solely of money, unrealized receivables, or inventory. Noncash property received will generally have a transferred basis, but limited to the partner's basis for the partnership interest.
Effect on entity	Generally gain as well as loss recognized on liquidating distributions of property to shareholders.	Same as for C corporations	Generally no gain or loss is recognized by partnership unless liquidating distribution is disproportionate and Sec. 751 applies.

KEY TERMS

Accumulated adjustments account. An S corporation account that reflects the cumulative total of undistributed net income previously taxed to shareholders. Distributions from the AAA are generally treated as nontaxable and are a return of a shareholder's stock basis.

Accumulated earnings tax. A penalty tax imposed on a corporation (in addition to regular income tax) if it accumulates earnings in excess of reasonable business needs in order to avoid a shareholder tax on dividend distributions. The tax is not self-assessing, and does not apply to personal holding companies.

Affiliated corporations. A parent-subsidiary chain of corporations in which at least 80% of the voting power (and total value) of stock is owned by includable corporations. An affiliated group may elect to file a consolidated tax return.

Controlled group. Two or more corporations owned by the same individuals or entities. Controlled groups include parent-subsidiary corporations, brother-sister corporations, and combined groups. The two or more corporations that make up a controlled group are in the aggregate limited to the tax benefits available to a single corporation.

Dividend. A corporate distribution of property to shareholders on their stock that is made from the corporation's current or accumulated earnings and profits.

Dividends received deduction (DRD). A deduction allowed a corporation for dividends received from other taxable domestic corporations. The percentage used varies according to the percentage of stock owned in the dividend paying corporation. If the stock ownership percentage is less than 20%, the DRD is 70% of the dividends received. If the stock ownership percentage is at least 20% but less than 80%, the DRD is 80% of the dividends received. If the stock ownership percentage is at least 80%, the DRD percentage is 100% (if a consolidated return is not filed).

Organizational expenditures. Include expenses of temporary directors and organizational meetings, state fees for incorporation, and accounting and legal service costs incident to incorporation. A corporation may immediately expense the first $5,000 (subject to phaseout) of organizational expenditures and generally amortize the remainder over a period of 180 months beginning with the month that business begins.

Personal holding company tax. A penalty tax imposed on a personal holding company (in addition to regular income tax) to discourage individuals from placing investment property in a corporation in order to have investment income taxed at lower corporate rates. The tax is self-assessing.

S corporation. A qualifying small business corporation for which an election has been made to be taxed under the provisions of Subchapter S of the IRC. An S corporation generally pays no corporate income tax and is treated as a pass-through entity. An S corporation's items of income, gain, loss, deduction, and credit pass through to shareholders and are reported on the tax returns of its shareholders.

Sec. 1244 stock. Stock issued by a qualifying small business corporation that entitles the original holder to deduct an ordinary loss (rather than a capital loss) if the stock is disposed of at a loss or becomes worthless. The annual ceiling on ordinary loss treatment is $50,000 ($100,000 for married individuals filing jointly).

Multiple-Choice Questions (1–161)

I.A. Transfers to a Controlled Corporation

1. Alan, Baker, and Carr formed Dexter Corporation during 2015. Pursuant to the incorporation agreement, Alan transferred property with an adjusted basis of $30,000 and a fair market value of $45,000 for 450 shares of stock, Baker transferred cash of $35,000 in exchange for 350 shares of stock, and Carr performed services valued at $25,000 in exchange for 250 shares of stock. Assuming the fair market value of Dexter Corporation stock is $100 per share, what is Dexter Corporation's tax basis for the property received from Alan?

a. $0
b. $30,000
c. $45,000
d. $65,000

2. Clark and Hunt organized Jet Corp. with authorized voting common stock of $400,000. Clark contributed $60,000 cash. Both Clark and Hunt transferred other property in exchange for Jet stock as follows:

| | Other property | | |
	Adjusted basis	Fair market value	Percentage of Jet stock acquired
Clark	$50,000	$100,000	40%
Hunt	120,000	240,000	60%

What was Clark's basis in Jet stock?

a. $0
b. $100,000
c. $110,000
d. $160,000

3. Adams, Beck, and Carr organized Flexo Corp. with authorized voting common stock of $100,000. Adams received 10% of the capital stock in payment for the organizational services that he rendered for the benefit of the newly formed corporation. Adams did not contribute property to Flexo and was under no obligation to be paid by Beck or Carr. Beck and Carr transferred property in exchange for stock as follows:

	Adjusted basis	Fair market value	Percentage of Flexo stock acquired
Beck	5,000	20,000	20%
Carr	60,000	70,000	70%

What amount of gain did Carr recognize from this transaction?

a. $40,000
b. $15,000
c. $10,000
d. $0

4. Jones incorporated a sole proprietorship by exchanging all the proprietorship's assets for the stock of Nu Co., a new corporation. To qualify for tax-free incorporation, Jones must be in control of Nu immediately after the exchange. What percentage of Nu's stock must Jones own to qualify as "control" for this purpose?

a. 50.00%
b. 51.00%
c. 66.67%
d. 80.00%

5. Feld, the sole stockholder of Maki Corp., paid $50,000 for Maki's stock in 2009. In 2015, Feld contributed a parcel of land to Maki but was not given any additional stock for this contribution. Feld's basis for the land was $10,000, and its fair market value was $18,000 on the date of the transfer of title. What is Feld's adjusted basis for the Maki stock?

a. $50,000
b. $52,000
c. $60,000
d. $68,000

6. Rela Associates, a partnership, transferred all of its assets, with a basis of $300,000, along with liabilities of $50,000, to a newly formed corporation in return for all of the corporation's stock. The corporation assumed the liabilities. Rela then distributed the corporation's stock to its partners in liquidation. In connection with this incorporation of the partnership, Rela recognizes

a. No gain or loss on the transfer of its assets nor on the assumption of Rela's liabilities by the corporation.
b. Gain on the assumption of Rela's liabilities by the corporation.
c. Gain or loss on the transfer of its assets to the corporation.
d. Gain, but **not** loss, on the transfer of its assets to the corporation.

7. Roberta Warner and Sally Rogers formed the Acme Corporation on October 1, 2015. On the same date Warner paid $75,000 cash to Acme for 750 shares of its common stock. Simultaneously, Rogers received 100 shares of Acme's common stock for services rendered. How much should Rogers include as taxable income for 2015 and what will be the basis of her stock?

	Taxable income	Basis of stock
a.	$0	$0
b.	$0	$10,000
c.	$10,000	$0
d.	$10,000	$10,000

I.B. Sec. 1244 Stock

8. Jackson, a single individual, inherited Bean Corp. common stock from Jackson's parents. Bean is a qualified small business corporation under Code Sec. 1244. The stock cost Jackson's parents $20,000 and had a fair market value of $25,000 at the parents' date of death. During the current year, Bean declared bankruptcy and Jackson was informed that the stock was worthless. What amount may Jackson deduct as an ordinary loss in the current year?

    a. $0
    b. $3,000
    c. $20,000
    d. $25,000

9. Which of the following is **not** a requirement for stock to qualify as Sec. 1244 small business corporation stock?

    a. The stock must be issued to an individual or to a partnership.
    b. The stock was issued for money or property (other than stock and securities).
    c. The stock must be common stock.
    d. The issuer must be a domestic corporation.

10. During the current year, Dinah sold Sec. 1244 small business corporation stock that she owned for a loss of $125,000. Assuming Dinah is married and files a joint income tax return for the current year, what is the character of Dinah's recognized loss from the sale of the stock?

    a. $125,000 capital loss.
    b. $25,000 capital loss; $100,000 ordinary loss.
    c. $75,000 capital loss; $50,000 ordinary loss.
    d. $0 capital loss; $125,000 ordinary loss.

11. Nancy, who is single, formed a corporation during 2009 using a tax-free asset transfer that qualified under Sec. 351. She transferred property having an adjusted basis of $80,000 and a fair market value of $60,000, and in exchange received Sec. 1244 small business corporation stock. During February 2015, Nancy sold all of her stock for $35,000. What is the amount and character of Nancy's recognized loss resulting from the sale of the stock in 2015?

    a. $0 ordinary loss; $45,000 capital loss.
    b. $25,000 ordinary loss; $10,000 capital loss.
    c. $25,000 ordinary loss; $20,000 capital loss.
    d. $45,000 ordinary loss; $0 capital loss.

I.C.1. Filing and Payment of Tax

12. A civil fraud penalty can be imposed on a corporation that underpays tax by

    a. Omitting income as a result of inadequate recordkeeping.
    b. Failing to report income it erroneously considered **not** to be part of corporate profits.
    c. Filing an incomplete return with an appended statement, making clear that the return is incomplete.

    d. Maintaining false records and reporting fictitious transactions to minimize corporate tax liability.

13. Bass Corp., a calendar-year C corporation, made qualifying 2014 estimated tax deposits based on its actual 2013 tax liability. On March 15, 2015, Bass filed a timely automatic extension request for its 2014 corporate income tax return. Estimated tax deposits and the extension payment totaled $7,600. This amount was 95% of the total tax shown on Bass' final 2014 corporate income tax return. Bass paid $400 additional tax on the final 2014 corporate income tax return filed before the extended due date. For the 2014 calendar year, Bass was subject to pay

  I. Interest on the $400 tax payment made in 2015.
  II. A tax delinquency penalty.

    a. I only.
    b. II only.
    c. Both I and II.
    d. Neither I nor II.

14. Edge Corp., a calendar-year C corporation, had a net operating loss and zero tax liability for its 2014 tax year. To avoid the penalty for underpayment of estimated taxes, Edge could compute its first quarter 2015 estimated income tax payment using the

	Annualized income method	Preceding year method
a.	Yes	Yes
b.	Yes	No
c.	No	Yes
d.	No	No

15. A corporation's tax year can be reopened after all statutes of limitations have expired if

  I. The tax return has a 50% nonfraudulent omission from gross income.
  II. The corporation prevails in a determination allowing a deduction in an open tax year that was taken erroneously in a closed tax year.

    a. I only.
    b. II only.
    c. Both I and II.
    d. Neither I nor II.

16. A corporation's penalty for underpaying federal estimated taxes is

    a. Not deductible.
    b. Fully deductible in the year paid.
    c. Fully deductible if reasonable cause can be established for the underpayment.
    d. Partially deductible.

17. Blink Corp., an accrual-basis calendar-year corporation, carried back a net operating loss for the tax year ended December 31, 2014. Blink's gross revenues have been under $500,000 since inception. Blink expects to have profits for the tax year ending December 31, 2015. Which method(s) of estimated tax payment can Blink use for its quarterly payments during the 2015 tax year to avoid underpayment of federal estimated taxes?

I. 100% of the preceding tax year method
II. Annualized income method

a. I only.
b. Both I and II.
c. II only.
d. Neither I nor II.

18. When computing a corporation's income tax expense for estimated income tax purposes, which of the following should be taken into account?

	Corporate tax credits	Alternative minimum tax
a.	No	No
b.	No	Yes
c.	Yes	No
d.	Yes	Yes

19. Finbury Corporation's taxable income for the year ended December 31, 2014, was $2,000,000 on which its tax liability was $680,000. In order for Finbury to escape the estimated tax underpayment penalty for the year ending December 31, 2015, Finbury's 2015 estimated tax payments must equal at least

a. 90% of the 2015 tax liability.
b. 93% of the 2015 tax liability.
c. 100% of the 2015 tax liability.
d. The 2014 tax liability of $680,000.

I.C.2.a. Regular Tax Rates

20. Kisco Corp.'s taxable income for 2015 before taking the dividends received deduction was $70,000. This includes $10,000 in dividends from a 15%-owned taxable domestic corporation. Given the following tax rates, what would Kisco's income tax be before any credits?

Taxable income partial rate table	Tax rate
Up to $50,000	15%
Over $50,000 but not over $75,000	25%

a. $10,000
b. $10,750
c. $12,500
d. $15,750

I.C.2.c. Alternative Minimum Tax (AMT)

21. Green Corp. was incorporated and began business in 2012. In computing its alternative minimum tax for 2013, it determined that it had adjusted current earnings (ACE) of $400,000 and alternative minimum taxable income (prior to the ACE adjustment) of $300,000. For 2014, it had adjusted current earnings of $100,000 and alternative minimum taxable income (prior to the ACE adjustment) of $300,000. What is the amount of Green Corp.'s adjustment for adjusted

current earnings that will be used in calculating its alternative minimum tax for 2014?

a. $75,000
b. $(75,000)
c. $(100,000)
d. $(150,000)

22. Eastern Corp., a calendar-year corporation, was formed during 2013. On January 3, 2014, Eastern placed five-year property in service. The property was depreciated under the general MACRS system. Eastern did not elect to use the straight-line method, and elected not to use bonus depreciation. The following information pertains to Eastern:

Eastern's 2014 taxable income	$300,000
Adjustment for the accelerated depreciation taken on 2014 5-year property	1,000
2014 tax-exempt interest from private activity bonds issued in 2008	5,000

What was Eastern's 2014 alternative minimum taxable income before the adjusted current earnings (ACE) adjustment?

a. $306,000
b. $305,000
c. $304,000
d. $301,000

23. If a corporation's tentative minimum tax exceeds the regular tax, the excess amount is

a. Carried back to the first preceding taxable year.
b. Carried back to the third preceding taxable year.
c. Payable in addition to the regular tax.
d. Subtracted from the regular tax.

24. Rona Corp.'s 2015 alternative minimum taxable income was $200,000. The exempt portion of Rona's 2015 alternative minimum taxable income was

a. $0
b. $12,500
c. $27,500
d. $52,500

25. A corporation's tax preference items that must be taken into account for 2015 alternative minimum tax purposes include

a. Use of the percentage-of-completion method of accounting for long-term contracts.
b. Casualty losses.
c. Tax-exempt interest on private activity bonds issued in 2008.
d. Capital gains.

26. In computing its 2015 alternative minimum tax, a corporation must include as an adjustment

a. The dividends received deduction.
b. The difference between regular tax depreciation and straight-line depreciation over forty years for real property placed in service in 1998.

c. Charitable contributions.
d. Interest expense on investment property.

27. A corporation will **not** be subject to the alternative minimum tax for calendar year 2015 if

    a. The corporation's net assets do not exceed $7.5 million.
    b. The corporation's average annual gross receipts do not exceed $10 million.
    c. The corporation has less than ten shareholders.
    d. 2014 is the corporation's first tax year.

28. Bradbury Corp., a calendar-year corporation, was formed on January 2, 2011, and had gross receipts for its first four taxable years as follows:

Year	Gross receipts
2011	$4,500,000
2012	9,000,000
2013	9,500,000
2014	6,500,000

What is the first taxable year that Bradbury Corp. is **not** **exempt** from the alternative minimum tax (AMT)?

    a. 2012
    b. 2013
    c. 2014
    d. Bradbury is exempt from AMT for its first four taxable years.

I.C.3. Gross Income

29. Which of the following entities must include in gross income 100% of dividends received from unrelated taxable domestic corporations in computing regular taxable income?

	Personal service corporations	Personal holding companies
a.	Yes	Yes
b.	No	No
c.	Yes	No
d.	No	Yes

30. Andi Corp. issued $1,000,000 face amount of bonds in 2005 and established a sinking fund to pay the debt at maturity. The bondholders appointed an independent trustee to invest the sinking fund contributions and to administer the trust. In the current year, the sinking fund earned $60,000 in interest on bank deposits and $8,000 in net long-term capital gains. All of the trust income is accumulated with Andi's periodic contributions so that the aggregate amount will be sufficient to pay the bonds when they mature. What amount of trust income was taxable to Andi for the current year?

    a. $0
    b. $8,000
    c. $60,000
    d. $68,000

31. The following information pertains to treasury stock sold by Lee Corp. to an unrelated broker in 2015:

Proceeds received	$50,000
Cost	30,000
Par value	9,000

What amount of capital gain should Lee recognize in 2015 on the sale of this treasury stock?

    a. $0
    b. $8,000
    c. $20,000
    d. $30,500

32. During the current year, Ral Corp. exchanged 5,000 shares of its own $10 par common stock for land with a fair market value of $75,000. As a result of this exchange, Ral should report in its current year tax return

    a. $25,000 Section 1245 gain.
    b. $25,000 Section 1231 gain.
    c. $25,000 ordinary income.
    d. No gain.

33. Pym, Inc., which had earnings and profits of $100,000, distributed land to Kile Corporation, a shareholder. Pym's adjusted basis for this land was $3,000. The land had a fair market value of $12,000 and was subject to a mortgage liability of $5,000, which was assumed by Kile Corporation. The dividend was declared and paid during March of the current year.

How much of the distribution would be reportable by Kile as a dividend, before the dividends received deduction?

    a. $0
    b. $3,000
    c. $7,000
    d. $12,000

I.C.4.b. Organizational Expenditures

34. Which of the following costs are deductible organizational expenditures?

    a. Professional fees to issue the corporation's stock.
    b. Commissions paid by the corporation to underwriters for stock issue.
    c. Printing costs to issue the corporation's stock.
    d. Expenses of temporary directors meetings.

35. Brown Corp., a calendar-year taxpayer, was organized and actively began operations on July 1, 2015, and incurred the following costs:

Legal fees to obtain corporate charter	$40,000
Commission paid to underwriter	25,000
Temporary directors' meetings	15,000
State incorporation fees	4,400

For 2015, what amount should Brown Corp. deduct for organizational expenses?

    a. $1,980
    b. $2,814

c. $5,940

d. $6,812

36. The costs of organizing a corporation during 2015

    a. May be deducted in full in the year in which these costs are incurred if they do not exceed $5,000.

    b. May be deducted only in the year in which these costs are paid.

    c. May be amortized over a period of 120 months even if these costs are capitalized on the company's books.

    d. Are nondeductible capital expenditures.

37. Silo Corp. was organized on March 1, 2015, began doing business on September 1, 2015, and elected to file its income tax return on a calendar-year basis. The following qualifying organizational expenditures were incurred in organizing the corporation:

July 1, 2015	$3,000
September 3, 2015	5,600

The maximum allowable deduction for organizational expenditures for 2015 is

    a. $600

    b. $3,000

    c. $5,000

    d. $5,080

I.C.4.c.   *Charitable Contributions*

38. During 2015, Jackson Corp. had the following income and expenses:

Gross income from operations	$100,000
Dividend income from taxable domestic 20%-owned corporations	10,000
Operating expenses	35,000
Officers' salaries	20,000
Contributions to qualified charitable organizations	8,000
Net operating loss carryforward from 2014	30,000

What is the amount of Jackson Corp.'s charitable contribution carryover to 2016?

    a. $0

    b. $2,500

    c. $5,500

    d. $6,300

39. In 2015, Cable Corp., a calendar-year C corporation, contributed $80,000 to a qualified charitable organization. Cable's 2015 taxable income before the deduction for charitable contributions was $820,000, after a $40,000 dividends received deduction. Cable also had carryover contributions of $10,000 from the prior year. In 2015, what amount can Cable deduct as charitable contributions?

    a. $90,000

    b. $86,000

    c. $82,000

    d. $80,000

40. Tapper Corp., an accrual-basis calendar-year corporation, was organized on January 2, 2014. During 2014, revenue was exclusively from sales proceeds and interest income. The following information pertains to Tapper:

Taxable income before charitable contributions for the year ended December 31, 2014	$500,000
Tapper's matching contribution to employee-designated qualified universities made during 2014	10,000
Board of Directors' authorized contribution to a qualified charity (authorized December 1, 2014, made February 1, 2015)	30,000

What is the maximum allowable deduction that Tapper may take as a charitable contribution on its tax return for the year ended December 31, 2014?

    a. $0

    b. $10,000

    c. $30,000

    d. $40,000

41. Lyle Corp. is a distributor of pharmaceuticals and sells only to retail drug stores. During the current year, Lyle received unsolicited samples of nonprescription drugs from a manufacturer. Lyle donated these drugs during the current to a qualified exempt organization and deducted their fair market value as a charitable contribution. What should be included as gross income in Lyle's current year return for receipt of these samples?

    a. Fair market value.

    b. Net discounted wholesale price.

    c. $25 nominal value assigned to gifts.

    d. $0.

42. During the current year, Nale Corp. received dividends of $1,000 from a 10%-owned taxable domestic corporation. When Nale computes the maximum allowable deduction for contributions in its current year return, the amount of dividends to be included in the computation of taxable income is

    a. $0

    b. $200

    c. $300

    d. $1,000

43. Gero Corp. had operating income of $160,000, after deducting $10,000 for contributions to State University, but not including dividends of $2,000 received from nonaffiliated taxable domestic corporations.

In computing the maximum allowable deduction for contributions, Gero should apply the percentage limitation to a base amount of

    a. $172,000

    b. $170,400

    c. $170,000

    d. $162,000

44. Norwood Corporation is an accrual-basis taxpayer. For the year ended December 31, 2014, it had book income before tax of $500,000 after deducting a charitable contribution of $100,000. The contribution was authorized by the Board of

Directors in December 2014, but was not actually paid until March 1, 2015. How should Norwood treat this charitable contribution for tax purposes to minimize its 2014 taxable income?

    a. It cannot claim a deduction in 2014, but must apply the payment against 2015 income.
    b. Make an election claiming a deduction for 2014 of $50,000 and carry the remainder over a maximum of five succeeding tax years.
    c. Make an election claiming a deduction for 2014 of $60,000 and carry the remainder over a maximum of five succeeding tax years.
    d. Make an election claiming a 2014 deduction of $100,000.

I.C.4.d. Dividends Received Deduction (DRD)

45. In 2015, Best Corp., an accrual-basis calendar-year C corporation, received $100,000 in dividend income from the common stock that it held in a 15%-owned domestic corporation. The stock was not debt-financed, and was held for over a year. Best recorded the following information for 2015:

Loss from Best's operations	$(10,000)
Dividends received	100,000
Taxable income (before dividends received deduction)	$90,000

Best's dividends received deduction on its 2015 tax return was

    a. $100,000
    b. $80,000
    c. $70,000
    d. $63,000

46. During the current year, Acorn, Inc. had the following items of income and expense:

Sales	$500,000
Cost of sales	250,000
Dividends received	25,000

The dividends were received from a corporation of which Acorn owns 30%. In Acorn's current year corporate income tax return, what amount should be reported as income before special deductions?

    a. $525,000
    b. $505,000
    c. $275,000
    d. $250,000

47. The corporate dividends received deduction

    a. Must exceed the applicable percentage of the recipient shareholder's taxable income.
    b. Is affected by a requirement that the investor corporation must own the investee's stock for a specified minimum holding period.
    c. Is unaffected by the percentage of the investee's stock owned by the investor corporation.
    d. May be claimed by S corporations.

48. For the current year, Ryan Corp. had the following income:

Income from operations	$300,000
Dividends from unrelated taxable domestic corporations less than 20% owned	2,000

Ryan had no portfolio indebtedness. In Ryan's current year taxable income, what amount should be included for the dividends received?

    a. $400
    b. $600
    c. $1,400
    d. $1,600

49. For the current year, Daly Corp. had the following income:

Profit from operations	$100,000
Dividends from 20%-owned taxable domestic corporation	1,000

In Daly's current year taxable income, how much should be included for the dividends received?

    a. $0
    b. $200
    c. $800
    d. $1,000

50. Cava Corp., which has **no** portfolio indebtedness, received the following dividends during the current year:

From a mutual savings bank	$1,500
From a 20%-owned unaffiliated domestic taxable corporation	7,500

How much of these dividends qualifies for the 80% dividends received deduction?

    a. $9,000
    b. $7,500
    c. $1,500
    d. $0

I.C.4.j. Losses

51. During 2015, Stark Corp. reported gross income from operations of $350,000 and operating expenses of $400,000. Stark also received dividend income of $100,000 (not included in gross income from operations) from an investment in a taxable domestic corporation in which it owns 10% of the stock. Additionally, Stark had a net operating loss carryover from 2014 of $30,000. What is the amount of Stark Corp.'s net operating loss for 2015?

    a. $0
    b. $(20,000)
    c. $(30,000)
    d. $(50,000)

52. A C corporation's net capital losses are

    a. Carried forward indefinitely until fully utilized.
    b. Carried back three years and forward five years.

c. Deductible in full from the corporation's ordinary income.

d. Deductible from the corporation's ordinary income only to the extent of $3,000.

53. For the year ended December 31, 2014, Taylor Corp. had a net operating loss of $200,000. Taxable income for the earlier years of corporate existence, computed without reference to the net operating loss, was as follows:

Taxable income	
2009	$5,000
2010	$10,000
2011	$20,000
2012	$30,000
2013	$40,000

If Taylor makes **no** special election to waive a net operating loss carryback period, what amount of net operating loss will be available to Taylor for the year ended December 31, 2015?

a. $200,000
b. $130,000
c. $110,000
d. $95,000

54. When a corporation has an unused net capital loss that is carried back or carried forward to another tax year,

a. It retains its original identity as short-term or long-term.
b. It is treated as a short-term capital loss whether or not it was short-term when sustained.
c. It is treated as a long-term capital loss whether or not it was long-term when sustained.
d. It can be used to offset ordinary income up to the amount of the carryback or carryover.

55. For the year ended December 31, 2015, Haya Corp. had gross business income of $600,000 and expenses of $800,000. Contributions of $5,000 to qualified charities were included in expenses. In addition to the expenses, Haya had a net operating loss carryover of $9,000. What was Haya's net operating loss for 2015?

a. $209,000
b. $204,000
c. $200,000
d. $195,000

56. Dorsett Corporation's income tax return for 2015 shows deductions exceeding gross income by $56,800. Included in the tax return are the following items:

Net operating loss deduction (carryover from 2014)	$15,000
Dividends received deduction	6,800

What is Dorsett's net operating loss for 2015?

a. $56,800
b. $50,000
c. $41,800
d. $35,000

57. Ram Corp.'s operating income for the year ended December 31, 2015, amounted to $100,000. Also in 2015, a machine owned by Ram was completely destroyed in an accident. This machine's adjusted basis immediately before the casualty was $15,000. The machine was not insured and had no salvage value.

In Ram's 2015 tax return, what amount should be deducted for the casualty loss?

a. $5,000
b. $5,400
c. $14,900
d. $15,000

I.C.6.　Reconcile Book and Taxable Income

58. For the year ended December 31, 2015, Kelly Corp. had net income per books of $300,000 before the provision for federal income taxes. Included in the net income were the following items:

Dividend income from a 5%-owned domestic taxable corporation (taxable income limitation does not apply and there is no portfolio indebtedness)	$50,000
Bad debt expense (represents the increase in the allowance for doubtful accounts)	80,000

Assuming no bad debt was written off, what is Kelly's taxable income for the year ended December 31, 2015?

a. $250,000
b. $330,000
c. $345,000
d. $380,000

59. For the year ended December 31, 2015, Maple Corp.'s book income, before federal income tax, was $100,000. Included in this $100,000 were the following:

Provision for state income tax	$1,000
Interest earned on US Treasury Bonds	6,000
Interest expense on bank loan to purchase US Treasury Bonds	2,000

Maple's taxable income for 2015 was

a. $96,000
b. $97,000
c. $100,000
d. $101,000

60. For the current year Dodd Corp. had net income per books of $100,000. Included in the computation of net income were the following items:

Provision for federal income tax	$27,000
Net long-term capital loss	5,000
Keyman life insurance premiums (corporation is beneficiary)	3,000

Dodd's current year taxable income was

a. $127,000
b. $130,000
c. $132,000
d. $135,000

61. For the year ended December 31, 2015, Bard Corp.'s income per accounting records, before federal income taxes, was $450,000 and included the following:

State corporate income tax refunds	$4,000
Life insurance proceeds on officer's death	15,000
Net loss on sale of securities bought for investment in 2013	20,000

Bard's 2015 taxable income was

a. $435,000
b. $451,000
c. $455,000
d. $470,000

62. Dewey Corporation's book income before federal income taxes was $520,000 for the year ended December 31, 2015. Dewey was incorporated during 2015 and began business in June. Organization costs of $257,400 were expensed for financial statement purposes during 2015. For tax purposes these costs are being written off over the minimum allowable period. For the year ended December 31, 2015, Dewey's taxable income was

a. $520,000
b. $747,900
c. $767,390
d. $778,000

63. Bishop Corporation reported taxable income of $700,000 on its federal income tax return for the current year. Selected information for the current year is available from Bishop's records as follows:

Provision for federal income tax per books	$280,000
Depreciation claimed on the tax return	130,000
Depreciation recorded in the books	75,000
Life insurance proceeds on death of corporate officer	100,000

Bishop reported net income per books for the current year of

a. $855,000
b. $595,000
c. $575,000
d. $475,000

64. For the current year, Ajax Corporation had net income per books of $1,200,000. Included in the determination of net income were the following items:

Interest income on municipal bonds	$40,000
Damages received from settlement of patent infringement lawsuit	200,000
Interest paid on loan to purchase municipal bonds	8,000
Provision for federal income tax	524,000

What should Ajax report as its taxable income for the current year?

a. $1,492,000
b. $1,524,000
c. $1,684,000
d. $1,692,000

I.C.6.c. Schedule M-1

65. For its taxable year 2015, Rogers Corp. had net income per books of $80,000, which included municipal bond interest of $5,000, dividend income of $10,000, a deduction for a net capital loss of $6,000, a deduction for business meals of $4,000, and a deduction for federal income taxes of $18,000. What is the amount of income that would be shown on the last line of Schedule M-1 (Reconciliation of Income [Loss] Per Books with Income [Loss] Per Return) of Rogers Corp.'s corporate income tax return for 2015?

a. $90,000
b. $93,000
c. $99,000
d. $101,000

66. For the current taxable year, Starke Corp., an accrual-basis calendar-year corporation, reported book income of $380,000. Included in that amount was $50,000 municipal bond interest income, $170,000 for federal income tax expense, and $2,000 interest expense on the debt incurred to carry the municipal bonds. What amount should Starke's taxable income be as reconciled on Starke's Schedule M-1 of Form 1120, US Corporation Income Tax Return?

a. $330,000
b. $500,000
c. $502,000
d. $550,000

67. Would the following expense items be reported on Schedule M-1 of the corporation income tax return (Form 1120) showing the reconciliation of income per books with income per return?

	Lodging expenses for executive out-of-town travel	Deduction for a net capital loss
a.	Yes	Yes
b.	No	No
c.	Yes	No
d.	No	Yes

68. In the reconciliation of income per books with income per return in Schedule M-1 of Form 1120

a. Only temporary differences are considered.
b. Only permanent differences are considered.
c. Both temporary and permanent differences are considered.
d. Neither temporary nor permanent differences are considered.

69. Media Corp. is an accrual-basis, calendar-year C corporation. Its 2015 reported book income included $6,000 in municipal bond interest income. Its expenses included $1,500 of interest incurred on indebtedness used to carry municipal bonds and $8,000 in advertising expense. What is Media's net M-1 adjustment on its 2015 Form 1120, US Corporation Income Tax Return, to reconcile to its 2015 taxable income?

    a. $(4,500)
    b. $1,500
    c. $3,500
    d. $9,500

I.C.6.d.   Schedule M-2

70. Barbaro Corporation's retained earnings at January 1, 2014, was $600,000. During 2014 Barbaro paid cash dividends of $150,000 and received a federal income tax refund of $26,000 as a result of an IRS audit of Barbaro's 2011 tax return. Barbaro's net income per books for the year ended December 31, 2014, was $274,900 after deducting federal income tax of $183,300. How much should be shown in the reconciliation Schedule M-2, of Form 1120, as Barbaro's retained earnings at December 31, 2014?

    a. $443,600
    b. $600,900
    c. $626,900
    d. $750,900

71. Olex Corporation's books disclosed the following data for the current taxable year:

Retained earnings at beginning of year	$50,000
Net income for year	70,000
Contingency reserve established at end of year	10,000
Cash dividends paid during year	8,000

What amount should appear on the last line of reconciliation Schedule M-2 of Form 1120?

    a. $102,000
    b. $120,000
    c. $128,000
    d. $138,000

I.D.   Affiliated and Controlled Corporations

72. Bank Corp. owns 80% of Shore Corp.'s outstanding capital stock. Shore's capital stock consists of 50,000 shares of common stock issued and outstanding. Shore's 2015 net income was $140,000. During 2015, Shore declared and paid dividends of $60,000. In conformity with generally accepted accounting principles, Bank recorded the following entries in 2015:

	Debit	Credit
Investment in Shore Corp. common stock	$112,000	
Equity in earnings of subsidiary		$112,000
Cash	48,000	
Investment in Shore Corp. common stock		48,000

In its 2015 consolidated tax return, Bank should report dividend revenue of

    a. $48,000
    b. $14,400
    c. $9,600
    d. $0

73. During the current year, Portal Corp. received $100,000 in dividends from Sal Corp., its 80%-owned subsidiary. What net amount of dividend income should Portal include in its current year consolidated tax return?

    a. $100,000
    b. $80,000
    c. $70,000
    d. $0

74. Potter Corp. and Sly Corp. file consolidated tax returns. In January 2014, Potter sold land, with a basis of $60,000 and a fair value of $100,000, to Sly for $100,000. Sly sold the land in June 2015 for $125,000. In its 2015 and 2014 tax returns, what amount of gain should be reported for these transactions in the consolidated return?

	2015	2014
a.	$25,000	$40,000
b.	$25,000	$0
c.	$40,000	$25,000
d.	$65,000	$0

75. When a consolidated return is filed by an affiliated group of includible corporations connected from inception through the requisite stock ownership with a common parent

    a. Intercompany dividends are excludable to the extent of 80%.
    b. Operating losses of one member of the group offset operating profits of other members of the group.
    c. Each of the subsidiaries is entitled to an alternative minimum tax exemption.
    d. Each of the subsidiaries is entitled to an accumulated earnings tax credit.

76. Dana Corp. owns stock in Seco Corp. For Dana and Seco to qualify for the filing of consolidated returns, at least what percentage of Seco's total voting power and total value of stock must be directly owned by Dana?

	Total voting power	Total value of stock
a.	51%	51%
b.	51%	80%
c.	80%	51%
d.	80%	80%

77. Consolidated returns may be filed

    a. Either by parent-subsidiary corporations or by brother-sister corporations.
    b. Only by corporations that formally request advance permission from the IRS.
    c. Only by parent-subsidiary affiliated groups.
    d. Only by corporations that issue their financial statements on a consolidated basis.

78. Parent Corporation and Subsidiary Corporation file consolidated returns on a calendar-year basis. In January 2014, Subsidiary sold land, which it had used in its business, to Parent for $50,000. Immediately before this sale, Subsidiary's basis for the land was $30,000. Parent held the land primarily for sale to customers in the ordinary course of business. In July 2015, Parent sold the land to Adams, an unrelated individual. In determining consolidated taxable income for 2015, how much should Subsidiary take into account as a result of the 2014 sale of the land from Subsidiary to Parent?

a. $0
b. $20,000
c. $30,000
d. $50,000

I.E. Dividends and Distributions

79. At the beginning of the year, Westwind, a C corporation, had a deficit of $45,000 in accumulated earnings and profits. For the current year, Westwind reported earnings and profits of $15,000. Westwind distributed $12,000 during the year. What was the amount of Westwind's accumulated earnings and profits deficit at year-end?

a. $(30,000)
b. $(42,000)
c. $(45,000)
d. $(57,000)

80. At the beginning of the year, Cable, a C corporation, had accumulated earnings and profits of $100,000. Cable reported the following items on its current year tax return:

Taxable income	$50,000
Federal income taxes paid	5,000
Current year charitable contributions in excess of 10% limitation	1,000
Net capital loss for current year	2,000

What is Cable's accumulated earnings and profits at the end of the year?

a. $142,000
b. $145,000
c. $147,000
d. $150,000

81. On January 1, 2015, Locke Corp., an accrual-basis, calendar-year C corporation, had $30,000 in accumulated earnings and profits. For 2015, Locke had current earnings and profits of $20,000 and made two $40,000 cash distributions to its shareholders, one in April and one in September of 2015. What amount of the 2015 distributions is classified as dividend income to Locke's shareholders?

a. $0
b. $20,000
c. $50,000
d. $80,000

82. Chicago Corp., a calendar-year C corporation, had accumulated earnings and profits of $100,000 as of January 1, 2014 and had a **deficit** in its current earnings and profits for the entire 2014 tax year in the amount of $140,000. Chicago Corp. distributed $30,000 cash to its shareholders on December 31, 2014. What would be the balance of Chicago Corp.'s accumulated earnings and profits as of January 1, 2015?

a. $0
b. $(30,000)
c. $(40,000)
d. $(70,000)

83. Salon, Inc. distributed cash and personal property to its sole shareholder. Using the following facts, determine the amount of gain that would be recognized by Salon, Inc. as the result of making the distribution to its shareholder?

Item	Amount
Cash	$20,000
Personal property:	
Fair market value	6,000
Adjusted basis	3,000
Liability on property assumed by shareholder	10,000

a. $3,000
b. $4,000
c. $7,000
d. $23,000

84. Kent Corp. is a calendar-year, accrual-basis C corporation. In 2014, Kent made a nonliquidating distribution of property with an adjusted basis of $150,000 and a fair market value of $200,000 to Reed, its sole shareholder. The following information pertains to Kent:

Reed's basis in Kent stock at January 1, 2014	$500,000
Accumulated earnings and profits at January 1, 2014	125,000
Current earnings and profits for 2014	60,000

What was taxable as dividend income to Reed for 2014?

a. $60,000
b. $150,000
c. $185,000
d. $200,000

85. Ridge Corp., a calendar-year C corporation, made a nonliquidating cash distribution to its shareholders of $1,000,000 with respect to its stock. At that time, Ridge's current and accumulated earnings and profits totaled $750,000 and its total paid-in capital for tax purposes was $10,000,000. Ridge had no corporate shareholders. Ridge's cash distribution

I. Was taxable as $750,000 of dividend income to its shareholders.
II. Reduced its shareholders' adjusted bases in Ridge stock by $250,000.

a. I only.
b. II only.
c. Both I and II.
d. Neither I nor II.

86. Tour Corp., which had earnings and profits of $400,000, made a nonliquidating distribution of property to its shareholders during the current year. This property, which had an adjusted basis of $30,000 and a fair market value of $20,000 at date of distribution, did not constitute assets used in the active conduct of Tour's business. How much loss did Tour recognize on this distribution?

a. $30,000
b. $20,000
c. $10,000
d. $0

87. On January 1, 2015, Kee Corp., a C corporation, had a $50,000 deficit in earnings and profits. For 2015 Kee had current earnings and profits of $10,000 and made a $30,000 cash distribution to its stockholders. What amount of the distribution is taxable as dividend income to Kee's stockholders?

a. $30,000
b. $20,000
c. $10,000
d. $0

88. Dahl Corp. was organized and commenced operations in 2003. At December 31, 2014, Dahl had accumulated earnings and profits of $9,000 before dividend declaration and distribution. On December 31, 2014, Dahl distributed cash of $9,000 and a vacant parcel of land to Green, Dahl's only stockholder. At the date of distribution, the land had a basis of $5,000 and a fair market value of $40,000. What was Green's taxable dividend income in 2014 from these distributions?

a. $9,000
b. $14,000
c. $44,000
d. $49,000

89. On June 30, 2015, Ral Corporation had retained earnings of $100,000. On that date, it sold a plot of land to a noncorporate shareholder for $50,000. Ral had paid $40,000 for the land in 2006, and it had a fair market value of $80,000 when the shareholder bought it. The amount of dividend income taxable to the shareholder in 2015 is

a. $0
b. $10,000
c. $20,000
d. $30,000

90. On December 1, 2014, Gelt Corporation declared a dividend and distributed to its sole shareholder a parcel of land that was not an inventory asset. On the date of the distribution, the following data were available:

Adjusted basis of land	$6,500
Fair market value of land	14,000
Mortgage on land	5,000

For the year ended December 31, 2014, Gelt had earnings and profits of $30,000 without regard to the dividend distribution. If the mortgage on the land was assumed by the sole shareholder, by how much should the dividend distribution reduce Gelt's earnings and profits?

a. $1,500
b. $6,500
c. $9,000
d. $14,000

I.E.3. Stock Redemptions

91. Two unrelated individuals, Mark and David, each own 50% of the stock of Pike Corporation, which has accumulated earnings and profits of $250,000. Because of his inactivity in the business in recent years, Mark has decided to retire from the business and wishes to sell his stock. Accordingly, Pike will distribute cash of $500,000 in redemption of all of the stock owned by Mark. If Mark's adjusted basis for his stock at date of redemption is $300,000, what will be the tax effect of the redemption to Mark?

a. $125,000 dividend.
b. $200,000 dividend.
c. $200,000 capital gain.
d. $250,000 dividend.

92. How does a noncorporate shareholder treat the gain on a redemption of stock that qualifies as a partial liquidation of the distributing corporation?

a. Entirely as capital gain.
b. Entirely as a dividend.
c. Partly as capital gain and partly as a dividend.
d. As a tax-free transaction.

93. In 2015, Kara Corp. incurred the following expenditures in connection with the repurchase of its stock from shareholders to avert a hostile takeover:

Interest on borrowings used to repurchase stock	$100,000
Legal and accounting fees in connection with the repurchase	400,000

The total of the above expenditures deductible in 2015 is

a. $0
b. $100,000
c. $400,000
d. $500,000

I.E.4. Complete Liquidations

94. A corporation was completely liquidated and dissolved during 2015. The filing fees, professional fees, and other expenditures incurred in connection with the liquidation and dissolution are

a. Deductible in full by the dissolved corporation.
b. Deductible by the shareholders and not by the corporation.

c. Treated as capital losses by the corporation.

d. Not deductible either by the corporation or shareholders.

95. What is the usual result to the shareholders of a distribution in complete liquidation of a corporation?

a. No taxable effect.

b. Ordinary gain to the extent of cash received.

c. Ordinary gain or loss.

d. Capital gain or loss.

96. Par Corp. acquired the assets of its wholly owned subsidiary, Sub Corp., under a plan that qualified as a tax-free complete liquidation of Sub. Which of the following of Sub's unused carryovers may be transferred to Par?

	Excess charitable contributions	**Net operating loss**
a.	No	Yes
b.	Yes	No
c.	No	No
d.	Yes	Yes

97. Kappes Corp. distributed marketable securities in a pro rata redemption of its stock in a complete liquidation. These securities, which had been purchased six years ago for $150,000, had a fair market value of $100,000 when distributed. What loss does Kappes recognize as a result of the distribution?

a. $0.

b. $50,000 long-term capital loss.

c. $50,000 Section 1231 loss.

d. $50,000 ordinary loss.

98. When a parent corporation completely liquidates its 80%-owned subsidiary, the parent (as stockholder) will ordinarily

a. Be subject to capital gains tax on 80% of the long-term gain.

b. Be subject to capital gains tax on 100% of the long-term gain.

c. Have to report any gain on liquidation as ordinary income.

d. Not recognize gain or loss on the liquidating distributions.

99. Lark Corp. and its wholly owned subsidiary, Day Corp., both operated on a calendar year. In January 2015, Day adopted a plan of complete liquidation. Two months later, Day paid all of its liabilities and distributed its remaining assets to Lark. These assets consisted of the following:

Cash	$50,000
Land (at cost)	10,000

Fair market value of the land was $30,000. Upon distribution of Day's assets to Lark, all of Day's capital stock was canceled. Lark's basis for the Day stock was $7,000.

Lark's recognized gain in 2015 on receipt of Day's assets in liquidation was

a. $0

b. $50,000

c. $53,000

d. $73,000

100. On June 1, 2015, Green Corp. adopted a plan of complete liquidation. On August 1, 2015, Green distributed to its stockholders installment notes receivable that Green had acquired in connection with the sale of land in 2014. The following information pertains to these notes:

Green's basis	$90,000
Fair market value	162,000
Face amount	185,000

How much gain must Green recognize in 2015 as a result of this distribution?

a. $0

b. $23,000

c. $72,000

d. $95,000

101. Carmela Corporation had the following assets on January 2, 2015, the date on which it adopted a plan of complete liquidation:

	Adjusted basis	**Fair market value**
Land	$75,000	$150,000
Inventory	43,500	66,000
Totals	$118,500	$216,000

The land was sold on June 30, 2015, to an unrelated party at a gain of $75,000. The inventory was sold to various customers during 2015 at an aggregate gain of $22,500. On December 10, 2015, the remaining asset (cash) was distributed to Carmela's stockholders, and the corporation was liquidated. What is Carmela's recognized gain in 2015?

a. $0

b. $22,500

c. $75,000

d. $97,500

102. Mintee Corp., an accrual-basis calendar-year C corporation, had no corporate shareholders when it liquidated during the current year. In cancellation of all their Mintee stock, each Mintee shareholder received a liquidation distribution of $2,000 cash and land with a tax basis of $5,000 and a fair market value of $10,500. Before the distribution, each shareholder's tax basis in Mintee stock was $6,500. What amount of gain should each Mintee shareholder recognize on the liquidating distribution?

a. $0

b. $500

c. $4,000

d. $6,000

I.F. Personal Holding Company and Accumulated Earnings Taxes

103. Edge Corp. met the stock ownership requirements of a personal holding company. What sources of income must Edge consider to determine if the income requirements for a personal holding company have been met?

I. Interest earned on tax-exempt obligations.
II. Dividends received from an unrelated domestic corporation.

    a. I only.
    b. II only.
    c. Both I and II.
    d. Neither I nor II.

104. Kane Corp. is a calendar-year domestic personal holding company. Which deduction(s) must Kane make from its current year taxable income to determine undistributed personal holding company income prior to the dividend-paid deduction?

	Federal income taxes	Net long-term capital gain less related federal income taxes
a.	Yes	Yes
b.	Yes	No
c.	No	Yes
d.	No	No

105. Dart Corp., a calendar-year domestic C corporation, is not a personal holding company. For purposes of the accumulated earnings tax, Dart has accumulated taxable income for 2014. Which step(s) can Dart take to eliminate or reduce any 2014 accumulated earnings tax?

I. Demonstrate that the "reasonable needs" of its business require the retention of all or part of the 2014 accumulated taxable income.
II. Pay dividends by March 15, 2015.

    a. I only.
    b. II only.
    c. Both I and II.
    d. Neither I nor II.

106. The accumulated earnings tax can be imposed

    a. On both partnerships and corporations.
    b. On companies that make distributions in excess of accumulated earnings.
    c. On personal holding companies.
    d. Regardless of the number of stockholders in a corporation.

107. Zero Corp. is an investment company authorized to issue only common stock. During the last half of the current year, Edwards owned 240 of the 1,000 outstanding shares of stock in Zero. Another 560 shares of stock outstanding were owned, 20 shares each, by 28 shareholders who are neither related to each other nor to Edwards. Zero could be a personal holding company if the remaining 200 shares of common stock were owned by

    a. An estate where Edwards is the beneficiary.
    b. Edwards' brother-in-law.
    c. A partnership where Edwards is not a partner.
    d. Edwards' cousin.

108. Arbor Corp. has nine common stockholders. Arbor derives all of its income from investments in stocks and securities, and regularly distributes 51% of its taxable income as dividends to its stockholders. Arbor is a

    a. Regulated investment company.
    b. Personal holding company.
    c. Corporation subject to the accumulated earnings tax.
    d. Corporation subject to tax on income not distributed to stockholders.

109. Kari Corp., a manufacturing company, was organized on January 2, 2014. Its 2014 federal taxable income was $400,000 and its federal income tax was $100,000. What is the maximum amount of accumulated taxable income that may be subject to the accumulated earnings tax for 2014 if Kari takes only the minimum accumulated earnings credit?

    a. $300,000
    b. $150,000
    c. $50,000
    d. $0

110. The following information pertains to Hull, Inc., a personal holding company, for the year ended December 31, 2014:

Undistributed personal holding company income	$100,000
Dividends paid during 2014	20,000
Consent dividends reported in the 2014 individual income tax returns of the holders of Hull's common stock, but **not** paid by Hull to its stockholders	10,000

In computing its 2014 personal holding company tax, what amount should Hull deduct for dividends paid?

    a. $0
    b. $10,000
    c. $20,000
    d. $30,000

111. Benson, a singer, owns 100% of the outstanding capital stock of Lund Corp. Lund contracted with Benson, specifying that Benson was to perform personal services for Magda Productions, Inc., in consideration of which Benson was to receive $50,000 a year from Lund. Lund contracted with Magda, specifying that Benson was to perform personal services for Magda, in consideration of which Magda was to pay Lund $1,000,000 a year. Personal holding company income will be attributable to

    a. Benson only.
    b. Lund only.

c. Magda only.

d. All three contracting parties.

112. The personal holding company tax

a. Qualifies as a tax credit that may be used by partners or stockholders to reduce their individual income taxes.

b. May be imposed on both corporations and partnerships.

c. Should be self-assessed by filing a separate schedule with the regular tax return.

d. May be imposed regardless of the number of equal stockholders in a corporation.

113. The accumulated earnings tax does **not** apply to

a. Corporations that have more than 100 stockholders.

b. Personal holding companies.

c. Corporations filing consolidated returns.

d. Corporations that have more than one class of stock.

114. The personal holding company tax may be imposed

a. As an alternative tax in place of the corporation's regularly computed tax.

b. If more than 50% of the corporation's stock is owned, directly or indirectly, by more than ten stockholders.

c. If at least 60% of the corporation's adjusted ordinary gross income for the taxable year is personal holding company income, and the stock ownership test is satisfied.

d. In conjunction with the accumulated earnings tax.

115. The accumulated earnings tax

a. Should be self-assessed by filing a separate schedule along with the regular tax return.

b. Applies only to closely held corporations.

c. Can be imposed on S corporations that do not regularly distribute their earnings.

d. Cannot be imposed on a corporation that has undistributed earnings and profits of less than $150,000.

116. Kee Holding Corp. has eighty unrelated equal stockholders. For the year ended December 31, 2014, Kee's income comprised the following:

Net rental income	$1,000
Commissions earned on sales of franchises	3,000
Dividends from taxable domestic corporations	90,000

Deductible expenses for 2014 totaled $10,000. Kee paid no dividends for the past three years. Kee's liability for personal holding company tax for 2014 will be based on undistributed personal holding company income of:

a. $12,000

b. $11,000

c. $9,000

d. $0

117. The accumulated earnings tax

a. Depends on a stock ownership test based on the number of stockholders.

b. Can be avoided by sufficient dividend distributions.

c. Is computed by the filing of a separate schedule along with the corporation's regular tax return.

d. Is imposed when the entity is classified as a personal holding company.

118. Where passive investment income is involved, the personal holding company tax may be imposed

a. On both partnerships and corporations.

b. On companies whose gross income arises solely from rentals, if the lessors render no services to the lessees.

c. If more than 50% of the company is owned by five or fewer individuals.

d. On small business investment companies licensed by the Small Business Administration.

119. In determining accumulated taxable income for the purpose of the accumulated earnings tax, which one of the following is allowed as a deduction?

a. Capital loss carryover from prior year.

b. Dividends received deduction.

c. Net operating loss deduction.

d. Net capital loss for current year.

120. The minimum accumulated earnings credit is

a. $150,000 for all corporations.

b. $150,000 for nonservice corporations only.

c. $250,000 for all corporations.

d. $250,000 for nonservice corporations only.

121. Daystar Corp. which is not a mere holding or investment company, derives its income from consulting services. Daystar had accumulated earnings and profits of $45,000 at December 31, 2013. For the year ended December 31, 2014, it had earnings and profits of $115,000 and a dividends-paid deduction of $15,000. It has been determined that $20,000 of the accumulated earnings and profits for 2014 is required for the reasonable needs of the business. How much is the allowable accumulated earnings credit at December 31, 2014?

a. $105,000

b. $205,000

c. $150,000

d. $250,000

I.G.   S Corporations

122. Stahl, an individual, owns 100% of Talon, an S corporation. At the beginning of the year, Stahl's basis in Talon was $65,000. Talon reported the following items from operations during the current year:

Ordinary loss	$10,000
Municipal interest income	6,000
Long-term capital gain	4,000
Short-term capital loss	9,000

What was Stahl's basis in Talon at year-end?

a. $50,000
b. $55,000
c. $56,000
d. $61,000

123. Baker, an individual, owned 100% of Alpha, an S corporation. At the beginning of the year, Baker's basis in Alpha Corp. was $25,000. Alpha realized ordinary income during the year in the amount of $1,000 and a long-term capital loss in the amount of $3,000 for this year. Alpha distributed $30,000 in cash to Baker during the year. What amount of the $30,000 cash distribution is taxable to Baker?

a. $0
b. $4,000
c. $7,000
d. $30,000

124. Lane Inc., an S corporation, pays single coverage health insurance premiums of $4,800 per year and family coverage premiums of $7,200 per year. Mill is a 10% shareholder-employee in Lane. On Mill's behalf, Lane pays Mill's family coverage under the health insurance plan. What amount of insurance premiums is includible in Mill's gross income?

a. $0
b. $720
c. $4,800
d. $7,200

125. Beck Corp. has been a calendar-year S corporation since its inception on January 2, 2009. On January 1, 2014, Lazur and Lyle each owned 50% of the Beck stock, in which their respective tax bases were $12,000 and $9,000. For the year ended December 31, 2014, Beck had $81,000 in ordinary business income and $10,000 in tax-exempt income. Beck made a $51,000 cash distribution to each shareholder on December 31, 2014. What was Lazur's tax basis in Beck after the distribution?

a. $1,500
b. $6,500
c. $52,500
d. $57,500

126. Graphite Corp. has been a calendar-year S corporation since its inception on January 2, 2009. On January 1, 2014, Smith and Tyler each owned 50% of the Graphite stock, in which their respective bases were $12,000 and $9,000. For the year ended December 31, 2014, Graphite had $80,000 in ordinary business income and $6,000 in tax-exempt income. Graphite made a $53,000 cash distribution to each shareholder on December 31, 2014. What total amount of income from Graphite is includible in Smith's 2014 adjusted gross income?

a. $96,000
b. $93,000
c. $43,000
d. $40,000

127. Dart Corp., a calendar-year S corporation, had 60,000 shares of voting common stock and 40,000 shares of nonvoting common stock issued and outstanding. On February 23,

2015, Dart filed a revocation statement with the consent of shareholders holding 30,000 shares of its voting common stock and 10,000 shares of its nonvoting common stock. Dart's S corporation election

a. Did not terminate.
b. Terminated as of January 1, 2015.
c. Terminated on February 23, 2015.
d. Terminates as of January 1, 2016.

128. Which one of the following statements concerning the eligibility requirements for S corporations is **not** correct?

a. An S corporation is permitted to own 90% of the stock of a C corporation.
b. An S corporation is permitted to own 100% of the stock of another S corporation.
c. An S corporation is permitted to be a partner in a partnership.
d. A partnership is permitted to be a shareholder of an S corporation.

129. Dart Corp., a calendar-year corporation, was formed in 2004 and made an S corporation election in 2006 that is still in effect. Its books and records for 2014 reflect the following information:

Accumulated earnings and profits at 1/1/14	$90,000
Accumulated adjustments account at 1/1/14	50,000
Ordinary income for 2014	200,000

Dart Corp. is solely owned by Robert, whose basis in Dart's stock was $100,000 on January 1, 2014. During 2014, Dart distributed $310,000 to Robert. What is the amount of the $310,000 distribution that Robert must report as dividend income for 2014 assuming no special elections were made with regard to the distribution?

a. $0
b. $60,000
c. $90,000
d. $140,000

130. Village Corp., a calendar-year corporation, began business in 2007. Village made a valid S Corporation election on September 5, 2014, with the unanimous consent of its shareholders. The eligibility requirements for S status continued to be met throughout 2014. On what date did Village's S status become effective?

a. January 1, 2014.
b. January 1, 2015.
c. September 5, 2014.
d. September 5, 2015.

131. A shareholder's basis in the stock of an S corporation is increased by the shareholder's pro rata share of income from

	Tax-exempt interest	Taxable interest
a.	No	No
b.	No	Yes
c.	Yes	No
d.	Yes	Yes

132. Zinco Corp. was a calendar-year S corporation. Zinco's S status terminated on April 1, 2015, when Case Corp. became a shareholder. During 2015 (365-day calendar year), Zinco had nonseparately computed income of $310,250. If no election is made by Zinco, what amount of the income, if any, should be allocated to the S short year for 2015?

a. $78,200
b. $77,350
c. $76,500
d. $0

133. Bristol Corp. was formed as a C corporation on January 1, 2003, and elected S corporation status on January 1, 2012. At the time of the election, Bristol had accumulated C corporation earnings and profits that have not been distributed. Bristol has had the same 25 shareholders throughout its existence. In 2015 Bristol's S election will terminate if it

a. Increases the number of shareholders to one hundred.
b. Adds a decedent's estate as a shareholder to the existing shareholders.
c. Takes a charitable contribution deduction.
d. Has passive investment income exceeding 90% of gross receipts in each of the three consecutive years ending December 31, 2014.

134. As of January 1, 2015, Kane owned all the 100 issued shares of Manning Corp., a calendar-year S corporation. On the 40th day of 2015, Kane sold 25 of the Manning shares to Rodgers. For the year ended December 31, 2015 (a 365-day calendar year), Manning had $73,000 in nonseparately stated income and made no distributions to its shareholders. What amount of nonseparately stated income from Manning should be reported on Kane's 2015 tax return?

a. $56,900
b. $56,750
c. $54,750
d. $48,750

135. On February 10, 2015, Ace Corp., a calendar-year corporation, elected S corporation status and all shareholders consented to the election. There was no change in shareholders in 2015. Ace met all eligibility requirements for S status during the pre-election portion of the year. What is the earliest date on which Ace can be recognized as an S corporation?

a. February 10, 2014.
b. February 10, 2015.
c. January 1, 2015.
d. January 1, 2016.

136. An S corporation has 30,000 shares of voting common stock and 20,000 shares of nonvoting common stock issued and outstanding. The S election can be revoked voluntarily with the consent of the shareholders holding, on the day of the revocation,

	Shares of voting stock	Shares of nonvoting stock
a.	0	20,000
b.	7,500	5,000
c.	10,000	16,000
d.	20,000	0

137. The Haas Corp., a calendar-year S corporation, has two equal shareholders. For the current year, Haas had income of $60,000, which included $50,000 from operations and $10,000 from investment interest income. There were no other transactions that year. As a result, each shareholder's basis in the stock of Haas will increase by

a. $50,000
b. $30,000
c. $25,000
d. $0

138. Which of the following conditions will prevent a corporation from qualifying as an S Corporation?

a. The corporation owns 100% of the stock of a C corporation.
b. The corporation is a partner in a partnership.
c. 30% of the corporation's stock is held by a voting trust.
d. The corporation has common voting stock and preferred nonvoting stock outstanding.

139. If an S corporation has no accumulated earnings and profits, the amount distributed to a shareholder

a. Must be returned to the S corporation.
b. Increases the shareholder's basis for the stock.
c. Decreases the shareholder's basis for the stock.
d. Has no effect on the shareholder's basis for the stock.

140. A corporation that has been an S corporation from its inception may

	Have both passive and non passive income	Be owned by a bankruptcy estate
a.	No	Yes
b.	Yes	No
c.	No	No
d.	Yes	Yes

141. Bern Corp., an S corporation, had an ordinary loss of $36,500 for the year ended December 31, 2015. At January 1, 2015, Meyer owned 50% of Bern's stock. Meyer held the stock for forty days in 2015 before selling the entire 50% interest to an unrelated third party. Meyer's basis for the stock was $10,000. Meyer was a full-time employee of Bern until the stock was sold. Meyer's share of Bern's 2015 loss was

a. $0
b. $2,000
c. $4,000
d. $18,300

142. A calendar-year corporation whose status as an S corporation was terminated during 2014 must wait how many years before making a new S election, in the absence of IRS consent to an earlier election?

a. Can make a new S election for calendar year 2015.
b. Must wait three years.
c. Must wait five years.
d. Must wait six years.

143. Which one of the following will render a corporation ineligible for S corporation status?

   a. One of the stockholders is a decedent's estate.
   b. One of the stockholders is a bankruptcy estate.
   c. The corporation has both voting and nonvoting common stock issued and outstanding.
   d. The corporation has 110 stockholders.

144. With regard to S corporations and their stockholders, the "at risk" rules applicable to losses

   a. Depend on the type of income reported by the S corporation.
   b. Are subject to the elections made by the S corporation's stockholders.
   c. Take into consideration the S corporation's ratio of debt to equity.
   d. Apply at the shareholder level rather than at the corporate level.

145. An S corporation may deduct

   a. Foreign income taxes.
   b. A net Section 1231 loss.
   c. Investment interest expense.
   d. The amortization of organizational expenditures.

146. An S corporation's accumulated adjustments account, which measures the amount of earnings that may be distributed tax-free

   a. Must be adjusted downward for the full amount of federal income taxes attributable to any taxable year in which the corporation was a C corporation.
   b. Must be adjusted upward for the full amount of federal income taxes attributable to any taxable year in which the corporation was a C corporation.
   c. Must be adjusted upward or downward for only the federal income taxes affected by capital gains or losses, respectively, for any taxable year in which the corporation was a C corporation.
   d. Is not adjusted for federal income taxes attributable to a taxable year in which the corporation was a C corporation.

147. If a calendar-year S corporation does not request an automatic six-month extension of time to file its income tax return, the return is due by

   a. January 31.
   b. March 15.
   c. April 15.
   d. June 30.

148. An S corporation is **not** permitted to take a deduction for

   a. Compensation of officers.
   b. Interest paid to individuals who are not stockholders of the S corporation.
   c. Charitable contributions.
   d. Employee benefit programs established for individuals who are not stockholders of the S corporation.

149. An S corporation may

   a. Have both common and preferred stock outstanding.
   b. Have a partnership as a shareholder.
   c. Have a nonresident alien as a shareholder.
   d. Have as many as 100 shareholders.

150. Which of the following is **not** a requirement for a corporation to elect S corporation status (Subchapter S)?

   a. Must be a member of a controlled group.
   b. Must confine stockholders to individuals, estates, and certain qualifying trusts.
   c. Must be a domestic corporation.
   d. Must have only one class of stock.

151. Brooke, Inc., an S corporation, was organized on January 2, 2014, with two equal stockholders who materially participate in the S corporation's business. Each stockholder invested $5,000 in Brooke's capital stock, and each loaned $15,000 to the corporation. Brooke then borrowed $60,000 from a bank for working capital. Brooke sustained an operating loss of $90,000 for the year ended December 31, 2014. How much of this loss can each stockholder claim on his 2014 income tax return?

   a. $5,000
   b. $20,000
   c. $45,000
   d. $50,000

I.H. Corporate Reorganizations

152. Jaxson Corp. has 200,000 shares of voting common stock issued and outstanding. King Corp. has decided to acquire 90% of Jaxson's voting common stock solely in exchange for 50% of its voting common stock and retain Jaxson as a subsidiary after the transaction. Which of the following statements is true?

   a. King must acquire 100% of Jaxson stock for the transaction to be a tax-free reorganization.
   b. The transaction will qualify as a tax-free reorganization.
   c. King must issue at least 60% of its voting common stock for the transaction to qualify as a tax-free reorganization.
   d. Jaxson must surrender assets for the transaction to qualify as a tax-free reorganization.

153. Ace Corp. and Bate Corp. combine in a qualifying reorganization and form Carr Corp., the only surviving corporation. This reorganization is tax-free to the

	Shareholders	Corporations
a.	Yes	Yes
b.	Yes	No
c.	No	Yes
d.	No	No

154. In a type B reorganization, as defined by the Internal Revenue Code, the

I. Stock of the target corporation is acquired solely for the voting stock of either the acquiring corporation or its parent.
II. Acquiring corporation must have control of the target corporation immediately after the acquisition.

    a. I only.
    b. II only.
    c. Both I and II.
    d. Neither I nor II.

155. Pursuant to a plan of corporate reorganization adopted during the current year, Gow exchanged 500 shares of Lad Corp. common stock that he had bought in January 2011 at a cost of $5,000 for 100 shares of Rook Corp. common stock having a fair market value of $6,000. Gow's recognized gain on this exchange was

    a. $1,000 long-term capital gain.
    b. $1,000 short-term capital gain.
    c. $1,000 ordinary income.
    d. $0

156. Which one of the following is a corporate reorganization as defined in the Internal Revenue Code?

    a. Mere change in place of organization of one corporation.
    b. Stock redemption.
    c. Change in depreciation method from accelerated to straight-line.
    d. Change in inventory costing method from FIFO to LIFO.

157. With regard to corporate reorganizations, which one of the following statements is correct?

    a. A mere change in identity, form, or place of organization of one corporation does **not** qualify as a reorganization.
    b. The reorganization provisions **cannot** be used to provide tax-free treatment for corporate transactions.
    c. Securities in corporations **not** parties to a reorganization are always "boot."
    d. A "party to the reorganization" does **not** include the consolidated company.

158. Which one of the following is **not** a corporate reorganization as defined in the Internal Revenue Code?

    a. Stock redemption.
    b. Recapitalization.
    c. Mere change in identity.
    d. Statutory merger.

159. Claudio Corporation and Stellar Corporation both report on a calendar-year basis. Claudio merged into Stellar on June 30, 2014. Claudio had an allowable net operating loss carryover of $270,000. Stellar's taxable income for the year ended December 31, 2014, was $360,000 before consideration of Claudio's net operating loss carryover. Claudio's fair market value before the merger was $1,500,000. The federal long-term tax-exempt rate is 3%. As a result of the merger, Claudio's former shareholders own 10% of Stellar's outstanding stock. How much of Claudio's net operating loss carryover can be used to offset Stellar's 2014 taxable income?

    a. $22,685
    b. $45,000
    c. $180,000
    d. $180,984

160. In 2011, Celia Mueller bought a $1,000 bond issued by Disco Corporation for $1,100. Instead of paying off the bondholders in cash, Disco issued 100 shares of preferred stock in 2015 for each bond outstanding. The preferred stock had a fair market value of $15 per share. What is the recognized gain to be reported by Mueller in 2015?

    a. $0.
    b. $400 dividend.
    c. $400 long-term capital gain.
    d. $500 long-term capital gain.

161. During the current year, in connection with a recapitalization of Oakbrook Corporation, Mary Roberts exchanged 500 shares that cost her $95,000 for 1,000 shares of new stock worth $91,000 and bonds in the principal amount of $10,000 with a fair market value of $10,500. What is the amount of Roberts' recognized gain for the current year?

    a. $0
    b. $6,500
    c. $10,000
    d. $10,500

Multiple-Choice Answers and Explanations

Answers

1. c __ __	29. a __ __	57. d __ __	85. c __ __	113. b __ __	141. b __ __
2. c __ __	30. d __ __	58. c __ __	86. d __ __	114. c __ __	142. c __ __
3. d __ __	31. a __ __	59. c __ __	87. c __ __	115. d __ __	143. d __ __
4. d __ __	32. d __ __	60. d __ __	88. c __ __	116. d __ __	144. d __ __
5. c __ __	33. c __ __	61. c __ __	89. d __ __	117. b __ __	145. d __ __
6. a __ __	34. d __ __	62. c __ __	90. a __ __	118. c __ __	146. d __ __
7. d __ __	35. a __ __	63. c __ __	91. c __ __	119. d __ __	147. b __ __
8. a __ __	36. a __ __	64. d __ __	92. a __ __	120. d __ __	148. c __ __
9. c __ __	37. d __ __	65. d __ __	93. b __ __	121. a __ __	149. d __ __
10. b __ __	38. c __ __	66. c __ __	94. a __ __	122. c __ __	150. a __ __
11. c __ __	39. b __ __	67. d __ __	95. d __ __	123. b __ __	151. b __ __
12. d __ __	40. d __ __	68. c __ __	96. d __ __	124. d __ __	152. b __ __
13. a __ __	41. a __ __	69. a __ __	97. b __ __	125. b __ __	153. a __ __
14. b __ __	42. d __ __	70. d __ __	98. d __ __	126. d __ __	154. c __ __
15. b __ __	43. a __ __	71. a __ __	99. a __ __	127. a __ __	155. d __ __
16. a __ __	44. c __ __	72. d __ __	100. c __ __	128. d __ __	156. a __ __
17. c __ __	45. d __ __	73. d __ __	101. d __ __	129. b __ __	157. c __ __
18. d __ __	46. c __ __	74. d __ __	102. d __ __	130. b __ __	158. a __ __
19. c __ __	47. b __ __	75. b __ __	103. b __ __	131. d __ __	159. a __ __
20. b __ __	48. b __ __	76. d __ __	104. a __ __	132. c __ __	160. a __ __
21. b __ __	49. b __ __	77. c __ __	105. c __ __	133. d __ __	161. b __ __
22. a __ __	50. b __ __	78. b __ __	106. d __ __	134. b __ __	
23. c __ __	51. b __ __	79. b __ __	107. a __ __	135. c __ __	
24. c __ __	52. b __ __	80. a __ __	108. b __ __	136. c __ __	
25. c __ __	53. b __ __	81. c __ __	109. c __ __	137. b __ __	
26. b __ __	54. b __ __	82. c __ __	110. d __ __	138. d __ __	
27. d __ __	55. d __ __	83. c __ __	111. b __ __	139. c __ __	1st: __/161 = __%
28. c __ __	56. c __ __	84. c __ __	112. c __ __	140. d __ __	2nd: __/161 = __%

Explanations

1. (c) The requirement is to determine Dexter Corporation's tax basis for the property received in the incorporation from Alan. Since Alan and Baker are the only transferors of property and they, in the aggregate, own only 800 of the 1,050 shares outstanding immediately after the incorporation, Sec. 351 does not apply to provide nonrecognition treatment for Alan's transfer of property. As a result, Alan is taxed on his realized gain of $15,000, and Dexter Corporation has a cost (i.e., FMV) basis of $45,000 for the transferred property.

2. (c) The requirement is to determine Clark's basis for the Jet Corp. stock received in exchange for a contribution of cash and other property. Generally, no gain or loss is recognized if property is transferred to a corporation solely in exchange for stock, if immediately after the transfer, the transferors of property are in control of the corporation. Since Clark and Hunt both transferred property solely in exchange for stock, and together own all of the corporation's stock, their realized gains on the "other property" transferred are not recognized. As a result, Clark's basis for his Jet stock is equal to the $60,000 of cash plus the $50,000 adjusted basis of other property transferred, or $110,000. Hunt's basis for his Jet stock is equal to the $120,000 adjusted basis of the other property that he transferred.

3. (d) The requirement is to determine Carr's recognized gain on the transfer of appreciated property in connection with the organization of Flexo Corp. No gain or loss is recognized if property is transferred to a corporation solely in exchange for stock, if the transferors of property are in control of the corporation immediately after the exchange. "Control" means that the transferors of property must, in the aggregate, own at least 80% of the corporation's stock immediately after the exchange. Since both Beck and Carr transferred property in exchange for stock, and in the aggregate they own 90% of Flexo's stock immediately after the exchange, the requirements for nonrecognition are met.

4. (d) The requirement is to determine the percentage of Nu's stock that Jones must own to qualify for a tax-free incorporation. No gain or loss is recognized if property is transferred to a corporation solely in exchange for stock and the transferor(s) are in control of the corporation immediately after the exchange. For this purpose, the term "control" means the ownership of at least 80% of the combined voting power of stock entitled to vote, and at least 80% of each class of nonvoting stock.

5. (c) The requirement is to determine Feld's stock basis following the contribution of a parcel of land to his solely owned corporation. When a shareholder makes a contribution to the capital of a corporation, no gain or loss is recognized to the shareholder, the corporation has a transferred (carryover) basis for the property, and the shareholder's original stock basis is increased by the adjusted basis of the additional property contributed. Here, Feld's beginning stock basis of $50,000 is increased by the $10,000 basis for the contributed land, resulting in a stock basis of $60,000.

6. (a) The requirement is to determine whether gain or loss is recognized on the incorporation of Rela Associates (a partnership). No gain or loss is recognized if property is transferred to a corporation solely in exchange for stock, if immediately after the transfer, the transferor is in control of the corporation. For purposes of determining whether consideration other than stock (boot) has been received, the assumption of liabilities by the transferee corporation is not to be treated as the receipt of money or other property by the transferor. Thus, Rela Associates recognizes no gain or loss on the transfer of its assets and liabilities to a newly formed corporation in return for all of the corporation's stock.

Also note that no gain or loss will be recognized by Rela Associates on the distribution of the corporation's stock to its partners in liquidation, and no gain or loss will be recognized by the partners when they receive the corporation's stock in liquidation of their partnership interests.

7. (d) The requirement is to determine the taxable income to Rogers and the basis of her stock. Since services are excluded from the definition of "property," Rogers' transfer does not fall under the nonrecognition provision of Sec. 351. Rogers must report $10,000 of compensation income and the basis for the stock is $10,000, the amount reported as income.

8. (a) The requirement is to determine the amount of ordinary loss that Jackson can deduct as a result of the worthlessness of the Bean Corp. stock that he inherited from his parents. Sec. 1244 permits a shareholder to deduct an ordinary loss of up to $50,000 per year ($100,000 if married filing jointly) if qualifying stock is sold, exchanged, or becomes worthless. The qualifying stock must have been issued in exchange for money or other property and must have been issued to the individual or partnership sustaining the loss. Ordinary loss treatment is not available if the shareholder sustaining the loss was **not** the original holder of the stock. As a result, an individual who acquires stock by purchase, gift, or inheritance from another shareholder is not entitled to ordinary loss treatment. Since Jackson inherited the Bean stock from his parents, Jackson does not qualify for ordinary loss treatment and his $25,000 loss will be recognized as a long-term capital loss.

9. (c) The requirement is to determine which statement is **not** a requirement for stock to qualify as Sec. 1244 small business corporation stock. To qualify as Sec. 1244 small business corporation stock, the stock must be issued by a domestic corporation to an individual or partnership in exchange for money or property (other than stock or

securities). Any type of stock can qualify, whether common or preferred, voting or nonvoting.

10. (b) The requirement is to determine the character of Dinah's recognized loss from the sale of Sec. 1244 stock to be reported on her joint income tax return for the current year. Sec. 1244 permits an individual to deduct an ordinary loss on the sale or worthlessness of stock. The amount of ordinary loss deduction is annually limited to $50,000 ($100,000 for a married taxpayer filing a joint return), with any excess loss treated as a capital loss. Since Dinah is married filing a joint return, her ordinary loss is limited to $100,000, with the remaining $25,000 recognized as a capital loss.

11. (c) The requirement is to determine the amount and character of Nancy's recognized loss resulting from the sale of Sec. 1244 stock for $35,000 in 2015. Sec. 1244 permits a single individual to annually deduct up to $50,000 of ordinary loss from the sale or exchange of small business corporation stock. Since Nancy acquired her stock in a tax-free asset transfer under Sec. 351, her stock's basis is $80,000 and the sale of the stock for $35,000 results in a loss of $45,000. However, because the property that Nancy transferred in exchange for the stock had an adjusted basis ($80,000) in excess of its fair market value ($60,000), the stock's basis must be reduced by the excess ($20,000) for purposes of determining the amount that can be treated as an ordinary loss. Thus, the amount of ordinary loss is limited to $60,000 – $35,000 = $25,000, with the remaining loss ($45,000 – $25,000 = $20,000) treated as a capital loss.

12. (d) The requirement is to determine the correct statement concerning the imposition of a civil fraud penalty on a corporation. If part of a tax underpayment is the result of fraud, a fraud penalty equal to 75% of the portion of the underpayment attributable to fraud will be assessed. Fraud differs from simple, honest mistakes and negligence. Fraud involves a taxpayer's actual, deliberate, or intentional wrongdoing with the specific purpose to evade a tax believed to be owing. Examples of conduct from which fraud may be inferred include keeping a double set of books; making false entries or alterations, false invoices or documents; destroying books or records; and, concealing assets or covering up sources of income. Answers (a), (b), and (c) are incorrect because omitting income as a result of inadequate recordkeeping, erroneously failing to report income, and filing an incomplete return with a statement attached making clear that the return is incomplete, do not constitute deliberate actions with the specific intent of evading tax.

13. (a) The requirement is to determine whether Bass Corp. has to pay interest on the $400 tax payment made in 2015 and/or a tax delinquency penalty. A corporation is generally required to make estimated tax payments and to pay all of its remaining tax liability on or before the original due date of its tax return. Filing for an extension of time to file the tax return does not extend the time to pay the tax liability. If any amount of tax is not paid by the original due date, interest must be paid from the due date until the tax is paid. Additionally, a failure-to-pay tax delinquency penalty will be owed if the amount of tax paid by the original due date of the return is less than 90% of the tax shown on the return. The failure-to-pay penalty is imposed at a rate of 0.5% per month (or fraction thereof), with a maximum penalty of 25%. The penalty is imposed on the amount of unpaid tax at the beginning of the month for which the penalty is being computed. Bass Corp. is not subject to the failure-to-pay delinquency penalty because it paid in 95% of the total tax shown on its return by the original due date of the return.

14. (b) The requirement is to determine whether Edge Corp. could compute its first quarter 2015 estimated income tax payment using the annualized income method and/or the preceding year method. A corporation generally must pay four installments of estimated tax, each equal to 25% of its required annual payment. A penalty for the underpayment of estimated taxes can be avoided if a corporation's quarterly estimated payments are at least equal to the least of (1) 100% of the tax shown on the current year's tax return, (2) 100% of the tax that would be due by placing the current year's income for specified monthly periods on an annualized basis, or (3) 100% of the tax shown on the corporation's return for the preceding year. However, the preceding year's tax liability cannot be used to determine estimated payments if no tax liability existed in the preceding year or a short-period tax return was filed for the preceding year.

15. (b) The requirement is to determine which statements are correct in regard to the reopening of a tax year after the statute of limitations have expired. The statute of limitations stipulate a time limit for the government's assessment of tax or a taxpayer's claim for refund. The normal period for the statute of limitations is the later of three years after a return is filed, or three years after the due date of the return. A six-year statute of limitations will apply if the gross income omitted from the return exceeds 25% of the gross income reported on the return. If a taxpayer's return was false or fraudulent with the intent to evade tax, or the taxpayer engaged in a willful attempt to evade tax, there is no statute of limitations. If a tax return has a 50% nonfraudulent omission from gross income, there would be a six-year statute of limitations. However, once the six-year period expired, the year could not be reopened. In contrast, a closed year can be reopened if a corporation prevails in a determination allowing a deduction in an open year that the taxpayer erroneously had taken in a closed tax year. This special rule for the reopening of a tax year is intended to prevent the double inclusion of an item of income, or the double allowance of a deduction or credit that would otherwise occur.

16. (a) Even though a corporation's penalty for underpaying federal estimated taxes is in the nature of interest, it is treated as an addition to tax, and as such, the penalty is not deductible.

17. (c) The requirement is to determine which methods of estimated tax payment can be used by Blink Corp. to avoid the penalty for underpayment of federal estimated taxes. Generally, to avoid a penalty for the underpayment of estimated taxes a corporation's quarterly estimated payments must be at least equal to the least of (1) 100% of the tax shown on the current year's tax return, (2) 100% of the tax that would be due by placing income for specified monthly periods on an annualized basis, or (3) 100% of the tax shown on the corporation's return for the preceding year, provided the

preceding year showed a positive tax liability and consisted of twelve months. In this case, Blink cannot base its estimated payments on its preceding year because Blink had a net operating loss for 2014.

18. (d) The requirement is to indicate whether corporate tax credits and the alternative minimum tax must be taken into account for purposes of computing a corporation's estimated income tax payments. A corporation must make estimated tax payments unless its tax liability can reasonably be expected to be less than $500. A corporation's estimated tax is its expected tax liability (including the alternative minimum tax) less its allowable tax credits.

19. (c) The requirement is to determine the minimum estimated tax payments that must be made by Finbury Corporation to avoid the estimated tax underpayment penalty for 2015. Since Finbury is a large corporation (i.e., a corporation with taxable income of $1,000,000 or more in any of its three preceding tax years), its estimated tax payments must be at least equal to 100% of its 2015 tax liability.

20. (b) The requirement is to determine Kisco's income tax before credits given $70,000 of taxable income before a dividends received deduction that included a $10,000 dividend from a 15%-owned taxable domestic corporation. Since the $10,000 dividend would be eligible for a 70% dividends received deduction, Kisco's taxable income would be reduced by $7,000, resulting in taxable income of $63,000. The computation of tax would be

$50,000	×	15%	=	$7,500
$13,000	×	25%	=	3,250
		Tax	=	$10,750

21. (b) The requirement is to determine the adjustment for adjusted current earnings (ACE) that will be used in the computation of Green Corp.'s alternative minimum tax for 2014. The ACE adjustment is equal to 75% of the difference between ACE and pre-ACE alternative minimum taxable income (AMTI). The ACE adjustment can be positive or negative, but a negative ACE adjustment is limited in amount to prior years' net positive ACE adjustments. For 2013, Green had a positive ACE adjustment of ($400,000 – $300,000) × 75% = $75,000. For 2014, Green's ACE is less than its pre-ACE AMTI leading to a negative ACE adjustment of ($100,000 – $300,000) × 75% = $150,000. However, this negative ACE adjustment is allowed only to the extent of $75,000, the amount of Green's net positive adjustment for prior years.

22. (a) The requirement is to determine Eastern's alternative minimum taxable income before the adjusted current earnings (ACE) adjustment. The starting point for computing a corporation's alternative minimum taxable income (AMTI) is its regular taxable income, which is then increased by tax preferences, and increased or decreased by specified adjustments. One tax preference that must be added to a corporation's regular taxable income is the amount of tax-exempt interest from private activity bonds. One adjustment that must be made to convert regular taxable income to

AMTI is the adjustment for depreciation on personal business property placed in service after 1986. For regular tax purposes, Eastern utilized the general MACRS depreciation system and would have used the 200% declining balance method for computing regular tax depreciation on the five-year property placed in service during 2014. However, for AMT purposes, depreciation on five-year property must be computed using the 150% declining balance method. In this case, it means that Eastern's regular tax depreciation exceeded its allowable AMT depreciation by $1,000, and this amount must be added back to regular taxable income to arrive at AMTI. Thus, Eastern's AMTI (before ACE adjustment) is its regular taxable income of $300,000, plus its $5,000 of tax-exempt interest from private activity bonds and $1,000 of depreciation adjustment, or $306,000.

23. (c) The requirement is to determine the correct statement regarding the amount of excess of a corporation's tentative minimum tax over its regular tax. If a corporation's tentative minimum tax exceeds its regular tax, the excess represents the corporation's alternative minimum tax and is payable in addition to its regular tax.

24. (c) The requirement is to determine the exempt portion of Rona Corp.'s alternative minimum taxable income (AMTI). A corporation is allowed an exemption of $40,000 in computing its AMTI. However, the $40,000 exemption is reduced by 25% of the corporation's AMTI in excess of $150,000. Here, the amount of exemption is $40,000 – [($200,000 – $150,000) × 25%] = $27,500.

25. (c) The requirement is to determine which item is a tax preference that must be included in the computation of a corporation's alternative minimum tax (AMT) for 2015. Tax-exempt interest on private activity bonds issued in 2008 is a tax preference item. Answer (a) is incorrect because it is the excess of income under the percentage-of-completion method over the amount reported using the completed-contract method that is a positive adjustment in computing the AMT. Answer (b) is incorrect because a deduction for casualty losses is allowed in the computation of AMT. Answer (d) is incorrect because capital gains are not a preference item in computing the AMT. Note that tax-exempt interest on private activity bonds issued in 2009 and 2010 is not a tax preference item.

26. (b) For real property that was placed in service before January 1, 1999, an AMT adjustment is necessary because for AMT purposes, real property must be depreciated using the straight-line method over a forty-year recovery period, rather than the thirty-nine year or twenty-seven and one-half year recovery period used for regular tax purposes. However, note that this adjustment has been eliminated for real property first placed in service after December 31, 1998. The dividends received deduction, charitable contributions, and investment interest expense are neither adjustments nor tax preference items.

27. (d) The requirement is to determine when a corporation will **not** be subject to the alternative minimum tax (AMT) for 2015. A corporation is exempt from AMT for its first tax year. After the first year, a corporation is exempt from AMT for each year that it passes a gross receipts test. A corporation is exempt for its second year if its gross receipts for the first year did not exceed $5 million. For all subsequent years, a corporation is exempt if its average annual gross receipts for the testing period do not exceed $7.5 million. Exemption from the AMT is not based on asset size nor number of shareholders.

28. (c) A corporation is exempt from the corporate AMT for its first tax year. It is exempt for its second year if its first year's gross receipts were $5 million or less. To be exempt for its third year, the corporation's average gross receipts for the first two years must be $7.5 million or less. To be exempt for the fourth year (and subsequent years), the corporation's average gross receipts for all prior three-year periods also must be $7.5 million or less. Here, Bradbury is exempt for 2013 because its average gross receipts for 2011–2012 were $6.75 million. However, Bradbury loses its exemption for 2014 and all subsequent years because its average gross receipts for 2011–2013 exceed $7.5 million ($7.67 million).

29. (a) The requirement is to indicate whether personal service corporations and personal holding companies must include 100% of dividends received from unrelated taxable domestic corporations in gross income in computing regular taxable income. Since the question concerns **gross income,** not taxable income, no part of the dividend income would be offset by a dividends received deduction. Therefore, both personal service corporations and personal holding companies must include 100% of dividends received from unrelated taxable domestic corporations in gross income.

30. (d) The requirement is to determine the amount of bond sinking fund trust income taxable to Andi Corp. for the current year. Since the trust income will be accumulated and benefit Andi Corp. by reducing the amount of future contributions that Andi must make to the bond sinking fund, all of the trust income, consisting of $60,000 of interest and $8,000 of long-term capital gain, is taxable to Andi Corp.

31. (a) The requirement is to determine the amount of capital gain recognized by Lee Corp. on the sale of its treasury stock. A corporation will never recognize gain or loss on the receipt of money or other property in exchange for its stock, including treasury stock.

32. (d) The requirement is to determine the amount of gain to be recognized by Ral Corp. when it issues its stock in exchange for land. No gain or loss is ever recognized by a corporation on the receipt of money or other property in exchange for its own stock (including treasury stock).

33. (c) The requirement is to determine the amount of dividend reportable by a corporate distributee on a property distribution. The amount of dividend to be reported by a corporate distributee is the FMV of the property less any liability assumed. Kile's dividend would be $12,000, reduced by the liability of $5,000 = $7,000.

34. (d) The requirement is to determine which costs are deductible organizational expenditures. Organizational expenditures include fees for accounting and legal services incident to incorporation (e.g., fees for drafting corporate charter, bylaws, terms of stock certificates), expenses of organizational meetings and of temporary directors meetings, and fees paid to the state of incorporation. However, the costs incurred in issuing and selling stock and securities (e.g., professional fees to issue stock, printing costs, underwriting commissions) do not qualify as organizational expenditures and are not tax deductible.

35. (a) The requirement is to determine the amount that Brown should deduct for organizational expenditures for 2015. A corporation may deduct up to $5,000 of organizational expenditures for the tax year in which the corporation begins business. The $5,000 amount must be reduced by the amount by which organizational expenditures exceed $50,000. Remaining expenditures are deducted ratably over the 180-month period beginning with the month in which the corporation begins business. Brown's qualifying organizational expenditures include the $40,000 of legal fees, $15,000 for temporary directors' meetings, and $4,400 of state incorporation fees, a total of $59,400. The $25,000 of underwriting commissions and other costs of issuing stock are not deductible, and merely reduce paid-in capital. Since Brown began business in July, Brown's deduction for 2015 is $59,400 × 6/180 = $1,980.

36. (a) The requirement is to determine the correct statement regarding the costs of organizing a corporation during 2015. A corporation's organizational expenditures (e.g., legal fees for drafting the corporate charter, bylaws, and terms of original stock certificates, necessary accounting services, expenses of temporary directors, fees paid to the state of incorporation) are incidental to the creation of the corporation. A corporation may deduct up to $5,000 of organizational expenditures for the tax year in which the corporation begins business. The $5,000 amount must be reduced by the amount by which organizational expenditures exceed $50,000. Remaining expenditures are deducted ratably over the 180-month period beginning with the month in which the corporation begins business.

37. (d) The requirement is to determine the maximum allowable deduction for organizational expenditures for 2015. A corporation may deduct up to $5,000 of organizational expenditures for the tax year in which the corporation begins business. The $5,000 amount must be reduced by the amount by which organizational expenditures exceed $50,000. Remaining expenditures are deducted ratably over the 180-month period beginning with the month in which the corporation begins business. Here, since organizational expenditures total $8,600, $5,000 can be deducted for 2015, with the remaining $3,600 deducted ratably over the 180-month period beginning with September (the month in which the corporation began business). Thus, the maximum deduction for 2015 would be $5,000 + ($3,600 × 4/180) = $5,080.

38. (c) The requirement is to determine the amount of Jackson Corp.'s charitable contributions carryover to 2016. A corporation's charitable contributions deduction is limited to 10% of its taxable income computed before the deduction for charitable contributions, the dividends received deduction, the deductions for a NOL carryback and capital loss carryback, and the domestic production activities deduction. Although the

limitation is computed before deducting NOL and capital loss carrybacks, NOL and capital loss carryforwards are deducted in arriving at the contribution base amount. Thus, of the $8,000 given to charitable organizations during 2015, $2,500 can be currently deducted, leaving $5,500 to be carried over to 2016.

Gross income from operations	$100,000
Dividend income	10,000
Operating expenses	(35,000)
Officers' salaries	(20,000)
NOL carryover from 2014	(30,000)
TI before contributions and DRD	$25,000
	× 10%
Contributions deduction for 2015	$2,500

39. (b) The requirement is to determine the amount that Cable Corp. can deduct for charitable contributions for 2015. A corporation's charitable contribution deduction is limited to 10% of its taxable income computed before the charitable contribution and dividends received deductions. Since Cable's taxable income of $820,000 already included a $40,000 dividends received deduction, $40,000 must be added back to arrive at Cable's contribution base of $860,000. Thus, Cable's maximum contribution deduction for 2015 would be limited to $860,000 × 10% = $86,000. Cable would deduct the $80,000 contributed during 2015, plus $6,000 of its $10,000 carryover from 2014. This means that Cable will have a $4,000 contributions carryover from 2014 to 2016.

40. (d) The requirement is to determine the **maximum** charitable contribution deduction that Tapper Corp. may take on its 2014 return. Since Tapper is an accrual method calendar-year corporation, it can deduct contributions actually made during 2014, plus Tapper can elect to deduct any contribution authorized by its board of directors during 2014, so long as the contribution is subsequently made no later than 2 1/2 months after the end of the tax year. Thus, to maximize its deduction for 2014, Tapper can deduct both the $10,000 contribution made during 2014 as well as the $30,000 contribution authorized during 2014 and paid on February 1, 2015. The total ($40,000) is deductible for 2014 since it is less than the limitation amount ($500,000 × 10% = $50,000).

41. (a) The requirement is to determine the amount to be included as gross income in Lyle Corp.'s current year return for the receipt of nonprescription drug samples that were later donated to an exempt organization. When unsolicited samples of items that are normally inventoried and sold in the ordinary course of business are received from a supplier, and later donated as a charitable contribution, the fair market value of the items received must be included in gross income. The taxpayer is then allowed a charitable contribution deduction equal to the fair market value of the items donated.

42. (d) The requirement is to determine the portion of the dividends received of $1,000 that is to be included in taxable income when Nale Corp. computes its maximum allowable deduction for contributions. A corporation's maximum allowable deduction for charitable contributions is limited to 10% of its taxable income before the charitable contributions and dividends received deductions. Thus, Nale must include all $1,000 of dividends in its taxable income for purposes of computing its maximum allowable deduction for contributions.

43. (a) The requirement is to determine the contribution base for purposes of computing Gero Corp.'s charitable contributions deduction. A corporation's contribution base is its taxable income before the charitable contributions deduction, the dividends received deduction, and before deductions for NOL and capital loss carrybacks. Since Gero had operating income of $160,000 after deducting $10,000 of contributions, its contribution base would be $160,000 + $10,000 + $2,000 dividends = $172,000.

44. (c) The requirement is to determine the maximum charitable contribution deduction for 2014. Since Norwood is an accrual-basis calendar-year corporation, it can elect to deduct a contribution authorized by its board of directors during 2014, so long as the contribution is subsequently paid no later than two and one-half months after year-end (i.e., by March 15th). Thus, to maximize its deduction for 2014, Norwood can elect to deduct the $10,000 contribution authorized during 2014 and paid on March 1, 2015, but its deduction is limited to 10% of taxable income before the charitable contribution deduction. The maximum amount deductible for 2014 is

	Book income	$500,000
+	Charitable contribution	100,000
	TI before CC deduction	$600,000
		× 10%
	Maximum CC deduction	$60,000

The remaining $40,000 can be carried over a maximum of five years.

45. (d) The requirement is to determine Best Corp.'s dividends received deduction for the $100,000 of dividends received from an unrelated domestic corporation. Dividends received from less than 20%-owned corporations are generally eligible for a 70% DRD (i.e., 70% × dividend). However, if the corporation's taxable income before the DRD is less than the amount of dividend, the DRD will be limited to 70% of taxable income, unless the full DRD (70% × dividend) creates or increases a net operating loss. Here, since taxable income before the DRD ($90,000) is less than the amount of dividends ($100,000), and the full DRD (70% × $100,000 = $70,000) would not create a NOL, the DRD is limited to 70% × $90,000 = $63,000.

46. (c) The requirement is to determine the amount to be reported as income before special deductions on Acorn's tax return. A corporation's taxable income before special deductions generally includes all income and all deductions except for the dividends received deduction. Thus, Acorn's income before special deductions would include the sales of $500,000 and dividend income of $25,000, less the cost of sales of $250,000, a total of $275,000.

47. (b) The requirement is to determine the correct statement regarding the corporate dividends received deduction (DRD). To qualify for a DRD, the investor corporation must own the

investee's stock for more than forty-five days (ninety days for preferred stock if the dividends received are in arrears for more than one year). Answer (a) is incorrect because the DRD may be limited to the applicable percentage of the investor corporation's taxable income. Answer (c) is incorrect because a 70% DRD applies to dividends from less-than-20%-owned corporations, an 80% DRD applies to dividends from unaffiliated corporations that are at least 20%-owned, while a 100% DRD applies to dividends from corporations that are at least 80%-owned when a consolidated tax return is not filed.

48. (b) The requirement is to determine the amount of dividends to be included in Ryan Corp.'s taxable income. Since the dividends were received from less than 20%-owned taxable domestic corporations, they are eligible for a 70% dividends received deduction. Thus, the amount of dividends to be included in taxable income is $2,000 – (70% × $2,000) = $600.

49. (b) The requirement is to determine the amount of dividends to be included in Daly Corp.'s **taxable income** for the current year. Since the dividends were received from 20%-owned taxable domestic corporations, they are eligible for an 80% dividends received deduction. Thus, the amount of dividends to be included in taxable income is $1,000 – (80% × $1,000) = $200.

50. (b) The requirement is to determine the amount of dividends that qualifies for the 80% dividends received deduction. Only dividends received from taxable domestic unaffiliated corporations that are at least 20%-owned qualify for the 80% dividends received deduction ($7,500). So-called "dividends" paid by mutual savings banks are reported as interest, and are not eligible for the dividends received deduction.

51. (b) The requirement is to determine Stark Corp.'s net operating loss (NOL) for 2015. A NOL carryover from 2014 would **not** be allowed in computing the 2015 NOL. In contrast, a dividends received deduction (DRD) is allowed in computing a NOL since a corporation's DRD is not subject to limitation if it creates or increases a NOL. Stark Corp.'s NOL would be computed as follows:

Gross income from operations	$350,000
Dividend income	100,000
Less operating expenses	(400,000)
TI before DRD	$50,000
DRD (70% × $100,000)	(70,000)
Net operating loss for 2015	$(20,000)

52. (b) The requirement is to determine the proper treatment of a C corporation's net capital losses. A corporation's capital losses can only be used to offset capital gains. If a corporation has a net capital loss, it cannot be currently deducted, but instead must be carried back three years and forward five years as a STCL to offset capital gains in those years.

53. (b) The requirement is to determine the amount of Taylor Corp.'s 2014 net operating loss (NOL) that is available for use in its 2015 return. A net operating loss is generally carried back two years and forward twenty years to offset taxable income in the carryback and carryforward years. Since Taylor Corp. made no election to waive a carryback period, the 2014 NOL would be used to offset Taylor's 2012 and 2013 taxable income in the two carryback years (a total of $70,000) leaving $200,000 – $70,000 = $130,000 to be carried forward as an NOL deduction in its 2015 return.

54. (b) The requirement is to determine the correct statement regarding the carryback or carryforward of an unused net capital loss. A corporation's unused net capital loss is carried back three years and forward for up to five years to offset capital gains in the carryback and carryforward years. An unused net capital loss is always carried back and forward as a short-term capital loss whether or not it was short-term when sustained.

55. (d) The requirement is to determine Haya Corporation's NOL for 2015. A deduction for a net operating loss carryover is not allowed in computing a NOL. Furthermore, a deduction for charitable contributions is generally not allowed, since the charitable contributions deduction is limited to 10% of taxable income before the charitable contributions and dividends received deductions. Thus, Haya's NOL for 2015 would be computed as follows:

Gross income	$600,000
Less expenses	(800,000)
	$(200,000)
Add back contributions included in expenses	5,000
NOL for 2015	$(195,000)

56. (c) The requirement is to determine the NOL for 2015 given that deductions in the tax return exceed gross income by $56,800. In computing the NOL for 2015, the DRD of $6,800 would be fully allowed, but the $15,000 NOL deduction (carryover from 2014) would not be allowed. $56,800 – $15,000 = $41,800.

57. (d) The requirement is to determine the amount of casualty loss deduction available to Ram Corp. due to the complete destruction of its machine. If business property is completely destroyed, the amount of casualty loss deduction is the property's adjusted basis immediately before the casualty. Note that the "$100 floor" and "10% of adjusted gross income" limitations that apply to personal casualty losses, do not apply to business casualty losses.

58. (c) The requirement is to determine Kelly Corp.'s taxable income given net income per books of $300,000, that included $50,000 of dividend income and an $80,000 deduction for bad debt expense. Since the dividends were received from a 5%-owned taxable domestic corporation, they are eligible for a 70% dividends received deduction ($50,000 × 70% = $35,000). Since no bad debts were actually written off and the reserve method cannot be used for tax purposes, the $80,000 of bad debt expense per books is not deductible for tax purposes and must be added back to book income to arrive at taxable income. Kelly's taxable income is $300,000 – $35,000 + $80,000 = $345,000.

59. (c) The requirement is to determine Maple Corp.'s taxable income given book income before federal income

taxes of $100,000. The provision for state income taxes of $1,000 that was deducted per books is also an allowable deduction in computing taxable income. The interest earned on US Treasury Bonds of $6,000 that was included in book income must also be included in computing taxable income. The $2,000 of interest expense on the bank loan to purchase the US Treasury Bonds was deducted per books and is also an allowable deduction in computing taxable income, because the interest income from the obligations is taxable. Since there are no differences between the book and tax treatment of these items, taxable income is the same as book income before federal income taxes, $100,000.

60. (d) The requirement is to determine Dodd Corp.'s taxable income given net income per books of $100,000. The $27,000 provision for federal income tax deducted per books is not deductible in computing taxable income. The $5,000 net capital loss deducted per books is not deductible in computing taxable income because a corporation can only use capital losses to offset capital gains. The life insurance premiums of $3,000 deducted per books are not deductible in computing taxable income because life insurance proceeds are excluded from gross income. Thus, Dodd Corp.'s taxable income is $100,000 + $27,000 + $5,000 + $3,000 = $135,000.

61. (c) The requirement is to determine Bard Corp.'s taxable income given book income of $450,000. No adjustment is necessary for the $4,000 of state corporate income tax refunds since they were included in book income and would also be included in taxable income due to the "tax benefit rule" (i.e., an item of deduction that reduces a taxpayer's income tax for a prior year must be included in gross income if later recovered). The life insurance proceeds of $15,000 must be subtracted from book income because they were included in book income, but would be excluded from taxable income. The net capital loss of $20,000 that was subtracted in computing book income must be added back to book income because a net capital loss is not deductible in computing taxable income. Thus, Bard Corp.'s taxable income would be $450,000 – $15,000 + $20,000 = $455,000.

62. (c) The requirement is to determine Dewey Corporation's taxable income, given that organization costs of $257,400 were deducted as an expense in arriving at book income of $520,000. A corporation may deduct up to $5,000 of organizational expenditures for the tax year in which the corporation begins business. The $5,000 amount must be reduced by the amount by which organizational expenditures exceed $50,000. Remaining expenditures are deducted ratably over the 180-month period beginning with the month in which the corporation begins business. Since Dewey began business in June, the allowable amortization for 2015 would be $257,400 × 7/180 = $10,010. Thus, adding back the $257,400 deduction for organization expense to book income, and subtracting the $10,010 of allowable amortization for tax purposes results in taxable income of $520,000 + $257,400 – $10,010 = $767,390.

63. (c) The requirement is to determine net income per books given TI of $700,000.

Taxable income	$700,000
Provision for federal income tax	– 280,000
Depreciation on tax return	+ 130,000
Depreciation per books	– 75,000
Life insurance proceeds	+ 100,000
Net income per books	$575,000

The provision for federal income tax is not deductible in computing TI but must be deducted per books. The life insurance proceeds are tax exempt, but must be included per books.

64. (d) The requirement is to compute Ajax's taxable income given book income of $1,200,000 and items included in the computation of book income. Book income must be adjusted for the tax-exempt interest (net of related expenses) and the provision for federal income tax:

Book income	$1,200,000
Municipal bond interest	(40,000)
Nondeductible interest expense (to produce tax-exempt interest income)	8,000
Provision for federal income tax	524,000
Taxable income	$1,692,000

The damages received for patent infringement that were included in book income are similarly included in taxable income, so no adjustment is necessary.

65. (d) The requirement is to determine the amount of income to be shown on the last line of Rodgers Corp.'s Schedule M-1 for 2015. Schedule M-1 provides a reconciliation of income reported per books with income reported on the tax return. Generally, items of income and deduction whose book and tax treatment differ, result in Schedule M-1 items. However, since Schedule M-1 reconciles to taxable income before the dividends received and net operating loss deductions, the dividends received deduction will not be a reconciling item on Schedule M-1. In this case, Rodgers Corp.'s $80,000 of book income would be increased by the $18,000 of federal income tax, $6,000 of net capital loss, and 50% of the $4,000 of business meals which were deducted per books, but are not deductible for tax purposes. Book income would be reduced by the $5,000 of municipal bond interest that is tax-exempt.

66. (c) The requirement is to determine Starke Corp.'s taxable income as reconciled on Schedule M-1 of Form 1120. Schedule M-1 provides a reconciliation of a corporation's book income with its taxable income before the dividends received and net operating loss deductions. Starke reported book income of $380,000 that included $50,000 of municipal bond interest income, and deductions for $170,000 of federal income tax expense and $2,000 of interest expense incurred to carry the municipal bonds. Since municipal bond interest is tax-exempt, the $50,000 of interest income must be subtracted from book income, and the $2,000 of interest expense incurred to carry the municipal bonds is not deductible and must be added back to book income. Similarly, the $170,000 of federal income tax expense is not deductible and must be added back

to book income. Thus, Starke's taxable income is $380,000 – $50,000 + $2,000 + $170,000 = $502,000.

67. (d) The requirement is to determine whether lodging expenses for out-of-town travel and the deduction of a net capital loss would be reported on Schedule M-1 of the US corporate income tax return (Form 1120). Schedule M-1 generally provides a reconciliation of a corporation's income per books with the corporation's taxable income before the NOL and dividends received deductions. Since a net capital loss deducted per books would not be deductible for tax purposes, the net capital loss would be added back to book income on Schedule M-1. However, since out-of-town lodging expenses are deductible for both book and tax purposes, the expenses would not appear on Schedule M-1.

68. (c) The reconciliation of income per books with income per return is accomplished on Schedule M-1 of Form 1120. Both temporary differences (e.g., accelerated depreciation on tax return and straight-line on books) and permanent differences (e.g., tax-exempt interest) must be considered to convert book income to taxable income.

69. (a) The requirement is to determine Media Corporation's net M-1 adjustment on its 2015 Form 1120. Generally, items of income and deduction whose book and tax treatment differ result in Schedule M-1 adjustments that reconcile income reported per books with taxable income. Media reported book income that included $6,000 in municipal bond interest income, and deductions that included $1,500 of interest expense incurred on debt to carry the municipal bonds, and $8,000 in advertising expense. Since municipal bond interest is tax-exempt, the $6,000 of interest income must be subtracted from book income. Additionally, since the $1,500 of interest expense to carry the municipal bonds is an expense incurred in the production of exempt income, it is not tax deductible and must be added back to book income. On the other hand, the $8,000 of advertising expense is deductible for book as well as taxable income purposes, and no Schedule M-1 adjustment is necessary. Thus, Media's net Schedule M-1 adjustment to reconcile book income to taxable income is $1,500 – $6,000 = ($4,500).

70. (d) The requirement is to determine the amount to be shown on Schedule M-2 of Form 1120 as Barbaro's retained earnings at December 31, 2014. Beginning with the balance at January 1, 2014, the end of year balance would be computed as follows:

Balance, 1/1/14	$600,000
Net income for year	+ 274,900
Federal income tax refund	+ 26,000
Cash dividends	– 150,000
Balance, 12/31/14	$750,900

71. (a) The requirement is to determine the amount that should appear on the last line of Schedule M-2 of Form 1120. Schedule M-2 is an "Analysis of Unappropriated Retained Earnings Per Books." Its first line is the balance at the beginning of the year and its last line is the balance at the end of the year. The end-of-year balance would be computed as follows:

Retained earnings, beginning	$50,000
Net income for year	+70,000
Contingency reserve	–10,000
Cash dividends	–8,000
Retained earnings, end of year	$102,000

72. (d) The requirement is to determine the amount of dividend revenue to be reported on Bank Corp.'s consolidated tax return for the $48,000 of dividends received from Bank Corp.'s 80%-owned subsidiary, Shore Corp. Instead of filing separate tax returns, an affiliated group of corporations (i.e., corporations connected through 80% or more stock ownership) can elect to file a consolidated tax return. If a consolidated return is filed, dividends received from affiliated group members are eliminated in the consolidation process, and are not reported on the consolidated tax return.

73. (d) The requirement is to determine the amount of net dividend income received from an affiliated corporation that should be included in Portal Corporation's current year consolidated tax return. When dividends are received from an affiliated corporation (i.e., at least 80%-owned subsidiary) during a consolidated return year, the intercompany dividends are eliminated in the consolidation process and are not included in gross income.

74. (d) The requirement is to determine the amount of gain to be reported in the 2015 and 2014 consolidated tax returns. Generally, gains and losses on intercompany transactions during consolidated return years are deferred and reported in subsequent years when a restoration event occurs. Since Potter and Sly filed a consolidated tax return for 2014, Potter's gain on the sale of land to Sly in 2014 is deferred and is reported when Sly sells the land outside of the affiliated group in 2015. Thus, the 2014 consolidated return will report no gain with regard to the land, while the 2015 consolidated return will report the aggregate amount of gain, $125,000 – $60,000 = $65,000.

75. (b) The requirement is to determine the correct statement regarding an affiliated group of includible corporations filing a consolidated return. One of the advantages of filing a consolidated return is that operating losses of one member of the group offset operating profits of other members of the group. Answer (a) is incorrect because intercompany dividends are eliminated in the consolidation process and are excluded from the return. Answers (c) and (d) are incorrect because an affiliated group of includible corporations is also a controlled group and is therefore limited to one alternative minimum tax exemption and one accumulated earnings credit.

76. (d) The requirement is to determine the stock ownership requirement that must be satisfied to enable Dana Corp. to elect to file a consolidated tax return that includes Seco Corp. For Dana and Seco to qualify for filing a consolidated tax return, Dana must directly own stock possessing at least 80% of the total voting power, and at least 80% of the total value of Seco stock.

77. (c) The requirement is to determine the correct statement regarding the filing of consolidated returns. The election to file consolidated returns is limited to affiliated corporations. Affiliated corporations are parent-subsidiary corporations that are connected through stock ownership wherein at least 80% of the combined voting power and value of all stock (except the common parent's) is directly owned by other includible corporations. Answer (a) is incorrect because brother-sister corporations are not affiliated corporations. Answer (b) is incorrect because no advance permission is required. Answer (d) is incorrect because an affiliated group's election to file consolidated returns is independent of its issuing financial statements on a consolidated basis.

78. (b) The requirement is to determine the amount of gain for 2015 that Subsidiary should take into account as a result of the 2014 sale of land to Parent. Since Parent and Subsidiary are filing consolidated tax returns, the $20,000 of gain to Subsidiary in 2014 is not recognized, but instead is deferred and recognized when the land is sold outside the affiliated group in 2015.

79. (b) The requirement is to determine Westwind's accumulated earnings and profits at year-end. Here, Westwind had a beginning deficit of $45,000, had current earnings and profits of $15,000, and distributed $12,000 cash during the year. As a result, Westwind's beginning deficit of $45,000 would be reduced by the $3,000 of current earnings and profits that were not distributed, resulting in a deficit of $42,000 at the end of the year.

80. (a) The requirement is to determine Cable's accumulated earnings and profits (AEP) at the end of the year. Cable's beginning AEP of $100,000 would be increased by its earnings and profits for the current tax year (CEP). The starting point for computing Cable's CEP would be its taxable income of $50,000. Taxable income would be reduced by the $5,000 of federal income taxes paid, and would also be reduced by the $1,000 of current year charitable contributions which would not be allowed as a deduction in computing taxable income because of the 10% of taxable income limitation. Additionally, CEP would be reduced by the current year net capital loss of $2,000 which would not be allowed as a deduction in computing current year taxable income because a corporation cannot deduct a net capital loss. As a result, Cable's CEP is $50,000 – ($5,000 + $1,000 + $2,000) = $42,000, and its AEP at the end of the current year is $100,000 + $42,000 = $142,000.

81. (c) The requirement is to determine the amount of the 2015 distributions classified as dividend income to Locke's shareholders. A corporation's distributions to shareholders on their stock are treated as a dividend to the extent of a corporation's current earnings and profits and/or accumulated earnings and profits. Here, the $80,000 distributed to shareholders would be treated as a dividend to the extent of Locke's current ($20,000) and accumulated ($30,000) earnings and profits, or $50,000.

82. (c) The requirement is to determine the balance of Chicago Corp.'s accumulated earnings and profits (AEP) at January 1, 2015. The AEP beginning balance of $100,000 would be reduced by the 2014 deficit of ($140,000), resulting in a deficit of ($40,000). Since distributions only pay out a corporation's positive AEP, and neither create nor increase a deficit in AEP, the AEP deficit of ($40,000) is not affected by the $30,000 distributed to shareholders.

83. (c) The requirement is to determine the amount of gain recognized by Salon, Inc. as a result of the distribution of property and liability to its sole shareholder. Generally, a corporation must recognize gain when it distributes appreciated property to a shareholder. The gain is measured by treating the corporation as if it had sold the property to the shareholder for its fair market value. However, if there is a liability on the property that is assumed by the shareholder and the amount of liability exceeds the property's fair market value, then the amount of liability is used to measure the gain. Here, Salon's recognized gain would total $10,000 liability – $3,000 basis = $7,000.

84. (c) The requirement is to determine the amount received from Kent Corp. that is taxable as dividend income to Reed for 2014. The term "dividend" means any distribution of property made by a corporation to its shareholders out of its current earnings and profits and/or accumulated earnings and profits. For distributions of property other than cash, the amount of distribution is the property's fair market value reduced by any liabilities that are assumed or liabilities to which the property is subject. In this case, the amount of distribution made by Kent Corp. to Reed is the property's fair market value of $200,000. This $200,000 of distribution is taxable as dividend income to Reed to the extent of Kent Corp.'s current earnings and profits ($60,000) and accumulated earnings and profits ($125,000), a total of $185,000. Note that this answer assumes that the gain that was recognized by Kent Corp. on the distribution ($200,000 FMV – $150,000 adjusted basis = $50,000) has already been included in the amount provided as Kent's current earnings and profits for 2014. This assumption can be made because the item indicates "Current earnings and profits for 2014," not "Current earnings and profits before the distribution." Also, note that the portion of the distribution that is not a dividend ($200,000 – $185,000 = $15,000) is a nontaxable return of Reed's stock basis, and reduces stock basis from $500,000 to $485,000.

85. (c) The requirement is to determine which statements are correct concerning Ridge Corp.'s cash distribution of $1,000,000 to its shareholders with respect to its stock. A corporation's distributions to shareholders on their stock will be taxed as dividend income to the extent of the corporation's current and accumulated earnings and profits. Any distributions in excess of earnings and profits are treated as a nontaxable return of stock basis, with any distributions in excess of a shareholder's stock basis treated as capital gain. Therefore, $750,000 of the distribution to Ridge's shareholders was taxable as a dividend, with the remaining $250,000 treated as a nontaxable return of stock basis.

86. (d) The requirement is to determine the amount of loss recognized by Tour Corporation on the nonliquidating distribution of property to shareholders. Although a gain would be recognized, no loss can be recognized on nonliquidating corporate distributions to shareholders.

87. (c) The requirement is to determine the amount taxable as a dividend to Kee's shareholders for 2015. Corporate distributions of property to shareholders on their stock are taxed as dividends to the extent of accumulated and/or current earnings and profits. Even though a corporation has an accumulated deficit in earnings and profits for prior years ($50,000 in this case), a distribution will nevertheless be taxed as a dividend to the extent of the corporation's earnings and profits for the current taxable year when measured at the end of the year. Thus, the $30,000 distribution will be taxed as a dividend to the extent of the current earnings and profits for 2015 of $10,000.

88. (c) The requirement is to determine the amount of taxable dividend income resulting from Dahl Corp.'s distribution of cash and land to Green. The amount of distribution received by Green equals the amount of cash ($9,000) plus the FMV of the land ($40,000), a total of $49,000. This $49,000 will be taxable as dividend income to Green to the extent that it is paid out of Dahl Corp.'s current and accumulated earnings and profits. Dahl had accumulated earnings and profits of $9,000 before consideration of the dividend declaration and distribution. Since a distributing corporation recognizes gain on the distribution of appreciated property, Dahl must recognize a gain of $40,000 – $5,000 = $35,000 on the distribution of the land. This $35,000 of gain increases Dahl Corp.'s available earnings and profits from $9,000 to $44,000. Thus, Green's $49,000 distribution will be taxed as a dividend to the extent of $44,000.

89. (d) The requirement is to determine the amount of dividend income taxable to the shareholder. If a corporation sells property to a shareholder for less than fair market value, the shareholder generally is considered to have received a constructive dividend to the extent of the difference between the fair market value of the property and the price paid. Thus, the shareholder's dividend income is $80,000 – $50,000 = $30,000.

90. (a) Distributions of property to shareholders reduce earnings and profits (E&P) by the greater of the property's adjusted basis, or its FMV at date of distribution. E&P must also be adjusted by any gain recognized to the distributing corporation, and any liabilities to which the property being distributed is subject. Gelt Corporation would recognize a gain of $7,500 on the distribution (i.e., $14,000 FMV – $6,500 basis). The adjustments to E&P (before tax) would be

	E&P
Gain recognized	$7,500
Distribution of property (FMV)	(14,000)
Distribution of liability	5,000
Net decrease in E&P (before tax)	$(1,500)

91. (c) The requirement is to determine the tax effect of Mark's stock redemption. Since the redemption is a complete redemption of all of Mark's stock ownership, the redemption proceeds of $500,000 qualify for exchange treatment. Thus, Mark will report a capital gain of $500,000 – $300,000 = $200,000.

92. (a) The requirement is to determine how the gain resulting from a stock redemption should be treated by a noncorporate shareholder if the redemption qualifies as a partial liquidation of the distributing corporation. A corporate stock redemption is treated as an exchange, generally resulting in capital gain or loss treatment to a shareholder if the redemption meets any one of five tests. Redemptions qualifying for exchange treatment include (1) a redemption that is not essentially equivalent to a dividend, (2) a redemption that is substantially disproportionate, (3) a redemption that completely terminates a shareholder's interest, (4) a redemption of a noncorporate shareholder in a partial liquidation, and (5) a redemption to pay death taxes. If none of the above five tests are met, the redemption proceeds are generally treated as a dividend.

93. (b) The requirement is to determine the amount of interest and legal and accounting fees that were incurred in connection with Kara Corp.'s stock repurchase that is deductible for 2015. No deduction is allowed for any amount paid or incurred by a corporation in connection with the redemption of its stock, except for interest expense on loans to repurchase stock. Thus, the $100,000 of interest expense on loans used to repurchase stock is deductible, while the $400,000 of legal and accounting fees incurred in connection with the repurchase of stock is not deductible.

94. (a) The requirement is to determine the correct statement regarding the expenses incurred in completely liquidating and dissolving a corporation. The general expenses incurred in the complete liquidation and dissolution of a corporation are deductible by the corporation as ordinary and necessary business expenses. These expenses include filing fees, professional fees, and other expenditures incurred in connection with the liquidation and dissolution.

95. (d) The requirement is to determine the usual result to the shareholders of a distribution in complete liquidation of a corporation. Amounts received by shareholders in complete liquidation of a corporation are treated as received in exchange for stock, generally resulting in capital gain or loss because the stock was held as an investment. Because liquidating distributions are generally treated as received in a taxable exchange, any property received by shareholders will have a basis equal to fair market value.

96. (d) The requirement is to determine whether the unused carryovers for excess charitable contributions and net operating loss of a wholly owned subsidiary carryover to a parent corporation as a result of a tax-free complete liquidation of the subsidiary. When a parent corporation completely liquidates its 80% or more owned subsidiary under Sec. 332, the liquidation is treated as a mere change in form and the parent corporation will not recognize any gain or loss on the receipt of liquidating distributions from its subsidiary. Similarly, the subsidiary corporation will not recognize any gain or loss on distributions to its parent corporation. As a result, there will be a carryover basis for all of the subsidiary's assets that are received by the parent corporation, as well as a carryover of all of the subsidiary's tax attributes to the parent corporation. The subsidiary's tax attributes that carryover to the parent include such items as earnings and profits, capital loss carryovers, accounting methods, and tax credit carryovers,

as well as unused excess charitable contributions, and net operating losses.

97. (b) The requirement is to determine the amount of Kappes Corp.'s recognized loss resulting from the distribution of marketable securities in complete liquidation. Generally, a corporation will recognize gain or loss on the distribution of its property in complete liquidation just as if the property were sold to the distributee for its fair market value. Since the marketable securities were a capital asset and held for more than one year, the distribution results in a long-term capital loss of $150,000 – $100,000 = $50,000.

98. (d) When a parent corporation liquidates its 80% or more owned subsidiary, the parent corporation (as stockholder) will ordinarily not recognize any gain or loss on the receipt of liquidating distributions from its subsidiary.

99. (a) The requirement is to determine the recognized gain to Lark Corp. on the complete liquidation of its wholly owned subsidiary, Day Corp. No gain or loss will be recognized by a parent corporation (Lark Corp.) on the receipt of property in complete liquidation of an 80% or more owned subsidiary (Day Corp.).

100. (c) The requirement is to determine the amount of gain to be recognized by Green Corp. as a result of the distribution of installment notes in the process of liquidation. A corporation generally recognizes gain on the distribution of appreciated property in the process of liquidation. Thus, Green Corp. must recognize gain on the distribution of the notes to the extent that the FMV of the notes ($162,000) exceeds the basis of the notes ($90,000), or $72,000.

101. (d) The requirement is to determine Carmela's recognized gain from the sale of assets during a complete liquidation. Gain or loss is generally recognized by a corporation on the sale of property following the adoption of a plan of complete liquidation. Carmela would recognize gain on the land of $75,000 ($150,000 – $75,000) and on the inventory of $22,500 ($66,000 – $43,500).

102. (d) The requirement is to determine the amount of gain that each Mintee Corp. shareholder should recognize as a result of a liquidating distribution from Mintee. Amounts received by noncorporate shareholders in complete liquidation of a corporation are treated as received in exchange for stock, generally resulting in capital gain or loss because the stock was held as an investment. Here the amount realized by each shareholder consists of $2,000 cash plus the $10,500 FMV of the land, for a total of $12,500. Since each shareholder's stock basis was $6,500, each shareholder has a gain of $12,500 – $6,500 = $6,000.

103. (b) The requirement is to determine what sources of income that Edge Corp. must consider to determine whether the income requirements for a personal holding company have been met. A corporation is a personal holding company if (1) five or fewer individuals own more than 50% of its stock at any time during the last half of its taxable year, and (2) at least 60% of its adjusted gross income is personal holding company income (e.g., dividends, interest, rent). The computation of the personal holding company income requirement includes only items that are included in gross income. Since interest on tax-exempt obligations would be excluded from gross income, tax-exempt interest would not be considered in determining whether the income requirement is met.

104. **(a)** The requirement is to determine which deduction(s) can be subtracted from taxable income in arriving at a corporation's undistributed personal holding company income (UPHCI). A series of adjustments must be made to a corporation's taxable income in order to arrive at UPHCI. These adjustments include the deduction of federal income taxes (including AMT and foreign income taxes), and the deduction for a net capital gain (i.e., the excess of NLTCG over NSTCL) less the amount of federal income taxes attributable to the net capital gain. This deduction prevents a personal holding company from paying the PHC tax on its net long-term capital gains.

105. **(c)** The requirement is to determine which step(s) Dart Corp. can take to eliminate or reduce any 2014 accumulated earnings tax (AET). The AET is a penalty tax that can be imposed (in addition to regular income tax) on a corporation if it accumulates earnings in excess of reasonable business needs. To avoid the AET, Dart can demonstrate that the reasonable needs of its business require the retention of all or part of the 2014 accumulated taxable income. Additionally, Dart can reduce its accumulated taxable income by paying a dividend to its shareholders. For this purpose, any dividends paid within the first 2 1/2 months of the tax year are treated as if paid on the last day of the preceding tax year. Thus, Dart's payment of dividends by March 15, 2015, would reduce its exposure to the AET for 2014.

106. **(d)** The requirement is to determine the correct statement regarding the accumulated earnings tax (AET). The AET is a penalty tax that can be imposed on a corporation if it accumulates earnings in excess of reasonable business needs, regardless of the number of shareholders that the corporation has. Answer (a) is incorrect because the AET cannot be imposed on partnerships. Answer (b) is incorrect because a corporation that distributes all of its accumulated earnings would not be subject to the AET. Answer (c) is incorrect because the AET cannot be imposed on personal holding companies.

107. **(a)** The requirement is to determine whose ownership of the remaining 200 shares of common stock could make Zero Corp. (with 1,000 outstanding shares) a personal holding company. A corporation is a personal holding company if (1) at least 60% of its adjusted ordinary gross income is derived from investment sources (e.g., interest, dividends, royalties), and (2) five or fewer individuals own more than 50% of the value of its stock at any time during the last half of its taxable year. In determining whether the more than 50% stock ownership requirement is met, the constructive ownership rules of Sec. 544 apply. Under these rules, an individual is considered as owning the stock owned by his family including only brothers and sisters, spouse, ancestors, and lineal descendants. Additionally, stock owned by a corporation, partnership, estate, or trust is considered as being owned proportionately by its shareholders, partners, or beneficiaries. Here, Edwards directly owns 240 shares and if he were the beneficiary of an

estate that owned 200 shares, Edwards would directly and constructively own 440 shares. Then with four other unrelated shareholders, each owning twenty shares, there would be five shareholders who directly or constructively own 520 shares, more than 50% of the corporation's outstanding stock.

108. **(b)** The requirement is to determine the status of Arbor Corp. A corporation is a personal holding company (PHC) if (1) five or fewer individuals own more than 50% of its stock during the last half of its taxable year, and (2) at least 60% of its adjusted gross income is derived from investment sources (e.g., dividends, interest, rents). Although the amount of dividends paid to its shareholders may affect the computation of the PHC tax, the amount of dividends paid has no effect on the determination of PHC status. Answer (a) is incorrect because a regulated investment company is a status obtained by registering under the Investment Company Act of 1940, and is not determined by the facts and circumstances present for any given year. Answer (c) is incorrect because the accumulated earnings tax does not apply to personal holding companies. Answer (d) is incorrect because all of Arbor's taxable income is subject to regular federal income tax.

109. **(c)** The requirement is to determine the maximum amount of accumulated taxable income that may be subject to the accumulated earnings tax for 2014 if Kari Corp. takes only the minimum accumulated earnings credit. Since Kari is a manufacturing company that was first organized in 2014, it is entitled to a minimum accumulated earnings credit of $250,000. To determine its potential exposure to the accumulated earnings tax, its 2014 taxable income of $400,000 must be reduced by its federal income taxes of $100,000 and its minimum accumulated earnings credit of $250,000, to arrive at its maximum exposure of $50,000.

110. **(d)** The requirement is to determine the amount that Hull, Inc. can deduct for dividends paid in the computation of its personal holding company (PHC) tax. The PHC tax is a penalty tax imposed at a 20% tax rate on a corporation's undistributed personal holding company income. A PHC is allowed a dividends paid deduction that is subtracted from its adjusted taxable income in arriving at its undistributed personal holding company income. Hull's dividends paid deduction consists of the $20,000 of dividends actually paid to its shareholders during 2014, plus the $10,000 of consent dividends reported in its shareholders' individual income tax returns for 2014.

Consent dividends are hypothetical dividends that are treated as if they were paid on the last day of the corporation's tax year. Since consent dividends are taxable to shareholders but not actually distributed, shareholders increase their stock basis by the amount of consent dividends included in their gross income. The consent dividend procedure has the same result as an actual dividend distribution, followed by the shareholders making a capital contribution of the dividend back to the corporation.

111. **(b)** The requirement is to determine the taxpayer to whom the personal holding company (PHC) income will be attributed. A corporation will be classified as a personal holding company if (1) it is more than 50% owned by five or fewer individuals, and (2) at least 60% of the corporation's adjusted ordinary gross income is PHC income. PHC income is generally passive income and includes dividends, interest, adjusted rents, adjusted royalties, compensation for the use of corporate property by a 25% or more shareholder, and certain personal service contracts involving a 25% or more shareholder. An amount received from a personal service contract is classified as PHC income if (1) some person other than the corporation has the right to designate, by name or by description, the individual who is to perform the services, and (2) the person so designated is (directly or constructively) a 25% or more shareholder. Here, since Benson owns 100% of Lund Corp. and Lund Corp. contracted with Magda specifying that Benson is to perform personal services for Magda, the income from the personal service contract will be personal holding company income to Lund Corp.

112. (c) The requirement is to determine the correct statement regarding the personal holding company (PHC) tax. The PHC tax should be self-assessed by filing a separate schedule 1120-PH along with the regular tax return Form 1120. Answer (a) is incorrect because the PHC tax is a penalty tax imposed in addition to regular federal income taxes. Answer (b) is incorrect because the PHC tax can only be imposed on corporations. Answer (d) is incorrect because the PHC tax can only be imposed if five or fewer individuals own more than 50% of the value of a corporation's stock. Thus, if a corporation's stock is owned by ten or more equal unrelated shareholders, the corporation cannot be a PHC.

113. (b) The requirement is to determine the correct statement regarding the accumulated earnings tax (AET). The AET does not apply to corporations that are personal holding companies. Answer (a) is incorrect because the AET can apply regardless of the number of shareholders that a corporation has. Answers (c) and (d) are incorrect because the AET applies to corporations that accumulate earnings in excess of their reasonable business needs and is not dependent upon whether a corporation files a consolidated return or the number of classes of stock that a corporation has.

114. (c) The requirement is to determine the correct statement concerning the personal holding company (PHC) tax. The personal holding company tax may be imposed if at least 60% of the corporation's adjusted ordinary gross income for the taxable year is personal holding company income, and the stock ownership test is satisfied. Answer (b) is incorrect because the stock ownership test is met if more than 50% of the corporation's stock is owned, directly or indirectly, by **five or fewer** stockholders. Answer (a) is incorrect because the PHC tax is a penalty tax imposed in addition to the regular corporate income tax. Answer (d) is incorrect because the PHC tax takes precedent over the accumulated earnings tax. The accumulated earnings tax does not apply to a personal holding company.

115. (d) The requirement is to determine the correct statement concerning the accumulated earnings tax (AET). Answer (d), "The accumulated earnings tax **cannot** be imposed on a corporation that has undistributed earnings and profits of less than $150,000," is correct because every corporation (even a personal service corporation) is eligible for an accumulated

earnings credit of at least $150,000. Answer (a) is incorrect because the AET is not self-assessing, but instead is assessed by the IRS after finding a tax avoidance intent on the part of the taxpayer. Answer (b) is incorrect because the AET may be imposed regardless of the number of shareholders that a corporation has. Answer (c) is incorrect because the AET cannot be imposed on a corporation for any year in which an S corporation election is in effect because an S corporation's earnings pass through and are taxed to shareholders regardless of whether the earnings are actually distributed.

116. (d) The requirement is to determine the amount on which Kee Holding Corp.'s liability for personal holding company (PHC) tax will be based. To be classified as a personal holding company, a corporation must meet both a "stock ownership test" and an "income test." The "stock ownership test" requires that more than 50% of the stock must be owned (directly or indirectly) by five or fewer individuals. Since Kee has eighty unrelated equal shareholders, the stock ownership test is not met. Thus, Kee is not a personal holding company and has no liability for the PHC tax.

117. (b) The accumulated earnings tax (AET) can be avoided by sufficient dividend distributions. The imposition of the AET does not depend on a stock ownership test, nor is it self-assessing requiring the filing of a separate schedule attached to the regular tax return. The AET cannot be imposed on personal holding companies.

118. (c) The personal holding company (PHC) tax may be imposed if more than 50% of a corporation's stock is owned by five or fewer individuals. The PHC tax cannot be imposed on partnerships. Additionally, small business investment companies licensed by the Small Business Administration are excluded from the tax. If a corporation's gross income arises solely from rents, the rents will not be PHC income (even though no services are rendered to lessees) and thus, the PHC tax cannot be imposed.

119. (d) A net capital loss for the current year is allowed as a deduction in determining accumulated taxable income for purposes of the accumulated earnings tax. A capital loss carryover from a prior year, a dividends received deduction, and a net operating loss deduction would all be added back to taxable income in arriving at accumulated taxable income.

120. (d) The minimum accumulated earnings credit is $250,000 for non service corporations; $150,000 for service corporations.

121. (a) The requirement is to determine Daystar's allowable accumulated earnings credit for 2014. The credit is the greater of (1) the earnings and profits of the tax year retained for reasonable business needs of $20,000; or (2) $150,000 less the accumulated earnings and profits at the end of the preceding year of $45,000. Thus, the credit is $150,000 – $45,000 = $105,000. Note that Daystar qualifies for only the $150,000 minimum credit (not the $250,000 credit) because it is a personal service corporation.

122. (c) The requirement is to determine Stahl's basis for his S corporation stock at the end of the year. A shareholder's basis for S corporation stock is increased by the pass-through of all income items (including tax-exempt income) and is decreased by distributions that are excluded from the shareholder's gross income, as well as the pass-through of all loss and deduction items (including nondeductible items). Here, Stahl's beginning stock basis of $65,000 is increased by the $6,000 of municipal interest income and $4,000 of long-term capital gain, and is decreased by the ordinary loss of $10,000 and short-term capital loss of $9,000, resulting in a stock basis of $56,000 at the end of the year.

123. (b) The requirement is to determine the amount of the $30,000 distribution from an S corporation that is taxable to Baker. If an S corporation has no accumulated earnings and profits from C years, distributions to shareholders are generally nontaxable and reduce a shareholder's stock basis. To the extent that distributions exceed stock basis, they result in capital gain. A shareholder's basis for S corporation stock is first increased by the pass through of income, then reduced by distributions that are excluded from gross income, and finally reduced by the pass through of losses and deductions. Here, Baker's beginning stock basis of $25,000 would first be increased by the pass through of the $1,000 of ordinary income, to $26,000. Then the $30,000 cash distribution would be a nontaxable return of stock basis to the extent of $26,000, with the remaining $4,000 in excess of stock basis taxable to Baker as capital gain. Baker will not be able to deduct the long-term capital loss of $3,000 this year because the cash distribution reduced his stock basis to zero. Instead, the $3,000 loss will be carried forward and will be available as a deduction when Baker has sufficient basis to absorb the loss.

124. (d) The requirement is to determine the amount of the $7,200 of health insurance premiums paid by Lane, Inc. (an S corporation) to be included in gross income by Mill. Compensation paid by an S corporation includes fringe benefit expenditures made on behalf of officers and employees owning more than 2% of the S corporation' stock. Since Mill is a 10% shareholder-employee, Mill's compensation income reported on his W-2 from Lane must include the $7,200 of health insurance premiums paid by Lane for health insurance covering Mill, his spouse, and dependents. Note that Mill may qualify to deduct 100% of the $7,200 for AGI as a self-employed health insurance deduction.

125. (b) The requirement is to determine Lazur's tax basis for the Beck Corp. stock after the distribution. A shareholder's basis for stock of an S corporation is increased by the pass-through of all income items (including tax-exempt income) and is decreased by distributions that are excluded from the shareholder's gross income. Here, Lazur's beginning basis of $12,000 is increased by his 50% share of Beck's ordinary business income ($40,500) and tax-exempt income ($5,000) and is decreased by the $51,000 cash distribution excluded from his gross income, resulting in a stock basis of $6,500.

126. (d) The requirement is to determine the amount of income from Graphite Corp. (an S corporation) that should be included in Smith's 2014 adjusted gross income. An S corporation is a pass-through entity and its items of income and deduction flow through to be reported on shareholders' returns. Since Smith is a 50% shareholder, half of the ordinary business income ($80,000 × 50% = $40,000) and half of the

tax-exempt interest ($6,000 × 50% = $3,000) would pass through to Smith. Since the income passed through to Smith would retain its character, Smith must include the $40,000 of ordinary income in gross income, while the $3,000 of tax-exempt interest retains its exempt characteristic and would be excluded from Smith's gross income. Smith's $12,000 of stock basis at the beginning of the year would be increased by the pass-through of the $40,000 of ordinary income as well as the $3,000 of tax-exempt income, to $55,000. As a result, the $53,000 cash distribution received by Smith would be treated as a nontaxable return of stock basis and would reduce the basis of Smith's stock to $2,000.

127. (a) The requirement is to determine the effect of the revocation statement on Dart Corp.'s S corporation election. A revocation of an S election will be effective if it is signed by shareholders owning more than 50% of the S corporation's outstanding stock. For this purpose, both voting and nonvoting shares are counted. Here Dart Corp. has a total of 100,000 shares outstanding. As a result, the revocation statement consented to by shareholders holding a total of 40,000 shares, would not be effective and would not terminate Dart Corp.'s S corporation election.

128. (d) The requirement is to determine the incorrect statement regarding S corporation eligibility requirements. The eligibility requirements restrict S corporation shareholders to individuals (other than nonresident aliens), estates, and certain trusts. Partnerships and C corporations are not permitted to own stock in an S corporation. However, an S corporation is permitted to be a partner in a partnership, and may own any percentage of stock of a C corporation, as well as own 100% of the stock of a qualified subchapter S subsidiary.

129. (b) The requirement is to determine the portion of the $310,000 distribution that must be reported as dividend income by Robert. Distributions from an S corporation are generally treated as first coming from its accumulated adjustment account (AAA), and then are treated as coming from its accumulated earnings and profits (AEP). A positive balance in an S corporation's AAA is generally nontaxable when distributed because it represents amounts that have already been taxed to shareholders during S years. In contrast, an S corporation's AEP represents earnings accumulated during C years that have never been taxed to shareholders, and must be reported as dividend income when received. In this case, the beginning balance in the AAA and shareholder stock basis must first be increased by the pass through of the $200,000 of ordinary income that is taxed to Robert for 2014. This permits the first $250,000 of the distribution to be nontaxable and will reduce the balance in the AAA to zero and Robert's stock basis to $50,000. The remaining $60,000 of distribution is a distribution of the corporation's AEP and must be reported as dividend income by Robert.

130. (b) The requirement is to determine the date on which Village Corp.'s S status became effective. A subchapter S election that is filed on or before the 15th day of the third month of a corporation's taxable year is generally effective as of the beginning of the taxable year in which filed. If the S election is filed after the 15th day of the third month, the election is generally effective as of the first day of the corporation's next taxable year. Here, Village Corp. uses a calendar year and its S election was filed on September 5, 2014, which is beyond the 15th day of the third month of the taxable year (March 15). As a result, Village's subchapter S status becomes effective as of the first day of its next taxable year, January 1, 2015.

131. (d) The requirement is to determine whether a shareholder's basis in the stock of an S corporation is increased by the shareholder's pro rata share of tax-exempt interest and taxable interest. An S corporation is a pass-through entity and its items of income and deduction pass through to be reported on shareholder returns. As a result, a shareholder's S corporation stock basis is increased by the pass through of all items of income, including both taxable as well as tax-exempt interest. An S shareholder's stock basis must be increased by tax-exempt interest in order to permit a later distribution of that interest to be nontaxable.

132. (c) The requirement is to determine the amount of income that should be allocated to Zinco Corp.'s short S year when its S election is terminated on April 1, 2015. When a corporation's subchapter S election is terminated during a taxable year, its income for the entire year must be allocated between the resulting S short year and C short year. If no special election is made, the income must be allocated on a daily basis between the S and C short years. In this case, the daily income equals $310,250/365 days = $850 per day. Since the election was terminated on April 1, there would be ninety days in the S short year, and $850 × 90 = $76,500 of income would be allocated to the tax return for the S short year to be passed through and taxed to shareholders.

133. (d) The requirement is to determine the correct statement regarding the termination of an S election. Answer (d) is correct because an S election will be terminated if an S corporation has passive investment income in excess of 25% of gross receipts for three consecutive taxable years, if the corporation also has subchapter C accumulated earnings and profits at the end of each of those three years. Answer (a) is incorrect because an S corporation is permitted to have a maximum of one hundred shareholders. Answer (b) is incorrect because a decedent's estate may be a shareholder of an S corporation. Answer (c) is incorrect because S corporations are allowed to make charitable contributions. Contributions separately pass through to shareholders and can be deducted as charitable contributions on shareholder returns.

134. (b) The requirement is to determine the amount of income from Manning (an S corporation) that should be reported on Kane's 2015 tax return. An S corporation's tax items are allocated to shareholders on a per share, per day basis. Since Manning had income of $73,000 for its entire year, its per day income is $73,000/365 = $200. Since there are 100 shares outstanding, Manning's daily income per share is $200/100 = $2. Since Kane sold 25 of his shares on the 40th day of 2015 and held his remaining seventy-five shares throughout the year, the amount of income to be reported on Kane's 2015 return would be determined as follows:

75 shares	×	$2	×	365 days	=	$54,750
25 shares	×	$2	×	40 days	=	2,000
						$56,750

135. (c) The requirement is to determine the earliest date on which Ace Corp. (a calendar-year corporation) can be recognized as an S corporation. Generally, an S election will be effective as of the first day of a taxable year if the election is made on or before the 15th day of the third month of the taxable year. Since there was no change in shareholders during the year, all of Ace's shareholders consented to the election, and Ace met all eligibility requirements during the pre-election portion of the year, its election filed on February 10, 2015, is effective as of January 1, 2015. Note that if either a shareholder who held stock during the taxable year and before the date of election did not consent to the election, or the corporation did not meet the eligibility requirements before the date of election, then an otherwise valid election would be treated as made for the following taxable year.

136. (c) The requirement is to determine the number of shares of voting and nonvoting stock that must be owned by shareholders making a revocation of an S election. A revocation of an S election may be filed by shareholders owning more than 50% of an S corporation's outstanding stock. For this purpose, both voting and nonvoting shares are counted. In this case, since the S corporation has a total of 50,000 voting and nonvoting shares outstanding, the shareholders consenting to the revocation must own more than 25,000 shares.

137. (b) The requirement is to determine the amount of increase for each shareholder's basis in the stock of Haas Corp., a calendar-year S corporation. An S corporation shareholder's basis for stock is increased by the pass through of all S corporation income items (including tax-exempt income), and is decreased by all loss and deduction items, as well as nondeductible expenses not charged to capital. Since Haas has two equal shareholders, each shareholder's stock basis will be increased by 50% of the operating income of $50,000, and 50% of the interest income of $10,000, resulting in an increase for each shareholder of $30,000.

138. (d) The requirement is to determine the condition that will prevent a corporation from qualifying as an S corporation. Certain eligibility requirements must be satisfied before a corporation can make a subchapter S election. Generally, in order to be an S corporation, a corporation must have only one class of stock outstanding and have no more than one hundred shareholders, who are either individuals, estates, or certain trusts. An S corporation may own any percentage of the stock of a C corporation, and 100% of the stock of a qualified subchapter S subsidiary.

139. (c) The requirement is to determine the correct statement regarding distributions to shareholders by an S corporation that has no accumulated earnings and profits. S corporations do not generate any earnings and profits, but may have accumulated earnings and profits from prior years as a C corporation. If accumulated earnings and profits are distributed to shareholders, the distributions will be taxed as dividend income to the shareholders. However, if an S corporation has no accumulated earnings and profits, distributions are generally nontaxable and reduce a shareholder's basis for stock. To the extent distributions exceed stock basis, they result in capital gain.

140. (**d**) The requirement is to determine whether a corporation that has been an S corporation from its inception may have both passive and nonpassive income, and be owned by a bankruptcy estate. To qualify as an S corporation, a corporation must have one hundred or fewer shareholders who are individuals (other than nonresident aliens), certain trusts, or estates (including bankruptcy estates). If a corporation has been an S corporation since its inception, there is no limitation on the amount or type of income that it generates, and it can have both passive and nonpassive income.

141. (**b**) The requirement is to determine Meyer's share of an S corporation's $36,500 ordinary loss. An S corporation's items of income and deduction are allocated on a daily basis to anyone who was a shareholder during the taxable year. Here, the $36,500 ordinary loss would be divided by 365 days to arrive at a loss of $100 per day. Since Meyer held 50% of the S corporation's stock for forty days, Meyer's share of the loss would be ($100 × 50%) × 40 days = $2,000.

142. (**c**) The requirement is to determine the period that a calendar-year corporation must wait before making a new S election following the termination of its S status during 2014. Generally, following the revocation or termination of an S election, a corporation must wait five years before reelecting subchapter S status unless the IRS consents to an earlier election.

143. (**d**) The requirement is to determine which will render a corporation ineligible for S corporation status. Answer (d) is correct because an S corporation is limited to 100 shareholders. Answers (a) and (b) are incorrect because a decedent's estate and a bankruptcy estate are allowed as S corporation shareholders. Although an S corporation may only have one class of stock issued and outstanding, answer (c) is incorrect because a difference in voting rights among outstanding common shares is not treated as having more than one class of stock outstanding.

144. (**d**) The requirement is to determine the correct statement with regard to the application of the "at-risk" rules to S corporations and their shareholders. The at-risk rules limit a taxpayer's deduction of losses to the amount that the taxpayer can actually lose (i.e., generally the amount of cash and the adjusted basis of property invested by the taxpayer, plus any liabilities for which the taxpayer is personally liable). The at-risk rules apply to S corporation shareholders rather than at the corporate level, with the result that the deduction of S corporation losses is limited to the amount of a shareholder's at-risk investment. The application of the at-risk rules does not depend on the type of income reported by the S corporation, are not subject to any elections made by S corporation shareholders, and are applied without regard to the S corporation's ratio of debt to equity.

145. (**d**) The requirement is to determine the item that may be deducted by an S corporation. Items having no special tax characteristics can be netted together in the computation of the S corporation's ordinary income or loss, with only the net amount passed through to shareholders. Thus, only ordinary items (e.g., amortization of organizational expenditures) can be deducted by an S corporation. Answer (a) is incorrect because foreign income taxes must be separately passed through to

shareholders so that the shareholders can individually elect to treat the payment of foreign income taxes as a deduction or as a credit. Answer (b) is incorrect because a net Sec. 1231 loss must be separately passed through to shareholders so that the Sec. 1231 netting process can take place at the shareholder level. Answer (c) is incorrect because investment interest expense must be separately passed through to shareholders so the deduction limitation (i.e., limited to net investment income) can be applied at the shareholder level.

146. (**d**) The requirement is to determine the correct statement regarding an S corporation's Accumulated Adjustments Account (AAA). An S corporation that has accumulated earnings and profits must maintain an AAA. The AAA represents the cumulative balance of all items of the undistributed net income and deductions for S corporation years beginning after 1982. The AAA is generally increased by all income items and is decreased by distributions and all loss and deduction items except no adjustment is made for tax-exempt income and related expenses, and no adjustment is made for federal income taxes attributable to a taxable year in which the corporation was a C corporation. The payment of federal income taxes attributable to a C corporation year would decrease an S corporation's accumulated earnings and profits (AEP). Note that the amounts represented in the AAA differ from AEP. A positive AEP balance represents earnings and profits accumulated in C corporation years that have never been taxed to shareholders. A positive AAA balance represents income from S corporation years that has already been taxed to shareholders but not yet distributed. An S corporation will not generate any earnings and profits for taxable years beginning after 1982.

147. (**b**) The requirement is to determine the due date of a calendar-year S corporation's tax return. An S corporation must file its federal income tax return (Form 1120-S) by the 15th day of the third month following the close of its taxable year. Thus, a calendar-year S corporation must file its tax return by March 15, if an automatic six-month extension of time is not requested.

148. (**c**) The requirement is to determine the item for which an S corporation is **not** permitted a deduction. Compensation of officers, interest paid to non shareholders, and employee benefits for non shareholders are deductible by an S corporation in computing its ordinary income or loss. However, charitable contributions, since they are subject to percentage limitations at the shareholder level, must be separately stated and are not deductible in computing an S corporation's ordinary income or loss.

149. (**d**) An S corporation may have as many as 100 shareholders. However, an S corporation cannot have both common and preferred stock outstanding because an S corporation is limited to a single class of stock. Similarly, a partnership is not permitted to be a shareholder in an S corporation because all S corporation shareholders must be individuals, estates, or certain trusts. Additionally, an S corporation cannot have a nonresident alien as a shareholder.

150. (**a**) The requirement is to determine which is **not** a requirement for a corporation to elect S corporation status. An S corporation must generally have only one class of stock, be a domestic corporation, and confine shareholders to individuals, estates, and certain trusts. An S corporation need **not** be a member of a controlled group.

151. (b) The requirement is to determine the amount of loss from an S corporation that can be deducted by each of two equal shareholders. An S corporation loss is passed through to shareholders and is deductible to the extent of a shareholder's basis for stock plus the basis for any debt owed the shareholder by the corporation. Here, each shareholder's allocated loss of $45,000 ($90,000/2) is deductible to the extent of stock basis of $5,000 plus debt basis of $15,000, or $20,000. The remainder of the loss ($25,000 for each shareholder) can be carried forward indefinitely by each shareholder and deducted when there is basis to absorb it.

152. (b) The requirement is to determine the correct statement regarding King Corp.'s acquisition of 90% of Jaxson Corp.'s voting common stock solely in exchange for 50% of King Corp.'s voting common stock. The acquisition by one corporation, in exchange **solely** for part of its voting stock, of stock of another corporation qualifies as a tax-free type B reorganization if immediately after the acquisition, the acquiring corporation is in control of the acquired corporation. The term **control** means the ownership of at least 80% of the acquired corporation's stock. Since King Corp. will use solely its voting stock to acquire 90% of Jaxson Corp. the acquisition will qualify as a tax-free type B reorganization. Answer (c) is incorrect because there is no requirement concerning the minimum percentage of King Corp. stock that must be used. Answer (d) is incorrect because a type B reorganization involves the acquisition of stock, not assets.

153. (a) The requirement is to determine whether a qualifying reorganization is tax-free to the corporations and their shareholders. Corporate reorganizations are generally nontaxable. As a result, a corporation will not recognize gain or loss on the transfer of its assets, and shareholders do not recognize gain or loss when they exchange stock and securities in parties to the reorganization. Here, Ace and Bate combine and form Carr, the only surviving corporation. This qualifies as a consolidation (Type A reorganization) and is tax-free to Ace and Bate on the transfer of their assets to Carr, and also is tax-free to the shareholders when they exchange their Ace and Bate stock for Carr stock. Similarly, the reorganization is tax-free to Carr when it issues its shares to acquire the Ace and Bate assets.

154. (c) The requirement is to determine whether the statements are applicable to type B reorganizations. In a type B reorganization, the acquiring corporation must use solely voting stock to acquire control of the target corporation immediately after the acquisition. The stock that is used to make the acquisition can be solely voting stock of the acquiring corporation, or solely voting stock of the parent corporation that is in control of the acquiring corporation, but not both. If a subsidiary uses its parent's stock to make the acquisition, the target corporation becomes a second-tier subsidiary of the parent corporation.

155. (d) The requirement is to determine Gow's recognized gain resulting from the exchange of Lad Corp. stock for Rook Corp. stock pursuant to a plan of corporate reorganization. No gain or loss is recognized to a shareholder if stock in one party to a reorganization (Lad Corp.) is exchanged **solely** for stock in another corporation (Rook Corp.) that is a party to the reorganization.

156. (a) The requirement is to determine the item that is defined in the Internal Revenue Code as a corporate reorganization. Corporate reorganizations generally receive nonrecognition treatment. Sec. 368 of the Internal Revenue Code defines seven types of reorganization, one of which is listed. An "F" reorganization is a mere change in identity, form, or place of organization of one corporation. A stock redemption is not a reorganization but instead results in dividend treatment or qualifies for exchange treatment. A change of depreciation method or inventory method is a change of an accounting method.

157. (c) The requirement is to determine the correct statement concerning corporate reorganizations. Answer (b) is incorrect because the reorganization provisions do provide for tax-free treatment for certain corporate transactions. Specifically, shareholders will not recognize gain or loss when they exchange stock or securities in a corporation that is a party to a reorganization solely for stock or securities in such corporation, or in another corporation that is also a party to the reorganization. Thus, securities in corporations not parties to the reorganization are always treated as "boot." Answer (d) is incorrect because the term "a party to the reorganization" includes a corporation resulting from the reorganization (i.e., the consolidated company). Answer (a) is incorrect because a mere change in identity, form, or place of organization of one corporation qualifies as a Type F reorganization.

158. (a) The requirement is to determine which is **not** a corporate reorganization. A corporate reorganization is specifically defined in Sec. 368 of the Internal Revenue Code. Sec. 368 defines seven types of reorganization, of which 3 are present in this item: Type A, a statutory merger; Type E, a recapitalization; and, Type F, a mere change in identity, form, or place of organization. Answer (a), a stock redemption, is the correct answer because it is not a reorganization as defined by Sec. 368 of the Code.

159. (a) The requirement is to determine the amount of Claudio's NOL carryover that can be used to offset Stellar's 2014 taxable income. The amount of Claudio's NOL ($270,000) that can be utilized by Stellar for 2014 is limited by Sec. 381 to the taxable income of Stellar for its full taxable year (before a NOL deduction) multiplied by the fraction

$$\frac{\text{Days after acquisition date}}{\text{Total days in the tax table year}}$$

This limitation is 184/365 days × $360,000 = $181,479. Additionally, since there was a more than fifty percentage point change in the ownership of Claudio, Sec. 382 limits the amount of Claudio's NOL carryover that can be utilized by Stellar to the fair market value of Claudio multiplied by the federal long-term tax-exempt rate. $1,500,000 × 3% =

$45,000. However, for purposes of applying this limitation for the year of acquisition, the limitation amount is only available to the extent allocable to the days in Stellar's taxable year after the acquisition date.

$$\$45,000 \times 184/365 \text{ days} = \$22,685$$

The remainder of Claudio's NOL ($270,000 − $22,685 = $247,315) can be carried forward and used to offset Stellar's taxable income (subject to the Sec. 382 limitation) in carry forward years.

160. (a) The requirement is to determine the recognized gain to be reported by Mueller on the exchange of her Disco bond for Disco preferred stock. The issuance by Disco Corporation of its preferred stock in exchange for its bonds is a nontaxable "Type E" reorganization (i.e., a recapitalization).

Since Mueller did not receive any boot, no part of her $400 realized gain is recognized.

161. (b) The requirement is to determine the amount of recognized gain in a recapitalization. Since a recapitalization is a reorganization, a realized gain will be recognized to the extent that consideration other than stock or securities is received, including the FMV of an excess principal amount of securities received over the principal amount of securities surrendered. Since no securities were surrendered, the entire $10,500 FMV of the securities received by Roberts is treated as boot. However, in this case, Roberts recognized gain is limited to her realized gain ($91,000 + $10,500) − $95,000 = $6,500.

Simulations

Task-Based Simulation 1

Concepts		
	Authoritative Literature	Help

Given below are terms appearing in the federal income tax code, regulations and explanations.

A. Accumulated earnings tax
B. Capital assets
C. Capital contribution
D. Claim of right
E. Consent divided
F. Constructive dividend
G. Constructive receipt
H. Deficiency dividend
I. Dividends paid deduction

J. Dividends received deduction
K. Earned income
L. Exchanged basis
M. Excise tax
N. Fair market value
O. Head of household
P. Nontaxable exchange
Q. Passive income
R. Personal holding company

S. Personal holding company tax
T. Personal service corporation
U. Portfolio income
V. Regulated investment company
W. Sec. 1231 assets
X. Surviving spouse
Y. Taxable exchange
Z. Transferred basis

Indicate your choice of the **best** term applying to each of the statements below. Each term may be selected once, more than once, or not at all.

1. A corporation whose income was derived solely from dividends, interest, and royalties, and during the last six months of its year more than 50% of the value of its outstanding stock is owned by five or fewer individuals.

2. The basis used to determine gain on sale of property that was received as a gift.

3. The trade-in of production machinery for new production machinery by a corporation, when the corporation pays additional cash.

4. An unmarried individual whose filing status enables the taxpayer to use a set of income tax rates that are lower than those applicable to other unmarried individuals, but are higher than those applicable to married persons filing a joint return.

5. If income is unqualifiedly available, it will be subject to the income tax even though it is not physically in the taxpayer's possession.

6. A special tax imposed on corporations that accumulate their earnings beyond the reasonable needs of the business.

7. The classification of income from interest, dividends, annuities, and certain royalties.

8. The classification of depreciable assets and real estate used in a trade or business and held for more than one year.

9. This deduction attempts to mitigate the triple taxation that would occur if one corporation paid dividends to a corporate shareholder who, in turn, distributed such amounts to its individual shareholders.

10. Sale of property to a corporation by a shareholder for a selling price that is in excess of the property's fair market value.

	(A) (B) (C) (D) (E) (F) (G) (H) (I) (J) (K) (L) (M) (N) (O) (P) (Q) (R) (S) (T) (U) (V) (W) (X) (Y) (Z)
1.	O O O O O O O O O O O O O O O O O O O O O O O O O O
2.	O O O O O O O O O O O O O O O O O O O O O O O O O O
3.	O O O O O O O O O O O O O O O O O O O O O O O O O O
4.	O O O O O O O O O O O O O O O O O O O O O O O O O O
5.	O O O O O O O O O O O O O O O O O O O O O O O O O O
6.	O O O O O O O O O O O O O O O O O O O O O O O O O O
7.	O O O O O O O O O O O O O O O O O O O O O O O O O O
8.	O O O O O O O O O O O O O O O O O O O O O O O O O O
9.	O O O O O O O O O O O O O O O O O O O O O O O O O O
10.	O O O O O O O O O O O O O O O O O O O O O O O O O O

Task-Based Simulation 2

Tax Return Amount		
	Authoritative Literature	Help

The following adjusted revenue and expense accounts appeared in the accounting records of Aviator, Inc., an accrual-basis taxpayer, for the year ended December 31, 2014:

Revenues	
Net sales	$2,000,000
Dividends	50,000
Interest	22,000
Gains on the sale of stock	20,000
Total	$2,092,000
Expenses	
Cost of goods sold	$1,000,000
Salaries and wages	400,000
Interest	25,000
Contributions	40,000
Depreciation (see note)	260,000
Losses on the sale of stock	30,000
Total	$1,755,000
Net Income	$337,000

NOTE: There is no Sec. 1245, Sec. 1250, or Sec. 291 recapture.

Additional information for 2014

(1) The dividends were received from a taxable domestic corporation, whose stock is traded on a major stock exchange.

(2) Interest expense consists of: $20,000 interest on funds borrowed for working capital and $5,000 interest on funds borrowed to purchase municipal bonds.

(3) Interest revenue consists of interest earned on

Corporate bonds purchased in 2014	$20,000
Municipal bonds purchased in 2014	2,000

(4) Contributions of $40,000 were made to qualified charitable organizations.

(5) On January 2, 2014, Aviator, Inc. commenced active operations. In connection with creating the business, Aviator incurred the following organizational expenditures:

Legal fees	$30,000
State incorporation fees	20,000
Brokers commission on the sale of stock	15,000

Aviator is taking the maximum amortization deduction for the above expenditures. The expenditures were erroneously excluded from the accounts shown above.

(6) Gains from the sale of stock arose from the following sales of stock of unrelated corporations:

Tech. Corp (bought February 2014; sold April 2014)	$15,000
Major Corp (bought June 2014; sold September 2014)	5,000

(7) All losses from the sale of stock are classified as long-term capital losses.

For **items 1 through 7** record the appropriate amount as it would appear on the Aviator, Inc. corporate tax return. On the exam, a list of numeric answers would be presented for the candidate to select from.

1. What is the amount of interest expense that Aviator, Inc. can deduct on its tax return?

2. What is the amount of interest income that must be included in Aviator's gross income?

3. What is the allowable amount of organizational expenditures that is deductible on Aviator's tax return?

4. How much of the capital gains must be included in Aviator's gross income?

5. How much of the capital losses can be deducted on Aviator's tax return?

6. What is the amount of Aviator's dividends received deduction?

7. What is Aviator's maximum charitable contributions deduction?

Task-Based Simulation 3

Schedule M-1		
	Authoritative Literature	Help

Aviator provides the following information for 2014:

Net income per books (after tax)	$310,000
Federal income tax liability deducted per books	104,150
Retained earnings at January 1, 2014	425,000
Interest income from municipal general obligation bonds	20,000
Cash dividends paid to shareholders	60,000
Life insurance proceeds received on death of Aviator's president (Aviator was the owner and beneficiary of the policy)	100,000
Premiums paid on policy insuring Aviator's president	5,000
Excess of capital losses over capital gains for 2014	7,000
Employee entertainment expenses reimbursed by Aviator	6,000
Dividend income received from 5%-owned taxable domestic corporation	10,000
MACRS depreciation for 2014 in excess of straight-time depreciation deducted per books	9,000
Retained earnings at December 31, 2014	645,000

Prepare Schedule M-1, which will reconcile Aviator's income reported per books for 2014 with its income reported on its 2014 tax return Form 1120.

Schedule M-1	**Reconciliation of Income (Loss) per Books With Income per Return**		
	Note: Schedule M-3 required instead of Schedule M-1 if total assets are $10 million or more—see instructions		
1 Net income (loss) per books		7 Income recorded on books this year not included on this return (itemize):	
2 Federal income tax per books		Tax-exempt interest $	
3 Excess of capital losses over capital gains			
4 Income subject to tax not recorded on books this year (itemize):		8 Deductions on this return not charged against book income this year (itemize):	
5 Expenses recorded on books this year not deducted on this return (itemize):		a Depreciation $	
a Depreciation $		b Charitable contributions $	
b Charitable contributions $			
c Travel and entertainment $		9 Add lines 7 and 8	
6 Add lines 1 through 5		10 Income (page 1, line 28)—line 6 less line 9	

Task-Based Simulation 4

Aviator's gains from the sale of stock investments totaled $20,000, while its losses from the sale of other stock investments totaled $30,000. What Internal Revenue Code section and subsection limits the deduction of a corporation's capital losses? Indicate the reference to that citation in the shaded boxes below.

Section	Subsection
§	( )

Task-Based Simulation 5

Situation

Ral Corp. is a calendar-year accrual method corporation. Following is their condensed income statement, before federal income tax, for the year ended December 31, 2014:

Sales		$1,000,000
Cost of sales		700,000
Gross profit		300,000
Operating expenses		220,000
Operating income		80,000
Other income (loss):		
Interest	$5,200	
Dividends	19,200	
Net long-term capital loss	(6,400)	18,000
Income before federal income tax		$98,000

Additional information

Interest arose from the following sources:

US Treasury notes	$3,000
Municipal arbitrage bonds	2,000
Other municipal bonds	200
Total interest	$5,200

Dividends arose from the following sources:

Taxable domestic corporation	Date stock acquired	Percent owned by Ral	
Clove Corp.	7/1/06	30.0	$7,000
Ramo Corp.	9/1/08	10.0	6,000
Sol Corp. (stock sold 1/10/15)	12/1/14	5.0	1,000
Real Estate Investment Trust	6/1/11	1.0	2,700
Mutual Fund Corp. (capital gains dividends only)	4/1/10	0.1	400
Money Market Fund (invests only in interest/paying securities)	3/1/09	0.1	2,100
Total dividends			$19,200

Operating expenses include the following:

Bonus of $5,000 paid to Ral's sales manager on January 31, 2015. This bonus was based on a percentage of Ral's 2014 sales and was computed on January 25, 2015, under a formula in effect in 2014.

Estimate of $10,000 for bad debts. Actual bad debts for the year amounted to $8,000.

Key man life insurance premiums of $4,000. Ral is the beneficiary of the policies.

State income taxes of $12,000.

During 2014, Ral made estimated federal income tax payments of $25,000. These payments were debited to prepaid tax expense on Ral's books.

Ral does not exercise significant influence over Clove and accordingly did **not** use the equity method of accounting for this investment.

Ral declared and paid dividends of $11,000 during 2014.

Corporate income tax rates are as follows:

Taxable income				
over	but not over	Pay	+ % on excess	Of the amount over
$0	$50,000	$0	15%	$0
50,000	75,000	7,500	25	50,000
75,000	100,000	13,750	34	75,000
100,000	335,000	22,250	39	100,000

Ral was not subject to the alternative minimum tax in 2014.

Items 1 through 14 below pertain to the computation of Ral Corp.'s 2014 federal income tax. For each item, select the appropriate amount. An amount may be selected once, more than once, or not at all.

Amount

A. $0	J. $3,000	S. $6,400
B. $280	K. $3,200	T. $7,000
C. $320	L. $4,000	U. $8,000
D. $1,000	M. $4,200	V. $10,000
E. $1,470	N. $4,800	W. $11,000
F. $1,680	O. $4,900	X. $12,000
G. $1,890	P. $5,000	Y. $13,750
H. $2,000	Q. $5,200	Z. $22,250
I. $2,200	R. $5,600	

Item for Ral's 2014 federal income tax

1. Amount of deduction for manager's $5,000 bonus for 2014.

2. Deduction for bad debts for 2014.

3. Deduction for keyman life insurance premiums for 2014.

4. Deduction for state income taxes for 2014.

5. Amount of interest to be included in gross income for 2014.

6. Dividends received deduction for dividends received from Clove Corp.

7. Dividends received deduction for dividends received from Ramo Corp.

8. Dividends received deduction for dividends received from Sol Corp.

9. Dividends received deduction for dividends received from Real Estate Investment Trust.

10. Dividends received deduction for dividends received from Mutual Fund Corp.

11. Dividends received deduction for dividends received from Money Market Fund.

12. Deduction for the $11,000 of dividends paid by Ral to its shareholders.

13. Deduction for net capital loss for 2014.

14. Ral's federal income tax for 2014 if taxable income were $100,000.

Task-Based Simulation 6

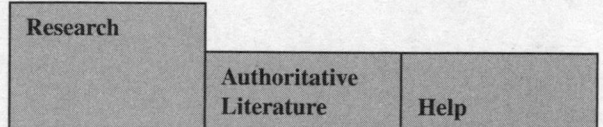

Dividends received from taxable domestic corporations are generally eligible for a dividends received deduction. What Internal Revenue Code section provides a special restriction on the dividends-received deduction if the stock investment is financed with debt? Indicate the reference to that citation in the shaded box below.

Task-Based Simulation 7

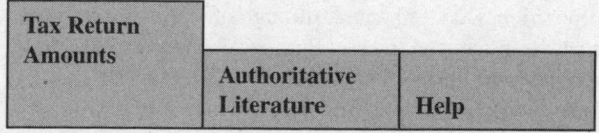

Situation

Lan Corp., an accrual-basis calendar-year repair service corporation, was formed and began business on January 6, 2015. Lan's valid S corporation election took effect retroactively on January 6, 2015. Since the question requires a numeric answer, a list of numeric amounts would be provided for the candidate to select from.

For **items 1 through 4,** determine the amount, if any, using the fact pattern for each item.

1. Assume the following facts:

Lan's 2015 books recorded the following items:

Gross receipts	$7,260
Interest income on investments	50
Charitable contributions	1,000
Supplies	1,120

What amount of net business income should Lan report on its 2015 Form 1120S, US Income Tax Return for an S Corporation, Schedule K?

2. Assume the following facts:

As of January 6, 2015, Taylor and Barr each owned 100 shares of the 200 issued shares of Lan stock. On January 31, 2015, Taylor and Barr each sold twenty shares to Pike. No election was made to terminate the tax year. Lan had net business income of $14,400 for the year ended December 31, 2015, and made no distributions to its shareholders. Lan's 2015 calendar year had 360 days.

What amount of net business income should have been reported on Pike's 2015 Schedule K-1 from Lan? (2015 is a 360-day tax year.) Round the answer to the nearest hundred.

3. Assume the following facts:

Pike purchased forty Lan shares on January 31, 2015, for $4,000. Lan made no distributions to shareholders, and Pike's 2015 Schedule K-1 from Lan reported

Ordinary business loss	$(1,000)
Municipal bond interest income	150

What was Pike's basis in his Lan stock at December 31, 2015?

4. Assume the following facts:

On January 6, 2015, Taylor and Barr each owned 100 shares of the 200 issued shares of Lan stock. Taylor's basis in Lan shares on that date was $10,000. Taylor sold all of his Lan shares to Pike on January 31, 2015, and Lan made a valid election to terminate its tax year. Taylor's share of ordinary income from Lan prior to the sale was $2,000. Lan made a cash distribution of $3,000 to Taylor on January 30, 2015.

What was Taylor's basis in Lan shares for determining gain or loss from the sale to Pike?

Task-Based Simulation 8

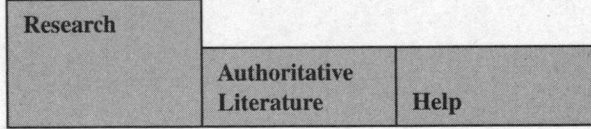

Mr. Perry is the sole shareholder of Arrow, Inc., a calendar-year S corporation. Due to the pass-through of losses in previous years, Perry's aggregate basis for the Arrow stock and debt that he owns has been reduced to zero. For its calendar year 2015, Arrow expects to incur another large loss which Perry wishes to deduct on his 2015 Form 1040 tax return. What Internal Revenue Code section and subsection limits a shareholder's deduction of an S corporation's losses to the shareholder's basis for stock and debt? Indicate the reference to that citation in the shaded boxes below.

Section	Subsection
§ [　　　]	([　　　])

Task-Based Simulation 9

| Schedule M-1 |
| Adjustments |
| | Authoritative Literature | Help |

Reliant Corp., an accrual-basis calendar-year C corporation, filed its 2014 federal income tax return on March 15, 2015. The following **two** responses are required for each of the **items 1 through 6**.

- Determine the amount of Reliant's 2014 Schedule M-1 adjustment.
- Indicate if the adjustment increases, decreases, or has no effect, on Reliant's 2014 taxable income.

Selections
I. Increases Reliant's 2014 taxable income.
D. Decreases Reliant's 2014 taxable income.
N. Has no effect on Reliant's 2014 taxable income.

	Schedule M-1 Adjustment	(I)	(D)	(N)
1. Reliant's disbursements included reimbursed employees' expenses in 2014 for travel of $100,000, and business meals of $30,000. The reimbursed expenses met the conditions of deductibility and were properly substantiated under an accountable plan. The reimbursement was not treated as employee compensation.	_____	O	O	O
2. Reliant's books expensed $7,000 in 2014 for the term life insurance premiums on the corporate officers. Reliant was the policy owner and beneficiary.	_____	O	O	O
3. Reliant's books indicated an $18,000 state franchise tax expense for 2014. Estimated state tax payments for 2014 were $15,000.	_____	O	O	O
4. Book depreciation on computers for 2014 was $10,000. These computers, which cost $50,000, were placed in service on January 2, 2013. Tax depreciation used MACRS with the half-year convention. No election was made to expense part of the computer cost and Reliant elected not to use bonus depreciation.	_____	O	O	O
5. For 2014, Reliant's books showed a $4,000 short-term capital gain distribution from a mutual fund corporation and a $5,000 loss on the sale of Retro stock that was purchased in 2012. The stock was an investment in an unrelated corporation. There were no other 2014 gains or losses and no loss carryovers from prior years.	_____	O	O	O
6. Reliant's 2014 taxable income before the charitable contribution and the dividends received deductions was $500,000. Reliant's books expensed $15,000 in board of director authorized charitable contributions that were paid on January 5, 2015. Charitable contributions paid and expensed during 2014 were $35,000. All charitable contributions were properly substantiated. There were no net operating losses or charitable contributions that were carried forward.	_____	O	O	O

Task-Based Simulation 10

| Deductibility |
| | Authoritative Literature | Help |

For the following, indicate if the expenses are fully deductible, partially deductible, or nondeductible for regular tax purposes on Reliant Corp.'s 2014 federal income tax return.

Selections

F. Fully deductible for regular tax purposes on Reliant's 2014 federal income tax return.
P. Partially deductible for regular tax purposes on Reliant's 2014 federal income tax return.
N. Nondeductible for regular tax purposes on Reliant's 2014 federal income tax return.

		(F)	(P)	(N)
1.	Reliant purchased theater tickets for its out of town clients. The performances took place after Reliant's substantial and bona fide business negotiations with its clients.	O	O	O
2.	Reliant accrued advertising expenses to promote a new product line. Ten percent of the new product line remained in ending inventory.	O	O	O
3.	Reliant incurred interest expense on a loan to purchase municipal bonds.	O	O	O
4.	Reliant paid a penalty for the underpayment of 2013 estimated taxes.	O	O	O
5.	On December 9, 2014, Reliant's board of directors voted to pay a $500 bonus to each nonstockholder employee for 2014. The bonuses were paid on February 3, 2015.	O	O	O

Task-Based Simulation 11

Taxability		
	Authoritative Literature	Help

For the following, indicate if the items are fully taxable, partially taxable, or nontaxable for regular tax purposes on Reliant Corp.'s 2014 federal income tax return. All transactions occurred during 2014.

Selections

F. Fully taxable for regular tax purposes on Reliant's 2014 federal income tax return.
P. Partially taxable for regular tax purposes on Reliant's 2014 federal income tax return.
N. Nontaxable for regular tax purposes on Reliant's 2014 federal income tax return.

Items 1 through 5 are based on the following:

Reliant filed an amended federal income tax return for 2012 and received a refund that included both the overpayment of the federal taxes and interest.

		(F)	(P)	(N)
1.	The portion of Reliant's refund that represented the overpayment of the 2012 federal taxes.	O	O	O
2.	The portion of Reliant's refund that is attributable to the interest on the overpayment of federal taxes.	O	O	O
3.	Reliant received dividend income from a mutual fund that solely invests in municipal bonds.	O	O	O
4.	Reliant, the lessor, benefited from the capital improvements made to its property by the lessee in 2014. The lease agreement is for one year ending December 31, 2014, and provides for a reduction in rental payments by the lessee in exchange for the improvements.	O	O	O
5.	Reliant collected the proceeds on the term life insurance policy on the life of a debtor who was not a shareholder. The policy was assigned to Reliant as collateral security for the debt. The proceeds exceeded the amount of the debt.	O	O	O

Task-Based Simulation 12

Alternative Minimum Tax		
	Authoritative Literature	Help

Indicate if the following items increase, decrease, or have no effect on Reliant Corp.'s 2014 alternative minimum taxable income (AMTI) **prior to** the adjusted current earnings adjustment (ACE).

Selections

I.   Increases Reliant's 2014 AMTI.
D.   Decreases Reliant's 2014 AMTI.
N.   Has no effect on Reliant's 2014 AMTI.

		(I)	(D)	(N)
1.	Reliant used the 70% dividends received deduction for regular tax purposes.	○	○	○
2.	Reliant received interest from a state's general obligation bonds.	○	○	○
3.	Reliant used MACRS depreciation on seven-year personal property placed into service January 3, 2014, for regular tax purposes. No expense election was made, and Reliant elected not to use bonus depreciation.	○	○	○
4.	Depreciation on nonresidential real property placed into service on January 3, 2014, was under the general MACRS depreciation system for regular tax purposes.	○	○	○
5.	Reliant had only cash charitable contributions for 2014.	○	○	○

Task-Based Simulation 13

Research		
	Authoritative Literature	Help

What Internal Revenue Code section, subsection, and paragraph limits a corporation's deduction for charitable contributions to a percentage of its taxable income before specified deductions? Indicate the reference to that citation in the shaded boxes below.

Section	Subsection	Paragraph
§ [＿＿]	([＿＿])	([＿＿])

Task-Based Simulation 14

Schedule M-1 Adjustments		
	Authoritative Literature	Help

Situation

Capital Corp., an accrual-basis calendar-year C corporation, began operations on January 2, 2012. Capital timely filed its 2014 federal income tax return on March 15, 2015.

The following items each require **two** responses:

- For each item below, determine the amount of Capital's 2014 Schedule M-1 adjustment necessary to reconcile book income to taxable income. On the CPA exam, a list of numeric answers would be presented for the candidate to select from.
- In addition, determine if the Schedule M-1 adjustment necessary to reconcile book income to taxable income increases, decreases, or has no effect on Capital's 2014 taxable income. An answer may be selected once, more than once, or not at all.

Selections

    I.   Increases Capital's 2014 taxable income.
    D.   Decreases Capital's 2014 taxable income.
    N.   Has no effect on Capital's 2014 taxable income.

	Amount of Adjustment	(I)	(D)	(N)
1. At its corporate inception in 2012, Capital incurred and paid $40,100 in organizational costs for legal fees to draft the corporate charter. In 2012, Capital correctly elected, for book purposes, to expense the organizational costs and to amortize the organizational expenditures over the minimum allowable period on its federal income tax return. For 2014, no organizational costs were deducted on its books.	_____	O	O	O
2. Capital's 2014 disbursements included $10,000 for reimbursed employees' expenses for business meals and entertainment. The reimbursed expenses met the conditions of deductibility and were properly substantiated under an accountable plan. The reimbursement was not treated as employee compensation.	_____	O	O	O
3. Capital's 2014 disbursements included $15,000 for life insurance premium expense paid for its executives as part of their taxable compensation. Capital is neither the direct nor the indirect beneficiary of the policy, and the amount of the compensation is reasonable.	_____	O	O	O
4. In 2014, Capital increased its allowance for uncollectible accounts by $10,000. No bad debt was written off in 2014.	_____	O	O	O

Task-Based Simulation 15

Taxability		
	Authoritative Literature	Help

Sunco Corp., an accrual-basis calendar-year C corporation, timely filed its 2014 federal income tax return on March 15, 2015. Determine if the following items are fully taxable, partially taxable, or nontaxable for regular income tax purposes on Sunco's 2014 federal income tax return. An answer may be selected once, more than once, or not at all.

Selections

    F.   Fully taxable for regular income tax purposes on Sunco's 2014 federal income tax return.
    P.   Partially taxable for regular income tax purposes on Sunco's 2014 federal income tax return.
    N.   Nontaxable for regular income tax purposes on Sunco's 2014 federal income tax return.

	(F)	(P)	(N)
1. In 2014, Sunco received dividend income from a 35%-owned domestic corporation. The dividends were not from debt-financed portfolio stock, and the taxable income limitation did not apply.	O	O	O
2. In 2014, Sunco received a $2,800 lease cancellation payment from a three-year lease tenant.	O	O	O

Task-Based Simulation 16

Deductibility		
	Authoritative Literature	**Help**

Quest Corp., an accrual-basis calendar-year C corporation, timely filed its 2014 federal income tax return on March 15, 2015. Determine if the following items are fully deductible, partially deductible, or nondeductible for regular income tax purposes on Quest's 2014 federal income tax return. An answer may be selected once, more than once, or not at all.

Selections
F. Fully deductible for regular income tax purposes on Quest's 2014 federal income tax return.
P. Partially deductible for regular income tax purposes on Quest's 2014 federal income tax return.
N. Nondeductible for regular income tax purposes on Quest's 2014 federal income tax return.

		(F)	(P)	(N)
1.	Quest's 2014 taxable income before charitable contributions and dividends received deduction was $200,000. Quest's Board of Directors authorized a $38,000 contribution to a qualified charity on December 1, 2014. The payment was made on February 1, 2015. All charitable contributions were properly substantiated.	○	○	○
2.	During 2014 Quest was assessed and paid a $300 uncontested penalty for failure to pay its 2013 federal income taxes on time.	○	○	○

Task-Based Simulation 17

Alternative Minimum Tax		
	Authoritative Literature	**Help**

On its 2014 federal income tax return, Gelco Corp., an accrual-basis calendar-year C corporation, reported the same amounts for regular income tax and alternative minimum tax purposes. Determine if each item, taken separately, contributes to overstating, understating, or correctly stating Gelco's 2014 alternative minimum taxable income (AMTI) prior to the adjusted current earnings adjustment (ACE). An answer may be selected once, more than once, or not at all.

Selections
O. Overstating Gelco's 2014 AMTI prior to the ACE.
U. Understating Gelco's 2014 AMTI prior to the ACE.
C. Correctly stating Gelco's 2014 AMTI prior to the ACE.

		(O)	(U)	(C)
1.	For regular tax purposes, Gelco deducted the maximum MACRS depreciation on seven-year personal property placed in service on January 2, 2014. Gelco did not elect to expense any part of the cost of the property under Sec. 179, and elected not to take bonus depreciation.	○	○	○
2.	For regular income tax purposes, Gelco depreciated nonresidential real property placed in service on January 2, 1998, under the general MACRS depreciation system for a thirty-nine-year depreciable life.	○	○	○
3.	Gelco excluded state highway construction general obligation bond interest income earned in 2014 for regular income tax and alternative minimum tax (AMT) purposes.	○	○	○

Task-Based Simulation 18

Dan King contacts you and indicates that he is considering incorporating a business by transferring investment property with a fair market value of $500,000 and an adjusted basis of $150,000. In the exchange, King would receive all of the corporation's stock.

Assuming King's transfer qualifies under Sec. 351 as a transfer to a corporation controlled by the transferor, what Internal Revenue Code section and paragraph determines whether King's holding period for the stock received will include his holding period for the property transferred? Indicate the reference to that citation in the shaded boxes below.

Task-Based Simulation 19

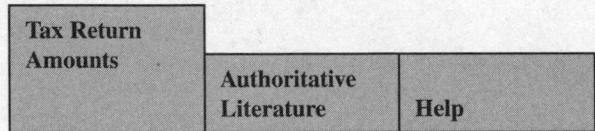

Situation

Kimberly Corp. is a calendar-year accrual-basis corporation that commenced operations on January 2, 2010. The following adjusted accounts appear on Kimberly's records for the year ended December 31, 2014. Kimberly is not subject to the uniform capitalization rules.

Revenues and gains	
Gross sales	$2,000,000
Dividends:	10,000
30%-owned domestic corporation	10,000
XYZ Corp.	
Interest:	26,000
US treasury bonds	25,000
Municipal bonds	
Insurance proceeds	40,000
Gain on sale:	20,000
Unimproved lot (1)	5,000
XYZ stock (2)	
State franchise tax refund	14,000
Total	2,150,000
Costs and expenses	
Cost of goods sold	350,000
Salaries and wages	470,000
Depreciation:	50,000
Real property	100,000
Personal property (3)	
Bad debt (4)	10,000
State franchise tax	25,000
Vacation expense	10,000
Interest expense (5)	16,000
Life insurance premiums	20,000
Federal income taxes	200,000
Entertainment expense	20,000
Other expenses	29,000
Total	1,300,000
Net income	$850,000

Additional information

(1)   Gain on the sale of unimproved lot: Purchased in 2012 for use in business for $50,000. Sold in 2014 for $70,000. Kimberly has never had any Sec. 1231 losses.

(2)   Gain on sale of XYZ Stock: Purchased in 2012.

(3)   Personal Property: The book depreciation is the same as tax depreciation for all the property that was placed in service before January 1, 2014. The book depreciation is straight-line over the useful life, which is the same as class life. Company policy is to use the half-year convention per books for personal property. Furniture and fixtures costing $56,000 were placed in service on January 2, 2014.

(4)   Bad Debt: Represents the increase in the allowance for doubtful accounts based on an aging of accounts receivable. Actual bad debts written off were $7,000.

(5)   Interest expense on

Mortgage loan	$10,000
Loan obtained to purchase municipal bonds	4,000
Line of credit loan	2,000

For **items 1 through 5,** determine the amount that should be reported on Kimberly Corporation's 2014 federal income tax return.

Items to be answered

1.   What amount of interest income is taxable from the US Treasury bonds?

2.   Determine the tax depreciation expense under the Modified Accelerated Cost Recovery System (MACRS), for the furniture and fixtures that were placed in service on January 2, 2014. Round the answer to the nearest thousand. Kimberly did not use the alternative depreciation system (ADS) or a straight-line method of depreciation. No election was made to expense part of the cost of the property, and Kimberly elected not to use bonus depreciation.

3.   Determine the amount of bad debt to be included as an expense item.

4.   Determine Kimberly's net long-term capital gain.

5.   What amount of interest expense is deductible?

Task-Based Simulation 20

Deductibility		
	Authoritative Literature	Help

For **items 1 through 5,** select whether the following expenses are fully deductible, partially deductible, or nondeductible, for regular tax purposes, on Kimberly's 2014 federal income tax return.

Selections
F.   Fully deductible for regular tax purposes on Kimberly Corp's 2014 federal income tax return.
P.   Partially deductible for regular tax purposes on Kimberly Corp's 2014 federal income tax return.
N.   Nondeductible for regular tax purposes on Kimberly Corp's 2014 federal income tax return.

	(F)	(P)	(N)
1. Organization expense incurred in January 2010 to draft the corporate charter. No deduction was taken for the organization expense in 2010.	O	O	O
2. Life insurance premiums paid by the corporation for its executives as part of their compensation for services rendered. The corporation is neither the direct nor the indirect beneficiary of the policy and the amount of compensation is reasonable.	O	O	O
3. Vacation pay earned by employees which vested under a plan by December 31, 2014, and was paid February 1, 2015.	O	O	O
4. State franchise tax liability that has accrued during the year and was paid on March 15, 2015.	O	O	O
5. Entertainment expense to lease a luxury skybox during football season to entertain clients. A bona fide business discussion precedes each game. The cost of regular seats would have been one-half the amount paid.	O	O	O

Simulation Solutions

Task-Based Simulation 1

1.   A corporation whose income was derived solely from dividends, interest, and royalties, and during the last six months of its year more than 50% of the value of its outstanding stock is owned by five or fewer individuals.

2.   The basis used to determine gain on sale of property that was received as a gift.

3.   The trade-in of production machinery for new production machinery by a corporation, when the corporation pays additional cash.

4.   An unmarried individual whose filing status enables the taxpayer to use a set of income tax rates that are lower than those applicable to other unmarried individuals, but are higher than those applicable to married persons filing a joint return.

5.   If income is unqualifiedly available, it will be subject to the income tax even though it is not physically in the taxpayer's possession.

6.   A special tax imposed on corporations that accumulate their earnings beyond the reasonable needs of the business.

7.   The classification of income from interest, dividends, annuities, and certain royalties.

8.   The classification of depreciable assets and real estate used in a trade or business and held for more than one year.

9.   This deduction attempts to mitigate the triple taxation that would occur if one corporation paid dividends to a corporate shareholder who, in turn, distributed such amounts to its individual shareholders.

10.   Sale of property to a corporation by a shareholder for a selling price that is in excess of the property's fair market value.

	(A)	(B)	(C)	(D)	(E)	(F)	(G)	(H)	(I)	(J)	(K)	(L)	(M)	(N)	(O)	(P)	(Q)	(R)	(S)	(T)	(U)	(V)	(W)	(X)	(Y)	(Z)
1.	○	○	○	○	○	○	○	○	○	○	○	○	○	○	○	○	○	●	○	○	○	○	○	○	○	○
2.	○	○	○	○	○	○	○	○	○	○	○	○	○	○	○	○	○	○	○	○	○	○	○	○	○	●
3.	○	○	○	○	○	○	○	○	○	○	○	○	○	○	○	●	○	○	○	○	○	○	○	○	○	○
4.	○	○	○	○	○	○	○	○	○	○	○	○	○	○	●	○	○	○	○	○	○	○	○	○	○	○
5.	○	○	○	○	○	○	●	○	○	○	○	○	○	○	○	○	○	○	○	○	○	○	○	○	○	○
6.	●	○	○	○	○	○	○	○	○	○	○	○	○	○	○	○	○	○	○	○	○	○	○	○	○	○
7.	○	○	○	○	○	○	○	○	○	○	○	○	○	○	○	○	○	○	●	○	○	○	○	○	○	○
8.	○	○	○	○	○	○	○	○	○	○	○	○	○	○	○	○	○	○	○	○	○	○	●	○	○	○
9.	○	○	○	○	○	○	○	○	○	●	○	○	○	○	○	○	○	○	○	○	○	○	○	○	○	○
10.	○	○	○	○	○	●	○	○	○	○	○	○	○	○	○	○	○	○	○	○	○	○	○	○	○	○

Explanations

1.   **(R)** To be classified as a personal holding company, a corporation must meet two requirements: (1) the corporation must receive at least 60% of its adjusted ordinary gross income as "personal holding company income" such as dividends, interest, rents, royalties, and other passive income; and (2) the corporation must have more than 50% of the value of its outstanding stock directly or indirectly owned by five or fewer individuals during any time in the last half of the tax year.

2. (**Z**) The transferred basis, equal to the basis of the donor plus any gift tax paid attributable to the net appreciation in the value of the gift, is the basis used to determine gain on sale of property that was received as a gift.

3. (**P**) A like-kind exchange, the exchange of business or investment property for property of a like-kind, qualifies as a nontaxable exchange. Thus, the exchange of production machinery for new production machinery when boot (money) is given is a nontaxable exchange.

4. (**O**) Head of household filing status applies to unmarried persons not qualifying for surviving spouse status who maintain a household for more than one-half of the taxable year for a dependent. The tax rates applicable to the head of household status are lower than those applicable to individuals filing as single, but are higher than rates applicable to married individuals filing a joint return.

5. (**G**) Under the doctrine of constructive receipt, income is includable in gross income and subject to income tax for the taxable year in which that income is made unqualifiedly available to the taxpayer without restriction, even though not physically in the taxpayer's possession.

6. (**A**) Corporations may be subject to an accumulated earnings tax, in addition to regular income tax, if a corporation accumulates earnings beyond reasonable business needs in order to avoid shareholder tax on dividend distributions.

7. (**U**) Portfolio income is defined as income from interest, dividends, annuities, and certain royalties.

8. (**W**) Section 1231 assets include depreciable assets and real estate used in a trade or business and held for more than one year.

9. (**J**) The dividends received deduction was enacted by Congress to mitigate the triple taxation that occurs when one corporation pays dividends to a corporate stockholder who, in turn, distributes such amounts to its individual stockholders.

10. (**F**) A constructive dividend results when a shareholder is considered to have received a dividend from a corporation, although the corporation did not specifically declare a dividend. This situation may occur when a shareholder/employee receives an excessive salary from a corporation, when there is a loan to a shareholder where there is no intent to repay the amount loaned, or when a corporation purchases shareholder property for an amount in excess of the property's fair market value. Constructive dividends often result when a transaction between a shareholder and corporation is not an arm's-length transaction.

Task-Based Simulation 2

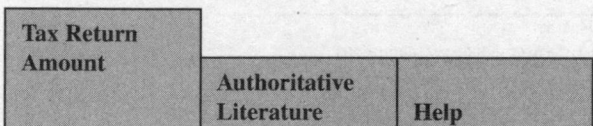

1. (**$20,000**) Interest on funds borrowed for working capital is deductible. However, interest incurred on borrowed funds to purchase municipal bonds is not deductible because the resulting income is exempt from tax.

2. (**$20,000**) Interest earned on corporate bonds must be included in gross income. However, interest earned on municipal bonds is excluded.

3. (**$8,000**) A corporation may deduct up to $5,000 of organizational expenditures for the tax year in which the corporation begins business. This $5,000 amount must be reduced by the amount by which organizational expenditures exceed $50,000. Remaining expenditures are deducted ratably over the 180-month period beginning with the month in which the corporation begins business. Aviator's qualifying expenditures include the legal fees and state incorporation fees, which total $50,000. However, the $15,000 commission for selling stock is neither deductible nor amortizable. The amount of Aviator's deduction for organizational expenditures for 2014 is $5,000 + ($45,000 × 12/180) = $8,000.

4. (**$20,000**) All of the capital gains would be included in Aviator's gross income.

5. (**$20,000**) Corporate capital losses can only be deducted to the extent of capital gains. Therefore, only $20,000 of capital losses can be deducted on the Aviator, Inc. tax return. Since this is Aviator's first year of existence, the excess of capital losses over capital gains ($10,000) will then be carried forward five years as a short-term capital loss, to offset capital gains.

6. (**$35,000**) The dividends received deduction will be based on 70% of its dividends received, since Aviator, Inc. owns less than 20% of the dividend-paying corporation.

7. (**$38,200**) A charitable contributions deduction is limited to a maximum of 10% of taxable income before the dividends received deduction and a charitable contributions deduction. Therefore, taxable income before these deductions needs to be calculated to determine the maximum allowable deduction. Taxable income is computed as follows:

Sales	$2,000,000
Dividends	50,000
Interest revenue	20,000
Gains on the sale of stock	20,000
Cost of goods sold	(1,000,000)
Salaries and wages	(400,000)
Depreciation	(260,000)
Losses on the sale of stock	(20,000)
Organizational expenditures	(8,000)
Interest expense	(20,000)
	$382,000

The charitable contributions deduction will be limited to $38,200 ($382,000 × 10%). The excess not allowed ($40,000 – $38,200 = $1,800) will be carried forward for up to five years.

Task-Based Simulation 3

Schedule M-1		
	Authoritative Literature	Help

Schedule M-1 of Form 1120 is used to reconcile a corporate taxpayer's income reported per books with income reported on the tax return. Generally, items of income or deduction whose book and tax treatment differ, result in Schedule M-1 items. However, since Schedule M-1 reconciles book income to taxable income before special deductions (line 28, page 1), the dividends received deduction and net operating loss deduction which are special deductions will never be reconciling items on Schedule M-1.

The beginning and ending balance of Retained Earnings and cash dividends paid to shareholders are neither deducted per books nor on the tax return and are not Schedule M-1 items. Instead they will be included on Schedule M-2 which provides an Analysis of Unappropriated Retained Earnings per books between the beginning and end of the year.

Schedule M-1   Reconciliation of Income (Loss) per Books With Income per Return

Note: Schedule M-3 required instead of Schedule M-1 if total assets are $10 million or more—see instructions

1	Net income (loss) per books	310,000	7	Income recorded on books this year not included on this return (itemize):	
2	Federal income tax per books	104,150		Tax-exempt interest $ 20,000	
3	Excess of capital losses over capital gains	7,000		Insurance proceeds 100,000	
4	Income subject to tax not recorded on books this year (itemize):				120,000
			8	Deductions on this return not charged against book income this year (itemize):	
5	Expenses recorded on books this year not deducted on this return (itemize):		a	Depreciation $ 9,000	
a	Depreciation $		b	Charitable contributions $	
b	Charitable contributions $				
c	Travel and entertainment $ 3,000				9,000
	Insurance premiums 5,000	8,000	9	Add lines 7 and 8	129,000
6	Add lines 1 through 5	429,150	10	Income (page 1, line 28)—line 6 less line 9	300,150

Line 2. The federal income taxes of $104,150 deducted per books is not deductible for tax purposes and is added back to book income.

Line 3. Since a corporation is not allowed to deduct a net capital loss, the $7,000 net capital loss deducted per books must be added back to book income.

Line 5c. Since only 50% of business meals and entertainment are deductible for tax purposes, 50% of the $6,000 of business entertainment expense deducted per books must be added back to book income. Additionally, the life insurance premiums of $5,000 on the president's life that were deducted per books represent an expense incurred in the production of tax-exempt income and are not deductible for tax purposes.

Line 7. The $20,000 of interest income from municipal bonds included per books is tax-exempt and must be subtracted from book income. Similarly, the $100,000 of life insurance proceeds received on the death of Aviator's president included in book income is not taxable and must be subtracted from book income.

Line 8a. Since Aviator's MACRS depreciation deductible for tax purposes exceeds the depreciation deducted for book purposes, the excess of $9,000 must be subtracted from book income.

Task-Based Simulation 4

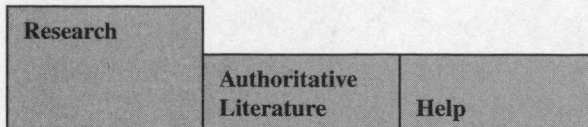

Internal Revenue Code Section 1211, subsection (a), provides that a corporation's capital losses are allowed only to the extent of capital gains. As a result, a corporation cannot deduct a net capital loss.

§	Section	Subsection
	1211	(a)

Task-Based Simulation 5

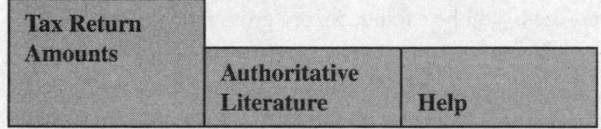

Item for Ral's 2014 federal income tax

1. Amount of deduction for manager's $5,000 bonus for 2014.

2. Deduction for bad debts for 2014.

3. Deduction for keyman life insurance premiums for 2014.

4. Deduction for state income taxes for 2014.

5. Amount of interest to be included in gross income for 2014.

6. Dividends received deduction for dividends received from Clove Corp.

7. Dividends received deduction for dividends received from Ramo Corp.

8. Dividends received deduction for dividends received from Sol Corp.

9. Dividends received deduction for dividends received from Real Estate Investment Trust.

10. Dividends received deduction for dividends received from Mutual Fund Corp.

11. Dividends received deduction for dividends received from Money Market Fund.

12. Deduction for the $11,000 of dividends paid by Ral to its shareholders.

13. Deduction for net capital loss for 2014.

14. Ral's federal income tax for 2014 if taxable income were $100,000.

	(A)	(B)	(C)	(D)	(E)	(F)	(G)	(H)	(I)	(J)	(K)	(L)	(M)	(N)	(O)	(P)	(Q)	(R)	(S)	(T)	(U)	(V)	(W)	(X)	(Y)	(Z)
1.	○	○	○	○	○	○	○	○	○	○	○	○	○	○	○	●	○	○	○	○	○	○	○	○	○	○
2.	○	○	○	○	○	○	○	○	○	○	○	○	○	○	○	○	○	○	○	○	●	○	○	○	○	○
3.	●	○	○	○	○	○	○	○	○	○	○	○	○	○	○	○	○	○	○	○	○	○	○	○	○	○
4.	○	○	○	○	○	○	○	○	○	○	○	○	○	○	○	○	○	○	○	○	○	○	○	●	○	○
5.	○	○	○	○	○	○	○	○	○	○	○	○	○	○	○	●	○	○	○	○	○	○	○	○	○	○
6.	○	○	○	○	○	○	○	○	○	○	○	○	○	○	○	○	○	●	○	○	○	○	○	○	○	○
7.	○	○	○	○	○	○	○	○	○	○	○	○	●	○	○	○	○	○	○	○	○	○	○	○	○	○
8.	●	○	○	○	○	○	○	○	○	○	○	○	○	○	○	○	○	○	○	○	○	○	○	○	○	○
9.	●	○	○	○	○	○	○	○	○	○	○	○	○	○	○	○	○	○	○	○	○	○	○	○	○	○
10.	●	○	○	○	○	○	○	○	○	○	○	○	○	○	○	○	○	○	○	○	○	○	○	○	○	○

	(A)	(B)	(C)	(D)	(E)	(F)	(G)	(H)	(I)	(J)	(K)	(L)	(M)	(N)	(O)	(P)	(Q)	(R)	(S)	(T)	(U)	(V)	(W)	(X)	(Y)	(Z)
11.	●	○	○	○	○	○	○	○	○	○	○	○	○	○	○	○	○	○	○	○	○	○	○	○	○	○
12.	●	○	○	○	○	○	○	○	○	○	○	○	○	○	○	○	○	○	○	○	○	○	○	○	○	○
13.	●	○	○	○	○	○	○	○	○	○	○	○	○	○	○	○	○	○	○	○	○	○	○	○	○	○
14.	○	○	○	○	○	○	○	○	○	○	○	○	○	○	○	○	○	○	○	○	○	○	○	○	○	●

Explanations

1. (**P**; **$5,000**) Ral is an accrual method taxpayer, the payment was based on a formula in effect for 2014, and the sales manager had performed the services in 2014.

2. (**U**; **$8,000**) Since taxpayers are required to use the direct charge-off method in computing taxable income, only the $8,000 of actual bad debts for 2014 can be deducted.

3. (**A**; **$0**) Since Ral is the beneficiary of the policies and the eventual proceeds will be excluded from gross income, the premium cannot be deducted in computing taxable income.

4. (**X**; **$12,000**) State income taxes are deductible in computing federal taxable income.

5. (**P**; **$5,000**) The $3,000 interest on US Treasury notes and $2,000 interest on municipal arbitrage bonds is taxable, while the $200 interest on municipal bonds is nontaxable.

6. (**R**; **$5,600**) Since Clove is at least 20% owned, the $7,000 of dividends are eligible for an 80% dividends received deduction.

7. (**M**; **$4,200**) Since Ramo is less than 20% owned, the $6,000 of dividends are eligible for an 70% dividends received deduction.

8. (**A**; **$0**) No dividends received deduction is allowed because the stock was not held for more than forty-five days.

9. (**A**; **$0**) No dividends received deduction is allowed because a real estate investment trust (REIT) is a pass-through entity with only one level of tax paid (by its shareholders).

10. (**A**; **$0**) The $400 of capital gains dividends pass through as capital gains and are not eligible for a dividends received deduction.

11. (**A**; **$0**) No dividends received deduction is allowed because Money Market Fund derived all of its income from investments in "interest paying securities," not dividend paying stocks.

12. (**A**; **$0**) No federal income tax deduction is allowed for corporate dividend payments to its own shareholders.

13. (**A**; **$0**) Ral's net capital loss is $6,400 – $400 capital gains dividends = $6,000. However, a corporation cannot deduct a net capital loss. Instead, it is carried back three years and forward five years to offset capital gains in those years.

14. (**Z**; **$22,250**) The tax rate schedule indicates that the tax on $100,000 of taxable income is $22,250.

Task-Based Simulation 6

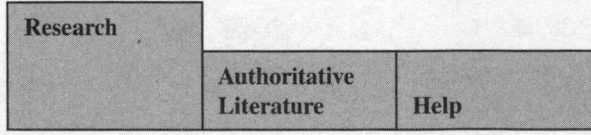

Internal Revenue Code Section 246A provides that a corporation's dividends received deduction will be reduced to the extent that its stock investment was financed by debt (e.g., if 40% of its investment was financed by debts its dividends received deduction will be reduced by 40%).

Task-Based Simulation 7

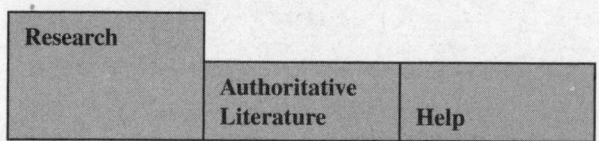

For **items 1 through 4,** candidates were asked to determine the amount for Lan Corp. (an accrual-basis calendar-year S corporation), using the fact pattern for each item.

1. ($6,140) The requirement is to determine the amount of net business income that Lan should report on Schedule K of Form 1120S. The term "net business income" corresponds to an S corporation's "ordinary income (loss) from trade or business activities." The computation of this amount excludes any item that must be separately stated and passed through to shareholders in order to retain the item's special tax characteristics. Here, the interest income on investments is portfolio income and must be separately stated and passed through to shareholders as interest income. Similarly, the charitable contributions must be separately stated and passed through to shareholders in order to apply the appropriate percentage limitations at the shareholder level. As a result, Lan's net business income consists of its $7,200 of gross receipts reduced by the $1,120 of supplies expense, or $6,140.

2. ($2,700) The requirements is to determine the amount of net business income to be reported on Pike's 2015 Schedule K-1 from Lan. If there is no election to terminate the tax year following the sale of stock, the income of an S corporation for the entire taxable year is allocated per share, per day to anyone who was a shareholder during the year. Lan was formed on January 6, 2015, and its tax year consists of 360 days. So its net business income per share, per day would be $14,400 ÷ 200 shares ÷ 360 days = $.20. Since Pike purchased his forty shares on January 31, he is considered to own his stock for a total of 334 days during the year (counting February 1 as the first day). Thus, the amount of net business income to be reported on Pike's Schedule K-1 is (40 shares × 334 days × $.20) = $2,672. Since the instructions indicated that the answer should be rounded to the nearest hundred, the correct answer is $2,700.

3. ($3,150) The requirement is to determine Pike's basis for his Lan stock at December 31, 2015, assuming that he had purchased the stock for $4,000. An S corporation's items of income and deduction pass through to be reported on shareholder returns even though no distributions are made. As a result, a shareholder's S corporation stock basis is increased by the pass through of all income items (including tax-exempt income), and is decreased by all loss and deduction items (including nondeductible expenses). In this case, Pike's beginning basis of $4,000 would be increased by the $150 of municipal bond interest income, and decreased by the $1,000 of ordinary business loss.

4. ($9,000) The requirement is to determine Taylor's basis in Lan shares for determining gain or loss from the sale of stock to Pike. Taylor's beginning stock basis of $10,000 must be increased by his $2,000 share of the ordinary income from Lan prior to the sale, and must be decreased by the $3,000 nontaxable cash distribution that Taylor received. Recall that distributions by S corporations without accumulated earnings and profits are treated as a return of stock basis and are excluded from gross income.

Task-Based Simulation 8

Internal Revenue Code section 1366, subsection (d) limits a shareholder's deduction of an S corporation's losses to the shareholder's basis for stock and debt.

Section	Subsection
§ 1366	(d)

Task-Based Simulation 9

Schedule M-1 Adjustments		
	Authoritative Literature	Help

> **NOTE:** Schedule M-1 is the schedule of the corporate income tax return that provides a reconciliation of net income (loss) per books with the corporation's taxable income before the net operating loss and dividends received deductions. If an item's treatment per books differs from its treatment for tax purposes, an M-1 adjustment will result.

		Schedule M-1 Adjustment	(I)	(D)	(N)
1.	Reliant's disbursements included reimbursed employees' expenses in 2014 for travel of $100,000, and business meals of $30,000. The reimbursed expenses met the conditions of deductibility and were properly substantiated under an accountable plan. The reimbursement was not treated as employee compensation.	$15,000	●	○	○
2.	Reliant's books expensed $7,000 in 2014 for the term life insurance premiums on the corporate officers. Reliant was the policy owner and beneficiary.	$7,000	●	○	○
3.	Reliant's books indicated an $18,000 state franchise tax expense for 2014. Estimated state tax payments for 2014 were $15,000.	$0	○	○	●
4.	Book depreciation on computers for 2014 was $10,000. These computers, which cost $50,000, were placed in service on January 2, 2013. Tax depreciation used MACRS with the half-year convention. No election was made to expense part of the computer cost and Reliant elected not to use bonus depreciation.	$6,000	○	●	○
5.	For 2014, Reliant's books showed a $4,000 short-term capital gain distribution from a mutual fund corporation and a $5,000 loss on the sale of Retro stock that was purchased in 2012. The stock was an investment in an unrelated corporation. There were no other 2014 gains or losses and no loss carryovers from prior years.	$5,000	●	○	○
6.	Reliant's 2014 taxable income before the charitable contribution and the dividends received deductions was $500,000. Reliant's books expensed $15,000 in board of director authorized charitable contributions that were paid on January 5, 2015. Charitable contributions paid and expensed during 2014 were $35,000. All charitable contributions were properly substantiated. There were no net operating losses or charitable contributions that were carried forward.	$0	○	○	●

Explanations

1. ($15,000; I) The $100,000 reimbursement for employee travel is deductible for both book and tax purposes and no adjustment is necessary. However, since only 50% of the $30,000 of reimbursed business meals that was deducted per books is deductible for tax purposes, an M-1 increase adjustment results in the amount of $15,000 ($30,000 × 50%).

2. ($7,000; I) The $7,000 of term life insurance premiums on corporate officers that was deducted per books is not deductible for tax purposes because Reliant was the policy owner and beneficiary. As a result there is an M-1 increase adjustment of $7,000.

3. ($0; N) The $18,000 of state franchise taxes and $15,000 of estimated state tax payments are fully deductible for both book and tax purposes and no M-1 adjustment is necessary.

4. ($6,000; D) Since the computers are five-year recovery property and Reliant used MACRS and the half-year convention, depreciation would be computed using the 200% declining balance method (i.e., twice the straight-line rate) and the tax depreciation for 2013 would be ($50,000 × 40% × 1/2) = $10,000. The tax depreciation for 2014 would then be ($50,000 – $10,000) × 40% = $16,000. Since book depreciation was only $10,000, the book to tax difference in depreciation would result in an M-1 decrease adjustment of $6,000.

5. ($5,000; I) Since only **long-term capital gain distributions** from a mutual fund pass through as capital gain, the $4,000 of **short-term capital gain distribution** from a mutual fund corporation must be reported by Reliant as ordinary dividend income, and cannot be netted against the $5,000 capital loss from the sale of the Retro stock held as an investment. As a result, Reliant's sale of the Retro stock results in a net capital loss of $5,000 for 2014. Since a corporation cannot deduct a net capital loss for tax purposes, the $5,000 of net capital loss deducted per books results in a book to tax difference and an M-1 increase adjustment of $5,000.

6. ($0; N) Since Reliant had taxable income before the charitable contribution deduction of $500,000 for 2014, Reliant can deduct a maximum of ($500,000 × 10%) = $50,000 of charitable contributions for tax purposes. Reliant can deduct the $35,000 of contributions made during 2014, as well as the $15,000 paid on January 5, 2015, because Reliant is an accrual-basis taxpayer, the $15,000 contribution was authorized by Reliant's board of directors, and the $15,000 was paid within 2 1/2 months after the end of 2014. Since Reliant is deducting $50,000 of contributions for both book and tax purposes, there is no M-1 adjustment.

Task-Based Simulation 10

Deductibility		
	Authoritative Literature	Help

		(F)	(P)	(N)
1.	Reliant purchased theater tickets for its out of town clients. The performances took place after Reliant's substantial and bona fide business negotiations with its clients.	○	●	○
2.	Reliant accrued advertising expenses to promote a new product line. Ten percent of the new product line remained in ending inventory.	●	○	○
3.	Reliant incurred interest expense on a loan to purchase municipal bonds.	○	○	●
4.	Reliant paid a penalty for the underpayment of 2013 estimated taxes.	○	○	●
5.	On December 9, 2014, Reliant's board of directors voted to pay a $500 bonus to each nonstockholder employee for 2014. The bonuses were paid on February 3, 2015.	●	○	○

Explanations

1. (P) The cost of the theater tickets qualifies as a business entertainment expense which is only 50% deductible for 2014.

2. (F) Indirect costs that do not directly benefit a particular activity or are not incurred because of a particular activity may be currently deducted and are not required to be capitalized as part of the cost of inventory. Indirect costs that can be currently deducted include such costs as marketing, selling, advertising, distribution, and general and administrative expenses.

3. (N) Since the proceeds of the loan were used to purchase municipal bonds which generate tax-exempt income, the interest expense on the loan is not deductible.

4. (N) No deduction is allowed for the penalty that results from the underpayment of estimated income tax.

5. (F) An accrual method taxpayer can deduct compensation for nonstockholder employees when there is an obligation to make payment, economic performance has occurred, the amount is reasonable, and payment is made not later than 2 1/2 months after the end of the tax year. Here, the amount of bonus was determined on December 9, 2014, and was paid February 3, 2015.

Task-Based Simulation 11

Taxability		
	Authoritative Literature	**Help**

		(F)	(P)	(N)
1.	The portion of Reliant's refund that represented the overpayment of the 2012 federal taxes.	○	○	●
2.	The portion of Reliant's refund that is attributable to the interest on the overpayment of federal taxes.	●	○	○
3.	Reliant received dividend income from a mutual fund that solely invests in municipal bonds.	○	○	●
4.	Reliant, the lessor, benefited from the capital improvements made to its property by the lessee in 2014. The lease agreement is for one year ending December 31, 2014, and provides for a reduction in rental payments by the lessee in exchange for the improvements.	●	○	○
5.	Reliant collected the proceeds on the term life insurance policy on the life of a debtor who was not a shareholder. The policy was assigned to Reliant as collateral security for the debt. The proceeds exceeded the amount of the debt.	○	●	○

Explanations

1. (N) Since the payment of federal income tax does not result in a deduction, a subsequent refund of federal income tax will be nontaxable.

2. (F) Interest is generally fully included in gross income, including the interest on an overpayment of federal taxes.

3. (N) A mutual fund that invests in tax-exempt municipal bonds is permitted to pass the tax exemption on the bond interest on to its shareholders when the tax-exempt interest is distributed in the form of dividends. To qualify, the mutual fund has to have at least 50% of the value of its total assets invested in tax-exempt municipal bonds at the close of each quarter of its taxable year.

4. (F) Generally, a lessor will not recognize any income as a result of the capital improvements made by a lessee that revert to the lessor at the expiration of the lease. However, if the parties intend the improvements to be, in whole or in part, a substitute for rental payments, then the lessor must recognize the improvements as rental income equal in amount to the reduction in rental payments.

5. (P) Since Reliant was a collateral assignee as a result of the insured's indebtedness, Reliant received the insurance proceeds as payment on the debt, rather than as life insurance proceeds paid "by reason of death of the insured." Consequently, the insurance proceeds are tax-free only to the extent of the amount of unpaid debt, and any proceeds in excess of the debt repayment must be included in Reliant's gross income.

Task-Based Simulation 12

Alternative Minimum Tax		
	Authoritative Literature	**Help**

		(I)	(D)	(N)
1.	Reliant used the 70% dividends received deduction for regular tax purposes.	○	○	●
2.	Reliant received interest from a state's general obligation bonds.	○	○	●
3.	Reliant used MACRS depreciation on seven-year personal property placed into service January 3, 2014 for regular tax purposes. No expense election was made, and Reliant elected not to use bonus depreciation.	●	○	○
4.	Depreciation on nonresidential real property placed into service on January 3, 2014, was under the general MACRS depreciation system for regular tax purposes.	○	○	●
5.	Reliant had only cash charitable contributions for 2014.	○	○	●

Explanations

1. **(N)** The dividends received deduction is not an adjustment in computing AMTI before the ACE adjustment. However, note that the 70% dividends received deduction is an increase adjustment in computing a corporation's ACE.

2. **(N)** The tax-exempt interest on a state's **general obligation** bonds is not an adjustment is computing AMTI before the ACE adjustment.

3. **(I)** Generally for seven-year property, the 200% declining balance method would be used under MACRS for regular tax purposes, while the 150% declining balance method must be used for AMT purposes, resulting in an increase adjustment in computing AMTI prior to the ACE adjustment for the year placed in service.

4. **(N)** For real property placed in service after December 31, 1998, the AMT adjustment has been eliminated because for AMT purposes, the recovery period is the same as that used for regular tax MACRS depreciation (e.g., 39 years or 27 1/2 years). On the other hand, for real property that was placed in service before January 1, 1999, an AMT adjustment is necessary because for AMT purposes, real property must be depreciated using the straight-line method over a 40-year recovery period, rather than the 39-year or 27 1/2-year period used for regular tax purposes.

5. **(N)** Allowable charitable contributions do not result in an adjustment in computing AMTI or ACE.

Task-Based Simulation 13

Research		
	Authoritative Literature	Help

Internal Revenue Code Section 170, subsection (b), paragraph (2), limits a corporation's deduction for charitable contributions to 10% of its taxable income before certain specified deductions.

Section	Subsection	Paragraph
§ 170	(b)	(2)

Task-Based Simulation 14

Schedule M-1 Adjustments		
	Authoritative Literature	Help

		Amount of Adjustment	(I)	(D)	(N)
1.	At its corporate inception in 2012, Capital incurred and paid $40,100 in organizational costs for legal fees to draft the corporate charter. In 2012, Capital correctly elected, for book purposes, to expense the organizational costs and to amortize the organizational expenditures over the minimum allowable period on its federal income tax return. For 2014, no organizational costs were deducted on its books.	$2,340	○	●	○
2.	Capital's 2014 disbursements included $10,000 for reimbursed employees' expenses for business meals and entertainment. The reimbursed expenses met the conditions of deductibility and were properly substantiated under an accountable plan. The reimbursement was not treated as employee compensation.	$5,000	●	○	○
3.	Capital's 2014 disbursements included $15,000 for life insurance premium expense paid for its executives as part of their taxable compensation. Capital is neither the direct nor the indirect beneficiary of the policy, and the amount of the compensation is reasonable.	$0	○	○	●
4.	In 2014, Capital increased its allowance for uncollectible accounts by $10,000. No bad debt was written off in 2014.	$10,000	●	○	○

Explanations

1. **($2,340; D)** $5,000 of Capital's organizational costs of $40,100 would have been deducted in 2012 with remainder amortized over 180 months (15 years) for tax purposes. As a result, the tax amortization of organizational costs results in a tax deduction of $35,100 × 12/180 = $2,340 for 2014. Since no organizational costs were deducted per books for 2014, a Schedule M-1 decrease adjustment is necessary for the $2,340 difference.

2. **($5,000; I)** Only 50% of reimbursed employees' expenses for business meals and entertainment is deductible for tax purposes. As a result, an M-1 increase adjustment of $5,000 is necessary to reflect the fact that 50% of the $10,000 of reimbursed business meals and entertainment that was deducted for book purposes is not deductible for tax purposes.

3. **($0; N)** The $15,000 of life insurance premiums treated as reasonable compensation is fully deductible for both book and tax purposes and no M-1 adjustment is necessary.

4. **($10,000; I)** The reserve method of accounting for bad debts is not allowed for tax purposes. Instead, a bad debt deduction can be taken only when a specific debt is determined to be uncollectible. Since no bad debt was written off during 2014, an M-1 increase adjustment is necessary for the $10,000 addition to the allowance for uncollectible accounts for 2014.

Task-Based Simulation 15

Taxability		
	Authoritative Literature	Help

		(F)	(P)	(N)
1.	In 2014, Sunco received dividend income from a 35%-owned domestic corporation. The dividends were not from debt-financed portfolio stock, and the taxable income limitation did not apply.	○	●	○
2.	In 2014, Sunco received a $2,800 lease cancellation payment from a three-year lease tenant.	●	○	○

Explanations

1. **(P)** Dividends received from a 35%-owned domestic corporation would be eligible for an 80% dividends received deduction. As a result, only 20% of the gross dividends received would be included in taxable income.

2. **(F)** A lease cancellation payment is treated as rent and must be fully included in income when received.

Task-Based Simulation 16

Deductibility		
	Authoritative Literature	Help

		(F)	(P)	(N)
1.	Quest's 2014 taxable income before charitable contributions and dividends received deduction was $200,000. Quest's Board of Directors authorized a $38,000 contribution to a qualified charity on December 1, 2014. The payment was made on February 1, 2015. All charitable contributions were properly substantiated.	○	●	○
2.	During 2014 Quest was assessed and paid a $300 uncontested penalty for failure to pay its 2013 federal income taxes on time.	○	○	●

Explanations

1. (P) Since Quest is an accrual method corporation, it can elect to deduct contributions authorized by its board of directors during 2014, so long as the contribution is actually paid no later than 2 1/2 months after the end of the tax year. Thus, to maximize its deduction for 2014, Quest can elect to treat the $38,000 contribution as a deduction for 2014 subject to the 10% of taxable income limitation that applies for 2014. Since Quest had 2014 taxable income of $200,000 before the charitable contributions and dividends received deductions, Quest's 2014 deduction for the $38,000 charitable contribution is limited to $200,000 × 10% = $20,000.

2. (N) A penalty that is paid for a failure to pay federal income taxes on time is not deductible.

Task-Based Simulation 17

Alternative Minimum Tax		
	Authoritative Literature	Help

		(O)	(U)	(C)
1.	For regular tax purposes, Gelco deducted the maximum MACRS depreciation on seven-year personal property placed in service on January 2, 2014. Gelco did not elect to expense any part of the cost of the property under Sec. 179, and elected not to take bonus depreciation.	○	●	○
2.	For regular income tax purposes, Gelco depreciated nonresidential real property placed in service on January 2, 1998, under the general MACRS depreciation system for a thirty-nine-year depreciable life.	○	●	○
3.	Gelco excluded state highway construction general obligation bond interest income earned in 2014 for regular income tax and alternative minimum tax (AMT) purposes.	○	○	●

Explanations

1. (U) Generally for seven-year property, the 200% declining balance method would be used for MACRS, while the 150% declining balance method must be used for AMT purposes. Therefore, the use of MACRS would have the effect of understating AMTI before the ACE adjustment, and would necessitate an increase adjustment to convert 2013 regular taxable income to AMTI.

2. (U) MACRS depreciation for nonresidential real property placed in service during 1998 would be computed using the straight-line method and a thirty-nine-year recovery period. For AMT purposes depreciation would have to be computed using the straight-line method over a forty-year recovery period. Therefore, regular tax depreciation would have the effect of understating AMTI before the ACE adjustment, and would necessitate an increase adjustment to convert 2014 regular taxable income to AMTI. However, note that for real property placed in service after December 31, 1998, the AMT adjustment has been eliminated because for AMT purposes, the recovery period is the same as that used for regular tax MACRS depreciation (e.g., 39 years or 27 1/2 years). Thus, if the building had instead been placed in service **after** December 31, 1998, no AMT adjustment would be necessary and the correct answer would be (C).

3. (C) Interest on a state's general obligation bonds is tax exempt for purposes of computing both regular taxable income, as well as for computing AMTI before the ACE adjustment, and would have the effect of correctly stating AMTI before the ACE adjustment. However, note that interest from a state's general obligation bonds is includible income for purposes of determining a corporation's ACE adjustment for 2014.

Task-Based Simulation 18

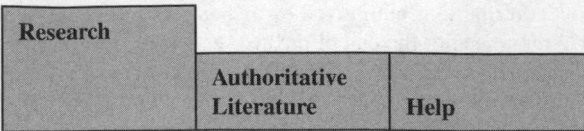

Internal Revenue Code Section 1223, paragraph (1), provides that the holding period of the stock will include the holding period of the property transferred if the transferred property was either a capital asset or a Section 1231 asset. Since King transferred investment property (a capital asset), King's holding period for the stock received includes his holding period for the investment property transferred.

Task-Based Simulation 19

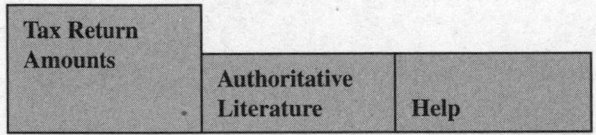

For **items 1 through 5,** candidates were required to determine the amount that should be reported on Kimberly Corp.'s 2014 Federal income tax return.

1.   ($26,000) All $26,000 of interest income from US Treasury bonds is taxable.

2.   ($8,000) The furniture and fixtures are classified as seven-year recovery property. Under MACRS, their cost of $56,000 will be recovered using the 200% declining balance method of depreciation and the half-year convention. Thus, the amount of depreciation for the year of acquisition would be $56,000 \times 2/7 \times 1/2 = $8,000.

3.   ($7,000) The bad debt deduction consists of the $7,000 of bad debts actually written off during the year. The reserve method, using the increase in the allowance for doubtful accounts based on an aging of accounts receivable, cannot be used for tax purposes.

4.   ($25,000) Since the unimproved lot was used in the business and held for more than one year, the $20,000 gain on its sale is classified as a Sec. 1231 gain. Since Kimberly had no previous nonrecaptured Sec. 1231 losses, the net Sec. 1231 gain is treated as a LTCG. Combining this $20,000 LTCG with the $5,000 LTCG from the sale of XYZ stock results in a net LTCG of $25,000.

5.   ($12,000) Deductible interest expense consists of the $10,000 interest on the mortgage loan and the $2,000 interest on the line of credit loan. The $4,000 of interest expense on the loan obtained to purchase municipal bonds is not deductible because the municipal bonds produce tax-exempt income.

Task-Based Simulation 20

Deductibility		
	Authoritative Literature	Help

	(F)	(P)	(N)
1. Organization expense incurred in January 2010 to draft the corporate charter. No deduction was taken for the organization expense in 2010.	○	○	●
2. Life insurance premiums paid by the corporation for its executives as part of their compensation for services rendered. The corporation is neither the direct nor the indirect beneficiary of the policy and the amount of compensation is reasonable.	●	○	○
3. Vacation pay earned by employees which vested under a plan by December 31, 2014, and was paid February 1, 2015.	●	○	○
4. State franchise tax liability that has accrued during the year and was paid on March 15, 2015.	●	○	○
5. Entertainment expense to lease a luxury skybox during football season to entertain clients. A bona fide business discussion precedes each game. The cost of regular seats would have been one-half the amount paid.	○	●	○

Explanations

1. (N) Corporate organizational expenditures may be amortized over a period of 180 months, beginning with the month that business begins. If no deduction is taken, the expenditures must be capitalized and can only be deducted when the corporation is liquidated. Here, the problem indicates that Kimberly was formed and commenced operations during 2010, and further states that no deduction was taken for the organization expense in 2010. As a result, no amortization deduction would be available for 2014.

2. (F) The life insurance premiums are fully deductible because Kimberly is neither the direct nor indirect beneficiary of the policy. The life insurance premiums are deductible as part of the reasonable compensation paid to its executives.

3. (F) An accrual method taxpayer can deduct vacation pay for employees **in the year earned** if (1) it is paid during the year, or (2) the vacation pay is vested and paid no later than 2 1/2 months after the end of the year. Here, the vacation pay was vested and paid on February 1, 2015.

4. (F) Corporate franchise taxes are deductible as a business expense. An accrual method corporation can take a deduction for franchise taxes in the year it becomes legally liable to pay the tax regardless of the year that the tax is based on, or the year it is paid. The item indicates that the franchise tax liability accrued during the year (2014).

5. (P) The cost to lease a skybox is disallowed as an entertainment expense to the extent that the amount paid exceeds the cost of the highest-priced non-luxury box seat tickets multiplied by the number of seats in the skybox. Since the item indicates that the cost of regular seats would have been one half the amount paid, only 50% of the cost of the skybox would qualify as an entertainment expense. Of this amount only 50% would be deductible for 2014.

Module 39: Other Taxation Topics

Overview

This module presents a review of several independent taxation topics. Coverage is first presented regarding the federal gift, estate, and generation-skipping transfer taxes. Next reviewed is the income taxation of estates and trusts. That is followed by coverage of exempt organizations. Multijurisdictional taxation is then reviewed, including state and local taxation (SALT) and international taxation. Next, the module provides a review of the sources of federal tax authority including the federal tax legislative process, as well as the Internal Revenue Code, regulations, and rulings. The module concludes with an overview of some tax-planning possibilities.

I. GIFT AND ESTATE TAXATION

The estate, gift, and generation-skipping transfer (GST) taxes form a unified transfer tax system. The estate tax is based on property transferred at an individual's death, while the gift tax is based on property transferred during an individual's lifetime. The generation-skipping transfer tax ensures that property does not skip a generation without a transfer tax being assessed. The estate tax, gift tax, and GST share a single progressive tax rate schedule.

The American Taxpayer Relief Act of 2012 permanently provides for a maximum federal gift and estate tax rate of 40 percent with an annually inflation-adjusted $5 million exclusion for gifts during an individual's lifetime and estates of decedents dying after December 31, 2012. Additionally, the estate of a surviving spouse is entitled to the unused portion of his or her predeceased spouse's applicable exclusion amount if the appropriate election was made by the predeceased.

A. The Gift Tax

1. Gift Tax Formula

Gross gifts (cash plus FMV of property at date of gift)		$xxx
Plus: One-half of spouse's gifts to third parties if gift splitting elected		x
Less:		
One-half of gifts to third parties treated as given by spouse if gift splitting elected	$ x	
Annual exclusion (up to $14,000 per donee)	x	
Unlimited exclusion for tuition or medical expenses paid on behalf of donee	x	
Unlimited exclusion for gifts to political organizations	x	
Charitable gifts (remainder of charitable gifts after annual exclusion)	x	
Marital deduction (remainder of gifts to spouse after annual exclusion)	x	xx
Taxable gifts for current year		$ xx
Add: Taxable gifts for prior years		x
Total taxable gifts		$ xx
Transfer tax on total taxable gifts		$ xx
Less: Transfer tax on taxable gifts made prior to current year		x
Transfer tax for current year		$ xx
Transfer tax credit	$ xx	
Less: Transfer tax credit used in prior years	x	x
Net gift tax liability		$ xx

2. A **gift** is a transfer for less than adequate consideration in money or money's worth. A gift *occurs* when a transfer becomes complete and is measured by its fair market value on that date. A gift becomes **complete** when the donor has relinquished dominion and control and no longer has the power to change its disposition, whether for the donor's benefit or for the benefit of another.

   a. The creation of joint ownership in property is treated as a gift to the extent the donor's contribution exceeds the donor's retained interest.

   b. The creation of a joint bank account is not a gift; but a gift results when the noncontributing tenant withdraws funds.

   c. The transfer of property to a revocable trust is not a completed gift because the transferor may demand the return of the property or change the beneficiaries of the trust.

3. Gross gifts less the following deductions equal taxable gifts:

   a. **Annual exclusion**—of up to $14,000 per donee is allowed for gifts of present interests (not future interests). A **present interest** is an unrestricted right to the immediate use, possession, or enjoyment of property or the income from property. A **future interest** includes reversions, remainders, and other interests that are limited to commence in use, possession, or enjoyment at some future date or time.

     (1) Trusts for minors (Sec. 2503(c) trusts) allow parents and other donors to obtain an annual exclusion for gifts to trusts for children under age twenty-one even though the trust does not distribute its income annually. To qualify, the trust must provide

       (a) Until the beneficiary reaches age twenty-one, the trustee **may** pay the income and/or the underlying assets to the beneficiary, and,

(b) Any income and assets not distributed must pass to the beneficiary when the beneficiary reaches age twenty-one. If the beneficiary dies before age twenty-one, the income and underlying assets are either payable to the beneficiary's estate, or are payable to any person the minor may appoint if the minor possesses a general power of appointment over the trust property.

(2) **Crummey** trusts allow a donor to obtain an annual exclusion upon funding a discretionary trust. This type of trust is more flexible than a Sec. 2503(c) trust because the beneficiary can be of any age and the trust can terminate at any age. To qualify, a beneficiary must have the power to demand a distribution equal to the lesser of the donor's annual exclusion ($14,000), or the beneficiary's pro rata share of the amount transferred to the trust each year

b. **Gift-splitting**—a gift by either spouse to a third party may be treated as made one-half by each, if both spouses consent to election. Gift-splitting has the advantage of using the other spouse's annual exclusion and unified transfer tax credit.

EXAMPLE

H is married and has three sons. H could give $28,000 to each of his sons during 2015 without making a taxable gift if H's spouse (W) consents to gift-splitting.

	H	W
Gifts	$84,000	
Gift-splitting	(42,000)	$42,000
Annual exclusion (3 × $14,000)	(42,000)	(42,000)
Taxable gifts	$ 0	$ 0

---

c. **Educational and medical exclusion**—an unlimited exclusion is available for amounts **paid on behalf of a donee** (1) as tuition to an educational organization, or (2) to a health care provider for medical care of donee.
d. **Political gifts**—an unlimited exclusion is available for the transfer of money or other property to a political organization.
e. **Charitable gifts**—(net of annual exclusion) are deductible without limitation.
f. **Marital deduction**—is allowed without limitation for gifts to a donor's spouse.

(1) The gift must not be a terminable interest (i.e., donee spouse's interest ends at death with no control over who receives remainder).
(2) If donor elects, a gift of **qualified terminable interest** property (i.e., property placed in trust with income to donee spouse for life and remainder to someone else at donee spouse's death) will qualify for the marital deduction if the income is paid at least annually to spouse and the property is not subject to transfer during the donee spouse's lifetime.
(3) In lieu of a marital deduction, gifts to an alien spouse are eligible for an annual exclusion of up to $145,000 for 2015 ($145,000 for 2014).

4. The **tax computation** reflects the **cumulative nature** of the gift tax. A tax is first computed on lifetime taxable gifts, then is reduced by the tax on taxable gifts made in prior years in order to tax the current year's gifts at applicable marginal rates. Any available transfer tax credit is then subtracted to arrive at the gift tax liability.

a. For 2015, the transfer tax credit is $2,117,800, which is equivalent to an exemption of the first $5.43 million of taxable gifts from the gift tax.
b. For 2014, the transfer tax credit is $2,081,800, which is equivalent to an exemption of the first $5.34 million of taxable gifts from the gift tax.

5. A **gift tax return** (Form 709 United States Gift [and Generation-Skipping Transfer] Tax Return) must be filed on a calendar-year basis, with the return due and tax paid on or before April 15th of the following year.

a. A donor who makes a gift to charity is not required to file a gift tax return if the entire value of the donated property qualifies for a gift tax charitable deduction.
b. If the donor dies, the gift tax return for the year of death is due not later than the due date for filing the decedent's federal estate tax return (generally nine months after date of death).

6. The **basis of property acquired by gift**

a. Basis for gain—basis of donor plus gift tax attributable to appreciation
b. Basis for loss—lesser of gain basis or FMV at date of gift
c. The increase in basis for gift tax paid is limited to the amount (not to exceed the gift tax paid) that bears the same ratio to the amount of gift tax paid as the net appreciation in value of the gift bears to the amount of the gift.

   (1) The amount of gift is reduced by any portion of the $14,000 annual exclusion allowable with respect to the gift.
   (2) Where more than one gift of a present interest is made to the same donee during a calendar year, the $14,000 exclusion is applied to gifts in chronological order.

EXAMPLE

Joan received property with an FMV of $60,000 and an adjusted basis of $80,000 as a gift. The donor paid a gift tax of $12,000 on the transfer. Since the property was not appreciated in value, no gift tax can be added in the basis computation. Joan's basis for computing a gain is $80,000, while her basis for computing a loss is $60,000.

NOW REVIEW MULTIPLE-CHOICE QUESTIONS 1 THROUGH 9

B. The Estate Tax

1. **Estate Tax Formula**

Gross estate (cash plus FMV of property at date of death, or alternate valuation date)		$xxx
Less:		
Funeral expenses	$x	
Administrative expenses	x	
Debts and mortgages	x	
Casualty losses	x	
State death taxes	x	
Charitable bequests (unlimited)	x	
Marital deduction (unlimited)	x	xx
Taxable estate		$xxx
Add: Post-76 adjusted taxable gifts		xx
Total taxable life and death transfers		$xxx
Transfer tax on total transfers		$ xx
Less:		
Post-76 gift taxes (specially computed at estate tax rates in effect at time of death)	$x	
Transfer tax credit ($2,117,800 for 2015)	x	
Foreign death and prior transfer tax credits	x	x
Net estate tax liability		$ xx

2. **Gross estate** includes the FMV of all property in which the decedent had an interest at time of death.

a. **Concurrently held property**

   (1) If property was held by tenancy in common, only the FMV of the decedent's share is included.
   (2) Include one-half the FMV of community property, and one-half the FMV of property held **by spouses** in joint tenancy or tenancy by the entirety.
   (3) Include one-half of FMV if the property held by two persons in joint tenancy was acquired by gift, bequest, or inheritance (1/3 if held by three persons, etc.).
   (4) If property held in joint tenancy was acquired by purchase by **other than spouses,** include the FMV of the property multiplied by the percentage of total cost furnished by the decedent.

b. The FMV of transfers with retained life estates and revocable transfers are included in the gross estate.

c. Include the FMV of transfers intended to take effect at death (i.e., the donee can obtain enjoyment only by surviving the decedent, and the decedent prior to death had a reversionary interest of more than 5% of the value of the property).

d. Include any property over which the decedent had a **general power of appointment** (i.e., decedent could appoint property in favor of decedent, decedent's estate, or creditors of decedent or decedent's estate).

e. Include the value of life insurance proceeds from policies payable to the estate, and policies over which the decedent possessed an "incident of ownership" (e.g., right to change beneficiary).

f. Include income in respect of a decedent.

g. Include gifts of life insurance within three years of the decedent's date of death.

h. Include gift tax paid on all transfers made within three years of death.

3. Property is included at **FMV** at **date of decedent's death**; or executor may elect to use FMV at **alternate valuation date** (generally a date six months subsequent to death), if such election will reduce both the gross estate and the federal estate tax liability.

a. If alternate valuation is elected, but property is distributed, sold, exchanged, or otherwise disposed of within six months of death, then use FMV on date of distribution, sale, exchange or other disposition.

b. Election is irrevocable and applies to all property in estate; cannot be made on an individual property basis.

4. **Estate tax deductions** include funeral expenses, administrative expenses, debts and mortgages, casualty losses during the estate administration, state death taxes, charitable bequests (no limit), and an unlimited marital deduction for the FMV of property passing to a surviving spouse.

a. A terminable interest granted to surviving spouse will not generally qualify for marital deduction.

b. If executor elects, the FMV of "qualified terminable interest property" is eligible for the marital deduction if the income from the property is paid at least annually to spouse and the property is not subject to transfer during the surviving spouse's lifetime.

c. Property passing to a surviving spouse who is not a US citizen is not eligible for the estate tax marital deduction, except for property passing to an alien spouse through a qualified domestic trust (QDT).

d. Property passing from a nonresident alien to a surviving spouse who is a US citizen is eligible for the estate tax marital deduction.

e. An unlimited charitable deduction is available for amounts transferred by bequest, devise, or legacy to qualified charitable organizations, including foreign charities. However, the amount of charitable deduction must be reduced by any estate, legacy, or inheritance taxes that are payable in whole or in part from the bequest, devise, or legacy.

f. The decedent's medical and funeral expenses are allowed as deductions on the estate tax return Form 706. However, if the decedent's medical expenses are paid within twelve months of death, they instead can be deducted on the decedent's final income tax return Form 1040 if the estate's executor makes the appropriate election to waive the deduction on the decedent's estate tax return. The decedent's medical and funeral expenses are never allowed as deductions on the estate's income tax return Form 1041.

5. Post-76 taxable gifts are added back to the taxable estate at date of gift FMV. Any gift tax paid is *not* added back.

6. A transfer tax is computed on total life and death transfers, then is reduced by the tax already paid on post-76 gifts, the unified tax credit, foreign death tax credit, and prior transfer tax credit (i.e., percentage of estate tax paid on the transfer to the present decedent from a transferor who died within past ten years).

7. **Portability of unused exclusion between spouses.** Effective for deaths occurring after 2010, the estate of a surviving spouse may qualify to utilize the unused portion of the estate tax applicable exclusion amount ($5.43 million for 2015) of his or her last predeceased spouse. To take advantage of this provision, a special election must have been made by the predeceased spouse's estate. Thus, even though an estate tax return is not required to be filed, it must be filed in order to make this election. The applicable exclusion amount for a surviving spouse will be the sum of a basic exclusion amount ($5.43 million for 2015), plus the aggregate deceased spousal unused exclusion amount. The provision applies to only the unused exclusion of the last deceased spouse. It is not possible for individuals who have been married multiple times to tack on multiple applicable exclusion amounts of their predeceased spouses.

EXAMPLE

Henry died in 2013 with a taxable estate of $2 million. An election is made on Henry's estate tax return to permit his wife, Wilma, to use his unused exclusion of $3.25 million. Wilma, who had not made any lifetime taxable gifts, dies in 2014 with a taxable estate of $9 million. The total applicable exclusion amount available to Wilma's estate will consist of her basic exclusion amount of $5.34 million plus the $3.25 million of Henry's unused exclusion amount, for a total exclusion of $8,590,000.

---

8. **Form 706** United States Estate (and Generation-Skipping Transfer) Tax Return must be filed if the decedent's **gross estate exceeds $5,430,000 for 2015 ($5,340,000 for 2014).** The return must be filed within **nine months** of decedent's death, unless an extension of time has been granted.
9. The **basis of property acquired from a decedent** is generally the FMV at date of decedent's death, or the alternate valuation date if elected for estate tax purposes.

    a. Use FMV on date of disposition if alternate valuation is elected and property is distributed, sold, or otherwise disposed of during the six-month period following death.
    b. FMV rule does not apply to appreciated property acquired by the decedent by gift within one year before death if such property then passes from the donee-decedent to the original donor or donor's spouse. The basis of such property to the original donor (or spouse) will be the adjusted basis of the property to the decedent immediately before death.

EXAMPLE

Son gives property with FMV of $40,000 (basis of $5,000) to terminally ill father within one year before father's death. The property is included in father's estate at FMV of $40,000. If property passes to son or son's spouse, basis will remain at $5,000. If passed to someone else, the property's basis will be $40,000.

II. GENERATION-SKIPPING TAX

This tax is imposed on transfers in addition to the federal gift and estate taxes and is designed to prevent individuals from escaping an entire generation of gift and estate taxes by transferring property to, or in trust for the benefit of, a person that is two or more generations younger than the donor or transferor.

A. The tax approximates the transfer tax that would be imposed if property were actually transferred to each successive generation, and is imposed on taxable distributions, taxable terminations, and direct skips to someone at least two generations below that of the donor or transferor.

    1. A taxable distribution is a distribution out of a trust's income or corpus to a beneficiary at least two generations below that of the grantor (unless the grandchild's parent is deceased and was a lineal descendant of the grantor) while an older generation beneficiary has an interest in the trust.
    2. A taxable termination means that by reason of death, expiration of time, or otherwise, the interest of a nonskip person terminates (i.e., someone less than two generations below the donor or transferor) and a skip person (i.e., someone at least two generations below the donor or transferor) becomes the recipient of the trust property or the only beneficiary.
    3. A direct skip occurs when one or more generations are bypassed altogether and property is transferred directly to, or in trust for, a skip person.

B. The generation-skipping transfer tax is imposed at a flat rate that equals the maximum unified transfer tax rate of 40%.
C. Exemptions available

    1. A $5,430,000 exemption per transferor for 2015 ($5,340,000 for 2014)
    2. An unlimited exemption is available for a direct skip to a grandchild if the grandchild's parent is deceased and was a lineal descendant of the transferor

---

NOW REVIEW MULTIPLE-CHOICE QUESTIONS 10 THROUGH 26

III. INCOME TAXATION OF ESTATES AND TRUSTS

Although estates and trusts are separate taxable entities, they will not pay an income tax if they distribute all of their income to beneficiaries. In this respect they act as a conduit, since the income taxed to beneficiaries will have the same character as it had for the estate or trust.

A. **US Income Tax Return for Estate or Trust (Form 1041)** must be filed by an estate if it has gross income of $600 or more, or has a beneficiary who is a nonresident alien. Form 1041 must be filed by a trust if it has gross income of $600 or more, any taxable income, or a beneficiary who is a nonresident alien.

1. Return is due by the 15th day of the fourth month following the close of the estate or trust's taxable year.
2. A **trust must adopt a calendar year** as its taxable year. An estate may adopt a calendar year or any fiscal year.
3. For 2015, estate and trusts are taxed as follows:

    a. First $2,500 of taxable income is taxed at 15%
    b. Over $2,500 but not over $5,900 is taxed at 25%
    c. Over $5,900 but not over $9,050 is taxed at 28%
    d. Over $9,050 but not over $12,300 is taxed at 33%
    e. Over $12,300 is taxed at 39.6%

4. The alternative minimum tax applies to estates and trusts and is computed in the same manner as for individuals. The AMT exemption for an estate or trust is $23,800 for 2015.
5. For tax years beginning after December 31, 2012, an estate or trust is subject to the 3.8% Medicare Contribution Tax on net investment income. The tax is imposed on the lessor of (a) an estate or trust's undistributed net investment income, or (b) the excess of an estate or trust's AGI over the dollar amount at which an estate or trust's highest income tax bracket begins ($12,300 for 2015).
6. Estates and trusts are generally required to make estimated tax payments using the rules applicable to individuals. However, estates do not have to make estimated payments for taxable years ending within two years of the decedent's death.

B. **Classification of Trusts**

1. **Simple trust** is one that (1) is required to distribute all of its income to beneficiaries each year, (2) cannot make charitable contributions, and (3) makes no distribution of trust corpus (i.e., principal) during the year.
2. **Complex trust** is any trust other than a simple trust.

C. **Computation of Estate or Trust Taxable Income**

1. **Gross income** for an estate or trust is generally the same as for individual taxpayers.

    a. Generally no gain or loss is recognized on the transfer of property to beneficiaries to satisfy specific bequests.
    b. Gain or loss is recognized on the transfer of property to beneficiaries in lieu of cash to satisfy specific cash bequests.

2. **Allowable deductions** for an estate or trust are generally the same as for an individual taxpayer. For example, an estate or trust is allowed deductions for expenses incurred in carrying on a trade or business, in the production of income or the management of income-producing property, in the determination of any tax, as well as amounts paid by a fiduciary for administration of the estate or trust.

    a. Some expenses incurred by an estate or non-grantor trust are subject to a 2% of AGI floor. Typically, these are costs that are included in the definition of miscellaneous itemized deductions, and commonly would be incurred by a hypothetical individual holding the same kind of property. Examples of costs subject to the 2% of AGI floor include fees for investment advice, the cost of property appraisals for insurance purposes, and the costs of preparing gift tax returns.
    b. Costs that are unique to an estate or trust, and not commonly incurred by an individual are not subject to the 2% of AGI floor. Costs not subject to the 2% of AGI floor include the costs of preparing the estate and generation-skipping transfer tax returns, fiduciary income tax returns, and the decedent's final individual tax return. Also, appraisal fees to determine the FMV of the decedent's assets as of date of death (or alternate valuation date), to determine the value for purposes of making distributions, or as otherwise required to properly prepare the estate or trust's tax returns are not subject to the 2% floor. Additionally, some fiduciary expenses are not subject to the 2% floor including probate costs, fiduciary bond premiums, legal publication costs of notices to creditors or heirs, and the cost of certified copies of the decedent's death certificate

    c. A personal **exemption** is allowed.

       (1) $600 for estate
       (2) $300 for trusts required to distribute all income currently
       (3) $100 for all other trusts

    d. Charitable contributions can be made by estates and trusts (other than simple trusts).

       (1) Contributions can be deducted without limitation if paid out of income.
       (2) Contributions are not deductible to the extent paid out of tax-exempt income.

    e. Expenses incurred in the production of tax exempt income are not deductible.
    f. Capital losses offset capital gains and a net capital loss of up to $3,000 can be deducted with the remainder carried forward.
    g. Any unused capital loss and net operating loss (NOL) carryovers from the decedent's final Form 1040 are not allowed as deductions.

  3. An **income distribution deduction** is allowed for distributions of income to beneficiaries.

    a. **Distributable net income (DNI)** is the maximum amount of deduction for distributions to beneficiaries in any taxable year and also determines the amounts and character of the income reported by the beneficiaries.
    b. Generally, DNI is the same as the estate's or trust's taxable income computed before the income distribution deduction with the following modifications:

       (1) Add

         (a) Personal exemption
         (b) Any net capital loss deduction (limited to $3,000)
         (c) Tax exempt interest (reduced by related nondeductible expenses)

       (2) Subtract

         (a) Net capital gains allocable to corpus
         (b) Extraordinary dividends and taxable stock dividends allocated to corpus of simple trust

    c. Deduction will be the lesser of DNI or the amount distributed to beneficiaries (i.e., taxable income required to be distributed, plus other amount of taxable income distributed).

D. Treatment of Simple Trust and Beneficiaries

  1. Income is taxed to beneficiaries, not to trust.
  2. Beneficiaries are taxed on the income required to be distributed (up to DNI), even though not actually distributed during the year.
  3. Income passes through to beneficiaries retaining its characteristics (e.g., tax-exempt income passes through retaining its exempt status).
  4. If multiple beneficiaries, DNI is prorated in proportion to the amount of required distribution to each beneficiary.

E. Treatment of Complex Trust and Beneficiaries

  1. A two-tier income distribution system is used.

    a. First tier: Distributions of the first tier are income amounts that are required to be distributed and include distributions that can be paid out of income or corpus, to the extent paid out of income.
    b. Second tier: Distributions of the second tier are all other amounts that are actually paid during the year or are required to be paid.

  2. DNI is first allocated to distributions in the first tier. Any remaining DNI is prorated to distributions in the second tier.

EXAMPLE

A trust has DNI of $9,000. The trust instrument requires that $6,000 of income be distributed annually to Alan. Further, it permits distributions to Baker and Carr of income or corpus in the trustee's discretion. For the current year, the trustee distributes $6,000 to Alan, $4,000 to Baker, and $2,000 to Carr.

    Since Alan's distribution is a first tier distribution, all $6,000 distributed is taxable to Alan. This leaves only $3,000 of DNI to be allocated to the second tier distributions to Baker and Carr. Since DNI would be allocated in proportion to the amounts distributed, $2,000 of Baker's distribution and $1,000 of Carr's distribution would be taxable.

F. Grantor Trusts are trusts over which the grantor (or grantor's spouse) retain substantial control. The income from a grantor trust is generally taxed to the grantor, not to the trust or beneficiaries. A grantor trust generally exists if any of the following conditions are present:

1. Trust income will, or in the grantor's or nonadverse party's discretion may be, distributed to the grantor or grantor's spouse (or used to pay life insurance premiums of either).
2. The grantor (or nonadverse party) has the power to revoke the trust.
3. The grantor (or grantor's spouse) holds a reversionary interest worth more than 5% of trust corpus.
4. The grantor (or nonadverse party) can deal with trust property in a nonfiduciary capacity (e.g., purchase trust assets for less than adequate consideration or borrow trust property at below market rate).
5. The grantor (or grantor's spouse) or nonadverse party controls the beneficial enjoyment of the trust (e.g., ability to change beneficiaries).

G. Termination of Estate or Trust

1. An estate or trust is not entitled to a personal exemption on its final return.
2. Any unused carryovers (e.g., NOL or capital loss) are passed through to beneficiaries for use on their individual tax returns.
3. Any excess deductions for its final year are passed through to beneficiaries and can be deducted as miscellaneous itemized deductions.

NOW REVIEW MULTIPLE-CHOICE QUESTIONS 27 THROUGH 41

IV. EXEMPT ORGANIZATIONS

A. Types of Organizations

1. Tax-exempt organizations are listed by class of organization in the Internal Revenue Code. Generally, an exempt organization serves some common good, is operated as a not-for-profit entity, its net earnings do not inure for the benefit of specified individuals, and the organization does not exert undue political influence. To obtain exempt status, the organization must be one of those specifically identified in the Code, and generally must apply for and receive an exemption.

IRC 501	Type of Organization	Description
(c) (1)	Federal and Regulated Agencies	Federal Credit Unions, FDIC, Federal Land Bank
(c) (2)	Title Holding Corporation for Exempt Organization	Corporation holding title to fraternity or sorority house
(c) (3)	Religious, Educational, Charitable, Scientific, Literary, Testing for Public Safety, Foster National or International Amateur Sports Competition, Prevention of Cruelty to Children or Animals Organizations	Activities of a nature implied by description of class of organization (e.g., church, school, museum, zoo, planetarium, Red Cross, Boy Scouts of America)
(c) (4)	Civic Leagues, Social Welfare Organizations, and Local Associations of Employees	Promotion of community welfare (e.g., community association, volunteer fire companies, garden club, League of Women Voters)
(c) (5)	Labor, Agricultural, and Horticultural Organizations	Educational or instructive, to improve conditions of work, and to improve products and efficiency (e.g., teacher's association)
(c) (6)	Business Leagues, Chamber of Commerce, Real Estate Boards, etc.	Improvement of business conditions of one or more lines of business (e.g., trade of professional associations, Chambers of Commerce)
(c) (7)	Social and Recreation Clubs	Recreation and social activities (e.g., country club, sailing club, tennis club)
(c) (8)	Fraternal Beneficiary Societies and Associations	Lodge providing for payment of life, sickness, accident, or other benefits to members
(c) (9)	Voluntary Employees' Beneficiary Associations	Providing for payment of life, sickness, accident, or other benefits to members

IRC 501	Type of Organization	Description
(c)(10)	Domestic Fraternal Societies and Associations	Lodge devoting its net earnings to charitable, fraternal, and other specified purposes, but no life, sickness, or accident benefits to members
(c)(11)	Teachers' Retirement Fund Associations	Payment of retirement benefits to teachers
(c)(12)	Benevolent Life Insurance Associations, Mutual or Cooperative Telephone Companies, etc.	Activities of a mutually beneficial nature
(c)(13)	Cemetery Companies	Operated for benefit of lot owners who purchase lots for burial
(c)(14)	State Chartered Credit Unions	Loans to members
(c)(15)	Mutual Insurance Companies or Associations	Providing insurance to members substantially at cost
(c)(16)	Farmers Cooperative Organizations to Finance Crop Operations	Financing of crop operations in conjunction with activities of marketing or purchasing association
(c)(17)	Supplemental Unemployment Benefit Trusts	Payment of supplemental unemployment compensation benefits
(c)(19)	Member of Armed Forces Post or Organization	Veterans of Foreign Wars (VFW)
(d)	Religious and Apostolic Associations	Communal religious community that conducts business activities. Members must include pro rata share of organization's income in their gross income
(e)	Cooperative Hospital Service Organizations	Performs cooperative service for hospitals (e.g., centralized purchasing organization)
(k)	Child Care Organizations	Provides care for children

2. **Sec. 501(c)(3) organizations** (religious, educational, charitable, etc.) generally must apply for exemption by filing Form 1023 within fifteen months from the end of the month in which they were organized. To qualify, (1) the organization must meet an organizational and operational test, (2) no part of the organization's net earnings can inure to the benefit of private shareholders or individuals, and (3) the organization cannot, as a substantial part of its activities, attempt to influence legislation (unless it elects an exception permitting certain lobby expenditures) or directly participate to any extent in a political campaign for or against any candidate for public office.

   a. Some organizations do not have to file for exemption (e.g., churches or an organization [other than a private foundation] normally having annual gross receipts of not more than $5,000). They automatically are exempt if they meet the requirements of Sec. 501(c)(3).

   b. The **organizational test** requires the articles of organization limit the organization's purposes to one or more exempt purposes described in Sec. 501(c)(3), and must not expressly empower the organization to engage in activities that are not in furtherance of its one or more exempt purposes, except as an insubstantial part of its activities.

   c. The **operational test** requires that an exempt organization be operated exclusively for an exempt purpose. An organization will be considered to be operated exclusively for an exempt purpose only if it engages primarily in activities that accomplish its exempt purpose. An organization will not be so regarded if more than an insubstantial part of its activities is not in furtherance of an exempt purpose.

   d. **Inurement** is private benefit provided to insiders who have the institutional opportunity to direct the organization's resources to themselves, to entities in which they have an interest, or to family members. Inurement issues may arise because of excessive compensation, payment of excessive rent, receipt of less than fair value from sales of property, and inadequately secured loans.

   e. An organization (other than churches and private foundations) can elect to replace the substantial part of activities test with a limit defined in terms of expenditures for influencing legislation. **Attempting to influence legislation** includes (1) any attempt to influence any legislation through an effort to affect the opinions of the general public (i.e., grassroots lobbying), and (2) any attempt to influence any legislation through communication with any member or employee of a legislative body, or with any government official or employee who may participate in the formulation of legislation (i.e., direct lobbying).

(1) Attempting to influence legislation does **not** include appearing before or communicating with any legislative body with respect to a possible decision of that body that might affect the powers, duties, exempt status, or the deduction of contributions to the organization.

(2) If the election to be subject to the lobbying expenditures limits (instead of the substantial part of activities test) is made, an organization will not lose its exempt status unless it normally makes lobbying expenditures in excess of 150% of lobbying nontaxable amount or normally makes grassroots expenditures in excess of 150% of grassroots nontaxable amount.

(3) If the election is made, an organization will be subject to a 25% excise tax on the excess of its lobbying and grassroots expenditures over the lobbying and grassroots nontaxable amounts.

3. Most organizations must apply for exemption using Form 1023, Application for Recognition of Exemption Under Section 501(c)(3) of the IRC. However, a shorter application Form 1023-EZ, Streamlined Application for Recognition of Exemption Under Section 501(c)(3) of the IRC, can be used by organizations with assets of $250,000 or less and annual gross receipts of $50,000 or less. An organization utilizing Form 1023-EZ must submit the form and applicable user fee online. Form 1023-EZ cannot be used by foreign organizations, churches, schools, hospitals, and private foundations.

4. **Private foundations** are Sec. 501(c)(3) organizations other than churches, educational organizations, hospitals or medical research organizations operated in conjunction with hospitals, endowment funds operated for the benefit of certain state and municipal colleges and universities, governmental units, and publicly supported organizations.

   a. An organization is **publicly supported** if it normally receives at least one-third of its total support from governmental units and the general public (e.g., support received in the form of gifts, grants, contributions, membership fees, gross receipts from admissions, sales of merchandise, etc.)

   b. Private foundations may be subject to taxes based on investment income, self-dealing, failure to distribute income, excess business holdings, investments that jeopardize charitable purposes, and taxable expenditures. The initial taxes (with the exception of the tax on investment income) are imposed because the organization engages in prohibited transactions. Additional taxes are imposed if the prohibited transactions are not corrected with a specified period.

5. **Feeder organizations** do not qualify for tax-exempt status. A feeder organization carries on a trade or business for the benefit of an exempt organization and remits its profits to the exempt organization.

B. Filing Requirements

1. Most exempt organizations must file an **annual information return** Form 990 (Return of Organization Exempt from Income Tax). Organizations **not** required to file Form 990 include churches, federal agencies, organizations whose annual gross receipts do not exceed $50,000, and private foundations.

2. Exempt organizations with **unrelated business income** must file Form 990-T (Exempt Organization Business Income Tax Return) if the organization has gross income of at least $1,000 from an unrelated trade or business. The obligation to file Form 990-T is in addition to the obligation to file Form 990. Additionally, Form 990-T may be required even though Form 990 is not required to be filed.

3. **Private foundations** must annually file Form 990-PF (Return of Private Foundation). If an organization is subject to any of the excise taxes imposed on private foundations, Form 4720 (Return of Certain Excise Taxes on Charities and Other Persons) must be filed with Form 990-PF.

4. Small exempt organizations whose gross receipts are $50,000 or less are required to annually file an electronic Form 990-N (e-Postcard). Organizations eligible to file the 990-N can instead elect to file Form 990.

5. Exempt organizations who are *not* eligible to file the 990-N but have gross receipts less than $200,000 and total assets less than $500,000 are required to file Form 990-EZ or Form 990.

6. Forms 990, 990-EZ, 990-T, 990-PF, and 990-N are generally due by the 15th day of the 5th month after the end of the tax year (e.g., May 15th for a calendar-year organization).

7. An exempt organization that fails to file its required return for three consecutive years will lose its tax-exempt status. The revocation of the organization's tax-exempt status will not take place until the filing due date for the third year.

NOW REVIEW MULTIPLE-CHOICE QUESTIONS 42 THROUGH 56

C. Unrelated Business Income (UBI)

1. **UBI** is income from a business that is (1) **regularly carried on**, and (2) is **unrelated** to the organization's exempt purpose. A business is substantially related only if the activity (not its proceeds) contributes importantly to the accomplishment of the exempt purposes of the organization.
2. Income derived from debt-financed property unrelated to the exempt function of the organization is included in UBI. The amount of such income to be included in UBI is based on the proportion of average acquisition indebtedness to the property's average adjusted basis.
3. Income from commercial product advertising in journals and other publications is generally UBI.
4. Activities specifically treated as resulting in **related income** (not UBI) include

   a. An activity where substantially all work is performed without compensation (e.g., a church runs a second-hand clothing store with all work performed by volunteers).
   b. A trade or business carried on for the convenience of students or members of a charitable, religious, or scientific organization (e.g., university bookstore).
   c. The sale of merchandise received as gifts or contributions.
   d. Income from dividends, interest, annuities, and royalties. However, such income will be included in UBI if it results from debt-financed investments.
   e. Income derived from renting real property. However, income derived from renting personal property is considered UBI unless the personal property is leased with the real property and personal property rents do not exceed 10% of total rents.
   f. Conducting bingo games if the games are not in violation of any state or local law, and are conducted in a jurisdiction that ordinarily confines bingo games to exempt organizations.

5. UBI is **taxed to the extent in excess of $1,000.** UBI is taxed at regular corporate rates if the organization is a corporation, taxed at rates applicable to trusts if the organization is a trust.
6. An organization must make estimated tax payments if it expects its tax for the year to be more than $500.

NOW REVIEW MULTIPLE-CHOICE QUESTIONS 57 THROUGH 64

V. MULTIJURISDICTIONAL TAXATION

A. State and Local Taxation (SALT)

1. There are various types of state and local taxes such as income, sales, use, property, franchise, employment, excise, severance, and estate and inheritance taxes. Each state controls the taxation of persons within its jurisdiction and may apply tax rules that differ from the rules that are applied in other states.
2. The US Constitution prohibits a state from taxing a nonresident unless the nonresident has sufficient connection to the state. The presence or activity required within a state before the state may tax a nonresident is referred to as **nexus**. There are different nexus standards for different types of taxes. Simply engaging in an activity or a business transaction within a state may be sufficient to result in nexus for income tax purposes in many states. Property ownership, derivation of income from sources within a state, or the presence of an office within a state also may produce nexus. On the other hand, nexus is generally *not* established merely because of the solicitation of sales of tangible personal property within a state.
3. For *state income tax*, many states conform to the federal income tax model, with a state relying on information from a federal return for its own tax base. As a result, a state income tax base might begin with federal taxable income which is then modified by adjustments required by state law (e.g., no deduction allowed for state income taxes).
4. When a business can be taxed by more than one state, it becomes necessary to develop rules that **allocate** particular types of income to specific states, and to **apportion** other types of income among the several states that can tax it.

   a. **The Uniform Division of Income for Tax Purposes Act (UDITPA)** provides rules for allocating and apportioning a multistate or multinational enterprise's nonbusiness and business income among states and foreign countries. The Multistate Tax Commission adopted model regulations that interpret the UDITPA provisions.
   b. Under UDITPA, **nonbusiness income** is allocated as follows:

      (1) Interest and dividends are allocated to the state of the taxpayer's commercial domicile.
      (2) Net rents and royalties from real property are allocated to the state in which the property is located.
      (3) Capital gains and losses from sales of real property are allocated to the state where the property is located.
      (4) Capital gains and losses from the sale of intangible personal property are allocated to the state of the taxpayer's commercial domicile.

(5) Net rents and royalties from tangible personal property are allocated to a state to the extent that the property is utilized within that state. Alternatively, all rents and royalties from tangible personal property will be allocated to the state of the taxpayer's commercial domicile if the taxpayer is not organized in or taxable in the state in which the property is utilized.

(6) Capital gains and losses from sales of tangible personal property are allocated to a state if the property was situated in that state at the time of sale. Alternatively, the gains and losses will be allocated to the state of the taxpayer's commercial domicile if the taxpayer is not taxable in the state in which the property was situated.

(7) Patent and copyright royalties are allocated to a state to the extent that the patent or copyright is utilized by the payer in the state. Alternatively, the royalties will be allocated to the state of the taxpayer's commercial domicile if the taxpayer is not taxable in the state in which the patent or copyright was utilized.

c. States use various formulas to apportion a taxpayer's **business income** derived from multistate operations. Although the formulas used may differ, the objective is to derive an apportionment percentage to determine the amount of income subject to tax in each state. UDITPA recommends a formula using three equally weighted factors: sales, payroll, and property. Business income is then apportioned to a state by multiplying the taxpayer's business income by a fraction; the numerator of which is the total of the sales factor plus the payroll factor plus the property factor, and the denominator is three (3), to average the factors. Many states that levy an income tax use a modified three-factor formula in which sales are double-weighted (i.e., the sales factor is counted twice and the factor total is divided by four). Some states use just one or two of the factors.

(1) The **sales factor** is the ratio of total sales to in-state customers divided by total sales from all sales made by the taxpayer. *Total sales* means total net sales after discounts and returns.

(2) The **payroll factor** is the ratio of compensation paid to employees working in a state divided by the total compensation paid by the taxpayer.

(3) The **property factor** is the ratio of the average cost of real and tangible personal property owned or rented and located in a state divided by the total average cost of all such property owned or rented by the taxpayer.

EXAMPLE

Assume Multistate Corp. conducts business in several states and provided relevant information as follows:

	Total	State A
Sales	$4,000,000	$1,000,000
Average property	5,000,000	2,000,000
Compensation	1,000,000	200,000
Business taxable income before apportionment	500,000	

State A uses the UDITPA apportionment formula to compute state taxable income for Multistate Corp.'s business income. The sales factor for State A would be $1,000,000 / $4,000,000 = 25%. The property factor would be $2,000,000 / $5,000,000 = 40%. The compensation factor would be $200,000 / $1,000,000 = 20%. The apportionment factor would be (25% + 40% + 20%) / 3 = 28.33%. As a result, $500,000 × 28.33% = $141,667 of Multistate Corp.'s business income would be taxed by State A.

EXAMPLE

Assume State A in the above example gives double weight to the sales factor. The apportionment factor would be (25% + 25% + 40% + 20%) / 4 = 27.5%.

---

5. Under the **unitary** concept, if one company in a group of entities has nexus with a state, the state's apportionment factor is applied to the unitary income of the entire group. A **unitary business** is a single economic enterprise that is made up either of separate parts of a single business entity, or of a commonly controlled group of business entities that are sufficiently interdependent, integrated, and interrelated through their activities. Whether business activities constitute a unitary business is subjective and the courts generally give states great latitude in deciding whether a particular set of activities constitute a unitary business. Under the factors-of-profitability test, business activities will be treated as a unitary business if they are functionally integrated, have centralized management, and show economies of scale.

6. Many states have enacted provisions that require **combined reporting** in applying the unitary business concept to related entities. In a combined return a taxpayer must apply the unitary concept to the combined income of the entities making up the unitary business. Most states have established a 50% ownership rule as the threshold for combined reporting purposes though some states have chosen to use a different percentage.

NOW REVIEW MULTIPLE-CHOICE QUESTIONS 65 AND 66

B. International Taxation

1. **US Taxation of Foreign Persons.** Nonresident foreign persons generally are subject to US tax on two categories of income: (1) *income that is effectively connected with a US trade or business (ECI)*, and (2) certain passive types of US source income commonly referred to as *fixed and determinable annual or periodical income (FDAP)*.

    a. A foreign person's **income that is effectively connected with a US trade or business (ECI)** is subject to tax at regular graduated income tax rates and deductions are allowed in computing the amount subject to tax. A trade or business generally is defined by case law as profit-oriented activities that are regular, substantial, and continuous. Effectively connected with a US trade or business means that (1) the income is derived from assets held for use in the conduct of a US business, and (2) the activity of the US business was a material factor in the realization of the income. Under an income tax treaty, the US may instead agree to tax business profits of a treaty resident only if the profits are attributable to a **permanent establishment** (PE) in the US. A PE is a fixed place of business through which business is wholly or partially carried on. Simply maintaining storage facilities within the US generally does not by itself amount to a PE.

    b. Generally, a nonresident alien who performs personal services within the US is considered to be engaged in a US trade or business. However, the performance of personal services will not constitute a US trade or business if (1) the nonresident alien is present in the US for 90 days or less during the tax year, (2) the amount of compensation received for US services is $3,000 or less, and (3) the nonresident alien works for either a foreign person who is not engaged in a US trade or business, or the foreign office of a US person.

    c. **Fixed and determinable annual or periodical income (FDAP)** is generally subject to a 30% withholding tax that is applied to the gross amount of income with no deductions allowed. Withholding of tax occurs at the source of payment (i.e., the person paying the income is required to withhold the tax and remit it to the IRS). FDAP primarily is from passive, nonbusiness activities *including* such items as interest, dividends, rents, royalties, and annuities. FDAP generally *excludes* gain from the sale or exchange of real or personal property, and income that is excluded from gross income by US persons. The 30% withholding tax rate may be reduced or even eliminated by an applicable income tax treaty.

    d. **Sourcing rules** are used to determine whether items of income will be deemed to be US source and consequently subject a nonresident foreign person to US taxation. Although the sourcing rules may be modified by tax treaty, the sourcing rules for specific types of income include

        (1) Interest—the domicile of the payor
        (2) Dividends—whether the payor is a US or foreign corporation
        (3) Rents—the location of the property
        (4) Royalties—the location where the property is used
        (5) Gain on sale of real property—the location of the property
        (6) Gain on sale of inventory—the location where title to the inventory passes
        (7) Services—the location where the services are performed

2. **US Taxation of US Persons on Foreign Activities.** US persons are subject to US tax on their worldwide income. A US person includes a citizen or resident of the US, a domestic partnership or corporation, and any estate or trust other than a foreign estate or trust

    a. A US corporation is subject to tax on its worldwide income, including the income of a *foreign branch*. In contrast, a US corporation is generally not taxed on the net income of a *foreign subsidiary* corporation until the income is repatriated in the form of dividends to the parent corporation.

EXAMPLE

A US corporation's foreign subsidiary has $1,000 of earnings but makes no distributions to its US parent during the year. The US corporation is not taxed on the $1,000 of earnings of its foreign subsidiary.

b. Certain types of income, referred to as **subpart F income**, of a *controlled foreign corporation* are subject to current US taxation even though the earnings are not distributed to the US parent corporation. **A controlled foreign corporation (CFC)** is a foreign corporation whose stock is more than 50% owned (by vote or value) by US shareholders that own at least 10% of the combined voting power of the foreign corporation's stock. The US shareholders get a corresponding basis increase for their CFC stock for the amount of subpart F income taxed to them but not received in the form of dividends. A later distribution of those earnings will be nontaxable and will reduce their basis for the CFC stock.

EXAMPLE

US corporation M owns all the stock of foreign subsidiary N which has $1,000 of earnings from subpart F income but makes no distributions to M during the year. M is currently taxed on the $1,000 of subpart F income of N, and increases its basis for its N stock by $1,000.

c. **Subpart F income** generally includes foreign passive income as well as certain types of foreign business income that can be readily shifted between taxing jurisdictions to take advantage of a lower foreign tax rate. Included in Subpart F income is income from a CFC's insurance of risks outside its country of creation or organization, foreign base company income, amounts attributable to international boycott participation, and amounts attributable to illegal bribes and kickbacks. Two examples of **foreign base company income** are *foreign personal holding company income,* and *foreign base company sales income.*

   (1) **Foreign personal holding company** income generally includes such items as dividends, interest, royalties, rents, annuities, and income from personal service contracts.
   (2) **Foreign base company sales income** generally consists of income attributable to sales of personal property if three requirements are met: (1) the subject purchase or sale must be to, from, or on behalf of, a related party (a related party includes all individuals and entities owning, directly or indirectly, more than 50% of the CFC's stock), (2) the purchase or sale must be for use, consumption, or disposition outside of the CFC's country of incorporation, and (3) the personal property must be manufactured, grown, produced, or extracted outside of the CFC's country of incorporation.

   As a result of the above requirements, certain sales of personal property will be excluded from foreign base company sales income. For example, Subpart F income does not include income from the sale of personal property that was manufactured, produced, or constructed by the CFC. Also, it does not include income from the purchase and sale of property if the property is used in the jurisdiction wherein the CFC is incorporated.

d. **A foreign tax credit** against US income tax, for income taxes paid to a foreign country, mitigates the double taxation of foreign-source income. However, the amount of allowable foreign tax credit is limited to the US income tax imposed on the foreign source income.

$$\text{Overall limitation is } \frac{\text{Foreign source taxable income}}{\text{Worldwide taxable income}} \times \text{(US income tax)}$$

   (1) The overall limit on the foreign tax credit must be computed on a separate basis for several income categories including passive category income such as interest and dividends, and general category income, which includes most income other than passive category income. As a result, the foreign tax credit cannot exceed the lesser of the amount of foreign income taxes paid or accrued, or the limitation amount, for each category.

(2) Foreign income taxes paid in excess of the overall limitation can be carried back 1 year and forward 10 years and used to the extent that the taxpayer is below the limitation in those years.

(3) An individual with $300 or less ($600 for married filing jointly) of creditable foreign income taxes in exempt from the overall limitation if all foreign-source income is passive investment income.

(4) Taxpayers have the option of deducting foreign income taxes in lieu of taking a credit.

e. In addition to the foreign taxes actually paid, a US corporation that receives dividends from a *10% or more owned foreign corporation* (based on voting stock) is entitled to a deemed paid foreign tax credit for the foreign income taxes paid by that foreign corporation with respect to such dividends. A corporation taking the **deemed paid credit** must *gross-up* (increase) the amount of dividend income that it received by the foreign income tax paid on those dividends. The deemed paid credit is subject to the FTC limitation.

EXAMPLE

A US corporation receives a dividend of $75 from a wholly owned foreign subsidiary that has paid $25 of foreign income taxes on the earnings to which the dividend relates. The US corporation's dividend income of $75 is grossed-up by the $25 of foreign income taxes paid by its subsidiary, to $100. The US corporation is then eligible for a foreign tax credit for the $25 of foreign income taxes that it is deemed to have paid.

---

3. **Transfers of Property to Foreign Corporations**

a. Gain (but not loss) is generally recognized on the transfer of property by a US person to a foreign corporation notwithstanding the deferral provision of Subchapter C that otherwise would apply. This prevents gains from escaping US taxation and is accomplished by providing that a "foreign corporation" shall not be considered a corporation for purposes of the Subchapter C provisions (e.g., Sec. 351 transfer to a controlled corporation, Sec. 332 liquidation of a subsidiary, Sec. 361 transfer of property pursuant to a corporate reorganization).

EXAMPLE

US Corporation P owns property with a value of $1 million that has a zero tax basis. Corporation P transfers title to the property to its foreign subsidiary, Corporation S, in exchange for all of the stock of Corporation S. If Sec. 351(a) applied, no gain would be recognized on the transfer of the appreciated property to S. Thereafter, S could sell the property and recognize the gain. Assuming that S does not distribute its earnings to P and that Subpart F does not apply, the gain would escape US taxation. However, since foreign Corporation S is not considered a corporation for purposes of applying Sec. 351, P's realized gain of $1 million on the transfer of property to S is recognized and subject to US taxation.

---

b. The above recognition rule does *not* apply to any property transferred to a foreign corporation for use by such foreign corporation in the active conduct of a trade or business outside of the US. Exceptions requiring gain recognition apply to transfers of certain types of property that are likely to be promptly resold or are highly fungible such as receivables, copyrights, inventory, installment obligations, foreign currency or foreign-currency-denominated investments, and interests in leased property.

4. **Transfer Pricing**

a. When businesses in different countries that are owned or controlled by the same interests sell products or services or make loans between themselves, they have the opportunity to affect each other's taxable income and thereby reduce the overall tax liability of the group. This can be accomplished by shifting taxable income from a high-tax country to a lower-tax country.

b. To restrict this artificial shifting of income, Code Sec. 482 gives the IRS the authority to apportion and allocate income, deductions, and credits as is necessary in order to prevent the evasion of taxes or to clearly reflect income.

c. Generally, Sec. 482 requires that organizations under common control conduct business between themselves as if they were unrelated. That is, in determining the taxable income of a taxpayer from transactions with related organizations, the standard to be applied is that of a taxpayer *dealing at arm's length with an unrelated taxpayer.*

EXAMPLE

A US Corporation causes income which it has earned by means of its property or activity to be received by its foreign subsidiary, and thus shields such income from US taxation. Sec. 482 empowers the IRS to allocate the income to the US corporation.

EXAMPLE

A US Corporation sells its product to an independent third party as well as to its foreign subsidiary, each of whom operate as distributors of its product in a foreign market. The unit price charged the independent distributor is $200, while the unit price charged its foreign subsidiary is $125. If the US corporation dealt with its subsidiary at "arm's length," then the unit price charged the foreign subsidiary would have been $200. The IRS may utilize Sec. 482 to allocate $75 of profit from the subsidiary to the US corporation.

---

d. Because it may be difficult for a taxpayer to determine what price might be used by unrelated taxpayers dealing at arm's length, the IRS permits taxpayers to enter into an Advance Pricing Agreement (APA) with the IRS on the best method for determining arm's length prices for transfers between taxpayers owned or controlled by the same interests. Pursuant to an APA, a taxpayer and the IRS agree as to the transfer pricing method to be used to determine the transfer prices for specified transactions.

NOW REVIEW MULTIPLE-CHOICE QUESTIONS 67 THROUGH 70

VI. SOURCES OF FEDERAL TAX AUTHORITY

A. **Primary authorities** are official sources of tax law generated by the legislative branch (e.g., Internal Revenue Code, committee reports), judicial branch (e.g., court decisions), and executive/administrative branch (e.g., Treasury regulations, revenue rulings, revenue procedures). Secondary authorities are unofficial tax authorities that interpret and explain the primary authorities such as tax research services, professional periodicals, and IRS publications.

B. **Federal Tax Legislative Process**

1. Tax legislation usually begins in the House of Representatives. Hearings are held before the Ways and Means Committee. Members of the Committee draft a bill, and after having been approved by the Committee, it is sent to the House for debate and vote by the full House membership. A tax bill passed by the House is sent to the Senate Finance Committee.

2. The Senate Finance Committee may amend bill or draft its own bill, and when approved by the Finance Committee, the bill is sent to the Senate floor for debate before the Senate and possible additional amendments.

3. If the House- and Senate-passed versions of the tax bill differ, the tax bill is sent to the House-Senate Conference Committee for resolution of any differences. The modified bill, when approved by the Conference Committee, is sent back to the House and Senate for approval in its final form.

4. The uniform bill, after passage by the House and Senate, goes to the president for signing. If the president signs the bill it becomes law. If the president vetoes the bill, at least a two-thirds vote of the House and at least a two-thirds vote of the Senate are needed to override the presidential veto for the tax bill to become law.

5. Most tax legislation simply amends the current Internal Revenue Code of 1986. Note that the IRS does *not* write the tax law, and the Internal Revenue Code was not written by the IRS. Tax legislation is passed by Congress and signed by the president to become law.

C. **The Internal Revenue Code (IRC)** is the basic foundation of federal tax law, and represents a codification of the federal tax laws of the United States.

1. A series of self-contained revenue acts were first codified into an organized framework with the Internal Revenue Code of 1939. Subsequently, the 1939 IRC was reorganized and replaced with the 1954 IRC. In 1986, the Code's name was changed to the IRC of 1986, and has been frequently amended since then (e.g., American Taxpayer Relief Act of 2012).

2. The Internal Revenue Code of 1986 is actually Title 26 of the United States Code, and is generally divided into an orderly framework as follows: Subtitles; Chapters; Subchapters; Parts; Subparts; Sections; and Subsections.

3. **Subtitles** are denoted with a capital letter, with most pertaining to a general area of tax law as follows:

Subtitle	Topic
A	Income Taxes
B	Estate and Gift Taxes
C	Employment Taxes
D	Miscellaneous Excise Taxes
E	Alcohol, Tobacco, and Certain Other Excise Taxes
F	Procedure and Administration
G	The Joint Committee on Taxation
H	Financing of Presidential Election Campaigns
I	Trust Fund Code
J	Coal Industry Health Benefits
K	Group Health Plan Requirements

4. Each subtitle generally contains a number of **chapters** that are numbered in ascending order throughout the Code. Each chapter generally contains the tax rules that relate to a more narrowly defined area of law than is addressed by a subtitle. For example, Subtitle A—Income Taxes is divided as follows:

Chapter	Topic
1	Normal Taxes and Surtaxes
2	Tax on Self-Employment Income
3	Withholding of Tax on Nonresident Aliens and Foreign Corporations
4	[Repealed]
5	[Repealed]
6	Consolidated Returns

5. Chapters of the IRC are further divided into **subchapters** with each subchapter pertaining to a more narrowly defined area of tax law than is addressed by a chapter. For example, Chapter 1, Normal Taxes and Surtaxes includes Subchapter C—corporate distributions and adjustments, Subchapter K—partners and partnerships, and Subchapter S—tax treatment of S corporations and shareholders.

6. Subchapters are generally divided into **parts,** which are then frequently divided into subparts. Additionally, subparts are divided into **sections** that represent the organizational division of the Internal Revenue Code to which persons dealing with tax matters most often refer (e.g., Sec. 351 transfers to a controlled corporation, Sec. 1231 gains and losses, Sec. 1245 recapture).

7. Code sections are often divided into smaller divisions that may include subsections, paragraphs, subparagraphs, and clauses. Sections are denoted by numbers (1, 2, 3, etc.), subsections by lowercase letters (a, b, c, etc.), paragraphs by numbers (1, 2, 3, etc.), subparagraphs by capital letters (A, B, C, etc.), and clauses by lowercase roman numerals (i, ii, iii, etc.). This organizational scheme is important because the IRC contains many cross references which indicate the scope or limit the application of a provision.

EXAMPLE

Sec. 7701 is a definitional section that begins. "When used in this title…" and then goes on to provide a series of definitions. As a result, a definition found in Sec. 7701 applies to all of the Internal Revenue of Code of 1986.

> **EXAMPLE**
>
> Code Sec. 311(b) provides a gain recognition rule that applies to a corporation when it distributes appreciated property to a shareholder. However, its application is limited in that it only applies to distributions described in Subpart A (i.e., Code Secs. 301 through 307). Code Sec. 311(b)'s position within the overall Code framework is as follows:
>
> Title: Internal Revenue Code of 1986
>
> Subtitle A: Income Taxes
>
> Chapter 1: Normal taxes and surtaxes
>
> Subchapter C: Corporate distributions and adjustments
>
> Part I: Distributions by corporations
>
> Subpart B: Effects on corporation
>
> Section 311: Tax liability of corporation on distributions
>
> Subsection (b): Distributions of appreciated property
>
> Paragraph (1): In general. If—
>
> Subparagraph (A): "a corporation distributes property…in a distribution to which Subpart A applies…"

D. The IRC gives the Treasury Department or its delegate (the Commissioner of Internal Revenue) the authority to issue **regulations** to provide administrative interpretation of the tax law. These regulations may be separated into two broad categories: legislative and interpretive. **Legislative regulations** are those issued by the IRS under a specific grant of authority to prescribe the operating rules for a statute (e.g., "the Secretary shall prescribe such regulations as he may deem necessary," or "under regulations prescribed by the Secretary") and have the force and effect of law. The consolidated tax return regulations are an example of legislative regulations. In contrast, **interpretive regulations** are issued pursuant to the general rule-making authority granted to the IRS under Sec. 7805(a) and provide guidance regarding the IRS's interpretation of a statute. Although interpretive regulations do not have the force and effect of law, they are generally accorded substantial weight by the courts.

1. Regulations may also be categorized as proposed, temporary, or final regulations. Regulations are generally issued as **Proposed regulations** allowing interested parties a period of time of at least thirty days to comment and suggest changes. As a result of the comments received, the IRS may make changes to a proposed regulation before being published as a final regulation. Proposed regulations do not carry the same authority as temporary or final regulations. **Temporary regulations** are generally issued following recent tax legislation to provide interim guidance until final regulations are adopted. Temporary regulations (issued after 11/20/88) must be concurrently issued as proposed regulations, and these temporary regulations expire no later than three years from date of issue. Prior to its expiration, a temporary regulation is given the same weight as a final regulation. **Final regulations** are issued after public comments on proposed regulations are evaluated. Final regulations supersede any existing temporary regulations.

2. Regulations are organized in a sequential system with numbers preceding and following a decimal point. The numbers preceding the decimal point indicate the type of regulation or applicable area of tax law to which they pertain, while the numbers immediately following a decimal point indicate the IRC section being interpreted. Some of the more common prefixes include

Number	Type
1	Income Tax
20	Estate Tax
25	Gift Tax
301	Administrative and Procedural Matters
601	Procedural Rules

The numbers and letters to the right of the section number indicate the regulation number and smaller divisions of the regulation (e.g., paragraph, subparagraph). These regulation numbers and paragraphs do not necessarily correspond to the subsection of the Code being interpreted. For example, Reg. 1.267(d)-1(a)(4) provides four examples of the application of Code Sec. 267(d) concerning the determination of recognized gain where a loss was previously disallowed. The citation represents subparagraph (4) of paragraph (a) of the first regulation interpreting Code Sec. 267(d). The citation of a temporary regulation includes a "T" which indicates the nature of the regulation as temporary. For example, 1.45D-1T is a temporary regulation that explains the rules and conditions for claiming the new markets tax credit of Code Sec. 45.

E. **Revenue rulings** have less force and effect than regulations, but are second to regulations as important administrative sources of federal tax law. A revenue ruling gives the IRS's interpretation of how the Code and regulations apply to a specific fact situation, and therefore indicates how the IRS will treat similar transactions. Revenue rulings can be relied upon as authority by all taxpayers, and are published in the Internal Revenue Bulletin and later in the Cumulative Bulletin. The current status of a revenue ruling can be checked in the most current index to the Cumulative Bulletin. **Revenue procedures** announce administrative practices followed by the IRS, and are published in the Internal Revenue Bulletin and later in the Cumulative Bulletin. Revenue procedures provide guidelines that taxpayers must meet in order to obtain a revenue ruling, and also indicate areas in which the IRS will not issue revenue rulings. A **private letter ruling** is a written statement issued to the taxpayer who requested advice concerning a specific transaction. Although issued only to a specific taxpayer, private letter rulings are useful because they indicate how the IRS may treat a similar transaction, and are included in the list of substantial authority upon which a taxpayer may rely to avoid certain statutory penalties.

VII. TAX PLANNING

Tax planning should not be done in isolation, but instead should be a part of a taxpayer's overall financial goals, and integrated with nontax considerations. Three general tax planning strategies involve (1) the timing of income and deductions, (2) the shifting of income and deductions between taxpayers, and (3) the conversion of the character of income and deductions.

A. **Timing**

The tax accounting period in which an expense is deducted or in which income is recognized effects the real tax savings or cost because of the time value of money. A simple tax planning strategy would be to accelerate a tax deduction to an earlier period, while deferring the recognition of income to a later period.

1. **Installment sale.** A taxpayer may want to structure the casual sale of an asset so that at least one payment is received in the year(s) following the year of sale. By using the installment method and spreading the gain over multiple years, the taxpayer's gain will be deferred and may be taxed in lower brackets

2. **Net operating loss.** A taxpayer should carefully consider whether to carry back an NOL or elect to forgo the carryback period. A taxpayer may want to only carry the loss forward if the taxpayer anticipates being in a higher marginal tax bracket in carryforward years.

3. **Casualty loss.** If a casualty loss is sustained in a presidentially declared disaster area, the taxpayer may make an election to deduct the loss in the year preceding the year in which the loss was incurred in order to obtain a more immediate tax benefit for the loss deduction.

4. **Medical expenses.** Because of the 10% (or 7.5%) of AGI threshold for deducting medical expenses, taxpayers often are unable to take a deduction for unreimbursed medical expenses. However, it may be possible to take a medical expense deduction if the expenses are bunched into one year. Medical expenses are generally deductible when paid, but can be deducted in the year charged to a credit card.

5. **Itemized deductions.** If a taxpayer's total itemized deductions are approximately the same as the standard deduction, a taxpayer may benefit from bunching itemized deductions into a year in which the taxpayer intends to itemize, with the intention of taking the standard deduction in the following year. By alternating standard deduction and itemized deductions years, the taxpayer may be able to maximize deductions over a multiyear time frame.

6. **Alternative minimum tax.** If a taxpayer is not subject to AMT in 2015 but expects to be in 2016, accelerate expenses that are not deductible for AMT into 2015. For example, consider paying off home equity debt since the interest expense is usually not deductible for AMT purposes. Alternatively, if the taxpayer expects to pay an AMT in 2015 but not in 2016, consider accelerating ordinary and short-term capital gain income into 2015 while deferring expenses not deductible for AMT into 2016 (e.g., state and local income taxes, real estate taxes, miscellaneous deductions in the 2% category).

7. **Short-term capital gain.** If a taxpayer has short-term capital gains (which are taxed at ordinary income tax rates), consider selling capital assets that will generate capital losses in order to offset the short-term capital gain. Taxpayers are allowed to deduct up to $3,000 of net capital loss against ordinary income each year, with any net capital loss in excess of $3,000 carried forward to future years.

8. **Estimated tax.** An exception that can be used to avoid an underpayment penalty for the current year is for a taxpayer to make estimated payments and withholdings which in total are at least equal to 100% (110% if prior year AGI was greater than $150,000) of the tax liability for the prior year. Income tax withholdings are considered paid equally throughout the year, even if the taxes are withheld near the end of the year. If a taxpayer anticipates that taxes for the current year are underpaid, consider adjusting withholdings for the remainder of the year to avoid the underpayment penalty.

B. Income and Deduction Shifting

This planning strategy seeks to take advantage of the differences in tax rates between taxpayers, or between taxing jurisdictions. The goal is to shift income from high-tax rate to low-tax rate taxpayers or jurisdictions, and to shift deductions from low-tax rate to high-tax rate taxpayers or jurisdictions.

1. **Children.** Parents can reduce their family's income tax by shifting income that would otherwise be taxed at higher rates to their children whose income is taxed at lower rates. Even if the kiddie tax applies, the first $2,100 of unearned (e.g., interest) income will be taxed at the child's rates. Additionally, if the child has no earned income (e.g., wages), the child's unearned income will be partially offset by a limited basic standard deduction of $1,050.

2. **Gift tax exclusion.** A taxpayer interested in family wealth planning may want to consider the annual gift tax exclusion when gifting appreciated assets to family members. There is an annual $14,000 exclusion per donee for gifts of a present interest. This means that up to $14,000 of gifts can be given to a donee without making a taxable gift. Additionally, if the appreciated assets are given to family members not subject to the kiddie tax who are in the lowest two brackets, the capital gain on sale of the assets will be taxed at a 0% rate as opposed to a 15% or 20% rate if sold by the parents.

3. **Sec. 529 plan.** A Sec. 529 educational savings plan could be established for a child or grandchild. Using a special election, a taxpayer could currently fund up to five years of annual exclusions into the plan without making a taxable gift. This would permit up to $70,000 to be deposited into a child's Section 529 plan where the principal would grow tax-deferred, and later distributions used for the child's college costs would be exempt from tax.

4. **Owners and their businesses.** Incorporating a business and thus shifting income from an individual to a C corporation may result in lower current taxation of the business income (e.g., first $50,000 of corporate taxable income taxed at 15% rate). Alternatively, business income could be shifted from a corporation to an owner through tax-deductible expenses paid to the owner (e.g., compensation, rent, interest) allowing the owner to avoid the double taxation of corporate profits. Additionally, corporate level taxes could generally be completely avoided by making an S corporation election which would shift all income and deductions to the S corporation's shareholders.

C. Conversion

This planning strategy involves converting ordinary income that would be taxed at regular rates into income that will be taxed at a preferential rate. Additionally, this strategy might be applied to convert deductions that would be subject to limitations into ordinary deductions that are deductible without limitation.

1. **Sale of a company.** If considering the sale of a business, a taxpayer may attempt to structure the transaction as a sale of the company's stock rather than a sale of the company's assets. A sale of the company's stock generally results in gain eligible for reduced capital-gains rates, as opposed to a sale of assets which may be taxed as ordinary income.

2. **Qualified dividends.** A taxpayer may want to consider replacing investments generating interest income taxed at regular rates, with stocks paying qualified dividends that are taxed at a reduced rate of 15% or 20%, or possibly 0% if the taxpayer is in the 10% or 15% bracket. In order to qualify for the reduced rate, the underlying stock upon which a dividend is paid must be held for at least 61 days during the 121-day period beginning 60 days before the ex-dividend date (91 days of the 181-day period for preferred stock).

3. **Passive activities.** A taxpayer may be able to increase participation in what would otherwise be a "passive activity" in order to classify the activity as an active business activity whose losses are currently deductible. Alternatively, a taxpayer might be able to decrease participation in a profitable business activity in order to classify the income as passive activity income that could then be sheltered by losses generated from other passive activities.

KEY TERMS

Estate tax. A tax imposed on the transfer of property at death. The tax is part of the unified transfer tax system and takes into account transfers an individual made during lifetime and at death.

Generation-skipping tax. A tax on the transfer of property to, or in trust for the benefit of, a person that is two or more generations younger than the donor or transferor and is designed to prevent individuals from escaping an entire generation of gift and estate taxes. It is imposed in addition to federal gift and estate taxes.

Gift tax. A tax imposed on the transfer of property during an individual's lifetime. The tax is imposed upon the donor of the gift and is based upon the fair market value of the property on the date of gift.

Grantor trust. A trust over which the grantor (or grantor's spouse) retains substantial control. The income of a grantor trust is taxed to the grantor, not to the trust or beneficiaries.

Revenue ruling. Gives the IRS's interpretation of how the IRC and regulations apply to a specific fact situation, and therefore indicates how the IRS will treat similar transactions.

Simple trust. A trust that is required to distribute all of its income to beneficiaries each year, cannot make charitable contributions, and makes no distributions of trust corpus (i.e., principal) during the year.

UDITPA. The Uniform Division of Income for Tax Purposes Act which provides rules for allocating and apportioning a multistate or multinational enterprise's nonbusiness and business income among states and foreign counties.

Unrelated business income. Income of an exempt organization from a business that is regularly carried on, and is unrelated to the organization's exempt purpose. UBI is subject to tax to the extent in excess of $1,000.

I.A. The Gift Tax

1. Steve and Kay Briar, US citizens, were married for the entire 2014 calendar year. In 2014, Steve gave a $32,000 cash gift to his sister. The Briars made no other gifts in 2014. They each signed a timely election to treat the $32,000 gift as made one-half by each spouse. Disregarding the applicable credit and estate tax consequences, what amount of the 2014 gift is taxable to the Briars?

   a. $30,000
   b. $6,000
   c. $4,000
   d. $0

2. In 2015, Sayers, who is single, gave an outright gift of $50,000 to a friend, Johnson, who needed the money to pay medical expenses. In filing the 2015 gift tax return, Sayers was entitled to a maximum exclusion of

   a. $0
   b. $13,000
   c. $14,000
   d. $50,000

3. During 2015, Blake transferred a corporate bond with a face amount and fair market value of $20,000 to a trust for the benefit of her sixteen-year old child. Annual interest on this bond is $2,000, which is to be accumulated in the trust and distributed to the child on reaching the age of twenty-one. The bond is then to be distributed to the donor or her successor-in-interest in liquidation of the trust. Present value of the total interest to be received by the child is $8,710. The amount of the gift that is excludable from taxable gifts is

   a. $20,000
   b. $14,000
   c. $8,710
   d. $0

4. Under the unified rate schedule for 2015,

   a. Lifetime taxable gifts are taxed on a noncumulative basis.
   b. Transfers at death are taxed on a noncumulative basis.
   c. Lifetime taxable gifts and transfers at death are taxed on a cumulative basis.
   d. The gift tax rates are 5% higher than the estate tax rates.

5. Which of the following requires filing a gift tax return, if the transfer exceeds the available annual gift tax exclusion?

   a. Medical expenses paid directly to a physician on behalf of an individual unrelated to the donor.
   b. Tuition paid directly to an accredited university on behalf of an individual unrelated to the donor.
   c. Payments for college books, supplies, and dormitory fees on behalf of an individual unrelated to the donor.
   d. Campaign expenses paid to a political organization.

6. On July 1, 2014, Vega made a transfer by gift in an amount sufficient to require the filing of a gift tax return. Vega was still alive in 2015. If Vega did **not** request an extension of time for filing the 2014 gift tax return, the due date for filing was

   a. March 15, 2015.
   b. April 15, 2015.
   c. June 15, 2015.
   d. June 30, 2015.

7. Jan, an unmarried individual, gave the following outright gifts in 2015:

Donee	Amount	Use by donee
Jones	$16,000	Down payment on house
Craig	15,000	College tuition
Kande	5,000	Vacation trip

Jan's 2015 exclusions for gift tax purposes should total

   a. $34,000
   b. $33,000
   c. $31,000
   d. $18,000

8. When Jim and Nina became engaged in April 2015, Jim gave Nina a ring that had a fair market value of $50,000. After their wedding in July 2015, Jim gave Nina $75,000 in cash so that Nina could have her own bank account. Both Jim and Nina are US citizens. What was the amount of Jim's 2015 marital deduction?

   a. $63,000
   b. $75,000
   c. $113,000
   d. $125,000

9. Raff created a joint bank account for himself and his friend's son, Dave. There is a gift to Dave when

   a. Raff creates the account.
   b. Raff dies.
   c. Dave draws on the account for his own benefit.
   d. Dave is notified by Raff that the account has been created.

I.B. The Estate Tax

10. Fred and Ethel (brother and sister), residents of a noncommunity property state, own unimproved land that they hold in joint tenancy with rights of survivorship. The land cost $100,000 of which Ethel paid $80,000 and Fred paid $20,000. Ethel died during 2015 when the land was worth $300,000, and $240,000 was included in Ethel's gross estate. What is Fred's basis for the property after Ethel's death?

   a. $140,000
   b. $240,000

c. $260,000
d. $300,000

11. Bell, a cash-basis calendar-year taxpayer, died on June 1, 2015. In 2015, prior to her death, Bell incurred $2,000 in medical expenses. The executor of the estate paid the medical expenses, which were a claim against the estate, on July 1, 2015. If the executor files the appropriate waiver, the medical expenses are deductible on

a. The estate tax return.
b. Bell's final income tax return.
c. The estate income tax return.
d. The executor's income tax return.

12. If the executor of a decedent's estate elects the alternate valuation date and none of the property included in the gross estate has been sold or distributed, the estate assets must be valued as of how many months after the decedent's death?

a. 12
b. 9
c. 6
d. 3

13. What amount of a decedent's taxable estate is effectively tax-free if the maximum basic exclusion amount is taken during 2015?

a. $1,000,000
b. $1,455,800
c. $5,340,000
d. $5,430,000

14. Which of the following credits may be offset against the gross estate tax to determine the net estate tax of a US citizen dying during 2015?

	Applicable credit	Credit for gift taxes paid on gifts made after 1976
a.	Yes	Yes
b.	No	No
c.	No	Yes
d.	Yes	No

15. Fred and Amy Kehl, both US citizens, are married. All of their real and personal property is owned by them as tenants by the entirety or as joint tenants with right of survivorship. The gross estate of the first spouse to die

a. Includes 50% of the value of all property owned by the couple, regardless of which spouse furnished the original consideration.
b. Includes only the property that had been acquired with the funds of the deceased spouse.
c. Is governed by the federal statutory provisions relating to jointly held property, rather than by the decedent's interest in community property vested by state law, if the Kehls reside in a community property state.
d. Includes one-third of the value of all real estate owned by the Kehls, as the dower right in the case of the wife or curtesy right in the case of the husband.

16. In connection with a "buy-sell" agreement funded by a cross-purchase insurance arrangement, business associate

Adam bought a policy on Burr's life to finance the purchase of Burr's interest. Adam, the beneficiary, paid the premiums and retained all incidents of ownership. On the death of Burr, the insurance proceeds will be

a. Includible in Burr's gross estate, if Burr owns 50% or more of the stock of the corporation.
b. Includible in Burr's gross estate only if Burr had purchased a similar policy on Adam's life at the same time and for the same purpose.
c. Includible in Burr's gross estate, if Adam has the right to veto Burr's power to borrow on the policy that Burr owns on Adam's life.
d. Excludible from Burr's gross estate.

17. Following are the fair market values of Wald's assets at the date of death:

Personal effects and jewelry	$1,750,000
Land bought by Wald with Wald's funds five years prior to death and held with Wald's sister as joint tenants with right of survivorship	3,800,000

The executor of Wald's estate did not elect the alternate valuation date. The amount includible as Wald's gross estate in the federal estate tax return is

a. $1,750,000
b. $3,800,000
c. $5,000,000
d. $5,550,000

18. Which one of the following is a valid deduction from a decedent's gross estate?

a. Foreign death taxes.
b. Income tax paid on income earned and received after the decedent's death.
c. Federal estate taxes.
d. Unpaid income taxes on income received by the decedent before death.

19. Eng and Lew, both US citizens, died in 2015. Eng made taxable lifetime gifts of $400,000 that are **not** included in Eng's gross estate. Lew made no lifetime gifts. At the dates of death, Eng's gross estate was $4,200,000, and Lew's gross estate was $5,300,000. A federal estate tax return must be filed for

	Eng	Lew
a.	No	No
b.	No	Yes
c.	Yes	No
d.	Yes	Yes

20. With regard to the federal estate tax, the alternate valuation date

a. Is required to be used if the fair market value of the estate's assets has increased since the decedent's date of death.
b. If elected on the first return filed for the estate, may be revoked in an amended return provided that the first return was filed on time.

c. Must be used for valuation of the estate's liabilities if such date is used for valuation of the estate's assets.

d. Can be elected only if its use decreases both the value of the gross estate and the estate tax liability.

21. Proceeds of a life insurance policy payable to the estate's executor, as the estate's representative, are

a. Includible in the decedent's gross estate only if the premiums had been paid by the insured.

b. Includible in the decedent's gross estate only if the policy was taken out within three years of the insured's death under the "contemplation of death" rule.

c. Always includible in the decedent's gross estate.

d. Never includible in the decedent's gross estate.

22. Ross, a calendar-year, cash-basis taxpayer who died in June 2015, was entitled to receive a $10,000 accounting fee that had not been collected before the date of death. The executor of Ross' estate collected the full $10,000 in July 2015. This $10,000 should appear in

a. Only the decedent's final individual income tax return.

b. Only the estate's fiduciary income tax return.

c. Only the estate tax return.

d. Both the fiduciary income tax return and the estate tax return.

Items 23 and 24 are based on the following data:

Alan Curtis, a US citizen, died on March 1, 2015, leaving an adjusted gross estate with a fair market value of $6,400,000 at the date of death. Under the terms of Alan's will, $3,000,000 was bequeathed outright to his widow, free of all estate and inheritance taxes. The remainder of Alan's estate was left to his mother. Alan made no taxable gifts during his lifetime.

23. Disregarding extensions of time for filing, within how many months after the date of Alan's death is the federal estate tax return due?

a. 2 1/2

b. 3 1/2

c. 9

d. 12

24. In computing the taxable estate, the executor of Alan's estate should claim a marital deduction of

a. $450,000

b. $780,800

c. $900,000

d. $3,000,000

25. In 2009, Edwin Ryan bought 100 shares of a listed stock for $5,000. In June 2015, when the stock's fair market value was $7,000, Edwin gave this stock to his sister, Lynn. No gift tax was paid. Lynn died in October 2015, bequeathing this stock to Edwin, when the stock's fair market value was $9,000. Lynn's executor did not elect the alternate valuation. What is Edwin's basis for this stock after he inherits it from Lynn's estate?

a. $0

b. $5,000

c. $7,000

d. $9,000

II. Generation-Skipping Tax

26. For 2015, the generation-skipping transfer tax is imposed

a. Instead of the gift tax.

b. Instead of the estate tax.

c. At the highest tax rate under the transfer tax rate schedule.

d. When an individual makes a gift to a grandparent.

III. Income Taxation of Estates and Trusts

27. Under the terms of the will of Melvin Crane, $10,000 a year is to be paid to his widow and $5,000 a year is to be paid to his daughter out of the estate's income during the period of estate administration. No charitable contributions are made by the estate. During 2015, the estate made the required distributions to Crane's widow and daughter and for the entire year the estate's distributable net income was $12,000. What amount of the $10,000 distribution received from the estate must Crane's widow include in her gross income for 2015?

a. $0

b. $4,000

c. $8,000

d. $10,000

Items 28 and 29 are based on the following:

Lyon, a cash-basis taxpayer, died on January 15, 2015. In 2015, the estate executor made the required periodic distribution of $9,000 from estate income to Lyon's sole heir. The following pertains to the estate's income and disbursements in 2015:

2015 Estate Income	
$20,000	Taxable interest
10,000	Net long-term capital gains allocable to corpus

2015 Estate Disbursements	
$5,000	Administrative expenses attributable to taxable income

28. For the 2015 calendar year, what was the estate's distributable net income (DNI)?

a. $15,000

b. $20,000

c. $25,000

d. $30,000

29. Lyon's executor does not intend to file an extension request for the estate fiduciary income tax return. By what date must the executor file the Form 1041, US Fiduciary Income Tax Return, for the estate's 2015 calendar year?

a. March 15, 2016.

b. April 15, 2016.

c. June 15, 2016.

d. September 15, 2016.

30. A distribution from estate income, that was **currently** required, was made to the estate's sole beneficiary during its calendar year. The maximum amount of the distribution to be included in the beneficiary's gross income is limited to the estate's

Module 39: Other Taxation Topics

a. Capital gain income.
b. Ordinary gross income.
c. Distributable net income.
d. Net investment income.

31. A distribution to an estate's sole beneficiary for the 2015 calendar year equaled $15,000, the amount currently required to be distributed by the will. The estate's 2015 records were as follows:

Estate income

$40,000   Taxable interest

Estate disbursements

$34,000   Expenses attributable to taxable interest

What amount of the distribution was taxable to the beneficiary?

a. $40,000
b. $15,000
c. $6,000
d. $0

32. With regard to estimated income tax, estates

a. Must make quarterly estimated tax payments starting no later than the second quarter following the one in which the estate was established.
b. Are exempt from paying estimated tax during the estate's first two taxable years.
c. Must make quarterly estimated tax payments only if the estate's income is required to be distributed currently.
d. Are not required to make payments of estimated tax.

33. A complex trust is a trust that

a. Must distribute income currently, but is prohibited from distributing principal during the taxable year.
b. Invests only in corporate securities and is prohibited from engaging in short-term transactions.
c. Permits accumulation of current income, provides for charitable contributions, or distributes principal during the taxable year.
d. Is exempt from payment of income tax since the tax is paid by the beneficiaries.

34. The 2015 standard deduction for a trust or an estate in the fiduciary income tax return is

a. $0
b. $650
c. $750
d. $800

35. Which of the following fiduciary entities are required to use the calendar year as their taxable period for income tax purposes?

	Estates	Trusts (except those that are tax exempt)
a.	Yes	Yes
b.	No	No
c.	Yes	No
d.	No	Yes

36. Ordinary and necessary administration expenses paid by the fiduciary of an estate are deductible

a. Only on the fiduciary income tax return (Form 1041) and never on the federal estate tax return (Form 706).
b. Only on the federal estate tax return and never on the fiduciary income tax return.
c. On the fiduciary income tax return only if the estate tax deduction is waived for these expenses.
d. On both the fiduciary income tax return and on the estate tax return by adding a tax computed on the proportionate rates attributable to both returns.

37. An executor of a decedent's estate that has only US citizens as beneficiaries is required to file a fiduciary income tax return, if the estate's gross income for the year is at least

a. $400
b. $500
c. $600
d. $1,000

38. The charitable contribution deduction on an estate's fiduciary income tax return is allowable

a. If the decedent died intestate.
b. To the extent of the same adjusted gross income limitation as that on an individual income tax return.
c. Only if the decedent's will specifically provides for the contribution.
d. Subject to the 2% threshold on miscellaneous itemized deductions.

39. On January 2, 2015, Carlt created a $300,000 trust that provided his mother with a lifetime income interest starting on January 2, 2015, with the remainder interest to go to his son. Carlt expressly retained the power to revoke both the income interest and the remainder interest at any time. Who will be taxed on the trust's 2015 income?

a. Carlt's mother.
b. Carlt's son.
c. Carlt.
d. The trust.

40. Astor, a cash-basis taxpayer, died on February 3. During the year, the estate's executor made a distribution of $12,000 from estate income to Astor's sole heir and adopted a calendar year to determine the estate's taxable income. The following additional information pertains to the estate's income and disbursements for the year:

Estate income

Taxable interest	$65,000
Net long-term capital gains allocable to corpus	5,000

Estate disbursements

Administrative expenses attributable to taxable income	14,000
Charitable contributions from gross income to a public charity, made under the terms of the will	9,000

For the calendar year, what was the estate's distributable net income (DNI)?

a. $39,000
b. $42,000
c. $58,000
d. $65,000

41. For income tax purposes, the estate's initial taxable period for a decedent who died on October 24

a. May be either a calendar year, or a fiscal year beginning on the date of the decedent's death.
b. Must be a fiscal year beginning on the date of the decedent's death.
c. May be either a calendar year, or a fiscal year beginning on October 1 of the year of the decedent's death.
d. Must be a calendar year beginning on January 1 of the year of the decedent's death.

IV. Exempt Organizations

42. The private foundation status of an exempt organization will terminate if it

a. Becomes a public charity.
b. Is a foreign corporation.
c. Does not distribute all of its net assets to one or more public charities.
d. Is governed by a charter that limits the organization's exempt purposes.

43. Which of the following exempt organizations would be eligible to satisfy its annual filing requirement by filing Form 990-N (e-Postcard)?

a. Church.
b. Private foundation.
c. An exempt organization with $20,000 of gross receipts.
d. An exempt organization with $3,500 of gross income from an unrelated business.

44. To qualify as an exempt organization other than a church or an employees' qualified pension or profit-sharing trust, the applicant

a. Cannot operate under the "lodge system" under which payments are made to its members for sick benefits.
b. Need not be specifically identified as one of the classes on which exemption is conferred by the Internal Revenue Code, provided that the organization's purposes and activities are of a nonprofit nature.
c. Is barred from incorporating and issuing capital stock.
d. Must file a written application with the Internal Revenue Service.

45. To qualify as an exempt organization, the applicant

a. May be organized and operated for the primary purpose of carrying on a business for profit, provided that all of the organization's net earnings are turned over to one or more tax exempt organizations.

b. Need not be specifically identified as one of the classes upon which exemption is conferred by the Internal Revenue Code, provided that the organization's purposes and activities are of a nonprofit nature.
c. Must not be classified as a social club.
d. Must not be a private foundation organized and operated exclusively to influence legislation pertaining to protection of the environment.

46. Carita Fund, organized and operated exclusively for charitable purposes, provides insurance coverage, at amounts substantially below cost, to exempt organizations involved in the prevention of cruelty to children. Carita's insurance activities are

a. Exempt from tax.
b. Treated as unrelated business income.
c. Subject to the same tax provisions as those applicable to insurance companies.
d. Considered "commercial-type" as defined by the Internal Revenue Code.

47. The filing of a return covering unrelated business income

a. Is required of all exempt organizations having at least $1,000 of unrelated business taxable income for the year.
b. Relieves the organization of having to file a separate annual information return.
c. Is not necessary if all of the organization's income is used exclusively for charitable purposes.
d. Must be accompanied by a minimum payment of 50% of the tax due as shown on the return, with the balance of tax payable six months later.

48. A condominium management association wishing to be treated as a homeowners association and to qualify as an exempt organization for a particular year

a. Need not file a formal election.
b. Must file an election as of the date the association was organized.
c. Must file an election at the beginning of the association's first taxable year.
d. Must file a separate election for each taxable year no later than the due date of the return for which the election is to apply.

49. An organization wishing to qualify as an exempt organization

a. Is prohibited from issuing capital stock.
b. Is limited to three prohibited transactions a year.
c. Must not have non-US citizens on its governing board.
d. Must be of a type specifically identified as one of the classes on which exemption is conferred by the Code.

50. Which one of the following statements is correct with regard to exempt organizations?

a. An organization is automatically exempt from tax merely by meeting the statutory requirements for exemptions.

b. Exempt organizations that are required to file annual information returns must disclose the identity of all substantial contributors, in addition to the amount of contributions received.

c. An organization will automatically forfeit its exempt status if any executive or other employee of the organization is paid compensation in excess of $150,000 per year, even if such compensation is reasonable.

d. Exempt status of an organization may not be retroactively revoked.

51. To qualify as an exempt organization, the applicant

a. Must fall into one of the specific classes upon which exemption is conferred by the Internal Revenue Code.

b. Cannot, under any circumstances, be a foreign corporation.

c. Cannot, under any circumstances, engage in lobbying activities.

d. Cannot be exclusively a social club.

52. To qualify as an exempt organization,

a. A written application need not be filed if no applicable official form is provided.

b. No employee of the organization is permitted to receive compensation in excess of $100,000 per year.

c. The applicant must be of a type specifically identified as one of the classes upon which exemption is conferred by the Code.

d. The organization is prohibited from issuing capital stock.

IV.A.2.   Sec. 501(c)(3) Organizations

53. Hope is a tax-exempt religious organization. Which of the following activities is (are) consistent with Hope's tax-exempt status?

I. Conducting weekend retreats for business organizations.

II. Providing traditional burial services that maintain the religious beliefs of its members.

a. I only.
b. II only.
c. Both I and II.
d. Neither I nor II.

54. The organizational test to qualify a public service charitable entity as tax-exempt requires the articles of organization to

I. Limit the purpose of the entity to the charitable purpose.

II. State that an information return should be filed annually with the Internal Revenue Service.

a. I only.
b. II only.
c. Both I and II.
d. Neither I nor II.

55. Which of the following activities regularly conducted by a tax-exempt organization will result in unrelated business income?

I. Selling articles made by handicapped persons as part of their rehabilitation, when the organization is involved exclusively in their rehabilitation.

II. Operating a grocery store almost fully staffed by emotionally handicapped persons as part of a therapeutic program.

a. I only.
b. II only.
c. Both I and II.
d. Neither I nor II.

56. An organization that operates for the prevention of cruelty to animals will fail to meet the operational test to qualify as an exempt organization if

	The organization engages in insubstantial nonexempt activities	The organization directly participates in any political campaign
a.	Yes	Yes
b.	Yes	No
c.	No	Yes
d.	No	No

IV.C.   Unrelated Business Income (UBI)

57. Which one of the following statements is correct with regard to unrelated business income of an exempt organization?

a. An exempt organization that earns any unrelated business income in excess of $100,000 during a particular year will lose its exempt status for that particular year.

b. An exempt organization is not taxed on unrelated business income of less than $1,000.

c. The tax on unrelated business income can be imposed even if the unrelated business activity is intermittent and is carried on once a year.

d. An unrelated trade or business activity that results in a loss is excluded from the definition of unrelated business.

58. Which of the following activities regularly carried out by an exempt organization will **not** result in unrelated business income?

a. The sale of laundry services by an exempt hospital to other hospitals.

b. The sale of heavy-duty appliances to senior citizens by an exempt senior citizen's center.

c. Accounting and tax services performed by a local chapter of a labor union for its members.

d. The sale by a trade association of publications used as course materials for the association's seminars that are oriented towards its members.

59. If an exempt organization is a corporation, the tax on unrelated business taxable income is

a. Computed at corporate income tax rates.

b. Computed at rates applicable to trusts.

c. Credited against the tax on recognized capital gains.

d. Abated.

60. During 2015, Help, Inc., an exempt organization, derived income of $15,000 from conducting bingo games. Conducting bingo games is legal in Help's locality and is confined to exempt organizations in Help's state. Which of the following statements is true regarding this income?

    a. The entire $15,000 is subject to tax at a lower rate than the corporation income tax rate.

    b. The entire $15,000 is exempt from tax on unrelated business income.

    c. Only the first $5,000 is exempt from tax on unrelated business income.

    d. Since Help has unrelated business income, Help automatically forfeits its exempt status for 2014.

61. Which of the following statements is correct regarding the unrelated business income of exempt organizations?

    a. If an exempt organization has any unrelated business income, it may result in the loss of the organization's exempt status.

    b. Unrelated business income relates to the performance of services, but not to the sale of goods.

    c. An unrelated business does not include any activity where all the work is performed for the organization by unpaid volunteers.

    d. Unrelated business income tax will not be imposed if profits from the unrelated business are used to support the exempt organization's charitable activities.

62. An incorporated exempt organization subject to tax on its unrelated business income

    a. Must make estimated tax payments if its tax can reasonably be expected to be $100 or more.

    b. Must comply with the Code provisions regarding installment payments of estimated income tax by corporations.

    c. Must pay at least 70% of the tax due as shown on the return when filed, with the balance of tax payable in the following quarter.

    d. May defer payment of the tax for up to nine months following the due date of the return.

63. If an exempt organization is a charitable trust, then unrelated business income is

    a. Not subject to tax.

    b. Taxed at rates applicable to corporations.

    c. Subject to tax even if such income is less than $1,000.

    d. Subject to tax only for the amount of such income in excess of $1,000.

64. With regard to unrelated business income of an exempt organization, which one of the following statements is true?

    a. If an exempt organization has any unrelated business income, such organization automatically forfeits its exempt status for the particular year in which such income was earned.

    b. When an unrelated trade or business activity results in a loss, such activity is excluded from the definition of unrelated business.

c. If an exempt organization derives income from conducting bingo games, in a locality where such activity is legal, and in a state that confines such activity to nonprofit organizations, then such income is exempt from the tax on unrelated business income.

d. Dividends and interest earned by all exempt organizations always are excluded from the definition of unrelated business income.

V.A. State and Local Taxation (SALT)

Items 65 and 66 are based on the following information:

Miramar Corp. has total business income of $1 million, and in State XY has a sales factor of 60%, a payroll factor of 50%, and a property factor of 49%.

65. What is Miramar's State XY UDITPA appointment factor and State XY business income?

    a. 60%; $600,000 business income

    b. 50%; $500,000 business income

    c. 53%; $530,000 business income

    d. 53%; $1,000,000 business income

66. What would be Miramar's State XY apportionment factor if State XY used an apportionment formula in which the property factor was double-weighted?

    a. 50%

    b. 52%

    c. 54.75%

    d. 60%

V.B. International Taxation

67. Which one of the following statements regarding the foreign operations of Glencoe Corporation (a domestic corporation) is correct?

    a. Glencoe's earnings from its foreign operations are not subject to US income tax.

    b. Glencoe may take a deduction, but not a credit, for the income taxes paid to a foreign country.

    c. Glencoe may take a credit, but not a deduction, for the income taxes paid to a foreign country.

    d. Glencoe may take either a deduction or a tax credit, but not both, for the income taxes paid to a foreign country.

Items 68 and 69 are based on the following information:

For the current year, Crocker Corp., a domestic corporation, has US taxable income of $700,000, which includes $100,000 from a foreign division. Crocker paid $40,000 of foreign income taxes on the income of the foreign division.

68. Assuming Crocker's US income tax for the current year before credits is $210,000, its maximum foreign tax credit for the current year is

    a. $6,400

    b. $30,000

    c. $35,000

    d. $40,000

69. Crocker Corp.'s unused foreign tax credit:

   a. Can be carried back two years and forward twenty years.

   b. Can be carried back one year and forward ten years.

   c. Can be carried back two years and forward five years.

   d. Cannot be carried to other tax years.

70. The following information pertains to Raubolt Corporation's operations for the current year:

Worldwide taxable income	$300,000
US source taxable income	180,000
US income tax before foreign tax credit	96,000
General category income	90,000
Foreign income tax paid on general category income	32,000
Foreign passive category income	30,000
Foreign income tax paid on passive category income	7,500

What amount of foreign tax credit may Raubolt Corporation claim for the current year?

   a. $32,000

   b. $36,300

   c. $38,400

   d. $39,500

Multiple-Choice Answers and Explanations

Answers

1.	c	__ __	17.	d	__ __	33.	c	__ __	49.	d	__ __	65.	c	__ __
2.	c	__ __	18.	d	__ __	34.	a	__ __	50.	b	__ __	66.	b	__ __
3.	d	__ __	19.	a	__ __	35.	d	__ __	51.	a	__ __	67.	d	__ __
4.	c	__ __	20.	d	__ __	36.	c	__ __	52.	c	__ __	68.	b	__ __
5.	c	__ __	21.	c	__ __	37.	c	__ __	53.	b	__ __	69.	b	__ __
6.	b	__ __	22.	d	__ __	38.	c	__ __	54.	a	__ __	70.	b	__ __
7.	b	__ __	23.	c	__ __	39.	c	__ __	55.	d	__ __			
8.	b	__ __	24.	d	__ __	40.	b	__ __	56.	c	__ __			
9.	c	__ __	25.	b	__ __	41.	a	__ __	57.	b	__ __			
10.	c	__ __	26.	c	__ __	42.	a	__ _.	58.	d	__ __			
11.	b	__ __	27.	c	__ __	43.	c	__ __	59.	a	__ __			
12.	c	__ __	28.	a	__ __	44.	d	__ __	60.	b	__ __			
13.	d	__ __	29.	b	__ __	45.	d	__ __	61.	c	__ __			
14.	d	__ __	30.	c	__ __	46.	a	__ __	62.	b	__ __			
15.	a	__ __	31.	c	__ __	47.	a	__ __	63.	d	__ __	1st:	__/70 = __%	
16.	d	__ __	32.	b	__ __	48.	d	__ __	64.	c	__ __	2nd:	__/70 = __%	

Explanations

1. (c) The requirement is to determine the amount of the $32,000 gift that is taxable to the Briars for 2014. Steve and Kay (his spouse) elected to split the gift made to Steve's sister, so each is treated as making a gift of $16,000. Since both Steve and Kay would be eligible for a $14,000 exclusion, each will have made a taxable gift of $16,000 – $14,000 exclusion = $2,000.

2. (c) The requirement is to determine the maximum exclusion available on Sayers' 2015 gift tax return for the $50,000 gift to Johnson who needed the money to pay medical expenses. The first $14,000 of gifts made to a donee during calendar year 2015 (except gifts of future interests) is excluded in determining the amount of the donor's taxable gifts for the year. Note that Sayers does not qualify for the unlimited exclusion for medical expenses paid on behalf of a donee, because Sayers did not pay the $50,000 to a medical care provider on Johnson's behalf.

3. (d) The requirement is to determine the amount of gift that is excludable from taxable gifts. Since the interest income resulting from the bond transferred to the trust will be accumulated and distributed to the child in the future upon reaching the age of twenty-one, the gift (represented by the $8,710 present value of the interest to be received by the child at age twenty-one) is a gift of a future interest and is not eligible to be offset by an annual exclusion.

4. (c) The requirement is to determine the correct statement regarding the unified transfer tax rate schedule. The unified transfer tax rate schedule applies on a cumulative basis to both life and death transfers. During a person's lifetime, a tax is first computed on cumulative lifetime taxable gifts, then is reduced by the tax on taxable gifts made in prior years in order to tax the current year's gifts at applicable marginal rates. At death, a unified transfer tax is computed on total life and death transfers, then is reduced by the tax already paid on post-1976

gifts, the unified transfer tax credit, foreign death taxes, and prior transfer taxes.

5. (c) The requirement is to determine which gift requires the filing of a gift tax return when the amount transferred exceeds the available annual gift tax exclusion. A gift in the form of payments for college books, supplies, and dormitory fees on behalf of an individual unrelated to the donor requires the filing of a gift tax return if the amount of payments exceeds the $14,000 annual exclusion contrast, no gift tax return need be filed for medical expenses or college tuition paid on behalf of a donee, and campaign expenses paid to a political organization, because there are unlimited exclusions available for these types of gifts after the annual exclusion has been used.

6. (b) The requirement is to determine the due date for filing a 2014 gift tax return (Form 709). A gift tax return must be filed on a calendar-year basis, with the return due and tax paid on or before April 15th of the following year. If the donor subsequently dies, the gift tax return is due not later than the date for filing the federal estate tax return (generally nine months after date of death). Here, since Vega was still living in 2015, the due date for filing the 2013 gift tax return is April 15, 2015.

7. (b) The requirement is to determine Jan's total exclusions for gift tax purposes for 2015. In computing a donor's gift tax, the first $14,000 of gifts made to a donee during calendar year 2015 is excluded in determining the amount of the donor's taxable gifts. Thus, $14,000 of the $16,000 given to Jones, $14,000 of the $15,000 given to Craig, and all $5,000 given to Kande can be excluded, resulting in a total exclusion of $33,000. Jan's gift to Craig does not qualify for the unlimited exclusion of educational gifts paid on behalf of a donee because the amount was paid directly to Craig. All $15,000 could have been excluded if Jan had made the tuition payment directly to the college.

8. (b) The requirement is to determine the amount of Jim's gift tax marital deduction for 2015. An unlimited marital deduction is allowed for gift tax purposes for gifts to a donee, who at the time of the gift is the donor's spouse. Thus, Jim's gift of $75,000 to Nina made after their wedding is eligible for the marital deduction, whereas the gift of the $50,000 engagement ring does not qualify because Jim and Nina were not married at date of gift. The gift tax annual exclusion of $14,000 applies to multiple gifts to the same donee in chronological order, reducing the taxable gift of the engagement ring to $50,000 – $14,000 = $36,000. Since there is no remaining annual exclusion to reduce the gift of the $75,000 bank account, it would be completely offset by a marital deduction of $75,000.

9. (c) The requirement is to determine when a gift occurs in conjunction with Raff's creation of a joint bank account for himself and his friend's son, Dave. A gift does not occur when Raff opens the joint account and deposits money into it. Instead, a gift results when the noncontributing tenant (Dave) withdraws money from the account for his own benefit.

10. (c) The requirement is to determine Fred's basis for the property after the death of the joint tenant (Ethel). When property is held in joint tenancy by other than spouses, the property's fair market value is included in a decedent's estate to the extent of the percentage that the decedent contributed toward the purchase. Since Ethel furnished 80% of the land's purchase price, 80% of its $300,000 fair market value, or $240,000 is included in Ethel's estate. Thus, Fred's basis is $240,000 plus the $20,000 of purchase price that he furnished, a total of $260,000.

11. (b) The requirement is to determine the correct treatment of medical expenses paid by the executor of Bell's estate if the executor files the appropriate waiver. The executor may elect to treat medical expenses paid by the decedent's estate for the decedent's medical care as paid by the decedent at the time the medical services were provided. To qualify for this election, the medical expenses must be paid within the one-year period after the decedent's death, and the executor must attach a waiver to the decedent's Form 1040 indicating that the expenses will not be claimed as a deduction on the decedent's estate tax return. Here, since Bell died during 2015, and the medical services were provided and paid for by Bell's estate during 2015, the medical expenses are deductible on Bell's final income tax return for 2015 provided that the executor attaches the appropriate waiver.

12. (c) If the executor of a decedent's estate elects the alternate valuation date and none of the assets have been sold or distributed, the estate assets must be included in the decedent's gross estate at their FMV as of six months after the decedent's death.

13. (d) The requirement is to determine the amount of a decedent's taxable estate that is effectively tax-free if the maximum basic exclusion amount is taken for 2015. The maximum estate tax credit is the equivalent of an exemption of $5,430,000 and effectively permits $5,430,000 of taxable estate to be free of tax.

14. (d) The requirement is to determine which of the credits may be offset against the gross estate tax in determining the net estate tax of a US citizen for 2015. In computing the net estate tax of a US citizen, the gross estate tax may be offset by the applicable tax credit, and credits for foreign death taxes, and prior transfer taxes. For 2015, the applicable tax credit is equivalent to an exemption of the first $5,430,000 of taxable gifts or taxable estate from the unified transfer tax. Only adjusted taxable gifts made after 1976 are added back to a donor's taxable estate in arriving at the tax base for the application of the federal estate tax at death. To the extent these taxable gifts exceeded the exemption equivalent of the applicable credit and required the payment of a gift tax during the donor's lifetime, such tax is then subtracted from a donor's tentative estate tax at death in arriving at the gross estate tax. Thus, although post-1976 gift taxes reduce the net estate tax, they are not subtracted as a tax credit from the gross estate tax.

15. (a) The requirement is to determine the correct statement with regard to the gross estate of the first spouse to die when property is owned by them as tenants by the entirety or as joint tenants with right of survivorship. Under the general rule for joint tenancies, 100% of the value of jointly held property is included in a deceased tenant's gross estate except to the extent that the surviving tenants can prove that they contributed to the cost of the property. However, under a special rule applicable to spouses who own property as tenants by the entirety or as joint tenants with right of survivorship, the gross estate of the first spouse to die automatically includes 50% of the value of the jointly held property, regardless of which spouse furnished the original consideration for the purchase of the property.

16. (d) The requirement is to determine the amount of insurance proceeds included in Burr's gross estate with regard to a policy on Burr's life purchased by Adam in connection with a "buy-sell" agreement funded by a cross-purchase insurance arrangement. The gross estate of a decedent includes the proceeds of life insurance on the decedent's life if (1) the insurance proceeds are payable to the estate, (2) the proceeds are payable to another for the benefit of the estate, or (3) the decedent possessed an incident of ownership in the policy. An "incident of ownership" not only means ownership of the policy in a legal sense, but also includes the power to change beneficiaries, to revoke an assignment, to pledge the policy for a loan, or to surrender or cancel the policy. Here, since the policy owned by Adam on Burr's life was not payable to or for the benefit of Burr's estate, and Burr had no incident of ownership in the policy, the full amount of insurance proceeds would be excluded from Burr's gross estate.

17. (d) The requirement is to determine the amount includible as Wald's gross estate for federal estate tax purposes. If an executor does not elect the alternate valuation date, all property in which the decedent possessed an ownership interest at time of death is included in the decedent's gross estate at its fair market value at date of death. If property was held in joint tenancy and was acquired by purchase by other than spouses, the property's total fair market value will be included in the decedent's gross estate except to the extent that the surviving tenant can prove that he/she contributed toward the purchase. Since Wald purchased the land with his own funds, the land's total fair market value ($3,800,000) must be included in Wald's gross estate together with Wald's personal effects and jewelry ($1,750,000), resulting in a gross estate of $5,550,000.

18. (d) The requirement is to determine the item that is deductible from a decedent's gross estate. Unpaid income taxes on income received by the decedent before death would be a liability of the estate and would be deductible from the gross estate. Foreign death taxes, income tax paid on income earned and received after the decedent's death, and federal estate taxes are not deductible in computing a decedent's taxable estate. Note that although foreign death taxes are not deductible in computing a decedent's taxable estate, a limited tax credit is allowed for foreign death taxes in computing the net estate tax payable.

19. (a) The requirement is to determine whether federal estate tax returns must be filed for the estates of Eng and Lew. For a decedent dying during 2015, a federal estate tax return (Form 706) must be filed if the decedent's gross estate exceeds $5,430,000. If a decedent made taxable lifetime gifts such that the decedent's applicable transfer tax credit was used to offset the gift tax, the ($5,430,000) exemption amount must be reduced by the amount of taxable lifetime gifts to determine whether a return is required to be filed.

Since Lew made no lifetime gifts and the value of Lew's gross estate was only $5,300,000, no federal estate tax return is required to be filed for Lew's estate. In Eng's case, the $5,430,000 exemption is reduced by Eng's $400,000 of taxable lifetime gifts to $5,030,000. However, since Eng's gross estate totaled only $4,200,000, no federal estate tax return is required to be filed for Eng's estate.

20. (d) The requirement is to determine the correct statement regarding the use of the alternate valuation date in computing the federal estate tax. An executor of an estate can elect to use the alternate valuation date (the date six months after the decedent's death) to value the assets included in a decedent's gross estate only if its use decreases both the value of the gross estate and the amount of estate tax liability. Answer (a) is incorrect because the alternate valuation date cannot be used if its use increases the value of the gross estate. Answer (b) is incorrect because the use of the alternate valuation date is an irrevocable election. Answer (c) is incorrect because the alternate valuation date is only used to value an estate's assets, not its liabilities.

21. (c) The requirement is to determine when the proceeds of life insurance payable to the estate's executor, as the estate's representative, are includible in the decedent's gross estate. The proceeds of life insurance on the decedent's life are always included in the decedent's gross estate if (1) they are receivable by the estate, (2) the decedent possessed any incident of ownership in the policy, or (3) they are receivable by another (e.g., the estate's executor) for the benefit of the estate.

22. (d) The requirement is to determine the proper income and estate tax treatment of an accounting fee earned by Ross before death, that was subsequently collected by the executor of Ross' estate. Since Ross was a calendar-year, cash-method taxpayer, the income would not be included on Ross' final individual income tax return because payment had not been received. Since the accounting fee would not be included in Ross' final income tax return because of Ross' cash method of accounting, the accounting fee would be "income in respect of a decedent." For estate tax purposes, income in respect of a decedent will be included in the decedent's gross estate at its fair market value on the appropriate valuation date. For income tax purposes, the income tax basis of the decedent (zero) transfers over to the estate or beneficiary who collects the fee. The recipient of the income must classify it in the same manner (i.e., ordinary income) as would have the decedent. Thus, the accounting fee must be included in Ross' gross estate and must also be included in the estate's fiduciary income tax return (Form 1041) because the fee was collected by the executor of Ross' estate.

23. (c) The requirement is to determine within how many months after the date of Alan's death his federal estate tax return should be filed. The federal estate tax return (Form 706) must be filed and the tax paid within nine months of the decedent's death, unless an extension of time has been granted.

24. (d) The requirement is to determine the amount of marital deduction that can be claimed in computing Alan's taxable estate. In computing the taxable estate of a decedent, an unlimited marital deduction is allowed for the portion of the decedent's estate that passes to the decedent's surviving spouse. Since $3,000,000 was bequeathed outright to Alan's widow, Alan's estate will receive a marital deduction of $3,000,000.

25. (b) The requirement is to determine Edwin's basis for the stock inherited from Lynn's estate. A special rule applies if a decedent (Lynn) acquires appreciated property as a gift within one year of death, and this property passes to the donor (Edwin) or donor's spouse. Then the donor's (Edwin's) basis is the basis of the property in the hands of the decedent (Lynn) before death. Since Lynn had received the stock as a gift, Lynn's basis before death ($5,000) becomes the basis of the stock to Edwin.

26. (c) The requirement is to determine the correct statement regarding the generation-skipping transfer tax. The generation-skipping transfer tax is imposed as a separate tax in addition to the federal gift and estate taxes, and is designed to prevent an individual from escaping an entire generation of gift and estate taxes by transferring property to a person that is two or more generations *below* that of the transferor. The tax is imposed at the highest tax rate (40% for 2015) under the transfer tax rate schedule.

27. (c) The requirement is to determine the amount of the estate's $10,000 distribution that must be included in gross income by Crane's widow. The maximum amount that is taxable to beneficiaries is limited to the estate's distributable net income (DNI). Since distributions to multiple beneficiaries exceed DNI, the estate's $12,000 of DNI must be prorated to distributions to determine the portion of each distribution that must be included in gross income. Since distributions to the widow and daughter totaled $15,000, the portion of the $10,000 distribution that must be included in the widow's gross income equals ($10,000/$15,000) × $12,000 = $8,000.

28. (a) The requirement is to determine the estate's distributable net income (DNI). An estate's DNI generally is its taxable income before the income distribution deduction, increased by its personal exemption, any net capital loss deduction, and tax-exempt interest (reduced by related nondeductible expenses), and decreased by any net capital gains allocable to corpus. Here, the estate's DNI is the $20,000 of taxable interest reduced by the $5,000 of administrative expenses attributable to taxable income, or $15,000.

29. (b) The requirement is to determine the due date for the Fiduciary Income Tax Return (Form 1041) for the estate's 2015 calendar year. Form 1041 is due on the 15th day of the fourth month following the end of the tax year. Thus, an estate's calendar-year return is generally due on April 15th of the following year.

30. (c) The requirement is to determine the maximum amount to be included in the beneficiary's gross income for a distribution from estate income that was currently required. Distributable net income (DNI) is the maximum amount of distributions that can be taxed to beneficiaries as well as the maximum amount of distributions deduction for an estate.

31. (c) The requirement is to determine the amount of the estate's $15,000 distribution that is taxable to the sole beneficiary. The maximum amount that is taxable to the beneficiary is limited to the estate's distributable net income (DNI). An estate's DNI is generally its taxable income before the income distribution deduction, increased by its exemption, a net capital loss deduction, and tax-exempt interest (reduced by related nondeductible expenses), and decreased by any net capital gains allocable to corpus. Here, the estate's DNI is its taxable interest of $40,000, reduced by the $34,000 of expenses attributable to taxable interest, or $6,000.

32. (b) The requirement is to determine the correct statement regarding an estate's estimated income taxes. Trusts and estates must make quarterly estimated tax payments, except that an estate is exempt from making estimated tax payments for taxable years ending within two years of the decedent's death.

33. (c) The requirement is to determine the correct statement regarding a complex trust. A simple trust is one that (1) is required to distribute all of its income to designated beneficiaries every year, (2) has no beneficiaries that are qualifying charitable organizations, and (3) makes no distributions of trust corpus (i.e., principal) during the year. A complex trust is any trust that is not a simple trust. Answer (a) is incorrect because a complex trust is not required to distribute income currently, nor is it prohibited from distributing trust principal. Answer (b) is incorrect because there are no investment restrictions imposed on a complex trust. Answer (d) is incorrect because an income tax is imposed on a trust's taxable income.

34. (a) The requirement is to determine the amount of *standard deduction* for a trust or an estate in the fiduciary income tax return (Form 1041). No standard deduction is available for a trust or an estate on the fiduciary income tax return. On the other hand, a personal exemption is allowed for an estate or trust on the fiduciary income tax return. The personal exemption is $600 for an estate, $300 for a trust required to distribute all income currently, and $100 for all other trusts.

35. (d) The requirement is to indicate whether estate and trusts are required to use the calendar year as their taxable year. All trusts (except those that are tax exempt) are generally required to use the calendar year for tax purposes. In contrast, an estate may adopt the calendar year, or any fiscal year as its taxable year.

36. (c) The requirement is to determine the proper treatment for ordinary and necessary administrative expenses paid by the fiduciary of an estate. Ordinary and necessary administrative expenses paid by the fiduciary of an estate can be deducted on either the estate's fiduciary income tax return, or on the estate's federal estate tax return. Although the expenses cannot be deducted twice, they can be allocated between the two returns in any manner that the fiduciary sees fit. If the administrative expenses are to be deducted on the fiduciary income tax return, the potential estate tax deduction must be waived for these expenses.

37. (c) The requirement is to determine when a fiduciary income tax return for a decedent's estate must be filed. The executor of a decedent's estate that has only US citizens as beneficiaries is required to file a fiduciary income tax return (Form 1041) if the estate's gross income is $600 or more. The return is due on or before the 15th day of the fourth month following the close of the estate's taxable year.

38. (c) The requirement is to determine the correct statement regarding the charitable contribution deduction on an estate's fiduciary income tax return (Form 1041). An estate is allowed a deduction for a contribution to a charitable organization if (1) the decedent's will specifically provides for the contribution, and (2) the recipient is a qualified charitable organization. The amount allowed as a charitable deduction is not subject to any percentage limitations, but must be paid from amounts included in the estate's gross income for the year of contribution.

39. (c) The requirement is to determine who will be taxed on the trust's 2015 income. During 2015, Carlt created a trust providing a lifetime income interest for his mother, with a remainder interest to go to his son, but he expressly retained the power to revoke both the income interest and remainder interest at any time. When the grantor of a trust retains substantial control over the trust, such as the power to revoke the income and remainder interests, the trust income will be taxed to the grantor and not to the trust or beneficiaries.

40. (b) The requirement is to determine the estate's distributable net income (DNI). An estate's DNI generally is its taxable income before the income distribution deduction, increased by its personal exemption, any net capital loss deduction, and tax-exempt income (reduced by related expenses), and decreased by any net capital gain allocable to corpus. Here, the estate's DNI is the $65,000 of taxable interest, reduced by the $14,000 of administrative expenses attributable to taxable income and the $9,000 of charitable contributions. Charitable contributions are allowed as a deduction if made under the terms of the decedent's will and are paid to qualified charitable organizations from amounts included in the estate's gross income.

41. (a) The requirement is to determine the correct statement for income tax purposes regarding the initial taxable period for the estate of a decedent who died on October 24. For income tax purposes, a decedent's estate is allowed to adopt a calendar year or any fiscal year beginning on the date of the decedent's death. Answer (b) is incorrect because an estate may adopt a calendar year and is not restricted to a fiscal year. Answer (c) is incorrect because the estate's first tax year would begin on October 24, not October 1. Answer (d) is incorrect because an estate is not restricted to a calendar year, and if it adopted a calendar year, its initial year would begin with the date of the decedent's death (October 24).

42. (a) The requirement is to determine what will terminate the private foundation status of an exempt organization. The private foundation status of an exempt organization will terminate if it becomes a public charity. Answer (b) is incorrect because a private foundation can be organized as a foreign corporation. Answer (c) is incorrect because private foundations are not required to distribute their assets to public charities. Answer (d) is incorrect because a private foundation's exempt purposes are already severely restricted by the Code.

43. (c) The requirement is to determine which exempt organization would be eligible to satisfy its annual filing requirement by filing Form 990-N (e-Postcard). Small exempt organizations whose gross receipts are $50,000 or less are generally eligible to annually file an electronic form 990-N (e-Postcard) listing the organization's legal name, mailing address, and employer identification number. Exceptions apply to churches and exempt organizations that are required to file a different form. Churches do not have to file an annual information return. A private foundation must annually file Form 990-PF Return of Private Foundation. An exempt organization having gross income of $1,000 or more from an unrelated business must file Form 990-T Exempt Organization Business Income Tax Return.

44. (d) Organizations that can qualify as exempt organizations are listed in Sec. 501 of the Internal Revenue Code, and can take the form of a trust or corporation. To receive exempt status, the organization must file a written application with the IRS. In no event will exempt status be conferred upon an organization unless the organization is one of those types of organizations specifically listed in the Code. A fraternal benefit society must operate under the lodge system. An organization operating under the lodge system carries on its activities under a form of organization that comprises local branches chartered by a parent organization and can be established to provide its members with sick benefits.

45. (d) The requirement is to determine the correct statement regarding qualification as an exempt organization. To qualify as an exempt organization, the applicant must not be a private foundation organized and operated exclusively to influence legislation pertaining to protection of the environment. Exempt status is specifically denied to organizations if a substantial part of their activities consists of "carrying on propaganda, or otherwise attempting, to influence legislation," if expenditures exceed certain amounts. Answer (a) is incorrect because an exempt organization cannot be organized for the primary purpose of carrying on a business for profit. Answer (b) is incorrect because an organization must be one of those classes upon which exemption is specifically conferred by the Internal Revenue Code. Answer (c) is incorrect because a social club organized for recreation will qualify for exemption if substantially all of the activities of the club are for such purposes and none of the profits inure to the benefit of any shareholder.

46. (a) The requirement is to determine the proper tax treatment of Carita Fund's insurance activities. An otherwise qualifying exempt organization will instead be subject to tax if a substantial part of its activities consists of providing commercial-type insurance. Sec. 501(m)(3) provides that "commercial-type insurance" does not include insurance provided at substantially below cost to a class of charitable recipients. Since Carita Fund was organized and operated exclusively for charitable purposes, and provided below cost insurance coverage to exempt organizations involved in the prevention of cruelty to children, its insurance activities are exempt from tax. The insurance activities do not constitute unrelated business income because the insurance activities were substantially related to the performance of the fund's exempt purpose. Answer (c) is incorrect because Carita Fund qualifies as an exempt organization.

47. (a) The filing of a return covering unrelated business income (Form 990-T) is required of all exempt organizations having at least $1,000 of unrelated business taxable income for the year. However, this does not relieve the organization of having to file a separate information return (Form 990) if it is otherwise required to file. Answer (c) is incorrect because in determining whether income is unrelated business income, the exempt organization's need for the income or the use it makes of the profits is irrelevant. Answer (d) is incorrect because the tax on unrelated business income of exempt organizations must be paid in full with the return.

48. (d) A condominium management association wishing to be treated as a homeowners association and thereby qualify as an exempt organization for a particular year must file a separate election for each taxable year no later than the due date of the tax return for which the election is to apply.

49. (d) An organization wishing to qualify as an exempt organization must be of a type specifically identified as one of the classes on which exemption is conferred by the Code. In no event will exempt status be conferred upon an organization unless the organization is one of those listed. Furthermore, in order to receive exempt status, the organization must file an application with the Internal Revenue Service. Answer (a) is incorrect since an exempt organization may be organized as a corporation. Answer (b) is incorrect because an exempt organization may lose its exempt status by engaging in any prohibited transaction. Answer (c) is incorrect because non-US citizens may be on an exempt organization's governing board.

50. (b) The requirement is to determine the correct statement regarding exempt organizations. With the exception chiefly of churches, an exempt organization (other than a private foundation) must nevertheless file an annual information return specifically stating items of gross income, receipts, and disbursements unless its gross receipts are normally not more than $25,000. An exempt organization required to file a return must annually report the total amount of contributions received as well as the identity of substantial contributors.

Answer (a) is incorrect because an organization can only achieve exempt status by filing an application for exemption with the Internal Revenue Service. Answer (c) is incorrect because there is no limitation on the amount of compensation that can be paid to an employee if the compensation is reasonable. Answer (d) is incorrect because exempt status can be retroactively revoked if an organization's character, purposes, or methods of operation are other than as stated in the application for exemption.

51. (a) The requirement is to determine the correct statement regarding qualification as an exempt organization. To qualify as an exempt organization, the applicant for exemption must fall into one of the specified classes of organizations that are listed in Sec. 501 as being exempt from tax. Answer (d) is incorrect because a social club can be an exempt organization as long as substantially all its activities are for such purposes and no part of its net earnings inures to the benefit of any private shareholder. Answer (c) is incorrect because most exempt organizations are permitted specified levels of lobbying expenditures, and can even elect to be subject to a tax equal to 25% of their excess lobbying expenditures to prevent loss of exempt status. Answer (b) is incorrect because foreign corporations can qualify as exempt organizations.

52. (c) Organizations that can qualify as exempt organizations are listed in Sec. 501 of the Internal Revenue Code. An exempt organization can take the form of a trust or a corporation. In order to receive exempt status, the organization must file an application with the Internal Revenue Service. In no event will exempt status be conferred upon an organization unless the organization is one of those listed in the Code. Answer (b) is incorrect because there is no limitation on the amount of salary that can be paid an employee.

53. (b) The requirement is to determine which of the activities is(are) consistent with Hope's tax-exempt status as a religious organization. An exempt organization must be operated exclusively for its exempt purpose, and other activities not in furtherance of its exempt purpose must be only an insubstantial part of its activities. A religious organization's providing traditional burial services that maintain the religious beliefs of its members would be consistent with its tax-exempt status as a religious organization. However, conducting recreational functions such as weekend retreats conducted for business organizations ordinarily would not be consistent with the tax-exempt status of a religious organization unless there were tightly scheduled religious activities and only limited free time for incidental recreation activities.

54. (a) The requirement is to determine which statements are correct in regard to the organizational test to qualify a public service charitable entity as tax-exempt. The term "articles of organization" includes the trust instrument, corporate charter, articles of association, or any other written instruments by which an organization is created. To satisfy the organizational test, the articles of organization (1) must limit the organization's purposes to one or more exempt purposes described in Sec. 501(c)(3); and, (2) must not expressly empower the organization to engage in activities that are not in furtherance of one or more exempt purposes, except as an insubstantial part of its activities.

55. (d) The requirement is to determine which of two activities (if any) will result in unrelated business income. Unrelated business income (UBI) is income derived from a trade or business, the conduct of which is not substantially related to the exercise or performance of an organization's exempt purpose. For a trade or business to be related, the conduct of the business activity must have a causal relationship to the achievement of the organization's exempt purpose. Selling articles made by handicapped persons as part of their rehabilitation would be substantially related to the exempt purpose of an organization exclusively involved in their rehabilitation. Similarly, operating a grocery store almost fully staffed by emotionally handicapped persons as part of a therapeutic program to allow the persons to become involved with society, assume responsibility, and to exercise business judgment, would be substantially related to the rehabilitation purposes of the exempt organization.

56. (c) The operational test requires that an exempt organization be operated exclusively for an exempt purpose. An organization will be considered to be operated exclusively for an exempt purpose only if it engages primarily in activities that accomplish its exempt purpose. An organization will not be so regarded if more than an insubstantial part of its activities is not in furtherance of an exempt purpose. Thus, an organization that engages in insubstantial nonexempt activities will not fail the operational test. In contrast, an organization that operates for the prevention of cruelty to animals will fail the operational test if it directly participates in any political campaign.

57. (b) The requirement is to determine the correct statement with regard to the unrelated business income of an exempt organization. An exempt organization is not taxed on unrelated business income of less than $1,000. Answer (a) is incorrect because the amount of unrelated business income will not cause the loss of exempt status. Answer (c) is incorrect because the tax will not apply to a business activity that is not regularly carried on. Answer (d) is incorrect because a loss from an unrelated trade or business activity is allowed in computing unrelated business taxable income.

58. (d) The requirement is to determine which one of the listed activities will not result in unrelated business income. Unrelated business income (UBI) is income derived from any trade or business, the conduct of which is not substantially related to the exercise or performance of an organization's exempt purpose. For a trade or business to be "related," the conduct of the business activity must have a causal relationship to the achievement of the exempt purpose. A business activity will be "substantially related" only if the causal relationship is a substantial one. Assuming that the development and improvement of its members is one of the purposes for which a trade association is granted an exemption, the sale of publications used as course materials for the association's seminars for its members would be substantially related.

Answer (a) is incorrect because even though a special rule permits an exempt hospital to perform services at cost for other hospitals with facilities to serve not more than 100 inpatients, the permitted services are limited to data processing, purchasing, warehousing, billing and collection, food, clinical, industrial engineering, laboratory, printing, communications, record center, and personnel services. Answer (b) is incorrect because even though an exempt senior citizen's center may operate a beauty parlor and barber shop for its members, selling major appliances to its members has been held to generate unrelated business income. Answer (c) is incorrect because the performance of accounting and tax services for its members would be unrelated to the exempt purpose of a labor union.

59. (a) The requirement is to determine the correct statement with regard to an exempt organization's unrelated business taxable income when the exempt organization is a corporation. An exempt organization's unrelated business income in excess of $1,000 is taxed at regular corporate income tax rates if the organization is a corporation. An exempt organization must be a trust in order for its unrelated business income to be taxed at the rates applicable to trusts.

60. (b) The requirement is to determine the correct statement regarding an exempt organization's income of $15,000 derived from conducting bingo games. If an exempt organization derives income from conducting bingo games, in a locality where such activity is legal, and in a state that confines such activity to nonprofit organizations, then such income is exempt from the tax on unrelated business income. Answer (d) is incorrect because unrelated business income will not cause the revocation or forfeiture of an organization's exempt status.

61. (c) The requirement is to determine the correct statement regarding the unrelated business income of exempt organizations. A tax-exempt organization may be subject to tax on its unrelated business income if the organization conducts a trade or business that is not substantially related to the exempt purpose of the organization, and the trade or business is regularly carried on by the organization. For an exempt organization, an unrelated business does not include any activity where all the work is performed for the organization by unpaid volunteers. Answer (a) is incorrect because although unrelated business income may result in a tax, it will not result in the loss of the organization's exempt status. Answer (b) is incorrect because the term "business" is broadly defined to include any activity conducted for the production of income through the sale of merchandise or the performance of services. Answer (d) is incorrect because using a trade or business to provide financial support for the organization's exempt purpose will not prevent an activity from being classified as an unrelated trade or business and being subject to the tax on unrelated business income.

62. (b) The requirement is to determine the correct statement regarding an exempt organization's payment of estimated taxes on its unrelated business income. An exempt organization subject to tax on its unrelated business income must comply with the Code provisions regarding installment payments of estimated income tax by corporations. This means that an exempt organization must make quarterly estimated

tax payments if it expects its estimated tax on its unrelated business income to be $500 or more. Answers (c) and (d) are incorrect because any tax on unrelated business income must be paid in full by the due date of the exempt organization's return.

63. (d) The requirement is to determine the correct statement regarding the taxability of unrelated business income (UBI) to an exempt organization that is a charitable trust. Answer (c) is incorrect because an exempt organization that is a charitable trust is subject to tax on its UBI only to the extent that its UBI exceeds $1,000. Answers (a) and (b) are incorrect because an exempt organization with UBI in excess of $1,000 is subject to tax at rates applicable to trusts if it is organized as a charitable trust.

64. (c) Unrelated business income (UBI) is gross income derived from any trade or business the conduct of which is not substantially related to the exercise or performance of an organization's exempt purpose. Although dividends and interest are generally excluded from UBI, they will be included if they result from debt-financed investments. Answer (d) is incorrect because it states that dividends and interest are always **excluded** from UBI. Answer (a) is incorrect because the Code only imposes a tax on UBI, it does not revoke an organization's exempt status. Answer (b) is incorrect because a net operating loss is allowed in computing unrelated business taxable income. Answer (c) is correct because Code Sec. 513(f) specifically excludes from UBI an exempt organization's conducting bingo games where such activity is legal.

65. (c) The requirement is to determine Miramar's UDITPA State XY apportionment factor and State XY business income. UDITPA recommends an apportionment formula that equally weighs sales, payroll, and property. Business income is then apportioned to a state by adding the three factors and then dividing by 3 to average the factors. Here the apportionment factor would be $(60\% + 50\% + 49\%) /3 = 53\%$, and would result in the apportionment of $530,000 of business income to State XY.

66. (b) The requirement is to determine Miramar's State XY apportionment factor if State XY used an apportionment formula in which the property factor was double-weighted. This means that the property factor would be counted twice and then the total would be divided by 4 to determine the average. The apportionment factor would then be $(60\% + 50\% + 49\% + 49\%)/4 = 52\%$.

67. (d) The requirement is to determine the correct statement regarding the foreign operations of Glencoe Corporation. Glencoe's foreign earnings are subject to US income tax. Since Glencoe may have already paid an income tax on those earnings to a foreign country, Glencoe may take either a deduction or a tax credit for the foreign income taxes paid which mitigates the double taxation of Glencoe's foreign-source earnings.

68. (b) The requirement is to determine Crocker's maximum foreign tax credit for the current year. Since US taxpayers are subject to US income tax on their worldwide income, they are allowed a credit for the income taxes paid to foreign countries. However, the amount of credit that can be currently used cannot exceed the amount of US tax that is attributable to the foreign income. This foreign tax credit limitation can be expressed as follows:

$$\frac{\text{Foreign TI}}{\text{Worldwide TI}} \times \quad (\text{US tax}) = \text{Foreign tax credit limitation}$$

In this case, the credit for the $40,000 of foreign income taxes paid is limited to the amount of US tax attributable to the foreign income, $30,000.

$$\frac{\$100,000}{\$700,000} \times \quad (\$210,000) = \$30,000$$

69. (b) The requirement is to determine the correct statement concerning Crocker Corp.'s unused foreign tax credit. The $40,000 – $30,000 = $10,000 of unused foreign tax credit resulting from the application of the limitation can be carried back one year and forward ten years and used to the extent that the taxpayer is below the limitation in those years.

70. (b) The requirement is to determine the amount of foreign tax credit that Raubolt Corporation may claim for the current year. Since US taxpayers are subject to US income tax on their worldwide income, they are allowed a credit for the income taxes paid to foreign countries. However, the amount of credit that can be currently used cannot exceed the amount of US tax that is attributable to the foreign income. This foreign tax credit limitation can be expressed as follows:

$$\frac{\text{Foreign TI}}{\text{Worldwide TI}} \times \quad (\text{US tax}) = \text{Foreign tax credit limitation}$$

One limitation must be computed for foreign passive category income (e.g., interest, dividends, royalties, rents, annuities), with a separate limitation computed for foreign general category income. In this case, the foreign income taxes paid on passive category income of $7,500 is fully usable as a credit because it is less than the applicable limitation amount of ($30,000/$300,000) × $96,000 = $9,600 (i.e., the amount of US tax attributable to the income).

On the other hand, the credit for the $32,000 of foreign income taxes paid on general category income is limited to the amount of US tax attributable to the foreign general category income of ($90,000/$300,000) × $96,000 = $28,800. Thus, Raubolt's foreign tax credit for the current year totals $28,800 + $7,500 = $36,300.

Simulations

Task-Based Simulation 1

Type of Gift		
	Authoritative Literature	**Help**

During 2015, various clients went to Rowe, CPA, for tax advice concerning possible gift tax liability on transfers they made throughout 2015. For each client, indicate whether the transfer of cash, the income interest, or the remainder interest is a gift of a present interest, a gift of a future interest, or not a completed gift.

Answer List

P. Present Interest
F. Future Interest
N. Not Completed

Assume the following facts:

Cobb created a $500,000 trust that provided his mother with an income interest for her life and the remainder interest to go to his sister at the death of his mother. Cobb expressly retained the power to revoke both the income interest and the remainder interest at any time.

Items to be answered

		(P)	(F)	(N)
1.	The income interest at the trust's creation.	○	○	○
2.	The remainder interest at the trust's creation.	○	○	○

Kane created a $100,000 trust that provided her nephew with the income interest until he reached forty-five years of age. When the trust was created, Kane's nephew was twenty-five. The income distribution is to start when Kane's nephew is twenty-nine. After Kane's nephew reaches the age of forty-five, the remainder interest is to go to Kane's niece.

		(P)	(F)	(N)
3.	The income interest.	○	○	○

During 2015, Hall, an unmarried taxpayer, made a $10,000 cash gift to his son in May and a further $12,000 cash gift to him in August.

		(P)	(F)	(N)
4.	The cash transfers.	○	○	○

During 2015, Yeats transferred property worth $20,000 to a trust with the income to be paid to her twenty-two-year-old niece Jane. After Jane reaches the age of thirty, the remainder interest is to be distributed to Yeats' brother. The income interest is valued at $9,700 and the remainder interest at $10,300.

		(P)	(F)	(N)
5.	The income interest.	○	○	○
6.	The remainder interest.	○	○	○

Tom and Ann Curry, US citizens, were married for the entire 2015 calendar year. Tom gave a $40,000 cash gift to his uncle, Grant. The Currys made no other gifts to Grant in 2015. Tom and Ann each signed a timely election stating that each made one-half of the $40,000 gift.

	(P)	(F)	(N)
7. The cash transfers.	O	O	O

Murray created a $1,000,000 trust that provided his brother with an income interest for ten years, after which the remainder interest passes to Murray's sister. Murray retained the power to revoke the remainder interest at any time. The income interest was valued at $600,000.

	(P)	(F)	(N)
8. The income interest.	O	O	O
9. The remainder interest.	O	O	O

Task-Based Simulation 2

Generation-Skipping Tax		
	Authoritative Literature	Help

Determine whether the transfer is subject to the generation skipping tax, the gift tax, or both taxes. Disregard the use of any exclusions and the unified credit.

Answer List
A.   Generation-Skipping Tax
B.   Gift Tax
C.   Both Taxes

	(A)	(B)	(C)
Martin's daughter, Kim, has one child, Dale. During 2015, Martin made an outright $6,000,000 gift to Dale.	O	O	O

Task-Based Simulation 3

Estate Tax Treatment		
	Authoritative Literature	Help

Situation

Before his death, Remsen, a US citizen, made cash gifts of $7,000 each to his four sisters. In 2015 Remsen also paid $20,000 in tuition directly to his grandchild's university on the grandchild's behalf. Remsen made no other lifetime transfers. Remsen died on January 9, 2015, and was survived by his wife and only child, both of whom were US citizens. The Remsens did not live in a community property state.

At his death Remsen owned

Cash	$ 650,000
Marketable securities (fair market value)	1,900,000
Life insurance policy with Remsen's wife named as the beneficiary (fair market value)	2,500,000

For **items 1 through 5,** identify the federal estate tax treatment for each item. A response may be selected once, more than once, or not at all.

Answer List
F. Fully includible in Remsen's gross estate.
P. Partially includible in Remsen's gross estate.
N. Not includible in Remsen's gross estate.

		(F)	(P)	(N)
1.	What is the estate tax treatment of the $7,000 cash gift to each sister?	O	O	O
2.	What is the estate tax treatment of the life insurance proceeds?	O	O	O
3.	What is the estate tax treatment of the marketable securities?	O	O	O
4.	What is the estate tax treatment of the $20,000 tuition payment?	O	O	O
5.	What is the estate tax treatment of the $650,000 cash?	O	O	O

Task-Based Simulation 4

Estate Tax Treatment		
	Authoritative Literature	Help

Situation

Remsen died on January 9, 2015, and was survived by his wife and only child, both of whom were US citizens. The Remsens did not live in a community property state.

At his death Remsen owned

Cash	$ 650,000
Marketable securities (fair market value)	1,900,000
Life insurance policy with Remsen's wife named as the beneficiary (fair market value)	2,500,000

Under the provisions of Remsen's will, the net cash, after payment of executor's fees and medical and funeral expenses, was bequeathed to Remsen's son. The marketable securities were bequeathed to Remsen's spouse. During 2015 Remsen's estate paid

Executor fees to distribute the decedent's property (deducted on the fiduciary tax return)	$50,000
Decedent's funeral expenses	12,000

The estate's executor extended the time to file the estate tax return. On December 3, 2015, the estate's executor paid the decedent's outstanding $10,000 medical expenses and filed the extended estate tax return.

For **items 1 through 5,** identify the federal estate tax treatment for each item. A response may be selected once, more than once, or not at all.

Answer List
G. Deductible from Remsen's gross estate to arrive at Remsen's taxable estate.
I. Deductible on Remsen's 2015 individual income tax return.
E. Deductible on either Remsen's estate tax return or Remsen's 2015 individual income tax return.
N. Not deductible on either Remsen's estate tax return or Remsen's 2015 individual income tax return.

		(G)	(I)	(E)	(N)
1.	What is the estate tax treatment of the executor's fees?	○	○	○	○
2.	What is the estate tax treatment of the cash bequest to Remsen's son?	○	○	○	○
3.	What is the estate tax treatment of the life insurance proceeds paid to Remsen's spouse?	○	○	○	○
4.	What is the estate tax treatment of the funeral expenses?	○	○	○	○
5.	What is the estate tax treatment of the $10,000 of medical expenses incurred before the decedent's death and paid by the executor on December 3, 2015?	○	○	○	○

Task-Based Simulation 5

Gift Tax Treatment		
	Authoritative Literature	Help

Situation

Scott Lane, an unmarried US citizen, made no lifetime transfers prior to 2015. During 2015, Lane made the following transfers:

- Gave a $14,000 cash gift to Kamp, a close friend.
- Made two separate $10,000 cash gifts to his only child.
- Created an **irrevocable** trust beginning in 2015 that provided his aunt with an income interest to be paid for the next five years. The remainder interest is to pass to Lane's sole cousin. The income interest is valued at $26,000 and the remainder interest is valued at $74,000.
- Paid $25,000 tuition directly to his grandchild's university on his grandchild's behalf.
- Created an **irrevocable** trust that provided his brother with a lifetime income interest beginning in 2017, after which a remainder interest passes to their sister.
- Created a **revocable** trust with his niece as the sole beneficiary. During 2015, the niece received $15,000 interest income from the trust.

For **items 1 through 7,** determine whether the tax transactions are fully taxable, partially taxable, or not taxable to Lane in 2015 for gift tax purposes after considering the gift tax annual exclusion. Ignore the transfer tax credit when answering the items. An answer may be selected once, more than once, or not at all.

Gift Tax Treatments
F. Fully taxable to Lane in 2015 for gift tax purposes.
P. Partially taxable to Lane in 2015 for gift tax purposes.
N. Not taxable to Lane in 2015 for gift tax purposes.

		(F)	(P)	(N)
1.	What is the gift tax treatment of Lane's gift to Kamp?	○	○	○
2.	What is the gift tax treatment of Lane's cash gifts to his child?	○	○	○
3.	What is the gift tax treatment of the trust's income interest to Lane's aunt?	○	○	○
4.	What is the gift tax treatment of the trust's remainder interest to Lane's cousin?	○	○	○
5.	What is the gift tax treatment of the tuition payment to Lane's grandchild's university?	○	○	○
6.	What is the gift tax treatment of the trust's income interest to Lane's brother?	○	○	○
7.	What is the gift tax treatment of the $14,000 interest income that Lane's niece received from the revocable trust?	○	○	○

Task-Based Simulation 6

Situation

Glen Moore inherited stock from his mother, Ruth. She had died on February 1, 2015, when the stock had a fair market value of $150,000. Ruth had acquired the stock on May 15, 2013, at a cost of $120,000. Ruth's estate was too small to require the filing of a federal estate tax return. Moore wants to know how much gross income he must report because of the receipt of his inheritance in 2015. Which code section and subsection provides the rule for determining whether Moore's inheritance must be included in his gross income? Indicate the reference to that citation in the shaded boxes below.

§	Section	Subsection
		( )

Simulation Solutions

Task-Based Simulation 1

Type of Gift		
	Authoritative Literature	Help

For items 1 through 9, candidates were asked to determine whether the transfer of cash, an income interest, or a remainder interest represents a gift of a present interest (P), a gift of a future interest (F), or not a completed gift (N).

		(P)	(F)	(N)
1.	The income interest at the trust's creation.	○	○	●
2.	The remainder interest at the trust's creation.	○	○	●
3.	The income interest.	○	●	○
4.	The cash transfers.	●	○	○
5.	The income interest.	●	○	○
6.	The remainder interest.	○	●	○
7.	The cash transfers.	●	○	○
8.	The income interest.	●	○	○
9.	The remainder interest.	○	○	●

Explanations

1. **(N)** Since Cobb expressly retained the power to revoke the income interest transferred to his mother at any time, he has not relinquished dominion and control and the transfer of the income interest is not a completed gift.

2. **(N)** Since Cobb expressly retained the power to revoke the remainder interest transferred to his sister at any time, he has not relinquished dominion and control and the transfer of the remainder interest is not a completed gift.

3. **(F)** Kane's transfer of an income interest to a nephew and a remainder interest to a niece are completed gifts because Kane has relinquished dominion and control. Since Kane's nephew was twenty-five years of age when the trust was created, but income distributions will not begin until the nephew is age twenty-nine, the transfer of the income interest is a gift of future interest and does not qualify for the annual exclusion.

4. **(P)** Since Hall's gifts of cash to his son were outright gifts, they are gifts of a present interest and qualify for the annual exclusion.

5. **(P)** Yeats' gift of the income interest to her twenty-two-year-old niece is a gift of a present interest qualifying for the annual exclusion since Jane has the unrestricted right to immediate enjoyment of the income. The fact that the value of the income interest does not exceed $14,000 does not affect its nature (i.e., completed gift of a present interest).

6. **(F)** Yeats' gift of the remainder interest to her brother is a completed gift of a future interest since the brother cannot enjoy the property or any of the income until Jane reaches age thirty.

7. **(P)** Tom's gift of $40,000 cash to his uncle is an outright gift of a present interest and qualifies for the annual exclusion. Since gift-splitting was elected and Tom and Ann would each receive a $14,000 annual exclusion, Tom and Ann each made a taxable gift of $20,000 – $14,000 exclusion = $6,000.

8. **(P)** Murray's gift of the income interest to his brother is a completed gift because Murray has relinquished dominion and control. It is a gift of a present interest qualifying for the annual exclusion since his brother has the unrestricted right to immediate enjoyment of the income.

9. **(N)** Since Murray retained the right to revoke the remainder interest transferred to his sister at any time, the transfer of the remainder interest does not result in a completed gift.

Task-Based Simulation 2

Generation-Skipping Tax		
	Authoritative Literature	Help

For this item, candidates were asked to determine whether the transfer is subject to the generation-skipping tax (A), the gift tax (B), or both taxes (C).

	(A)	(B)	(C)
Martin's daughter, Kim, has one child, Dale. During 2015, Martin made an outright $6,000,000 gift to Dale.	○	○	●

Explanation

(C) Since Martin made an outright gift of $6,000,000 to Dale, the transfer is a gift of a present interest and is subject to the gift tax. Since Dale happens to be Martin's grandchild, the gift also is subject to the generation-skipping tax. The generation-skipping tax on the transfer of property is imposed in addition to federal gift and estates taxes and is designed to prevent individuals from escaping an entire generation of gift and estate taxes by transferring property to, or in trust for the benefit of, a person that is two or more generations younger than the donor or transferor. The tax approximates the transfer tax that would be imposed if the property were actually transferred to each successive generation.

Task-Based Simulation 3

Estate Tax Treatment I		
	Authoritative Literature	Help

For **items 1 through 5,** candidates were asked to identify the federal tax treatment for each item by indicating whether the item was fully includible in Remsen's gross estate (F), partially includible in Remsen's gross estate (P), or not includible in Remsen's gross estate (N).

		(F)	(P)	(N)
1.	What is the estate tax treatment of the $7,000 cash gift to each sister?	○	○	●
2.	What is the estate tax treatment of the life insurance proceeds?	●	○	○
3.	What is the estate tax treatment of the marketable securities?	●	○	○
4.	What is the estate tax treatment of the $20,000 tuition payment?	○	○	●
5.	What is the estate tax treatment of the $650,000 cash?	●	○	○

Explanations

1. **(N)** Generally, gifts made before death are not includible in the decedent's gross estate, even though the gifts were made within three years of death.

2. **(F)** The gross estate includes the value of all property in which the decedent had a beneficial interest at time of death. Here, the life insurance proceeds must be included in Remsen's gross estate because the problem indicates that Remsen was the owner of the policy.

3. (**F**) The fair market value of the marketable securities must be included in Remsen's gross estate because Remsen was the owner of the securities at the time of his death.

4. (**N**) Generally, gifts made before death are not includible in the decedent's gross estate.

5. (**F**) The $650,000 cash that Remsen owned must be included in Remsen's gross estate.

Task-Based Simulation 4

Estate Tax Treatment		
	Authoritative Literature	Help

For **items 1 through 5,** candidates were asked to identify the federal tax treatment for each item by indicating whether the item was deductible from Remsen's gross estate to arrive at Remsen's taxable estate (G), deductible on Remsen's 2015 individual income tax return (I), deductible on either Remsen's estate tax return or Remsen's 2015 individual income tax return (E), or not deductible on either Remsen's estate tax return or Remsen's 2015 individual income tax return (N).

		(G)	(I)	(E)	(N)
1.	What is the estate tax treatment of the executor's fees?	○	○	○	●
2.	What is the estate tax treatment of the cash bequest to Remsen's son?	○	○	○	●
3.	What is the estate tax treatment of the life insurance proceeds paid to Remsen's spouse?	●	○	○	○
4.	What is the estate tax treatment of the funeral expenses?	●	○	○	○
5.	What is the estate tax treatment of the $10,000 of medical expenses incurred before the decedent's death and paid by the executor on December 3, 2015?	○	○	●	○

Explanations

1. (**N**) The $50,000 of executor's fees to distribute the decedent's property are deductible on **either** the federal estate tax return (Form 706) or the estate's fiduciary income tax return (Form 1041). Such expenses **cannot** be deducted twice. Since the problem indicates that these expenses were deducted on the fiduciary tax return (Form 1041), they cannot be deducted on the estate tax return.

2. (**N**) A decedent's gross estate is reduced by funeral and administrative expenses, debts and mortgages, casualty and theft losses, charitable bequests, and a marital deduction for the value of property passing to the decedent's surviving spouse. There is no deduction for bequests to beneficiaries other than the decedent's surviving spouse.

3. (**G**) Generally, property included in a decedent's gross estate will be eligible for an unlimited marital deduction if the property passes to the decedent's surviving spouse. Here, the life insurance proceeds paid to Remsen's spouse were included in Remsen's gross estate because Remsen owned the policy, and are deductible from Remsen's gross estate as part of the marital deduction in arriving at Remsen's taxable estate.

4. (**G**) Funeral expenses are deductible only on the estate tax return and include a reasonable allowance for a tombstone, monument, mausoleum, or burial lot.

5. (**E**) The executor of a decedent's estate may elect to treat medical expenses paid by the estate for the decedent's medical care as paid by the decedent at the time the medical services were provided. To qualify for this election, the medical expenses must be paid within the one-year period after the decedent's death, and the executor must attach a waiver to the decedent's Form 1040 indicating that the expenses will not be claimed as a deduction on the decedent's estate tax return. In this case, the medical expenses qualify for the election because Remsen died on January 9, 2015, and the expenses were paid on December 3, 2015.

Task-Based Simulation 5

Gift Tax Treatment		
	Authoritative Literature	Help

For **items 1 through 7,** candidates were asked to identify the federal gift tax treatment for each item by indicating whether the item is fully taxable (F), partially taxable (P), or not taxable (N) to Lane in 2015 for gift tax purposes after considering the gift tax annual exclusion.

		(F)	(P)	(N)
1.	What is the gift tax treatment of Lane's gift to Kamp?	○	○	●
2.	What is the gift tax treatment of Lane's cash gifts to his child?	○	●	○
3.	What is the gift tax treatment of the trust's income interest to Lane's aunt?	○	●	○
4.	What is the gift tax treatment of the trust's remainder interest to Lane's cousin?	●	○	○
5.	What is the gift tax treatment of the tuition payment to Lane's grandchild's university?	○	○	●
6.	What is the gift tax treatment of the trust's income interest to Lane's brother?	●	○	○
7.	What is the gift tax treatment of the $15,000 interest income that Lane's niece received from the revocable trust?	○	●	○

Explanations

1. (**N**) There is no taxable gift because the $14,000 cash gift is a gift of a present interest and is fully offset by a $14,000 annual exclusion.

2. (**P**) The $20,000 of cash gifts given to his child would be partially offset by a $14,000 annual exclusion, resulting in a taxable gift of $6,000.

3. (**P**) The gift of the income interest valued at $26,000 to his aunt is a gift of a present interest and would be partially offset by a $14,000 annual exclusion, resulting in a taxable gift of $12,000.

4. (**F**) Since the remainder interest will pass to Lane's cousin after the expiration of five years, the gift of the remainder interest is a gift of a future interest and is not eligible for an annual exclusion. As a result, the $74,000 value of the remainder interest is fully taxable.

5. (**N**) An unlimited exclusion is available for medical expenses and tuition paid on behalf of a donee. Since Lane paid the $25,000 of tuition directly to his grandchild's university on his grandchild's behalf, the gift is fully excluded and not subject to gift tax.

6. (**F**) Since Lane created the irrevocable trust in 2015 but his brother will not begin receiving the income until 2017, the gift of the income interest to his brother is a gift of a future interest and cannot be offset by an annual exclusion. As a result, the gift is fully taxable for gift tax purposes.

7. (**P**) The creation of a revocable trust is not a completed gift and trust income is taxable to the grantor (Lane). As a result, a gift occurs only as the trust income is actually paid to the beneficiary. Here, the $15,000 of interest income received by the niece during 2015 is a gift of a present interest and would be partially offset by a $14,000 annual exclusion.

Task-Based Simulation 6

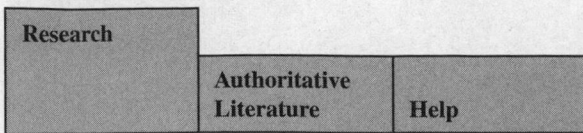

Internal Revenue Code Sec. 102, subsection (a) provides that gross income does not include the value of property acquired by gift, bequest, devise, or inheritance.

APPENDICES

The following appendices provide you with additional practice for the exam.

Appendix A: Regulation Sample Examination

Testlet 1

1. Able, Bray, and Carry form a general partnership to produce and sell widgets. Able is a CPA, Bray has an MBA, and Carry has few skills. In their partnership agreement, they decide to split any profits they have in the following respective proportions: 45%, 45%, and 10%. They fail to agree on how they will share any losses. At the end of the first year of operations they have a large loss. Assuming each of the partners has sufficient assets to cover the loss of their partnership, how will they split the losses between Able, Bray, and Carry, respectively?

    a. 45%, 45%, and 10%.
    b. Equally.
    c. It cannot be determined yet until they agree upon a loss-sharing plan.
    d. A court of law will have to decide upon the way they will each share the loss.

2. CPAs must be concerned with their responsibilities in the performance of professional services. In performing an audit, a CPA

    a. Is strictly liable for failure to exercise due professional care.
    b. Is strictly liable for failure to detect management fraud.
    c. Is **not** liable unless the CPA is found to be grossly negligent.
    d. Is strictly liable for failure to detect illegal acts.

3. The Apex Surety Company wrote a general fidelity bond covering defalcations by the employees of Watson, Inc. Thereafter, Grand, an employee of Watson, embezzled $18,900 of company funds. When his activities were discovered, Apex paid Watson the full amount in accordance with the terms of the fidelity bond, and then sought recovery against Watson's auditors, Kane & Dobbs, CPAs. Which of the following would be Kane & Dobbs' best defense?

    a. Apex is not in privity of contract.
    b. The shortages were the result of clever forgeries and collusive fraud that would not be detected by an examination made in accordance with generally accepted auditing standards.
    c. Kane & Dobbs were not guilty either of gross negligence or fraud.
    d. Kane & Dobbs were not aware of the Apex-Watson surety relationship.

4. If a stockholder sues a CPA for common law fraud based on false statements contained in the financial statements audited by the CPA, which of the following, if present, would be the CPA's best defense?

    a. The stockholder lacks privity to sue.
    b. The false statements were immaterial.
    c. The CPA did **not** financially benefit from the alleged fraud.
    d. The contributory negligence of the client.

5. Mathews is an agent for Sears with the express authority to solicit orders from customers in a geographic area assigned by Sears. Mathews has no authority to grant discounts or to collect payment on orders solicited. Mathews secured an order from Davidson for $1,000 less a 10% discount if Davidson makes immediate payment. Davidson had previously done business with Sears through Mathews but this was the first time that a discount-payment offer had been made. Davidson gave Mathews a check for $900 and, thereafter, Mathews turned in both the check and the order to Sears. The order clearly indicated that a 10% discount had been given by Mathews. Sears shipped the order and cashed the check. Later, Sears attempted to collect $100 as the balance owed on the order from Davidson. Which of the following is correct?

    a. Sears can collect the $100 from Davidson because Mathews contracted outside the scope of his express or implied authority.
    b. Sears **cannot** collect the $100 from Davidson because Mathews, as an agent with express authority to solicit orders, had implied authority to give discounts and collect.
    c. Sears **cannot** collect the $100 from Davidson as Sears has ratified the discount granted and made to Mathews.
    d. Sears **cannot** collect the $100 from Davidson because, although Mathews had **no** express or implied authority to grant a discount and collect, Mathews had apparent authority to do so.

6. Regulation D of the Securities Act of 1933 is available to issuers without regard to the dollar amount of an offering only when the

    a. Purchasers are all accredited investors.
    b. Number of purchasers who are nonaccredited is thirty-five or less.
    c. Issuer is **not** a reporting company under the Securities Exchange Act of 1934.
    d. Issuer is **not** an investment company.

7. Nat purchased a typewriter from Rob. Rob is not in the business of selling typewriters. Rob tendered delivery of the typewriter after receiving payment in full from Nat. Nat informed Rob that he was unable to take possession of the typewriter at that time, but would return later that day. Before

Nat returned, the typewriter was destroyed by a fire. The risk of loss

    a. Passed to Nat upon Rob's tender of delivery.
    b. Remained with Rob, since Nat had not yet received the typewriter.
    c. Passed to Nat at the time the contract was formed and payment was made.
    d. Remained with Rob, since title had **not** yet passed to Nat.

8. On April 14, 2010, Seeley Corp. entered into a written agreement to sell to Boone Corp. 1,200 cartons of certain goods at $.40 per carton, delivery within 30 days. The agreement contained no other terms. On April 15, 2010, Boone and Seeley orally agreed to modify their April 14 agreement so that the new quantity specified was 1,500 cartons, same price and delivery terms. What is the status of this modification?

    a. Enforceable.
    b. Unenforceable under the statute of frauds.
    c. Unenforceable for lack of consideration.
    d. Unenforceable because the change is substantial.

9. Purdy purchased real property from Hart and received a warranty deed with full covenants. Recordation of this deed is

    a. Not necessary if the deed provides that recordation is not required.
    b. Necessary to vest the purchaser's legal title to the property conveyed.
    c. Required primarily for the purpose of providing the local taxing authorities with the information necessary to assess taxes.
    d. Irrelevant if the subsequent party claiming superior title had actual notice of the unrecorded deed.

10. Richard Brown, who retired on May 31, 2014, receives a monthly pension benefit of $700 payable for life. His life expectancy at the date of retirement is ten years. The first pension check was received on June 15, 2014. During his years of employment, Brown contributed $12,000 to the cost of his company's pension plan. How much of the pension amounts received may Brown exclude from taxable income for the years 2014, 2015, and 2016?

	2014	2015	2016
a.	$0	$0	$0
b.	$4,900	$4,900	$4,900
c.	$700	$1,200	$1,200
d.	$4,900	$8,400	$8,400

11. Lee, an attorney, uses the cash receipts and disbursements method of reporting. In 2014, a client gave Lee 500 shares of a listed corporation's stock in full satisfaction of a $10,000 legal fee the client owed to Lee. This stock had a fair market value of $8,000 on the date it was given to Lee. The client's basis for this stock was $6,000. Lee sold the stock for cash in January 2015. In Lee's 2014 income tax return, what amount of income should be reported in connection with the receipt of the stock?

    a. $10,000
    b. $8,000

    c. $6,000
    d. $0

12. Don Wolf became a general partner in Gata Associates on January 1, 2014, with a 5% interest in Gata's profits, losses, and capital. Gata is a distributor of auto parts. Wolf does not materially participate in the partnership business. For the year ended December 31, 2015, Gata had an operating loss of $100,000. In addition, Gata earned interest of $20,000 on a temporary investment. Gata has kept the principal temporarily invested while awaiting delivery of equipment that is presently on order. The principal will be used to pay for this equipment. Wolf's passive loss for 2015 is

    a. $0
    b. $4,000
    c. $5,000
    d. $6,000

13. For the current year, Don Mills, a single taxpayer, had $70,000 in taxable income before personal exemptions. Mills had no tax preferences. His itemized deductions were as follows:

State and local income taxes	$5,000
Home mortgage interest on loan to acquire residence	6,000
Miscellaneous deductions that exceed 2% of adjusted gross income	2,000

What amount did Mills report as alternative minimum taxable income before the AMT exemption?

    a. $72,000
    b. $75,000
    c. $77,000
    d. $83,000

14. An accuracy-related penalty applies to the portion of tax underpayment attributable to

    I. Negligence or a disregard of the tax rules or regulations.
    II. Any substantial understatement of income tax.

    a. I only.
    b. II only.
    c. Both I and II.
    d. Neither I nor II.

15. Smith, an individual calendar-year taxpayer, purchased 100 shares of Core Co. common stock for $15,000 on November 15, 2014, and an additional 100 shares for $13,000 on December 30, 2014. On January 3, 2015, Smith sold the shares purchased on November 15, 2014, for $13,000. What amount of loss from the sale of Core's stock is deductible on Smith's 2014 and 2015 income tax returns?

	2014	2015
a.	$0	$0
b.	$0	$2,000
c.	$1,000	$1,000
d.	$2,000	$0

16. Strom acquired a 25% interest in Ace Partnership by contributing land having an adjusted basis of $16,000 and a fair market value of $50,000. The land was subject to a $24,000 mortgage, which was assumed by Ace. No other liabilities existed at the time of the contribution. What was Strom's basis in Ace?

    a. $0
    b. $16,000
    c. $26,000
    d. $32,000

Items 17 and 18 are based on the following data:

Mike Reed, a partner in Post Co., received the following distribution from Post:

	Post's basis	Fair market value
Cash	$11,000	$11,000
Land	5,000	12,500

Before this distribution, Reed's basis in Post was $25,000.

17. If this distribution were nonliquidating, Reed's recognized gain or loss on the distribution would be

    a. $11,000 gain.
    b. $9,000 loss.
    c. $1,500 loss.
    d. $0.

18. If this distribution were in complete liquidation of Reed's interest in Post, Reed's basis for the land would be

    a. $14,000
    b. $12,500
    c. $5,000
    d. $1,500

19. Finbury Corporation's taxable income for the year ended December 31, 2014, was $2,000,000 on which its tax liability was $680,000. In order for Finbury to escape the estimated tax underpayment penalty for the year ending December 31, 2015, Finbury's 2015 estimated tax payments must equal at least

    a. 90% of the 2015 tax liability.
    b. 93% of the 2015 tax liability.
    c. 100% of the 2015 tax liability.
    d. The 2014 tax liability of $680,000.

20. Barbaro Corporation's retained earnings at January 1, 2015, was $600,000. During 2015 Barbaro paid cash dividends of $150,000 and received a federal income tax refund of $26,000 as a result of an IRS audit of Barbaro's 2012 tax return. Barbaro's net income per books for the year ended December 31, 2015, was $274,900 after deducting federal income tax of $183,300. How much should be shown in the reconciliation Schedule M-2, of Form 1120, as Barbaro's retained earnings at December 31, 2015?

    a. $443,600
    b. $600,900
    c. $626,900
    d. $750,900

21. Brooke, Inc., an S corporation, was organized on January 2, 2015, with two equal stockholders who materially participate in the S corporation's business. Each stockholder invested $5,000 in Brooke's capital stock, and each loaned $15,000 to the corporation. Brooke then borrowed $60,000 from a bank for working capital. Brooke sustained an operating loss of $90,000 for the year ended December 31, 2015. How much of this loss can each stockholder claim on his 2015 income tax return?

    a. $5,000
    b. $20,000
    c. $45,000
    d. $50,000

22. When Jim and Nina became engaged in April 2015, Jim gave Nina a ring that had a fair market value of $50,000. After their wedding in July 2015, Jim gave Nina $75,000 in cash so that Nina could have her own bank account. Both Jim and Nina are US citizens. What was the amount of Jim's 2015 marital deduction?

    a. $0
    b. $75,000
    c. $115,000
    d. $125,000

23. Ross, a calendar-year, cash-basis taxpayer who died in June 2015, was entitled to receive a $10,000 accounting fee that had not been collected before the date of death. The executor of Ross' estate collected the full $10,000 in July 2015. This $10,000 should appear in

    a. Only the decedent's final individual income tax return.
    b. Only the estate's fiduciary income tax return.
    c. Only the estate tax return.
    d. Both the fiduciary income tax return and the estate tax return.

24. Kopel was engaged to prepare Raff's 2014 federal income tax return. During the tax preparation interview, Raff told Kopel that he paid $3,000 in property taxes in 2014. Actually, Raff's property taxes amounted to only $600. Based on Raff's word, Kopel deducted the $3,000 on Raff's return, resulting in an understatement of Raff's tax liability. Kopel had no reason to believe that the information was incorrect. Kopel did not request underlying documentation and was reasonably satisfied by Raff's representation that Raff had adequate records to support the deduction. Which of the following statements is correct?

    a. To avoid the preparer penalty for willful understatement of tax liability, Kopel was obligated to examine the underlying documentation for the deduction.
    b. To avoid the preparer penalty for willful understatement of tax liability, Kopel would be required to obtain Raff's representation in writing.
    c. Kopel is **not** subject to the preparer penalty for willful understatement of tax liability because the deduction that was claimed was more than 25% of the actual amount that should have been deducted.
    d. Kopel is **not** subject to the preparer penalty for willful understatement of tax liability because Kopel was justified in relying on Raff's representation.

Hints for Testlet 1

1. Losses are essentially negative profits.

2. Professionals must exercise due professional care.

3. Compliance with GAAS indicates due care.

4. Recall proof requirements.

5. The principal accepted the benefits of the unauthorized act.

6. Recall the requirements for a private placement.

7. Rob is **not** a merchant.

8. After modification, contract is for >$500.

9. Notice can be constructive or actual.

10. Each payment is part income and part a return of Brown's investment.

11. The amount of compensation is determined from the value of the property received.

12. Interest is generally considered portfolio income.

13. Qualified residence interest in the form of acquisition indebtedness is deductible for AMT purposes.

14. The items listed are two components of the accuracy-related penalty.

15. The acquisition of substantially identical stock within a thirty-day period before or after the date of the loss results in a wash sale.

16. The 75% net reduction in liability is treated as a deemed cash distribution.

17. No loss can be recognized in a non liquidating distribution.

18. No loss can be recognized in a liquidating distribution if property other than cash, receivables, or inventory is received.

19. Because of taxable income in excess of $1 million, Finbury cannot use its tax for the preceding year as a safe estimate.

20. Schedule M-2 provides a reconciliation of unappropriated retained earnings per books.

21. Shareholders do not receive basis for the corporation's debts to third parties.

22. The taxpayer must be married on the date of gift to qualify for the marital deduction.

23. The fee qualifies as income in respect of a decedent.

24. A preparer is not required to audit or examine a client's books and records.

Answers to Testlet 1

1. a	4. b	7. a	10. c	13. c	16. a	19. c	22. b
2. a	5. c	8. b	11. b	14. c	17. d	20. d	23. d
3. b	6. b	9. d	12. c	15. a	18. a	21. b	24. d

Explanations

1. (a) If partners agree on unequal profit sharing but are silent on loss sharing, losses are shared based on the profit-sharing proportions.

2. (a) CPAs are required ethically and legally to exercise due professional care in the performance of all services.

3. (b) The surety with respect to this loss is given the same rights as the client under common law and may sue for ordinary negligence. The CPAs' best defense is that an audit performed in accordance with professional standards would not have detected the fraud.

4. (b) Under common law, the shareholder has the right to sue for fraud on the part of the auditor. The auditor's best defense is to show that the false statements are not material.

5. (c) Sears cannot collect from Davidson because Sears ratified the discount granted by shipping the goods and cashing the check.

6. (b) Rule 506 allows private placement of unlimited amounts of securities if the number of unaccredited investors is no more than 35.

7. (a) Risk of loss passes to the buyer on tender of delivery unless the seller is a merchant.

8. (b) Modification of contract must be in writing if contract, as modified, is covered by the Statue of Frauds (i.e., sale of goods for $500 or more).

9. (d) Under a notice-type statute, a subsequent purchaser, whether he or she records or not, prevails over a previous purchaser who did not record before that subsequent purchase.

10. (c) The amount that is not taxable is based on the ratio of contribution to total expected benefits. This ratio is $12,000/(120 months × $700), which is equal to $12,000/$84,000 or 1/7. In 2014, the nontaxable amount would equal $700 [1/7 × ($700 × 7 months)]. In 2015 and 2016, the nontaxable amount would equal $1,200 [1/7 × ($700 × 12)].

11. (b) The stock should be recognized as revenue at its fair market value when it is received.

12. (c) The interest income is portfolio income. Therefore, Wolf would have a passive loss of $5,000.

13. (c) The alternative minimum taxable income is $77,000 ($70,000 + $5,000 + $2,000). Since the mortgage interest was from a loan used to acquire a personal residence, it does not have to be added back.

14. (c) An accuracy-related penalty applies to both situations.

15. (a) The sale is a wash sale and the loss is not deductible.

16. (a) The basis of a partner's partnership interest is increased by the adjusted basis of the property contributed. Since the basis of the property ($16,000) is less than the amount of the mortgage assumed by the partnership ($24,000), the partner's basis is $0.

17. (d) A partner recognizes gain only to the extent that the money received exceeds the partner's partnership basis.

18. (a) The land absorbs Reed's basis in the partnership after adjusting for the receipt of the cash, or $14,000 ($25,000 basis – $11,000 cash received).

19. (c) No penalty will be assessed if the estimated tax payments are equal to at least 100% of the current year's tax.

20. (d) Retained earnings at year end should be shown as $750,900 ($600,000 + $274,900 net income + $26,000 tax refund – $150,000 dividends).

21. (b) The shareholders are limited to their basis in the corporation ($5,000 cash contributed + $15,000 loan to the corporation).

22. (b) The marital deduction is generally unlimited. Therefore, the entire $75,000 is a deduction. The value of the ring is not considered because the individuals were not married when the gift was made.

23. (d) The amount would be included in both returns.

24. (d) The preparer is not required to audit the information and may accept the taxpayer's representation unless it is unreasonable.

Testlet 2

1. Three partners have formed a general partnership that they desire to last for several years. They have not agreed to any specified time period. Which of the following is true under the Revised Uniform Partnership Act?

    a. The partnership agreement is required to be in writing.

    b. All three partners are required to share profits or losses equally.

    c. Each of the three partners has an equal right to participate in the management of the partnership.

    d. A partner may assign his or her interest in the partnership only if the other two agree.

2. Which of the following is true concerning the rights of shareholders?

    a. Shareholders have the right to receive dividends when the corporation makes a profit.

    b. Shareholders have the right to manage the corporation.

    c. Shareholders have no right to inspect the books and records of the corporation.

    d. Shareholders can vote by proxy when they have voting rights.

3. Rhodes Corp. desired to acquire the common stock of Harris Corp. and engaged Johnson & Co., CPAs, to audit the financial statements of Harris Corp. Johnson failed to discover a significant liability in performing the audit. In a common law action against Johnson, Rhodes at a minimum must prove

    a. Gross negligence on the part of Johnson.

    b. Negligence on the part of Johnson.

    c. Fraud on the part of Johnson.

    d. Johnson knew that the liability existed.

4. A debtor will be denied a discharge in bankruptcy if the debtor

    a. Failed to timely list a portion of his debts.

    b. Unjustifiably failed to preserve his books and records which could have been used to ascertain the debtor's financial condition.

    c. Has negligently made preferential transfers to favored creditors within ninety days of the filing of the bankruptcy petition.

    d. Has committed several willful and malicious acts that resulted in bodily injury to others.

5. Which of the following is a part of the social security law?

    a. A self-employed person must contribute an annual amount that is equal to the combined contributions of an employee and his or her employer.

    b. Upon the death of an employee prior to his retirement, his estate is entitled to receive the amount attributable to his contributions as a death benefit.

    c. Social security benefits must be fully funded and payments, current and future, must constitutionally come only from social security taxes.

    d. Social security benefits are taxable as income when they exceed the individual's total contributions.

6. Duval Manufacturing Industries, Inc. orally engaged Harris as one of its district sales managers for an eighteen-month period commencing April 1, 2009. Harris commenced work on that date and performed his duties in a highly competent manner for several months. On October 1, 2009, the company gave Harris a notice of termination as of November 1, 2009, citing a downturn in the market for its products. Harris sues seeking either specific performance or damages for breach of contract. Duval pleads the Statute of Frauds and/or a justified dismissal due to the economic situation. What is the probable outcome of the lawsuit?

    a. Harris will prevail because he has partially performed under the terms of the contract.

    b. Harris will lose because his termination was caused by economic factors beyond Duval's control.

    c. Harris will lose because such a contract must be in writing and signed by a proper agent of Duval.

    d. Harris will prevail because the Statute of Frauds does **not** apply to contracts such as his.

7. Kent, a wholesale distributor of cameras, entered into a contract with Williams. Williams agreed to purchase 100 cameras with certain optional attachments. The contract was made on March 1, 2009, for delivery by March 15, 2009; terms: 2/10, net 30. Kent shipped the cameras on March 6, and they were delivered on March 10. The shipment did not conform to the contract, in that one of the attachments was not included. Williams immediately notified Kent that he was rejecting the goods. For maximum legal advantage Kent's most appropriate action is to

    a. Bring an action for the price less an allowance for the missing attachment.

    b. Notify Williams promptly of his intention to cure the defect and make a conforming delivery by March 15.

    c. Terminate his contract with Williams and recover for breach of contract.

    d. Sue Williams for specific performance.

8. Wilmont owned a tract of waterfront property on Big Lake. During Wilmont's ownership of the land, several frame bungalows were placed on the land by tenants who rented the land from Wilmont. In addition to paying rent, the tenants paid for the maintenance and insurance of the bungalows, repaired, altered and sold them, without permission or hindrance from Wilmont. The bungalows rested on surface cinderblock and were not bolted to the ground. The buildings could be removed without injury to either the buildings or the land. Wilmont sold the land to Marsh. The deed to Marsh recited that Wilmont sold the land, with buildings thereon, "subject to the rights of tenants, if any, . . ." When the tenants attempted to remove the bungalows, Marsh claimed ownership of them. In deciding who owns the bungalows, which of the following is least significant?

a. The leasehold agreement itself, to the extent it manifested the intent of the parties.

b. The mode and degree of annexation of the buildings to the land.

c. The degree to which removal would cause injury to the buildings or the land.

d. The fact that the deed included a general clause relating to the buildings.

9. Tremont Enterprises, Inc. needed some additional working capital to develop a new product line. It decided to obtain intermediate term financing by giving a second mortgage on its plant and warehouse. Which of the following is true with respect to the mortgages?

a. If Tremont defaults on both mortgages and a bankruptcy proceeding is initiated, the second mortgagee has the status of general creditor.

b. If the second mortgagee proceeds to foreclose on its mortgage, the first mortgagee must be satisfied completely before the second mortgagee is entitled to repayment.

c. Default on payment to the second mortgagee will constitute default on the first mortgage.

d. Tremont **cannot** prepay the second mortgage prior to its maturity without the consent of the first mortgagee.

10. Frank Lanier is a resident of a state that imposes a tax on income. The following information pertaining to Lanier's state income taxes is available:

Taxes withheld in 2015	$3,500
Refund received in 2015 of 2014 tax	400
Deficiency assessed and paid in 2015 for 2013:	
Tax	600
Interest	100

What amount should Lanier utilize as state and local income taxes in calculating itemized deductions for his 2015 federal tax return?

a. $3,500
b. $3,700
c. $4,100
d. $4,200

11. Ace Rentals, Inc., an accrual-basis taxpayer, reported rent receivable of $35,000 and $25,000 in its 2015 and 2014 balance sheets, respectively. During 2015, Ace received $50,000 in rent payments and $5,000 in nonrefundable rent deposits. In Ace's 2015 corporate income tax return, what amount should Ace include as rent revenue?

a. $50,000
b. $55,000
c. $60,000
d. $65,000

12. Sol and Julia Crane (both age 41) are married, and filed a joint return for 2014. Sol earned a salary of $125,000 in 2014 from his job at Troy Corp., where Sol is covered by his employer's pension plan. In addition, Sol and Julia earned interest of $3,000 in 2015 on their joint savings account. Julia is not employed, and the couple had no other income. On January 15, 2015, Sol contributed $4,000 to an IRA for himself, and $4,000 to an IRA for his spouse. The allowable IRA deduction in the Cranes' 2015 joint return is

a. $0
b. $5,000
c. $6,000
d. $10,000

13. Spencer, who itemizes deductions, had adjusted gross income of $60,000 in 2015. The following additional information is available for 2015:

Cash contribution to church	$4,000
Purchase of art object at church bazaar (with a fair market value of $800 on the date of purchase)	1,200
Donation of used clothing to Salvation Army (fair value evidenced by receipt received)	600

What is the maximum amount Spencer can claim as a deduction for charitable contributions in 2015?

a. $5,400
b. $5,200
c. $5,000
d. $4,400

14. The following information pertains to Wald Corp.'s operations for the year ended December 31, 2015:

Worldwide taxable income	$300,000
US source taxable income	180,000
US income tax before foreign tax credit	96,000
Foreign nonbusiness-related interest earned	30,000
Foreign income taxes paid on nonbusiness-related interest earned	12,000
Other foreign source taxable income	90,000
Foreign income taxes paid on other foreign source taxable income	27,000

What amount of foreign tax credit may Wald claim for 2015?

a. $28,800
b. $36,600
c. $38,400
d. $39,000

15. Platt owns land that is operated as a parking lot. A shed was erected on the lot for the related transactions with customers. With regard to capital assets and Section 1231 assets, how should these assets be classified?

	Land	Shed
a.	Capital	Capital
b.	Section 1231	Capital
c.	Capital	Section 1231
d.	Section 1231	Section 1231

16. At partnership inception, Black acquires a 50% interest in Decorators Partnership by contributing property with an adjusted basis of $80,000. Black recognizes a gain if

   I. The fair market value of the contributed property exceeds its adjusted basis.
  II. The property is encumbered by a mortgage with a balance of $100,000.

   a. I only.
   b. II only.
   c. Both I and II.
   d. Neither I nor II.

Items 17 and 18 are based on the following data:

The partnership of Hager, Mazer & Slagle had the following cash-basis balance sheet at December 31, 2014:

	Adjusted basis per books	Fair market value
Assets		
Cash	$51,000	$ 51,000
Accounts receivable	--	210,000
Totals	$51,000	$261,000
Liabilities and Capital		
Note payable	$30,000	$ 30,000
Capital accounts:		
Hager	7,000	77,000
Mazer	7,000	77,000
Slagle	7,000	77,000
Totals	$51,000	$261,000

Slagle, an equal partner, sold his partnership interest to Burns, an outsider, for $77,000 cash on January 1, 2015. In addition, Burns assumed Slagle's share of partnership liabilities.

17. What was the total amount realized by Slagle on the sale of his partnership interest?

   a. $67,000
   b. $70,000
   c. $77,000
   d. $87,000

18. How much ordinary income should Slagle report in his 2015 income tax return on the sale of his partnership interest?

   a. $0
   b. $10,000
   c. $70,000
   d. $77,000

19. Eastern Corp., a calendar-year corporation, was formed in 2014. On January 2, 2015, it placed five-year property in service. The property was depreciated under the general MACRS system. Eastern did not elect to use the straight-line method. The following information pertains to Eastern:

Eastern's 2015 taxable income $300,000

Adjustment for the accelerated depreciation taken on 2015 five-year property	1,000
2015 tax-exempt interest from specified private activity bonds issued in 2007	5,000

What was Eastern's 2015 alternative minimum taxable income before the adjusted current earnings (ACE) adjustment?

   a. $306,000
   b. $305,000
   c. $304,000
   d. $301,000

20. Bank Corp. owns 80% of Shore Corp.'s outstanding capital stock. Shore's capital stock consists of 50,000 shares of common stock issued and outstanding. Shore's 2015 net income was $140,000. During 2015, Shore declared and paid dividends of $60,000. In conformity with generally accepted accounting principles, Bank recorded the following entries in 2015:

	Debit	Credit
Investment in Shore Corp. common stock	$112,000	
Equity in earnings of subsidiary		$112,000
Cash	48,000	
Investment in Shore Corp. common stock		48,000

In its 2015 consolidated tax return, Bank should report dividend revenue of

   a. $48,000
   b. $14,400
   c. $9,600
   d. $0

21. Kari Corp., a manufacturing company, was organized on January 2, 2015. Its 2015 federal taxable income was $400,000 and its federal income tax was $100,000. What is the maximum amount of accumulated taxable income that may be subject to the accumulated earnings tax for 2015 if Kari takes only the minimum accumulated earnings credit?

   a. $300,000
   b. $150,000
   c. $50,000
   d. $0

22. On February 10, 2015, Ace Corp., a calendar-year corporation, elected S corporation status and all shareholders consented to the election. There was no change in shareholders in 2015. Ace met all eligibility requirements for S status during the pre-election portion of the year. What is the earliest date on which Ace can be recognized as an S corporation?

   a. February 10, 2015.
   b. February 10, 2016.
   c. January 1, 2015.
   d. January 1, 2016.

23. Lyon, a cash-basis taxpayer, died on January 15, 2015. In 2015, the estate executor made the required periodic distribution of $9,000 from estate income to Lyon's sole heir. The following pertains to the estate's income and disbursements in 2015:

2015 Estate Income

$20,000	Taxable interest
10,000	Net long-term capital gains allocable to corpus

2015 Estate Disbursements

$5,000	Administrative expenses attributable to taxable income

For the 2015 calendar year, what was the estate's distributable net income (DNI)?

a. $15,000
b. $20,000
c. $25,000
d. $30,000

24. A tax return preparer may disclose or use tax return information without the taxpayer's consent to

a. Facilitate a supplier's or lender's credit evaluation of the taxpayer.
b. Accommodate the request of a financial institution that needs to determine the amount of taxpayer's debt to it, to be forgiven.
c. Be evaluated by a quality or peer review.
d. Solicit additional nontax business.

Hints for Testlet 2

1. Partners have many rights in a partnership unless they give up those rights.

2. Shareholders may assign their voting rights.

3. Rhodes Corp. is the client, not Harris Corp.

4. Preferential transfers will simply be set aside.

5. There is no other party to split the payments with.

6. The agreement cannot be performed within one year.

7. Kent is subject to the perfect tender rule.

8. Recall factors determining whether item is a fixture.

9. First mortgage has priority.

10. Include amounts withheld or actually paid during the year.

11. Try setting up a "T" account and analyzing the journal entries that would have been made.

12. The deduction is subject to a special phase-out since Sol (but not Julia) is a participant in a qualified employer retirement plan.

13. The amount of contribution includes the excess of the amount paid over the value of the object received.

14. A separate FTC limitation applies to non-business-related interest.

15. The definition of capital assets excludes property used in a trade or business.

16. Generally no gain is recognized when property is transferred in exchange for a partnership interest.

17. The amount realized includes the buyer's assumption of the seller's share of partnership liabilities.

18. Ordinary income must be reported to the extent of the seller's share of unrealized receivables and appreciated inventory.

19. The 150% declining balance method of depreciation must be used for AMT purposes.

20. Intercompany dividends from affiliated group members are eliminated in the consolidation process.

21. The minimum accumulated earnings credit is $250,000 for non service corporations.

22. An election is generally effective at the beginning of a corporation's tax year.

23. The computation of DNI excludes capital gains allocable to corpus.

24. Only one answer choice merits disclosure.

Answers to Testlet 2

1. c	4. b	7. b	10. c	13. c	16. d	19. a	22. c
2. d	5. a	8. d	11. d	14. b	17. d	20. d	23. a
3. b	6. c	9. b	12. b	15. d	18. c	21. c	24. c

Explanations

1. (c) In a general partnership all general partners have a right to participate in management.

2. (d) Shareholders have the right to vote by proxy at shareholder meetings. The other items are not rights and would require action by the board of directors.

3. (b) Since Rhodes engaged Johnson, Rhodes is the client and in privity of contract. Therefore, Johnson could be held liable for ordinary negligence.

4. (b) Failing to keep books of account or records will bar the discharge of all debts.

5. (a) A self-employed individual must pay both halves of the required contribution.

6. (c) Agreements that cannot be performed within one year from the date of the agreement must be in writing to be enforceable under the Statute of Fraud.

7. (b) To get maximum legal advantage, the buyer must notify the seller of rejection of the goods on a timely basis.

8. (d) A general clause in the deed would have the least significance.

9. (b) The first mortgage has priority before repayment of any portion of the second mortgage.

10. (c) The taxes paid in 2015 are equal to $4,100 ($3,500 withheld and $600 for deficiency). The refund is included in income and the interest is not deductible.

11. (d) The amount of rent revenue is equal to $65,000 ($50,000 received – $25,000 beginning receivable + $35,000 ending receivable + $5,000 nonrefundable deposits).

12. (b) Julia's $5,000 contribution is allowable but Sol's is not because he is a participant in a pension plan and their combined compensation is greater than $116,000.

13. (c) The maximum is $5,000 ($4,000 cash contribution + $400 excess of purchase price over fair value of art object + $600 clothing contribution).

14. (b) The amount of credit that can be currently used cannot exceed the amount of US tax that is attributable to the foreign income. This foreign tax credit limitation can be expressed as follows:

$$\frac{\text{Foreign TI}}{\text{Worldwide TI}} \times (\text{US tax}) = \text{Foreign tax credit limitation}$$

One limitation must be computed for foreign source passive income (e.g., interest, dividends, royalties, rents, annuities), with a separate limitation computed for all other foreign source taxable income.

In this case, the foreign income taxes paid on other foreign source taxable income of $27,000 is fully usable as a credit in 2015 because it is less than the applicable limitation amount (i.e., the amount of US tax attributable to the income).

$$\frac{\$90,000}{\$300,000} \times (\$96,000) = \$28,000$$

On the other hand, the credit for the $12,000 of foreign income taxes paid on non-business-related interest is limited to the amount of US tax attributable to the foreign interest income, $9,600.

$$\frac{\$30,000}{\$300,000} \times (\$96,000) = \$9,600$$

Thus, Wald Corp.'s foreign tax credit for 2015 totals $27,000 + $9,600 = $36,600. The $12,000 – $9,600 = $2,400 of unused foreign tax credit resulting from the application of the limitation of foreign taxes attributable to foreign source interest income can be carried back one year and forward ten years to offset US income tax in those years.

15. (d) Both of the assets are Section 1231 property.

16. (d) No gain is recognized on the transfer. A gain would only be recognized if the decrease in the partner's liability exceeds his or her partnership basis.

17. (d) The amount realized is $87,000 ($77,000 cash received + $10,000 liability assumed).

18. (c) The ordinary income would be equal to his share of the unrealized receivables or $70,000 ($210,000 × 1/3). The remainder would be capital gain.

19. (a) The amount of alternative minimum taxable income before ACE adjustment is equal to $306,000 ($300,000 taxable income + $5,000 tax-exempt private activity bond interest + $1,000 excess depreciation).

20. (d) On the consolidated tax return intercompany dividends are eliminated.

21. (c) The accumulated taxable income that may be subject to the accumulated earnings tax is $50,000 ($400,000 taxable income – $100,000 income tax – $250,000 accumulated earnings credit). The credit is equal to $250,000 ($250,000 – the accumulated earnings and profits at the end of the prior year which is $0).

22. (c) Since the election was filed on or before the fifteenth day of the third month of the year, it is effective as of the beginning of that year.

23. (a) DNI would be net income $25,000 ($20,000 + $10,000 – $5,000) minus $10,000 net capital gains allocable to corpus, which equals $15,000.

24. (c) The only allowed use of the information is if the preparer is being evaluated under a quality or peer review.

Testlet 3

1. Which of the following is (are) included in the Articles of Incorporation when a corporation is formed?

    a. The number of authorized shares of stock.
    b. The name of the registered agent of the corporation.
    c. The names and addresses of the incorporators.
    d. All of the above.

2. Which of the following is (are) true under the Americans with Disabilities Act?

    I. The Act requires companies to make reasonable accommodations for disabled persons unless this results in undue hardship on the operations of the company.
    II. The Act requires that companies with 100 or more employees set up a plan to hire Americans with disabilities.

    a. Both I and II.
    b. Neither I nor II.
    c. I only.
    d. II only.

3. The partnership of Maxim & Rose, CPAs, has been engaged by their largest client, a limited partnership, to examine the financial statements in connection with the offering of 2,000 limited-partnership interests to the public at $5,000 per subscription. Under these circumstances, which of the following is true?

    a. Maxim & Rose may disclaim any liability under the Federal Securities Acts by an unambiguous, boldfaced disclaimer of liability on its audit report.
    b. Under the Securities Act of 1933, Maxim & Rose has responsibility only for the financial statements as of the close of the fiscal year in question.
    c. The dollar amount in question is sufficiently small so as to provide an exemption from the Securities Act of 1933.
    d. The Securities Act of 1933 requires a registration despite the fact that the client is not selling stock or another traditional "security."

4. One of the major purposes of federal security regulation is to

    a. Establish the qualifications for accountants who are members of the profession.
    b. Eliminate incompetent attorneys and accountants who participate in the registration of securities to be offered to the public.
    c. Provide a set of uniform standards and tests for accountants, attorneys, and others who practice before the Securities and Exchange Commission.
    d. Provide sufficient information to the investing public who purchases securities in the marketplace.

5. Which of the following statements is (are) true of the National Environment Policy Act?

    I. The Act provides tax breaks for those companies that help accomplish national environmental policy.
    II. Enforcement of the Act is primarily accomplished by litigation of persons who decide to challenge federal government decisions.

    a. I only.
    b. II only.
    c. Both I and II.
    d. Neither I nor II.

6. Your client has in its possession the following instrument:

$700.000	Provo, Utah	May 1, 2002

Thirty days after date I promise to pay to the order of

    _____ Cash _____

    _____ Seven hundred _____ Dollars

at   _____ Boise, Idaho _____

Value received with interest at the rate of 10% per annum.
This instrument is secured by a conditional sales contract.

No. 20   Due June 1, 2002   *Len Bowie*

This instrument is

    a. A negotiable time draft.
    b. A nonnegotiable note since it states that it is secured by a conditional sales contract.
    c. Not negotiable until June 1, 2002.
    d. A negotiable bearer note.

7. In which of the following situations would an oral agreement without any consideration be binding under the Uniform Commercial Code?

    a. A renunciation of a claim or right arising out of an alleged breach.
    b. A firm offer by a merchant to sell or buy goods which gives assurance that it will be held open.
    c. An agreement that is a requirements contract.
    d. An agreement that modifies an existing sales contract.

8. A dispute has arisen between two merchants over the question of who has the risk of loss in a given sales transaction. The contract does not specifically cover the point. The goods were shipped to the buyer who rightfully rejected them. Which of the following factors will be the most important factor in resolving their dispute?

    a. Who has title to the goods.
    b. The shipping terms.
    c. The credit terms.
    d. The fact that a breach has occurred.

9. Moch sold her farm to Watkins and took back a purchase money mortgage on the farm. Moch failed to record the mortgage. Moch's mortgage will be valid against all of the following parties **except**

    a. The heirs or estate of Watkins.
    b. A subsequent mortgagee who took a second mortgage since he had heard there was a prior mortgage.
    c. A subsequent bona fide purchaser from Watkins.
    d. A friend of Watkins to whom the farm was given as a gift and who took without knowledge of the mortgage.

10. For the year ended December 31, 2014, Don Raff earned $1,000 interest at Ridge Savings Bank on a certificate of deposit scheduled to mature in 2015. In January 2015, before filing his 2014 income tax return, Raff incurred a forfeiture penalty of $500 for premature withdrawal of the funds. Raff should treat this $500 forfeiture penalty as a

    a. Reduction of interest earned in 2014, so that only $500 of such interest is taxable on Raff's 2014 return.
    b. Deduction from 2015 adjusted gross income, deductible only if Raff itemizes his deductions for 2015.
    c. Penalty **not** deductible for tax purposes.
    d. Deduction from gross income in arriving at 2015 adjusted gross income.

11. Axis Corp. is an accrual-basis calendar-year corporation. On December 13, 2014, the Board of Directors declared a 2% of profits bonus to all employees for services rendered during 2014 and notified them in writing. None of the employees own stock in Axis. The amount represents reasonable compensation for services rendered and was paid on March 13, 2015. Axis' bonus expense may

    a. Not be deducted on Axis' 2014 tax return because the per share employee amount **cannot** be determined with reasonable accuracy at the time of the declaration of the bonus.
    b. Be deducted on Axis' 2014 tax return.
    c. Be deducted on Axis' 2015 tax return.
    d. Not be deducted on Axis' tax return because payment is a disguised dividend.

12. On August 1, 2015, Graham purchased and placed into service an office building costing $264,000 including $30,000 for the land. What was Graham's MACRS deduction for the office building in 2015?

    a. $9,600
    b. $6,000
    c. $3,600
    d. $2,250

13. This item is based on the following selected 2015 information pertaining to Sam and Ann Hoyt, who filed a joint federal income tax return for the calendar year 2015. The Hoyts had adjusted gross income of $34,000 and itemized their deductions for 2015. Among the Hoyts' cash expenditures during 2015 were the following:

    • $2,500 repairs in connection with 2015 fire damage to the Hoyt residence. This property has a basis of $50,000. Fair market value was $60,000 before the fire

and $55,000 after the fire. Insurance on the property had lapsed in 2014 for nonpayment of premium.
    • $800 appraisal fee to determine amount of fire loss.

What amount of fire loss were the Hoyts entitled to deduct as an itemized deduction on their 2015 return?

    a. $5,000
    b. $2,500
    c. $1,500
    d. $1,100

14. A calendar-year taxpayer filed an individual tax return for 2014 on March 20, 2015. The taxpayer neither committed fraud nor omitted amounts in excess of 25% of gross income on the tax return. What is the latest date that the Internal Revenue Service can assess tax and assert a notice of deficiency?

    a. March 20, 2018.
    b. March 20, 2017.
    c. April 15, 2018.
    d. April 15, 2017.

15. During the current year, Riley exchanged investment real property, with an adjusted basis of $160,000 and subject to a mortgage of $70,000, and received from Wilson $30,000 cash and other investment real property having a fair market value of $250,000. Wilson assumed the mortgage. What is Riley's recognized gain on the exchange?

    a. $30,000
    b. $70,000
    c. $90,000
    d. $100,000

16. In 2013, Martha received as a gift several shares of Good Corporation stock. The donor's basis of this stock was $2,800, and he paid gift tax of $50. On the date of the gift, the fair market value of the stock was $2,600. If Martha sells this stock in 2015 for $2,700, what amount and type of gain or loss should Martha report in her 2015 income tax return?

    a. $50 long-term capital gain.
    b. $100 long-term capital gain.
    c. $100 long-term capital loss.
    d. No gain or loss.

17. Hall and Haig are equal partners in the firm of Arosa Associates. On January 1, 2015, each partner's adjusted basis in Arosa was $40,000. During 2015 Arosa borrowed $60,000, for which Hall and Haig are personally liable. Arosa sustained an operating loss of $10,000 for the year ended December 31, 2015. The basis of each partner's interest in Arosa at December 31, 2015, was

    a. $35,000
    b. $40,000
    c. $65,000
    d. $70,000

18. Clark and Hunt organized Jet Corp. with authorized voting common stock of $400,000. Clark contributed $60,000 cash. Both Clark and Hunt transferred other property in exchange for Jet stock as follows:

Other property

	Adjusted basis	Fair market value	Percentage of Jet stock acquired
Clark	$50,000	$100,000	40%
Hunt	120,000	240,000	60%

What was Clark's basis in Jet stock?

a. $0
b. $100,000
c. $110,000
d. $160,000

19. Roberta Warner and Sally Rogers formed the Acme Corporation on October 1, 2015. On the same date Warner paid $75,000 cash to Acme for 750 shares of its common stock. Simultaneously, Rogers received 100 shares of Acme's common stock for services rendered. How much should Rogers include as taxable income for 2015 and what will be the basis of her stock?

	Taxable income	Basis of stock
a.	$0	$0
b.	$0	$10,000
c.	$10,000	$0
d.	$10,000	$10,000

20. The following information pertains to Hull, Inc., a personal holding company, for the year ended December 31, 2015:

Undistributed personal holding company income	$100,000
Dividends paid during 2015	20,000
Consent dividends reported in the 2015 individual income tax returns of the holders of Hull's common stock, but **not** paid by Hull to its stockholders	10,000

In computing its 2015 personal holding company tax, what amount should Hull deduct for dividends paid?

a. $0
b. $10,000
c. $20,000
d. $30,000

21. Bern Corp., an S corporation, had an ordinary loss of $36,500 for the year ended December 31, 2014. At January 1,

2015, Meyer owned 50% of Bern's stock. Meyer held the stock for forty days in 2015 before selling the entire 50% interest to an unrelated third party. Meyer's basis for the stock was $10,000. Meyer was a full-time employee of Bern until the stock was sold. Meyer's share of Bern's 2015 loss was

a. $0
b. $2,000
c. $10,000
d. $18,300

22. On July 1, 2015, in connection with a recapitalization of Yorktown Corporation, Robert Moore exchanged 1,000 shares of stock that cost him $95,000 for 1,000 shares of new stock worth $108,000 and bonds in the principal amount of $10,000 with a fair market value of $10,500. What is the amount of Moore's recognized gain during 2015?

a. $0
b. $10,500
c. $23,000
d. $23,500

23. Steve and Kay Briar, US citizens, were married for the entire 2015 calendar year. In 2015, Steve gave a $32,000 cash gift to his sister. The Briars made no other gifts in 2015. They each signed a timely election to treat the $30,000 gift as made one-half by each spouse. Disregarding the unified credit and estate tax consequences, what amount of the 2015 gift is taxable to the Briars?

a. $18,000
b. $6,000
c. $4,000
d. $0

24. Following are the fair market values of Wald's assets at the date of death:

Personal effects and jewelry	$1,400,000
Land bought by Wald with Wald's funds five years prior to death and held with Wald's sister as joint tenants with right of survivorship	4,900,000

The executor of Wald's estate did not elect the alternate valuation date. The amount includible as Wald's gross estate in the federal estate tax return is

a. $1,400,000
b. $3,850,000
c. $4,900,000
d. $6,300,000

Hints for Testlet 3

1. The Articles of Incorporation contain much important information.

2. ADA applies to employers with at least fifteen employees; forbidding discrimination.

3. Must comply with **all** requirements of the 1933 Act.

4. The goal is to help investors avoid fraudulent offerings.

5. The EPA ensures compliance with environmental protection laws.

6. A note is a two-party instrument.

7. Review Module 24, Section A.2.d.

8. Risk of loss is independent of title under UCC.

9. To prevail, subsequent party must give value and must not have notice.

10. The interest forfeiture results in a deduction.

11. The amount must be fixed by a predetermined formula.

12. Remember to use the midmonth averaging convention.

13. Remember to subtract a $100 floor and 10% of AGI.

14. A return filed early is treated as filed on its due date for statute of limitations purposes.

15. The assumption of Riley's mortgage is treated as boot received.

16. The basis for gain is $2,800, and the basis for loss is $2,600.

17. An increase in partnership liabilities is treated as a deemed cash contribution.

18. Clark's basis must reflect his non recognition of gain.

19. The shares received as compensation are worth $100 per share.

20. Consent dividends are included as part of the corporation's dividends paid deduction.

21. S corporation items are allocated per share, per day to shareholders.

22. The definition of boot (other property) includes the FMV of an excess principal amount of security received.

23. The gift is treated as made one-half by each spouse.

24. In the case of jointly held property by other than spouses, the property is included in the gross estate except to the extent that the surviving tenant contributed toward the purchase.

Answers to Testlet 3

1. d	4. d	7. d	10. d	13. c	16. d	19. d	22. b
2. c	5. b	8. d	11. b	14. c	17. c	20. d	23. c
3. d	6. d	9. c	12. d	15. d	18. c	21. b	24. d

Explanations

1. (d) The Articles of Incorporation include the number of authorized shares of stock, the name of the registered agent, and the names and addresses of the incorporators, among other information.

2. (c) The Americans with Disabilities Act requires companies to make reasonable accommodations for disabled persons. It also prohibits discrimination but does not require setting up plans to hire disabled persons.

3. (d) The Securities Act of 1933 covers sales of limited-partnership interests to the public.

4. (d) One of the major purposes of federal security regulation is to assure full and fair disclosure of information to the investing public.

5. (b) The National Environment Policy Act enforcement is primarily accomplished by litigation of persons who decide to challenge federal government decisions.

6. (d) The instrument is a negotiable bearer note because it is payable to the bearer (cash), unconditional, payable on a fixed date, and specifies a certain amount of cash.

7. (d) The only oral agreement that would be binding without consideration would be an agreement that modifies an existing sales contract.

8. (d) Risk of loss transfers when title passes unless there is a breach of contract.

9. (c) A subsequent bona fide purchaser would take the property over a previous mortgage holder who fails to record.

10. (d) The penalty may be deducted from gross income in arriving at 2015 adjusted gross income.

11. (b) The bonuses are deductible provided that they are paid within 2½ months of the close of the tax year.

12. (d) The depreciation allowed is $2,250 ($234,000 × 4.5 ÷ 468 months). Notice that the midmonth convention is used.

13. (c) The casualty loss is equal to $5,000 ($60,000 FMV before the casualty – $55,000 FMV after the casualty). The

deductible loss is equal to $1,500 ($5,000 loss – $100 floor – $3,400 [10% of adjusted gross income]).

14. (c) The normal period for assessment of a tax deficiency is three years after the date of the return or three years after the return is filed, whichever is later.

15. (d) The gain is equal to $100,000, which is the amount of boot received in the like-kind exchange. The boot is equal to the $30,000 cash received plus the $70,000 liability assumed.

16. (d) Martha's basis for a gain is the basis of the donor increased by any gift tax paid, or $2,850. The basis for a loss is the lesser of gain basis ($2,850) or the FMV on the date of gift ($2,600). Therefore, no gain or loss is recognized.

17. (c) The basis of each partner's interest was $65,000 ($40,000 January 1 basis + $30,000 share of liability – $5,000 share of loss).

18. (c) Clark's basis is equal to $110,000 ($60,000 cash + $50,000 adjusted basis of property contributed).

19. (d) Rogers must include the FMV of the stock at the date of receipt in his taxable income. The basis of the investment in the stock also is the FMV of the stock at date of receipt.

20. (d) The corporation may deduct both regular and consent dividends.

21. (b) The amount of ordinary loss is $2,000 [$36,500 × 50% × (40 days/365 days)].

22. (b) The FMV of the bonds represents boot in the reorganization. Therefore, the recognized gain is $10,500.

23. (c) The amount taxable is $4,000 ($32,000 – $28,000 [two annual exclusions of $14,000 each]).

24. (d) The gross estate is equal to $6,300,000. The entire FMV of the land is included because it is held in joint tenancy and acquired by purchase by other than spouses.

Testlet 4

Task-Based Simulation 1

Schedule SE

| | Authoritative Literature | Help |

Sara Padilla (social security #123-45-6789) works as a financial consultant and had a net profit from her sole proprietorship reported on Schedule C, line 31, of $70,000 for 2014. Sara also worked a second job as an employee and had social security wages of $60,000 for 2014.

Complete the following 2014 Form 1040 Schedule SE to compute Sara's self-employment tax and her self-employment tax deduction.

Schedule SE (Form 1040) 2014		Attachment Sequence No. **17**		Page **2**

Name of person with **self-employment** income (as shown on Form 1040 or Form 1040NR) | Social security number of person with **self-employment** income ▶

Section B—Long Schedule SE
Part I   **Self-Employment Tax**

Note. If your only income subject to self-employment tax is **church employee income**, see instructions. Also see instructions for the definition of church employee income.

A	If you are a minister, member of a religious order, or Christian Science practitioner **and** you filed Form 4361, but you had $400 or more of **other** net earnings from self-employment, check here and continue with Part I . . . . ▶ ☐			
1a	Net farm profit or (loss) from Schedule F, line 34, and farm partnerships, Schedule K-1 (Form 1065), box 14, code A. **Note.** Skip lines 1a and 1b if you use the farm optional method (see instructions)	**1a**		
b	If you received social security retirement or disability benefits, enter the amount of Conservation Reserve Program payments included on Schedule F, line 4b, or listed on Schedule K-1 (Form 1065), box 20, code Z	**1b**	(	)
2	Net profit or (loss) from Schedule C, line 31; Schedule C-EZ, line 3; Schedule K-1 (Form 1065), box 14, code A (other than farming); and Schedule K-1 (Form 1065-B), box 9, code J1. Ministers and members of religious orders, see instructions for types of income to report on this line. See instructions for other income to report. **Note.** Skip this line if you use the nonfarm optional method (see instructions)	**2**		
3	Combine lines 1a, 1b, and 2	**3**		
4a	If line 3 is more than zero, multiply line 3 by 92.35% (.9235). Otherwise, enter amount from line 3	**4a**		
	Note. If line 4a is less than $400 due to Conservation Reserve Program payments on line 1b, see instructions.			
b	If you elect one or both of the optional methods, enter the total of lines 15 and 17 here . .	**4b**		
c	Combine lines 4a and 4b. If less than $400, **stop**; you do not owe self-employment tax. **Exception.** If less than $400 and you had **church employee income,** enter -0- and continue ▶	**4c**		
5a	Enter your **church employee income** from Form W-2. See instructions for definition of church employee income . . .	**5a**		
b	Multiply line 5a by 92.35% (.9235). If less than $100, enter -0-	**5b**		
6	Add lines 4c and 5b	**6**		
7	Maximum amount of combined wages and self-employment earnings subject to social security tax or the 6.2% portion of the 7.65% railroad retirement (tier 1) tax for 2014	**7**	117,000	00
8a	Total social security wages and tips (total of boxes 3 and 7 on Form(s) W-2) and railroad retirement (tier 1) compensation. If $117,000 or more, skip lines 8b through 10, and go to line 11	**8a**		
b	Unreported tips subject to social security tax (from Form 4137, line 10)	**8b**		
c	Wages subject to social security tax (from Form 8919, line 10)	**8c**		
d	Add lines 8a, 8b, and 8c	**8d**		
9	Subtract line 8d from line 7. If zero or less, enter -0- here and on line 10 and go to line 11 ▶	**9**		
10	Multiply the **smaller** of line 6 or line 9 by 12.4% (.124)	**10**		
11	Multiply line 6 by 2.9% (.029)	**11**		
12	**Self-employment tax.** Add lines 10 and 11. Enter here and on **Form 1040, line 57,** or **Form 1040NR, line 55**	**12**		
13	**Deduction for one-half of self-employment tax.** Multiply line 12 by 50% (.50). Enter the result here and on **Form 1040, line 27,** or **Form 1040NR, line 27**	**13**		

Part II   **Optional Methods To Figure Net Earnings** (see instructions)

Farm Optional Method. You may use this method **only** if **(a)** your gross farm income[1] was not more than $7,200, **or (b)** your net farm profits[2] were less than $5,198.

14	Maximum income for optional methods	**14**	4,800	00
15	Enter the **smaller** of: two-thirds (2/3) of gross farm income[1] (not less than zero) **or** $4,800. Also include this amount on line 4b above	**15**		

Nonfarm Optional Method. You may use this method **only** if **(a)** your net nonfarm profits[3] were less than $5,198 and also less than 72.189% of your gross nonfarm income,[4] **and (b)** you had net earnings from self-employment of at least $400 in 2 of the prior 3 years. **Caution.** You may use this method no more than five times.

16	Subtract line 15 from line 14	**16**		
17	Enter the **smaller** of: two-thirds (2/3) of gross nonfarm income[4] (not less than zero) **or** the amount on line 16. Also include this amount on line 4b above	**17**		

[1] From Sch. F, line 9, and Sch. K-1 (Form 1065), box 14, code B.
[2] From Sch. F, line 34, and Sch. K-1 (Form 1065), box 14, code A—minus the amount you would have entered on line 1b had you not used the optional method.
[3] From Sch. C, line 31; Sch. C-EZ, line 3; Sch. K-1 (Form 1065), box 14, code A; and Sch. K-1 (Form 1065-B), box 9, code J1.
[4] From Sch. C, line 7; Sch. C-EZ, line 1; Sch. K-1 (Form 1065), box 14, code C; and Sch. K-1 (Form 1065-B), box 9, code J2.

Schedule SE (Form 1040) 2014

Task-Based Simulation 2

Form 2441		
	Authoritative Literature	**Help**

Charles (social security #123-45-6789) and Susan Mead were married and gainfully employed throughout 2014. Charles earned $24,000 and Susan earned $16,000 in wages during the year. The couple have a son, Alan (social security #123-54-6789), who is sent to an after-school child care center (Happy Times Child Care, 123 Anywhere Road, Nowhere, USA 12345, EIN #11-1111111) to enable the Meads to work. The Meads paid Happy Times $5,200 during the year for the care of Alan, but did not receive any employer-provided dependent care benefits. The Meads' adjusted gross income reported on Form 1040, line 38, was $41,600 for 2014, while their tax before credits shown on the Meads' Form 1040, line 46, was $1,749. The Meads had no foreign tax credit on Form 1040, line 47.

Complete the following Form 2441 to determine the Meads' available credit for child and dependent care expenses for 2014.

Form **2441**

Child and Dependent Care Expenses

1040 / 1040A / 1040NR   2441

OMB No. 1545-0074

20**14**

▶ Attach to Form 1040, Form 1040A, or Form 1040NR.

Department of the Treasury
Internal Revenue Service (99)

▶ Information about Form 2441 and its separate instructions is at *www.irs.gov/form2441*.

Attachment Sequence No. **21**

Name(s) shown on return

Your social security number

Part I **Persons or Organizations Who Provided the Care**—You **must** complete this part.
(If you have more than two care providers, see the instructions.)

1	(a) Care provider's name	(b) Address (number, street, apt. no., city, state, and ZIP code)	(c) Identifying number (SSN or EIN)	(d) Amount paid (see instructions)

Did you receive dependent care benefits?	No ⟶ Complete only Part II below.
	Yes ⟶ Complete Part III on the back next.

Caution. If the care was provided in your home, you may owe employment taxes. If you do, you cannot file Form 1040A. For details, see the instructions for Form 1040, line 60a, or Form 1040NR, line 59a.

Part II **Credit for Child and Dependent Care Expenses**

2   Information about your **qualifying person(s).** If you have more than two qualifying persons, see the instructions.

(a) Qualifying person's name		(b) Qualifying person's social security number	(c) **Qualified expenses** you incurred and paid in 2014 for the person listed in column (a)
First	Last		

3	Add the amounts in column (c) of line 2. **Do not** enter more than $3,000 for one qualifying person or $6,000 for two or more persons. If you completed Part III, enter the amount from line 31	**3**
4	Enter your **earned income.** See instructions	**4**
5	If married filing jointly, enter your spouse's earned income (if you or your spouse was a student or was disabled, see the instructions); **all others,** enter the amount from line 4	**5**
6	Enter the **smallest** of line 3, 4, or 5	**6**
7	Enter the amount from Form 1040, line 38; Form 1040A, line 22; or Form 1040NR, line 37. . . . . . **7**	

8   Enter on line 8 the decimal amount shown below that applies to the amount on line 7

If line 7 is:				If line 7 is:		
Over	But not over	Decimal amount is		Over	But not over	Decimal amount is
$0—15,000		.35		$29,000—31,000		.27
15,000—17,000		.34		31,000—33,000		.26
17,000—19,000		.33		33,000—35,000		.25
19,000—21,000		.32		35,000—37,000		.24
21,000—23,000		.31		37,000—39,000		.23
23,000—25,000		.30		39,000—41,000		.22
25,000—27,000		.29		41,000—43,000		.21
27,000—29,000		.28		43,000—No limit		.20

8 X .

9	Multiply line 6 by the decimal amount on line 8. If you paid 2013 expenses in 2014, see the instructions	**9**
10	Tax liability limit. Enter the amount from the Credit Limit Worksheet in the instructions. **10**	
11	**Credit for child and dependent care expenses.** Enter the **smaller** of line 9 or line 10 here and on Form 1040, line 49; Form 1040A, line 31; or Form 1040NR, line 47	**11**

For Paperwork Reduction Act Notice, see your tax return instructions.   Cat. No. 11862M   Form **2441** (2014)

Task-Based Simulation 3

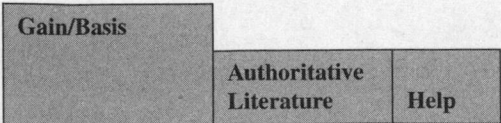

Miller, Smith, and Tucker decided to form a partnership to perform engineering services. All of the partners have extensive experience in the engineering field and now wish to pool their resources and client contacts to begin their own firm. The new entity, Sabre Consulting, will begin operations on April 1, 2015, and will use the calendar year for reporting purposes.

All of the partners expect to work full time for Sabre and each will contribute cash and other property to the company sufficient to commence operations. The partners have agreed to share all income and losses of the partnership equally. A written partnership agreement, duly executed by the partners, memorializes this agreement among the partners.

The table below shows the estimated values for assets contributed to Sabre by each partner. None of the contributed assets' costs have been previously recovered for tax purposes.

Partner	Cash contribution	Estimated FMV of noncash property contributed	Basis in noncash property contributed
Miller	$15,000	$11,000	$10,000
Smith	10,000	17,000	15,000
Tucker	20,000	6,500	5,000
Totals	45,000	34,500	30,000

Complete the shaded cells in the following table by entering the gain or loss recognized by each partner on the property contributed to Sabre Consulting, the partner's basis in the partnership interest, and Sabre's basis in the contributed property. Loss amounts should be recorded as a negative number.

NOTE: To use a formula in the spreadsheet, it must be preceded by an equals sign (e.g., =B1+B2).

E16	▼	fx		
	A	**B**	**C**	**D**
1		Parner's gain or loss on property transferred	Partner's basis in partnership interest	Partnership's basis in property contributed
2	Miller			
3	Smith			
4	Tucker			

Task-Based Simulation 4

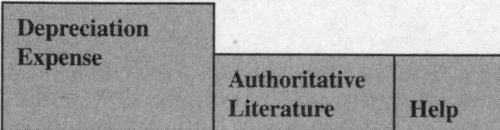

Assume that Wilson Partners (a general partnership) had only the items of income and expense shown in the following table for the 2015 tax year. Complete the remainder of the table by properly classifying each item of income and expense as ordinary business income that is reportable on page 1, Form 1065, or as a separately stated item that is reportable on Schedule K, Form 1065. Some entries may appear in both columns.

NOTE: To use a formula in the spreadsheet, it must be preceded by an equals sign (e.g., =B1+B2).

	G15	▼	fx		
	A	B	C	D
1			Ordinary Income	Separately stated items
2	Sales revenue	$500,000		
3	Interest income	4,000		
4	Depreciation expense	(7,500)		
5	Operating expenses	(426,000)		
6	Charitable contributions	(3,000)		
7				
8	Total net ordinary income			

Task-Based Simulation 5

Depreciation Expense — Authoritative Literature — Help

Wilson, Martin, and Keller form a general partnership, Express Supply Company, and each partner contributed property as described below. Using the MACRS table (which can be found by clicking the Resources tab), complete the following table to determine Express Supply's tax depreciation expense for 2015. Assume that none of the original cost of any asset was expensed by the partnership under the provisions of Section 179, and that the partnership elected not to take bonus depreciation.

NOTE: To use a formula in the spreadsheet, it must be preceded by an equals sign (e.g., =B1+B2).

D15	▼	*fx*		
	A	B	C	D
1	Partner	Asset type	Depreciable basis	2015 Depreciation expense
2	Wilson	Office furniture	$10,000	
3	Martin	Pickup truck used 100% for business purposes	$15,000	
4	Keller	Computers and printers	$5,000	

Task-Based Simulation 6

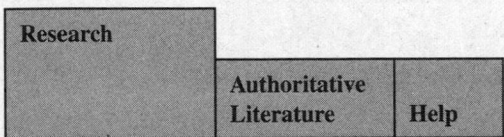

The credit for expenses for household and dependent care services necessary for gainful employment is allowed for expenses incurred for qualifying individuals. What Internal Revenue Code section and subsection defines a "qualified individual" for purposes of the child and dependent care credit?

Indicate the reference to that citation in the shaded boxes below.

Solutions to Testlet 4

Solution to Task-Based Simulation 1

Schedule SE		
	Authoritative Literature	Help

Schedule SE (Form 1040) 2014   Attachment Sequence No. **17**   Page **2**

Name of person with **self-employment** income (as shown on Form 1040 or Form 1040NR)   Social security number of person with **self-employment** income ▶

Section B—Long Schedule SE

Part I   Self-Employment Tax

Note. If your only income subject to self-employment tax is **church employee income,** see instructions. Also see instructions for the definition of church employee income.

A   If you are a minister, member of a religious order, or Christian Science practitioner **and** you filed Form 4361, but you had $400 or more of **other** net earnings from self-employment, check here and continue with Part I . . . . ▶ ☐

1a   Net farm profit or (loss) from Schedule F, line 34, and farm partnerships, Schedule K-1 (Form 1065), box 14, code A. **Note.** Skip lines 1a and 1b if you use the farm optional method (see instructions)   **1a**

   b   If you received social security retirement or disability benefits, enter the amount of Conservation Reserve Program payments included on Schedule F, line 4b, or listed on Schedule K-1 (Form 1065), box 20, code Z   **1b** (   )

2   Net profit or (loss) from Schedule C, line 31; Schedule C-EZ, line 3; Schedule K-1 (Form 1065), box 14, code A (other than farming); and Schedule K-1 (Form 1065-B), box 9, code J1. Ministers and members of religious orders, see instructions for types of income to report on this line. See instructions for other income to report. **Note.** Skip this line if you use the nonfarm optional method (see instructions) **2**

3   Combine lines 1a, 1b, and 2 . . . .   **3**

4a   If line 3 is more than zero, multiply line 3 by 92.35% (.9235). Otherwise, enter amount from line 3   **4a**
     Note. If line 4a is less than $400 due to Conservation Reserve Program payments on line 1b, see instructions.

   b   If you elect one or both of the optional methods, enter the total of lines 15 and 17 here . .   **4b**

   c   Combine lines 4a and 4b. If less than $400, **stop**; you do not owe self-employment tax. **Exception.** If less than $400 and you had **church employee income,** enter -0- and continue ▶   **4c**

5a   Enter your **church employee income** from Form W-2. See instructions for definition of church employee income . . .   **5a**

   b   Multiply line 5a by 92.35% (.9235). If less than $100, enter -0- **5b**

6   Add lines 4c and 5b **6**

7   Maximum amount of combined wages and self-employment earnings subject to social security tax or the 6.2% portion of the 7.65% railroad retirement (tier 1) tax for 2014 . . . . . .   **7**   117,000 | 00

8a   Total social security wages and tips (total of boxes 3 and 7 on Form(s) W-2) and railroad retirement (tier 1) compensation. If $117,000 or more, skip lines 8b through 10, and go to line 11   **8a**

   b   Unreported tips subject to social security tax (from Form 4137, line 10)   **8b**

   c   Wages subject to social security tax (from Form 8919, line 10)   **8c**

   d   Add lines 8a, 8b, and 8c **8d**

9   Subtract line 8d from line 7. If zero or less, enter -0- here and on line 10 and go to line 11 ▶   **9**

10   Multiply the **smaller** of line 6 or line 9 by 12.4% (.124) **10**

11   Multiply line 6 by 2.9% (.029) **11**

12   **Self-employment tax.** Add lines 10 and 11. Enter here and on **Form 1040, line 57,** or **Form 1040NR, line 55**   **12**

13   **Deduction for one-half of self-employment tax.** Multiply line 12 by 50% (.50). Enter the result here and on **Form 1040, line 27,** or **Form 1040NR, line 27** **13**

Part II   Optional Methods To Figure Net Earnings (see instructions)

Farm Optional Method. You may use this method **only** if **(a)** your gross farm income[1] was not more than $7,200, **or (b)** your net farm profits[2] were less than $5,198.

14   Maximum income for optional methods . . . .   **14**   4,800 | 00

15   Enter the **smaller** of: two-thirds (²/₃) of gross farm income[1] (not less than zero) **or** $4,800. Also include this amount on line 4b above **15**

Nonfarm Optional Method. You may use this method **only** if **(a)** your net nonfarm profits[3] were less than $5,198 and also less than 72.189% of your gross nonfarm income,[4] **and (b)** you had net earnings from self-employment of at least $400 in 2 of the prior 3 years. **Caution.** You may use this method no more than five times.

16   Subtract line 15 from line 14 . . . .   **16**

17   Enter the **smaller** of: two-thirds (²/₃) of gross nonfarm income[4] (not less than zero) **or** the amount on line 16. Also include this amount on line 4b above **17**

---

[1] From Sch. F, line 9, and Sch. K-1 (Form 1065), box 14, code B.

[2] From Sch. F, line 34, and Sch. K-1 (Form 1065), box 14, code A—minus the amount you would have entered on line 1b had you not used the optional method.

[3] From Sch. C, line 31; Sch. C-EZ, line 3; Sch. K-1 (Form 1065), box 14, code A; and Sch. K-1 (Form 1065-B), box 9, code J1.

[4] From Sch. C, line 7; Sch. C-EZ, line 1; Sch. K-1 (Form 1065), box 14, code C; and Sch. K-1 (Form 1065-B), box 9, code J2.

Schedule SE (Form 1040) 2014

Solution to Task-Based Simulation 2

Form 2441

Authoritative Literature	**Help**

Form **2441**

Child and Dependent Care Expenses

► Attach to Form 1040, Form 1040A, or Form 1040NR.

► Information about Form 2441 and its separate instructions is at *www.irs.gov/form2441*.

Department of the Treasury
Internal Revenue Service (99)

| 1040 |
| 1040A |
| 1040NR |
| 2441 |

OMB No. 1545-0074

20**13**

Attachment
Sequence No. **21**

Name(s) shown on return

Charles and Susan Mead

Your social security number

123-45-6789

Part I **Persons or Organizations Who Provided the Care**—You **must** complete this part.
(If you have more than two care providers, see the instructions.)

1	(a) Care provider's name	(b) Address (number, street, apt. no., city, state, and ZIP code)	(c) Identifying number (SSN or EIN)	(d) Amount paid (see instructions)
	Happy Times Child Care	123 Anywhere Road Nowhere, USA 12345	11-1111111	5,200

Did you receive dependent care benefits?	→ No →	Complete only Part II below.
	→ Yes →	Complete Part III on the back next.

Caution. If the care was provided in your home, you may owe employment taxes. If you do, you cannot file Form 1040A. For details, see the instructions for Form 1040, line 59a, or Form 1040NR, line 58a.

Part II **Credit for Child and Dependent Care Expenses**

2   Information about your **qualifying person(s).** If you have more than two qualifying persons, see the instructions.

(a) Qualifying person's name		(b) Qualifying person's social security number	(c) **Qualified expenses** you incurred and paid in 2013 for the person listed in column (a)
First	Last		
Alan	Mead	123-54-6789	5,200

3	Add the amounts in column (c) of line 2. **Do not** enter more than $3,000 for one qualifying person or $6,000 for two or more persons. If you completed Part III, enter the amount from line 31	**3**		3,000
4	Enter your **earned income.** See instructions	**4**		24,000
5	If married filing jointly, enter your spouse's earned income (if you or your spouse was a student or was disabled, see the instructions); **all others,** enter the amount from line 4 .	**5**		16,000
6	Enter the **smallest** of line 3, 4, or 5	**6**		3,000
7	Enter the amount from Form 1040, line 38; Form 1040A, line 22; or Form 1040NR, line 37 . . . . . . [7] 41,600			

8   Enter on line 8 the decimal amount shown below that applies to the amount on line 7

If line 7 is:			If line 7 is:		
Over	But not over	Decimal amount is	Over	But not over	Decimal amount is
$0—15,000		.35	$29,000—31,000		.27
15,000—17,000		.34	31,000—33,000		.26
17,000—19,000		.33	33,000—35,000		.25
19,000—21,000		.32	35,000—37,000		.24
21,000—23,000		.31	37,000—39,000		.23
23,000—25,000		.30	39,000—41,000		.22
25,000—27,000		.29	41,000—43,000		.21
27,000—29,000		.28	43,000—No limit		.20

8   X . 21

9	Multiply line 6 by the decimal amount on line 8. If you paid 2012 expenses in 2013, see the instructions	**9**	630
10	Tax liability limit. Enter the amount from the Credit Limit Worksheet in the instructions. . . . . . . [10] 1,749		
11	**Credit for child and dependent care expenses.** Enter the **smaller** of line 9 or line 10 here and on Form 1040, line 48; Form 1040A, line 29; or Form 1040NR, line 46	**11**	630

For Paperwork Reduction Act Notice, see your tax return instructions.   Cat. No. 11862M   Form **2441** (2013)

Solution to Task-Based Simulation 3

Gain/Basis

| | Authoritative Literature | Help |

| E16 | ▼ | *fx* | | ⧉ ✄ ⧉ |

	A	B	C	D
1	**Partner**	**Partner's gain or loss on property transferred**	**Partner's basis in partnership interest**	**Partnership's basis in property contributed**
2	Miller	$0	**$25,000**	**$10,000**
3	Smith	$0	**$25,000**	**$15,000**
4	Tucker	$0	**$25,000**	**$5,000**

Generally, no gain or loss is recognized on the contribution of property in exchange for a partnership interest. As a result, a partner's initial basis for a partnership interest consists of the amount of cash plus the adjusted basis of noncash property contributed. Similarly, a partnership receives a transferred basis for contributed noncash property equal to the partner's basis for the property prior to contribution. Miller's initial partnership basis consists of the $15,000 cash plus the $10,000 adjusted basis of noncash property contributed, or $25,000. Smith's partnership basis consists of the $10,000 cash plus the $15,000 basis of noncash property contributed, or $25,000. Tucker's partnership basis consists of the $20,000 cash plus the $5,000 basis of noncash property contributed, or $25,000.

Solution to Task-Based Simulation 4

Distributive Share

| | Authoritative Literature | Help |

| G15 | ▼ | *fx* | | ⧉ ✄ ⧉ |

	A	B	C	D
1			**Ordinary Income**	**Separately stated items**
2	Sales revenue	$500,000	**$500,000**	
3	Interest income	4,000		**$4,000**
4	Depreciation expense	(7,500)	**(7,500)**	
5	Operating expenses	(426,000)	**(426,000)**	
6	Charitable contributions	(3,000)		**(3,000)**
7				
8	Total net ordinary income		**$66,500**	

Partnership items having special tax characteristics (e.g., passive activity losses, deductions subject to dollar or percentage limitations, etc.) must be separately stated and shown on Schedules K and K-1 so that their special characteristics are preserved when reported on partners' returns. In contrast, partnership ordinary income and deduction items having no special tax characteristics can be netted together in the computation of a partnership's ordinary income and deductions from trade or business activities on page 1 of Form 1065. Here, assuming the $4,000 of interest income is from investments, it represents portfolio income and must be separately stated on Schedule K. Similarly, the charitable contributions of $3,000 must be separately stated so that the appropriate percentage limitations can be applied when passed through to partners. Sales, depreciation, and operating expenses are ordinary items and result in net ordinary income of $66,500.

Solution to Task-Based Simulation 5

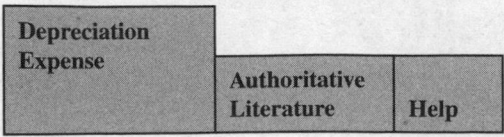

	A	B	C	D
	Partner	**Asset type**	**Depreciable basis**	**2015 Depreciation expense**
1				
2	Wilson	Office furniture	$10,000	$1,429
3	Martin	Pickup truck used 100% for business purposes	$15,000	$3,000
4	Keller	Computers and printers	$5,000	$1,000

The office furniture has a 7-year recovery period, while the pickup truck and computers and printers have a 5–year recovery period. The MACRS depreciation table that was provided is based on the 200% declining-balance method and already incorporates the half-year convention which permits just a half-year of depreciation for the year that depreciable personalty is placed in service. Thus, the 2015 depreciation expense for the office furniture is $10,000 × 14.29% = $1,429 (i.e., $10,000 × 2/7 × 1/2). The 2015 depreciation for the pickup truck is $15,000 × 20% = $3,000 (i.e., $15,000 × 2/5 × 1/2). The 2015 depreciation expense for the computers and printers is $5,000 × 20% = $1,000 (i.e., $5,000 × 2/5 × 1/2).

Solution to Task-Based Simulation 6

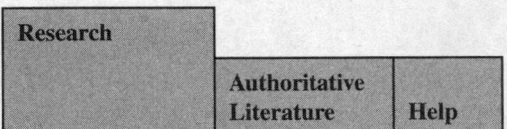

Internal Revenue Code Section 21, subsection (b), defines a qualifying individual for purposes of the child and dependent care credit.

Appendix B: Regulation Sample Testlet Released by AICPA

1. Which of the following statements concerning the similarities between a general partnership and a corporation are correct?

    a. Corporate stockholders and general partners have limited personal liability.

    b. Corporations and general partnerships have perpetual existence.

    c. Corporations and general partnerships can declare bankruptcy.

    d. Corporations and general partnerships are recognized as taxpayers for federal income tax purposes.

1. (c) The requirement is to identify the similarity between a general partnership and a corporation. Answer (c) is correct because under the federal securities laws both a corporation and a general partnership may file for bankruptcy. Answer (a) is incorrect because general partners do not have limited liability for partnership debts. Answer (b) is incorrect because while corporations have perpetual existence, general partnerships do not. Answer (d) is incorrect because while a corporation is a taxpaying entity, a partnership is a flow-through entity. The partners of the partnership pay the taxes.

2. Furl Corp., a corporation organized under the laws of State X, sued Row, a customer residing in State Y, for nonpayment for goods sold. Row attempted to dismiss the suit brought by Furl in State Y on the grounds that Furl was conducting business in State Y but had not obtained a certificate of authority from State Y to transact business therein. Which of the following actions by Furl would generally result in the court ruling that Furl was conducting business in State Y?

    a. Maintaining bank accounts in State Y.

    b. Shipping goods across state lines into State Y.

    c. Owning and operating a small manufacturing plant in State Y.

    d. Holding board of directors meetings in State Y.

2. (c) The requirement is to identify the actions that would result in Furl Corp. legally conducting business in a state. Furl Corp. is a domestic corporation in State X because Furl incorporated there. Furl is a foreign corporation in State Y because it was not incorporated in that state. When Furl is conducting business in State Y, Furl may be denied access to the courts to sue persons residing in State Y unless it qualified to do business in State Y by obtaining a certificate of authority from that state. Therefore, an important issue that the court examines is whether Furl was conducting business in State Y since Furl sued Row, a customer residing in this state. Generally a foreign corporation is ruled as conducting business in a state if the corporation's transactions are continuous rather than isolated. Owning and operating even a small manufacturing plant in the state would generally result in a ruling that Furl is conducting business in that state. Answer (a) is incorrect because merely maintaining a bank account in the state does not meet the definition of conducting business in that state. Answer (b) is incorrect because solely shipping goods across state lines into State Y does not meet the definition of conducting business in that state. Answer (d) is incorrect because Furl Corp. may hold its meetings for the board of directors in a state without meeting the definition of conducting business in that state.

3. Which of the following rights is a holder of a public corporation's cumulative preferred stock always entitled to?

    a. Conversion of the preferred stock into common stock.

    b. Voting rights.

    c. Dividend carryovers from years in which dividends were **not** paid, to future years.

    d. Guaranteed dividends.

3. (c) Preferred shares of stock are shares that have a contractual preference over other classes of stock as to liquidations and dividends. If a preferred stock is cumulative, the shareholder would be entitled to dividend carryovers from years in which dividends were not paid, to future years and would receive all dividends in arrears before any dividend is paid to owners of common stock. Answers (a) and (b) are incorrect because in order for a shareholder to be entitled to convert preferred stock into common stock or to have voting rights, it must be stated in the articles of incorporation. These are not rights that a holder of preferred stock would always be entitled to. Answer (d) is incorrect because although a preferred stockholder has preference over other classes of stock as to declared dividends, the board of directors' power to declare dividends is discretionary and thus dividends are not guaranteed.

4. Leker exchanged a van that was used exclusively for business and had an adjusted tax basis of $20,000 for a new van. The new van had a fair market value of $10,000, and Leker also received $3,000 in cash. What was Leker's tax basis in the acquired van?

   a. $20,000
   b. $17,000
   c. $13,000
   d. $7,000

4. (b) The requirement is to determine the basis for Leker's new van. The exchange of Leker's old van with a basis of $20,000 that was used exclusively for business, for a new van worth $10,000 plus $3,000 cash qualified as a like-kind exchange. Since it is a like-kind exchange, Leker's realized loss of $20,000 − ($10,000 + $3,000) = $7,000 cannot be recognized, but instead is reflected in the basis of the new van. The new van's basis is the adjusted basis of Leker's old van of $20,000 reduced by the $3,000 of cash boot received, resulting in a basis of $17,000.

5. If a corporation's charitable contributions exceed the limitation for deductibility in a particular year, the excess

   a. Is **not** deductible in any future or prior year.
   b. May be carried back or forward for one year at the corporation's election.
   c. May be carried forward to a maximum of five succeeding years.
   d. May be carried back to the third preceding year.

5. (c) The requirement is to select the correct statement regarding a corporation's charitable contributions in excess of the limitation for deductibility in a particular year. Corporate charitable contributions in excess of the 10% of taxable income limitation may be carried forward to a maximum of 5 succeeding years, subject to a 10% limitation in those years.

6. Strom acquired a 25% interest in Ace Partnership by contributing land having an adjusted basis of $16,000 and a fair market value of $50,000. The land was subject to a $24,000 mortgage, which was assumed by Ace. No other liabilities existed at the time of the contribution. What was Strom's basis in Ace?

   a. $0
   b. $16,000
   c. $26,000
   d. $32,000

6. (a) The requirement is to determine Strom's initial basis for the 25% interest in Ace Partnership that was received in exchange for land, subject to a mortgage that was assumed by Ace. Strom's initial basis for the 25% partnership interest received consists of the $16,000 basis of the land contributed, less the net reduction in Strom's liabilities resulting from the partnership's assumption of the $24,000 mortgage. Since Strom received a 25% partnership interest, the **net** reduction in Strom's liability is $24,000 × 75% = $18,000. Since Strom cannot have a negative basis, his basis for his 25% interest in Ace is $16,000 − $18,000 = $0. Additionally, note that Strom must recognize a $2,000 gain because the liability reduction exceeded the basis of the transferred land.

7. Which of the following statements concerning the similarities between a general partnership and a corporation is correct?

   a. Corporate stockholders and general partners have limited personal liability.
   b. Corporations and general partnerships have perpetual existence.
   c. Corporations and general partnerships can declare bankruptcy.
   d. Corporations and general partnerships are recognized as taxpayers for federal income tax purposes.

7. (c) The requirement is to identify the similarity between a general partnership and a corporation. Answer (c) is correct because under the federal securities laws both a corporation and a general partnership may file for bankruptcy. Answer (a) is incorrect because general partners do not have limited liability for partnership debts. Answer (b) is incorrect because while corporations have perpetual existence general partnerships do not. Answer (d) is incorrect because while a corporation is a taxpaying entity, a partnership is a flow-through entity. The partners of the partnership pay the taxes.

Task-Based Simulation 1

Gain/Basis		
	Authoritative Literature	**Help**

Miller, Smith, and Tucker decided to form a partnership to perform engineering services. All of the partners have extensive experience in the engineering field and now wish to pool their resources and client contacts to begin their own firm. The new entity, Sabre Consulting, will begin operations on April 1, 2015, and will use the calendar year for reporting purposes.

All of the partners expect to work full time for Sabre and each will contribute cash and other property to the company sufficient to commence operations. The partners have agreed to share all income and losses of the partnership equally. A written partnership agreement, duly executed by the partners, memorializes this agreement among the partners.

The table below shows the estimated values for assets contributed to Sabre by each partner. None of the contributed assets' costs have been previously recovered for tax purposes.

Partner	Cash contribution	Estimated FMV of noncash property contributed	Basis in noncash property contributed
Miller	$15,000	$11,000	$10,000
Smith	10,000	17,000	15,000
Tucker	20,000	6,500	5,000
Totals	45,000	34,500	30,000

Complete the shaded cells in the following table by entering the gain or loss recognized by each partner on the property contributed to Sabre Consulting, the partner's basis in the partnership interest, and Sabre's basis in the contributed property. Loss amounts should be recorded as a negative number.

> **NOTE:** To use a formula in the spreadsheet, it must be preceded by an equals sign (e.g., =B1+B2).

E16	▾	*fx*		
	A	**B**	**C**	**D**
1		Partner's gain or loss on property transferred	Partner's basis in partnership interest	Partnership's basis in property contributed
2	Miller			
3	Smith			
4	Tucker			

Solution to Task-Based Simulation 1

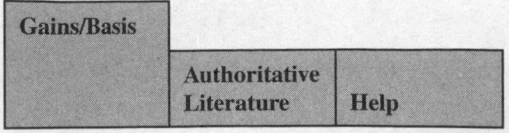

	A	B	C	D
1	**Partner**	**Partner's gain or loss on property transferred**	**Partner's basis in partnership interest**	**Partnership's basis in property contributed**
2	Miller	$0	$25,000	$10,000
3	Smith	$0	$25,000	$15,000
4	Tucker	$0	$25,000	$ 5,000

Generally, no gain or loss is recognized on the contribution of property in exchange for a partnership interest. As a result, a partner's initial basis for a partnership interest consists of the amount of cash plus the adjusted basis of noncash property contributed. Similarly, a partnership receives a transferred basis for contributed noncash property equal to the partner's basis for the property prior to contribution. Miller's initial partnership basis consists of the $15,000 cash plus the $10,000 adjusted basis of noncash property contributed, or $25,000. Smith's partnership basis consists of the $10,000 cash plus the $15,000 basis of noncash property contributed, or $25,000. Tucker's partnership basis consists of the $20,000 cash plus the $5,000 basis of noncash property contributed, or $25,000.

Task-Based Simulation 2

Miller, Smith, and Tucker decided to form a partnership to perform engineering services. All of the partners have extensive experience in the engineering field and now wish to pool their resources and client contacts to begin their own firm. The new entity, Sabre Consulting, will begin operations on April 1, 2015, and will use the calendar year for reporting purposes.

All of the partners expect to work full time for Sabre and each will contribute cash and other property to the company sufficient to commence operations. The partners have agreed to share all income and losses of the partnership equally. A written partnership agreement, duly executed by the partners, memorializes this agreement among the partners.

The table below shows the estimated values for assets contributed to Sabre by each partner. None of the contributed assets' costs have been previously recovered for tax purposes.

Partner	Cash contribution	Estimated FMV of noncash property contributed	Basis in noncash property contributed
Miller	$15,000	$11,000	$10,000
Smith	10,000	17,000	15,000
Tucker	20,000	6,500	5,000
Totals	45,000	34,500	30,000

Using the MACRS table (which can be found by clicking the Resources tab) and the partnership basis in the contributed assets calculated on the prior tab, complete the following table to determine Sabre's tax depreciation expense for 2015. Assume that none of the original cost of any asset was expensed by the partnership under the provisions of Section 179, and that the partnership elected not to take bonus depreciation.

NOTE: To use a formula in the spreadsheet, it must be preceded by an equals sign (e.g., =B1+B2).

D15	▼	*fx*		🗐 ✂ 🗐
	A	**B**	**C**	**D**
1	**Partner**	**Asset type**	**Depreciable basis**	**2015 Depreciation expense**
2	Miller	Office furniture		
3	Smith	Pickup truck used 100% for business purposes		
4	Tucker	Computers and printers		

Solution to Task-Based Simulation 2

Depreciation Expense		
	Authoritative Literature	Help

D15	▼	*fx*		🗐 ✂ 🗐
	A	**B**	**C**	**D**
1	**Partner**	**Asset type**	**Depreciable basis**	**2015 Depreciation expense**
2	Miller	Office furniture	**$10,000**	**$1,429**
3	Smith	Pickup truck used 100% for business purposes	**$15,000**	**$3,000**
4	Tucker	Computers and printers	**$5,000**	**$1,000**

The Sabre partnership's depreciable basis for the contributed property is a transferred basis equal to the contributing partner's basis for the property prior to contribution. The office furniture has a 7-year recovery period, while the pickup truck and computers and printers have a 5-year recovery period. The MACRS depreciation table that was provided is based on the 200% declining-balance method and already incorporates the half-year convention which permits just a half-year of depreciation for the year that depreciable personalty is placed in service. Thus, the 2015 depreciation expense for the office furniture is $10,000 × 14.29% = $1,429 (i.e., $10,000 × 2/7 × 1/2). The 2015 depreciation for the pickup truck is $15,000 × 20% = $3,000 (i.e., $15,000 × 2/5 × 1/2). The 2015 depreciation expense for the computers and printers is $5,000 × 20% = $1,000 (i.e., $5,000 × 2/5 × 1/2).

Task-Based Simulation 3

Distributive Share		
	Authoritative Literature	Help

Assume that Sabre (a partnership) had only the items of income and expense shown in the following table for the 2015 tax year. Complete the remainder of the table by properly classifying each item of income and expense as ordinary business income that is reportable on page 1, Form 1065, or as a separately stated item that is reportable on Schedule K, Form 1065. Some entries may appear in both columns.

	A	B	C	D
	G15	▼ *fx*		
	A	B	Ordinary income	Separately stated items
2	Sales revenue	$500,000		
3	Interest income	4,000		
4	Depreciation expense	(7,500)		
5	Operating expenses	(426,000)		
6	Charitable contributions	(3,000)		
7				
8	Total net ordinary income			

Solution to Task-Based Simulation 3

Distributive Share | Authoritative Literature | Help

	A	B	C	D
	G15	▼ *fx*		
1			Ordinary Income	Separately stated items
2	Sales revenue	$500,000	$500,000	
3	Interest income	4,000		$4,000
4	Depreciation expense	(7,500)	(7,500)	
5	Operating expenses	(426,000)	(426,000)	
6	Charitable contributions	(3,000)		(3,000)
7				
8	Total net ordinary income		$66,500	

Partnership items having special tax characteristics (e.g., passive activity losses, deductions subject to dollar or percentage limitations, etc.) must be separately stated and shown on Schedules K and K-1 so that their special characteristics are preserved when reported on partners' returns. In contrast, partnership ordinary income and deduction items having no special tax characteristics can be netted together in the computation of a partnership's ordinary income and deductions from trade or business activities on page 1 of Form 1065. Here, assuming the $4,000 of interest income is from investments, it represents portfolio income and must be separately stated on Schedule K. Similarly, the charitable contributions of $3,000 must be separately stated so that the appropriate percentage limitations can be applied when passed through to partners. Sales, depreciation, and operating expenses are ordinary items and result in net ordinary income of $66,500.

Task-Based Simulation 4

Liquidating Distributions		
	Authoritative Literature	Help

The partners have decided to liquidate Sabre Consulting at December 31, 2015. On that date, Tucker received the following asset as a liquidating distribution in exchange for his entire partnership interest. There were no partnership liabilities at the date of liquidation. Tucker's basis in the partnership interest at the date of liquidation was $3,000.

	Cost	Accumulated depreciation	Estimated FMV
Drafting equipment	$12,000	$8,000	$6,000

Based on the foregoing information, complete the following table. Loss amounts should be recorded as a negative number.

NOTE: To use a formula in the spreadsheet, it must be preceded by an equals sign (e.g., =B1+B2).

D15	▼	fx		
		A		B
1	Gain or loss recognized by partnership on the liquidating distribution			
2	Gain or loss recognized by Tucker on the liquidating distribution			
3	Tucker's basis in the asset received as part of the liquidating distribution			

Solution to Task-Based Simulation 4

Liquidation Distributions		
	Authoritative Literature	Help

D15	▼	fx		
		A		B
1	Gain or loss recognized by partnership on the liquidating distribution			$0
2	Gain or loss recognized by Tucker on the liquidating distribution			$0
3	Tucker's basis in the asset received as part of the liquidating distribution			$3,000

Generally, no gain or loss is recognized by a partnership on the distribution of noncash property in complete liquidation of the partnership. Similarly, no gain or loss is generally recognized by a distributee partner when noncash property is received in complete liquidation of the partner's partnership interest. Here, Sabre recognizes no gain when it distributes drafting equipment with an FMV of $6,000 and an adjusted basis of $4,000, and Tucker recognizes no gain when he receives the drafting equipment in liquidation of his partnership interest. Although distributed property generally has a transferred basis, the basis of the drafting equipment to Tucker is limited to his $3,000 basis for his partnership interest before the distribution.

Task-Based Simulation 5

Use the research materials available to you by clicking the Authoritative Literature button to research the answer to the following questions. Find the code section that addresses the question, and enter the section citation in the shaded boxes below. Give the most precise a citation possible (i.e., both code section and subsection, if applicable). Do **not** copy the actual text of the citation.

During its initial tax year, Sabre Consulting incurred $2,000 of legal fees and $750 of accounting fees to organize the partnership. What code section and subsection permits the partnership to deduct these expenses for federal tax purposes?

Solution to Task-Based Simulation 5

Code Sec. 709(b) allows a partnership to deduct up to $5,000 of organizational expenditures for the tax year in which the partnership begins business. The $5,000 amount must be reduced by the amount by which organizational expenditures exceed $50,000. Remaining expenditures are deducted ratably over the 180-month period beginning with the month in which the partnership begins business.

1. The IRS requested client records from a CPA who does not have possession or control of the records. According to Treasury Circular 230, the CPA must

    a. Notify the IRS of the identity of any person who, according to the CPA's belief, could have the records.

    b. Require the client to submit the records to the IRS or withdraw from the engagement.

    c. Obtain the records from the client and submit them to the IRS.

    d. Contact all third parties associated with the records, such as banks and employers, to obtain the requested records for submission to the IRS.

2. Under Treasury Circular 230, which of the following correctly represents the requirements related to the communication of fee information from a tax practitioner to a taxpayer:

    a. It may be communicated only through the confidential engagement letter between the tax practitioner and the taxpayer.

    b. It may be communicated in a number of ways, including in professional lists, telephone directories, mailings, and electronic mail.

    c. It must be communicated as an estimate before the engagement begins, with the understanding that the actual amount of the fee will **not** be determined until the engagement ends.

    d. It may **not** be communicated by television, radio, or hand-delivered flyers.

3. A taxpayer wants to take a position on a tax return that the CPA determines is frivolous. However, the CPA and the taxpayer determine that the possibility of the return being selected for audit is remote and that even if the return is selected for audit the issue most likely will not be raised. According to the AICPA *Statements on Standards for Tax Services*, under these circumstances the CPA

    a. Can sign or prepare the return with this position as long as the CPA advises the taxpayer that the position is frivolous.

    b. Cannot sign or prepare the return with this position.

    c. Can sign or prepare the return with this position because there is a realistic possibility that the position will **not** be challenged.

    d. Can sign or prepare the return with this position if the taxpayer signs a tax preparer waiver of liability.

4. Which of the following types of debtor are **not** eligible for relief under Chapter 11 of the Bankruptcy Code?

    a. Individuals.

    b. Railroads.

    c. Airlines.

    d. Stockbrokers.

1. (a) The requirement is to determine what a CPA should do if the IRS requests client records that are not in possession or control of the CPA. In that case, a tax practitioner must notify the IRS of the identity of any person who the practitioner believes may have possession or control of the requested records or information. Also, the practitioner must make reasonable inquiry of the client regarding the identity of any person who may have possession or control of the requested records or information, but the practitioner is not required to make inquiry of any other person or independently verify any information provided by the practitioner's client regarding the identity of such persons.

2. (b) The requirement is to determine the correct statement regarding the communication of fee information from a tax practitioner to a taxpayer. A tax practitioner may publish a fee schedule including fixed fees for specific services, hourly rates, ranges of fees for specific services, and the fee charged for an initial consultation. Fee information may be communicated in professional lists, telephone directories, print media, mailings, and electronic mail, facsimile, hand delivered flyers, radio, television, and any other method.

3. (b) The requirement is to determine the correct statement regarding a CPA's response when a client wants the CPA to take a frivolous position on the client's tax return. According to the AICPA Statements on Standards for Tax Services, a CPA should not recommend a position unless there is a realistic probability of it being sustained if it is challenged. A realistic probability implies at least a one-third likelihood of being sustained. Since a frivolous position implies a less than 10% chance of being sustained, a CPA cannot prepare or sign a tax return containing a frivolous position.

4. (b) The requirement is to identify the type of debtor that is not eligible for relief under Chapter 11. Answer (b) is correct because Railroads are specifically prohibited from using Chapter 11. Answers (a), (c) and (d) are incorrect because they are all eligible for relief under Chapter 11.

5. Which of the following statements is correct regarding the taxes payable under the Federal Unemployment Tax Act (FUTA)?

    a. Liability arises only when wages are actually, **not** constructively, paid to employees.

    b. Credits for this tax are allowed to employers for certain state unemployment taxes paid by the employer.

    c. The amount is withheld from the wages of all employees.

    d. The amount is determined as a percentage of all compensation paid to an employee.

6. In a principal-agent relationship that is **not** contractual, which of the following remedies is **not** available to the agent whose principal is guilty of violating a duty owed the agent?

    a. Recovery for past services.

    b. Recovery for future damages.

    c. Specific performance.

    d. Withholding further performance.

7. An individual client asks a CPA to determine whether the client is solvent for federal tax purposes. The client has assets consisting of cash and marketable securities with a basis of $250,000 and a fair market value of $155,000. The client has liabilities of $175,000, which include $130,000 of non dischargeable liabilities under the Bankruptcy Code. Which of the following statements is correct?

    a. The client is insolvent since the client's liabilities exceed the fair market value of the client's assets by $20,000.

    b. The CPA is unable to determine whether the client is solvent or insolvent because the CPA is **not** an accredited appraiser.

    c. The client is solvent because the fair market value of the client's assets exceeds the client's non dischargeable debt by $25,000.

    d. The client is solvent because the basis of the client's assets totals $250,000 and exceeds the client's liabilities by $75,000.

8. In which of the following situations will a controlled foreign corporation located in Ireland be deemed to have Subpart F income?

    a. Services are provided by an Irish company in England under a contract entered into by its U.S. parent.

    b. Property is produced in Ireland by the Irish company and sold outside its country of incorporation.

    c. Services are performed in Ireland by the Irish company under a contract entered into by its U.S. parent.

    d. Property is bought from the controlled foreign corporation's U.S. parent and is sold by an Irish company for use in an Irish manufacturing plant.

5. (b) The requirement is to determine the correct statement regarding the FUTA tax. The FUTA tax is imposed on employers and applies to the first $7,000 of wages paid to an employee during a calendar year. The full rate of tax is 6 percent, but the employer is allowed a partial credit (up to 5.4%) against this tax based on the employer's state unemployment insurance tax liability.

6. (c) The requirement is to identify the remedies available to the agent when a principal violates a duty owed to the agent. Answer (c) is correct because the agent may not hold the principal to specific performance. Answers (a), (b), and (d) are incorrect because these are all remedies available to the agent.

7. (a) The requirement is to determine the correct statement regarding whether a client is solvent for federal tax purposes. A taxpayer is considered insolvent for federal tax purposes if the taxpayer's total liabilities exceed the total FMV of the taxpayer's assets. Here, the client has $175,000 of liabilities and $155,000 of assets indicating that the client is insolvent to the extent of $20,000.

8. (a) The requirement is to determine in which situation a controlled foreign corporation (CFC) located in Ireland will be deemed to have Subpart F income. Subpart F income of a CFC is subject to US taxation even though the earnings are not distributed to the US parent corporation. Subpart F targets transactions whereby income is shifted between taxing jurisdictions to take advantage of lower tax rates, and generally applies to a CFC's transactions producing income that has little or no economic connection with the CFC's country of incorporation. Subpart F income includes foreign personal holding company income, foreign base company sales income, and foreign base company services income. Foreign base company services income is income derived from services performed by a CFC for or on behalf of a related party (e.g., US parent) and performed outside the country in which the CFC is organized. Thus, services performed by an Irish CFC in England under a contract entered into by its US parent would be Subpart F income. Answer (b) is not correct because the sold property was produced in Ireland. Answer (c) is not correct because the services are performed in Ireland, the CFC's country of incorporation. Answer (d) is not correct because the purchased property is sold for use in Ireland, the CFC country of incorporation.

9. Kuo sells residential rental property to his son, Karl for $100,000. Karl gives Kuo $1,000 and an installment note for the balance of $99,000. Kuo's basis is $50,000. Karl pays Kuo $4,000 in year 1. In year 2, after paying Kuo $5,000, Karl sells the property for $70,000. Which of the following statements about this situation is correct?

    a. Kuo should report the entire gain of $50,000 in year 1 because installment sales of depreciable property are **not** allowed between related parties.

    b. Kuo should report $2,500 gain in year 1.

    c. Kuo should report the entire gain of $50,000 in year 1 because Karl disposed of the land within two years of purchase.

    d. Kuo should report a $49,000 gain in year 2.

9. (b) The requirement is to determine the amount of gain to be reported by Kuo following the installment sale of residential rental property to his son. The installment method generally applies to gains where at least one payment is to be received after the year of sale. Under the installment method, the gross profit from the sale is reported as payments are received. Here, Kuo's gross profit is $100,000 − $50,000 = $50,000. Since the payments to be received total 100,000, $50,000 / $100,000 = ½ of each payment received must be included in income. Since Kuo received payments totaling $5,000 in year 1, $5,000 × ½ = $2,500 of gain must be reported by Kuo in year 1.

Answer (a) is not correct because installment sales of depreciable property are generally allowed between related taxpayers, and are only prohibited if the related taxpayer is a controlled entity. Answer (c) is not correct because the disposition by Karl in year 2 will not affect the amount of gain already reported by Kuo in year 1. Answer (d) is not correct because there is only $50,000 − $2,500 = $47,500 of gain to be reported by Kuo after year 1.

10. A husband and wife agree to split monetary gifts to their relatives. The husband gives his daughter $20,500, and the wife gives her niece $17,000. The annual exclusion is $12,000. What amount is the taxable gift for the husband and wife?

    a. $0.

    b. $13,500.

    c. $17,000.

    d. $37,500.

10. (a) The requirement is to determine the amount of taxable gift for the husband and wife when gift splitting is elected. With the gift splitting election, each spouse is treated as making one-half of each gift. As a result, each spouse is treated as making a gift of $10,250 to the daughter, and $8,500 to the niece. Since each spouse would receive a $12,000 exclusion for the gift to the daughter, as well as a $12,000 exclusion for the gift to the niece, there would be no taxable gift.

11. If a security becomes worthless in the current taxable year, it is treated as sold or exchanged on

    a. The last day of the preceding taxable year.

    b. The last day of the current taxable year.

    c. The date it is deemed worthless.

    d. The first day of the current taxable year.

11. (b) The requirement is to determine the date on which a worthless security is treated as sold or exchanged. A loss from a worthless security is treated as occurring on the last day of the taxable year is which the security becomes worthless.

12. Mike and Carol, a married couple, have two assets at the time of Mike's death: a $10,000,000 life insurance policy owned by Mike naming Carol as the sole beneficiary, and $8,000,000 of real estate owned by the couple as joint tenants with right of survivorship. What is the amount of the marital deduction to Mike's estate for these two assets?

    a. $9,000,000.

    b. $10,000,000.

    c. $14,000,000.

    d. $18,000,000.

12. (c) The requirement is to determine the amount of marital deduction for Mike's estate for the two assets left to Mike's spouse. In computing the taxable estate of a decedent, an unlimited marital deduction is allowed for the portion of a decedent's estate that passes to the decedent's surviving spouse. The $10,000,000 life insurance policy owned by Mike would be included in Mike's gross estate and would be eligible for a marital deduction since Carol is the beneficiary. Since the real estate was owned in joint tenancy with Carol, 50% of $8,000,000 = $4,000,000 would be included in Mike's gross estate and would be eligible for a marital deduction since ownership passes to Carol. As a result, the amount of marital deduction for Mike's estate would be $14,000,000.

13. Logan, an employee of Argon Industries, earned a salary of $60,000 in year 2. In addition, the following two transactions between Logan and Argon occurred in year 2: Logan received a bonus of 100 shares of publicly-traded stock worth $13,000 with a basis to Argon of $8,000, and Logan purchased 1,000 shares of unrestricted Argon stock pursuant to a nonqualifying stock option plan for $10 per share when stock

13. (c) The requirement is to determine the amount of compensation that Argon should report in Logan's Form W-2 for year 2. Logan's compensation to be reported on his W-2 would consist of the $60,000 salary, the bonus in the form of stock worth $13,000, and the bargain element resulting from the exercise of the nonqualifying stock option ($25 − $10) × 1,000 shares = $15,000, a total of $88,000.

was valued at $25 per share. What amount of compensation should Argon report in Logan's Form W-2 for year 2?

    a. $60,000
    b. $73,000
    c. $88,000
    d. $93,000

14. Flowers, a married taxpayer, purchased an annuity for $64,400 that will pay $700 per month over the life of Flowers and Flowers' spouse. At the time of purchase the couple's joint life expectancy was 23 years. Flowers received payment beginning April 1, year 1 amounting to $6,300 in the first year of the annuity contract. How much is includible in Flowers' gross income in the first year?

    a. $0
    b. $2,100
    c. $4,200
    d. $6,300

14. (c) The requirement is to determine the amount of annuity payment includible in Flowers' gross income for the first year. The $64,400 cost of the annuity will be recovered pro rata over the life of the annuity. This results in an exclusion ratio to be applied to each annuity payment of $64,400 / ($700 \times 12 \times 23) = 1/3$. Therefore, the amount includible in gross income for the first year is $6,300 \times 2/3 = $4,200$.

15. Four years ago, an individual taxpayer purchased silver coins at face value for $200. The coins were stolen in the current year, when their fair market value was $1,000. The coins were not covered by insurance. Without considering the limit based on AGI, what is the maximum amount of loss that the taxpayer can deduct on the current-year's tax return?

    a. $100
    b. $200
    c. $900
    d. $1,000

15. (a) The requirement is to determine the maximum amount of loss that an individual can deduct as a result of the theft of the coins. The amount of a personal (nonbusiness) casualty or theft loss is the lesser of the property's basis ($200), or the decline in value resulting from the casualty or theft ($1,000). This amount of $200 would then be reduced by a $100 floor which applies to each casualty or theft resulting in a maximum amount of loss of $100 (before the 10% of AGI limitation).

16. An S corporation had the following income and expenses:

Sales	$240,000
Rent expense	25,000
Entertainment expense	5,000
Interest income	1,500
Contributions to qualifying charities	600
Section 179 expense	3,000
Depreciation expense	1,800

What would be reported as ordinary income on the corporation's income tax return?

    a. $206,100
    b. $208,600
    c. $210,700
    d. $213,200

16. (c) The requirement is to determine an S corporation's ordinary income on the corporation's tax return. The computation of ordinary income would include the sales of $240,000, rent expense of $25,000, 50% of the entertainment expense of $5,000, and the depreciation expense of $1,800, resulting in $210,700 of ordinary income. The computation excludes the items that must be separately stated and passed through to shareholders that consist of the interest income, contributions, Sec. 179 expense, and the nondeductible 50% portion of the entertainment expense.

17. Dove and Eagle formed a business entity in which they are equal owners. Dove contributed cash of $100,000, and Eagle contributed land with a basis of $40,000 and fair market value of $100,000. For its first year of operations, the entity had taxable income of $60,000 and made no distributions. At year end it had outstanding recourse liabilities to third parties of $10,000. Eagle had a basis of $70,000 in the entity at the end of the first year of operations. What type of entity was formed?

    a. C corporation.
    b. S corporation.
    c. General partnership.
    d. Limited liability company (LLC).

17. (b) The requirement is to determine the type of entity that was formed given Eagle's basis of $40,000 at the beginning of the year and $70,000 of basis at the end of the year. The entity is an S corporation since Eagle's $40,000 beginning basis was increased by Eagle's 50% share of the S corporation's taxable income (50% \times $60,000 = $30,000). The entity is not a C corporation because a C corporation's taxable income does not increase a shareholder's basis. Also, the entity is not a general partnership nor is it an LLC because in that case Eagle's basis would have been increased by half of the year-end liabilities to third parties.

18. Jetson and Tomson are equal partners in JT Partnership, which has the following income and expense items:

Sales	$100,000
Interest income from checking account	1,000
Charitable contributions	3,000
Employee wages	4,000
Cost of goods sold	50,000

What is the nonseparately stated partnership income?

   a. $43,000
   b. $44,000
   c. $46,000
   d. $47,000

18. (c) The requirement is to determine the amount of nonseparately stated (ordinary) partnership income. The partnership's ordinary income consists of the $100,000 of sales, less the employee wages of $4,000, and the cost of goods sold of $50,000, which results in a total of $46,000 of ordinary income. The charitable contributions and interest income (portfolio income) are excluded from the computation of ordinary income and must be separately passed through to partners.

19. Borasco Corp. owns land with a fair market value of $200,000. Borasco purchased the land 10 years ago for $65,000 and owes a liability of $50,000 as of August 2 of the current year. Alvo Corp. owns 100% of Borasco. Borasco is completely liquidated on August 2 of the current year, according to a plan adopted on June 18 of the current year. As a result, the land is transferred to Alvo in complete cancellation of Borasco's stock. What basis does Alvo have in the land it receives?

   a. $15,000
   b. $65,000
   c. $150,000
   d. $200,000

19. (b) The requirement is to determine Alvo Corp.'s basis for the land it receives in the complete liquidation of Borasco Corp. Since Alvo owns at least 80% of Borasco, the liquidation of Borasco is a nontaxable Sec. 332 liquidation. No gain is recognized by Borasco, and Alvo has a transferred basis of $65,000 for the land it receives.

20. What is the tax rate for an S corporation that pays tax on built-in gains?

   a. The calculated income tax rate of the corporation.
   b. The income tax rate of the shareholder.
   c. The highest individual income tax rate.
   d. The highest corporate income tax rate.

20. (d) The requirement is to determine the tax rate that applies to an S corporation's built-in gains. The applicable rate that applies to an S corporation's net recognized built-in gain is the highest corporate rate (currently 35%).

21. The partnership of Rodgers & Higgs, CPAs, performed audits of Alt Corp., a publicly-traded company, for the past several years. After issuing the current year's audit report, the CFO of Alt confessed to having committed fraud against Alt. Under which of the following statutes would the investors most likely bring suit against Rodgers & Higgs?

   a. Securities Act of 1933, if they can prove ordinary negligence.
   b. Securities Act of 1933, if they can prove gross negligence.
   c. Securities Exchange Act of 1934, if they can prove ordinary negligence.
   d. Securities Exchange Act of 1934, if they can prove *scienter*.

21. (d) The requirement is to identify the statute most likely to be used by the investors. Answer (d) is correct because the Securities and Exchange Act of 1934 would apply and the investors must prove scienter on the part of Rodgers & Higgs. Answers (a) and (b) are incorrect because the 1933 Act applies to initial security offerings. Answer (c) is incorrect because under the 1934 Act the investors must prove scienter on the part of Rodges & Higgs.

22. In which of the following circumstances would a tax return preparer be prohibited from disclosing a client's tax return information?

   a. The information will be needed for a peer review.
   b. The information will be provided in response to a court order.
   c. The information will be provided to a section 501(c)(3) charity.
   d. The information will be used to prepare state or local tax returns.

22. (c) The requirement is to determine the circumstances in which a return preparer would be prohibited from disclosing a client's tax return information. A return preparer would be subject to penalty if the preparer knowingly disclosed a client's tax return information to a Sec. 501(c)(3) charitable organization. On the other hand, tax return information can be disclosed by the preparer without penalty if the information is needed for the preparer's peer review, is furnished in response to a court order, or the information is used to prepare state or local tax returns.

23. Under the *Statements on Standards for Tax Services*, what is a CPA's responsibility for verifying information furnished by the taxpayer or third parties?

- a. A CPA need **not** make additional inquiries if the information furnished appears to be incorrect, incomplete, or inconsistent with other facts known to the CPA.
- b. A CPA need **not** consider implications of information furnished if the information comes directly from a third party.
- c. A CPA may, in good faith, rely on information furnished by the taxpayer or by third parties without verification.
- d. A CPA should **not** refer to the taxpayer's previous tax returns **unless** the returns report transactions that affect the current tax period.

24. Which of the following contractual assignments is prohibited?

- a. The right to receive royalties.
- b. The right to be insured under a liability insurance policy.
- c. The right to receive installment payments.
- d. The rights under an option contract.

25. Under which of the following circumstances would a promoter be relieved of personal liability on contracts entered into while engaged in forming a corporation?

- a. When the bylaws of the corporation expressly adopt all preincorporation contracts without novation.
- b. When the corporation unknowingly accepts the benefits of the contract.
- c. When the contracting party verbally agrees to relieve the promoter.
- d. When the third party, the corporation, and the promoter enter into an agreement to substitute the corporation for the promoter.

26. Under the Negotiable Instruments Article of the UCC, which of the following defenses could be successfully asserted by the drawer of a draft against a holder in due course of that draft?

- a. The drawer issued the draft to the payee because of the payee's fraudulent representations concerning the value of the property the payee was transferring to the drawer in return for the draft.
- b. The drawer issued the draft as a gift to the original payee, without the drawer receiving any consideration or value for it.
- c. The drawer was discharged from the obligation in bankruptcy after the issuance of the draft.
- d. The drawer issued the draft as bearer paper, and it was transferred by the original holder to the next holder without an endorsement.

23. (c) The requirement is to determine a CPA's responsibility to verify information furnished by the taxpayer or third parties. A CPA may, in good faith, reply on information furnished by the taxpayer or by third parties without verification. However, a CPA should make additional inquiries if the information furnished appears to be incorrect, incomplete, or inconsistent with other facts known to the CPA, and should consider the implications of information directly furnished by third parties. Additionally, a CPA should refer to the client's previous returns when preparing the return for the current year.

24. (b) The requirement is to identify the contractual assignment that is prohibited. Answer (b) is correct because insurance contracts cannot be assigned because it alters the risk of the contract. Answers (a), (c), and (d) are incorrect because they are all contractual assignments that are allowed.

25. (d) The requirement is to identify the circumstance in which a promoter would be relieved of personal liability on contracts. Answer (d) is correct because the third party and the corporation must enter into an agreement to substitute the corporation for the promoter. Answer (a), (b), and (c) are incorrect because the third party and the corporation must agree to substitute the corporation for the promoter in the contract.

26. (c) The requirement is to identify the defense that may successfully be asserted against a holder in due course. Answer (c) is correct because discharge of the debt in bankruptcy is a successful defense. Answers (a), (b), and (d) are incorrect because they are not valid defenses.

27. The two equal shareholders of a C corporation are thinking of filing an election to have the company treated as an S corporation. Which of the following consequences is an advantage of this election?

    a. The corporation's net operating loss carryovers from prior years are immediately deductible by the shareholders.

    b. The corporation's tax-free fringe benefits for the shareholders will be deductible by the corporation.

    c. The shareholders of the S corporation will be taxed only on distributions from the corporation.

    d. The corporation's capital losses can be claimed on the tax returns of the shareholders.

28. Benson exchanged a van, used exclusively for business and with an adjusted basis of $100,000, for a new van with a fair market value of $120,000 and received $5,000 in cash. What amount of gain did Benson recognize from the transaction?

    a. $0

    b. $5,000

    c. $20,000

    d. $25,000

29. Which of the following items qualifies for treatment under Section 1231 (Property Used in the Trade or Business and Involuntary Conversions)?

    a. Copyright used in the business, held for 10 years.

    b. Building used in the business, held for six months.

    c. Machinery used in the business, held for eleven months.

    d. Computer used in the business, held for four years.

30. A personal service corporation may deduct payments made to owner-employees only in the year in which the

    a. Corporation is formed.

    b. Expense is accrued on the books and records of the corporation.

    c. Corporation makes a valid subchapter S election.

    d. Owner-employee includes it in income.

31. An individual taxpayer reports the following information:

U.S. Treasury bond income	$ 100
Municipal bond income	200
Rental income	500
Investment interest expense	1,000

What amount of investment interest can the taxpayer deduct in the current year?

    a. $100

    b. $300

    c. $800

    d. $1,000

27. (d) The requirement is to determine the advantage of an S corporation election. An S corporation is a pass-through entity and its capital losses pass through and can be claimed on the tax returns of its shareholders. Answer (a) is not correct because a C corporation's net operating loss carryovers cannot pass through to shareholders during an S year. Answer (b) is not correct because fringe benefits provided for shareholders (as opposed to employees) are not deductible by the S corporation. Fringe benefits provided to shareholder-employees owning 2% or less of the S corporation's stock are deductible as fringe benefits, while fringe benefits provided to shareholder-employees owning more than 2% of the S corporation's stock are deductible as compensation by the S corporation, but must be reported as compensation income by the shareholder-employees. Answer (c) is not correct because the income of an S corporation is taxed to shareholders regardless of whether the income is distributed.

28. (b) The requirement is to determine the amount of Benson's recognized gain from the transaction. The exchange of a business van for a new business van qualifies as a like-kind exchange. Benson's realized gain is ($120,000 new van + $5,000 cash) − $100,000 basis = $25,000. However, $5,000 of gain must be recognized because of the $5,000 of cash boot received.

29. (d) The requirement is to determine which property qualifies as Sec. 1231 property. Sec. 1231 property generally includes depreciable and nondepreciable property used in a trade or business and held for more than one year. A business computer held for four years is Sec. 1231 property, but property held for one year or less, as well as inventory, accounts receivable, notes receivable, and copyrights are excluded from Sec. 1231 treatment.

30. (d) The requirement is to determine when a personal service corporation can deduct payments made to owner-employees. A personal service corporation (PSC) and any of its owner-employees are considered related taxpayers regardless of the amount of the corporation's stock owned by the owner-employee. Thus, a PSC is not allowed to deduct payments made to an owner-employee before the tax year in which such person must include the payment in gross income.

31. (a) The requirement is to determine the amount of the $1,000 of investment interest expense that can be deducted for the current year. The deduction for investment interest expense is limited to an individual's net investment income. Here, the investment income includes only the $100 of U.S. Treasury bond income. Municipal bond interest is tax-exempt and is excluded from investment income. Additionally, rental income attributable to a passive activity or a rental real estate activity is excluded from investment income.

32. As a result of a divorce, a taxpayer received the following during the current year:

Cash from the property settlement	$100,000
Child support	12,000
Alimony payments	30,000

What amount, if any, must be included in gross income for the current year?

    a. $0
    b. $30,000
    c. $130,000
    d. $142,000

32. (b) The requirement is to determine the amount that must be included in gross income. Alimony must be included in gross income by the payee and is deductible by the payor. Property settlements and child support payments are not alimony. Those payments are neither deductible by the payor, nor taxable to the payee.

33. Thompson's spouse died in year 1. Thompson did not remarry in year 2 and lived alone the entire year. What is Thompson's year 2 filing status?

    a. Married filing jointly.
    b. Surviving spouse.
    c. Head of household.
    d. Single.

33. (d) The requirement is to determine Thompson's year 2 filing status. Since Thompson did not remarry and lived alone the entire year 2, he does not qualify as married filing jointly, as a surviving spouse, or as a head of household for year 2. As a result, Thompson's filing status for year 2 is a single taxpayer.

34. Paige, a 25% shareholder in an S corporation, had a stock basis of $10,000 at the beginning of the year. The corporation had ordinary income of $200,000 for the year. There were no separately stated items. Paige received wages from the corporation of $25,000 and a distribution of $30,000. What was Paige's basis in the stock at year end?

    a. $0
    b. $5,000
    c. $30,000
    d. $35,000

34. (c) The requirement is to determine a 25% shareholder's basis for S corporation stock at year end. The beginning stock basis of $10,000 would be increased by the 25% × $200,000 = $50,000 pass-through of income taxed to the shareholder, and would be reduced by the nontaxable distribution of $30,000, resulting in an ending stock basis of $30,000. Also note that the amount taxed to the shareholder for the year would consist of the $25,000 of wages plus the $50,000 pass-through of ordinary income, a total of $75,000.

35. Kline and Salomon form the KS Partnership as 50/50 partners. Kline contributes equipment that has a fair market value of $60,000 and an adjusted basis of $45,000. In addition, the equipment is subject to a $10,000 loan that KS Partnership is assuming. What amount represents Kline's initial basis in the partnership?

    a. $35,000
    b. $40,000
    c. $45,000
    d. $60,000

35. (b) The requirement is to determine Kline's initial basis for the 50% partnership interest. Kline's initial basis would consist of the $45,000 adjusted basis of contributed property less the net reduction in his liability that results from having the partnership assume the $10,000 liability. As a result, Kline is in effect transferring 50% of his liability to the other partner, and Kline's initial basis for the partnership interest would be $45,000 – (50% × $10,000) = $40,000.

36. Parent company X and subsidiary company Y file a calendar year consolidated federal income tax return. Company X reported a $120,000 tax loss, which included a $10,000 dividend from Y. Company Y reported $140,000 of taxable income, which included $30,000 of dividends received from less than 20% owned stock investments. Neither company took into account any applicable dividends received deduction. What is the group's consolidated tax loss for the year?

    a. ($1,000)
    b. ($4,000)
    c. ($11,000)
    d. ($20,000)

36. (c) The requirement is to determine X and Y's consolidated tax loss for the year. Since Companies X and Y are filing a consolidated tax return, the $10,000 dividend that Y paid to X would be eliminated in determining the group's consolidated taxable income or loss. Since X reported a $120,000 tax loss which included the $10,000 dividend as income, X's tax loss would be $130,000 when the dividend is eliminated. Additionally, the $30,000 of dividends received by Y from less than 20% owned stock investments would be eligible for a 70% dividends received deduction when computing the group's consolidated taxable income or loss. As a result, X and Y's consolidated tax loss would be $140,000 – $130,000 – (70%)($30,000) = ($11,000).

37. Which of the following is a disadvantage of a revocable trust?

    a. The grantor will be subject to gift taxes on the transfer of property to the trust.
    b. The trust assets are subject to being probated upon the death of the grantor.
    c. The grantor loses power to control the trust funds for federal estate tax purposes.
    d. The trust is included in the gross estate of the grantor.

38. IRC Section 263A requires the capitalization of certain indirect costs related to inventory when a qualifying business is manufacturing tangible personal property. Which of the following costs is **not** required to be capitalized as part of this adjustment?

    a. Marketing.
    b. Recruiting.
    c. Payroll.
    d. Securities services.

39. A company terminated its S corporation status for the current tax year. When can the company reelect S status?

    a. Immediately.
    b. Third year from the current tax year.
    c. Fifth year from the current tax year.
    d. Cannot reelect in future.

40. The CPA was preparing the financial statement for a limited liability company. To which of the following would the CPA's report be addressed?

    a. Member.
    b. Shareholder
    c. General partner.
    d. Limited partner.

37. (d) The requirement is determine the disadvantage of a revocable trust. If a grantor creates a trust and reserves the power to revoke it, the grantor is treated as the owner of the property in the trust and the income of the trust is treated as the grantor's income. Since the grantor is treated as the owner of the trust, the trust will be included in the gross estate of the grantor at death. An advantage of a revocable trust is that the transfer of property to the trust is an incomplete transfer and is not subject to Federal gift tax. Another advantage of a revocable trust is that the trust property will not be subject to probate upon the grantor's death. Finally, note that the grantor of a revocable trust retains the right to change the trustee and beneficiaries and therefore retains the power to control the trust property at death.

38. (a) The requirement is to determine which cost is not required to be capitalized under the rules of Sec. 263A. Sec. 263A requires that specified indirect costs must be capitalized as part of the cost of inventory including factory repairs and maintenance, factory administration and officer salaries related to production, taxes (other than income taxes), payroll, warehousing costs, and service support including human resources, purchasing, payroll, and services rendered in conjunction with securities. Nonmanufacturing costs such as selling, advertising, and other marketing costs are not required to be included in inventory.

39. (c) The requirement is to determine when a corporation can reelect S status if it terminates its election in the current year. Following the revocation or termination of an S election, a corporation generally must wait five years before reelecting subchapter S status unless the IRS consents to an earlier election.

40. (a) The requirement is to determine to whom a CPA's report should be addressed in the case of a financial statement prepared for a limited liability company (LLC). An LLC is a pass-through entity, and a multi-owner LLC is generally considered to be a partnership for Federal tax purposes. However, the owners of an LLC are technically considered to be "members" rather than partners or shareholders.

Task-Based Simulation 1

Asset Valuation	Authoritative Literature	Help

Scroll down to complete all parts of this task.

Clients have approached your firm inquiring about various dates related to the filing of an income tax return. For each scenario, select the applicable date from the list provided. A selection may be used once, more than once, or not at all.

	A	B
1	**Scenario**	**Date**
2	What is the due date for filing of a federal income tax return for a C corporation with a fiscal year of 6/10/year 2 that has not filed a request for extension?	
3	What is the due date for filling of a federal income tax return for a calendar year C corporation for year 1 that has filed a timely request for an extension?	
4	A calendar year C corporation discovers an error resulting in overpayment of tax on the return for year 1 filed on 2/17/year 2. When does the statute of limitations for filing an amended return expire?	
5	An individual hand delivers his original tax returns for the calendar years 1, 2, and 3 on 4/15/year 5. When does the statute of limitations for assessment of tax on the earliest year expire?	
6	A partnership with a fiscal year end of 9/30/year 1 files a timely federal income tax return (without extension). What is the due date of this return?	
7	An individual files a tax return of calendar year 1 on 4/15/year 2 showing taxes due of $57,000. The individual made no payment with the return. When would the statute of limitations for collection after assessment of this tax expire?	
8	An individual files for an automatic extension before April 15, year 2. The individual files the income tax return on July 31, year 2, and pays the tax due. When does the statute of limitations expire on this return?	

Selection List—Column B, Tax Return Dates (all MOs)

Select Item
4/15/year 1
9/15/year 1
1/15/year 2
3/15/year 2
4/15/year 2
4/30/year 2
7/31/year 2
9/15/year 2
9/30/year 2
4/15/year 4

3/15/year 5
3/30/year 5
4/15/year 5
7/31/year 5
4/15/year 6
4/15/year 7
4/15/year 8
4/15/year 10
4/15/year 12

Solution to Task-Based Simulation 1

Asset Valuation	Authoritative Literature	Help

	A	B
1	**Scenario**	**Date**
2	What is the due date for filing of a federal income tax return for a C corporation with a fiscal year of 6/10/year 2 that has not filed a request for extension?	9/15/year 2
3	What is the due date for filling of a federal income tax return for a calendar year C corporation for year 1 that has filed a timely request for an extension?	9/15/year 2
4	A calendar year C corporation discovers an error resulting in overpayment of tax on the return for year 1 filed on 2/17/year 2. When does the statute of limitations for filing an amended return expire?	3/15/year 5
5	An individual hand delivers his original tax returns for the calendar years 1, 2, and 3 on 4/15/year 5. When does the statute of limitations for assessment of tax on the earliest year expire?	4/15/year 8
6	A partnership with a fiscal year end of 9/30/year 1 files a timely federal income tax return (without extension). What is the due date of this return?	1/15/ year 2
7	An individual files a tax return of calendar year 1 on 4/15/year 2 showing taxes due of $57,000. The individual made no payment with the return. When would the statute of limitations for collection after assessment of this tax expire?	4/15/year 12
8	An individual files for an automatic extension before April 15, year 2. The individual files the income tax return on July 31, year 2, and pays the tax due. When does the statute of limitations expire on this return?	7/31/year 5

Rationale

2. A corporate return Form 1120 must be filed by the fifteenth day of the third month following the close of a corporation's taxable year. Since the tax year ended 6/30/year2, the return due date is 9/15/year2.

3. A corporation can use Form 7004 to obtain an automatic 6-month extension for filing its tax return. Since a corporation's calendar-year year 1 return would be due 3/15/year2, the extended due date of the return would be 9/15/year2.

4. A refund claim must be filed within three years from the date the return was filed, or two years from payment of tax, whichever is later. If a return is filed before the due date, the return is treated as filed on the due date. Since the due date for early filed year 1 return would be 3/15/year2, an amended return would have to be filed by 3/15/year5.

5. The statute of limitations does not run if a return is not filed. Thus, the statute of limitations for assessment for a year 1 return that was filed on 4/15/year5 would not end until 4/15/year8.

6. A partnership return Form 1065 must be filed by the fifteenth day of the fourth month following the close of a partnership's taxable year. Since the year ended 9/30/year1, the due date for the year 1 return would be 1/15/year2.

7. If a taxpayer files a return but does not pay the tax on the return, the period for collection of tax by levy or a proceeding in court would end 10 years after assessment. Since the year 1 return was filed on 4/15/year2, the statute of limitations for collection would expire on 4/15/year12.

8. The normal statute of limitations is three years after the original due date of the return or three years after the return is filed, whichever is later. Since the year 1 return was not filed until July 31 year 2, the statute of limitations would end on 7/31/year5.

Task-Based Simulation 2

Corporate Formation		
	Authoritative Literature	Help

Scroll down to complete all parts of this task.

Clay, Finch, Lark and Token formed Amber Co., a C corporation. The shareholders made the following contributions to the corporation in exchange for stock on January 2, year 1.

		Shareholder ownership of stock	Shareholder contributions
	Clay	40%	$20,000 in cash, property worth $60,000 ($40,000 basis).
	Finch	20%	$10,000 in cash, property worth $50,000 ($30,000 basis), with related assumed recourse liability of $20,000.
	Lark	25%	Property worth $60,000 ($50,000 basis), received $10,000 in cash from Amber Co.
	Token	15%	$10,000 in cash property worth $40,000 ($5,000 basis), with a related assumed recourse liability of $20,000

D3 × ✓ fx					
	A	**B**	**C**	**D**	**E**
1	**Shareholder**	**Shareholder tax basis in Amber Co. stock**	**Shareholder gain realized**	**Shareholder gain recognized**	**Amber Co.'s tax basis in noncash property received from shareholder**
2	Clay				
3	Finch				
4	Lark				
5	Token				

Solution to Task-Based Simulation 2

Corporate Formation	
	Authoritative Literature	**Help**

D3 × ✓ fx					
	A	**B**	**C**	**D**	**E**
1	**Shareholder**	**Shareholder tax basis in Amber Co. stock**	**Shareholder gain realized**	**Shareholder gain recognized**	**Amber Co.'s tax basis in noncash property received from shareholder**
2	Clay	60,000		0	
3	Finch	20,000			30,000
4	Lark		10,000		60,000
5	Token		35,000	5,000	

Rationale

The requirement is to determine the amount of gain realized, gain recognized, and the tax basis for stock as well as assets as a result of transfers of property as part of the incorporation of Amber Co.

The transfers of property to Amber Co. in exchange for Amber stock qualify for Sec. 351 treatment because the transferors in the aggregate own at least 80% of the Amber Co. stock immediately after the exchange. Under Sec. 351 a realized gain is generally recognized only to the extent that consideration other than stock is received.

2. Clay realizes a gain of $60,000 – $40,000 = $20,000, but it is not recognized because no consideration other than stock was received. Clay's stock basis must reflect his deferred gain of $20,000. As a result, Clay's stock basis is equal to the $20,000 of cash plus the $40,000 basis of other property transferred, resulting in a stock basis of $60,000. Amber Co.'s basis for the other property would be $40,000.

3. Finch realizes a gain of $50,000 – $30,000 = $20,000, but it is not recognized because no consideration other than stock was received. Finch's stock basis must reflect his deferred gain of $20,000. As a result, Finch's stock basis is equal to the $10,000 cash plus the $30,000 basis of other property transferred, less the $20,000 liability that was assumed by Amber, or $20,000. Amber Co.'s basis for the other property is its transferred basis of $30,000.

4. Lark realizes a gain of $60,000 – $50,000 = $10,000, which must be recognized because of the $10,000 of cash received. Amber Co.'s basis for the property is its basis of $50,000 increased by the $10,000 of gain recognized to Lark, or $60,000. Lark's basis for his stock is the $50,000 basis of property transferred, plus the $10,000 of gain recognized, less the $10,000 cash received, or $50,000.

5. Token realizes a gain of $40,000 − $5,000 = $35,000 on the transfer of property. Token must recognize a gain of $5,000 because the $20,000 liability assumed by Amber exceeds the $15,000 total of the $10,000 cash plus $5,000 basis of other property transferred by Token. [$20,000 − ($10,000 + $5,000)] = $5,000 recognized gain. Amber's basis for the property is its transferred basis of $5,000 increased by the recognized gain of $5,000, or $10,000. Token's basis for the stock equals the $10,000 cash plus the $5,000 basis of property transferred, plus the $5,000 gain recognized, reduced by the $20,000 of liability assumed by Amber, or zero.

Task-Based Simulation 3

A client received a Form 1099-DIV showing only a portion of the total distribution as qualified dividends. Which section and subsection of the Internal Revenue Code defines the tax rates to be imposed on qualified dividends?

Enter your response in the answer fields below. Guidance on correctly structuring your response appears above and below the answer fields.

Solution to Task-Based Simulation 3

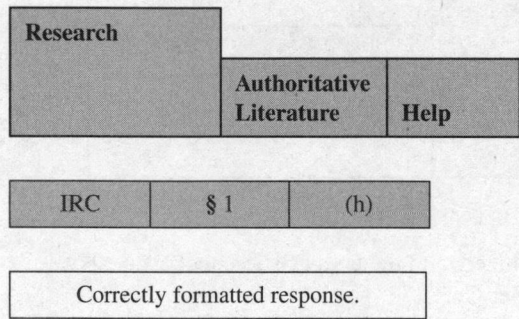

Index

A

AAA (Accumulated Adjustments Account), 726, 732
"Above the line" deductions (taxes), 489–494
  alimony or separate maintenance payments, 494
  discrimination suit costs, 494
  interest on education loans, 493
  jury duty pay remitted to employer, 494
  moving expenses, 490–491
  penalties for time deposit premature withdrawals, 494
  property held for production of rents or royalties, 489–490
  qualified tuition and related expenses, 494
  reimbursed employee business expenses, 489
  retirement plan contributions, 491–493
  self-employed premiums for medical insurance, 490
  self-employment tax paid, 490
  teachers' expenses, 494
Accelerated death benefits, 462
Acceptance:
  contracts, 173–175
  defined, 196
  sales contracts, 217–218
Accident benefits, 463
Accommodation:
  negotiable instruments, 266–267
  sales contracts, 218
Accountants' responsibilities, 43–54
  common law liability to clients, 43–47
  common law liability to third parties (nonclients), 47–49
  disciplinary systems, 42–43
  legal considerations affecting, 52–54
  regulation of the profession, 41–42
  statutory liability against, 49–59
  statutory liability to third parties, 49–52
Accounting method, 526
Accounting periods:
  defined, 526
  individual taxation, 472–473
Accrual method, 474

Accumulated Adjustments Account (AAA), 726, 732
Accumulated earnings and profits (AEP), 716
Accumulated earnings credit, 719–720
Accumulated earnings tax (AET), 719–720, 732
Accuracy-related tax penalty, 525
Acquisition, of personal property, 422–423
Acquisition indebtedness, tax deduction for, 498
Acts of employees, 53
Actual authority, 369, 373
ADA (Americans with Disabilities Act), 391, 408
ADEA (Age Discrimination in Employment Act), 391, 408
Adjusted basis, 630
Adjusted gross income (AGI):
  defined, 526
  itemized deductions from, 494–506
    charitable contributions, 499–501, 503
    interest expense, 497–499
    medical and dental expenses, 495–496
    miscellaneous deductions, 505–506
    personal casualty and theft gains and losses, 503–504
    reduction of total itemized deductions, 506
    taxes, 496–497
Adoption expenses:
  as gross income exclusion, 463
  tax credit for, 519
ADS (alternative depreciation system), 484
Adverse possession, 437
AEP (accumulated earnings and profits), 716
AET (accumulated earnings tax), 719–720, 732
Affiliated corporations, 713, 732
Age Discrimination in Employment Act (ADEA), 391, 408
Agency, 365–373
  characteristics of, 365
  duties and rights, 368

  examples of principals and agents, 365–367
  key terms, 373
  liability to third parties, 369–371
  methods of creation, 367–368
  multiple-choice answers and explanations, 377–379
  multiple-choice questions, 374–376
  simulations, 380
  simulation solutions, 381
  termination of principal-agent relationship, 371–373
Agents:
  defined, 373
  duties to principal, 368
  examples of, 365–367
  termination of principal-agent relationship, 371–373
AGI, *see* Adjusted gross income
AICPA *Code of Professional Conduct,* 41–42
Alcohol fuels tax credit, 515
Alimony:
  as "above the line" tax deduction, 494
  included in gross income, 468–469
Alimony recapture, 468–469
Alternate valuation date (estate tax), 803
Alternative depreciation system (ADS), 484
Alternative minimum tax (AMT):
  for corporations, 702–704
  for individuals, 511–512
  tax planning for, 818
Alternative minimum taxable income (AMTI), 702–704
American Opportunity Credit (AOC), 519–520
Americans with Disabilities Act (ADA), 391, 408
Amortization (individual taxation), 487
Amount realized, 526
AMT, *see* Alternative minimum tax
AMTI (alternative minimum taxable income), 702–704
Annual exclusion (gift tax), 800
Annuities:
  as gross income exclusion, 462
  included in gross income, 469–470

on sale or disposition of property between related taxpayers, 619
Express contracts, 170
Express warranties, 224–225

F
Face value, 272
Fair Credit and Charge Card Disclosure Act, 346
Fair Credit Billing Act, 346
Fair Credit Reporting Act, 346
Fair Debt Collection Practices Act, 345
Fair disclosure, Securities Exchange Act of 1934 requirements, 87–88
Fair Labor Standards Act (FLSA), 392, 409
Fair use doctrine, 425, 442
Family and Medical Leave Act, 392, 409
Family Educational Rights and Privacy Act, 430
Family partnerships, 657
Farming income and expenses, 522–523
Faxed contracts, 187
FDAP (fixed and determinable annual or periodical income), 812
Federal Anticybersquatting Consumer Protection Act, 429
Federal Environmental Pesticide Control Act, 398
Federal Insecticide, Fungicide, and Rodenticide Act, 397–398
Federal Insurance Contributions Act (FICA), 384, 409
Federal securities acts, 87–102
electronic signatures and electronic records, 102
exemptions for smaller and emerging companies, 101–102
Internet Securities Offering, 102
key terms, 102
multiple-choice answers and explanations, 108–111
multiple-choice questions, 103–107
Sarbanes-Oxley Act of 2002, 99–100, 393–394
professional and legal responsibilities under, 56–59
requirements for officers and directors, 143
Securities Act of 1933, 87–95
antifraud provisions, 94
civil liability, 94–95
criminal liability, 54–55, 95
defined, 65
definitions under, 88–90

exemptions for small and emerging companies, 101
exempt securities, 91–92
exempt transactions or offerings, 92–94
liability to third parties, 49–50
purposes of, 87–88
registration requirements, 90–91
whistle-blower protection, 95
Securities Exchange Act of 1934, 95–99
antifraud provisions, 97–98
civil liability, 98
criminal liability, 54–55, 98–99
defined, 65
disclosures required by, 96
exemptions for small and emerging companies, 101
exempt securities, 96
and Foreign Corrupt Practices Act, 99
insider reporting requirements, 99
liability to third parties, 51–52
proxy solicitations, 96–97
purposes, 95–96
registration requirements, 96
Regulation Fair Disclosure, 99
remedies against violators of, 99
sanctions available to SEC under, 96
SEC reports required by, 96
short-swing profits, 97
statute of limitations for securities fraud, 99
tender offers, 97
simulations, 112–114
simulation solutions, 115–117
and state "blue-sky" laws, 102
Wall Street Reform and Consumer Protection (Dodd-Frank) Act of 2010, 100–102
Federal tax authority, sources of, 815–818
Federal tax legislative process, 815
Federal Telecommunications Act, 400, 431
Federal Trade Commission Act of 1914, 407
Federal unemployment tax, computation of, 512
Federal Unemployment Tax Act (FUTA), 384–385, 409
Feeder organizations, 809
Fees, bankruptcy, 328
Fee simple, 431–432
Fellowships, 466
FICA, *see* Federal Insurance Contributions Act
Fictitious payee rule, 268
Fiduciary duties, 368, 373

Field warehousing (secured transactions), 297
52-53 week year, 472
50% reduction rule, 477
Filing requirements:
for corporations, 701–702
for exempt organizations, 809
Filing status, 495, 510
Final regulations, 817
Financial Modernization (Gramm-Leach Bliley) Act of 1999, 53
Financial structure (corporations), 138–140
Financing statement, 302
Firm offer, 232
Fiscal year, 472, 660
Fitness for a particular purpose, warranty of, 225
Fixed and determinable annual or periodical income (FDAP), 812
Fixtures, 422
Floating lien, 302
FLSA (Fair Labor Standards Act), 392, 409
Foreign activities, US taxation of US persons on, 812–814
Foreign base company income, 813
Foreign base company sales income, 813
Foreign corporations, 136
Foreign corporations, transfer of property to, 814
Foreign Corrupt Practices Act, 99
Foreign earned income exclusion, 467
Foreign persons, US taxation of, 812
Foreign personal holding company, 813
Foreign tax credit, 518, 813–814
Foreseeable party, 48
Foreseen party, 47–48
Forged endorsements, 267–268
Form 706, 804
Form 1120 schedules, 711–712
Form 1120S filing, 722
Formation defenses:
contracts, 175–178
defined, 196
Foundations, 809
Fraud:
contracts, 175–177
defined, 64
liability to clients for, 46–47
Fringe benefits:
as gross income exclusion, 463–464
S corporation taxation, 727

on involuntary conversions of property, 615

on liquidation of subsidiaries, 718

ordinary:

on business property held one year or less, 624

as corporate deductions, 709

on SBC stock, 700–701

partnership, 653–655

from passive activities, 482

personal casualty, 503–504, 624

realized, 526

risk of, 222–224

on sale of partnership interest, 662–664

on sales and other dispositions of property, 611–612

deposits in insolvent financial institutions, 618

between related taxpayers, 618–619

of S corporations, 725

in transfers to controlled corporations, 699

Low-income housing tax credit, 515

M

Mailbox Rule, 174

Majority rule, 47, 48

Maker:

defined, 272

forged signature of, 267

negotiable instruments, 251

Mandatory adjustments to basis of partnership property, 667

Marine Protection, Research, and Sanctuaries Act, 399

Marital deduction (gift taxes), 801

Market discount bonds, 617

Material facts, 49

Materialman's lien, 343

Material participation, 526

Meals (business expense):

as gross income exclusion, 463

tax rules for, 477

Mechanic's lien, 343

Medical expenses:

tax deductions for, 495–496

tax planning for, 818

Medical gift exclusion, 801

Medical insurance, self-employed premiums for, 490

Medical savings accounts (MSAs), 463

Merchant, 216, 232

Mergers, 405–406

as change in corporate structure, 146

defined, 409

of partnerships, 662

Minimum tax credit (corporations), 704

Minister's allowances, 466

Minors:

and contracts, 180–181

defined, 196

Minority rule, 47

Mirror image rule, 173, 196

Misrepresentation (contracts), 177

Mistakes (contracts), 177

Mitigation of damages, 196

Model Statutory Close Corporation Supplement, 136–137

Modification of contracts:

sales contracts, 218, 219

under UCC, 185–186

Monetary damages (contracts), 194–195

Money laundering, 407–408

Money Laundering Control Act of 1986, 408

Money order, 268

Monopolization, 403–404, 409

Monopoly power, 409

More likely than not standard, 63

Mortgages, 438–440, 442

Mortgagee, 439, 440, 442

Mortgagor, 439, 440, 442

Moving expenses:

as "above the line" tax deduction, 490–491

as gross income exclusion, 464

MSAs (medical savings accounts), 463

Multijurisdictional taxation, 810–815

Multiple support agreement (taxes), 507

Municipal bonds interest, 464

Mutual assent, 196

N

National Environmental Policy Act, 395

National Labor Relations Act (NLRA), 392–393, 409

Negligence:

defined, 64

liability to clients for, 45–46

product liability, 226

Negligence penalty (taxes), 525

Negligent misrepresentation, 177

Negotiable, 273

Negotiable instruments, 249–273

agencies involved in banking, 272

banks, 269–270

drafts (bills of exchange), 250, 268

Electronic Fund Transfer Act, 270

functions of, 249–250

fund transfers under UCC, 270

holder in due course, 259–264

interpretation of ambiguities in, 255–256

key terms, 272–273

liability of parties, 264–268

multiple-choice answers and explanations, 281–285

multiple-choice questions, 274–280

negotiation of, 256–258

notes (promissory notes), 251

Regulation E, 270

requirements of, 251–255

simulations, 286–288

simulation solutions, 289–292

transfer of documents of title, 271–272

types of checks, 268–269

Negotiation:

defined, 273

negotiable instruments, 256–258

NET Act (No Electronic Theft Act), 425

Net assets, 139

Net capital loss, 623–624

Net investment income tax (NIIT), 513–514

Net operating loss (NOL):

of acquired corporations, 730

for corporations, 709

tax deductions for, 479–480

tax planning for, 818

NIIT (net investment income tax), 513–514

Ninety-day letter, 523

NLRA (National Labor Relations Act), 392–393, 409

No additional-cost services, 464

No Electronic Theft Act (NET Act), 425

Noise Control Act, 397

NOL, *see* Net operating loss

Nonbusiness bad debts, deduction of, 478

Nonbusiness income, 810–811

Nondischargeable debts, 324–325

Non-pro rata distributions from partnership, 666

Nonqualified stock options, 470

Nontaxable exchanges, 612–617

No-par stock, 138

Notes (promissory notes), 251, 273

Notice:

deed recording, 436

negotiable instruments, 260

Notice-race statute:

defined, 443

mortgages, 439

recording deeds, 436

Notice statute, 442

Novation (mortgages), 439

Nuclear Waste Policy Act, 398–399

Index